M000007106

Justice Antonin Scalia Dissents

Edited by Robert Dittmer

"We do not reject Conan Doyle's method of statutory interpretation only to embrace Lewis Carroll's."

-Justice Scalia's dissent in Chisom v. Roemer (June 20, 1991)

Text Copyright © 2018 Robert Dittmer
All Rights Reserved

Note on the text: most italics and bold has been removed.

Acknowledgements

Websites (in no particular order):

www.law.cornell.edu
supreme.justia.com
caselaw.findlaw.com
law.resource.org
openjurist.org
scholar.google.com
en.wikipedia.org

    " "Attention all citizens. To assure the fairness of elections by preventing disproportionate expression of the views of any single powerful group, your Government has decided that the following associations of persons shall be prohibited from speaking or writing in support of any candidate: ___." In permitting Michigan to make private corporations the first object of this Orwellian announcement, the Court today endorses the principle that too much speech is an evil that the democratic majority can proscribe. I dissent because that principle is contrary to our case law and incompatible with the absolutely central truth of the First Amendment: that government cannot be trusted to assure, through censorship, the "fairness" of political debate."

    -Justice Scalia's dissent in Austin v. Michigan State Chamber of Commerce (March 27, 1990)

    "The injury-discovery rule applied by the Court of Appeals is bad wine of recent vintage."

    -Justice Scalia's concurrence in TRW, Inc. v. Andrews (November 13, 2001)

Table of Contents

Contents

Judge Scalia's dissent in Community for Creative Non-Violence v. Watt (DC Circuit Court) (March 9, 1983)

SCALIA, Circuit Judge, dissenting, with whom Circuit Judges MacKINNON and BORK concur:

I concur with the principal dissent in this case because I agree that, if traditional First Amendment analysis is applied to this sleeping, on the assumption that it is a fully protected form of expression, the appellants would nonetheless lose. I write separately to express my willingness to grasp the nettle which the principal dissent leaves untouched, and which the opinions supporting the court's disposition consider untouchable — that is, flatly to deny that sleeping is or can ever be speech for First Amendment purposes. That this should seem a bold assertion is a commentary upon how far judicial and scholarly discussion of this basic constitutional guarantee has strayed from common and common-sense understanding.

I start from the premise that when the Constitution said "speech" it meant speech and not all forms of expression. Otherwise, it would have been unnecessary to address "freedom of the press" separately — or, for that matter, "freedom of assembly," which was obviously directed at facilitating expression. The effect of the speech and press guarantees is to provide special protection against all laws that impinge upon spoken or written communication (which I will, for the sake of simplicity, refer to generically as "speech") even if they do so for purposes that have nothing to do with communication, such as the suppression of noise or the elimination of litter. But to extend equivalent protection against laws that affect actions which happen to be conducted for the purpose of "making a point" is to stretch the Constitution not only beyond its meaning but beyond reason, and beyond the capacity of any legal system to accommodate.

The cases find within the First Amendment some protection for "expressive conduct" apart from spoken and written thought. The nature and effect of that protection, however, is quite different from the guarantee of freedom of speech narrowly speaking. It involves a significantly different balancing of private rights and public interests, and does not always call for the detailed "First Amendment analysis" characteristic of the speech cases and applied by the majority opinions here. Specifically, what might be termed the more generalized guarantee of freedom of expression makes the communicative nature of conduct an inadequate basis for singling out that conduct for proscription. A law directed at the communicative nature of conduct must, like a law directed at speech itself, be justified by the substantial showing of need that the First Amendment requires. But a law proscribing conduct for a reason having nothing to do with its communicative character need only meet the ordinary minimal requirements of the equal protection clause.[1] In other words, the only "First Amendment analysis"[2] applicable to laws that do not directly or indirectly impede speech is the threshold inquiry of whether the purpose of the law is to suppress communication. If not, that is the end of the matter so far as First Amendment guarantees are concerned; if so, the court then proceeds to determine whether there is substantial justification for the proscription, just as it does in free-speech cases.

Thus, the First Amendment's protection of free speech invalidates laws that happen to inhibit speech even though they are directed at some other activity (sound amplification,[3] campaign contributions,[4] littering[5]). The more limited guarantee of freedom of expression, by contrast, does not apply to accidental intrusion upon expressiveness but only to purposeful restraint of expression. It would not invalidate a law generally prohibiting the extension of limbs from the windows of moving vehicles; it would invalidate a law prohibiting only the extension of clenched fists.

I believe the foregoing analysis is consistent with all of the Supreme Court's holdings in this field. I would be content to consign marching and picketing, as the principal dissent suggests, to a category of traditionally expressive conduct which itself qualifies as speech, and thus does not require a showing of expression-suppressing intent. I do not think that exception is necessary, however, to explain the cases. The marching and picketing holdings represent not conduct protected because it is in itself expressive, but rather what the cases and commentators call "speech-plus"[6] — conduct "intertwined"[7] or "intermingled"[8] with speech. The union organizer, for example, cannot convey his spoken or written message to the relevant audience if he is not allowed to be present at the entrance to the employer's place of business. Those cases differ only in degree from the sound-amplification, campaign-contribution and littering cases referred to above: They deal with laws which, by prohibiting an essential concomitant of effective speech, infringe upon speech itself, and thus call forth the full First Amendment standard of justification.[9] (It may be difficult to determine what particular conduct beyond the physical presence involved in the marching and picketing cases, or the distribution of literature involved in the littering case, is constitutionally deemed an essential concomitant of effective speech; but I consider it self-evident that on-site sleeping is not.)

It is only such cases as Stromberg v. California, 283 U.S. 359, 51 S.Ct. 532, 75 L.Ed. 1117 (1931) (flying of a red flag), Brown v. Louisiana, 383 U.S. 131, 86 S.Ct. 719, 15 L.Ed.2d 637 (1966) (silent sit-in), United States v. O'Brien, 391 U.S. 367, 88 S.Ct. 1673, 20 L.Ed.2d 672 (1968) (burning of a draft card), Tinker v. Des Moines School District, 393 U.S. 503, 89 S.Ct. 733, 21 L.Ed.2d 731 (1969) (black arm-bands), and Spence v. Washington, 418 U.S. 405, 94 S.Ct. 2727, 41 L.Ed.2d 842 (1974) (defacing the United States flag), that clearly present situations in which speech — that is, the spoken or written word — is not necessarily involved.[10] The holdings of all these cases support the analysis set forth above. Every proscription of expressive conduct struck down by the Supreme Court was aimed precisely at the communicative effect of the conduct. The only reason to ban the flying of a red flag (Stromberg) was the revolutionary sentiment that symbol expressed.[11] The only reason for applying the "breach of the peace" statute to the silent presence of black protestors in the library in Brown was the effect which the communicative content of that presence had upon onlookers.[12] The only reason for singling out black armbands for a dress proscription (Tinker) was precisely their expressive content, allegedly causing classroom disruption.[13] The only reason to prevent the attachment of symbols to the United States flag (Spence) was related to the communicative content of the flag.[14] In O'Brien, on the other hand, where the Supreme Court upheld a ban on the destruction of draft cards, the law was not directed against the communicative nature of that activity.[15]

I do not suggest that the dicta of all the expressive conduct cases, as opposed to their holdings, support the distinction set forth above. Some of the opinions merely label the conduct "expressive" and proceed at once to application of First Amendment standards. Only O'Brien, however, really raises the question (though leaves it unanswered)[16] of what it is that avoids required application of those standards in every case. It is true that O'Brien appears to prescribe an inquiry, identical to that which I have described, as one of the four tests to be applied after it is determined that full First Amendment protections obtain. That would be inconsistent with my analysis if the O'Brien formulation were directed exclusively at "expressive conduct" cases — for a test triggered by the protection could hardly be the very test applied to determine whether the protection exists in the first place. In fact, however, the O'Brien discussion is directed at the tests to be applied in order to validate a statute impinging upon any activity protected by the First Amendment — not just expressive conduct, but also conduct "intertwined with speech," and indeed even religiously motivated or associational conduct.[17] For most of these categories the test would not be duplicative; it is only the governmental restriction of purely expressive conduct that escapes the necessity of First Amendment analysis if it is not aimed at repressing expression. This explanation is confirmed by the Supreme Court's later per curiam opinion in Spence, which, in the context of expressive conduct, describes the inquiry into expression-suppressing purpose — as I have — as a test preliminary to the application of O'Brien's four-step analysis.[18]

I find O'Brien supportive of my view since it shows the importance of statutory purpose in the Court's thinking. The distinction here proposed is described explicitly in the following passage:

The case at bar is therefore unlike one where the alleged governmental interest in regulating conduct arises in some measure because the communication allegedly integral to the conduct is itself thought to be harmful. In Stromberg v. California, 283 U.S. 359 [51 S.Ct. 532, 75 L.Ed. 1117] (1931), for example, this Court struck down a statutory phrase which punished people who expressed their "opposition to organized government" by displaying "any flag, badge, banner, or device." Since the statute there was aimed at suppressing communication it could not be sustained as a regulation of noncommunicative conduct. 391 U.S. at 382, 88 S.Ct. at 1681. To the same effect is the following statement in Buckley v. Valeo, 424 U.S. 1, 17, 96 S.Ct. 612, 633, 46 L.Ed.2d 659 (1976):

Even if the categorization of the expenditure of money as conduct were accepted, the limitations challenged here would not meet the O'Brien test because the governmental interests advanced in support of the Act involve "suppressing communication." The interests served by the Act include restricting the voices of people and interest groups who have money to spend and reducing the overall scope of federal election campaigns. Although the Act does not focus on the ideas expressed by persons or groups subject to its regulations, it is aimed in part at equalizing the relative ability of all voters to affect electoral outcomes by placing a ceiling on expenditures for political expression by citizens and groups. Unlike O'Brien, where the Selective Service System's administrative interest in the preservation of draft cards was wholly unrelated to their use as a means of communication, it is beyond dispute that the interest in regulating the alleged "conduct" of giving or spending money "arises in some measure because the communication allegedly integral to conduct is itself thought to be harmful." 391 U.S. at 382, 88 S.Ct. at 1681.

The effect of the rule I think to be the law may be to permit the prohibition of some expressive conduct that might be desirable. Perhaps symbolic campsites[19] or symbolic fire bases[20] are a good idea. But it is not the function of the Constitution to make such fine judgments; nor is it within the practical power of the courts to apply them. There is a gap between what the Constitution requires and what perfect governance might sometimes suggest, in the area of expression as in other fields. So long as the Park Service is held to even-handed application of its rules, I doubt that the political pressures generated in a representative democracy will tolerate the proscription of all expressive conduct, in Lafayette Park or anywhere else. The Park Service's judgment will not be distorted, however — nor its time and ours consumed — in the mistaken pursuit of a supposed constitutional answer.

Where expressive conduct unrelated to speech is at issue, I think it worthwhile to engage in the preliminary step of analysis that separates conduct-prohibiting from expression-prohibiting laws and exempts the former from rigorous First Amendment scrutiny. The government argued in the present case, with some justification, that the posture in which it now finds itself — prohibiting sleep, but permitting all of the external manifestations of sleeping, including tents — is attributable to its efforts to comply with the directives of this court relating to the special justification needed to prohibit expressive conduct. See Women Strike for Peace v. Morton, 472 F.2d 1273 (D.C.Cir.1972). The Park Service has in effect been required to split each of its regulations into two: one that applies to people who are not engaging in the prohibited conduct for an expressive purpose, which can be enforced as written; the other that applies to demonstrators, which can be enforced only if supported by the substantial governmental interest that the First Amendment requires. That necessity may be unavoidable with regard to the relatively narrow range of conduct essential to effective speech. But to expand it to all conduct, even including sleep, seems to me unreasonable and unlikely to work. Park Service officers who have even less assurance of the proper application of the O'Brien four-part test than the various opinions of this court display will (against their sound administrative judgment) permit "symbolic" intrusions that need not be allowed; and the rule for demonstrators will inevitably (and perhaps rightly) tend to become the rule for the public at large — all with needlessly harmful effect upon the agreeability of our parks and public places. The unfortunate result is described by Justice Jackson's statement in Saia v. New York, supra, 334 U.S. at 566, 68 S.Ct. at 1152, which I take the liberty of adapting to the facts of this case: "I dissent from this decision, which seems to me to endanger the great right of free speech by making it ridiculous and obnoxious, more than the Park Service regulation in question menaces free speech by proscribing sleep."

Notes

[1] For a description of those requirements, see, e.g., City of New Orleans v. Dukes, 427 U.S. 297, 303, 96 S.Ct. 2513, 2516, 49 L.Ed.2d 511 (1976).

[2] I refer here only to the First Amendment's guarantees of freedom of speech and press — not to other guarantees, such as freedom of religion or the right of personal autonomy or privacy which some cases have rested in part upon the First Amendment. See, e.g., Stanley v. Georgia, 394 U.S. 557, 564, 89 S.Ct. 1243, 1247, 22 L.Ed.2d 542 (1969); Griswold v. Connecticut, 381 U.S. 479, 482-83, 85 S.Ct. 1678, 1680-1681, 14 L.Ed.2d 510 (1965).

[3] See Saia v. New York, 334 U.S. 558, 561, 68 S.Ct. 1148, 1150, 92 L.Ed. 1574 (1948) ("Loudspeakers are today indispensable instruments of effective public speech").

[4] See Buckley v. Valeo, 424 U.S. 1, 16, 96 S.Ct. 612, 633, 46 L.Ed.2d 659 (1976):

We cannot share the view that the present Act's contribution and expenditure limitations are comparable to the restrictions on conduct upheld in O'Brien. The expenditure of money simply cannot be equated with such conduct as destruction of a draft card. Some forms of communication made possible by the giving and spending of money involve speech alone, some involve conduct primarily, and some involve a combination of the two. Yet this Court has never suggested that the dependence of a communication on the expenditure of money operates itself to introduce a nonspeech element or to reduce the exacting scrutiny required by the First Amendment.

[5] See Schneider v. State, 308 U.S. 147, 163, 60 S.Ct. 146, 151, 84 L.Ed. 155 (1939):

It is argued that the circumstance that in the actual enforcement of the Milwaukee ordinance the distributor is arrested only if those who receive the literature throw it in the streets, renders it valid. But, even as thus construed, the ordinance cannot be enforced without unconstitutionally abridging the liberty of free speech. As we have pointed out, the public convenience in respect of cleanliness of the streets does not justify an exertion of the police power which invades the free communication of information and opinion secured by the Constitution.

[6] See American Radio Ass'n v. Mobile Steamship Ass'n, 419 U.S. 215, 231, 95 S.Ct. 409, 418, 42 L.Ed.2d 911 (1974); W. LOCKHART, Y. KAMISAR, & J. CHOPER, CONSTITUTIONAL LAW 1136 (1980).

[7] See, e.g., Cameron v. Johnson, 390 U.S. 611, 617, 88 S.Ct. 1335, 1338, 20 L.Ed.2d 182 (1968); Cox v. Louisiana, 379 U.S. 559, 563, 85 S.Ct. 476, 480, 13 L.Ed.2d 487

(1965).

[8] See, e.g., Amalgamated Food Employees Union Local 590 v. Logan Valley Plaza, Inc., 391 U.S. 308, 313, 88 S.Ct. 1601, 1605, 20 L.Ed.2d 603 (1968).

[9] These cases would be compatible with the analysis I have set forth, even if they were to be regarded as involving not "speech-plus" but purely nonspeech expressive conduct. The picketing cases, for example, do not invalidate general prohibitions against walking back and forth, or against obstructing entrances, but rather banning such activities when engaged in for the (expressive) purpose of inducing people to refrain from trading or working. See, e.g., Thornhill v. Alabama, 310 U.S. 88, 91-92 [60 S.Ct. 736, 738-739, 84 L.Ed. 1093] (1940), where the statute forbade "[a]ny person ... [to] go near to or loiter about the premises or place of business of any other person ... for the purpose, or with the intent of influencing, or inducing other persons not to trade with, buy from, sell to, have business dealings with, or be employed by such persons ...." See also Carlson v. California, 310 U.S. 106 [60 S.Ct. 746, 84 L.Ed. 1104] (1940). The marching cases typically turn upon the use of a vague ordinance for the very purpose of suppressing only expressive activity. See, e.g., Shuttlesworth v. City of Birmingham, 394 U.S. 147, 153, 89 S.Ct. 935, 940, 22 L.Ed.2d 162 (1969); Edwards v. South Carolina, 372 U.S. 229, 236, 83 S.Ct. 680, 683, 9 L.Ed.2d 697 (1963).

[10] In my view, the nude entertainment holdings do not deal with mere expressive conduct. Schad v. Borough of Mount Ephraim, 452 U.S. 61, 101 S.Ct. 2176, 68 L.Ed.2d 671 (1981), struck down the challenged ordinance on overbreadth grounds, since it included all live entertainment — including spoken entertainment. Southeastern Promotions, Ltd. v. Conrad, 420 U.S. 546, 95 S.Ct. 1239, 43 L.Ed.2d 448 (1975), involved a prohibition not of nudity alone, but of the entire stage production "Hair" because it included nudity. It stands for the well-established principle that a spoken or written work which has "serious artistic value" cannot be banned simply because it includes matter which, in isolation, might be proscribable. In California v. LaRue, 409 U.S. 109, 118, 93 S.Ct. 390, 397, 34 L.Ed.2d 342 (1972), the Court said that "at least some of the performances" covered by the regulation banning nudity and sexual acts "are within the limits of the constitutional protection of freedom of expression" (the case in any event upheld the regulation); and in Doran v. Salem Inn, Inc., 422 U.S. 922, 932, 95 S.Ct. 2561, 2568, 45 L.Ed.2d 648 (1975), it said that the nude barroom dancing might be protected "under some circumstances." Both these cases may have had in mind only nudity in connection with a spoken or sung performance. In any case, I find it difficult to believe that exhibitory nudity will, on the ground that it is independently "communicative," be accorded greater constitutional protection than the nondemonstrative sort, such as nude bathing, see, e.g., Chapin v. Town of Southampton, 457 F.Supp. 1170 (E.D.N.Y.1978). In other words, to the extent the nude entertainment cases speak to nudity apart from spoken or sung performances they seem to me based upon the "personal autonomy" rather than the "free speech" line of cases. See note 2, supra.

[11] The statute in Stromberg forbade the flying of "a red flag, banner or badge ...

as a sign, symbol or emblem of opposition to organized government ...." 283 U.S. at 361, 51 S.Ct. at 532.

[12] "The statute was deliberately and purposefully applied solely to terminate the reasonable, orderly, and limited exercise of the right to protest the unconstitutional segregation of a public facility." 383 U.S. at 142, 86 S.Ct. at 724.

[13] "The school officials banned and sought to punish petitioners for a silent, passive expression of opinion unaccompanied by any disorder or disturbance on the part of petitioners." 393 U.S. at 508, 89 S.Ct. at 737.

[14] "If [Washington's interest in preserving the national flag as an unalloyed symbol of our country] is valid, we note that it is directly related to expression in the context of activity like that undertaken by appellant. For that reason and because no other governmental interest unrelated to expression has been advanced or can be supported on this record, the four-step analysis of United States v. O'Brien ... is inapplicable." 418 U.S. at 414 n. 8, 94 S.Ct. at 2732 n. 8 (citation omitted).

[15] "[B]oth the governmental interest and the operation of the 1965 Amendment [banning draft card burning] are limited to the noncommunicative aspect of O'Brien's conduct." 391 U.S. at 381-82, 88 S.Ct. at 1681-1682.

[16] "We cannot accept the view that an apparently limitless variety of conduct can be labeled `speech' whenever the person engaging in the conduct intends thereby to express an idea. However, even on the assumption that the alleged communicative element in O'Brien's conduct is sufficient to bring into play the First Amendment, it does not necessarily follow that the destruction of a registration certificate is constitutionally protected activity." 391 U.S. at 376, 88 S.Ct. at 1678.

[17] See the cases cited at 391 U.S. at 376-77 nn. 22-27, 88 S.Ct. at 1678-1679 nn. 22-27.

[18] See note 14, supra.

[19] See Vietnam Veterans Against the War v. Morton, 506 F.2d 53 (D.C.Cir.1974) (per curiam).

[20] See Reply to Appellees' Opposition to Appellants' Emergency Motion for Injunction Pending Appeal and Opposition to Appellants' Motion for Summary Affirmance at 46 (Dec. 14, 1982) (description of Vietnam Veterans' May 1982 demonstration).

Judge Scalia's concurrence in Hirschey v. FERC (DC Circuit Court) (Nov 15, 1985)

SCALIA, Circuit Judge, concurring:

Although I dissented in Hirschey II, believing that the EAJA did not apply to the present case, since the court held otherwise I have participated in this subsequent consideration of what the amount of the EAJA award should be. I join the court's opinion with the exception of the dictum discussed below. I write separately principally to clarify several points in the current opinion related to my earlier dissent.

I agree that the petitioner can be compensated for the attorneys' fees expended in litigating her right to attorneys' fees, even though the "substantial justification" defense to the assessment of EAJA fees, see 28 U.S.C. § 2412(d)(1)(A) (1982), literally applies to the conduct of the fee litigation as well as to the conduct of the substantive suit, and even though in my view (as my earlier dissent suggests) FERC's litigation of the fee issues was amply justified. The defense of substantial justification for the fee litigation was not asserted by the government, and as I understand the opinion, Maj. op. at 3 n. 15, we have declined to resolve the applicability of that defense here, just as we have declined to resolve it in other cases where the point was not argued, see Cinciarelli v. Reagan, 729 F.2d 801, 810 (D.C.Cir.1984); Martin v. Lauer, 740 F.2d 36, 44-45 n. 15 (D.C.Cir.1984). I further note that there was not argued, and we have not considered, the effect of the fact that in the present case the fees awarded for litigating fee issues substantially exceeded the value of the litigated fees themselves — or, to put it another way, the fees awarded for litigating fees substantially exceeded the fees awarded for litigating petitioner's substantive grievance. The Supreme Court currently has before it the analogous question of whether there must be some proportionality between the fees awarded and the recovery in the underlying case. See City of Riverside v. Rivera, 763 F.2d 1580 (9th Cir.1985), cert. granted, ____ U.S. ____, 106 S.Ct. 244, 88 L.Ed.2d 253 (1985).

While not contesting that Hirschey II is now the law of this circuit, I must nonetheless dissociate myself from the dictum of the court — which may be given effect in other circuits — that the legislative history of the 1985 EAJA amendments "ratifies the holding of the majority opinion in Hirschey II." Maj. op. at 2 n. 9. Hirschey II and the three decisions of other circuits reaching the same result (two of which, like Hirschey II itself, were accompanied by dissents), present a conflict with the contrary holding of the Ninth Circuit in Tulalip Tribes v. FERC, 749 F.2d 1367, 1369 (9th Cir.1984), rather than the sort of uniform judicial interpretation that Congress, by unamended reenactment of the subject provision, may be deemed to have approved. See, e.g., Lorillard v. Pons, 434 U.S. 575, 580-81, 98 S.Ct. 866, 869-70, 55 L.Ed.2d 40 (1978). The entire case for the majority's asserted "ratification" of Hirschey II rests upon the following statement in the House Committee Report:

> The language of section 2412(d)(1)(A) expresses the view that prevailing parties shall be awarded attorney's fees and, when available, costs as well. This interpretation ratifies the approach taken by four circuits. [Citing, inter alia, Hirschey II.] ... Thus, the Committee rejects the interpretations of the statute by the 9th Circuit. See Tulalip Tribes....

H.R. REP. No. 120, 99th Cong., 1st Sess. 17 (1985), 1985 U.S.CODE CONG. & AD.NEWS 132, 145. It is most interesting that the House Committee rejected the interpretation of the Ninth Circuit, and perhaps that datum should be accorded the weight of an equivalently unreasoned law review article. But the authoritative, as opposed to the persuasive, weight of the Report depends entirely upon how reasonable it is to assume that

that rejection was reflected in the law which Congress adopted. I frankly doubt that it is ever reasonable to assume that the details, as opposed to the broad outlines of purpose, set forth in a committee report come to the attention of, much less are approved by, the house which enacts the committee's bill.[1] And I think it time for courts to become concerned about the fact that routine deference to the detail of committee reports, and the predictable expansion in that detail which routine deference has produced, are converting a system of judicial construction into a system of committee-staff prescription. But the authority of the committee report in the present case is even more suspect than usual. Where a committee-generated report deals with the meaning of a committee-generated text, one can at least surmise that someone selected these statutory words to convey this intended meaning. The portion of the report at issue here, however, comments upon language drafted in an earlier Congress, and reenacted, unamended so far as is relevant to the present point, in the 1985 law. We are supposed to believe that the legislative action recommended by the Committee and adopted by the Congress, in order to resolve a difficult question of interpretation that had produced a conflict in the circuits and internal disagreement within three of the five courts that had considered it, was reenactment of the same language unchanged! Such a supposition is absurd on its face; and doubly absurd since the precise section was amended in 1985 on such a point of minute detail as changing an "and" to "or." Pub.L. No. 99-80, § 2(a)(1), 99 Stat. 183, 184 (1985).

In sum, even if the 1985 EAJA amendments had been relevant to our determination in Hirschey II, I think the question should still have been resolved, as it was, not on the basis of what the committee report said, but on the basis of what we judged to be the most rational reconciliation of the relevant provisions of law Congress had adopted. I was disappointed that the court did not reconcile them as I would have, but I at least had the comfort, which implementation of the dictum here under discussion would deny me, of thinking that the court was wrong for the right reason.

Notes

[1] Several years ago, the following illuminating exchange occurred between members of the Senate, in the course of floor debate on a tax bill:

Mr. ARMSTRONG. ... My question, which may take [the chairman of the Committee on Finance] by surprise, is this: Is it the intention of the chairman that the Internal Revenue Service and the Tax Court and other courts take guidance as to the intention of Congress from the committee report which accompanies this bill?

Mr. DOLE. I would certainly hope so....

Mr. ARMSTRONG. Mr. President, will the Senator tell me whether or not he wrote the committee report?

Mr. DOLE. Did I write the committee report?

Mr. ARMSTRONG. Yes.

Mr. DOLE. No; the Senator from Kansas did not write the committee report.

Mr. ARMSTRONG. Did any Senator write the committee report?

Mr. DOLE. I have to check.

Mr. ARMSTRONG. Does the Senator know of any Senator who wrote the committee report?

Mr. DOLE. I might be able to identify one, but I would have to search. I was here all during the time it was written, I might say, and worked carefully with the staff as they worked....

Mr. ARMSTRONG. Mr. President, has the Senator from Kansas, the chairman of the Finance Committee, read the committee report in its entirety?

Mr. DOLE. I am working on it. It is not a bestseller, but I am working on it.

Mr. ARMSTRONG. Mr. President, did members of the Finance Committee vote on the committee report?

Mr. DOLE. No.

Mr. ARMSTRONG. Mr. President, the reason I raise the issue is not perhaps apparent on the surface, and let me just state it: .... The report itself is not considered by the Committee on Finance. It was not subject to amendment by the Committee on Finance. It is not subject to amendment now by the Senate.

....

... If there were matter within this report which was disagreed to by the Senator from Colorado or even by a majority of all Senators, there would be no way for us to change the report. I could not offer an amendment tonight to amend the committee report.

... [F]or any jurist, administrator, bureaucrat, tax practitioner, or others who might chance upon the written record of this proceeding, let me just make the point that this is not the law, it was not voted on, it is not subject to amendment, and we should discipline ourselves to the task of expressing congressional intent in the statute.

128 CONG.REC. S8659 (daily ed. July 19, 1982).

Justice Scalia's dissent in Tashjian, Secretary of State of Connecticut v. Republican Party of Connecticut (Dec 10, 1986)

JUSTICE SCALIA, with whom THE CHIEF JUSTICE and JUSTICE O'CONNOR join, dissenting.

Both the right of free political association and the State's authority to establish arrangements that assure fair and effective party participation in the election process are essential to democratic government. Our cases make it clear that the accommodation of these two vital interests does not lend itself to bright-line rules, but requires careful inquiry into the extent to which the one or the other interest is inordinately impaired under the facts of the particular case. See Anderson v. Celebrezze, 460 U. S. 780, 460 U. S. 788-790 (1983); Storer v. Brown, 415 U. S. 724, 415 U. S. 730 (1974). Even so, the conclusion reached on the individuated facts of one case sheds some measure of light upon the conclusion that will be reached on the individuated facts of the next. Since this is an area, moreover, in which the predictability of decisions is important, I think it worth noting that, for me, today's decision already exceeds the permissible limit of First Amendment restrictions upon the States' ordering of elections.

In my view, the Court's opinion exaggerates the importance of the associational interest at issue, if indeed it does not see one where none exists. There is no question here of restricting the Republican Party's ability to recruit and enroll Party members by offering them the ability to select Party candidates; Conn.Gen.Stat. § 9-56 (1985) permits an independent voter to join the Party as late as the day before the primary. Cf. Kusper v. Pontikes, 414 U. S. 51 (1973). Nor is there any question of restricting the ability of the Party's members to select whatever candidate they desire. Appellees' only complaint is that the Party cannot leave the selection of its candidate to persons who are not members of the Party, and are unwilling to become members. It seems to me fanciful to refer to this as an interest in freedom of association between the members of the Republican Party and the putative independent voters. The Connecticut voter who, while steadfastly refusing to register as a Republican, casts a vote in the Republican primary, forms no more meaningful an "association" with the Party than does the independent or the registered Democrat who responds to questions by a Republican Party pollster. If the concept of freedom of association is extended to such casual contacts, it ceases to be of any analytic use. See Democratic Party of United States v. Wisconsin ex rel. La Follette, 450 U. S. 107, 450 U. S. 130-131 (1981) (POWELL, J., dissenting) ("[Not] every conflict between state law and party rules concerning participation in the nomination process creates a burden on associational rights"; one must "look closely at the nature of the intrusion, in light of the nature of the association involved, to see whether we are presented with a real limitation on First Amendment freedoms").

The ability of the members of the Republican Party to select their own candidate, on the other hand, unquestionably implicates an associational freedom -- but it can hardly be thought that that freedom is unconstitutionally impaired here. The Party is entirely free to put forward, if it wishes, that candidate who has the highest degree of support among Party members and independents combined. The State is under no obligation, however, to let its party primary be used, instead of a party-funded opinion poll, as the means by which the party identifies the relative popularity of its potential candidates among independents. Nor is there any reason apparent to me why the State cannot insist that this decision to support what might be called the independents' choice be taken by the party membership in a democratic fashion, rather than through a process that permits the members' votes to be diluted -- and perhaps even absolutely outnumbered -- by the votes of outsiders.

The Court's opinion characterizes this, disparagingly, as an attempt to "protec[t] the integrity of the Party against the Party itself." Ante at 479 U. S. 224. There are two problems with this characterization. The first, and less important, is that it is not true. We have no way of knowing that a majority of the Party's members is in favor of allowing ultimate selection of its candidates for federal and statewide office to be determined by persons outside the Party. That decision was not made by democratic ballot, but by the Party's state convention -- which, for all we know, may have been dominated by officeholders and office seekers whose evaluation of the merits of assuring election of the Party's candidates, vis-a-vis the merits of proposing candidates faithful to the Party's political philosophy, diverged significantly from the views of the Party's rank and file. I had always thought it was a major purpose of state-imposed party primary requirements to protect the general party membership against this sort of minority control. See Nader v. Schaffer, 417 F.Supp. 837, 843 (Conn.), summarily aff'd, 429 U.S. 989 (1976). Second and more important, however, even if it were the fact that the majority of the Party's members wanted its candidates to be determined by outsiders, there is no reason why the State is bound to honor that desire -- any more than it would be bound to honor a party's democratically expressed desire that its candidates henceforth be selected by convention rather than by primary, or by the party's executive committee in a smoke-filled room. In other words, the validity of the state-imposed primary requirement itself, which we have hitherto considered "too plain for argument," American Party of Texas v. White, 415 U. S. 767, 415 U. S. 781 (1974), presupposes that the State has the right "to protect the Party against the Party itself." Connecticut may lawfully require that significant elements of the democratic election process be democratic -- whether the Party wants that or not. It is beyond my understanding why the Republican Party's delegation of its democratic choice to a Republican Convention can be proscribed, but its delegation of that choice to nonmembers of the Party cannot.

In the case before us, Connecticut has said no more than this: Just as the Republican Party may, if it wishes, nominate the candidate recommended by the Party's executive committee, so long as its members select that candidate by name in a democratic vote; so also it may nominate the independents' choice, so long as its members select him by name in a democratic vote. That seems to me plainly and entirely constitutional.

I respectfully dissent.

Notes

[1] Article I, § 2, cl. 1, provides:

"The House of Representatives shall be composed of Members chosen every second Year by the People of the several States, and the Electors in each State shall have the Qualifications requisite for Electors of the most numerous Branch of the State Legislature."

[2] "The electors in each State shall have the qualifications requisite for electors of the most numerous branch of the State legislatures."

[3] James Wilson referred to this part of the Report of the Committee on Detail as "well considered," and "he did not think it could be changed for the better. It was difficult to form any uniform rule of qualifications, for all the States." J. Madison, Journal of the Federal Convention 467 (E. Scott ed. 1893).

[4] See opinion of Justice Harlan, 400 U.S. at 400 U. S. 152, 400 U. S. 212-213

(concurring in part and dissenting in part), and opinion of Justice Stewart, id. at 281, 287-289 (joined by Burger, C. J., and BLACKMUN, J.).

[5] See opinion of Justice Douglas, id. at 400 U. S. 135, 400 U. S. 141-144, and the joint opinion, id. at 400 U. S. 229, 400 U. S. 280-281 (opinion of BRENNAN, WHITE, and MARSHALL, JJ.).

[6] This was certainly the view of Justice Harlan, see id. at 400 U. S. 210-211, and of Justice Stewart and the two Justices who joined his opinion, see id. at 400 U. S. 287-290. As Justice Stewart observed: "The Constitution thus adopts as the federal standard the standard which each State has chosen for itself." Id. at 400 U. S. 288. The opinions of Justice Douglas and JUSTICE BRENNAN are silent on the issue.

Justice Scalia's dissent in California Coastal Comm'n v. Granite Rock Co. (March 24, 1987)

JUSTICE SCALIA, with whom JUSTICE WHITE joins, dissenting.

I agree with the Court that this case is live because of continuing dispute over California's ability to assert a reclamation claim, ante at 480 U. S. 578. [1] In my view, however, the merits of this case must be decided on simpler and narrower grounds than those addressed by the Court's opinion. It seems to me ultimately irrelevant whether state environmental regulation has been preempted with respect to federal lands, since the exercise of state power at issue here is not environmental regulation, but land use control. The Court errs in entertaining the Coastal Commission's contention that "its permit requirement is an exercise of environmental regulation," ante at 480 U. S. 589, and mischaracterizes the issue when it describes it to be whether "any state permit requirement, whatever its conditions, [is] per se preempted by federal law," ante at 480 U. S. 593. We need not speculate as to what the nature of this permit requirement was. We are not dealing with permits in the abstract, but with a specific permit, purporting to require application of particular criteria, mandated by a numbered section of a known California law. That law is plainly a land use statute, and the permit that statute requires Granite Rock to obtain is a land use control device. Its character as such is not altered by the fact that the State may now be agreeable to issuing it so long as environmental concerns are satisfied. Since, as the Court's opinion quite correctly assumes, ante at 480 U. S. 585, state exercise of land use authority over federal lands is preempted by federal law, California's permit requirement must be invalid.

The permit at issue here is a "coastal development permit," required by the California Coastal Act, Cal.Pub.Res.Code Ann. § 30000 et seq. (West 1986). It is provided for by § 30600 of Chapter 7 of that Act (entitled "Development Controls"), which states that a person wishing to undertake any "development" in the coastal zone -- a term defined to include construction mining, and "change in the density or intensity of use of land," § 30106 -- must obtain a coastal development permit from a local government or the California Coastal Commission. The permit is to be granted if the proposed development is in conformity with a state-approved local coastal program or, where no such program yet exists, if the proposed development

"is in conformity with the provisions of Chapter 3 . . . and . . . will not prejudice the ability of the local government to prepare a local coastal program that is in conformity with Chapter 3."

§ 30604. The "local coastal programs" to which these provisions refer consist of two parts: (1) a land use plan, and (2) zoning ordinances, zoning maps, and other implementing actions. §§ 30511(b), 30512, 30513. Chapter 3 of the Act, with which these local coastal programs must comply, consists largely of land use prescriptions -- for example, that developments providing public recreational opportunities shall be preferred, § 30213; that oceanfront land suitable for recreational use shall be protected for recreational use and development, § 30221; that commercial recreational facilities shall have priority over private residential, general industrial, or general commercial development, but not over agriculture or coastal-dependent industry, § 30222; that oceanfront land suitable for coastal-dependent aquaculture shall be protected for that use, § 30222.5; that facilities serving the commercial fishing and recreational boating industries shall be protected and, where feasible, upgraded, § 30234; that the maximum amount of prime agricultural land shall be maintained in agricultural production, § 30241; that all other lands suitable for agricultural use shall not be converted to nonagricultural use except in specified circumstances, § 30242; that conversions of coastal commercial timberlands in units of commercial size to other uses shall be limited to providing for necessary timber processing and related facilities, § 30243; that the location and amount of new development should maintain and enhance public access to the coast, § 30252; that coastal-dependent developments shall have priority over other developments on or near the shoreline, § 30255; and that coastal-dependent industrial facilities shall be encouraged to locate or expand within existing sites, § 30260. [2]

It could hardly be clearer that the California Coastal Act is land use regulation. To compound the certainty, California has designated its Coastal Act as the State's coastal management program for purposes of the Coastal Zone Management Act (CZMA), 16 U.S.C. § 1451 et seq. Cal.Pub.Res.Code Ann. § 30008 (West 1986). The requirements for such a program include "[a] definition of what shall constitute permissible land uses and water uses within the coastal zone," 16 U.S.C. § 1454(b)(2), and "[a]n identification of the means by which the state proposes to exert control over [those] land uses and water uses." § 1454(b)(4).

The § 30600 permit requirement, of course, is one of those means of control -- and, whenever a permit application is evaluated pursuant to the statutory standards, land (or water) use management is afoot. Even if, as the State has argued before us and as the Court has been willing to postulate, California intended to employ the land use permit in this case only as a device for exacting environmental assurances, the power to demand that permit nevertheless hinges upon the State's power to do what the statutory permitting requirements authorize: to control land use. The legal status of the matter is that Granite

Rock, having received land use approval from the Federal Government, has been requested to obtain land use approval from the State of California. If state land use regulation is in fact preempted in this location, there is no justification for requiring Granite Rock to go through the motions of complying with that ultra vires request on the chance that permission will be granted with no more than environmental limitations. It is inconceivable that, if a labor union federally certified as an authorized bargaining agent sought injunctive or declaratory relief against a requirement that it submit to state certification for the same purpose, we would say that,

"[b]y choosing to seek . . . relief against the . . . requirement before discovering what conditions the [State] would have placed on the [certification], [the union] has lost the possibility"

of prevailing. Ante at 480 U. S. 588. I see no basis for making the equivalent statement here. In the one case as in the other, the demand for state approval is, in and of itself, invalid. As the Ninth Circuit said in a similar case that we summarily affirmed:

"The issue is whether [the State] has the power of ultimate control over the Government's lessee, and this issue persists whether or not a use permit would eventually be granted."

Ventura County v. Gulf Oil Corp., 601 F.2d 1080, 1085 (1979), summarily aff'd, 445 U.S. 947 (1980). Even on the assumption, therefore, that California was only using its land use permit requirement as a means of enforcing its environmental laws, Granite Rock was within its rights to ignore that requirement -- unless California has land use authority over the federal lands in question.

In fact, however, this case is even more straightforward than that, for there is no reason to believe that California was seeking anything less than what the Coastal Act requires: land use regulation. The Commission's letter to Granite Rock demanding a permit application read as follows:

"Because of the significant control and authority enjoyed by Granite Rock Company over the land subject to its mining claims at Pico Blanco and the concommitant [sic] significant diminution of federal discretionary control, this land cannot be included among the federal lands excluded from the coastal zone by the CZMA. . . . Consequently, because the land is located seaward of the coastal zone boundary established by the state legislature effective January 1, 1977, it is subject to the permit requirements of the California Coastal Act."

"This letter will serve to notify Granite Rock of its obligation to apply to the Coastal Commission for a coastal development permit for any development, as defined in Section 30106 of the Coastal Act, at the site undertaken after the date of this letter."

App. 22. This letter contains no hint that only environmental constraints are at issue, as opposed to compliance with all of the requirements of the State's coastal management program. Even in the litigation stage -- both in the District Court and in the Court of Appeals -- the argument that California was (or might be) seeking to enforce only environmental controls was merely an alternative position. The Commission's more sweeping contention was that the land in question is not excluded from the CZMA, and that the CZMA permits designated state coastal management programs to override the Mining Act. See App. to Juris. Statement A-4, A-12, A-24. That argument has not been pressed here, having been rejected by both lower courts. 768 F.2d 1077, 1080-1081 (CA9 1985); 590 F.Supp. 1361, 1370-1371 (ND Cal.1984). It is perfectly clear, however, that the assertion that the State is only enforcing its environmental laws is purely a litigating position -- and a late-asserted one at that.

On any analysis, therefore, the validity of California's demand for permit application, and the lawfulness of Granite Rock's refusal, depend entirely upon whether California has authority to regulate land use at Pico Blanco. The Court is willing to assume that California lacks such authority on account of the National Forest Management Act of 1976 (NFMA), 16 U.S.C. § 1600 et seq. (1982 ed. and Supp. III), and the Federal Land Policy and Management Act of 1976 (FLPMA), 43 U.S.C. § 1701 et seq. (1982 ed. and Supp. III). Ante at 480 U. S. 585. I believe that assumption is correct. Those statutes, as well as the CZMA, require federal officials to coordinate and consult with the States regarding use of federal lands in order to assure consistency with state land use plans to the maximum extent compatible with federal law and objectives. 16 U.S.C. §§ 1456(c)(3)(A), 1604(a); 43 U.S.C. § 1712(c). Those requirements would be superfluous, and the limitation upon federal accommodation meaningless, if the States were meant to have independent land use authority over federal lands. The Court is quite correct that the CZMA did not purport to change the status quo with regard to state authority over the use of federal lands. Ante at 480 U. S. 589-593. But as the CZMA's federal lands exclusion, 16 U.S.C. § 1453(1), and consistency review provisions, 16 U.S.C. § 1456(c)(3)(A), clearly demonstrate, that status quo was assumed to be exclusive federal regulation.

Finally, any lingering doubt that exercise of Coastal Act authority over federal lands is an exercise of land use authority preempted by federal laws is removed by the fact that that is not only the view of the federal agencies in charge of administering those laws, see Brief for United States as Amicus Curiae, but also was the original view of California, which until 1978 excluded from the Coastal Act in language exactly mirroring that of the federal lands exclusion from the CZMA, 16 U.S.C. § 1453(1),

"lands the use of which is by law subject solely to the discretion of or which is held in trust by the federal government, its officers or agents."

1976 Cal.Stats., ch. 1331, § 1, as amended by 1978 Cal.Stats., ch. 1075, § 2, codified at Cal.Pub.Res.Code Ann. § 30008 (West 1986).

Any competent lawyer, faced with a demand from the California Coastal Commission that Granite Rock obtain a § 30600 coastal development permit for its Pico Blanco operations, would have responded precisely as Granite Rock's lawyers essentially did: Our use of federal land has been approved by the Federal Government, thank you, and does not require the approval of the State. We should not allow California to claim, in the teeth of the plain language of its legislation, and in violation of the assurance it gave to the Federal Government by designating its Coastal Act as a coastal management program under the CZMA, that it would use the permitting requirement to achieve, not land use management, but only environmental controls. We should particularly not give ear to that claim since it was not the representation made to Granite Rock when application for the permit was demanded. If environmental control is, as California now assures us, its limited objective in this case, then it must simply achieve that objective by means other than a land use control scheme. If and when it does so, we may have occasion to decide (as we need not today) whether state environmental controls are also preempted. More likely, however, the question will not arise in the future, as it has not arisen in the past, because of the Federal Government's voluntary accommodation of state environmental concerns -- an accommodation that could not occur here only because California neglected to participate in the proceedings. Ante at 480 U. S. 576-577, n. 1, 591.

I would affirm the court below on the ground that the California Coastal Act permit requirement constitutes a regulation of the use of federal land, and is therefore preempted by federal law.

Notes

[1] I would not rely upon the alternative ground that the dispute between these parties is "capable of repetition, yet evading review." Ante at 480 U. S. 578. Assuming that Granite Rock submits a new 5-year plan to the Forest Service and that California again seeks to require it to comply with the coastal permitting requirements, I see no reason why that action would evade our review. See Weinstein v. Bradford, 423 U. S. 147, 423 U. S. 149 (1975). Moreover, for a dispute to be "capable of repetition," there must be a "reasonable expectation that the same complaining party [will] be subjected to the same action again." Ibid. The Court may be correct that it is possible that California will seek to enforce its permit requirement directly again, ante at 480 U. S. 578; but since California may well be able to accomplish what it wants through the Coastal Zone Management Act's consistency review procedures, 16 U.S.C. § 1456(c)(3)(A), I do not think it likely that it will do so.

[2] The State Coastal Commission is responsible for issuing coastal development permits until the Commission has certified a local land use plan, Cal.Pub.Res.Code Ann. § 30600.5(b) (West 1986), at which time the responsibility devolves upon the local government, ibid. Regardless of which governmental entity has the authority to issue the permit, the requirements for its issuance are those set forth in Chapter 3 of the California Coastal Act, discussed supra. These apply directly if a local coastal program has not been certified, § 30604(a), or by enforcement of the requirements of the local coastal program, § 30604(b), whose land use plan must conform with that Chapter in order to be certified, §§ 30512(c), 30512.1(c), 30512.2. Because local coastal programs consist of such classic land use regulation tools as a land use plan, zoning maps, zoning ordinances, and other implementing devices, §§ 30511(b), 30512, permits issued upon a showing of consistency with a local coastal program may be even more obviously land use control devices than permits issued upon a showing of consistency with the provisions of Chapter 3. But under

the plain terms of the statute, the latter no less than the former are permits for land use. To establish the contrary proposition, which is essential to its holding, the majority relies upon nothing more substantial than the statement of counsel for the Commission, in oral argument before us, that "[T]he Coastal Commission issues permits based upon compliance with the environmental criteria in the Coastal Act itself." Tr. of Oral Arg. 52, quoted ante at 480 U. S. 586, n. 2. Read literally (i.e., without inferring the adverb "exclusively"), the statement is true (the Act does contain some environmental criteria), but unhelpful to the majority's case. If, however, counsel meant to imply that the Commission's permits could not be conditioned upon compliance with the land use criteria, the statement would not only contradict the plain language of the Act, but would also be inconsistent with the litigating position taken by the Commission in the previous stages of this lawsuit, see infra at 480 U. S. 611-612.

Justice Scalia's dissent in Johnson v. Transportation Agency (March 25, 1987)

JUSTICE SCALIA, with whom THE CHIEF JUSTICE joins, and with whom JUSTICE WHITE joins in Parts I and II, dissenting.

With a clarity which, had it not proven so unavailing, one might well recommend as a model of statutory draftsmanship, Title VII of the Civil Rights Act of 1964 declares:

"It shall be an unlawful employment practice for an employer -- "

"(1) to fail or refuse to hire or to discharge any individual, or otherwise to discriminate against any individual with respect to his compensation, terms, conditions, or privileges of employment, because of such individual's race, color, religion, sex, or national origin; or "

"(2) to limit, segregate, or classify his employees or applicants for employment in any way which would deprive or tend to deprive any individual of employment opportunities or otherwise adversely affect his status as an employee, because of such individual's race, color, religion, sex, or national origin."

42 U.S.C. § 2000e-2(a). The Court today completes the process of converting this from a guarantee that race or sex will not be the basis for employment determinations to a guarantee that it often will. Ever so subtly, without even alluding to the last obstacles preserved by earlier opinions that we now push out of our path, we effectively replace the goal of a discrimination-free society with the quite incompatible goal of proportionate representation by race and by sex in the workplace. Part I of this dissent will describe the nature of the plan that the Court approves, and its effect upon this petitioner. Part II will discuss prior holdings that are tacitly overruled, and prior distinctions that are disregarded. Part III will describe the engine of discrimination we have finally completed.

I

On October 16, 1979, the County of Santa Clara adopted an Affirmative Action Program (County plan) which sought the

"attainment of a County workforce whose composition . . . includes women, disabled persons and ethnic minorities in a ratio in all job categories that reflects their distribution in the Santa Clara County area workforce."

App. 113. In order to comply with the County plan and various requirements imposed by federal and state agencies, the Transportation Agency adopted, effective December 18, 1978, the Equal Employment Opportunity Affirmative Action Plan (Agency plan or plan) at issue here. Its stated long-range goal was the same as the County plan's:

"to attain a workforce whose composition in all job levels and major job classifications approximates the distribution of women, minority and handicapped persons in the Santa Clara County workforce."

Id. at 54. The plan called for the establishment of a procedure by which Division Directors would review the ethnic and sexual composition of their workforces whenever they sought to fill a vacancy, which procedure was expected to include

"a requirement that Division Directors indicate why they did not select minorities, women and handicapped persons if such persons were on the list of eligibles considered and if the Division had an underrepresentation of such persons in the job classification being filled."

Id. at 75 (emphasis in original).

Several salient features of the plan should be noted. Most importantly, the plan's purpose was assuredly not to remedy prior sex discrimination by the Agency. It could not have been, because there was no prior sex discrimination to remedy. The majority, in cataloging the Agency's alleged misdeeds, ante at 480 U. S. 624, n. 5, neglects to mention the District Court's finding that the Agency

"has not discriminated in the past, and does not discriminate in the present against women in regard to employment opportunities in general and promotions in particular."

App. to Pet. for Cert. 13a. This finding was not disturbed by the Ninth Circuit.

Not only was the plan not directed at the results of past sex discrimination by the Agency, but its objective was not to achieve the state of affairs that this Court has dubiously assumed would result from an absence of discrimination -- an overall workforce "more or less representative of the racial and ethnic composition of the population in the community." Teamsters v. United States, 431 U. S. 324, 431 U. S. 340, n. 20 (1977). Rather, the oft-stated goal was to mirror the racial and sexual composition of the entire county labor force, not merely in the Agency workforce as a whole, but in each and every individual job category at the Agency. In a discrimination-free world, it would obviously be a statistical oddity for every job category to match the racial and sexual composition of even that portion of the county workforce qualified for that job; it would be utterly miraculous for each of them to match, as the plan expected, the composition of the entire workforce.

Quite obviously, the plan did not seek to replicate what a lack of discrimination would produce, but rather imposed racial and sexual tailoring that would, in defiance of normal expectations and laws of probability, give each protected racial and sexual group a governmentally determined "proper" proportion of each job category.

That the plan was not directed at remedying or eliminating the effects of past discrimination is most clearly illustrated by its description of what it regarded as the "Factors Hindering Goal Attainment" -- i.e., the existing impediments to the racially and sexually representative workforce that it pursued. The plan noted that it would be "difficult," App. 55, to attain its objective of across-the-board statistical parity in at least some job categories, because:

"a. Most of the positions require specialized training and experience. Until recently, relatively few minorities, women and handicapped persons sought entry into these positions. Consequently, the number of persons from these groups in the area labor force who possess the qualifications required for entry into such job classifications is limited."

"* * * *"

"c. Many of the Agency positions where women are underrepresented involve heavy labor; e.g., Road Maintenance Worker. Consequently, few women seek entry into these positions."

"* * * *"

"f. Many women are not strongly motivated to seek employment in job classifications where they have not been traditionally employed because of the limited opportunities that have existed in the past for them to work in such classifications."

Id. at 56-57. That is, the qualifications and desires of women may fail to match the Agency's Platonic ideal of a workforce. The plan concluded from this, of course, not that the ideal should be reconsidered, but that its attainment could not be immediate.

Id. at 58-60. It would, in any event, be rigorously pursued, by giving

"special consideration to Affirmative Action requirements in every individual hiring action pertaining to positions where minorities, women and handicapped persons continue to be underrepresented."

Id. at 60. [1]

Finally, the one message that the plan unmistakably communicated was that concrete results were expected, and supervisory personnel would be evaluated on the basis of the affirmative action numbers they produced. The plan's implementation was expected to

"result in a statistically measurable yearly improvement in the hiring, training and promotion of minorities, women and handicapped persons in the major job classifications utilized by the Agency where these groups are underrepresented."

Id. at 35. Its Preface declared that

"[t]he degree to which each Agency Division attains the Plan's objectives will provide a direct measure of that Division Director's personal commitment to the EEO Policy,"

ibid. (emphasis added), and the plan itself repeated that

"[t]he degree to which each Division attains the Agency Affirmative Action employment goals will provide a measure of that Director's commitment and effectiveness in carrying out the Division's EEO Affirmative Action requirements."

Id. at 44 (emphasis added). As noted earlier, supervisors were reminded of the need to give attention to affirmative action in every employment decision, and to explain their reasons for failing to hire women and minorities whenever there was an opportunity to do so.

The petitioner in the present case, Paul E. Johnson, had been an employee of the Agency since 1967, coming there from a private company where he had been a road dispatcher for 17 years. He had first applied for the position of Road Dispatcher at the Agency in 1974, coming in second. Several years later, after a reorganization resulted in a downgrading of his Road Yard Clerk II position, in which Johnson "could see no future," Tr. 127, he requested and received a voluntary demotion from Road Yard Clerk II to Road Maintenance Worker, to increase his experience and thus improve his chances for future promotion. When the Road Dispatcher job next became vacant, in 1979, he was the leading candidate -- and indeed was assigned to work out of class full-time in the vacancy, from September 1979 until June 1980. There is no question why he did not get the job.

The fact of discrimination against Johnson is much clearer, and its degree more shocking, than the majority and JUSTICE O'CONNOR'S concurrence would suggest -- largely because neither of them recites a single one of the District Court findings that govern this appeal, relying instead upon portions of the transcript which those findings implicitly rejected, and even upon a document (favorably comparing Joyce to Johnson), ante at 480 U. S. 625, that was prepared after Joyce was selected. See App. 27-28; Tr. 223-227. Worth mentioning, for example, is the trier of fact's determination that, if the Affirmative Action Coordinator had not intervened, "the decision as to whom to promote . . . would have been made by [the Road Operations Division Director]," App. to Pet. for Cert. 12a, who had recommended that Johnson be appointed to the position. Ibid. [2] Likewise, the even more extraordinary findings that James Graebner, the Agency Director who made the appointment, "did not inspect the applications and related examination records of either [Paul Johnson] or Diane Joyce before making his decision," ibid., and indeed

"did little or nothing to inquire into the results of the interview process and conclusions which [were] described as of critical importance to the selection process."

Id. at 3a. In light of these determinations, it is impossible to believe (or to think that the District Court believed) Graebner's self-serving statements relied upon by the majority and JUSTICE O'CONNOR's concurrence, such as the assertion that he

"tried to look at the whole picture, the combination of [Joyce's] qualifications and Mr. Johnson's qualifications, their test scores, their expertise, their background, affirmative action matters, things like that,"

Tr. 68 (quoted ante at 480 U. S. 625; ante at 480 U. S. 655 (O'CONNOR, J., concurring in judgment)). It was evidently enough for Graebner to know that both candidates (in the words of Johnson's counsel, to which Graebner assented) "met the

M.Q.'s, the minimum. Both were minimally qualified." Tr. 25. When asked whether he had "any basis," ibid., for determining whether one of the candidates was more qualified than the other, Graebner candidly answered, "No. . . . As I've said, they both appeared, and my conversations with people tended to corroborate, that they were both capable of performing the work." Ibid.

After a 2-day trial, the District Court concluded that Diane Joyce's gender was "the determining factor," App. to Pet. for Cert. 4a, in her selection for the position. Specifically, it found that,

"[b]ased upon the examination results and the departmental interview, [Mr. Johnson] was more qualified for the position of Road Dispatcher than Diane Joyce,"

id. at 12a; that, "[b]ut for [Mr. Johnson's] sex, male, he would have been promoted to the position of Road Dispatcher," id. at 13a; and that, "[b]ut for Diane Joyce's sex, female, she would not have been appointed to the position. . . ." Ibid. The Ninth Circuit did not reject these factual findings as clearly erroneous, nor could it have done so on the record before us. We are bound by those findings under Federal Rule of Civil Procedure 52(a).

II

The most significant proposition of law established by today's decision is that racial or sexual discrimination is permitted under Title VII when it is intended to overcome the effect, not of the employer's own discrimination, but of societal attitudes that have limited the entry of certain races, or of a particular sex, into certain jobs. Even if the societal attitudes in question consisted exclusively of conscious discrimination by other employers, this holding would contradict a decision of this Court rendered only last Term. Wygant v. Jackson Board of Education, 476 U. S. 267 (1986), held that the objective of remedying societal discrimination cannot prevent remedial affirmative action from violating the Equal Protection Clause. See id. at 476 U. S. 276; id. at 476 U. S. 288 (O'CONNOR, J., concurring in part and concurring in judgment); id. at 476 U. S. 296 (WHITE, J., concurring in judgment). While Mr. Johnson does not advance a constitutional claim here, it is most unlikely that Title VII was intended to place a lesser restraint on discrimination by public actors than is established by the Constitution. The Court has already held that the prohibitions on discrimination in Title VI, 42 U.S.C. § 2000d, are at least as stringent as those in the Constitution. See Regents of University of California v. Bakke, 438 U. S. 265, 438 U. S. 286-287 (1978) (opinion of POWELL, J.) (Title VI embodies constitutional restraints on discrimination); id. at 438 U. S. 329-340 (opinion of BRENNAN, WHITE, MARSHALL, and BLACKMUN, JJ.) (same); id. at 438 U. S. 416 (opinion of STEVENS, J., joined by Burger, C.J., and Stewart and REHNQUIST, JJ.) (Title VI "has independent force, with language and emphasis in addition to that found in the Constitution") (emphasis added). There is no good reason to think that Title VII, in this regard, is any different from Title VI. [3] Because, therefore, those justifications (e.g., the remedying of past societal wrongs) that are inadequate to insulate discriminatory action from the racial discrimination prohibitions of the Constitution are also inadequate to insulate it from the racial discrimination prohibitions of Title VII; and because the portions of Title VII at issue here treat race and sex equivalently; Wygant, which dealt with race discrimination, is fully applicable precedent, and is squarely inconsistent with today's decision. [4]

Likewise, on the assumption that the societal attitudes relied upon by the majority consist of conscious discrimination by employers, today's decision also disregards the limitations carefully expressed in last Term's opinions in Sheet Metal Workers v. EEOC, 478 U. S. 421 (1986). While those limitations were dicta, it is remarkable to see them so readily (and so silently) swept away. The question in Sheet Metal Workers was whether the remedial provision of Title VII, 42 U.S.C. § 2000e-5(g), empowers courts to order race-conscious relief for persons who were not identifiable victims of discrimination. Six Members of this Court concluded that it does, under narrowly confined circumstances. The plurality opinion for four Justices found that race-conscious relief could be ordered at least when

"an employer or a labor union has engaged in persistent or egregious discrimination, or where necessary to dissipate the lingering effects of pervasive discrimination."

478 U.S. at 478 U. S. 445 (opinion of BRENNAN, J., joined by MARSHALL, BLACKMUN, and STEVENS, JJ.). See also id. at 478 U. S. 476. JUSTICE POWELL concluded that race-conscious relief can be ordered "in cases involving particularly egregious conduct," id. at 476 U. S. 483 (concurring in part and concurring in judgment), and JUSTICE WHITE similarly limited his approval of race-conscious remedies to "unusual cases." Id. at 476 U. S. 499 (dissenting). See also Firefighters v. Cleveland, 478 U. S. 501, 478 U. S. 533 (1986) (WHITE, J., dissenting) ("I also agree with JUSTICE BRENNAN's opinion in Sheet Metal Workers . . . that, in Title VII cases, enjoining discriminatory practices and granting relief only to victims of past discrimination is the general rule, with relief for nonvictims being reserved for particularly egregious conduct"). There is no sensible basis for construing Title VII to permit employers to engage in race- or sex-conscious employment practices that courts would be forbidden from ordering them to engage in following a judicial finding of discrimination. As JUSTICE WHITE noted last Term:

"There is no statutory authority for concluding that, if an employer desires to discriminate against a white applicant or employee on racial grounds, he may do so without violating Title VII, but may not be ordered to do so if he objects. In either case, the harm to the discriminatee is the same, and there is no justification for such conduct other than as a permissible remedy for prior racial discrimination practiced by the employer involved."

Id. at 478 U. S. 533. The Agency here was not seeking to remedy discrimination -- much less "unusual" or "egregious" discrimination. Firefighters, like Wygant, is given only the most cursory consideration by the majority opinion.

In fact, however, today's decision goes well beyond merely allowing racial or sexual discrimination in order to eliminate the effects of prior societal discrimination. The majority opinion often uses the phrase "traditionally segregated job category" to describe the evil against which the plan is legitimately (according to the majority) directed. As originally used in Steelworkers v. Weber, 443 U. S. 193 (1979), that phrase described skilled jobs from which employers and unions had systematically and intentionally excluded black workers -- traditionally segregated jobs, that is, in the sense of conscious, exclusionary discrimination. See id. at 443 U. S. 197-198. But that is assuredly not the sense in which the phrase is used here. It is absurd to think that the nationwide failure of road maintenance crews, for example, to achieve the Agency's ambition of 36.4% female representation is attributable primarily, if even substantially, to systematic exclusion of women eager to shoulder pick and shovel. It is a "traditionally segregated job category" not in the Weber sense, but in the sense that, because of longstanding social attitudes, it has not been regarded by women themselves as desirable work. Or as the majority opinion puts the point, quoting approvingly the Court of Appeals:

"'A plethora of proof is hardly necessary to show that women are generally underrepresented in such positions, and that strong social pressures weigh against their participation.'"

Ante at 480 U. S. 634, n. 12 (quoting 748 F.2d 1308, 1313 (CA9 1984)). Given this meaning of the phrase, it is patently false to say that

"[t]he requirement that the 'manifest imbalance' relate to a 'traditionally segregated job category' provides assurance . . . that sex or race will be taken into account in a manner consistent with Title VII's purpose of eliminating the effects of employment discrimination."

Ante at 480 U. S. 632. There are, of course, those who believe that the social attitudes which cause women themselves to avoid certain jobs and to favor others are as nefarious as conscious, exclusionary discrimination. Whether or not that is so (and there is assuredly no consensus on the point equivalent to our national consensus against intentional discrimination), the two phenomena are certainly distinct. And it is the alteration of social attitudes, rather than the elimination of discrimination, which today's decision approves as justification for state-enforced discrimination. This is an enormous expansion, undertaken without the slightest justification or analysis.

III

I have omitted from the foregoing discussion the most obvious respect in which today's decision o'erleaps, without analysis, a barrier that was thought still to be overcome. In Weber, this Court held that a private-sector affirmative action training program that overtly discriminated against white applicants did not violate Title VII. However, although the majority does not advert to the fact, until today the applicability of Weber to public employers remained an open question. In Weber itself, see 443 U.S. at 443 U. S. 200, 443 U. S. 204, and in later decisions, see Firefighters v. Cleveland, supra, at 478 U. S. 517; Wygant, 476 U.S. at 476 U. S. 282, n. 9 (opinion of POWELL, J.), this Court has repeatedly emphasized that Weber involved only a private employer. See Williams v. New Orleans,

729 F.2d 1554, 1565 (CA5 1984) (en banc) (Gee, J., concurring) ("Writing for the Court in Weber, Justice Brennan went out of his way, on at least eleven different occasions, to point out that what was there before the Court was private affirmative action") (footnote omitted). This distinction between public and private employers has several possible justifications. Weber rested in part on the assertion that the 88th Congress did not wish to intrude too deeply into private employment decisions. See 443 U.S. at 443 U. S. 206-207. See also Firefighters v. Cleveland, supra, at 478 U. S. 519-521. Whatever validity that assertion may have with respect to private employers (and I think it negligible), it has none with respect to public employers or to the 92d Congress that brought them within Title VII. See Equal Employment Opportunity Act of 1972, Pub. L. 92-261, § 2, 86 Stat. 103, 42 U.S.C. § 2000e(a). Another reason for limiting Weber to private employers is that state agencies, unlike private actors, are subject to the Fourteenth Amendment. As noted earlier, it would be strange to construe Title VII to permit discrimination by public actors that the Constitution forbids.

In truth, however, the language of 42 U.S.C. § 2000e-2 draws no distinction between private and public employers, and the only good reason for creating such a distinction would be to limit the damage of Weber. It would be better, in my view, to acknowledge that case as fully applicable precedent, and to use the Fourteenth Amendment ramifications -- which Weber did not address and which are implicated for the first time here -- as the occasion for reconsidering and overruling it. It is well to keep in mind just how thoroughly Weber rewrote the statute it purported to construe. The language of that statute, as quoted at the outset of this dissent, is unambiguous: it is an unlawful employment practice

"to fail or refuse to hire or to discharge any individual, or otherwise to discriminate against any individual with respect to his compensation, terms, conditions, or privileges of employment, because of such individual's race, color, religion, sex, or national origin."

42 U.S.C. § 2000e-2(a). Weber disregarded the text of the statute, invoking instead its "spirit,'" 443 U.S. at 443 U. S. 201 (quoting Holy Trinity Church v. United States, 143 U. S. 457, 143 U. S. 459 (1892)), and "practical and equitable [considerations] only partially perceived, if perceived at all, by the 88th Congress," 443 U.S. at 443 U. S. 209 (BLACKMUN, J., concurring). It concluded, on the basis of these intangible guides, that Title VII's prohibition of intentional discrimination on the basis of race and sex does not prohibit intentional discrimination on the basis of race and sex, so long as it is "designed to break down old patterns of racial [or sexual] segregation and hierarchy," "does not unnecessarily trammel the interests of the white [or male] employees," "does not require the discharge of white [or male] workers and their replacement with new black [or female] hirees," "does [not] create an absolute bar to the advancement of white [or male] employees," and "is a temporary measure . . . not intended to maintain racial [or sexual] balance, but simply to eliminate a manifest racial [or sexual] imbalance." Id. at 443 U. S. 208. In effect, Weber held that the legality of intentional discrimination by private

employers against certain disfavored groups or individuals is to be judged not by Title VII, but by a judicially crafted code of conduct, the contours of which are determined by no discernible standard, aside from (as the dissent convincingly demonstrated) the divination of congressional "purposes" belied by the face of the statute and by its legislative history. We have been recasting that self-promulgated code of conduct ever since -- and what it has led us to today adds to the reasons for abandoning it.

The majority's response to this criticism of Weber, ante at 480 U. S. 629, n. 7, asserts that, since

"Congress has not amended the statute to reject our construction, . . . we . . . may assume that our interpretation was correct."

This assumption, which frequently haunts our opinions, should be put to rest. It is based, to begin with, on the patently false premise that the correctness of statutory construction is to be measured by what the current Congress desires, rather than by what the law as enacted meant. To make matters worse, it assays the current Congress' desires with respect to the particular provision in isolation, rather than (the way the provision was originally enacted) as part of a total legislative package containing many quids pro quo. Whereas the statute as originally proposed may have presented to the enacting Congress a question such as "Should hospitals be required to provide medical care for indigent patients, with federal subsidies to offset the cost?," the question theoretically asked of the later Congress, in order to establish the "correctness" of a judicial interpretation that the statute provides no subsidies, is simply "Should the medical care that hospitals are required to provide for indigent patients be federally subsidized?" Hardly the same question -- and many of those legislators who accepted the subsidy provisions in order to gain the votes necessary for enactment of the care requirement would not vote for the subsidy in isolation, now that an unsubsidized care requirement is, thanks to the judicial opinion, safely on the books. But even accepting the flawed premise that the intent of the current Congress, with respect to the provision in isolation, is determinative, one must ignore rudimentary principles of political science to draw any conclusions regarding that intent from the failure to enact legislation. The "complicated check on legislation," The Federalist No. 62, p. 378 (C. Rossiter ed. 1961), erected by our Constitution creates an inertia that makes it impossible to assert with any degree of assurance that congressional failure to act represents (1) approval of the status quo, as opposed to (2) inability to agree upon how to alter the status quo, (3) unawareness of the status quo, (4) indifference to the status quo, or even (5) political cowardice. It is interesting to speculate on how the principle that congressional inaction proves judicial correctness would apply to another issue in the civil rights field, the liability of municipal corporations under § 1983. In 1961, we held that that statute did not reach municipalities. See Monroe v. Pape, 365 U. S. 167, 365 U. S. 187 (1961). Congress took no action to overturn our decision, but we ourselves did, in Monell v. New York City Dept. of Social Services, 436 U. S. 658, 436 U. S. 663 (1978). On the majority's logic, Monell was wrongly decided, since Congress' 17 years of silence established that Monroe had not "misperceived the political will," and one could therefore "assume that [Monroe's] interpretation was correct." On the other hand, nine years have now gone by since Monell, and Congress again has not amended § 1983. Should we now "assume that [Monell's] interpretation was correct"? Rather, I think we should admit that vindication by congressional inaction is a canard.

JUSTICE STEVENS' concurring opinion emphasizes the "undoubted public interest in stability and orderly development of the law,'" ante at 480 U. S. 644 (citation omitted), that often requires adherence to an erroneous decision. As I have described above, however, today's decision is a demonstration not of stability and order, but of the instability and unpredictable expansion which the substitution of judicial improvisation for statutory text has produced. For a number of reasons, stare decisis ought not to save Weber. First, this Court has applied the doctrine of stare decisis to civil rights statutes less rigorously than to other laws. See Maine v. Thiboutot, 448 U. S. 1, 448 U. S. 33 (1980) (POWELL, J., dissenting); Monroe v. Pape, supra, at 365 U. S. 221-222 (Frankfurter, J., dissenting in part). Second, as JUSTICE STEVENS acknowledges in his concurrence, ante at 480 U. S. 644, Weber was itself a dramatic departure from the Court's prior Title VII precedents, and can scarcely be said to be "so consistent with the warp and woof of civil rights law as to be beyond question." Monell v. New York City Dept. of Social Services, supra, at 436 U. S. 696. Third, Weber was decided a mere seven years ago, and has provided little guidance to persons seeking to conform their conduct to the law, beyond the proposition that Title VII does not mean what it says. Finally,

"even under the most stringent test for the propriety of overruling a statutory decision . . . -- 'that it appear beyond doubt . . . that [the decision] misapprehended the meaning of the controlling provision,'"

436 U.S. at 436 U. S. 700 (quoting Monroe v. Pape, supra, at 365 U. S. 192 (Harlan, J., concurring)), Weber should be overruled.

In addition to complying with the commands of the statute, abandoning Weber would have the desirable side effect of eliminating the requirement of willing suspension of disbelief that is currently a credential for reading our opinions in the affirmative action field -- from Weber itself, which demanded belief that the corporate employer adopted the affirmative action program "voluntarily," rather than under practical compulsion from government contracting agencies, see 443 U.S. at 443 U. S. 204; to Bakke, a Title VI case cited as authority by the majority here, ante at 480 U. S. 638, which demanded belief that the University of California took race into account as merely one of the many diversities to which it felt it was educationally important to expose its medical students, see 438 U.S. at 438 U. S. 311-315; to today's opinion, which -- in the face of a plan obviously designed to force promoting officials to prefer candidates from the favored racial and sexual classes, warning them that their "personal commitment" will be determined by how successfully they "attain" certain numerical goals, and in the face of a particular promotion awarded to the less qualified applicant by an official who "did little or nothing" to inquire into sources "critical" to determining the final candidates' relative qualifications other than their sex -- in the face of all this, demands belief that we are dealing here with no more than a program that "merely authorizes that consideration be given to affirmative action concerns when evaluating qualified applicants." Ante at 480 U. S. 638. Any line of decisions rooted so firmly in naivete must be wrong.

The majority emphasizes, as though it is meaningful, that "No persons are automatically excluded from consideration; all are able to have their qualifications weighed against those of other applicants." Ibid. One is reminded of the exchange from Shakespeare's King Henry the Fourth, Part I:

"GLENDOWER: I can call Spirits from the vasty Deep."

"HOTSPUR: Why, so can I, or so can any man. But will they come when you do call for them?"

Act III, Scene I, lines 53-55. Johnson was indeed entitled to have his qualifications weighed against those of other applicants -- but more to the point, he was virtually assured that, after the weighing, if there was any minimally qualified applicant from one of the favored groups, he would be rejected.

Similarly hollow is the Court's assurance that we would strike this plan down if it "failed to take distinctions in qualifications into account," because that "would dictate mere blind hiring by the numbers." Ante at 480 U. S. 636. For what the Court means by "taking distinctions in qualifications into account" consists of no more than eliminating from the applicant pool those who are not even minimally qualified for the job. Once that has been done, once the promoting officer assures himself that all the candidates before him are "M.Q.'s" (minimally qualifieds), he can then ignore, as the Agency Director did here, how much better than minimally qualified some of the candidates may be, and can proceed to appoint from the pool solely on the basis of race or sex, until the affirmative action "goals" have been reached. The requirement that the employer "take distinctions in qualifications into account" thus turns out to be an assurance, not that candidates' comparative merits will always be considered, but only that none of the successful candidates selected over the others solely on the basis of their race or sex will be utterly unqualified. That may be of great comfort to those concerned with American productivity; and it is undoubtedly effective in reducing the effect of affirmative action discrimination upon those in the upper strata of society, who (unlike road maintenance workers, for example) compete for employment in professional and semiprofessional fields where, for many reasons, including most notably the effects of past discrimination, the numbers of "M.Q." applicants from the favored groups are substantially less. But I fail to see how it has any relevance to whether selecting among final candidates solely on the basis of race or sex is permissible under Title VII, which prohibits discrimination on the basis of race or sex. [5]

Today's decision does more, however, than merely reaffirm Weber, and more than merely extend it to public actors. It is impossible not to be aware that the practical effect of our holding is to accomplish de facto what the law -- in language even plainer than that ignored in Weber, see 42 U.S.C. § 2000e-2(j) -- forbids anyone from accomplishing de jure: in many contexts, it effectively requires employers, public as well as private, to engage in intentional discrimination on the basis of race or sex. This Court's prior interpretations of Title VII, especially the decision in Griggs v. Duke Power Co., 401 U. S. 424 (1971), subject employers to a potential Title VII suit whenever there is a noticeable imbalance in the representation of minorities or women in the employer's workforce. Even the employer who is confident of ultimately prevailing in such a suit must contemplate the expense and adverse publicity of a trial, because the extent of the imbalance, and the "job relatedness" of his selection criteria, are questions of fact to be explored through rebuttal and counterrebuttal of a "prima facie case" consisting of no more than the showing that the employer's selection process "selects those from the protected class at a significantly' lesser rate than their counterparts." B. Schlei & P. Grossman, Employment Discrimination Law 91 (2d ed. 1983). If, however, employers are free to discriminate through affirmative action, without fear of "reverse discrimination" suits by their nonminority or male victims, they are offered a threshold defense against Title VII liability premised on numerical disparities. Thus, after today's decision, the failure to engage in reverse discrimination is economic folly, and arguably a breach of duty to shareholders or taxpayers, wherever the cost of anticipated Title VII litigation exceeds the cost of hiring less capable (though still minimally capable) workers. (This situation is more likely to obtain, of course, with respect to the least skilled jobs -- perversely creating an incentive to discriminate against precisely those members of the nonfavored groups least likely to have profited from societal discrimination in the past.) It is predictable, moreover, that this incentive will be greatly magnified by economic pressures brought to bear by government contracting agencies upon employers who refuse to discriminate in the fashion we have now approved. A statute designed to establish a color-blind and gender-blind workplace has thus been converted into a powerful engine of racism and sexism, not merely permitting intentional race- and sex-based discrimination, but often making it, through operation of the legal system, practically compelled.

It is unlikely that today's result will be displeasing to politically elected officials, to whom it provides the means of quickly accommodating the demands of organized groups to achieve concrete, numerical improvement in the economic status of particular constituencies. Nor will it displease the world of corporate and governmental employers (many of whom have filed briefs as amici in the present case, all on the side of Santa Clara) for whom the cost of hiring less qualified workers is often substantially less -- and infinitely more predictable -- than the cost of litigating Title VII cases and of seeking to convince federal agencies by nonnumerical means that no discrimination exists. In fact, the only losers in the process are the Johnsons of the country, for whom Title VII has been not merely repealed, but actually inverted. The irony is that these individuals -- predominantly unknown, unaffluent, unorganized -- suffer this injustice at the hands of a Court fond of thinking itself the champion of the politically impotent. I dissent.

Notes

[1] This renders utterly incomprehensible the majority's assertion that

"the Agency acknowledged that [its long-term goal] could not by itself necessarily justify taking into account the sex of applicants for positions in all job categories."

Ante at 480 U. S. 635.

[2] The character of this intervention, and the reasoning behind it, was described by the Agency Director in his testimony at trial:

"Q. How did you happen to become involved in this particular promotional opportunity?"

"A. I . . . became aware that there was a difference of opinion between specifically the Road Operations people [Mr. Shields] and the Affirmative Action Director [Mr. Morton] as to the desirability of certain of the individuals to be promoted."

"* * * *"

". . . Mr. Shields felt that Mr. Johnson should be appointed to that position."

"Q. Mr. Morton felt that Diane Joyce should be appointed?"

"A. Mr. Morton was less interested in the particular individual; he felt that this was an opportunity for us to take a step toward meeting our affirmative action goals, and because there was only one person on the [eligibility] list who was one of the protected groups, he felt that this afforded us an opportunity to meet those goals through the appointment of that member of a protected group."

Tr. 16-18.

[3] To support the proposition that Title VII is more narrow than Title VI, the majority repeats the reasons for the dictum to that effect set forth in Steelworkers v. Weber, 443 U. S. 193, 443 U. S. 206, n. 6 (1979) -- a case which, as JUSTICE O'CONNOR points out, ante at 480 U. S. 651-652, could reasonably be read as consistent with the constitutional standards of Wygant. Those reasons are unpersuasive, consisting only of the existence in Title VII of 42 U.S.C. § 2000e-2(j) (the implausibility of which, as a restriction upon the scope of Title VII, was demonstrated by CHIEF JUSTICE REHNQUIST's literally unanswered Weber dissent) and the fact that Title VI pertains to recipients of federal funds, while Title VII pertains to employers generally. The latter fact, while true and perhaps interesting, is not conceivably a reason for giving to virtually identical categorical language the interpretation, in one case, that intentional discrimination is forbidden, and, in the other case, that it is not. Compare 42 U.S.C. § 2000d ("No person . . . shall, on the ground of race, color, or national origin, be . . . subjected to discrimination"), with § 2000e-2(a)(1) (no employer shall "discriminate against any individual . . . because of such individual's race, color, religion, sex, or national origin").

[4] JUSTICE O'CONNOR's concurrence at least makes an attempt to bring this Term into accord with last. Under her reading of Title VII, an employer may discriminate affirmatively, so to speak, if he has a "firm basis" for believing that he might be guilty of (nonaffirmative) discrimination under the Act, and if his action is designed to remedy that suspected prior discrimination. Ante at 480 U. S. 649. This is something of a halfway house between leaving employers scot-free to discriminate against disfavored groups, as the majority opinion does, and prohibiting discrimination, as do the words of Title VII. In

the present case, although the District Court found that in fact no sex discrimination existed, JUSTICE O'CONNOR would find a "firm basis" for the agency's belief that sex discrimination existed in the "inexorable zero": the complete absence, prior to Diane Joyce, of any women in the Agency's skilled positions. There are two problems with this: First, even positing a "firm basis" for the Agency's belief in prior discrimination, as I have discussed above, the plan was patently not designed to remedy that prior discrimination, but rather to establish a sexually representative workforce. Second, even an absolute zero is not "inexorable." While it may inexorably provide "firm basis" for belief in the mind of an outside observer, it cannot conclusively establish such a belief on the employer's part, since he may be aware of the particular reasons that account for the zero. That is quite likely to be the case here, given the nature of the jobs we are talking about and the list of "Factors Hindering Goal Attainment" recited by the Agency plan. See supra at 480 U. S. 622. The question is in any event one of fact, which, if it were indeed relevant to the outcome, would require a remand to the District Court, rather than an affirmance.

[5] In a footnote purporting to respond to this dissent's (nonexistent) "predict[ion] that today's decision will loose a flood of less qualified' minorities and women upon the workforce," ante at 480 U. S. 641, n. 17, the majority accepts the contention of the American Society for Personnel Administration that there is no way to determine who is the best qualified candidate for a job such as Road Dispatcher. This effectively constitutes appellate reversal of a finding of fact by the District Court in the present case ("[P]laintiff was more qualified for the position of Road Dispatcher than Diane Joyce," App. to Pet. for Cert. 12a). More importantly, it has staggering implications for future Title VII litigation, since the most common reason advanced for failing to hire a member of a protected group is the superior qualification of the hired individual. I am confident, however, that the Court considers this argument no more enduring than I do.

Justice Scalia's dissent in Arkansas Writers' Project v. Ragland (April 22, 1987)

JUSTICE SCALIA, with whom THE CHIEF JUSTICE joins, dissenting.

All government displays an enduring tendency to silence, or to facilitate silencing, those voices that it disapproves. In the case of the Judicial Branch of Government, the principal restraint upon that tendency, as upon other judicial error, is the requirement that judges write opinions providing logical reasons for treating one situation differently from another. I dissent from today's decision because it provides no rational basis for distinguishing the subsidy scheme here under challenge from many others that are common and unquestionably lawful. It thereby introduces into First Amendment law an element of arbitrariness that ultimately erodes, rather than fosters, the important freedoms at issue.

The Court's opinion does not dispute, and I think it evident, that the tax exemption in this case has a rational basis sufficient to sustain the tax scheme against ordinary equal protection attack, see, e.g., Massachusetts Board of Retirement v. Murgia, 427 U. S. 307, 427 U. S. 312 (1976) (per curiam). Though assuredly not "narrowly tailored," it is reasonably related to the legitimate goals of encouraging small publishers with limited audiences and advertising revenues (a category which in the State's judgment includes most publishers of religious, professional, trade, and sports magazines) and of avoiding the collection of taxes where administrative cost exceeds tax proceeds. See Brief for Appellee 15-16. The exemption is found invalid, however, because it does not pass the "strict scrutiny" test applicable to discriminatory restriction or prohibition of speech, namely, that it be "necessary to serve a compelling state interest and . . . narrowly drawn to achieve that end." Ante at 481 U. S. 231; cf. Police Department of Chicago v. Mosley, 408 U. S. 92, 408 U. S. 101 (1972) (discriminatory ban on picketing); Carey v. Brown, 447 U. S. 455, 447 U. S. 461-462 (1980) (same).

Here, as in the Court's earlier decision in Minneapolis Star & Tribune Co. v. Minnesota Comm'r of Revenue, 460 U. S. 575 (1983), application of the "strict scrutiny" test rests upon the premise that for First Amendment purposes denial of exemption from taxation is equivalent to regulation. That premise is demonstrably erroneous, and cannot be consistently applied. Our opinions have long recognized -- in First Amendment contexts as elsewhere -- the reality that tax exemptions, credits, and deductions are "a form of subsidy that is administered through the tax system," and the general rule that

"a legislature's decision not to subsidize the exercise of a fundamental right does not infringe the right, and thus is not subject to strict scrutiny."

Regan v. Taxation With Representation of Washington, 461 U. S. 540, 461 U. S. 544, 461 U. S. 549 (1983) (upholding denial of tax exemption for organization engaged in lobbying even though veterans' organizations received exemption regardless of lobbying activities). See also Cammarano v. United States, 358 U. S. 498, 358 U. S. 513 (1959) (deduction for lobbying activities); Buckley v. Valeo, 424 U. S. 1, 424 U. S. 93-95 (1976) (declining to apply strict scrutiny to campaign finance law that excludes certain candidates); Harris v. McRae, 448 U. S. 297, 448 U. S. 324-326 (1980) (declining to apply strict scrutiny to legislative decision not to subsidize abortions even though other medical procedures were subsidized); Maher v. Roe, 432 U. S. 464 (1977) (same).

The reason that denial of participation in a tax exemption or other subsidy scheme does not necessarily "infringe" a fundamental right is that -- unlike direct restriction or prohibition -- such a denial does not, as a general rule, have any significant coercive effect. It may, of course, be manipulated so as to do so, in which case the courts will be available to provide relief. But that is not remotely the case here. It is implausible that the 4% sales tax, generally applicable to all sales in the State with the few enumerated exceptions, was meant to inhibit, or had the effect of inhibiting, this appellant's publication.

Perhaps a more stringent, prophylactic rule is appropriate, and can consistently be applied, when the subsidy pertains to the expression of a particular viewpoint on a matter of political concern -- a tax exemption, for example, that is expressly available only to publications that take a particular point of view on a controversial issue of foreign policy.

Political speech has been accorded special protection elsewhere. See, e.g., FCC v. League of Women Voters of California, 468 U. S. 364, 468 U. S. 375-376 (1984) (invalidating ban on editorializing by recipients of grants from the Corporation for Public Broadcasting, in part on ground that political speech "is entitled to the most exacting degree of First Amendment protection"); Connick v. Myers, 461 U. S. 138, 461 U. S. 143-146 (1983) (discussing history of First Amendment protection for political speech by public employees); Red Lion Broadcasting Co. v. FCC, 395 U. S. 367 (1969) (upholding FCC's "fairness doctrine," which imposes special obligations upon broadcasters with regard to "controversial issues of public importance"). There is no need, however, and it is realistically quite impossible, to extend to all speech the same degree of protection against exclusion from a subsidy that one might think appropriate for opposing shades of political expression.

By seeking to do so, the majority casts doubt upon a wide variety of tax preferences and subsidies that draw distinctions based upon subject matter. The United States Postal Service, for example, grants a special bulk rate to written material disseminated by certain nonprofit organizations -- religious, educational, scientific, philanthropic, agricultural, labor, veterans', and fraternal organizations. See Domestic Mail Manual § 623 (1985). Must this preference be justified by a "compelling governmental need" because a nonprofit organization devoted to some other purpose -- dissemination of information about boxing, for example -- does not receive the special rate? The Kennedy Center, which is subsidized by the Federal Government in the amount of up to $23 million per year, see 20 U.S.C. § 76n(a), is authorized by statute to "present classical and contemporary music, opera, drama, dance, and poetry." § 76j. Is this subsidy subject to strict scrutiny because other kinds of expressive activity, such as learned lectures and political speeches, are excluded? Are government research grant programs or the funding activities of the Corporation for Public Broadcasting, see 47 U.S.C. § 396(g)(2), subject to strict scrutiny because they provide money for the study or exposition of some subjects, but not others?

Because there is no principled basis to distinguish the subsidization of speech in these areas -- which we would surely uphold -- from the subsidization that we strike down here, our decision today places the granting or denial of protection within our own idiosyncratic discretion. In my view, that threatens First Amendment rights infinitely more than the tax exemption at issue. I dissent.

Justice Scalia's dissent in Edwards v. Aguillard (June 19, 1987) [Notes omitted]

JUSTICE SCALIA, with whom THE CHIEF JUSTICE joins, dissenting.

Even if I agreed with the questionable premise that legislation can be invalidated under the Establishment Clause on the basis of its motivation alone, without regard to its effects, I would still find no justification for today's decision. The Louisiana legislators who passed the "Balanced Treatment for Creation-Science and Evolution-Science Act" (Balanced Treatment Act), La.Rev.Stat.Ann. §§ 17:286.1-17:286.7 (West 1982), each of whom had sworn to support the Constitution, [n1] were well aware of the potential Establishment Clause problems, and considered that aspect of the legislation with great care. After seven hearings and several months of study, resulting in substantial revision of the original proposal, they approved the Act overwhelmingly, and specifically articulated the secular purpose they meant it to serve. Although the record contains abundant evidence of the sincerity of that purpose (the only issue pertinent to this case), the Court today holds, essentially on the basis of "its visceral knowledge regarding what must have motivated the legislators," 778 F.2d 225, 227 (CA5 1985) (Gee, J., dissenting) (emphasis added), that the members of the Louisiana Legislature knowingly violated their oaths and then lied about it. I dissent. Had requirements of the Balanced Treatment Act that are not apparent on its face been clarified by an interpretation of the Louisiana Supreme Court, or by the manner of its implementation, the Act might well be found unconstitutional; but the question of its constitutionality cannot rightly be disposed of on the gallop, by impugning the motives of its supporters.

I

This case arrives here in the following posture: the Louisiana Supreme Court has never been given an opportunity to interpret the Balanced Treatment Act, State officials have never attempted to implement it, and it has never been the subject of a full evidentiary hearing. We can only guess at its meaning. We know that it forbids instruction in either "creation science" or "evolution science" without instruction in the other, § 17:286.4A, but the parties are sharply divided over what creation science consists of. Appellants insist that it is a collection of educationally valuable scientific data that has been censored from classrooms by an embarrassed scientific establishment. Appellees insist it is not science at all, but thinly veiled religious doctrine. Both interpretations of the intended meaning of that phrase find considerable support in the legislative history.

At least at this stage in the litigation, it is plain to me that we must accept appellants' view of what the statute means. To begin with, the statute itself defines "creation science" as "the scientific evidences for creation and inferences from those scientific evidences." § 17:286.3(2) (emphasis added). If, however, that definition is not thought sufficiently helpful, the means by which the Louisiana Supreme Court will give the term more precise content is quite clear -- and again, at this stage in the litigation, favors the appellants' view. "Creation science" is unquestionably a "term of art," see Brief for 72 Nobel Laureates et al. as Amici Curiae 20, and thus, under Louisiana law, is "to be interpreted according to [its] received meaning and acceptation with the learned in the art, trade or profession to which [it] refer[s]." La.Civ.Code Ann., Art. 15 (West 1952). [n2] The only evidence in the record of the "received meaning and acceptation" of "creation science" is found in five affidavits filed by appellants. In those affidavits, two scientists, a philosopher, a theologian, and an educator, all of whom claim extensive knowledge of creation science, swear that it is essentially a collection of scientific data supporting the theory that the physical universe and life within it appeared suddenly, and have not changed substantially since appearing. See App. to Juris. Statement A-19 (Kenyon); id. at A-36 (Morrow); id. at A-41 (Miethe). These experts insist that creation science is a strictly scientific concept that can be presented without religious reference. See id. at A-19 - A-20, A-35 (Kenyon); id. at A-36 - A-38 (Morrow); id. at A-40, A-41, A-43 (Miethe); id. at A-47, A-48 (Most); id. at A-49 (Clinkert). At this point, then, we must assume that the Balanced Treatment Act does not require the presentation of religious doctrine.

Nothing in today's opinion is plainly to the contrary, but what the statute means and what it requires are of rather little concern to the Court. Like the Court of Appeals, 765 F.2d 1251, 1253, 1254 (CA5 1985), the Court finds it necessary to consider only the motives of the legislators who supported the Balanced Treatment Act, ante at 482 U.S. 586"]586, 593-594, 596. After examining the statute, its legislative history, and its historical and social context, the Court holds that the Louisiana Legislature acted without "a secular legislative purpose," and that the Act therefore fails the "purpose" prong of the three-part test set forth in 586, 593-594, 596. After examining the statute, its legislative history, and its historical and social context, the Court holds that the Louisiana Legislature acted without "a secular legislative purpose," and that the Act therefore fails the "purpose" prong of the three-part test set forth in Lemon v. Kurtzman, 403 U.S. 602, 612 (1971). As I explain below, infra at 636-640, I doubt whether that "purpose" requirement of Lemon is a proper interpretation of the Constitution; but even if it were, I could not agree with the Court's assessment that the requirement was not satisfied here.

This Court has said little about the first component of the Lemon test. Almost invariably, we have effortlessly discovered a secular purpose for measures challenged under the Establishment Clause, typically devoting no more than a sentence or two to the matter. See, e.g., Witters v. Washington Dept. of Services for Blind, 474 U.S. 481, 485-486 (1986); Grand Rapids School District v. Ball, 473 U.S. 373, 383 (1985); Mueller v. Allen, 463 U.S. 388, 394-395 (1983); Larkin v. Grendel's Den, Inc., 459 U.S. 116, 123-124 (1982); Widmar v. Vincent, 454 U.S. 263, 271 (1981); Committee for Public Education & Religious Liberty v. Regan, 444 U.S. 646, 654, 657 (1980); Wolman v. Walter, 433 U.S. 229, 236 (1977) (plurality opinion); Meek v. Pittenger, 421 U.S. 349, 363 (1975); Committee for Public Education & Religious Liberty v. Nyquist, 413 U.S. 756, 773 (1973); Levitt v. Committee for Public Education & Religious Liberty, 413 U.S. 472, 479-480, n. 7 (1973); Tilton v. Richardson, 403 U.S. 672, 678-679 (1971) (plurality opinion); Lemon v. Kurtzman, supra, at 613. In fact, only once before deciding Lemon, and twice since, have we invalidated a law for lack of a secular purpose. See Wallace v. Jaffree, 472 U.S. 38 (1985); Stone v. Graham, 449 U.S. 39 (1980) (per curiam); Epperson v. Arkansas, 393 U.S. 97 (1968).

Nevertheless, a few principles have emerged from our cases, principles which should, but to an unfortunately large extent do not, guide the Court's application of Lemon today. It is clear, first of all, that regardless of what "legislative purpose" may mean in other contexts, for the purpose of the Lemon test, it means the "actual" motives of those responsible for the challenged action. The Court recognizes this, see ante at 585, as it has in the past, see, e.g., Witters v. Washington Dept. of Services for Blind, supra, at 486; Wallace v. Jaffree, supra, at 56. Thus, if those legislators who supported the Balanced Treatment Act in fact acted with a "sincere" secular purpose, ante at 587, the Act survives the first component of the Lemon test, regardless of whether that purpose is likely to be achieved by the provisions they enacted.

Our cases have also confirmed that, when the Lemon Court referred to "a secular . . . purpose," 403 U.S. at 403 U.S. 612"]612, it meant "a secular purpose." The author of Lemon, writing for the Court, has said that invalidation under the purpose prong is appropriate when "there [is] no question that the statute or activity was motivated wholly by religious considerations." 612, it meant "a secular purpose." The author of Lemon, writing for the Court, has said that invalidation under the purpose prong is appropriate when "there [is] no question that the statute or activity was motivated wholly by religious considerations." Lynch v. Donnelly, 465 U.S. 668, 680 (1984) (Burger, C.J.) (emphasis added); see also id. at 681, n. 6; Wallace v. Jaffree, supra, at 56 ("[T]he First Amendment requires that a statute must be invalidated if it is entirely motivated by a purpose to advance religion") (emphasis added; footnote omitted). In all three cases in which we struck down laws under the Establishment Clause for lack of a secular purpose, we found that the legislature's sole motive was to promote religion. See Wallace v. Jaffree, supra, at 56, 57, 60; Stone v. Graham, supra, at 41, 43, n. 5; Epperson v. Arkansas, supra, at 103, 107-108; see also Lynch v. Donnelly, supra, at 680 (describing Stone and Epperson as cases in which we invalidated laws "motivated wholly by religious considerations"). Thus, the majority's invalidation of the Balanced Treatment Act is defensible only if the record indicates that the Louisiana Legislature had no secular purpose.

It is important to stress that the purpose forbidden by Lemon is the purpose to "advance religion." 403 U.S. at 613; accord, ante at 585 ("promote" religion); Witters v. Washington Dept. of Services for Blind, supra, at 486 ("endorse religion"); Wallace v. Jaffree, 472 U.S. at 56 ("advance religion"); ibid. ("endorse . . . religion"); Committee for Public Education & Religious Liberty v. Nyquist, supra, at 788 ("'advancing' . . . religion"); Levitt v. Committee for Public Education & Religious Liberty, supra, at 481 ("advancing religion"); Walz v. Tax Comm'n of New York City, 397 U.S. 664, 674 (1970) ("establishing, sponsoring, or supporting religion"); Board of Education v. Allen, 392 U.S. 236, 243 (1968) ("'advancement or inhibition of religion'") (quoting Abington School Dist. v. Schempp, 374 U.S. 203, 222 (1963)). Our cases in no way imply that the Establishment Clause forbids legislators merely to act upon their religious convictions. We surely would not strike down a law providing money to feed the hungry or shelter the homeless if it could be demonstrated that, but for the religious beliefs of the legislators, the funds would not have been approved. Also, political activism by the religiously motivated is part of our heritage. Notwithstanding the majority's implication to the contrary, ante at 589-591, we do not presume that the sole purpose of a law is to advance religion merely because it was supported strongly by organized religions or by adherents of particular faiths. See Walz v.

Tax Comm'n of New York City, supra, at 670; cf. Harris v. McRae, 448 U.S. 297, 319-320 (1980). To do so would deprive religious men and women of their right to participate in the political process. Today's religious activism may give us the Balanced Treatment Act, but yesterday's resulted in the abolition of slavery, and tomorrow's may bring relief for famine victims.

Similarly, we will not presume that a law's purpose is to advance religion merely because it "'happens to coincide or harmonize with the tenets of some or all religions,'" Harris v. McRae, supra, at 319 (quoting McGowan v. Maryland, 366 U.S. 420, 442 (1961)), or because it benefits religion, even substantially. We have, for example, turned back Establishment Clause challenges to restrictions on abortion funding, Harris v. McRae, supra, and to Sunday closing laws, McGowan v. Maryland, supra, despite the fact that both "agre[e] with the dictates of [some] Judaeo-Christian religions," id. at 442.

In many instances, the Congress or state legislatures conclude that the general welfare of society, wholly apart from any religious considerations, demands such regulation.

Ibid. On many past occasions, we have had no difficulty finding a secular purpose for governmental action far more likely to advance religion than the Balanced Treatment Act. See, e.g., Mueller v. Allen, 463 U.S. at 394-395 (tax deduction for expenses of religious education); Wolman v. Walter, 433 U.S. at 236 (plurality opinion) (aid to religious schools); Meek v. Pittenger, 421 U.S. at 363 (same); Committee for Public Education & Religious Liberty v. Nyquist, 413 U.S. at 773 (same); Lemon v. Kurtzman, 403 U.S. at 613 (same); Walz v. Tax Comm'n of New York City, supra, at 672 (tax exemption for church property); Board of Education v. Allen, supra, at 243 (textbook loans to students in religious schools). Thus, the fact that creation science coincides with the beliefs of certain religions, a fact upon which the majority relies heavily, does not itself justify invalidation of the Act.

Finally, our cases indicate that even certain kinds of governmental actions undertaken with the specific intention of improving the position of religion do not "advance religion" as that term is used in Lemon. 403 U.S. at 613. Rather, we have said that, in at least two circumstances, government must act to advance religion, and that, in a third, it may do so.

First, since we have consistently described the Establishment Clause as forbidding not only state action motivated by the desire to advance religion, but also that intended to "disapprove," "inhibit," or evince "hostility" toward religion, see, e.g., ante at 585 ("'disapprove'") (quoting Lynch v. Donnelly, supra, at 690 (O'CONNOR, J., concurring)); Lynch v. Donnelly, supra, at 673 ("hostility"); Committee for Public Education & Religious Liberty v. Nyquist, supra, at 788 ("'inhibi[t]'"); and since we have said that governmental "neutrality" toward religion is the preeminent goal of the First Amendment, see, e.g., Grand Rapids School District v. Ball, 473 U.S. at 382; Roemer v. Maryland Public Works Bd., 426 U.S. 736, 747 (1976) (plurality opinion); Committee for Public Education & Religious Liberty v. Nyquist, supra, at 792-793; a State which discovers that its employees are inhibiting religion must take steps to prevent them from doing so, even though its purpose would clearly be to advance religion. Cf. Walz v. Tax Comm'n of New York City, supra, at 673. Thus, if the Louisiana Legislature sincerely believed that the State's science teachers were being hostile to religion, our cases indicate that it could act to eliminate that hostility without running afoul of Lemon's purpose test.

Second, we have held that intentional governmental advancement of religion is sometimes required by the Free Exercise Clause. For example, in Hobbie v. Unemployment Appeals Comm'n of Fla., 480 U.S. 136 (1987); Thomas v. Review Bd., Indiana Employment Security Div., 450 U.S. 707 (1981); Wisconsin v. Yoder, 406 U.S. 205 (1972); and Sherbert v. Verner, 374 U.S. 398 (1963), we held that, in some circumstances, States must accommodate the beliefs of religious citizens by exempting them from generally applicable regulations. We have not yet come close to reconciling Lemon and our Free Exercise cases, and typically we do not really try. See, e.g., Hobbie v. Unemployment Appeals Comm'n of Fla., supra, at 144-145; Thomas v. Review Bd., Indiana Employment Security Div., supra, at 719-720. It is clear, however, that members of the Louisiana Legislature were not impermissibly motivated for purposes of the Lemon test if they believed that approval of the Balanced Treatment Act was required by the Free Exercise Clause.

We have also held that, in some circumstances, government may act to accommodate religion, even if that action is not required by the First Amendment. See Hobbie v. Unemployment Appeals Comm'n of Fla., supra, at 144-145. It is well established that

[t]he limits of permissible state accommodation to religion are by no means coextensive with the noninterference mandated by the Free Exercise Clause.

Walz v. Tax Comm'n of New York City, supra, at 673; see also Gillette v. United States, 401 U.S. 437, 453 (1971). We have implied that voluntary governmental accommodation of religion is not only permissible, but desirable. See, e.g., ibid. Thus, few would contend that Title VII of the Civil Rights Act of 1964, which both forbids religious discrimination by private sector employers, 78 Stat. 255, 42 U.S.C. § 2000e-2(a)(1), and requires them reasonably to accommodate the religious practices of their employees, § 2000e(j), violates the Establishment Clause, even though its "purpose" is, of course, to advance religion, and even though it is almost certainly not required by the Free Exercise Clause. While we have warned that, at some point, accommodation may devolve into "an unlawful fostering of religion," Hobbie v. Unemployment Appeals Comm'n of Fla., supra, at 145, we have not suggested precisely (or even roughly) where that point might be. It is possible, then, that, even if the sole motive of those voting for the Balanced Treatment Act was to advance religion, and its passage was not actually required, or even believed to be required, by either the Free Exercise or Establishment Clauses, the Act would nonetheless survive scrutiny under Lemon's purpose test.

One final observation about the application of that test: although the Court's opinion gives no hint of it, in the past we have repeatedly affirmed "our reluctance to attribute unconstitutional motives to the States." Mueller v. Allen, supra, at 394; see also Lynch v. Donnelly, 465 U.S. at 699 (BRENNAN, J., dissenting). We "presume that legislatures act in a constitutional manner." Illinois v. Krull, 480 U.S. 340, 351 (1987); see also Clements v. Fashing, 457 U.S. 957, 963 (1982) (plurality opinion); Rostker v. Goldberg, 453 U.S. 57, 64 (1981); McDonald v. Board of Election Comm'rs of Chicago, 394 U.S. 802, 809 (1969). Whenever we are called upon to judge the constitutionality of an act of a state legislature,

we must have "due regard to the fact that this Court is not exercising a primary judgment, but is sitting in judgment upon those who also have taken the oath to observe the Constitution and who have the responsibility for carrying on government."

Rostker v. Goldberg, supra, at 64 (quoting Joint Anti-Fascist Refugee Committee v. McGrath, 341 U.S. 123, 164 (1951) (Frankfurter, J., concurring)). This is particularly true, we have said, where the legislature has specifically considered the question of a law's constitutionality. Ibid.

With the foregoing in mind, I now turn to the purposes underlying adoption of the Balanced Treatment Act.

II

A

We have relatively little information upon which to judge the motives of those who supported the Act. About the only direct evidence is the statute itself and transcripts of the seven committee hearings at which it was considered. Unfortunately, several of those hearings were sparsely attended, and the legislators who were present revealed little about their motives. We have no committee reports, no floor debates, no remarks inserted into the legislative history, no statement from the Governor, and no postenactment statements or testimony from the bill's sponsor or any other legislators. Cf. Wallace v. Jaffree, 472 U.S. at 43, 56-57. Nevertheless, there is ample evidence that the majority is wrong in holding that the Balanced Treatment Act is without secular purpose.

At the outset, it is important to note that the Balanced Treatment Act did not fly through the Louisiana Legislature on wings of fundamentalist religious fervor -- which would be unlikely, in any event, since only a small minority of the State's citizens belong to fundamentalist religious denominations. See B. Quinn, H. Anderson, M. Bradley, P. Goetting, & P. Shriver, Churches and Church Membership in the United States 16 (1982). The Act had its genesis (so to speak) in legislation introduced by Senator Bill Keith in June, 1980. After two hearings before the Senate Committee on Education, Senator Keith asked that his bill be referred to a study commission composed of members of both Houses of the Louisiana Legislature. He expressed hope that the joint committee would give the bill careful consideration and determine whether his arguments were "legitimate." 1 App. E-29 - E-30. The committee met twice during the interim, heard testimony (both for and against the bill) from several witnesses, and received staff reports. Senator Keith introduced his bill again when the legislature reconvened. The Senate Committee on Education held two more hearings, and approved the bill after substantially amending it (in part over Senator Keith's objection). After approval by the full Senate, the bill was referred to the House Committee on Education. That committee conducted a lengthy hearing, adopted further amendments, and sent the bill on to the full House, where it received favorable consideration. The Senate concurred in the House amendments, and, on July 20, 1981, the Governor signed the bill into law.

Senator Keith's statements before the various committees that considered the bill hardly reflect the confidence of a man preaching to the converted. He asked his colleagues to "keep an open mind," and not to be "biased" by misleading characterizations of creation science. Id. at E-33. He also urged them to "look at this subject on its merits, and not on some preconceived idea." Id. at E-34; see also 2 id. at E-491. Senator Keith's reception was not especially warm. Over his strenuous objection, the Senate Committee on Education voted 5-1 to amend his bill to deprive it of any force; as amended, the bill merely gave teachers permission to balance the teaching of creation science or evolution with the other. 1 id. at E-442 - E-461. The House Committee restored the "mandatory" language to the bill by a vote of only 6-5, 2 id. at E-626 - E-627, and both the full House (by vote of 52-35), id. at E-700 - E-706, and full Senate (23-15), id. at E-735 - E-738, had to repel further efforts to gut the bill.

The legislators understood that Senator Keith's bill involved a "unique" subject, 1 id. at E-106 (Rep. M. Thompson), and they were repeatedly made aware of its potential constitutional problems, see, e.g., id. at E-26 - E-28 (McGehee); id. at E-38 - E-39 (Sen. Keith); id. at E-241 - E-242 (Rossman); id. at E-257 (Probst); id. at E-261 (Beck); id. at E-282 (Sen. Keith). Although the Establishment Clause, including its secular purpose requirement, was of substantial concern to the legislators, they eventually voted overwhelmingly in favor of the Balanced Treatment Act: the House approved it 71-19 (with 15 members absent), 2 id. at E-716 - E-722; the Senate 26-12 (with all members present), id. at E-741 - E-744. The legislators specifically designated the protection of "academic freedom" as the purpose of the Act. La.Rev.Stat.Ann. § 17:286.2 (West 1982). We cannot accurately assess whether this purpose is a "sham," ante at 587, until we first examine the evidence presented to the legislature far more carefully than the Court has done.

Before summarizing the testimony of Senator Keith and his supporters, I wish to make clear that I by no means intend to endorse its accuracy. But my views (and the views of this Court) about creation science and evolution are (or should be) beside the point. Our task is not to judge the debate about teaching the origins of life, but to ascertain what the members of the Louisiana Legislature believed. The vast majority of them voted to approve a bill which explicitly stated a secular purpose; what is crucial is not their wisdom in believing that purpose would be achieved by the bill, but their sincerity in believing it would be.

Most of the testimony in support of Senator Keith's bill came from the Senator himself, and from scientists and educators he presented, many of whom enjoyed academic credentials that may have been regarded as quite impressive by members of the Louisiana Legislature. To a substantial extent, their testimony was devoted to lengthy, and, to the layman, seemingly expert, scientific expositions on the origin of life. See, e.g., 1 App. E-11 - E-18 (Sunderland); id. at E-50 - E-60 (Boudreaux); id. at E-86 - E-89 (Ward); id. at E-130 - E-153 (Boudreaux paper); id. at E-321 - E-326 (Boudreaux); id. at E-423 - E-428 (Sen. Keith). These scientific lectures touched upon, inter alia, biology, paleontology, genetics, astronomy, astrophysics, probability analysis, and biochemistry. The witnesses repeatedly assured committee members that "hundreds and hundreds" of highly respected, internationally renowned scientists believed in creation science, and would support their testimony. See, e.g., id. at E-5 (Sunderland); id. at E-76 (Sen. Keith); id. at E-100 - E-101 (Reiboldt); id. at E-327 - E-328 (Boudreaux); 2 id. at E-503 - E-504 (Boudreaux).

Senator Keith and his witnesses testified essentially as set forth in the following numbered paragraphs:

(1) There are two and only two scientific explanations for the beginning of life [n3] -- evolution and creation science. 1 id. at E-6 (Sunderland); id. at E-34 (Sen. Keith); id. at E-280 (Sen. Keith); id. at E-417 - E-418 (Sen. Keith). Both are bona fide "sciences." Id. at E-6 - E-7 (Sunderland); id. at E-12 (Sunderland); id. at E-416 (Sen. Keith); id. at E-427 (Sen. Keith); 2 id. at E-491 - E-492 (Sen. Keith); id. at E-497 - E-498 (Sen. Keith). Both posit a theory of the origin of life, and subject that theory to empirical testing. Evolution posits that life arose out of inanimate chemical compounds and has gradually evolved over millions of years. Creation science posits that all life forms now on earth appeared suddenly and relatively recently, and have changed little. Since there are only two possible explanations of the origin of life, any evidence that tends to disprove the theory of evolution necessarily tends to prove the theory of creation science, and vice versa. For example, the abrupt appearance in the fossil record of complex life, and the extreme rarity of transitional life forms in that record, are evidence for creation science. 1 id. at E-7 (Sunderland); id. at E-12 - E-18 (Sunderland); id. at E-45 - E-60 (Boudreaux); id. at E-67 (Harlow); id. at E-130 - E-153 (Boudreaux paper); id. at E-423 - E-428 (Sen. Keith).

(2) The body of scientific evidence supporting creation science is as strong as that supporting evolution. In fact, it may be stronger. Id. at E-214 (Young statement); id. at E-310 (Sen. Keith); id. at E-416 (Sen. Keith); 2 id. at E-492 (Sen. Keith). The evidence for evolution is far less compelling than we have been led to believe. Evolution is not a scientific "fact," since it cannot actually be observed in a laboratory. Rather, evolution is merely a scientific theory or "guess." 1 id. at E-20 - E-21 (Morris); id. at E-85 (Ward); id. at E-100 (Reiboldt); id. at E-328 - E-329 (Boudreaux); 2 id. at E-506 (Boudreaux). It is a very bad guess at that. The scientific problems with evolution are so serious that it could accurately be termed a "myth." 1 id. at E-85 (Ward); id. at E-92 - E-93 (Kalivoda); id. at E-95 - E-97 (Sen. Keith); id. at E-154 (Boudreaux paper); id. at E-329 (Boudreaux); id. at E-453 (Sen. Keith); 2 id. at E-505 - E-506 (Boudreaux); id. at E-516 (Young).

(3) Creation science is educationally valuable. Students exposed to it better understand the current state of scientific evidence about the origin of life. 1 id. at E-19 (Sunderland); id. at E-39 (Sen. Keith); id. at E-79 (Kalivoda); id. at E-308 (Sen. Keith); 2 id. at E-513 - E-514 (Morris). Those students even have a better understanding of

evolution. 1 id. at E-19 (Sunderland). Creation science can and should be presented to children without any religious content. Id. at E-12 (Sunderland); id. at E-22 (Sanderford); id. at E-35 - E-36 (Sen. Keith); id. at E-101 (Reiboldt); id. at E-279 - E-280 (Sen. Keith); id. at E-282 (Sen. Keith).

(4) Although creation science is educationally valuable and strictly scientific, it is now being censored from or misrepresented in the public schools. Id. at E-19 (Sunderland); id. at E-21 (Morris); id. at E-34 (Sen. Keith); id. at E-37 (Sen. Keith); id. at E-42 (Sen. Keith); id. at E-92 (Kalivoda); id. at E-97 - E-98 (Reiboldt); id. at E-214 (Young statement); id. at E-218 (Young statement); id. at E-280 (Sen. Keith); id. at E-309 (Sen. Keith); 2 id. at E-513 (Morris). Evolution, in turn, is misrepresented as an absolute truth. 1 id. at E-63 (Harlow); id. at E-74 (Sen. Keith); id. at E-81 (Kalivoda); id. at E-214 (Young statement); 2 id. at E-507 (Harlow); id. at E-513 (Morris); id. at E-516 (Young). Teachers have been brainwashed by an entrenched scientific establishment composed almost exclusively of scientists to whom evolution is like a "religion." These scientists discriminate against creation scientists, so as to prevent evolution's weaknesses from being exposed. 1 id. at E-61 (Boudreaux); id. at E-63 - E-64 (Harlow); id. at E-78 - E-79 (Kalivoda); id. at E-80 (Kalivoda); id. at E-95 - E-97 (Sen. Keith); id. at E-129 (Boudreaux paper); id. at E-218 (Young statement); id. at E-357 (Sen. Keith); id. at E-430 (Boudreaux).

(5) The censorship of creation science has at least two harmful effects. First, it deprives students of knowledge of one of the two scientific explanations for the origin of life, and leads them to believe that evolution is proven fact; thus, their education suffers, and they are wrongly taught that science has proved their religious beliefs false. Second, it violates the Establishment Clause. The United States Supreme Court has held that secular humanism is a religion. Id. at E-36 (Sen. Keith) (referring to Torcaso v. Watkins, 367 U.S. 488, 495, n. 11 (1961));1 App. E-418 (Sen. Keith); 2 id. at E-499 (Sen. Keith). Belief in evolution is a central tenet of that religion. 1 id. at E-282 (Sen. Keith); id. at E-312 - E-313 (Sen. Keith); id. at E-317 (Sen. Keith); id. at E-418 (Sen. Keith); 2 id. at E-499 (Sen. Keith). Thus, by censoring creation science and instructing students that evolution is fact, public school teachers are now advancing religion in violation of the Establishment Clause. 1 id. at E-2 - E-4 (Sen. Keith); id. at E-36 - E-37, E-39 (Sen. Keith); id. at E-154 - E-155 (Boudreaux paper); id. at E-281 - E-282 (Sen. Keith); id. at E-313 (Sen. Keith); id. at E-315 - E-316 (Sen. Keith); id. at E-317 (Sen. Keith); 2 id. at E-499 - E-500 (Sen. Keith).

Senator Keith repeatedly and vehemently denied that his purpose was to advance a particular religious doctrine. A t the outset of the first hearing on the legislation, he testified:

We are not going to say today that you should have some kind of religious instructions in our schools. . . . We are not talking about religion today. . . . I am not proposing that we take the Bible in each science class and read the first chapter of Genesis.

1 id. at E-35. At a later hearing, Senator Keith stressed:

[T]o . . . teach religion and disguise it as creationism . . . is not my intent. My intent is to see to it that our textbooks are not censored.

Id. at E-280. He made many similar statements throughout the hearings. See, e.g., id. at E-41; id. at E-282; id. at E-310; id. at E-417; see also id. at E-44 (Boudreaux); id. at E-80 (Kalivoda).

We have no way of knowing, of course, how many legislators believed the testimony of Senator Keith and his witnesses. But in the absence of evidence to the contrary, [n4] we have to assume that many of them did. Given that assumption, the Court today plainly errs in holding that the Louisiana Legislature passed the Balanced Treatment Act for exclusively religious purposes.

B

Even with nothing more than this legislative history to go on, I think it would be extraordinary to invalidate the Balanced Treatment Act for lack of a valid secular purpose. Striking down a law approved by the democratically elected representatives of the people is no minor matter.

The cardinal principle of statutory construction is to save, and not to destroy. We have repeatedly held that, as between two possible interpretations of a statute, by one of which it would be unconstitutional and by the other valid, our plain duty is to adopt that which will save the act.

NLRB v. Jones & Laughlin Steel Corp., 301 U.S. 1, 30 (1937). So, too, it seems to me, with discerning statutory purpose. Even if the legislative history were silent or ambiguous about the existence of a secular purpose -- and here it is not -- the statute should survive Lemon's purpose test. But even more validation than mere legislative history is present here. The Louisiana Legislature explicitly set forth its secular purpose ("protecting academic freedom") in the very text of the Act. La.Rev.Stat. § 17:286.2 (West 1982). We have in the past repeatedly relied upon or deferred to such expressions, see, e.g., Committee for Public Education & Religious Liberty v. Regan, 444 U.S. at 654; Meek v. Pittenger, 421 U.S. at 363, 367-368; Committee for Public Education & Religious Liberty v. Nyquist, 413 U.S. at 773; Levitt v. Committee for Public Education & Religious Liberty, 413 U.S. at 479-480, n. 7; Tilton v. Richardson, 403 U.S. at 678-679 (plurality opinion); Lemon v. Kurtzman, 403 U.S. at 613; Board of Education v. Allen, 392 U.S. at 243.

The Court seeks to evade the force of this expression of purpose by stubbornly misinterpreting it, and then finding that the provisions of the Act do not advance that misinterpreted purpose, thereby showing it to be a sham. The Court first surmises that "academic freedom" means "enhancing the freedom of teachers to teach what they will," ante at 586 -- even though "academic freedom" in that sense has little scope in the structured elementary and secondary curriculums with which the Act is concerned. Alternatively, the Court suggests that it might mean "maximiz[ing] the comprehensiveness and effectiveness of science instruction," ante at 588 -- though that is an exceedingly strange interpretation of the words, and one that is refuted on the very face of the statute. See § 17:286.5. Had the Court devoted to this central question of the meaning of the legislatively expressed purpose a small fraction of the research into legislative history that produced its quotations of religiously motivated statements by individual legislators, it would have discerned quite readily what "academic freedom" meant: students' freedom from indoctrination. The legislature wanted to ensure that students would be free to decide for themselves how life began, based upon a fair and balanced presentation of the scientific evidence -- that is, to protect "the right of each [student] voluntarily to determine what to believe (and what not to believe) free of any coercive pressures from the State." Grand Rapids School District v. Ball, 473 U.S. at 385. The legislature did not care whether the topic of origins was taught; it simply wished to ensure that, when the topic was taught, students would receive "'all of the evidence.'" Ante at 586 (quoting Tr. of Oral Arg. 60).

As originally introduced, the "purpose" section of the Balanced Treatment Act read:

This Chapter is enacted for the purposes of protecting academic freedom . . . of students . . . and assisting students in their search for truth.

1 App. E-292 (emphasis added). Among the proposed findings of fact contained in the original version of the bill was the following:

Public school instruction in only evolution science . . . violates the principle of academic freedom because it denies students a choice between scientific models, and instead indoctrinates them in evolution science alone.

Id. at E-295 (emphasis added). [n5] Senator Keith unquestionably understood "academic freedom" to mean "freedom from indoctrination." See id. at E-36 (purpose of bill is "to protect academic freedom by providing student choice"); id. at E-283 (purpose of bill is to protect "academic freedom" by giving students a "choice," rather than subjecting them to "indoctrination on origins").

If one adopts the obviously intended meaning of the statutory term "academic freedom," there is no basis whatever for concluding that the purpose they express is a "sham." Ante at 587. To the contrary, the Act pursues that purpose plainly and consistently. It requires that, whenever the subject of origins is covered, evolution be "taught as a theory, rather than as proven scientific fact," and that scientific evidence inconsistent with the theory of evolution (viz., "creation science") be taught as well. La.Rev.Stat.Ann. § 17:286.4A (West 1982). Living up to its title of "Balanced Treatment for Creation-Science and Evolution-Science Act," § 17.286.1, it treats the teaching of creation the same way. It does not mandate instruction in creation science, § 17:286.5; forbids teachers to present creation science "as proven scientific fact," § 17:286.4A; and bans the teaching of creation science unless the theory is (to use the Court's terminology) "discredit[ed] ' . . . at every turn'" with the teaching of evolution. Ante at 589 (quoting 765 F.2d at 1257). It surpasses understanding how the Court can see in this a purpose "to restructure the science curriculum to conform with a particular religious viewpoint," ante at 593, "to provide a persuasive advantage to a particular religious doctrine," ante at 592, "to promote the theory of creation science which embodies a particular religious tenet," ante at 593, and "to endorse a particular religious doctrine," ante at 594.

The Act's reference to "creation" is not convincing evidence of religious purpose.

The Act defines creation science as "scientific evidenc[e]," § 17:286.3(2) (emphasis added), and Senator Keith and his witnesses repeatedly stressed that the subject can and should be presented without religious content. See supra, at 623. We have no basis on the record to conclude that creation science need be anything other than a collection of scientific data supporting the theory that life abruptly appeared on earth. See n. 4, supra. Creation science, its proponents insist, no more must explain whence life came than evolution must explain whence came the inanimate materials from which it says life evolved. But even if that were not so, to posit a past creator is not to posit the eternal and personal God who is the object of religious veneration. Indeed, it is not even to posit the "unmoved mover" hypothesized by Aristotle and other notably nonfundamentalist philosophers. Senator Keith suggested this when he referred to "a creator, however you define a creator." 1 App. E-280 (emphasis added).

The Court cites three provisions of the Act which, it argues, demonstrate a "discriminatory preference for the teaching of creation science" and no interest in "academic freedom." Ante at 482 U.S. 588"]588. First, the Act prohibits discrimination only against creation scientists and those who teach creation science. § 17:286.4C. Second, the Act requires local school boards to develop and provide to science teachers "a curriculum guide on presentation of creation-science." § 17:286.7A. Finally, the Act requires the Governor to designate seven creation scientists who shall, upon request, assist local school boards in developing the curriculum guides. § 17:286.7B. But none of these provisions casts doubt upon the sincerity of the legislators' articulated purpose of "academic freedom" -- unless, of course, one gives that term the obviously erroneous meanings preferred by the Court. The Louisiana legislators had been told repeatedly that creation scientists were scorned by most educators and scientists, who themselves had an almost religious faith in evolution. It is hardly surprising, then, that, in seeking to achieve a balanced, "nonindoctrinating" curriculum, the legislators protected from discrimination only those teachers whom they thought were suffering from discrimination. (Also, the legislators were undoubtedly aware of 588. First, the Act prohibits discrimination only against creation scientists and those who teach creation science. § 17:286.4C. Second, the Act requires local school boards to develop and provide to science teachers "a curriculum guide on presentation of creation-science." § 17:286.7A. Finally, the Act requires the Governor to designate seven creation scientists who shall, upon request, assist local school boards in developing the curriculum guides. § 17:286.7B. But none of these provisions casts doubt upon the sincerity of the legislators' articulated purpose of "academic freedom" -- unless, of course, one gives that term the obviously erroneous meanings preferred by the Court. The Louisiana legislators had been told repeatedly that creation scientists were scorned by most educators and scientists, who themselves had an almost religious faith in evolution. It is hardly surprising, then, that, in seeking to achieve a balanced, "nonindoctrinating" curriculum, the legislators protected from discrimination only those teachers whom they thought were suffering from discrimination. (Also, the legislators were undoubtedly aware of Epperson v. Arkansas, 393 U.S. 97 (1968), and thus could quite reasonably have concluded that discrimination against evolutionists was already prohibited.) The two provisions respecting the development of curriculum guides are also consistent with "academic freedom" as the Louisiana Legislature understood the term. Witnesses had informed the legislators that, because of the hostility of most scientists and educators to creation science, the topic had been censored from or badly misrepresented in elementary and secondary school texts. In light of the unavailability of works on creation science suitable for classroom use (a fact appellees concede, see Brief for Appellees 27, 40) and the existence of ample materials on evolution, it was entirely reasonable for the legislature to conclude that science teachers attempting to implement the Act would need a curriculum guide on creation science, but not on evolution, and that those charged with developing the guide would need an easily accessible group of creation scientists. Thus, the provisions of the Act of so much concern to the Court support the conclusion that the legislature acted to advance "academic freedom."

The legislative history gives ample evidence of the sincerity of the Balanced Treatment Act's articulated purpose. Witness after witness urged the legislators to support the Act so that students would not be "indoctrinated," but would instead be free to decide for themselves, based upon a fair presentation of the scientific evidence, about the origin of life. See, e.g., 1 App. E-18 (Sunderland) ("all that we are advocating" is presenting "scientific data" to students and "letting [them] make up their own mind[s]"); id. at E-19 - E-20 (Sunderland) (Students are now being "indoctrinated" in evolution through the use of "censored school books. . . . All that we are asking for is [the] open unbiased education in the classroom . . . your students deserve"); id. at E-21 (Morris) ("A student cannot [make an intelligent decision about the origin of life] unless he is well informed about both [evolution and creation science]"); id. at E-22 (Sanderford) ("We are asking very simply [that] . . . creationism [be presented] alongside . . . evolution, and let people make their own mind[s] up"); id. at E-23 (Young) (the bill would require teachers to live up to their "obligation to present all theories," and thereby enable "students to make judgments themselves"); id. at E-44 (Boudreaux) ("Our intention is truth, and, as a scientist, I am interested in truth"); id. at E-60 - E-61 (Boudreaux) ("[W]e [teachers] are guilty of a lot of rainwashing. . . . We have a duty to . . . [present the] truth" to students "at all levels from grade school on through the college level"); id. at E-79 (Kalivoda) ("This [hearing] is being held, I think, to determine whether children will benefit from freedom of information, or if they will be handicapped educationally by having little or no information about creation"); id. at E-80 (Kalivoda) ("I am not interested in teaching religion in schools. . . . I am interested in the truth, and [students'] having the opportunity to hear more than one side"); id. at E-98 (Reiboldt) ("The students have a right to know there is an alternate creationist point of view. They have a right to know the scientific evidences which suppor[t] that alternative"); id. at E-218 (Young statement) (passage of the bill will ensure that "communication of scientific ideas and discoveries may be unhindered"); 2 id. at E-514 (Morris) ("[A]re we going to allow [students] to look at evolution, to look at creationism, and to let one or the other stand or fall on its own merits, or will we, by failing to pass this bill, . . . deny students an opportunity to hear another viewpoint?"); id. at E-516 - E-517 (Young) ("We want to give the children here in this state an equal opportunity to see both sides of the theories"). Senator Keith expressed similar views. See, e.g., 1 id. at E-36; id. at E-41; id. at E-280; id. at E-283.

Legislators other than Senator Keith made only a few statements providing insight into their motives, but those statements cast no doubt upon the sincerity of the Act's articulated purpose. The legislators were concerned primarily about the manner in which the subject of origins was presented in Louisiana schools -- specifically, about whether scientifically valuable information was being censored, and students misled about evolution. Representatives Cain, Jenkins, and F. Thompson seemed impressed by the scientific evidence presented in support of creation science. See 2 id. at E-530 (Rep. F. Thompson); id. at E-533 (Rep. Cain); id. at E-613 (Rep. Jenkins). At the first study commission hearing, Senator Picard and Representative M. Thompson questioned Senator Keith about Louisiana teachers' treatment of evolution and creation science. See 1 id. at E-71 - E-74. At the close of the hearing, Representative M. Thompson told the audience:

We, as members of the committee, will also receive from the staff information of what is currently being taught in the Louisiana public schools. We really want to see [it]. I . . . have no idea in what manner [biology] is presented, and in what manner the creationist theories [are] excluded in the public school[s]. We want to look at what the status of the situation is.

Id. at E-104. Legislators made other comments suggesting a concern about censorship and misrepresentation of scientific information. See, e.g., id. at E-386 (Sen. McLeod); 2 id. at E-527 (Rep. Jenkins); id. at E-528 (Rep. M. Thompson); id. at E-534 (Rep. Fair).

It is undoubtedly true that what prompted the legislature to direct its attention to the misrepresentation of evolution in the schools (rather than the inaccurate presentation of other topics) was its awareness of the tension between evolution and the religious beliefs of many children. But even appellees concede that a valid secular purpose is not rendered impermissible simply because its pursuit is prompted by concern for religious sensitivities. Tr. of Oral Arg. 43, 56. If a history teacher falsely told her students that the bones of Jesus Christ had been discovered, or a physics teacher that the Shroud of Turin had been conclusively established to be inexplicable on the basis of natural causes, I cannot believe (despite the majority's implication to the contrary, see ante at 592-593) that legislators or school board members would be constitutionally prohibited from taking corrective action simply because that action was prompted by concern for the religious beliefs of the misinstructed students.

In sum, even if one concedes, for the sake of argument, that a majority of the Louisiana Legislature voted for the Balanced Treatment Act partly in order to foster (rather than merely eliminate discrimination against) Christian fundamentalist beliefs, our cases establish that that, alone, would not suffice to invalidate the Act, so long as there was a genuine secular purpose as well. We have, moreover, no adequate basis for disbelieving the secular purpose set forth in the Act itself, or for concluding that it is a sham enacted to conceal the legislators' violation of their oaths of office. I am astonished by the Court's unprecedented readiness to reach such a conclusion, which I can only attribute to an intellectual predisposition created by the facts and the legend of Scopes v. State, 154 Tenn. 105, 289 S.W. 363 (1927) -- an instinctive reaction that any governmentally imposed requirements bearing upon the teaching of evolution must be a manifestation of Christian fundamentalist repression. In this case, however, it seems to me the Court's position is the repressive one. The people of Louisiana, including those who are Christian fundamentalists, are quite entitled, as a secular matter, to have whatever scientific evidence there may be against evolution presented in their schools, just as Mr. Scopes was entitled to present whatever scientific evidence there was for it. Perhaps what the Louisiana Legislature has done is unconstitutional because there is no such evidence, and the scheme they have established will amount to no more than a presentation of the Book of Genesis. But we cannot say that on the evidence before us in this summary judgment context, which includes ample uncontradicted testimony that "creation science" is a body of scientific knowledge, rather than revealed belief. Infinitely less can we say (or should we say) that the scientific evidence for evolution is so conclusive that no one could be gullible enough to believe that there is any real scientific evidence to the contrary, so that the legislation's stated purpose must be a lie. Yet that illiberal judgment, that Scopes-in-reverse, is ultimately the basis on which the Court's facile rejection of the Louisiana Legislature's purpose must rest.

Since the existence of secular purpose is so entirely clear, and thus dispositive, I will not go on to discuss the fact that, even if the Louisiana Legislature's purpose were exclusively to advance religion, some of the well-established exceptions to the impermissibility of that purpose might be applicable -- the validating intent to eliminate a perceived discrimination against a particular religion, to facilitate its free exercise, or to accommodate it. See supra, at 617-618. I am not, in any case, enamored of those amorphous exceptions, since I think them no more than unpredictable correctives to what is (as the next Part of this opinion will discuss) a fundamentally unsound rule. It is surprising, however, that the Court does not address these exceptions, since the context of the legislature's action gives some reason to believe they may be applicable. [n6]

Because I believe that the Balanced Treatment Act had a secular purpose, which is all the first component of the Lemon test requires, I would reverse the judgment of the Court of Appeals and remand for further consideration.

III

I have to this point assumed the validity of the Lemon "purpose" test. In fact, however, I think the pessimistic evaluation that THE CHIEF JUSTICE made of the totality of Lemon is particularly applicable to the "purpose" prong: it is

a constitutional theory [that] has no basis in the history of the amendment it seeks to interpret, is difficult to apply, and yields unprincipled results. . . .

Wallace v. Jaffree, 472 U.S. at 112 (REHNQUIST, J., dissenting).

Our cases interpreting and applying the purpose test have made such a maze of the Establishment Clause that even the most conscientious governmental officials can only guess what motives will be held unconstitutional. We have said essentially the following: government may not act with the purpose of advancing religion, except when forced to do so by the Free Exercise Clause (which is now and then); or when eliminating existing governmental hostility to religion (which exists sometimes); or even when merely accommodating governmentally uninhibited religious practices, except that at some point (it is unclear where) intentional accommodation results in the fostering of religion, which is of course unconstitutional. See supra, at 614-618.

But the difficulty of knowing what vitiating purpose one is looking for is as nothing compared with the difficulty of knowing how or where to find it. For while it is possible to discern the objective "purpose" of a statute (i.e., the public good at which its provisions appear to be directed), or even the formal motivation for a statute where that is explicitly set forth (as it was, to no avail, here), discerning the subjective motivation of those enacting the statute is, to be honest, almost always an impossible task. The number of possible motivations, to begin with, is not binary, or indeed even finite. In the present case, for example, a particular legislator need not have voted for the Act either because he wanted to foster religion or because he wanted to improve education. He may have thought the bill would provide jobs for his district, or may have wanted to make amends with a faction of his party he had alienated on another vote, or he may have been a close friend of the bill's sponsor, or he may have been repaying a favor he owed the majority leader, or he may have hoped the Governor would appreciate his vote and make a fund-raising appearance for him, or he may have been pressured to vote for a bill he disliked by a wealthy contributor or by a flood of constituent mail, or he may have been seeking favorable publicity, or he may have been reluctant to hurt the feelings of a loyal staff member who worked on the bill, or he may have been settling an old score with a legislator who opposed the bill, or he may have been mad at his wife, who opposed the bill, or he may have been intoxicated and utterly unmotivated when the vote was called, or he may have accidentally voted "yes" instead of "no," or, of course, he may have had (and very likely did have) a combination of some of the above and many other motivations. To look for the sole purpose of even a single legislator is probably to look for something that does not exist.

Putting that problem aside, however, where ought we to look for the individual legislator's purpose? We cannot, of course, assume that every member present (if, as is unlikely, we know who or even how many they were) agreed with the motivation expressed in a particular legislator's preenactment floor or committee statement. Quite obviously, "[w]hat motivates one legislator to make a speech about a statute is not necessarily what motivates scores of others to enact it." United States v. O'Brien, 391 U.S. 367, 384 (1968). Can we assume, then, that they all agree with the motivation expressed in the staff-prepared committee reports they might have read -- even though we are unwilling to assume that they agreed with the motivation expressed in the very statute that they voted for? Should we consider postenactment floor statements? Or postenactment testimony from legislators, obtained expressly for the lawsuit? Should we consider media reports on the realities of the legislative bargaining? All of these sources, of course, are eminently manipulable. Legislative histories can be contrived and sanitized, favorable media coverage orchestrated, and postenactment recollections conveniently distorted. Perhaps most valuable of all would be more objective indications -- for example, evidence regarding the individual legislators' religious affiliations. And if that, why not evidence regarding the fervor or tepidity of their beliefs?

Having achieved, through these simple means, an assessment of what individual legislators intended, we must still confront the question (yet to be addressed in any of our cases) how many of them must have the invalidating intent. If a state senate approves a bill by vote of 26 to 25, and only one of the 26 intended solely to advance religion, is the law unconstitutional? What if 13 of the 26 had that intent? What if 3 of the 26 had the impermissible intent, but 3 of the 25 voting against the bill were motivated by religious hostility, or were simply attempting to "balance" the votes of their impermissibly motivated colleagues? Or is it possible that the intent of the bill's sponsor is alone enough to invalidate it -- on a theory, perhaps, that even though everyone else's intent was pure, what they produced was the fruit of a forbidden tree?

Because there are no good answers to these questions, this Court has recognized from Chief Justice Marshall, see Fletcher v. Peck, 6 Cranch 87, 130 (1810), to Chief Justice Warren, United States v. O'Brien, supra, at 383-384, that determining the subjective intent of legislators is a perilous enterprise. See also Palmer v. Thompson, 403 U.S. 217, 224-225 (1971); Epperson v. Arkansas, 393 U.S. at 113 (Black, J., concurring). It is perilous, I might note, not just for the judges who will very likely reach the wrong result, but also for the legislators who find that they must assess the validity of proposed legislation -- and risk the condemnation of having voted for an unconstitutional measure -- not on the basis of what the legislation contains, nor even on the basis of what they themselves intend, but on the basis of what others have in mind.

Given the many hazards involved in assessing the subjective intent of governmental decisionmakers, the first prong of Lemon is defensible, I think, only if the text of the Establishment Clause demands it. That is surely not the case. The Clause states that "Congress shall make no law respecting an establishment of religion." One could argue, I suppose, that any time Congress acts with the intent of advancing religion, it has enacted a "law respecting an establishment of religion"; but, far from being an unavoidable reading, it is quite an unnatural one. I doubt, for example, that the Clayton Act, 38 Stat. 730, as amended, 15 U.S.C. § 12 et seq., could reasonably be described as a "law respecting an establishment of religion" if bizarre new historical evidence revealed that it lacked a secular purpose, even though it has no discernible nonsecular effect. It is, in short, far from an inevitable reading of the Establishment Clause that it forbids all governmental action intended to advance religion; and, if not inevitable, any reading with such untoward consequences must be wrong.

In the past, we have attempted to justify our embarrassing Establishment Clause jurisprudence [n7] on the ground that it "sacrifices clarity and predictability for flexibility." Committee for Public Education & Religious Liberty v. Regan, 444 U.S. at 662. One commentator has aptly characterized this as "a euphemism . . . for . . . the absence of any principled rationale." Choper, supra, n. 7, at 681. I think it time that we sacrifice some "flexibility" for "clarity and predictability." Abandoning Lemon's purpose test -- a test which exacerbates the tension between the Free Exercise and Establishment Clauses, has no basis in the language or history of the Amendment, and, as today's decision shows, has wonderfully flexible consequences -- would be a good place to start.

Justice Scalia's dissent in Rankin v. McPherson (June 24, 1987)

JUSTICE SCALIA, with whom THE CHIEF JUSTICE, JUSTICE WHITE, and JUSTICE O'CONNOR join, dissenting.

I agree with the proposition, felicitously put by Constable Rankin's counsel, that no law enforcement agency is required by the First Amendment to permit one of its employees to "ride with the cops and cheer for the robbers." App. 94. The issue in this case is whether Constable Rankin, a law enforcement official, is prohibited by the First Amendment from preventing his employees from saying of the attempted assassination of President Reagan -- on the job and within hearing of other employees -- "If they go for him again, I hope they get him." The Court, applying the two-prong analysis of Connick v. Myers, 461 U. S. 138 (1983), holds that McPherson's statement was protected by the First Amendment because (1) it "addressed a matter of public concern," and (2) McPherson's interest in making the statement outweighs Rankin's interest in suppressing it. In so doing, the Court significantly and irrationally expands the definition of "public concern"; it also carves out a new and very large class of employees -- i.e., those in "nonpolicymaking" positions -- who, if today's decision is to be believed, can never be disciplined for statements that fall within the Court's expanded definition. Because I believe the Court's conclusions rest upon a distortion of both the record and the Court's prior decisions, I dissent.

I

To appreciate fully why the majority errs in reaching its first conclusion, it is necessary to recall the origins and purposes of Connick's "public concern" requirement. The Court long ago rejected Justice Holmes' approach to the free speech rights of public employees, that "[a policeman] may have a constitutional right to talk politics, but he has no constitutional right to be a policeman," McAuliffe v. Mayor of New Bedford, 155 Mass. 216, 220, 29 N.E. 517 (1892). We have, however, recognized that the government's power as an employer to make hiring and firing decisions on the basis of what its employees and prospective employees say has a much greater scope than its power to regulate expression by the general public. See, e.g., Pickering v. Board of Education, 391 U. S. 563, 391 U. S.

568 (1968).

Specifically, we have held that the First Amendment's protection against adverse personnel decisions extends only to speech on matters of "public concern," Connick, supra, at 461 U. S. 147-149, which we have variously described as those matters dealing in some way with "the essence of self-government," Garrison v. Louisiana, 379 U. S. 64, 379 U. S. 74-75 (1964), matters as to which "free and open debate is vital to informed decisionmaking by the electorate," Pickering, supra, at 391 U. S. 571-572, and matters as to which "debate . . . [must] be uninhibited, robust, and wide-open,'" Dun & Bradstreet, Inc. v. Greenmoss Builders, Inc., 472 U. S. 749, 472 U. S. 755 (1985) (plurality opinion) (quoting New York Times Co. v. Sullivan, 376 U. S. 254, 376 U. S. 270 (1964)). In short, speech on matters of public concern is that speech which lies "at the heart of the First Amendment's protection," First Nat. Bank v. Bellotti, 435 U. S. 765, 435 U. S. 776 (1978). If, but only if, an employee's speech falls within this category, a public employer seeking to abridge or punish it must show that the employee's interest is outweighed by the government's interest, "as an employer, in promoting the efficiency of the public services it performs through its employees." Pickering, supra, at 391 U. S. 568.

McPherson fails this threshold requirement. The statement for which she was fired -- and the only statement reported to the Constable -- was, "If they go for him again, I hope they get him." It is important to bear in mind the District Judge's finding that this was not hyperbole. The Court's opinion not only does not clarify that point, but beclouds it by a footnote observing that the District Judge did not explicitly resolve the conflict in testimony as to whether McPherson told the Constable that she "meant" what she had said. Ante at 483 U. S. 382, n 4. He did not. But he assuredly found that, whether McPherson later said she meant it or not, and whether she even meant it at the time or not, the idea she expressed was not just an exaggerated expression of her disapproval for the President's policies, but a voicing of the hope that, next time, the President would be killed. The District Judge rejected McPherson's argument that her statement was "mere political hyperbole," finding, to the contrary, that it was, "in context," "violent words." 786 F.2d 1233, 1235 (CA5 1986).

"This is not,' he said, 'the situation where one makes an idle threat to kill someone for not picking them [sic] up on time, or not picking up their [sic] clothes. It was more than that."

Ibid. He ruled against McPherson at the conclusion of the second hearing because "I don't think it is a matter of public concern to approve even more to [sic] the second attempt at assassination." App. 119. The Court's opinion does not attempt to set aside this finding as to the import of the statement, and there is indeed no basis for doing so, since it is entirely reasonable and supported by the evidence.

Given the meaning of the remark, there is no basis for the Court's suggestion, ante at 483 U. S. 386-387, that McPherson's criticisms of the President's policies that immediately preceded the remark can illuminate it in such fashion as to render it constitutionally protected. Those criticisms merely reveal the speaker's motive for expressing the desire that the next attempt on the President's life succeed, in the same way that a political assassin's remarks to his victim before pulling the trigger might reveal a motive for that crime. The majority's magical transformation of the motive for McPherson's statement into its content is as misguided as viewing a political assassination preceded by a harangue as nothing more than a strong denunciation of the victim's political views.

That McPherson's statement does not constitute speech on a matter of "public concern" is demonstrated by comparing it with statements that have been found to fit that description in prior decisions involving public employees. McPherson's statement is a far cry from the question by the Assistant District Attorney in Connick whether her coworkers "ever [felt] pressured to work in political campaigns," Connick, 461 U.S. at 461 U. S. 149; from the letter written by the public school teacher in Pickering criticizing the Board of Education's proposals for financing school construction, Pickering, supra, at 391 U. S. 566; from the legislative testimony of a state college teacher in Perry v. Sindermann, 408 U. S. 593, 408 U. S. 595 (1972), advocating that a particular college be elevated to 4-year status; from the memorandum given by a teacher to a radio station in Mt. Healthy City Board of Ed. v. Doyle, 429 U. S. 274, 429 U. S. 282 (1977), dealing with teacher dress and appearance; and from the complaints about school board policies and practices at issue in Givhan v. Western Line Consolidated School Dist., 439 U. S. 410, 439 U. S. 413 (1979). See Connick, supra, at 461 U. S. 145-146.

McPherson's statement is indeed so different from those that it is only one step removed from statements that we have previously held entitled to no First Amendment protection even in the nonemployment context -- including assassination threats against the President (which are illegal under 18 U.S.C. § 871), see Frohwerk v. United States, 249 U. S. 204, 249 U. S. 206 (1919); "fighting' words," Chaplinsky v. New Hampshire, 315 U. S. 568, 315 U. S. 572 (1942); epithets or personal abuse, Cantwell v. Connecticut, 310 U. S. 296, 310 U. S. 309-310 (1940); and advocacy of force or violence, Harisiades v. Shaughnessy, 342 U. S. 580, 342 U. S. 591-592 (1952). A statement lying so near the category of completely unprotected speech cannot fairly be viewed as lying within the "heart" of the First Amendment's protection; it lies within that category of speech that can neither be characterized as speech on matters of public concern nor properly subject to criminal penalties, see Connick, supra, at 461 U. S. 147. Once McPherson stopped explicitly criticizing the President's policies and expressed a desire that he be assassinated, she crossed the line.

The Court reaches the opposite conclusion only by distorting the concept of "public concern." It does not explain how a statement expressing approval of a serious and violent crime -- assassination of the President -- can possibly fall within that category. It simply rehearses the "context" of McPherson's statement, which, as we have already seen, is irrelevant here, and then concludes that, because of that context, and because the statement "came on the heels of a news bulletin regarding what is certainly a matter of heightened public attention: an attempt on the life of the President," the statement "plainly dealt with a matter of public concern." Ante at 483 U. S. 386. I cannot respond to this progression of reasoning except to say I do not understand it. Surely the Court does not mean to adopt the reasoning of the court below, which was that McPherson's statement was "addressed to a matter of public concern" within the meaning of Connick because the public would obviously be "concerned" about the assassination of the President. That is obviously untenable: the public would be "concerned" about a statement threatening to blow up the local federal building or demanding a $1 million extortion payment, yet that kind of "public concern" does not entitle such a statement to any First Amendment protection at all.

II

Even if I agreed that McPherson's statement was speech on a matter of "public concern," I would still find it unprotected. It is important to be clear on what the issue is in this part of the case. It is not, as the Court suggests, whether "Rankin's interest in discharging [McPherson] outweighed her rights under the First Amendment." Ante at 483 U. S. 392 (emphasis added). Rather, it is whether his interest in preventing the expression of such statements in his agency outweighed her First Amendment interest in making the statement. We are not deliberating, in other words (or at least should not be), about whether the sanction of dismissal was, as the concurrence puts it, "an . . . intemperat[e] employment decision." It may well have been -- and personally I think it was. But we are not sitting as a panel to develop sound principles of proportionality for adverse actions in the state civil service. We are asked to determine whether, given the interests of this law enforcement office, McPherson had a right to say what she did -- so that she could not only not be fired for it, but could not be formally reprimanded for it, or even prevented from repeating it endlessly into the future. It boggles the mind to think that she has such a right.

The Constable testified that he "was very concerned that this remark was made." App. 81. Rightly so. As a law enforcement officer, the Constable obviously has a strong interest in preventing statements by any of his employees approving, or expressing a desire for, serious, violent crimes -- regardless of whether the statements actually interfere with office operations at the time they are made or demonstrate character traits that make the speaker unsuitable for law enforcement work. In Connick, we upheld the dismissal of an Assistant District Attorney for circulating among her coworkers a questionnaire implicitly criticizing her superiors. Although we held that one of the questions -- dealing with pressure in the office to participate in political campaigns -- satisfied the "public concern" requirement, we held that the discharge nonetheless did not violate the First Amendment because the questionnaire itself "carrie[d] the clear potential for undermining office relations." Connick, supra, at 461 U. S. 152. Statements like McPherson's obviously carry a similar potential in an office devoted to law enforcement. Although that proposition is, in my view, evident on its face, we have actual evidence of it in the present record: the only reason McPherson's remark was brought to the Constable's attention was that one of his deputies, Captain Levrier, had overheard the remark and, according to the Constable, "was very upset because of [it]." App. 80.*

Statements by the Constable's employees to the effect that, "if they go for the President again, I hope they get him" might also, to put it mildly, undermine public confidence in the Constable's office. A public employer has a strong interest in preserving its reputation with the public. See, e.g., Snepp v. United States, 444 U. S. 507, 444 U. S. 509, n. 3 (1980); CSC v. Letter Carriers, 413 U. S. 548, 413 U. S. 564-565 (1973). We know -- from undisputed testimony -- that McPherson had or might have had some occasion to deal with the public while carrying out her duties. See App. 73 (answering telephone inquiries); id. at 78-79 (personal assistance).

The Court's sweeping assertion (and apparent holding) that, where an employee "serves no confidential, policymaking, or public contact role, the danger to the agency's successful functioning from that employee's private speech is minimal," ante at 483 U. S. 390-391, is simply contrary to reason and experience. Nonpolicymaking employees (the Assistant District Attorney in Connick, for example) can hurt working relationships and undermine public confidence in all organization every bit as much as policymaking employees. I, for one, do not look forward to the new First Amendment world the Court creates, in which nonpolicymaking employees of the Equal Employment Opportunity Commission must be permitted to make remarks on the job approving of racial discrimination, nonpolicymaking employees of the Selective Service System to advocate noncompliance with the draft laws, and (since it is really quite difficult to contemplate anything more absurd than the present case itself), nonpolicymaking constable's deputies to express approval for the assassination of the President.

In sum, since Constable Rankin's interest in maintaining both an esprit de corps and a public image consistent with his office's law enforcement duties outweighs any interest his employees may have in expressing on the job a desire that the President be killed, even assuming that such an expression addresses a matter of public concern, it is not protected by the First Amendment from suppression. I emphasize once again that that is the issue here -- and not, as both the Court's opinion and especially the concurrence seem to assume, whether the means used to effect suppression (viz., firing) were excessive. The First Amendment contains no "narrow tailoring" requirement that speech the government is entitled to suppress must be suppressed by the mildest means possible. If Constable Rankin was entitled (as I think any reasonable person would say he was) to admonish McPherson for saying what she did on the job, within hearing of her coworkers, and to warn her that, if she did it again a formal censure would be placed in her personnel file, then it follows that he is entitled to rule that particular speech out of bounds in that particular work environment -- and that is the end of the First Amendment analysis. The "intemperate" manner of the permissible suppression is an issue for another forum, or at least for a more plausibly relevant provision of the Constitution.

Because the statement at issue here did not address a matter of public concern, and because, even if it did, a law enforcement agency has adequate reason not to permit such expression, I would reverse the judgment of the court below.

* The majority errs in asserting that

"Constable Rankin testified that the possibility of interference with the functions of the Constable's office had not been a consideration in his discharge of respondent."

Ante at 483 U. S. 389. In fact, the statement on which the majority relies for that proposition merely affirms that the Constable did not base his decision "on whether the work was interrupted or not.'" See ante at 483 U. S. 389, n. 14, quoting Tr. (Jan. 21, 1985), p. 45. That says nothing about his perceptions of the effect of such statements upon office morale and efficiency.

Justice Scalia's dissent in Honig v. Doe (January 20, 1988)

JUSTICE SCALIA, with whom JUSTICE O'CONNOR joins, dissenting.

Without expressing any views on the merits of this case, I respectfully dissent because, in my opinion, we have no authority to decide it. I think the controversy is moot.

The Court correctly acknowledges that we have no power under Art. III of the Constitution to adjudicate a case that no longer presents an actual, ongoing dispute between the named parties. Ante at 484 U. S. 317, citing Nebraska Press Assn. v. Stuart, 427 U. S. 539, 427 U. S. 546 (1976); Preiser v. Newkirk, 422 U. S. 395, 422 U. S. 401 (1975). Here, there is obviously no present controversy between the parties, since both respondents are no longer in school, and therefore no longer subject to a unilateral "change in placement." The Court concedes mootness with respect to respondent John Doe, who is now too old to receive the benefits of the Education of the Handicapped Act (EHA). Ante at 484 U. S. 318. It concludes, however, that the case is not moot as to respondent Jack Smith, who has two more years of eligibility, but is no longer in the public schools, because the controversy is "capable of repetition, yet evading review." Ante at 484 U. S. 318-323.

Jurisdiction on the basis that a dispute is "capable of repetition, yet evading review" is limited to the "exceptional situatio[n]," Los Angeles v. Lyons, 461 U. S. 95, 461 U. S. 109 (1983), where the following two circumstances simultaneously occur:

"'(1) the challenged action [is] in its duration too short to be fully litigated prior to its cessation or expiration, and (2) there [is] a reasonable expectation that the same complaining party would be subjected to the same action again.'"

Murphy v. Hunt, 455 U. S. 478, 455 U. S. 482 (1982) (per curiam), quoting Weinstein v. Bradford, 423 U. S. 147, 423 U. S. 149 (1975) (per curiam). The second of these requirements is not met in this case.

For there to be a "reasonable expectation" that Smith will be subjected to the same action again, that event must be a "demonstrated probability." Murphy v. Hunt, supra, at 455 U. S. 482, 455 U. S. 483; Weinstein v. Bradford, supra, at 423 U. S. 149. I am surprised by the Court's contention, fraught with potential for future mischief, that "reasonable expectation" is satisfied by something less than "demonstrated probability." Ante at 484 U. S. 318-319, n. 6. No one expects that to happen which he does not think probable, and his expectation cannot be shown to be reasonable unless the probability is demonstrated. Thus, as the Court notes, our cases recite the two descriptions side by side ("a reasonable expectation' or a `demonstrated probability,'" Hunt, supra, at 455 U. S. 482). The Court asserts, however, that these standards are "described . . . in the disjunctive," ante at 484 U. S. 318-319, n. 6 -- evidently believing that the conjunction "or" has no accepted usage except a disjunctive one, i.e., "expressing an alternative, contrast, or opposition," Webster's Third New International Dictionary 651 (1981). In fact, however, the conjunction is often used

"to indicate . . . (3) the synonymous, equivalent, or substitutive character of two words or phrases (fell over a precipice [or] cliff) (the off [or] far side) (lessen [or] abate); (4) correction or greater exactness of phrasing or meaning (these essays, [or] rather rough sketches) (the present king had no children -- [or] no legitimate children . . .)."

Id. at 1585. It is obvious that, in saying "a reasonable expectation or a demonstrated probability," we have used the conjunction in one of the latter, or nondisjunctive, senses. Otherwise (and according to the Court's exegesis), we would have been saying that a controversy is sufficiently likely to recur if either a certain degree of probability exists or a higher degree of probability exists. That is rather like a statute giving the vote to persons who are "18 or 21." A bare six years ago, the author of today's opinion and one other Member of the majority plainly understood "reasonable expectation" and "demonstrated probability" to be synonymous. Cf. Edgar v. MITE Corp., 457 U. S. 624, 457 U. S. 662, and n. 11 (1982) (MARSHALL, J., dissenting, joined by BRENNAN, J.) (using the two terms here at issue interchangeably, and concluding that the case is moot because "there is no demonstrated probability that the State will have occasion to prevent MITE from making a takeover offer for some other corporation") (emphasis added).

The prior holdings cited by the Court in a footnote, see ante at 484 U. S. 319, n. 6, offer no support for the novel proposition that less than a probability of recurrence is sufficient to avoid mootness. In Burlington Northern R. Co. v. Maintenance of Way Employes, 481 U. S. 429, 481 U. S. 436, n. 4 (1987), we found that the same railroad and union were "reasonably likely" to find themselves in a recurring dispute over the same issue. Similarly, in California Coastal Comm'n v. Granite Rock Co., 480 U. S. 572, 480 U. S. 578 (1987), we found it "likely" that the plaintiff mining company would submit new plans which the State would seek to subject to its coastal permit requirements. See Webster's Third New International Dictionary 1310 (1981) (defining "likely" as "of such a nature or so circumstanced as to make something probable[;] . . . seeming to justify belief or expectation[;] . . . in all probability"). In the cases involving exclusion orders issued to prevent the press from attending criminal trials, we found that "[i]t can reasonably be assumed" that a news organization covering the area in which the defendant court sat will again be subjected to that court's closure rules. Press-Enterprise Co. v. Superior Court of Cal., Riverside County, 478 U. S. 1, 478 U. S. 6 (1986); Globe Newspaper Co. v. Superior Court of Norfolk County, 457 U. S. 596, 457 U. S. 603 (1982). In these and other cases, one may quarrel, perhaps, with the accuracy of the Court's probability assessment; but there is no doubt that assessment was regarded as necessary to establish jurisdiction.

In Roe v. Wade, 410 U. S. 113, 410 U. S. 125 (1973), we found that the "human gestation period is so short that the pregnancy will come to term before the usual appellate process is complete," so that "pregnancy litigation seldom will survive much beyond the trial stage, and appellate review will be effectively denied." Roe, at least one other abortion case, see Doe v. Bolton, 410 U. S. 179, 410 U. S. 187 (1973), and some of our election law decisions, see Rosario v. Rockefeller, 410 U. S. 752, 410 U. S. 756, n. 5 (1973); Dunn v. Blumstein, 405 U. S. 330, 405 U. S. 333, n. 2 (1972), differ from the body of our mootness jurisprudence not in accepting less than a probability that the issue will recur, in a manner evading review, between the same parties; but in dispensing with the same-party requirement entirely, focusing instead upon the great likelihood that the issue will recur between the defendant and the other members of the public at large without ever reaching us. Arguably, those cases have been limited to their facts, or to the narrow areas of abortion and election rights, by our more recent insistence that, at least in the absence of a class action, the "capable of repetition" doctrine applies only where "there [is] a reasonable expectation'" that the "same complaining party" would be subjected to the same action again. Hunt, 455 U.S. at 455 U. S. 482 (emphasis added), quoting Weinstein, 423 U.S. at 423 U. S. 149; see Burlington Northern R. Co., supra, at 481 U. S. 436, n. 4; Illinois Elections Bd. v. Socialist Workers Party, 440 U. S. 173, 440 U. S. 187 (1979). If those earlier cases have not been so limited, however, the conditions for their application do not in any event exist here. There is no extraordinary improbability of the present issue's reaching us as a traditionally live controversy. It would have done so in this very case if Smith had not chosen to leave public school. In sum, on any analysis, the proposition the Court asserts in the present case -- that probability need not be shown in order to establish the "same-party-recurrence" exception to mootness -- is a significant departure from settled law.

II

If our established mode of analysis were followed, the conclusion that a live controversy exists in the present case would require a demonstrated probability that all of the following events will occur: (1) Smith will return to public school; (2) he will be placed in an educational setting that is unable to tolerate his dangerous behavior; (3) he will again engage in dangerous behavior; and (4) local school officials will again attempt unilaterally to change his placement, and the state defendants will fail to prevent such action. The Court spends considerable time establishing that the last two of these events are likely to recur, but relegates to a footnote its discussion of the first event, upon which all others depend, and only briefly alludes to the second. Neither the facts in the record, nor even the extrarecord assurances of counsel, establish a demonstrated probability of either of them.

With respect to whether Smith will return to school, at oral argument, Smith's counsel forthrightly conceded that she "cannot represent whether in fact either of these students will ask for further education from the Petitioners." Tr. of Oral Arg. 23. Rather, she observed, respondents would "look to [our decision in this case] to find out what will happen after that." Id. at 23-24. When pressed, the most counsel would say was that, in her view, the 20-year-old Smith could seek to return to public school because he has not graduated, he is handicapped, and he has a right to an education. Id. at 27. I do not perceive the principle that would enable us to leap from the proposition that Smith could reenter public school to the conclusion that it is a demonstrated probability he will do so.

The Court nevertheless concludes that "there is, at the very least, a reasonable expectation" that Smith will return to school. Ante at 484 U. S. 319, n. 6. I cannot possibly dispute that on the basis of the Court's terminology. Once it is accepted that a "reasonable expectation" can exist without a demonstrable probability that the event in question will occur, the phrase has been deprived of all meaning, and the Court can give it whatever application it wishes, without fear of effective contradiction. It is worth pointing out, however, how slim are the reeds upon which this conclusion of "reasonable expectation" (whatever that means) rests. The Court bases its determination on three observations from the record and oral argument. First, it notes that Smith has been pressing this lawsuit since 1980. It suffices to observe that the equivalent argument can be made in every case that remains active and pending; we have hitherto avoided equating the existence of a case or controversy with the existence of a lawsuit. Second, the Court observes that Smith has "as great a need of a high school education and diploma as any of his peers." Ibid. While this is undoubtedly good advice, it hardly establishes that the 20-year-old Smith is likely to return to high school, much less to public high school. Finally, the Court notes that counsel "advises us that [Smith] is awaiting the outcome of this case to decide whether to pursue his degree." Ibid. Not only do I not think this establishes a current case or controversy, I think it a most conclusive indication that no current case or controversy exists. We do not sit to broaden decisionmaking options, but to adjudicate the lawfulness of acts that have happened or, at most, are about to occur.

The conclusion that the case is moot is reinforced, moreover, when one considers that, even if Smith does return to public school, the controversy will still not recur unless he is again placed in an educational setting that is unable to tolerate his behavior. It seems to me not only not demonstrably probable, but indeed quite unlikely, given what is now known about Smith's behavioral problems, that local school authorities would again place him in an educational setting that could not control his dangerous conduct, causing a suspension that would replicate the legal issues in this suit. The majority dismisses this further contingency by noting that the school authorities have an obligation under the EHA to provide an "appropriate" education in "the least restrictive environment." Ante at 484 U. S. 321. This means, however, the least restrictive environment appropriate for the particular child. The Court observes that "the preparation of an [individualized educational placement]" is "an inexact science, at best," ibid., thereby implying that the school authorities are likely to get it wrong. Even accepting this assumption, which seems to me contrary to the premises of the Act, I see no reason further to assume that they will get it wrong by making the same mistake they did last time -- assigning Smith to too unrestrictive an environment, from which he will thereafter be suspended -- rather than by assigning him to too restrictive an environment. The latter, which seems to me more likely than the former (though both combined are much less likely than a correct placement), might produce a lawsuit, but not a lawsuit involving the issues that we have before us here.

III

THE CHIEF JUSTICE joins the majority opinion on the ground, not that this case is not moot, but that, where the events giving rise to the mootness have occurred after we have granted certiorari, we may disregard them, since mootness is only a prudential doctrine, and not part of the "case or controversy" requirement of Art. III. I do not see how that can be. There is no more reason to intuit that mootness is merely a prudential doctrine than to intuit that initial standing is. Both doctrines have equivalently deep roots in the common law understanding, and hence the constitutional understanding, of what makes a matter appropriate for judicial disposition. See Flast v. Cohen, 392 U. S. 83, 392 U. S. 95 (1968) (describing mootness and standing as various illustrations of the requirement of "justiciability" in Art. III).

THE CHIEF JUSTICE relies upon the fact that an 1895 case discussing mootness, Mills v. Green, 159 U. S. 651, makes no mention of the Constitution. But there is little doubt that the Court believed the doctrine called into question the Court's power, and not merely its prudence, for (in an opinion by the same Justice who wrote Mills) it had said two years earlier:

"[T]he court is not empowered to decide moot questions or abstract propositions, or to declare . . . principles or rules of law which cannot affect the result as to the thing in issue in the case before it. No stipulation of parties or counsel . . . can enlarge the power, or affect the duty, of the court in this regard."

California v. San Pablo & Tulare R. Co., 149 U. S. 308, 149 U. S. 314 (1893) (Gray, J.) (emphasis added). If it seems peculiar to the modern lawyer that our 19th-century mootness cases make no explicit mention of Art. III, that is a peculiarity shared with our 19th-century, and even our early 20th-century, standing cases. As late as 1919, in dismissing a suit for lack of standing, we said simply:

"Considerations of propriety, as well as long-established practice, demand that we refrain from passing upon the constitutionality of an act of Congress unless obliged to do so in the proper performance of our judicial function, when the question is raised by a party whose interests entitle him to raise it."

Blair v. United States, 250 U. S. 273, 250 U. S. 279. See also, e.g., Standard Stock Food Co. v. Wright, 225 U. S. 540, 225 U. S. 550 (1912); Southern R. Co. v. King, 217 U. S. 524, 217 U. S. 534 (1910); Turpin v. Lemon, 187 U. S. 51, 187 U. S. 60-61 (1902); Tyler v. Judges of Court of Registration, 179 U. S. 405, 179 U. S. 409 (1900). The same is also true of our early cases dismissing actions lacking truly adverse parties, that is, collusive actions. See, e.g., 66 U. S. Chamberlain, 1 Black 419, 66 U. S. 425-426 (1862); Lord v. Veazie, 8

How. 251, 49 U. S. 254-256 (1850). The explanation for this ellipsis is that the courts simply chose to refer directly to the traditional, fundamental limitations upon the powers of common law courts, rather than referring to Art. III, which, in turn, adopts those limitations through terms ("The judicial Power"; "Cases"; "Controversies") that have virtually no meaning except by reference to that tradition. The ultimate circularity, coming back in the end to tradition, is evident in the statement by Justice Field:

"By cases and controversies are intended the claims of litigants brought before the courts for determination by such regular proceedings as are established by law or custom for the protection or enforcement of rights, or the prevention, redress, or punishment of wrongs. Whenever the claim of a party under the constitution, laws, or treaties of the United States takes such a form that the judicial power is capable of acting upon it, then it has become a case."

In re Pacific Railway Comm'n, 32 F. 241, 255 (CC ND Cal.1887).

See also 2 M. Farrand, Records of the Federal Convention of 1787, p. 430 (rev. ed.1966):

"Docr. Johnson moved to insert the words 'this Constitution and the' before the word 'laws.'"

"Mr. Madison doubted whether it was not going too far to extend the jurisdiction of the Court generally to cases arising Under the Constitution, & whether it ought not to be limited to cases of a Judiciary Nature. The right of expounding the Constitution in cases not of this nature ought not to be given to that Department."

"The motion of Docr. Johnson was agreed to nem: con: it being generally supposed that the jurisdiction given was constructively limited to cases of a Judiciary nature."

In sum, I cannot believe that it is only our prudence, and nothing inherent in the understood nature of "The judicial Power," U.S.Const., Art. III, § 1, that restrains us from pronouncing judgment in a case that the parties have settled, or a case involving a nonsurviving claim where the plaintiff has died, or a case where the law has been changed so that the basis of the dispute no longer exists, or a case where conduct sought to be enjoined has ceased, and will not recur. Where the conduct has ceased for the time being, but there is a demonstrated probability that it will recur, a real-life controversy between parties with a personal stake in the outcome continues to exist, and Art. III is no more violated than it is violated by entertaining a declaratory judgment action. But that is the limit of our power. I agree with THE CHIEF JUSTICE to this extent: the "yet evading review" portion of our "capable of repetition, yet evading review" test is prudential; whether or not that criterion is met, a justiciable controversy exists. But the probability of recurrence between the same parties is essential to our jurisdiction as a court, and it is that deficiency which the case before us presents.

It is assuredly frustrating to find that a jurisdictional impediment prevents us from reaching the important merits issues that were the reason for our agreeing to hear this case. But we cannot ignore such impediments for purposes of our appellate review without simultaneously affecting the principles that govern district courts in their assertion or retention of original jurisdiction. We thus do substantial harm to a governmental structure designed to restrict the courts to matters that actually affect the litigants before them.

Justice Scalia's concurrence and dissent in Pennell v. City of San Jose (Feb 24, 1988)

JUSTICE SCALIA, with whom JUSTICE O'CONNOR joins, concurring in part and dissenting in part.

I agree that the tenant hardship provision of the Ordinance does not, on its face, violate either the Due Process Clause or the Equal Protection Clause of the Fourteenth Amendment. I disagree, however, with the Court's conclusion that appellants' takings claim is premature. I would decide that claim on the merits, and would hold that the tenant hardship provision of the Ordinance effects a taking of private property without just compensation in violation of the Fifth and Fourteenth Amendments.

I

Appellants contend that any application of the tenant hardship provision of the San Jose Ordinance would effect an uncompensated taking of private property because that provision does not substantially advance legitimate state interests and because it improperly imposes a public burden on individual landlords. I can understand how such a claim -- that a law applicable to the plaintiffs is, root and branch, invalid -- can be readily rejected on the merits by merely noting that at least some of its applications may be lawful. But I do not understand how such a claim can possibly be avoided by considering it "premature." Suppose, for example, that the feature of the rental ordinance under attack was a provision allowing a hearing officer to consider the race of the apartment owner in deciding whether to allow a rent increase. It is inconceivable that we would say judicial challenge must await demonstration that this provision has actually been applied to the detriment of one of the plaintiffs. There is no difference, it seems to me, when the facial, root-and-branch challenge rests upon the Takings Clause, rather than the Equal Protection Clause.

The Court confuses the issue by relying on cases, and portions of cases, in which the Takings Clause challenge was not (as here) that the law in all its applications took property without just compensation, but was rather that the law's application in regulating the use of particular property so severely reduced the value of that property as to constitute a taking. It is in that context, and not (as the Court suggests) generally, that takings analysis involves an "essentially ad hoc, factual inquir[y]," Kaiser Aetna v. United States, 444 U. S. 164, 444 U. S. 175 (1979). We said as much less than a year ago, and it is surprising that we have so soon forgotten:

"In addressing petitioners' claim, we must not disregard the posture in which this case comes before us. The District Court granted summary judgment to respondents only on the facial challenge to the Subsidence Act. The court explained that ' . . . the only question before this court is whether the mere enactment of the statutes and regulations constitutes a taking.' . . ."

"The posture of the case is critical, because we have recognized an important distinction between a claim that the mere enactment of a statute constitutes a taking and a claim that the particular impact of government action on a specific piece of property requires the payment of just compensation. This point is illustrated by our decision in Hodel v. Virginia Surface Mining & Reclamation Assn., Inc., 452 U. S. 264 (1981), in which we rejected a preenforcement challenge to the constitutionality of the Surface Mining Control and Reclamation Act of 1977. . . . The Court [there] explained:"

"* * * *"

"Because appellees' taking claim arose in the context of a facial challenge, it presented no concrete controversy concerning either application of the Act to particular surface mining operations or its effect on specific parcels of land. Thus, the only issue properly before the District Court and, in turn, this Court, is whether the 'mere enactment' of the Surface Mining Act constitutes a taking. . . . The test to be applied in considering this facial challenge is straightforward. A statute regulating the uses that can be made of property effects a taking if it 'denies an owner economically viable use of his land.'. . ."

"Petitioners thus face an uphill battle in making a facial attack on the Act as a taking."

Keystone Bituminous Coal Assn. v. DeBenedictis, 480 U. S. 470, 480 U. S. 493-495 (1987). While the battle was "uphill" in Keystone, we allowed it to be fought, and did not declare it "premature."

The same was true of the facial takings challenge in Hodel v. Virginia Surface Mining & Reclamation Assn., Inc., supra. It is remarkable that the Court should point to that case in support of its position, describing the holding as follows:

"In Virginia Surface Mining, for example, we found that a challenge to the Surface Mining Control and Reclamation Act . . . was 'premature,' . . . and 'not ripe for judicial resolution,' . . . because the property owners in that case had not identified any property that had allegedly been taken by the Act, nor had they sought administrative relief from the Act's restrictions on surface mining."

Ante at 485 U. S. 10. But this holding in Virginia Surface Mining applied only to "the taking issue decided by the District Court," 452 U.S. at 452 U. S. 297, which was the issue of the statute's validity as applied. Having rejected that challenge as premature, the Court then continued (in the language we quoted in Keystone):

"Thus, the only issue properly before the District Court and, in turn, this Court, is whether the 'mere enactment' of the Surface Mining Act constitutes a taking."

452 U.S. at 452 U. S. 295. That issue was not rejected as premature, but was decided on its merits, id. at 452 U. S. 295-297, just as it was in Keystone, and as it was before that in Agins v. Tiburon, 447 U. S. 255, 447 U. S. 260-263 (1980).

In sum, it is entirely clear from our cases that a facial takings challenge is not premature even if it rests upon the ground that the ordinance deprives property owners of all economically viable use of their land -- a ground that is, as we have said, easier to establish in an "as-applied" attack. It is, if possible, even more clear that the present facial challenge is not premature, because it does not rest upon a ground that would even profit from consideration in the context of particular application. As we said in Agins, a zoning law

"effects a taking if the ordinance does not substantially advance legitimate state interests, . . . or denies an owner economically viable use of his land."

Id. at 447 U. S. 260. The present challenge is of the former sort. Appellants contend that providing financial assistance to impecunious renters is not a state interest that can legitimately be furthered by regulating the use of property. Knowing the nature and character of the particular property in question, or the degree of its economic impairment, will in no way assist this inquiry. Such factors are as irrelevant to the present claim as we have said they are to the claim that a law effects a taking by authorizing a permanent physical invasion of property. See Loretto v. Teleprompter Manhattan CATV Corp., 458 U. S. 419 (1982). So even if we were explicitly to overrule cases such as Agins, Virginia Surface Mining, and Keystone, and to hold that a facial challenge will not lie where the issue can be more forcefully presented in an "as-applied" attack, there would still be no reason why the present challenge should not proceed.

Today's holding has no more basis in equity than it does in precedent. Since the San Jose Ordinance does not require any specification of how much reduction in rent is attributable to each of the various factors that the hearing officer is allowed to take into account, it is quite possible that none of the many landlords affected by the Ordinance will ever be able to meet the Court's requirement of a "showing in a particular case as to the consequences of [the hardship factor] in the ultimate determination of the rent." Ante at 10. There is no reason thus to shield alleged constitutional injustice from judicial scrutiny. I would therefore consider appellants' takings claim on the merits.

II

The Fifth Amendment of the United States Constitution, made applicable to the States through the Fourteenth Amendment, Chicago, B. & Q. R. Co. v. Chicago, 166 U. S. 226, 166 U. S. 239 (1897), provides that "private property [shall not] be taken for public use, without just compensation." We have repeatedly observed that the purpose of this provision is

"to bar Government from forcing some people alone to bear public burdens which, in all fairness and justice, should be borne by the public as a whole."

Armstrong v. United States, 364 U. S. 40, 364 U. S. 49 (1960); See also First English Evangelical Lutheran Church of Glendale v. Los Angeles County, 482 U.S. 304, 482 U. S. 318-319 (1987); Webb's Fabulous Pharmacies, Inc. v. Beckwith, 449 U. S. 155, 449 U. S. 163 (1980); Agins v. Tiburon, supra, at 447 U. S. 260; Penn Central Transportation Co. v. New York City, 438 U. S. 104, 438 U. S. 123 (1978); Monongahela Navigation Co. v. United States, 148 U. S. 312, 148 U. S. 325 (1893).

Traditional land-use regulation (short of that which totally destroys the economic value of property) does not violate this principle because there is a cause-and-effect relationship between the property use restricted by the regulation and the social evil that the regulation seeks to remedy. Since the owner's use of the property is (or, but for the regulation, would be) the source of the social problem, it cannot be said that he has been singled out unfairly. Thus, the common zoning regulations requiring subdividers to observe lot-size and set-back restrictions, and to dedicate certain areas to public streets, are in accord with our constitutional traditions because the proposed property use would otherwise be the cause of excessive congestion. The same cause-and-effect relationship is popularly thought to justify emergency price regulation: when commodities have been priced at a level that produces exorbitant returns, the owners of those commodities can be viewed as responsible for the economic hardship that occurs. Whether or not that is an accurate perception of the way a free market economy operates, it is at least true that the owners reap unique benefits from the situation that produces the economic hardship, and in that respect singling them out to relieve it may not be regarded as "unfair." That justification might apply to the rent regulation in the present case, apart from the single feature under attack here.

Appellants do not contest the validity of rent regulation in general. They acknowledge that the city may constitutionally set a "reasonable rent" according to the statutory minimum and the six other factors that must be considered by the hearing officer (cost of debt servicing, rental history of the unit, physical condition of the unit, changes in housing services, other financial information provided by the landlord, and market value rents for similar units). San Jose Municipal Ordinance 19696, § 5703.28(c) (1979). Appellants' only claim is that a reduction of a rent increase below what would otherwise be a "reasonable rent" under this scheme may not, consistently with the Constitution, be based on consideration of the seventh factor -- the hardship to the tenant as defined in § 5703.29. I think they are right.

Once the other six factors of the Ordinance have been applied to a landlord's property, so that he is receiving only a reasonable return, he can no longer be regarded as a "cause" of exorbitantly priced housing; nor is he any longer reaping distinctively high profits from the housing shortage. The seventh factor, the "hardship" provision, is invoked to meet a quite different social problem: the existence of some renters who are too poor to afford even reasonably priced housing. But that problem is no more caused or exploited by landlords than it is by the grocers who sell needy renters their food, or the department stores that sell them their clothes, or the employers who pay them their wages, or the citizens of San Jose holding the higher paying jobs from which they are excluded. And even if the neediness of renters could be regarded as a problem distinctively attributable to landlords in general, it is not remotely attributable to the particular landlords that the Ordinance singles out -- namely, those who happen to have a "hardship" tenant at the present time, or who may happen to rent to a "hardship" tenant in the future, or whose current or future affluent tenants may happen to decline into the "hardship" category.

The traditional manner in which American government has met the problem of those who cannot pay reasonable prices for privately sold necessities -- a problem caused by the society at large -- has been the distribution to such persons of funds raised from the public at large through taxes, either in cash (welfare payments) or in goods (public housing, publicly subsidized housing, and food stamps). Unless we are to abandon the guiding principle of the Takings Clause that "public burdens . . . should be borne by the public as a whole," Armstrong, 364 U.S. at 364 U. S. 49, this is the only manner that our Constitution permits. The fact that government acts through the landlord-tenant relationship does not magically transform general public welfare, which must be supported by all the public, into mere "economic regulation," which can disproportionately burden particular individuals. Here the city is not "regulating" rents in the relevant sense of preventing rents that are excessive; rather, it is using the occasion of rent regulation (accomplished by the rest of the Ordinance) to establish a welfare program privately funded by those landlords who happen to have "hardship" tenants.

Of course all economic regulation effects wealth transfer. When excessive rents are forbidden, for example, landlords as a class become poorer and tenants as a class (or at least incumbent tenants as a class) become richer. Singling out landlords to be the transferors may be within our traditional constitutional notions of fairness, because they can plausibly be regarded as the source or the beneficiary of the high-rent problem. Once such a connection is no longer required, however, there is no end to the social transformations that can be accomplished by so-called "regulation," at great expense to the democratic process.

The politically attractive feature of regulation is not that it permits wealth transfers to be achieved that could not be achieved otherwise; but rather that it permits them to be achieved "off budget," with relative invisibility, and thus relative immunity from normal democratic processes. San Jose might, for example, have accomplished something like the result here by simply raising the real estate tax upon rental properties and using the additional revenues thus acquired to pay part of the rents of "hardship" tenants. It seems to me doubtful, however, whether the citizens of San Jose would allow funds in the municipal treasury, from wherever derived, to be distributed to a family of four with income as high as $32,400 a year -- the generous maximum necessary to qualify automatically as a "hardship" tenant under the rental Ordinance. * The voters might well see other, more pressing, social priorities. And of course what $32,400-a-year renters can acquire through spurious "regulation," other groups can acquire as well. Once the door is opened, it is not unreasonable to expect price regulations requiring private businesses to give special discounts to senior citizens (no matter how affluent), or to students, the handicapped, or war veterans. Subsidies for these groups may well be a good idea, but because of the operation of the Takings Clause our governmental system has required them to be applied, in general, through the process of taxing and spending, where both economic effects and competing priorities are more evident.

That fostering of an intelligent democratic process is one of the happy effects of the constitutional prescription -- perhaps accidental, perhaps not. Its essence, however, is simply the unfairness of making one citizen pay, in some fashion other than taxes, to remedy a social problem that is none of his creation. As the Supreme Court of New Jersey said in finding unconstitutional a scheme displaying, among other defects, the same vice I find dispositive here:

"A legislative category of economically needy senior citizens is sound, proper and sustainable as a rational classification. But compelled subsidization by landlords or by tenants who happen to live in an apartment building with senior citizens is an improper and unconstitutional method of solving the problem."

Property Owners Assn. v. North Bergen, 74 N.J. 327, 339, 378 A.2d 25, 31 (1977).

I would hold that the seventh factor in § 5703.28(c) of the San Jose Ordinance effects a taking of property without just compensation.

* Under the San Jose Ordinance, "hardship" tenants include (though are not limited to) those whose "household income and monthly housing expense meets [sic] the criteria" for assistance under the existing housing provisions of § 8 of the Housing and Community Development Act of 1974, 42 U.S.C. § 1437f (1982 ed. and Supp. III). The United States Department of Housing and Urban Development currently limits assistance under these provisions for families of four in the San Jose area to those who earn $32,400 or less per year. Memorandum from U.S. Dept. of Housing and Urban Development, Assistant Secretary for Housing-Federal Housing Comm'r, Income Limits for Lower Income and Very Low-Income Families Under the Housing Act of 1937 (Jan. 15, 1988).

Justice Scalia's dissent in K Mart Corp. v. Cartier, Inc. (March 7, 1988)

JUSTICE SCALIA, with whom THE CHIEF JUSTICE and JUSTICE O'CONNOR join, dissenting.

In a Court that selects its docketed cases on the basis of the general importance of the issues they present, jurisdictional questions tend to get short shrift. The central issue in this suit, the so-called "gray market" issue, which may have immediate and substantial effects on the national economy, has provoked no less than 15 amici briefs; while the jurisdictional question, which could have the undesirable consequence of preventing our immediate resolution of the merits, has been briefed in only 11 pages by petitioners and 6 pages by respondents. Understandably enough, no one, myself included, is eager to conclude that we are powerless to resolve the issue that is this suit's claim to national attention.

Even so, we must carefully review any question that asks us to determine the limits of a federal court's power, particularly when, as in this suit, two different sets of courts have concluded that they have exclusive jurisdiction over the subject of the suit. Compare Vivitar Corp. v. United States, 761 F.2d 1552, 1557-1560 (CA Fed.1985), cert. denied, 474 U.S. 1055 (1986); with cases below, 252 U.S.App.D.C. 342, 344-346, 790 F.2d

903, 905-907 (1986); and Olympus Corp. v. United States, 792 F.2d 315, 317-319 (CA2 1986). Moreover, while the gray market question is of greater immediate economic importance (though we would soon enough have another occasion to address it), the jurisdictional question, if decided incorrectly, may generate uncertainty, and hence litigation, into the indefinite future. In my view, the Court's resolution of this question strains the plain language of the statute and blurs a clear jurisdictional line that Congress has established.

The Court of International Trade's exclusive jurisdiction extends to any civil action against the United States, its agencies or officers,

"that arises out of any law of the United States providing for . . . embargoes or other quantitative restrictions on the importation of merchandise for reasons other than the protection of the public health or safety."

28 U.S.C. § 1581(i)(3). The statute does not define "embargo," and there is no reason to give it anything other than its ordinary meaning. An embargo is "a prohibition imposed by law upon commerce either in general or in one or more of its branches," Webster's Third New International Dictionary 738 (1981), a "[g]overnment order prohibiting commercial trade with individuals or businesses of other nations," Black's Law Dictionary 468 (5th ed.1979), an "[a]uthoritative stoppage of foreign commerce or of any special trade," Funk & Wagnalls New International Dictionary of the English Language 411 (1984).

The present lawsuit challenges a Customs Service regulation, 19 CFR § 133.21(c) (1987), that implements § 526(a) of the Tariff Act of 1930, 19 U.S.C. § 1526(a). That statutory provision, which begins with the caption "(a) Importation prohibited," excludes from the United States foreign-made merchandise bearing a trademark owned and recorded by a United States citizen or corporation. Section 526(a) is, to borrow language from the Senate debate, "an embargo against any foreign country shipping goods here where an American claims he has a trade-mark upon them." 62 Cong.Rec. 11603 (1922) (remarks of Sen. Kellogg) (emphasis added). Because this suit against the United States arises out of a law providing for an embargo, I would hold that it is within the exclusive jurisdiction of the Court of International Trade.

The Court acknowledges that the term "embargo" means a "governmentally imposed" import prohibition, ante at 185, but it seems to me that its analysis departs from that truth. Surely § 526(a) prohibits imports, and that prohibition, enacted by Congress and enforced by an executive agency, is surely governmentally imposed. One might argue that the privately invocable exception to § 526(a) causes it not to be an absolute governmental prohibition, and that only absolute governmental prohibitions qualify as embargoes. The Court rightly avoids that line of analysis, however, since many of the provisions commonly regarded as embargoes contain privately invocable exceptions, such as exemptions for certain privately determined uses. See, e.g., 19 U.S.C.A. § 1202, p. 265, Schedule 1, Part 4, Subpart E; 19 CFR §§ 12.80(b)(v), (vi) (1987). But if, despite its privately invocable exception, § 526(a) meets the requirement of being a prohibition, it unquestionably meets the requirement of being a governmentally imposed one. Here, as with other embargoes, the availability of a privately invocable exception affects the extent of the prohibition; but the residual prohibition, whatever its extent, is governmental.

The Court seeks to set § 526(a) apart from other embargoes with privately invocable exceptions by observing that

"rather than reflecting a governmental restriction on the quantity of a particular product that will enter, it merely provides a mechanism by which a private party might, at its own option, enlist the Government's aid in restricting the quantity of imports in order to enforce a private right."

Ante at 485 U. S. 185. Perhaps it is meant to provide such a mechanism, but that relates not to whether it is a governmental prohibition, but to what the purpose of the governmental prohibition happens to be. It is no more in accord with common usage to say that a provision cannot be an embargo if its purpose is to protect private rights than to say (as did the Court of Appeals in the analysis that the Court readily rejects, ibid.,) that it cannot be an embargo if its purpose is something other than trade policy. Embargoes are imposed for many different purposes, including sometimes the protection of private rights. Assuredly those which have the latter purpose are different from those that do not, but it is beyond me why that purpose, any more than any other one, would cause them not to be governmentally imposed import prohibitions. In my view, for example, the prohibition on the importation of art stolen from a private nonprofit museum, see 19 CFR §§ 12.104-12.104h (1987), is unquestionably an embargo. Moreover, since the lever that the Court is using for its analysis is the prohibition's asserted lack of "governmental" character, it should make no difference whether the objective of the prohibition is to protect a private "right," or to protect some other private interest, or the interest of some nonprivate entity other than the Government itself. Thus, on the Court's analysis, there would be excluded from the term "embargo" the prohibition on importing pre-Columbian sculptures or murals, which does not apply if the importer produces a certificate issued by the country of origin stating that the goods were not unlawfully exported. 19 U.S.C. § 2092; 19 CFR § 12.107 (1987). This is simply not in accord with normal understanding.

The Court seeks to establish the inherently "nonembargo" character of a prohibition protecting private property rights by noting that a court injunction enforcing a contractual import prohibition is not an embargo. Ante at 485 U. S. 185. I agree that an injunction is not an embargo, but that conclusion does not follow from the fact that the injunction issued at the instance of a private individual to protect property rights. A court injunction issued at the instance of a Government agency, to prevent importation that was part of a conspiracy in violation of the Sherman Act, would likewise not generally be thought of as an embargo -- because the word is normally applied only to prohibitions imposed by the Legislative or Executive Branches of Government.

The short of the matter is that an "embargo" is an import regulation that takes the form of a governmental prohibition on imports, regardless of any exceptions it may contain and regardless of its ultimate purpose -- just as quotas, tariffs, and conditions on importation are identifiable forms of import regulation regardless of their exceptions and purposes. The Court points out, ante at 485 U. S. 187, that it may sometimes be difficult to distinguish a condition on importation from a prohibition on importation containing exceptions. That may be true, but since we are agreed that only prohibitions, and not conditions, come within the meaning of embargo, that ambiguity will have to be grappled with under the Court's view of things no less than under mine. It is irrelevant to the present issue, unless the existence of one ambiguity within a statute justifies the needless creation of another. Under my analysis, when a provision has been identified as an import prohibition (however difficult that may be -- and it is neither difficult nor contested here), that is an end of the matter. Under the Court's analysis, one must proceed further to examine the exceptions to the prohibition and its purpose.

Today's decision leaves some doubt as to what prohibitions on importation other than § 526(a) are not governmental, and hence not embargoes, because they benefit private parties and are avoidable by private consent. Even if the Court's holding can be limited to prohibitions that protect private "rights," then at least the status of the prohibitions on the importation of goods that infringe trademarks or copyrights is called into question. See 15 U.S.C. § 1124; 17 U.S.C. §§ 601-603. And since, as noted earlier, the purpose of protecting private "rights" (whatever that might mean) is logically no more invalidating than the purpose of protecting private "interests," or even, more broadly, nongovernmental interests, the status of other import prohibitions is cast in doubt as well.

These uncertainties arise from today's particular departure from the meaning of "embargo" as "a governmental prohibition on importation." Much greater, unfortunately, are the uncertainties that arise from today's acknowledgment of the principle that departure is permissible. Having cast § 526(a) loose from the moorings of its language, we leave it to drift on the currents of lawyerly invention. It remains to be seen what other limitations on the ordinary meaning of "embargo," no more apparent to the naked mind than the present one, may exist.

Justice Scalia's concurrence in Bendix Autolite Corp. v. Midwesco Enterprises, Inc. (June 17, 1988)

JUSTICE SCALIA, concurring in the judgment.

I cannot confidently assess whether the Court's evaluation and balancing of interests in this case is right or wrong. Although the Court labels the effect of exposure to the general jurisdiction of Ohio's courts "a significant burden" on commerce, I am not sure why that is. In precise terms, it is the burden of defending in Ohio (rather than some other forum) any lawsuit having all of the following features: (1) the plaintiff desires to bring it in Ohio, (2) it has so little connection to Ohio that service could not otherwise be made under Ohio's long-arm statute, and (3) it has a great enough connection to Ohio that it is not subject to dismissal on forum non conveniens grounds. The record before us supplies no indication as to how many suits fit this description (even the present suit is not an example since appellee Midwesco Enterprises was subject to long-arm service, ante, at 894), and frankly I have no idea how one would go about estimating the number. It may well be "significant," but for all we know it is "negligible."

A person or firm that takes the other alternative, by declining to appoint a general agent for service, will remain theoretically subject to suit in Ohio (as the Court says) "in perpetuity" — at least as far as the statute of limitations is concerned. But again, I do not know how we assess how significant a burden this is, unless anything that is theoretically perpetual must be significant. It seems very unlikely that anyone would intentionally wait to sue later rather than sooner — not only because the prospective defendant may die or dissolve, but also because prejudgment interest is normally not awarded, and the staleness of evidence generally harms the party with the burden of proof. The likelihood of an unintentionally delayed suit brought under this provision that could not be brought without it seems not enormously large. Moreover, whatever the likelihood is, it does not seem terribly plausible that any real-world deterrent effect on interstate transactions will be produced by the incremental cost of having to defend a delayed suit rather than a timely suit. But the point is, it seems to me we can do no more than speculate.

On the other side of the scale, the Court considers the benefit of the Ohio scheme to local interests. These are, presumably, to enable the preservation of claims against defendants who have placed themselves beyond the personal jurisdiction of Ohio courts, and (by encouraging appointment of an agent) to facilitate service upon out-of-state defendants who might otherwise be difficult to locate. See G. D. Searle & Co. v. Cohn, 455 U. S. 404, 410 (1982) (it is "a reasonable assumption that unrepresented foreign corporations, as a general rule, may not be so easy to find and serve"). We have no way of knowing how often these ends are in fact achieved, and the Court thus says little about them except to call them "an important factor to consider." Ante, at 893.

Having evaluated the interests on both sides as roughly as this, the Court then proceeds to judge which is more important. This process is ordinarily called "balancing," Pike v. Bruce Church, Inc., 397 U. S. 137, 142 (1970), but the scale analogy is not really appropriate, since the interests on both sides are incommensurate. It is more like judging whether a particular line is longer than a particular rock is heavy. All I am really persuaded of by the Court's opinion is that the burdens the Court labels "significant" are more determinative of its decision than the benefits it labels "important." Were it not for the brief implication that there is here a discrimination unjustified by any state interest, see ante, at 894, I suggest an opinion could as persuasively have been written coming out the opposite way. We sometimes make similar "balancing" judgments in determining how far the needs of the State can intrude upon the liberties of the individual, see, e. g., Boos v. Barry, 485 U. S. 312, 324 (1988), but that is of the essence of the courts' function as the nonpolitical branch. Weighing the governmental interests of a State against the needs of interstate commerce is, by contrast, a task squarely within the responsibility of Congress, see U. S. Const., Art. I, § 8, cl. 3, and "ill suited to the judicial function." CTS Corp. v. Dynamics Corp. of America, 481 U. S. 69, 95 (1987) (SCALIA, J., concurring in part and concurring in judgment).

I would therefore abandon the "balancing" approach to these negative Commerce Clause cases, first explicitly adopted 18 years ago in Pike v. Bruce Church, Inc., supra, and leave essentially legislative judgments to the Congress. Issues already decided I would leave untouched, but would adopt for the future an analysis more appropriate to our role and our abilities. This does no damage to the interests protected by the doctrine of stare decisis. Since the outcome of any particular still-undecided issue under the current methodology is in my view not predictable — except within the broad range that would in any event come out the same way under the test I would apply — no expectations can possibly be upset. To the contrary, the ultimate objective of the rule of stare decisis will be furthered. Because the outcome of the test I would apply is considerably more clear, confident expectations will more readily be able to be entertained.

In my view, a state statute is invalid under the Commerce Clause if, and only if, it accords discriminatory treatment to interstate commerce in a respect not required to achieve a lawful state purpose. When such a validating purpose exists, it is for Congress and not us to determine it is not significant enough to justify the burden on commerce. The Ohio tolling statute, Ohio Rev. Code Ann. § 2305.15 (Supp. 1987), is on its face discriminatory because it applies only to out-of-state corporations. That facial discrimination cannot be justified on the basis that "it advances a legitimate local purpose that cannot be adequately served by reasonable nondiscriminatory alternatives," New Energy Co. of Indiana v. Limbach, ante, at 278. A tolling statute that operated only against persons beyond the reach of Ohio's long-arm statute, or against all persons that could not be found for mail service, would be narrowly tailored to advance the legitimate purpose of preserving claims; but the present statute extends the time for suit even against corporations which (like Midwesco Enterprises) are fully suable within Ohio, and readily reachable through the mails.

Because the present statute discriminates against interstate commerce by applying a disadvantageous rule against nonresidents for no valid state purpose that requires such a rule, I concur in the judgment that the Ohio statute violates the Commerce Clause.

Justice Scalia's dissent in Stewart Organization, Inc. v. Ricoh Corp. (June 20, 1988)

JUSTICE SCALIA, dissenting.

I agree with the opinion of the Court that the initial question before us is whether the validity between the parties of a contractual forum-selection clause falls within the scope of 28 U. S. C. § 1404(a). See ante, at 26-27, 29. I cannot agree, however, that the answer to that question is yes. Nor do I believe that the federal courts can, consistent with the twin-aims test of Erie R. Co. v. Tompkins, 304 U. S. 64 (1938), fashion a judge-made rule to govern this issue of contract validity.

I

When a litigant asserts that state law conflicts with a federal procedural statute or formal Rule of Procedure, a court's first task is to determine whether the disputed point in question in fact falls within the scope of the federal statute or Rule. In this case, the Court must determine whether the scope of § 1404(a) is sufficiently broad to cause a direct collision with state law or implicitly to control the issue before the Court, i. e., validity between the parties of the forum-selection clause, thereby leaving no room for the operation of state law. See Burlington Northern R. Co. v. Woods, 480 U. S. 1, 4-5 (1987). I conclude that it is not.

Although the language of § 1404(a) provides no clear answer, in my view it does provide direction. The provision vests the district courts with authority to transfer a civil action to another district "[f]or the convenience of parties and witnesses, in the interest of justice." This language looks to the present and the future. As the specific reference to convenience of parties and witnesses suggests, it requires consideration of what is likely to be just in the future, when the case is tried, in light of things as they now stand. Accordingly, the courts in applying § 1404(a) have examined a variety of factors, each of which pertains to facts that currently exist or will exist: e. g., the forum actually chosen by the plaintiff, the current convenience of the parties and witnesses, the current location of pertinent books and records, similar litigation pending elsewhere, current docket conditions, and familiarity of the potential courts with governing state law. See 15 C. Wright, A. Miller, & E. Cooper, Federal Practice and Procedure §§ 3848-3849, 3851, 3853-3854 (2d ed. 1986). In holding that the validity between the parties of a forum-selection clause falls within the scope of § 1404(a), the Court inevitably imports, in my view without adequate textual foundation, a new retrospective element into the court's deliberations, requiring examination of what the facts were concerning, among other things, the bargaining power of the parties and the presence or absence of overreaching at the time the contract was made. See ante, at 28, and n. 7, 29.

The Court largely attempts to avoid acknowledging the novel scope it gives to § 1404(a) by casting the issue as how much weight a district court should give a forum-selection clause as against other factors when it makes its determination under § 1404(a). I agree that if the weight-among-factors issue were before us, it would be governed by § 1404 (a). That is because, while the parties may decide who between them should bear any inconvenience, only a court can decide how much weight should be given under § 1404(a) to the factor of the parties' convenience as against other relevant factors such as the convenience of witnesses. But the Court's description of the issue begs the question: what law governs whether the forum-selection clause is a valid or invalid allocation of any inconvenience between the parties. If it is invalid, i. e., should be voided, between the parties, it cannot be entitled to any weight in the § 1404(a) determination. Since under Alabama law the forum-selection clause should be voided, see Redwing Carriers, Inc. v. Foster, 382 So. 2d 554, 556 (Ala. 1980), in this case the question of what weight should be given the forum-selection clause can be reached only if as a preliminary matter federal law controls the issue of the validity of the clause between the parties.[*]

Second, § 1404(a) was enacted against the background that issues of contract, including a contract's validity, are nearly always governed by state law. It is simply contrary to the practice of our system that such an issue should be wrenched from state control in absence of a clear conflict with federal law or explicit statutory provision. It is particularly instructive in this regard to compare § 1404(a) with another provision, enacted by the same Congress a year earlier, that did pre-empt state contract law, and in precisely the same field of agreement regarding forum selection. Section 2 of the Federal Arbitration Act, 9 U. S. C. § 2, provides:

"A written provision in . . . a contract evidencing a transaction involving commerce to settle by arbitration a controversy thereafter arising out of such contract or transaction, or the refusal to perform the whole or any part thereof, or an agreement in writing to submit to arbitration an existing controversy arising out of such a contract, transaction, or refusal, shall be valid, irrevocable, and enforceable, save upon such grounds as exist at law or in equity for the revocation of any contract."

We have said that an arbitration clause is a "kind of forum-selection clause," Scherk v. Alberto-Culver Co., 417 U. S. 506, 519 (1974), and the contrast between this explicit pre-emption of state contract law on the subject and § 1404(a) could not be more stark. Section 1404(a) is simply a venue provision that nowhere mentions contracts or agreements, much less that the validity of certain contracts or agreements will be matters of federal law. It is difficult to believe that state contract law was meant to be pre-empted by this provision that we have said "should be regarded as a federal judicial housekeeping measure," Van Dusen v. Barrack, 376 U. S. 612, 636-637 (1964), that we have said did not change "the relevant factors" which federal courts used to consider under the doctrine of forum non conveniens, Norwood v. Kirkpatrick, 349 U. S. 29, 32 (1955), and that we have held can be applied retroactively because it is procedural, Ex parte Collett, 337 U. S. 55, 71 (1949). It seems to me the generality of its language — "[f]or the convenience of parties and witnesses, in the interest of justice" — is plainly insufficient to work the great change in law asserted here.

Third, it has been common ground in this Court since Erie, 304 U. S., at 74-77, that when a federal procedural statute or Rule of Procedure is not on point, substantial uniformity of predictable outcome between federal and state courts in adjudicating claims should be striven for. See also Klaxon Co. v. Stentor Electric Mfg. Co., 313 U. S. 487, 496 (1941). This rests upon a perception of the constitutional and congressional plan underlying the creation of diversity and pendent jurisdiction in the lower federal courts, which should quite obviously be carried forward into our interpretation of ambiguous statutes relating to the exercise of that jurisdiction. We should assume, in other words, when it is fair to do so, that Congress is just as concerned as we have been to avoid significant differences between state and federal courts in adjudicating claims. Cf. Southland Corp. v. Keating, 465 U. S. 1, 15 (1984) (interpreting Federal Arbitration Act to apply to claims brought in state courts in order to discourage forum shopping). Thus, in deciding whether a federal procedural statute or Rule of Procedure encompasses a particular issue, a broad reading that would create significant disuniformity between state and federal courts should be avoided if the text permits. See, e. g., Walker v. Armco Steel Corp., 446 U. S. 740, 750-751 (1980); Cohen v. Beneficial Industrial Loan Corp., 337 U. S. 541, 556 (1949); Palmer v. Hoffman, 318 U. S. 109, 117 (1943); cf. P. Bator, D. Meltzer, P. Mishkin, & D. Shapiro, Hart and Wechsler's The Federal Courts and the Federal System 828 (3d ed. 1988) ("The Supreme Court has continued since Hanna to interpret the federal rules to avoid conflict with important state regulatory policies"). As I have shown, the interpretation given § 1404(a) by the Court today is neither the plain nor the more natural meaning; at best, § 1404(a) is ambiguous. I would therefore construe it to avoid the significant encouragement to forum shopping that will inevitably be provided by the interpretation the Court adopts today.

II

Since no federal statute or Rule of Procedure governs the validity of a forum-selection clause, the remaining issue is whether federal courts may fashion a judge-made rule to govern the question. If they may not, the Rules of Decision Act, 28 U. S. C. § 1652, mandates use of state law. See Erie, supra, at 72-73; Hanna v. Plumer, 380 U. S. 460, 471-472 (1965) (if federal courts lack authority to fashion a rule, "state law must govern because there can be no other law"); DelCostello v. Teamsters, 462 U. S. 151, 174, n. 1 (1983) (O'CONNOR, J., dissenting) (Rules of Decision Act "simply requires application of state law unless federal law applies"); see also id., at 159, n. 13.

In general, while interpreting and applying substantive law is the essence of the "judicial Power" created under Article III of the Constitution, that power does not encompass the making of substantive law. Cf. Erie, supra, at 78-79. Whatever the scope of the federal courts' authority to create federal common law in other areas, it is plain that the mere fact that petitioner company here brought an antitrust claim, ante, at 24, does not empower the federal courts to make common law on the question of the validity of the forum-selection clause. See Campbell v. Haverhill, 155 U. S. 610, 616 (1895) (Rules of Decision Act "itself neither contains nor suggests . . . a distinction" between federal-question cases and diversity cases); DelCostello, supra, at 173, n. 1 (STEVENS, J., dissenting) (same); cf. Texas Industries, Inc. v. Radcliff Materials, Inc., 451 U. S. 630 (1981). The federal courts do have authority, however, to make procedural rules that govern the practice before them. See 28 U. S. C. § 2071 (federal courts may make rules "for the conduct of their business"); Fed. Rule Civ. Proc. 83 (districts courts have authority to "regulate their practice"); see generally Sibbach v. Wilson & Co., 312 U. S. 1, 9-10 (1941).

In deciding what is substantive and what is procedural for these purposes, we have adhered to a functional test based on the "twin aims of the Erie rule: discouragement of forum-shopping and avoidance of inequitable administration of the laws." Hanna, supra, at 468; see also ante, at 27, n. 6; Walker v. Armco Steel Corp., supra, at 747. Moreover, although in reviewing the validity of a federal procedural statute or Rule of Procedure we inquire only whether Congress or the rulemakers have trespassed beyond the wide latitude given them to determine that a matter is procedural, see Burlington Northern R. Co. v. Woods, 480 U. S., at 5; Hanna, supra, at 471-474, in reviewing the lower courts' application of the twin-aims test we apply our own judgment as a matter of law.

Under the twin-aims test, I believe state law controls the question of the validity of a forum-selection clause between the parties. The Eleventh Circuit's rule clearly encourages forum shopping. Venue is often a vitally important matter, as is shown by the frequency with which parties contractually provide for and litigate the issue. Suit might well not be pursued, or might not be as successful, in a significantly less convenient forum. Transfer to such a less desirable forum is, therefore, of sufficient import that plaintiffs will base their decisions on the likelihood of that eventuality when they are choosing whether to sue in state or federal court. With respect to forum-selection clauses, in a State with law unfavorable to validity, plaintiffs who seek to avoid the effect of a clause will be encouraged to sue in state court, and non-resident defendants will be encouraged to shop for more favorable law by removing to federal court. In the reverse situation — where a State has law favorable to enforcing such clauses — plaintiffs will be encouraged to sue in federal court. This significant encouragement to forum shopping is alone sufficient to warrant application of state law. Cf. Walker v. Armco Steel Corp., supra, at 753 (failure to meet one part of the twin-aims test suffices to warrant application of state law).

I believe creating a judge-made rule fails the second part of the twin-aims test as well, producing inequitable administration of the laws. The best explanation of what constitutes inequitable administration of the laws is that found in Erie itself: allowing an unfair discrimination between noncitizens and citizens of the forum state. 304 U. S., at 74-75; see also Hanna, 380 U. S., at 468, n. 9. Whether discrimination is unfair in this context largely turns on how important is the matter in question. See id., at 467-468, and n. 9. The decision of an important legal issue should not turn on the accident of diversity of citizenship, see, e. g., Walker, supra, at 753, or the presence of a federal question unrelated to that issue. It is difficult to imagine an issue of more importance, other than one that goes to the very merits of the lawsuit, than the validity of a contractual forum-selection provision. Certainly, the Erie doctrine has previously been held to require the application of state law on subjects of similar or obviously lesser importance. See, e. g., Walker, supra (whether filing of complaint or service tolls statute of limitations); Bernhardt v. Polygraphic Co. of America, 350 U. S. 198, 202-204 (1956) (arbitrability); Cohen v. Beneficial Industrial Loan Corp., 337 U. S., at 555-556 (indemnity bond for litigation expenses). Nor can or should courts ignore that issues of contract validity are traditionally matters governed by state law.

For the reasons stated, I respectfully dissent.

[*] Contrary to the opinion of the Court, there is nothing unusual about having "the applicability of a federal statute depend on the content of state law." Ante, at 31, n. 10. We have recognized that precisely this is required when the application of the federal

statute depends, as here, on resolution of an underlying issue that is fundamentally one of state law. See Commissioner v. Estate of Bosch, 387 U. S. 456, 457, 464-465 (1967); cf. Budinich v. Becton Dickinson & Co., 486 U. S. 196, 199 (1988) (dictum). Nor is the approach I believe is required undermined by the fact that there would still be some situations where the state-law rule on the validity of a forum-selection clause would not be dispositive of the issue of transfer between federal courts. When state law would hold a forum-selection clause invalid the federal court could nonetheless order transfer to another federal court under § 1404(a), but it could do so only if such transfer was warranted without regard to the forum-selection clause. This is not at all remarkable since whether to transfer a case from one federal district court to another for reasons other than the contractual agreement of the parties is plainly made a matter of federal law by § 1404(a). When, on the other hand, state law would hold a forum-selection clause valid, I agree with JUSTICE KENNEDY'S concurrence that under § 1404(a) such a valid forum-selection clause is to be "given controlling weight in all but the most exceptional cases." Ante, at 33. And even in those exceptional cases where a forum-selection clause is valid under state law but transfer is unwarranted because of some factor other than the convenience of the parties, the district court should give effect to state contract law by dismissing the suit.

Justice Scalia's dissent in Houston v. Lack (June 24, 1988)

JUSTICE SCALIA, with whom THE CHIEF JUSTICE, JUSTICE O'CONNOR, and JUSTICE KENNEDY join, dissenting.

Today's decision obliterates the line between textual construction and textual enactment. It would be within the realm of normal judicial creativity (though in my view wrong) to interpret the phrase "filed with the clerk" to mean "mailed to the clerk," or even "mailed to the clerk or given to a person bearing an obligation to mail to the clerk." But interpreting it to mean "delivered to the clerk or, if you are a prisoner, delivered to your warden" is no more acceptable than any of an infinite number of variants, such as: "delivered to the clerk or, if you are out of the country, delivered to a United States consul"; or "delivered to the clerk or, if you are a soldier on active duty in a war zone, delivered to your commanding officer"; or "delivered to the clerk or, if you are held hostage in a foreign country, meant to be delivered to the clerk." Like these other examples, the Court's rule makes a good deal of sense. I dissent only because it is not the rule that we have promulgated through congressionally prescribed procedures.

I

This case requires us to construe one statutory provision and two provisions of the Federal Rules of Appellate Procedure. The former is 28 U. S. C. § 2107, which sets a statutory, jurisdictional deadline for the filing of notices of appeal in civil actions such as this habeas proceeding. It provides:

"[N]o appeal shall bring any judgment, order or decree in an action, suit, or proceeding of a civil nature before a court of appeals for review unless notice of appeal is filed, within thirty days after the entry of such judgment, order or decree" (emphasis added).

Although the statute itself does not define when a notice of appeal has been "filed" or designate with whom it must be filed, the Federal Rules of Appellate Procedure fill in these details. Federal Rule of Appellate Procedure 3(a) provides:

"An appeal permitted by law as of right from a district court to a court of appeals shall be taken by filing a notice of appeal with the clerk of the district court within the time allowed by Rule 4" (emphasis added).

This is supplemented by Federal Rule of Appellate Procedure 4(a)(1), which provides:

"In a civil case in which an appeal is permitted by law as of right from a district court to a court of appeals the notice of appeal required by Rule 3 shall be filed with the clerk of the district court within 30 days after the date of entry of the judgment or order appealed from . . ." (emphasis added).

It is clear, then, that there was a notice of appeal effective to give the Court of Appeals jurisdiction in this case if, and only if, it was "filed with the clerk of the district court" within the 30-day period.

The Court observes that "filed with the clerk" could mean many different things, including merely "mailed to the clerk." Ante, at 272-274. That is unquestionable. But it is the practice in construing such a phrase to pick a single meaning, and not to impart first one, and then another, as the judicially perceived equities of individual cases might require. Some statutory terms, such as "restraint of trade," Business Electronics Corp. v. Sharp Electronics Corp., 485 U. S. 717, 731-733 (1988), invite judicial judgment from case to case; but a provision establishing a deadline upon which litigants are supposed to rely is not of that sort. That is why we adopted the proviso in Rule 28.2 of our own Rules, which the Court unexpectedly invokes in support of its position. Rule 28.2 reads:

"To be timely filed, a document must be received by the Clerk within the time specified for filing, except that any document shall be deemed timely filed if it has been deposited in a United States post office or mailbox, with first-class postage prepaid, and properly addressed to the Clerk of this Court, within the time allowed for filing, and if there is filed with the Clerk a notarized statement by a member of the Bar of this Court, setting forth the details of the mailing, and stating that to his knowledge the mailing took place on a particular date within the permitted time." (Emphasis added.)

Since "received by the Clerk" must, in the context of such a rule, reasonably be understood to have a unitary meaning, which would of course normally be actual receipt, we felt constrained to specify an exception in which mailing would suffice. It would have been as inappropriate (though no less possible) there as in the present case to create the exception through interpretation — reasoning that the Post Office can be deemed the agent of the addressee, Household Fire & Carriage Accident Ins. Co. v. Grant, 4 Ex. D. 216 (1879) ("[P]ost office [is] the agent of both parties"), and hence it is theoretically possible to consider the document "received by" the Clerk when it is mailed, and the policy considerations usually militating in favor of a rule of actual receipt are well enough satisfied by an affidavit from a member of our Bar, etc.

If the need for a uniform meaning is apparent even with respect to ordinary statutory deadlines, and indeed even with respect to court-created rules that can be amended at the judges' discretion, it is even more apparent when a statutory deadline bearing upon the very jurisdiction of the courts is at issue. In that context, allowing courts to give different meanings from case to case allows them to expand and contract the scope of their own competence. That this is not envisioned is plain (if any citation is needed) from Rule 26(b) of the Federal Rules of Appellate Procedure, which specifically excepts from the courts' broad equitable power to "suspend the requirements or provisions of any of these rules in a particular case," Fed. Rule App. Proc. 2, the power to "enlarge the time for filing a notice of appeal." When we adopted Rules 3 and 4 of the Federal Rules of Appellate Procedure we delayed, as required by law, their effective date until 90 days after they were "reported to Congress by the Chief Justice," 28 U. S. C. § 2072, so that Congress might consider whether it wished to legislate any changes in them. Surely Congress could not have imagined that "filing . . . with the clerk" in Rule 3(a) and "filed with the clerk" in Rule 4(a)(1) could have a meaning as remote from plain English as "delivered to the warden of a prison" — or whatever else might be held in the future to fit today's announced "rationale . . . that the appellant has no control over delays," ante, at 273.

The Court seeks to have it both ways, at one and the same time abandoning a unitary interpretation of "filed" for purposes of the present decision, yet purporting "not [to] disturb" the many cases stating that a notice of appeal is filed when received, "[t]o the extent these cases state the general rule." Ante, at 274. See, e. g., Parissi v. Telechron, Inc., 349 U. S. 46, 47 (1955) (holding that timely receipt satisfies 28 U. S. C. § 2107); United States v. Lombardo, 241 U. S. 73, 76 (1916) ("A paper is filed when it is delivered to the proper official and by him received and filed"); Haney v. Mizell Memorial Hospital, 744 F. 2d 1467, 1472 (CA11 1984); In re LBL Sports Center, Inc., 684 F. 2d 410, 413 (CA6 1982); In re Robinson, 640 F. 2d 737, 738 (CA5 1981); In re Ramsey, 612 F. 2d 1220, 1223 (CA9 1980); In re Bad Bubba Racing Products, Inc., 609 F. 2d 815, 816 (CA5 1980); Ward v. Atlantic Coast Line R. Co., 265 F. 2d 75, 80 (CA5 1959), rev'd on other grounds, 362 U. S. 396 (1960); Allen v. Schnuckle, 253 F. 2d 195, 197 (CA9 1958). It seems to me that to leave them undisturbed only "to the extent [they] state the general rule" is to disturb them profoundly. The rationale of today's decision is that any of various theoretically possible meanings of "filed with the clerk" may be adopted — even one as remote as "addressed to the clerk and given to the warden" — depending upon what equity requires. It may turn out that we will not often agree that equity requires anything other than "received by the clerk," but parties will often argue it, and the lower courts will sometimes hold it. Thus is wasteful litigation in our appellate courts multiplied.

Petitioner Prentiss Houston's notice of appeal in this case was stamped received 31 days after the District Court's judgment was entered — that is, one day after the expiration of the 30-day filing period set out in Federal Rule of Appellate Procedure 4(a)(1). Since there is no legal warrant for creating a special exception to the rule of receipt for the benefit of incarcerated pro se appellants, I cannot join the Court in reversing the judgment on that basis.

II

Petitioner advanced several additional arguments supporting reversal which the Court did not have to reach. Ante, at 276-277, n. 4. I must consider them, and, having done so, find that none of them has merit.

First, petitioner asserts that his untimeliness in filing his notice of appeal should be excused because he "did all he could under the circumstances," as required by Fallen v. United States, 378 U. S. 139, 144 (1964). This argument fails because there is no warrant for equitable tolling of filing deadlines in the civil context of this habeas proceeding as there was in the criminal context that was at issue in Fallen. The bar erected by § 2107 in civil cases is jurisdictional, and this Court is without power to waive it, no matter what the equities of a particular case. As noted above, this is made explicit in Rule 26(b) of the Federal Rules of Appellate Procedure. In Fallen, by contrast, there was no jurisdictional statute at issue, and the relevant Federal Rule of Criminal Procedure 2 provided that a "just determination" should be achieved. See 378 U. S., at 142.

Second, petitioner maintains that he was lulled into thinking that his appeal was timely by the issuance of a certificate of probable cause and briefing schedule, and thus did not move for an extension of time within the 30-day grace period, see Fed. Rule App. Proc. 4(a)(5). This, he suggests, constitutes a "unique circumstance" of the sort recognized in Harris Truck Lines, Inc. v. Cherry Meat Packers, Inc., 371 U. S. 215, 217 (1962); Thompson v. INS, 375 U. S. 384, 387 (1964); and Wolfsohn v. Hankin, 376 U. S. 203 (1964). Petitioner asserts that those cases establish an equitable doctrine that sometimes permits the late filing of notices of appeal. Our later cases, however, effectively repudiate the Harris Truck Lines approach, affirming that the timely filing of a notice of appeal is "mandatory and jurisdictional." Griggs v. Provident Consumer Discount Co., 459 U. S. 56, 58, 61 (1982); see also Browder v. Director, Dept. of Corrections of Illinois, 434 U. S. 257 (1978). As we observed in United States v. Locke, 471 U. S. 84, 100-101 (1985):

"Filing deadlines, like statutes of limitations, necessarily operate harshly and arbitrarily with respect to individuals who fall just on the other side of them, but if the concept of a filing deadline is to have any content, the deadline must be enforced. `Any less rigid standard would risk encouraging a lax attitude toward filing dates,' United States v. Boyle, 469 U. S. [241,] 249 [(1985)]. A filing deadline cannot be complied with, substantially or otherwise, by filing late — even by one day."

Finally, petitioner asserts that his notice of appeal should be treated as a motion for extension of time under Federal Rule of Appellate Procedure 4(a)(5). That Rule, however, was specifically amended to require that a motion must be filed with the district court to obtain an extension, and its text precludes treating a late filed notice as being a motion. As revised, the Rule explicitly states:

"The district court, upon a showing of excusable neglect or good cause, may extend the time for filing a notice of appeal upon motion filed not later than 30 days after the expiration of the time prescribed by this Rule 4(a)" (emphasis added).

The Advisory Committee's Notes on Appellate Rule 4(a)(5) explain:

"Under the present rule there is a possible implication that prior to the time the initial appeal time has run, the district court may extend the time on the basis of an informal application. The amendment would require that the application must be made by motion, though the motion may be made ex parte. After the expiration of the initial time a motion for the extension of the time must be made in compliance with the F. R. C. P. and local rules of the district court." 28 U. S. C. App., p. 469.

The courts below were therefore without power to treat petitioner's late filed notice of appeal as a motion for extension of time under Federal Rule of Appellate Procedure 4(a)(5).

　　　　＊ ＊ ＊

Twenty-four years ago Justice Clark, joined by Justices Harlan, Stewart, and WHITE, said in the dissent in Thompson:

"Rules of procedure are a necessary part of an orderly system of justice. Their efficacy, however, depends upon the willingness of the courts to enforce them according to their terms. Changes in rules whose inflexibility has turned out to work hardship should be effected by the process of amendment, not by ad hoc relaxations by this Court in particular cases. Such dispensations in the long run actually produce mischievous results, undermining the certainty of the rules and causing confusion among the lower courts and the bar." 375 U. S., at 390.

That could not be more correct, nor more applicable to the present case. The filing rule the Court supports today seems to me a good one, but it is fully within our power to adopt it by an amendment of the Rules. Doing so instead in the present fashion not only evades the statutory requirement that changes be placed before Congress so that it may reject them by legislation before they become effective, 28 U. S. C. § 2072, but destroys the most important characteristic of filing requirements, which is the certainty of their application. It is hard to understand why the Court felt the need to short-circuit the orderly process of rule amendment in order to provide immediate relief in the present case. Petitioner delivered his notice of appeal to the warden three days before it was due to be filed with the Clerk. It would have been imprudent even to place it in a mailbox with the deadline so close at hand.

For the reasons stated, I respectfully dissent.

Justice Scalia's concurrence in US v. Taylor (June 24, 1988)

Justice SCALIA, concurring in part.

I join the opinion of the Court except Part II-A, which is largely devoted to establishing, through the floor debate in the House, (1) that prejudice to the defendant is one of the factors that the phrase "among others" in § 3162(a)(2) refers to, and (2) that that factor is not necessarily determinative. Both these points seem to me so utterly clear from the text of the legislation that there is no justification for resort to the legislative history. Assume that there was nothing in the legislative history except statements that, unless the defendant had been harmed by the delay, dismissal with prejudice could not be granted. Would we permit that to govern, even though the text of the provision does not consider that factor dominant enough to be mentioned specifically, but just includes it within the phrase "among othe[r] [factors]," or perhaps within the phrase "facts and circumstances of the case which led to the dismissal"? Or assume the opposite, that there was nothing in the legislative history except statements that harm to the defendant could not be considered at all. Would we permit that to govern, even though impairment of the accused's defense is so obviously one of the "other factors" highly relevant to whether the Government should be permitted to reinstitute the prosecution?

I think the answer to both these questions is obviously no. The text is so unambiguous on these points that it must be assumed that what the Members of the House and the Senators thought they were voting for, and what the President thought he was approving when he signed the bill, was what the text plainly said, rather than what a few Representatives, or even a Committee Report, said it said. Where we are not prepared to be governed by what the legislative history says—to take, as it were, the bad with the good—we should not look to the legislative history at all. This text is eminently clear, and we should leave it at that.

It should not be thought that, simply because adverting to the legislative history produces the same result we would reach anyway, no harm is done. By perpetuating the view that legislative history can alter the meaning of even a clear statutory provision, we produce a legal culture in which the following statement could be made—taken from a portion of the floor debate alluded to in the Court's opinion:

> "Mr. DENNIS. . . .
> * * * * *
>
> "I have an amendment here in my hand which could be offered, but if we can make up some legislative history which would do the same thing, I am willing to do it." 120 Cong.Rec. 41795 (1974).

We should not make the equivalency between making legislative history and making an amendment so plausible. It should not be possible, or at least should not be easy, to be sure of obtaining a particular result in this Court without making that result apparent on the face of the bill which both Houses consider and vote upon, which the President approves, and which, if it becomes law, the people must obey. I think we have an obligation to conduct our exegesis in a fashion which fosters that democratic process.

Justice Scalia's dissent in Morrison v. Olson (June 29, 1988) [Notes omitted]

Justice Scalia, dissenting.

It is the proud boast of our democracy that we have "a government of laws and not of men." Many Americans are familiar with that phrase; not many know its derivation. It comes from Part the First, Article XXX, of the Massachusetts Constitution of 1780, which reads in full as follows:

"In the government of this Commonwealth, the legislative department shall never exercise the executive and judicial powers, or either of them: The executive shall never exercise the legislative and judicial powers, or either of them: The judicial shall never exercise the legislative and executive powers, or either of them: to the end it may be a government of laws and not of men."

The Framers of the Federal Constitution similarly viewed the principle of separation of powers as the absolutely central guarantee of a just Government. In No. 47 of The Federalist, Madison wrote that "[n]o political truth is certainly of greater intrinsic value, or is stamped with the authority of more enlightened patrons of liberty." The Federalist No. 47, p. 301 (C. Rossiter ed. 1961) (hereinafter Federalist). Without a secure structure of separated powers, our Bill of Rights would be worthless, as are the bills of rights of many nations of the world that have adopted, or even improved upon, the mere words of ours.

The principle of separation of powers is expressed in our Constitution in the first section of each of the first three Articles. Article I, 1, provides that "[a]ll legislative Powers herein granted shall be vested in a Congress of the United States, which shall consist of a Senate and House of Representatives." Article III, 1, provides that "[t]he judicial Power of the United States, shall be vested in one supreme Court, and in such inferior Courts as the Congress may from time to time ordain and establish." And the provision at issue here, Art. II, 1, cl. 1, provides that "[t]he executive Power shall be vested in a President of the United States of America."

But just as the mere words of a Bill of Rights are not self-effectuating, the Framers recognized "[t]he insufficiency of a mere parchment delineation of the boundaries" to achieve the separation of powers. Federalist No. 73, p. 442 (A. Hamilton). "[T]he great security," wrote Madison, "against a gradual concentration of the several powers in the same department consists in giving to those who administer each department the necessary constitutional means and personal motives to resist encroachments of the others. The provision for defense must in this, as in all other cases, be made commensurate to the danger of attack." Federalist No. 51, pp. 321-322. Madison continued:

"But it is not possible to give to each department an equal power of self-defense. In republican government, the legislative authority necessarily predominates. The remedy for this inconveniency is to divide the legislature into different branches; and to render them, by different modes of election and different principles of action, as little connected with each other as the nature of their common functions and their common dependence on the society will admit. . . . As the weight of the legislative authority requires that it should be thus divided, the weakness of the executive may require, on the other hand, that it should be fortified." Id., at 322-323.

The major "fortification" provided, of course, was the veto power. But in addition to providing fortification, the Founders conspicuously and very consciously declined to sap the Executive's strength in the same way they had weakened the Legislature: by dividing the executive power. Proposals to have multiple executives, or a council of advisers with separate authority were rejected. See 1 M. Farrand, Records of the Federal Convention of 1787, pp. 66, 71-74, 88, 91-92 (rev. ed. 1966); 2 id., at 335-337, 533, 537, 542. Thus, while "[a]ll legislative Powers herein granted shall be vested in a Congress of the United States, which shall consist of a Senate and House of Representatives," U.S. Const., Art. I, 1 (emphasis added), "[t]he executive Power shall be vested in a President of the United States," Art. II, 1, cl. 1 (emphasis added).

That is what this suit is about. Power. The allocation of power among Congress, the President, and the courts in such fashion as to preserve the equilibrium the Constitution sought to establish - so that "a gradual concentration of the several powers in the same department," Federalist No. 51, p. 321 (J. Madison), can effectively be resisted. Frequently an issue of this sort will come before the Court clad, so to speak, in sheep's clothing: the potential of the asserted principle to effect important change in the equilibrium of power is not immediately evident, and must be discerned by a careful and perceptive analysis. But this wolf comes as a wolf.

I

The present case began when the Legislative and Executive Branches became "embroiled in a dispute concerning the scope of the congressional investigatory power," United States v. House of Representatives of United States, 556 F. Supp. 150, 152 (DC 1983), which - as is often the case with such interbranch conflicts - became quite acrimonious. In the course of oversight hearings into the administration of the Superfund by the Environmental Protection Agency (EPA), two Subcommittees of the House of Representatives requested and then subpoenaed numerous internal EPA documents. The President responded by personally directing the EPA Administrator not to turn over certain of the documents, see Memorandum of November 30, 1982, from President Reagan for the Administrator, Environmental Protection Agency, reprinted in H. R. Rep. No. 99-435, pp. 1166-1167 (1985), and by having the Attorney General notify the congressional Subcommittees of this assertion of executive privilege, see Letters of November 30, 1982, from Attorney General William French Smith to Hon. John D. Dingell and Hon. Elliott H. Levitas, reprinted, id., at 1168-1177. In his decision to assert executive privilege, the President was counseled by appellee Olson, who was then Assistant Attorney General of the Department of Justice for the Office of Legal Counsel, a post that has traditionally had responsibility for providing legal advice to the President (subject to approval of the Attorney General). The House's response was to pass a resolution citing the EPA Administrator, who had possession of the documents, for contempt. Contempt of Congress is a criminal offense. See 2 U.S.C. 192. The United States

Attorney, however, a member of the Executive Branch, initially took no steps to prosecute the contempt citation. Instead, the Executive Branch sought the immediate assistance of the Third Branch by filing a civil action asking the District Court to declare that the EPA Administrator had acted lawfully in withholding the documents under a claim of executive privilege. See ibid. The District Court declined (in my view correctly) to get involved in the controversy, and urged the other two branches to try "[c]ompromise and cooperation, rather than confrontation." 556 F. Supp., at 153. After further haggling, the two branches eventually reached an agreement giving the House Subcommittees limited access to the contested documents.

Congress did not, however, leave things there. Certain Members of the House remained angered by the confrontation, particularly by the role played by the Department of Justice. Specifically, the Judiciary Committee remained disturbed by the possibility that the Department had persuaded the President to assert executive privilege despite reservations by the EPA; that the Department had "deliberately and unnecessarily precipitated a constitutional confrontation with Congress"; that the Department had not properly reviewed and selected the documents as to which executive privilege was asserted; that the Department had directed the United States Attorney not to present the contempt certification involving the EPA Administrator to a grand jury for prosecution; that the Department had made the decision to sue the House of Representatives; and that the Department had not adequately advised and represented the President, the EPA, and the EPA Administrator. H. R. Rep. No. 99-435, p. 3 (1985) (describing unresolved "questions" that were the basis of the Judiciary Committee's investigation). Accordingly, staff counsel of the House Judiciary Committee were commissioned (apparently without the knowledge of many of the Committee's members, see id., at 731) to investigate the Justice Department's role in the controversy. That investigation lasted 2 1/2 years, and produced a 3,000-page report issued by the Committee over the vigorous dissent of all but one of its minority-party members. That report, which among other charges questioned the truthfulness of certain statements made by Assistant Attorney General Olson during testimony in front of the Committee during the early stages of its investigation, was sent to the Attorney General along with a formal request that he appoint an independent counsel to investigate Mr. Olson and others.

As a general matter, the Act before us here requires the Attorney General to apply for the appointment of an independent counsel within 90 days after receiving a request to do so, unless he determines within that period that "there are no reasonable grounds to believe that further investigation or prosecution is warranted." 28 U.S.C. 592(b)(1). As a practical matter, it would be surprising if the Attorney General had any choice (assuming this statute is constitutional) but to seek appointment of an independent counsel to pursue the charges against the principal object of the congressional request, Mr. Olson. Merely the political consequences (to him and the President) of seeming to break the law by refusing to do so would have been substantial. How could it not be, the public would ask, that a 3,000-page indictment drawn by our representatives over 2 1/2 years does not even establish "reasonable grounds to believe" that further investigation or prosecution is warranted with respect to at least the principal alleged culprit? But the Act establishes more than just practical compulsion. Although the Court's opinion asserts that the Attorney General had "no duty to comply with the [congressional] request," ante, at 694, that is not entirely accurate. He had a duty to comply unless he could conclude that there were "no reasonable grounds to believe," not that prosecution was warranted, but merely that "further investigation" was warranted, 28 U.S.C. 592(b)(1) (1982 ed., Supp. V) (emphasis added), after a 90-day investigation in which he was prohibited from using such routine investigative techniques as grand juries, plea bargaining, grants of immunity, or even subpoenas, see 592(a)(2). The Court also makes much of the fact that "the courts are specifically prevented from reviewing the Attorney General's decision not to seek appointment, 592(f)." Ante, at 695. Yes, 1 but Congress is not prevented from reviewing it. The context of this statute is acrid with the smell of threatened impeachment. Where, as here, a request for appointment of an independent counsel has come from the Judiciary Committee of either House of Congress, the Attorney General must, if he decides not to seek appointment, explain to that Committee why. See also 28 U.S.C. 595(c) (1982 ed., Supp. V) (independent counsel must report to the House of Representatives information "that may constitute grounds for an impeachment").

Thus, by the application of this statute in the present case, Congress has effectively compelled a criminal investigation of a high-level appointee of the President in connection with his actions arising out of a bitter power dispute between the President and the Legislative Branch. Mr. Olson may or may not be guilty of a crime; we do not know. But we do know that the investigation of him has been commenced, not necessarily because the President or his authorized subordinates believe it is in the interest of the United States, in the sense that it warrants the diversion of resources from other efforts, and is worth the cost in money and in possible damage to other governmental interests; and not even, leaving aside those normally considered factors, because the President or his authorized subordinates necessarily believe that an investigation is likely to unearth a violation worth prosecuting; but only because the Attorney General cannot affirm, as Congress demands, that there are no reasonable grounds to believe that further investigation is warranted. The decisions regarding the scope of that further investigation, its duration, and, finally, whether or not prosecution should ensue, are likewise beyond the control of the President and his subordinates.

II

If to describe this case is not to decide it, the concept of a government of separate and coordinate powers no longer has meaning. The Court devotes most of its attention to such relatively technical details as the Appointments Clause and the removal power, addressing briefly and only at the end of its opinion the separation of powers. As my prologue suggests, I think that has it backwards. Our opinions are full of the recognition that it is the principle of separation of powers, and the inseparable corollary that each department's "defense must . . . be made commensurate to the danger of attack,"

Federalist No. 51, p. 322 (J. Madison), which gives comprehensible content to the Appointments Clause, and determines the appropriate scope of the removal power. Thus, while I will subsequently discuss why our appointments and removal jurisprudence does not support today's holding, I begin with a consideration of the fountainhead of that jurisprudence, the separation and equilibration of powers.

First, however, I think it well to call to mind an important and unusual premise that underlies our deliberations, a premise not expressly contradicted by the Court's opinion, but in my view not faithfully observed. It is rare in a case dealing, as this one does, with the constitutionality of a statute passed by the Congress of the United States, not to find anywhere in the Court's opinion the usual, almost formulary caution that we owe great deference to Congress' view that what it has done is constitutional, see, e. g., Rostker v. Goldberg, 453 U.S. 57, 64 (1981); Fullilove v. Klutznick, 448 U.S. 448, 472 (1980) (opinion of Burger, C. J.); Columbia Broadcasting System, Inc. v. Democratic National Committee, 412 U.S. 94, 102 (1973); United States v. National Dairy Products Corp., 372 U.S. 29, 32 (1963), and that we will decline to apply the statute only if the presumption of constitutionality can be overcome, see Fullilove, supra, at 473; Columbia Broadcasting, supra, at 103. That caution is not recited by the Court in the present case because it does not apply. Where a private citizen challenges action of the Government on grounds unrelated to separation of powers, harmonious functioning of the system demands that we ordinarily give some deference, or a presumption of validity, to the actions of the political branches in what is agreed, between themselves at least, to be within their respective spheres. But where the issue pertains to separation of powers, and the political branches are (as here) in disagreement, neither can be presumed correct. The reason is stated concisely by Madison: "The several departments being perfectly co-ordinate by the terms of their common commission, neither of them, it is evident, can pretend to an exclusive or superior right of settling the boundaries between their respective powers . . . ." Federalist No. 49, p. 314. The playing field for the present case, in other words, is a level one. As one of the interested and coordinate parties to the underlying constitutional dispute, Congress, no more than the President, is entitled to the benefit of the doubt.

To repeat, Article II, 1, cl. 1, of the Constitution provides:

"The executive Power shall be vested in a President of the United States."

As I described at the outset of this opinion, this does not mean some of the executive power, but all of the executive power. It seems to me, therefore, that the decision of the Court of Appeals invalidating the present statute must be upheld on fundamental separation-of-powers principles if the following two questions are answered affirmatively: (1) Is the conduct of a criminal prosecution (and of an investigation to decide whether to prosecute) the exercise of purely executive power? (2) Does the statute deprive the President of the United States of exclusive control over the exercise of that power? Surprising to say, the Court appears to concede an affirmative answer to both questions, but seeks to avoid the inevitable conclusion that since the statute vests some purely executive power in a person who is not the President of the United States it is void.

The Court concedes that "[t]here is no real dispute that the functions performed by the independent counsel are `executive'," though it qualifies that concession by adding "in the sense that they are law enforcement functions that typically have been undertaken by officials within the Executive Branch." Ante, at 691. The qualifier adds nothing but atmosphere. In what other sense can one identify "the executive Power" that is supposed to be vested in the President (unless it includes everything the Executive Branch is given to do) except by reference to what has always and everywhere - if conducted by government at all - been conducted never by the legislature, never by the courts, and always by the executive. There is no possible doubt that the independent counsel's functions fit this description. She is vested with the "full power and independent authority to exercise all investigative and prosecutorial functions and powers of the Department of Justice [and] the Attorney General." 28 U.S.C. 594(a) (1982 ed., Supp. V) (emphasis added). Governmental investigation and prosecution of crimes is a quintessentially executive function. See Heckler v. Chaney, 470 U.S. 821, 832 (1985); Buckley v. Valeo, 424 U.S. 1, 138 (1976); United States v. Nixon, 418 U.S. 683, 693 (1974).

As for the second question, whether the statute before us deprives the President of exclusive control over that quintessentially executive activity: The Court does not, and could not possibly, assert that it does not. That is indeed the whole object of the statute. Instead, the Court points out that the President, through his Attorney General, has at least some control. That concession is alone enough to invalidate the statute, but I cannot refrain from pointing out that the Court greatly exaggerates the extent of that "some" Presidential control. "Most importan[t]" among these controls, the Court asserts, is the Attorney General's "power to remove the counsel for `good cause.'" Ante, at 696. This is somewhat like referring to shackles as an effective means of locomotion. As we recognized in Humphrey's Executor v. United States, 295 U.S. 602 (1935) - indeed, what Humphrey's Executor was all about - limiting removal power to "good cause" is an impediment to, not an effective grant of, Presidential control. We said that limitation was necessary with respect to members of the Federal Trade Commission, which we found to be "an agency of the legislative and judicial departments," and "wholly disconnected from the executive department," id., at 630, because "it is quite evident that one who holds his office only during the pleasure of another, cannot be depended upon to maintain an attitude of independence against the latter's will." Id., at 629. What we in Humphrey's Executor found to be a means of eliminating Presidential control, the Court today considers the "most importan[t]" means of assuring Presidential control. Congress, of course, operated under no such illusion when it enacted this statute, describing the "good cause" limitation as "protecting the independent counsel's ability to act independently of the President's direct control" since it permits removal only for "misconduct." H. R. Conf. Rep. 100-452, p. 37 (1987).

Moving on to the presumably "less important" controls that the President retains, the Court notes that no independent counsel may be appointed without a specific request from the Attorney General. As I have discussed above, the condition that renders such a request mandatory (inability to find "no reasonable grounds to believe" that further investigation is warranted) is so insubstantial that the Attorney General's discretion is severely confined. And once the referral is made, it is for the Special Division to determine the scope and duration of the investigation. See 28 U.S.C. 593(b) (1982 ed., Supp. V). And in any event, the limited power over referral is irrelevant to the question whether, once appointed, the independent counsel exercises executive power free from the President's control. Finally, the Court points out that the Act directs the independent counsel to abide by general Justice Department policy, except when not "possible." See 28 U.S.C. 594(f) (1982 ed., Supp. V). The exception alone shows this to be an empty promise. Even without that, however, one would be hard put to come up with many investigative or prosecutorial "policies" (other than those imposed by the Constitution or by Congress through law) that are absolute. Almost all investigative and prosecutorial decisions - including the ultimate decision whether, after a technical violation of the law has been found, prosecution is warranted - involve the balancing of innumerable legal and practical considerations. Indeed, even political considerations (in the nonpartisan sense) must be considered, as exemplified by the recent decision of an independent counsel to subpoena the former Ambassador of Canada, producing considerable tension in our relations with that country. See N. Y. Times, May 29, 1987, p. A12, col. 1. Another pre-eminently political decision is whether getting a conviction in a particular case is worth the disclosure of national security information that would be necessary. The Justice Department and our intelligence agencies are often in disagreement on this point, and the Justice Department does not always win. The present Act even goes so far as specifically to take the resolution of that dispute away from the President and give it to the independent counsel. 28 U.S.C. 594(a)(6) (1982 ed., Supp. V). In sum, the balancing of various legal, practical, and political considerations, none of which is absolute, is the very essence of prosecutorial discretion. To take this away is to remove the core of the prosecutorial function, and not merely "some" Presidential control.

As I have said, however, it is ultimately irrelevant how much the statute reduces Presidential control. The case is over when the Court acknowledges, as it must, that "[i]t is undeniable that the Act reduces the amount of control or supervision that the Attorney General and, through him, the President exercises over the investigation and prosecution of a certain class of alleged criminal activity." Ante, at 695. It effects a revolution in our constitutional jurisprudence for the Court, once it has determined that (1) purely executive functions are at issue here, and (2) those functions have been given to a person whose actions are not fully within the supervision and control of the President, nonetheless to proceed further to sit in judgment of whether "the President's need to control the exercise of [the independent counsel's] discretion is so central to the functioning of the Executive Branch" as to require complete control, ante, at 691 (emphasis added), whether the conferral of his powers upon someone else "sufficiently deprives the President of control over the independent counsel to interfere impermissibly with [his] constitutional obligation to ensure the faithful execution of the laws," ante, at 693 (emphasis added), and whether "the Act give[s] the Executive Branch sufficient control over the independent counsel to ensure that the President is able to perform his constitutionally assigned duties," ante, at 696 (emphasis added). It is not for us to determine, and we have never presumed to determine, how much of the purely executive powers of government must be within the full control of the President. The Constitution prescribes that they all are.

The utter incompatibility of the Court's approach with our constitutional traditions can be made more clear, perhaps, by applying it to the powers of the other two branches. Is it conceivable that if Congress passed a statute depriving itself of less than full and entire control over some insignificant area of legislation, we would inquire whether the matter was "so central to the functioning of the Legislative Branch" as really to require complete control, or whether the statute gives Congress "sufficient control over the surrogate legislator to ensure that Congress is able to perform its constitutionally assigned duties"? Of course we would have none of that. Once we determined that a purely legislative power was at issue we would require it to be exercised, wholly and entirely, by Congress. Or to bring the point closer to home, consider a statute giving to non-Article III judges just a tiny bit of purely judicial power in a relatively insignificant field, with substantial control, though not total control, in the courts - perhaps "clear error" review, which would be a fair judicial equivalent of the Attorney General's "for cause" removal power here. Is there any doubt that we would not pause to inquire whether the matter was "so central to the functioning of the Judicial Branch" as really to require complete control, or whether we retained "sufficient control over the matters to be decided that we are able to perform our constitutionally assigned duties"? We would say that our "constitutionally assigned duties" include complete control over all exercises of the judicial power - or, as the plurality opinion said in Northern Pipeline Construction Co. v. Marathon Pipe Line Co., 458 U.S. 50, 58 -59 (1982): "The inexorable command of [Article III] is clear and definite: The judicial power of the United States must be exercised by courts having the attributes prescribed in Art. III." We should say here that the President's constitutionally assigned duties include complete control over investigation and prosecution of violations of the law, and that the inexorable command of Article II is clear and definite: the executive power must be vested in the President of the United States.

Is it unthinkable that the President should have such exclusive power, even when alleged crimes by him or his close associates are at issue? No more so than that Congress should have the exclusive power of legislation, even when what is at issue is its own exemption from the burdens of certain laws. See Civil Rights Act of 1964, Title VII, 42 U.S.C. 2000e et seq. (prohibiting "employers," not defined to include the United States, from discriminating on the basis of race, color, religion, sex, or national origin). No more so than that this Court should have the exclusive power to pronounce the final decision on justiciable cases and controversies, even those pertaining to the constitutionality of a statute reducing the salaries of the Justices. See United States v. Will, 449 U.S. 200, 211 - 217 (1980). A system of separate and coordinate powers necessarily involves an acceptance of exclusive power that can theoretically be abused. As we reiterate this very day, "[i]t is a truism that constitutional protections have costs." Coy v. Iowa, post, at 1020. While the separation of powers may prevent us from righting every wrong, it does so in order to ensure that we do not lose liberty. The checks against any branch's abuse of its exclusive powers are twofold: First, retaliation by one of the other branch's use of its exclusive powers: Congress, for example, can impeach the executive who willfully fails to enforce the laws; the executive can decline to prosecute under unconstitutional statutes, cf. United States v. Lovett, 328 U.S. 303 (1946); and the courts can dismiss malicious prosecutions. Second, and ultimately, there is the political check that the people will replace those in the political branches (the branches more "dangerous to the political rights of the Constitution," Federalist No. 78, p. 465) who are guilty of abuse. Political pressures produced special prosecutors - for Teapot Dome and for Watergate, for example - long before this statute created the independent counsel. See Act of Feb. 8, 1924, ch. 16, 43 Stat. 5-6; 38 Fed. Reg. 30738 (1973).

The Court has, nonetheless, replaced the clear constitutional prescription that the executive power belongs to the President with a "balancing test." What are the standards to determine how the balance is to be struck, that is, how much removal of Presidential power is too much? Many countries of the world get along with an executive that is much weaker than ours - in fact, entirely dependent upon the continued support of the legislature. Once we depart from the text of the Constitution, just where short of that do we stop? The most amazing feature of the Court's opinion is that it does not even purport to give an answer. It simply announces, with no analysis, that the ability to control the decision whether to investigate and prosecute the President's closest advisers, and indeed the President himself, is not "so central to the functioning of the Executive Branch" as to be constitutionally required to be within the President's control. Apparently that is so because we say it is so. Having abandoned as the basis for our decisionmaking the text of Article II that "the executive Power" must be vested in the President, the Court does not even attempt to craft a substitute criterion - a "justiciable standard," see, e. g., Baker v. Carr, 369 U.S. 186, 210 (1962); Coleman v. Miller, 307 U.S. 433, 454 -455 (1939), however remote from the Constitution - that today governs, and in the future will govern, the decision of such questions. Evidently, the governing standard is to be what might be called the unfettered wisdom of a majority of this Court, revealed to an obedient people on a case-by-case basis. This is not only not the government of laws that the Constitution established; it is not a government of laws at all.

In my view, moreover, even as an ad hoc, standardless judgment the Court's conclusion must be wrong. Before this statute was passed, the President, in taking action disagreeable to the Congress, or an executive officer giving advice to the President or testifying before Congress concerning one of those many matters on which the two branches are from time to time at odds, could be assured that his acts and motives would be adjudged - insofar as the decision whether to conduct a criminal investigation and to prosecute is concerned - in the Executive Branch, that is, in a forum attuned to the interests and the policies of the Presidency. That was one of the natural advantages the Constitution gave to the Presidency, just as it gave members of Congress (and their staffs) the advantage of not being prosecutable for anything said or done in their legislative capacities. See U.S. Const., Art. I, 6, cl. 1; Gravel v. United States, 408 U.S. 606 (1972). It is the very object of this legislation to eliminate that assurance of a sympathetic forum. Unless it can honestly be said that there are "no reasonable grounds to believe" that further investigation is warranted, further investigation must ensure; and the conduct of the investigation, and determination of whether to prosecute, will be given to a person neither selected by nor subject to the control of the President - who will in turn assemble a staff by finding out, presumably, who is willing to put aside whatever else they are doing, for an indeterminate period of time, in order to investigate and prosecute the President or a particular named individual in his administration. The prospect is frightening (as I will discuss at some greater length at the conclusion of this opinion) even outside the context of a bitter, interbranch political dispute. Perhaps the boldness of the President himself will not be affected - though I am not even sure of that. (How much easier it is for Congress, instead of accepting the political damage attendant to the commencement of impeachment proceedings against the President on trivial grounds - or, for that matter, how easy it is for one of the President's political foes outside of Congress - simply to trigger a debilitating criminal investigation of the Chief Executive under this law.) But as for the President's high-level assistants, who typically have no political base of support, it is as utterly unrealistic to think that they will not be intimidated by this prospect, and that their advice to him and their advocacy of his interests before a hostile Congress will not be affected, as it would be to think that the Members of Congress and their staffs would be unaffected by replacing the Speech or Debate Clause with a similar provision. It deeply wounds the President, by substantially reducing the President's ability to protect himself and his staff. That is the whole object of the law, of course, and I cannot imagine why the Court believes it does not succeed.

Besides weakening the Presidency by reducing the zeal of his staff, it must also be obvious that the institution of the independent counsel enfeebles him more directly in his constant confrontations with Congress, by eroding his public support. Nothing is so politically effective as the ability to charge that one's opponent and his associates are not merely wrongheaded, naive, ineffective, but, in all probability, "crooks." And nothing so effectively gives an appearance of validity to such charges as a Justice Department investigation and, even better, prosecution. The present statute provides ample means for that sort of attack, assuring that massive and lengthy investigations will occur, not merely when the Justice Department in the application of its usual standards believes they are called for, but whenever it cannot be said that there are "no reasonable grounds to believe" they are called for. The statute's highly visible procedures assure, moreover, that unlike most investigations these will be widely known and prominently displayed. Thus, in the 10 years since the institution of the independent counsel was established by law, there have been nine highly publicized investigations, a source of constant political damage to two administrations. That they could not remotely be described as merely the application of "normal" investigatory and prosecutory standards is demonstrated by, in addition to the language of the statute ("no reasonable grounds to believe"), the following facts: Congress appropriates approximately $50 million annually for general legal activities, salaries, and expenses of the Criminal Division of the Department of Justice. See 1989 Budget Request of the Department of Justice, Hearings before a Subcommittee of the House Committee on Appropriations, 100th Cong., 2d Sess., pt. 6, pp. 284-285 (1988) (DOJ Budget Request). This money is used to support "[f]ederal appellate activity," "[o]rganized crime prosecution," "[p]ublic integrity" and "[f]raud" matters, "[n]arcotic & dangerous drug prosecution," "[i]nternal security," "[g]eneral litigation and legal advice," "special investigations," "[p]rosecution support," "[o]rganized crime drug enforcement," and "[m]anagement & administration." Id., at 284. By comparison, between May 1986 and August 1987, four independent counsel (not all of whom were operating for that entire period of time) spent almost $5 million (one-tenth of the amount annually appropriated to the entire Criminal Division), spending almost $1 million in the month of August 1987 alone. See Washington Post, Oct. 21, 1987, p. A21, col. 5. For fiscal year 1989, the Department of Justice has requested $52 million for the entire Criminal Division, DOJ Budget Request 285, and $7 million to support the activities of independent counsel, id., at 25.

In sum, this statute does deprive the President of substantial control over the prosecutory functions performed by the independent counsel, and it does substantially affect the balance of powers. That the Court could possibly conclude otherwise demonstrates both the wisdom of our former constitutional system, in which the degree of reduced control and political impairment were irrelevant, since all purely executive power had to be in the President; and the folly of the new system of standardless judicial allocation of powers we adopt today.

III

As I indicated earlier, the basic separation-of-powers principles I have discussed are what give life and content to our jurisprudence concerning the President's power to appoint and remove officers. The same result of unconstitutionality is therefore plainly indicated by our case law in these areas.

Article II, 2, cl. 2, of the Constitution provides as follows:

"[The President] shall nominate, and by and with the Advice and Consent of the the Senate, shall appoint Ambassadors, other public Ministers and Consuls, Judges of the supreme Court, and all other Officers of the United States, whose Appointments are not herein otherwise provided for, and which shall be established by Law: but the Congress may by Law vest the Appointment of such inferior Officers, as they think proper, in the President alone, in the Courts of Law, or in the Heads of Departments."

Because appellant (who all parties and the Court agree is an officer of the United States, ante, at 671, n. 12) was not appointed by the President with the advice and consent of the Senate, but rather by the Special Division of the United States Court of Appeals, her appointment is constitutional only if (1) she is an "inferior" officer within the meaning of the above Clause, and (2) Congress may vest her appointment in a court of law.

As to the first of these inquiries, the Court does not attempt to "decide exactly" what establishes the line between principal and "inferior" officers, but is confident that, whatever the line may be, appellant "clearly falls on the `inferior officer' side" of it. Ante, at 671. The Court gives three reasons: First, she "is subject to removal by a higher Executive Branch official," namely, the Attorney General. Ibid. Second, she is "empowered by the Act to perform only certain, limited duties." Ibid. Third, her office is "limited in jurisdiction" and "limited in tenure." Ante, at 672.

The first of these lends no support to the view that appellant is an inferior officer. Appellant is removable only for "good cause" or physical or mental incapacity. 28 U.S.C. 596(a) (1) (1982 ed., Supp. V). By contrast, most (if not all) principal officers in the Executive Branch may be removed by the President at will. I fail to see how the fact that appellant is more difficult to remove than most principal officers helps to establish that she is an inferior officer. And I do not see how it could possibly make any difference to her superior or inferior status that the President's limited power to remove her must be exercised through the Attorney General. If she were removable at will by the Attorney General, then she would be subordinate to him and thus properly designated as inferior; but the Court essentially admits that she is not subordinate. See ante, at 671. If it were common usage to refer to someone as "inferior" who is subject to removal for cause by another, then one would say that the President is "inferior" to Congress.

The second reason offered by the Court - that appellant performs only certain, limited duties - may be relevant to whether she is an inferior officer, but it mischaracterizes the extent of her powers. As the Court states: "Admittedly, the Act delegates to appellant [the] `full power and independent authority to exercise all investigative and prosecutorial functions and powers of the Department of Justice.'" Ibid., quoting 28 U.S.C. 594(a) (1982 ed., Supp. V) (emphasis added). 2 Moreover, in addition to this general grant of power she is given a broad range of specifically enumerated powers, including a power not even the Attorney General possesses: to "contes[t] in court . . . any claim of privilege or attempt to withhold evidence on grounds of national security." 594(a)(6). 3 Once all of this is "admitted," it seems to me impossible to maintain that appellant's authority is so "limited" as to render her an inferior officer. The Court seeks to brush this away by asserting that the independent counsel's power does not include any authority to "formulate policy for the Government or the Executive Branch." Ante, at 671. But the same could be said for all officers of the Government, with the single exception of the President. All of them only formulate policy within their respective spheres of responsibility - as does the independent counsel, who must comply with the policies of the Department of Justice only to the extent possible. 594(f).

The final set of reasons given by the Court for why the independent counsel clearly is an inferior officer emphasizes the limited nature of her jurisdiction and tenure. Taking the latter first, I find nothing unusually limited about the independent counsel's tenure. To the contrary, unlike most high ranking Executive Branch officials, she continues to serve until she (or the Special Division) decides that her work is substantially completed. See 596(b)(1), (b)(2). This particular independent prosecutor has already served more than two years, which is at least as long as many Cabinet officials. As to the scope of her jurisdiction, there can be no doubt that is small (though far from unimportant). But within it she exercises more than the full power of the Attorney General. The Ambassador to Luxembourg is not anything less than a principal officer, simply because Luxembourg is small. And the federal judge who sits in a small district is not for that reason "inferior in rank and authority." If the mere fragmentation of executive responsibilities into small compartments suffices to render the heads of each of those compartments inferior officers, then Congress could deprive the President of the right to appoint his chief law enforcement officer by dividing up the Attorney General's responsibilities among a number of "lesser" functionaries.

More fundamentally, however, it is not clear from the Court's opinion why the factors it discusses - even if applied correctly to the facts of this case - are determinative of the question of inferior officer status. The apparent source of these factors is a statement in United States v. Germaine, 99 U.S. 508, 511 (1879) (discussing United States v. Hartwell, 6 Wall. 385, 393 (1868)), that "the term [officer] embraces the ideas of tenure, duration, emolument, and duties." See ante, at 672. Besides the fact that this was dictum, it was dictum in a case where the distinguishing characteristics of inferior officers versus superior officers were in no way relevant, but rather only the distinguishing characteristics of an "officer of the United States" (to which the criminal statute at issue applied) as opposed to a mere employee. Rather than erect a theory of who is an inferior officer on the foundation of such an irrelevancy, I think it preferable to look to the text of the Constitution and the division of power that it establishes. These demonstrate, I think, that the independent counsel is not an inferior officer because she is not subordinate to any officer in the Executive Branch (indeed, not even to the President). Dictionaries in use at the time of the Constitutional Convention gave the word "inferiour" two meanings which it still bears today: (1) "[l]ower in place, . . . station, . . . rank of life, . . . value or excellency," and (2) "[s]ubordinate." S. Johnson, Dictionary of the English Language (6th ed. 1785). In a document dealing with the structure (the constitution) of a government, one would naturally expect the word to bear the latter meaning - indeed, in such a context it would be unpardonably careless to use the word unless a relationship of subordination was intended. If what was meant was merely "lower in station or rank," one would use instead a term such as "lesser officers." At the only other point in the Constitution at which the word "inferior" appears, it plainly connotes a relationship of subordination. Article III vests the judicial power of the United States in "one supreme Court, and in such inferior Courts as the Congress may from time to time ordain and establish." U.S. Const., Art. III, 1 (emphasis added). In Federalist No. 81, Hamilton pauses to describe the "inferior" courts authorized by Article III as inferior in the sense that they are "subordinate" to the Supreme Court. See id., at 485, n., 490, n.

That "inferior" means "subordinate" is also consistent with what little we know about the evolution of the Appointments Clause. As originally reported to the Committee on Style, the Appointments Clause provided no "exception" from the standard manner of appointment (President with the advice and consent of the Senate) for inferior officers. 2 M. Farrand, Records of the Federal Convention of 1787, pp. 498-499, 599 (rev. ed. 1966). On September 15, 1787, the last day of the Convention before the proposed Constitution was signed, in the midst of a host of minor changes that were being considered, Gouverneur Morris moved to add the exceptions clause. Id., at 627. No great debate ensued; the only disagreement was over whether it was necessary at all. Id., at 627-628. Nobody thought that it was a fundamental change, excluding from the President's appointment power and the Senate's confirmation power a category of officers who might function on their own, outside the supervision of those appointed in the more cumbersome fashion. And it is significant that in the very brief discussion Madison mentions (as in apparent contrast to the "inferior officers" covered by the provision) "Superior Officers." Id., at 637. Of course one is not a "superior officer" without some supervisory responsibility, just as, I suggest, one is not an "inferior officer" within the meaning of the provision under discussion unless one is subject to supervision by a "superior officer." It is perfectly obvious, therefore, both from the relative brevity of the discussion this addition received, and from the content of that discussion, that it was intended merely to make clear (what Madison thought already was clear, see id., at 627) that those officers appointed by the President with Senate approval could on their own appoint their subordinates, who would, of course, by chain of command still be under the direct control of the President.

This interpretation is, moreover, consistent with our admittedly sketchy precedent in this area. For example, in United States v. Eaton, 169 U.S. 331 (1898), we held that the appointment by an Executive Branch official other than the President of a "vice-consul," charged with the duty of temporarily performing the function of the consul, did not violate the Appointments Clause. In doing so, we repeatedly referred to the "vice-consul" as a "subordinate" officer. Id., at 343. See also United States v. Germaine, supra, at 511 (comparing "inferior" commissioners and bureau officers to heads of department, describing the former as "mere . . . subordinates") (dicta); United States v. Hartwell, supra, at 394 (describing clerk appointed by Assistant Treasurer with approval of Secretary of the Treasury as a "subordinate office[r]") (dicta). More recently, in United States v. Nixon, 418 U.S. 683 (1974), we noted that the Attorney General's appointment of the Watergate Special Prosecutor was made pursuant to the Attorney General's "power to appoint subordinate officers to assist him in the discharge of his duties." Id., at 694 (emphasis added). The Court's citation of Nixon as support for its view that the independent counsel is an inferior officer is simply not supported by a reading of the case. We explicitly stated that the Special Prosecutor was a "subordinate office[r]," ibid., because, in the end, the President or the Attorney General could have removed him at any time, if by no other means than amending or revoking the regulation defining his authority. Id., at 696. Nor are any of the other cases cited by the Court in support of its view inconsistent with the natural reading that an inferior officer must at least be subordinate to another officer of the United States. In Ex parte Siebold, 100 U.S. 371 (1880), we upheld the appointment by a court of federal "Judges of Election," who were charged with various duties involving the overseeing of local congressional elections. Contrary to the Court's assertion, see ante, at 673, we did not specifically find that these officials were inferior officers for purposes of the Appointments Clause, probably because no one had contended that they were principal officers. Nor can the case be said to represent even an assumption on our part that they were inferior without being subordinate. The power of assisting in the judging of elections that they were exercising was assuredly not a purely executive power, and if we entertained any assumption it was probably that they, like the marshals who assisted them, see Siebold, 100 U.S., at 380, were subordinate to the courts, see id., at 397. Similarly, in GoBart Importing Co. v. United States, 282 U.S. 344 (1931), where we held that United States commissioners were inferior officers, we made plain that they were subordinate to the district courts which appointed them: "The commissioner acted not as a court, or as a judge of any court, but as a mere officer of the district court in proceedings of which that court had authority to take control at any time." Id., at 354.

To be sure, it is not a sufficient condition for "inferior" officer status that one be subordinate to a principal officer. Even an officer who is subordinate to a department head can be a principal officer. That is clear from the brief exchange following Gouverneur Morris' suggestion of the addition of the exceptions clause for inferior officers. Madison responded:

"It does not go far enough if it be necessary at all - Superior Officers below Heads of Departments ought in some cases to have the appointment of the lesser offices." 2 M. Farrand, Records of the Federal Convention, of 1787, p. 627 (rev. ed. 1966) (emphasis added).

But it is surely a necessary condition for inferior officer status that the officer be subordinate to another officer.

The independent counsel is not even subordinate to the President. The Court essentially admits as much, noting that "appellant may not be `subordinate' to the Attorney General (and the President) insofar as she possesses a degree of independent discretion to exercise the powers delegated to her under the Act." Ante, at 671. In fact, there is no doubt about it. As noted earlier, the Act specifically grants her the "full power and independent authority to exercise all investigative and prosecutorial functions of the Department of Justice," 28 U.S.C. 594(a) (1982 ed., Supp. V), and makes her removable only for "good cause," a limitation specifically intended to ensure that she be independent of, not subordinate to, the President and the Attorney General. See H. R. Conf. Rep. No. 100-452, p. 37 (1987).

Because appellant is not subordinate to another officer, she is not an "inferior" officer and her appointment other than by the President with the advice and consent of the

Senate is unconstitutional.

IV

I will not discuss at any length why the restrictions upon the removal of the independent counsel also violate our established precedent dealing with that specific subject. For most of it, I simply refer the reader to the scholarly opinion of Judge Silberman for the Court of Appeals below. See In re Sealed Case, 267 U.S. App. D.C. 178, 838 F.2d 476 (1988). I cannot avoid commenting, however, about the essence of what the Court has done to our removal jurisprudence today.

There is, of course, no provision in the Constitution stating who may remove executive officers, except the provisions for removal by impeachment. Before the present decision it was established, however, (1) that the President's power to remove principal officers who exercise purely executive powers could not be restricted, see Myers v. United States, 272 U.S. 52, 127 (1926), and (2) that his power to remove inferior officers who exercise purely executive powers, and whose appointment Congress had removed from the usual procedure of Presidential appointment with Senate consent, could be restricted, at least where the appointment had been made by an officer of the Executive Branch, see ibid.; United States v. Perkins, 116 U.S. 483, 485 (1886). 4

The Court could have resolved the removal power issue in this case by simply relying upon its erroneous conclusion that the independent counsel was an inferior officer, and then extending our holding that the removal of inferior officers appointed by the Executive can be restricted, to a new holding that even the removal of inferior officers appointed by the courts can be restricted. That would in my view be a considerable and unjustified extension, giving the Executive full discretion in neither the selection nor the removal of a purely executive officer. The course the Court has chosen, however, is even worse.

Since our 1935 decision in Humphrey's Executor v. United States, 295 U.S. 602 - which was considered by many at the time the product of an activist, anti-New Deal Court bent on reducing the power of President Franklin Roosevelt - it has been established that the line of permissible restriction upon removal of principal officers lies at the point at which the powers exercised by those officers are no longer purely executive. Thus, removal restrictions have been generally regarded as lawful for so-called "independent regulatory agencies," such as the Federal Trade Commission, see ibid.; 15 U.S.C. 41, the Interstate Commerce Commission, see 49 U.S.C. 10301(c) (1982 ed., Supp. IV), and the Consumer Product Safety Commission, see 15 U.S.C. 2053(a), which engage substantially in what has been called the "quasi-legislative activity" of rulemaking, and for members of Article I courts, such as the Court of Military Appeals, see 10 U.S.C. 867(a)(2), who engage in the "quasi-judicial" function of adjudication. It has often been observed, correctly in my view, that the line between "purely executive" functions and "quasi-legislative" or "quasi-judicial" functions is not a clear one or even a rational one. See ante, at 689-691; Bowsher v. Synar, 478 U.S. 714, 761, n. 3 (1986) (WHITE, J., dissenting); FTC v. Ruberoid Co., 343 U.S. 470, 487 -488 (1952) (Jackson, J., dissenting). But at least it permitted the identification of certain officers, and certain agencies, whose functions were entirely within the control of the President. Congress had to be aware of that restriction in its legislation. Today, however, Humphrey's Executor is swept into the dustbin of repudiated constitutional principles. "[O]ur present considered view," the Court says, "is that the determination of whether the Constitution allows Congress to impose a `good cause'-type restriction on the President's power to remove an official cannot be made to turn on whether or not that official is classified as `purely executive.'" Ante, at 689. What Humphrey's Executor (and presumably Myers) really means, we are now told, is not that there are any "rigid categories of those officials who may or may not be removed at will by the President," but simply that Congress cannot "interefere with the President's exercise of the `executive power' and his constitutionally appointed duty to `take care that the laws be faithfully executed,'" ante, at 689-690.

One can hardly grieve for the shoddy treatment given today to Humphrey's Executor, which, after all, accorded the same indignity (with much less justification) to Chief Justice Taft's opinion 10 years earlier in Myers v. United States, 272 U.S. 52 (1926) - gutting, in six quick pages devoid of textual or historical precedent for the novel principle it set forth, a carefully researched and reasoned 70-page opinion. It is in fact comforting to witness the reality that he who lives by the ipse dixit dies by the ipse dixit. But one must grieve for the Constitution. Humphrey's Executor at least had the decency formally to observe the constitutional principle that the President had to be the repository of all executive power, see 295 U.S., at 627 -628, which, as Myers carefully explained, necessarily means that he must be able to discharge those who do not perform executive functions according to his liking. As we noted in Bowsher, once an officer is appointed "`it is only the authority that can remove him, and not the authority that appointed him, that he must fear and, in the performance of his functions, obey.'" 478 U.S., at 726, quoting Synar v. United States, 626 F. Supp. 1374, 1401 (DC 1986) (Scalia, Johnson, and Gasch, JJ.). By contrast, "our present considered view" is simply that any executive officer's removal can be restricted, so long as the President remains "able to accomplish his constitutional role." Ante, at 690. There are now no lines. If the removal of a prosecutor, the virtual embodiment of the power to "take care that the laws be faithfully executed," can be restricted, what officer's removal cannot? This is an open invitation for Congress to experiment. What about a special Assistant Secretary of State, with responsibility for one very narrow area of foreign policy, who would not only have to be confirmed by the Senate but could also be removed only pursuant to certain carefully designed restrictions? Could this possibly render the President "[un]able to accomplish his constitutional role"? Or a special Assistant Secretary of Defense for Procurement? The possibilities are endless, and the Court does not understand what the separation of powers, what "[a]mbition . . . counteract[ing] ambition." Federalist No. 51, p. 322 (Madison), is all about, if it does not expect Congress to try them. As far as I can discern from the Court's opinion, it is now open season upon the President's removal power for all executive officers, with not even the superficially principled restriction of Humphrey's Executor as cover. The Court essentially says to the President: "Trust us. We will make sure that you are able to accomplish your constitutional role." I think the Constitution gives the President - and the people - more protection than that.

V

The purpose of the separation and equilibration of powers in general, and of the unitary Executive in particular, was not merely to assure effective government but to preserve individual freedom. Those who hold or have held offices covered by the Ethics in Government Act are entitled to that protection as much as the rest of us, and I conclude my discussion by considering the effect of the Act upon the fairness of the process they receive.

Only someone who has worked in the field of law enforcement can fully appreciate the vast power and the immense discretion that are placed in the hands of a prosecutor with respect to the objects of his investigation. Justice Robert Jackson, when he was Attorney General under President Franklin Roosevelt, described it in a memorable speech to United States Attorneys, as follows:

"There is a most important reason why the prosecutor should have, as nearly as possible, a detached and impartial view of all groups in his community. Law enforcement is not automatic. It isn't blind. One of the greatest difficulties of the position of prosecutor is that he must pick his cases, because no prosecutor can even investigate all of the cases in which he receives complaints. If the Department of Justice were to make even a pretense of reaching every probable violation of federal law, ten times its present staff will be inadequate. We know that no local police force can strictly enforce the traffic laws, or it would arrest half the driving population on any given morning. What every prosecutor is practically required to do is to select the cases for prosecution and to select those in which the offense is the most flagrant, the public harm the greatest, and the proof the most certain.

"If the prosecutor is obliged to choose his case, it follows that he can choose his defendants. Therein is the most dangerous power of the prosecutor: that he will pick people that he thinks he should get, rather than cases that need to be prosecuted. With the law books filled with a great assortment of crimes, a prosecutor stands a fair chance of finding at least a technical violation of some act on the part of almost anyone. In such a case, it is not a question of discovering the commission of a crime and then looking for the man who has committed it, it is a question of picking the man and then searching the law books, or putting investigators to work, to pin some offense on him. It is in this realm - in which the prosecutor picks some person whom he dislikes or desires to embarrass, or selects some group of unpopular persons and then looks for an offense, that the greatest danger of abuse of prosecuting power lies. It is here that law enforcement becomes personal, and the real crime becomes that of being unpopular with the predominant or governing group, being attached to the wrong political views, or being personally obnoxious to or in the way of the prosecutor himself." R. Jackson, The Federal Prosecutor, Address Delivered at the Second Annual Conference of United States Attorneys, April 1,

1940.

Under our system of government, the primary check against prosecutorial abuse is a political one. The prosecutors who exercise this awesome discretion are selected and can be removed by a President, whom the people have trusted enough to elect. Moreover, when crimes are not investigated and prosecuted fairly, nonselectively, with a reasonable sense of proportion, the President pays the cost in political damage to his administration. If federal prosecutors "pick people that [they] thin[k] [they] should get, rather than cases that need to be prosecuted," if they amass many more resources against a particular prominent individual, or against a particular class of political protesters, or against members of a particular political party, than the gravity of the alleged offenses or the record of successful prosecutions seems to warrant, the unfairness will come home to roost in the Oval Office. I leave it to the reader to recall the examples of this in recent years. That result, of course, was precisely what the Founders had in mind when they provided that all executive powers would be exercised by a single Chief Executive. As Hamilton put it, "[t]he ingredients which constitute safety in the republican sense are a due dependence on the people, and a due responsibility." Federalist No. 70, p. 424. The President is directly dependent on the people, and since there is only one President, he is responsible. The people know whom to blame, whereas "one of the weightiest objections to a plurality in the executive . . . is that it tends to conceal faults and destroy responsibility." Id., at 427.

That is the system of justice the rest of us are entitled to, but what of that select class consisting of present or former high-level Executive Branch officials? If an allegation is made against them of any violation of any federal criminal law (except Class B or C misdemeanors or infractions) the Attorney General must give it his attention. That in itself is not objectionable. But if, after a 90-day investigation without the benefit of normal investigatory tools, the Attorney General is unable to say that there are "no reasonable grounds to believe" that further investigation is warranted, a process is set in motion that is not in the full control of persons "dependent on the people," and whose flaws cannot be blamed on the President. An independent counsel is selected, and the scope of his or her authority prescribed, by a panel of judges. What if they are politically partisan, as judges have been known to be, and select a prosecutor antagonistic to the administration, or even to the particular individual who has been selected for this special treatment? There is no remedy for that, not even a political one. Judges, after all, have life tenure, and appointing a surefire enthusiastic prosecutor could hardly be considered an impeachable offense. So if there is anything wrong with the selection, there is effectively no one to blame. The independent counsel thus selected proceeds to assemble a staff. As I observed earlier, in the nature of things this has to be done by finding lawyers who are willing to lay aside their current careers for an indeterminate amount of time, to take on a job that has no prospect of permanence and little prospect for promotion. One thing is certain, however: it involves investigating and perhaps prosecuting a particular individual. Can one imagine a less equitable manner of fulfilling the executive responsibility to investigate and prosecute?

What would be the reaction if, in an area not covered by this statute, the Justice Department posted a public notice inviting applicants to assist in an investigation and possible prosecution of a certain prominent person? Does this not invite what Justice Jackson described as "picking the man and then searching the law books, or putting investigators to work, to pin some offense on him"? To be sure, the investigation must relate to the area of criminal offense specified by the life-tenured judges. But that has often been (and nothing prevents it from being) very broad - and should the independent counsel or his or her staff come up with something beyond that scope, nothing prevents him or her from asking the judges to expand his or her authority or, if that does not work, referring it to the Attorney General, whereupon the whole process would recommence and, if there was "reasonable basis to believe" that further investigation was warranted, that new offense would be referred to the Special Division, which would in all likelihood assign it to the same independent counsel. It seems to me not conducive to fairness. But even if it were entirely evident that unfairness was in fact the result - the judges hostile to the administration, the independent counsel an old foe of the President, the staff refugees from the recently defeated administration - there would be no one accountable to the public to whom the blame could be assigned.

I do not mean to suggest that anything of this sort (other than the inevitable self-selection of the prosecutory staff) occurred in the present case. I know and have the highest regard for the judges on the Special Division, and the independent counsel herself is a woman of accomplishment, impartiality, and integrity. But the fairness of a process must be adjudged on the basis of what it permits to happen, not what it produced in a particular case. It is true, of course, that a similar list of horribles could be attributed to an ordinary Justice Department prosecution - a vindictive prosecutor, an antagonistic staff, etc. But the difference is the difference that the Founders envisioned when they established a single Chief Executive accountable to the people: the blame can be assigned to someone who can be punished.

The above described possibilities of irresponsible conduct must, as I say, be considered in judging the constitutional acceptability of this process. But they will rarely occur, and in the average case the threat to fairness is quite different. As described in the brief filed on behalf of three ex-Attorneys General from each of the last three administrations:

"The problem is less spectacular but much more worrisome. It is that the institutional environment of the Independent Counsel - specifically, her isolation from the Executive Branch and the internal checks and balances it supplies - is designed to heighten, not to check, all of the occupational hazards of the dedicated prosecutor; the danger of too narrow a focus, of the loss of perspective, of preoccupation with the pursuit of one alleged suspect to the exclusion of other interests." Brief for Edward H. Levi, Griffin B. Bell, and William French Smith as Amici Curiae 11.

It is, in other words, an additional advantage of the unitary Executive that it can achieve a more uniform application of the law. Perhaps that is not always achieved, but the mechanism to achieve it is there. The mini-Executive that is the independent counsel, however, operating in an area where so little is law and so much is discretion, is intentionally cut off from the unifying influence of the Justice Department, and from the perspective that multiple responsibilities provide. What would normally be regarded as a technical violation (there are no rules defining such things), may in his or her small world assume the proportions of an indictable offense. What would normally be regarded as an investigation that has reached the level of pursuing such picayune matters that it should be concluded, may to him or her be an investigation that ought to go on for another year. How frightening it must be to have your own independent counsel and staff appointed, with nothing else to do but to investigate you until investigation is no longer worthwhile - with whether it is worthwhile not depending upon what such judgments usually hinge on, competing responsibilities. And to have that counsel and staff decide, with no basis for comparison, whether what you have done is bad enough, willful enough, and provable enough, to warrant an indictment. How admirable the constitutional system that provides the means to avoid such a distortion. And how unfortunate the judicial decision that has permitted it.

* * *

The notion that every violation of law should be prosecuted, including - indeed, especially - every violation by those in high places, is an attractive one, and it would be risky to argue in an election campaign that that is not an absolutely overriding value. Fiat justitia, ruat coelum. Let justice be done, though the heavens may fall. The reality is, however, that it is not an absolutely overriding value, and it was with the hope that we would be able to acknowledge and apply such realities that the Constitution spared us, by life tenure, the necessity of election campaigns. I cannot imagine that there are not many thoughtful men and women in Congress who realize that the benefits of this legislation are far outweighed by its harmful effect upon our system of government, and even upon the nature of justice received by those men and women who agree to serve in the Executive Branch. But it is difficult to vote not to enact, and even more difficult to vote to repeal, a statute called, appropriately enough, the Ethics in Government Act. If Congress is controlled by the party other than the one to which the President belongs, it has little incentive to repeal it; if it is controlled by the same party, it dare not. By its shortsighted action today, I fear the Court has permanently encumbered the Republic with an institution that will do it great harm.

Worse than what it has done, however, is the manner in which it has done it. A government of laws means a government of rules. Today's decision on the basic issue of fragmentation of executive power is ungoverned by rule, and hence ungoverned by law. It extends into the very heart of our most significant constitutional function the "totality of the circumstances" mode of analysis that this Court has in recent years become fond of. Taking all things into account, we conclude that the power taken away from the President here is not really too much. The next time executive power is assigned to someone other than the President we may conclude, taking all things into account, that it is too much.

That opinion, like this one, will not be confined by any rule. We will describe, as we have today (though I hope more accurately) the effects of the provision in question, and will authoritatively announce: "The President's need to control the exercise of the [subject officer's] discretion is so central to the functioning of the Executive Branch as to require complete control." This is not analysis; it is ad hoc judgment. And it fails to explain why it is not true that - as the text of the Constitution seems to require, as the Founders seemed to expect, and as our past cases have uniformly assumed - all purely executive power must be under the control of the President.

The ad hoc approach to constitutional adjudication has real attraction, even apart from its work-saving potential. It is guaranteed to produce a result, in every case, that will make a majority of the Court happy with the law. The law is, by definition, precisely what the majority thinks, taking all things into account, it ought to be. I prefer to rely upon the judgment of the wise men who constructed our system, and of the people who approved it, and of two centuries of history that have shown it to be sound. Like it or not, that judgment says, quite plainly, that "[t]he executive Power shall be vested in a President of the United States."

Justice Scalia's dissent in Thompson v. Oklahoma (June 29, 1988) [Excerpt]

Justice Scalia, with whom Chief Justice Rehnquist and Justice White join, dissenting.

If the issue before us today were whether an automatic death penalty for conviction of certain crimes could be extended to individuals younger than 16 when they commit the crimes, thereby preventing individualized consideration of their maturity and moral responsibility, I would accept the plurality's conclusion that such a practice is opposed by a national consensus, sufficiently uniform and of sufficiently long standing, to render it cruel and unusual punishment within the meaning of the Eighth Amendment. We have already decided as much, and more, in Lockett v. Ohio, 438 U.S. 586 (1978). I might even agree with the plurality's conclusion if the question were whether a person under 16 when he commits a crime can be deprived of the benefit of a rebuttable presumption that he is not mature and responsible enough to be punished as an adult. The question posed here, however, is radically different from both of these. It is whether there is a national consensus that no criminal so much as one day under 16, after individuated consideration of his circumstances, including the overcoming of a presumption that he should not be tried as an adult, can possibly be deemed mature and responsible enough to be punished with death for any crime. [. . .]

Justice Scalia's dissent in Bowen v. Massachusetts (June 29, 1988) [Notes omitted]

JUSTICE SCALIA, with whom THE CHIEF JUSTICE and JUSTICE KENNEDY join, dissenting.

The Court holds for the State because it finds that these suits do not seek money damages, and involve claims for which there is no "adequate remedy" in the Claims Court. I disagree with both propositions, and therefore respectfully dissent.

I

"The States of the Union, like all other entities, are barred by federal sovereign immunity from suing the United States in the absence of an express waiver of this immunity by Congress." Block v. North Dakota ex rel. Bd. of Univ. and School Lands, 461 U. S. 273, 280 (1983). For this waiver, the Commonwealth of Massachusetts (hereafter respondent) relies on a provision added to § 10 of the Administrative Procedure Act (APA) in 1976:

"An action in a court of the United States seeking relief other than money damages and stating a claim that an agency or an officer or employee thereof acted or failed to act in an official capacity or under color of legal authority shall not be dismissed nor relief therein be denied on the ground that it is against the United States or that the United States is an indispensable party." 5 U. S. C. § 702 (emphasis added).

The Government contends that respondent's lawsuits seek "money damages" and therefore § 702 is unavailing.

In legal parlance, the term "damages" refers to money awarded as reparation for injury resulting from breach of legal duty. Webster's Third New International Dictionary 571 (1981); Black's Law Dictionary 351-352 (5th ed. 1979); D. Dobbs, Law of Remedies § 3.1, p. 135 (1973); W. Hale, Law of Damages 1 (Cooley 2d ed. 1912). Thus the phrase "money damages" is something of a redundancy, but it is, nonetheless, a common usage and refers to one of the two broad categories of judicial relief in the common-law system. The other, of course, is denominated "specific relief." Whereas damages compensate the plaintiff for a loss, specific relief prevents or undoes the loss — for example, by ordering return to the plaintiff of the precise property that has been wrongfully taken, or by enjoining acts that would damage the plaintiff's person or property. See 5A A. Corbin, Contracts § 1141, p. 113 (1964); Dobbs, supra, at 135.

The use of the term "damages" (or "money damages") in a context dealing with legal remedies would naturally be thought to advert to this classic distinction. This interpretation is reinforced by the desirability of reading § 702 in pari materia with the Tucker Act, 28 U. S. C. § 1491, which grants the Claims Court jurisdiction over certain suits against the Government. Although the Tucker Act is not expressly limited to claims for money damages, it "has long been construed as authorizing only actions for money judgments and not suits for equitable relief against the United States. See United States v. Jones, 131 U. S. 1 (1889). The reason for the distinction flows from the fact that the Court of Claims has no power to grant equitable relief. . . ." Richardson v. Morris, 409 U. S. 464, 465 (1973) (per curiam); see Lee v. Thornton, 420 U. S. 139, 140 (1975) (per curiam) (Tucker Act jurisdiction empowers courts "to award damages but not to grant injunctive or declaratory relief"); United States v. King, 395 U. S. 1, 3 (1969) (relief the Claims Court can give is "limited to actual, presently due money damages from the United States"); Glidden Co. v. Zdanok, 370 U. S. 530, 557 (1962) (Harlan, J., announcing the judgment of the Court) ("From the beginning [the Court of Claims] has been given jurisdiction only to award damages, not specific relief"). Since under the Tucker Act the absence of Claims Court jurisdiction generally turns upon the distinction between money damages and specific relief,[1] it is sensible, if possible (and here it is not only possible but most natural), to interpret § 702 so that the presence of district court jurisdiction will turn upon the same distinction. Otherwise, there would be a gap in the scheme of relief — an utterly irrational gap, which we have no reason to believe was intended.

The Court agrees that "the words `money damages' [were not intended to] have any meaning other than the ordinary understanding of the term as used in the common law for centuries," ante, at 897, and that § 702 encompasses "the time-honored distinction between damages and specific relief," ibid. It concludes, however, that respondent's suits seek the latter and not the former. The first theory the Court puts forward to support this conclusion is that, "insofar as [respondent's] complaints sought declaratory and injunctive relief, they were certainly not actions for money damages," ante, at 893, and since the District Court simply reversed the decision of the Departmental Grant Appeals Board, "neither of [its] orders in this case was a `money judgment,' " ante, at 909. I cannot agree (nor do I think the Court really agrees) with this reasoning. If the jurisdictional division established by Congress is not to be reduced to an absurdity, the line between damages and specific relief must surely be drawn on the basis of the substance of the claim, and not its mere form. It does not take much lawyerly inventiveness to convert a claim for payment of a past due sum (damages) into a prayer for an injunction against refusing to pay the sum, or for a declaration that the sum must be paid, or for an order reversing the agency's decision not to pay. It is not surprising, therefore, that "in the `murky' area of Tucker Act jurisprudence. . . one of the few clearly established principles is that the substance of the pleadings must prevail over their form," Amoco Production Co. v. Hodel, 815 F. 2d 352, 361 (CA5 1987), cert. pending, No. 87-372. All the Courts of Appeals that to my knowledge have addressed the issue, 12 out of 13, are unanimous that district court jurisdiction is not established merely because a suit fails to pray for a money judgment. See, e. g., Massachusetts v. Departmental Grant Appeals Bd. of Health and Human Services, 815 F. 2d 778, 783 (CA1 1987); B. K. Instrument, Inc. v. United States, 715 F. 2d 713, 727 (CA2 1983); Hahn v. United States, 757 F. 2d 581, 589 (CA3 1985); Portsmouth Redevelopment & Housing Authority v. Pierce, 706 F. 2d 471, 474 (CA4), cert. denied, 464 U. S. 960 (1983); Alabama Rural Fire Ins. Co. v. Naylor, 530 F. 2d 1221, 1228-1230 (CA5 1976); Tennessee ex rel. Leech v. Dole, 749 F. 2d 331, 336 (CA6 1984), cert. denied, 472 U. S. 1018 (1985); Clark v. United States, 596 F. 2d 252, 253-254 (CA7 1979) (per curiam); Minnesota ex rel. Noot v. Heckler, 718 F. 2d 852, 859, n. 12 (CA8 1983); Rowe v. United States, 633 F. 2d 799, 802 (CA9 1980); United States v. Kansas City, 761 F. 2d 605, 608-609 (CA10 1985); Megapulse, Inc. v. Lewis, 217 U. S. App. D. C. 397, 405, 672 F. 2d 959, 967 (1982); Chula Vista City School Dist. v. Bennett, 824 F. 2d 1573, 1579 (CA Fed. 1987).

The Court cannot intend to stand by a theory that obliterates § 702's jurisdictional requirements, that permits every Claims Court suit to be brought in district court merely because the complaint prays for injunctive relief, and that is contrary to the law of all 12 Circuits that have addressed the issue. Therefore, although the Court describes this first theory as an "independent reaso[n]" for its conclusion, ante, at 909, I must believe that its decision actually rests on different grounds.

The Court's second theory is that "the monetary aspects of the relief that the State sought are not `money damages' as that term is used in the law," ante, at 893; see ante, at 910. This at least focuses on the right question: whether the claim is in substance one for money damages. But the reason the Court gives for answering the question negatively, that respondent's suits are not "seeking money in compensation for the damage sustained by the failure of the Federal Government to pay as mandated," ante, at 900, is simply wrong. Respondent sought money to compensate for the monetary loss (damage) it sustained by expending resources to provide services to the mentally retarded in reliance on the Government's statutory duty to reimburse, just as a Government contractor's suit seeks compensation for the loss the contractor sustains by expending resources to provide services to the Government in reliance on the Government's contractual duty to pay. Respondent's lawsuits thus precisely fit the classic definition of suits for money damages.[2] It is true, of course, that they also fit a general description of a suit for specific relief, since the award of money undoes a loss by giving respondent the very thing (money) to which it was legally entitled. As the Court recognizes, however, the terms "damages" and "specific relief" have been "used in the common law for centuries," ante, at 897, and have meanings well established by tradition. Part of that tradition was that a suit seeking to recover a past due sum of money that does no more than compensate a plaintiff's loss is a suit for damages, not specific relief; a successful plaintiff thus obtains not a decree of specific performance requiring the defendant to pay the sum due on threat of punishment for contempt, but rather a money judgment permitting the plaintiff to order "the sheriff to seize and sell so much of the defendant's property as was required to pay the plaintiff." Farnsworth, Legal Remedies for Breach of Contract, 70 Colum. L. Rev. 1145, 1152 (1970). Those rare suits for a sum of money that were not suits for money damages (and that resulted at common law in an order to the defendant rather than a judgment executable by the sheriff) did not seek to compensate the plaintiff for a past loss in the amount awarded, but rather to prevent future losses that were either incalculable or would be greater than the sum awarded. Id., at 1154; 5A A. Corbin, Contracts § 1142, pp. 117-126 (1964); H. McClintock, Principles of Equity § 60, p. 149 (2d ed 1948); T. Waterman, Specific Performance of Contracts § 20, p. 25 (1881). Specific relief was available, for example, to enforce a promise to loan a sum of money when the unavailability of alternative financing would leave the plaintiff with injuries that are difficult to value; or to enforce an obligor's duty to make future monthly payments, after the obligor had consistently refused to make past payments concededly due, and thus threatened the obligee with the burden of bringing multiple damages actions. Almost invariably, however, suits seeking (whether by judgment, injunction, or declaration) to compel the defendant to pay a sum of money[3] to the plaintiff are suits for "money damages," as that phrase has traditionally been applied, since they seek no more than compensation for loss resulting from the defendant's breach of legal duty. The present cases are quite clearly of this usual sort.

The Court's second theory, that "the monetary aspects of the relief that the State sought are not `money damages,' " ante, at 893, is not only wrong, but it produces the same disastrous consequences as the first theory. As discussed above, see supra, at 913-915, and as the Court recognizes, see ante, at 905, and n. 40, the Claims Court has jurisdiction only to award damages, not specific relief. But if actions seeking past due sums are actions for specific relief, since "they undo the [Government's] refusal" to pay the plaintiff, ante, at 910, then the Claims Court is out of business. Almost its entire docket fits this description. In the past, typical actions have included suits by Government employees to obtain money allegedly due by statute which the Government refused to pay. See, e. g., Ellis v. United States, 222 Ct. Cl. 65, 610 F. 2d 760 (1979) (claim under 5 U. S. C. § 8336(c), entitling law enforcement officers and firefighters to special retirement benefits); Friedman v. United States, 159 Ct. Cl. 1, 30-31, 310 F. 2d 381, 396-397 (1962) (claim under 10 U. S. C. § 1201 et seq., entitling servicemen to disability retirement benefits), cert. denied sub nom. Lipp v. United States, 373 U. S. 932 (1963); Smykowski v. United States, 227 Ct. Cl. 284, 285, 647 F. 2d 1103, 1104 (1981) (claim under 42 U. S. C. §§ 3796-3796c, granting survivors' death benefits for public safety officers). Another large category of the Claims Court's former jurisdiction consisted of suits for money allegedly due under Government grant programs that the Government refused to pay. See, e. g., Missouri Health & Medical Organization, Inc. v. United States, 226 Ct. Cl. 274, 277-279, 641 F. 2d 870, 873 (1981) (grant awarded by Public Health Service); Idaho Migrant Council, Inc. v. United States, 9 Cl. Ct. 85, 88 (1985) ("The United States, for public purposes, has undertaken numerous programs to make grant funds available to various governmental and private organizations. Many hundreds of grants are made each year to states, municipalities, schools and colleges and other public and private organizations. . . . Obligations of the United States assumed in [grant] programs . . . are within this court's Tucker Act jurisdiction"). All these suits, and even actions for tax refunds, see, e. g., Yamamoto v. United States, 9 Cl. Ct. 207 (1985), are now disclosed to be actions for specific relief and beyond the Claims Court's jurisdiction, since they merely seek "to enforce the statutory mandate . . . which happens to be one for the payment of money," ante, at 900.

Most of these suits will now have to be brought in the district courts, as suits for specific relief "to undo the Government's refusal to pay." Alas, however, not all can be. The most regrettable consequence of the Court's analysis is its effect upon suits for a sum owed under a contract with the Government. In the past, the Claims Court has routinely exercised jurisdiction over a seller's action for the price. See, e. g., Dairylea Cooperative, Inc. v. United States, 210 Ct. Cl. 46, 535 F. 2d 24 (1976); Northern Helex Co. v. United States, 197 Ct. Cl. 118, 455 F. 2d 546 (1972); Paisner v. United States, 138 Ct. Cl. 420, 150

F. Supp. 835 (1957), cert. denied, 355 U. S. 941 (1958); R. M. Hollingshead Corp. v. United States, 124 Ct. Cl. 681, 111 F. Supp. 285 (1953). But since, on the Court's theory, such a suit is not a suit for money damages but rather for specific relief, that jurisdiction will have to be abandoned. Unfortunately, however, those suits will not lie in district court either. It is settled that sovereign immunity bars a suit against the United States for specific performance of a contract, see Larson v. Domestic & Foreign Commerce Corp., 337 U. S. 682 (1949), and that this bar was not disturbed by the 1976 amendment to § 702, see Spectrum Leasing Corp., v. United States, 246 U. S. App. D. C. 258, 260, and n. 2, 262, 764 F. 2d 891, 893, and n. 2, 895 (1985); Sea-Land Service, Inc. v. Brown, 600 F. 2d 429, 432-433 (CA3 1979); American Science & Engineering, Inc. v. Califano, 571 F. 2d 58, 63 (CA1 1978). Thus, the Court of Appeals for the District of Columbia Circuit, applying the logic (which the Court has today specifically adopted as its own, ante, at 894-896, 901) of its earlier decision in Maryland Dept. of Human Resources v. Department of Health and Human Services, 246 U. S. App. D. C. 180, 763 F. 2d 1441 (1985), has held that a contractor cannot sue the Government in district court for the amount due under a contract, not because that would be a suit for money damages within the exclusive jurisdiction of the Claims Court, but because it is a suit for specific performance of the contract. Spectrum Leasing Corp. v. United States, supra, at 262, 764 F. 2d, at 895. But since the Claims Court is also barred from granting specific performance, the Court's theory, in addition to leaving the Claims Court without a docket, leaves the contractor without a forum.

I am sure, however, that neither the judges of the Claims Court nor Government contractors need worry. The Court cannot possibly mean what it says today — except, of course, the judgment. What that leaves, unfortunately, is a judgment without a reason.

II

I agree with the Court that sovereign immunity does not bar respondent's actions insofar as they seek injunctive or declaratory relief with prospective effect. An action seeking an order that will prevent the wrongful disallowance of future claims is an action seeking specific relief and not damages, since no damage has yet occurred. Cf. United States v. Testan, 424 U. S. 392, 403 (1976) (distinguishing "between prospective reclassification, on the one hand, and retroactive reclassification resulting in money damages, on the other").

I do not agree, however, that respondent can pursue these suits in district court, as it has sought to, under the provisions of the APA, since in my view they are barred by 5 U. S. C. § 704, which is entitled "Actions reviewable," and which reads in relevant part:

"Agency action made reviewable by statute and final agency action for which there is no other adequate remedy in a court are subject to judicial review."

The purpose and effect of this provision is to establish that the APA "does not provide additional judicial remedies in situations where the Congress has provided special and adequate review procedures." Attorney General's Manual on the Administrative Procedure Act § 10(c), p. 101 (1947); see Estate of Watson v. Blumenthal, 586 F. 2d 925,

934 (CA2 1978); Alabama Rural Fire Ins. Co. v. Naylor, 530 F. 2d, at 1230; International Engineering Co. v. Richardson, 167 U. S. App. D. C. 396, 403, 512 F. 2d 573, 580 (1975); Warner v. Cox, 487 F. 2d 1301, 1304 (CA5 1974); Mohawk Airlines, Inc. v. CAB, 117 U. S. App. D. C. 326, 329 F. 2d 894 (1964); Ove Gustavsson Contracting Co. v. Floete, 278 F. 2d 912, 914 (CA2 1960); K. Davis, Administrative Law § 211, p. 720 (1951). Respondent has an adequate remedy in a court and may not proceed under the APA in the District Court because (1) an action for reimbursement may be brought in the Claims Court pursuant to the Tucker Act, and (2) that action provides all the relief respondent seeks.

The Tucker Act grants the Claims Court

"jurisdiction to render judgment upon any claim against the United States founded either upon the Constitution, or any Act of Congress or any regulation of an executive department, or upon any express or implied contract with the United States, or for liquidated or unliquidated damages in cases not sounding in tort." 28 U. S. C. § 1491(a)(1).

The Claims Court has not always clearly identified which of the several branches of jurisdiction recited in this provision it is proceeding under. It has held that Government grant instruments, although not formal contracts, give rise to enforceable obligations analogous to contracts. See, e. g., Missouri Health & Medical Organization, Inc. v. United States, 226 Ct. Cl., at 278, 641 F. 2d, at 873; Idaho Migrant Council, Inc. v. United States, 9 Cl. Ct., at 89. The Medicaid Act itself can be analogized to a unilateral offer for contract — offering to pay specified sums in return for the performance of specified services and inviting the States to accept the offer by performance. But regardless of the propriety of invoking the Claims Court's contractual jurisdiction, I agree with the Secretary that respondent can assert a claim "founded . . . upon [an] Act of Congress," to wit, the Medicaid provision mandating that "the Secretary (except as otherwise provided in this section) shall pay to each State which has a plan approved under this subchapter" the amounts specified by statutory formula. 42 U. S. C. § 1396b(a) (emphasis added).

We have held that a statute does not create a cause of action for money damages unless it " `can fairly be interpreted as mandating compensation by the Federal Government for the damage sustained.' " United States v. Testan, supra, at 400, quoting Eastport S. S. Corp. v. United States, 178 Ct. Cl. 599, 607, 372 F. 2d 1002, 1009 (1967). Although § 1396b(a) does not, in so many words, mandate damages, a statute commanding the payment of a specified amount of money by the United States impliedly authorizes (absent other indication) a claim for damages in the defaulted amount. See, e. g., Bell v. United States, 366 U. S. 393, 398 (1961) (claim brought under statute providing that captured soldiers "shall be entitled to receive" specified amounts); Sullivan v. United States, 4 Cl. Ct. 70, 72 (1983) (claim brought under 5 U. S. C. § 5595(b)(2), providing that employees are "entitled to be paid severance pay" in specified amounts), aff'd, 742 F. 2d 628 (CA Fed. 1984) (per curiam); Ellis v. United States, 222 Ct. Cl. 65, 610 F. 2d 760 (1979) (claim under 5 U. S. C. § 8336(c), entitling law enforcement officers and firefighters to special retirement benefits); Friedman v. United States, 159 Ct. Cl., at 30-31, 310 F. 2d, at 396-397 (claim under 10 U. S. C. § 1201 et seq., entitling servicemen to disability retirement benefits), cert. denied sub nom. Lipp v. United States, 373 U. S. 932 (1963); Smykowski v. United States, 227 Ct. Cl., at 285, 647 F. 2d, at 1104 (claim under 42 U. S. C. §§ 3796-3796c, granting survivors' death benefits for public safety officers); Biagioli v. United States, 2 Cl. Ct. 304, 306-307 (1983) (claim brought under 5 U. S. C. § 5596, providing that employees subject to unjustified personnel action are "entitled . . . to receive" backpay); see also Testan, supra, at 406 (dicta) ("Congress . . . has provided specifically. . . in the Back Pay Act [5 U. S. C. § 5596] for the award of money damages for a wrongful deprivation of pay").

I conclude, therefore, that respondent may bring an action in the Claims Court based on § 1396b(a). The Court does not disagree with this conclusion but does comment that "[i]t seems likely that while Congress intended `shall pay' language in statutes such as the Back Pay Act to be self-enforcing — i. e., to create both a right and a remedy — it intended similar language in § 1396b(a) of the Medicaid Act to provide merely a right, knowing that the APA provided for review of this sort of agency action." Ante, at 906, n. 42. I fail to understand this reasoning, if it is intended as reasoning rather than as an unsupported conclusion. The only basis the Court provides for treating differently statutes with identical language is that Congress knew "that the APA provided for review of this sort of agency action [i. e., denial of Medicare reimbursement]." Ibid. But that does not distinguish the Medicaid Act from any statute enacted after 1946 when the APA became effective, including the Back Pay Act, 5 U. S. C. § 5596, and most other statutory bases for Claims Court jurisdiction.

There remains to be considered whether the relief available in the Claims Court, damages for failure to pay a past due allocation, is an "adequate remedy" within the meaning of § 704. Like the term "damages," the phrase "adequate remedy" is not of recent coinage. It has an established, centuries-old, common-law meaning in the context of specific relief — to wit, that specific relief will be denied when damages are available and are sufficient to make the plaintiff whole. See, e. g., 1 W. Holdsworth, A History of English Law 457 (7th ed. 1956) (by the 18th century "it was settled that equity would only grant specific relief if damages were not an adequate remedy"). Thus, even though a plaintiff may often prefer a judicial order enjoining a harmful act or omission before it occurs, damages after the fact are considered an "adequate remedy" in all but the most extraordinary cases. See, e. g., Schoenthal v. Irving Trust Co., 287 U. S. 92, 94 (1932); Gaines v. Miller, 111 U. S. 395, 397-398 (1884); 5A A. Corbin, Contracts § 1136, pp. 95-96, § 1142, pp. 117-120 (1964); H. Hunter, Modern Law of Contracts: Breaches and Remedies ¶ 6.01[3], pp. 6-7 to 6-8 (1986); Farnsworth, 70 Colum. L. Rev. 1154; cf. Ruckelshaus v. Monsanto Co., 467 U. S. 986, 1017 (1984). There may be circumstances in which damages relief in the Claims Court is available, but is not an adequate remedy. For example, if a State could prove that the Secretary intended in the future to deny Medicaid reimbursement in bad faith, forcing the State to commence a new suit for each disputed period, an action for injunctive relief in district court would lie. See, e. g., Franklin

Telegraph Co. v. Harrison, 145 U. S. 459, 474 (1892). Or if a State wished to set up a new program providing certain services that the Secretary had made clear his intention to disallow for reimbursement, an action seeking a declaration as to the correct interpretation of the statute would lie, since it would be necessary to prevent the irreparable injury of either forgoing a reimbursable program or mistakenly expending state funds that will not be reimbursed. But absent such unusual circumstances, the availability of damages in the Claims Court precludes suit in district court under the provision of the APA permitting review of "agency action for which there is no other adequate remedy." See Estate of Watson v. Blumenthal, 586 F. 2d, at 934 (emphasis omitted); Warner v. Cox, 487 F. 2d, at 1304; Mohawk Airlines, Inc. v. CAB, 117 U. S. App. D. C. 326, 329 F. 2d 894 (1964); Ove Gustavsson Contracting Co. v. Floete, 278 F. 2d, at 914; cf. Monsanto, supra, at 1019 (equitable relief to enjoin taking barred since Tucker Act provides an "adequate remedy").[4]

The Court does not dispute that in the present cases an action in Claims Court would provide respondent complete relief. Respondent can assert immediately a claim for money damages in Claims Court, which if successful will as effectively establish its rights as would a declaratory judgment in district court. Since there is no allegation that the Secretary will not honor in the future a Claims Court judgment that would have not only precedential but collateral-estoppel effect, see Montana v. United States, 440 U. S. 147, 157-158, 162-163 (1979), the ability to bring an action in Claims Court with regard to disallowance decisions already made provides effective prospective relief as well.

Rather than trying to argue that the Claims Court remedy is inadequate in this case, the Court declares in a footnote that "[s]ince, as a category of case, alleged `improper Medicaid disallowances' cannot always be adequately remedied in the Claims Court, as a jurisdictional, or threshold matter, these actions should proceed in the district court." Ante, at 907, n. 43. This novel approach completely ignores the well-established meaning of "adequate remedy," which refers to the adequacy of a remedy for a particular plaintiff in a particular case rather than the adequacy of a remedy for the average plaintiff in the average case of the sort at issue. Although the Court emphasizes that the phrase "money damages" should be interpreted according to "the ordinary understanding of the term as used in the common law for centuries," ante, at 897, it appears to forget that prescription when it turns to the equally ancient phrase "adequate remedy." Evidently, whether to invoke "ordinary understanding" rather than novel meaning depends on the task at hand. In any event, were the Court's rationale taken seriously, it would (like the Court's novel analysis of "money damages" in § 702) divest the Claims Court of the bulk of its docket. It is difficult to think of a category of case that can "always be adequately remedied in the Claims Court." Nor is a categorical rule for challenges to Medicaid disallowance decisions justifiable on the basis that in most (not just some) such cases prospective or injunctive relief is required, and therefore it is efficient to have a bright-line rule. The traditional legal presumption (and the common-sense presumption) with respect to all other statutes that obligate the Government to pay money is that money damages are ordinarily an adequate remedy. I am aware of no empirical evidence to rebut that presumption with respect to Medicaid. Among the reported disallowance decisions, there appear to be none where a State has asserted a basis for prospective injunctive relief.

Nor can Medicaid disallowance cases be singled out for special treatment as a group because, as the Court declares, "[m]anaging the relationships between States and the Federal Government that occur over time and that involve constantly shifting balance sheets requires a different sort of review and relief process" than is provided in Claims Court, ante, at 904-905, n. 39, since the Medicaid Act is a "complex scheme . . . that governs a set of intricate, ongoing relationships between the States and the Federal Government," ante, at 901, n. 31. All aspects of this assertion are without foundation. The area of law involved here, Medicaid, is indistiguishable for all relevant purposes from many other areas of law the Claims Court routinely handles. Medicaid statutes and regulations are not more complex than, for example, the federal statutes and regulations governing income taxation or Government procurement, and the Government's relationship with the States is neither more intricate and ongoing nor uses a different kind of balance sheet than its relationship with many defense contractors or with large corporate taxpayers subject to perpetual audit. And I cannot imagine in what way district courts adjudicating Medicaid disallowance claims would apply "a different sort of review and relief process" so as to "manag[e] the relationships between States and Federal Governments." Just like the Claims Court, district courts adjudicate concrete cases, one at at a time, that present discrete factual and legal disputes.

Finally, the Court suggests that Medicaid disallowance suits are more suitably heard in district court with appeal to the regional courts of appeals than in the Claims Court with appeal to the Court of Appeals for the Federal Circuit, because (1) disallowance decisions have "state-law aspects" over which the regional courts of appeals have a better grasp, ante, at 908, (2) it is anomalous to have Medicaid compliance decisions reviewed in the regional courts of appeals while reviewing disallowance decisions in Claims Court, ibid., and (3) it is "highly unlikely that Congress intended to designate an Article I court as the primary forum for judicial review of agency action that may involve questions of policy," ante, at 908, n. 46. I do not see how these points have anything to do with the question before us (whether the Claims Court can provide an adequate remedy in these cases), but even if relevant they seem to me wrong. (1) Adjudicating a disallowance decision does not directly implicate state law. As the present cases illustrate, the typical dispute involves only the interpretation of federal statutes and regulations. I suppose it is conceivable that a state-law issue could sometimes be relevant — for example, the Government might contend that the State was, under state law, entitled to reimbursement for a particular expenditure from some third party and thus could not claim it against the Government. But there is no area of federal law that does not contain these incidental references to state law, and perhaps none does so as much as federal tax law, which is, of course, routinely adjudicated in the Claims Court. (2) It is not at all anomalous for the Claims Court to share jurisdiction over controversies arising from Medicaid. In fact, quite to the contrary, the Claims Court never exercises exclusive jurisdiction over any body of law, but only over particular types of claims. (3) It is not more likely that Congress intended disputes involving "questions of policy" to be heard in district court before appeal to an Article III court, since it is the business neither of district courts nor of Article III appellate courts to determine questions of policy. It is the norm for Congress to designate an Article I judge, usually an administrative law judge, as the initial forum for resolving policy disputes (to the extent they are to resolved in adjudication rather than by rulemaking), with the first stop in an Article III court being a court of appeals such as the Federal Circuit — where, of course, the policy itself would not be reviewed but merely its legality and the procedures by which it was pronounced. Ordinarily, when Congress creates a special judicial review mechanism using district courts, it is to get an independent adjudication of the facts, not an unconstitutional judicial determination of policy. See, e. g., 42 U. S. C. § 405(g).

   * * *

  Nothing is more wasteful than litigation about where to litigate, particularly when the options are all courts within the same legal system that will apply the same law. Today's decision is a potential cornucopia of waste. Since its reasoning cannot possibly be followed where it leads, the jurisdiction of the Claims Court has been thrown into chaos. On the other hand, perhaps this is the opinion's greatest strength. Since it cannot possibly be followed where it leads, the lower courts may have the sense to conclude that it leads nowhere, and to limit it to the single type of suit before us. Even so, because I think there is no justification in law for treating this single type of suit differently, I dissent.

Justice Scalia's dissent in Mistretta v. US (Jan. 18, 1989)

  Justice Scalia, dissenting.

  While the products of the Sentencing Commission's labors have been given the modest name "Guidelines," see 28 U.S.C. 994(a)(1) (1982 ed., Supp. IV); United States Sentencing Commission Guidelines Manual (June 15, 1988), they have the force and effect of laws, prescribing the sentences criminal defendants are to receive. A judge who disregards them will be reversed, 18 U.S.C. 3742 (1982 ed., Supp. IV). I dissent from today's decision because I can find no place within our constitutional system for an agency created by Congress to exercise no governmental power other than the making of laws.

  * There is no doubt that the Sentencing Commission has established significant, legally binding prescriptions governing application of governmental power against private individuals indeed, application of the ultimate governmental power, short of capital punishment. 1 Statutorily permissible sentences for particular crimes cover as broad a range as zero years to life, see, e.g., 18 U.S.C. 1201 (1982 ed. and Supp. IV) (kidnaping), and within those ranges the Commission was given broad discretion to prescribe the "correct" sentence, 28 U.S.C. 994(b)(2) (1982 ed., Supp. IV). Average prior sentences were to be a starting point for the Commission's inquiry, § 994(m), but it could and regularly

did deviate from those averages as it thought appropriate. It chose, for example, to prescribe substantial increases over average prior sentences for white-collar crimes such as public corruption, antitrust violations, and tax evasion. Guidelines, at 2.31, 2.133, 2.140. For antitrust violations, before the Guidelines only 39% of those convicted served any imprisonment, and the average imprisonment was only 45 days, id., at 2.133, whereas the Guidelines prescribe base sentences (for defendants with no prior criminal conviction) ranging from 2-to-8 months to 10-to-16 months, depending upon the volume of commerce involved. See id., at 2.131, 5.2.

The Commission also determined when probation was permissible, imposing a strict system of controls because of its judgment that probation had been used for an "inappropriately high percentage of offenders guilty of certain economic crimes." Id., at 1.8. Moreover, the Commission had free rein in determining whether statutorily authorized fines should be imposed in addition to imprisonment, and if so, in what amounts. It ultimately decided that every nonindigent offender should pay a fine according to a schedule devised by the Commission. Id., at 5.18. Congress also gave the Commission discretion to determine whether 7 specified characteristics of offenses, and 11 specified characteristics of offenders, "have any relevance," and should be included among the factors varying the sentence. 28 U.S.C. 994(c), (d) (1982 ed., Supp. IV). Of the latter, it included only three among the factors required to be considered, and declared the remainder not ordinarily relevant. Guidelines, at 5.29-5.31.

It should be apparent from the above that the decisions made by the Commission are far from technical, but are heavily laden (or ought to be) with value judgments and policy assessments. This fact is sharply reflected in the Commission's product, as described by the dissenting Commissioner:

"Under the guidelines, the judge could give the same sentence for abusive sexual contact that puts the child in fear as for unlawfully entering or remaining in the United States. Similarly, the guidelines permit equivalent sentences for the following pairs of offenses: drug trafficking and a violation of the Wild Free-Roaming Horses and Burros Act; arson with a destructive device and failure to surrender a cancelled naturalization certificate; operation of a common carrier under the influence of drugs that causes injury and alteration of one motor vehicle identification number; illegal trafficking in explosives and trespass; interference with a flight attendant and unlawful conduct relating to contraband cigarettes; aggravated assault and smuggling $11,000 worth of fish." Dissenting View of Commissioner Paul H. Robinson on the Promulgation of the Sentencing Guidelines by the United States Sentencing Commission 6-7 (May 1, 1987) (citations omitted).

Petitioner's most fundamental and far-reaching challenge to the Commission is that Congress' commitment of such broad policy responsibility to any institution is an unconstitutional delegation of legislative power. It is difficult to imagine a principle more essential to democratic government than that upon which the doctrine of unconstitutional delegation is founded: Except in a few areas constitutionally committed to the Executive

Branch, the basic policy decisions governing society are to be made by the Legislature. Our Members of Congress could not, even if they wished, vote all power to the President and adjourn sine die.

But while the doctrine of unconstitutional delegation is unquestionably a fundamental element of our constitutional system, it is not an element readily enforceable by the courts. Once it is conceded, as it must be, that no statute can be entirely precise, and that some judgments, even some judgments involving policy considerations, must be left to the officers executing the law and to the judges applying it, the debate over unconstitutional delegation becomes a debate not over a point of principle but over a question of degree. As Chief Justice Taft expressed the point for the Court in the landmark case of J.W. Hampton, Jr., & Co. v. United States, 276 U.S. 394, 406, 48 S.Ct. 348, 351, 72 L.Ed. 624 (1928), the limits of delegation "must be fixed according to common sense and the inherent necessities of the governmental co-ordination." Since Congress is no less endowed with common sense than we are, and better equipped to inform itself of the "necessities" of government; and since the factors bearing upon those necessities are both multifarious and (in the nonpartisan sense) highly political—including, for example, whether the Nation is at war, see Yakus v. United States, 321 U.S. 414, 64 S.Ct. 660, 88 L.Ed. 834 (1944), or whether for other reasons "emergency is instinct in the situation," Amalgamated Meat Cutters and Butcher Workmen of North America v. Connally, 337 F.Supp. 737, 752 (DC 1971) (three-judge court)—it is small wonder that we have almost never felt qualified to second-guess Congress regarding the permissible degree of policy judgment that can be left to those executing or applying the law. As the Court points out, we have invoked the doctrine of unconstitutional delegation to invalidate a law only twice in our history, over half a century ago. See Panama Refining Co. v. Ryan, 293 U.S. 388, 55 S.Ct. 241, 79 L.Ed. 446 (1935); A.L.A. Schechter Poultry Corp. v. United States, 295 U.S. 495, 55 S.Ct. 837, 79 L.Ed. 1570 (1935). What legislated standard, one must wonder, can possibly be too vague to survive judicial scrutiny, when we have repeatedly upheld, in various contexts, a "public interest" standard? See, e.g., National Broadcasting Co. v. United States, 319 U.S. 190, 216-217, 63 S.Ct. 997, 1009-1010, 87 L.Ed. 1344 (1943); New York Central Securities Corp. v. United States, 287 U.S. 12, 24-25, 53 S.Ct. 45, 48, 77 L.Ed. 138 (1932).

In short, I fully agree with the Court's rejection of petitioner's contention that the doctrine of unconstitutional delegation of legislative authority has been violated because of the lack of intelligible, congressionally prescribed standards to guide the Commission.

II

Precisely because the scope of delegation is largely uncontrollable by the courts, we must be particularly rigorous in preserving the Constitution's structural restrictions that deter excessive delegation. The major one, it seems to me, is that the power to make law cannot be exercised by anyone other than Congress, except in conjunction with the lawful exercise of executive or judicial power.

The whole theory of lawful congressional "delegation" is not that Congress is sometimes too busy or too divided and can therefore assign its responsibility of making law to someone else; but rather that a certain degree of discretion, and thus of lawmaking, inheres in most executive or judicial action, and it is up to Congress, by the relative specificity or generality of its statutory commands, to determine—up to a point—how small or how large that degree shall be. Thus, the courts could be given the power to say precisely what constitutes a "restraint of trade," see Standard Oil Co. of New Jersey v. United States, 221 U.S. 1, 31 S.Ct. 502, 55 L.Ed. 619 (1911), or to adopt rules of procedure, see Sibbach v. Wilson & Co., 312 U.S. 1, 22, 61 S.Ct. 422, 429, 85 L.Ed. 479 (1941), or to prescribe by rule the manner in which their officers shall execute their judgments, Wayman v. Southard,, 23 U.S. 1, 10 Wheat. 1, 45, 6 L.Ed. 253 (1825), because that "lawmaking" was ancillary to their exercise of judicial powers. And the Executive could be given the power to adopt policies and rules specifying in detail what radio and television licenses will be in the "public interest, convenience or necessity," because that was ancillary to the exercise of its executive powers in granting and policing licenses and making a "fair and equitable allocation" of the electromagnetic spectrum. See Federal Radio Comm'n v. Nelson Brothers Bond & Mortgage Co., 289 U.S. 266, 285, 53 S.Ct. 627, 636, 77 L.Ed. 1166 (1933). 2 Or to take examples closer to the case before us: Trial judges could be given the power to determine what factors justify a greater or lesser sentence within the statutorily prescribed limits because that was ancillary to their exercise of the judicial power of pronouncing sentence upon individual defendants. And the President, through the Parole Commission subject to his appointment and removal, could be given the power to issue Guidelines specifying when parole would be available, because that was ancillary to the President's exercise of the executive power to hold and release federal prisoners. See 18 U.S.C. 4203(a)(1) and (b); 28 CFR § 2.20 (1988).

As Justice Harlan wrote for the Court in Field v. Clark, 143 U.S. 649, 12 S.Ct. 495, 36 L.Ed. 294 (1892):

" 'The true distinction . . . is between the delegation of power to make the law, which necessarily involves a discretion as to what it shall be, and conferring authority or discretion as to its execution, to be exercised under and in pursuance of the law. The first cannot be done; to the latter no valid objection can be made.' " Id., at 693-694, 12 S.Ct., at 505 (emphasis added), quoting Cincinnati, W. & Z.R. Co. v. Commissioners of Clinton County, 1 Ohio St. 77, 88-89 (1852).

" 'Half the statutes on our books are in the alternative, depending on the discretion of some person or persons to whom is confided the duty of determining whether the proper occasion exists for executing them. But it cannot be said that the exercise of such discretion is the making of the law.' " Id., at 694, 12 S.Ct. at 505 (emphasis added), quoting Moers v. Reading, 21 Pa. 188, 202 (1853).

In United States v. Grimaud, 220 U.S. 506, 517, 31 S.Ct. 480, 483, 55 L.Ed. 563 (1911), which upheld a statutory grant of authority to the Secretary of Agriculture to make rules and regulations governing use of the public forests he was charged with managing, the Court said: "From the beginning of the Government various acts have been passed conferring upon executive officers power to make rules and regulations—not for the government of their departments, but for administering the laws which did govern. None of these statutes could confer legislative power." (Emphasis added.)

Or, finally, as Chief Justice Taft described it in Hampton & Co., 276 U.S., at 406, 48 S.Ct., at 351:

"The field of Congress involves all and many varieties of legislative action, and Congress has found it frequently necessary to use officers of the Executive Branch, within defined limits, to secure the exact effect intended by its acts of legislation, by vesting discretion in such officers to make public regulations interpreting a statute and directing the details of its execution, even to the extent of providing for penalizing a breach of such regulations." (Emphasis added.)

The focus of controversy, in the long line of our so-called excessive delegation cases, has been whether the degree of generality contained in the authorization for exercise of executive or judicial powers in a particular field is so unacceptably high as to amount to a delegation of legislative powers. I say "so-called excessive delegation" because although that convenient terminology is often used, what is really at issue is whether there has been any delegation of legislative power, which occurs (rarely) when Congress authorizes the exercise of executive or judicial power without adequate standards. Strictly speaking, there is no acceptable delegation of legislative power. As John Locke put it almost 300 years ago, "the power of the legislative being derived from the people by a positive voluntary grant and institution, can be no other, than what the positive grant conveyed, which being only to make laws, and not to make legislators, the leg- islative can have no power to transfer their authority of making laws, and place it in other hands." J. Locke, Second Treatise of Government 87 (R. Cox ed.1982) (emphasis added). Or as we have less epigrammatically said: "That Congress cannot delegate legislative power to the President is a principle universally recognized as vital to the integrity and maintenance of the system of government ordained by the Constitution." Field v. Clark, supra, 143 U.S. at 692, 12 S.Ct., at 504. In the present case, however, a pure delegation of legislative power is precisely what we have before us. It is irrelevant whether the standards are adequate, because they are not standards related to the exercise of executive or judicial powers; they are, plainly and simply, standards for further legislation.

The lawmaking function of the Sentencing Commission is completely divorced from any responsibility for execution of the law or adjudication of private rights under the law. It is divorced from responsibility for execution of the law not only because the Commission is not said to be "located in the Executive Branch" (as I shall discuss presently, I doubt whether Congress can "locate" an entity within one Branch or another for constitutional purposes by merely saying so); but, more importantly, because the Commission neither exercises any executive power on its own, nor is subject to the control of the President who does. The only functions it performs, apart from prescribing the law, 28 U.S.C. 994(a)(1), (3) (1982 ed., Supp. IV), conducting the investigations useful and necessary for prescribing the law, e.g., §§ 995(a)(13), (15), (16), (21), and clarifying the intended application of the law that it prescribes, e.g., §§ 994(a)(2), 995(a)(10), are data collection and intragovernmental advice giving and education, e.g., §§ 995(a)(8), (9), (12), (17), (18), (20). These latter activities—similar to functions performed by congressional agencies and even congressional staff—neither determine nor affect private rights, and do not constitute an exercise of governmental power. See Humphrey's Executor v. United States, 295 U.S. 602, 628, 55 S.Ct. 869, 874, 79 L.Ed. 1611 (1935). And the Commission's lawmaking is completely divorced from the exercise of judicial powers since, not being a court, it has no judicial powers itself, nor is it subject to the control of any other body with judicial powers. The power to make law at issue here, in other words, is not ancillary but quite naked. The situation is no different in principle from what would exist if Congress gave the same power of writing sentencing laws to a congressional agency such as the General Accounting Office, or to members of its staff.

The delegation of lawmaking authority to the Commission is, in short, unsupported by any legitimating theory to explain why it is not a delegation of legislative power. To disregard structural legitimacy is wrong in itself—but since structure has purpose, the disregard also has adverse practical consequences. In this case, as suggested earlier, the consequence is to facilitate and encourage judicially uncontrollable delegation. Until our decision last Term in Morrison v. Olson, 487 U.S. 654, 108 S.Ct. 2597, 101 L.Ed.2d 569 (1988), it could have been said that Congress could delegate lawmaking authority only at the expense of increasing the power of either the President or the courts. Most often, as a practical matter, it would be the President, since the judicial process is unable to conduct the investigations and make the political assessments essential for most policymaking. Thus, the need for delegation would have to be important enough to induce Congress to aggrandize its primary competitor for political power, and the recipient of the policymaking authority, while not Congress itself, would at least be politically accountable. But even after it has been accepted, pursuant to Morrison, that those exercising executive power need not be subject to the control of the President, Congress would still be more reluctant to augment the power of even an independent executive agency than to create an otherwise powerless repository for its delegation. Moreover, assembling the full-time senior personnel for an agency exercising executive powers is more difficult than borrowing other officials (or employing new officers on a short-term basis) to head an organization such as the Sentencing Commission.

By reason of today's decision, I anticipate that Congress will find delegation of its lawmaking powers much more attractive in the future. If rulemaking can be entirely unrelated to the exercise of judicial or executive powers, I foresee all manner of "expert" bodies, insulated from the political process, to which Congress will delegate various portions of its lawmaking responsibility. How tempting to create an expert Medical Commission (mostly M.D.'s, with perhaps a few Ph.D.'s in moral philosophy) to dispose of such thorny, "no-win" political issues as the withholding of life-support systems in federally funded hospitals, or the use of fetal tissue for research. This is an undemocratic precedent that we set—not because of the scope of the delegated power, but because its recipient is not one of the three Branches of Government. The only governmental power the Commission possesses is the power to make law; and it is not the Congress.

III

The strange character of the body that the Court today approves, and its incompatibility with our constitutional institutions, is apparent from that portion of the Court's opinion entitled "Location of the Commission." This accepts at the outset that the Commission is a "body within the Judicial Branch," ante, at 385, and rests some of its analysis upon that asserted reality. Separation-of-powers problems are dismissed, however, on the ground that "the Commission's powers are not united with the powers of the Judiciary in a way that has meaning for separation-of-powers analysis," since the Commission "is not a court, does not exercise judicial power, and is not controlled by or accountable to members of the Judicial Branch," ante, at 393. In light of the latter concession, I am at a loss to understand why the Commission is "within the Judicial Branch" in any sense that has relevance to today's discussion. I am sure that Congress can divide up the Government any way it wishes, and employ whatever terminology it desires, for non constitutional purposes—for example, perhaps the statutory designation that the Commission is "within the Judicial Branch" places it outside the coverage of certain laws which say they are inapplicable to that Branch, such as the Freedom of Information Act, see 5 U.S.C. 552(f) (1982 ed., Supp. IV). For such statutory purposes, Congress can define the term as it pleases. But since our subject here is the Constitution, to admit that that congressional designation "has no meaning for separation-of-powers analysis" is to admit that the Court must therefore decide for itself where the Commission is located for purposes of separation-of-powers analysis.

It would seem logical to decide the question of which Branch an agency belongs to on the basis of who controls its actions: If Congress, the Legislative Branch; if the President, the Executive Branch; if the courts (or perhaps the judges), the Judicial Branch. See, e.g., Bowsher v. Synar, 478 U.S. 714, 727-732, 106 S.Ct. 3181, 3188-3191, 92 L.Ed.2d 583 (1986). In Humphrey's Executor v. United States, 295 U.S. 602, 55 S.Ct. 869, 79 L.Ed. 1611 (1935), we approved the concept of an agency that was controlled by (and thus within) none of the Branches. We seem to have assumed, however, that that agency (the old Federal Trade Commission, before it acquired many of its current functions) exercised no governmental power whatever, but merely assisted Congress and the courts in the performance of their functions. See Id., at 628, 55 S.Ct., at 874. Where no governmental power is at issue, there is no strict constitutional impediment to a "branchless" agency, since it is only "all legislative Powers," Art. I, § 1, "the executive Power," Art. II, § 1, and "the judicial Power," Art. III, § 1, which the Constitution divides into three departments. (As an example of a "branchless" agency exercising no governmental powers, one can conceive of an Advisory Commission charged with reporting to all three Branches, whose members are removable only for cause and are thus subject to the control of none of the Branches.) Over the years, however, Humphrey's Executor has come in general contemplation to stand for something quite different—not an "independent agency" in the sense of an agency independent of all three Branches, but an "independent agency" in the sense of an agency within the Executive Branch (and thus authorized to exercise executive powers) independent of the control of the President.

We approved that concept last Term in Morrison. See 487 U.S., at 688-691, 108 S.Ct., at 2617-2619. I dissented in that case, essentially because I thought that concept illogical and destructive of the structure of the Constitution. I must admit, however, that today's next step—recognition of an independent agency in the Judicial Branch—makes Morrison seem, by comparison, rigorously logical. "The Commission," we are told, "is an independent agency in every relevant sense." Ante, at 393. There are several problems with this. First, once it is acknowledged that an "independent agency" may be within any of the three Branches, and not merely within the Executive, then there really is no basis for determining what Branch such an agency belongs to, and thus what governmental powers it may constitutionally be given, except (what the Court today uses) Congress' say-so. More importantly, however, the concept of an "independent agency" simply does not translate into the legislative or judicial spheres. Although the Constitution says that "the executive Power shall be vested in a President of the United States of America," Art. II, § 1, it was never thought that the President would have to exercise that power personally. He may generally authorize others to exercise executive powers, with full effect of law, in his place. See, e.g., Wolsey v. Chapman, 101 U.S. 755, 25 L.Ed. 915 (1880); Williams v. United States, 1 How. 290, 11 L.Ed. 135 (1843). It is already a leap from the proposition that a person who is not the President may exercise executive powers to the proposition we accepted in Morrison that a person who is neither the President nor subject to the President's control may exercise executive powers. But with respect to the exercise of judicial powers (the business of the Judicial Branch) the platform for such a leap does not even exist. For unlike executive power, judicial and legislative powers have never been thought delegable. A judge may not leave the decision to his law clerk, or to a master. See United States v. Raddatz, 447 U.S. 667, 683, 100 S.Ct. 2406, 2416, 65 L.Ed.2d 424 (1980); cf. Runkle v. United States, 122 U.S. 543, 7 S.Ct. 1141, 30 L.Ed. 1167 (1887). Senators and Members of the House may not send delegates to consider and vote upon bills in their place. See Rules of the House of Representatives, Rule VIII(3); Standing Rules of the United States Senate, Rule XII. Thus, however well established may be the "independent agencies" of the Executive Branch, here we have an anomaly beyond equal: an independent agency exercising governmental power on behalf of a Branch where all governmental power is supposed to be exercised personally by the judges of courts. 3

Today's decision may aptly be described as the Humphrey's Executor of the Judicial Branch, and I think we will live to regret it. Henceforth there may be agencies "within the Judicial Branch" (whatever that means), exercising governmental powers, that are neither courts nor controlled by courts, nor even controlled by judges. If an "independent agency" such as this can be given the power to fix sentences previously exercised by district courts, I must assume that a similar agency can be given the powers to adopt rules of procedure and rules of evidence previously exercised by this Court. The bases for distinction would be thin indeed.

* * *

Today's decision follows the regrettable tendency of our recent separation-of-powers jurisprudence, see Morrison, supra; Young v. United States ex rel. Vuitton et Fils S.A., 481 U.S. 787, 107 S.Ct. 2124, 95 L.Ed.2d 740 (1987), to treat the Constitution as though it were no more than a generalized prescription that the functions of the Branches should not be commingled too much—how much is too much to be determined, case-by-case, by this Court. The Constitution is not that. Rather, as its name suggests, it is a prescribed structure, a framework, for the conduct of government. In designing that structure, the Framers themselves considered how much commingling was, in the generality of things, acceptable, and set forth their conclusions in the document. That is the meaning of the statements concerning acceptable commingling made by Madison in defense of the proposed Constitution, and now routinely used as an excuse for disregarding it. When he said, as the Court correctly quotes, that separation of powers " 'does not mean that these three departments ought to have no partial agency in, or no controul over the acts of each other,' " ante, at 380—381, quoting The Federalist No. 47, pp. 325-326 (J. Cooke ed.1961), his point was that the commingling specifically provided for in the structure that he and his colleagues had designed—the Presidential veto over legislation, the Senate's confirmation of executive and judicial officers, the Senate's ratification of treaties, the Congress' power to impeach and remove executive and judicial officers—did not violate a proper understanding of separation of powers. He would be aghast, I think, to hear those words used as justification for ignoring that carefully designed structure so long as, in the changing view of the Supreme Court from time to time, "too much commingling" does not occur. Consideration of the degree of commingling that a particular disposition produces may be appropriate at the margins, where the outline of the framework itself is not clear; but it seems to me far from a marginal question whether our constitutional structure allows for a body which is not the Congress, and yet exercises no governmental powers except the making of rules that have the effect of laws.

I think the Court errs, in other words, not so much because it mistakes the degree of commingling, but because it fails to recognize that this case is not about commingling, but about the creation of a new Branch altogether, a sort of junior-varsity Congress. It may well be that in some circumstances such a Branch would be desirable; perhaps the agency before us here will prove to be so. But there are many desirable dispositions that do not accord with the constitutional structure we live under. And in the long run the improvisation of a constitutional structure on the basis of currently perceived utility will be disastrous.

I respectfully dissent from the Court's decision, and would reverse the judgment of the District Court.

Notes

1. It is even arguable that the Commission has authority to establish guidelines and procedures for imposing the death penalty, thus reinstituting that sanction under federal statutes for which (by reason of our recent decisions) it has been thought unusable because of constitutionally inadequate procedures. The Justice Department believes such authority exists, and has encouraged the Commission to exercise it. See Gubiensio-Ortiz v. Kanahele, 857 F.2d 1245, 1256 (CA9 1988).

2. An executive agency can, of course, be created with no power other than the making of rules, as long as that agency is subject to the control of the President and the President has executive authority related to the rulemaking. In such circumstances, the rulemaking is ultimately ancillary to the President's executive powers.

3. There are of course agencies within the Judicial Branch (because they operate under the control of courts or judges) which are not themselves courts, see, e.g., 28 U.S.C. 601 et seq. (Administrative Office of the United States Courts), just as there are agencies within the Legislative Branch (because they operate under the control of Congress) which are not themselves Senators or Representatives, see, e.g., 31 U.S.C. 701 et seq. (General Accounting Office). But these agencies, unlike the Sentencing Commission, exercise no governmental powers, that is, they establish and determine neither private rights nor the prerogatives of the other Branches. They merely assist the courts and the Congress in their exercise of judicial and legislative powers.

Justice Scalia's dissent in Texas Monthly, Inc. v. Bullock (Feb 21, 1989) [Notes omitted]

JUSTICE SCALIA, with whom THE CHIEF JUSTICE and JUSTICE KENNEDY join, dissenting.

As a judicial demolition project, today's decision is impressive. The machinery employed by the opinions of JUSTICE BRENNAN and JUSTICE BLACKMUN is no more substantial than the antinomy that accommodation of religion may be required but not permitted, and the bold but unsupportable assertion (given such realities as the text of the Declaration of Independence, the national Thanksgiving Day proclaimed by every President since Lincoln, the inscriptions on our coins, the words of our Pledge of Allegiance, the invocation with which sessions of our Court are opened and, come to think of it, the discriminatory protection of freedom of religion in the Constitution) that government may not "convey a message of endorsement of religion." With this frail equipment, the Court topples an exemption for religious publications of a sort that expressly appears in the laws of at least 15 of the 45 States that have sales and use taxes [1] -- States from Maine to Texas, from Idaho to New Jersey. [2] In practice, a similar exemption may well exist in even more States than that, since until today our case law has suggested that it is not only permissible but perhaps required. See Follett v. McCormick, 321 U. S. 573 (1944); Murdock v. Pennsylvania, 319 U. S. 105 (1943). I expect, for example, that, even in States without express exemptions, many churches and many tax assessors have thought sales taxes inapplicable to the religious literature typically offered for sale in church foyers.

When one expands the inquiry to sales taxes on items other than publications and to other types of taxes such as property, income, amusement, and motor vehicle taxes -- all of which are likewise affected by today's holding -- the Court's accomplishment is even more impressive. At least 45 States provide exemptions for religious groups without analogous exemptions for other types of nonprofit institutions. [3] For over half a century, the federal Internal Revenue Code has allowed "minister[s] of the gospel" (a term interpreted broadly enough to include cantors and rabbis) to exclude from gross income the rental value of their parsonages. 26 U.S.C. § 107; see also § 213(b)(11) of the Revenue Act of 1921, ch. 136, 42 Stat. 239. In short, religious tax exemptions of the type the Court invalidates today permeate the state and federal codes, and have done so for many years.

I dissent because I find no basis in the text of the Constitution, the decisions of this Court, or the traditions of our people for disapproving this longstanding and widespread practice.

I

The opinions of JUSTICE BRENNAN and JUSTICE BLACKMUN proceed as though this were a matter of first impression. It is not. Nineteen years ago, in Walz v. Tax Comm'n of New York City, 397 U. S. 664 (1970), we considered and rejected an Establishment Clause challenge that was in all relevant respects identical. Since today's opinions barely acknowledge the Court's decision in that case (as opposed to the separate concurrences of Justices BRENNAN and Harlan), it requires some discussion here. Walz involved New York City's grant of tax exemptions, pursuant to a state statute and a provision of the State Constitution, to "religious organizations for religious properties used solely for religious worship." Id. at 397 U. S. 666-667, and n. 1. In upholding the exemption, we conducted an analysis that contains the substance of the three-pronged "test" adopted the following Term in Lemon v. Kurtzman, 403 U. S. 602 (1971). First, we concluded that "[t]he legislative purpose of the property tax exemption is neither the advancement nor the inhibition of religion." 397 U.S. at 397 U. S. 672. We reached that conclusion because past cases and the historical record established that property tax exemption "constitutes a reasonable and balanced attempt to guard against" the "latent dangers" of government hostility to religion. Id. at 397 U. S. 673. We drew a distinction between an unlawful intent to favor religion and a lawful intent to "accommodat[e] the public service to [the people's] spiritual needs,'" id. at 397 U. S. 672 (quoting Zorach v. Clauson, 343 U. S. 306, 343 U. S. 314 (1952)), and found only the latter to be involved in "sparing the exercise of religion from the burden of property taxation levied on private profit institutions," 397 U.S. at 397 U. S. 673.

We further concluded that the exemption did not have the primary effect of sponsoring religious activity. We noted that, although tax exemptions may have the same economic effect as state subsidies, for Establishment Clause purposes, such "indirect economic benefit" is significantly different.

"The grant of a tax exemption is not sponsorship, since the government does not transfer part of its revenue to churches, but simply abstains from demanding that the church support the state. . . . There is no genuine nexus between tax exemption and establishment of religion."

Id. at 397 U. S. 675.

JUSTICE BRENNAN also recognized this distinction in his concurring opinion:

"Tax exemptions and general subsidies, however, are qualitatively different. Though both provide economic assistance, they do so in fundamentally different ways. A subsidy involves the direct transfer of public monies to the subsidized enterprise, and uses resources exacted from taxpayers as a whole. An exemption, on the other hand, involves no such transfer."

Id. at 397 U. S. 690 (footnote omitted). See also id. at 397 U. S. 691 ("Tax exemptions . . . constitute mere passive state involvement with religion, and not the affirmative involvement characteristic of outright governmental subsidy").

Third, we held that the New York exemption did not produce unacceptable government entanglement with religion. In fact, quite to the contrary. Since the exemptions avoided the "tax liens, tax foreclosures, and the direct confrontations and conflicts that follow in the train of those legal processes," id. at 397 U. S. 674, we found that their elimination would increase government's involvement with religious institutions, id. at 397 U. S. 674-676. See also id. at 397 U. S. 691 (BRENNAN, J., concurring) ("[I]t cannot realistically be said that termination of religious tax exemptions would quantitatively lessen the extent of state involvement with religion").

We recognized in Walz that the exemption of religion from various taxes had existed without challenge in the law of all 50 States and the National Government before, during, and after the framing of the First Amendment's Religion Clauses, and had achieved "undeviating acceptance" throughout the 200-year history of our Nation. "Few concepts," we said,

"are more deeply embedded in the fabric of our national life, beginning with pre-Revolutionary colonial times, than for the government to exercise at the very least this kind of benevolent neutrality toward churches and religious exercise generally, so long as none was favored over others and none suffered interference."

Id. at 397 U. S. 676-677. See also id. at 397 U. S. 681 (BRENNAN, J., concurring) (noting the "the undeviating acceptance given religious tax exemptions from our earliest days as a Nation").

It should be apparent from this discussion that Walz, which we have reaffirmed on numerous occasions in the last two decades, e.g., Corporation of Presiding Bishop of Church of Jesus Christ of Latter-day Saints v. Amos, 483 U. S. 327 (1987), is utterly dispositive of the Establishment Clause claim before us here. The Court invalidates § 151.312 of the Texas Tax Code only by distorting the holding of that case, and radically altering the well-settled Establishment Clause jurisprudence which that case represents.

JUSTICE BRENNAN explains away Walz by asserting that

"[t]he breadth of New York's property tax exemption was essential to our holding that it was 'not aimed at establishing, sponsoring, or supporting religion.'"

Ante at 489 U. S. 12 (quoting Walz, 397 U.S. at 397 U. S. 674). This is not a plausible reading of the opinion. At the outset of its discussion concerning the permissibility of the legislative purpose, the Walz Court did discuss the fact that the New York tax exemption applied not just to religions, but to certain other "nonprofit" groups, including "hospitals, libraries, playgrounds, scientific, professional, historical, and patriotic groups." Id. at 397 U. S. 673. The finding of valid legislative purpose was not rested upon that, however, but upon the more direct proposition that "exemption constitutes a reasonable and balanced attempt to guard against" the "latent dangers" of governmental hostility towards religion "inherent in the imposition of property taxes." Ibid. The venerable federal legislation that the Court cited to support its holding was not legislation that exempted religion along with other things, but legislation that exempted religion alone. See, e.g., ch. 17, 6 Stat. 116 (1813) (remitting duties paid on the importation of plates for printing Bibles); ch. 91, 6 Stat. 346 (1826) (remitting duties paid on the importation of church vestments, furniture, and paintings); ch. 259, 6 Stat. 600 (1834) (remitting duties paid on the importation of church bells). Moreover, if the Court had intended to rely upon a "breadth of coverage" rationale, it would have had to identify some characteristic that rationally placed religion within the same policy category as the other institutions. JUSTICE BRENNAN's concurring opinion in Walz conducted such an analysis, finding the New York exemption permissible only because religions, like the other types of nonprofit organizations exempted, "contribute to the wellbeing of the community in a variety of nonreligious ways," 397 U.S. at 397 U. S. 687, and (incomprehensibly) because they "uniquely contribute to the pluralism of American society by their religious activities," id. at 397 U. S. 689. (I say incomprehensibly because to favor religion for its "unique contribution" is to favor religion as religion.) Justice Harlan's opinion conducted a similar analysis, finding that the New York statute

"defined a class of nontaxable entities whose common denominator is their nonprofit pursuit of activities devoted to cultural and moral improvement and the doing of 'good works' by performing certain social services in the community that might otherwise have to be assumed by government."

Id. at 397 U. S. 696. The Court's opinion in Walz, however, not only failed to conduct such an analysis, but -- seemingly in reply to the concurrences -- explicitly and categorically disavowed reliance upon it, concluding its discussion of legislative purpose with a paragraph that begins as follows:

"We find it unnecessary to justify the tax exemption on the social welfare services or 'good works' that some churches perform for parishioners and others,"

id. at 397 U. S. 674. This should be compared with today's rewriting of Walz:

"[W]e concluded that the State might reasonably have determined that religious groups generally contribute to the cultural and moral improvement of the community, perform useful social services, and enhance a desirable pluralism of viewpoint and enterprise, just as do the host of other nonprofit organizations that qualified for the exemption."

Ante at 489 U. S. 12, n. 2. This is a marvelously accurate description of what Justices BRENNAN and Harlan believed, and what the Court specifically rejected.

The Court did not approve an exemption for charities that happened to benefit religion; it approved an exemption for religion as an exemption for religion.

Today's opinions go beyond misdescribing Walz, however. In repudiating what Walz in fact approved, they achieve a revolution in our Establishment Clause jurisprudence, effectively overruling other cases that were based, as Walz was, on the "accommodation of religion" rationale. According to JUSTICE BRENNAN's opinion, no law is constitutional whose "benefits [are] confined to religious organizations," ante at 489 U. S. 11 -- except, of course, those laws that are unconstitutional unless they contain benefits confined to religious organizations, see ante at 489 U. S. 17-18. See also JUSTICE BLACKMUN's opinion, ante at 489 U. S. 28. Our jurisprudence affords no support for this unlikely proposition. Walz is just one of a long line of cases in which we have recognized that

"the government may (and sometimes must) accommodate religious practices, and that it may do so without violating the Establishment Clause."

Hobbie v. Unemployment Appeals Comm'n of Fla., 480 U. S. 136, 480 U. S. 144-145 (1987); see McConnell, Accommodation of Religion, 1985 S.Ct.Rev. 1, 3. In such cases as Sherbert v. Verner, 374 U. S. 398 (1963), Wisconsin v. Yoder, 406 U. S. 205 (1972), Thomas v. Review Bd. of Indiana Employment Security Div., 450 U. S. 707 (1981), and Hobbie v. Unemployment Appeals Comm'n of Fla., supra, we held that the Free Exercise Clause of the First Amendment required religious beliefs to be accommodated by granting religion-specific exemptions from otherwise applicable laws. We have often made clear, however, that

"[t]he limits of permissible state accommodation to religion are by no means coextensive with the noninterference mandated by the Free Exercise Clause."

Walz, 397 U.S. at 397 U. S. 673. See also Hobbie, supra, at 480 U. S. 144-145, and n. 10; Gillette v. United States, 401 U. S. 437, 401 U. S. 453 (1971); Braunfeld v. Brown, 366 U. S. 599, 366 U. S. 605-608 (1961) (plurality opinion); Wallace v. Jaffree, 472 U. S. 38, 472 U. S. 82 (1985) (O'CONNOR, J., concurring).

We applied the accommodation principle, to permit special treatment of religion that was not required by the Free Exercise Clause, in Zorach v. Clauson, 343 U. S. 306 (1952), where we found no constitutional objection to a New York City program permitting public school children to absent themselves one hour a week for "religious observance and education outside the school grounds," id. at 343 U. S. 308, n. 1. We applied the same principle only two Terms ago in Corporation of Presiding Bishop, where, citing Zorach and Walz, we upheld a section of the Civil Rights Act of 1964 exempting religious groups (and only religious groups) from Title VII's antidiscrimination provisions. We found that

"it is a permissible legislative purpose to alleviate significant governmental interference with the ability of religious organizations to define and carry out their religious missions."

483 U.S. at 483 U. S. 335. We specifically rejected the District Court's conclusion identical to that which a majority of the Court endorses today: that invalidity followed from the fact that the exemption

"singles out religious entities for a benefit, rather than benefiting a broad grouping of which religious organizations are only a part."

Id. at 483 U. S. 333. We stated that the Court "has never indicated that statutes that give special consideration to religious groups are per se invalid." Id. at 483 U. S. 338. As discussed earlier, it was this same principle of permissible accommodation that we applied in Walz.

The novelty of today's holding is obscured by JUSTICE BRENNAN's citation and description of many cases in which "breadth of coverage" was relevant to the First Amendment determination. See ante at 489 U. S. 10-11. Breadth of coverage is essential to constitutionality whenever a law's benefiting of religious activity is sought to be defended not specifically (or not exclusively) as an intentional and reasonable accommodation of religion, but as merely the incidental consequence of seeking to benefit all activity that achieves a particular secular goal. But that is a different rationale -- more commonly invoked than accommodation of religion but, as our cases show, not preclusive of it. Where accommodation of religion is the justification, by definition religion is being singled out. The same confusion of rationales explains the facility with which JUSTICE BRENNAN's opinion can portray the present statute as violating the first prong of the Lemon test, which is usually described as requiring a "secular legislative purpose." Lemon, 403 U.S. at 403 U. S. 612. That is an entirely accurate description of the governing rule when, as in Lemon and most other cases, government aid to religious institutions is sought to be justified on the ground that it is not religion per se that is the object of assistance, but rather the secular functions that the religious institutions, along with other institutions, provide. But as I noted earlier, the substance of the Lemon test (purpose, effect, entanglement) was first roughly set forth in Walz -- and in that context, the "accommodation of religion" context, the purpose was said to be valid so long as it was "neither the advancement nor the inhibition of religion; . . . neither sponsorship nor hostility." 397 U.S. at 397 U. S. 672. Of course, rather than reformulating the Lemon test in "accommodation" cases (the text of Lemon is not, after all, a statutory enactment), one might instead simply describe the protection of free exercise concerns, and the maintenance of the necessary neutrality, as "secular purpose and effect," since they are a purpose and effect approved, and indeed to some degree mandated, by the Constitution. However the reconciliation with the Lemon terminology is achieved, our cases make plain that it is permissible for a State to act with the purpose and effect of "limiting governmental interference with the exercise of religion." Corporation of Presiding Bishop, 483 U.S. at 483 U. S. 339.

It is not always easy to determine when accommodation slides over into promotion, and neutrality into favoritism, but the withholding of a tax upon the dissemination of religious materials is not even a close case. The subjects of the exemption before us consist exclusively of "writings promulgating the teaching of the faith" and "writings sacred to a religious faith." If there is any close question, it is not whether the exemption is permitted, but whether it is constitutionally compelled in order to avoid "interference with the dissemination of religious ideas." Gillette, supra, at 401 U. S. 462. In Murdock v. Pennsylvania, 319 U. S. 105 (1943), we held that it was unconstitutional to apply a municipal license tax on door-to-door solicitation to sellers of religious books and pamphlets. One Term later, in Follett v. McCormick, 321 U. S. 573 (1944), we held that it was unconstitutional to apply to such persons a municipal license tax on "[a]gents selling books." Those cases are not as readily distinguishable as JUSTICE BRENNAN suggests. I doubt whether it would have made any difference (as he contends) if the municipalities had attempted to achieve the same result of burdening the religious activity through a sales tax, rather than a license tax; surely such a distinction trivializes the holdings. And the other basis of distinction he proposes -- that the persons taxed in those cases were "religious missionaries whose principal work is preaching" -- is simply not available with respect to the first part of the statute at issue here (which happens to be the portion upon which petitioner placed its exclusive reliance). Unlike the Texas exemption for sacred books, which, on its face at least, applies to all sales, the exemption for periodicals applies to material that not only "consist[s] wholly of writings promulgating the teaching of [a religious] faith," but also is "published or distributed by [that] faith." Surely this is material distributed by missionaries. Unless, again, one wishes to trivialize the earlier cases, whether they are full-time or part-time missionaries can hardly make a difference, nor can the fact that they conduct their proselytizing through the mail or from a church or store, instead of door-to-door.

I am willing to acknowledge, however, that Murdock and Follett are narrowly distinguishable. But what follows from that is not the facile conclusion that therefore the State has no "compelling interest in avoiding violations of the Free Exercise and Establishment Clauses," ante at 489 U. S. 17, and thus the exemption is invalid. This analysis is yet another expression of JUSTICE BRENNAN's repudiation of the accommodation principle -- which, as described earlier, consists of recognition that

"[t]he limits of permissible state accommodation to religion are by no means coextensive with the noninterference mandated by the Free Exercise Clause."

Walz, 397 U.S. at 397 U. S. 673. By saying that what is not required cannot be allowed, JUSTICE BRENNAN would completely block off the already narrow

"channel between the Scylla [of what the Free Exercise Clause demands] and the Charybdis [of what the Establishment Clause forbids] through which any state or federal action must pass in order to survive constitutional scrutiny."

Thomas, 450 U.S. at 450 U. S. 721 (REHNQUIST, J., dissenting). The proper lesson to be drawn from the narrow distinguishing of Murdock and Follett is quite different: if the exemption comes so close to being a constitutionally required accommodation, there is no doubt that it is at least a permissible one.

Although JUSTICE BRENNAN's opinion places almost its entire reliance upon the "purpose" prong of Lemon, it alludes briefly to the second prong as well, finding that § 151.312 has the impermissible "effect of sponsoring certain religious tenets or religious belief in general," ante at 489 U. S. 17. Once again, Walz stands in stark opposition to this assertion, but it may be useful to explain why. Quite obviously, a sales tax exemption aids religion, since it makes it less costly for religions to disseminate their beliefs. Cf. Murdock, supra, at 319 U. S. 112-113. But that has never been enough to strike down an enactment under the Establishment Clause. "A law is not unconstitutional simply because it allows churches to advance religion, which is their very purpose." Corporation of Presiding Bishop, supra, at 483 U. S. 337 (emphasis in original). The Court has consistently rejected "the argument that any program which in some manner aids an institution with a religious affiliation" violates the Establishment Clause. Mueller v. Allen, 463 U. S. 388, 463 U. S. 393 (1983) (quoting Hunt v. McNair, 413 U. S. 734, 413 U. S. 742 (1973)). To be sure, we have set our face against the subsidizing of religion -- and in other contexts we have suggested that tax exemptions and subsidies are equivalent. E.g., Bob Jones University v. United States, 461 U. S. 574, 461 U. S. 591 (1983); Regan v. Taxation With Representation of Wash., 461 U. S. 540, 461 U. S. 544 (1983). We have not treated them as equivalent, however, in the Establishment Clause context, and with good reason.

"In the case of direct subsidy, the state forcibly diverts the income of both believers and nonbelievers to churches. In the case of an exemption, the state merely refrains from diverting to its own uses income independently generated by the churches through voluntary contributions."

Giannella, Religious Liberty, Nonestablishment, and Doctrinal Development, 81 Harv.L.Rev. 513, 553 (1968). In Walz, we pointed out that the primary effect of a tax exemption was not to sponsor religious activity, but to "restric[t] the fiscal relationship between church and state" and to "complement and reinforce the desired separation insulating each from the other." 397 U.S. at 397 U. S. 676; see also id. at 397 U. S. 690-691 (BRENNAN, J., concurring).

Finally, and least persuasively of all, JUSTICE BRENNAN suggests that § 151.312 violates the "excessive government entanglement" aspect of Lemon, 403 U.S. at 403 U. S. 613. Ante at 489 U. S. 20-21. It is plain that the exemption does not foster the sort of "comprehensive, discriminating, and continuing state surveillance" necessary to run afoul of that test. 403 U.S. at 403 U. S. 619. A State does not excessively involve itself in religious affairs merely by examining material to determine whether it is religious or secular in nature. Mueller v. Allen, supra, at 463 U. S. 403; Meek v. Pittenger, 421 U. S. 349, 421 U. S. 359-362 (1975) (upholding loans of nonreligious textbooks to religious schools); Board of Education of Central School Dist. No. 1, v. Allen, 392 U. S. 236 (1968) (same). In Mueller, for instance, we held that state officials' examination of textbooks to determine whether they were "books and materials used in the teaching of religious tenets, doctrines or worship" did not constitute excessive entanglement. 463 U.S. at 463 U. S.

403. I see no material distinction between that inquiry and the one Texas officials must make in this case. Moreover, here as in Walz, see 397 U.S. at 397 U. S. 674, it is all but certain that elimination of the exemption will have the effect of increasing government's involvement with religion. The Court's invalidation of § 151.312 ensures that Texas churches selling publications that promulgate their religion will now be subject to numerous statutory and regulatory impositions, including audits, Tex.Tax Code Ann. § 151.023 (1982 and Supp.1988-1989), requirements for the filing of security, § 151.251 et seq., reporting requirements, § 151.401 et seq., writs of attachment without bond, § 151.605, tax liens, § 151.608, and the seizure and sale of property to satisfy tax delinquencies, § 151.610.

II

Having found that this statute does not violate the Establishment Clause of the First Amendment, I must consider whether it violates the Press Clause, pursuant to our decision two Terms ago in Arkansas Writers' Project, Inc. v. Ragland, 481 U. S. 221 (1987). Although I dissented in Ragland, even accepting it to be correct I cannot conclude as readily as does JUSTICE WHITE, ante at 489 U. S. 26, that it applies here.

The tax exemption at issue in Ragland, which we held to be unconstitutional because content-based, applied to trade publications and sports magazines, along with religious periodicals and sacred writings, and hence could not be justified as an accommodation of religion. If the purpose of accommodating religion can support action that might otherwise violate the Establishment Clause, I see no reason why it does not also support action that might otherwise violate the Press Clause or the Speech Clause. To hold otherwise would be to narrow the accommodation principle enormously, leaving it applicable to only nonexpressive religious worship. I do not think that is the law. Just as the Constitution sometimes requires accommodation of religious expression despite not only the Establishment Clause but also the Speech and Press Clauses, so also it sometimes permits accommodation despite all those Clauses. Such accommodation is unavoidably content-based -- because the Freedom of Religion Clause is content-based.

It is absurd to think that a State which chooses to prohibit booksellers from making stories about seduction available to children of tender years cannot make an exception for stories contained in sacred writings (e.g., the story of Susanna and the Two Elders, Daniel 13:1-65). And it is beyond imagination that the sort of tax exemption permitted (indeed, required) by Murdock and Follett would have to be withdrawn if door-to-door salesmen of commercial magazines demanded equal treatment with Seventh-day Adventists on Press Clause grounds. And it is impossible to believe that the State is constitutionally prohibited from taxing Texas Monthly magazine more heavily than the Holy Bible.

* * * *

Today's decision introduces a new strain of irrationality in our Religion Clause jurisprudence. I have no idea how to reconcile it with Zorach (which seems a much harder case of accommodation), with Walz (which seems precisely in point), and with

Corporation of Presiding Bishop (on which the ink is hardly dry). It is not right -- it is not constitutionally healthy -- that this Court should feel authorized to refashion anew our civil society's relationship with religion, adopting a theory of church and state that is contradicted by current practice, tradition, and even our own case law. I dissent.

Justice Scalia's dissent in Treasury Employees v. Von Raab (March 21, 1989)

Justice Scalia, with whom Justice Stevens joins, dissenting.

The issue in this case is not whether Customs Service employees can constitutionally be denied promotion, or even dismissed, for a single instance of unlawful drug use, at home or at work. They assuredly can. The issue here is what steps can constitutionally be taken to detect such drug use. The Government asserts it can demand that employees perform "an excretory function traditionally shielded by great privacy," Skinner v. Railway Labor Executives' Assn., ante, at 626, while "a monitor of the same sex . . . remains close at hand to listen for the normal sounds," ante, at 661, and that the excretion thus produced be turned over to the Government for chemical analysis. The Court agrees that this constitutes a search for purposes of the Fourth Amendment - and I think it obvious that it is a type of search particularly destructive of privacy and offensive to personal dignity.

Until today this Court had upheld a bodily search separate from arrest and without individualized suspicion of wrong-doing only with respect to prison inmates, relying upon the uniquely dangerous nature of that environment. See Bell v. Wolfish, 441 U.S. 520, 558 -560 (1979). Today, in Skinner, we allow a less intrusive bodily search of railroad employees involved in train accidents. I joined the Court's opinion there because the demonstrated frequency of drug and alcohol use by the targeted class of employees, and the demonstrated connection between such use and grave harm, rendered the search a reasonable means of protecting society. I decline to join the Court's opinion in the present case because neither frequency of use nor connection to harm is demonstrated or even likely. In my view the Customs Service rules are a kind of immolation of privacy and human dignity in symbolic opposition to drug use.

The Fourth Amendment protects the "right of the people to be secure in their persons, houses, papers, and effects, against unreasonable searches and seizures." While there are some absolutes in Fourth Amendment law, as soon as those have been left behind and the question comes down to whether a particular search has been "reasonable," the answer depends largely upon the social necessity that prompts the search. Thus, in upholding the administrative search of a student's purse in a school, we began with the observation (documented by an agency report to Congress) that "[m]aintaining order in the classroom has never been easy, but in recent years, school disorder has often taken particularly ugly forms: drug use and violent crime in the schools have become major social problems." New Jersey v. T. L. O., 469 U.S. 325, 339 (1985). When we approved fixed checkpoints near the Mexican border to stop and search cars for illegal aliens, we observed at the outset that "the Immigration and Naturalization Service now suggests there may be as many as 10 or 12 million aliens illegally in the country," and that "[i]nterdicting the flow of illegal entrants from Mexico poses formidable law enforcement problems." United States v. Martinez-Fuerte, 428 U.S. 543, 551 -552 (1976). And the substantive analysis of our opinion today in Skinner begins, "[t]he problem of alcohol use on American railroads is as old as the industry itself," and goes on to cite statistics concerning that problem and the accidents it causes, including a 1979 study finding that "23% of the operating personnel were `problem drinkers.'" Skinner, ante, at 606, and 607, n. 1.

The Court's opinion in the present case, however, will be searched in vain for real evidence of a real problem that will be solved by urine testing of Customs Service employees. Instead, there are assurances that "[t]he Customs Service is our Nation's first line of defense against one of the greatest problems affecting the health and welfare of our population," ante, at 668; that "[m]any of the Service's employees are often exposed to [drug smugglers] and to the controlled substances [they seek] to smuggle into the country," ante, at 669; that "Customs officers have been the targets of bribery by drug smugglers on numerous occasions, and several have been removed from the Service for accepting bribes and other integrity violations," ibid.; that "the Government has a compelling interest in ensuring that front-line interdiction personnel are physically fit, and have unimpeachable integrity and judgment," ante, at 670; that the "national interest in self-protection could be irreparably damaged if those charged with safeguarding it were, because of their own drug use, unsympathetic to their mission of interdicting narcotics," ibid.; and that "the public should not bear the risk that employees who may suffer from impaired perception and judgment will be promoted to positions where they may need to employ deadly force," ante, at 671. To paraphrase Churchill, all this contains much that is obviously true, and much that is relevant; unfortunately, what is obviously true is not relevant, and what is relevant is not obviously true. The only pertinent points, it seems to me, are supported by nothing but speculation, and not very plausible speculation at that. It is not apparent to me that a Customs Service employee who uses drugs is significantly more likely to be bribed by a drug smuggler, any more than a Customs Service employee who wears diamonds is significantly more likely to be bribed by a diamond smuggler - unless, perhaps, the addiction to drugs is so severe, and requires so much money to maintain, that it would be detectable even without benefit of a urine test. Nor is it apparent to me that Customs officers who use drugs will be appreciably less "sympathetic" to their drug-interdiction mission, any more than police officers who exceed the speed limit in their private cars are appreciably less sympathetic to their mission of enforcing the traffic laws. (The only difference is that the Customs officer's individual efforts, if they are irreplaceable, can theoretically affect the availability of his own drug supply - a prospect so remote as to be an absurd basis of motivation.) Nor, finally, is it apparent to me that urine tests will be even marginally more effective in preventing gun-carrying agents from risking "impaired perception and judgment" than is their current knowledge that, if impaired, they may be shot dead in unequal combat with unimpaired smugglers - unless, again, their addiction is so severe that no urine test is needed for detection.

What is absent in the Government's justifications - notably absent, revealingly absent, and as far as I am concerned dispositively absent - is the recitation of even a single instance in which any of the speculated horribles actually occurred: an instance, that is, in which the cause of bribetaking, or of poor aim, or of unsympathetic law enforcement, or of compromise of classified information, was drug use. Although the Court points out that several employees have in the past been removed from the Service for accepting bribes and other integrity violations, and that at least nine officers have died in the line of duty since 1974, ante, at 669, there is no indication whatever that these incidents were related to drug use by Service employees. Perhaps concrete evidence of the severity of a problem is unnecessary when it is so well known that courts can almost take judicial notice of it; but that is surely not the case here. The Commissioner of Customs himself has stated that he "believe[s] that Customs is largely drug-free," that "[t]he extent of illegal drug use by Customs employees was not the reason for establishing this program," and that he "hope[s] and expect[s] to receive reports of very few positive findings through drug screening." App. 10, 15. The test results have fulfilled those hopes and expectations. According to the Service's counsel, out of 3, 600 employees tested, no more than 5 tested positive for drugs. See ante, at 673.

The Court's response to this lack of evidence is that "[t]here is little reason to believe that American workplaces are immune from [the] pervasive social problem" of drug abuse. Ante, at 674. Perhaps such a generalization would suffice if the workplace at issue could produce such catastrophic social harm that no risk whatever is tolerable - the secured areas of a nuclear power plant, for example, see Rushton v. Nebraska Public Power District, 844 F.2d 562 (CA8 1988). But if such a generalization suffices to justify demeaning bodily searches, without particularized suspicion, to guard against the bribing or blackmailing of a law enforcement agent, or the careless use of a firearm, then the Fourth Amendment has become frail protection indeed. In Skinner, Bell, T. L. O., and Martinez-Fuerte, we took pains to establish the existence of special need for the search or seizure - a need based not upon the existence of a "pervasive social problem" combined with speculation as to the effect of that problem in the field at issue, but rather upon well-known or well-demonstrated evils in that field, with well-known or well-demonstrated consequences. In Skinner, for example, we pointed to a long history of alcohol abuse in the railroad industry, and noted that in an 8-year period 45 train accidents and incidents had occurred because of alcohol- and drug-impaired railroad employees, killing 34 people, injuring 66, and causing more than $28 million in property damage. Ante, at 608. In the present case, by contrast, not only is the Customs Service thought to be "largely drug-free," but the connection between whatever drug use may exist and serious social harm is entirely speculative. Except for the fact that the search of a person is much more intrusive than the stop of a car, the present case resembles Delaware v. Prouse, 440 U.S. 648 (1979), where we held that the Fourth Amendment prohibited random stops to check drivers' licenses and motor vehicle registrations. The contribution of this practice to highway safety, we concluded, was "marginal at best" since the number of licensed drivers that must be stopped in order to find one unlicensed one "will be large indeed." Id., at 660.

Today's decision would be wrong, but at least of more limited effect, if its approval of drug testing were confined to that category of employees assigned specifically to drug interdiction duties. Relatively few public employees fit that description. But in extending approval of drug testing to that category consisting of employees who carry firearms, the Court exposes vast numbers of public employees to this needless indignity. Logically, of course, if those who carry guns can be treated in this fashion, so can all others whose work, if performed under the influence of drugs, may endanger others - automobile drivers, operators of other potentially dangerous equipment, construction workers, school crossing guards. A similarly broad scope attaches to the Court's approval of drug testing for those with access to "sensitive information." 1 Since this category is not limited to Service employees with drug interdiction duties, nor to "sensitive information" specifically relating to drug traffic, today's holding apparently approves drug testing for all federal employees with security clearances - or, indeed, for all federal employees with valuable confidential information to impart. Since drug use is not a particular problem in the Customs Service, employees throughout the Government are no less likely to violate the public trust by taking bribes to feed their drug habit, or by yielding to blackmail. Moreover, there is no reason why this super-protection against harms arising from drug use must be limited to public employees; a law requiring similar testing of private citizens who use dangerous instruments such as guns or cars, or who have access to classified information, would also be constitutional.

There is only one apparent basis that sets the testing at issue here apart from all these other situations - but it is not a basis upon which the Court is willing to rely. I do not believe for a minute that the driving force behind these drug-testing rules was any of the feeble justifications put forward by counsel here and accepted by the Court. The only plausible explanation, in my view, is what the Commissioner himself offered in the concluding sentence of his memorandum to Customs Service employees announcing the program: "Implementation of the drug screening program would set an important example in our country's struggle with this most serious threat to our national health and security." App. 12. Or as respondent's brief to this Court asserted: "[I]f a law enforcement agency and its employees do not take the law seriously, neither will the public on which the agency's effectiveness depends." Brief for Respondent 36. What better way to show that the Government is serious about its "war on drugs" than to subject its employees on the front line of that war to this invasion of their privacy and affront to their dignity? To be sure, there is only a slight chance that it will prevent some serious public harm resulting from Service employee drug use, but it will show to the world that the Service is "clean," and - most important of all - will demonstrate the determination of the Government to eliminate this scourge of our society! I think it obvious that this justification is unacceptable; that the impairment of individual liberties cannot be the means of making a point; that symbolism, even symbolism for so worthy a cause as the abolition of unlawful drugs, cannot validate an otherwise unreasonable search.

There is irony in the Government's citation, in support of its position, of Justice Brandeis' statement in Olmstead v. United States, 277 U.S. 438, 485 (1928) that "[f]or good or for ill, [our Government] teaches the whole people by its example." Brief for Respondent 36. Brandeis was there dissenting from the Court's admission of evidence obtained through an unlawful Government wiretap. He was not praising the Government's example of vigor and enthusiasm in combatting crime, but condemning its example that "the end justifies the means," 277 U.S., at 485 . An even more apt quotation from that famous Brandeis dissent would have been the following:

"[I]t is . . . immaterial that the intrusion was in aid of law enforcement. Experience should teach us to be most on our guard to protect liberty when the Government's purposes are beneficent. Men born to freedom are naturally alert to repel invasion of their liberty by evil-minded rulers. The greatest dangers to liberty lurk in insidious encroachment by men of zeal, well-meaning but without understanding." Id., at 479.

Those who lose because of the lack of understanding that be-got the present exercise in symbolism are not just the Customs Service employees, whose dignity is thus offended, but all of us - who suffer a coarsening of our national manners that ultimately give the Fourth Amendment its content, and who become subject to the administration of federal officials whose respect for our privacy can hardly be greater than the small respect they have been taught to have for their own.

Notes

[1] The Court apparently approves application of the urine tests to personnel receiving access to "sensitive information." Ante, at 677. Since, however, it is unsure whether "classified material" is "sensitive information," it remands with instructions that the Court of Appeals "examine the criteria used by the Service in determining what materials are classified and in deciding whom to test under this rubric." Ante, at 678. I am not sure what these instructions mean. Surely the person who classifies information always considers it "sensitive" in some sense - and the Court does not indicate what particular sort of sensitivity is crucial. Moreover, it seems to me most unlikely that "the criteria used by the Service in determining what materials are classified" are any different from those prescribed by the President in his Executive Order on the subject, see Exec. Order No. 12356, 3 CFR 166 (1982 Comp.) - and if there is a difference it is probably unlawful, see 5.4(b)(2), id., at 177. In any case, whatever idiosyncratic standards for classification the Customs Service might have would seem to be irrelevant, inasmuch as the rule at issue here is not limited to material classified by the Customs Service, but includes (and may well apply principally to) material classified elsewhere in the Government - for example, in the Federal Bureau of Investigation, the Drug Enforcement Administration, or the State Department - and conveyed to the Service. See App. 24-25.

Justice Scalia's concurrence in Green v. Bock Laundry Machine (May 22, 1989)

Justice Scalia, concurring in the judgment.

We are confronted here with a statute which, if interpreted literally, produces an absurd, and perhaps unconstitutional, result. Our task is to give some alternative meaning to the word "defendant" in Federal Rule of Evidence 609(a)(1) that avoids this consequence; and then to determine whether Rule 609(a)(1) excludes the operation of Federal Rule of Evidence 403.

I think it entirely appropriate to consult all public materials, including the background of Rule 609(a)(1) and the legislative history of its adoption, to verify that what seems to us an unthinkable disposition (civil defendants but not civil plaintiffs receive the benefit of weighing prejudice) was indeed unthought-of, and thus to justify a departure from the ordinary meaning of the word "defendant" in the Rule. For that purpose, however, it would suffice to observe that counsel have not provided, nor have we discovered, a shred of evidence that anyone has ever proposed or assumed such a bizarre disposition. The Court's opinion, however, goes well beyond this. Approximately four-fifths of its substantive analysis is devoted to examining the evolution of Federal Rule of Evidence 609, from the 1942 Model Code of Evidence, to the 1953 Uniform Rules of Evidence, to the 1965 Luck case and the 1970 statute overruling it, to the Subcommittee, Committee, and Conference Committee Reports, and to the so-called floor debates on Rule 609 -- all with the evident purpose not merely of confirming that the word "defendant" cannot have been meant literally, but of determining what, precisely, the Rule does mean.

I find no reason to believe that any more than a handful of the Members of Congress who enacted Rule 609 were aware of its interesting evolution from the 1942 Model Code; or that any more than a handful of them (if any) voted, with respect to their understanding of the word "defendant" and the relationship between Rule 609 and Rule 403, on the basis of the referenced statements in the Subcommittee, Committee, or Conference Committee Reports, or floor debates -- statements so marginally relevant, to such minute details, in such relatively inconsequential legislation. The meaning of terms on the statute books ought to be determined not on the basis of which meaning can be shown to have been understood by a larger handful of the Members of Congress, but rather on the basis of which meaning is (1) most in accord with context and ordinary usage, and thus most likely to have been understood by the whole Congress which voted on the words of the statute (not to mention the citizens subject to it), and (2) most compatible with the surrounding body of law into which the provision must be integrated -- a compatibility which, by a benign fiction, we assume Congress always has in mind. I would not permit any of the historical and legislative material discussed by the Court, or all of it combined, to lead me to a result different from the one that these factors suggest.

I would analyze this case, in brief, as follows:

(1) The word "defendant" in Rule 609(a)(1) cannot rationally (or perhaps even constitutionally) mean to provide the benefit of prejudice-weighing to civil defendants and not civil plaintiffs. Since petitioner has not produced, and we have not ourselves discovered, even a snippet of support for this absurd result, we may confidently assume that the word was not used (as it normally would be) to refer to all defendants, and only all defendants.

(2) The available alternatives are to interpret "defendant" to mean (a) "civil plaintiff, civil defendant, prosecutor, and criminal defendant," (b) "civil plaintiff and defendant and criminal defendant," or (c) "criminal defendant." Quite obviously, the last does least violence to the text. It adds a qualification that the word "defendant" does not contain, but, unlike the others, does not give the word a meaning ("plaintiff" or "prosecutor") it simply will not bear. The qualification it adds, moreover, is one that could understandably have been omitted by inadvertence -- and sometimes is omitted in normal conversation ("I believe strongly in defendants' rights"). Finally, this last interpretation is consistent with the policy of the law in general and the Rules of Evidence in particular of providing special protection to defendants in criminal cases. *

(3) As well described by the Court, the "structure of the Rules," ante at 525, makes it clear that Rule 403 is not to be applied in addition to Rule 609(a)(1).

I am frankly not sure that, despite its lengthy discussion of ideological evolution and legislative history, the Court's reasons for both aspects of its decision are much different from mine. I respectfully decline to join that discussion, however, because it is natural for the bar to believe that the juridical importance of such material matches its prominence in our opinions -- thus producing a legal culture in which, when counsel arguing before us assert that "Congress has said" something, they now frequently mean, by "Congress," a committee report; and in which it was not beyond the pale for a recent brief to say the following:

"Unfortunately, the legislative debates are not helpful. Thus, we turn to the other guidepost in this difficult area, statutory language."

Brief for Petitioner in Jett v. Dallas Independent School District, O.T. 1988, No. 87-2084, p. 21.

For the reasons stated, I concur in the judgment of the Court.

* Acknowledging the statutory ambiguity, the dissent would read "defendant" to mean "any party" because, it says, this interpretation "extend[s] the protection of judicial supervision to a larger class of litigants" than the interpretation the majority and I favor, which "takes protection away from litigants." Post at 490 U. S. 534-535. But neither side in this dispute can lay claim to generosity without begging the policy question whether judicial supervision is better than the automatic power to impeach. We could as well say -- and with much more support in both prior law, see ante at 490 U. S. 511-512, and this Court's own recommendation, see ante at 490 U. S. 517 -- that our reading "extend[s] the protection of [the right to impeach with prior felony convictions] to a larger class of litigants" than the dissent's interpretation, which "takes protection away from litigants."

Justice Scalia's dissent in Jones v. Thomas (June 19, 1989)

JUSTICE SCALIA, with whom JUSTICE STEVENS joins, and with whom JUSTICE BRENNAN and JUSTICE MARSHALL join as to all but the footnote, dissenting.

This is not the first time we have been called upon to consider whether a criminal defendant's satisfaction of one of two alternative penalties prevents a court from imposing (or reimposing) the second penalty in a subsequent proceeding. In Ex parte Lange, 18 Wall. 163 (1874), the first case to recognize the Double Jeopardy Clause's protection against multiple punishment, petitioner was convicted of stealing mailbags from the Post Office, under a statute carrying a punishment of either imprisonment for up to one year or a fine of up to $200. The presiding judge erroneously imposed the maximum of both punishments. After petitioner had paid his fine (which was remitted by the Clerk of Court to the United States Treasury) and had spent five days in prison, the judge realized his mistake and entered an order vacating the former judgment and resentencing petitioner to one year in prison. This Court stated that because petitioner had "fully performed, completed, and endured one of the alternative punishments which the law prescribed for that offence," id., at 176, the court's "power to punish for that offence was at an end," ibid. (emphasis added). Holding that the judge's second order violated petitioner's rights under the Double Jeopardy Clause, the Court ordered that petitioner be freed.

More recently, in In re Bradley, 318 U. S. 50 (1943), a District Judge found petitioner guilty of contempt and sentenced him to six months in prison and a $500 fine. Petitioner began serving his prison sentence, and his attorney paid the fine to the Clerk of the Court three days later. The fine was not paid into the Treasury. Later that day, having discovered that the relevant statute permitted imprisonment or fine, but not both, the court issued a new order amending the sentence to omit the fine and instructed the Clerk to return the $500 to petitioner. Petitioner refused to accept the money. We held that order to be "a nullity." Id., at 52.

"When, on October 1, the fine was paid to the clerk and receipted for by him, the petitioner had complied with a portion of the sentence which could lawfully have been imposed. As the judgment of the court was thus executed so as to be a full satisfaction of one of the two alternative penalties of the law, the power of the court was at an end." Ibid.

The present case is indistinguishable from Lange and Bradley. Here, as there, only one of two available punishments could lawfully be imposed for the conduct in question; and here, as there, the defendant fully satisfied one of the two. Under the law of the State of Missouri, respondent's actions in the Reid Auto Parts store on November 8, 1972, allowed the State to convict him of attempted armed robbery, with a maximum penalty of 15 years in prison, or of felony murder, with a maximum penalty of life imprisonment. The State could not convict him or punish him for both offenses. Therefore, once respondent "fully suffered one of the alternative punishments to which alone the law subjected him, the power of the court to punish further was gone." Ex parte Lange, supra, at 176. In the present case, as in Bradley, the State attempted in a second proceeding to "give back" the detriment respondent had suffered as a result of the fully satisfied alternative — by crediting the 15-year sentence for attempted armed robbery that he had already served against the second (life) sentence that had been imposed. But I see no more reason to allow a crediting here than there was to allow a refund in Bradley. Does this produce, as the Court alleges, an "anomalous resul[t]," ante, at 386, and an "unjustified windfal[l]," ante, at 387? Undoubtedly. Just as it did in Bradley. And just as the Double Jeopardy Clause often does (to an even greater degree) in other contexts — where, for example, a prosecutorial error after the jury has been impaneled permits the defendant to go off scot free. E. g., Downum v. United States, 372 U. S. 734, 737-738 (1963).

The Court candidly recognizes that a "[s]trict application of Bradley," ante, at 383, compels the conclusion that requiring respondent to serve the life sentence after completion of the 15-year sentence violates the Double Jeopardy Clause. It advances three related arguments, however, to explain why "strict application" can be avoided. I find none of them persuasive.

Most readily answered is the contention that "Bradley and Lange both involved alternative punishments that were prescribed by the legislature for a single criminal act." Ante, at 384. This in no way distinguishes those cases, since it describes the facts of this case just as well. Although the sentencing court undoubtedly thought attempted armed robbery and felony murder "to be separately punishable offenses," ibid., that court, we now know, was wrong. Under the correct view of Missouri law, the 15-year sentence and the life sentence were "alternative punishments . . . prescribed by the legislature for a single criminal act," ibid. The Court states that "[i]t cannot be suggested seriously that the legislature intended an attempted robbery conviction to suffice as an alternative sanction for murder," ante, at 384-385. Perhaps not, but it might also have been said in Lange that the legislature did not intend a mere $200 fine for the gravity of offense at issue there. Just as the judge in that case frustrated the probable legislative intent by inadvertently imposing the lesser penalty that was available, unaware that it would preclude the greater, so the judge in the present case frustrated the probable legislative intent by inadvertently entering the lesser conviction and sentence, unaware that it would preclude the greater. But that is beside the point.

The Double Jeopardy Clause is not a device designed to assure effectuation of legislative intent — but to the contrary is often the means of frustrating it. The relevant question pertaining to legislative intent is not whether the Missouri Legislature intended an attempted armed robbery sentence for the crime of murder, but whether it intended that both a felony-murder sentence and an attempted armed robbery sentence could be imposed for the same crime. The Missouri Supreme Court has said not. See State v. Morgan, 612 S. W. 2d 1 (1981); State v. Olds, 603 S. W. 2d 501, 510 (1980). That being so, if respondent has served one of the two alternative sentences that could lawfully be imposed, he cannot be required to serve the other as well.

Second, the Court distinguishes Bradley on the ground that there "[t]he alternative sentences . . . were of a different type, fine and imprisonment," ante, at 384, so that it would not have been possible to credit the satisfied fine against the as-yet-unserved sentence. It is difficult to imagine, however, why the difference between a credit and a refund (which could have been made in Bradley) should be of constitutional dimensions insofar as the Double Jeopardy Clause is concerned. Bradley, of course, did not rely upon any difference in the nature of the two punishments, but upon the mere fact that one of them had been completely executed. "As the judgment of the court was thus executed so as to be a full satisfaction of one of the alternative punishments of the law, the power of the court was at an end." 318 U. S., at 52. Likewise Lange:

"[I]n that very case, and for that very offence, the prisoner had fully performed, completed, and endured one of the alternative punishments which the law prescribed. . . . [T]hus . . . [the court's] power to punish for that offence was at an end. . . . [T]he authority of the court to punish the prisoner was gone. The power was exhausted; its further exercise was prohibited." 18 Wall., at 176.

Finally, the Court states that in the multiple punishments context, " `the Double Jeopardy Clause does no more than prevent the sentencing court from prescribing greater punishment than the legislature intended.' " Ante, at 381, quoting Missouri v. Hunter, 459 U. S. 359, 366 (1983). If that were true it would certainly permit proceedings quite foreign to our criminal-law tradition. If, for example, a judge imposed only a 15-year sentence under a statute that permitted 15 years to life, he could — as far as the Court's understanding of the Double Jeopardy Clause is concerned — have second thoughts after the defendant has served that time, and add on another 10 years. I am sure that cannot be done, because the Double Jeopardy Clause is a statute of repose for sentences as well as for proceedings. Done is done. The Court is able to quote Hunter for this unusual result only because its quotation is incomplete. What we said in that case, and have subsequently repeated in other cases, is that "[w]ith respect to cumulative sentences imposed in a single trial, the Double Jeopardy Clause does no more than prevent the sentencing court from prescribing greater punishment than the legislature intended." Ibid. See also id., at 368 (The Double Jeopardy Clause does not "preclud[e] the imposition, in a single trial, of cumulative punishments pursuant to those statutes") (emphasis added); id., at 368-369 ("Where . . . a legislature specifically authorizes cumulative punishment under two statutes . . . the prosecutor may seek and the trial court or jury may impose cumulative punishment under such statutes in a single trial") (emphasis added).

In both of the cases in which we have applied the Court's "legislative intent" formulation of the Double Jeopardy Clause to uphold the imposition of multiple penalties, the penalties had been imposed (or would have been imposed) in a single proceeding. See Missouri v. Hunter, supra (defendant convicted of both armed criminal action and the underlying felony of armed robbery in single trial); Ohio v. Johnson, 467 U. S. 493 (1984) (defendant pleaded guilty to two lesser offenses and trial court dismissed three greater offenses, stating that prosecution would be barred under Double Jeopardy Clause). But when the added punishment, even though authorized by the legislature, was imposed in a later proceeding, we held that the Double Jeopardy Clause was a bar. In United States v. Halper, 490 U. S. 435, 451, n. 10 (1989), we said:

"That the Government seeks the civil penalty in a second proceeding is critical in triggering the protections of the Double Jeopardy Clause. Since a legislature may authorize cumulative punishment under two statutes for a single course of conduct, the multiple-punishment inquiry in the context of a single proceeding focuses on whether the legislature actually authorized the cumulative punishment. See Ohio v. Johnson, 467 U. S. 493, 499-500 (1984). On the other hand, when the Government has already imposed a criminal penalty and seeks to impose additional punishment in a second proceeding, the Double Jeopardy Clause protects against the possibility that the Government is seeking the second punishment because it is dissatisfied with the sanction obtained in the first proceeding."

See also id., at 450 ("In a single proceeding the multiple punishment issue would be limited to ensuring that the total punishment did not exceed that authorized by the legislature") (emphasis added); ibid. ("Nor does the decision [in Halper] prevent the Government from seeking and obtaining both the full civil penalty and the full range of statutorily authorized civil penalties in the same proceeding") (emphasis added).

In the present case, of course, it was not the same proceeding but a second proceeding that added time to the 15-year sentence the defendant had already satisfied for his crime. In those circumstances, our cases establish that the relevant double jeopardy criterion is not only whether the total punishment authorized by the legislature has been exceeded, but also whether the addition upsets the defendant's legitimate "expectation of finality in the original sentence," United States v. DiFrancesco, 449 U. S. 117, 139 (1980). In the latter case we upheld against a double jeopardy challenge a statute that allowed the Government to appeal as inadequate a District Court's sentence for a "dangerous special offender." We did so because, by reason of the appeal provision itself, the defendant had no legitimate expectation of finality in the original sentence. See id., at 136-137.

We applied the same rule in Pennsylvania v. Goldhammer, 474 U. S. 28 (1985) (per curiam). There the defendant was convicted of 56 counts of forgery and 56 counts of theft. The trial court sentenced him to a term of imprisonment on one theft count and a term of probation on one forgery count, and suspended sentence on the remaining counts. On appeal, the Supreme Court of Pennsylvania held that the theft count on which the defendant had been sentenced was barred by the applicable statute of limitations, and denied, on double jeopardy grounds, the State's request that the case be remanded for resentencing on the nonbarred theft counts. We did not reverse that disposition outright, but remanded so that the Supreme Court of Pennsylvania might consider, pursuant to DiFrancesco, "whether the Pennsylvania laws in effect at the time allowed the State to obtain review of the sentences on the counts for which the sentence had been suspended." 474 U. S., at 30. It is clear from DiFrancesco and Goldhammer that when a sentence is increased in a second proceeding "the application of the double jeopardy clause . . . turns on the extent and legitimacy of a defendant's expectation of finality in that sentence. If a defendant has a legitimate expectation of finality, then an increase in that sentence is prohibited . . . ." United States v. Fogel, 264 U. S. App. D. C. 292, 302, 829 F. 2d 77, 87 (1987) (Bork, J.).

The principle enunciated in DiFrancesco also explains our decision in Bozza v. United States, 330 U. S. 160 (1947).

There the defendant was convicted of operating an illegal still, a crime which carried a mandatory sentence of a $100 fine and a term in prison. The trial court originally sentenced the defendant only to the term of imprisonment. When the court realized its mistake five hours later, it recalled the defendant for resentencing and imposed the $100 fine as well. We held that the resentencing did not violate the defendant's rights under the Double Jeopardy Clause. There, as in DiFrancesco, the defendant could not argue that his legitimate expectation of finality in the original sentence had been violated, because he was charged with knowledge that the court lacked statutory authority to impose the subminimum sentence in the first instance. See 330 U. S., at 166, 167. See also United States v. Arrellano-Rios, 799 F. 2d 520, 524 (CA9 1986) (stating that defendant can have no legitimate expectation of finality in an illegal sentence); United States v. Edmondson, 792 F. 2d 1492, 1496, n. 4 (CA9 1986) (same).

Applying DiFrancesco and Bozza here, it seems to me respondent must prevail. There is no doubt that the court had authority to impose the 15-year sentence, and respondent therefore had a legitimate expectation of its finality. There are only two grounds on which that could possibly be contested: (1) that the court had authority to impose a 15-year sentence, but not both a 15-year sentence and life, or (2) that his legitimate expectation was not necessarily 15 years, but rather either 15 years (on the one sentence) or life (on the other sentence). But at least where, as here, the one sentence has been fully served, these alternative approaches to defining his legitimate expectation are ruled out by Bradley. There also it could have been said that the court had no authority to impose both the $500 fine and the six months' imprisonment; and there also it could have been said that the defendant's legitimate expectation was not necessarily a $500 fine, but either a $500 fine or six months' imprisonment. But we in effect rejected those approaches, holding that once the fine had been paid a subsequent proceeding could not replace it with the alternative penalty. There is simply no basis for departing from that holding here.

The Double Jeopardy Clause is and has always been, not a provision designed to assure reason and justice in the particular case, but the embodiment of technical, prophylactic rules that require the Government to turn square corners. Whenever it is applied to release a criminal deserving of punishment it frustrates justice in the particular case, but for the greater purpose of assuring repose in the totality of criminal prosecutions and sentences. There are many ways in which these technical rules might be designed. We chose one approach in Bradley — undoubtedly not the only possible approach, but also not one that can be said to be clearly wrong. (The fact that it produces a "windfall" separates it not at all from other applications of the double jeopardy guarantee.) With technical rules, above all others, it is imperative that we adhere strictly to what we have stated the rules to be. A technical rule with equitable exceptions is no rule at all. Three strikes is out. The State broke the rules here, and must abide by the result.

For these reasons, I believe the Court of Appeals was correct to set aside respondent's life sentence. I would therefore affirm the judgment of the Court of Appeals, and respectfully dissent from the Court's disposition of this case.[*]

[*] I agree with the Court, ante, at 384-385, n. 3, that the Court of Appeals erred in saying that the State could not resentence or retry respondent for a non-jeopardy-barred lesser included offense, see Morris v. Mathews, 475 U. S. 237 (1986). Since it is undisputed, however, that the State has made no attempt to do that, that portion of the Court of Appeals' opinion was the purest dictum, and no basis for reversal of its judgment.

Justice Scalia's dissent in John Doe Agency v. John Doe Corp. (Dec. 11, 1989)

Justice Scalia, with whom Justice Marshall joins, dissenting.

I fear today's decision confuses more law than it clarifies. From the prior opinions of this Court, I had thought that at least this much about the Freedom of Information Act was clear: its exemptions were to be "narrowly construed." United States Dept. of Justice v. Julian, 486 U. S. 1 (1988); FBI v. Abramson, 456 U. S. 615, 456 U. S. 630 (1982); Department of the Air Force v. Rose, 425 U. S. 352, 425 U. S. 361 (1976); cf. United States Dept. of Justice v. Reporters Committee for Freedom of the Press, 489 U. S. 749 (1989) (Act mandates "full agency disclosure unless information is exempted under clearly delineated statutory language" (citations and inner quotations omitted)); Federal Open Market Committee v. Merrill, 443 U. S. 340, 443 U. S. 351-352 (1979). We use the same language again today, ante at 493 U. S. 152, but demonstrate by our holding that it is a formula to be recited, rather than a principle to be followed.

Narrow construction of an exemption means, if anything, construing ambiguous language of the exemption in such fashion that the exemption does not apply. The word "compiled" is ambiguous -- not, as the Court suggests (and readily dismisses), because one does not know whether it means "compiled originally" or "ever compiled," see ante at 493 U. S. 154-155. Rather, it is ambiguous because "compiled" does not always refer simply to "the process of gathering," or "the assembling," ante at 493 U. S. 154, but often has the connotation of a more creative activity. When we say that a statesman has "compiled an enviable record of achievement," or that a baseball pitcher has "compiled a 1.87 earned run average," we do not mean that those individuals have pulled together papers that show those results, but rather that they have generated or produced those results. Thus, Roget's Thesaurus of Synonyms and Antonyms includes "compile" in the following listing of synonyms:

"compose, constitute, form, make; make up, fill up, build up; weave, construct, fabricate; compile; write, draw; set up (printing); enter into the composition of etc. (be a component)."

Roget's Thesaurus 13 (Galahad ed. 1972).

If used in this more generative sense, the phrase "records or information compiled for law enforcement purposes" would mean material that the government has acquired or produced for those purposes -- and not material acquired or produced for other reasons, which it later shuffles into a law enforcement file. The former meaning is not only entirely possible; several considerations suggest that it is the preferable one. First of all, the word "record" (unlike the word "file," which used to be the subject of this provision, see Freedom of Information Act Amendments of 1974, Pub.L. 93-502, § 2(b)) can refer to a single document containing a single item of information. There is no apparent reason to deprive such an item of Exemption 7 protection simply because, at the time of the request, it happens to be the only item in the file. It is unnatural, however, to refer to a single item as having been "compiled" in the Court's sense of "assembled" or "gathered" -- though quite natural to refer to it as having been "compiled" in the generative or acquisitive sense I have described.

Secondly, the regime that the Court's interpretation establishes lends itself to abuse so readily that it is unlikely to have been intended. The only other documents I am aware of that can go from being available under FOIA to being unavailable, simply on the basis of an agency's own action, are records containing national defense or foreign policy information. Exemption 1 is inapplicable to records of that description that have not been classified, but it can be rendered applicable, even after the FOIA request has been filed, by the mere act of classification. See, e.g., Goldberg v. Department of State, 818 F.2d 71, 77 (CADC 1987), cert. denied, 485 U.S. 904 (1988). In that context, however, Congress has greatly reduced the possibility of abuse by providing that the classification must be proper under criteria established by Executive order. There is no such check upon sweeping requested material into a "law enforcement" file -- which term may include, I might note, not just criminal enforcement but civil and regulatory enforcement as well. See, e.g., Pope v. United States, 599 F.2d 1383, 1386 (CA5 1979). I suppose a court could disregard such a "compilation" that has been made in bad faith, but it is hard to imagine what bad faith could consist of in this context, given the loose standard of need that will justify opening an investigation, and the loose standard of relevance that will justify including material in the investigatory file. Compare Pratt v. Webster, 673 F.2d 408, 420-421 (CADC 1982) (FBI acts for "law enforcement purposes" when its investigation concerns "a possible security risk or violation of federal law" and has "at least a colorable claim' of rationality"), with Williams v. FBI, 730 F.2d 882, 883 (CA2 1984) (FBI's investigatory records are exempt from disclosure "whether or not the reviewing judicial tribunal believes there was a sound law enforcement basis for the particular investigation"); cf. United States v. Bisceglia, 420 U. S. 141, 420 U. S. 148-151 (1975) (IRS investigative authority includes power to subpoena bank records even in the absence of suspicion that a particular taxpayer has broken the law); Blair v. United States, 250 U. S. 273, 250 U. S. 282 (1919) (grand jury subpoena cannot be resisted by raising "questions of propriety or forecasts of the probable result of the investigation, or . . . doubts whether any particular individual will be found properly subject to an accusation of crime"). It is particularly implausible that Congress was creating this potential for abuse in its revision of Exemption 7 at the same time that it was adding the "properly classified" requirement to Exemption 1 in order to eliminate the potential for similar abuse created by our decision in EPA v. Mink, 410 U. S. 73 (1973). The Court's only response is that "[e]vasional commingling . . . would be prevented" by the requirement that a document cannot be withheld under Exemption 7 unless, if disclosed, it "would effectuate one or more of the six specified harms." Ante at 493 U. S. 156-157. But that begs the question. Congress did not extend protection to all documents that produced one of the six specified harms, but only to such documents "compiled for law enforcement purposes." The latter requirement is readily evaded (or illusory) if it requires nothing more than gathering up documents the Government does not wish to disclose, with a plausible law enforcement purpose in mind. That is a hole one can drive a truck through.

But even if the meaning of "compiled" I suggest is not necessarily the preferable one, it is unquestionably a reasonable one; and that creates an ambiguity; and our doctrine of "narrowly construing" FOIA exemptions requires that ambiguity to be resolved in favor of disclosure. The Court asserts that we have "consistently . . . taken a practical approach" to the interpretation of FOIA, by which it means achieving "a workable balance between the interests of the public . . . and the needs of the Government." Ante at 493 U. S. 157. It seems to me, however, that what constitutes a workable balance is Congress's decision and not ours; and that the unambiguous provisions of FOIA are so remote from establishing what most people would consider a reasonable "workable balance" that there is no cause to believe such a standard permeates the Act. Consider, for example, FOIA's disequilibrous disposition with regard to information that "could reasonably be expected to endanger the life or physical safety of any individual" -- namely, that such information is not withholdable in all cases, but only if it has been "compiled for law enforcement purposes." See 5 U.S.C. § 552(b)(7)(F). "Workable balance" is not a workable criterion in the interpretation of this law. In my view, a "practical approach" to FOIA consists of following the clear provisions of its text and adhering to the rules we have enunciated regarding interpretation of the unclear ones -- thereby reducing the volume of litigation and making it inescapably clear to Congress what changes need to be made. I find today's decision most impractical, because it leaves the lower courts to guess whether they must follow what we say (exemptions are to be "narrowly construed") or what we do (exemptions are to be construed to produce a "workable balance").

I respectfully dissent.

Justice Scalia's dissent in NLRB v. Curtin Matheson Scientific (April 17, 1990) [Notes omitted]

Justice SCALIA, with whom Justice O'CONNOR and Justice KENNEDY join, dissenting.

The Court makes heavy weather out of what is, under well established principles of administrative law, a straightforward case. The National Labor Relations Board (NLRB or Board) has established as one of the central factual determinations to be made in § 8(a)(5) unfair labor practice adjudications, whether the employer had a reasonable, good faith doubt concerning the majority status of the union at the time it requested to bargain. The Board held in the present case that such a doubt was not established by a record showing that, at the time of the union's request, a majority of the bargaining unit were strike replacements, and containing no affirmative evidence that any of those replacements supported the union. The question presented is whether that factual finding is supported by substantial evidence. Since the principal employment-related interest of strike replacements (to retain their jobs) is almost invariably opposed to the principal interest of the striking union (to replace them with its striking members), it seems to me impossible to conclude on this record that the employer did not have a reasonable good faith doubt regarding the union's majority status. The Board's factual finding being unsupported by substantial evidence, it cannot stand. I therefore dissent from the judgment reversing the Fifth Circuit's refusal to enforce the Board's order.

I

As the Court describes, the union was certified in 1970. In 1979, before the strike, the bargaining unit was composed of 27 employees. After the strike began, 5 employees crossed the picket line and 29 new employees were hired to replace the strikers. On July 16, the union offered to return to work under the terms of respondent's last prestrike proposal. On July 20, respondent rejected this offer, withdrew recognition from the union, and refused to bargain further, stating that it doubted that the union represented a majority of the employees in the bargaining unit. On that date, according to the Board, the bargaining unit consisted of 49 employees: 19 strikers, 5 employees who had crossed the picket line to return to work, and 25 strike replacements. The union filed an unfair labor practice charge with the Board, and the Board's General Counsel filed a complaint charging that respondent had violated § 8(a)(5) (and thereby § 8(a)(1)) of the National Labor Relations Act (NLRA), 49 Stat. 452, as amended, 29 U.S.C. § 158(a)(1) and (5) (1982 ed.). After a formal hearing, the Administrative Law Judge (ALJ) found that respondent, at the time it withdrew recognition, had an objectively reasonable, good faith doubt that the union represented a majority of the employees in the bargaining unit. The General Counsel introduced no evidence that the union in fact commanded the support of a majority of the employees, and the ALJ dismissed the complaint.

The Board reversed, and entered an order finding that respondent had violated the Act. The Board began by reciting its longstanding rule that

"'[a]n employer who wishes to withdraw recognition after a year may do so . . . by presenting evidence of a sufficient objective basis for a reasonable doubt of the union's majority status at the time the employer refused to bargain.'"

287 N.L.R.B. 350, 352 (1987) (quoting Station KKHI, 284 N.L. R.B. 1339, 1340 (1987)).

Purporting to evaluate respondent's action under this standard, the Board concluded that respondent had not established a reasonable basis for doubting the union's majority status. First, the Board stated that there was no cause to doubt that the five strikers who crossed the picket line to return to work supported the union, because "[t]he failure of employees to join an economic strike may indicate their economic concerns, rather than a lack of support for the union." 287 N.L.R.B. at 352. Second, relying on its decision in Station KKHI, the Board stated that the fact that 25 employees in the bargaining unit were strike replacements provided "no evidentiary basis for reasonably inferring the union sentiments of the replacement employees as a group." Id. at 352-353. Third, the Board discounted the statements of six employees criticizing the union, because,

"[e]ven attributing to them the meaning most favorable to the Respondent, it would merely signify that 6 employees of a total of approximately 50 did not desire to keep the Union as the collective bargaining representative."

Id. at 353 (footnote omitted).

The Fifth Circuit denied enforcement of the Board's order on the ground that respondent "was justified in doubting that the striker replacements supported the union," and that the Board's contrary conclusion was not supported by substantial evidence. 859 F.2d 362, 365, 367 (1988).

II

An NLRB unfair labor practice action is the form of administrative proceeding known as formal adjudication, governed by the Administrative Procedure Act (APA), 5 U.S.C. §§ 556, 557. See 5 U.S.C. § 554(a). In fact, it is even somewhat more judicialized than ordinary formal adjudication, since it is governed in addition by the procedural provisions of the NLRA itself, which provide, inter alia, that the proceeding

"shall, so far as practicable, be conducted in accordance with the rules of evidence applicable in the district courts of the United States under the rules of civil procedure for the district courts of the United States,"

29 U.S.C. § 160(b) (1982 ed.). Among the attributes of formal adjudication relevant here, the agency opinion must contain "findings and conclusions, and the reasons or basis therefor, on all the material issues of fact, law, or discretion presented on the record," 5 U.S.C. § 557(c), and a reviewing court must "hold unlawful and set aside agency action, findings, and conclusions found to be . . . unsupported by substantial evidence," 5 U.S.C. § 706(2)(E); accord, 29 U.S.C. § 160(f) (1982 ed.) ("the findings of the Board with respect to questions of fact if supported by substantial evidence on the record considered as a whole shall . . . be conclusive").

The Board's factual finding challenged in the present case is that there was no "sufficient objective basis for a reasonable doubt of the union's majority status at the time of the employer refused to bargain.'" 287 N.L.R.B. at 385 (quoting Station KKHI, 284 N.L.R.B. at 1340). The Board has held for many years that an employer's reasonable, good faith doubt as to a certified union's continued majority status is a defense to an unfair labor practice charge for refusal to bargain, in the sense that it shifts to the General

Counsel the burden to

"come forward with evidence that, on the refusal-to-bargain date, the union in fact did represent a majority of employees in the appropriate unit."

Stoner Rubber Co., 123 N.L.R.B. 1440, 1445 (1959) (emphasis in original). The leading case on the subject, cited approvingly in the Station KKHI opinion that formed the basis for the Board's holding here, described the good faith doubt defense as follows:

"We believe that the answer to the question whether the Respondent violated Section 8(a)(5) of the Act . . . depends not on whether there was sufficient evidence to rebut the presumption of the Union's continuing majority status or to demonstrate that the Union in fact did not represent the majority of the employees, but upon whether the Employer in good faith believed that the Union no longer represented the majority of the employees. . . ."

"* * * *"

"By its very nature, the issue of whether an employer has questioned a union's majority in good faith cannot be resolved by resort to any simple formula. It can only be answered in the light of the totality of all the circumstances involved in a particular case. But among such circumstances, two factors would seem to be essential prerequisites to any finding that the employer raised the majority issue in good faith in cases in which a union had been certified. There must, first of all, have been some reasonable grounds for believing that the union had lost its majority status since its certification. And secondly, the majority issue must not have been raised by the employer in a context of illegal antiunion activities. . . ."

Celanese Corp. of America, 95 N.L.R.B. 664, 671-673 (1951). The Board purported to be proceeding on the basis that Celanese was still the law, and thus that "the totality of all [sic] the circumstances" in the present case did not establish reasonable grounds for doubting majority status. The precise question presented is whether there was substantial evidence to support this factual finding. There plainly was not.

As described above, of the 49 employees in the bargaining unit at the time of respondent's refusal to bargain, a majority (25) were strike replacements, and another 5 were former employees who had crossed the union's picket line. It may well be doubtful whether the latter group could be thought to support the union, but it suffices to focus upon the 25 strike replacements, who must be thought to oppose the union if the Board's own policies are to be believed. There was a deep and inherent conflict between the interests of these employees and the interests of the union. As the Board's cases have explained:

"Strike replacements can reasonably foresee that, if the union is successful, the strikers will return to work and the strike replacements will be out of a job. It is understandable that unions do not look with favor on persons who cross their picket lines and perform the work of strikers."

Leveld Wholesale, Inc., 218 N.L.R.B. 1344, 1350 (1975).

"The Union had been bargaining agent for those discharged employees, and there can be no question that the Union's loyalty lay with these employees. The interests of the discharged employees were diametrically opposed to those of the strike replacements. If the discharged employees returned to work, the strike replacements would lose their jobs."

Beacon Upholstery Co., 226 N.L. R.B. 1360, 1368 (1976) (footnote omitted). The Board relies upon this reality of "diametrically opposed" interests as the basis for two of its rules: First, that an employer does not commit an unfair labor practice by refusing to negotiate with the incumbent union regarding the terms and conditions of the replacements' employment. See Service Electric Co., 281 N.L.R.B. 633, 641 (1986). Second, that the union's duty of fair representation does not require it to negotiate in the best interests of the strike replacements regarding the terms and conditions of their employment -- in other words, that the union may propose "negotiations leading to replacements being terminated to make way for returning strikers," ibid. See id. at 639 ("it is not logical to expect [the striking bargaining] representative to negotiate in the best interests of strike replacements during the pendency of a strike") (internal quotation; citation omitted); id. at 641 (even after the strike has ended, the "inherent conflict between the two groups remains" until the underlying contractual dispute has been resolved); Leveld Wholesale, supra, at 1350 ("It would be asking a great deal of any union to require it to negotiate in the best interests of strike replacements during the pendency of a strike, where the strikers are on the picket line").

The respondent in this case, therefore, had an employee bargaining unit a majority of whose members (1) were not entitled to have their best interests considered by the complainant union, (2) would have been foolish to expect their best interests to be considered by that union, and indeed, (3) in light of their status as breakers of that union's strike, would have been foolish not to expect their best interests to be subverted by that union wherever possible. There was, moreover, not a shred of affirmative evidence that any strike replacement supported, or had reason to support, the union. On those facts, any reasonable factfinder must conclude that the respondent possessed, not necessarily a certainty, but at least a reasonable, good faith doubt, that the union did not have majority support. At least three Circuit Courts of Appeals have effectively agreed with this assessment, considering strike replacements as opposed to the union in reversing Board findings of no reasonable, good faith doubt. See Soule Glass & Glazing Co. v. NLRB, 652 F.2d 1055, 1110 (CA1 1981); National Car Rental System, Inc. v. NLRB, 594 F.2d 1203, 1206-1207 (CA8 1979); NLRB v. Randle-Eastern Ambulance Service, Inc., 584 F.2d 720, 728-729 (CA5 1978).

In making its no-reasonable doubt finding, the Board relied upon its decision in Station KKHI, which stated:

"[T]he hiring of permanent replacements who cross a picket line, in itself, does not support an inference that the replacements repudiate the union as collective bargaining representative. . . . In this regard, an employee may be forced to work for financial reasons, or may disapprove of the strike in question but still desire union representation and would support other union initiatives. The presumption of union disfavor is therefore not factually compelling."

284 N.L.R.B. at 1344 (footnotes omitted).

The Court finds this reasoning persuasive:

"Economic concerns, for instance, may force a replacement employee to work for a struck employer even though he otherwise supports the union and wants the benefits of union representation."

Ante at 494 U. S. 789. These responses are entirely inadequate. The question is not whether replacement employees accept employment for economic reasons. Undoubtedly they do -- the same economic reasons that would lead them to oppose the union that will likely seek to terminate their employment. Nor is the question whether replacements would like to be represented by a union. Some perhaps would. But what the employer is required to have a good faith doubt about is majority support, not for "union representation" in the abstract, but for representation by this particular complainant union, at the time the employer withdrew recognition from the union.

Also embarrassingly wide of the mark is the Court's observation that "[u]nions do not inevitably demand displacement of all strike replacements." Ante at 494 U. S. 790. It is not necessary to believe that unions inevitably demand displacement of all strike replacements in order to doubt (as any reasonable person must) that strike replacements support a union that is under no obligation to take their employment interests into account, and that is almost certain to demand displacement of as many strike replacements as is necessary to reinstate former employees. The Court does not accurately describe my position, therefore, when it suggests that I seek "to force the Board to apply a presumption based on the premise that unions always make such demands." Ante at 494 U. S. 793, n. 11. I seek to force the Board, as the APA requires, to give objectively reasonable probative effect to the reality (expressed in the Board's own opinions and made the basis for rules of law it has adopted) that unions almost always make such demands, and that replacement employees know that. That is enough to establish this employer's good faith doubt.

The Court asserts that "the facts of this case" belie the proposition that a union "is almost certain to demand the displacement of as many strike replacements as is necessary to reinstate former employees," because the union in this case "did not negotiate for the discharge of replacements as a condition for settling the strike." Ante at 494 U. S. 808, n. 9. That is not true, and even if it were true, it would not be determinative of the issue here. According to the Board, this is what happened:

"On 16 July, the Union, on behalf of the striking employees, made an unconditional offer to return to work, thereby ending the strike. Later on the same day, the Union notified the Respondent that the bargaining unit employees had accepted the Respondent's 25 May collective bargaining proposal."

287 N.L.R.B. at 351 (emphasis added). Surely an offer "on behalf of the striking employees . . . to return to work" can only be accepted by allowing the striking employees to return to work. Does the Court really mean to interpret the Union's action as agreement

that the strike replacements shall stay on the job under the terms of the May 25 collective bargaining proposal, and the strikers remain unemployed? Or as a proposal that the employer should double its work force, paying both the replacement workers and the returning strikers under the terms of the May 25 offer? Surely the very most that can be said is that the Union's offer left the status of the replacement workers for later negotiation. No more is necessary to establish a reasonable doubt that the replacement workers would support the union -- which, in any such negotiations, could be expected (indeed, would have a legal obligation) to seek displacement of the strikebreakers by the returning strikers. As the Board said in Service Electric:

"[E]ven if the strike be deemed to have ended by virtue of the Union's announcement that it had been terminated, there is no basis for concluding that the Union suddenly is better able 'to negotiate in the best interests of strike replacements,' Leveld Wholesale, . . . 218 NLRB 1344, than it previously had been able to do. The inherent conflict between the two groups remains."

281 N.L.R.B. at 641.

The Court mentions only as an afterthought the fundamental conflict of interests that is at the center of this case:

"Moreover, even if the interests of strikers and replacements conflict during the strike, those interests may converge after the strike, once job rights have been resolved. Thus, while the strike continues, a replacement worker whose job appears relatively secure might well want the union to continue to represent the unit regardless of the union's bargaining posture during the strike."

Ante at 494 U. S. 792 (emphasis in original). The trouble with this is that it posits a species of replacement worker that will rarely exist unless and until the union has agreed (as it had not in this case) to accept the replacements' employment status -- i.e., until "job rights have been resolved." How can there be "a replacement worker whose job appears relatively secure" when the employer agrees to negotiate in good faith with a union that will surely seek the reinstatement of all its strikers? Even a replacement worker who has clear seniority over other replacement workers, and who somehow knows (by what means I cannot imagine) that some of the striking workers no longer want their jobs back, [1] has no means of assurance that the union will do him the favor of bargaining for the employer to honor his seniority among strikebreakers. It seems overwhelmingly likely that the union will want its returning members to have their old jobs back, or better jobs, regardless of the relative seniority of the strikebreakers who would thereby be displaced. I do not dispute that "replacement workers are capable of looking past the strike in considering whether or not they desire representation by the union," ante at 494 U. S. 792 -- in the same way that a man who is offered one million dollars to jump off a cliff is capable of looking past the probable consequence of his performance to contemplate how much fun he would have with one million dollars if he should survive. Surely the benefits strike replacements anticipate from their post-strike representation by this particular union must be expected to weigh much less heavily in their calculus than the reality that, if this particular union does the bargaining and gets its way, they will not have post-strike jobs.

The Court's only response to this is that the union's ability to achieve displacement of the strike replacements will depend upon its bargaining power. Its bargaining power could conceivably be so weak, and a strike replacement might conceivably so prefer this union over other alternatives, that he would be willing to take the chance that the union will try to oust him. Ante at 494 U. S. 790-791. I suppose so. It might also be that one of the strike replacements hopes the union will continue as the bargaining representative because, as the employer knows, the union president is his son-in-law. The Board Counsel is entirely free to introduce such special circumstances. But unless they appear in the record, the reasonableness of the employer's doubt must be determined on the basis of how a reasonable person would assess the probabilities -- and it is overwhelmingly improbable that a strikebreaking replacement so much prefers the incumbent union to some other union, or to no union at all, that he will bet his job the union is not strong enough to replace him. The wager is particularly bad because it is so unnecessary, since he and his fellow replacements could achieve the same objective, without risking their jobs in the least, by simply voting for that union, after the strike is over, in a new certification election.

I reiterate that the burden upon the employer here was not to demonstrate 100% assurance that a majority of the bargaining unit did not support the union, but merely "reasonable doubt" that they did so. It seems to me absurd to deny that it sustained that burden.

III

The Court never directly addresses the question whether there was substantial evidence to support the Board's conclusion that respondent had not established a reasonable good faith doubt of the union's majority status. Indeed, it asserts that that question is not even at issue, since

"[t]he question on which we granted the Board's petition for certiorari is whether, in assessing whether a particular employer possessed a good faith doubt, the Board must adopt a general presumption of replacement opposition to the union."

Ante at 494 U. S. 778, n. 2. That is the equivalent of characterizing the appeal of a criminal conviction, in which the defendant asserts that the indictment should have been dismissed because all the evidence demonstrated that he was not at the scene of the crime, as involving, not the adequacy of the evidence, but rather the question whether the jury was required to adopt the general presumption that a person cannot be in two places at the same time. No more in administrative law than in criminal law is the underlying question altered by characterizing factual probabilities as presumptions. The two are one and the same. The only reason respondents assert, and the Fifth Circuit held, that the Board had to adopt the "presumption" of replacement opposition to the union (I place the word in quotation marks because, as I shall describe, that terminology is misleading) is that to refuse to apply that "presumption" for the reason the Board gave (viz., that it is not in fact an accurate assessment of probabilities) is to deny evidence its inherently probative effect, and thus to produce a decision that is not supported by substantial evidence. The Board's framing of the question presented, like its opinion in this case, invites us to confuse factfinding with policymaking. The Court should not so readily have accepted the invitation.

Prior to its decision in Station KKHI, the Board well understood the inevitable logic set forth in Part II above, and had held that an employer has an objectively reasonable basis for doubting the union's majority status when the majority of employees in the bargaining unit are permanent replacements, and there is no other indication regarding the replacements' sentiments toward the union. See Beacon Upholstery Co., 226 N.L.R.B. at 1368; Titan Metal Mfg. Co., 135 N.L.R.B. 196, 215 (1962); Stoner Rubber Co., supra, at 1445. In a case called Cutten Supermarket, 220 N.L.R.B. 507 (1975), the Board departed, in dictum, from this well established precedent. There, as the Board describes the case in Station KKHI, 284 N.L.R.B. at 1341, the Board "inexplicably stated," with respect to strike replacements:

"[I]t is a well-settled principle that new employees are presumed to support the union in the same ratio as those whom they have replaced."

220 N.L.R.B. at 509. This dictum became a Board holding in Pennco, Inc., 250 N.L.R.B. 716 (1980), where the Board stated:

"The Board has long held that [the presumption of strike replacement support for the union] applies as a matter of law, and it is incumbent upon Respondent to rebut it even, and perhaps especially, in the event of a strike."

Id. at 717 (emphasis added). As the Board acknowledged in Station KKHI:

"The Board in Pennco cited no cases in support of its assertion that the presumption in question was 'long held.' Indeed, . . . this presumption was not 'long held' at all, but in fact was not articulated in any fashion until Cutten Supermarket in 1975, only 5 years prior to Pennco, and even then (i.e., in Cutten) in dictum and without supporting rationale or precedent."

284 N.L.R.B. at 1343. Unsurprisingly, given the feeble support for this presumption, the Circuit Courts (I am still repeating the account in Station KKHI) "uniformly rejected it." Ibid.

In Station KKHI, which is the case that established the framework of reasoning for the decision we review today, the principal issue before the Board was the Pennco presumption of replacement support for the union. See 284 N.L.R.B. at 1340. The Board abandoned it. See id. at 1344. The Board went further, however, and here is the error that infects the present opinion:

"On the other hand, we find the contrary presumption equally unsupportable. Thus, the hiring of permanent replacements who cross a picket line, in itself, does not support an inference that the replacements repudiate the union as collective bargaining representative."

Ibid. The mistake here is to treat as equivalent elements of decisionmaking the presumption that strike replacements do support the union, and the evidentiary inference that strike replacements do not support the union. They are not different applications of the same device, and it does not display a commitment to be governed only by the "real facts" to reject both the one and the other. The former was applied "as a matter of law," Pennco, supra, at 717, and not as the product of inference, which is "[a] process of reasoning by which a fact or proposition sought to be established is deduced as a logical consequence from other facts, or a state of facts, already proved or admitted." Black's Law Dictionary 700 (5th ed. 1979). One can refer to the product of an inference as a presumption: If one knows the identity of the sole Englishman in a certain remote part of Africa, and encounters there a white man in pith helmet sipping a gin and tonic, it is perfectly appropriate to say "Dr. Livingston, I presume." But that sort of presumption, which the text writers used to call "presumption of fact," see 9 J. Wigmore, Evidence § 2491, p. 304 (J. Chadbourn rev. ed. 1981), is quite different from the Pennco-type "presumption of law" insofar as concerns both agency power and judicial review, as I shall proceed to explain.

It is the proper business of the Board, as of most agencies, to deal in both presumptions (i.e., presumptions of law) and inferences (presumptions of fact). The former it may create and apply in the teeth of the facts, as means of implementing authorized law or policy in the course of adjudication. An example is the virtually irrebuttable presumption of majority support for the union during the year following the union's certification by the Board, Station KKHI, 284 N.L.R.B. at 1340. The latter, however -- inferences (or presumptions of fact) -- are not creatures of the Board, but its masters, representing the dictates of reason and logic that must be applied in making adjudicatory factual determinations. Whenever an agency's action is reversed in court for lack of "substantial evidence," the reason is that the agency has ignored inferences that reasonably must be drawn, or has drawn inferences that reasonably cannot be. As I have discussed above, that is what happened here. [2]

Of course, the Board may choose to implement authorized law or policy in adjudication by forbidding a rational inference, just as it may do so by requiring a nonrational one (which is what a presumption of law is). And perhaps it could lawfully have reached the outcome it did here in that fashion -- saying that, even though it must reasonably be inferred that an employer has good faith doubt of majority status when more than half of the bargaining unit are strike replacements whose job rights have not been resolved, we will not permit that inference to be made. (This would produce an effect close to a rule of law eliminating the good faith doubt defense except for cases in which the employer can demonstrate, by employee statements, lack of support for the union.) But that is not what the agency did here. It relied on the reasoning of Station KKHI, which rested upon the conclusion that, as a matter of logic and reasoning,

"the hiring of permanent replacements who cross a picket line, in itself, does not support an inference that the replacements repudiate the union as collective bargaining representative."

Id. at 1344. That is simply false. It is bad factfinding, and must be reversed under the "substantial evidence" test.

It is true that Station KKHI added, seemingly as a make-weight:

"Moreover, adoption of this presumption would disrupt the balance of competing economic weapons long established in strike situations and substantially impair the employees' right to strike by adding to the risk of replacement the risk of loss of the bargaining representative as soon as replacements equal in number to the strikers are willing to cross the picket line."

Ibid. There are several reasons why we cannot allow this seeming policy justification to suffice for sustaining the agency's action.

First of all, it is set forth as a reason for not adopting a counter-factual presumption, rather than (what would have been necessary to validate the agency's action) a reason for ignoring legitimate factual inferences. It is one thing to say:

"The facts do not support conclusion X, and we decline to impose conclusion X as a matter of law, since that would have adverse policy consequences."

It is quite another thing to say: "Even though the facts require conclusion X, we reject it for policy reasons." The former is what the Board has said here, and the latter is what it would have to say to support its decision properly on policy grounds. The agency has set forth a reason for rejecting the suggestion that it ignore the facts; having found that, on the record, the facts were the opposite of what the agency believed (i.e., there was reasonable good faith doubt), we have no idea whether the agency would regard the same reason as adequate basis for now accepting a suggestion that it ignore the facts. Under long-established principles of judicial review, we cannot make that yet-to-be-made decision on the agency's behalf, but must remand so that the Board may do so. SEC v. Chenery Corp., 318 U. S. 80, 318 U. S. 88 (1943).

Second, by upholding as a counterfactual policy determination a ruling that was made, and defended before the Fifth Circuit, as ordinary factfinding plus the refusal to adopt a counterfactual policy determination, we would be depriving respondent of possible legal defenses that it had no occasion to present to the courts. Section 8(a)(5) of the NLRA is violated only if the employer refuses to bargain "with the representatives" of his employees. 29 U.S.C. § 158(a)(5) (1982 ed.). The Act does not define the term "representatives," except to say that it "includes any individual or labor organization." 29 U.S.C. § 152(4) (1982 ed.). Specifically, it does not say or anywhere suggest that a certified union is the "representative" for purposes of § 158(a)(5) unless and until it is decertified. Because the Board has long acknowledged the good faith doubt defense, there has been no occasion to test in the courts the proposition that the employer can be liable for refusing to bargain with a certified union that patently does not have majority support. The only presumption of law that is applied to effect a policy exception to this defense -- the almost irrebuttable presumption of union support for one year after its certification -- is arguably authorized as an implementation of the policy of 29 U.S.C. § 159(e)(2) (1982 ed.), which precludes certification elections more frequently than annually. Even if, moreover, the Board can generally require the employer to bargain with a union that is not a "representative" in the sense of having majority support, there is the further question whether it can require him to bargain with a union that is a "representative" neither in that sense nor in the sense that it is obligated to bargain in the best interests of the majority of employees. See my earlier discussion of the Board's rule that the union has no duty to represent the interest of replacement employees, supra, at 494 U. S. 806-807. The Board did not have to confront these issues in the present case, because it did not purport to be deciding the case on the assumption that the union lacked majority support. It found respondent guilty of an unfair labor practice on the ground that there was, in fact, no reasonable doubt of the union's majority status; and it is exclusively that finding which respondent challenged, both here and in the Fifth Circuit. If we permitted the Board's order to be enforced on the quite different ground that it does not matter whether respondent had a reasonable, good faith doubt, we not only would be making for the Board a decision it has not yet reached, but also would be depriving respondent of judicial review of that decision. [3]

* * * *

Despite the fact that the NLRB has explicit rulemaking authority, see 29 U.S.C. § 156 (1982 ed.), it has chosen -- unlike any other major agency of the federal government -- to make almost all its policy through adjudication. It is entitled to do that, see NLRB v. Bell Aerospace Co., 416 U. S. 267, 416 U. S. 294-295 (1974), but it is not entitled to disguise policymaking as factfinding, and thereby to escape the legal and political limitations to which policymaking is subject. Thus, when the Board purports to find no good faith doubt because the facts do not establish it, the question for review is whether there is substantial evidence to support that determination. Here there is not, and the Board's order should not be enforced. What the Court has permitted the Board to accomplish in this case recalls Chief Justice Hughes' description of the unscrupulous administrator's prayer: "Let me find the facts for the people of my country, and I care little who lays down the general principles.'" Address before Federal Bar Association, February 12, 1931, quoted by Frank, J. in United States v. Forness, 125 F.2d 928, 942 (CA2 1942), reprinted in 13 The Owl of Sigma Nu Phi 9, 12 (1931). I respectfully dissent.

Justice Scalia's dissent in Rutan v. Republican Party of Illinois (June 21, 1990)

Justice Scalia, with whom The Chief Justice and Justice Kennedy join, and with whom Justice O'Connor joins as to Parts II and III, dissenting.

Today the Court establishes the constitutional principle that party membership is not a permissible factor in the dispensation of government jobs, except those jobs for the performance of which party affiliation is an "appropriate requirement." Ante, at 1. It is hard to say precisely (or even generally) what that exception means, but if there is any category of jobs for whose performance party affiliation is not an appropriate requirement, it is the job of being a judge, where partisanship is not only unneeded but positively undesirable. It is, however, rare that a federal administration of one party will appoint a judge from another party. And it has always been rare. See Marbury v. Madison, 1 Cranch 137 (1803). Thus, the new principle that the Court today announces will be enforced by a corps of judges (the Members of this Court included) who overwhelmingly owe their office to its violation. Something must be wrong here, and I suggest it is the Court.

The merit principle for government employment is probably the most favored in modern America, having been widely adopted by civil-service legislation at both the state and federal levels. But there is another point of view, described in characteristically Jacksonian fashion by an eminent practitioner of the patronage system, George Washington Plunkitt of Tammany Hall:

"I ain't up on sillygisms, but I can give you some arguments that nobody can answer.

"First, this great and glorious country was built up by political parties; second, parties can't hold together if their workers don't get offices when they win; third, if the parties go to pieces, the government they built up must go to pieces, too; fourth, then there'll be hell to pay." W. Riordon, Plunkitt of Tammany Hall 13 (1963).

It may well be that the Good Government Leagues of America were right, and that Plunkitt, James Michael Curley and their ilk were wrong; but that is not entirely certain. As the merit principle has been extended and its effects increasingly felt; as the Boss Tweeds, the Tammany Halls, the Pender gast Machines, the Byrd Machines and the Daley Machines have faded into history; we find that political leaders at all levels increasingly complain of the helplessness of elected government, unprotected by "party discipline," before the demands of small and cohesive interest-groups.

The choice between patronage and the merit principle — or, to be more realistic about it, the choice between the desirable mix of merit and patronage principles in widely varying federal, state, and local political contexts — is not so clear that I would be prepared, as an original matter, to chisel a single, inflexible prescription into the Constitution. Fourteen years ago, in Elrod v. Burns, 427 U.S. 347 (1976), the Court did that. Elrod was limited however, as was the later decision of Branti v. Finkel, 445 U.S. 507 (1980), to patronage firings, leaving it to state and federal legislatures to determine when and where political affiliation could be taken into account in hirings and promotions. Today the Court makes its constitutional civil-service reform absolute, extending to all decisions regarding government employment. Because the First Amendment has never been thought to require this disposition, which may well have disastrous consequences for our political system, I dissent.

I

The restrictions that the Constitution places upon the government in its capacity as lawmaker, i.e., as the regulator of private conduct, are not the same as the restrictions that it places upon the government in its capacity as employer. We have recognized this in many contexts, with respect to many different constitutional guarantees. Private citizens perhaps cannot be prevented from wearing long hair, but policemen can. Kelley v.

Johnson, 425 U.S. 238, 247 (1976). Private citizens cannot have their property searched without probable cause, but in many circumstances government employees can. O'Connor v. Ortega, 480 U.S. 709, 723 (1987) (plurality opinion); id., at 732 (Scalia, J., concurring in judgment). Private citizens cannot be punished for refusing to provide the government information that may incriminate them, but government employees can be dismissed when the incriminating information that they refuse to provide relates to the performance of their job. Gardner v. Broderick, 392 U.S. 273, 277-278 (1968). With regard to freedom of speech in particular: Private citizens cannot be punished for speech of merely private concern, but government employees can be fired for that reason. Connick v. Myers, 461 U.S. 138, 147 (1983). Private citizens cannot be punished for partisan political activity, but federal and state employees can be dismissed and otherwise punished for that reason. Public Workers v. Mitchell, 330 U.S. 75, 101 (1947); CSC v. Letter Carriers, 413 U.S. 548, 556 (1973); Broadrick v. Oklahoma, 413 U.S. 601, 616-617 (1973).

Once it is acknowledged that the Constitution's prohibition against laws "abridging the freedom of speech" does not apply to laws enacted in the government's capacity as employer the same way it does to laws enacted in the government's capacity as regulator of private conduct, it may sometimes be difficult to assess what employment practices are permissible and what are not. That seems to me not a difficult question, however, in the present context. The provisions of the Bill of Rights were designed to restrain transient majorities from impairing long-recognized personal liberties. They did not create by implication novel individual rights overturning accepted political norms. Thus, when a practice not expressly prohibited by the text of the Bill of Rights bears the endorsement of a long tradition of open, widespread, and unchallenged use that dates back to the beginning of the Republic, we have no proper basis for striking it down. [n.1] Such a venerable and accepted tradition is not to be laid on the examining table and scrutinized for its conformity to some abstract principle of First-Amendment adjudication devised by this Court. To the contrary, such traditions are themselves the stuff out of which the Court's principles are to be formed. They are, in these uncertain areas, the very points of reference by which the legitimacy or illegitimacy of other practices are to be figured out. When it appears that the latest "rule," or "three-part test," or "balancing test" devised by the Court has placed us on a collision course with such a landmark practice, it is the former that must be recalculated by us, and not the latter that must be abandoned by our citizens. I know of no other way to formulate a constitutional jurisprudence that reflects, as it should, the principles adhered to, over time, by the American people, rather than those favored by the personal (and necessarily shifting) philosophical dispositions of a majority of this Court.

I will not describe at length the claim of patronage to landmark status as one of our accepted political traditions. Justice Powell discussed it in his dissenting opinions in Elrod and Branti. Elrod, 427 U.S., at 378-379 (Powell, J., dissenting); Branti, 445 U.S., at 522, n.1 (Powell, J., dissenting). Suffice it to say that patronage was, without any thought that it could be unconstitutional, a basis for government employment from the earliest days of the Republic until Elrod — and has continued unabated since Elrod, to the extent still permitted by that unfortunate decision. See, e.g., D. Price, Bringing Back the Parties 24, 32 (1984); Gardner, A Theory of the Spoils System, 54 Public Choice 171, 181 (1987); Toinet & Glenn, Clientelism and Corruption in the "Open" Society: The Case of the United States, in Private Patronage and Public Power 193, 202 (C. Clapham ed. 1982). Given that unbroken tradition regarding the application of an ambiguous constitutional text, there was in my view no basis for holding that patronage-based dismissals violated the First Amendment — much less for holding, as the Court does today, that even patronage hiring does so. [n.2]

II

Even accepting the Court's own mode of analysis, however, and engaging in "balancing" a tradition that ought to be part of the scales, Elrod, Branti, and today's extension of them seem to me wrong.

A

The Court limits patronage on the ground that the individual's interest in uncoerced belief and expression outweighs the systemic interests invoked to justify the practice. Ante, at 68-72. The opinion indicates that the government may prevail only if it proves that the practice is "narrowly tailored to further vital government interests." Ante, at 74.

That strict-scrutiny standard finds no support in our cases. Although our decisions establish that government employees do not lose all constitutional rights, we have consistently applied a lower level of scrutiny when "the governmental function operating ... [is] not the power to regulate or license, as lawmaker, an entire trade or profession, or to control an entire branch of private business, but, rather, as proprietor, to manage [its] internal operatio[ns] ...." Cafeteria & Restaurant Workers v. McElroy, 367 U.S. 886, 896 (1961). When dealing with its own employees, the government may not act in a manner that is "patently arbitrary or discriminatory," id., at 898, but its regulations are valid if they bear a "rational connection" to the governmental end sought to be served, Kelley v. Johnson, 425 U.S., at 247.

In particular, restrictions on speech by public employees are not judged by the test applicable to similar restrictions on speech by nonemployees. We have said that "[a] governmental employer may subject its employees to such special restrictions on free expression as are reasonably necessary to promote effective government." Brown v. Glines, 444 U.S. 348, 356, n.13 (1980). In Public Workers v. Mitchell, 330 U.S., at 101, upholding provisions of the Hatch Act which prohibit political activities by federal employees, we said that "it is not necessary that the act regulated be anything more than an act reasonably deemed by Congress to interfere with the efficiency of the public service." We reaffirmed Mitchell in CSC v. Letter Carriers, 413 U.S., at 556, over a dissent by Justice Douglas arguing against application of a special standard to government employees, except insofar as their "job performance" is concerned, id., at 597. We did not say that the Hatch Act was narrowly tailored to meet the government's interest, but merely deferred to the judgment of Congress, which we were not "in any position to dispute." Id., at 567. Indeed, we recognized that the Act was not indispensably necessary to achieve those ends, since we repeatedly noted that "Congress at some time [may] come to a different view." Ibid., see also id., at 555, 564. In Broadrick v. Oklahoma, 413 U.S. 601 (1973), we upheld similar restrictions on state employees, though directed "at political expression which if engaged in by private persons would plainly be protected by the First and Fourteenth Amendments," Id., at 616.

To the same effect are cases that specifically concern adverse employment action taken against public employees because of their speech. In Pickering v. Board of Education of Township High School Dist., 391 U.S. 563, 568 (1968), we recognized:

"[T]he State has interests as an employer in regulating the speech of its employees that differ significantly from those it possesses in connection with regulation of the speech of the citizenry in general. The problem in any case is to arrive at a balance between the interests of the [employee], as a citizen, in commenting upon matters of public concern and the interests of the State, as an employer, in promoting the efficiency of the public services it performs through its employees."

Because the restriction on speech is more attenuated when the government conditions employment than when it imposes criminal penalties, and because "government offices could not function if every employment decision became a constitutional matter," Connick v. Myers, 461 U.S., at 143, we have held that government employment decisions taken on the basis of an employee's speech do not "abridg[e] the freedom of speech," U.S. Const., Amdt. 1, merely because they fail the narrow-tailoring and compelling-interest tests applicable to direct regulation of speech. We have not subjected such decisions to strict scrutiny, but have accorded "a wide degree of deference to the employer's judgment" that an employee's speech will interfere with close working relationships. 461 U.S., at 152.

When the government takes adverse action against an employee on the basis of his political affiliation (an interest whose constitutional protection is derived from the interest in speech), the same analysis applies. That is why both the Elrod plurality, 427 U.S., at 359, and the opinion concurring in the judgment, id., at 375, as well as Branti, 445 U.S., at 514-515, and the Court today, ante, at 89, rely on Perry v. Sindermann, 408 U.S. 593 (1972), a case that applied the test announced in Pickering, not the strict-scrutiny test applied to restrictions imposed on the public at large. Since the government may dismiss an employee for political speech "reasonably deemed by Congress to interfere with the efficiency of the public service," Public Workers v. Mitchell, supra, at 101, it follows a fortiori that the government may dismiss an employee for political affiliation if "reasonably necessary to promote effective government." Brown v. Glines, supra, at 356, n.13.

While it is clear from the above cases that the normal "strict scrutiny" that we accord to government regulation of speech is not applicable in this field, [n.3] the precise test that replaces it is not so clear; we have used various formulations. The one that appears in the case dealing with an employment practice closest in its effects to patronage is whether the practice could be "reasonably deemed" by the enacting legislature to further a legitimate goal. Public Workers v. Mitchell, supra, at 101. For purposes of my ensuing discussion, however, I will apply a less permissive standard that seems more in accord with our general "balancing" test: can the governmental advantages of this employment practice reasonably be deemed to outweigh its "coercive" effects?

B

Preliminarily, I may observe that the Court today not only declines, in this area replete with constitutional ambiguities, to give the clear and continuing tradition of our people the dispositive effect I think it deserves, but even declines to give it substantial weight in the balancing. That is contrary to what the Court has done in many other contexts. In evaluating so-called "substantive due process" claims we have examined our history and tradition with respect to the asserted right. See, e.g., Michael H. v. Gerald D., 491 U.S. (1989); Bowers v. Hardwick, 478 U.S. 186, 192-194 (1986). In evaluating claims that a particular procedure violates the Due Process Clause we have asked whether the procedure is traditional. See, e.g., Burnham v. Superior Court of California, Marin County, 495 U.S. (1990). And in applying the Fourth Amendment's reasonableness test we have looked to the history of judicial and public acceptance of the type of search in question. See, e.g., Camara v. Municipal Court of San Francisco, 387 U.S. 523, 537 (1967). See also Press-Enterprise Co. v. Superior Court of California, Riverside County, 478 U.S. 1, 8 (1986) (tradition of accessibility to judicial proceedings implies judgment of experience that individual's interest in access outweighs government's interest in closure); Richmond Newspapers, Inc. v. Virginia, 448 U.S. 555, 589 (1980) (Brennan, J., concurring in judgment) ("Such a tradition [of public access] commands respect in part because the Constitution carries the gloss of history"); Walz v. Tax Comm'n of New York, 397 U.S. 664, 678 (1970) ("unbroken practice of according the [property tax] exemption to churches" demonstrates that it does not violate Establishment Clause).

But even laying tradition entirely aside, it seems to me our balancing test is amply met. I assume, as the Court's opinion assumes, that the balancing is to be done on a generalized basis, and not case-by-case. The Court holds that the governmental benefits of patronage cannot reasonably be thought to outweigh its "coercive" effects (even the lesser "coercive" effects of patronage hiring as opposed to patronage firing) not merely in 1990 in the State of Illinois, but at any time in any of the numerous political subdivisions of this vast country. It seems to me that that categorical pronouncement reflects a naive vision of politics and an inadequate appreciation of the systemic effects of patronage in promoting political stability and facilitating the social and political integration of previously powerless groups.

The whole point of my dissent is that the desirability of patronage is a policy question to be decided by the people's representatives; I do not mean, therefore, to endorse that system. But in order to demonstrate that a legislature could reasonably determine that its benefits outweigh its "coercive" effects, I must describe those benefits as the proponents of patronage see them: As Justice Powell discussed at length in his Elrod dissent, patronage stabilizes political parties and prevents excessive political fragmentation — both of which are results in which States have a strong governmental interest. Party strength requires the efforts of the rank-and-file, especially in "the dull periods between elections," to perform such tasks as organizing precincts, registering new voters, and providing constituent services. Elrod, 427 U.S., at 385 (dissenting opinion). Even the most enthusiastic supporter of a party's program will shrink before such drudgery, and it is folly to think that ideological conviction alone will motivate sufficient numbers to keep the party going through the off-years. "For the most part, as every politician knows, the hope of some reward generates a major portion of the local political activity supporting parties." Ibid. Here is the judgment of one such politician, Jacob Arvey (best known as the promoter of Adlai Stevenson): Patronage is "'a necessary evil if you want a strong organization, because the patronage system permits of discipline, and without discipline, there's no party organization.'" Quoted in M. Tolchin & S. Tolchin, To the Victor 36 (1971). A major study of the patronage system describes the reality as follows:

"[A]lthough men have many motives for entering political life ... the vast underpinning of both major parties is made up of men who seek practical rewards. Tangible advantages constitute the unifying thread of most successful political practitioners" Id., at 22.

"With so little patronage cement, party discipline is relatively low; the rate of participation and amount of service the party can extract from [Montclair] county committeemen are minuscule compared with Cook County. The party considers itself lucky if 50 percent of its committeemen show up at meetings — even those labeled 'urgent' — while even lower percentages turn out at functions intended to produce crowds for visiting candidates." Id., at 123.

See also W. Grimshaw, The Political Economy of Machine Politics, 4 Corruption and Reform 15, 30 (1989); G. Pomper, Voters, Elections, and Parties 255 (1988); Wolfinger, Why Political Machines Have Not Withered Away and Other Revisionist Thoughts, 34 J. Politics 365, 384 (1972).

The Court simply refuses to acknowledge the link between patronage and party discipline, and between that and party success. It relies (as did the plurality in Elrod, 427 U.S., at 369, n.23) on a single study of a rural Pennsylvania county by Professor Sorauf, ante, at 13 — a work that has been described as "more persuasive about the ineffectuality of Democratic leaders in Centre County than about the generaliz ability of [its] findings." Wolfinger, supra, at 384, n.39. It is unpersuasive to claim, as the Court does, that party workers are obsolete because campaigns are now conducted through media and other money-intensive means. Ante, at 13. Those techniques have supplemented but not supplanted personal contacts. See Price, Bringing Back the Parties, at 25. Certainly they have not made personal contacts unnecessary in campaigns for the lower-level offices that are the foundations of party strength, nor have they replaced the myriad functions performed by party regulars not directly related to campaigning. And to the extent such techniques have replaced older methods of campaigning (partly in response to the limitations the Court has placed on patronage), the political system is not clearly better off. See Elrod, supra, at 384 (Powell, J., dissenting); Branti, 445 U.S., at 528 (Powell, J., dissenting). Increased reliance on money-intensive campaign techniques tends to entrench those in power much more effectively than patronage — but without the attendant benefit of strengthening the party system. A challenger can more easily obtain the support of party-workers (who can expect to be rewarded even if the candidate loses — if not this year, then the next) than the financial support of political action committees (which will generally support incumbents, who are likely to prevail).

It is self-evident that eliminating patronage will significantly undermine party discipline; and that as party discipline wanes, so will the strength of the two-party system. But, says the Court, "[p]olitical parties have already survived the substantial decline in patronage employment practices in this century." Ante, at 1213. This is almost verbatim what was said in Elrod, see 427 U.S., at 369. Fourteen years later it seems much less convincing. Indeed, now that we have witnessed, in 18 of the last 22 years, an Executive Branch of the Federal Government under the control of one party while the Congress is entirely or (for two years) partially within the control of the other party; now that we have undergone the most recent federal election, in which 98" of the incumbents, of whatever party, were returned to office; and now that we have seen elected officials changing their political affiliation with unprecedented readiness, Washington Post, Apr. 10, 1990, p.A1, the statement that "political parties have already survived" has a positively whistling-in-the-graveyard character to it. Parties have assuredly survived — but as what? As the forges upon which many of the essential compromises of American political life are hammered out? Or merely as convenient vehicles for the conducting of national presidential elections?

The patronage system does not, of course, merely foster political parties in general; it fosters the two-party system in particular. When getting a job, as opposed to effectuating a particular substantive policy, is an available incentive for party-workers, those attracted by that incentive are likely to work for the party that has the best chance of displacing the "ins," rather than for some splinter group that has a more attractive political philosophy but little hope of success. Not only is a two-party system more likely to emerge, but the differences between those parties are more likely to be moderated, as each has a relatively greater interest in appealing to a majority of the electorate and a relatively lesser interest in furthering philosophies or programs that are far from the mainstream. The stabilizing effects of such a system are obvious. See Toinet & Glenn, Clientelism and Corruption in the "Open" Society, at 208. In the context of electoral laws we have approved the States' pursuit of such stability, and their avoidance of the "splintered parties and unrestrained factionalism [that] may do significant damage to the fabric of government." Storer v. Brown, 415 U.S. 724, 736 (1974) (upholding law disqualifying persons from running as independents if affiliated with a party in the past year).

Equally apparent is the relatively destabilizing nature of a system in which candidates cannot rely upon patronage-based party loyalty for their campaign support, but must attract workers and raise funds by appealing to various interest-groups. See Tolchin & Tolchin, To the Victor, at 127-130. There is little doubt that our decisions in Elrod and Branti, by contributing to the decline of party strength, have also contributed to the growth of interest-group politics in the last decade. See, e.g., Fitts, The Vice of Virtue, 136 U. Pa. L. Rev. 1567, 1603-1607 (1988). Our decision today will greatly accelerate the trend. It is not only campaigns that are affected, of course, but the subsequent behavior of politicians once they are in power. The replacement of a system firmly based in party discipline with one in which each office-holder comes to his own accommodation with competing interest groups produces "a dispersion of political influence that may inhibit a political party from enacting its programs into law." Branti, supra, at 531 (Powell, J., dissenting). [n.4]

Patronage, moreover, has been a powerful means of achieving the social and political integration of excluded groups. See, e.g., Elrod, supra, at 379 (Powell, J., dissenting); Cornwell, Bosses, Machines and Ethnic Politics, in Ethnic Group Politics 190, 195-197 (H. Bailey, Jr., & E. Katz eds. 1969). By supporting and ultimately dominating a particular party "machine," racial and ethnic minorities have — on the basis of their politics rather than their race or ethnicity — acquired the patronage awards the machine had power to confer. No one disputes the historical accuracy of this observation, and there is no reason to think that patronage can no longer serve that function. The abolition of patronage, however, prevents groups that have only recently obtained political power, especially blacks, from following this path to economic and social advancement.

"'Every ethnic group that has achieved political power in American cities has used the bureaucracy to provide jobs in return for political support. It's only when Blacks begin to play the same game that the rules get changed. Now the use of such jobs to build political bases becomes an "evil" activity, and the city insists on taking the control back "downtown."'" New York Amsterdam News, Apr. 1, 1978, p. A-4, quoted in Hamilton, The Patron-Recipient Relationship and Minority Politics in New York City, 94 Pol. Sci. Q. 211, 212 (1979).

While the patronage system has the benefits argued for above, it also has undoubted disadvantages. It facilitates financial corruption, such as salary kickbacks and partisan political activity on government-paid time. It reduces the efficiency of government, because it creates incentives to hire more and less-qualified workers and because highly qualified workers are reluctant to accept jobs that may only last until the next election. And, of course, it applies some greater or lesser inducement for individuals to join and work for the party in power.

To hear the Court tell it, this last is the greatest evil. That is not my view, and it has not historically been the view of the American people. Corruption and inefficiency, rather than abridgement of liberty, have been the major criticisms leading to enactment of the civil-service laws — for the very good reason that the patronage system does not have as harsh an effect upon conscience, expression, and association as the Court suggests. As described above, it is the nature of the pragmatic, patronage-based, two-party system to build alliances and to suppress rather than foster ideological tests for participation in the division of political "spoils." What the patronage system ordinarily demands of the party worker is loyalty to, and activity on behalf of, the organization itself rather than a set of political beliefs. He is generally free to urge within the organization the adoption of any political position; but if that position is rejected he must vote and work for the party nonetheless. The diversity of political expression (other than expression of party loyalty) is channeled, in other words, to a different stage — to the contests for party endorsement rather than the partisan elections. It is undeniable, of course, that the patronage system entails some constraint upon the expression of views, particularly at the partisan-election stage, and considerable constraint upon the employee's right to associate with the other party. It greatly exaggerates these, however, to describe them as a general "'coercion of belief,'" ante, at 9, quoting Branti, 445 U.S., at 516; see also ante, at 11-12; Elrod, 427 U.S., at 355 (plurality opinion). Indeed, it greatly exaggerates them to call them "coercion" at all, since we generally make a distinction between inducement and compulsion. The public official offered a bribe is not "coerced" to violate the law, and the private citizen offered a patronage job is not "coerced" to work for the party. In sum, I do not deny that the patronage system influences or redirects, perhaps to a substantial degree, individual political expression and political association. But like the many generations of Americans that have preceded us, I do not consider that a significant impairment of free speech or free association.

In emphasizing the advantages and minimizing the disadvantages (or at least minimizing one of the disadvantages) of the patronage system, I do not mean to suggest that that system is best. It may not always be; it may never be. To oppose our Elrod-Branti jurisprudence, one need not believe that the patronage system is necessarily desirable; nor even that it is always and everywhere arguably desirable; but merely that it is a political arrangement that may sometimes be a reasonable choice, and should therefore be left to the judgment of the people's elected representatives. The choice in question, I emphasize, is not just between patronage and a merit-based civil service, but rather among various combinations of the two that may suit different political units and different eras: permitting patronage hiring, for example, but prohibiting patronage dismissal; permitting patronage in most municipal agencies but prohibiting it in the police department; or permitting it in the mayor's office but prohibiting it everywhere else. I find it impossible to say that, always and everywhere, all of these choices fail our "balancing" test.

C

The last point explains why Elrod and Branti should be overruled, rather than merely not extended. Even in the field of constitutional adjudication, where the pull of stare decisis is at its weakest, see Glidden Co. v. Zdanok, 370 U.S. 530, 543 (1962) (opinion of Harlan, J.), one is reluctant to depart from precedent. But when that precedent is not only wrong, not only recent, not only contradicted by a long prior tradition, but also has proved unworkable in practice, then all reluctance ought to disappear. In my view that is the situation here. Though unwilling to leave it to the political process to draw the line between desirable and undesirable patronage, the Court has neither been prepared to rule that no such line exists (i.e., that all patronage is unconstitutional) nor able to design the line itself in a manner that judges, lawyers, and public employees can understand. Elrod allowed patronage dismissals of persons in "policymaking" or "confidential" positions. 427 U.S., at 367 (plurality opinion); id., at 375 (Stewart, J., concurring). Branti retreated from that formulation, asking instead "whether the hiring authority can demonstrate that party affiliation is an appropriate requirement for the effective performance of the public office involved." 445 U.S., at 518. What that means is anybody's guess. The Courts of Appeals have devised various tests for determining when "affiliation is an appropriate requirement." See generally Martin, A Decade of Branti Decisions: A Government Officials' Guide to Patronage Dismissals, 39 Am. U. L. Rev. 11, 23-42 (1989). These interpretations of Branti are not only significantly at variance with each other; they are still so general that for most positions it is impossible to know whether party affiliation is a permissible requirement until a court renders its decision.

A few examples will illustrate the shambles Branti has produced. A city cannot fire a deputy sheriff because of his political affiliation, [n.5] but then again perhaps it can, [n.6] especially if he is called the "police captain." [n.7] A county cannot fire on that basis its attorney for the department of social services, [n.8] nor its assistant attorney for family court, [n.9] but a city can fire its solicitor and his assistants, [n.10] or its assistant city attorney, [n.11] or its assistant state's attorney, [n.12] or its corporation counsel. [n.13] A city cannot discharge its deputy court clerk for his political affiliation, [n.14] but it can fire its legal assistant to the clerk on that basis. [n.15] Firing a juvenile court bailiff seems impermissible, [n.16] but it may be permissible if he is assigned permanently to a single judge. [n.17] A city cannot fire on partisan grounds its director of roads, [n.18] but it can fire the second in command of the water department. [n.19] A government cannot discharge for political reasons the senior vice president of its development bank, [n.20] but it can discharge the regional director of its rural housing administration. [n.21]

The examples could be multiplied, but this summary should make obvious that the "tests" devised to implement Branti have produced inconsistent and unpredictable results. That uncertainty undermines the purpose of both the nonpatron age rule and the exception. The rule achieves its objective of preventing the "coercion" of political affiliation, see supra, at, only if the employee is confident that he can engage in (or refrain from) political activities without risking dismissal. Since the current doctrine leaves many employees utterly in the dark about whether their jobs are protected, they are likely to play it safe. On the other side, the exception was designed to permit the government to implement its electoral mandate. Elrod, supra, at 367 (plurality opinion). But unless the government is fairly sure that dismissal is permitted, it will leave the politically uncongenial official in place, since an incorrect decision will expose it to lengthy litigation and a large damage award, perhaps even against the responsible officials personally.

This uncertainty and confusion are not the result of the fact that Elrod, and then Branti, chose the wrong "line." My point is that there is no right line — or at least no right line that can be nationally applied and that is known by judges. Once we reject as the criterion a long political tradition showing that party-based employment is entirely permissible, yet are unwilling (as any reasonable person must be) to replace it with the principle that party-based employment is entirely impermissible, we have left the realm of law and entered the domain of political science, seeking to ascertain when and where the undoubted benefits of political hiring and firing are worth its undoubted costs. The answer to that will vary from State to State, and indeed from city to city, even if one rejects out of hand (as the Branti line does) the benefits associated with party stability. Indeed, the answer will even vary from year to year. During one period, for example, it may be desirable for the manager of a municipally owned public utility to be a career specialist, insulated from the political system. During another, when the efficient operation of that utility or even its very existence has become a burning political issue, it may be desirable that he be hired and fired on a political basis. The appropriate "mix" of party-based employment is a political question if there ever was one, and we should give it back to the voters of the various political units to decide, through civil-service legislation crafted to suit the time and place, which mix is best.

III

Even were I not convinced that Elrod and Branti were wrongly decided, I would hold that they should not be extended beyond their facts, viz., actual discharge of employees for their political affiliation. Those cases invalidated patronage firing in order to prevent the "restraint it places on freedoms of belief and association." Elrod, 427 U.S., at 355 (plurality opinion); see also id., at 357 (patronage "compels or restrains" and "inhibits" belief and association). The loss of one's current livelihood is an appreciably greater constraint than such other disappointments as the failure to obtain a promotion or selection for an uncongenial transfer. Even if the "coercive" effect of the former has been held always to outweigh the benefits of party-based employment decisions, the "coercive" effect of the latter should not be. We have drawn a line between firing and other employment decisions in other contexts, see Wygant v. Jackson Bd. of Education, 476 U.S. 267, 282-283 (1986) (plurality opinion), and should do so here as well.

I would reject the alternative that the Seventh Circuit adopted in this case, which allows a cause of action if the employee can demonstrate that he was subjected to the "substantial equivalent of dismissal." 868 F. 2d 943, 950, 954 (CA7 1989). The trouble with that seemingly reasonable standard is that it is so imprecise that it will multiply yet again the harmful uncertainty and litigation that Branti has already created. If Elrod and Branti are not to be reconsidered in light of their demonstrably unsatisfactory consequences, I would go no further than to allow a cause of action when the employee has lost his position, that is, his formal title and salary. That narrow ground alone is enough to resolve the constitutional claims in the present case. Since none of the plaintiffs has alleged loss of his position because of affiliation, [n.22] I would affirm the Seventh

Circuit's judgment insofar as it affirmed the dismissal of petitioner Moore's claims, and would reverse the Seventh Circuit's judgment insofar as it reversed the dismissal of the claims of other petitioners and cross-respondents.

The Court's opinion, of course, not only declines to confine Elrod and Branti to dismissals in the narrow sense I have proposed, but, unlike the Seventh Circuit, even extends those opinions beyond "constructive" dismissals — indeed, even beyond adverse treatment of current employees — to all hiring decisions. In the long run there may be cause to rejoice in that extension. When the courts are flooded with litigation under that most unmanageable of standards (Branti) brought by that most persistent and tenacious of suitors (the disappointed office-seeker) we may be moved to reconsider our intrusion into this entire field.

In the meantime, I dissent.

Notes

1 The customary invocation of Brown v. Board of Education, 347 U.S. 483 (1954) as demonstrating the dangerous consequences of this principle, see ante, at 4 (Stevens, J., concurring), is unsupportable. I argue for the role of tradition in giving content only to ambiguous constitutional text; no tradition can supersede the Constitution. In my view the Fourteenth Amendment's requirement of "equal protection of the laws," combined with the Thirteenth Amendment's abolition of the institution of black slavery, leaves no room for doubt that laws treating people differently because of their race are invalid. Moreover, even if one does not regard the Fourteenth Amendment as crystal clear on this point, a tradition of unchallenged validity did not exist with respect to the practice in Brown. To the contrary, in the 19th century the principle of "separate-but-equal" had been vigorously opposed on constitutional grounds, litigated up to this Court, and upheld only over the dissent of one of our historically most respected Justices. See Plessy v. Ferguson, 163 U.S. 537, 555-556 (1896) (Harlan, J., dissenting).

2 Justice Stevens seeks to counteract this tradition by relying upon the supposed "unequivocal repudiation" of the right-privilege distinction. Ante, at 5. That will not do. If the right-privilege distinction was once used to explain the practice, and if that distinction is to be repudiated, then one must simply devise some other theory to explain it. The order of precedence is that a constitutional theory must be wrong if its application contradicts a clear constitutional tradition; not that a clear constitutional tradition must be wrong if it does not conform to the current constitutional theory. On Justice Stevens' view of the matter, this Court examines a historical practice, endows it with an intellectual foundation, and later, by simply undermining that foundation, relegates the constitutional tradition to the dustbin of history. That is not how constitutional adjudication works. Cf. Burnham v. Superior Court of California, Marin County, 495 U.S. (1990) (opinion of Scalia, J.). I am not sure, in any event, that the right-privilege distinction has been as unequivocally rejected as Justice Stevens supposes. It has certainly been recognized that the fact that the government need not confer a certain benefit does not mean that it can

attach any conditions whatever to the conferral of that benefit. But it remains true that certain conditions can be attached to benefits that cannot be imposed as prescriptions upon the public at large. If Justice Stevens chooses to call this something other than a right-privilege distinction, that is fine and good — but it is in any case what explains the nonpatronage restrictions upon federal employees that the Court continues to approve, and there is no reason why it cannot support patronage restrictions as well.

3 The Court calls our description of the appropriate standard of review "questionable," and suggests that these cases applied strict scrutiny ("even were Justice Scalia correct that less-than-strict scrutiny is appropriate"). Ante, at 7, n.4 (emphasis added). This suggestion is incorrect, does not aid the Court's argument, and if accepted would eviscerate the strict-scrutiny standard. It is incorrect because even a casual perusal of the cases reveals that the governmental actions were sustained, not because they were shown to be "narrowly tailored to further vital government interests," ante, at 1011, but because they were "reasonably" deemed necessary to promote effective government. It does not aid the Court's argument, moreover, because whatever standard those cases applied must be applied here, and if the asserted interests in patronage are as weighty as those proffered in the previous cases, then Elrod and Branti were wrongly decided. It eviscerates the standard, finally, because if the practices upheld in those cases survived strict scrutiny, then the so-called "strict scrutiny" test means nothing. Suppose a State made it unlawful for an employee of a privately owned nuclear power plant to criticize his employer. Can there be any doubt that we would reject out of hand the State's argument that the statute was justified by the compelling interest in maintaining the appearance that such employees are operating nuclear plants properly, so as to maintain public confidence in the plants' safety? But cf. CSC v. Letter Carriers, 413 U.S. 548, 565 (1973) (Hatch Act justified by need for government employees to "appear to the public to be avoiding [political partiality], if confidence in the system of representative Government is not to be eroded"). Suppose again that a State prohibited a private employee from speaking on the job about matters of private concern. Would we even hesitate before dismissing the State's claim that the compelling interest in fostering an efficient economy overrides the individual's interest in speaking on such matters? But cf. Connick v. Myers, 461 U.S. 138, 147 (1983) ("[W]hen a public employee speaks ... upon matters only of personal interest, absent the most unusual circumstances, a federal court is not the appropriate forum in which to review the wisdom of a personnel decision taken by a public agency allegedly in reaction to the employee's behavior"). If the Court thinks that strict scrutiny is appropriate in all these cases, then it should forthrightly admit that Public Workers v. Mitchell, 330 U.S. 75 (1947), Letter Carriers, Pickering v. Board of Education of Township High School Dist., 391 U.S. 563 (1968), Connick, and similar cases were mistaken and should be overruled; if it rejects that course, then it should admit that those cases applied, as they said they did, a reasonableness test.

The Court's further contention that these cases are limited to the "interests that the government has in its capacity as an employer," ante, at 7, n. 4, as distinct from its interests "in the structure and functioning of society as a whole," ibid., is neither true nor relevant. Surely a principal reason for the statutes that we have upheld preventing political activity by government employees — and indeed the only substantial reason, with respect to those employees who are permitted to be hired and fired on a political basis — is to prevent the party in power from obtaining what is considered an unfair advantage in political campaigns. That is precisely the type of governmental interest at issue here. But even if the Court were correct, I see no reason in policy or principle why the government would be limited to furthering only its interests "as employer." In fact, we have seemingly approved the furtherance of broader governmental interests through employment restrictions. In Hampton v. Mow Sun Wong, 426 U.S. 88 (1976), we held unlawful a Civil Service Commission regulation prohibiting the hiring of aliens on the ground that the Commission lacked the requisite authority. We were willing, however, to "assume ... that if the Congress or the President had expressly imposed the citizenship requirement, it would be justified by the national interest in providing an incentive for aliens to become naturalized, or possibly even as providing the President with an expendable token for treaty negotiating purposes." Id., at 105. Three months after our opinion, the President adopted the restriction by Executive Order. Exec. Order No.11935, 3 CFR 146 (1976 Comp.). On remand, the lower courts denied the Mow Sun Wong plaintiffs relief, on the basis of this new Executive Order and relying upon the interest in providing an incentive for citizenship. Mow SunWong v. Hampton, 435 F. Supp. 37 (ND Cal. 1977), aff'd, 626 F. 2d 739 (CA9 1980). We denied certiorari, sub nom. Lum v. Campbell, 450 U.S. 959 (1981). In other cases, the lower federal courts have uniformly reached the same result. See, e.g., Jalil v. Campbell, 192 U.S. App. D.C. 4, 7, 590 F. 2d 1120, 1123, n.3 (1978); Vergara v. Hampton, 581 F. 2d 1281 (CA7 1978), cert. denied, 441 U.S. 905 (1979); Santin Ramos v. United States Civil Service Comm'n, 430 F. Supp. 422 (PR 1977) (three-judge court).

4 Justice Stevens discounts these systemic effects when he characterizes patronage as fostering partisan, rather than public, interests. Ante, at 9. But taking Justice Stevens at his word, one wonders why patronage can ever be an "appropriate requirement for the position involved," ante, at 1.

5 Jones v. Dodson, 727 F. 2d 1329, 1338 (CA4 1984).

6 McBee v. Jim Hogg County, Texas, 730 F. 2d 1009, 1014-1015 (CA5 1984) (en banc).

7 Joyner v. Lancaster, 553 F. Supp. 809, 818 (MDNC 1982), later proceeding, 815 F. 2d 20, 24 (CA4), cert. denied, 484 U.S. 830 (1987).

8 Layden v. Costello, 517 F. Supp. 860, 862 (NDNY 1981).

9 Tavano v. County of Niagara, New York, 621 F. Supp. 345, 349-350 (WDNY 1985), aff'd mem., 800 F. 2d 1128 (CA2 1986).

10 Ness v. Marshall, 660 F. 2d 517, 521-522 (CA3 1981); Montaquila v. St. Cyr, 433 A. 2d 206, 211 (R.I. 1981).

11 Finkelstein v. Barthelemy, 678 F. Supp. 1255, 1265 (ED La 1988).

12 Livas v. Petka, 711 F. 2d 798, 800-801 (CA7 1983).

13 Bavoso v. Harding, 507 F. Supp. 313, 316 (SDNY 1980).

14 Barnes v. Bosley, 745 F. 2d 501, 508 (CA8 1984), cert. denied, 471 U.S. 1017 (1985).

15 Bauer v. Bosley, 802 F. 2d 1058, 1063 (CA8 1986), cert. denied, 481 U.S. 1038 (1987).

16 Elrod v. Burns, 427 U.S. 347, 351 (1976).

17 Balogh v. Charron, 855 F. 2d 356 (CA6 1988).

18 Abraham v. Pekarski, 537 F. Supp. 858, 865 (ED Pa 1982), aff'd in part and dismissed in part, 728 F. 2d 167 (CA3), cert. denied, 467 U.S. 1242 (1984).

19 Tomczak v. Chicago, 765 F. 2d 633 (CA7), cert. denied, 474 U.S. 946 (1985).

20 De Choudens v. Government Development Bank of Puerto Rico, 801 F. 2d 5, 10 (CA1 1986) (en banc), cert. denied, 481 U.S. 1013 (1987).

21 Rosario Nevarez v. Torres Gaztambide, 820 F. 2d 525 (CA1 1987).

22 Standefer and O'Brien do not allege that their political affiliation was the reason they were laid off, but only that it was the reason they were not recalled. Complaint 9, 21-22, App. to Respondent's Brief in Opposition; 641 F. Supp. 249, 256, 257 (CDIll. 1986). Those claims are essentially identical to the claims of persons wishing to be hired; neither fall within the narrow rule of Elrod and Branti against patronage firing.

Justice Scalia's dissent in Maryland v. Craig (June 27, 1990)

Justice Scalia, with whom Justice Brennan, Justice Marshall, and Justice Stevens join, dissenting.

Seldom has this Court failed so conspicuously to sustain a categorical guarantee of the Constitution against the tide of prevailing current opinion. The Sixth Amendment provides, with unmistakable clarity, that "[i]n all criminal prosecutions, the accused shall enjoy the right . . . to be confronted with the witnesses against him." The purpose of enshrining this protection in the Constitution was to assure that none of the many policy interests from time to time pursued by statutory law could overcome a defendant's right to face his or her accusers in court. The Court, however, says:

"We ... conclude today that a State's interest in the physical and psychological well-being of child abuse victims may be sufficiently important to outweigh, at least in some cases, a defendant's right to face his or her accusers in court. That a significant majority of States has enacted statutes to protect child witnesses from the trauma of giving testimony in child abuse cases attests to the widespread belief in the importance of such a public policy." Ante, at 13.

Because of this subordination of explicit constitutional text to currently favored public policy, the following scene can be played out in an American courtroom for the first time in two centuries: A father whose young daughter has been given over to the exclusive custody of his estranged wife, or a mother whose young son has been taken into custody by the State's child welfare department, is sentenced to prison for sexual abuse on the basis of testimony by a child the parent has not seen or spoken to for many months; and the guilty verdict is rendered without giving the parent so much as the opportunity to sit in the presence of the child, and to ask, personally or through counsel, "it is really not true, is it, that I — your father (or mother) whom you see before you — did these terrible things?" Perhaps that is a procedure today's society desires; perhaps (though I doubt it) it is even a fair procedure; but it is assuredly not a procedure permitted by the Constitution.

Because the text of the Sixth Amendment is clear, and because the Constitution is meant to protect against, rather than conform to, current "widespread belief," I respectfully dissent.

I

According to the Court, "we cannot say that [face-to-face] confrontation [with witnesses appearing at trial] is an in dispensable element of the Sixth Amendment's guarantee of the right to confront one's accusers." Ante, at 10. That is rather like saying "we cannot say that being tried before a jury is an indispensable element of the Sixth Amendment's guarantee of the right to jury trial." The Court makes the impossible plausible by recharacterizing the Confrontation Clause, so that confrontation (redesignated "face-to-face confrontation") becomes only one of many "elements of confrontation." Ante, at 7. The reasoning is as follows: The Confrontation Clause guarantees not only what it explicitly provides for — "face-to-face" confrontation — but also implied and collateral rights such as cross-examination, oath, and observation of demeanor (TRUE); the purpose of this entire cluster of rights is to ensure the reliability of evidence (TRUE); the Maryland procedure preserves the implied and collateral rights (TRUE), which adequately ensure the reliability of evidence (perhaps TRUE); therefore the Confrontation Clause is not violated by denying what it explicitly provides for — "face-to-face" confrontation (unquestionably FALSE). This reasoning abstracts from the right to its purposes, and then eliminates the right. It is wrong because the Confrontation Clause does not guarantee reliable evidence; it guarantees specific trial procedures that were thought to assure reliable evidence, undeniably among which was "face-to-face" confrontation. Whatever else it may mean in addition, the defendant's constitutional right "to be confronted with the witnesses against him" means, always and everywhere, at least what it explicitly says: the "`right to meet face to face all those who appear and give evidence at trial.'" Coy v. Iowa, 487 U.S. 1012, 1016 (1988), quoting California v. Green, 399 U.S. 149, 175 (1970) (Harlan, J. concurring).

The Court supports its antitextual conclusion by cobbling together scraps of dicta from various cases that have no bearing here. It will suffice to discuss one of them, since they are all of a kind: Quoting Ohio v. Roberts, 448 U.S. 56, 63 (1980), the Court says that "[i]n sum, our precedents es tablish that `the Confrontation Clause reflects a preference for face-to-face confrontation at trial,'" ante, at 10 (emphasis added by the Court). But Roberts, and all the other "precedents" the Court enlists to prove the implausible, dealt with the implications of the Confrontation Clause, and not its literal, unavoidable text. When Roberts said that the Clause merely "reflects a preference for face-to-face confrontation at trial," what it had in mind as the nonpreferred alternative was not (as the Court implies) the appearance of a witness at trial without confronting the defendant. That has been, until today, not merely "nonpreferred" but utterly unheardof. What Roberts had in mind was the receipt of other-than-first-hand testimony from witnesses at trial — that is, witnesses' recounting of hearsay statements by absent parties who, since they did not appear at trial, did not have to endure face-to-face confrontation. Rejecting that, I agree, was merely giving effect to an evident constitutional preference; there are, after all, many exceptions to the Confrontation Clause's hearsay rule. But that the defendant should be confronted by the witnesses who appear at trial is not a preference "reflected" by the Confrontation Clause; it is a constitutional right unqualifiedly guaranteed.

The Court claims that its interpretation of the Confron tation Clause "is consistent with our cases holding that other Sixth Amendment rights must also be interpreted in the context of the necessities of trial and the adversary process." Ante, at 1011. I disagree. It is true enough that the "necessities of trial and the adversary process" limit the manner in which Sixth Amendment rights may be exercised, and limit the scope of Sixth Amendment guarantees to the extent that scope is textually indeterminate. Thus (to describe the cases the Court cites): The right to confront is not the right to confront in a manner that disrupts the trial. Illinois v. Allen, 397 U.S. 337 (1970). The right "to have compulsory process for obtaining witnesses" is not the right to call witnesses in a manner that violates fair and orderly procedures. Taylor v. United States, 484 U.S. 400 (1988). The scope of the right "to have the assistance of counsel" does not include consultation with counsel at all times during the trial. Perry v. Leeke, 488 U.S. 272 (1989). The scope of the right to cross-examine does not include access to the State's investigative files. Pennsylvania v. Ritchie, 480 U.S. 39 (1987). But we are not talking here about denying expansive scope to a Sixth Amendment provision whose scope for the purpose at issue is textually unclear; "to confront" plainly means to encounter face-to-face, whatever else it may mean in addition. And we are not talking about the manner of arranging that face-to-face encounter, but about whether it shall occur at all. The "necessities of trial and the adversary process" are irrelevant here, since they cannot alter the constitutional text.

II

Much of the Court's opinion consists of applying to this case the mode of analysis we have used in the admission of hearsay evidence. The Sixth Amendment does not literally contain a prohibition upon such evidence, since it guarantees the defendant only the right to confront "the witnesses against him." As applied in the Sixth Amendment's context of a prosecution, the noun "witness" — in 1791 as today — could mean either (a) one "who knows or sees any thing; one personally present" or (b) "one who gives testimony" or who "testifies," i.e., "[i]n judicial proceedings, [one who] make[s] a solemn declaration under oath, for the purpose of establishing or making proof of some fact to a court." 2 N.Webster, An American Dictionary of the English Language (1828) (emphasis added). See also J.Buchanan, Linguae Britannicae Vera Pronunciatio (1757). The former meaning (one "who knows or sees") would cover hearsay evidence, but is excluded in the

Sixth Amendment by the words following the noun: "witnesses against him." The phrase obviously refers to those who give testimony against the defendant at trial. We have nonetheless found implicit in the Confrontation Clause some limitation upon hearsay evidence, since otherwise the Government could subvert the confrontation right by putting on witnesses who know nothing except what an absent declarant said. And in determining the scope of that implicit limitation, we have focused upon whether the reliability of the hearsay statements (which are not expressly excluded by the Confrontation Clause) "is otherwise assured." Ante, at 11. The same test cannot be applied, however, to permit what is explicitly forbidden by the constitutional text; there is simply no room for interpretation with regard to "the irreducible literal meaning of the Clause." Coy, supra, at 1020-1021.

Some of the Court's analysis seems to suggest that the children's testimony here was itself hearsay of the sort permissible under our Confrontation Clause cases. See ante, at 12. That cannot be. Our Confrontation Clause conditions for the admission of hearsay have long included a "general requirement of unavailability" of the declarant. Idaho v. Wright, ante, p.8. "In the usual case ..., the prosecution must either produce or demonstrate the unavailability of, the declarant whose statement it wishes to use against the defendant." Ohio v. Roberts, 448 U.S., at 65. We have permitted a few exceptions to this general rule — e.g., for co-conspirators' statements, whose effect cannot be replicated by live testimony because they "derive [their] significance from the circumstances in which [they were] made," United States v. Inadi, 475 U.S. 387, 395 (1986). "Live" closed-circuit television testimony, however — if it can be called hearsay at all — is surely an example of hearsay as "a weaker substitute for live testimony," id., at 394, which can be employed only when the genuine article is unavailable. "When two versions of the same evidence are available, longstanding principles of the law of hearsay, applicable as well to Confrontation Clause analysis, favor the better evidence." Ibid. See also Roberts, supra (requiring unavailability as precondition for admission of prior testimony); Barber v. Page, 390 U.S. 719 (1968) (same).

The Court's test today requires unavailability only in the sense that the child is unable to testify in the presence of the defendant. [n.1] That cannot possibly be the relevant sense. If unconfronted testimony is admissible hearsay when the witness is unable to confront the defendant, then presumably there are other categories of admissible hearsay consisting of unsworn testimony when the witness is unable to risk perjury, uncross-examined testimony when the witness is unable to undergo hostile questioning, etc. California v. Green, 399 U.S. 149 (1970), is not precedent for such a silly system. That case held that the Confrontation Clause does not bar admission of prior testimony when the declarant is sworn as a witness but refuses to answer. But in Green, as in most cases of refusal, we could not know why the declarant refused to testify. Here, by contrast, we know that it is precisely because the child is unwilling to testify in the presence of the defendant. That unwillingness cannot be a valid excuse under the Confrontation Clause, whose very object is to place the witness under the sometimes hostile glare of the defendant. "That face-to-face presence may, unfortunately, upset the truthful rape victim or abused child; but by the same token it may confound and undo the false accuser, or reveal the child coached by a malevolent adult." Coy, 487 U.S., at 1020. To say that a defendant loses his right to confront a witness when that would cause the witness not to testify is rather like saying that the defendant loses his right to counsel when counsel would save him, or his right to subpoena witnesses when they would exculpate him, or his right not to give testimony against himself when that would prove him guilty.

III

The Court characterizes the State's interest which "outweigh[s]" the explicit text of the Constitution as an "interest in the physical and psychological well-being of child abuse victims," ante, at 13, an "interest in protecting" such victims "from the emotional trauma of testifying," ante, at 16. That is not so. A child who meets the Maryland statute's requirement of suffering such "serious emotional distress" from confrontation that he "cannot reasonably communicate" would seem entirely safe. Why would a prosecutor want to call a witness who cannot reasonably communicate? And if he did, it would be the State's own fault. Protection of the child's interest — as far as the Confrontation Clause is concerned [n.2] — is entirely within Maryland's control. The State's interest here is in fact no more and no less than what the State's interest always is when it seeks to get a class of evidence admitted in criminal proceedings: more convictions of guilty defendants. That is not an unworthy interest, but it should not be dressed up as a humanitarian one.

And the interest on the other side is also what it usually is when the State seeks to get a new class of evidence admitted: fewer convictions of innocent defendants — specifically, in the present context, innocent defendants accused of particularly heinous crimes. The "special" reasons that exist for suspending one of the usual guarantees of reliability in the case of children's testimony are perhaps matched by "special" reasons for being particularly insistent upon it in the case of children's testimony. Some studies show that children are substantially more vulnerable to suggestion than adults, and often unable to separate recollected fantasy (or suggestion) from reality. See Lindsay & Johnson, Reality Monitoring and Suggestibility: Children's Ability to Discriminate Among Memories From Different Sources, in Children's Eyewitness Memory 92 (S.Ceci, M.Toglia, & D.Ross eds. 1987); Feher, The Alleged Molestation Victim, The Rules of Evidence, and the Constitution: Should Children Really Be Seen and Not Heard?, 14 Am. J. Crim. L. 227, 230-233 (1987); Christian sen, The Testimony of Child Witnesses: Fact, Fantasy, and the Influence of Pretrial Interviews, 62 Wash. L. Rev. 705, 708-711 (1987). The injustice their erroneous testimony can produce is evidenced by the tragic Scott County investigations of 1983-1984, which disrupted the lives of many (as far as we know) innocent people in the small town of Jordan, Minnesota. At one stage those investigations were pursuing allegations by at least eight children of multiple murders, but the prosecutions actually initiated charged only sexual abuse. Specifically, 24 adults were charged with molesting 37 children. In the course of the investigations, 25 children were placed in foster homes. Of the 24 indicted defendants, one pleaded guilty, two were acquitted at trial, and the charges against the remaining 21 were voluntarily dismissed. See Feher, supra, at 239-240. There is no doubt that some sexual abuse took place in Jordan; but there is no reason to believe it was as widespread as charged. A report by the Minnesota Attorney General's office, based on inquiries conducted by the Minnesota Bureau of Criminal Apprehension and the Federal Bureau of Investigation, concluded that there was an "absence of credible testimony and [a] lack of significant corroboration" to support reinstitution of sex-abuse charges, and "no credible evidence of murders." H. Humphrey, report on Scott County Investigation 8, 7 (1985). The report describes an investigation full of well-intentioned techniques employed by the prosecution team, police, child protection workers, and foster parents, that distorted and in some cases even coerced the children's recollection. Children were interrogated repeatedly, in some cases as many as 50 times, id., at 9; answers were suggested by telling the children what other witnesses had said, id., at 11; and children (even some who did not at first complain of abuse) were separated from their parents for months, id., at 9. The report describes the consequences as follows:

"As children continued to be interviewed the list of accused citizens grew. In a number of cases, it was only after weeks or months of questioning that children would `admit' their parents abused them.

"In some instances, over a period of time, the allegations of sexual abuse turned to stories of mutilations, and eventually homicide." Id., at 10-11.

The value of the confrontation right in guarding against a child's distorted or coerced recollections is dramatically evident with respect to one of the misguided investigative techniques the report cited: some children were told by their foster parents that reunion with their real parents would be hastened by "admission" of their parents' abuse. Id., at 9.Is it difficult to imagine how unconvincing such a testimonial admission might be to a jury that witnessed the child's delight at seeing his parents in the courtroom? Or how devastating it might be if, pursuant to a psychiatric evaluation that "trauma would impair the child's ability to communicate" in front of his parents, the child were permitted to tell his story to the jury on closed-circuit television?

In the last analysis, however, this debate is not an appropriate one. I have no need to defend the value of confrontation, because the Court has no authority to question it. It is not within our charge to speculate that, "where face-to-face confrontation causes significant emotional distress in a child witness," confrontation might "in fact disserve the Confrontation Clause's truth-seeking goal." Ante, at 17. If so, that is a defect in the Constitution — which should be amended by the procedures provided for such an eventuality, but cannot be corrected by judicial pronouncement that it is archaic, contrary to "widespread belief" and thus null and void. For good or bad, the Sixth Amendment requires confrontation, and we are not at liberty to ignore it. To quote the document one last time (for it plainly says all that need be said): "In all criminal prosecutions, the accused shall enjoy the right ... to be confronted with the witnesses against him" (emphasis added).

＊ ＊ ＊

The Court today has applied "interest-balancing" analysis where the text of the Constitution simply does not permit it. We are not free to conduct a cost-benefit analysis of clear and explicit constitutional guarantees, and then to adjust their meaning to comport with our findings. The Court has convincingly proved that the Maryland procedure serves a valid interest, and gives the defendant virtually everything the Confrontation Clause guarantees (everything, that is, except confrontation). I am persuaded, therefore, that the Maryland procedure is virtually constitutional. Since it is not, however, actually constitutional I would affirm the judgment of the Maryland Court of Appeals reversing the judgment of conviction.

Notes

1 I presume that when the Court says "trauma would impair the child's ability to communicate," ante, at 18, it means that trauma would make it impossible for the child to communicate. That is the requirement of the Maryland law at issue here: "serious emotional distress such that the child cannot reasonably communicate." Md. Cts. & Jud. Proc. Code Ann. 9-102(a)(1)(ii) (1989). Any implication beyond that would in any event be dictum.

2 A different situation would be presented if the defendant sought to call the child. In that event, the State's refusal to compel the child to appear, or its insistence upon a procedure such as that set forth in the Maryland statute as a condition of its compelling him to do so, would call into questioning — itially, at least, and perhaps exclusively — the scope of the defendant's Sixth Amendment right "to have compulsory process for obtaining witnesses in his favor."

Justice Scalia's dissent in Minnick v. Mississippi (Dec 3, 1990)

Justice Scalia, with whom The Chief Justice joins, dissenting.

The Court today establishes an irrebuttable presumption that a criminal suspect, after invoking his Miranda right to counsel, can never validly waive that right during any policeinitiated encounter, even after the suspect has been provided multiple Miranda warnings and has actually consulted his attorney. This holding builds on foundations already established in Edwards v. Arizona, 451 U.S. 477 (1981), but "the rule of Edwards is our rule, not a constitutional command; and it is our obligation to justify its expansion." Arizona v. Roberson, 486 U.S. 675, 688 (1988) (Kennedy, J., dissenting). Because I see no justification for applying the Edwards irrebuttable presumption when a criminal suspect has actually consulted with his attorney, I respectfully dissent.

I

Some recapitulation of pertinent facts is in order, given the Court's contention that "[t]he case before us well illustrates the pressures, and abuses, that may be concomitants of custody." Ante, at 7. It is undisputed that the FBI agents who first interviewed Minnick on Saturday, August 23, 1986, advised him of his Miranda rights before any questioning began. Although he refused to sign a waiver form, he agreed to talk to the agents, and described his escape from prison in Mississippi and the ensuing events. When he came to what happened at the trailer, however, Minnick hesitated. The FBI agents then reminded him that he did not have to answer questions without a lawyer present. Minnick indicated that he would finish his account on Monday, when he had a lawyer, and the FBI agents terminated the interview forthwith.

Minnick was then provided with an attorney, with whom he consulted several times over the weekend. As Minnick testified at a subsequent suppression hearing:

"I talked to [my attorney] two different times and — it might have been three different times. . . . He told me that first day that he was my lawyer and that he was appointed to me and not to talk to nobody and not tell nobody nothing and to not sign no waivers and not sign no extradition papers or sign anything and that he was going to get a court order to have any of the police — I advised him of the FBI talking to me and he advised me not to tell anybody anything that he was going to get a court order drawn up to restrict anybody talking to me outside of the San Diego Police Department." App. 46-47.

On Monday morning, Minnick was interviewed by Deputy Sheriff J. C. Denham, who had come to San Diego from Mississippi. Before the interview, Denham reminded Minnick of his Miranda rights. Minnick again refused to sign a waiver form, but he did talk with Denham, and did not ask for his attorney. As Minnick recalled at the hearing, he and Denham

"went through several different conversations about — first, about how everybody was back in the county jail and what everybody was doing, had he heard from Mama and had he went and talked to Mama and had he seen my brother, Tracy, and several different other questions pertaining to such things as that. And, we went off into how the escape went down at the county jail . . . ." App. 50.

Minnick then proceeded to describe his participation in the double murder at the trailer.

Minnick was later extradited and tried for murder in Mississippi. Before trial, he moved to suppress the statements he had given the FBI agents and Denham in the San Diego jail. The trial court granted the motion with respect to the statements made to the FBI agents, but ordered a hearing on the admissibility of the statements made to Denham. After receiving testimony from both Minnick and Denham, the court concluded that Minnick's confession had been "freely and voluntarily given from the evidence beyond a reasonable doubt," id., at 25, and allowed Denham to describe Minnick's confession to the jury.

The Court today reverses the trial court's conclusion. It holds that, because Minnick had asked for counsel during the interview with the FBI agents, he could not — as a matter of law — validly waive the right to have counsel present during the conversation initiated by Denham. That Minnick's original request to see an attorney had been honored, that Minnick had consulted with his attorney on several occasions, and that the attorney had specifically warned Minnick not to speak to the authorities, are irrelevant. That

Minnick was familiar with the criminal justice system in general or Miranda warnings in particular (he had previously been convicted of robbery in Mississippi and assault with a deadly weapon in California) is also beside the point. The confession must be suppressed, not because it was "compelled," nor even because it was obtained from an individual who could realistically be assumed to be unaware of his rights, but simply because this Court sees fit to prescribe as a "systemic assuranc[e]," ante, at 9, that a person in custody who has once asked for counsel cannot thereafter be approached by the police unless counsel is present. Of course the Constitution's proscription of compelled testimony does not remotely authorize this incursion upon state practices; and even our recent precedents are not a valid excuse.

II

In Miranda v. Arizona, 384 U.S. 436 (1966), this Court declared that a criminal suspect has a right to have counsel present during custodial interrogation, as a prophylactic assurance that the "inherently compelling pressures," id. at 467, of such interrogation will not violate the Fifth Amendment. But Miranda did not hold that these "inherently compelling pressures" precluded a suspect from waiving his right to have counsel present. On the contrary, the opinion recognized that a State could establish that the suspect "knowingly and intelligently waived . . . his right to retained or appointed counsel." Id., at 475. For this purpose, the Court expressly adopted the "high standar[d] of proof for the waiver of constitutional rights," ibid., set forth in Johnson v. Zerbst, 304 U.S. 458 (1938).

The Zerbst waiver standard, and the means of applying it, are familiar: Waiver is "an intentional relinquishment or abandonment of a known right or privilege," id., at 464; and whether such a relinquishment or abandonment has occurred depends "in each case, upon the particular facts and circumstances surrounding that case, including the background, experience, and conduct of the accused," ibid. We have applied the Zerbst approach in many contexts where a State bears the burden of showing a waiver of constitutional criminal procedural rights. See, e. g., Faretta v. California, 422 U.S. 806, 835 (1975) (right to the assistance of counsel at trial); Brookhart v. Janis, 384 U.S. 1, 4 (1966) (right to confront adverse witnesses); Adams v. United States ex rel. McCann, 317 U.S. 269, 275-280 (1942) (right to trial by jury).

Notwithstanding our acknowledgment that Miranda rights are "not themselves rights protected by the Constitution but . . . instead measures to insure that the right against compulsory self-incrimination [is] protected," Michigan v. Tucker, 417 U.S. 433, 444 (1974), we have adhered to the principle that nothing less than the Zerbst standard for the waiver of constitutional rights applies to the waiver of Miranda rights. Until Edwards, however, we refrained from imposing on the States a higher standard for the waiver of Miranda rights. For example, in Michigan v. Mosley, 423 U.S. 96 (1975), we rejected a proposed irrebuttable presumption that a criminal suspect, after invoking the Miranda right to remain silent, could not validly waive the right during any subsequent questioning by the police. In North Carolina v. Butler, 441 U.S. 369 (1979) we rejected a proposed rule that waivers of Miranda rights must be deemed involuntary absent an explicit assertion of waiver by the suspect. And in Fare v. Michael C., 442 U.S. 707, 723-727 (1979) we declined to hold that waivers of Miranda rights by juveniles are per se involuntary.

Edwards, however, broke with this approach, holding that a defendant's waiver of his Miranda right to counsel, made in the course of a police-initiated encounter after he had requested counsel but before counsel had been provided, was per se involuntary. The case stands as a solitary exception to our waiver jurisprudence. It does, to be sure, have the desirable consequences described in today's opinion. In the narrow context in which it applies, it provides 100" assurance against confessions that are "the result of coercive pressures," ante, at 4; it " `prevent[s] police from badgering a defendant,' " ibid. (quoting Michigan v. Harvey, 494 U. S. —, — (1990)); it "conserves judicial resources which would otherwise be expended in making difficult determinations of voluntariness," ante, at 4; and it provides " ` "clear and unequivocal" guidelines to the law enforcement profession,' " ibid. (quoting Arizona v. Roberson, 486 U. S., at 682). But so would a rule that simply excludes all confessions by all persons in police custody. The value of any prophylactic rule (assuming the authority to adopt a prophylactic rule) must be assessed not only on the basis of what is gained, but also on the basis of what is lost. In all other contexts we have thought the above-described consequences of abandoning Zerbst outweighed by " `the need for police questioning as a tool for effective enforcement of criminal laws,' " Moran v. Burbine, 475 U.S. 412, 426 (1986). "Admissions of guilt," we have said, "are more than merely `desirable'; they are essential to society's compelling interest in finding, convicting, and punishing those who violate the law." Ibid. (citation omitted).

III

In this case, of course, we have not been called upon to reconsider Edwards, but simply to determine whether its irrebuttable presumption should continue after a suspect has actually consulted with his attorney. Whatever justifications might support Edwards are even less convincing in this context.

Most of the Court's discussion of Edwards — which stresses repeatedly, in various formulations, the case's emphasis upon "the `right to have counsel present during custodial interrogation,' " ante, at 5, quoting 451 U. S., at 482 (emphasis added by the Court) — is beside the point. The existence and the importance of the Miranda-created right "to have counsel present" are unquestioned here. What is questioned is why a State should not be given the opportunity to prove (under Zerbst) that the right was voluntarily waived by a suspect who, after having been read his Miranda rights twice and having consulted with counsel at least twice, chose to speak to a police officer (and to admit his involvement in two murders) without counsel present.

Edwards did not assert the principle that no waiver of the Miranda right "to have counsel present" is possible. It simply adopted the presumption that no waiver is voluntary in certain circumstances, and the issue before us today is how broadly those circumstances are to be defined. They should not, in my view, extend beyond the circumstances present in Edwards itself — where the suspect in custody asked to consult an attorney, and was interrogated before that attorney had ever been provided. In those circumstances, the Edwards rule rests upon an assumption similar to that of Miranda itself: that when a suspect in police custody is first questioned he is likely to be ignorant of his rights and to feel isolated in a hostile environment. This likelihood is thought to justify special protection against unknowing or coerced waiver of rights. After a suspect has seen his request for an attorney honored, however, and has actually spoken with that attorney, the probabilities change. The suspect then knows that he has an advocate on his side, and that the police will permit him to consult that advocate. He almost certainly also has a heightened awareness (above what the Miranda warning itself will provide) of his right to remain silent — since at the earliest opportunity "any lawyer worth his salt will tell the suspect in no uncertain terms to make no statement to the police under any circumstances." Watts v. Indiana, 338 U.S. 49, 59 (1949) (Opinion of Jackson, J.).

Under these circumstances, an irrebuttable presumption that any police-prompted confession is the result of ignorance of rights, or of coercion, has no genuine basis in fact. After the first consultation, therefore, the Edwards exclusionary rule should cease to apply. Does this mean, as the Court implies, that the police will thereafter have license to "badger" the suspect? Only if all one means by "badger" is asking, without such insistence or frequency as would constitute coercion, whether he would like to reconsider his decision not to confess. Nothing in the Constitution (the only basis for our intervention here) prohibits such inquiry, which may often produce the desirable result of a voluntary confession. If and when post-consultation police inquiry becomes so protracted or threatening as to constitute coercion, the Zerbst standard will afford the needed protection.

One should not underestimate the extent to which the Court's expansion of Edwards constricts law enforcement. Today's ruling, that the invocation of a right to counsel permanently prevents a police-initiated waiver, makes it largely impossible for the police to urge a prisoner who has initially declined to confess to change his mind — or indeed, even to ask whether he has changed his mind. Many persons in custody will invoke the Miranda right to counsel during the first interrogation, so that the permanent prohibition will attach at once. Those who do not do so will almost certainly request or obtain counsel at arraignment. We have held that a general request for counsel, after the Sixth Amendment right has attached, also triggers the Edwards prohibition of policesolicited confessions, see Michigan v. Jackson, 475 U.S. 625 (1986), and I presume that the perpetuality of prohibition announced in today's opinion applies in that context as well. "Perpetuality" is not too strong a term, since, although the Court rejects one logical moment at which the Edwards presumption might end, it suggests no alternative. In this case Minnick was reapproached by the police three days after he requested counsel, but the result would presumably be the same if it had been three months, or three years, or even three decades. This perpetual irrebuttable presumption will apply, I might add, not merely to interrogations involving the original crime but to those involving other subjects as well. See Arizona v. Roberson, 486 U.S. 675 (1988).

Besides repeating the uncontroverted proposition that the suspect has a "right to have counsel present," the Court stresses the clarity and simplicity that are achieved by today's holding. Clear and simple rules are desirable, but only in pursuance of authority that we possess. We are authorized by the Fifth Amendment to exclude confessions that are "compelled," which we have interpreted to include confessions that the police obtain from a suspect in custody without a knowing and voluntary waiver of his right to remain silent. Undoubtedly some bright-line rules can be adopted to implement that principle, marking out the situations in which knowledge or voluntariness cannot possibly be established — for example, a rule excluding confessions obtained after five hours of continuous interrogation. But a rule excluding all confessions that follow upon even the slightest police inquiry cannot conceivably be justified on this basis. It does not rest upon a reasonable prediction that all such confessions, or even most such confessions, will be unaccompanied by a knowing and voluntary waiver.

It can be argued that the same is true of the category of confessions excluded by the Edwards rule itself. I think that is so, but, as I have discussed above, the presumption of involuntariness is at least more plausible for that category. There is, in any event, a clear and rational line between that category and the present one, and I see nothing to be said for expanding upon a past mistake. Drawing a distinction between police-initiated inquiry before consultation with counsel and police-initiated inquiry after consultation with counsel is assuredly more reasonable than other distinctions Edwards has already led us into — such as the distinction between police-initiated inquiry after assertion of the Miranda right to remain silent, and police-initiated inquiry after assertion of the Miranda right to counsel, see Kamisar, The Edwards and Bradshaw Cases: The Court Giveth and the Court Taketh Away, in 5 The Supreme Court: Trends and Developments 157 (J. Choper, Y. Kamisar, & L. Tribe eds. 1984) ("[E]ither Mosley was wrongly decided or Edwards was"); or the distinction between what is needed to prove waiver of the Miranda right to have counsel present and what is needed to prove waiver of rights found in the Constitution.

The rest of the Court's arguments can be answered briefly. The suggestion that it will either be impossible or ethically impermissible to determine whether a "consultation" between the suspect and his attorney has occurred is alarmist. Since, as I have described above, the main purpose of the consultation requirement is to eliminate the suspect's feeling of isolation and to assure him the presence of legal assistance, any discussion between him and an attorney whom he asks to contact, or who is provided to him, in connection with his arrest, will suffice. The precise content of the discussion is irrelevant.

As for the "irony" that "the suspect whose counsel is prompt would lose the protection of Edwards, while the one whose counsel is dilatory would not," ante, at 9: There seems to me no irony in applying a special protection only when it is needed. The Edwards rule is premised on an (already tenuous) assumption about the suspect's psychological state, and when the event of consultation renders that assumption invalid the rule should no longer apply. One searching for ironies in the state of our law should consider, first, the irony created by Edwards itself: The suspect in custody who says categorically "I do not wish to discuss this matter" can be asked to change his mind; but if he should say, more tentatively, "I do not think I should discuss this matter without my attorney present" he can no longer be approached. To that there is added, by today's decision, the irony that it will be far harder for the state to establish a knowing and voluntary waiver of Fifth Amendment rights by a prisoner who has already consulted with counsel than by a newly arrested suspect.

Finally, the Court's concern that "Edwards' protection could pass in and out of existence multiple times," ante, at 8, does not apply to the resolution of the matter I have proposed. Edwards would cease to apply, permanently, once consultation with counsel has occurred.

* * *

Today's extension of the Edwards prohibition is the latest stage of prophylaxis built upon prophylaxis, producing a veritable fairyland castle of imagined constitutional restriction upon law enforcement. This newest tower, according to the Court, is needed to avoid "inconsisten[cy] with [the] purpose" of Edwards' prophylactic rule, ante, at 8, which was needed to protect Miranda's prophylactic right to have counsel present, which was needed to protect the right against compelled self-incrimination found (at last!) in the Constitution.

It seems obvious to me that, even in Edwards itself but surely in today's decision, we have gone far beyond any genuine concern about suspects who do not know their right to remain silent, or who have been coerced to abandon it. Both holdings are explicable, in my view, only as an effort to protect suspects against what is regarded as their own folly. The sharp-witted criminal would know better than to confess; why should the dull-witted suffer for his lack of mental endowment? Providing him an attorney at every stage where he might be induced or persuaded (though not coerced) to incriminate himself will even the odds. Apart from the fact that this protective enterprise is beyond our authority under the Fifth Amendment or any other provision of the Constitution, it is unwise. The procedural protections of the Constitution protect the guilty as well as the innocent, but it is not their objective to set the guilty free. That some clever criminals may employ those protections to their advantage is poor reason to allow criminals who have not done so to escape justice.

Thus, even if I were to concede that an honest confession is a foolish mistake, I would welcome rather than reject it; a rule that foolish mistakes do not count would leave most offenders not only unconvicted but undetected. More fundamentally, however, it is wrong, and subtly corrosive of our criminal justice system, to regard an honest confession as a "mistake." While every person is entitled to stand silent, it is more virtuous for the wrongdoer to admit his offense and accept the punishment he deserves. Not only for society, but for the wrongdoer himself, "admissio[n] of guilt . . ., if not coerced, [is] inherently desirable," United States v. Washington, 431 U.S. 181, 187 (1977), because it advances the goals of both "justice and rehabilitation." Michigan v. Tucker, 417 U. S., at

448, n. 23 (emphasis added). A confession is rightly regarded by the sentencing guidelines as warranting a reduction of sentence, because it "demonstrates a recognition and affirmative acceptance of personal responsibility for . . . criminal conduct," U. S. Sentencing Commission, Guidelines Manual 3E1.1 (1988), which is the beginning of reform. We should, then, rejoice at an honest confession, rather than pity the "poor fool" who has made it; and we should regret the attempted retraction of that good act, rather than seek to facilitate and encourage it. To design our laws on premises contrary to these is to abandon belief in either personal responsibility or the moral claim of just government to obedience. Cf. Caplan, Questioning Miranda, 38 Vand. L. Rev. 1417, 1471-1473 (1985). Today's decision is misguided, it seems to me, in so readily exchanging, for marginal, super-Zerbst protection against genuinely compelled testimony, investigators' ability to urge, or even ask, a person in custody to do what is right.

Justice Scalia's dissent in Edmonson v. Leesville Concrete (June 3, 1991)

Justice Scalia, dissenting.

I join Justice O'Connor's dissent, which demonstrates that today's opinion is wrong in principle. I write to observe that it is also unfortunate in its consequences.

The concrete benefits of the Court's newly discovered constitutional rule are problematic. It will not necessarily be a net help rather than hindrance to minority litigants in obtaining racially diverse juries. In criminal cases, Batson v. Kentucky, 476 U.S. 79 (1986), already prevents the prosecution from using race-based strikes. The effect of today's decision (which logically must apply to criminal prosecutions) will be to prevent the defendant from doing so â€" so that the minority defendant can no longer seek to prevent an all-white jury, or to seat as many jurors of his own race as possible. To be sure, it is ordinarily more difficult to prove race-based strikes of white jurors, but defense counsel can generally be relied upon to do what we say the Constitution requires. So in criminal cases, today's decision represents a net loss to the minority litigant. In civil cases that is probably not true â€" but it does not represent an unqualified gain either. Both sides have peremptory challenges, and they are sometimes used to assure rather than to prevent a racially diverse jury.

The concrete costs of today's decision, on the other hand, are not at all doubtful; and they are enormous. We have now added to the duties of already-submerged state and federal trial courts the obligation to assure that race is not included among the other factors (sex, age, religion, political views, economic status) used by private parties in exercising their peremptory challenges. That responsibility would be burden enough if it were not to be discharged through the adversary process; but of course it is. When combined with our decision this Term in Powers v. Ohio, 499 U.S. Z (1991), which held that the party objecting to an allegedly race-based peremptory challenge need not be of the same race as the challenged juror, today's decision means that both sides, in all civil jury cases, no matter what their race (and indeed, even if they are artificial entities such as corporations), may lodge racial-challenge objections and, after those objections have been considered and denied, appeal the denials â€" with the consequence, if they are successful, of having the judgments against them overturned. Thus, yet another complexity is added to an increasingly Byzantine system of justice that devotes more and more of its energy to sideshows and less and less to the merits of the case. Judging by the number of Batson claims that have made their way even as far as this Court under the pre-Powers regime, it is a certainty that the amount of judges' and lawyers' time devoted to implementing today's newly discovered Law of the Land will be enormous. That time will be diverted from other matters, and the overall system of justice will certainly suffer. Alternatively, of course, the States and Congress may simply abolish peremptory challenges, which would cause justice to suffer in a different fashion. See Holland v. Illinois, 493 U.S. 474, 484 (1990).

Although today's decision neither follows the law nor produces desirable concrete results, it certainly has great symbolic value. To overhaul the doctrine of state action in this fashion â€" what a magnificent demonstration of this institution's uncompromising hostility to race-based judgments, even by private actors! The price of the demonstration is, alas, high, and much of it will be paid by the minority litigants who use our courts. I dissent.

Justice Scalia's dissent in Chambers v. Nasco (June 6, 1991)

JUSTICE SCALIA, dissenting.

I agree with the Court that Article III courts, as an independent and coequal Branch of Government, derive from the Constitution itself, once they have been created and their jurisdiction established, the authority to do what courts have traditionally done in order to accomplish their assigned tasks. Some elements of that inherent authority are so essential to "[t]he judicial Power," U. S. Const., Art. III, § 1, that they are indefeasible, among which is a court's ability to enter orders protecting the integrity of its proceedings.

"Certain implied powers must necessarily result to our Courts of justice from the nature of their institution.... To fine for contempt—imprison for contumacy—inforce the observance of order, &c. are powers which cannot be dispensed with in a Court, because they are necessary to the exercise of all others: and so far our Courts no doubt possess powers not immediately derived from statute...." United States v. Hudson, 7 Cranch 32, 34 (1812).

I think some explanation might be useful regarding the "bad-faith" limitation that the Court alludes to today, see ante, at 47. Since necessity does not depend upon a litigant's state of mind, the inherent sanctioning power must extend to situations involving less than bad faith. For example, a court has the power to dismiss when counsel fails to appear for trial, even if this is a consequence of negligence rather than bad faith.

"The authority of a court to dismiss sua sponte for lack of prosecution has generally been considered an `inherent power,' governed not by rule or statute but by the control necessarily vested in courts to manage their own affairs so as to achieve the orderly and expeditious disposition of cases." Link v. Wabash R. Co., 370 U. S. 626, 630-631 (1962).

However, a "bad-faith" limitation upon the particular sanction of attorney's fees derives from our jurisprudence regarding the so-called American Rule, which provides that the prevailing party must bear his own attorney's fees and cannot have them assessed against the loser. See Alyeska Pipeline Service Co. v. Wilderness Society, 421 U. S. 240, 247 (1975). That rule, "deeply rooted in our history and in congressional policy," id., at 271, prevents a court (without statutory authorization) from engaging in what might be termed substantive fee shifting, that is, fee shifting as part of the merits award. It does not in principle bar fee shifting as a sanction for procedural abuse, see id., at 258-259. We have held, however—in my view as a means of preventing erosion or evasion of the American Rule—that even fee shifting as a sanction can only be imposed for litigation conduct characterized by bad faith. See Roadway Express, Inc. v. Piper, 447 U. S. 752, 766 (1980). But that in no way means that all sanctions imposed under the courts' inherent authority require a finding of bad faith. They do not. See Redfield v. Ystalyfera Iron Co., 110 U. S. 174, 176 (1884) (dismissal appropriate for unexcused delay in prosecution); cf. Link, supra.

Just as Congress may to some degree specify the manner in which the inherent or constitutionally assigned powers of the President will be exercised, so long as the effectiveness of those powers is not impaired, cf. Myers v. United States, 272 U. S. 52, 128 (1926), so also Congress may prescribe the means by which the courts may protect the integrity of their proceedings. A court must use the prescribed means unless for some reason they are inadequate. In the present case they undoubtedly were. JUSTICE KENNEDY concedes that some of the impairments of the District Court's proceedings in the present case were not sanctionable under the Federal Rules. I have no doubt of a court's authority to go beyond the Rules in such circumstances. And I agree with the Court that an overall sanction resting at least in substantial portion upon the court's inherent power need not be broken down into its component parts, with the actions sustainable under the Rules separately computed. I do not read the Rules at issue here to require that, and it is unreasonable to import such needless complication by implication.

I disagree, however, with the Court's statement that a court's inherent power reaches conduct "beyond the court's confines" that does not "`interfer[e] with the conduct of trial,'" ante, at 44 (quoting Young v. United States ex rel. Vuitton et Fils S. A., 481 U. S. 787, 798 (1987)). See id., at 819-822 (SCALIA, J., concurring in judgment); Bank of Nova Scotia v. United States, 487 U. S. 250, 264 (1988) (SCALIA, J., concurring). I emphatically agree with JUSTICE KENNEDY, therefore, that the District Court here had no power to impose any sanctions for petitioner's flagrant, bad-faith breach of contract; and I agree with him that it appears to have done so. For that reason, I dissent.

JUSTICE KENNEDY, with whom THE CHIEF JUSTICE and JUSTICE SOUTER join, dissenting.

Today's decision effects a vast expansion of the power of federal courts, unauthorized by Rule or statute. I have no doubt petitioner engaged in sanctionable conduct that warrants severe corrective measures. But our outrage at his conduct should not obscure the boundaries of settled legal categories.

With all respect, I submit the Court commits two fundamental errors. First, it permits the exercise of inherent sanctioning powers without prior recourse to controlling Rules and statutes, thereby arrogating to federal courts Congress' power to regulate fees and costs. Second, the Court upholds the wholesale shift of respondent's attorney's fees to petitioner, even though the District Court opinion reveals that petitioner was sanctioned at least in part for his so-called bad-faith breach of contract. The extension of inherent authority to sanction a party's prelitigation conduct subverts the American Rule and turns the Erie doctrine upside down by punishing petitioner's primary conduct contrary to Louisiana law. Because I believe the proper exercise of inherent powers requires exhaustion of express sanctioning provisions and much greater caution in their application to redress prelitigation conduct, I dissent.

I

The Court's first error lies in its failure to require reliance, when possible, on the panoply of express sanctioning provisions provided by Congress.

A

The American Rule prohibits federal courts from awarding attorney's fees in the absence of a statute or contract providing for a fee award. Alyeska Pipeline Service Co. v. Wilderness Society, 421 U. S. 240, 258-259 (1975). The Rule recognizes that Congress defines the procedural and remedial powers of federal courts, Sibbach v. Wilson & Co., 312 U. S. 1, 9-10 (1941); McIntire v. Wood, 7 Cranch 504, 505-506 (1813), and controls the costs, sanctions, and fines available there, Kaiser Aluminum & Chemical Corp. v. Bonjorno, 494 U. S. 827, 835 (1990) ("[T]he allocation of the costs accruing from litigation is a matter for the legislature, not the courts"); Alyeska Pipeline Co., supra, at 262 ("[T]he circumstances under which attorney's fees are to be awarded and the range of discretion of the courts in making those awards are matters for Congress to determine").

By direct action and delegation, Congress has exercised this constitutional prerogative to provide district courts with a comprehensive arsenal of Federal Rules and statutes to protect themselves from abuse. A district court can punish contempt of its authority, including disobedience of its process, by fine or imprisonment, 18 U. S. C. § 401; award costs, expenses, and attorney's fees against attorneys who multiply proceedings vexatiously, 28 U. S. C. § 1927; sanction a party and/or the party's attorney for filing groundless pleadings, motions, or other papers, Fed. Rule Civ. Proc. 11; sanction a party and/or his attorney for failure to abide by a pretrial order, Fed. Rule Civ. Proc. 16(f); sanction a party and/or his attorney for baseless discovery requests or objections, Fed. Rule Civ. Proc. 26(g); award expenses caused by a failure to attend a deposition or to serve a subpoena on a party to be deposed, Fed. Rule Civ. Proc. 30(g); award expenses when a party fails to respond to discovery requests or fails to participate in the framing of a discovery plan, Fed. Rules Civ. Proc. 37(d) and (g); dismiss an action or claim of a party that fails to prosecute, to comply with the Federal Rules, or to obey an order of the court, Fed. Rule Civ. Proc. 41(b); punish any person who fails to obey a subpoena, Fed. Rule Civ. Proc. 45(f); award expenses and/or contempt damages when a party presents an affidavit in a summary judgment motion in bad faith or for the purpose of delay, Fed. Rule Civ. Proc. 56(g); and make rules governing local practice that are not inconsistent with the Federal Rules, Fed. Rule Civ. Proc. 81. See also 28 U. S. C. § 1912 (power to award just damages and costs on affirmance); Fed. Rule App. Proc. 38 (power to award damages and costs for frivolous appeal).

The Court holds nonetheless that a federal court may ignore these provisions and exercise inherent power to sanction bad-faith misconduct "even if procedural rules exist which sanction the same conduct." Ante, at 49. The Court describes the relation between express sanctioning provisions and inherent power to shift fees as a sanction for bad-faith conduct in a number of ways. At one point it states that where "neither the statute nor the Rules are up to the task [i. e., cover all the sanctionable conduct], the court may safely rely on its inherent power." Ante, at 50. At another it says that courts may place exclusive reliance on inherent authority whenever "conduct sanctionable under the Rules was intertwined within conduct that only the inherent power could address." Ante, at 51. While the details of the Court's rule remain obscure, its general approach is clear: When express Rules and statutes provided by Congress do not reach the entirety of a litigant's bad-faith conduct, including conduct occurring before litigation commenced, a district court may disregard the requirements of otherwise applicable Rules and statutes and instead exercise inherent power to impose sanctions. The only limitation on this sanctioning authority appears to be a finding at some point of "bad faith," a standard the Court fails to define.

This explanation of the permitted sphere of inherent powers to shift fees as a sanction for bad-faith litigation conduct is as illegitimate as it is unprecedented. The American Rule recognizes that the Legislature, not the Judiciary, possesses constitutional responsibility for defining sanctions and fees; the bad-faith exception to the Rule allows courts to assess fees not provided for by Congress "in narrowly defined circumstances." Roadway Express, Inc. v. Piper, 447 U. S. 752, 765 (1980). By allowing courts to ignore express Rules and statutes on point, however, the Court treats inherent powers as the norm and textual bases of authority as the exception. And although the Court recognizes that Congress in theory may channel inherent powers through passage of sanctioning Rules, it relies on Weinberger v. Romero-Barcelo, 456 U. S. 305 (1982), a decision that has nothing to do with inherent authority, to create a powerful presumption against congressional control of judicial sanctions. Ante, at 47.

The Court has the presumption backwards. Inherent powers are the exception, not the rule, and their assertion requires special justification in each case. Like all applications of inherent power, the authority to sanction bad-faith litigation practices can be exercised only when necessary to preserve the authority of the court. See Roadway Express, Inc. v. Piper, supra, at 764 (inherent powers "are those which `are necessary to the exercise of all others'"); Young v. United States ex rel. Vuitton et Fils S. A., 481 U. S. 787, 819-820 (1987) (SCALIA, J., concurring in judgment) (inherent powers only those "necessary to permit the courts to function").

The necessity limitation, which the Court brushes aside almost without mention, ante, at 43, prescribes the rule for the correct application of inherent powers. Although this case does not require articulation of a comprehensive definition of the term "necessary," at the very least a court need not exercise inherent power if Congress has provided a mechanism to achieve the same end. Consistent with our unaltered admonition that inherent powers must be exercised "with great caution," Ex parte Burr, 9 Wheat. 529, 531 (1824), the necessity predicate limits the exercise of inherent powers to those exceptional instances in which congressionally authorized powers fail to protect the processes of the court. Inherent powers can be exercised only when necessary, and there is no necessity if a Rule or statute provides a basis for sanctions. It follows that a district court should rely on text-based authority derived from Congress rather than inherent power in every case where the text-based authority applies.

Despite the Court's suggestion to the contrary, ante, at 48-49, our cases recognize that Rules and statutes limit the exercise of inherent authority. In Societe Internationale pour Participations Industrielles et Commerciales, S. A. v. Rogers, 357 U. S. 197 (1958), we rejected the Court of Appeals' reliance on inherent powers to uphold a dismissal of a complaint for failure to comply with a production order. Noting that "[r]eliance upon ... `inherent power' can only obscure analysis of the problem," we held that "whether a court has power to dismiss a complaint because of non-compliance with a production order depends exclusively upon Rule 37." Id., at 207. Similarly, in Bank of Nova Scotia v. United States, 487 U. S. 250, 254 (1988), we held that a federal court could not invoke its inherent supervisory power to circumvent the harmless-error inquiry prescribed by Federal Rule of Criminal Procedure 52(a). And Ex parte Robinson, 19 Wall. 505 (1874), the very case the Court cites for the proposition that "`[t]he power to punish for contempts is inherent in all courts,'" ante, at 44, held that Congress had defined and limited this inherent power through enactment of the contempt statute. "The enactment is a limitation upon the manner in which the [contempt] power shall be exercised." 19 Wall., at 512.

The Court ignores these rulings and relies instead on two decisions which "indicat[e] that the inherent power of a court can be invoked even if procedural rules exist which sanction the same conduct." Ante, at 49. The "indications" the Court discerns in these decisions do not withstand scrutiny. In Roadway Express, Inc. v. Piper, supra, we held that the costs recoverable under a prior version of 28 U. S. C. § 1927 for discovery abuse did not include attorney's fees. In the remand instruction, the Court mentioned that the District Court might consider awarding attorney's fees under either Federal Rule of Civil Procedure 37 or its inherent authority to sanction bad-faith litigation practices. 447 U. S., at 767-768. The decision did not discuss the relation between Rule 37 and the inherent power of federal courts, and certainly did not suggest that federal courts could rely on inherent powers to the exclusion of a Federal Rule on point.

The Court also misreads Link v. Wabash R. Co., 370 U. S. 626 (1962). Link held that a Federal District Court possessed inherent power to dismiss a case sua sponte for failure to prosecute. The majority suggests that this holding contravened a prior version of Federal Rule of Civil Procedure 41(b), which the Court today states "appeared to require a motion from a party," ante, at 49 (emphasis added). Contrary to the Court's characterization, the holding in Link turned on a determination that Rule 41(b) contained "permissive language ... which merely authorizes a motion by the defendant," 370 U. S., at 630 (emphasis added). Link reasoned that "[n]either the permissive language of the Rule ... nor its policy" meant that the Rule "abrogate[d]" the inherent power of federal courts to dismiss sua sponte. The permissive language at issue in Link distinguishes it from the present context, because some sanctioning provisions, such as Rules 11 and 26(g), are cast in mandatory terms.

In addition to dismissing some of our precedents and misreading others, the Court ignores the commands of the Federal Rules of Civil Procedure, which support the conclusion that a court should rely on rules, and not inherent powers, whenever possible. Like the Federal Rules of Criminal Procedure, the Federal Rules of Civil Procedure are "as binding as any statute duly enacted by Congress, and federal courts have no more discretion to disregard the Rule[s'] mandate than they do to disregard constitutional or statutory provisions." Bank of Nova Scotia v. United States, supra, at 255. See also Fed. Rule Civ. Proc. 1 (Federal Rules "govern the procedure in the United States district courts in all suits of a civil nature") (emphasis added). Two of the most prominent sanctioning provisions, Rules 11 and 26(g), mandate the imposition of sanctions when litigants violate the Rules' certification standards. See Fed. Rule Civ. Proc. 11 (court "shall impose ... an appropriate sanction" for violation of certification standard); Fed. Rule Civ. Proc. 26(g) (same); see also Business Guides, Inc. v. Chromatic Communications Enterprises, Inc., 498 U. S. 533, 543 (1991) (Rule 11 "requires that sanctions be imposed where a signature is present but fails to satisfy the certification standard").

The Rules themselves thus reject the contention that they may be discarded in a court's discretion. Disregard of applicable Rules also circumvents the rulemaking procedures in 28 U. S. C. § 2071 et seq., which Congress designed to assure that procedural innovations like those announced today "shall be introduced only after mature consideration of informed opinion from all relevant quarters, with all the opportunities for comprehensive and integrated treatment which such consideration affords." Miner v. Atlass, 363 U. S. 641, 650 (1960).

B

Upon a finding of bad faith, courts may now ignore any and all textual limitations on sanctioning power. By inviting district courts to rely on inherent authority as a substitute for attention to the careful distinctions contained in the Rules and statutes, today's decision will render these sources of authority superfluous in many instances. A number of pernicious practical effects will follow.

The Federal Rules establish explicit standards for, and explicit checks against, the exercise of judicial authority. Rule 11 provides a useful illustration. It requires a district court to impose reasonable sanctions, including attorney's fees, when a party or attorney violates the certification standards that attach to the signing of certain legal papers. A district court must (rather than may) issue sanctions under Rule 11 when particular individuals (signers) file certain types (groundless, unwarranted, vexatious) of documents (pleadings, motions and papers). Rule 11's certification requirements apply to all signers of documents, including represented parties, see Business Guides, Inc. v. Chromatic Communications Enterprises, Inc., supra, but law firms are not responsible for the signatures of their attorneys, see Pavelic & LeFlore v. Marvel Entertainment Group, 493 U. S. 120, 125-127 (1989), and the Rule does not apply to papers filed in fora other than district courts, see Cooter & Gell v. Hartmarx Corp., 496 U. S. 384, 405-409 (1990). These definite standards give litigants notice of proscribed conduct and make possible meaningful review for misuse of discretion—review which focuses on the misapplication of legal standards. See id., at 402 (misuse of discretion standard does "not preclude the appellate court's correction of a district court's legal errors").

By contrast, courts apply inherent powers without specific definitional or procedural limits. True, if a district court wishes to shift attorney's fees as a sanction, it must make a finding of bad faith to circumvent the American Rule. But today's decision demonstrates how little guidance or limitation the undefined bad-faith predicate provides. The Court states without elaboration that courts must "comply with the mandates of due process ... in determining that the requisite bad faith exists," ante, at 50, but the Court's bad-faith standard, at least without adequate definition, thwarts the first requirement of due process, namely, that "[a]ll are entitled to be informed as to what the State commands or forbids." Lanzetta v. New Jersey, 306 U. S. 451, 453 (1939). This standardless exercise of judicial power may appear innocuous in this litigation between commercial actors. But the same unchecked power also can be applied to chill the advocacy of litigants attempting to vindicate all other important federal rights.

In addition, the scope of sanctionable conduct under the bad-faith rule appears unlimited. As the Court boasts, "whereas each of the other mechanisms [in Rules and statutes] reaches only certain individuals or conduct, the inherent power extends to a full range of litigation abuses." Ante, at 46. By allowing exclusive resort to inherent authority whenever "conduct sanctionable under the Rules was intertwined within conduct that only the inherent power could address," ante, at 51, the Court encourages all courts in the federal system to find bad-faith misconduct in order to eliminate the need to rely on specific textual provisions. This will ensure the uncertain development of the meaning and scope of these express sanctioning provisions by encouraging their disuse, and will defeat, at least in the area of sanctions, Congress' central goal in enacting the Federal Rules— "`uniformity in the federal courts.'" Hanna v. Plumer, 380 U. S. 460, 472 (1965). Finally, as Part IV of the Court's opinion demonstrates, the lack of any legal requirement other than the talismanic recitation of the phrase "bad faith" will foreclose meaningful review of sanctions based on inherent authority. See Cooter & Gell v. Hartmarx Corp., supra, at 402.

Despite these deficiencies, the Court insists that concern about collateral litigation requires courts to place exclusive reliance on inherent authority in cases, like this one, which involve conduct sanctionable under both express provisions and inherent authority:

"In circumstances such as these in which all of a litigant's conduct is deemed santionable, requiring a court first to apply Rules and statutes containing sanctioning provisions to discrete occurrences before invoking inherent power to address remaining instances of sanctionable conduct would serve only to foster extensive and needless satellite litigation, which is contrary to the aim of the Rules themselves." Ante, at 51.

We are bound, however, by the Rules themselves, not their "aim," and the Rules require that they be applied, in accordance with their terms, to much of the conduct in this case. We should not let policy concerns about the litigation effects of following the Rules distort their clear commands.

Nothing in the foregoing discussion suggests that the fee-shifting and sanctioning provisions in the Federal Rules and Title 28 eliminate the inherent power to impose sanctions for certain conduct. Limitations on a power do not constitute its abrogation. Cases can arise in which a federal court must act to preserve its authority in a manner not provided for by the Federal Rules or Title 28. But as the number and scope of Rules and statutes governing litigation misconduct increase, the necessity to resort to inherent authority—a predicate to its proper application—lessens. Indeed, it is difficult to imagine a case in which a court can, as the District Court did here, rely on inherent authority as the exclusive basis for sanctions.

C

The District Court's own findings concerning abuse of its processes demonstrate that the sanctionable conduct in this case implicated a number of Rules and statutes upon which it should have relied. Rule 11 is the principal provision on point. The District Court found that petitioner and his counsel filed a number of "frivolous pleadings" (including "baseless, affirmative defenses and counterclaims") that contained "deliberate untruths and fabrications." NASCO, Inc. v. Calcasieu Television & Radio, Inc., 124 F. R. D. 120, 127-128, 135 (WD La. 1989). Rule 11 sanctions extend to "the person who signed [a paper], a represented party, or both." The court thus had a nondefeasible duty to impose sanctions under Rule 11.

The Court concedes that Rule 11 applied to some of the conduct in this case, ante, at 50, and even hints that the Rule might have sufficed as a basis for all of the sanctions imposed, ante, at 42, n. 8. It fails to explain, however, why the District Court had the discretion to ignore Rule 11's mandatory langnage and not impose sanctions under the Rule against Chambers. Nor does the Court inform us why Chambers' attorneys were not sanctioned under Rule 11. Although the District Court referred to Chambers as the "strategist" for the abusive conduct, it made plain that petitioner's attorneys as well as petitioner were responsible for the tactics. For example, the District Court stated:

"[Petitioner's] attorneys, without any investigation whatsoever, filed [the baseless charges and counterclaims].

We find ... that these attorneys knew, at the time that they were filed, that they were false." 124 F. R. D., at 128.

The court further stressed that "Chambers, through his attorneys, filed answers and counterclaims ... which both Chambers and his attorneys knew were false at the time they were filed." Id., at 143. In light of Rule 11's mandatory language, the District Court had a duty to impose at least some sanctions under Rule 11 against Chambers' attorneys.

The District Court should have relied as well upon other sources of authority to impose sanctions. The court found that Chambers and his attorneys requested "[a]bsolutely needless depositions" as well as "continuances of trial dates, extensions of deadlines and deferments of scheduled discovery" that "were simply part of the sordid scheme of deliberate misuse of the judicial process ... to defeat NASCO's claim by harassment, repeated and endless delay, mountainous expense and waste of financial resources." Id., at 128. The intentional pretrial delays could have been sanctioned under Federal Rule of Civil Procedure 16(f), which enables courts to impose sanctions, including attorney's fees, when a party or attorney "fails to participate in good faith" in certain pretrial proceedings; the multiple discovery abuses should have been redressed by "an appropriate sanction, ... including a reasonable attorney's fee," under Federal Rule of Civil Procedure 26(g). The District Court also could have sanctioned Chambers and his attorneys for the various bad-faith affidavits they presented in their summary judgment motions, see 124 F. R. D., at 128, 135, under Federal Rule of Civil Procedure 56(g), a Rule that permits the award of expenses and attorney's fees and the additional sanction of contempt. In addition, the District Court could have relied to a much greater extent on 18 U. S. C. § 401 to punish the "contempt of its authority" and "[d]isobedience ... to its ... process" that petitioner and his counsel displayed throughout the proceedings.

Finally, the District Court was too quick to dismiss reliance on 28 U. S. C. § 1927, which allows it to award costs and attorney's fees against an "attorney ... who ... multiplies the proceedings in any case unreasonably and vexatiously." The District Court refused to apply the provision because it did not reach petitioner's conduct as a nonattorney. 124 F. R. D., at 138-139. While the District Court has discretion not to apply § 1927, it cannot disregard the statute in the face of attorney misconduct covered by that provision to rely instead on inherent powers which by definition can be invoked only when necessary.

II

When a District Court imposes sanctions so immense as here under a power so amorphous as inherent authority, it must ensure that its order is confined to conduct under its own authority and jurisdiction to regulate. The District Court failed to discharge this obligation, for it allowed sanctions to be awarded for petitioner's prelitigation breach of contract. The majority, perhaps wary of the District Court's authority to extend its inherent power to sanction prelitigation conduct, insists that "the District Court did not attempt to sanction petitioner for breach of contract, but rather imposed sanctions for the fraud he perpetrated on the court and the bad faith he displayed toward both his adversary and the court throughout the course of the litigation." Ante, at 54 (footnote omitted).

Based on this premise, the Court appears to disclaim that its holding reaches prelitigation conduct. Ante, at 54, and nn. 16-17. This does not make the opinion on this point correct, of course, for the District Court's opinion, in my view, sanctioned petitioner's prelitigation conduct in express terms. Because I disagree with the Court's characterization of the District Court opinion, and because I believe the Court's casual analysis of inherent authority portends a dangerous extension of that authority to prelitigation conduct, I explain why inherent authority should not be so extended and why the District Court's order should be reversed.

The District Court's own candid and extensive opinion reveals that the bad faith for which petitioner was sanctioned extended beyond the litigation tactics and comprised as well what the District Court considered to be bad faith in refusing to perform the underlying contract three weeks before the lawsuit began. The court made explicit reference, for instance, to "this massive and absolutely unnecessary lawsuit forced on NASCO by Chambers' arbitrary and arrogant refusal to honor and perform this perfectly legal and enforceable contract." 124 F. R. D., at 136. See also id., at 143 ("Chambers arbitrarily and without legal cause refused to perform, forcing NASCO to bring its suit for specific performance"); ibid. ("Chambers, knowing that NASCO had a good and valid contract, hired Gray to find a defense and arbitrarily refused to perform, thereby forcing NASCO to bring its suit for specific performance and injunctive relief"); id., at 125 (petitioner's "unjustified and arbitrary refusal to file" the FCC application "was in absolute bad faith"). The District Court makes the open and express concession that it is sanctioning petitioner for his breach of contract:

"[T]he balance of ... fees and expenses included in the sanctions, would not have been incurred by NASCO if Chambers had not defaulted and forced NASCO to bring this suit. There is absolutely no reason why Chambers should not reimburse in full all attorney's fees and expenses that NASCO, by Chambers' action, was forced to pay." Id., at 143.

The trial court also explained that "[t]he attorney's fees and expenses charged to NASCO by its attorneys ... flowed from and were a direct result of this suit. We shall include them in the attorney's fees sanctions." Id., at 142 (emphasis added).

Despite the Court's equivocation on the subject, ante, at 54, n. 16, it is impermissible to allow a District Court acting pursuant to its inherent authority to sanction such prelitigation primary conduct. A court's inherent authority extends only to remedy abuses of the judicial process. By contrast, awarding damages for a violation of a legal norm, here the binding obligation of a legal contract, is a matter of substantive law, see Marek v. Chesny, 473 U. S. 1, 35 (1985) ("right to attorney's fees is `substantive' under any reasonable definition of that term"); see also Alyeska, 421 U. S., at 260-261, and n. 33, which must be defined either by Congress (in cases involving federal law) or by the States (in diversity cases).

The American Rule recognizes these principles. It bars a federal court from shifting fees as a matter of substantive policy, but its bad-faith exception permits fee shifting as a sanction to the extent necessary to protect the judicial process. The Rule protects each person's right to go to federal court to define and to vindicate substantive rights. "[S]ince litigation is at best uncertain one should not be penalized for merely defending or prosecuting a lawsuit." Fleischmann Distilling Corp. v. Maier Brewing Co., 386 U. S. 714, 718 (1967). When a federal court, through invocation of its inherent powers, sanctions a party for bad-faith prelitigation conduct, it goes well beyond the exception to the American Rule and violates the Rule's careful balance between open access to the federal court system and penalties for the willful abuse of it.

By exercising inherent power to sanction prelitigation conduct, the District Court exercised authority where Congress gave it none. The circumstance that this exercise of power occurred in a diversity case compounds the error. When a federal court sits in diversity jurisdiction, it lacks constitutional authority to fashion rules of decision governing primary contractual relations. See Erie R. Co. v. Tompkins, 304 U. S. 64, 78 (1938); Hanna v. Plumer, 380 U. S., at 471-472. See generally Ely, The Irrepressible Myth of Erie, 87 Harv. L. Rev. 693, 702-706 (1974). The Erie principle recognizes that "[e]xcept in matters governed by the Federal Constitution or by Acts of Congress, the law to be applied in any [diversity] case is the law of the State." 304 U. S., at 78. The inherent power exercised here violates the fundamental tenet of federalism announced in Erie by regnlating primary behavior that the Constitution leaves to the exclusive province of States.

The full effect of the District Court's encroachment on state prerogatives can be appreciated by recalling that the rationale for the bad-faith exception is punishment. Hall v. Cole, 412 U. S. 1, 5 (1973). To the extent that the District Court imposed sanctions by reason of the so-called bad-faith breach of contract, its decree is an award of punitive damages for the breach. Louisiana prohibits punitive damages "unless expressly authorized by statute," International Harvester Credit Corp. v. Seale, 518 So. 2d 1039, 1041 (La. 1988); and no Louisiana statute authorizes attorney's fees for breach of contract as a part of damages in an ordinary case, Ogea v. Loffland Brothers Co., 622 F. 2d 186, 190 (CA5 1980); Rutherford v. Impson, 366 So. 2d 944, 947 (La. App. 1978). One rationale for Louisiana's policy is its determination that "an award of compensatory damages will serve the same deterrent purpose as an award of punitive damages." Ricard v. State, 390 So. 2d 882, 886 (La. 1980). If respondent had brought this suit in state court it would not have recovered extra damages for breach of contract by reason of the so-called willful character of the breach. Respondent's decision to bring this suit in federal rather than state court resulted in a significant expansion of the substantive scope of its remedy. This is the result prohibited by Erie and the principles that flow from it.

As the Court notes, there are some passages in the District Court opinion suggesting its sanctions were confined to litigation conduct. See ante, at 55, n. 17. ("[T]he sanctions imposed `appl[ied] only to sanctionable acts which occurred in connection with the proceedings in the trial Court'"). But these passages in no way contradict the other statements by the trial court which make express reference to prelitigation conduct. At most, these passages render the court's order ambiguous, for the District Court appears to have adopted an expansive definition of "acts which occurred in connection with" the litigation. There is no question but that some sanctionable acts did occur in court. The problem is that the District Court opinion avoids any clear delineation of the acts being sanctioned and the power invoked to do so. This confusion in the premises of the District Court's order highlights the mischief caused by reliance on undefined inherent powers rather than on Rules and statutes that proscribe particular behavior. The ambiguity of the scope of the sanctionable conduct cannot be resolved against petitioner alone, who, despite the conceded bad-faith conduct of his attorneys, has been slapped with all of respondent's not inconsiderable attorney's fees. At the very least, adherence to the rule of law requires the case to be remanded to the District Court for clarification on the scope of the sanctioned conduct.

III

My discussion should not be construed as approval of the behavior of petitioner and his attorneys in this case. Quite the opposite. Our Rules permit sanctions because much of the conduct of the sort encountered here degrades the profession and disserves justice. District courts must not permit this abuse and must not hesitate to give redress through the Rules and statutes prescribed. It may be that the District Court could have imposed the full million dollar sanction against petitioner through reliance on Federal Rules and statutes, as well as on a proper exercise of its inherent authority. But we should remand here because a federal court must decide cases based on legitimate sources of power. I would reverse the Court of Appeals with instructions to remand to the District Court for a reassessment of sanctions consistent with the principles here set forth. For these reasons, I dissent.

Justice Scalia's dissent in Chisom v. Roemer (June 20, 1991)

JUSTICE SCALIA, with whom THE CHIEF JUSTICE and JUSTICE KENNEDY join, dissenting.

Section 2 of the Voting Rights Act is not some all-purpose weapon for well-intentioned judges to wield as they please in the battle against discrimination. It is a statute. I thought we had adopted a regular method for interpreting the meaning of language in a statute: first, find the ordinary meaning of the language in its textual context; and second, using established canons of construction, ask whether there is any clear indication that some permissible meaning other than the ordinary one applies. If not -- and especially if a good reason for the ordinary meaning appears plain -- we apply that ordinary meaning. See, e.g., West Virginia University Hospitals, Inc. v. Casey, 499 U. S. 83, 499 U. S. 98-99 (1991); Demarest v. Manspeaker, 498 U. S. 184, 498 U. S. 190 (1991); United States v. Ron Pair Enterprises, Inc., 489 U. S. 235, 489 U. S. 241 (1989); Pennsylvania Dept. of Public Welfare v. Davenport, 495 U. S. 552, 495 U. S. 552 (1990); Caminetti v. United States, 242 U. S. 470, 242 U. S. 485 (1917); Public Citizen v.

Department of Justice, 491 U. S. 440, 491 U. S. 470 (1989) (KENNEDY, J., concurring in judgment).

Today, however, the Court adopts a method quite out of accord with that usual practice. It begins not with what the statute says, but with an expectation about what the statute must mean absent particular phenomena ("we are convinced that, if Congress had . . . an intent [to exclude judges], Congress would have made it explicit in the statute, or at least some of the Members would have identified or mentioned it at some point in the unusually extensive legislative history," ante at 501 U. S. 396 (emphasis added)); and the Court then interprets the words of the statute to fulfill its expectation. Finding nothing in the legislative history affirming that judges were excluded from the coverage of § 2, the Court gives the phrase "to elect representatives" the quite extraordinary meaning that covers the election of judges.

As method, this is just backwards, and however much we may be attracted by the result it produces in a particular case, we should in every case resist it. Our job begins with a text that Congress has passed and the President has signed. We are to read the words of that text as any ordinary Member of Congress would have read them, see Holmes, The Theory of Legal Interpretation, 12 Harv.L.Rev. 417 (1899), and apply the meaning so determined. In my view, that reading reveals that § 2 extends to vote dilution claims for the elections of representatives only, and judges are not representatives.

I

As the Court suggests, the 1982 amendments to the Voting Rights Act were adopted in response to our decision in City of Mobile v. Bolden, 446 U. S. 55 (1980), which had held that the scope of the original Voting Rights Act was coextensive with the Fifteenth Amendment, and thus proscribed intentional discrimination only. I agree with the Court that that original legislation, directed towards intentional discrimination, applied to all elections, for it clearly said so:

"No voting qualification or prerequisite to voting, or standard, practice, or procedure shall be imposed or applied by any State or political subdivision to deny or abridge the right of any citizen of the United States to vote on account of race or color."

79 Stat. 437.

The 1982 amendments, however, radically transformed the Act. As currently written, the statute proscribes intentional discrimination only if it has a discriminatory effect, but proscribes practices with discriminatory effect, whether or not intentional. This new "results" criterion provides a powerful, albeit sometimes blunt, weapon with which to attack even the most subtle forms of discrimination. The question we confront here is how broadly the new remedy applies. The foundation of the Court's analysis, the itinerary for its journey in the wrong direction, is the following statement:

"It is difficult to believe that Congress, in an express effort to broaden the protection afforded by the Voting Rights Act, withdrew, without comment, an important category of elections from that protection."

Ante at 501 U. S. 404. There are two things wrong with this. First is the notion that Congress cannot be credited with having achieved anything of major importance by simply saying it, in ordinary language, in the text of a statute, "without comment" in the legislative history. As the Court colorfully puts it, if the dog of legislative history has not barked, nothing of great significance can have transpired. Ante at 501 U. S. 396, n. 23. Apart from the questionable wisdom of assuming that dogs will bark when something important is happening, see 1 T. Livius, The History of Rome 411-413 (1892) (D. Spillan translation), we have forcefully and explicitly rejected the Conan Doyle approach to statutory construction in the past. See Harrison v. PPG Industries, Inc., 446 U. S. 578, 446 U. S. 592 (1980) ("In ascertaining the meaning of a statute, a court cannot, in the manner of Sherlock Holmes, pursue the theory of the dog that did not bark"). We are here to apply the statute, not legislative history, and certainly not the absence of legislative history. Statutes are the law though sleeping dogs lie. See, e.g., Sedima, S.P.R.L. v. Imrex Co., 473 U. S. 479, 473 U. S. 495-496, n. 13 (1985); Williams v. United States, 458 U. S. 279, 458 U. S. 294-295 (1982) (MARSHALL, J., dissenting).

The more important error in the Court's starting-point, however, is the assumption that the effect of excluding judges from the revised § 2 would be to "withdr[aw] . . . an important category of elections from [the] protection [of the Voting Rights Act]." Ante at 501 U. S. 404. There is absolutely no question here of withdrawing protection. Since the pre-1982 content of § 2 was coextensive with the Fifteenth Amendment, the entirety of that protection subsisted in the Constitution, and could be enforced through the other provisions of the Voting Rights Act. Nothing was lost from the prior coverage; all of the new "results" protection was an add-on. The issue is not, therefore, as the Court would have it, ante at 501 U. S. 395-396, whether Congress has cut back on the coverage of the Voting Rights Act; the issue is how far it has extended it. Thus, even if a court's expectations were a proper basis for interpreting the text of a statute, while there would be reason to expect that Congress was not "withdrawing" protection, there is no particular reason to expect that the supplemental protection it provided was any more extensive than the text of the statute said.

What it said, with respect to establishing a violation of the amended § 2, is the following:

"A violation . . . is established if . . . it is shown that the political processes leading to nomination or election . . . are not equally open to participation by members of a [protected] class . . . in that its members have less opportunity than other members of the electorate to participate in the political process and to elect representatives of their choice."

42 U.S.C. § 1973(b) (emphasis added). Though this text nowhere speaks of "vote dilution," Thornburg v. Gingles, 478 U. S. 30 (1986), understood it to proscribe practices which produce that result, identifying as the statutory basis for a dilution claim the second of the two phrases highlighted above -- "to elect representatives of their choice." [1] Under this interpretation, the other highlighted phrase -- "to participate in the political process" -- is left for other, non-dilution § 2 violations. If, for example, a county permitted vote

registration for only three hours one day a week, and that made it more difficult for blacks to register than whites, blacks would have less opportunity "to participate in the political process," than whites, and § 2 would therefore be violated -- even if the number of potential black voters was so small that they would, on no hypothesis, be able to elect their own candidate, see Blumstein, Proving Race Discrimination, 69 Va.L.Rev. 633, 706-707 (1983).

The Court, however, now rejects Thornburg's reading of the statute, and asserts that, before a violation of § 2 can be made out, both conditions of § 2(b) must be met. As the Court explains,

"As the statute is written, . . . the inability to elect representatives of their choice is not sufficient to establish a violation unless, under the totality of the circumstances, it can also be said that the members of the protected class have less opportunity to participate in the political process. The statute does not create two separate and distinct rights. . . . It would distort the plain meaning of the sentence to substitute the word 'or' for the word 'and.' Such radical surgery would be required to separate the opportunity to participate from the opportunity to elect."

Ante at 501 U. S. 397. This is unquestionably wrong. If both conditions must be violated before there is any § 2 violation, then minorities who form such a small part of the electorate in a particular jurisdiction that they could on no conceivable basis "elect representatives of their choice" would be entirely without § 2 protection. Since, as the Court's analysis suggests, the "results" test of § 2 judges a violation of the "to elect" provision on the basis of whether the practice in question prevents actual election, then a protected class that with or without the practice will be unable to elect its candidate can be denied equal opportunity "to participate in the political process" with impunity. The Court feels compelled to reach this implausible conclusion of a "singular right" because the "to participate" clause and the "to elect" clause are joined by the conjunction "and." It is unclear to me why the rules of English usage require that conclusion here, any more than they do in the case of the First Amendment -- which reads

"Congress shall make no law . . . abridging . . . the right of the people peaceably to assemble, and to petition the Government for a redress of grievances."

This has not generally been thought to protect the right peaceably to assemble only when the purpose of the assembly is to petition the Government for a redress of grievances. So also here, one is deprived of an equal "opportunity . . . to participate . . . and to elect" if either the opportunity to participate or the opportunity to elect is unequal. The point is, in any event, not central to the present case -- and it is sad to see the Court repudiate Thornburg, create such mischief in the application of § 2, and even cast doubt upon the First Amendment, merely to deprive the State of the argument that elections for judges remain covered by § 2 even though they are not subject to vote dilution claims. [2]

The Court, petitioners, and petitioners' amici have labored mightily to establish that there is a meaning of "representatives" that would include judges, see, e.g., Brief for Lawyers Committee for Civil Rights as Amicus Curiae 10-11, and no doubt there is. But our job is not to scavenge the world of English usage to discover whether there is any possible meaning of "representatives" which suits our preconception that the statute includes judges; our job is to determine whether the ordinary meaning includes them, and if it does not, to ask whether there is any solid indication in the text or structure of the statute that something other than ordinary meaning was intended.

There is little doubt that the ordinary meaning of "representatives" does not include judges, see Webster's Second New International Dictionary 2114 (1950). The Court's feeble argument to the contrary is that "representatives" means those who "are chosen by popular election." Ante at 501 U. S. 399. On that hypothesis, the fan-elected members of the baseball All-Star teams are "representatives" -- hardly a common, if even a permissible, usage. Surely the word "representative" connotes one who is not only elected by the people, but who also, at a minimum, acts on behalf of the people. Judges do that in a sense -- but not in the ordinary sense. As the captions of the pleadings in some States still display, it is the prosecutor who represents "the People"; the judge represents the Law -- which often requires him to rule against the People. It is precisely because we do not ordinarily conceive of judges as representatives that we held judges not within the Fourteenth Amendment's requirement of "one person, one vote." Wells v. Edwards, 347 F.Supp. 453 (MD La.1972), aff'd, 409 U. S. 1095 (1973). The point is not that a State could not make judges in some senses representative, or that all judges must be conceived of in the Article III mold, but rather, that giving "representatives" its ordinary meaning, the ordinary speaker in 1982 would not have applied the word to judges, see Holmes, The Theory of Legal Interpretation, 12 Harv.L.Rev. 417 (1899). It remains only to ask whether there is good indication that ordinary meaning does not apply.

There is one canon of construction that might be applicable to the present case which, in some circumstances, would counter ordinary meaning -- but here it would only have the effect of reinforcing it. We applied that canon to another case this Term, concerning, curiously enough, the very same issue of whether state judges are covered by the provisions of a federal statute. In Gregory v. Ashcroft, post, p. 501 U. S. 452, we say that, unless it was clear that the term "appointee[s] on the policymaking level" did not include judges, we would construe it to include them, since the contrary construction would cause the statute to intrude upon the structure of state government, establishing a federal qualification for state judicial office. Such intrusion, we said, requires a "plain statement" before we will acknowledge it. See also Will v. Michigan Dept. of State Police, 491 U. S. 58, 491 U. S. 65 (1989); Atascadero State Hospital v. Scanlon, 473 U. S. 234, 473 U. S. 242 (1985); Pennhurst State School and Hospital v. Halderman, 465 U. S. 89, 465 U. S. 99 (1984). If the same principle were applied here, we would have double reason to give "representatives" its ordinary meaning. It is true, however, that, in Gregory, interpreting the statute to include judges would have made them the only high-level state officials affected, whereas here the question is whether judges were excluded from a general imposition upon state elections that unquestionably exists; and, in Gregory, it was questionable whether Congress was invoking its powers under the Fourteenth

Amendment (rather than merely the Commerce Clause), whereas here it is obvious. Perhaps those factors suffice to distinguish the two cases. Moreover, we tacitly rejected a "plain statement" rule as applied to the unamended § 2 in City of Rome v. United States, 446 U. S. 156, 446 U. S. 178-180 (1980), though arguably that was before the rule had developed the significance it currently has. I am content to dispense with the "plain statement" rule in the present case, cf. Pennsylvania v. Union Gas Co., 491 U. S. 1, 491 U. S. 41-42 (1989) (opinion of SCALIA, J.) -- but it says something about the Court's approach to today's decision that the possibility of applying that rule never crossed its mind.

While the "plain statement" rule may not be applicable, there is assuredly nothing whatever that points in the opposite direction, indicating that the ordinary meaning here should not be applied. Far from that, in my view, the ordinary meaning of "representatives" gives clear purpose to congressional action that otherwise would seem pointless. As an initial matter, it is evident that Congress paid particular attention to the scope of elections covered by the "to elect" language. As the Court suggests, that language, for the most part, tracked this Court's opinions in White v. Regester, 412 U. S. 755, 412 U. S. 766 (1973), and Whitcomb v. Chavis, 403 U. S. 124, 403 U. S. 149 (1971), but the word "legislators" was not copied. Significantly, it was replaced not with the more general term "candidates" used repeatedly elsewhere in the Act, see, e.g., 42 U.S.C. §§ 1971(b), (e); 1973i(c), 1973l(c); 1973ff-2; 1974; 1974e, but with the term "representatives," which appears nowhere else in the Act (except as a proper noun referring to Members of the federal lower House, or designees of the Attorney General). The normal meaning of this term is broader than "legislators" (it includes, for example, school boards and city councils as well as senators and representatives), but narrower than "candidates."

The Court says that the seemingly significant refusal to use the term "candidate" and selection of the distinctive term "representative" are really inconsequential, because "candidate" could not have been used. According to the Court, since "candidate" refers to one who has been nominated but not yet elected, the phrase "to elect candidates" would be a contradiction in terms. Ante at 501 U. S. 399-400. The only flaw in this argument is that it is not true, as repeated usage of the formulation "to elect candidates" by this Court itself amply demonstrates. See, e.g., Davis v. Bandemer, 478 U. S. 109, 478 U. S. 131 (1986); Rogers v. Lodge, 458 U. S. 613, 458 U. S. 624 (1982); id. at 458 U. S. 639, n. 18, 458 U. S. 641, n. 22, 458 U. S. 649 (STEVENS, J., dissenting); City of Mobile v. Bolden, 446 U.S. at 446 U. S. 75; United Jewish Organizations of Williamsburgh, Inc. v. Carey, 430 U. S. 144, 430 U. S. 158 (1977); Moore v. Ogilvie, 394 U. S. 814, 394 U. S. 819 (1969); Allen v. State Board of Elections, 393 U. S. 544, 393 U. S. 569 (1969). We even used the phrase repeatedly in Thornburg. Thornburg v. Gingles, 478 U.S. at 478 U. S. 40, 478 U. S. 44, 478 U. S. 50, 478 U. S. 54, 478 U. S. 80; id. at 478 U. S. 86, 478 U. S. 103 (O'CONNOR, J., concurring in judgment); id. at 478 U. S. 107 (opinion of STEVENS, J.). And the phrase is used in the Complaint of the minority plaintiffs in the other § 2 case decoded today. Houston Lawyers' Assn. v. Attorney General of Texas, post, p. 501 U. S. 419. App. in Nos.

90-813, 90-974, p. 22a. In other words, far from being an impermissible choice, "candidates" would have been the natural choice, even if it had not been used repeatedly elsewhere in the statute. It is quite absurd to think that Congress went out of its way to replace that term with "representatives," in order to convey what "candidates" naturally suggests (viz., coverage of all elections) and what "representatives" naturally does not.

A second consideration confirms that "representatives" in § 2 was meant in its ordinary sense. When given its ordinary meaning, it causes the statute to reproduce an established, eminently logical, and perhaps practically indispensable limitation upon the availability of vote dilution claims. Whatever other requirements may be applicable to elections for "representatives" (in the sense of those who are not only elected by but act on behalf of the electorate), those elections, unlike elections for all office-holders, must be conducted in accordance with the equal protection principle of "one person, one vote." And it so happens -- more than coincidentally, I think -- that in every case in which, prior to the amendment of § 2, we recognized the possibility of a vote dilution claim, the principle of "one person, one vote" was applicable. See, e.g., Fortson v. Dorsey, 379 U. S. 433, 379 U. S. 436 (1965); Burns v. Richardson, 384 U. S. 73, 384 U. S. 88 (1966); Whitcomb v. Chavis, supra, 403 U.S. at 403 U. S. 149-150; White v. Regester, supra, 412 U.S. at 412 U. S. 765-767; see also Davis v. Bandemer, 478 U. S. 109, 478 U. S. 131-132 (1986). Indeed, it is the principle of "one person, one vote" that gives meaning to the concept of "dilution." One's vote is diluted if it is not, as it should be, of the same practical effect as everyone else's. Of course the mere fact that an election practice satisfies the constitutional requirement of "one person, one vote" does not establish that there has been no vote dilution for Voting Rights Act purposes, since that looks not merely to equality of individual votes, but also to equality of minority blocs of votes. (White itself, which dealt with a multi-member district, demonstrates this point. See also City of Mobile v. Bolden, supra, 446 U.S. at 446 U. S. 65.) But "one person, one vote" has been the premise and the necessary condition of a vote dilution claim, since it establishes the baseline for computing the voting strength that the minority bloc ought to have. As we have suggested, the first question in a dilution case is whether the "one person, one vote" standard is met, and if it is, the second is whether voting structures nonetheless operate to "minimize or cancel out the voting strength of racial or political elements of the voting population.'" Burns v. Richardson, supra, 384 U.S. at 384 U. S. 88. See also Note, Fair and Effective Voting Strength Under Section 2 of the Voting Rights Act: The Impact of Thornburg v. Gingles on Minority Vote Dilution Litigation, 34 Wayne L.Rev. 303, 323-324 (1987).

Well before Congress amended § 2, we had held that the principle of "one person, one vote" does not apply to the election of judges, Wells v. Edwards, 347 F.Supp. 453 (MD La.1972), aff'd, 409 U. S. 1095 (1973). If Congress was (through use of the extremely inapt word "representatives") making vote dilution claims available with respect to the election of judges, it was, for the first time, extending that remedy to a context in which "one person, one vote" did not apply. That would have been a significant change in the law, and, given the need to identify some other baseline for computing "dilution," that is a matter which those who believe in barking dogs should be astounded to find unmentioned in the legislative history. If "representatives" is given its normal meaning, on the other hand, there is no change in the law (except elimination of the intent requirement), and the silence is entirely understandable.

I frankly find it very difficult to conceive how it is to be determined whether "dilution" has occurred, once one has eliminated both the requirement of actual intent to disfavor minorities and the principle that 10,000 minority votes throughout the State should have as much practical "electability" effect as 10,000 nonminority votes. How does one begin to decide, in such a system, how much elective strength a minority bloc ought to have? I do not assert that it is utterly impossible to impose "vote dilution" restrictions upon an electoral regime that is not based on the "one person, one vote" principle. Congress can define "vote dilution" to be whatever it will, within constitutional bounds. But my point is that "one person, one vote" is inherent in the normal concept of "vote dilution," and was an essential element of the preexisting, judicially crafted definition under § 2; that Congress did not adopt any new definition; that creating a new definition is a seemingly standardless task; and that the word Congress selected ("representative") seems specifically designed to avoid these problems. The Court is stoic about the difficulty of defining "dilution" without a standard of purity, expressing its resolve to stand up to that onerous duty inescapably thrust upon it:

"Even if serious problems lie ahead in applying the 'totality of the circumstances' described in § 2(b), that task, difficult as it may prove to be, cannot justify a judicially created limitation on the coverage of the broadly worded statute, as enacted and amended by Congress."

Ante at 501 U. S. 403. One would think that Congress had said "candidates," rather than "representatives." In reality, however, it is the Court, rather than Congress, that leads us -- quite unnecessarily and indeed with stubborn persistence -- into this morass of unguided and perhaps unguidable judicial interference in democratic elections. The Court attributes to Congress not only the intent to mean something other than what it said, but also the intent to let district courts invent (for there is no precedent where "one person, one vote" did not apply that Congress could have been consulting) what in the world constitutes dilution of a vote that does not have to be equal.

Finally, the Court suggests that there is something "anomalous" about extending coverage under § 5 of the Voting Rights Act to the election of judges, while not extending coverage under § 2 to the same elections. Ante at 501 U. S. 402. This simply misconceives the different roles of § 2 and § 5. The latter requires certain jurisdictions to preclear changes in election methods before those changes are implemented; it is a means of assuring in advance the absence of all electoral illegality, not only that which violates the Voting Rights Act but that which violates the Constitution as well. In my view, judges are within the scope of § 2 for nondilution claims, and thus for those claims, § 5 preclearance would enforce the Voting Rights Act with respect to judges. Moreover, intentional discrimination in the election of judges, whatever its form, is constitutionally prohibited, and the preclearance provision of § 5 gives the government a method by which to prevent that. The scheme makes entire sense without the need to bring judges within the "to elect" provision.

All this is enough to convince me that there is sense to the ordinary meaning of "representative" in § 2(b) -- that there is reason to Congress's choice -- and since there is, then, under our normal presumption, that ordinary meaning prevails. I would read § 2 as extending vote dilution claims to elections for "representatives," but not to elections for judges. For other claims under § 2, however -- those resting on the "to participate in the political process" provision, rather than the "to elect" provision -- no similar restriction would apply. Since the claims here are exclusively claims of dilution, I would affirm the judgment of the Fifth Circuit.

* * * *

As I said at the outset, this case is about method. The Court transforms the meaning of § 2 not because the ordinary meaning is irrational, or inconsistent with other parts of the statute, see, e.g., Green v. Bock Laundry, 490 U. S. 504, 490 U. S. 510-511 (1989); Public Citizen v. Department of Justice, 491 U.S. at 491 U. S. 470 (KENNEDY, J., concurring in judgment), but because it does not fit the Court's conception of what Congress must have had in mind. When we adopt a method that psychoanalyzes Congress, rather than reads its laws, when we employ a tinkerer's toolbox, we do great harm. Not only do we reach the wrong result with respect to the statute at hand, but we poison the well of future legislation, depriving legislators of the assurance that ordinary terms, used in an ordinary context, will be given a predictable meaning. Our highest responsibility in the field of statutory construction is to read the laws in a consistent way, giving Congress a sure means by which it may work the people's will. We have ignored that responsibility today. I respectfully dissent.

Notes

[1] As the Gingles Court noted, the plaintiffs' allegation was

"that the redistricting scheme impaired black citizens' ability to elect representatives of their choice in violation of . . . § 2 of the Voting Rights Act,"

478 U.S. at 478 U. S. 35. See also id. at 478 U. S. 46, n. 12 ("The claim we address in this opinion is . . . that their ability to elect the representatives of their choice was impaired by the selection of a multi-member electoral structure"). And as we explained the requirement for recovery in the case:

"Minority voters who contend that the multi-member form of districting violates § 2 must prove that the use of a multi-member electoral structure operates to minimize or cancel out their ability to elect their preferred candidates."

Id. at 478 U. S. 48 (emphasis added). While disagreeing with the Court's formulation of a remedy, the concurrence acknowledged that this structure underlay the Court's analysis, pointing out that, in the Court's view, "minority voting strength is to be assessed solely in terms of the minority group's ability to elect candidates it prefers. . . . Under this approach, the essence of a vote dilution claim is that the State has created single-member or multi-member districts that unacceptably impair the minority group's ability to elect the candidates its members prefer."

Id. at 478 U. S. 88 (emphasis added and deleted).

[2] The Court denies this conclusion follows, because, as it claims, it "rests on the erroneous assumption that a small group of voters can never influence the outcome of an election." Ante at 501 U. S. 397 n. 24. I make no such assumption. I only assume that, by "to elect," the statute does not mean "to influence," just as I assume that, by "representatives," the statute does not mean "judges." We do not reject Conan Doyle's method of statutory interpretation only to embrace Lewis Carroll's.

Justice Scalia's concurrence in Freytag v. Comm'r (June 27, 1991) [Notes omitted]

JUSTICE SCALIA, with whom JUSTICE O'CONNOR, JUSTICE KENNEDY, and JUSTICE SOUTER join, concurring in part and concurring in the judgment.

I agree with the Court that 26 U.S.C. § 7443A allows the Chief Judge of the Tax Court to assign special trial judges to preside over proceedings like those involved here, and join Parts I, II, and III of its opinion. I disagree, however, with the Court's decision to reach, as well as its resolution of, the Appointments Clause issue.

I

As an initial matter, I think the Court errs by entertaining petitioners' constitutional challenge on the merits. Petitioners not only failed to object at trial to the assignment of their case to a special trial judge, but expressly consented to that assignment. It was only after the judge ruled against them that petitioners developed their current concern over whether his appointment violated Article II, § 2, cl. 2, of the Constitution. They raised this important constitutional question for the first time in their appeal to the Fifth Circuit. That court concluded that petitioners had "waived this objection" by consenting to the assignment of their case. 904 F.2d 1011, 1015, n. 9 (1990). When we granted certiorari, we asked the parties to brief and argue the following additional question:

"Does a party's consent to have its case heard by a special tax judge constitute a waiver of any right to challenge the appointment of that judge on the basis of the Appointments Clause, Art. II, § 2, cl. 2?"

498 U.S. 1066 (1991).

Petitioners would have us answer that question "no" by adopting a general rule that "structural" constitutional rights, as a class, simply cannot be forfeited, and that litigants are entitled to raise them at any stage of litigation. The Court neither accepts nor rejects that proposal -- and, indeed, does not even mention it, though the opinion does dwell upon the structural nature of the present constitutional claim, ante at 501 U. S. 878-880. Nor does the Court in any other fashion answer the question we specifically asked to be briefed, choosing instead to say that, in the present case, it will "exercise our discretion" to entertain petitioners' constitutional claim. Ante at 501 U. S. 879. Thus, when there occurs a similar forfeiture of an Appointments Clause objection -- or of some other allegedly structural constitutional deficiency -- the Courts of Appeals will remain without guidance as to whether the forfeiture must, or even may, be disregarded. (The Court refers to this case as "one of th[e] rare" ones in which forfeiture will be ignored, ibid. -- but since all forfeitures of Appointments Clause rights, and arguably even all forfeitures of structural constitutional rights, can be considered "rare," this is hardly useful guidance.) Having asked for this point to be briefed and argued, and having expended our time in considering it, we should provide an answer. In my view, the answer is that Appointments Clause claims, and other structural constitutional claims, have no special entitlement to review. A party forfeits the right to advance on appeal a nonjurisdictional claim, structural or otherwise, that he fails to raise at trial. Although I have no quarrel with the proposition that appellate courts may, in truly exceptional circumstances, exercise discretion to hear forfeited claims, I see no basis for the assertion that the structural nature of a constitutional claim, in and of itself, constitutes such a circumstance; nor do I see any other exceptional circumstance in the present case. Cf. Peretz v. United States, post at 501 U. S. 954-955 (SCALIA, J., dissenting). I would therefore reject petitioners' sweeping proposition that structural constitutional rights, as a class, cannot be waived or forfeited, and would refuse to entertain the constitutional challenge presented here. [1]

"No procedural principle is more familiar to this Court than that a constitutional right may be forfeited in criminal as well as civil cases by the failure to make timely assertion of the right before a tribunal having jurisdiction to determine it."

Yakus v. United States, 321 U. S. 414, 321 U. S. 444 (1944); see also United States v. Socony-Vacuum Oil Co., 310 U. S. 150, 310 U. S. 238-239 (1940). Forfeiture [2] is "not a mere technicality, and is essential to the orderly administration of justice." 9 C. Wright & A. Miller, Federal Practice and Procedure § 2472, p. 455 (1971). In the federal judicial system, the rules generally governing the forfeiture of claims are set forth in Federal Rules of Criminal Procedure 51 and 52(b) and Federal Rule of Civil Procedure 46. The Tax Court, which is not an Article III court, has adopted a rule virtually identical to the latter, Tax Court Rule 144. These rules reflect the principle that a trial on the merits, whether in a civil or criminal case, is the "main event," and not simply a "tryout on the road" to appellate review. Cf. Wainwright v. Sykes, 433 U. S. 72, 433 U. S. 90 (1977). The very word "review" presupposes that a litigant's arguments have been raised and considered in the tribunal of first instance. To abandon that principle is to encourage the practice of "sandbagging": suggesting or permitting, for strategic reasons, that the trial court pursue a certain course, and later -- if the outcome is unfavorable -- claiming that the course followed was reversible error.

The blanket rule that

"argument[s] premised on the Constitution's structural separation of powers [are] not a matter of personal rights, and therefore [are] not waivable,"

Brief for Petitioners 43-44, would erode this cardinal principle of sound judicial administration. It has no support in principle or in precedent or in policy.

As to principle: personal rights that happen to bear upon governmental structure are no more laden with public interest (and hence inherently nonwaivable by the individual) than many other personal rights one can conceive of. First Amendment free speech rights, for example, or the Sixth Amendment right to a trial that is "public," provide benefits to the entire society more important than many structural guarantees; but if the litigant does not assert them in a timely fashion, he is foreclosed. See, e.g., Head v. New Mexico Bd. of Examiners in Optometry, 374 U. S. 424, 374 U. S. 432-433, n. 12 (1963) (First Amendment); Levine v. United States, 362 U. S. 610, 362 U. S. 619 (1960) (Sixth Amendment). Nor is it distinctively true of structural guarantees that litigants often may undervalue them. Many criminal defendants, for example, would prefer a trial from which the press is excluded.

It is true, of course, that a litigant's prior agreement to a judge's expressed intention to disregard a structural limitation upon his power cannot have any legitimating effect -- i.e., cannot render that disregard lawful. Even if both litigants not only agree to, but themselves propose, such a course, the judge must tell them no. But the question before us here involves the effect of waiver not ex ante, but ex post -- its effect not upon right, but upon remedy: must a judgment already rendered be set aside because of an alleged structural error to which the losing party did not properly object? There is no reason in principle why that should always be so. It will sometimes be so -- not, however, because the error was structural, but because, whether structural or not, it deprived the federal court of its requisite subject matter jurisdiction. Such an error may be raised by a party, and indeed must be noticed sua sponte by a court, at all points in the litigation, see, e.g., American Fire & Casualty Co. v. Finn, 341 U. S. 6, 341 U. S. 17-18 (1951); Mansfield, C. & L. M. R. Co. v. Swan, 111 U. S. 379, 111 U. S. 382 (1884); Capron v. Van Noorden, 2 Cranch 126, 6 U. S. 127 (1804). Since such a jurisdictional defect deprives not only the initial court but also the appellate court of its power over the case or controversy, to permit the appellate court to ignore it because of waiver would be to give the waiver legitimating, as opposed to merely remedial, effect, i.e., the effect of approving, ex ante, unlawful action by the appellate court itself. That this, rather than any principle of perpetual remediability of structural defects, is the basis for the rule of "nonwaivability" of lack of subject matter jurisdiction is demonstrated by the fact that a final judgment cannot be attacked collaterally -- i.e., before a court that does have jurisdiction -- on the ground that a subject matter jurisdictional limitation (structural or not) was ignored. See, e.g., Insurance Corp. of Ireland v. Compagnie des Bauxites de Guinee, 456 U. S. 694, 456 U. S. 702, n. 9 (1982).

As to precedent: Petitioners place primary reliance on some broad language in Commodity Futures Trading Comm'n v. Schor, 478 U. S. 833 (1986). We said in that case that, "[w]hen these Article III limitations are at issue" (referring not to all structural limitations of the Constitution, but only to those of Article III, §§ 1 and 2), "notions of consent and waiver cannot be dispositive." 478 U.S. at 478 U. S. 851. But the claim before us in Schor involved a particular sort of structural defect (a tribunal's exceeding its subject matter jurisdiction) which, as I have just described, had traditionally been held nonwaivable on appeal in the context of Article III tribunals. To extend the same treatment to similar defects in the context of non-Article III tribunals is quite natural, whether or not it is analytically required. Cf., e.g., Clapp v. Commissioner, 875 F.2d 1396, 1399 (CA9 1989) ("While the Tax Court is an Article I court, . . . the few cases discussing the differences between the Tax Court and an Article III court indicate that questions of Tax Court jurisdiction are to be resolved in the same manner as for an Article III court"). It is clear from our opinion in Schor that we had the analogy to Article III subject matter jurisdiction in mind. "To the extent that this structural principle is implicated in a given case," we said,

"the parties cannot by consent cure the constitutional difficulty for the same reason that the parties by consent cannot confer on federal courts subject matter jurisdiction beyond the limitations imposed by Article III, § 2. 478 U.S. at 478 U. S. 850-851. [3] I would not extend that nonwaiver rule -- a traditional rule in its application to Article III courts, and understandably extended to other federal adjudicative tribunals -- to structural defects that do not call into question the jurisdiction of the forum. The subject matter jurisdiction of the forum that issued the judgment, the Tax Court, is not in question in the present case."

Petitioners only other appeal to precedent is Glidden Co. v. Zdanok, 370 U. S. 530 (1962). That case did address a nonjurisdictional structural defect that had not been raised below. As the Court explains, however, that was a structural defect that went to the validity of the very proceeding under review, ante at 501 U. S. 879, as opposed to one that merely affected the validity of the claim -- for example, improper appointment of the Executive officer who issued the regulation central to the controversy. That was considered significant by the only opinion in the case (that of Justice Harlan, joined by Justices Brennan and Stewart) to address the waiver point. ("The alleged defect of authority here relates to basic constitutional protections designed in part for the benefit of litigants." Id. at 370 U. S. 536 (emphasis added).) The formulation petitioners advance, of course, is much broader than that. ("[A]n argument premised on the Constitution's structural separation of powers is not a matter of personal rights and therefore is not waivable." Brief for Petitioners 43-44 (emphasis added). "There can be no hierarchy among separation of powers principles, in which some are fundamental and nonwaivable, while the vindication of others may be relegated to the vagaries of individual litigation strategies." Id. at 45.) Even more important, Justice Harlan's plurality opinion in Glidden does not stand for the proposition that forfeiture can never be imposed, but rather the more limited proposition, which the Court reiterates today, that forfeiture need not always be imposed.

Several recent opinions flatly contradict petitioners' blanket assertion that structural claims cannot be waived. Surely under our jurisprudence the so-called negative Commerce Clause is structural. See Dennis v. Higgins, 498 U. S. 439, 498 U. S. 447 (1991). And surely the supposed guarantee against waivability must apply in state courts as well as in federal courts, since, according to petitioners, it emanates from the structural rights themselves. Yet only last Term, in Jimmy Swaggart Ministries v. Board of Equalization of California, 493 U. S. 378, 493 U. S. 397 (1990), we declined to consider a negative Commerce Clause challenge to a state tax because state courts had found the issue procedurally barred as a result of petitioner's failure to raise it in his administrative proceeding for tax refund. And in G. D. Searle & Co. v. Cohn, 455 U. S. 404, 455 U. S. 414 (1982), we declined to reach a negative Commerce Clause claim in litigation arising in the federal courts; we remanded the case for consideration of that issue by the Court of Appeals, "if it was properly raised below." (Emphasis added.) The Federal Courts of Appeals (even after Schor) have routinely applied the ordinary rules of forfeiture to structural claims not raised below. See, e.g., United States v. Doremus, 888 F.2d 630, 633, n. 3 (CA9 1989) (separation of powers claims), cert. denied, 498 U.S. 1046 (1991); Opdyke Investment Co. v. Detroit, 883 F.2d 1265, 1276 (CA6 1989) (same); Interface Group, Inc. v. Massachusetts Port Authority, 816 F.2d 9, 16 (CA1 1987) (Breyer, J.) (Supremacy and Commerce Clause claims).

Finally, as to policy: the need for the traditional forfeiture rule -- in cases involving structural claims as in all others -- is obvious. Without that incentive to raise legal objections as soon as they are available, the time of lower court judges and of juries would frequently be expended uselessly, and appellate consideration of difficult questions would be less informed and less complete. Besides inviting these evils, the categorical rule petitioners advance would require the development of a whole new body of jurisprudence concerning which constitutional provisions are "structural" -- a question whose answer is by no means clear. Cf. Sunstein, Government Control of Information, 74 Calif.L.Rev. 889, 915 (1986) (arguing that the First Amendment is structural). Moreover, since that rigid rule would cut so much against the grain of reason and practice, it would have the side effect of distorting substantive law. The maxim volenti non fit injuria has strong appeal in human affairs, and, by requiring it to be absolutely and systematically disregarded in cases involving structural protections of the Constitution, we would incline ourselves towards finding that no such structural protection exists.

Thus, the structural nature of the claim here is not sufficient reason to ignore its forfeiture -- and the Court (though it discusses the virtues of structure at some length) does not pretend otherwise. There must be some additional reason, then, why the Court "exercise[s] our discretion," ante at 501 U. S. 879, to disregard the forfeiture. To disregard it without sufficient reason is the exercise not of discretion, but of whimsy. Yet beyond its discussion of structure, the only reason the Court gives is no reason at all: "we are faced with a constitutional challenge that is neither frivolous nor disingenuous," ibid. That describes the situation with regard to the vast majority of forfeited claims raised on appeal. As we make clear in another case decided this very day, waiver generally extends not merely to "frivolous" and "disingenuous" challenges, but even to "[t]he most basic rights of criminal defendants." Peretz, post at 501 U. S. 936. Here, petitioners expressly consented to the Special Trial Judge. Under 26 U.S.C. § 7443A, the Chief Judge of that court has broad discretion to assign cases to special trial judges. Any party who objects to such an assignment, if so inclined, can easily raise the constitutional issue pressed today. Under these circumstances, I see no reason why this should be included among those "rare cases in which we should exercise our discretion," ante at 501 U. S. 879, to hear a forfeited claim.

II

Having struggled to reach petitioners' Appointments Clause objection, the Court finds it invalid. I agree with that conclusion, but the reason the Court assigns is, in my view, both wrong and full of danger for the future of our system of separate and coequal powers.

The Appointments Clause provides:

"[T]he Congress may by Law vest the Appointment of such inferior Officers, as they think proper, in the President alone, in the Courts of Law, or in the Heads of Departments."

Art. II, § 2, cl. 2. I agree with the Court that a special trial judge is an "inferior Office[r]" within the meaning of this Clause, with the result that, absent Presidential appointment, he must be appointed by a court of law or the head of a department. I do not agree, however, with the Court's conclusion that the Tax Court is a "Cour[t] of Law" within the meaning of this provision. I would find the appointment valid because the Tax Court is a "Departmen[t]" and the Chief Judge is its head.

A

A careful reading of the Constitution and attention to the apparent purpose of the Appointments Clause make it clear that the Tax Court cannot be one of those "Courts of Law" referred to there. The Clause does not refer generally to "Bodies exercising judicial Functions," or even to "Courts" generally, or even to "Courts of Law" generally. It refers to "the Courts of Law." Certainly this does not mean any "Cour[t] of Law" (the Supreme Court of Rhode Island would not do). The definite article "the" obviously narrows the class of eligible "Courts of Law" to those courts of law envisioned by the Constitution. Those are Article III courts, and the Tax Court is not one of them.

The Court rejects this conclusion because the Appointments Clause does not (in the style of the Uniform Commercial Code) contain an explicit cross-reference to Article III. Ante at 501 U. S. 888-889. This is no doubt true, but irrelevant. It is equally true that Article I, § 8, cl. 9, which provides that Congress may "constitute Tribunals inferior to the supreme Court," does not explicitly say "Tribunals under Article III, below." Yet this power "plainly relates to the 'inferior Courts' provided for in Article III, § 1; it has never been relied on for establishment of any other tribunals." Glidden Co. v. Zdanok, 370 U.S. at 370 U. S. 543 (opinion of Harlan, J.); see also 3 J. Story, Commentaries on the Constitution of the United States § 1573, p. 437 (1833). Today's Court evidently does not appreciate, as

Chief Justice Marshall did, that the Constitution does not "partake of the prolixity of a legal code," McCulloch v. Maryland, 4 Wheat. 316, 17 U. S. 407 (1819). It does not, like our opinions, bristle with "supras," "infras," and footnotes. Instead of insisting upon such legalisms, we should, I submit, follow the course mapped out in Buckley v. Valeo, 424 U. S. 1, 424 U. S. 124 (1976) (per curiam), and examine the Appointments Clause of the Constitution in light of the "cognate provisions" of which it is a central feature: Article I, Article II, and Article III. The only "Courts of Law" referred to there are those authorized by Article III, § 1, whose judges serve during good behavior with undiminishable salary. Art. III, § 1. See Glidden Co. v. Zdanok, supra at 370 U. S. 543 (opinion of Harlan, J.); United States v. Mouat, 124 U.S. 303, 124 U. S. 307 (1888) ("courts of justice") (dictum). The Framers contemplated no other national judicial tribunals.

"According to the plan of the convention, all judges who may be appointed by the United States are to hold their offices during good behavior. . . ."

The Federalist No. 78, p. 465 (C. Rossiter ed.1961) (A. Hamilton) (second emphasis in original).

We recognized this in Buckley, supra, and it was indeed an essential part of our reasoning. Responding to the argument that a select group of Congressmen was a "Department," we said:

"The phrase 'Heads of Departments,' used as it is in conjunction with the phrase 'Courts of Law,' suggests that the Departments referred to are themselves in the Executive Branch or at least have some connection with that branch. While the Clause expressly authorizes Congress to vest the appointment of certain officers in the 'Courts of Law,' the absence of similar language to include Congress must mean that neither Congress nor its officers were included within the language 'Heads of Departments' in this part of cl. 2."

"Thus, with respect to four of the six voting members of the Commission, neither the President, the head of any department, nor the Judiciary has any voice in their selection."

Id. at 424 U. S. 127 (emphasis added). The whole point of this passage is that "the Heads of Departments" must reasonably be understood to refer exclusively to the Executive Branch (thereby excluding officers of Congress) because "the Courts of Law" obviously refers exclusively to the Judicial Branch. We were right in Buckley, and the Court is wrong today.

Even if the Framers had no particular purpose in making the Appointments Clause refer only to Article III courts, we would still of course be bound by that disposition. In fact, however, there is every reason to believe that the Appointments Clause's limitation to Article III tribunals was adopted with calculation and forethought, faithfully implementing a considered political theory for the appointment of officers.

The Framers' experience with post-revolutionary self-government had taught them that combining the power to create offices with the power to appoint officers was a recipe for legislative corruption. [4] The foremost danger was that legislators would create offices with the expectancy of occupying them themselves. This was guarded against by the

Incompatibility and Ineligibility Clauses, Article I, § 6, cl. 2. See Buckley, supra at 424 U. S. 124. But real, if less obvious, dangers remained. Even if legislators could not appoint themselves, they would be inclined to appoint their friends and supporters. This proclivity would be unchecked because of the lack of accountability in a multimember body – as James Wilson pointed out in his criticism of a multimember executive:

"[A]re impartiality and fine discernment likely to predominate in a numerous [appointing] body? In proportion to their own number, will be the number of their friends, favorites and dependents. An office is to be filled. A person nearly connected, by some of the foregoing ties, with one of those who [is] to vote in filling it, is named as a candidate. . . . Every member, who gives, on his account, a vote for his friend, will expect the return of a similar favor on the first convenient opportunity. In this manner, a reciprocal intercourse of partiality, of interestedness, of favoritism, perhaps of venality, is established; and in no particular instance, is there a practicability of tracing the poison to its source. Ignorant, vicious, and prostituted characters are introduced into office; and some of those, who voted, and procured others to vote for them, are the first and loudest in expressing their astonishment that the door of admission was ever opened to men of their infamous description. The suffering people are thus wounded and buffeted, like Homer's Ajax, in the dark; and have not even the melancholy satisfaction of knowing by whom the blows are given."

1 Works of James Wilson 359-360 (J. Andrews ed. 1896). See also Essex Result, in Memoir of Theophilus Parsons 381-382 (1859); The Federalist No. 76, pp. 455-457 (C. Rossiter ed.1961) (A. Hamilton). And not only would unaccountable legislatures introduce their friends into necessary offices, they would create unnecessary offices into which to introduce their friends. As James Madison observed:

"The power of the Legislature to appoint any other than their own officers departs too far from the Theory which requires a separation of the great Departments of Government. One of the best securities against the creation of unnecessary offices or tyrannical powers is an exclusion of the authors from all share in filling the one, or influence in the execution of the other."

Madison's Observations on Jefferson's Draft of a Constitution for Virginia, reprinted in 6 Papers of Thomas Jefferson 308, 311 (J. Boyd ed.1952).

For these good and sufficient reasons, then, the federal appointment power was removed from Congress. The Framers knew, however, that it was not enough simply to define in writing who would exercise this power or that.

"After discriminating . . . in theory, the several classes of power, as they may in their nature be legislative, executive, or judiciary, the next and most difficult task [was] to provide some practical security for each, against the invasion of the others."

The Federalist No. 48, p. 308 (C. Rossiter ed.1961) (J. Madison). Invasion by the Legislature, of course, was the principal threat, since the "legislative authority . . . possesses so many means of operating on the motives of the other departments." Id. No. 49, p. 314 (J. Madison). It can "mask, under complicated and indirect measures, the encroachments which it makes on the co-ordinate departments," id. No. 48, p. 310 (J. Madison), and thus control the nominal actions (e.g., appointments) of the other branches. Cf. T. Jefferson, Notes on the State of Virginia 120 (W. Peden ed.1955).

Thus, it was not enough simply to repose the power to execute the laws (or to appoint) in the President; it was also necessary to provide him with the means to resist legislative encroachment upon that power. The means selected were various, including a separate political constituency, to which he alone was responsible, and the power to veto encroaching laws, see Art. I, § 7, or even to disregard them when they are unconstitutional. See Easterbrook, Presidential Review, 40 Case W.Res.L.Rev. 905, 920-924 (1990). One of the most obvious and necessary, however, was a permanent salary. Art. II, § 1. Without this, "the separation of the executive from the legislative department would be merely nominal and nugatory. The legislature, with a discretionary power over the salary and emoluments of the Chief Magistrate, could render him as obsequious to their will as they might think proper to make him." The Federalist No. 73, p. 441 (C. Rossiter ed.1961) (A. Hamilton). See also id. No. 51, p. 321 (J. Madison); Mass.Const., Part The Second, Chapter II, § 1, Art. XIII (1780).

A power of appointment lodged in a President surrounded by such structural fortifications could be expected to be exercised independently, and not pursuant to the manipulations of Congress. The same is true, to almost the same degree, of the appointment power lodged in the heads of departments. Like the President, these individuals possess a reputational stake in the quality of the individuals they appoint; and though they are not themselves able to resist congressional encroachment, they are directly answerable to the President, who is responsible to his constituency for their appointments and has the motive and means to assure faithful actions by his direct lieutenants.

Like the President, the Judicial Branch was separated from Congress not merely by a paper assignment of functions, but by endowment with the means to resist encroachment -- foremost among which, of course, are life tenure (during "good behavior") and permanent salary. These structural accoutrements not only assure the fearless adjudication of cases and controversies, see The Federalist Nos. 78, 79 (A. Hamilton); Northern Pipeline Constr. Co. v. Marathon Pipe Line Co., 458 U. S. 50, 458 U. S. 57-60 (1982) (opinion of Brennan, J.); they also render the Judiciary a potential repository of appointment power free of congressional (as well as Presidential) influence. In the same way that depositing appointment power in a fortified President and his lieutenants ensures an actual exclusion of the legislature from appointment, so too does reposing such power in an Article III court. The Court's holding, that Congress may deposit such power in "legislative courts," without regard to whether their personnel are either Article III judges or "Heads of Departments," utterly destroys this carefully constructed scheme. And the Court produces this result, I remind the reader, not because of, but in spite of, the apparent meaning of the phrase "the Courts of Law."

B

Having concluded, against all odds, that "the Courts of Law" referred to in Article II, § 2, are not the courts of law established by Article III, the Court is confronted with the difficult problem of determining what courts of law they are. It acknowledges that they must be courts which exercise "the judicial power of the United States" and concludes that the Tax Court is such a court -- even though it is not an Article III court. This is quite a feat, considering that Article III begins "The judicial Power of the United States" -- not "Some of the judicial Power of the United States," or even "Most of the judicial Power of the United States" -- "shall be vested in one supreme Court, and in such inferior Courts as the Congress may from time to time ordain and establish." Despite this unequivocal text, the Court sets forth the startling proposition that "the judicial power of the United States is not limited to the judicial power defined under Article III." Ante at 501 U. S. 889. It turns out, however -- to our relief, I suppose it must be said -- that this is really only a pun. "The judicial power," as the Court uses it, bears no resemblance to the constitutional term of art we are all familiar with, but means only "the power to adjudicate in the manner of courts." So used, as I shall proceed to explain, the phrase covers an infinite variety of individuals exercising executive, rather than judicial, power (in the constitutional sense), and has nothing to do with the separation of powers or with any other characteristic that might cause one to believe that is what was meant by "the Courts of Law." As far as I can tell, the only thing to be said for this approach is that it makes the Tax Court a "Cour[t] of Law" -- which is perhaps the object of the exercise.

I agree with the unremarkable proposition that "Congress [has] wide discretion to assign the task of adjudication in cases arising under federal law to legislative tribunals." Ante at 501 U. S. 889. Congress may also assign that task to subdivisions of traditional executive departments, as it did in 1924 when it created the Tax Court's predecessor, the Tax Board of Appeals -- or to take a more venerable example, as it did in 1791 when it created within the Treasury Department the Comptroller of the United States, who "decide[d] on appeal, without further review by the Secretary, all claims concerning the settlement of accounts." Casper, An Essay in Separation of Powers: Some Early Versions and Practices, 30 Wm. & Mary L.Rev. 211, 238 (1989); see 1 Stat. 66. Such tribunals, like any other administrative board, exercise the executive power, not the judicial power of the United States. They are, in the words of the great Chief Justice, "incapable of receiving [the judicial power]" -- unless their members serve for life during good behavior and receive permanent salary. American Ins. Co. v. Canter, 1 Pet. 511, 26 U. S. 546 (1828) (Marshall, C.J.).

It is no doubt true that all such bodies "adjudicate," i.e., they determine facts, apply a rule of law to those facts, and thus arrive at a decision. But there is nothing "inherently judicial" about "adjudication." To be a federal officer and to adjudicate are necessary but not sufficient conditions for the exercise of federal judicial power, as we recognized almost a century and a half ago.

"That the auditing of the accounts of a receiver of public moneys may be, in an enlarged sense, a judicial act, must be admitted. So are all those administrative duties the performance of which involves an inquiry into the existence of facts and the application to them of rules of law. In this sense the act of the President in calling out the militia under the act of 1795, [Martin v. Mott,] 12 Wheat. 19 [(1827)], or of a commissioner who makes a certificate for the extradition of a criminal, under a treaty, is judicial. But it is not sufficient to bring such matters under the judicial power, that they involve the exercise of judgment upon law and fact."

Murray's Lessee v. Hoboken Land & Improvement Co., 18 How. 272, 59 U. S. 280 (1856). Accord, Bator, The Constitution as Architecture: Legislative and Administrative Courts Under Article III, 65 Ind. L.J. 233, 264-265 (1990). The first Patent Board, which consisted of Thomas Jefferson, Henry Knox, and Edmund Randolph in their capacities as Secretary of State, Secretary of War, and Attorney General, respectively, 1 Stat. 109, 110 (1790), adjudicated the patentability of inventions, sometimes hearing argument by petitioners. See 18 J. Pat.Off.Soc. 68-69 (July 1936). They were exercising the executive power. See Easterbrook, "Success" and the Judicial Power, 65 Ind. L.J. 277, 280 (1990). Today, the Federal Government has a corps of administrative law judges numbering more than 1,000, whose principal statutory function is the conduct of adjudication under the Administrative Procedure Act (APA), see 5 U.S.C. §§ 554, 3105. They are all executive officers. "Adjudication," in other words, is no more an "inherently" judicial function than the promulgation of rules governing primary conduct is an "inherently" legislative one. See Standard Oil Co. of New Jersey v. United States, 221 U. S. 1 (1911); APA, 5 U.S.C. § 553 ("Rule making").

It is true that Congress may commit the sorts of matters administrative law judges and other executive adjudicators now handle to Article III courts -- just as some of the matters now in Article III courts could instead be committed to executive adjudicators.

"[T]here are matters, involving public rights, which may be presented in such form that the judicial power is capable of acting on them, and which are susceptible of judicial determination, but which Congress may or may not bring within the cognizance of the courts of the United States, as it may deem proper."

Murray's Lessee, supra at 59 U. S. 284. See also Ex parte Bakelite Corp., 279 U. S. 438, 279 U. S. 451 (1929). Congress could, for instance, allow direct review by the Courts of Appeals of denials of Social Security benefits. It could instead establish the Social Security Court -- composed of judges serving 5-year terms -- within the Social Security Administration. Both tribunals would perform identical functions, but only the former would exercise the judicial power.

In short, given the performance of adjudicatory functions by a federal officer, it is the identity of the officer -- not something intrinsic about the mode of decisionmaking or type of decision -- that tells us whether the judicial power is being exercised. "[O]ur cases demonstrate [that] a particular function, like a chameleon, will often take on the aspect of the office to which it is assigned." Bowsher v. Synar, 478 U. S. 714, 478 U. S. 749 (1986) (STEVENS, J., concurring in judgment). Cf. INS v. Chadha, 462 U. S. 919, 462 U. S. 953, n. 16 (1983). Where adjudicative decisionmakers do not possess life tenure and a permanent salary, they are "incapable of exercising any portion of the judicial power." Ex parte Randolph, 20 F.Cas. (No. 11,558) 242, 254 (CC Va. 1833) (Marshall, C.J.).

The Tax Court is indistinguishable from my hypothetical Social Security Court. It reviews determinations by Executive Branch officials (the Internal Revenue Service) that this much or that much tax is owed -- a classic executive function. For 18 years its predecessor, the Board of Tax Appeals, did the very same thing, see H. Dubroff, The United States Tax Court 47-175 (1979), and no one suggested that body exercised "the judicial power." We held just the opposite:

"The Board of Tax Appeals is not a court. It is an executive or administrative board, upon the decision of which the parties are given an opportunity to base a petition for review to the courts after the administrative inquiry of the Board has been had and decided."

Old Colony Trust Co. v. Commissioner, 279 U. S. 716, 279 U. S. 725 (1929) (Taft, C.J.). Though renamed "the Tax Court of the United States" in 1942, it remained "an independent agency in the Executive Branch," 26 U.S.C. § 1100 (1952 ed.), and continued to perform the same function. As an executive agency, it possessed many of the accoutrements the Court considers "quintessentially judicial," ante at 501 U. S. 891. It administered oaths, for example, and subpoenaed and examined witnesses, § 1114; its findings were reviewed "in the same manner and to the same extent as decisions of the district courts in civil actions tried without a jury," § 1141(a). This Court continued to treat it as an administrative agency, akin to the Federal Communications Commission (FCC) or the National Labor Relations Board (NLRB). See Dobson v. Commissioner, 320 U. S. 489, 320 U. S. 495-501 (1943).

When the Tax Court was statutorily denominated an "Article I Court" in 1969, its judges did not magically acquire the judicial power. They still lack life tenure; their salaries may still be diminished; they are still removable by the President for "inefficiency, neglect of duty, or malfeasance in office." 26 U.S.C. § 7443(f). (In Bowsher v. Synar, supra at 478 U. S. 729, we held that these latter terms are "very broad" and "could sustain removal . . . for any number of actual or perceived transgressions.") How anyone with these characteristics can exercise judicial power "independent . . . [of] the Executive Branch" is a complete mystery. It seems to me entirely obvious that the Tax Court, like the Internal Revenue Service, the FCC, and the NLRB, exercises executive power. Amar, Marbury, Section 13, and the Original Jurisdiction of the Supreme Court, 56 U.Chi.L.Rev. 443, 451, n. 43 (1989). See also Northern Pipeline, 458 U.S. at 458 U. S. 113 (WHITE, J., dissenting) (equating administrative agencies and Article I courts); Samuels, Kramer & Co. v. Commissioner, 930 F.2d 975, 992-993 (CA2 1991) (collecting academic authorities for same proposition).

In seeking to establish that "judicial power" in some constitutionally significant sense -- in a sense different from the adjudicative exercise of executive power -- can be exercised by someone other than an Article III judge, the Court relies heavily upon the existence of territorial courts. Ante at 501 U. S. 889-891. Those courts have nothing to do with the issue before us. [5] I agree that they do not exercise the national executive power -- but neither do they exercise any national judicial power. They are neither Article III courts nor Article I courts, but Article IV courts -- just as territorial governors are not Article I executives but Article IV executives.

"These Courts, then, are not constitutional Courts, in which the judicial power conferred by the Constitution on the general government, can be deposited. They are incapable of receiving it. They are legislative Courts, created in virtue of the general right of sovereignty which exists in the government, or in virtue of that clause which enables Congress to make all needful rules and regulations, respecting the territory belonging to the United States. . . . In legislating for them, Congress exercises the combined powers of the general, and of a state government."

American In. Co. v. Canter, 1 Pet. at 26 U. S. 546 (Marshall, C.J.) (emphasis added).

Or as the Court later described it:

"[Territories] are not organized under the Constitution, nor subject to its complex distribution of the powers of government, as the organic law; but are the creations, exclusively, of the legislative department, and subject to its supervision and control."

Benner v. Porter, 9 How. 235, 50 U. S. 242 (1850). Thus, Congress may endow territorial governments with a plural executive; it may allow the executive to legislate; it may dispense with the legislature or judiciary altogether. It should be obvious that the powers exercised by territorial courts tell us nothing about the nature of an entity, like the Tax Court, which administers the general laws of the Nation. See Northern Pipeline, supra at 458 U. S. 75-76 (opinion of Brennan, J.).

The Court claims that there is a "longstanding practice" of permitting Article I courts to appoint inferior officers. Ante at 501 U. S. 890. I am unaware of such a practice. Perhaps the Court means to refer not to Article I courts but to the territorial courts just discussed, in which case the practice would be irrelevant. As I shall discuss below, an Article I court (such as the Tax Court) that is not within any other department would be able to have its inferior officers appointed by its chief judge -- not under the "Courts of Law" provision of Article II, § 2, but under the "Heads of Departments" provision; perhaps it is that sort of practice the Court has in mind. It is certain, in any case, that no decision of ours has ever approved the appointment of an inferior officer by an Article I court. Ex parte Hennen, 13 Pet. 230 (1839), which the Court cites, involved appointment by an Article III tribunal.

III

Since the Tax Court is not a court of law, unless the Chief Judge is the head of a department, the appointment of the Special Trial Judge was void. Unlike the Court, I think he is.

I have already explained that the Tax Court, like its predecessors, exercises the executive power of the United States. This does not, of course, suffice to market a "Departmen[t]" for purposes of the Appointments Clause. If, for instance, the Tax Court were a subdivision of the Department of the Treasury -- as the Board of Tax Appeals used to be -- it would not qualify. In fact, however, the Tax Court is a freestanding, self-contained entity in the Executive Branch, whose Chief Judge is removable by the President (and, save impeachment, no one else). Nevertheless, the Court holds that the Chief Judge is not the head of a department.

It is not at all clear what the Court's reason for this conclusion is. I had originally thought that the Court was adopting petitioners' theory -- wrong, but at least coherent -- that "Heads of Departments" means Cabinet officers. This is suggested by the Court's reliance upon the dictum in Burnap v. United States, 252 U. S. 512, 252 U. S. 515 (1920), to the effect that the head of a department must be

"'the Secretary in charge of a great division of the executive branch of the Government, like the State, Treasury, and War, who is a member of the Cabinet,'"

ante at 501 U. S. 886 (emphasis added); by the Court's observation that "[t]he Cabinet-level departments are limited in number and easily identified," ibid.; and by its reliance upon the fact that, in the Twenty-fifth Amendment, "the term department' refers to Cabinet-level entities," ante at 501 U. S. 887. Elsewhere, however, the Court seemingly disclaims Cabinet status as the criterion, see ante at 501 U. S. 887, n. 4, and says that the term "Departmen[t]" means "executive divisions like the Cabinet-level departments," ante at 501 U. S. 886 (emphasis added). Unfortunately, it never specifies what characteristic it is that causes an agency to be "like a Cabinet-level department," or even provides any intelligible clues as to what it might have in mind. It quotes a congressional Committee Report that seemingly equates Cabinet status with inclusion within the statutory definition of "'department'" in 5 U.S.C. § 101, ante at 501 U. S. 887 (quoting H.R.Rep. No. 203, 89th Cong., 1st Sess., 3 (1965)), but this hint is canceled by a footnote making it clear that "Cabinet-like" character, whatever it is, is not "strictly limit[ed] by that provision," ante at 501 U. S. 887, n. 4. Its approving quotation of Burnap's reference to "a great division of the executive branch" might invite the guess that numerosity is the key -- but the Department of Education has fewer than 5,000 employees, and the FCC, which the Court also appears willing to consider such a "'great division,'" ante at 501 U. S. 886, fewer than 1,800. See Employment and Trends as of March, 1991, Office of Personnel Management, Table 2. The Court reserves the right to consider as "Cabinet-like," and hence as "Departments," those agencies which, above all others, are at the farthest remove from Cabinet status, and whose heads are specifically designed not to have the quality that the Court earlier thinks important, of being "subject to the exercise of political oversight and shar[ing] the President's accountability to the people," ante at 501 U. S. 886 -- namely, independent regulatory agencies such as the Federal Trade Commission and the Securities and Exchange Commission, ante at 501 U. S. 887, n. 4. Indeed, lest any conceivable improbability be excluded, the Court even reserves the right to consider as a "Departmen[t]" an entity that is not headed by an officer of the United States -- the Federal Reserve Bank of St. Louis, whose president is appointed in none of the manners constitutionally permitted for federal officers, but rather by a Board of Directors, two-thirds of whom are elected by regional banks, see 12 U.S.C. §§ 302, 304, and 341. It is as impossible to respond to this random argumentation as it is to derive a comprehensible theory of the appointments power from it. I shall address, therefore, what was petitioners' point, what I originally took to be the point of the Court's opinion, and what is the only trace of a flesh-and-blood point that subsists: the proposition that "Departmen[t]" means "Cabinet-level agency."

There is no basis in text or precedent for this position. The term "Cabinet" does not appear in the Constitution, the Founders having rejected proposals to create a Cabinet-like entity. See H. Learned, The President's Cabinet 74-94 (1912); E. Corwin, The President 97, 238-240 (5th rev. ed.1984). The existence of a Cabinet, its membership, and its prerogatives (except to the extent the Twenty-fifth Amendment speaks to them), are entirely matters of Presidential discretion. Nor does any of our cases hold that "the Heads of Departments" are Cabinet members. In United States v. Germaine, 99 U. S. 508 (1879), we merely held that the Commissioner of Pensions, an official within the Interior Department, was not the head of a department. And, in Burnap, supra, we held that the Bureau of Public Buildings and Grounds, a bureau within the War Department, was not a department.

The Court's reliance on the Twenty-fifth Amendment is misplaced. I accept that the phrase "the principal officers of the executive departments" is limited to members of the Cabinet. It is the structural composition of the phrase, however, and not the single word "departments," which gives it that narrow meaning -- "the principal officers" of the "executive departments" in gross, rather than (as in the Opinions Clause) "the principal Officer in each of the executive Departments," or (in the Appointments Clause) simply "the Heads" (not "principal Heads") "of Departments."

The only history on the point also militates against the Court's conclusion. The 1792 Congress passed an "Act to establish the Post-Office and Post Roads within the United States," creating a Postmaster General and empowering him to appoint "an assistant, and deputy postmasters, at all places where such may be found necessary." § 3, 1 Stat. 234. President Washington did not bring the Postmaster into his Cabinet. See Learned, supra at 233-249. It seems likely that the Assistant Postmaster General and Deputy Postmasters were inferior officers -- which means either that "the Heads of Departments" include principal officers other than the Cabinet, or that the Second Congress and President Washington did not understand the Appointments Clause. In any case, it is silly to think that the Second Congress (or any later Congress) was supposed to guess whether the President would bring the new agency into his Cabinet in order to determine how the appointment of its inferior officers could be made.

Modern practice as well as original practice refutes the distinction between Cabinet and non-Cabinet agencies. Congress has empowered non-Cabinet agencies to appoint inferior officers for quite some time. See, e.g., 47 U.S.C. § 155(f) (FCC -- managing director); 15 U.S.C. § 78d(b) (Securities and Exchange Commission -- "such officers . . . as may be necessary"); 15 U.S.C. § 42 (Federal Trade Commission -- secretary); 7 U.S.C. §

4a(c) (Commodity Futures Trading Commission -- general counsel). In fact, I know of very few inferior officers in the independent agencies who are appointed by the President, and of none who is appointed by the head of a Cabinet department. The Court's interpretation of "Heads of Departments" casts into doubt the validity of many appointments and a number of explicit statutory authorizations to appoint.

A number of factors support the proposition that "Heads of Departments" includes the heads of all agencies immediately below the President in the organizational structure of the Executive Branch. It is quite likely that the "Departments" referred to in the Opinions Clause ("The President . . . may require the Opinion, in writing, of the principal Officer in each of the executive Departments," Art. II, § 2) are the same as the "Departments" in the Appointments Clause. See Germaine, supra at 99 U. S. 511. In the former context, it seems to me, the word must reasonably be thought to include all independent establishments. The purpose of the Opinions Clause, presumably, was to assure the President's ability to get a written opinion on all important matters. But if the "Departments" it referred to were only Cabinet departments, it would not assure the current President the ability to receive a written opinion concerning the operations of the Central Intelligence Agency, an agency that is not within any other department, and whose Director is not a member of the Cabinet.

This evident meaning -- that the term "Departments" means all independent executive establishments -- is also the only construction that makes sense of Article II, § 2's sharp distinction between principal officers and inferior officers. The latter, as we have seen, can by statute be made appointable by "the President alone, . . . the Courts of Law, or . . . the Heads of Departments." Officers that are not "inferior Officers," however, must be appointed (unless the Constitution itself specifies otherwise, as it does, for example, with respect to officers of Congress) by the President, "by and with the Advice and Consent of the Senate." The obvious purpose of this scheme is to make sure that all the business of the Executive will be conducted under the supervision of officers appointed by the President with Senate approval; only officers "inferior," i.e., subordinate, to those can be appointed in some other fashion. If the Appointments Clause is read as I read it, all inferior officers can be made appointable by their ultimate (sub-Presidential) superiors; as petitioners would read it, only those inferior officers whose ultimate superiors happen to be Cabinet members can be. All the other inferior officers, if they are to be appointed by an Executive official at all, must be appointed by the President himself or (assuming cross-department appointments are permissible) by a Cabinet officer who has no authority over the appointees. This seems to me a most implausible disposition, particularly since the makeup of the Cabinet is not specified in the Constitution, or indeed the concept even mentioned. It makes no sense to create a system in which the inferior officers of the Environmental Protection Agency, for example -- which may include, inter alios, bureau chiefs, the general counsel, and administrative law judges -- must be appointed by the President, the courts of law, or the "Secretary of Something Else."

In short, there is no reason, in text, judicial decision, history, or policy, to limit the phrase "the Heads of Departments" in the Appointments Clause to those officials who are members of the President's Cabinet. I would give the term its ordinary meaning, something which Congress has apparently been doing for decades without complaint. As an American dictionary roughly contemporaneous with adoption of the Appointments Clause provided, and as remains the case, a department is "[a] separate allotment or part of business; a distinct province, in which a class of duties are allotted to a particular person. . . ." 1 N. Webster, American Dictionary 58 (1828). I readily acknowledge that applying this word to an entity such as the Tax Court would have seemed strange to the Founders, as it continues to seem strange to modern ears. But that is only because the Founders did not envision that an independent establishment of such small size and specialized function would be created. They chose the word "Departmen[t]," however, not to connote size or function (much less Cabinet status), but separate organization -- a connotation that still endures even in colloquial usage today ("that is not my department"). The Constitution is clear, I think, about the chain of appointment and supervision that it envisions: principal officers could be permitted by law to appoint their subordinates. That should subsist, however much the nature of federal business or of federal organizational structure may alter.

I must confess that, in the case of the Tax Court, as with some other independent establishments (notably, the so-called "independent regulatory agencies" such as the FCC and the Federal Trade Commission) permitting appointment of inferior officers by the agency head may not ensure the high degree of insulation from congressional control that was the purpose of the appointments scheme elaborated in the Constitution. That is a consequence of our decision in Humphrey's Executor v. United States, 295 U. S. 602 (1935), which approved congressional restriction upon arbitrary dismissal of the heads of such agencies by the President, a scheme avowedly designed to made such agencies less accountable to him, and hence he less responsible for them. Depending upon how broadly one reads the President's power to dismiss "for cause," it may be that he has no control over the appointment of inferior officers in such agencies; and if those agencies are publicly regarded as beyond his control -- a "headless Fourth Branch" -- he may have less incentive to care about such appointments. It could be argued, then, that much of the raison d'etre for permitting appointive power to be lodged in "Heads of Departments," see supra at 501 U. S. 903-908, does not exist with respect to the heads of these agencies, because they, in fact, will not be shored up by the President, and are thus not resistant to congressional pressures. That is a reasonable position -- though I tend to the view that adjusting the remainder of the Constitution to compensate for Humphrey's Executor is a fruitless endeavor. But, in any event, it is not a reasonable position that supports the Court's decision today -- both because a "Cour[t] of Law" artificially defined as the Court defines it is even less resistant to those pressures, and because the distinction between those agencies that are subject to full Presidential control and those that are not is entirely unrelated to the distinction between Cabinet agencies and non-Cabinet agencies, and to all the other distinctions that the Court successively embraces. (The Central Intelligence

Agency and the Environmental Protection Agency, for example, though not Cabinet agencies or components of Cabinet agencies, are not "independent" agencies in the sense of independence from Presidential control.)

In sum, whatever may be the distorting effects of later innovations that this Court has approved, considering the Chief Judge of the Tax Court to be the head of a department seems to me the only reasonable construction of Article II, § 2.

For the above reasons, I concur in the judgment that the decision below must be affirmed.

Justice Scalia's concurrence in US v. R. L. C. (March 24, 1992)

Justice Scalia, with whom Justice Kennedy and Justice Thomas join, concurring in part and concurring in the judgment.

In my view it is not consistent with the rule of lenity to construe a textually ambiguous penal statute against a criminal defendant on the basis of legislative history. Because Justice Souter's opinion assumes the contrary, I join only Parts I, II A, and III, and concur in the judgment.

The Court begins its analysis, quite properly, by examining the language of 18 U.S.C. § 5037(c)(1)(B) — which proves to be ambiguous. Reasonable doubt remains, the Court concludes, as to whether the provision refers (i) to the maximum punishment that could be imposed if the juvenile were being sentenced under the United States Sentencing Guidelines (15-21 months) or (ii) to the maximum punishment authorized by the statute defining the offense, see 18 U.S.C. § 1112(a) (36 months). Ante, at 5. With that conclusion I agree — and that conclusion should end the matter. The rule of lenity, in my view, prescribes the result when a criminal statute is ambiguous: the more lenient interpretation must prevail.

Yet the plurality continues. Armed with its warrant of textual ambiguity, the plurality conducts a search of § 5037's legislative history to determine whether that clarifies the statute. Happily for this defendant, the plurality's extratextual inquiry is benign: It uncovers evidence that the "better understood" reading of § 5037 is the more lenient one. Ante, at 12. But this methodology contemplates as well a different ending, one in which something said in a Committee Report causes the criminal law to be stricter than the text of the law displays. According to the plurality, "we resort to the [rule of lenity] only when `a reasonable doubt persists about a statute's intended scope even after resort to "the language and structure, legislative history, and motivating policies" of the statute.' " Ante, at 12 (quoting Moskal v. United States, 498 U.S. ____ (1990) (slip op., at 4)) (citation omitted). I doubt that Moskal accurately characterizes the law in this area, and I am certain that its treatment of "the venerable rule of lenity," ante, at 12, does not venerate the important values the old rule serves.

The Moskal formulation of the rule, in approving reliance on a statute's "motivating policies" (an obscure phrase), seems contrary to our statement in Hughey v.

United States, 495 U.S. 411, 422 (1990), that "[e]ven [where] the statutory language . . . [is] ambiguous, longstanding principles of lenity . . . preclude our resolution of the ambiguity against [the criminal defendant] on the basis of general declarations of policy in the statute and legislative history." And insofar as Moskal requires consideration of legislative history at all, it compromises what we have described to be purposes of the lenity rule. "[A] fair warning," we have said, "should be given to the world in language that the common world will understand, of what the law intends to do if a certain line is passed. To make the warning fair, so far as possible the line should be clear." McBoyle v. United States, 283 U.S. 25, 27 (1931). "[T]he rule of lenity ensures that criminal statutes will provide fair warning concerning conduct rendered illegal." Liparota v. United States, 471 U.S. 419, 427 (1985). It may well be true that in most cases the proposition that the words of the United States Code or the Statutes at Large give adequate notice to the citizen is something of a fiction, see McBoyle, supra, at 27, albeit one required in any system of law; but necessaryfiction descends to needless farce when the public is charged even with knowledge of Committee Reports.

Moskal's mode of analysis also disserves the rule of lenity's other purpose: assuring that the society, through its representatives, has genuinely called for the punishment to be meted out. "[B]ecause of the seriousness of criminal penalties, and because criminal punishment usually represents the moral condemnation of the community, legislatures and not courts should define criminal activity." United States v. Bass, 404 U.S. 336, 348 (1971). See also Liparota, supra, at 427; United States v. Wiltberger, 5 Wheat. 76, 95 (1820). The rule reflects, as the plurality acknowledges, " ` "the instinctive distaste against men languishing in prison unless the lawmaker has clearly said they should." ' " Ante, at 12 (quoting Bass, supra, at 348, and H. Friendly, Benchmarks 209 (1967)). But legislative history can never provide assurance against that unacceptable result. After all, "[a] statute is a statute," ante, at 12, n. 5, and no matter how "authoritative" the history may be — even if it is that veritable Rosetta Stone of legislative archaeology, a crystal clear Committee Report — one can never be sure that the legislators who voted for the text of the bill were aware of it. The only thing that was authoritatively adopted for sure was the text of the enactment; the rest is necessarily speculation. Where it is doubtful whether the text includes the penalty, the penalty ought not be imposed. "[T]he moral condemnation of the community," Bass, supra, at 348, is no more reflected in the views of a majority of a single committee of congressmen (assuming, of course, they have genuinely considered what their staff has produced) than it is reflected in the views of a majority of an appellate court; we should feel no less concerned about "men languishing in prison" at the direction of the one than of the other.

We have in a number of cases other than Moskal done what the plurality has done here: inquired into legislative history and invoked it to support or at least permit themore lenient reading. But only once, to my knowledge, have we relied on legislative history to "clarify" a statute, explicitly found to be facially ambiguous, against the interest of a criminal defendant. In Dixson v. United States, 465 U.S. 482, 500-501, n. 19 (1984), the

Court relied on legislative history to determine that defendants, officers of a corporation responsible for administering federal block grants, were "public officials" within the meaning of 18 U.S.C. § 201(a). The opinion does not trouble to discuss the "fair warning" or "condemnation of the community" implications of its decision, and both of the cases it cites in supposed support of its holding found the statute at hand not to be facially ambiguous. See United States v. Moore, 423 U.S. 122, 131 (1975) ("By its terms § 841 reaches `any person" and "does not exempt (as it could have) `all registrants' or `all persons registered under this Act' "); United States v. Brown, 333 U.S. 18, 22 (1948) ("The legislation reflects an unmistakable intention to provide punishment for escape or attempted escape to be superimposed upon the punishment meted out for previous offenses. This appears from the face of the statute itself"). I think Dixson weak (indeed, utterly unreasoned) foundation for a rule of construction that permits legislative history to satisfy the ancient requirement that criminal statutes speak "plainly and unmistakably," United States v. Gradwell, 243 U.S. 476, 485 (1917); see also Bass, supra, at 348.

In sum, I would not embrace, as the plurality does, the Moskal formulation of this canon of construction, lest lower courts take the dictum to heart. I would acknowledge the tension in our precedents, the absence of an examination of the consequences of the Moskal mode of analysis, and the consequent conclusion that Moskal may not be good law.

Justice Scalia's dissent in Eastman Kodak v. Image Technical Services (June 8, 1992)

Justice Scalia, with whom Justice O'Connor and Justice Thomas join, dissenting.

This is not, as the Court describes it, just "another case that concerns the standard for summary judgment in an antitrust controversy." Ante, at 1. Rather, the case presents a very narrow — but extremely important — question of substantive antitrust law: whether, for purposes of applying our per se rule condemning "ties," and for purposes of applying our exacting rules governing the behavior of would-be monopolists, a manufacturer's conceded lack of power in the interbrand market for its equipment is somehow consistent with its possession of "market," or even "monopoly," power in wholly derivative aftermarkets for that equipment. In my view, the Court supplies an erroneous answer to this question, and I dissent.

I

Per se rules of antitrust illegality are reserved for those situations where logic and experience show that the risk of injury to competition from the defendant's behavior is so pronounced that it is needless and wasteful to conduct the usual judicial inquiry into the balance between the behavior's procompetitive benefits and its anticompetitive costs. See, e. g., Arizona v. Maricopa County Medical Society, 457 U.S. 332, 350-351 (1982). "The character of the restraint produced by [behavior to which a per se ruleapplies] is considered a sufficient basis for presuming unreasonableness without the necessity of any analysis of the market context in which the [behavior] may be found." Jefferson Parish Hospital Dist. No. 2 v. Hyde, 466 U.S. 2, 9 (1984). The per se rule against tying is just such a rule: Where the conditions precedent to application of the rule are met, i.e., where the tying arrangement is backed up by the defendant's market power in the "tying" product, the arrangement is adjudged in violation of § 1 of the Sherman Act, 15 U.S.C. § 1 without any inquiry into the practice's actual effect on competition and consumer welfare. But see United States v. Jerrold Electronics Corp., 187 F. Supp. 545, 560 (ED Pa. 1960), aff'd per curiam, 365 U.S. 567 (1961) (accepting affirmative defense to per se tying allegation).

Despite intense criticism of the tying doctrine in academic circles, see, e. g., R. Bork, The Antitrust Paradox 365-381 (1978), the stated rationale for our per se rule has varied little over the years. When the defendant has genuine "market power" in the tying product — the power to raise price by reducing output — the tie potentially enables him to extend that power into a second distinct market, enhancing barriers to entry in each. In addition:

"[T]ying arrangements may be used to evade price control in the tying product through clandestine transfer of the profit to the tied product; they may be used as a counting device to effect price discrimination; and they may be used to force a full line of products on the customer so as to extract more easily from him a monopoly return on one unique product in the line." Fortner Enterprises, Inc. v. United States Steel Corp., 394 U.S. 495, 513-514 (1969) (Fortner I) (White, J., dissenting) (footnotes omitted).

For these reasons, as we explained in Jefferson Parish, "the law draws a distinction between the exploitation of market power by merely enhancing the price of the tying product, on the one hand, and by attempting to impose restraints oncompetition in the market for a tied product, on the other." 466 U. S., at 14.

Our Section 2 monopolization doctrines are similarly directed to discrete situations in which a defendant's possession of substantial market power, combined with his exclusionary or anticompetitive behavior, threatens to defeat or forestall the corrective forces of competition and thereby sustain or extend the defendant's agglomeration of power. See United States v. Grinnell Corp., 384 U.S. 563, 570-571 (1966). Where a defendant maintains substantial market power, his activities are examined through a special lens: Behavior that might otherwise not be of concern to the antitrust laws — or that might even be viewed as procompetitive — can take on exclusionary connotations when practiced by a monopolist. 3 P. Areeda & D. Turner, Antitrust Law ◆ 813, pp. 300-302 (1978) (hereinafter 3 Areeda & Turner).

The concerns, however, that have led the courts to heightened scrutiny both of the "exclusionary conduct" practiced by a monopolist and of tying arrangements subject to per se prohibition, are completely without force when the participants lack market power. As to the former, "[t]he [very] definition of exclusionary conduct," as practiced by a monopolist, ". . . [is] predicated on the existence of substantial market power." Id., at ◆ 813, p. 301 (1978); see, e. g., Walker Process Equipment, Inc. v. Food Machinery & Chemical Corp., 382 U.S. 172, 177-178 (1965) (fraudulent patent procurement); Standard

Oil Co. of N.J. v. United States, 221 U.S. 1, 75 (1911) (acquisition of competitors); 3 Areeda and Turner ◆ 724, at 195-197 (vertical integration). And with respect to tying, we have recognized that bundling arrangements not coerced by the heavy hand of market power can serve the procompetitive functions of facilitating new entry into certain markets, see, e. g., Brown Shoe Co. v. United States, 370 U.S. 294, 330 (1962), permitting "clandestine price cutting in products which otherwise would have no price competition at all because of fear ofretaliation from the few other producers dealing in the market," Fortner I, supra, at 514, n. 9 (White, J., dissenting), assuring quality control, see, e. g., Standard Oil Co. of Cal. v. United States, 337 U.S. 293, 306 (1949), and, where "the tied and tying products are functionally related, . . . reduc[ing] costs through economies of joint production and distribution." Fortner I, supra, at 514, n. 9 (White, J., dissenting). "Accordingly, we have [only] condemned tying arrangements [under the per se rule] when the seller has some special ability — usually called `market power' — to force a purchaser to do something that he would not do in a competitive market." Jefferson Parish, supra, at 13-14.

The Court today finds in the typical manufacturer's inherent power over its own brand of equipment — over the sale of distinctive repair parts for that equipment, for example — the sort of "monopoly power" sufficient to bring the sledgehammer of § 2 into play. And, not surprisingly in light of that insight, it readily labels single brand power over aftermarket products "market power" sufficient to permit an antitrust plaintiff to invoke the per se rule against tying. In my opinion, this makes no economic sense. The holding that market power can be found on the present record causes these venerable rules of selective proscription to extend well beyond the point where the reasoning that supports them leaves off. Moreover, because the sort of power condemned by the Court today is possessed by every manufacturer of durable goods with distinctive parts, the Court's opinion threatens to release a torrent of litigation and a flood of commercial intimidation that will do much more harm than good to enforcement of the antitrust laws and to genuine competition. I shall explain, in Parts II and III, respectively, how neither logic nor experience suggests, let alone compels, application of the per se tying prohibition and monopolization doctrine to a seller's behavior in its single brand aftermarkets, when that seller is without power at the interbrand level.

II

On appeal in the Ninth Circuit, respondents, having waived their "rule of reason" claim, were limited to arguing that the record, construed in the light most favorable to them, Anderson v. Liberty Lobby, Inc., 477 U.S. 242, 255 (1986), supported application of the per se tying prohibition to Kodak's restrictive parts and service policy. See Image Technical Services, Inc. v. Eastman Kodak Co., 903 F. 2d 612, 615, n. 1 (CA9 1990). As the Court observes, in order to survive Kodak's motion for summary judgment on this claim, respondents bore the burden of proffering evidence on which a reasonable trier of fact could conclude that Kodak possesses power in the market for the alleged "tying" product. See ante, at 10; Jefferson Parish Hospital Dist. No. 2 v. Hyde, 466 U. S., at 13-14.

A

We must assume, for purposes of deciding this case, that petitioner is without market, much less monopoly, power in the interbrand markets for its micrographics and photocopying equipment. See ante, at 11-12, n. 10; Oklahoma City v. Tuttle, 471 U.S. 808, 816 (1985). In the District Court, respondents did, in fact, include in their complaint an allegation which posited the interbrand equipment markets as the relevant markets; in particular, they alleged a § 1 "tie" of micrographics and photocopying equipment to the parts and service for those machines. 1 App. 22-23. Though this allegation was apparently abandoned in pursuit of § 1 and § 2 claims focused exclusively on the parts and service aftermarkets (about which more later), I think it helpful to analyze how that claim would have fared under the per se rule.

Had Kodak — from the date of its entry into the micrographics and photocopying equipment markets — included a lifetime parts and service warranty with all original equipment, or required consumers to purchase a lifetime parts and service contract with each machine, that bundling of equipment, parts and service would no doubt constitute a tie under the tests enunciated in Jefferson Parish Hospital Dist. No. 2 v. Hyde, supra. Nevertheless, it would be immune from per se scrutiny under the antitrust laws because the tying product would be equipment, a market in which (we assume) Kodak has no power to influence price or quantity. See Jefferson Parish, supra, at 13-14; United States Steel Corp. v. Fortner Enterprises, Inc., 429 U.S. 610, 620 (1977) (Fortner II); Northern Pacific R. Co. v. United States, 356 U.S. 1, 6-7 (1958). The same result would obtain, I think, had Kodak — from the date of its market entry — consistently pursued an announced policy of limiting parts sales in the manner alleged in this case, so that customers bought with the knowledge that aftermarket support could be obtained only from Kodak. The foreclosure of respondents from the business of servicing Kodak's micrographics and photocopying machines in these illustrations would be undeniably complete — as complete as the foreclosure described in respondents' complaint. Nonetheless, we would inquire no further than to ask whether Kodak's market power in the equipment market effectively forced consumers to purchase Kodak micrographics or photocopying machines subject to the company's restrictive aftermarket practices. If not, that would end the case insofar as the per se rule was concerned. See Jefferson Parish, supra, at 13-14; 9 P. Areeda, Antitrust Law � 1709c5, pp. 101-102 (1991); Klein & Saft, The Law and Economics of Franchise Tying Contracts, 28 J. Law & Econ. 345, 356 (1985). The evils against which the tying prohibition is directed would simply not be presented. Interbrand competition would render Kodak powerless to gain economic power over an additional class of consumers, to price discriminate by charging each customer a "system" price equal to the system's economic value to that customer, or to raise barriers to entry in the interbrand equipment markets. See 3 Areeda and Turner � 829d, at 331-332.

I have described these illustrations as hypothetical, but in fact they are not far removed from this case. The record below is consistent — in large part — with just this sort of bundling of equipment on the one hand, with parts and service on the other. The restrictive parts policy, with respect to micrographics equipment at least, was not even alleged to be anything but prospective. See 1 App. 17. As respondents summarized their factual proffer below:

"Under this policy, Kodak cut off parts on new products to Kodak micrographics ISOs. The effect of this, of course, was that as customers of Kodak micrographics ISOs obtained new equipment, the ISOs were unable to service the equipment for that customer, and, service for these customers was lost by the Kodak ISOs. Additionally, as equipment became obsolete, and the equipment population became all "new equipment" (post April 1985 models), Kodak micrographics ISOs would be able to service no equipment at all." 2 id., at 360.

As to Kodak copiers, Kodak's restrictive parts policy had a broader foundation: Considered in the light most favorable to respondents, see Anderson, supra, at 255, the record suggests that, from its inception, the policy was applied to new and existing copier customers alike. But at least all post-1985 purchasers of micrographics equipment, like all post-1985 purchasers of new Kodak copiers, could have been aware of Kodak's parts practices. The only thing lacking to bring all of these purchasers (accounting for the vast bulk of the commerce at issue here) squarely within the hypotheticals we have described is concrete evidence that the restrictive parts policy was announced or generally known. Thus, under the Court's approach the existence vel non of such evidence is determinative of the legal standard (the per se rule versus the rule of reason) under which the alleged tie is examined. In my judgment, this makes no sense. It is quite simply anomalous that a manufacturer functioning in a competitive equipment market should be exempt from the per se rule when it bundles equipment with parts and service, but not when it bundles parts with service. This vast difference in the treatment of what will ordinarily be economically similar phenomena is alone enough to call today's decision into question.

B

In the Court of Appeals, respondents sought to sidestep the impediment posed by interbrand competition to their invocation of the per se tying rule by zeroing in on the parts and service "aftermarkets" for Kodak equipment. By alleging a tie of parts to service, rather than of equipment to parts and service, they identified a tying product in which Kodak unquestionably held a near monopoly share: the parts uniquely associated with Kodak's brand of machines. See Jefferson Parish, 466 U. S., at 17. The Court today holds that such a facial showing of market share in a single brand aftermarket is sufficient to invoke the per se rule. The existence of even vibrant interbrand competition is no defense. See ante, at 17-18.

I find this a curious form of market power on which to premise the application of a per se proscription. It is enjoyed by virtually every manufacturer of durable goods requiring aftermarket support with unique, or relatively unique, goods. See P. Areeda & H. Hovenkamp, Antitrust Law � 525.1, p. 563 (Supp. 1991). "[S]uch reasoning makes every maker of unique parts for its own product a holder of market power no matter how unimportant its product might be in the market." Ibid. (emphasis added). [n.1] Under theCourt's analysis, the per se rule may now be applied to single brand ties effected by the most insignificant players in fully competitive interbrand markets, as long as the arrangement forecloses aftermarket competitors from more than a de minimis amount of business, Fortner I, 394 U. S., at 501. This seems to me quite wrong. A tying arrangement "forced" through the exercise of such power no more implicates the leveraging and price discrimination concerns behind the per se tying prohibition than does a tie of the foremarket brand to its aftermarket derivatives, which — as I have explained — would not be subject to per se condemnation. [n.2] As implemented, the Kodak arrangement challengedin this case may have implicated truth in advertising or other consumer protection concerns, but those concerns do not alone suggest an antitrust prohibition. See, e. g., Town Sound and Custom Tops, Inc. v. Chrysler Motors Corp., 959 F.2d 468 (CA3 1992) (en banc).

In the absence of interbrand power, a seller's predominant or monopoly share of its single brand derivative markets does not connote the power to raise derivative market prices generally by reducing quantity. As Kodak and its principal amicus, the United States, point out, a rational consumer considering the purchase of Kodak equipment will inevitably factor into his purchasing decision the expected cost of aftermarket support. "[B]oth the price of the equipment and the price of parts and service over the life of the equipment are expenditures that are necessary to obtain copying and micrographic services." Brief for United States as Amicus Curiae 13. If Kodak set generally supracompetitive prices for either spare parts or repair services without making an offsetting reduction in the price of its machines, rational consumers would simply turn to Kodak's competitors for photocopying and micrographic systems. See, e. g., Grappone, Inc. v. Subaru of New England, Inc., 858 F. 2d 792, 796-798 (CA1 1988). True, there are — as the Court notes, see ante, at 21" the occasional irrational consumers that consider only the hardware cost at the time of purchase (a category that regrettably includes the Federal Government, whose "purchasing system," we are told, assigns foremarket purchases and aftermarket purchases to different entities). But we have never before premised the application of antitrust doctrine on the lowest common denominator of consumer.

The Court attempts to counter this theoretical point with theory of its own. It says that there are "information costs" — the costs and inconvenience to the consumer of acquiring and processing life cycle pricing data for Kodak machines — that "could create a less responsive connection between service and parts prices and equipment sales." Ante, at 19. But this truism about the functioning of markets for sophisticated equipment cannot create "market power" of concern to the antitrust laws where otherwise there is none. "Information costs," or, more accurately, gaps in the availability and quality of consumer information, pervade real world markets; and because consumers generally make do with "rough cut" judgments about price in such circumstances, in virtually any market there are zones within which otherwise competitive suppliers may overprice their products without losing appreciable market share. We have never suggested that the principal players in a market with such commonplace informational deficiencies (and, thus, bands of apparent consumer pricing indifference) exercise market power in any sense relevant to the antitrust laws. "While [such] factors may generate `market power' in some abstract sense, they do not generate the kind of market power that justifies condemnation of tying." Jefferson Parish Hospital Dist. No. 2 v. Hyde, 466 U. S., at 27; see, e.g., Town Sound and Custom Tops, Inc. v. Chrysler Motors Corp., supra.

Respondents suggest that, even if the existence of interbrand competition prevents Kodak from raising prices generally in its single brand aftermarkets, there remain certain consumers who are necessarily subject to abusive Kodak pricing behavior by reason of their being "locked in" to their investments in Kodak machines. The Court agrees; indeed, it goes further by suggesting that even a generalpolicy of supracompetitive aftermarket prices might be profitable over the long run because of the "lock in" phenomenon. "[A] seller profitably could maintain supracompetitive prices in the aftermarket," the Court explains, "if the switching costs were high relative to the increase in service prices, and the number of locked in customers were high relative to the number of new purchasers." Ante, at 23. In speculating about this latter possibility, the Court is essentially repudiating the assumption on which we are bound to decide this case, viz., Kodak's lack of any power whatsoever in the interbrand market. If Kodak's general increase in aftermarket prices were to bring the total "system" price above competitive levels in the interbrand market, Kodak would be wholly unable to make further foremarket sales — and would find itself exploiting an ever dwindling aftermarket, as those Kodak micrographic and photocopying machines already in circulation passed into disuse.

The Court's narrower point, however, is undeniably true. There will be consumers who, because of their capital investment in Kodak equipment, "will tolerate some level of service price increases before changing equipment brands," ante, at 23; this is necessarily true for "every maker of unique parts for its own product." Areeda & Hovenkamp, Antitrust Law ◆ 525.1b, at 563. But this "circumstantial" leverage created by consumer investment regularly crops up in smoothly functioning, even perfectly competitive, markets, and in most — if not all — of its manifestations, it is of no concern to the antitrust laws. The leverage held by the manufacturer of a malfunctioning refrigerator (which is measured by the consumer's reluctance to walk away from his initial investment in that device) is no different in kind or degree from the leverage held by the swimming pool contractor when he discovers a 5 ton boulder in his customer's backyard and demands an additional sum of money to remove it; or the leverage held by an airplane manufacturer over an airline that has "standardized" its fleet around the manufacturer's models; or the leverage held by a drill press manufacturer whose customers have built their production lines around the manufacturer's particular style of drill press; the leverage held by an insurance company over its independent sales force that has invested in company specific paraphernalia; or the leverage held by a mobile home park owner over his tenants, who are unable to transfer their homes to a different park except at great expense, see generally Yee v. Escondido, 503 U. S. ____ (1992). Leverage, in the form of circumstantial power, plays a role in each of these relationships; but in none of them is the leverage attributable to the dominant party's market power in any relevant sense. Though that power can plainly work to the injury of certain consumers, it produces only "a brief perturbation in competitive conditions — not the sort of thing the antitrust laws do or should worry about." Parts & Elec. Motors, Inc. v. Sterling Elec., Inc., 866 F. 2d 228, 236 (CA7 1988) (Posner, J., dissenting).

The Court correctly observes that the antitrust laws do not permit even a natural monopolist to project its monopoly power into another market, i.e., to " `exploi[t] his dominant position in one market to expand his empire into the next.' " Ante, at 27, n. 29 (quoting Times Picayune Publishing Co. v. United States, 345 U.S. 594, 611 (1953)). However, when a manufacturer uses its control over single branded parts to acquire influence in single branded service, the monopoly "leverage" is almost invariably of no practical consequence, because of perfect identity between the consumers in each of the subject aftermarkets (those who need replacement parts for Kodak equipment, and those who need servicing of Kodak equipment). When that condition exists, the tie does not permit the manufacturer to project power over a class of consumers distinct from that which it is already able to exploit (and fully) without the inconvenience of the tie. Cf., e. g., Bowman, Tying Arrangements and the Leverage Problem, 67 Yale L. J. 19, 21-27 (1957).

We have never before accepted the thesis the Court today embraces: that a seller's inherent control over the unique parts for its own brand amounts to "market power" of a character sufficient to permit invocation of the per se rule against tying. As the Court observes, ante, at 27, n. 29, we have applied the per se rule to manufacturer ties of foremarket equipment to aftermarket derivatives — but only when the manufacturer's monopoly power in the equipment, coupled with the use of derivative sales as "counting devices" to measure the intensity of customer equipment usage, enabled the manufacturer to engage in price discrimination, and thereby more fully exploit its interbrand power. See International Salt Co. v. United States, 332 U.S. 392 (1947); International Business Machines Corp. v. United States, 298 U.S. 131 (1936); United Shoe Machinery Corp. v. United States, 258 U.S. 451 (1922). That sort of enduring opportunity to engage in price discrimination is unavailable to a manufacturer — like Kodak — that lacks power at the interbrand level. A tie between two aftermarket derivatives does next to nothing to improve a competitive manufacturer's ability to extract monopoly rents from its consumers. [n.3]

Nor has any court of appeals (save for the Ninth Circuit panel below) recognized single branded aftermarket power as a basis for invoking the per se tying prohibition. See Virtual Maintenance, Inc. v. Prime Computer, Inc., 957 F.2d 1318, 1328 (CA6 1992) ("Defining the market by customer demand after the customer has chosen a single supplierfails to take into account that the supplier . . . must compete with other similar suppliers to be designated the sole source in the first place"); Grappone, Inc. v. Subaru of New England, Inc., 858 F. 2d 792, 798 (CA1 1988) ("[W]e do not see how such dealer investment [in facilities to sell Subaru products] . . . could easily translate into Subaru market power of a kind that, through tying, could ultimately lead to higher than competitive prices for consumers"); A.I. Root Co. v. Computer/Dynamics, Inc., 806 F. 2d

673, 675-677, and n. 3 (CA6 1986) (competition at "small business computer" level precluded assertion of computer manufacturer's power over software designed for use only with manufacturer's brand of computer); General Business Systems v. North American Philips Corp., 699 F. 2d 965, 977 (CA9 1983) ("To have attempted to impose significant pressure to buy [aftermarket hardware] by use of the tying service only would have hastened the date on which Philips surrendered to its competitors in the small business computer market"). See also Parts & Elec. Motors, Inc. v. Sterling Elec., Inc., 866 F. 2d, at 233 (law of the case doctrine compelled finding of market power in replacement parts for single brand engine).

We have recognized in closely related contexts that the deterrent effect of interbrand competition on the exploitation of intrabrand market power should make courts exceedingly reluctant to apply rules of per se illegality to intrabrand restraints. For instance, we have refused to apply a rule of per se illegality to vertical nonprice restraints "because of their potential for a simultaneous reduction of intrabrand competition and stimulation of interbrand competition," Continental T.V., Inc. v. GTE Sylvania Inc., 433 U.S. 36, 51-52 (1977), the latter of which we described as "the primary concern of antitrust law." Id., at 52, n. 19. We noted, for instance, that "new manufacturers and manufacturers entering new markets can use the restrictions in order to induce competent and aggressive retailers to make the kind of investment of capital and labor that is often required in the distribution of products unknown to the consumer," and that "[e]stablished manufacturers can use them to induce retailers to engage in promotional activities or to provide service and repair facilities necessary to the efficient marketing of their products." Id., at 55. See also Business Electronics Corp. v. Sharp Electronics Corp., 485 U.S. 717, 726 (1988). The same assumptions, in my opinion, should govern our analysis of ties alleged to have been "forced" solely through intrabrand market power. In the absence of interbrand power, a manufacturer's bundling of aftermarket products may serve a multitude of legitimate purposes: It may facilitate manufacturer efforts to ensure that the equipment remains operable and thus protect the seller's business reputation, see United States v. Jerrold Electronics Corp., 187 F. Supp., at 560, aff'd per curiam, 365 U.S. 567 (1961); it may create the conditions for implicit consumer financing of the acquisition cost of the tying equipment through supracompetitively priced aftermarket purchases, see, e. g., A. Oxenfeldt, Industrial Pricing and Market Practices 378 (1951); and it may, through the resultant manufacturer control of aftermarket activity, "yield valuable information about component or design weaknesses that will materially contribute to product improvement," 3 Areeda & Turner ◆ 733c, at 258-259; see also id. ◆ 829d, at 331-332. Because the interbrand market will generally punish intrabrand restraints that consumers do not find in their interest, we should not — under the guise of a per se rule — condemn such potentially procompetitive arrangements simply because of the antitrust defendant's inherent power over the unique parts for its own brand.

I would instead evaluate the aftermarket tie alleged in this case under the rule of reason, where the tie's actual anticompetitive effect in the tied product market, together with its potential economic benefits, can be fully captured in the analysis, see, e. g., Jefferson Parish Hospital Dist. No. 2 v. Hyde, 466 U. S., at 41 (O'Connor, J., concurring injudgment). Disposition of this case does not require such an examination, however, as respondents apparently waived any rule of reason claim they may have had in the District Court. I would thus reverse the Ninth Circuit's judgment on the tying claim outright.

III

These considerations apply equally to respondents' § 2 claims. An antitrust defendant lacking relevant "market power" sufficient to permit invocation of the per se prohibition against tying a fortiori lacks the monopoly power that warrants heightened scrutiny of his allegedly exclusionary behavior. Without even so much as asking whether the purposes of § 2 are implicated here, the Court points to Kodak's control of "100% of the parts market and 80% to 95% of the service market," markets with "no readily available substitutes," ante, at 28, and finds that the proffer of such statistics is sufficient to fend off summary judgment. But this showing could easily be made, as I have explained, with respect to virtually any manufacturer of differentiated products requiring aftermarket support. By permitting antitrust plaintiffs to invoke § 2 simply upon the unexceptional demonstration that a manufacturer controls the supplies of its single branded merchandise, the Court transforms § 2 from a specialized mechanism for responding to extraordinary agglomerations (or threatened agglomerations) of economic power to an all purpose remedy against run of the mill business torts.

In my view, if the interbrand market is vibrant, it is simply not necessary to enlist § 2's machinery to police a seller's intrabrand restraints. In such circumstances, the interbrand market functions as an infinitely more efficient and more precise corrective to such behavior, rewarding the seller whose intrabrand restraints enhance consumer welfare while punishing the seller whose control of the aftermarkets is viewed unfavorably by interbrand consumers. See Business Electronics Corp., supra, at 725; Continental T.V., Inc., supra, at 52, n. 19, 54. Because this case comes to us on the assumption that Kodak is without such interbrand power, I believe we are compelled to reverse the judgment of the Court of Appeals. I respectfully dissent.

Notes

1 That there exist innumerable parts and service firms in such industries as the automobile industry, see Brief for Automotive Warehouse Distributors Assn., et al., as Amici Curiae 2-3, does not detract from this point. The question whether power to control an aftermarket exists is quite distinct from the question whether the power has been exercised. Manufacturers in some markets have no doubt determinedthat exclusionary intrabrand conduct works to their disadvantage at the competitive interbrand level, but this in no way refutes the self evident reality that control over unique replacement parts for single branded goods is ordinarily available to such manufacturers for the taking. It confounds sound analysis to suggest, as respondents do, see Brief for Respondents 5, 37, that the asserted fact that Kodak manufactures only 10% of its replacement parts, and

purchases the rest from original equipment manufacturers, casts doubt on Kodak's possession of an inherent advantage in the aftermarkets. It does no such thing, any more than Kodak's contracting with others for the manufacture of all constituent parts included in its original equipment would alone suggest that Kodak lacks power in the interbrand micrographics and photocopying equipment markets. The suggestion implicit in respondents' analysis — that if a seller chooses to contract for the manufacture of its branded merchandise, it must permit the contractors to compete in the sale of that merchandise — is plainly unprecedented.

2 Even with interbrand power, I may observe, it is unlikely that Kodak could have incrementally exploited its position through the tie of parts to service alleged here. Most of the "service" at issue is inherently associated with the parts, i.e., that service involved in incorporating the parts into Kodak equipment, and the two items tend to be demanded by customers in fixed proportions (one part with one unit of service necessary to install the part). When that situation obtains, "no revenue can be derived from setting a higher price for the tied product which could not have been made by setting the optimum price for the tying product." P. Areeda & L. Kaplow, Antitrust Analysis ❖ 426 (a), p. 706 (4th ed. 1988) (quoting Bowman, Tying Arrangements and the LeverageProblem, 67 Yale L. J. 19 (1957)). These observations strongly suggest that Kodak parts and the service involved in installing them should not be treated as distinct products for antitrust tying purposes. See Jefferson Parish, 466 U.S. 2, 39 (O'Connor, J., concurring in judgment) ("For products to be treated as distinct, the tied product must, at a minimum, be one that some consumers might wish to purchase separately without also purchasing the tying product") (emphasis in original) (footnote omitted); Ross, The Single Product Issue in Antitrust Tying: A Functional Approach, 23 Emory L. J. 963, 1009-1010 (1974).

3 The Court insists that the record in this case suggests otherwise, i.e., that a tie between parts and service somehow does enable Kodak to increase overall monopoly profits. See ante, at 27, n. 29. Although the Court does not identify the record evidence on which it relies, the suggestion, apparently, is that such a tie facilitates price discrimination between sophisticated, "high volume" users of Kodak equipment and their unsophisticated counterparts. The sophisticated users (who, the Court presumes, invariably self service their equipment) are permitted to buy Kodak parts without also purchasing supracompetitively priced Kodak service, while the unsophisticated are — through the imposition of the tie — compelled to buy both. See ante, at 22-23.

While superficially appealing, at bottom this explanation lacks coherence. Whether they self service their equipment or not, rational foremarket consumers (those consumers who are not yet "locked in" to Kodak hardware) will be driven to Kodak's competitors if the price of Kodak equipment, together with the expected cost of aftermarket support, exceeds competitive levels. This will be true no matter how Kodak distributes the total system price among equipment, parts, and service. See supra, at 10. Thus, as to these consumers, Kodak's lack of interbrand power wholly prevents it from employing a tie between parts and service as a vehicle for price discrimination. Nor does a tie between parts and service offer Kodak incremental exploitative power over those consumers — sophisticated or not — who have the supposed misfortune of being "locked in" to Kodak equipment. If Kodak desired to exploit its circumstantial power over this wretched class by pressing them up to the point where the cost to each consumer of switching equipment brands barely exceeded the cost of retaining Kodak equipment and remaining subject to Kodak's abusive practices, it could plainly do so without the inconvenience of a tie, through supracompetitive parts pricing alone. Since the locked in sophisticated parts purchaser is as helpless as the locked in unsophisticated one, I see nothing to be gained by price discrimination in favor of the former. If such price discrimination were desired, however, it would not have to be accomplished indirectly, through a tie of parts to service. Section 2(a) of the Robinson Patman Act, 15 U.S.C. § 13(a), would prevent giving lower parts prices to the sophisticated customers only "where the effect of such discrimination may be substantially to lessen competition or tend to create a monopoly in any line of commerce, or to injure, destroy, or prevent competition with any person who either grants or knowingly receives the benefit of such discrimination, or with customers of either of them . . . ." Ibid.; see, e. g., Falls City Industries, Inc. v. Vanco Beverage, Inc., 460 U.S. 428, 434-435 (1983). That prohibited effect often occurs when price discriminated goods are sold for resale (i.e., to purchasers who are necessarily in competition with one another). E. g., Federal Trade Commission v. Morton Salt Co., 334 U.S. 37, 47 (1948); see P. Areeda & L. Kaplow, Antitrust Analysis ¶ 600, p. 923 (1988) ("Secondary line injury arises [under the Robinson Patman Act] when a powerful firm buying supplies at favorable prices thereby gains a decisive advantage over its competitors that are forced to pay higher prices for their supplies"). It rarely occurs where, as would be the case here, the price discriminated goods are sold to various businesses for consumption.

Justice Scalia's dissent in American Nat. Red Cross v. SG (June 19, 1992) [Notes omitted]

Justice Scalia, with whom The Chief Justice, Justice O'Connor, and Justice Kennedy join, dissenting.

The Court today concludes that whenever a statute granting a federally chartered corporation the "power to sue and be sued" specifically mentions the federal courts (as opposed to merely embracing them within general language), the law will be deemed not only to confer on the corporation the capacity to bring and suffer suit (which is all that the words say), but also to confer on federal district courts jurisdiction over any and all controversies to which that corporation is a party. This wonderland of linguistic confusion—in which words are sometimes read to mean only what they say and other times read also to mean what they do not say—is based on the erroneous premise that our cases in this area establish a "magic words" jurisprudence that departs from ordinary rules of English usage. In fact, our cases simply reflect the fact that the natural reading of some "sue and be sued" clauses is that they confer both capacity and jurisdiction. Since the natural reading of the Red Cross Charter is that it confers only capacity, I respectfully dissent.

I

Section 2 of the Red Cross Charter, 36 U. S. C. § 2, sets forth the various powers of the corporation, such as the power "to have and to hold . . . real and personal estate"; "to adopt a seal"; "to ordain and establish bylaws and regulations"; and to "do all such acts and things as may be necessary to . . . promote [its] purposes."[1] The second item on this list is "the power to sue and be sued in courts of law and equity, State or Federal, within the jurisdiction of the United States." Ibid. The presence of this language amidst a list of more or less ordinary corporate powers confirms what the words themselves suggest: It merely establishes that the Red Cross is a juridical person which may be party to a lawsuit in an American court, and that the Red Cross—despite its status as a federally chartered corporation—does not share the Government's general immunity from suit. Cf. Fed. Rule Civ. Proc. 17(b) ("The capacity of a corporation to sue or be sued shall be determined by the law under which it was organized"); 4 Thompson on Corporations § 3161, p. 975 (3d ed. 1927) ("[The power to sue and be sued] is expressly conferred in practically every incorporating act"); Loeffler v. Frank, 486 U. S. 549, 554-557 (1988) ("sue and be sued" clause waives sovereign immunity).

It is beyond question that nothing in the language of this provision suggests that it has anything to do with regulating the jurisdiction of the federal courts. The grant of corporate power to sue and be sued in no way implies a grant of federal-court jurisdiction; it merely places the corporation on the same footing as a natural person, who must look elsewhere to establish grounds for getting his case into court. Words conferring authority upon a corporation are a most illogical means of conferring jurisdiction upon a court, and would not normally be understood that way. Moreover, it would be extraordinary to confer a new subject-matter jurisdiction upon "federal courts" in general, rather than upon a particular federal court or courts.

The Court apparently believes, see ante, at 256, n. 8, that the language of § 2 is functionally equivalent to a specific reference to the district courts, since no other court could reasonably have been intended to be the recipient of the jurisdictional grant. Perhaps so, but applying that intuition requires such a random butchering of the text that it is much more reasonable to assume that no court was the intended recipient. The Red Cross is clearly granted the capacity to sue and be sued in all federal courts, so that it could appear, for example, as a party in a third-party action in the Court of International Trade, see 28 U. S. C. § 1583, and in an action before the United States Claims Court, see Claims Court Rule 14(a) (Mar. 15, 1991). There is simply no textual basis, and no legal basis except legal intuition, for saying that it must in addition establish an independent basis of jurisdiction to proceed in those courts, though it does not in the district courts.

In fact, the language of this provision not only does not distinguish among federal courts, it also does not treat federal courts differently from state courts; the Red Cross is granted the "power" to sue in both. This parallel treatment of state and federal courts even further undermines a jurisdictional reading of the statute, since the provision cannot reasonably be read as allowing the Red Cross to enter a state court without establishing the independent basis of jurisdiction appropriate under state law. Such a reading would present serious constitutional questions. Cf. Brown v. Gerdes, 321 U. S. 178, 188 (1944) (Frankfurter, J., concurring); Howlett v. Rose, 496 U. S. 356, 372 (1990); Herb v. Pitcairn, 324 U. S. 117, 120-121 (1945); Minneapolis & St. Louis R. Co. v. Bombolis, 241 U. S. 211, 222-223 (1916); but cf. Sandalow, Henry v. Mississippi and the Adequate State Ground: Proposals for a Revised Doctrine, 1965 S. Ct. Rev. 187, 207, n. 84. Since the language of the Red Cross Charter cannot fairly be read to create federal jurisdiction but not state jurisdiction, we should not construe it as creating either. Edward J. DeBartolo Corp. v. NLRB, 463 U. S. 147, 157 (1983); NLRB v. Catholic Bishop of Chicago, 440 U. S. 490, 500— 501 (1979).

I therefore conclude—indeed, I do not think it seriously contestable—that the natural reading of the "sue and be sued" clause of 36 U. S. C. § 2 confers upon the Red Cross only the capacity to "sue and be sued" in state and federal courts; it does not confer jurisdiction upon any court, state or federal.

II

I do not understand the Court to disagree with my analysis of the ordinary meaning of the statutory language. Its theory is that, regardless of ordinary meaning, our cases have created what might be termed a "phrase of art," whereby a "sue and be sued" clause confers federal jurisdiction "if, but only if, it specifically mentions the federal courts." Ante, at 255. Thus, while the uninitiated would consider the phrase "sue and be sued in any court in the United States" to mean the same thing as "sue and be sued in any court, state or federal," the Court believes that our cases have established the latter (but not the former) as a shorthand for "sue and be sued in any court, state or federal, and the federal district courts shall have jurisdiction over any such action. " Congress is assumed to have used this cleverly crafted code in enacting the charter provision at issue here. Ante, at 251-252. In my view, our cases do not establish the cryptology the Court attributes to them. Rather, the four prior cases in which we have considered the jurisdictional implications of "sue and be sued" clauses are best understood as simply applications of conventional rules of statutory construction.

In Bank of the United States v. Deveaux, 5 Cranch 61 (1809), we held that a provision of the Act establishing the first Bank of the United States which stated that the Bank was "made able and capable in law . . . to sue and be sued. . . in courts of record, or any other place whatsoever," 1 Stat. 192, did not confer jurisdiction on the federal courts to adjudicate suits brought by the Bank. Construing the statutory terms in accordance with their ordinary meaning, we concluded (as I conclude with respect to the Red Cross Charter) that the provision merely gave "a capacity to the corporation to appear, as a corporation, in any court which would, by law, have cognisance of the cause, if brought by individuals." 5 Cranch, at 85-86 (emphasis added). We expressly noted (as I have in this case) that the Act's undifferentiated mention of all courts compelled the conclusion that the provision was not jurisdictional: "If jurisdiction is given by this clause to the federal courts, it is equally given to all courts having original jurisdiction, and for all sums however small they may be. " Id., at 86 (emphasis added). That statement is immediately followed by contrasting this provision with another section of the Act which provided that certain actions against the directors of the Bank "may . . . be brought . . . in any court of record of the United States, or of either of them." 1 Stat. 194. That provision, we said, "expressly authorizes the bringing of that action in the federal or state courts," which "evinces the opinion of congress, that the right to sue does not imply a right to sue in the courts of the union, unless it be expressed." 5 Cranch, at 86. It is clear, I think, that the reason the Court thought the right to have been "expressed" under the directors-suit provision, but not "expressed" under the provision before it, was not that the former happened to mention courts "of the United States." For that would have provided no contrast to the argument against jurisdiction (italicized above) that the Court had just made. Reference to suits "in any court of record of the United States, or of either of them," is no less universal in its operative scope than reference to suits "in courts of record," and hence is subject to the same objection (to which the Court was presumably giving a contrasting example) that jurisdiction was indiscriminately conferred on all courts of original jurisdiction and for any and all amounts.

Deveaux establishes not, as the Court claims, the weird principle that mention of the federal courts in a "sue and be sued" clause confers jurisdiction; but rather, the quite different (and quite reasonable) proposition that mention of the federal courts in a provision allowing a particular cause of action to be brought does so. The contrast between the "sue and be sued" clause and the provision authorizing certain suits against the directors lay, not in the mere substitution of one broad phrase for another, but in the fact that the latter provision, by authorizing particular actions to be brought in federal court, could not reasonably be read not to confer jurisdiction. A provision merely conferring a general capacity to bring actions, however, cannot reasonably be read to confer jurisdiction.[2]

This reading of Deveaux is fully consistent with our subsequent decision in Osborn v. Bank of United States, 9 Wheat. 738 (1824), which construed the "sue and be sued" clause of the second Bank's charter as conferring jurisdiction on federal circuit courts. The second charter provided that the Bank was "made able and capable, in law . . . to sue and be sued . . . in all state courts having competent jurisdiction, and in any circuit court of the United States," 3 Stat. 269. By granting the Bank power to sue, not in all courts generally (as in Deveaux), but in particular federal courts, this suggested a grant of jurisdiction rather than merely of capacity to sue. And that suggestion was strongly confirmed by the fact that the Bank was empowered to sue in state courts "having competent jurisdiction," but in federal circuit courts simpliciter. If the statute had jurisdiction in mind as to the one, it must as to the other as well. Our opinion in Osborn did not invoke the "magic words" approach adopted by the Court today, but concluded that the charter language "admit[ted] of but one interpretation" and could not "be made plainer by explanation." 9 Wheat., at 817.

In distinguishing Deveaux, Osborn noted, and apparently misunderstood as the Court today does, that case's contrast between the "express grant of jurisdiction to the federal courts" over suits against directors and the "general words" of the "sue and be sued" clause, "which [did] not mention those courts." 9 Wheat., at 818. All it concluded from that, however, was that Deveaux established that "a general capacity in the bank to sue, without mentioning the courts of the Union, may not give a right to sue in those courts." 9 Wheat., at 818. There does not logically follow from that the rule which the Court announces today: that any grant of a general capacity to sue with mention of federal courts will suffice to confer jurisdiction. The Court's reading of this language from Osborn as giving talismanic significance to any "mention" of federal courts is simply inconsistent with the fact that Osborn (like Deveaux) did not purport to confer on the words of the clause any meaning other than that suggested by their natural import.

This reading of Deveaux and Osborn is confirmed by our later decision in Bankers Trust Co. v. Texas & Pacific R. Co., 241 U. S. 295 (1916). There we held it to be "plain" that a railroad charter provision stating that the corporation "shall be able to sue and be sued . . . in all courts of law and equity within the United States," 16 Stat. 574, did not confer jurisdiction on any court. 241 U. S., at 303. Had our earlier cases stood for the "magic words" rule adopted by the Court today, we could have reached that conclusion simply by noting that the clause at issue did not contain a specific reference to the federal courts. That is not, however, what we did. Indeed, the absence of such specific reference was not even mentioned in the opinion. See id., at 303-305. Instead, as before, we sought to determine the sense of the provision by considering the ordinary meaning of its language in context. We concluded that "Congress would have expressed [a] purpose [to confer jurisdiction] in altogether different words" than these, id., at 303, which had "the same generality and natural import as did those in the earlier bank act [in Deveaux]," id., at 304 (emphasis added). Considered in their context of a listing of corporate powers, these words established that

"Congress was not then concerned with the jurisdiction of courts but with the faculties and powers of the corporation which it was creating; and evidently all that was intended was to render this corporation capable of suing and being sued by its corporate name in any court of law or equity —Federal, state, or territorial —whose jurisdiction as otherwise competently defined was adequate to the occasion." Id., at 303 (emphasis added).

That paraphrasing of the railroad charter, in terms that would spell jurisdiction under the key the Court adopts today, belies any notion that Bankers Trust was using the same code book.[3]

The fourth and final case relied upon by the Court is D'Oench, Duhme & Co. v. FDIC, 315 U. S. 447 (1942). In that case, we granted certiorari to consider whether a federal court in a nondiversity action must apply the conflict-of-laws rules of the forum

State. We ultimately did not address that question (because we concluded that the rule of decision was provided by federal, rather than state, law, see id., at 456), but in the course of setting forth the question presented, we noted that, as all parties had conceded, the jurisdiction of the federal district court did not rest on diversity:

> "Respondent, a federal corporation, brings this suit under an Act of Congress authorizing it to sue or be sued `in any court of law or equity, State or Federal.' Sec. 12 B, Federal Reserve Act; 12 U. S. C. § 264(j).[2]
>
> "2 That subdivision of the Act further provides: `All suits of a civil nature at common law or in equity to which the Corporation shall be a party shall be deemed to arise under the laws of the United States . . . .' "

Id., at 455-456.

The Court relies heavily on this case, which it views as holding that a statute granting a corporation the power "`to sue or be sued "in any court of law or equity, State or Federal"` " establishes jurisdiction in federal district courts. Ante, at 254-255. Even if the quoted language did say that, it would be remarkable to attribute such great significance to a passing comment on a conceded point. But in my view it does not say that anyway, since the footnote must be read together with the text as explaining the single basis of jurisdiction (rather than, as the Court would have it, explaining two separate bases of jurisdiction in a case where even the explanation of one is obiter). The language quoted in the footnote is not, as the Court says, from "another part of the same statute," ante, at 254, but is the continuation of the provision quoted in the text, see 12 U. S. C. § 264(j) (1940 ed.). And the complaint in D'Oench, Duhme expressly predicated jurisdiction on the fact that the action was one "aris[ing] under the laws of the United States." Tr. of Record in D'Oench, Duhme & Co. v. Federal Deposit Ins. Corp., O. T. 1941, No. 206, p. 3. The language in this case is a thin reed upon which to rest abandonment of the rudimentary principle (followed even in other "sue and be sued" cases) that a statute should be given the meaning suggested by the "natural import" of its terms. Bankers Trust, supra, at 304.

III

Finally, the Court argues that a jurisdictional reading of the Red Cross Charter is required by the canon of construction that an amendment to a statute ordinarily should not be read as having no effect. Ante, at 263. The original "sue and be sued" clause in the Red Cross Charter did not contain the phrase "State or Federal," and the Court argues that its reading—which gives decisive weight to that addition— is therefore strongly to be preferred. Ibid. I do not agree. Even if it were the case that my reading of the clause rendered this phrase superfluous, I would consider that a small price to pay for adhering to the competing (and more important) canon that statutory language should be construed in accordance with its ordinary meaning. And it would seem particularly appropriate to run the risk of surplusage here, since the amendment in question was one of a number of technical changes in a comprehensive revision. Ch. 50, § 3, 61 Stat. 80, 81 (1947).

But in any event, a natural-meaning construction of the "sue and be sued" clause does not render the 1947 amendment superfluous. The addition of the words "State or

Federal" eliminates the possibility that the language "courts of law and equity within the jurisdiction of the United States" that was contained in the original charter, see ch. 23, § 2, 33 Stat. 600 (emphasis added), might be read to limit the grant of capacity to sue in federal court. State courts are not within the "jurisdiction" of the United States unless "jurisdiction" is taken in the relatively rare sense of referring to territory rather than power. The addition of the words "State or Federal" removes this ambiguity.

The Court rejects this argument on the ground that there is "no evidence of such an intent." Ante, at 264, n. 15. The best answer to that assertion is that it is irrelevant: To satisfy the canon the Court has invoked, it is enough that there be a reasonable construction of the old and amended statutes that would explain why the amendment is not superfluous. Another answer to the assertion is that it is wrong. As the Court notes elsewhere in its opinion, ante, at 261, n. 13, one of the only comments made by a Member of Congress on this amendment was Senator George's statement, during the hearings, that the purpose of the provision was to confirm the Red Cross' capacity to sue in state court. See Hearings on S. 591 before the Senate Committee on Foreign Relations, 80th Cong., 1st Sess., 11 (1947).[4]

　　　* * *

Because the Red Cross Charter contains no language suggesting a grant of jurisdiction, I conclude that it grants only the capacity to "sue or be sued" in a state or federal court of appropriate jurisdiction. In light of this conclusion, I find it unnecessary to reach the constitutional question addressed in Part V of the Court's opinion. I would affirm the judgment of the Court of Appeals.

Justice Scalia's concurrence and dissent in Planned Parenthood of Southeastern Pa. v. Casey (June 29, 1992) [Excerpt]

Justice Scalia, with whom the Chief Justice, Justice White, and Justice Thomas join, concurring in the judgment in part and dissenting in part.

[. . .] The States may, if they wish, permit abortion on demand, but the Constitution does not require them to do so. The permissibility of abortion, and the limitations upon it, are to be resolved like most important questions in our democracy: by citizens trying to persuade one another and then voting. As the Court acknowledges, "where reasonable people disagree the government can adopt one position or the other." Ante, at 8. The Court is correct in adding the qualification that this "assumes a state of affairs in which the choice does not intrude upon a protected liberty," ante, at 9--but the crucial part of that qualification is the penultimate word. A State's choice between two positions on which reasonable people can disagree is constitutional even when (as is often the case) it intrudes upon a "liberty" in the absolute sense. Laws against bigamy, for example--which entire societies of reasonable people disagree with--intrude upon men and women's liberty to marry and live with one another. But bigamy happens not to be a liberty specially "protected" by the Constitution.

That is, quite simply, the issue in this case: not whether the power of a woman to abort her unborn child is a "liberty" in the absolute sense; or even whether it is a liberty of great importance to many women. Of course it is both. The issue is whether it is a liberty protected by the Constitution of the United States. I am sure it is not. I reach that conclusion not because of anything so exalted as my views concerning the "concept of existence, of meaning, of the universe, and of the mystery of human life." Ibid. Rather, I reach it for the same reason I reach the conclusion that bigamy is not constitutionally protected--because of two simple facts: (1) the Constitution says absolutely nothing about it, and (2) the longstanding traditions of American society have permitted it to be legally proscribed. [n.1] Akron II, supra, at 520 (Scalia, J., concurring).

The Court destroys the proposition, evidently meant to represent my position, that "liberty" includes "only those practices, defined at the most specific level, that were protected against government interference by other rules of law when the Fourteenth Amendment was ratified," ante, at 5 (citing Michael H. v. Gerald D., 491 U.S. 110, 127, n. 6 (1989) (opinion of Scalia, J.). That is not, however, what Michael H. says; it merely observes that, in defining "liberty," we may not disregard a specific, "relevant tradition protecting, or denying protection to, the asserted right," 491 U. S., at 127, n. 6. But the Court does not wish to be fettered by any such limitations on its preferences. The Court's statement that it is "tempting" to acknowledge the authoritativeness of tradition in order to "cur[b] the discretion of federal judges," ante, at 5, is of course rhetoric rather than reality; no government official is "tempted" to place restraints upon his own freedom of action, which is why Lord Acton did not say "Power tends to purify." The Court's temptation is in the quite opposite and more natural direction--towards systematically eliminating checks upon its own power; and it succumbs. [. . .]

We should get out of this area, where we have no right to be, and where we do neither ourselves nor the country any good by remaining.

Justice Scalia's concurrence in Herrera v. Collins (Jan 23, 1993) [Excerpt]

Justice Scalia, with whom Justice Thomas joins, concurring.

[. . .] With any luck, we shall avoid ever having to face this embarrassing question again, since it is improbable that evidence of innocence as convincing as today's opinion requires would fail to produce an executive pardon.

My concern is that in making life easier for ourselves we not appear to make it harder for the lower federal courts, imposing upon them the burden of regularly analyzing newly discovered evidence of innocence claims in capital cases (in which event such federal claims, it can confidently be predicted, will become routine and even repetitive). [. . .]

Justice Scalia's concurrence and dissent in Withrow v. Williams (April 21, 1993)

Justice Scalia, with whom Justice Thomas joins, concurring in part and dissenting in part.

The issue in this case-whether the extraordinary remedy of federal habeas corpus should routinely be available for claimed violations of Miranda rights-involves not jurisdiction to issue the writ, but the equity of doing so. In my view, both the Court and JUSTICE O'CONNOR disregard the most powerful equitable consideration: that Williams has already had full and fair opportunity to litigate this claim. He had the opportunity to raise it in the Michigan trial court; he did so and lost. He had the opportunity to seek review of the trial court's judgment in the Michigan Court of Appeals; he did so and lost. Finally, he had the opportunity to seek discretionary review of that Court of Appeals judgment in both the Michigan Supreme Court and this Court; he did so and review was denied. The question at this stage is whether, given all that, a federal habeas court should now reopen the issue and adjudicate the Miranda claim anew. The answer seems to me obvious: it should not. That would be the course followed by a federal habeas court reviewing a federal conviction; it mocks our federal system to accord state convictions less respect.

I

By statute, a federal habeas court has jurisdiction over any claim that a prisoner is "in custody in violation of the Constitution or laws" of the United States. See 28 U.S.C. §§ 2241(c)(3), 2254(a), 2255. While that jurisdiction does require a claim of legal error in the original proceedings, compare Herrera v. Collins, 506 U. S. ___ (1993), it is otherwise sweeping in its breadth. As early as 1868, this Court described it in these terms:

"This legislation is of the most comprehensive character. It brings within the habeas corpus jurisdiction of every court and of every judge every possible case of privation of liberty contrary to the National Constitution, treaties, or laws. It is impossible to widen this jurisdiction." Ex parte McCardle, 6 Wall. 318, 325-326 (1868).

Our later case law has confirmed that assessment. Habeas jurisdiction extends, we have held, to federal claims for which an opportunity for full and fair litigation has already been provided in state or federal court, see Brown v. Allen, 344 U.S. 443, 458-459 (1953); Kaufman v. United States, 394 U.S. 217, 223-224 (1969); to procedurally defaulted federal claims, including those over which this Court would have no jurisdiction on direct review, see Fay v. Noia, 372 U.S. 391, 426, 428-429 (1963); Kaufman, supra, at 223; Wainwright v. Sykes, 433 U.S. 72, 90-91 (1977); Coleman v. Thompson, 501 U. S. ___, ___ (1991) (slip op., at 24-25); and to federal claims of a state criminal defendant awaiting trial, see Ex parte Royall, 117 U.S. 241, 251 (1886).

But with great power comes great responsibility. Habeas jurisdiction is tempered by the restraints that accompany the exercise of equitable discretion. This is evident from the text of the federal habeas statute, which provides that writs of habeas corpus "may be granted"--not that they shall be granted--and enjoins the court to "dispose of the matter as law and justice require." 28 U.S.C. §§ 2241(a), 2243 (emphases added). That acknowledgment of discretion is merely the continuation of a long historic tradition. In English law, habeas corpus was one of the so called "prerogative" writs, which included the writs of mandamus, certiorari, and prohibition. Duker, The English Origins of the Writ of Habeas Corpus: A Peculiar Path to Fame, 53 N. Y. U. L. Rev. 983, 984 n. 2 (1978); 3 W. Blackstone, Commentaries 132 (1768). "[A]s in the case of all other prerogative writs," habeas would not issue "as of mere course," but rather required a showing "why the extraordinary power of the crown is called in to the party's assistance." Ibid. And even where the writ was issued to compel production of the prisoner in court, the standard applied to determine whether relief would be accorded was equitable: the court was to "determine whether the case of [the prisoner's] commitment be just, and thereupon do as to justice shall appertain." 1 id., at 131.

This Court has frequently rested its habeas decisions on equitable principles. In one of the earliest federal habeas cases, Ex parte Watkins, 3 Pet. 193, 201 (1830), Chief Justice Marshall wrote: "No doubt exists respecting the power [of the Court to issue the writ]; the question is, whether this be a case in which it ought to be exercised." And in Ex parte Royall, the Court, while affirming that a federal habeas court had %the power" to discharge a state prisoner awaiting trial, held that it was "not bound in every case to exercise such a power," 117 U. S., at 251. The federal habeas statute did "not deprive the court of discretion," which "should be exercised in the light of the relations existing, under our system of government, between the judicial tribunals of the Union and of the States," ibid.

This doctrine continues to be reflected in our modern cases. In declining to extend habeas relief to all cases of state procedural default, the Court in Fay v. Noia said: "Discretion is implicit in the statutory command that the judge . . . `dispose of the matter as law and justice require,' 28 U.S.C. § 2243; and discretion was the flexible concept employed by the federal courts in developing the exhaustion rule." 372 U. S., at 438. See also Wainwright v. Sykes, supra, at 88. In fashioning this Court's retroactivity doctrine, the plurality in Teague v. Lane, 489 U.S. 288, 308-310 (1989), also relied on equitable considerations. And in a case announced today, holding that the harmless error standard for habeas corpus is less onerous than the one for direct review, the Court carries on this tradition by expressly considering equitable principles such as "finality," "comity," and "federalism." Brecht v. Abrahamson, ____ U. S. ____, ____ (1993) (slip op., at 14-15). Indeed, as Justice O'Connor notes, this Court's jurisprudence has defined the scope of habeas corpus largely by means of such equitable principles. See ante, at 2-4. The use of these principles, which serve as "gateway[s]" through which a habeas petitioner must pass before proceeding to the merits of a constitutional claim, "is grounded in the `equitable discretion' of habeas courts." Herrera v. Collins, supra, at ____ (slip op., at 12-13).

As the Court today acknowledges, see ante, at 4-5, the rule of Stone v. Powell, 428 U.S. 465 (1976), is simply one application of equitable discretion. It does not deny a federal habeas court jurisdiction over Fourth Amendment claims, but merely holds that the court ought not to entertain them when the petitioner has already had an opportunity to litigate them fully and fairly. See id., at 495, n. 37. It is therefore not correct to say that applying Stone to the present case involves "eliminating review of Miranda claims" from federal habeas, ante, at 11, or that the Court is being "asked to exclude a substantive category of issues from relitigation on habeas," ante, at 4 (opinion of O'Connor, J.). And it is therefore unnecessary to discuss at length the value of Mirandarights, as though it has been proposed that since they are particularly worthless they deserve specially disfavored treatment. The proposed rule would treat Miranda claims no differently from all other claims, taking account of all equitable factors, including the opportunity for full and fair litigation, in determining whether to provide habeas review. Wherein Miranda and Fourth Amendment claims differ from some other claims, is that the most significant countervailing equitable factor (possibility that the assigned error produced the conviction of an innocent person) will ordinarily not exist.

At common law, the opportunity for full and fair litigation of an issue at trial and (if available) direct appeal was not only a factor weighing against reaching the merits of an issue on habeas; it was a conclusive factor, unless the issue was a legal issue going to the jurisdiction of the trial court. See Ex parte Watkins, supra, at 202-203; W. Church, Habeas Corpus § 363 (1884). Beginning in the late 19th century, however, that rule was gradually relaxed, by the device of holding that various illegalities deprived the trial court of jurisdiction. See, e. g., Ex parte Lange, 18 Wall. 163, 176 (1874) (no jurisdiction to impose second sentence in violation of Double Jeopardy Clause); Ex parte Siebold, 100 U.S. 371, 376-377 (1880) (no jurisdiction to try defendant for violation of unconstitutional statute); Frank v. Mangum, 237 U.S. 309 (1915) (no jurisdiction to conduct trial in atmosphere of mob domination); Moore v. Dempsey, 261 U.S. 86 (1923) (same); Johnson v. Zerbst, 304 U.S. 458, 468 (1938) (no jurisdiction to conduct trial that violated defendant's Sixth Amendment right to counsel). See generally Wright v. West, 505 U. S. ____, ____ (1992) (slip op., at 6-7) (opinion of Thomas, J.); Fay, supra, at 450-451 (Harlan, J., dissenting). Finally, the jurisdictional line was openly abandoned in Waley v. Johnston, 316 U.S. 101, 104-105 (1942). See P. Bator, D. Meltzer, P. Mishkin & D. Shapiro, Hart and Wechsler'sThe Federal Courts and the Federal System 1502 (3d ed. 1988) (hereinafter Hart and Wechsler).

But to say that prior opportunity for full and fair litigation no longer automatically precludes from consideration even nonjurisdictional issues is not to say that such prior opportunity is no longer a relevant equitable factor. Reason would suggest that it must be, and Stone v. Powell, 428 U.S. 465 (1976), establishes that it is. Thus, the question before us is not whether a holding unique to Fourth Amendment claims (and resting upon nothing more principled than our estimation that Fourth Amendment exclusion claims are not very important) should be expanded to some other arbitrary category beyond that; but rather, whether the general principle that is the only valid justification for Stone v. Powell should for some reason not be applied to Miranda claims. I think the answer to that question is clear: Prior opportunity to litigate an issue should be an important equitable consideration in any habeas case, and should ordinarily preclude the court from reaching the merits of a claim, unless it goes to the fairness of the trial process or to the accuracy of the ultimate result.

Our case law since Stone is entirely consistent with this view. As the Court notes, ante, at 5-6, we have held that the rule in Stone does not apply in three cases. Kimmelman v. Morrison, 477 U.S. 365 (1986) involved alleged denial of the Sixth Amendment right to counsel, which unquestionably goes to the fairness of the trial process. Rose v. Mitchell, 443 U.S. 545 (1979) involved alleged discrimination by the trial court in violation of the Fourteenth Amendment. We concluded that since the "same trial court will be the court that initially must decide the merits of such a claim," and since the claim involved an assertion that "the state judiciary itself has purposely violated the Equal Protection Clause," no opportunity for a full and fair state hearing existed. Id, at 561; see also id., at 563. And Jackson v. Virginia, 443 U.S. 307 (1979) involved a claim that "no rational trier of fact could have found proof of guilt beyond a reasonable doubt," id., at 324, which is obviously a direct challenge to the accuracy of the ultimate result.

The rule described above--or indeed a rule even somewhat more limiting of habeas review than that--is followed in federal postconviction review of federal convictions under 28 U.S.C. § 2255. In Kaufman v. United States, 394 U.S. 217 (1969), which held that res judicata does not bar § 2255 habeas review of constitutional issues, we stated that a district court had "discretion" to refuse to reach the merits of a constitutional claim that had already been raised and resolved against the prisoner at trial and on direct review. Id., at 227, n. 8. Since Kaufman, federal courts have uniformly held that, absent countervailing considerations, district courts may refuse to reach the merits of a constitutional claim previously raised and rejected on direct appeal. See, e. g., Giacalone v. United States, 739 F. 2d 40, 42-43 (CA2 1984); United States v. Orejuela, 639 F. 2d 1055, 1057 (CA3 1981); Stephan v. United States, 496 F. 2d 527, 528-529 (CA6 1974), cert denied sub nom. Marchesani v. United States, 423 U.S. 861 (1975); see also 3 C. Wright, Federal Practice and Procedure § 593, p. 439, n. 26 (1982); Note, Developments in the Law--Federal Habeas Corpus, 83 Harv. L. Rev. 1038, 1064-1066 (1970). Thus, a prior opportunity for full and fair litigation is normally dispositive of a federal prisoner's habeas claim. If the claim was raised and rejected on direct review, the habeas court will not readjudicate it absent countervailing equitable considerations; if the claim was not raised, it is procedurally defaulted and the habeas court will not adjudicate it absent countervailing equitable considerations (e. g., actual innocence or cause and prejudice, see United States v. Frady, 456 U.S. 152 (1982)).

Because lower federal courts have not generally recognized their discretion to deny habeas relief in state cases where opportunity for full and fair litigation was accorded, the peculiar state of current federal habeas practice is this: State courts routinely see their criminal convictions vacated by federal district judges, but federal courts see their criminal convictions afforded a substantial measure of finality and respect. See Hart and Wechsler 1585. Only one theory can possibly justify this disparity--the theory advanced in Fay v. Noia, that a federal forum must be afforded for every federal claim of a state criminal defendant. [n.1] See 372 U. S., at 418. In my view, that theory is profoundly wrong for several reasons.

First, it has its origin in a misreading of our early precedents. Fay interpreted the holding of Ex parte Royall--that federal courts had discretion not to entertain the habeas claims of state prisoners prior to the conclusion of state court proceedings--as containing the implication that after conclusion of those proceedings there would be plenary federal review of all constitutional claims. 372 U. S., at 420. In fact, however, Royall had noted and affirmed the common law rule that claims of error not going to the jurisdiction of the convicting court could ordinarily be entertained only on writ of error, not on habeas corpus. 117 U. S., at 253. See Fay, 372 U. S., at 453-454 (Harlan, J., dissenting). See also Schneckloth v. Bustamonte, 412 U.S. 218, 255 (1973) (Powell, J., concurring). Royall contained no hint of a suggestion that a federal habeas court should afford state court judgments less respect than federal court judgments. To the contrary, it maintained the traditional view that federal and state courts have equal responsibility for the protection of federal constitutional rights. The discretion of the federal habeas court "should be exercised," it said, "in the light of the relations existing, under our system of government, between the judicial tribunals of the Union and of the States, . . . courts equally bound to guard and protect rights secured by the Constitution." 117 U. S., at 251. And in describing the proper disposition of a federal habeas petition filed after state conviction, Royall cited Ex parte Lange, 18 Wall. 163 (1874), which involved a federal habeas attack on a federal conviction. See 117 U. S., at 253. Thus, Royall is properly understood as saying that the federal habeas statute guaranteed state prisoners, not a federal forum for all their federal claims, but rather the same rights to federal habeas relief that federal prisoners possessed.

Worse than misreading case precedent, however, the federal right/federal forum theory misperceives the basic structure of our national system. That structure establishes this Court as the supreme judicial interpreter of the Federal Constitution and laws, but gives other federal courts no higher or more respected a role than state courts in applying that "Law of the Land"--which it says all state courts are bound by, and all state judges must be sworn to uphold. U. S. Const., Art. VI. See Robb v. Connolly, 111 U.S. 624, 637 (1884); Ex parte Royall, supra, at 251; Brown, 344 U. S., at 499 (opinion of Frankfurter, J.). It would be a strange constitution that regards state courts as second rate instruments for the vindication of federal rights and yet makes no mandatory provision for lower federal courts (as our Constitution does not). And it would be an unworkable constitution that requires redetermination in federal courts of all issues of pervasive federal constitutional law that arise in state court litigation.

Absent indication to the contrary, state courts should be presumed to have applied federal law as faithfully as federal courts. See Ex parte Royall, supra, at 252; Brecht v. Abrahamson, ____ U. S., at ____ (slip op., at 15). A federal court entertaining collateral attack against a state criminal conviction should accord the same measure of respect and finality as it would to a federal criminal conviction. As it exercises equitable discretion to determine whether the merits of constitutional claims will be reached in the one, it should exercise a similar discretion for the other. The distinction that has arisen in lower court practice is unsupported in law, utterly impractical and demeaning to the States in its consequences, and must be eliminated.

* * *

While I concur in Part III of the Court's opinion, I cannot agree with the rest of its analysis. I would reverse the judgment of the Court of Appeals and remand the case for a determination whether, given that respondent has already been afforded an opportunity for full and fair litigation in the courts of Michigan, any unusual equitable factors counsel in favor of readjudicating the merits of his Miranda claim on habeas corpus.

Notes

1 Of course a federal forum is theoretically available in this Court, by writ of certiorari. Quite obviously, however, this mode of review cannot be generally applied due to practical limitations. See, Stone v. Powell, 428 U.S. 465, 526 (1976) (Brennan, J., dissenting).

Justice Scalia's dissent in Smith v. US (June 1, 1993)

Justice Scalia, with whom Justice Stevens and Justice Souter join, dissenting.

In the search for statutory meaning, we give nontechnical words and phrases their ordinary meaning. See Chapman v. United States, 500 U. S. ___, ___ (1991) (slip op., at 7); Perrin v. United States, 444 U.S. 37, 42 (1979); Minor v. Mechanics Bank of Alexandria, 1 Pet. 46, 64 (1828). To use an instrumentality ordinarily means to use it for its intended purpose. When someone asks "Do you use a cane?" he is not inquiring whether you have your grandfather's silver handled walking stick on display in the hall; he wants to know whether you walk with a cane. Similarly, to speak of "using a firearm" is to speak of using it for its distinctive purpose, i.e., as a weapon. To be sure, "one can use a firearm in a number of ways," ante, at 7, including as an article of exchange, just as one can "use" a cane as a hall decoration--but that is not the ordinary meaning of "using" the one or the other. [n.1] The Court does not appear to grasp the distinction between how a word can be used and how it ordinarily is used. It would, indeed, be "both reasonable and normal to say that petitioner `used' his MAC-10 in his drug trafficking offense by trading it for cocaine." Ibid. It would also be reasonable and normal to say that he "used" it to scratch his head. When one wishes to describe the action of employing the instrument of a firearm for such unusual purposes, "use" is assuredly a verb one could select. But that says nothing about whether the ordinary meaning of the phrase "uses a firearm" embraces such extraordinary employments. It is unquestionably not reasonable and normal, I think, to say simply "do not use firearms" when one means to prohibit selling or scratching with them.

The normal usage is reflected, for example, in the United States Sentencing Guidelines, which provide for enhanced sentences when firearms are "discharged," "brandished, displayed, or possessed," or "otherwise used." See, e. g., United States Sentencing Commission, Guidelines Manual § 2B3.1(b)(2) (Nov. 1992). As to the latter term, the Guidelines say: " `Otherwise used' with reference to a dangerous weapon (including a firearm) means that the conduct did not amount to the discharge of a firearm but was more than brandishing, displaying, or possessing a firearm or other dangerous weapon." USSG § 1B1.1, comment., n. 1(g) (definitions). "Otherwise used" in this provision obviously means "otherwise used as a weapon." [n.2]

Given our rule that ordinary meaning governs, and given the ordinary meaning of "uses a firearm," it seems to me inconsequential that "the words `as a weapon' appear nowhere in the statute," ante, at 5; they are reasonably implicit. Petitioner is not, I think, seeking to introduce an "additional requirement" into the text, ante, at 6, but is simply construing the text according to its normal import.

The Court seeks to avoid this conclusion by referring to the next subsection of the statute, § 924(d), which does not employ the phrase "uses a firearm," but provides for the confiscation of firearms that are "used in" referenced offenses which include the crimes of transferring, selling, or transporting firearms in interstate commerce. The Court concludes from this that whenever the term appears in this statute, "use" of a firearm must include nonweapon use. See ante, at 10-12. I do not agree. We are dealing here not with a technical word or an "artfully defined" legal term, compare Dewsnup v. Timm, 502 U. S. ___, ___ (1992) (Scalia, J., dissenting) (slip op., at 2-4), but with common words that are, as I have suggested, inordinately sensitive to context. Just as adding the direct object "a firearm" to the verb "use" narrows the meaning of that verb (it can no longer mean "partake of"), so also adding the modifier "in the offense of transferring, selling, or transporting firearms" to the phrase "use a firearm" expands the meaning of that phrase (it then includes, as it previously would not, nonweapon use). But neither the narrowing nor the expansion should logically be thought to apply to all appearances of the affected word or phrase. Just as every appearance of the word "use" in the statute need not be given the narrow meaning that word acquires in the phrase "use a firearm," so also every appearance of the phrase "use a firearm" need not be given the expansive connotation that phrase acquires in the broader context "use a firearm in crimes such as unlawful sale of firearms." When, for example, the statute provides that its prohibition on certain transactions in firearms "shall not apply to the loan or rental of a firearm to any person for temporary use for lawful sporting purposes," 18 U.S.C. §§ 922(a)(5)(B), (b)(3)(B), I have no doubt that the "use" referred to is only use as a sporting weapon, and not the use of pawning the firearm to pay for a ski trip. Likewise when, in § 924(c)(1), the phrase "uses . . . a firearm" is not employed in a context that necessarily envisions the unusual "use" of a firearm as a commodity, the normally understood meaning of the phrase should prevail.

Another consideration leads to the same conclusion: § 924(c)(1) provides increased penalties not only for one who "uses" a firearm during and in relation to any crime of violence or drug trafficking crime, but also for one who "carries" a firearm in those circumstances. The interpretation I would give the language produces an eminently reasonable dichotomy between "using a firearm" (as a weapon) and "carrying a firearm" (which in the context "uses or carries a firearm" means carrying it in such manner as to be ready for use as a weapon). The Court's interpretation, by contrast, produces a strange dichotomy between "using a firearm for any purpose whatever, including barter," and "carrying a firearm." [n.3]

Finally, although the present prosecution was brought under the portion of § 924(c)(1) pertaining to use of a firearm "during and in relation to any . . . drug trafficking crime," I think it significant that that portion is affiliated with the pre-existing provision pertaining to use of a firearm "during and in relation to any crime of violence," rather than with the firearm trafficking offenses defined in § 922 and referenced in § 924(d). The word "use" in the "crime of violence" context has the unmistakable import of use as a weapon, and that import carries over, in my view, to the subsequently added phrase "or drug trafficking crime." Surely the word "use" means the same thing as to both, and surely the 1986 addition of "drug trafficking crime" would have been a peculiar way to expand its meaning (beyond "use as a weapon") for crimes of violence.

Even if the reader does not consider the issue to be as clear as I do, he must at least acknowledge, I think, that it is eminently debatable--and that is enough, under the rule of lenity, to require finding for the petitioner here. "At the very least, it may be said that the issue is subject to some doubt. Under these circumstances, we adhere to the familiar rule that, `where there is ambiguity in a criminal statute, doubts are resolved in favor of the defendant.' " Adamo Wrecking Co. v. United States, 434 U.S. 275, 284-285 (1978), quoting United States v. Bass, 404 U. S.

336, 348 (1971). [n.4]

For the foregoing reasons, I respectfully dissent.

Notes

1 The Court asserts that the "significant flaw" in this argument is that "to say that the ordinary meaning of `uses a firearm' includes using a firearm as a weapon" is quite different from saying that the ordinary meaning "also excludes any other use." Ante, at 6 (emphases in original). The two are indeed different--but it is precisely the latter that I assert to be true: The ordinary meaning of "uses a firearm" does not include using it as an article of commerce. I think it perfectly obvious, for example, that the objective falsity requirement for a perjury conviction would not be satisfied if a witness answered "no" to a prosecutor's inquiry whether he had ever "used a firearm," even though he had once sold his grandfather's Enfield rifle to a collector.

2 The Court says that it is "not persuaded that [its] construction of the phrase `uses . . . a firearm' will produce anomalous applications." Ante, at 9. But as proof it points only to the fact that § 924(c)(1) fortuitously contains other language--the requirement that the use be "during and in relation to any crime of violence or drug trafficking crime"--that happens to prevent untoward results. Ibid. That language does not, in fact, prevent all untoward results: Though it excludes an enhanced penalty for the burglar who scratches

his head with the barrel of a gun, it requires one for the burglar who happens to use a gun handle, rather than a rock, to break the window affording him entrance--hardly a distinction that ought to make a sentencing difference if the gun has no other connection to the crime. But in any event, an excuse that turns upon the language of § 924(c)(1) is good only for that particular statute. The Court cannot avoid "anomalous applications" when it applies its anomalous meaning of "use a firearm" in other contexts--for example, the Guidelines provision just described in text.

In a vain attempt to show the contrary, it asserts that the phrase "otherwise used" in the Guidelines means used for any other purpose at all (the Court's preferred meaning of "use a firearm"), so long as it is more %culpable" than brandishing. See ante, at 8. But whence does it derive that convenient limitation? It appears nowhere in the text--as well it should not, since the whole purpose of the Guidelines is to take out of the hands of individual judges determinations as to what is "more culpable" and "less culpable." The definition of "otherwise used" in the Guidelines merely says that it means "more than" brandishing and less than firing. The Court is confident that "scratching one's head" with a firearm is not "more than" brandishing it. See ante, at 9. I certainly agree--but only because the "more" use referred to is more use as a weapon. Reading the Guidelines as they are written (rather than importing the Court's deusex machina of a culpability scale), and interpreting "use a firearm" in the strange fashion the Court does, produces, see ante, at 8, a full seven point upward sentence adjustment for firing a gun at a storekeeper during a robbery; a mere five point adjustment for pointing the gun at the storekeeper (which falls within the Guidelines' definition of "brandished," see USSG § 1B1.1, comment., n. 1(c)); but an intermediate six%point adjustment for using the gun to pry open the cash register or prop open the door. Quite obviously ridiculous. When the Guidelines speak of "otherwise us[ing]" a firearm, they mean, in accordance with normal usage, otherwise "using" it as a weapon--for example, placing the gun barrel in the mouth of the storekeeper to intimidate him.

3 The Court responds to this argument by abandoning all pretense of giving the phrase "uses a firearm" even a permissible meaning, much less its ordinary one. There is no problem, the Court says, because it is not contending that "uses a firearm" means "uses for any purpose," only that it means "uses as a weapon or for trade." See ante, at 12-13. Unfortunately, that is not one of the options that our mother tongue makes available. "Uses a firearm" can be given a broad meaning ("uses for any purpose") or its more ordinary narrow meaning ("uses as a weapon"); but it can not possibly mean "uses as a weapon or for trade."

4 The Court contends that giving the language its ordinary meaning would frustrate the purpose of the statute, since a gun "can be converted instantaneously from currency to cannon," ante, at 17. Stretching language in order to write a more effective statute than Congress devised is not an exercise we should indulge in. But in any case, the ready ability to use a gun that is at hand as a weapon is perhaps one of the reasons the statute sanctions not only using a firearm, but carrying one. Here, however, the

Government chose not to indict under that provision. See ante, at 4.

Justice Scalia's concurrence in Lamb's Chapel v. Center Moriches Union Free School District (June 7, 1993) [Excerpt]

JUSTICE SCALIA, with whom JUSTICE THOMAS joins, concurring in the judgment.

[. . .] As to the Court's invocation of the Lemon test: like some ghoul in a late-night horror movie that repeatedly sits up in its grave and shuffles abroad after being repeatedly killed and buried, Lemon stalks our Establishment Clause jurisprudence once again, frightening the little children and school attorneys of Center Moriches Union Free School District. Its most recent burial, only last Term, was, to be sure, not fully six-feet under: our decision in Lee v. Weisman, 505 U.S. ____ (1992), conspicuously avoided using the supposed "test," but also declined the invitation to repudiate it. [. . .]

The secret of the Lemon test's survival, I think, is that it is so easy to kill. It is there to scare us (and our audience) when we wish it to do so, but we can command it to return to the tomb at will. See, e.g., Lynch v. Donnelly, 465 U.S. 668, 679 (1984) (noting instances in which Court has not applied Lemon test). When we wish to strike down a practice it forbids, we invoke it, see, e.g., Aguilar v. Fenton, 473 U.S. 402 (1985) (striking down state remedial education program administered in part in parochial schools); when we wish to uphold a practice it forbids, we ignore it entirely, see Marsh v. Chambers, 463 U.S. 783 (1983) (upholding state legislative chaplains). Sometimes, we take a middle course, calling its three prongs "no more than helpful signposts," Hunt v. McNair, 413 U.S. 734, 741 (1973). Such a docile and useful monster is worth keeping around, at least in a somnolent state; one never knows when one might need him.

For my part, I agree with the long list of constitutional scholars who have criticized Lemon and bemoaned the strange Establishment Clause geometry of crooked lines and wavering shapes its intermittent use has produced. [. . .]

Justice Scalia's concurrence in US v. Carlton (June 13, 1994) [Excerpt]

Justice Scalia, with whom Justice Thomas joins, concurring in the judgment.

If I thought that "substantive due process" were a constitutional right rather than an oxymoron, I would think it violated by bait-and-switch taxation.

[. . .]

The picking and choosing among various rights to be accorded "substantive due process" protection is alone enough to arouse suspicion; but the categorical and inexplicable exclusion of so called "economic rights" (even though the Due Process Clause explicitly applies to "property") unquestionably involves policymaking rather than neutral legal analysis. I would follow the text of the Constitution, which sets forth certain substantive rights that cannot be taken away, and adds, beyond that, a right to due process when life, liberty, or property is to be taken away.

Justice Scalia's dissent in Simmons v. South Carolina (June 17, 1994) [Notes omitted]

Justice Scalia, with whom Justice Thomas joins, dissenting.

Today's judgment certainly seems reasonable enough as a determination of what a capital sentencing jury should be permitted to consider. That is not, however, what it purports to be. It purports to be a determination that any capital sentencing scheme that does not permit jury consideration of such material is so incompatible with our national traditions of criminal procedure that it violates the Due Process Clause of the Constitution of the United States. There is really no basis for such a pronouncement, neither in any near uniform practice of our people, nor in the jurisprudence of this Court.

With respect to the former I shall discuss only current practice, since the parties and amici have addressed only that, and since traditional practice may be relatively uninformative with regard to the new schemes of capital sentencing imposed upon the States by this Court's recent jurisprudence. The overwhelming majority of the 32 States that permit juries to impose or recommend capital sentences do not allow specific information regarding parole to be given to the jury. To be sure, in many of these States the sentencing choices specifically include "life without parole," so that the jury charge itself conveys the information whether parole is available. In at least eight of those States, however, the jury's choice is not merely between "life without parole" and "death," but among some variation of (parole eligible) "life," "life without parole," and "death"[1]—so that the precise date of availability of parole is relevant to the jury's choice. Moreover, even among those States that permit the jury to choose only between "life" (unspecified) and "death," South Carolina is not alone in keeping parole information from the jury. Four other States in widely separated parts of the country follow that same course,[2] and there are other States that lack any clear practice.[3] By contrast, the parties and their amici point to only 10 States that arguably employ the procedure which, according to today's opinions, the Constitution requires.[4] This picture of national practice falls far short of demonstrating a principle so widely shared that it is part of even a current and temporary American consensus.

As for our prior jurisprudence: The opinions of Justice Blackmun and Justice O'Connor rely on the Fourteenth Amendment's guarantee of due process, rather than on the Eighth Amendment's "cruel and unusual punishments" prohibition, as applied to the States by the Fourteenth Amendment. But cf. ante, at 172 (Souter, J., concurring). The prior law applicable to that subject indicates that petitioner's due process rights would be violated if he was "sentenced to death `on the basis of information which he had no opportunity to deny or explain.' " Skipper v. South Carolina, 476 U. S. 1, 5, n. 1 (1986), quoting Gardner v. Florida, 430 U. S. 349, 362 (1977). Both opinions try to bring this case within that description, but it does not fit.

The opinions paint a picture of a prosecutor who repeatedly stressed that petitioner would pose a threat to society upon his release. The record tells a different story.

Rather than emphasizing future dangerousness as a crucial factor, the prosecutor stressed the nature of petitioner's crimes: the crime that was the subject of the prosecution, the brutal murder of a 79-year-old woman in her home, and three prior crimes confessed to by petitioner, all rapes and beatings of elderly women, one of them his grandmother. I am sure it was the sheer depravity of those crimes, rather than any specific fear for the future, which induced the South Carolina jury to conclude that the death penalty was justice.

Not only, moreover, was future dangerousness not emphasized, but future dangerousness outside of prison was not even mentioned. The trial judge undertook specifically to prevent that, in response to the broader request of petitioner's counsel that the prosecutor be prevented from arguing future dangerousness at all:

"Obviously, I will listen carefully to the argument of the solicitor to see if it contravenes the actual factual circumstance. Certainly, I recognize the right of the State to argue concerning the defendant's dangerous propensity. I will not allow the solicitor, for example, to say to the jury anything that would indicate that the defendant is not going to be jailed for the period of time that is encompassed within the actual law. The fact that we do not submit the parole eligibility to the jury does not negate the fact that the solicitor must stay within the trial record." App. 56-57.

As I read the record, the prosecutor followed this admonition—and the Due Process Clause requires nothing more.

Both Justice Blackmun and Justice O'Connor focus on two portions of the prosecutor's final argument to the jury in the sentencing phase. First, they stress that the prosecutor asked the jury to answer the question of "what to do with [petitioner] now that he is in our midst." That statement, however, was not made (as they imply) in the course of an argument about future dangerousness, but was a response to petitioner's mitigating evidence. Read in context, the statement is not even relevant to the issue in this case:

"The defense in this case as to sentence . . . [is] a diversion. It's putting the blame on society, on his father, on his grandmother, on whoever else he can, spreading it out to avoid that personal responsibility. That he came from a deprived background. That he didn't have all of the breaks in life and certainly that helps shape someone. But we are not concerned about how he got shaped. We are concerned about what to do with him now that he is in our midst." Id. , at 110.

Both opinions also seize upon the prosecutor's comment that the jury's verdict would be "an act of self-defense." That statement came at the end of admonition of the jury to avoid emotional responses and enter a rational verdict:

"Your verdict shouldn't be returned in anger. Your verdict shouldn't be an emotional catharsis. Your verdict shouldn't be . . . a response to that eight-year-old kid [testifying in mitigation] and really shouldn't be a response to the gruesome grotesque handiwork of [petitioner]. Your verdict should be a response of society to someone who is a threat. Your verdict will be an act of self-defense." Id. , at 109-110.

This reference to "self-defense" obviously alluded, neither to defense of the jurors' own persons, nor specifically to defense of persons outside the prison walls, but to defense of all members of society against this individual, wherever he or they might be. Thus, as I read the record (and bear in mind that the trial judge was on the lookout with respect to this point), the prosecutor did not invite the jury to believe that petitioner would be eligible for parole—he did not mislead the jury.

The rule the majority adopts in order to overturn this sentence therefore goes well beyond what would be necessary to counteract prosecutorial misconduct (a disposition with which I might agree). It is a rule at least as sweeping as this: that the Due Process Clause overrides state law limiting the admissibility of information concerning parole whenever the prosecution argues future dangerousness. Justice Blackmun appears to go even further, requiring the admission of parole ineligibility even when the prosecutor does not argue future dangerousness. See ante, at 163-164; but see ante, at 174 (Ginsburg, J., concurring). I do not understand the basis for this broad prescription. As a general matter, the Court leaves it to the States to strike what they consider the appropriate balance among the many factors— probative value, prejudice, reliability, potential for confusion, among others—that determine whether evidence ought to be admissible. Even in the capital punishment context, the Court has noted that "the wisdom of the decision to permit juror consideration of [postsentencing contingencies] is best left to the States." California v. Ramos, 463 U. S. 992, 1014 (1983). "[T]he States, and not this Court, retain `the traditional authority' to determine what particular evidence . . . is relevant." Skipper v. South Carolina, 476 U. S., at 11 (Powell, J., concurring in judgment). One reason for leaving it that way is that a sensible code of evidence cannot be invented piecemeal. Each item cannot be considered in isolation, but must be given its place within the whole. Preventing the defense from introducing evidence regarding parolability is only half of the rule that prevents the prosecution from introducing it as well. If the rule is changed for defendants, many will think that evenhandedness demands a change for prosecutors as well. State's attorneys ought to be able to say that if, ladies and gentlemen of the jury, you do not impose capital punishment upon this defendant (or if you impose anything less than life without parole) he may be walking the streets again in eight years! Many would not favor the admission of such an argument—but would prefer it to a state scheme in which defendants can call attention to the unavailability of parole, but prosecutors cannot note its availability. This Court should not force state legislators into such a difficult choice unless the isolated state evidentiary rule that the Court has before it is not merely less than ideal, but beyond a high threshold of unconstitutionality.

The low threshold the Court constructs today is difficult to reconcile with our almost simultaneous decision in Romano v. Oklahoma, ante, p. 1. There, the Court holds that the proper inquiry when evidence is admitted in contravention of a state law is "whether the admission of evidence. . . so infected the sentencing proceeding with unfairness as to render the jury's imposition of the death penalty a denial of due process."

Ante, at 12. I do not see why the unconstitutionality criterion for excluding evidence in accordance with state law should be any less demanding than the unconstitutionality criterion Romano recites for admitting evidence in violation of state law: "fundamental unfairness." And "fundamentally unfair" the South Carolina rule is assuredly not. The notion that the South Carolina jury imposed the death penalty "just in case" Simmons might be released on parole seems to me quite farfetched. And the notion that the decision taken on such grounds would have been altered by information on the current state of the law concerning parole (which could of course be amended) is even more farfetched. And the scenario achieves the ultimate in farfetchedness when there is added the fact that, according to uncontroverted testimony of prison officials in this case, even current South Carolina law (as opposed to discretionary prison regulations) does not prohibit furloughs and work-release programs for life-without-parole inmates. See App. 16-17.

When the prosecution has not specifically suggested parolability, I see no more reason why the United States Constitution should compel the admission of evidence showing that, under the State's current law, the defendant would be nonparolable, than that it should compel the admission of evidence showing that parolable life-sentence murderers are in fact almost never paroled, or are paroled only after age 70; or evidence to the effect that escapes of life-without-parole inmates are rare; or evidence showing that, though under current law the defendant will be parolable in 20 years, the recidivism rate for elderly prisoners released after long incarceration is negligible. All of this evidence may be thought relevant to whether the death penalty should be imposed, and a petition raising the last of these claims has already arrived. See Pet. for Cert. in Rudd v. Texas, O. T. 1993, No. 93-7955.

As I said at the outset, the regime imposed by today's judgment is undoubtedly reasonable as a matter of policy, but I see nothing to indicate that the Constitution requires it to be followed coast to coast. I fear we have read today the first page of a whole new chapter in the "death-is-different" jurisprudence which this Court is in the apparently continuous process of composing. It adds to our insistence that state courts admit "all relevant mitigating evidence," see, e. g., Eddings v. Oklahoma, 455 U. S. 104 (1982); Lockett v. Ohio, 438 U. S. 586 (1978), a requirement that they adhere to distinctive rules, more demanding than what the Due Process Clause normally requires, for admitting evidence of other sorts—Federal Rules of Death Penalty Evidence, so to speak, which this Court will presumably craft (at great expense to the swiftness and predictability of justice) year by year. The heavily outnumbered opponents of capital punishment have successfully opened yet another front in their guerilla war to make this unquestionably constitutional sentence a practical impossibility.

I dissent.

Justice Scala's dissent in Board of Education of Kiryas Joel Village School District v. Louis Grumet (June 27, 1994) [Notes omitted]

Justice Scalia, with whom The Chief Justice and Justice Thomas join, dissenting.

The Court today finds that the Powers That Be, up in Albany, have conspired to effect an establishment of the Satmar Hasidim. I do not know who would be more surprised at this discovery: the Founders of our Nation or Grand Rebbe Joel Teitelbaum, founder of the Satmar. The Grand Rebbe would be astounded to learn that after escaping brutal persecution and coming to America with the modest hope of religious toleration for their ascetic form of Judaism, the Satmar had become so powerful, so closely allied with Mammon, as to have become an "establishment" of the Empire State. And the Founding Fathers would be astonished to find that the Establishment Clause-which they designed "to insure that no one powerful sect or combination of sects could use political or governmental power to punish dissenters," Zorach v. Clauson, 343 U. S. 306, 319 (1952) (Black, J., dissenting)-has been employed to prohibit characteristically and admirably American accommodation of the religious practices (or more precisely, cultural peculiarities) of a tiny minority sect. I, however, am not surprised. Once this Court has abandoned text and history as guides, nothing prevents it from calling religious toleration the establishment of religion.

I

Unlike most of our Establishment Clause cases involving education, these cases involve no public funding, however slight or indirect, to private religious schools. They do not involve private schools at all. The school under scrutiny is a public school specifically designed to provide a public secular education to handicapped students. The superintendent of the school, who is not Hasidic, is a 20 year veteran of the New York City public school system, with expertise in the area of bilingual, bicultural, special education. The teachers and therapists at the school all live outside the village of Kiryas Joel. While the village's private schools are profoundly religious and strictly segregated by sex, classes at the public school are co ed and the curriculum secular. The school building has the bland appearance of a public school, unadorned by religious symbols or markings; and the school complies with the laws and regulations governing all other New York State public schools. There is no suggestion, moreover, that this public school has gone too far in making special adjustments to the religious needs of its students. Cf. Zorach v. Clauson, supra, at 312-315 (approving a program permitting early release of public school students to attend religious instruction). In sum, these cases involve only public aid to a school that is public as can be. The only thing distinctive about the school is that all the students share the same religion.

None of our cases has ever suggested that there is anything wrong with that. In fact, the Court has specifically approved the education of students of a single religion on a neutral site adjacent to a private religious school. See Wolman v. Walter, 433 U.S. 229, 247-248 (1977). In that case, the Court rejected the argument that "any program that isolates the sectarian pupils is impermissible," id., at 246, and held that, "[t]he fact that a unit on a neutral site on occasion may serve only sectarian pupils does not provoke [constitutional] concerns," id., at 247. And just last Term, the Court held that the State could permit public employees to assist students in a Catholic school. See Zobrest v. Catalina Foothills School Dist., 509 U. S. ____, ____ (1993) (slip op., at 11-12) (sign language translator for deaf student). If a State can furnish services to a group of sectarian students on a neutral site adjacent to a private religious school, or even within such a school, how can there be any defect in educating those same students in a public school? As the Court noted in Wolman, the constitutional dangers of establishment arise "from the nature of the institution, not from the nature of the pupils," Wolman, supra, at 248. There is no danger in educating religious students in a public school.

For these very good reasons, Justice Souter's opinion does not focus upon the school, but rather upon the school district and the New York Legislature that created it. His arguments, though sometimes intermingled, are two: that reposing governmental power in the Kiryas Joel School District is the same as reposing governmental power in a religious group; and that in enacting the statute creating the district, the New YorkState Legislature was discriminating on the basis of religion, i.e., favoring the Satmar Hasidim over others. I shall discuss these arguments in turn.

For his thesis that New York has unconstitutionally conferred governmental authority upon the Satmar sect, Justice Souter relies extensively, and virtually exclusively, upon Larkin v. Grendel's Den, Inc., 459 U.S. 116 (1982). Justice Souter believes that the present case "resembles" Grendel's Den because that cases "teaches that a state may not delegate its civic authority to a group chosen according to a religious criterion," ante, at 9 (emphasis added). That misdescribes both what that case taught (which is that a state may not delegate its civil authority to a church), and what this case involves (which is a group chosen according to cultural characteristics). The statute at issue there gave churches veto power over the State's authority to grant a liquor license to establishments in the vicinity of the church. The Court had little difficulty finding the statute unconstitutional. "The Framers did not set up a system of government in which important, discretionary governmental powers would be delegated to or shared with religious institutions." Id., at 127.

Justice Souter concedes that Grendel's Den "presented an example of united civic and religious authority, an establishment rarely found in such straightforward form in modern America." Ante, at 9. The uniqueness of the case stemmed from the grant of governmental power directly to a religious institution, and the Court's opinion focused on that fact, remarking that the transfer of authority was to "churches" (10 times), the "governing body of churches" (twice), "religious institutions" (twice) and "religious bodies" (once). Astonishingly, however, Justice Souter dismisses the difference between atransfer of government power to citizens who share a common religion as opposed to "the officers of its sectarian organization"--the critical factor that made Grendel's Den unique and "rar[e]"--as being "one of form, not substance." Ante, at 10.

Justice Souter's steamrolling of the difference between civil authority held by a church, and civil authority held by members of a church, is breathtaking. To accept it, one must believe that large portions of the civil authority exercised during most of our history were unconstitutional, and that much more of it than merely the Kiryas Joel School District is unconstitutional today. The history of the populating of North America is in no small measure the story of groups of people sharing a common religious and cultural heritage striking out to form their own communities. See, e.g., W. Sweet, The Story of Religion in America 9 (1950). It is preposterous to suggest that the civil institutions of these communities, separate from their churches, were constitutionally suspect. And if they were, surely Justice Souter cannot mean that the inclusion of one or two nonbelievers in the community would have been enough to eliminate the constitutional vice. If the conferral of governmental power upon a religious institution as such (rather than upon American citizens who belong to the religious institution) is not the test of Grendel's Den invalidity, there is no reason why giving power to a body that is overwhelmingly dominated by the members of one sect would not suffice to invoke the Establishment Clause. That might have made the entire States of Utah and New Mexico unconstitutional at the time of their admission to the Union, [n.1] and would undoubtedlymake many units of local government unconstitutional today. [n.2]

Justice Souter's position boils down to the quite novel proposition that any group of citizens (say, the residents of Kiryas Joel) can be invested with political power, but not if they all belong to the same religion. Of course such disfavoring of religion is positively antagonistic to the purposes of the Religion Clauses, and we have rejected it before. In McDaniel v. Paty, 435 U.S. 618 (1978), we invalidated a state constitutional amendment that would have permitted all persons to participate in political conventions, except ministers. We adopted James Madison's view that the State could not " `punis[h] a religious profession with the privation of a civil right.' " Id., at 626 (opinion of Burger, C. J.), quoting 5 Writings of James Madison 288 (G. Hunt ed. 1904). Or as Justice Brennan put it in his opinion concurring in judgment: "Religionists no less than members of any other group enjoy the full measure of protection afforded speech, association, and political activity generally." Id., at 641; see also Widmar v.Vincent, 454 U.S. 263 (1981). I see no reason why it is any less pernicious to deprive a group rather than an individual of its rights simply because of its religious beliefs.

Perhaps appreciating the startling implications for our constitutional jurisprudence of collapsing the distinction between religious institutions and their members, Justice Souter tries to limit his "unconstitutional conferral of civil authority" holding by pointing out several features supposedly unique to the present case: that the "boundary lines of the school district divide residents according to religious affiliation," ante, at 11 (emphasis added); that the school district was created by "a special act of the legislature," ante, at 12; and that the formation of the school district ran counter to the legislature's trend of consolidating districts in recent years, ante, at 11-12. Assuming all these points to be true (and they are not), they would certainly bear upon whether the legislature had an impermissible religious motivation in creating the district (which is Justice Souter's next point, in the discussion of which I shall reply to these arguments). But they have nothing to do with whether conferral of power upon a group of citizens can be the conferral of power upon a religious institution. It can not. Or if it can, our Establishment Clause jurisprudence has been transformed.

I turn, next, to Justice Souter's second justification for finding an establishment of religion: his facile conclusion that the New York Legislature's creation of the Kiryas Joel School District was religiously motivated. But in the Land of the Free, democratically adopted laws are not so easily impeached by unelected judges. To establish the unconstitutionality of a facially neutral law on the mere basis of its asserted religiously preferential (or discriminatory) effects--or at least to establish it in conformity with our precedents--Justice Souter "must be able to show the absence of a neutral, secular basis" for the law. Gillette v. United States, 401 U.S. 437, 452 (1971); see also Arlington Heights v. Metropolitan Housing Development Corp., 429 U.S. 252, 266 (1977) (facially race neutral laws can be invalidated on the basis of their effects only if "unexplainable on grounds other than race").

There is of course no possible doubt of a secular basis here. The New York Legislature faced a unique problem in Kiryas Joel: a community in which all the non handicapped children attend private schools, and the physically and mentally disabled children who attend public school suffer the additional handicap of cultural distinctiveness. It would be troublesome enough if these peculiarly dressed, handicapped students were sent to the next town, accompanied by their similarly clad but unimpaired classmates. But all the unimpaired children of Kiryas Joel attend private school. The handicapped children suffered sufficient emotional trauma from their predicament that their parents kept them home from school. Surely the legislature could target this problem, and provide a public education for these students, in the same way it addressed, by a similar law, the unique needs of children institutionalized in a hospital. See e.g., 1970 N. Y. Laws, ch. 843 (authorizing a union free school district for the area owned by Blythedale Children's Hospital).

Since the obvious presence of a neutral, secular basis renders the asserted preferential effect of this law inadequate to invalidate it, Justice Souter is required to come forward with direct evidence that religious preference was the objective. His case could scarcely be weaker. It consists, briefly, of this: The People of New York created the Kiryas Joel Village School District in order to further the Satmar religion, rather than for anyproper secular purpose, because (1) they created the district in an extraordinary manner--by special Act of the legislature, rather than under the State's general laws governing school district reorganization; (2) the creation of the district ran counter to a State trend towards consolidation of school districts; and (3) the District includes only adherents of the Satmar religion. On this indictment, no jury would convict.

One difficulty with the first point is that it is not true. There was really nothing so "special" about the formation of a school district by an Act of the New York Legislature. The State has created both large school districts, see e.g., 1972 N. Y. Laws, ch. 928 (creating the Gananda School District out of land previously in two other districts), and small specialized school districts for institutionalized children, see e.g., 1972 N. Y. Laws, ch. 559 (creating a union free school district for the area owned by Abbott House), through these special Acts. But in any event all that the first point proves, and the second point as well (countering the trend toward consolidation), [n.3] is that New York regarded Kiryas Joelas a special case, requiring special measures. I should think it obvious that it did, and obvious that it should have. But even if the New York Legislature had never before created a school district by special statute (which is not true), and even if it had done nothing but consolidate school districts for over a century (which is not true), how could the departure from those past practices possibly demonstrate that the legislature had religious favoritism in mind? It could not. To be sure, when there is no special treatment there is no possibility of religious favoritism; but it is not logical to suggest that when there is special treatment there is proof of religious favoritism.

Justice Souter's case against the statute comes down to nothing more, therefore, than his third point: the fact that all the residents of the Kiryas Joel Village School District are Satmars. But all its residents also wear unusual dress, have unusual civic customs, and have not much to do with people who are culturally different from them. (The Court recognizes that "the Satmars prefer to live together `to facilitate individual religious observance and maintain social, cultural and religious values,' but that it is not `against their religion' to interact with others." Ante, at 18, n. 9, quoting Brief for Petitioners in No. 93-517, p. 4, n. 1.) On what basis does Justice Souter conclude that it is the theological distinctiveness rather than the cultural distinctiveness that was the basis for New York State's decision? The normal assumption would be that it was the latter, since it was not theology but dress, language, and cultural alienation that posed the educational problem for the children. Justice Souter not only does not adopt the logical assumption, he does not even give the New York Legislature the benefit of the doubt. The following is the level of his analysis:

"Not even the special needs of the children in this community can explain the legislature's unusual Act, for the State could have responded to the concerns of the Satmar parents [by other means]." Ante, at 14.

In other words, we know the legislature must have been motivated by the desire to favor the Satmar Hasidim religion, because it could have met the needs of these children by a method that did not place the Satmar Hasidim in a separate school district. This is not a rational argument proving religious favoritism; it is rather a novel Establishment Clause principle to the effect that no secular objective may be pursued by a means that might also be used for religious favoritism if some other means is available.

I have little doubt that Justice Souter would laud this humanitarian legislation if all of the distinctiveness of the students of Kiryas Joel were attributable to the fact that their parents were nonreligious commune dwellers, or American Indians, or gypsies. The creation of a special, one culture school district for the benefit of those children would pose no problem. The neutrality demanded by the Religion Clauses requires the same indulgence towards cultural characteristics that are accompanied by religious belief. "The Establishment Clause does not license government to treat religion and those who teach or

practice it, simply by virtue of their status as such, as . . . subject to unique disabilities."
McDaniel v. Paty, supra, at 641 (Brennan, J., concurring in judgment).

Even if Justice Souter could successfully establish that the cultural distinctiveness
of the Kiryas Joel students (which is the problem the New York Legislature addressed) was
an essential part of their religious belief rather than merely an accompaniment of their
religious belief, that would not discharge his heavy burden. In order to invalidate a facially
neutral law, Justice Souter would have to show not only that legislators were aware that
religion caused the problems addressed, but also that the legislature's proposed solution
was motivated by a desire to disadvantage or benefit a religious group (i.e. to disadvantage
or benefit them because of their religion). For example, if the city of Hialeah, knowing of
the potential health problems raised by the Santeria religious practice of animal sacrifice,
were to provide by ordinance a special, more frequent, municipal garbage collection for
the carcasses of dead animals, we would not strike the ordinance down just because the
city council was aware that a religious practice produced the problem the ordinance
addressed. See Church of Lukumi Babalu Aye, Inc. v. Hialeah, 508 U. S. ____, ____%____
(1993) (slip op., at 15-19). Here a facially neutral statute extends an educational benefit to
the one area where it was not effectively distributed. Whether or not the reason for the
ineffective distribution had anything to do with religion, it is a remarkable stretch to say
that the Act was motivated by a desire to favor or disfavor a particular religious group. The
proper analogy to Chapter 748 is not the Court's hypothetical law providing school buses
only to Christian students, see ante, at 21, but a law providing extra buses to rural school
districts (which happen to be predominantly Southern Baptist).

At various times Justice Souter intimates, though he does not precisely say, that
the boundaries of the school district were intentionally drawn on the basis of religion. He
refers, for example, to "[t]he State's manipulation of the franchise for this district . . . ,
giving the sect exclusive control of the political subdivision," ante, at10--implying that the
"giving" of political power to the religious sect was the object of the "manipulation." There
is no evidence of that. The special district was created to meet the special educational
needs of distinctive handicapped children, and the geographical boundaries selected for
that district were (quite logically) those that already existed for the village. It sometimes
appears as though the shady "manipulation" Justice Souter has in mind is that which
occurred when the village was formed, so that the drawing of its boundaries infected the
coterminous boundaries of the district. He says, for example, that "[i]t is undisputed that
those who negotiated the village boundaries when applying the general village
incorporation statute drew them so as to exclude all but Satmars." Ante, at 11. It is indeed.
But non Satmars were excluded, not (as he intimates) because of their religion, but--as
Justice O'Connor clearly describes, see ante, at 1-2--because of their lack of desire for the
high density zoning that Satmars favored. It was a classic drawing of lines on the basis of
communality of secular governmental desires, not communality of religion. What
happened in the creation of the village is in fact precisely what happened in the creation of
the school district, so that the former cannot possibly infect the latter, as Justice Souter

tries to suggest. Entirely secular reasons (zoning for the village, cultural alienation of students for the school district) produced a political unit whose members happened to share the same religion. There is no evidence (indeed, no plausible suspicion) of the legislature's desire to favor the Satmar religion, as opposed to meeting distinctive secular needs or desires of citizens who happened to be Satmars. If there were, Justice Souter would say so; instead, he must merely insinuate.

But even if Chapter 748 were intended to create a special arrangement for the Satmars because of their religion (not including, as I have shown in Part I, any conferral of governmental power upon a religious entity), it would be a permissible accommodation. "This Court has long recognized that the government may (and sometimes must) accommodate religious practices and that it may do so without violating the Establishment Clause." Hobbie v. Unemployment Appeals Comm'n of Fla., 480 U.S. 136, 144-145 (1987). Moreover, "there is ample room for accommodation of religion under the Establishment Clause," Corporation for Presiding Bishop of Church of Jesus of Latter day Saints v. Amos, 483 U.S. 327, 338 (1987), and for "play in the joints productive of a benevolent neutrality which will permit religious exercise to exist without sponsorship and without interference," Walz v. Tax Comm'n of N. Y. City, 397 U.S. 664, 669 (1970). Accommodation is permissible, moreover, even when the statute deals specifically with religion, see, e.g., Zorach v. Clauson, 343 U. S., at 312-315, and even when accommodation is not commanded by the Free Exercise Clause, see, e.g., Walz, supra, at 673.

When a legislature acts to accommodate religion, particularly a minority sect, "it follows the best of our traditions." Zorach, supra, at 314. The Constitution itself contains an accommodation of sorts. Article VI, cl. 3, prescribes that executive, legislative and judicial officers of the Federal and State Governments shall bind themselves to support the Constitution "by Oath or Affirmation." Although members of the most populous religions found no difficulty in swearing an oath to God, Quakers, Moravians, and Mennonites refused to take oaths based on Matthew 5:34's injunction "swear not at all." The option of affirmation was added to accommodate these minority religions and enable their membersto serve in government. See 1 A. Stokes, Church and State in The United States 524-527 (1950). Congress, from its earliest sessions, passed laws accommodating religion by refunding duties paid by specific churches upon the importation of plates for the printing of Bibles, see 6 Stat. 116 (1813), vestments, 6 Stat. 346 (1816), and bells, 6 Stat. 675 (1836). Congress also exempted church property from the tax assessments it levied on residents of the District of Columbia; and all 50 States have had similar laws. See Walz, supra, at 676-678.

This Court has also long acknowledged the permissibility of legislative accommodation. In one of our early Establishment Clause cases, we upheld New York City's early release program, which allowed students to be released from public school during school hours to attend religious instruction or devotional exercises. See Zorach, supra, at 312-315. We determined that the early release program "accommodates the public service to . . . spiritual needs," and noted that finding it unconstitutional would "show a callous indifference to religious groups." 343 U. S., at 314. In Walz, supra, we upheld a property tax exemption for religious organizations, observing that it was part of a salutary tradition of "permissible state accommodation to religion." Id., at 672-673. And in Presiding Bishop, supra, we upheld a section of the Civil Rights Act of 1964 exempting religious groups from the antidiscrimination provisions of Title VII. We concluded that it was "a permissible legislative purpose to alleviate significant governmental interference with the ability of religious organizations to define and carry out their religious missions." Id., at 335.

In today's opinion, however, the Court seems uncomfortable with this aspect of our constitutional tradition. Although it acknowledges the concept of accommodation, it quickly points out that it is "not a principle without limits," ante, at 18, and then gives reasons why thepresent case exceeds those limits, reasons which simply do not hold water. "[W]e have never hinted," the Court says, "that an otherwise unconstitutional delegation of political power to a religious group could be saved as a religious accommodation." Ante, at 19. Putting aside the circularity inherent in referring to a delegation as "otherwise unconstitutional" when its constitutionality turns on whether there is an accommodation, if this statement is true, it is only because we have never hinted that delegation of political power to citizens who share a particular religion could be unconstitutional. This is simply a replay of the argument we rejected in Part II, supra.

The second and last reason the Court finds accommodation impermissible is, astoundingly, the mere risk that the State will not offer accommodation to a similar group in the future, and that neutrality will therefore not be preserved. Returning to the ill fitted crutch of Grendel's Den, the Court suggests that by acting through this special statute the New York Legislature has eliminated any " `effective means of guaranteeing' that governmental power will be and has been neutrally employed." Ante, at 15, quoting Grendel's Den, 459 U. S., at 125. How misleading. That language in Grendel's Den was an expression of concern not (as the context in which it is quoted suggests) about the courts' ability to assure the legislature's future neutrality, but about the legislature's ability to assure the neutrality of the churches to which it had transferred legislative power. That concern is inapposite here; there is no doubt about the legislature's capacity to control what transpires in a public school.

At bottom, the Court's "no guarantee of neutrality" argument is an assertion of this Court's inability to control the New York Legislature's future denial of comparable accommodation. We have "no assurance," the Court says, "that the next similarly situated groupseeking a school district of its own will receive one," since "a legislature's failure to enact a special lawis . . . unreviewable." Ante, at 16; see also ante, at 6 (O'Connor, J., concurring in part and concurring in judgment). [n.4] That is true only in the technical (and irrelevant) sense that the later group denied an accommodation may need to challenge the grant of the first accommodation in light of the later denial, rather than challenging the denial directly. But one way or another, "even if [an administrative agency is] not empowered or obliged to act, [a litigant] would be entitled to a judicial audience.

Ultimately the courts cannot escape the obligation to address [a] plea that the exemption [sought] is mandated by the first amendment's religion clauses." Olsen v. Drug Enforcement Admin., 878 F. 2d 1458, 1461 (CADC 1989) (R. B. Ginsburg, J.).

The Court's demand for "up front" assurances of a neutral system is at war with both traditional accommodation doctrine and the judicial role. As we have described, supra, at 15, Congress's earliest accommodations exempted duties paid by specific churches on particular items. See, e.g., 6 Stat. 346 (1816) (exempting vestments imported by "bishop of Bardstown"). Moreover, most efforts at accommodation seek to solve a problem that applies to members of only one or a few religions. Not every religion uses wine in its sacraments, but that does not make an exemption from Prohibition for sacramental wine use impermissible, accord, Church of Lukumi Babalu Aye, Inc. v. Hialeah,508 U. S., at ___, n. 2 (slip op., at 3, n. 2) (Souter, J., concurring in judgment), nor does it require the State granting such an exemption to explain in advance how it will treat every other claim for dispensation from its controlled substances laws. Likewise, not every religion uses peyote in its services, but we have suggested that legislation which exempts the sacramental use of peyote from generally applicable drug laws is not only permissible, but desirable, see Employment Div., Ore. Dept of Human Resources v. Smith, 494 U.S. 872, 890 (1990), without any suggestion that some "up front" legislative guarantee of equal treatment for sacramental substances used by other sects must be provided. The record is clear that the necessary guarantee can and will be provided, after the fact, by the courts. See, e.g., Olsen v. Drug Enforcement Admin., supra, (rejecting claim that peyote exemption requires marijuana exemption for Ethiopian Zion Coptic Church); Olsen v. Iowa, 808 F. 2d 652 (CA8 1986) (same); Kennedy v. Bureau of Narcotics and Dangerous Drugs, 459 F. 2d 415 (CA9 1972) (accepting claim that peyote exemption for Native American Church requires peyote exemption for other religions that use that substance in their sacraments). [n.5]

Contrary to the Court's suggestion, ante, at 20-22, I do not think that the Establishment Clause prohibits formally established "state" churches and nothing more. I have always believed, and all my opinions are consistent with the view, that the Establishment Clause prohibits the favoring of one religion over others. In this respect, it is the Court that attacks lions of straw. What I attack is the Court's imposition of novel "up front" procedural requirements on state legislatures. Making law (and making exceptions) one case at a time, whether through adjudication or through highly particularized rulemaking or legislation, violates, ex ante, no principle of fairness, equal protection, or neutrality, simply because it does not announce in advance how all future cases (and all future exceptions) will be disposed of. If it did, the manner of proceeding of this Court itself would be unconstitutional. It is presumptuous for this Court to impose--out of nowhere--an unheard of prohibition against proceeding in this manner upon the Legislature of New York State. I never heard of such a principle, nor has anyone else, nor will it ever be heard of again. Unlike what the New York Legislature has done, this is a special rule to govern only the Satmar Hasidim.

A few words in response to the separate concurrences: Justice Stevens adopts, for these cases, a rationale that is almost without limit. The separate Kiryas Joel school district is problematic in his view because "[t]he isolation of these children, while it may protect them from `panic, fear and trauma,' also unquestionably increased the likelihood that they would remain within the fold, faithful adherents of their parents' religious faith." Ante, at 2. So much for family values. If the Constitution forbids any state action that incidentally helps parents to raise their children in their own religious faith, it would invalidate a release program permitting public school children to attend the religious instruction program of their parents' choice, of the sort we approved in Zorach, supra; [n.6] indeed, it would invalidate state laws according parents physical control over their children, at least insofar as that is used to take the little fellows to church or synagogue. Justice Stevens' statement is less a legal analysis than a manifesto of secularism. It surpasses mere rejection of accommodation, and announces a positive hostility to religion--which, unlike all other noncriminal values, the state must not assist parents in transmitting to their offspring.

Justice Kennedy's "political line drawing" approach founders on its own terms. He concedes that the Constitution does not prevent people who share a faith from forming their own villages and towns, and suggests that the formation of the village of Kiryas Joel was free from defect. Ante, at 9-10. He also notes that States are free to draw political lines on the basis of history and geography. Ante, at 10. I do not see, then, how a school district drawn to mirror the boundaries of an existing village (an existing geographic line), which itself is not infirm, can violate the Constitution. Thus, while Justice Kennedy purports to share my criticism (Part IV, supra) of the Court's unprecedented insistence that the New York Legislature make its accommodations only by general legislation, see ante, at 1-2, 6, his own approach is little different. He says the village is constitutional because it was formed (albeit by members of a single religious sect) under a general New York law; but he finds the school district unconstitutional because it was the product of a specific enactment. In the end, his analysis is no different from the Court's.

Justice Kennedy expresses the view that School Dist. of Grand Rapids v. Ball, 473 U.S. 373 (1985), and Aguilar v. Felton, 473 U.S. 402 (1985)--the cases that created the need for the Kiryas Joel legislation by holding unconstitutional state provision of supplemental educational services in sectarian schools--"may have been erroneous," and he suggests that "it may be necessary for us to reconsider them at a later date." Ante, at 11. Justice O'Connor goes even further and expresses the view that Aguilar should be overruled. Ante, at 7. I heartily agree that these cases, so hostile to our national tradition of accommodation, should be overruled at the earliest opportunity; but meanwhile, today's opinion causes us to lose still further ground, and in the same anti accommodationist direction.

Finally, Justice O'Connor observes that the Court's opinion does not focus on the so called Lemon test, see Lemon v. Kurtzman, 403 U.S. 602 (1971), and she urges that that test be abandoned, at least as a "unitary approach" to all Establishment Clause claims, ante, at 11. I have previously documented the Court's convenient relationship with Lemon, which it cites only when useful, see Lamb's Chapel v. Center Moriches Union Free School Dist., 508 U. S. ____, ____ (1993) (slip op., at 1-5) (Scalia, J., concurring in judgment), and I no longer take any comfort in the Court's failure to rely on it in any particular case, as I once mistakenly did, see Lee v. Weisman, 505 U. S. ____, ____ (1992) (Scalia, J., dissenting). But the Court's snub of Lemon today (it receives only two "see also" citations, in the course of the opinion's description of Grendel's Den) is particularly noteworthy because all three courts below (who are not free to ignore Supreme Court precedent at will) relied on it, and the parties (also bound by our case law) dedicated over 80 pages of briefing to the application and continued vitality of the Lemon test. In addition to the other sound reasons for abandoning Lemon, see e.g., Edwards v. Aguillard, 482 U.S. 578, 636-640 (1987) (Scalia, J., dissenting); Wallace v. Jaffree, 472 U.S. 38, 108-112 (1985) (Rehnquist, J., dissenting), it seems quite inefficient for this Court, which in reaching its decisions relies heavily on the briefing of the parties and, to a lesser extent, the opinions of lower courts, to mislead lower courts and parties about the relevance of the Lemon test. Compare ante (ignoring Lemon despite lower courts' reliance) with Lamb's Chapel, supra (applying Lemon despite failure of lower court to mention it).

Unlike Justice O'Connor, however, I would not replace Lemon with nothing, and let the case law "evolve" into a series of situation specific rules (government speech on religious topics, government benefits to particular groups, etc.) unconstrained by any "rigid influence," ante, at 11. The problem with (and the allure of) Lemon has not been that it is "rigid," but rather that in many applications it has been utterly meaningless, validating whatever result the Court would desire. See Lamb's Chapel, supra, at ____ (slip op., at 2-3) (Scalia, J., concurring in judgment); Wallace, supra, at 110-111 (Rehnquist, J., dissenting). To replace Lemon with nothing is simply to announce that we are now so bold that we no longer feel the need even to pretend that our haphazard course of Establishment Clause decisions is governed by any principle. The foremost principle I would apply is fidelity to the longstanding traditions of our people, which surely provide the diversity of treatment that Justice O'Connor seeks, but do not leave us to our own devices.

* * *

The Court's decision today is astounding. Chapter 748 involves no public aid to private schools and does not mention religion. In order to invalidate it, the Court casts aside, on the flimsiest of evidence, the strong presumption of validity that attaches to facially neutral laws, and invalidates the present accommodation because it does not trust New York to be as accommodating toward other religions (presumably those less powerful than the Satmar Hasidim) in the future. This is unprecedented--except that it continues, and takes to new extremes, a recent tendency in the opinions of this Court to turn the Establishment Clause into a repealer of our Nation's tradition of religious toleration. I dissent.

Justice Scalia's dissent in US v. X-citement Video (November 29, 1994)

Justice Scalia, with whom Justice Thomas joins, dissenting.

Today's opinion is without antecedent. None of the decisions cited as authority support interpreting an explicit statutory scienter requirement in a manner that its language simply will not bear. Staples v. United States, 511 U. S. ____ (1994), discussed ante, at 7, and United States v. United States Gypsum Co., 438 U.S. 422 (1978), discussed ante, at 6, applied the background common law rule of scienter to a statute that said nothing about the matter. Morissette v. United States, 342 U.S. 246 (1952), discussed ante, at 5-6, applied that same background rule to a statute that did contain the word "knowingly," in order to conclude that "knowingly converts" requires knowledge not merely of the fact of one's assertion of dominion over property, but also knowledge of the fact that that assertion is a conversion, i.e., is wrongful. [n.*] Liparota v. United States, 471 U.S. 419 (1985), discussed ante, at 6, again involved a statute that did contain the word " `knowingly,' " used in such a fashion that it could reasonably and grammatically be thought to apply (1) only to the phrase " `uses, transfers, acquires, alters, or possesses' " (which would cause a defendant to be liable without wrongful intent), or (2) also to the later phrase " `in any manner not authorized by [the statute].' " Once again applying the background rule of scienter, the latter reasonable and permissible reading was preferred.

There is no way in which any of these cases, or all of them in combination, can be read to stand for the sweeping proposition that "the presumption in favor of a scienter requirement should apply to each of the statutory elements which criminalize otherwise innocent conduct," ante, at 8, even when the plain text of the statute says otherwise. All those earlier cases employ the presumption as a rule of interpretation which applies when Congress has not addressed the question of criminal intent (Staples and Gypsum), or when the import of what it has said on that subject is ambiguous (Morissette and Liparota). Today's opinion converts the rule of interpretation into a rule of law, contradicting the plain import of what Congress has specifically prescribed regarding criminal intent.

In United States v. Thomas, 893 F. 2d 1066, 1070 (CA9), cert. denied, 498 U.S. 826 (1990), the Ninth Circuit interpreted 18 U.S.C. § 2252 to require knowledge of neither the fact that the visual depiction portrays sexually explicit conduct, nor the fact that a participant in that conduct was a minor. The panel in the present case accepted that interpretation. See 982 F. 2d 1285, 1289 (CA9 1992). To say, as the Court does, that this interpretation is "the most grammatical reading," ante, at 5, or "[t]he most natural grammatical reading," ante, at 4, is understatement to the point of distortion--rather like saying that the ordinarily preferred total for 2 plus 2 is 4. The Ninth Circuit's interpretation is in fact and quite obviously the only grammatical reading. If one were to rack his brains for a way to express the thought that the knowledge requirement in subsection (a)(1) applied only to the transportation or shipment of visual depiction in interstate or foreign commerce, and not to the fact that that depiction was produced by use of a minor engaging in sexually explicit conduct, and was a depiction of that conduct, it would be impossible to construct a sentence structure that more clearly conveys that thought, and that thought alone. The word "knowingly" is contained, not merely in a distant phrase, but in an entirely separate clause from the one into which today's opinion inserts it. The equivalent, in expressing a simpler thought, would be the following: "Anyone who knowingly double parks will be subject to a $200 fine if that conduct occurs during the 4:30 to 6:30 rush hour." It could not be clearer that the scienter requirement applies only to the double parking, and not to the time of day. So also here, it could not be clearer that it applies only to the transportation or shipment of visual depiction in interstate or foreign commerce. There is no doubt. There is no ambiguity. There is no possible "less natural" but nonetheless permissible reading.

I have been willing, in the case of civil statutes, to acknowledge a doctrine of "scrivener's error" that permits a court to give an unusual (though not unheard of) meaning to a word which, if given its normal meaning, would produce an absurd and arguably unconstitutional result. See Green v. Bock Laundry Machine Co., 490 U.S. 504, 527 (1989) (Scalia, J., concurring). Even if I were willing to stretch that doctrine so as to give the problematic text a meaning it cannot possibly bear; and even if I were willing to extend the doctrine to criminal cases in which its application would produce conviction rather than acquittal; it would still have no proper bearing here. For the sine qua non of any "scrivener's error" doctrine, it seems to me, is that the meaning genuinely intended but inadequately expressed must be absolutely clear; otherwise we might be rewriting the statute rather than correcting a technical mistake. That condition is not met here.

The Court acknowledges that "it is a good deal less clear from the Committee Reports and floor debates that Congress intended that the requirement [of scienter] extend . . . to the age of the performers." Ante, at 14. That is surely so. In fact it seems to me that the dominant (if not entirely uncontradicted) view expressed in the legislative history is that set forth in the statement of the Carter Administration Justice Department which introduced the original bill: "[T]he defendant's knowledge of the age of the child is not an element of the offense but . . . the bill is not intended to apply to innocent transportation with no knowledge of the nature or character of the material involved." S. Rep. No. 95-438, p. 29 (1977). As applied to the final bill, this would mean that the scienter requirement applies to the element of the crime that the depiction be of "sexually explicit conduct," but not to the element that the depiction "involv[e] the use of a minor engaging" in such conduct. See 18 U.S.C. §§ 2252(a)(1)(A) and (a)(2)(A). This is the interpretation that was argued by the United States before the Ninth Circuit. See 982 F. 2d, at 1289.

The Court rejects this construction of the statute for two reasons: First, because "as a matter of grammar it is difficult to conclude that the word `knowingly' modifies one of the elements in (1)(A) and (2)(A), but not the other." Ante, at 14. But as I have described, "as a matter of grammar" it is also difficult (nay, impossible) to conclude that the word "knowingly" modifies both of those elements. It is really quite extraordinary for the Court, fresh from having, as it says ibid., "emancipated"the adverb from the grammatical restriction that renders it inapplicable to the entire conditional clause, suddenly to insist that the demands of syntax must prevail over legislative intent--thus producing an end result that accords neither with syntax nor with supposed intent. If what the statute says must be ignored, one would think we might settle at least for what the statute was meant to say; but alas, we are told, what the statute says prevents this.

The Court's second reason is even worse: "[A] statute completely bereft of a scienter requirement as to the age of the performers would raise serious constitutional doubts." Ante, at 14. In my view (as in the apparent view of the Government before the Court of Appeals) that is not true. The Court derives its "serious constitutional doubts" from the fact that "sexually explicit materials involving persons over the age of 18 are protected by the First Amendment," ante, at 8. We have made it entirely clear, however, that the First Amendment protection accorded to such materials is not as extensive as that accorded to other speech. "[T]here is surely a less vital interest in the uninhibited exhibition of material that is on the borderline between pornography and artistic expression than in the free dissemination of ideas of social and political significance ¡ . . ." Young v. American Mini Theatres, Inc., 427 U.S. 50, 61 (1976). See also id., at 70-71 ("[E]ven though we recognize that the First Amendment will not tolerate the total suppression of erotic materials that have some arguably artistic value, it is manifest that society's interest in protecting this type of expression is of a wholly different, and lesser, magnitude than the interest in untrammeled political debate . . .") (opinion of Stevens, J., joined by Burger, C. J., and White and Rehnquist, JJ.). Cf. FCC v. Pacifica Foundation, 438 U.S. 726, 743 (1978) (While some broadcasts of patently offensive references to excretory and sexual organs andactivities may be protected, "they surely lie at the periphery of First Amendment concern"). Let us be clear about what sort of pictures are at issue here. They are not the sort that will likely be found in a catalog of the National Gallery or the Metropolitan Museum of Art. " `[S]exually explicit conduct,' " as defined in the statute, does not include mere nudity, but only conduct that consists of "sexual intercourse . . . between persons of the same or opposite sex," "bestiality," "masturbation," "sadistic or masochistic abuse," and "lascivious exhibition of the genitals or pubic area." See 18 U.S.C. § 2256(2). What is involved, in other words, is not the clinical, the artistic, nor even the risqu◆, but hard core pornography. Indeed, I think it entirely clear that all of what is involved constitutes not merely pornography but fully proscribable obscenity, except to the extent it is joined with some other material (or perhaps some manner of presentation) that has artistic or other social value. See Miller v. California, 413 U.S. 15, 24 (1973). (Such a requirement cannot be imposed, of course, upon fully protected speech: one can shout "Down with the Republic!," "Hooray for Mozart!," or even "Twenty Three Skidoo!," whether or not that expression is joined with something else of social value.) And whereas what is on one side of the balance in the present case is this material of minimal First Amendment concern, the Court has described what is on the other side-- %prevention of sexual exploitation and abuse of children"--as "a government objective of surpassing importance." New York v. Ferber, 458 U.S. 747, 757 (1982).

I am not concerned that holding the purveyors and receivers of this material absolutely liable for supporting the exploitation of minors will deter any activity the United States Constitution was designed to protect. But I am concerned that the Court's suggestion of the unconstitutionality of such absolute liability will cause Congress to leave the world's children inadequately protected against the depredations of the pornography trade. As we recognized in Ferber, supra, at 766, n. 19, the producers of these materials are not always readily found, and are often located abroad; and knowledge of the performers' age by the dealers who specialize in child pornography, and by the purchasers who sustain that market, is obviously hard to prove. The First Amendment will lose none of its value to a free society if those who knowingly place themselves in the stream of pornographic commerce are obliged to make sure that they are not subsidizing child abuse. It is no more unconstitutional to make persons who knowingly deal in hard core pornography criminally liable for the underage character of their entertainers than it is to make men who engage in consensual fornication criminally liable (in statutory rape) for the underage character of their partners.

I would dispose of the present case, as the Ninth Circuit did, by reading the statute as it is written: to provide criminal penalties for the knowing transportation or shipment of a visual depiction in interstate or foreign commerce, and for the knowing receipt or distribution of a visual depiction so transported or shipped, if that depiction was (whether the defendant knew it or not) a portrayal of a minor engaging in sexually explicit conduct. I would find the statute, as so interpreted, to be unconstitutional since, by imposing criminal liability upon those not knowingly dealing in pornography, it establishes a severe deterrent, not narrowly tailored to its purposes, upon fully protected First Amendment activities. See Smith v. California, 361 U.S. 147, 153-154 (1959). This conclusion of unconstitutionality is of course no ground for going back to reinterpret the statute, making it say something that it does not say, but that is constitutional. Not every construction, but only " `every reasonable construction must be resorted to, in order to save a statute from unconstitutionality.' " Edward J. DeBartolo Corp. v. Florida Gulf Coast Building & Construction Trades Council, 485 U.S. 568, 575 (1988) (quoting Hooper v. California, 155 U.S. 648, 657 (1895)) (emphasis added). " `Although this Court will often strain to construe legislation so as to save it against constitutional attack, it must not and will not carry this to the point of perverting the purpose of a statute . . .' or judicially rewriting it." Commodity Futures Trading Comm'n v. Schor, 478 U.S. 833, 841 (1986) (quoting Aptheker v. Secretary of State, 378 U.S. 500, 515 (1964)). Otherwise, there would be no such thing as an unconstitutional statute. As I have earlier discussed, in the present case no reasonable alternative construction exists, neither any that can be coaxed from the text nor any that can be substituted for the text on "scrivener's error" grounds. I therefore agree with the Ninth Circuit that respondent's conviction cannot stand.

I could understand (though I would not approve of) a disposition which, in order to uphold this statute, departed from its text as little as possible in order to sustain its constitutionality--i.e., a disposition applying the scienter requirement to the pornographic nature of the materials, but not to the age of the performers. I can neither understand nor approve of the disposition urged by the United States before this Court and adopted today, which not only rewrites the statute, but (1) rewrites it more radically than its constitutional survival demands, and (2) raises baseless constitutional doubts that will impede congressional enactment of a law providing greater protection for the child victims of the pornography industry. The Court today saves a single conviction by putting in place a relatively toothless child pornography law that Congress did not enact, and by rendering congressional strengthening of that new law more difficult. I respectfully dissent.

Notes

* The case did not involve, as the Court claims, a situation in which, "even more obviously than in the statute presently before us, the word `knowingly' in its isolated position suggested that it only attached to the verb `converts' " ante, at 6, and we nonetheless applied it as well to another word. The issue was simply the meaning of "knowingly converts."

Justice Scalia's dissent in McIntyre v. Ohio Elections Comm'n (April 19, 1995)

Justice Scalia, with whom The Chief Justice joins, dissenting.

At a time when both political branches of Government and both political parties reflect a popular desire to leave more decision making authority to the States, today's decision moves in the opposite direction, adding to the legacy of inflexible central mandates (irrevocable even by Congress) imposed by this Court's constitutional jurisprudence. In an opinion which reads as though it is addressing some peculiar law like the Los Angeles municipal ordinance at issue in Talley v. California, 362 U. S. 60 (1960), the Court invalidates a species of protection for the election process that exists, in a variety of forms, in every State except California, and that has a pedigree dating back to the end of the 19th century. Preferring the views of the English utilitarian philosopher John Stuart Mill, ante, at 357, to the considered judgment of the American people's elected representatives from coast to coast, the Court discovers a hitherto unknown right-to-be-unknown while engaging in electoral politics. I dissent from this imposition of free-speech imperatives that are demonstrably not those of the American people today, and that there is inadequate reason to believe were those of the society that begat the First Amendment or the Fourteenth.

I

The question posed by the present case is not the easiest sort to answer for those who adhere to the Court's (and the society's) traditional view that the Constitution bears its original meaning and is unchanging. Under that view, "[o]n every question of construction, [we should] carry ourselves back to the time when the Constitution was adopted; recollect the spirit manifested in the debates; and instead of trying [to find] what meaning may be squeezed out of the text, or invented against it, conform to the probable one in which it was passed." T. Jefferson, Letter to William Johnson (June 12, 1823), in 15 Writings of Thomas Jefferson 439, 449 (A. Lipscomb ed. 1904). That technique is simple of application when government conduct that is claimed to violate the Bill of Rights or the Fourteenth Amendment is shown, upon investigation, to have been engaged in without objection at the very time the Bill of Rights or the Fourteenth Amendment was adopted. There is no doubt, for example, that laws against libel and obscenity do not violate "the freedom of speech" to which the First Amendment refers; they existed and were universally approved in 1791. Application of the principle of an unchanging Constitution is also simple enough at the other extreme, where the government conduct at issue was not engaged in at the time of adoption, and there is ample evidence that the reason it was not engaged in is that it was thought to violate the right embodied in the constitutional guarantee. Racks and thumbscrews, well known instruments for inflicting pain, were not in use because they were regarded as cruel punishments.

The present case lies between those two extremes. Anonymous electioneering was not prohibited by law in 1791 or in 1868. In fact, it was widely practiced at the earlier date, an understandable legacy of the revolutionary era in which political dissent could produce governmental reprisal. I need not dwell upon the evidence of that, since it is described at length in today's concurrence. See ante, at 3-13 (Thomas, J., concurring in judgment). The practice of anonymous electioneering may have been less general in 1868, when the Fourteenth Amendment was adopted, but at least as late as 1837 it was respectable enough to be engaged in by Abraham Lincoln. See 1 A. Beveridge, Abraham Lincoln 1809-1858, pp. 215-216 (1928); 1 Uncollected Works of Abraham Lincoln 155-161 (R. Wilson ed. 1947).

But to prove that anonymous electioneering was used frequently is not to establish that it is a constitutional right. Quite obviously, not every restriction upon expression that did not exist in 1791 or in 1868 is ipso facto unconstitutional, or else modern election laws such as those involved in Burson v. Freeman, 504 U.S. 191 (1992), and Buckley v. Valeo, 424 U.S. 1 (1976), would be prohibited, as would (to mention only a few other categories) modern anti noise regulation of the sort involved in Kovacs v. Cooper, 336 U.S. 77 (1949), and Ward v. Rock Against Racism, 491 U.S. 781 (1989), and modern parade permitting regulation of the sort involved in Cox v. New Hampshire, 312 U.S. 569 (1941).

Evidence that anonymous electioneering was regarded as a constitutional right is sparse, and as far as I am aware evidence that it was generally regarded as such is nonexistent. The concurrence points to "freedom of the press" objections that were made against the refusal of some Federalist newspapers to publish unsigned essays opposing the proposed constitution (on the ground that they might be the work of foreign agents). See ante, at 7-9 (Thomas, J., concurring in judgment). But of course if every partisan cry of "freedom of the press" were accepted as valid, our Constitution would be unrecognizable; and if one were to generalize from these particular cries, the First Amendment would be not only a protection for newspapers but a restriction upon them. Leaving aside, however, the fact that no governmental action was involved, the Anti Federalists had a point, inasmuch as the editorial proscription of anonymity applied only to them, and thus had the vice of viewpoint discrimination. (Hence the comment by Philadelphiensis, quoted in the concurrence: " `Here we see pretty plainly through [the Federalists'] excellent regulation of the press, how things are to be carried on after the adoption of the new constitution.' " Ante, at 8 (quoting Philadelphiensis, Essay I, Independent Gazetteer, Nov. 7, 1787, in 3 Complete Anti Federalist 103 (H. Storing ed. 1981)).)

The concurrence recounts other pre-and post-Revolution examples of defense of anonymity in the name of "freedom of the press," but not a single one involves the context of restrictions imposed in connection with a free, democratic election, which is all that is at issue here. For many of them, moreover, such as the 1735 Zenger trial, ante, at 3-4, the 1779 "Leonidas" controversy in the Continental Congress, ante, at 4, and the 1779 action by the New Jersey Legislative Council against Isaac Collins, ante, at 5, the issue of anonymity was incidental to the (unquestionably free speech) issue of whether criticism of the government could be punished by the state.

Thus, the sum total of the historical evidence marshalled by the concurrence for the principle of constitutional entitlement to anonymous electioneering is partisan claims in the debate on ratification (which was almost like an election) that a viewpoint based restriction on anonymity by newspaper editors violates freedom of speech. This absence of historical testimony concerning the point before us is hardly remarkable. The issue of a governmental prohibition upon anonymous electioneering in particular (as opposed to a government prohibition upon anonymous publication in general) simply never arose. Indeed, there probably never arose even the abstract question of whether electoral openness and regularity was worth such a governmental restriction upon the normal right to anonymous speech. The idea of close government regulation of the electoral process is a more modern phenomenon, arriving in this country in the late 1800's. See Burson v. Freeman, supra, at 203-205.

What we have, then, is the most difficult case for determining the meaning of the Constitution. No accepted existence of governmental restrictions of the sort at issue here demonstrates their constitutionality, but neither can their nonexistence clearly be attributed to constitutional objections. In such a case, constitutional adjudication necessarily involves not just history but judgment: judgment as to whether the government action under challenge is consonant with the concept of the protected freedom (in this case, the freedom of speech and of the press) that existed when the constitutional protection was accorded. In the present case, absent other indication I would be inclined to agree with the concurrence that a society which used anonymous political debate so regularly would not regard as constitutional even moderate restrictions made to improve the election process. (I would, however, want further evidence of common practice in 1868, since I doubt that the Fourteenth Amendment time warped the post-Civil War States back to the Revolution.)

But there is other indication, of the most weighty sort: the widespread and longstanding traditions of our people. Principles of liberty fundamental enough to have been embodied within constitutional guarantees are not readily erased from the Nation's consciousness. A governmental practice that has become general throughout the United States, and particularly one that has the validation of long, accepted usage, bears a strong presumption of constitutionality. And that is what we have before us here. Section 3599.09(A) was enacted by the General Assembly of the State of Ohio almost 80 years ago. See Act of May 27, 1915, 1915 Ohio Leg. Acts 350. Even at the time of its adoption, there was nothing unique or extraordinary about it. The earliest statute of this sort was adopted by Massachusetts in 1890, little more than 20 years after the Fourteenth Amendment was ratified. No less than 24 States had similar laws by the end of World War I, [n.1] and today every State of the Union except California has one, [n.2] as does the District of Columbia, see D. C. Code Ann. §1-1420 (1992), and as does the Federal Government where advertising relating to candidates for federal office is concerned, see 2 U.S.C. § 441d(a). Such a universal [n.3] and long established American legislative practice must be given precedence, I think, over historical and academic speculation regarding a restriction that assuredly does not go to the heart of free speech.

It can be said that we ignored a tradition as old, and almost as widespread, in Texas v. Johnson, 491 U.S. 397 (1989), where we held unconstitutional a state law prohibiting desecration of the United States flag. See also United States v. Eichman, 496 U.S. 310 (1990). But those cases merely stand for the proposition that post-adoption tradition cannot alter the core meaning of a constitutional guarantee. As we said in Johnson, "[i]f there is a bedrock principle underlying the First Amendment, it is that the government may not prohibit the expression of an idea simply because society finds the idea itself offensive or disagreeable." 491 U. S., at 414. Prohibition of expression of contempt for the flag, whether by contemptuous words, see Street v. New York, 394 U.S. 576 (1969), or by burning the flag, came, we said, within that "bedrock principle." The law at issue here, by contrast, forbids the expression of no idea, but merely requires identification of the speaker when the idea is uttered in the electoral context. It is at the periphery of the First Amendment, like the law at issue in Burson, where we took guidance from tradition in upholding against constitutional attack restrictions upon electioneering in the vicinity of polling places, see 504 U. S., at 204-206 (plurality opinion); id., at 214-216 (Scalia, J., concurring in judgment).

The foregoing analysis suffices to decide this case for me. Where the meaning of a constitutional text (such as "the freedom of speech") is unclear, the widespread and long accepted practices of the American people are the best indication of what fundamental beliefs it was intended to enshrine. Even if I were to close my eyes to practice, however, and were to be guided exclusively by deductive analysis from our case law, I would reach the same result.

Three basic questions must be answered to decide this case. Two of them are readily answered by our precedents; the third is readily answered by common sense and by a decent regard for the practical judgment of those more familiar with elections than we are. The first question is whether protection of the election process justifies limitations upon speech that cannot constitutionally be imposed generally. (If not, Talley v. California, which invalidated a flat ban on all anonymous leafletting, controls the decision here.) Our cases plainly answer that question in the affirmative--indeed, they suggest that no justification for regulation is more compelling than protection of the electoral process. "Other rights, even the most basic, are illusory if the right to vote is undermined." Wesberry v. Sanders, 376 U.S. 1, 17 (1964). The State has a "compelling interest in preserving the integrity of its election process." Eu v. San Francisco Cty. Democratic Central Comm., 489 U.S. 214, 231 (1989). So significant have we found the interest in protecting the electoral process to be that we have approved the prohibition of political speech entirely in areas that would impede that process. Burson, supra, at 204-206 (plurality opinion).

The second question relevant to our decision is whether a "right to anonymity" is such a prominent value in our constitutional system that even protection of the electoral process cannot be purchased at its expense. The answer, again, is clear: no. Several of our cases have held that in peculiar circumstances the compelled disclosure of a person's identity would unconstitutionally deter the exercise of First Amendment associational rights. See, e.g., Brown v. Socialist Workers '74 Campaign Comm. (Ohio), 459 U.S. 87 (1982); Bates v. Little Rock, 361 U.S. 516 (1960); NAACP v. Alabama ex rel. Patterson, 357 U.S. 449 (1958). But those cases did not acknowledge any general right to anonymity, or even any right on the part of all citizens to ignore the particular laws under challenge. Rather, they recognized a right to an exemption from otherwise valid disclosure requirements on the part of someone who could show a "reasonable probability" that the compelled disclosure would result in "threats, harassment, or reprisals from either Government officials or private parties." This last quotation is from Buckley v. Valeo, 424 U.S. 1, 74 (1976) (per curiam), which prescribed the safety valve of a similar exemption in upholding the disclosure requirements of the Federal Election Campaign Act. That is the answer our case law provides to the Court's fear about the "tyranny of the majority," ante, at 23, and to its concern that " `[p]ersecuted groups and sects from time to time throughout history have been able to criticize oppressive practices and laws either anonymously or not at all,' " ante, at 8 (quoting Talley, 362 U. S., at 64). Anonymity can still be enjoyed by those who require it, without utterly destroying useful disclosure laws. The record in this case contains not even a hint that Mrs. McIntyre feared "threats, harassment, or reprisals"; indeed, she placed her name on some of her fliers and meant to place it on all of them. See App. 12, 36-40.

The existence of a generalized right of anonymity in speech was rejected by this Court in Lewis Publishing Co. v. Morgan, 229 U.S. 288 (1913), which held that newspapers desiring the privilege of second class postage could be required to provide to the Postmaster General, and to publish, a statement of the names and addresses of their editors, publishers, business managers and owners. We rejected the argument that the First Amendment forbade the requirement of such disclosure. Id., at 299. The provision that gave rise to that case still exists, see 39 U.S.C. § 3685 and is still enforced by the

Postal Service. It is one of several federal laws seemingly invalidated by today's opinion.

The Court's unprecedented protection for anonymous speech does not even have the virtue of establishing a clear (albeit erroneous) rule of law. For after having announced that this statute, because it "burdens core political speech," requires "exacting scrutiny" and must be "narrowly tailored to serve an overriding state interest," ante, at 13 (ordinarily the kiss of death), the opinion goes on to proclaim soothingly (and unhelpfully) that "a State's enforcement interest might justify a more limited identification requirement." Ante, at 19. See also ante, at 2 (Ginsburg, J., concurring) ("We do not . . . hold that the State may not in other, larger circumstances, require the speaker to disclose its interest by disclosing its identity.") Perhaps, then, not all the State statutes I have alluded to are invalid, but just some of them; or indeed maybe all of them remain valid in "larger circumstances"! It may take decades to work out the shape of this newly expanded right to speak incognito, even in the elections field. And in other areas, of course, a whole new boutique of wonderful First Amendment litigation opens its doors. Must a parade permit, for example, be issued to a group that refuses to provide its identity, or that agrees to do so only under assurance that the identity will not be made public? Must a municipally owned theater that is leased for private productions book anonymously sponsored presentations? Must a government periodical that has a "letters to the editor" column disavow the policy that most newspapers have against the publication of anonymous letters? Must a public university that makes its facilities available for a speech by Louis Farrakhan or David Duke refuse to disclose the on campus or off campus group that has sponsored or paid for the speech? Must a municipal "public access" cable channel permit anonymous (and masked) performers? The silliness that follows upon a generalized right to anonymous speech has no end.

The third and last question relevant to our decision is whether the prohibition of anonymous campaigning is effective in protecting and enhancing democratic elections. In answering this question no, the Justices of the majority set their own views--on a practical matter that bears closely upon the real life experience of elected politicians and not upon that of unelected judges--up against the views of 49 (and perhaps all 50, see n. 4, supra) state legislatures and the federal Congress. We might also add to the list on the other side the legislatures of foreign democracies: Australia, Canada, and England, for example, all have prohibitions upon anonymous campaigning. See, e.g., Commonwealth Electoral Act 1918, §328 (Australia); Canada Elections Act, R.S.C., ch. E-2, §261 (1985); Representation of the People Act, 1983, §110 (England). How is it, one must wonder, that all of these elected legislators, from around the country and around the world, could not see what six Justices of this Court see so clearly that they are willing to require the entire Nation to act upon it: that requiring identification of the source of campaign literature does not improve the quality of the campaign?

The Court says that the State has not explained "why it can more easily enforce the direct bans on disseminating false documents against anonymous authors and distributors than against wrongdoers who might use false names and addresses in an attempt to avoid detection." Ante, at 19. I am not sure what this complicated comparison means. I am sure, however, that (1) a person who is required to put his name to a document is much less likely to lie than one who can lie anonymously, and (2) the distributor of a leaflet which is unlawful because it is anonymous runs much more risk of immediate detection and punishment than the distributor of a leaflet which is unlawful because it is false. Thus, people will be more likely to observe a signing requirement than a naked "no falsity" requirement; and, having observed that requirement, will then be significantly less likely to lie in what they have signed.

But the usefulness of a signing requirement lies not only in promoting observance of the law against campaign falsehoods (though that alone is enough to sustain it). It lies also in promoting a civil and dignified level of campaign debate--which the State has no power to command, but ample power to encourage by such undemanding measures as a signature requirement. Observers of the past few national elections have expressed concern about the increase of character assassination--"mudslinging" is the colloquial term--engaged in by political candidates and their supporters to the detriment of the democratic process. Not all of this, in fact not much of it, consists of actionable untruth; most is innuendo, or demeaning characterization, or mere disclosure of items of personal life that have no bearing upon suitability for office. Imagine how much all of this would increase if it could be done anonymously. The principal impediment against it is the reluctance of most individuals and organizations to be publicly associated with uncharitable and uncivil expression. Consider, moreover, the increased potential for "dirty tricks." It is not unheard of for campaign operatives to circulate material over the name of their opponents or their opponents' supporters (a violation of election laws) in order to attract or alienate certain interest groups. See, e.g., B. Felknor, Political Mischief: Smear, Sabotage, and Reform in U. S. Elections 111-112 (1992) (fake United Mine Workers' newspaper assembled by the National Republican Congressional Committee); New York v. Duryea, 76 Misc. 2d 948, 351 N. Y. S. 2d 978 (Sup. 1974) (letters purporting to be from the "Action Committee for the Liberal Party" sent by Republicans). How much easier--and sanction free!--it would be to circulate anonymous material (for example, a really tasteless, though not actionably false, attack upon one's own candidate) with the hope and expectation that it will be attributed to, and held against, the other side.

The Court contends that demanding the disclosure of the pamphleteer's identity is no different from requiring the disclosure of any other information that may reduce the persuasiveness of the pamphlet's message. See ante, at 14-15. It cites Miami Herald Publishing Co. v. Tornillo, 418 U.S. 241 (1974), which held it unconstitutional to require a newspaper that had published an editorial critical of a particular candidate to furnish space for that candidate to reply. But it is not usual for a speaker to put forward the best arguments against himself, and it is a great imposition upon free speech to make him do so. Whereas it is quite usual--it is expected--for a speaker to identify himself, and requiring that is (at least when there are no special circumstances present) virtually no imposition at all.

We have approved much more onerous disclosure requirements in the name of fair elections. In Buckley v. Valeo, 424 U.S. 1 (1976), we upheld provisions of the Federal Election Campaign Act that required private individuals to report to the Federal Election Commission independent expenditures made for communications advocating the election or defeat of a candidate for federal office. Id., at 80. Our primary rationale for upholding this provision was that it served an "informational interest" by "increas[ing] the fund of information concerning those who support the candidates," id., at 81. The provision before us here serves the same informational interest, as well as more important interests, which I have discussed above. The Court's attempt to distinguish Buckley, see ante, at 22-23, would be unconvincing, even if it were accurate in its statement that the disclosure requirement there at issue "reveals far less information" than requiring disclosure of the identity of the author of a specific campaign statement. That happens not to be accurate, since the provision there at issue required not merely "[d]isclosure of an expenditure and its use, without more," ante, at 22. It required, among other things:

"the identification of each person to whom expenditures have been made . . . within the calendar year in an aggregate amount or value in excess of $100, the amount, date, and purpose of each such expenditure and the name and address of, and office sought by, each candidate on whose behalf such expenditure was made." 2 U.S.C. § 434(b)(9) (1970 ed., Supp. IV) (emphasis added). See also 2 U.S.C. § 434(e) (1970 ed., Supp. IV). (Both reproduced in Appendix to Buckley, 424 U. S., at 158, 160).

Surely in many if not most cases, this information will readily permit identification of the particular message that the would be anonymous campaigner sponsored. Besides which the burden of complying with this provision, which includes the filing of quarterly reports, is infinitely more onerous than Ohio's simple requirement for signature of campaign literature. If Buckley remains the law, this is an easy case.

* * *

I do not know where the Court derives its perception that "anonymous pamphleteering is not a pernicious, fraudulent practice, but an honorable tradition of advocacy and of dissent." Ante, at 23. I can imagine no reason why an anonymous leaflet is any more honorable, as a general matter, than an anonymous phone call or an anonymous letter. It facilitates wrong by eliminating accountability, which is ordinarily the very purpose of the anonymity. There are of course exceptions, and where anonymity is needed to avoid "threats, harassment, or reprisals" the First Amendment will require an exemption from the Ohio law. Cf. NAACP v. Alabama ex rel. Patterson, 357 U.S. 449 (1958). But to strike down the Ohio law in its general application--and similar laws of 48 other States and the Federal Government--on the ground that all anonymous communication is in our society traditionally sacrosanct, seems to me a distortion of the past that will lead to a coarsening of the future.

I respectfully dissent.

Notes

1 See Act of June 19, 1915, No. 171, §9, 1915 Ala. Acts 250, 254-255; Act of Mar. 12, 1917, ch. 47, §1, 1917 Ariz. Sess. Laws 62, 62-63; Act of Apr. 2, 1913, No. 308, §6, 1913 Ark. Gen. Acts 1252, 1255; Act of Mar. 15, 1901, ch. 138, §1, 1901 Cal. Stats. 297; Act of June 6, 1913, ch. 6470, §9, 1913 Fla. Laws 268, 272-273; Act of June 26, 1917, §1, 1917 Ill. Laws 456, 456-457; Act of Mar. 14, 1911, ch. 137, §1, 1911 Kan. Sess. Laws 221; Act of July 11, 1912, No. 213, §14, 1912 La. Acts 447, 454; Act of June 3, 1890, ch. 381, 1890 Mass. Laws 342; Act of June 20, 1912, Ex. Sess. ch. 3, §7, 1912 Minn. Laws 23, 26; Act of Apr. 21, 1906, S. B. No. 191, 1906 Miss. Gen. Laws 295 (enacting Miss. Code §3728 (1906)); Act of Apr. 9, 1917, §1, 1917 Mo. Laws 272, 273; Act of Nov. 1912, §35, 1912 Mont. Laws 593, 608; Act of Mar. 31, 1913, ch. 282, §34, 1913 Nev. Stats. 476, 486-487; Act of Apr. 21, 1915, ch. 169, §7, 1915 N. H. Laws 234, 236; Act of Apr. 20, 1911, ch. 188, §9, 1911 N. J. Laws 329, 334; Act of Mar. 12, 1913, ch. 164, §1(k), 1913 N. C. Sess. Laws 259, 261; Act of May 27, 1915, 1915 Ohio Leg. Acts 350; Act of June 23, 1908, ch. 3, §35, 1909 Ore. Laws 15, 30; Act of June 26, 1895, No. 275, 1895 Pa. Laws 389; Act of Mar. 13, 1917, ch. 92, §23, 1917 Utah Laws 258, 267; Act of Mar. 12, 1909, ch. 82, §8, 1909 Wash. Laws 169, 177-178; Act of Feb. 20, 1915, ch. 27, §13, 1915 W. Va. Acts 246, 255; Act of July 11, 1911, ch. 650, §§94-14 to 94-16, 1911 Wis. Laws 883, 890.

2 See Ala. Code §17-22A%13 (Supp. 1994); Alaska Stat. Ann. §15.56.010 (1988); Ariz. Rev. Stat. Ann. §16-912 (Supp. 1994); Ark. Code Ann. §7-1-103 (1993); Colo. Rev. Stat. §1-13-108 (Supp. 1994); Conn. Gen. Stat. §9-333w (Supp. 1994); Del. Code Ann., Tit. 15, §§8021, 8023 (1993); Fla. Stat. §§106.143 and 106.1437 (1992); Ga. Code Ann. §21-2-415 (1993); Haw. Rev. Stat. §11-215 (1988); Idaho Code §67-6614A (Supp. 1994); Ill. Comp. Stat. §5/29-14 (1993); Ind. Code §3-14-1-4 (Supp. 1994); Iowa Code §56.14 (1991); Kan. Stat. Ann. §§25-2407 and 25-4156 (Supp. 1991); Ky. Rev. Stat. Ann. §121.190 (Baldwin Supp. 1994); La. Rev. Stat. Ann. §18:1463 (West Supp. 1994); Me. Rev. Stat. Ann., Tit. 21-A, §1014 (1993); Md. Ann. Code, Art. 33, §26-17 (1993); Mass. Gen. Laws §41 (1990); Mich. Comp. Laws Ann. §169.247 (West 1989); Minn. Stat. §211B.04 (1994); Miss. Code Ann. §23-15-899 (1990); Mo. Rev. Stat. §130.031 (Supp. 1994); Mont. Code Ann. §13-35-225 (1993); Neb. Rev. Stat. §49-1474.01 (1993); Nev. Rev. Stat. §294A.320 (Supp. 1993); N. H. Rev. Stat. Ann. §664:14 (Supp. 1992); N. J. Stat. Ann. §19:34-38.1 (1989); N. M. Stat. Ann. §§1-19-16 and 1-19-17 (1991); N. Y. Elec. Law §14-106 (McKinney 1978); N. C. Gen. Stat. §163-274 (Supp. 1994); N. D. Cent. Code §16.1-10-04.1 (1981); Ohio Rev. Code Ann. §3599.09(A) (1988); Okla. Stat., Tit. 21, §1840 (Supp. 1995); Ore. Rev. Stat. §260.522 (1991); 25 Pa. Cons. Stat. §3258 (1994); R. I. Gen. Laws §17-23-2 (1988); S. C. Code Ann. §8-13-1354 (Supp. 1993); S. D. Comp. Laws Ann. §12-25-4.1 (Supp. 1994); Tenn. Code Ann. §2-19-120 (Supp. 1994); Tex. Elec. Code Ann. §255.001 (Supp. 1995); Utah Code Ann. §20-14-24 (Supp. 1994); Vt. Stat. Ann., Tit. 17, §2022 (1982); Va. Code Ann. §24.2-1014 (1993); Wash. Rev. Code §42.17.510 (Supp. 1994); W. Va. Code §3-8-12 (1994); Wis. Stat. §11.30 (Supp. 1994); Wyo. Stat. §22-25-110 (1992).

Courts have declared some of these laws unconstitutional in recent years, relying upon our decision in Talley v. California, 362 U.S. 60 (1960). See, e.g., State v. Burgess,

543 So. 2d 1332 (La. 1989); State v. North Dakota Ed. Assn., 262 N. W. 2d 731 (N. D. 1978); People v. Duryea, 76 Misc. 2d 948, 351 N. Y. S. 2d 978 (Sup.), aff'd, 44 App. Div. 2d 663, 354 N. Y. S. 2d 129 (1974). Other decisions, including all pre-Talley decisions I am aware of, have upheld the laws. See, e.g., Commonwealth v. Evans, 156 Pa. Super. 321, 40 A. 2d 137 (1944); State v. Freeman, 143 Kan. 315, 55 P. 2d 362 (1936); State v. Babst, 104 Ohio St. 167, 135 N. E. 525 (1922).

3 It might be accurate to say that, insofar as the judicially unconstrained judgment of American legislatures is concerned, approval of the law before us here is universal. California, although it had enacted an election disclosure requirement as early as 1901, see Act of Mar. 15, 1901, ch. 138, §1, 1901 Cal. Stats. 297, abandoned its law (then similar to Ohio's) in 1983, see Act of Sept. 11, 1983, ch. 668, 1983 Cal. Stats. 2621, after a California Court of Appeal, relying primarily on our decision in Talley, had declared the provision unconstitutional, see Schuster v. Imperial County Municipal Court, 109 Cal. App. 3d 887, 167 Cal. Rptr. 447 (1980), cert. denied, 450 U.S. 1042 (1981).

Justice Scalia's dissent in Kyles v. Whitley (April 19, 1995)

Justice Scalia, with whom the Chief Justice, Justice Kennedy, and Justice Thomas join, dissenting.

In a sensible system of criminal justice, wrongful conviction is avoided by establishing, at the trial level, lines of procedural legality that leave ample margins of safety (for example, the requirement that guilt be proved beyond a reasonable doubt)-not by providing recurrent and repetitive appellate review of whether the facts in the record show those lines to have been narrowly crossed. The defect of the latter system was described, with characteristic candor, by Justice Jackson:

"Whenever decisions of one court are reviewed by another, a percentage of them are reversed. That reflects a difference in outlook normally found between personnel comprising different courts. However, reversal by a higher court is not proof that justice is thereby better done." Brown v. Allen, 344 U.S. 443, 540 (1953) (Jackson, J., concurring).

Since this Court has long shared Justice Jackson's view, today's opinion--which considers a fact bound claim of error rejected by every court, state and federal, that previously heard it--is, so far as I can tell, wholly unprecedented. The Court has adhered to the policy that, when the petitioner claims only that a concededly correct view of the law was incorrectly applied to the facts, certiorari should generally (i.e., except in cases of the plainest error) be denied. United States v. Johnston, 268 U.S. 220, 227 (1925). That policy has been observed even when the fact bound assessment of the federal court of appeals has differed from that of the district court, Sumner v. Mata, 449 U.S. 539, 543 (1981); and under what we have called the "two court rule," the policy has been applied with particular rigor when district court and court of appeals are in agreement as to what conclusion the record requires. See, e.g., Graver Tank & Mfg. Co. v. Linde Air Products Co., 336 U.S. 271, 275 (1949). How much the more should the policy be honored in this case, a federal habeas proceeding where not only both lower federal courts but also the state courts on post conviction review have all reviewed and rejected precisely the fact specific claim before us. Cf. 28 U.S.C. § 2254(d) (requiring federal habeas courts to accord a presumption of correctness to state court findings of fact); Sumner, supra, at 550, n. 3. Instead, however, the Court not only grants certiorari to consider whether the Court of Appeals (and all the previous courts that agreed with it) was correct as to what the facts showed in a case where the answer is far from clear, but in the process of such consideration renders new findings of fact and judgments of credibility appropriate to a trial court of original jurisdiction. See, e.g., ante, at 5 ("Beanie seemed eager to cast suspicion on Kyles"); ante, at 23, n. 12 ("Record photographs of Beanie . . . depict a man possessing a medium build"); ante, at 30-31, n. 18 ("the record photograph of the homemade holster indicates . . .").

The Court says that we granted certiorari "[b]ecause `[o]ur duty to search for constitutional error with painstaking care is never more exacting than it is in a capital case,' Burger v. Kemp, 483 U.S. 776, 785(1987)." Ante, at 2. The citation is perverse, for the reader who looks up the quoted opinion will discover that the very next sentence confirms the traditional practice from which the Court today glaringly departs: "Nevertheless, when the lower courts have found that [no constitutional error occurred], . . . deference to the shared conclusion of two reviewing courts prevent[s] us from substituting speculation for their considered opinions." Burger v. Kemp, 483 U.S. 776, 785 (1987).

The greatest puzzle of today's decision is what could have caused this capital case to be singled out for favored treatment. Perhaps it has been randomly selected as a symbol, to reassure America that the United States Supreme Court is reviewing capital convictions to make sure no factual error has been made. If so, it is a false symbol, for we assuredly do not do that. At, and during the week preceding, our February 24 Conference, for example, we considered and disposed of 10 petitions in capital cases, from seven States. We carefully considered whether the convictions and sentences in those cases had been obtained in reliance upon correct principles of federal law; but if we had tried to consider, in addition, whether those correct principles had been applied, not merely plausibly, but accurately, to the particular facts of each case, we would have done nothing else for the week. The reality is that responsibility for factual accuracy, in capital cases as in other cases, rests elsewhere--with trial judges and juries, state appellate courts, and the lower federal courts; we do nothing but encourage foolish reliance to pretend otherwise.

Straining to suggest a legal error in the decision below that might warrant review, the Court asserts that "[t]here is room to debate whether the two judges in the majority in the Court of Appeals made an assessment of the cumulative effect of the evidence," ante, at 21. In support of this it quotes isolated sentences of the opinion below that supposedly "dismiss[ed] particular items of evidence as immaterial," ibid. This claim of legal error does not withstand minimal scrutiny. The Court of Appeals employed precisely the same legal standard that the Court does. Compare 5 F. 3d 806, 811 (CA5 1993) ("We apply the

[United States v.] Bagley [473 U.S. 667 (1985)] standard here by examining whether it is reasonably probable that, had the undisclosed information been available to Kyles, the result would have been different") with ante, at 22 ("In this case, disclosure of the suppressed evidence to competent counsel would have made a different result reasonably probable"). Nor did the Court of Appeals announce a rule of law, that might have precedential force in later cases, to the effect that Bagley requires a series of independent materiality evaluations; in fact, the court said just the contrary. See 5 F. 3d, at 817 ("We are not persuaded that it is reasonably probable that the jury would have found in Kyles' [sic] favor if exposed to any or all of the undisclosed materials") (emphasis added). If the decision is read, shall we say, cumulatively, it is clear beyond cavil that the court assessed the cumulative effect of the Brady evidence in the context of the whole record. See 5 F. 3d, at 807 (basing its rejection of petitioner's claim on "a complete reading of the record"); id., at 811 ("Rather than reviewing the alleged Brady materials in the abstract, we will examine the evidence presented at trial and how the extra materials would have fit"); id., at 813 ("We must bear [the eyewitness testimony] in mind while assessing the probable effect of other undisclosed information"). It is, in other words, the Court itself which errs in the manner that it accuses the Court of Appeals of erring: failing to consider the material under review as a whole. The isolated snippets it quotes from the decision merely do what the Court's own opinion acknowledges must be done: to "evaluate the tendency and force of the undisclosed evidence item by item; there is no other way." Ante, at 17, n. 10. Finally, the Court falls back on this: "The result reached by the Fifth Circuit majority is compatible with a series of independent materiality evaluations, rather than the cumulative evaluation required by Bagley," ante, at 22. In other words, even though the Fifth Circuit plainly enunciated the correct legal rule, since the outcome it reached would not properly follow from that rule, the Fifth Circuit must in fact (and unbeknownst to itself) have been applying an incorrect legal rule. This effectively eliminates all distinction between mistake in law and mistake in application.

What the Court granted certiorari to review, then, is not a decision on an issue of federal law that conflicts with a decision of another federal or state court; nor even a decision announcing a rule of federal law that because of its novelty or importance might warrant review despite the lack of a conflict; nor yet even a decision that patently errs in its application of an old rule. What we have here is an intensely fact specific case in which the court below unquestionably applied the correct rule of law and did not unquestionably err--precisely the type of case in which we are most inclined to deny certiorari. But despite all of that, I would not have dissented on the ground that the writ of certiorari should be dismissed as improvidently granted. Since the majority is as aware of the limits of our capacity as I am, there is little fear that the grant of certiorari in a case of this sort will often be repeated-- which is to say little fear that today's grant has any generalizable principle behind it. I am still forced to dissent, however, because, having improvidently decided to review the facts of this case, the Court goes on to get the facts wrong. Its findings are in my view clearly erroneous, cf. Fed. R. Civ. Proc. 52(a), and the Court's verdict would be reversed if there were somewhere further to appeal.

Before proceeding to detailed consideration of the evidence, a few general observations about the Court's methodology are appropriate. It is fundamental to the discovery rule of Brady v. Maryland, 373 U.S. 83 (1963), that the materiality of a failure to disclose favorable evidence "must be evaluated in the context of the entire record." United States v. Agurs, 427 U.S. 97, 112 (1976). It is simply not enough to show that the undisclosed evidence would have allowed the defense to weaken, or even to "destro[y]," ante, at 22, the particular prosecution witnesses or items of prosecution evidence to which the undisclosed evidence relates. It is petitioner's burden to show that in light of all the evidence, including that untainted by the Brady violation, it is reasonably probable that a jury would have entertained a reasonable doubt regarding petitioner's guilt. See United States v. Bagley, 473 U.S. 667, 682 (1985); Agurs, supra, at 112-113. The Court's opinion fails almost entirely to take this principle into account. Having spent many pages assessing the effect of the Brady material on two prosecution witnesses and a few items of prosecution evidence, ante, at 22-33, it dismisses the remainder of the evidence against Kyles in a quick page and a half, ante, at 33-35. This partiality is confirmed in the Court's attempt to "recap . . . the suppressed evidence and its significance for the prosecution," ante, at 35 (emphasis added), which omits the required comparison between that evidence and the evidence that was disclosed. My discussion of the record will present the half of the analysis that the Court omits, emphasizing the evidence concededly unaffected by the Brady violation which demonstrates the immateriality of the violation.

In any analysis of this case, the desperate implausibility of the theory that petitioner put before the jury must be kept firmly in mind. The first half of that theory-- designed to neutralize the physical evidence (Mrs. Dye's purse in his garbage, the murder weapon behind his stove)--was that petitioner was the victim of a "frame up" by the police informer and evil genius, Beanie. Now it is not unusual for a guilty person who knows that he is suspected of a crime to try to shift blame to someone else; and it is less common, but not unheard of, for a guilty person who is neither suspected nor subject to suspicion (because he has established a perfect alibi), to call attention to himself by coming forward to point the finger at an innocent person. But petitioner's theory is that the guilty Beanie, who could plausibly be accused of the crime (as petitioner's brief amply demonstrates), but who was not a suspect any more than Kyles was (the police as yet had no leads, see ante, at 4), injected both Kyles and himself into the investigation in order to get the innocent Kyles convicted. [n.1] If this were not stupid enough, the wicked Beanie is supposed to have suggested that the police search his victim's premises a full day before he got around to planting the incriminating evidence on the premises.

The second half of petitioner's theory was that he was the victim of a quadruple coincidence, in which four eyewitnesses to the crime mistakenly identified him as the murderer--three picking him out of a photo array without hesitation, and all four affirming their identification in open court after comparing him with Beanie. The extraordinary mistake petitioner had to persuade the jury these four witnesses made was not simply to mistake the real killer, Beanie, for the very same innocent third party (hard enough to believe), but in addition to mistake him for the very man Beanie had chosen to frame--the last and most incredible level of coincidence. However small the chance that the jury would believe any one of those improbable scenarios, the likelihood that it would believe them all together is far smaller. The Court concludes that it is "reasonably probable" the undisclosed witness interviews would have persuaded the jury of petitioner's implausible theory of mistaken eyewitness testimony, and then argues that it is "reasonably probable" the undisclosed information regarding Beanie would have persuaded the jury of petitioner's implausible theory regarding the incriminating physical evidence. I think neither of those conclusions is remotely true, but even if they were the Court would still be guilty of a fallacy in declaring victory on each implausibility in turn, and thus victory on the whole, without considering the infinitesimal probability of the jury's swallowing the entire concoction of implausibility squared.

This basic error of approaching the evidence piecemeal is also what accounts for the Court's obsessive focus on the credibility or culpability of Beanie, who did not even testify at trial and whose credibility or innocence the State has never once avowed. The Court's opinion reads as if either petitioner or Beanie must be telling the truth, and any evidence tending to inculpate or undermine the credibility of the one would exculpate or enhance the credibility of the other. But the jury verdict in this case said only that petitioner was guilty of the murder. That is perfectly consistent with the possibilities that Beanie repeatedly lied, ante, at 27, that he was an accessory after the fact, cf. ibid, or even that he planted evidence against petitioner, ante, at 29-30. Even if the undisclosed evidence would have allowed the defense to thoroughly impeach Beanie and to suggest the above possibilities, the jury could well have believed all of those things and yet have condemned petitioner because it could not believe that all four of the eyewitnesses were similarly mistaken. [n.2]

Of course even that much rests on the premise that competent counsel would run the terrible risk of calling Beanie, a witness whose "testimony almost certainly would have inculpated [petitioner]" and whom "any reasonable attorney would perceive . . . as a `loose cannon.'" 5 F. 3d, at 818. Perhaps because that premise seems so implausible, the Court retreats to the possibility that petitioner's counsel, even if not calling Beanie to the stand, could have used the evidence relating to Beanie to attack "the reliability of the investigation." Ante, at 27. But that is distinctly less effective than substantive evidence bearing on the guilt or innocence of the accused. In evaluating Brady claims, we assume jury conduct that is both rational and obedient to the law. We do not assume that even though the whole mass of the evidence, both disclosed and undisclosed, shows petitioner guilty beyond a reasonable doubt, the jury will punish sloppy investigative techniques by setting the defendant free. Neither Beanie nor the police were on trial in this case. Petitioner was, and no amount of collateral evidence could have enabled his counsel to move the mountain of direct evidence against him.

The undisclosed evidence does not create a " `reasonable probability' of a different result." Ante, at 15 (quoting United States v. Bagley, 473 U. S., at 682). To begin with the eyewitness testimony: Petitioner's basic theory at trial was that the State's four eyewitnesses happened to mistake Beanie, the real killer, for petitioner, the man whom Beanie was simultaneously trying to frame. Police officers testified to the jury, and petitioner has never disputed, that three of the four eyewitnesses (Territo, Smallwood, and Williams) were shown a photo lineup of six young men four days after the shooting and, without aid or duress, identified petitioner as the murderer; and that all of them, plus the fourth eyewitness, Kersh, reaffirmed their identifications at trial after petitioner and Beanie were made to stand side by side.

Territo, the first eyewitness called by the State, was waiting at a red light in a truck 30 or 40 yards from the Schwegmann's parking lot. He saw petitioner shoot Mrs. Dye, start her car, drive out onto the road and pull up just behind Territo's truck. When the light turned green petitioner pulled beside Territo and stopped while waiting to make a turn. Petitioner looked Territo full in the face. Territo testified, "I got a good look at him. If I had been in the passenger seat of the little truck, I could have reached out and not even stretched my arm out, I could have grabbed hold of him." Tr. 13-14 (Dec. 6, 1984). Territo also testified that a detective had shown him a picture of Beanie and asked him if the picture "could have been the guy that did it. I told him no." Id., at 24. The second eyewitness, Kersh, also saw petitioner shoot Mrs. Dye. When asked whether she got "a good look" at him as he drove away, she answered "yes." Id., at 32. She also answered "yes" to the question whether she "got to see the side of his face," id., at 31, and said that while petitioner was stopped she had driven to within reaching distance of the driver's side door of Mrs. Dye's car and stopped there. Id., at 34. The third eyewitness, Smallwood, testified that he saw petitioner shoot Mrs. Dye, walk to the car, and drive away. Id., at 42. Petitioner drove slowly by, within a distance of 15 or 25 feet, id., at 43-45, and Smallwood saw his face from the side. Id., at 43. The fourth eyewitness, Williams, who had been working outside the parking lot, testified that "the gentleman came up the side of the car," struggled with Mrs. Dye, shot her, walked around to the driver's side of the car, and drove away. Id., at 52. Williams not only "saw him before he shot her," id., at 54, but watched petitioner drive slowly by "within less than ten feet." Ibid. When asked "[d]id you get an opportunity to look at him good?", Williams said, "I did." Id., at 55.

The Court attempts to dispose of this direct, unqualified and consistent eyewitness testimony in two ways. First, by relying on a theory so implausible that it was apparently not suggested by petitioner's counsel until the oral argument cum%evidentiary hearing held before us, perhaps because it is a theory that only the most removed appellate court could love. This theory is, that there is a reasonable probability that the jury would have changed its mind about the eyewitness identification because the Brady material would have permitted the defense to argue that the eyewitnesses only got a good look at the killer when he was sitting in Mrs. Dye's car, and thus could identify him, not by his height and build, but only by his face. Never mind, for the moment, that this is factually false, since the Brady material showed that only one of the four eyewitnesses, Smallwood, did not see the killer outside the car. [n.3] And never mind, also, the dubious premise that the build of a man six feet tall (like petitioner) is indistinguishable, when seated behind the wheel, from that of a man less than five and one half feet tall (like Beanie). To assert that unhesitant and categorical identification by four witnesses who viewed the killer, close up and with the sun high in the sky, would not eliminate reasonable doubt if it were based only on facial characteristics, and not on height and build, is quite simply absurd. Facial features are the primary means by which human beings recognize one another. That is why police departments distribute "mug" shots of wanted felons, rather than Ivy League type posture pictures; it is why bank robbers wear stockings over their faces instead of floor length capes over their shoulders; it is why the Lone Ranger wears a mask instead of a poncho; and it is why a criminal defense lawyer who seeks to destroy an identifying witness by asking "You admit that you saw only the killer's face?" will be laughed out of the courtroom.

It would be different, of course, if there were evidence that Kyles's and Beanie's faces looked like twins, or at least bore an unusual degree of resemblance. That facial resemblance would explain why, if Beanie committed the crime, all four witnesses picked out Kyles at first (though not why they continued to pick him out when he and Beanie stood side by side in court), and would render their failure to observe the height and build of the killer relevant. But without evidence of facial similarity, the question "You admit that you saw only the killer's face?" draws no blood; it does not explain any witness's identification of petitioner as the killer. While the assumption of facial resemblance between Kyles and Beanie underlies all of the Court's repeated references to the partial concealment of the killer's body from view, see, e.g., ante, at 24, 25, n. 14, 26, 36, the Court never actually says that such resemblance exists. That is because there is not the slightest basis for such a statement in the record. No court has found that Kyles and Beanie bear any facial resemblance. In fact, quite the opposite: every federal and state court that has reviewed the record photographs, or seen the two men, has found that they do not resemble each other in any respect. See 5 F. 3d, at 813 ("Comparing photographs of Kyles and Beanie, it is evident that the former is taller, thinner, and has a narrower face"); App. 181 (District Court opinion) ("The court examined all of the pictures used in the photographic line up and compared Kyles' and Beanie's pictures; it finds that they did not resemble one another"); id., at 36 (state trial court findings on post conviction review) ("[Beanie] clearly and distinctly did not resemble the defendant in this case") (emphasis in original). The District Court's finding controls because it is not clearly erroneous, Fed. R. Civ. Proc. 52(a), and the state court's finding, because fairly supported by the record, must be presumed correct on habeas review. See 28 U.S.C. § 2254(d).

The Court's second means of seeking to neutralize the impressive and unanimous eyewitness testimony uses the same "build is everything" theory to exaggerate the effect of the State's failure to disclose the contemporaneous statement of Henry Williams. That statement would assuredly have permitted a sharp cross examination, since it contained estimations of height and weight that fit Beanie better than petitioner. Ante, at 22-23. But

I think it is hyperbole to say that the statement would have "substantially reduced or destroyed" the value of Williams' testimony. Id., at 22. Williams saw the murderer drive slowly by less than 10 feet away, Tr. 54, and unhesitatingly picked him out of the photo lineup. The jury might well choose to give greater credence to the simple fact of identification than to the difficult estimation of height and weight.

The Court spends considerable time, see ante, at 24-25, showing how Smallwood's testimony could have been discredited to such a degree as to "rais[e] a substantial implication that the prosecutor had coached him to give it." Ibid. Perhaps so, but that is all irrelevant to this appeal, since all of that impeaching material (except the "facial identification" point I have discussed above) was available to the defense independently of the Brady material. See ante, at 25, n. 14. In sum, the undisclosed statements, credited with everything they could possibly have provided to the defense, leave two prosecution witnesses (Territo and Kersh) totally untouched; one prosecution witness (Smallwood) barely affected (he saw "only" the killer's face); and one prosecution witness (Williams) somewhat impaired (his description of the killer's height and weight did not match Kyles). We must keep all this in due perspective, remembering that the relevant question in the materiality inquiry is not how many points the defense could have scored off the prosecution witnesses, but whether it is reasonably probable that the new evidence would have caused the jury to accept the basic thesis that all four witnesses were mistaken. I think it plainly is not. No witness involved in the case ever identified anyone but petitioner as the murderer. Their views of the crime and the escaping criminal were obtained in bright daylight from close at hand; and their identifications were reaffirmed before the jury. After the side by side comparison between Beanie and Kyles, the jury heard Territo say that there was "[n]o doubt in my mind" that petitioner was the murderer, Tr. 378 (Dec. 7, 1984); heard Kersh say "I know it was him. . . . I seen his face and I know the color of his skin. I know it. I know it's him," id., at 383; heard Smallwood say "I'm positive . . . [b]ecause that's the man who I seen kill that woman," id., at 387; and heard Williams say "[n]o doubt in my mind." id., at 391. With or without the Brady evidence, there could be no doubt in the mind of the jury either.

There remains the argument that is the major contribution of today's opinion to Brady litigation; with our endorsement, it will surely be trolled past appellate courts in all future failure to disclose cases. The Court argues that "the effective impeachment of one eyewitness can call for a new trial even though the attack does not extend directly to others, as we have said before." Ante, at 26 (citing Agurs v. United States, 427 U. S., at 112-113, n. 21). It would be startling if we had "said [this] before," since it assumes irrational jury conduct. The weakening of one witness's testimony does not weaken the unconnected testimony of another witness; and to entertain the possibility that the jury will give it such an effect is incompatible with the whole idea of a materiality standard, which presumes that the incriminating evidence that would have been destroyed by proper disclosure can be logically separated from the incriminating evidence that would have remained unaffected. In fact we have said nothing like what the Court suggests. The opinion's only authority for its theory, the cited footnote from Agurs, was appended to the proposition that "[a Brady] omission must be evaluated in the context of the entire record," 427 U. S., at 112. In accordance with that proposition, the footnote recited a hypothetical that shows how a witness's testimony could have been destroyed by withheld evidence that contradicts the witness. [n.4] That is worlds apart from having it destroyed by the corrosive effect of withheld evidence that impeaches (or, as here, merely weakens) some other corroborating witness.

The physical evidence confirms the immateriality of the nondisclosures. In a garbage bag outside petitioner's home the police found Mrs. Dye's purse and other belongings. Inside his home they found, behind the kitchen stove, the .32 caliber revolver used to kill Mrs. Dye; hanging in a wardrobe, a homemade shoulder holster that was "a perfect fit" for the revolver, Tr. 74 (Dec. 6, 1984) (Detective Dillman); in a dresser drawer in the bedroom, two boxes of gun cartridges, one containing only .32 caliber rounds of the same brand found in the murder weapon, another containing .22, .32, and .38 caliber rounds; in a kitchen cabinet, eight empty Schwegmann's bags; and in a cupboard underneath that cabinet, one Schwegmann's bag containing 15 cans of pet food. Petitioner's account at trial was that Beanie planted the purse, gun and holster, that petitioner received the ammunition from Beanie as collateral for a loan, and that petitioner had bought the pet food the day of the murder. That account strains credulity to the breaking point.

The Court is correct that the Brady material would have supported the claim that Beanie planted Mrs. Dye's belongings in petitioner's garbage and (to a lesser degree) that Beanie planted the gun behind petitioner's stove. Ante, at 29-30. But we must see the whole story that petitioner presented to the jury. Petitioner would have it that Beanie did not plant the incriminating evidence until the day after he incited the police to search petitioner's home. Moreover, he succeeded in surreptitiously placing the gun behind the stove, and the matching shoulder holster in the wardrobe, while at least 10 and as many as 19 people were present in petitioner's small apartment. [n.5] Beanie, who was wearing blue jeans and either a "tank top" shirt, Tr. 302 (Dec. 7, 1984) (Cathora Brown), or a short sleeved shirt, id., at 351 (petitioner), would have had to be concealing about his person not only the shoulder holster and the murder weapon, but also a different gun with tape wrapped around the barrel that he showed to petitioner. Id., at 352. Only appellate judges could swallow such a tale. Petitioner's only supporting evidence was Johnny Burns's testimony that he saw Beanie stooping behind the stove, presumably to plant the gun. Id., at 262-263. Burns's credibility on the stand can perhaps best be gauged by observing that the state judge who presided over petitioner's trial stated, in a postconviction proceeding, that "[I] ha[ve] chosen to totally disregard everything that [Burns] has said," App. 35. See also id., at 165 (District Court opinion) ("Having reviewed the entire record, this court without hesitation concurs with the trial court's determination concerning the credibility of [Burns]"). Burns, by the way, who repeatedly stated at trial that Beanie was his "best friend," Tr. 279 (Dec. 7, 1984), has since been tried and convicted for killing Beanie. See

State v. Burnes, 533 So.2d 1029 (La. App. 1988). [n.6]

Petitioner did not claim that the ammunition had been planted. The police found a .22 caliber rifle under petitioner's mattress and two boxes of ammunition, one containing .22, .32, and .38 caliber rounds, another containing only .32 caliber rounds of the same brand as those found loaded in the murder weapon. Petitioner's story was that Beanie gave him the rifle and the .32 caliber shells as security for a loan, but that he had taken the .22 caliber shells out of the box. Tr. 353, 355 (Dec. 7, 1984). Put aside that the latter detail was contradicted by the facts; but consider the inherent implausibility of Beanie's giving petitioner collateral in the form of a box containing only .32 shells, if it were true that petitioner did not own a .32 caliber gun. As the Fifth Circuit wrote, "[t]he more likely inference, apparently chosen by the jury, is that [petitioner] possessed .32 caliber ammunition because he possessed a .32 caliber firearm." 5 F. 3d, at 817.

We come to the evidence of the pet food, so mundane and yet so very damning. Petitioner's confused and changing explanations for the presence of 15 cans of pet food in a Schwegmann's bag under the sink must have fatally undermined his credibility before the jury. See App. 36 (trial judge finds that petitioner's "obvious lie" concerning the pet food "may have been a crucial bit of evidence in the minds of the jurors which caused them to discount the entire defense in this case"). The Court disposes of the pet food evidence as follows:

"The fact that pet food was found in Kyles's apartment was consistent with the testimony of several defense witnesses that Kyles owned a dog and that his children fed stray cats. The brands of pet food found were only two of the brands that Dye typically bought, and these two were common, whereas the one specialty brand that was found in Dye's apartment after her murder, Tr. 180 (Dec. 7, 1984), was not found in Kyles's apartment, id., at 188. Although Kyles was wrong in describing the cat food as being on sale the day he said he bought it, he was right in describing the way it was priced at Schwegmann's market, where he commonly shopped." Ante, at 33-34; see also id., at 34, n. 20.

The full story is this. Mr. and Mrs. Dye owned two cats and a dog, Tr. 178 (Dec. 7, 1984), for which she regularly bought varying brands of pet food, several different brands at a time. Id., at 179, 180. Found in Mrs. Dye's home after her murder were the brands Nine Lives, Kalkan and Puss n' Boots. Id., at 180. Found in petitioner's home were eight cans of Nine Lives, four cans of Kalkan, and three cans of Cozy Kitten. Id., at 188. Since we know that Mrs. Dye had been shopping that day and that the murderer made off with her goods, petitioner's possession of these items was powerful evidence that he was the murderer. Assuredly the jury drew that obvious inference. Pressed to explain why he just happened to buy 15 cans of pet food that very day (keep in mind that petitioner was a very poor man, see id., at 329, who supported a common law wife, a mistress, and four children), petitioner gave the reason that "it was on sale." Id., at 341. The State, however, introduced testimony from the Schwegmann's advertising director that the pet food was not on sale that day. Id., at 395. The dissenting judge below tried to rehabilitate petitioner's testimony by interpreting the "on sale" claim as meaning "for sale," a reference to the pricing of the pet food (e.g., "3 for 89 cents"), which petitioner claimed to have read on a shelf sign in the store. Id., at 343. But unless petitioner was parodying Sir Edmund Hillary, "because it was for sale" would have been an irrational response to the question it was given in answer to: Why did you buy so many cans? In any event, the Schwegmann's employee also testified that store policy was not to put signs on the shelves at all. Id., at 398-399. The sum of it is that petitioner, far from explaining the presence of the pet food, doubled the force of the State's evidence by perjuring himself before the jury, as the state trial judge observed. See supra, at 19. [n.7]

I will not address the list of cars in the Schwegmann's parking lot and the receipt, found in the victim's car, that bore petitioner's fingerprints. These were collateral matters that provided little evidence of either guilt or innocence. The list of cars, which did not contain petitioner's automobile, would only have served to rebut the State's introduction of a photograph purporting to show petitioner's car in the parking lot; but petitioner does not contest that the list was not comprehensive, and that the photograph was taken about six hours before the list was compiled. See 5 F. 3d, at 816. Thus its rebuttal value would have been marginal at best. The receipt--although it showed that petitioner must at some point have been both in Schwegmann's and in the murdered woman's car--was as consistent with petitioner's story as with the State's. See ante, at 34.

* * *

The State presented to the jury a massive core of evidence (including four eyewitnesses) showing that petitioner was guilty of murder, and that he lied about his guilt. The effect that the Brady materials would have had in chipping away at the edges of the State's case can only be called immaterial. For the same reasons I reject petitioner's claim that the Brady materials would have created a "residual doubt" sufficient to cause the sentencing jury to withhold capital punishment.

I respectfully dissent.

Notes

1 The Court tries to explain all this by saying that Beanie mistakenly thought that he had become a suspect. The only support it provides for this is the fact that, after having come forward with the admission that he had driven the dead woman's car, Beanie repeatedly inquired whether he himself was a suspect. See ante, at 23, n. 13. Of course at that point he well should have been worried about being a suspect. But there is no evidence that he erroneously considered himself a suspect beforehand. Moreover, even if he did, the notion that, a guilty person would, on the basis of such an erroneous belief, come forward for the reward or in order to "frame" Kyles (rather than waiting for the police to approach him first) is quite simply implausible.

2 There is no basis in anything I have said for the Court's charge that "the dissent appears to assume that Kyles must lose because there would still have been adequate [i.e. sufficient] evidence to convict even if the favorable evidence had been disclosed." Ante, at

16, n. 8. I do assume, indeed I expressly argue, that petitioner must lose because there was, is, and will be overwhelming evidence to convict, so much evidence that disclosure would not "have made a different result reasonably probable." Ante, at 22.

3 Smallwood and Williams were the only eyewitnesses whose testimony was affected by the Brady material, and Williams's was affected not because it showed he did not observe the killer standing up, but to the contrary because it showed that his estimates of height and weight based on that observation did not match Kyles. The other two witnesses did observe the killer in full. Territo testified that he saw the killer running up to Mrs. Dye before the struggle began, and that after the struggle he watched the killer bend down, stand back up, and then "stru[t]" over to the car. Tr. 12 (Dec. 6, 1984). Kersh too had a clear opportunity to observe the killer's body type; she testified that she saw the killer and Mrs. Dye arguing, and that she watched him walk around the back of the car after Mrs. Dye had fallen. Id., at 29-30.

4 " `If, for example, one of only two eyewitnesses to a crime had told the prosecutor that the defendant was definitely not its perpetrator and if this statement was not disclosed to the defense, no court would hesitate to reverse a conviction resting on the testimony of the other eyewitness. But if there were fifty eyewitnesses, forty nine of whom identified the defendant, and the prosecutor neglected to reveal that the other, who was without his badly needed glasses on the misty evening of the crime, had said that the criminal looked something like the defendant but he could not be sure as he had only a brief glimpse, the result might well be different.' " Agurs, 427 U. S., at 112, n. 21 (quoting Comment, Brady v. Maryland and The Prosecutor's Duty to Disclose, 40 U. Chi. L. Rev. 112, 125 (1972)).

5 The estimates varied. See Tr. 269 (Dec. 7, 1984) (Johnny Burns) (18 or 19 people); id., at 298 (Cathora Brown) (6 adults, 4 children); id., at 326 (petitioner) ("about 16 . . . about 18 or 19"); id., at 340 (petitioner) (13 people).

6 The Court notes that "neither observation could possibly have affected the jury's appraisal of Burns's credibility at the time of Kyles's trials." Ante, at 31-32, n. 19. That is obviously true. But it is just as obviously true that because we have no findings about Burns's credibility from the jury and no direct method of asking what they thought, the only way that we can assess the jury's appraisal of Burns's credibility is by asking (1) whether the state trial judge, who saw Burns's testimony along with the jury, thought it was credible; and (2) whether Burns was in fact credible--a question on which his later behavior towards his "best friend" is highly probative.

7 I have charitably assumed that petitioner had a pet or pets in the first place, although the evidence tended to show the contrary. Petitioner claimed that he owned a dog or puppy, that his son had a cat, and that there were "seven or eight more cats around there." Tr. 325 (Dec. 7, 1984). The dog, according to petitioner, had been kept "in the country" for a month and half, and was brought back just the week before petitioner was arrested. Id., at 337-338. Although petitioner claimed to have kept the dog tied up in a yard behind his house before it was taken to the country, id., at 336-337, two defense

witnesses contradicted this story. Donald Powell stated that he had not seen a dog at petitioner's home since at least six months before the trial, id., at 254, while Cathora Brown said that although Pinky, petitioner's wife, sometimes fed stray pets, she had no dog tied up in the back yard. Id., at 304-305. The police found no evidence of any kind that any pets lived in petitioner's home at or near the time of the murder. Id., at 75.

Justice Scalia's concurrence in Adarand Constructors v. Pena (June 12, 1995)

JUSTICE SCALIA, concurring in part and concurring in the judgment.

I join the opinion of the Court, except ____Part III-C, and except insofar as it may be inconsistent with the following: in my view, government can never have a "compelling interest" in discriminating on the basis of race in order to "make up" for past racial discrimination in the opposite direction. See Richmond v. J. A. Croson Co., 488 U.S. 469, 520 (1989) (SCALIA, J., concurring in judgment). Individuals who have been wronged by unlawful racial discrimination should be made whole, but, under our Constitution, there can be no such thing as either a creditor or a debtor race. That concept is alien to the Constitution's focus upon the individual, see Amdt. 14, § 1 ("[N]or shall any State . . . deny to any person" the equal protection of the laws) (emphasis added), and its rejection of dispositions based on race, see Amdt. 15, § 1 (prohibiting abridgment of the right to vote "on account of race") or based on blood, see Art. III, § 3 ("[N]o Attainder of Treason shall work Corruption of Blood"); Art. I, § 9 ("No Title of Nobility shall be granted by the United States"). To pursue the concept of racial entitlement -- even for the most admirable and benign of purposes -- is to reinforce and preserve for future mischief the way of thinking that produced race slavery, race privilege and race hatred. In the eyes of government, we are just one race here. It is American.

It is unlikely, if not impossible, that the challenged program would survive under this understanding of strict scrutiny, but I am content to leave that to be decided on remand.

Justice Scalia's dissent in Babbitt v. Sweet Home Chapter, Communities for Great Ore. (June 29, 1995)

Justice Scalia, with whom The Chief Justice and Justice Thomas join, dissenting.

I think it unmistakably clear that the legislation at issue here (1) forbade the hunting and killing of endangered animals, and (2) provided federal lands and federal funds for the acquisition of private lands, to preserve the habitat of endangered animals. The Court's holding that the hunting and killing prohibition incidentally preserves habitat on private lands imposes unfairness to the point of financial ruin—not just upon the rich, but upon the simplest farmer who finds his land conscripted to national zoological use. I respectfully dissent.

I

The Endangered Species Act of 1973 (Act), 16 U. S. C. § 1531 et seq. (1988 ed. and Supp. V), provides that "it is unlawful for any person subject to the jurisdiction of the United States to—. . . take any [protected] species within the United States." § 1538(a)(1)(B). The term "take" is defined as "to harass, harm, pursue, hunt, shoot, wound, kill, trap, capture, or collect, or to attempt to engage in any such conduct." § 1532(19) (emphasis added). The challenged regulation defines "harm" thus:

"Harm in the definition of `take' in the Act means an act which actually kills or injures wildlife. Such act may include significant habitat modification or degradation where it actually kills or injures wildlife by significantly impairing essential behavioral patterns, including breeding, feeding or sheltering." 50 CFR § 17.3 (1994).

In my view petitioners must lose—the regulation must fall— even under the test of Chevron U. S. A. Inc. v. Natural Resources Defense Council, Inc., 467 U. S. 837, 843 (1984), so I shall assume that the Court is correct to apply Chevron. See ante, at 703-704, and n. 18.

The regulation has three features which, for reasons I shall discuss at length below, do not comport with the statute. First, it interprets the statute to prohibit habitat modification that is no more than the cause-in-fact of death or injury to wildlife. Any "significant habitat modification" that in fact produces that result by "impairing essential behavioral patterns" is made unlawful, regardless of whether that result is intended or even foreseeable, and no matter how long the chain of causality between modification and injury. See, e. g., Palila v. Hawaii Dept. of Land and Natural Resources, 852 F. 2d 1106, 1108-1109 (CA9 1988) (Palila II) (sheep grazing constituted "taking" of palila birds, since although sheep do not destroy full-grown mamane trees, they do destroy mamane seedlings, which will not grow to full-grown trees, on which the palila feeds and nests). See also Davison, Alteration of Wildlife Habitat as a Prohibited Taking under the Endangered Species Act, 10 J. Land Use & Envtl. L. 155, 190 (1995) (regulation requires only causation-in-fact).

Second, the regulation does not require an "act": The Secretary's officially stated position is that an omission will do. The previous version of the regulation made this explicit. See 40 Fed. Reg. 44412, 44416 (1975) ("`Harm' in the definition of `take' in the Act means an act or omission which actually kills or injures wildlife . . ."). When the regulation was modified in 1981 the phrase "or omission" was taken out, but only because (as the final publication of the rule advised) "the [Fish and Wildlife] Service feels that `act' is inclusive of either commissions or omissions which would be prohibited by section [1538(a)(1)(B)]." 46 Fed. Reg. 54748, 54750 (1981). In their brief here petitioners agree that the regulation covers omissions, see Brief for Petitioners 47 (although they argue that "[a]n `omission' constitutes an `act' . . . only if there is a legal duty to act"), ibid.

The third and most important unlawful feature of the regulation is that it encompasses injury inflicted, not only upon individual animals, but upon populations of the protected species. "Injury" in the regulation includes "significantly impairing essential behavioral patterns, including breeding, " 50 CFR § 17.3 (1994) (emphasis added).

Impairment of breeding does not "injure" living creatures; it prevents them from propagating, thus "injuring" a population of animals which would otherwise have maintained or increased its numbers. What the face of the regulation shows, the Secretary's official pronouncements confirm. The Final Redefinition of "Harm" accompanying publication of the regulation said that "harm" is not limited to "direct physical injury to an individual member of the wildlife species," 46 Fed. Reg. 54748 (1981), and refers to "injury to a population, " id., at 54749 (emphasis added). See also Palila II, supra, at 1108; Davison, supra, at 190, and n. 177, 195; M. Bean, The Evolution of National Wildlife Law 344 (1983).[1]

None of these three features of the regulation can be found in the statutory provisions supposed to authorize it. The term "harm" in § 1532(19) has no legal force of its own. An indictment or civil complaint that charged the defendant with "harming" an animal protected under the Act would be dismissed as defective, for the only operative term in the statute is to "take." If "take" were not elsewhere defined in the Act, none could dispute what it means, for the term is as old as the law itself. To "take," when applied to wild animals, means to reduce those animals, by killing or capturing, to human control. See, e. g., 11 Oxford English Dictionary (1933) ("Take . . . To catch, capture (a wild beast, bird, fish, etc.)"); Webster's New International Dictionary of the English Language (2d ed. 1949) (take defined as "to catch or capture by trapping, snaring, etc., or as prey"); Geer v. Connecticut, 161 U. S. 519, 523 (1896) ("`[A]ll the animals which can be taken upon the earth, in the sea, or in the air, that is to say, wild animals, belong to those who take them' ") (quoting the Digest of Justinian); 2 W. Blackstone, Commentaries 411 (1766) ("Every man . . . has an equal right of pursuing and taking to his own use all such creatures as are ferae naturae "). This is just the sense in which "take" is used elsewhere in federal legislation and treaty. See, e. g., Migratory Bird Treaty Act, 16 U. S. C. § 703 (1988 ed., Supp. V) (no person may "pursue, hunt, take, capture, kill, [or] attempt to take, capture, or kill" any migratory bird); Agreement on the Conservation of Polar Bears, Nov. 15, 1973, Art. I, 27 U. S. T. 3918, 3921, T. I. A. S. No. 8409 (defining "taking" as "hunting, killing and capturing"). And that meaning fits neatly with the rest of § 1538(a)(1), which makes it unlawful not only to take protected species, but also to import or export them, § 1538(a)(1)(A); to possess, sell, deliver, carry, transport, or ship any taken species, § 1538(a)(1)(D); and to transport, sell, or offer to sell them in interstate or foreign commerce, §§ 1538(a)(1)(E), (F). The taking prohibition, in other words, is only part of the regulatory plan of § 1538(a)(1), which covers all the stages of the process by which protected wildlife is reduced to man's dominion and made the object of profit. It is obvious that "take" in this sense—a term of art deeply embedded in the statutory and common law concerning wildlife—describes a class of acts (not omissions) done directly and intentionally (not indirectly and by accident) to particular animals (not populations of animals).

The Act's definition of "take" does expand the word slightly (and not unusually), so as to make clear that it includes not just a completed taking, but the process of taking, and all of the acts that are customarily identified with or accompany that process ("to harass, harm, pursue, hunt, shoot, wound, kill, trap, capture, or collect"); and so as to include attempts. § 1532(19). The tempting fallacy—which the Court commits with abandon, see ante, at 697-698, n. 10—is to assume that once defined, "take" loses any significance, and it is only the definition that matters. The Court treats the statute as though Congress had directly enacted the § 1532(19) definition as a self-executing prohibition, and had not enacted § 1538(a)(1)(B) at all. But § 1538(a)(1)(B) is there, and if the terms contained in the definitional section are susceptible of two readings, one of which comports with the standard meaning of "take" as used in application to wildlife, and one of which does not, an agency regulation that adopts the latter reading is necessarily unreasonable, for it reads the defined term "take"—the only operative term—out of the statute altogether.[2]

That is what has occurred here. The verb "harm" has a range of meaning: "to cause injury" at its broadest, "to do hurt or damage" in a narrower and more direct sense. See, e. g., 1 N. Webster, An American Dictionary of the English Language (1828) ("Harm, v.t. To hurt; to injure; to damage; to impair soundness of body, either animal or vegetable") (emphasis added); American College Dictionary 551 (1970) ("harm . . . n. injury; damage; hurt: to do him bodily harm "). In fact the more directed sense of "harm" is a somewhat more common and preferred usage; "harm has in it a little of the idea of specially focused hurt or injury, as if a personal injury has been anticipated and intended." J. Opdycke, Mark My Words: A Guide to Modern Usage and Expression 330 (1949). See also American Heritage Dictionary 662 (1985) ("Injure has the widest range. . . . Harm and hurt refer principally to what causes physical or mental distress to living things"). To define "harm" as an act or omission that, however remotely, "actually kills or injures" a population of wildlife through habitat modification is to choose a meaning that makes nonsense of the word that "harm" defines—requiring us to accept that a farmer who tills his field and causes erosion that makes silt run into a nearby river which depletes oxygen and thereby "impairs [the] breeding" of protected fish has "taken" or "attempted to take" the fish. It should take the strongest evidence to make us believe that Congress has defined a term in a manner repugnant to its ordinary and traditional sense.

Here the evidence shows the opposite. "Harm" is merely one of 10 prohibitory words in § 1532(19), and the other 9 fit the ordinary meaning of "take" perfectly. To "harass, pursue, hunt, shoot, wound, kill, trap, capture, or collect" are all affirmative acts (the provision itself describes them as "conduct," see § 1532(19)) which are directed immediately and intentionally against a particular animal—not acts or omissions that indirectly and accidentally cause injury to a population of animals. The Court points out that several of the words ("harass," "pursue," "wound," and "kill") "refer to actions or effects that do not require direct applications of force. " Ante, at 701 (emphasis added). That is true enough, but force is not the point. Even "taking" activities in the narrowest sense, activities traditionally engaged in by hunters and trappers, do not all consist of direct applications of force; pursuit and harassment are part of the business of "taking" the prey even before it has been touched. What the nine other words in § 1532(19) have in common—and share with the narrower meaning of "harm" described above, but not with the Secretary's ruthless dilation of the word— is the sense of affirmative conduct intentionally directed against a particular animal or animals.

I am not the first to notice this fact, or to draw the conclusion that it compels. In 1981 the Solicitor of the Fish and Wildlife Service delivered a legal opinion on § 1532(19) that is in complete agreement with my reading:

"The Act's definition of `take' contains a list of actions that illustrate the intended scope of the term . . . . With the possible exception of `harm,' these terms all represent forms of conduct that are directed against and likely to injure or kill individual wildlife. Under the principle of statutory construction, ejusdem generis, . . . the term `harm' should be interpreted to include only those actions that are directed against, and likely to injure or kill, individual wildlife." Memorandum of Apr. 17, reprinted in 46 Fed. Reg. 29490, 29491 (1981) (emphasis in original).

I would call it noscitur a sociis, but the principle is much the same: The fact that "several items in a list share an attribute counsels in favor of interpreting the other items as possessing that attribute as well," Beecham v. United States, 511 U. S. 368, 371 (1994). The Court contends that the canon cannot be applied to deprive a word of all its "independent meaning," ante, at 702. That proposition is questionable to begin with, especially as applied to long lawyers' listings such as this. If it were true, we ought to give the word "trap" in the definition its rare meaning of "to clothe" (whence "trappings")— since otherwise it adds nothing to the word "capture." See Moskal v. United States, 498 U. S. 103, 120 (1990) (Scalia, J., dissenting). In any event, the Court's contention that "harm" in the narrow sense adds nothing to the other words underestimates the ingenuity of our own species in a way that Congress did not. To feed an animal poison, to spray it with mace, to chop down the very tree in which it is nesting, or even to destroy its entire habitat in order to take it (as by draining a pond to get at a turtle), might neither wound nor kill, but would directly and intentionally harm.

The penalty provisions of the Act counsel this interpretation as well. Any person who "knowingly" violates § 1538(a)(1)(B) is subject to criminal penalties under § 1540(b)(1) and civil penalties under § 1540(a)(1); moreover, under the latter section, any person "who otherwise violates" the taking prohibition (i. e., violates it un knowingly) may be assessed a civil penalty of $500 for each violation, with the stricture that "[e]ach such violation shall be a separate offense." This last provision should be clear warning that the regulation is in error, for when combined with the regulation it produces a result that no legislature could reasonably be thought to have intended: A large number of routine private activities—for example, farming, ranching, roadbuilding, construction and logging—are subjected to strict-liability penalties when they fortuitously injure protected wildlife, no matter how remote the chain of causation and no matter how difficult to foresee (or to disprove) the "injury" may be (e. g., an "impairment" of breeding). The Court says that "[the strict-liability provision] is potentially sweeping, but it would be so with or without the Secretary's `harm' regulation." Ante, at 696, n. 9. That is not correct. Without the regulation, the routine "habitat modifying" activities that people conduct to make a daily living would not carry exposure to strict penalties; only acts directed at animals, like those described by the other words in § 1532(19), would risk liability.

The Court says that "[to] read a requirement of intent or purpose into the words used to define `take' . . . ignore[s] [§ 1540's] express provision that a `knowin[g]' action is enough to violate the Act." Ante, at 701-702. This presumably means that because the reading of § 1532(19) advanced here ascribes an element of purposeful injury to the prohibited acts, it makes superfluous (or inexplicable) the more severe penalties provided for a "knowing" violation. That conclusion does not follow, for it is quite possible to take protected wildlife purposefully without doing so knowingly. A requirement that a violation be "knowing" means that the defendant must "know the facts that make his conduct illegal," Staples v. United States, 511 U. S. 600, 606 (1994). The hunter who shoots an elk in the mistaken belief that it is a mule deer has not knowingly violated § 1538(a)(1)(B)— not because he does not know that elk are legally protected (that would be knowledge of the law, which is not a requirement, see ante, at 696-697, n. 9), but because he does not know what sort of animal he is shooting. The hunter has nonetheless committed a purposeful taking of protected wildlife, and would therefore be subject to the (lower) strict-liability penalties for the violation.

So far I have discussed only the immediate statutory text bearing on the regulation. But the definition of "take" in § 1532(19) applies "[f]or the purposes of this chapter," that is, it governs the meaning of the word as used everywhere in the Act. Thus, the Secretary's interpretation of "harm" is wrong if it does not fit with the use of "take" throughout the Act. And it does not. In § 1540(e)(4)(B), for example, Congress provided for the forfeiture of "[a]ll guns, traps, nets, and other equipment . . . used to aid the taking, possessing, selling, [etc.]" of protected animals. This listing plainly relates to "taking" in the ordinary sense. If environmental modification were part (and necessarily a major part) of taking, as the Secretary maintains, one would have expected the list to include "plows, bulldozers, and backhoes." As another example, § 1539(e)(1) exempts "the taking of any endangered species" by Alaskan Indians and Eskimos "if such taking is primarily for subsistence purposes"; and provides that "[n]on-edible byproducts of species taken pursuant to this section may be sold . . . when made into authentic native articles of handicrafts and clothing." Surely these provisions apply to taking only in the ordinary sense, and are meaningless as applied to species injured by environmental modification. The Act is full of like examples. See, e. g., § 1538(a)(1)(D) (prohibiting possession, sale, and transport of "species taken in violation" of the Act). "[I]f the Act is to be interpreted as a symmetrical and coherent regulatory scheme, one in which the operative words have a consistent meaning throughout," Gustafson v. Alloyd Co., 513 U. S. 561, 569 (1995), the regulation must fall.

The broader structure of the Act confirms the unreasonableness of the regulation. Section 1536 provides:

"Each Federal agency shall . . . insure that any action authorized, funded, or carried out by such agency . . . is not likely to jeopardize the continued existence of any endangered species or threatened species or result in the destruction or adverse modification of habitat of such species which is determined by the Secretary . . . to be critical." 16 U. S. C. § 1536(a)(2) (emphasis added).

The Act defines "critical habitat" as habitat that is "essential to the conservation of the species," §§ 1532(5)(A)(i), (A)(ii), with "conservation" in turn defined as the use of methods necessary to bring listed species "to the point at which the measures provided pursuant to this chapter are no longer necessary," § 1532(3).

These provisions have a double significance. Even if §§ 1536(a)(2) and 1538(a)(1)(B) were totally independent prohibitions—the former applying only to federal agencies and their licensees, the latter only to private parties—Congress's explicit prohibition of habitat modification in the one section would bar the inference of an implicit prohibition of habitat modification in the other section. "[W]here Congress includes particular language in one section of a statute but omits it in another . . . , it is generally presumed that Congress acts intentionally and purposely in the disparate inclusion or exclusion." Keene Corp. v. United States, 508 U. S. 200, 208 (1993) (internal quotation marks omitted). And that presumption against implicit prohibition would be even stronger where the one section which uses the language carefully defines and limits its application. That is to say, it would be passing strange for Congress carefully to define "critical habitat" as used in § 1536(a)(2), but leave it to the Secretary to evaluate, willy-nilly, impermissible "habitat modification" (under the guise of "harm") in § 1538(a)(1)(B).

In fact, however, §§ 1536(a)(2) and 1538(a)(1)(B) do not operate in separate realms; federal agencies are subject to both, because the "person[s]" forbidden to take protected species under § 1538 include agencies and departments of the Federal Government. See § 1532(13). This means that the "harm" regulation also contradicts another principle of interpretation: that statutes should be read so far as possible to give independent effect to all their provisions. See Ratzlaf v. United States, 510 U. S. 135, 140-141 (1994). By defining "harm" in the definition of "take" in § 1538(a)(1)(B) to include significant habitat modification that injures populations of wildlife, the regulation makes the habitat-modification restriction in § 1536(a)(2) almost wholly superfluous. As "critical habitat" is habitat "essential to the conservation of the species," adverse modification of "critical" habitat by a federal agency would also constitute habitat modification that injures a population of wildlife.

Petitioners try to salvage some independent scope for § 1536(a)(2) by the following contortion: Because the definition of critical habitat includes not only "the specific areas within the geographical area occupied by the species [that are] essential to the conservation of the species," § 1532(5)(A)(i), but also "specific areas outside the geographical area occupied by the species at the time it is listed [as a protected species] . . . [that are] essential to the conservation of the species," § 1532A(5)(ii), there may be some agency modifications of critical habitat which do not injure a population of wildlife. See

Brief for Petitioners 41, and n. 27. This is dubious to begin with. A principal way to injure wildlife under the Secretary's own regulation is to "significantly impai[r] ... breeding," 50 CFR § 17.3 (1994). To prevent the natural increase of a species by adverse modification of habitat suitable for expansion assuredly impairs breeding. But even if true, the argument only narrows the scope of the superfluity, leaving as so many wasted words the § 1532(a)(5)(i) definition of critical habitat to include currently occupied habitat essential to the species' conservation. If the Secretary's definition of "harm" under § 1538(a)(1)(B) is to be upheld, we must believe that Congress enacted § 1536(a)(2) solely because in its absence federal agencies would be able to modify habitat in currently unoccupied areas. It is more rational to believe that the Secretary's expansion of § 1538(a)(1)(B) carves out the heart of one of the central provisions of the Act.

II

The Court makes four other arguments. First, "the broad purpose of the [Act] supports the Secretary's decision to extend protection against activities that cause the precise harms Congress enacted the statute to avoid." Ante, at 698.

I thought we had renounced the vice of "simplistically ... assum[ing] that whatever furthers the statute's primary objective must be the law." Rodriguez v. United States, 480 U. S. 522, 526 (1987) (per curiam) (emphasis in original). Deduction from the "broad purpose" of a statute begs the question if it is used to decide by what means (and hence to what length) Congress pursued that purpose; to get the right answer to that question there is no substitute for the hard job (or, in this case, the quite simple one) of reading the whole text. "The Act must do everything necessary to achieve its broad purpose" is the slogan of the enthusiast, not the analytical tool of the arbiter.[3]

Second, the Court maintains that the legislative history of the 1973 Act supports the Secretary's definition. See ante, at 704-706. Even if legislative history were a legitimate and reliable tool of interpretation (which I shall assume in order to rebut the Court's claim); and even if it could appropriately be resorted to when the enacted text is as clear as this, but see Chicago v. Environmental Defense Fund, 511 U. S. 328, 337 (1994); here it shows quite the opposite of what the Court says. I shall not pause to discuss the Court's reliance on such statements in the Committee Reports as "`[t]ake' is defined . . . in the broadest possible manner to include every conceivable way in which a person can `take' or attempt to `take' any fish or wildlife.' " S. Rep. No. 93-307, p. 7 (1973) (quoted ante, at 704). This sort of empty flourish—to the effect that "this statute means what it means all the way"— counts for little even when enacted into the law itself. See Reves v. Ernst & Young, 507 U. S. 170, 183-184 (1993).

Much of the Court's discussion of legislative history is devoted to two items: first, the Senate floor manager's introduction of an amendment that added the word "harm" to the definition of "take," with the observation that (along with other amendments) it would "`help to achieve the purposes of the bill' "; second, the relevant Committee's removal from the definition of a provision stating that "take" includes "`the destruction, modification or curtailment of [the] habitat or range' " of fish and wildlife. See ante, at

705. The Court inflates the first and belittles the second, even though the second is on its face far more pertinent. But this elaborate inference from various pre-enactment actions and inactions is quite unnecessary, since we have direct evidence of what those who brought the legislation to the floor thought it meant—evidence as solid as any ever to be found in legislative history, but which the Court banishes to a footnote. See ante, at 706-707, n. 19.

Both the Senate and House floor managers of the bill explained it in terms which leave no doubt that the problem of habitat destruction on private lands was to be solved principally by the land acquisition program of § 1534, while § 1538 solved a different problem altogether—the problem of takings. Senator Tunney stated:

"Through [the] land acquisition provisions, we will be able to conserve habitats necessary to protect fish and wildlife from further destruction.

"Although most endangered species are threatened primarily by the destruction of their natural habitats, a significant portion of these animals are subject to preda- tion by man for commercial, sport, consumption, or other purposes. The provisions of [the bill] would prohibit the commerce in or the importation, exportation, or taking of endangered species . . . ." 119 Cong. Rec. 25669 (1973) (emphasis added).

The House floor manager, Representative Sullivan, put the same thought in this way:

"[T]he principal threat to animals stems from destruction of their habitat. . . .[The bill] will meet this prob- lem by providing funds for acquisition of critical habitat. . . . It will also enable the Department of Agriculture to cooperate with willing landowners who desire to assist in the protection of endangered species, but who are understandably unwilling to do so at excessive cost to themselves.

"Another hazard to endangered species arises from those who would capture or kill them for pleasure or profit. There is no way that the Congress can make it less pleasurable for a person to take an animal, but we can certainly make it less profitable for them to do so." Id., at 30162 (emphasis added).

Habitat modification and takings, in other words, were viewed as different problems, addressed by different provisions of the Act. The Court really has no explanation for these statements. All it can say is that "[n]either statement even suggested that [the habitat acquisition funding provision in § 1534] would be the Act's exclusive remedy for habitat modification by private landowners or that habitat modification by private landowners stood outside the ambit of [§ 1538]." Ante, at 707, n. 19. That is to say, the statements are not as bad as they might have been. Little in life is. They are, however, quite bad enough to destroy the Court's legislative-history case, since they display the clear understanding (1) that habitat modification is separate from "taking," and (2) that habitat destruction on private lands is to be remedied by public acquisition, and not by making particular unlucky landowners incur "excessive cost to themselves." The Court points out triumphantly that they do not display the understanding (3) that the land acquisition program is "the [Act's] only response to habitat modification." Ibid. Of course not, since that is not so (all public lands are subject to habitat-modification restrictions); but (1) and (2) are quite enough to exclude the Court's interpretation. They identify the land acquisition program as the Act's only response to habitat modification by private landowners, and thus do not in the least "contradic[t]," ibid., the fact that § 1536 prohibits habitat modification by federal agencies.

Third, the Court seeks support from a provision that was added to the Act in 1982, the year after the Secretary promulgated the current regulation. The provision states:

"[T]he Secretary may permit, under such terms and conditions as he shall prescribe—

. . . . .

"any taking otherwise prohibited by section 1538 (a)(1)(B) . . . if such taking is incidental to, and not the purpose of, the carrying out of an otherwise lawful activity." 16 U. S. C. § 1539(a)(1)(B).

This provision does not, of course, implicate our doctrine that reenactment of a statutory provision ratifies an extant judicial or administrative interpretation, for neither the taking prohibition in § 1538(a)(1)(B) nor the definition in § 1532(19) was reenacted. See Central Bank of Denver, N. A. v. First Interstate Bank of Denver, N. A., 511 U. S. 164, 185 (1994). The Court claims, however, that the provision "strongly suggests that Congress understood [§ 1538(a)(1)(B)] to prohibit indirect as well as deliberate takings." Ante, at 700. That would be a valid inference if habitat modification were the only substantial "otherwise lawful activity" that might incidentally and nonpurposefully cause a prohibited "taking." Of course it is not. This provision applies to the many otherwise lawful takings that incidentally take a protected species—as when fishing for unprotected salmon also takes an endangered species of salmon, see Pacific Northwest Generating Cooperative v. Brown, 38 F. 3d 1058, 1067 (CA9 1994).

Congress has referred to such "incidental takings" in other statutes as well—for example, a statute referring to "the incidental taking of . . . sea-turtles in the course of . . .harvesting [shrimp]" and to the "rate of incidental taking of sea turtles by United States vessels in the course of such harvesting," 103 Stat. 1038, § 609(b)(2), note following 16 U. S. C. § 1537 (1988 ed., Supp. V); and a statute referring to "the incidental taking of marine mammals in the course of commercial fishing operations," 108 Stat. 546, § 118(a). The Court shows that it misunderstands the question when it says that "[n]o one could seriously request an `incidental' take permit to avert . . . liability for direct, deliberate action against a member of an endangered or threatened species. " Ante, at 700-701 (emphasis added). That is not an incidental take at all.[4]

This is enough to show, in my view, that the 1982 permit provision does not support the regulation. I must acknowledge that the Senate Committee Report on this provision, and the House Conference Committee Report, clearly contemplate that it will enable the Secretary to permit environmental modification. See S. Rep. No. 97-418, p. 10 (1982); H. R. Conf. Rep. No. 97-835, pp. 30-32 (1982). But the text of the amendment cannot possibly bear that asserted meaning, when placed within the context of an Act that must be interpreted (as we have seen) not to prohibit private environmental modification. The neutral language of the amendment cannot possibly alter that interpretation, nor can its legislative history be summoned forth to contradict, rather than clarify, what is in its totality an unambiguous statutory text. See Chicago v. Environmental Defense Fund, 511 U. S. 328 (1994). There is little fear, of course, that giving no effect to the relevant portions of the Committee Reports will frustrate the real-life expectations of a majority of the Members of Congress. If they read and relied on such tedious detail on such an obscure point (it was not, after all, presented as a revision of the statute's prohibitory scope, but as a discretionary-waiver provision) the Republic would be in grave peril.

Fourth and lastly, the Court seeks to avoid the evident shortcomings of the regulation on the ground that the respondents are challenging it on its face rather than as applied. See ante, at 699; see also ante, at 709 (O'Connor, J., concurring). The Court seems to say that even if the regulation dispenses with the foreseeability of harm that it acknowledges the statute to require, that does not matter because this is a facial challenge: So long as habitat modification that would foreseeably cause harm is prohibited by the statute, the regulation must be sustained. Presumably it would apply the same reasoning to all the other defects of the regulation: The regulation's failure to require injury to particular animals survives the present challenge, because at least some environmental modifications kill particular animals. This evisceration of the facial challenge is unprecedented. It is one thing to say that a facial challenge to a regulation that omits statutory element x must be rejected if there is any set of facts on which the statute does not require x. It is something quite different—and unlike any doctrine of "facial challenge" I have ever encountered—to say that the challenge must be rejected if the regulation could be applied to a state of facts in which element x happens to be present. On this analysis, the only regulation susceptible to facial attack is one that not only is invalid in all its applications, but also does not sweep up any person who could have been held liable under a proper application of the statute. That is not the law. Suppose a statute that prohibits "premeditated killing of a human being," and an implementing regulation that prohibits "killing a human being." A facial challenge to the regulation would not be rejected on the ground that, after all, it could be applied to a killing that happened to be premeditated. It could not be applied to such a killing, because it does not require the factfinder to find premeditation, as the statute requires. In other words, to simplify its task the Court today confuses lawful application of the challenged regulation with lawful application of a different regulation, i. e., one requiring the various elements of liability that this regulation omits.

III

In response to the points made in this dissent, the Court's opinion stresses two points, neither of which is supported by the regulation, and so cannot validly be used to uphold it. First, the Court and the concurrence suggest that the regulation should be read to contain a requirement of proximate causation or foreseeability, principally because the statute does —and "[n]othing in the regulation purports to weaken those requirements [of the statute]." See ante, at 696-697, n. 9; 700, n. 13; see also ante, at 711-713 (O'Connor, J., concurring). I quite agree that the statute contains such a limitation, because the verbs of purpose in § 1538(a)(1)(B) denote action directed at animals. But the Court has rejected that reading. The critical premise on which it has upheld the regulation is that, despite the weight of the other words in § 1538(a)(1)(B), "the statutory term `harm' encompasses indirect as well as direct injuries," ante, at 697-698. See also ante, at 698, n. 11 (describing "the sense of indirect causation that `harm' adds to the statute"); ante, at 702 (stating that the Secretary permissibly interprets "`harm'" to include "indirectly injuring endangered animals"). Consequently, unless there is some strange category of causation that is indirect and yet also proximate, the Court has already rejected its own basis for finding a proximate-cause limitation in the regulation. In fact "proximate" causation simply means "direct" causation. See, e. g., Black's Law Dictionary 1103 (5th ed. 1979) (defining "[p]roximate" as "Immediate; nearest; direct ") (emphasis added); Webster's New International Dictionary 1995 (2d ed. 1949) ("[P]roximate cause. A cause which directly, or with no mediate agency, produces an effect") (emphasis added).

The only other reason given for finding a proximate-cause limitation in the regulation is that "by use of the word `actually,' the regulation clearly rejects speculative or conjectural effects, and thus itself invokes principles of proximate causation." Ante, at 712 (O'Connor, J., concurring); see also ante, at 700, n. 13 (majority opinion). Non sequitur, of course. That the injury must be "actual" as opposed to "potential" simply says nothing at all about the length or foreseeability of the causal chain between the habitat modification and the "actual" injury. It is thus true and irrelevant that "[t]he Secretary did not need to include `actually' to connote `but for' causation," ibid.; "actually" defines the requisite injury, not the requisite causality.

The regulation says (it is worth repeating) that "harm" means (1) an act that (2) actually kills or injures wildlife. If that does not dispense with a proximate-cause requirement, I do not know what language would. And changing the regulation by judicial invention, even to achieve compliance with the statute, is not permissible. Perhaps the agency itself would prefer to achieve compliance in some other fashion. We defer to reasonable agency interpretations of ambiguous statutes precisely in order that agencies, rather than courts, may exercise policymaking discretion in the interstices of statutes. See Chevron, 467 U. S., at 843-845. Just as courts may not exercise an agency's power to adjudicate, and so may not affirm an agency order on discretionary grounds the agency has not advanced, see SEC v. Chenery Corp., 318 U. S. 80 (1943), so also this Court may not exercise the Secretary's power to regulate, and so may not uphold a regulation by adding to it even the most reasonable of elements it does not contain.

The second point the Court stresses in its response seems to me a belated mending of its holding. It apparently concedes that the statute requires injury to particular animals rather than merely to populations of animals. See ante, at 700, n. 13; ante, at 696 (referring to killing or injuring "members of [listed] species" (emphasis added)). The Court then rejects my contention that the regulation ignores this requirement, since, it says, "every term in the regulation's definition of `harm' is subservient to the phrase `an act which actually kills or injures wildlife.' " Ante, at 700, n. 13. As I have pointed out, see supra, at 716-717, this reading is incompatible with the regulation's specification of impairment of "breeding" as one of the modes of "kill[ing] or injur[ing] wildlife."[5]

But since the Court is reading the regulation and the statute incorrectly in other respects, it may as well introduce this novelty as well—law à la carte. As I understand the regulation that the Court has created and held consistent with the statute that it has also created, habitat modification can constitute a "taking," but only if it results in the killing or harming of individual animals, and only if that consequence is the direct result of the modification. This means that the destruction of privately owned habitat that is essential, not for the feeding or nesting, but for the breeding, of butterflies, would not violate the Act, since it would not harm or kill any living butterfly. I, too, think it would not violate the Act—not for the utterly unsupported reason that habitat modifications fall outside the regulation if they happen not to kill or injure a living animal, but for the textual reason that only action directed at living animals constitutes a "take."

* * *

The Endangered Species Act is a carefully considered piece of legislation that forbids all persons to hunt or harm endangered animals, but places upon the public at large, rather than upon fortuitously accountable individual landowners, the cost of preserving the habitat of endangered species. There is neither textual support for, nor even evidence of congressional consideration of, the radically different disposition contained in the regulation that the Court sustains. For these reasons, I respectfully dissent.

Notes

[1] The Court and Justice O'Connor deny that the regulation has the first or the third of these features. I respond to their arguments in Part III, infra.

[2] The Court suggests halfheartedly that "take" cannot refer to the taking of particular animals, because § 1538(a)(1)(B) prohibits "tak[ing] any [endangered] species. " Ante, at 697, n. 10. The suggestion is halfhearted because that reading obviously contradicts the statutory intent. It would mean no violation in the intentional shooting of a single bald eagle—or, for that matter, the intentional shooting of 1,000 bald eagles out of the extant 1,001. The phrasing of § 1538(a)(1)(B), as the Court recognizes elsewhere, see, e. g., ante, at 696, is shorthand for "take any [member of an endangered] species."

[3] This portion of the Court's opinion, see ante, at 699, n. 12, discusses and quotes a footnote in TVA v. Hill, 437 U. S. 153, 184-185, n. 30 (1978), in which we described the then-current version of the Secretary's regulation, and said that the habitat modification undertaken by the federal agency in the case would have violated the regulation. Even if we had said that the Secretary's regulation was authorized by § 1538, that would have been utter dictum, for the only provision at issue was § 1536. See id., at 193. But in fact we simply opined on the effect of the regulation while assuming its validity, just as courts always do with provisions of law whose validity is not at issue.

[4] The statutory requirement of a "conservation plan" is as consistent with this construction as with the Court's. See ante, at 700, and n.14. The commercial fisherman who is in danger of incidentally sweeping up protected fish in his nets can quite reasonably be required to "minimize and mitigate" the "impact" of his activity. 16 U. S. C. § 1539(a)(2)(A).

[5] Justice O'Connor supposes that an "impairment of breeding" intrinsically injures an animal because "to make it impossible for an animal to reproduce is to impair its most essential physical functions and to render that animal, and its genetic material, biologically obsolete." Ante, at 710 (concurring opinion). This imaginative construction does achieve the result of extending "impairment of breeding" to individual animals; but only at the expense of also expanding "injury" to include elements beyond physical harm to individual animals. For surely the only harm to the individual animal from impairment of that "essential function" is not the failure of issue (which harms only the issue), but the psychic harm of perceiving that it will leave this world with no issue (assuming, of course, that the animal in question, perhaps an endangered species of slug, is capable of such painful sentiments). If it includes that psychic harm, then why not the psychic harm of not being able to frolic about—so that the draining of a pond used for an endangered animal's recreation, but in no way essential to its survival, would be prohibited by the Act? That the concurrence is driven to such a dubious redoubt is an argument for, not against, the proposition that "injury" in the regulation includes injury to populations of animals. Even more so with the concurrence's alternative explanation: that "impairment of breeding" refers to nothing more than concrete injuries inflicted by the habitat modification on the animal who does the breeding, such as "physical complications [suffered] during gestation," ibid. Quite obviously, if "impairment of breeding" meant such physical harm to an individual animal, it would not have had to be mentioned.

The concurrence entangles itself in a dilemma while attempting to explain the Secretary's commentary to the harm regulation, which stated that "harm" is not limited to "direct physical injury to an individual member of the wildlife species," 46 Fed. Reg. 54748 (1981). The concurrence denies that this means that the regulation does not require injury to particular animals, because "one could just as easily emphasize the word `direct' in this sentence as the word `individual.' " Ante, at 711. One could; but if the concurrence does, it thereby refutes its separate attempt to exclude indirect causation from the regulation's coverage, see ante, at 711— 713. The regulation, after emerging from the concurrence's analysis, has acquired both a proximate-cause limitation and a particular-animals limitation—precisely the one meaning that the Secretary's quoted declaration will not allow, whichever part of it is emphasized.

Justice Scalia's dissent in Morse v. Republican Party of Virginia (March 27, 1996)

Justice Scalia, with whom Justice Thomas joins, dissenting.

"Any interference with the freedom of a party is simultaneously an interference with the freedom of its adherents." Sweezy v. New Hampshire, 354 U.S. 234, 250 (1957). For that reason, we have always treated government assertion of control over the internal affairs of political parties--which, after all, are simply groups of like minded individual voters--as a matter of the utmost constitutional consequence. See, e.g., Democratic Party of United States, v. La Follette, 450 U.S. 107, 121-122 (1981); Cousins v. Wigoda, 419 U.S. 477, 487-488 (1975); O'Brien v. Brown, 409 U.S. 1, 4-5 (1972) (per curiam). What is at issue in this case, therefore, is not merely interpretation of §5 of the Voting Rights Act, 42 U.S.C. § 1973c but, inextricably bound up with that interpretation, the First Amendment freedom of political association.

There are several respects in which both Justice Stevens' and Justice Breyer's opinion constitute remarkable departures from the settled course of our First Amendment jurisprudence. The most obvious, perhaps, is their refusal to consider the present application of §5 unconstitutional on the basis of "hypothetical cases unrelated to the facts of this case [that] might implicate First Amendment concerns." Stevens, J., at 42. [n.1] Instead, they "leave consideration of hypothetical concerns for another day," id., at 43, and reserve such "difficult" questions "for a case that squarely presents them," Breyer, J., at 5. That is a luxury our precedents do not allow. It has been a constant of our free speech jurisprudence that claimants whose First Amendment rights are affected may challenge a statute, not merely on the ground that its specific application to them is unconstitutional, but also on the ground that its application is void in a substantial number of other contexts that arguably fall within its scope. This principle of "overbreadth" has been applied not only in the context of freedom of speech narrowly speaking, but also in the context of the freedom to associate for the purpose of political speech. See, e.g., United States v. Robel, 389 U.S. 258, 265-266 (1967); Elfbrandt v. Russell, 384 U.S. 11, 18-19 (1966).

Thus, to satisfy oneself that the particular practice challenged here lies "well outside the area of greatest `associational' concern," Breyer, J., at 5, is to take only the first and smallest step in treating the weighty constitutional question posed by application of §5 to political parties. In this First Amendment context, to "go no further than necessary to decide the case at hand" means going far enough to assure against overbreadth. We must do that whenever "rights of association [are] ensnared in statutes which, by their broad sweep, might result in burdening innocent associations." Broadrick v. Oklahoma, 413 U.S. 601, 612 (1973) (citing, inter alia, Keyishian v. Board of Regents of Univ. of State of N. Y., 385 U.S. 589 (1967)). Justice Stevens does not assert that applying §5 to party activity passes First Amendment muster except "in the case before us," ante, at 42-43, and Justice Breyer acknowledges that the First Amendment may bar application of §5 to other convention activity, see ante, at 5. Yet despite these indications of overbreadth, neither opinion attempts to provide what our cases require: a "limiting construction or partial invalidation" that will "remove the seeming threat or deterrence to constitutionally protected expression," Broadrick, supra, at 613.

Besides flouting the doctrine of overbreadth, the opinions' refusal to provide "[f]urther definition" of §5's application to political parties, Breyer, J., at 6, leaves political parties without guidance as to "when [their] activities are, in effect, substitutes for state nominating primaries," id., at 4, and as to "which party nominating convention practices fall within the scope of the Act," ibid. [n.2] Before today, this Court has not tolerated such uncertainty in rules bearing upon First Amendment activities, because it causes persons to refrain from engaging in constitutionally protected conduct for fear of violation. See, e.g., Baggett v. Bullitt, 377 U.S. 360,372 (1964). Surely such an effect can be expected here. Party officials will at least abstain from proceeding with certain convention activities without notification; and in light of the high degree of uncertainty they may well decide to hold no conventions at all.

Another respect in which the Court today diverges from our free speech jurisprudence is even more astounding, if possible, than its disregard of the doctrines of overbreadth and vagueness. From reading the majority's two opinions, one would surmise that the only constitutional question at issue is whether the First Amendment permits the Federal Government to make unlawful and set aside party rule changes designed to hinder racial minorities' full participation in election related functions. But this statute does not present only that question, any more than a statute establishing a Board of Obscenity Censors, to which films or books must be submitted for approval before publication, presents only the question whether the First Amendment permits the prohibition of obscenity. See, e.g., Freedman v. Maryland, 380 U.S. 51 (1965); Bantam Books, Inc. v. Sullivan, 372 U.S. 58 (1963). A point entirely ignored by Justices Stevens and Breyer is that this case involves a classic prior restraint.

Our cases have heavily disfavored all manner of prior restraint upon the exercise of freedoms guaranteed by the First Amendment. Although most often imposed upon speech, prior restraints are no less noxious, and have been no less condemned, when directed against associational liberty (with which, we have said, freedom of speech "overlap[s] and blend[s]," Citizens Against Rent Control/Coalition for Fair Housing v. City of Berkeley, 454 U.S. 290, 300 (1981)). See Thomas v. Collins, 323 U.S. 516, 539-540 (1945); Carroll v. President and Comm'rs of Princess Anne, 393 U.S. 175, 180-185 (1968); cf. Healy v. James, 408 U.S. 169, 184 (1972). Today, however, a majority of the Court readily accepts the proposition that §5 can subject this First Amendment freedom to a permit system, requiring its exercise to be "precleared" with the Government even when it is not being used unlawfully. The Court thus makes citizens supplicants in the exercise of their First Amendment rights.

As the five Justices who support the judgment of the Court choose to read this statute, a political party (or at least one that the State has awarded a place on the ballot [n.3]) can make no change in its practices or procedures that might affect a voter's capacity to have his candidate elected--no matter how race neutral in purpose and effect--unless it first obtains prior clearance by the Government, see Stevens, J., at 16-19; Breyer, J., at 3-5. Any change not precleared--after a proceeding in which the burden rests on the party to show absence of discriminatory purpose and effect, see City of Rome v. United

States, 446 U.S. 156, 172-173, 183, n. 18 (1980))--can be enjoined. Given that political parties are organized with the near exclusive purpose of influencing the outcomes of elections, I think it obvious that as construed today, §5 requires political parties to submit for prior Government approval, and bear the burden of justifying, virtually every decision of consequence regarding their internal operations. That is the most outrageous tyranny. A freedom of political association that must await the Government's favorable response to a "Mother, may I?" is no freedom of political association at all.

There would be reason enough for astonishment and regret if today's judgment upheld a statute clearly imposing a prior restraint upon private, First Amendment conduct. But what makes today's action astonishing and regrettable beyond belief is that this Court itself is the architect of a prior restraint that the law does not clearly express. And here is yet another respect in which today's opinions ignore established law: their total disregard of the doctrine that, where ambiguity exists, statutes should be construed to avoid substantial constitutional questions. That has been our practice because we presume that "Congress, which also has sworn to protect the Constitution, would intend to err on the side of fundamental constitutional liberties when its legislation implicates those liberties." Regan v. Time, Inc., 468 U.S. 641, 697 (1984) (Stevens, J., concurring in judgment in part and dissenting in part). We have in the past relied upon this canon to construe statutes narrowly, so as not to impose suspect prior restraints. For example, in Lowe v. SEC, 472 U.S. 181 (1985), we held that a statute requiring all "investment advisors" to register with the Securities and Exchange Commission, see 15 U.S.C. § 80b-3, does not extend to persons who publish "nonpersonalized" investment advice such as periodic market commentary--thereby avoiding the question whether Congress could constitutionally require such persons to register. Lowe, supra, at 190, 204-205, and n. 50. How insignificant that prior restraint when compared with the requirement for preclearance of all changes in self governance by political parties.

What drives the majority to find a prior restraint where the text does not demand (or even suggest) it is the notion that it "strains credulity" to think that Congress would enact a Voting Rights Act that did not reach political party activity, Stevens, J., at 30. Congress, the majority believes, "could not have intended" such a result, Breyer, J., at 5. I doubt the validity of that perception; the assumption it rests upon--that a legislature never adopts half way measures, never attacks the easy part of a problem without attacking the more sensitive part as well--seems to me quite false. Indeed, the one step at a time doctrine that we regularly employ in equal protection cases is based on precisely the opposite assumption. See, e.g., Williamson v. Lee Optical of Okla., Inc., 348 U.S. 483, 488-489 (1955).

Moreover, even if one were to accept the majority's question begging assumption that Congress must have covered political party activity, and even if one were to credit the majority's sole textual support for such coverage, today's decision to impose a prior restraint upon purely private, political party activity would still be incomprehensible. The sole textual support adduced by the two opinions consists of §14's reference to elections for "party office," and §2's reference to "the political processes leading to nomination or election." See Stevens, J., at 20-22; Breyer, J., at 2. Justice Thomas gives compelling reasons why these phrases cannot bear the meaning the majority would ascribe, see post, at 27-32. But even accepting that they mean what the majority says, all that the phrase in §14 shows is that some portion of the Act reaches private, political party conduct; and all that the phrase in §2 shows is that (at least in some circumstances) §2 does so. Nothing in the text, nor anything in the assumption that Congress must have addressed political party activity, compels the conclusion that Congress addressed political party activity in the preclearance, prior restraint scheme of §5, [n.4] which is of course the only question immediately before us. Thus, the only real credulity strainer involved here is the notion that Congress would impose a restraint bearing a "heavy presumption against its constitutional validity," Bantam Books, 372 U. S., at 70, in such a backhanded fashion-- saying simply "State[s]" and "political subdivision[s]" in §5, but meaning political parties as well. Because I find that impossible to believe, I respectfully dissent.

Notes

1 For brevity's sake, I cite each of today's opinions by the name of its author.

2 Justice Breyer apparently thinks that the First Amendment concerns raised by appellees are minimal because many activities engaged in by a party at its convention "are very likely not subject to preclearance." Ante, at 4. Of course, a mere "very likelihood" that failure to preclear a particular activity will not result in nullification of the work of the convention is hardly sufficient to induce a party organizer to take the chance. In any event, I find curious the proposition that certain subsidiary determinations of the convention, such as " `adoption of resolutions or platforms outlining the philosophy [of the party],' " ibid., are not subject to Government oversight, whereas the determination of who may attend the convention--upon which all else depends--is subject to Government oversight. That is a good bargain for the tyrant.

3 Justice Stevens makes much of the fact that the nominee selected by the Republican Party of Virginia, by reason of the outcome of prior elections, had automatically been given a place on the primary ballot, see ante, at 6-11, but he also explains his interpretation of §5 as "follow[ing] directly from our decision in Terry [v. Adams, 345 U.S. 461 (1953)]," ante, at 28, a case in which the private party's nominating election "did not involve the State's electoral apparatus in even the slightest way," ibid. Justice Breyer alludes to Virginia's election laws, see ante, at 4, but they are plainly incidental to his analysis, see ante, at 1-4. So one must assume that what the Court today holds for parties whose nominees are automatically listed is true for other parties as well.

4 The Court majority would respond, perhaps, that the phrase "State or political subdivision" in §5 should be read to have the same meaning that it has in §2. Of course it normally should. But if the majority fancies itself confronted with the choice between departing from that general rule of construction (which, like all rules of construction, can be overcome by other indication of statutory intent, see, e.g., Helvering v. Stockholms

Enskilda Bank, 293 U.S. 84, 86-88 (1934)) and violating the inflexible principle that courts should not needlessly interpret a statute to impose a prior restraint upon private political activity, it is not debatable where the outcome must lie. Of course, the imagined conflict between the rule and the principle disappears if "State or political subdivision" is given its natural meaning in both §5 and §2, subjecting political parties to neither.

Justice Scalia's dissent in BMW of North America v. Gore (May 20, 1996)

Justice Scalia, with whom Justice Thomas joins, dissenting.

Today we see the latest manifestation of this Court's recent and increasingly insistent "concern about punitive damages that `run wild.'" Pacific Mut. Life Ins. Co. v. Haslip, 499 U. S. 1, 18 (1991). Since the Constitution does not make that concern any of our business, the Court's activities in this area are an unjustified incursion into the province of state governments.

In earlier cases that were the prelude to this decision, I set forth my view that a state trial procedure that commits the decision whether to impose punitive damages, and the amount, to the discretion of the jury, subject to some judicial review for "reasonableness," furnishes a defendant with all the process that is "due." See TXO Production Corp. v. Alliance Resources Corp., 509 U.S. 443, 470 (1993) (Scalia, J., concurring in judgment); Haslip, supra, at 25-28 (Scalia, J., concurring in judgment); cf. Honda Motor Co. v. Oberg, 512 U. S. ____, ____ (1994) (slip op., at 1-2) (Scalia, J., concurring). I do not regard the Fourteenth Amendment's Due Process Clause as a secret repository of substantive guarantees against "unfairness"--neither the unfairness of an excessive civil compensatory award, nor the unfairness of an "unreasonable" punitive award. What the Fourteenth Amendment's procedural guarantee assures is an opportunity to contest the reasonableness of a damages judgment in state court; but there is no federal guarantee a damages award actually be reasonable. See TXO, supra, at 471 (Scalia, J., concurring in judgment).

This view, which adheres to the text of the Due Process Clause, has not prevailed in our punitive damages cases. See TXO Production Corp. v. Alliance Resources Corp., 509 U. S., at 453-462 (plurality opinion); id., at 478-481 (O'Connor, J., dissenting); Haslip, supra, at 18. When, however, a constitutional doctrine adopted by the Court is not only mistaken but also insusceptible of principled application, I do not feel bound to give it stare decisis effect--indeed, I do not feel justified in doing so. See, e.g., Witte v. United States, 515 U. S. ____, ____ (1995) (Scalia, J., concurring in judgment); Walton v. Arizona, 497 U.S. 639, 673 (1990) (Scalia, J., concurring in judgment in part and dissenting in part). Our punitive damages jurisprudence compels such a response. The Constitution provides no warrant for federalizing yet another aspect of our Nation's legal culture (no matter how much in need of correction it may be), and the application of the Court's new rule of constitutional law is constrained by no principle other than the Justices' subjective assessment of the "reasonableness" of the award in relation to the conduct for which it was assessed.

Because today's judgment represents the first instance of this Court's invalidation of a state court punitive assessment as simply unreasonably large, I think it a proper occasion to discuss these points at some length.

The most significant aspects of today's decision--the identification of a "substantive due process" right against a "grossly excessive" award, and the concomitant assumption of ultimate authority to decide anew a matter of "reasonableness" resolved in lower court proceedings--are of course not new. Haslip and TXO revived the notion, moribund since its appearance in the first years of this century, that the measure of civil punishment poses a question of constitutional dimension to be answered by this Court. Neither of those cases, however, nor any of the precedents upon which they relied, actually took the step of declaring a punitive award unconstitutional simply because it was "too big." At the time of adoption of the Fourteenth Amendment, it was well understood that punitive damages represent the assessment by the jury, as the voice of the community, of the measure of punishment the defendant deserved. See, e.g., Barry v. Edmunds, 116 U.S. 550, 565 (1886); Missouri Pacific R. Co. v. Humes, 115 U.S. 512, 521 (1885); Day v. Woodworth, 13 How. 363, 371 (1852). See generally Haslip, supra, at 25-27 (Scalia, J., concurring in judgment). Today's decision, though dressed up as a legal opinion, is really no more than a disagreement with the community's sense of indignation or outrage expressed in the punitive award of the Alabama jury, as reduced by the State Supreme Court. It reflects not merely, as the concurrence candidly acknowledges, "a judgment about a matter of degree," ante, at 12; but a judgment about the appropriate degree of indignation or outrage, which is hardly an analytical determination.

There is no precedential warrant for giving our judgment priority over the judgment of state courts and juries on this matter. The only support for the Court's position is to be found in a handful of errant federal cases, bunched within a few years of one other, which invented the notion that an unfairly severe civil sanction amounts to a violation of constitutional liberties. These were the decisions upon which the TXO plurality relied in pronouncing that the Due Process Clause "imposes substantive limits `beyond which penalties may not go,' " 509 U. S., at 454 (quoting Seaboard Air Line R. Co. v. Seegers, 207 U.S. 73, 78 (1907)); see also 509 U. S., at 478-481 (O'Connor, J., dissenting); Haslip, 499 U. S., at 18. Although they are our precedents, they are themselves too shallowly rooted to justify the Court's recent undertaking. The only case relied upon in which the Court actually invalidated a civil sanction does not even support constitutional review for excessiveness, since it really concerned the validity, as a matter of procedural due process, of state legislation that imposed a significant penalty on a common carrier which lacked the means of determining the legality of its actions before the penalty was imposed. See Southwestern Telegraph & Telephone Co. v. Danaher, 238 U.S. 482, 489-491 (1915). The amount of the penalty was not a subject of independent scrutiny. As for the remaining cases, while the opinions do consider arguments that statutory penalties can, by reason of their excessiveness, violate due process, not a single one of these judgments invalidates a damages award. See Seaboard, supra, at 78-79; Waters Pierce Oil Co. v. Texas (No. 1), 212 U.S. 86, 111-112 (1909); Standard Oil Co. of Ind. v. Missouri, 224 U.S. 270, 286, 290 (1912); St. Louis, I. M. & S. R. Co. v. Williams, 251 U.S. 63, 66-67 (1919).

More importantly, this latter group of cases--which again are the sole precedential foundation put forward for the rule of constitutional law espoused by today's Court-- simply fabricated the "substantive due process" right at issue. Seaboard assigned no precedent to its bald assertion that the Constitution imposes "limits beyond which penalties may not go," 207 U. S., at 78. Waters Pierce cited only Coffey v. County of Harlan, 204 U.S. 659 (1907), a case which inquired into the constitutionality of state procedure, id., at 662-663. Standard Oil simply cited Waters Pierce, and St. Louis, I. M. &S. R. Co. offered in addition to these cases only Collins v. Johnston, 237 U.S. 502 (1915), which said nothing to support the notion of a "substantive due process" right against excessive civil penalties, but to the contrary asserted that the prescribing and imposing of criminal punishment were "functions peculiarly belonging to the several States," id., at 509-510. Thus, the only authority for the Court's position is simply not authoritative. These cases fall far short of what is needed to supplant this country's longstanding practice regarding exemplary awards, see, e.g., Haslip, 499 U. S., at 15-18; id., at 25-28 (Scalia, J., concurring in judgment).

One might understand the Court's eagerness to enter this field, rather than leave it with the state legislatures, if it had something useful to say. In fact, however, its opinion provides virtually no guidance to legislatures, and to state and federal courts, as to what a "constitutionally proper" level of punitive damages might be.

We are instructed at the outset of Part II of the Court's opinion--the beginning of its substantive analysis--that "the federal excessiveness inquiry . . . begins with an identification of the state interests that a punitive award is designed to serve." Ante, at 7. On first reading this, one is faced with the prospect that federal punitive damages law (the new field created by today's decision) will be beset by the sort of "interest analysis" that has laid waste the formerly comprehensible field of conflict of laws. The thought that each assessment of punitive damages, as to each offense, must be examined to determine the precise "state interests" pursued, is most unsettling. Moreover, if those "interests" are the most fundamental determinant of an award, one would think that due process would require the assessing jury to be instructed about them.

It appears, however (and I certainly hope), that all this is a false alarm. As Part II of the Court's opinion unfolds, it turns out to be directed, not to the question "How much punishment is too much?" but rather to the question "Which acts can be punished?" "Alabama does not have the power," the Court says, "to punish BMW for conduct that was lawful where it occurred and that had no impact on Alabama or its residents." Ante, at 12. That may be true, though only in the narrow sense that a person cannot be held liable to be punished on the basis of a lawful act. But if a person has been held subject to punishment because he committed an unlawful act, the degree of his punishment assuredly can be increased on the basis of any other conduct of his that displays his wickedness, unlawful or not. Criminal sentences can be computed, we have said, on the basis of "information concerning every aspect of a defendant's life," Williams v. New York, 337 U.S. 241, 250-252 (1949). The Court at one point seems to acknowledge this, observing that, although a sentencing court "[cannot] properly punish lawful conduct," it may in assessing the penalty "consider . . . lawful conduct that bears on the defendant's character." Ante, at 12, n. 19. That concession is quite incompatible, however, with the later assertion that, since "neither the jury nor the trial court was presented with evidence that any of BMW's out of state conduct was unlawful," the Alabama Supreme Court "therefore properly eschewed reliance on BMW's out of state conduct, . . . and based its remitted award solely on conduct that occurred within Alabama." Ante, at 13. Why could the Supreme Court of Alabama not consider lawful (but disreputable) conduct, both inside and outside Alabama, for the purpose of assessing just how bad an actor BMW was?

The Court follows up its statement that "Alabama does not have the power . . . to punish BMW for conduct that was lawful where it occurred" with the statement: "Nor may Alabama impose sanctions on BMW in order to deter conduct that is lawful in other jurisdictions." Ante, at 12. The Court provides us no citation of authority to support this proposition--other than the barely analogous cases cited earlier in the opinion, see ante, at 10-11--and I know of none.

These significant issues pronounced upon by the Court are not remotely presented for resolution in the present case. There is no basis for believing that Alabama has sought to control conduct elsewhere. The statutes at issue merely permit civil juries to treat conduct such as petitioner's as fraud, and authorize an award of appropriate punitive damages in the event the fraud is found to be "gross, oppressive, or malicious," Ala. Code §6-11-20(b)(1) (1993). To be sure, respondent did invite the jury to consider out of state conduct in its calculation of damages, but any increase in the jury's initial award based on that consideration is not a component of the remitted judgment before us. As the Court several times recognizes, in computing the amount of the remitted award the Alabama Supreme Court--whether it was constitutionally required to or not--"expressly disclaimed any reliance on acts that occurred in other jurisdictions." Ante, at 6 (internal quotation marks omitted); see also ante, at 13. [n.*] Thus, the only question presented by this case is whether that award, limited to petitioner's Alabama conduct and viewed in light of the factors identified as properly informing the inquiry, is excessive. The Court's sweeping (and largely unsupported) statements regarding the relationship of punitive awards to lawful or unlawful out of state conduct are the purest dicta.

In Part III of its opinion, the Court identifies "[t]hree guideposts" that lead it to the conclusion that the award in this case is excessive: degree of reprehensibility, ratio between punitive award and plaintiff's actual harm, and legislative sanctions provided for comparable misconduct. Ante, at 14-25. The legal significance of these "guideposts" is nowhere explored, but their necessary effect is to establish federal standards governing the hitherto exclusively state law of damages. Apparently (though it is by no means clear) all three federal "guideposts" can be overridden if "necessary to deter future misconduct," ante, at 25--a loophole that will encourage state reviewing courts to uphold awards as necessary for the "adequat[e] protect[ion]" of state consumers, ibid. By effectively requiring state reviewing courts to concoct rationalizations--whether within the "guideposts" or through the loophole--to justify the intuitive punitive reactions of state juries, the Court accords neither category of institution the respect it deserves.

Of course it will not be easy for the States to comply with this new federal law of damages, no matter how willing they are to do so. In truth, the "guideposts" mark a road to nowhere; they provide no real guidance at all. As to "degree of reprehensibility" of the defendant's conduct, we learn that " `nonviolent crimes are less serious than crimes marked by violence or the threat of violence,' " ante, at 15 (quoting Solem v. Helm, 463 U.S. 277, 292-293 (1983)), and that " `trickery and deceit' " are "more reprehensible than negligence," ante, at 15. As to the ratio of punitive to compensatory damages, we are told that a " `general concer[n] of reasonableness . . . enter[s] into the constitutional calculus,' " ante, at 23 (quoting TXO, supra, at 458)--though even "a breathtaking 500 to 1" will not necessarily do anything more than " `raise a suspicious judicial eyebrow,' " ante, at 23 (quoting TXO, supra, at 481 (O'Connor, J., dissenting), an opinion which, when confronted with that "breathtaking" ratio, approved it). And as to legislative sanctions provided for comparable misconduct, they should be accorded " `substantial deference,' " ibid. (quoting Browning Ferris Industries of Vt., Inc. v. Kelco Disposal, Inc., 492 U.S. 257, 301 (O'Connor, J., concurring in part and dissenting in part)). One expects the Court to conclude: "To thine own self be true."

These crisscrossing platitudes yield no real answers in no real cases. And it must be noted that the Court nowhere says that these three "guideposts" are the only guideposts; indeed, it makes very clear that they are not--explaining away the earlier opinions that do not really follow these "guideposts" on the basis of additional factors, thereby "reiterat[ing] our rejection of a categorical approach." Ante, at 23. In other words, even these utter platitudes, if they should ever happen to produce an answer, may be overridden by other unnamed considerations. The Court has constructed a framework that does not genuinely constrain, that does not inform state legislatures and lower courts-- that does nothing at all except confer an artificial air of doctrinal analysis upon its essentially ad hoc determination that this particular award of punitive damages was not "fair."

The Court distinguishes today's result from Haslip and TXO partly on the ground that "the record in this case discloses no deliberate false statements, acts of affirmative misconduct, or concealment of evidence of improper motive, such as were present in Haslip and TXO." Ante, at 19. This seemingly rejects the findings necessarily made by the jury--that petitioner had committed a fraud that was "gross, oppressive, or malicious," Ala. Code §6-11-20(b)(1) (1996). Perhaps that rejection is intentional; the Court does not say.

The relationship between judicial application of the new "guideposts" and jury findings poses a real problem for the Court, since as a matter of logic there is no more justification for ignoring the jury's determination as to how reprehensible petitioner's conduct was (i.e., how much it deserves to be punished), than there is for ignoring its determination that it was reprehensible at all (i.e., that the wrong was willful and punitive damages are therefore recoverable). That the issue has been framed in terms of a constitutional right against unreasonably excessive awards should not obscure the fact that the logical and necessary consequence of the Court's approach is the recognition of a constitutional right against unreasonably imposed awards as well. The elevation of "fairness" in punishment to a principle of "substantive due process" means that every punitive award unreasonably imposed is unconstitutional; such an award is by definition excessive, since it attaches a penalty to conduct undeserving of punishment. Indeed, if the Court is correct, it must be that every claim that a state jury's award of compensatory damages is "unreasonable" (because not supported by the evidence) amounts to an assertion of constitutional injury. See TXO, supra, at 471 (Scalia, J. concurring in judgment). And the same would be true for determinations of liability. By today's logic, every dispute as to evidentiary sufficiency in a state civil suit poses a question of constitutional moment, subject to review in this Court. That is a stupefying proposition.

For the foregoing reasons, I respectfully dissent.

Notes

* The Alabama Supreme Court said:

"[W]e must conclude that the award of punitive damages was based in large part on conduct that happened in other jurisdictions. . . . Although evidence of similar acts in other jurisdictions is admissible as to the issue of `pattern and practice' of such acts, . . . this jury could not use the number of similar acts that a defendant has committed in other jurisdictions as a multiplier when determining the dollar amount of a punitive damages award. Such evidence may not be considered in setting the size of the civil penalty, because neither the jury nor the trial court had evidence before it showing in which states the conduct was wrongful." 646 So. 2d 619, 627 (1994).

Justice Scalia's dissent in Romer v. Evans (May 20, 1996) [Excerpt]

Justice Scalia, with whom The Chief Justice and Justice Thomas join, dissenting.

The Court has mistaken a Kulturkampf for a fit of spite. The constitutional amendment before us here is not the manifestation of a "`bare . . . desire to harm'" homosexuals, ante, at 13, but is rather a modest attempt by seemingly tolerant Coloradans to preserve traditional sexual mores against the efforts of a politically powerful minority to revise those mores through use of the laws. [. . .]

Justice Scalia's dissent in Gasperini v. Center for Humanities (June 24, 1996)

JUSTICE SCALIA, with whom THE CHIEF JUSTICE and JUSTICE THOMAS join, dissenting.

Today the Court overrules a longstanding and well-reasoned line of precedent that has for years prohibited federal appellate courts from reviewing refusals by district courts to set aside civil jury awards as contrary to the weight of the evidence. One reason is given for overruling these cases: that the Courts of Appeals have, for some time now, decided to ignore them. Such unreasoned capitulation to the nullification of what was long regarded as a core component of the Bill of Rights-the Seventh Amendment's prohibition on appellate reexamination of civil jury awards is wrong. It is not for us, much less for the Courts of Appeals, to decide that the Seventh Amendment's restriction on federal-court review of jury findings has outlived its usefulness.

The Court also holds today that a state practice that relates to the division of duties between state judges and juries must be followed by federal courts in diversity cases. On this issue, too, our prior cases are directly to the contrary.

As I would reverse the judgment of the Court of Appeals, I respectfully dissent.

Because the Court and I disagree as to the character of the review that is before us, I recount briefly the nature of the New York practice rule at issue. Section 5501(c) of the N. Y. Civ. Prac. Law and Rules (CPLR) (McKinney 1995) directs New York intermediate appellate courts faced with a claim "that the award is excessive or inadequate and that a new trial should have been granted" to determine whether the jury's award "deviates materially from what would be reasonable compensation." In granting respondent a new trial under this standard, the Court of Appeals necessarily engaged in a two step process. As it has explained the application of §5501(c), that provision "requires the reviewing court to determine the range it regards as reasonable, and to determine whether the particular jury award deviates materially from that range." Consorti v. Armstrong World Industries, Inc., 72 F. 3d 1003, 1013 (1995) (amended). The first of these two steps--the determination as to "reasonable" damages--plainly requires the reviewing court to reexamine a factual matter tried by the jury: the appropriate measure of damages, on the evidence presented, under New York law. The second step--the determination as to the degree of difference between "reasonable" damages and the damages found by the jury (whether the latter "deviates materially" from the former)--establishes the degree of judicial tolerance for awards found not to be reasonable, whether at the trial level or by the appellate court. No part of this exercise is appropriate for a federal court of appeals, whether or not it is sitting in a diversity case.

Granting appellate courts authority to decide whether an award is "excessive or inadequate" in the manner of CPLR §5501(c) may reflect a sound understanding of the capacities of modern juries and trial judges. That is to say, the people of the State of New York may well be correct that such a rule contributes to a more just legal system. But the practice of federal appellate reexamination of facts found by a jury is precisely what the People of the several States considered not to be good legal policy in 1791. Indeed, so fearful were they of such a practice that they constitutionally prohibited it by means of the Seventh Amendment.

That Amendment was Congress's response to one of the principal objections to the proposed Constitution raised by the Anti Federalists during the ratification debates: its failure to ensure the right to trial by jury in civil actions in federal court. The desire for an explicit constitutional guarantee against reexamination of jury findings was explained by Justice Story, sitting as Circuit Justice in 1812, as having been specifically prompted by Article III's conferral of "appellate Jurisdiction, both as to Law and Fact" upon the Supreme Court. "[O]ne of the most powerful objections urged against [the Constitution]," he recounted, was that this authority "would enable that court, with or without a new jury, to re examine the whole facts, which had been settled by a previous jury." United States v. Wonson, 28 F. Cas. 745, 750 (No. 16,750) (CC Mass). [n.1]

The second clause of the Amendment responded to that concern by providing that "[i]n [s]uits at common law . . . no fact tried by a jury, shall be otherwise re examined in any Court of the United States, than according to the rules of the common law." U. S. Const., Amdt. 7. The Reexamination Clause put to rest "apprehensions" of "new trials by the appellate courts," Wonson, 28 F. Cas., at 750, by adopting, in broad fashion, "the rules of the common law" to govern federal court interference with jury determinations. [n.2] The content of that law was familiar and fixed. See, e.g., ibid. ("[T]he common law here alluded to is not the common law of any individual state, (for it probably differs in all), but it is the common law of England, the grand reservoir of all our jurisprudence"); Dimick v. Schiedt, 293 U.S. 474, 487 (1935) (Seventh Amendment "in effect adopted the rules of the common law, in respect of trial by jury, as these rules existed in 1791"). It quite plainly barred reviewing courts from entertaining claims that the jury's verdict was contrary to the evidence.

At common law, review of judgments was had only on writ of error, limited to questions of law. See, e.g., Wonson, supra, at 748; 3 W. Blackstone, Commentaries on the Laws of England 405 (1768) ("The writ of error only lies upon matter of law arising upon the face of the proceedings; so that no evidence is required to substantiate or support it"); 1 W. Holdsworth, History of English Law 213-214 (7th ed. 1956); cf. Ross v. Rittenhouse, 2 Dall. 160, 163 (Pa. 1792) (McKean, C. J.). That principle was expressly acknowledged by this Court as governing federal practice in Parsons v. Bedford, 3 Pet. 433 (1830) (Story, J.). There, the Court held that no error could be assigned to a district court's refusal to allow transcription of witness testimony "to serve as a statement of facts in case of appeal," notwithstanding the right to such transcription under state practices made applicable to federal courts by Congress. This was so, the Court explained, because "[t]he whole object" of the transcription was "to present the evidence here in order to establish the error of the verdict in matters of fact," id., at 445" a mode of review simply unavailable on writ of error, see id., at 446, 448. The Court concluded that Congress had not directed federal courts to follow state practices that would change "the effect or conclusiveness of the verdict of the jury upon the facts litigated at the trial," id., at 449, because it had "the most serious doubts whether [that] would not be unconstitutional" under the Seventh Amendment, id., at 448.

"This is a prohibition to the courts of the United States to re examine any facts tried by a jury in any other manner. The only modes known to the common law to re examine such facts, are the granting of a new trial by the court where the issue was tried, or to which the record was properly returnable; or the award of a venire facias de novo, by an appellate court, for some error of law which intervened in the proceedings.

. . . . .

"[I]f the evidence were now before us, it would not be competent for this court to reverse the judgment for any error in the verdict of the jury at the trial . . . ." Id., at 447-449.

Nor was the common law proscription on reexamination limited to review of the correctness of the jury's determination of liability on the facts. No less than the existence of liability, the proper measure of damages "involves only a question of fact," St. Louis, I. M. & S. R. Co. v. Craft, 237 U.S. 648, 661 (1915), as does a "motio[n] for a new trial based on the ground that the damages . . . are excessive," Metropolitan R. Co. v. Moore, 121 U.S. 558, 574 (1887). As appeals from denial of such motions necessarily pose a factual question, courts of the United States are constitutionally forbidden to entertain them.

"No error of law appearing upon the record, this court cannot reverse the judgment because, upon examination of the evidence, we may be of the opinion that the jury should have returned a verdict for a less amount. If the jury acted upon a gross mistake of facts, or were governed by some improper influence or bias, the remedy therefore rested with the court below, under its general power to set aside the verdict. . . . Whether [the refusal to exercise that power] was erroneous or not, our power is restricted by the Constitution to the determination of the questions of law arising upon the record. Our authority does not extend to a re examination of facts which have been tried to the jury under instructions correctly defining the legal rights of parties. Parsons v. Bedford, [supra] . . . ." Railroad Co. v. Fraloff, 100 U.S. 24, 31-32 (1879).

This view was for long years not only unquestioned in our cases, but repeatedly affirmed. [n.3]

Respondent's principal response to these cases, which is endorsed by Justice Stevens, see ante, at 5-7, is that our forebears were simply wrong about the English common law. The rules of the common law practice incorporated in the Seventh Amendment, it is claimed, did not prevent judges sitting in an appellate capacity from granting a new trial on the ground that an award was contrary to the weight of the evidence. This claim simply does not withstand examination of the actual practices of the courts at common law. The weight of the historical record strongly supports the view of the common law taken in our early cases.

At common law, all major civil actions were initiated before panels of judges sitting at the courts of Westminster. Trial was not always held at the bar of the court, however. The inconvenience of having jurors and witnesses travel to Westminster had given rise to the practice of allowing trials to be held in the countryside, before a single itinerant judge. This nisi prius trial, as it was called, was limited to the jury's deciding a matter of fact in dispute; once that was accomplished, the verdict was entered on the record which--along with any exceptions to the instructions or rulings of the nisi prius judge--was then returned to the en banc court at Westminster. See generally 1 Holdsworth, History of English Law, at 223-224, 278-282; G. Radcliffe & G. Cross, The English Legal System 90-91, 183-186 (3d ed. 1954). Requests for new trials were made not to the nisi prius judge, but to the en banc court, prior to further proceedings and entry of judgment. See 1 Holdsworth, supra, at 282; Riddell, New Trial at the Common Law, 26 Yale L. J. 49, 53, 57 (1916). Such motions were altogether separate from appeal on writ of error, which followed the entry of judgment. 1 Holdsworth, supra, at 213-214; Radcliffe & Cross, supra, at 210-212. [n.4]

Nonetheless, respondent argues, the role of the en banc court at Westminster was essentially that of an appellate body, reviewing the proceedings below; and those appellate judges were capable of examining the evidence, and of granting a new trial when, in their view, the verdict was contrary to the weight of the evidence. See Blume, Review of Facts in Jury Cases-- The Seventh Amendment, 20 J. Am. Jud. Soc. 130, 131 (1936); Riddell, supra, at 55-57, 60. There are two difficulties with this argument. The first is the characterization of the court at Westminster as an appellate body. The court's role with respect to the initiation of the action, the entertaining of motions for new trial, and the entry of judgment was the same in all cases--whether the cause was tried at the bar or at nisi prius. To regard its actions in deciding a motion for a new trial as "appellate" in the latter instance supposes a functional distinction where none existed. The second difficulty is that when the trial had been held at nisi prius, the judges of the en banc court apparently would order a new trial only if the nisi prius judge certified that he was dissatisfied with the verdict. To be sure, there are many cases where no mention is made of the judge's certificate, but there are many indications that it was a required predicate to setting aside a verdict rendered at nisi prius, and respondent has been unable to identify a single case where a new trial was granted in the absence of such certification. In short, it would seem that a new trial could not be had except upon the approval of the judge who presided over the trial and heard the evidence. [n.5]

I am persuaded that our prior cases were correct that, at common law, "reexamination" of the facts found by a jury could be undertaken only by the trial court, and that appellate review was restricted to writ of error which could challenge the judgment only upon matters of law. Even if there were some doubt on the point, we should be hesitant to advance our view of the common law over that of our forbears, who were far better acquainted with the subject than we are. But in any event, the question of how to apply the "rules of the common law" to federal appellate consideration of motions for new trials is one that has already been clearly and categorically answered, by our precedents. As we said in Dimick v. Schiedt, 293 U.S. 474 (1935), in discussing the status of remittitur under "the rules of the common law," a doctrine that "has been accepted as the law for more than a hundred years and uniformly applied in the federal courts during that time" and "finds some support in the practice of the English courts prior to the adoption of the

Constitution" will not lightly "be reconsidered or disturbed," id., at 484-485. The time to question whether orders on motions for a new trial were in fact reviewable at common law has long since passed. Cases of this Court reaching back into the early 19th century establish that the Constitution forbids federal appellate courts to "reexamine" a fact found by the jury at trial; and that this prohibition encompasses review of a district court's refusal to set aside a verdict as contrary to the weight of the evidence.

The Court, as is its wont of late, all but ignores the relevant history. It acknowledges that federal appellate review of district court refusals to set aside jury awards as against the weight of the evidence was "once deemed inconsonant with the Seventh Amendment's re examination clause," ante, at 18, but gives no indication of why ever we held that view; and its citation of only one of our cases subscribing to that proposition fails to convey how long and how clearly it was a fixture of federal practice, see ibid. (citing only Lincoln v. Power, 151 U.S. 436 (1894)). That our earlier cases are so poorly recounted is not surprising, however, given the scant analysis devoted to the conclusion that "appellate review for abuse of discretion is reconcilable with the Seventh Amendment," ante, at 19.

No precedent of this Court affirmatively supports that proposition. The cases upon which the Court relies neither affirmed nor rejected the practice of appellate weight of the evidence review that has been adopted by the courts of appeals--a development that, in light of our past cases, amounts to studied waywardness by the intermediate appellate bench. Our unaccountable reluctance, in Grunenthal v. Long Island R. Co., 393 U.S. 156, 158 (1968), and Neese v. Southern R. Co., 350 U.S. 77 (1955), to stand by our precedents, and the undeniable illogic of our disposition of those two cases--approving ourselves a district court denial of a new trial motion, so as not to have to confront the lawfulness of reversal by the court of appeals--is authority of only the weakest and most negative sort. Nor can any weight be assigned to our statement in Browning Ferris Industries of Vt., Inc. v. Kelco Disposal, Inc., 492 U.S. 257, 279 (1989), seemingly approving appellate abuse of discretion review of denials of new trials where punitive damages are claimed to be excessive. Browning Ferris, like Grunenthal and Neese, explicitly avoided the question that is before us today, see 492 U. S., at 279, n. 25. Even more significantly, Browning Ferris involved review of a jury's punitive damages award. Unlike the measure of actual damages suffered, which presents a question of historical or predictive fact, see, e.g., Craft, 237 U. S., at 661, the level of punitive damages is not really a "fact" "tried" by the jury. In none of our cases holding that the Reexamination Clause prevents federal appellate review of claims of excessive damages does it appear that the damages had a truly "punitive" component.

In any event, it is not this Court's statements that the Court puts forward as the basis for dispensing with our prior cases. Rather, it is the Circuit Courts of Appeals' unanimous "agree[ment]" that they may review trial court refusals to set aside jury awards claimed to be against the weight of the evidence. Ante, at 19. This current unanimity is deemed controlling, notwithstanding the "relatively late" origin of the practice, ante, at 18, and without any inquiry into the reasoning set forth in those Court of Appeals decisions. [n.6] The Court contents itself with citations of two federal appellate cases and the assurances of two leading treatises that the view (however meager its intellectual provenance might be) is universally held. See ante, at 19-20. To its credit, one of those treatises describes the "dramatic change in doctrine" represented by appellate abuse of discretion review of denials of new trial orders generally as having been "accomplished by a blizzard of dicta" that, through repetition alone, has "given legitimacy to a doctrine of doubtful constitutionality." 11 C. Wright, A. Miller, & M. Kane, Federal Practice and Procedure §2819, pp. 200, 204 (2d ed. 1995). [n.7]

The Court's only suggestion as to what rationale might underlie approval of abuse of discretion review is to be found in a quotation from Dagnello v. Long Island R. Co., 289 F. 2d 797 (CA2 1961), to the effect that review of denial of a new trial motion, if conducted under a sufficiently deferential standard, poses only " `a question of law.' " Ante, at 19 (quoting Dagnello, supra, at 806). But that is not the test that the Seventh Amendment sets forth. Whether or not it is possible to characterize an appeal of a denial of new trial as raising a "legal question," it is not possible to review such a claim without engaging in a "reexamin[ation]" of the "facts tried by the jury" in a manner "otherwise" than allowed at common law. Determining whether a particular award is excessive requires that one first determine the nature and extent of the harm--which undeniably requires reviewing the facts of the case. That the court's review also entails application of a legal standard (whether "shocks the conscience," "deviates materially," or some other) makes no difference, for what is necessarily also required is reexamination of facts found by the jury.

In the last analysis, the Court frankly abandons any pretense at faithfulness to the common law, suggesting that "the meaning" of the Reexamination Clause was not "fixed at 1791," ante, at 20, n. 20, contrary to the view that all our prior discussions of the Reexamination Clause have adopted, see supra, at 4-7. The Court believes we can ignore the very explicit command that "no fact tried by a jury shall be otherwise reexamined in any Court of the United States, than according to the rules of the common law" because, after all, we have not insisted that juries be all male, or consist of 12 jurors, as they were at common law. Ante, at 20, n. 20. This is a desperate analogy, since there is of course no comparison between the specificity of the command of the Reexamination Clause and the specificity of the command that there be a "jury." The footnote abandonment of our traditional view of the Reexamination Clause is a major step indeed. [n.8]

The Court's holding that federal courts of appeals may review district court denials of motions for new trials for error of fact is not the only novel aspect of today's decision. The Court also directs that the case be remanded to the District Court, so that it may "test the jury's verdict against CPLR §5501(c)'s `deviates materially' standard," ante, at 23. This disposition contradicts the principle that "[t]he proper role of the trial and appellate courts in the federal system in reviewing the size of jury verdicts is . . . a matter of federal law." Donovan v. Penn Shipping Co., 429 U.S. 648, 649 (1977) (per curiam).

The Court acknowledges that state procedural rules cannot, as a general matter, be permitted to interfere with the allocation of functions in the federal court system, see ante, at 21. Indeed, it is at least partly for this reason that the Court rejects direct application of §5501(c) at the appellate level as inconsistent with an " `essential characteristic' " of the federal court system-- by which the Court presumably means abuse of discretion review of denials of motions for new trials. See ante, at 15, 21-22. But the scope of the Court's concern is oddly circumscribed. The "essential characteristic" of the federal jury, and, more specifically, the role of the federal trial court in reviewing jury judgments, apparently counts for little. The Court approves the "accommodat[ion]" achieved by having district courts review jury verdicts under the "deviates materially" standard, because it regards that as a means of giving effect to the State's purposes "without disrupting the federal system," ante, at 21. But changing the standard by which trial judges review jury verdicts does disrupt the federal system, and is plainly inconsistent with "the strong federal policy against allowing state rules to disrupt the judge jury relationship in federal court." Byrd v. Blue Ridge Rural Elec. Cooperative, Inc., 356 U.S. 525, 538 (1958). [n.9] The Court's opinion does not even acknowledge, let alone address, this dislocation.

We discussed precisely the point at issue here in Browning Ferris Industries of Vt., Inc. v. Kelco Disposal, Inc., 492 U.S. 257 (1989), and gave an answer altogether contrary to the one provided today. Browning Ferris rejected a request to fashion a federal common law rule limiting the size of punitive damages awards in federal courts, reaffirming the principle of Erie R. Co. v. Tompkins, 304 U.S. 64 (1938), that "[i]n a diversity action, or in any other lawsuit where state law provides the basis of decision, the propriety of an award of punitive damages . . . and the factors the jury may consider in determining their amount, are questions of state law." 492 U. S., at 278. But the opinion expressly stated that "[f]ederal law . . . will control on those issues involving the proper review of the jury award by a federal district court and court of appeals." Id., at 278-279. "In reviewing an award of punitive damages," it said, "the role of the district court is to determine whether the jury's verdict is within the confines of state law, and to determine, by reference to federal standards developed under Rule 59, whether a new trial or remittitur should be ordered." Id., at 279. The same distinction necessarily applies where the judgment under review is for compensatory damages: State substantive law controls what injuries are compensable and in what amount; but federal standards determine whether the award exceeds what is lawful to such degree that it may be set aside by order for new trial or remittitur. [n.10]

The Court does not disavow those statements in Browning Ferris (indeed, it does not even discuss them), but it presumably overrules them, at least where the state rule that governs "whether a new trial or remittitur should be ordered" is characterized as "substantive" in nature. That, at any rate, is the reason the Court asserts for giving §5501(c) dispositive effect. The objective of that provision, the Court states, "is manifestly substantive," ante, at 13, since it operates to "contro[l] how much a plaintiff can be awarded" by "tightening the range of tolerable awards," ante, at 9. Although "less readily classified" as substantive than "a statutory cap on damages," it nonetheless "was designed to provide an analogous control," ante, at 12, by making a new trial mandatory when the award "deviat[es] materially" from what is reasonable, see ante, at 12-13.

I do not see how this can be so. It seems to me quite wrong to regard this provision as a "substantive" rule for Erie purposes. The "analog[y]" to "a statutory cap on damages," ante, at 12, fails utterly. There is an absolutely fundamental distinction between a rule of law such as that, which would ordinarily be imposed upon the jury in the trial court's instructions, and a rule of review, which simply determines how closely the jury verdict will be scrutinized for compliance with the instructions. A tighter standard for reviewing jury determinations can no more plausibly be called a "substantive" disposition than can a tighter appellate standard for reviewing trial court determinations. The one, like the other, provides additional assurance that the law has been complied with; but the other, like the one, leaves the law unchanged.

The Court commits the classic Erie mistake of regarding whatever changes the outcome as substantive, see ante, at 12-14. That is not the only factor to be considered. See Byrd, 356 U. S., at 537 ("[W]ere `outcome' the only consideration, a strong case might appear for saying that the federal court should follow the state practice. But there are affirmative countervailing considerations at work here"). Outcome determination "was never intended to serve as a talisman," Hanna v. Plumer, 380 U.S. 460, 466-467 (1965), and does not have the power to convert the most classic elements of the process of assuring that the law is observed into the substantive law itself. The right to have a jury make the findings of fact, for example, is generally thought to favor plaintiffs, and that advantage is often thought significant enough to be the basis for forum selection. But no one would argue that Erie confers a right to a jury in federal court wherever state courts would provide it; or that, were it not for the Seventh Amendment, Erie would require federal courts to dispense with the jury whenever state courts do so.

In any event, the Court exaggerates the difference that the state standard will make. It concludes that different outcomes are likely to ensue depending on whether the law being applied is the state "deviates materially" standard of §5501(c) or the "shocks the conscience" standard. See ante, at 12-14. Of course it is not the federal appellate standard but the federal district court standard for granting new trials that must be compared with the New York standard to determine whether substantially different results will obtain-- and it is far from clear that the district court standard ought to be "shocks the conscience." [n.11] Indeed, it is not even clear (as the Court asserts) that "shocks the conscience" is the standard (erroneous or not) actually applied by the district courts of the Second Circuit. The Second Circuit's test for reversing a grant of a new trial for an excessive verdict is whether the award was "clearly within the maximum limit of a reasonable range," Ismail v. Cohen, 899 F. 2d 183, 186 (CA2 1990) (internal quotation marks omitted), so any district court that uses that standard will be affirmed. And while many district court decisions express the "shocks the conscience" criterion, see, e.g., Koerner v. Club Mediterranee, S. A., 833 F. Supp. 327, 333 (SDNY 1993), some have used a standard of "indisputably egregious," Banff v. Express, Inc., 921 F. Supp. 1065, 1069 (SDNY 1995), or have adopted the inverse of the Second Circuit's test for reversing a grant of new trial, namely, "clearly outside the maximum limit of a reasonable range," Paper Corp. v. Schoeller Technical Papers, Inc., 807 F. Supp. 337, 350-351 (SDNY 1992). Moreover, some decisions that say "shocks the conscience" in fact apply a rule much less stringent. One case, for example, says that any award that would not be sustained under the New York "deviates materially" rule "shocks the conscience." See In re Joint Eastern & S. Dist. Asbestos Litigation, 798 F. Supp. 925, 937 (E&SDNY 1992), rev'd on other grounds, 995 F. 2d 343, 346 (CA2 1993). In sum, it is at least highly questionable whether the consistent outcome differential claimed by the Court even exists. What seems to me far more likely to produce forum shopping is the consistent difference between the state and federal appellate standards, which the Court leaves untouched. Under the Court's disposition, the Second Circuit reviews only for abuse of discretion, whereas New York's appellate courts engage in a de novo review for material deviation, giving the defendant a double shot at getting the damages award set aside. The only result that would produce the conformity the Court erroneously believes Erie requires is the one adopted by the Second Circuit and rejected by the Court: de novo federal appellate review under the §5501(c) standard.

To say that application of §5501(c) in place of the federal standard will not consistently produce disparate results is not to suggest that the decision the Court has made today is not a momentous one. The principle that the state standard governs is of great importance, since it bears the potential to destroy the uniformity of federal practice and the integrity of the federal court system. Under the Court's view, a state rule that directed courts "to determine that an award is excessive or inadequate if it deviates in any degree from the proper measure of compensation" would have to be applied in federal courts, effectively requiring federal judges to determine the amount of damages de novo, and effectively taking the matter away from the jury entirely. Cf. Byrd, 356 U. S., at 537-538. Or consider a state rule that allowed the defendant a second trial on damages, with judgment ultimately in the amount of the lesser of two jury awards. Cf. United States v. Wonson, 28 F. Cas., at 747-748 (describing Massachusetts practice by which a second jury trial could be had on appeal). Under the reasoning of the Court's opinion, even such a rule as that would have to be applied in the federal courts.

The foregoing describes why I think the Court's Erie analysis is flawed. But in my view, one does not even reach the Erie question in this case. The standard to be applied by a district court in ruling on a motion for a new trial is set forth in Rule 59 of the Federal Rules of Civil Procedure, which provides that "[a] new trial may be granted . . . for any of the reasons for which new trials have heretofore been granted in actions at law in the courts of the United States" (emphasis added). That is undeniably a federal standard. [n.12] Federal district courts in the Second Circuit have interpreted that standard to permit the granting of new trials where " `it is quite clear that the jury has reached a seriously erroneous result' " and letting the verdict stand would result in a " `miscarriage of justice.' " Koerner v. Club Mediterranee, S. A., 833 F. Supp. 327 (SDNY 1993) (quoting Bevevino v. Saydjari, 574 F. 2d 676, 684 (CA2 1978)). Assuming (as we have no reason to question) that this is a correct interpretation of what Rule 59 requires, it is undeniable that the federal rule is " `sufficiently broad' to cause a `direct collision' with the state law or, implicitly, to `control the issue' before the court, thereby leaving no room for the operation of that law." Burlington Northern R. Co. v. Woods, 480 U.S. 1, 4-5 (1987). It is simply not possible to give controlling effect both to the federal standard and the state standard in reviewing the jury's award. That being so, the court has no choice but to apply the Federal Rule, which is an exercise of what we have called Congress's "power to regulate matters which, though falling within the uncertain area between substance and procedure, are rationally capable of classification as either," Hanna, 380 U. S., at 472.

* * *

There is no small irony in the Court's declaration today that appellate review of refusals to grant new trials for error of fact is "a control necessary and proper to the fair administration of justice," ante, at 19. It is objection to precisely that sort of "control" by federal appellate judges that gave birth to the Reexamination Clause of the Seventh Amendment. Alas, those who drew the Amendment, and the citizens who approved it, did not envision an age in which the Constitution means whatever this Court thinks it ought to mean--or indeed, whatever the courts of appeals have recently thought it ought to mean.

When there is added to the revision of the Seventh Amendment the Court's precedent setting disregard of Congress's instructions in Rule 59, one must conclude that this is a bad day for the Constitution's distinctive Article III courts in general, and for the role of the jury in those courts in particular. I respectfully dissent.

Notes

1 This objection was repeatedly made following the Constitutional Convention, see, e.g., Martin, Genuine Information, in 3 Records of the Federal Convention of 1787, pp. 172, 221-222 (M. Farrand ed. 1911); Gerry, Reply to a Landholder, id., at 298, 299, and at the ratifying conventions in the States, see, e.g., 3 J. Elliot, Debates on the Federal Constitution 525, 540-541, 544-546 (1863) (Virginia Convention, statements of Mr. Mason and Mr. Henry); 4 id., at 151, 154 (North Carolina Convention, statements of Mr. Bloodworth and Mr. Spencer).

Prior to adoption of the Amendment, these concerns were addressed by Congress in the Judiciary Act of 1789, 1 Stat. 73, which expressly directed, in providing for "reexamin[ation]" of civil judgments "upon a writ of error," that "there shall be no reversal in either [the Circuit or Supreme Court] . . . for any error of fact." §22, 1 Stat. 84-85. That restriction remained in place until the 1948 revisions of the Judicial Code. See 62 Stat. 963, 28 U.S.C. § 2105 (1994).

2 The Amendment was relied upon at least twice to prevent actual new trials. In Wonson itself, Justice Story rejected the United States' claim of right to retry, on appeal, a matter unsuccessfully put before a jury in the District Court--notwithstanding acceptance of such a practice under local law. The court based its ruling on statutory grounds, but its interpretation of its statutory jurisdiction was dictated by its view that a contrary

interpretation would contravene the Seventh Amendment. 28 F. Cas., at 750. And in The Justices v. Murray, 9 Wall. 274, 281 (1870), this Court relied on Wonson in invalidating under the Seventh Amendment a federal habeas statute that provided for removal of certain judgments from state courts for purposes of retrial in federal court.

3 See, e.g., Wabash R. Co. v. McDaniels, 107 U.S. 454, 456 (1883) ("That we are without authority to disturb the judgment upon the ground that the damages are excessive cannot be doubted. Whether the order overruling the motion for a new trial based upon that ground was erroneous or not, our power is restricted to the determination of questions of law arising upon the record. Railroad Company v. Fraloff, 100 U.S. 24 [(1879)]"); Arkansas Valley Land & Cattle Co. v. Mann, 130 U.S. 69, 75 (1889) ("[H]owever it was ascertained by the court that the verdict was too large . . . , the granting or refusing a new trial in a Circuit Court of the United States is not subject to review by this court") (citing Parsons v. Bedford, 3. Pet. 433 (1830); Railroad Co. v. Fraloff, 100 U.S. 24 (1879)); Lincoln v. Power, 151 U.S. 436, 437-438 (1894) ("[I]t is not permitted for this court, sitting as a court of errors, in a case wherein damages have been fixed by the verdict of a jury, to take notice of [a claim of excessive damages] where the complaint is only of the action of the jury. . . . [W]here there is no reason to complain of the instructions, an error of the jury in allowing an unreasonable amount is to be redressed by a motion for a new trial") (citing Parsons, supra; Fraloff, supra); Chicago, B. & Q. R. Co. v. Chicago, 166 U.S. 226, 242-246 (1897); Southern Railway Carolina Div. v. Bennett, 233 U.S. 80, 87 (1914) ("[A] case of mere excess upon the evidence is a matter to be dealt with by the trial court. It does not present a question for reexamination here upon a writ of error") (citing Lincoln, supra); Fairmount Glass Works v. Cub Fork Coal Co., 287 U.S. 474, 481-482 (1933) ("The rule that this Court will not review the action of a federal trial court in granting or denying a motion for a new trial for error of fact has been settled by a long and unbroken line of decisions; and has been frequently applied where the ground of the motion was that the damages awarded by the jury were excessive or were inadequate") (footnotes omitted).

4 The grounds for granting a new trial were "want of notice of trial; or any flagrant misbehavior of the party prevailing toward the jury, which may have influenced their verdict; or of any gross misbehavior of the jury among themselves: also if it appears by the judge's report, certified to the court, that the jury have brought in a verdict without or contrary to evidence, so that he is reasonably dissatisfied therewith; or if they have given exorbitant damages; or if the judge himself has misdirected the jury, so that they found an unjustifiable verdict." 3 W. Blackstone, Commentaries on the Laws of England 387 (1768) (footnotes omitted; emphases omitted).

5 See ibid. (new trial would be granted "if it appears by the judge's report, certified to the court, that the jury have brought in a verdict without or contrary to evidence, so that he is reasonably dissatisfied therewith"). See, e.g., Berks v. Mason, Say. 264, 265, 96 Eng. Rep. 874, 874-875 (K. B. 1756); Bright v. Eynon, 1 Burr. 390, 390, 97 Eng. Rep. 365 (K. B. 1757); see also Note, Limitations on Trial by Jury in Illinois, 19 Chi. Kent L. Rev. 91, 92 (1940) ("An exhaustive examination of the early English cases has revealed not a single

case where an English court at common law ever granted a new trial, as being against the evidence, unless the judge or judges who sat with the jury stated in open court, or certified, that the verdict was against the evidence and he was dissatisfied with the verdict").

Justice Stevens understands Blackstone to say that new trials were granted for excessiveness even where the nisi prius judge was not dissatisfied with the damages awarded, see ante, at 6-7. Blackstone's phrasing certainly allows for this reading, see n. 4, supra, but what indications we have suggest that the dissatisfaction of the presiding judge played the same role where the motion for new trial was based on a claim of excessive damages as where based on a claim of an erroneous verdict. See, e.g., Boulsworth v. Pilkington, Jones, T. 200, 84 Eng. Rep. 1216 (K. B. 1685); Anonymous, 1 Wils. K. B. 22, 95 Eng. Rep. 470 (K. B. 1743); Redshaw v. Brook, 2 Wils. K. B. 405, 95 Eng. Rep. 887 (C. P. 1769); Sharpe v. Brice, 2 Black. W. 942, 96 Eng. Rep. 557 (C. P. 1774). The cases cited by Justice Stevens, ante, at 7, n. 5, are not at all to the contrary: In one, the case was tried at the bar of the court, so that there was no nisi prius judge, see Wood v. Gunston, Sty. 466, 82 Eng. Rep. 867 (K. B. 1655); in the other, the judge who had presided at trial was on the panel that ruled on the new trial motion, and recommended a new trial, see Bright v. Eynon, supra, at 390" 391, 396-397, Eng. Rep., at 365, 368.

6 The Second Circuit, notwithstanding its practice with respect to excessiveness claims, will not review a district court's determination that the jury's liability ruling was supported by the weight of the evidence, see Stonewall Ins. Co. v. Asbestos Claims Management, 73 F. 3d 1178, 1199 (1995) (such a decision is "one of those few rulings that is simply unavailable for appellate review"), and the Eighth Circuit has questioned whether the Seventh Amendment permits appellate review of such determinations, see Thongvanh v. Thalacker, 17 F. 3d 256, 259-260 (1994); see also White v. Pence, 961 F. 2d 776, 782 (1992).

7 I am at a loss to understand the Court's charge that keeping faith with our precedents--and requiring that the courts of appeals do likewise--would " `destroy the uniformity of federal practice,' " ante, at 20, n. 19. I had thought our decisions established uniformity. And as for commentators' observations that it would be "`astonishing'" for us actually to heed our precedents, see ibid., quoting 11 C. Wright, A. Miller, & M. Kane, Federal Practice and Procedure §2820, p. 212 (2d ed. 1995), they are no more than a prediction of inconstancy--which the Court today fulfills.

8 Gasoline Products Co. v. Champlin Refining Co., 283 U.S. 494 (1931), is the only case cited in the Court's footnote that arguably involved the slightest departure from common law practices regarding review of jury findings. It held, to be sure, that new trial could be ordered on damages alone, even though at common law there was no practice of setting a verdict aside in part. But it did so only after satisfying itself that the change was one of "form" rather than "substance," quoting Lord Mansfield to the effect that "`for form's sake, we must set aside the whole verdict.'" Id., at 498 (quoting Edie v. East India Co., 1 Black W. 295, 298, 96 Eng. Rep. 166 (K. B. 1761)). It can hardly be maintained that whether or not a jury's damages award may be set aside on appeal is a matter of form. The

footnote also cites 9A C. Wright & A. Miller, Federal Practice and Procedure §2522 (2d ed. 1995) for its discussion of Federal Rule of Civil Procedure 50(b), which permits post-trial motion for judgment as a matter of law. The Court neglects to mention that that discussion states: "The Supreme Court held that reservation of the decision in this fashion had been recognized at common law . . . ." Id., §2522, at 245.

9 Since I reject application of the New York standard on other grounds, I need not consider whether it constitutes "reexamination" of a jury's verdict in a manner "otherwise . . . than according to the rules of the common law."

10 Justice Stevens thinks that if an award "exceeds what is lawful," the result is "legal error" that "may be corrected" by the appellate court. Ante, at 5, n. 2. But the sort of "legal error" involved here is the imposition of legal consequences (in this case, damages) in light of facts that, under the law, may not warrant them. To suggest that every fact may be reviewed, because what may ensue from an erroneous factual determination is a "legal error," is to destroy the notion that there is a factfinding function reserved to the jury.

11 That the "shocks the conscience" standard was not the traditional one would seem clear from the opinion of Justice Story, quoted approvingly by the Court, ante, at 17, to the effect that remittitur should be granted "if it should clearly appear that the jury . . . have given damages excessive in relation to the person or the injury." Blunt v. Little, 3 F. Cas. 760, 761-762 (CC Mass. 1822).

12 I agree with the Court's entire progression of reasoning in its footnote 22, ante, at 21-22, leading to the conclusion that state law must determine "[w]hether damages are excessive." But the question of whether damages are excessive is quite separate from the question of when a jury award may be set aside for excessiveness. See supra, at 17. It is the latter that is governed by Rule 59; as Browning Ferris said, district courts are "to determine, by reference to federal standards developed under Rule 59, whether a new trial or remittitur should be ordered," 492 U. S., at 279 (emphasis added).

Justice Scalia's dissent in US v. Virginia (June 26, 1996) [Excerpt]

Justice Scalia, dissenting.

Much of the Court's opinion is devoted to deprecating the closed mindedness of our forebears with regard to women's education, and even with regard to the treatment of women in areas that have nothing to do with education. Closed minded they were--as every age is, including our own, with regard to matters it cannot guess, because it simply does not consider them debatable. The virtue of a democratic system with a First Amendment is that it readily enables the people, over time, to be persuaded that what they took for granted is not so, and to change their laws accordingly. That system is destroyed if the smug assurances of each age are removed from the democratic process and written into the Constitution. So to counterbalance the Court's criticism of our ancestors, let me say a word in their praise: they left us free to change. The same cannot be said of this most illiberal Court, which has embarked on a course of inscribing one after another of the current preferences of the society (and in some cases only the counter majoritarian preferences of the society's law trained elite) into our Basic Law. Today it enshrines the notion that no substantial educational value is to be served by an all men's military academy--so that the decision by the people of Virginia to maintain such an institution denies equal protection to women who cannot attend that institution but can attend others. Since it is entirely clear that the Constitution of the United States--the old one-- takes no sides in this educational debate, I dissent. [. . .]

Justice Scalia's dissent in Board of Commissioners, Wabaunsee County, Kansas v. Umbehr (June 28, 1996)

Justice Scalia, with whom Justice Thomas joins, dissenting.

Taken together, today's decisions in Board of Comm'rs, Waubansee Cty. v. Umbehr, ante, p. ___, and O'Hare Truck Service, Inc. v. Northlake, ante, p. ___, demonstrate why this Court's Constitution making process can be called "reasoned adjudication" only in the most formalistic sense.

Six years ago, by the barest of margins, the Court expanded Elrod v. Burns, 427 U.S. 347 (1976), and Branti v. Finkel, 445 U.S. 507 (1980), which had held that public employees cannot constitutionally be fired on the basis of their political affiliation, to establish the new rule that applicants for public employment cannot constitutionally be rejected on the basis of their political affiliation. Rutan v. Republican Party of Ill., 497 U.S. 62 (1990). The four dissenters argued that "the desirability of patronage is a policy question to be decided by the people's representatives" and "a political question if there ever was one." Id., at 104, 114 (Scalia, J., dissenting). They were "convinced" that Elrod and Branti had been "wrongly decided," 497 U. S., at 114; indeed, that those cases were "not only wrong, not only recent, not only contradicted by a long prior tradition, but also . . . unworkable in practice" and therefore "should be overruled," id., at 110-111. At the very least, the dissenters maintained, Elrod and Branti "should not be extended beyond their facts," 497 U. S., at 114.

Today, with the addition to the Court of another Justice who believes that we have no basis for proscribing as unconstitutional practices that do not violate any explicit text of the Constitution and that have been regarded as constitutional ever since the framing, see, e.g., Bennis v. Michigan, 516 U. S. ___, ___ (1996) (slip op., at 1-2) (Thomas, J., concurring), one would think it inconceivable that Elrod and Branti would be extended far beyond Rutan to the massive field of all government contracting. Yet amazingly, that is what the Court does in these two opinions--and by lopsided votes, at that. It is profoundly disturbing that the varying political practices across this vast country, from coast to coast, can be transformed overnight by an institution whose conviction of what the Constitution means is so fickle.

The basic reason for my dissent today is the same as one of the reasons I gave (this one not joined by Justice O'Connor) in Rutan:

"[W]hen a practice not expressly prohibited by the text of the Bill of Rights bears the endorsement of a long tradition of open, widespread, and unchallenged use that dates back to the beginning of the Republic, we have no proper basis for striking it down. Such a venerable and accepted tradition is not to be laid on the examining table and scrutinized for its conformity to some abstract principle of First Amendment adjudication devised by this Court. To the contrary, such traditions are themselves the stuff out of which the Court's principles are to be formed. They are, in these uncertain areas, the very points of reference by which the legitimacy or illegitimacy of other practices is to be figured out. When it appears that the latest `rule,' or `three part test,' or `balancing test' devised by the Court has placed us on a collision course with such a landmark practice, it is the former that must be recalculated by us, and not the latter that must be abandoned by our citizens. I know of no other way to formulate a constitutional jurisprudence that reflects, as it should, the principles adhered to, over time, by the American people, rather than those favored by the personal (and necessarily shifting) philosophical dispositions of a majority of this Court." Rutan, supra, at 95-96 (Scalia, J., dissenting) (footnote omitted).

There can be no dispute that, like rewarding one's allies, the correlative act of refusing to reward one's opponents--and at bottom both of today's cases involve exactly that--is an American political tradition as old as the Republic. This is true not only with regard to employment matters, as Justice Powell discussed in his dissenting opinions in Elrod, supra, at 377-379, and Branti, supra, at 522, n. 1, but also in the area of government contracts, see, e.g., M. Tolchin & S. Tolchin, To the Victor: Political Patronage from the Clubhouse to the White House 14-15, 61, 233-241, 273-277 (1971); A. Heard, The Costs of Democracy 143-145 (1960); R. Caro, The Power Broker: Robert Moses and the Fall of New York 723-726, 738, 740-741, 775, 799, 927 (1975); M.Royko, Boss: Richard J. Daley of Chicago 69 (1971); Wolfinger, Why Political Machines Have Not Withered Away and Other Revisionist Thoughts, 34 J. Politics 365, 367-368, 372, 389 (1972); The Bond Game Remains the Same, Nat'l L. J., July 1, 1996, pp. A1, A20-A21. If that long and unbroken tradition of our people does not decide these cases, then what does? The constitutional text is assuredly as susceptible of one meaning as of the other; in that circumstance, what constitutes a "law abridging the freedom of speech" is either a matter of history or else it is a matter of opinion. Why are not libel laws such an "abridgment"? The only satisfactory answer is that they never were. What secret knowledge, one must wonder, is breathed into lawyers when they become Justices of this Court, that enables them to discern that a practice which the text of the Constitution does not clearly proscribe, and which our people have regarded as constitutional for 200 years, is in fact unconstitutional?

The Court seeks to avoid the charge that it ignores the centuries old understandings and practices of our people by recounting, Umbehr, ante, at 13-14, shocking examples of raw political patronage in contracting, most of which would be unlawful under the most rudimentary bribery law. (It selects, of course, only the worst examples from the sources I have cited, omitting the more common practices that permit one author to say, with undeniable accuracy, that "honorable and prudent businessmen competing for government ventures make campaign contributions" out of "a desire to do what [is] thought necessary to remain eligible," and that "[m]any contractors routinely do so to both parties." Heard, supra, at 145.) These "examples of covert, widely condemned and sometimes illegal government action," it says, do not "legitimize the government discrimination." Umbehr, ante, at 14. But of course it is not the County's or City's burden (or mine) to "legitimize" all patronage practices; it is Umbehr's and O'Hare's (and the Court's) to show that all patronage practices are not only "illegitimate" in some vague moral or even precise legal sense, but that they are unconstitutional. It suffices to demonstrate the error of the Court's opinions that many contracting patronage practices have been open, widespread, and unchallenged since the beginning of the Republic; and that those that have been objected to have not been objected to on constitutional grounds. That the Court thinks it relevant that many patronage practices are "covert, widely condemned and sometimes illegal" merely displays its persistent tendency to equate those many things that are or should be proscribed as a matter of social policy with those few things that we have the power to proscribe under the Constitution. The relevant and inescapable point is this: No court ever held, and indeed no one ever thought, prior to our decisions in Elrod and Branti, that patronage contracting could violate the First Amendment. The Court's attempt to contest this point, or at least to becloud the issue, by appeal to obnoxious and universally condemned patronage practices simply displays the feebleness of its case.

In each case today, the Court observes that we "have long since rejected Justice Holmes' famous dictum, that a policeman `may have a constitutional right to talk politics, but he has no constitutional right to be a policeman.'" Umbehr, ante, at 5 (quoting McAuliffe v. Mayor of New Bedford, 155 Mass. 216, 220, 29 N. E. 517 (1892)); see O'Hare, ante, at 3 (quoting same). But this activist Court also repeatedly rejects a more important aphorism of Justice Holmes, which expresses a fundamental philosophy that was once an inseparable part of our approach to constitutional law. In a case challenging the constitutionality of a federal estate tax on the ground that it was an unapportioned direct tax in violation of Article I, §9, Justice Holmes wrote:

"[The] matter . . . is disposed of . . ., not by an attempt to make some scientific distinction, which would be at least difficult, but on an interpretation of language by its traditional use--on the practical and historical ground that this kind of tax always has been regarded as the antithesis of a direct tax . . . . Upon this point a page of history is worth a volume of logic." New York Trust Co. v. Eisner, 256 U.S. 345, 349 (1921) (emphasis added).

The Court's decision to enter this field cannot be justified by the consideration (if it were ever a justification) that the democratic institutions of government have not been paying adequate attention to the problems it presents. The American people have evidently decided that political influence in government contracting, like many other things that are entirely constitutional, is not entirely desirable, and so they have set about passing laws to prohibit it in some but not all instances. As a consequence, government contracting is subject to the most extraordinary number of laws and regulations at the federal, state, and local levels.

The United States Code contains a categorical statutory prohibition on political contributions by those negotiating for or performing contracts with the Federal Government, 2 U.S.C. § 441c competitive bidding requirements for contracts with executive agencies, 41 U.S.C. §§ 252-253, public corruption and bribery statutes, e.g., 18 U.S.C. § 201 and countless other statutory requirements that restrict government officials' discretion in awarding contracts. "There are already over four thousand individual statutory provisions that affect the [Defense Department's] procurement process." Pyatt, Procurement Competition at Work: The Navy's Experience, 6 Yale J. Reg. 319, 319-320 (1989). Federal regulations are even more widespread. As one handbook in the area has explained, "[t]heir procedural and substantive requirements dictate, to an oftentimes astonishing specificity, how the entire contracting process will be conducted." ABA General Practice Section, Federal Procurement Regulations: Policy, Practice and Procedures 1 (1987). That is why it is no surprise in this area to find a 253-page book just setting forth "fundamentals," E. Massengale, Fundamentals of Federal Contract Law (1991), or a mere "deskbook" that runs 436 pages, ABA Section of Public Contract Law, Government Contract Law: The Deskbook for Procurement Professionals (1995). Such "summaries" are indispensable when, for example, the regulations that comprise the "Federal Acquisition Regulations System" total some 5,037 pages of fine print. See Title 48 CFR (1995).

Similar systems of detailed statutes and regulations exist throughout the States. In addition to the various statutes criminalizing bribes to government officials and other forms of public corruption, all 50 States have enacted legislation imposing competitive bidding requirements on various types of contracts with the government. [n.1] Government contracting is such a standard area for state regulation that a model procurement code has been developed, which is set forth in a 265-page book complete with proposed statutes, regulations, and explanations. See ABA Section of Urban, State and Local Government Law, Model Procurement Code for State and Local Governments (1981). As of 1989, 15 States had enacted legislation based on the model code. See ABA Section of Urban, State and Local Government Law, Annotations to the Model Procurement Code, at vii-viii (2d ed. 1992) (and statutes cited).

By 1992, more than 25 local jurisdictions had also adopted legislation based on the Model Procurement Code, see id., at ix, and thousands of other counties and municipalities have over time devised their own measures. New York City, for example, which "[e]ach year . . . enter[s] into approximately 40,000 contracts worth almost $6.5 billion," has regulated the public contracting process by a myriad of codes and regulations that seek to assure "scrupulous neutrality in choosing contractors and [consequently impose] multiple layers of investigation and accountability." Anechiarico & Jacobs, Purging Corruption from Public Contracting: The `Solutions' Are Now Part of the Problem, 40 N. Y. L. S. L. Rev. 143, 143-144 (1995) (hereinafter Anechiarico & Jacobs).

These examples of federal, state, and local statutes, codes, ordinances, and regulations could be multiplied to fill many volumes. They are the way in which government contracts have been regulated, and the way in which public policy problems that arise in the area have been addressed, since the founding of the Republic. See, e.g., Federal Procurement Regulations: Policy, Practice and Procedures, at 11-196 (describing the history of federal government procurement regulation). But these laws and regulations have brought to the field a degree of discrimination, discernment, and predictability that cannot be achieved by the blunt instrument of a constitutional prohibition.

Title 48 of the Code of Federal Regulations would not contain the 5,000+ pages it does if it did not make fine distinctions, permitting certain actions in some government acquisition areas and prohibiting them in others. Similarly, many of the competitive bidding statutes that I have cited contain exceptions for, or are simply written not to include, contracts under a particular dollar amount, [n.2] or those covering certain subject matters, [n.3] or those that are time sensitive. [n.4] A political unit's decision not to enact contracting regulations, or to suspend the regulations in certain circumstances, amounts to a decision to permit some degree of political favoritism. As I shall discuss shortly, O'Hare's and Umbehr's First Amendment permits no such selectivity--or at least none that can be known before litigation is over.

If inattention by the democratic organs of government is not a plausible reason for the Court's entry into the field, then what is? I believe the Court accepts (any sane person must accept) the premise that it is utterly impossible to erect, and enforce through litigation, a system in which no citizen is intentionally disadvantaged by the government because of his political beliefs. I say the Court accepts that, because the O'Hare opinion, in a rare brush with the real world, points out that "O'Hare was not part of a constituency that must take its chance of being favored or ignored in the larger political process--for example, by residing or doing business in a region the government rewards or spurns in the construction of public works." Ante, at 8. Of course. Government favors those who agree with its political views, and disfavors those who disagree, every day--in where it builds its public works, in the kinds of taxes it imposes and collects, in its regulatory prescriptions, in the design of its grant and benefit programs--in a million ways, including the letting of contracts for government business. What good reason has the Court given for separating out this last way, and declaring it to be (as all the others for some reason are not) an "abridgment of the freedom of speech"?

As I have explained, I would separate the permissible from the impermissible on the basis of our Nation's traditions, which is what I believe sound constitutional adjudication requires. In Elrod and Branti, the Court rejected this criterion--but if what it said did not make good constitutional law, at least it made some sense: the loss of one's job is a powerful price to pay for one's politics. But the Court then found itself on the fabled slippery slope that Justice Holmes's aphorism about history and logic warned about: one logical proposition detached from history leads to another, until the Court produces a result that bears no resemblance to the America that we know. The next step was Rutan, which extended the prohibition of political motivation from firing to hiring. The third step is today's Umbehr, which extends it to the termination of a government contract. And the fourth step (as I shall discuss anon) is today's O'Hare, which extends it to the refusal to enter into contractual relationships.

If it is to be possible to dig in our cleats at some point on this slope--before we end up holding that the First Amendment requires the City of Chicago to have as few potholes in Republican wards (if any) as in Democratic ones--would not the most defensible point of termination for this indefensible exercise be public employment? A public employee is always an individual, and a public employee below the highest political level (which is exempt from Elrod) is virtually always an individual who is not rich; the termination or denial of a public job is the termination or denial of a livelihood. A public contractor, on the other hand, is usually a corporation; and the contract it loses is rarely its entire business, or even an indispensable part of its entire business. As Judge Posner put it:

"Although some business firms sell just to government, most government contractors also have private customers. If the contractor does not get the particular government contract on which he bids, because he is on the outs with the incumbent and the state does not have laws requiring the award of the contract to the low bidder (or the laws are not enforced), it is not the end of the world for him; there are other government entities to bid to, and private ones as well. It is not like losing your job." LaFalce v. Houston, 712 F. 2d 292, 294 (CA7 1983).

Another factor that suggests we should stop this new enterprise at government employment is the much greater volume of litigation that its extension to the field of contracting entails. The government contracting decisions worth litigating about are much more numerous than the number of personnel hirings and firings in that category; and the litigation resources of contractors are infinitely more substantial than those of fired employees or rejected applicants. Anyone who has had even brief exposure to the intricacies of federal contracting law knows that a lawsuit is often used as a device to stay or frustrate the award of a contract to a competitor. See, e.g., Delta Data Systems Corp. v. Webster, 744 F. 2d 197 (CADC 1984); Delta Data Systems Corp. v. Webster, 755 F. 2d 938 (CADC 1985). What the Court's decisions today mean is that all government entities, no matter how small, are at risk of §1983 lawsuits for violation of constitutional rights, unless they adopt (at great cost in money and efficiency) the detailed and cumbersome procedures that make a claim of political favoritism (and a §1983 lawsuit) easily defended against.

The Court's opinion in O'Hare shrugs off this concern with the response that "[w]e have no reason to believe that governments cannot bear a like burden [to that in the employment context] in defending against suits alleging the denial of First Amendment freedoms to public contractors." Ante, at 12. The burden is, as I have suggested, likely much greater than that in the employment context; and the relevant question (if one rejects history as the determinant) is not simply whether the governments "can bear" it, but whether the inconvenience of bearing it is outbalanced by the degree of abridgment of supposed First Amendment rights (of corporate shareholders, for the most part) that would occur if the burden were not imposed. [n.5] The Court in Umbehr dismisses the risk of litigation, not by analogy to the employment context, but by analogy to the many government contracting laws of the type I have discussed. "We are aware," it says, "of no evidence of excessive or abusive litigation under such provisions." Umbehr, ante, at 15. I am not sure the Court would be aware of such evidence if it existed, but if in fact litigation has been "nonexcessive" (a conveniently imprecise term) under these provisions, that is scant indication that it will be "nonexcessive" under the First Amendment. Uncertainty breeds litigation. Government contracting laws are clear and detailed, and whether they have been violated is typically easy to ascertain: the contract was put out for bid, or it was not. Umbehr's new First Amendment, by contrast, requires a sensitive "balancing" in each case; and the factual question of whether political affiliation or disfavored speech was the reason for the award or loss of the contract will usually be litigable. In short, experience under the government contracting laws has little predictive value.

The Court additionally asserts that the line cannot be drawn between employment and independent contracting, because " `the applicability of a provision of the Constitution has never depended on the vagaries of state or federal law.' " Umbehr, ante, at 11 (quoting Browning Ferris Industries of Vt., Inc. v. Kelco Disposal, Inc., 492 U.S. 257, 299 (1989) (O'Connor, J., concurring in part and dissenting in part)); see also Umbehr, ante, at 10-11 (citing other cases). That is not so. State law frequently plays a dispositive role in the issue of whether a constitutional provision is applicable. In fact, before we invented the First Amendment right not to be fired for political views, most litigation in this very field of government employment revolved around the Fourteenth Amendment's Due Process Clause, and asked whether the firing had deprived the plaintiff of a "property" interest without due process. And what is a property interest entitled to Fourteenth Amendment protection? " [P]roperty interests," we said, "are not created by the Constitution. Rather, they are created and their dimensions are defined by existing rules or understandings that stem from an independent source such as state law . . . . If it is the law of Texas that a teacher in the respondent's position has no contractual or other claim to job tenure, the respondent's [federal constitutional] claim would be defeated." Perry v. Sindermann, 408 U.S. 593, 602, n. 7 (1972) (internal quotation marks and citation omitted). See also Mt. Healthy City Bd. of Ed. v. Doyle, 429 U.S. 274, 280-281 (1977) (whether a government entity possesses Eleventh Amendment immunity "depends, at least in part, upon the nature of the entity created by state law").

I have spoken thus far as though the only problem involved here were a practical one: as though, in the best of all possible worlds, if our judicial system and the resources of our governmental entities could only manage it, it would be desirable for an individual to suffer no disadvantage whatever at the hands of the government solely because of his political views--no denial of employment, no refusal of contracts, no discrimination in social programs, not even any potholes. But I do not believe that. The First Amendment guarantees that you and I can say and believe whatever we like (subject to a few tradition based exceptions, such as obscenity and "fighting words") without going to jail or being fined. What it ought to guarantee beyond that is not at all the simple question the Court assumes. The ability to discourage eccentric views through the mild means that have historically been employed, and that the Court has now set its face against, may well be important to social cohesion. To take an uncomfortable example from real life: An organization (I shall call it the White Aryan Supremacist Party, though that was not the organization involved in the actual incident I have in mind) is undoubtedly entitled, under the Constitution, to maintain and propagate racist and antisemitic views. But when the Department of Housing and Urban Development lets out contracts to private security forces to maintain law and order in units of public housing, must it really treat this bidder the same as all others? Or may it determine that the views of this organization are not political views that it wishes to "subsidize" with public funds, nor political views that it wishes to hold up as an exemplar of the law to the residents of public housing?

The state and local regulation I described earlier takes account of this reality. Even where competitive bidding requirements are applicable (which is far from always), they almost invariably require that a contract be awarded not to the lowest bidder but to the "lowest responsible bidder." [n.6] "The word `responsible' is as important as the word `lowest,' " H. Cohen, Public Construction Contracts and the Law 81 (1961), and has been interpreted in some States to permit elected officials to exercise political discretion. "Some New York courts," for example, "have upheld agency refusals to award a contract to a low bidder because the contractor, while technically and financially capable, was not morally responsible." Anechiarico & Jacobs 146-147. In the leading case of Picone v. New York, 176 Misc. 967, 29 N. Y. S. 2d 539 (Sup. Ct. N. Y. Cty. 1941), the court stated that in determining whether a lowest bidder for a particular contract was the "lowest responsible bidder," New York City officials had permissibly considered "whether [the bidder] possessed integrity and moral worth." Id., at 969, 29 N. Y. S. 2d, at 541. The New Jersey Supreme Court has similarly said "[i]t is settled that the legislative mandate that a bidder be `responsible' embraces moral integrity just as surely as it embraces a capacity to supply labor and materials." Trap Rock Industries, Inc. v. Kohl, 59 N. J. 471, 481, 284 A. 2d 161, 166 (1971). In the future, presumably, this will be permitted only if the disfavored moral views of the bidder have never been verbalized, for otherwise the First Amendment will produce entitlement to the contract, or at least guarantee a lawsuit.

In treading into this area, "we have left the realm of law and entered the domain of political science." Rutan, 497 U. S., at 113 (Scalia, J., dissenting). As Judge Posner rightly perceived, the issue that the Court today disposes of like some textbook exercise in logic "raises profound questions of political science that exceed judicial competence to answer." LaFalce v. Houston, 712 F. 2d, at 294.

If, however, the Court is newly to announce that it has discovered that the granting or withholding of a contract is a First Amendment issue, a coherent statement of the new law is the least that those who labor in the area are entitled to expect. They do not get it from today's decisions, which contradict each other on a number of fundamental points.

The decision in Umbehr appears to be an improvement on our Elrod-Branti-Rutan trilogy in one sense. Rutan, the most recent of these decisions, provided that the government could justify patronage employment practices only if it proved that such patronage was "narrowly tailored to further vital governmental interests." Rutan, supra, at 74. The four of us in dissent explained that "[t]hat strict scrutiny standard finds no support in our cases," and we argued that, if the new constitutional right was to be invented, the criterion for violation should be "the test announced in Pickering [v. Board of Ed. of Township High School Dist. 205, Will Cty., 391 U.S. 563 (1968)]." Rutan, supra, at 98, 100 (Scalia, J., dissenting). It thus appears a happy development that the Court in Umbehr explicitly rejects the suggestion, urged by Umbehr and by the United States as amicus curiae, that "on proof of viewpoint based retaliation for contractors' political speech, the government should be required to justify its actions as narrowly tailored to serve a compelling state interest," Umbehr, ante, at 7; accord, ante, at 9, and instead holds "that the Pickering balancing test, adjusted to weigh the government's interests as contractor rather than as employer, determines the extent of [independent contractors'] protection" under the First Amendment, ante, at 4. Pickering balancing, of course, requires a case by case assessment of the government's and the contractor's interests. "Pickering and its progeny . . . involve a post hoc analysis of one employee's speech and its impact on that employee's public responsibilities." United States v. Treasury Employees, 513 U. S. ___, ___ (1995) (slip op., at 11). See also id., at ___ (slip op., at 2) (O'Connor, J., concurring in judgment in part and dissenting in part) (Pickering requires "case by case application"); Rankin v. McPherson, 483 U.S. 378, 388-392 (1987); Connick v. Myers, 461 U.S. 138, 150-154 (1983); Pickering v. Board of Ed. of Township High School Dist. 205, Will Cty., 391 U.S. 563, 568-573 (1968). It is clear that this is what the Court's opinion in Umbehr anticipates: "a fact sensitive and deferential weighing of the government's legitimate interests," ante, at 8-9 (emphasis added), which accords "[d]eference . . . to the government's reasonable assessments of its interests as contractor," ante, at 9 (emphasis removed). "[S]uch a nuanced approach," Umbehr says, "which recognizes the variety of interests that may arise in independent contractor cases, is superior to a bright line rule." Ante, at 9-10.

What the Court sets down in Umbehr, however, it rips up in O'Hare. In Part III of that latter opinion, where the Court makes its application of the First Amendment to the facts of the case, there is to be found not a single reference to Pickering. See O'Hare, ante, at 7-13. Indeed, what is quite astonishing, the Court concludes that it "need not inquire" into any government interests that patronage contracting may serve--even generally, much less in the particular case at hand--"for Elrod and Branti establish that patronage does not justify the coercion of a person's political beliefs and associations." O'Hare, ante, at 5. Leaving aside that there is no coercion here, [n.7] the assertion obviously contradicts the need for "balancing" announced in the companion Umbehr decision. This rejection of "balancing" is evident elsewhere in O'Hare--as when the Court rejects as irrelevant the

Seventh Circuit's observation in LaFalce v. Houston, 712 F. 2d 292 (1983), that some contractors elect to "curr[y] favor with diverse political parties," on the ground that the fact "[t]hat some citizens [thus] find a way to mitigate governmental overreaching, or refrain from complaining, does not excuse wrongs done to those who exercise their rights." O'Hare, ante, at 11. But whether the government action at issue here is a "wrong" is precisely the issue in this case, which we thought (per Umbehr) was to be determined by "balancing."

One would have thought these two opinions the products of the courts of last resort of two different legal systems, presenting fertile material for a comparative law course on freedom of speech . . . were it not for a single paragraph in O'Hare, a veritable deus ex machina of legal analysis, which reconciles the irreconcilable. The penultimate paragraph of that portion of the O'Hare opinion which sets forth the general principles of law governing the case, see ante, at 6-7, advises that henceforth "the freedom of speech" alluded to in the Bill of Rights will be divided into two categories: (1) the "right of free speech," where "we apply the balancing test from Pickering," and (since this "right of free speech" presumably does not exhaust the Free Speech Clause), (2) "political affiliation," where we apply the rigid rule of Elrod and Branti. The Court (or at least the O'Hare Court) says that "[t]here is an advantage in so confining the inquiry where political affiliation alone is concerned, for one's beliefs and allegiances ought not to be subject to probing or testing by the government." O'Hare, ante, at 6.

Frankly, the only "advantage" I can discern in this novel distinction is that it provides some explanation (no matter how difficult to grasp) of how these two opinions can issue from the same Court on the same day. It raises many questions. Does the "right of free speech" (category (1), that is) come into play if the contractor not only is a Republican, but says "I am a Republican"? (At that point, of course, the fatal need for "probing or testing" his allegiance disappears.) Or is the "right of free speech" at issue only if he goes still further, and says "I believe in the principles set forth in the Republican platform"? Or perhaps one must decide whether the Rubicon between the "right of free speech" and the more protected "political affiliation" has been crossed on the basis of the contracting authority's motivation, so that it does not matter whether the contractor says he is a Republican, or even says that he believes in the Republican platform, so long as the reason he is disfavored is simply that (whatever he says or believes) he is a Republican. But the analysis would change, perhaps, if the contracting authority really has nothing against Republicans as such, but can't stand people who believe what the Republican platform stands for. Except perhaps it would not change if the contractor never actually said he was a Republican--or perhaps only if he never actually said that he believed in the Republican platform. The many variations will provide endless diversion for the courts of appeals.

If one is so sanguine as to believe that facts involving the "right of free speech" and facts involving "political affiliation" can actually be segregated into separate categories, there arises, of course, the problem of what to do when both are involved. One would expect the more rigid test (Elrod nonbalancing) to prevail. That is certainly what happens elsewhere in the law. If one is categorically liable for a defamatory statement, but liable for a threatening statement only if it places the subject in immediate fear of physical harm, an utterance that which combines both ("Sir, I shall punch you in your lying mouth!") would be (at least as to the defamatory portion) categorically actionable. Not so, however, with our new First Amendment law. Where, we are told, "specific instances of the employee's speech or expression, which require balancing in the Pickering context, are intermixed with a political affiliation requirement," balancing rather than categorical liability will be the result. O'Hare, ante, at 6-7.

Were all this confusion not enough, the explanatory paragraph makes doubly sure it is not setting forth any comprehensible rule by adding, immediately after its description of how Elrod, rather than the Pickering balancing test, applies in "political affiliation" cases, the following: "It is true, on the other hand, . . . that the inquiry is whether the affiliation requirement is a reasonable one, so it is inevitable that some case by case adjudication will be required even where political affiliation is the test the government has imposed." O'Hare, ante, at 6. As I said in Rutan, "[w]hat that means is anybody's guess." 497 U. S., at 111 (Scalia, J., dissenting). Worse still, we learn that O'Hare itself, where the Court does not conduct balancing, may "perhaps [be] includ[ed]" among "those many cases . . . which require balancing" because it is one of the "intermixed" cases I discussed in the paragraph immediately above. O'Hare, ante, at 6. Why, then, one is inclined to ask, did not the Court conduct balancing?

The answer is contained in the next brief paragraph of the O'Hare opinion:

"The Court of Appeals, based on its understanding of the pleadings, considered this simply an affiliation case, and held, based on circuit precedent, there was no constitutional protection for one who was simply an outside contractor. We consider the case in those same terms, but we disagree with the Court of Appeals' conclusion." Ante, at 7.

This is a deus ex machina sent in to rescue the Court's deus ex machina, which was itself overwhelmed by the plot of this tragedy of inconsistency. Unfortunately, this adjutor adjutoris (to overextend, perhaps, my classical analogy) is also unequal to the task: The respondent in this case is entitled to defend the judgment in its favor on the basis of the facts as they were alleged, not as the Court of Appeals took them to be. When, as here, "the decision we review adjudicated a motion to dismiss, we accept all of the factual allegations in petitioners' complaint as true and ask whether, in these circumstances, dismissal of the complaint was appropriate." Berkovitz v. United States, 486 U.S. 531, 540 (1988) (emphasis added). It is at least highly arguable that the complaint alleged what the Court calls a violation of the "right of free speech" rather than merely the right of "political affiliation." The count at issue was entitled " FREEDOM OF SPEECH," see App. in No. 95-191, p. 15, and contended that petitioners had been retaliated against because of "the exercise of their constitutional right of freedom of speech," id., at 17. One of the two central factual allegations is the following: "John A. Gratzianna openly supported Paxson's opponent for the office of Mayor. Campaign posters for Paxson's opponent were displayed at plaintiff O'Hare's place of business." Id., at 16. It is particularly inexcusable to hide behind the Court of Appeals' treatment of this litigation as "simply an affiliation case," since when the Court of Appeals wrote its opinion the world had not yet learned that the Free Speech Clause is divided into the two categories of "right of free speech" and "political affiliation." As far as that court knew, it could have substituted "freedom of speech" for "freedom of political affiliation" whenever it used the term, with no effect on the outcome. It did not, in other words, remotely make a "finding" that the case involves only the right of political affiliation. Unavoidably, therefore, if what the O'Hare Court says in its first explanatory paragraph is to be believed--that is, what it says in the latter part of that paragraph, to the effect that "intermixed" cases are governed by Pickering--there is simply no basis for reversing the Court of Appeals without balancing, and directing that the case proceed, effectively depriving the City of its right to judgment on the pleadings.

Unless, of course, Pickering balancing can never support the granting of a motion to dismiss. That is the proposition that today's O'Hare opinion, if it is not total confusion, must stand for. Nothing else explains how the Court can (1) assert that an "intermixed" case requires Pickering balancing, (2) acknowledge that the complaint here may set forth an "intermixed" case, and yet (3) reverse the dismissal without determining whether the complaint does set forth an "intermixed" case and, if so, proceeding to conduct at least a preliminary Pickering balancing. There is of course no reason in principle why this particular issue should be dismissal proof, and the consequence of making it so, given the burdens of pre-trial discovery (to say nothing of trial itself) will be to make litigation on this subject even more useful as a device for harassment and weapon of commercial competition. It must be acknowledged, however, that proceeding this way in the present case has one unquestionable advantage: it leaves it entirely to the district court to clean up, without any guidance or assistance from us, the mess that we have made--to figure out whether saying "Vote against Paxson," or "Paxson is a hack," or "Paxson's project for a 100,000-seat municipal stadium is wasteful," or whatever else Mr. Gratzianna's campaign posters might have said, removes this case from the Political Affiliation Clause of the Constitution and places it within the Right of Free Speech Clause.

One final observation about the sweep of today's holdings. The opinion in Umbehr, having swallowed the camel of First Amendment extension into contracting, in its penultimate paragraph demonstrates the Court's deep down judicial conservatism by ostentatiously straining out the following gnat: "Finally, we emphasize the limited nature of our decision today. Because Umbehr's suit concerns the termination of a pre-existing commercial relationship with the government, we need not address the possibility of suits by bidders or applicants for new government contracts who cannot rely on such a relationship." Umbehr, ante, at 17. The facts in Umbehr, of course, involved the termination of nothing so vague as a "commercial relationship with the government"; the Board of Commissioners had terminated Umbehr's contract. The fuzzier terminology is used, presumably, because O'Hare did not involve termination of a contract. As far as appears, O'Hare had not paid or promised anything to be placed on a list of tow truck operators who would be offered individual contracts as they came up. The company had no right to sue if the city failed to call it, nor the city any right to sue if the company turned down an offered tow. It had, in short, only what might be called (as an infinity of things might be called) "a pre-existing commercial relationship" with the city: it was one of the tow truck operators they regularly called. The quoted statement in Umbehr invites the bar to believe, therefore, that the Court which declined to draw the line of First Amendment liability short of firing from government employment (Elrod and Branti); short of nonhiring for government employment (Rutan); short of termination of a government contract (Umbehr); and short of denial of a government contract to someone who had a "pre existing commercial relationship with the government" (O'Hare); may take a firm stand against extending the Constitution into every little thing when it comes to denying a government contract to someone who had no "pre existing commercial relationship." Not likely; in fact, not even believable.

This Court has begun to make a habit of disclaiming the natural and foreseeable jurisprudential consequences of its pathbreaking (i.e., Constitution making) opinions. Each major step in the abridgment of the people's right to govern themselves is portrayed as extremely limited or indeed sui juris. In Romer v. Evans, 517 U. S. ___, ___ (1996) (slip op. at 11, 12), announced last month, the Court asserted that the Colorado constitutional amendment at issue was so distinctive that it "defies . . . conventional inquiry" and "confounds [the] normal process of judicial review." In United States v. Virginia, ante, at ___ n. 7 (1996), announced two days ago, the Court purported to address "specifically and only an educational opportunity recognized by the District Court and the Court of Appeals as `unique.' " And in the cases announced today, "we emphasize the limited nature of our decision." Umbehr, ante, at 17. The people should not be deceived. While the present Court sits, a major, undemocratic restructuring of our national institutions and mores is constantly in progress.

    * * *

They say hard cases make bad law. The cases before the Court today set the blood boiling, with the arrogance that they seem to display on the part of elected officials. Shall the American System of Justice let insolent, petty tyrant politicians get away with this? What one tends to forget is that we have heard only the plaintiffs' tale. These suits were dismissed before trial, so the "facts" the Court recites in its opinions assume the truth of the allegations made (or the preliminary evidence presented) by the plaintiffs. We have no idea whether the allegations are true or false--but if they are true, they are certainly highly unusual. Elected officials do not thrive on arrogance.

For every extreme case of the sort alleged here, I expect there are thousands of contracts awarded on a "favoritism" basis that no one would get excited about. The Democratic mayor gives the city's municipal bond business to what is known to be a solid Democratic law firm--taking it away from the solid Republican law firm that had the business during the previous, Republican, administration. What else is new? Or he declines to give the construction contract for the new municipal stadium to the company that opposed the bond issue for its construction, and that in fact tried to get the stadium built across the river in the next State. What else would you expect? Or he awards the cable monopoly, not to the (entirely responsible) Johnny come lately, but to the local company that has always been a "good citizen"--which means it has supported with money, and the personal efforts of its management, civic initiatives that the vast majority of the electorate favor, though some oppose. Hooray! Favoritism such as this happens all the time in American political life, and no one has ever thought that it violated--of all things--the First Amendment to the Constitution of the United States.

The Court must be living in another world. Day by day, case by case, it is busy designing a Constitution for a country I do not recognize. Depending upon which of today's cases one chooses to consider authoritative, it has either (O'Hare) thrown out vast numbers of practices that are routine in American political life in order to get rid of a few bad apples; or (Umbehr) with the same purpose in mind subjected those routine practices to endless, uncertain, case by case, balance all the factors and who knows who will win litigation.

I dissent.

Notes

1 See, e.g., Ala. Code §11-43C%70 (1989); id., §24-1-83 (1992); id., §41-16-20 (Supp. 1995); Alaska Stat. Ann. §36.30.100 (1992); Ariz. Rev. Stat. Ann. §41-2533 (1992); Ark. Code Ann. §§14-47-120, 14-47-138, 14-48-117, 14-48-129 (1987); Cal. Pub. Cont. Code Ann. §§10302, 10309, 10373, 10501, 10507.7, 20723, 20736, 20751, 20803, 20921, 21501, 21631 (West 1985 and Supp. 1996); Cal. Pub. Util. Code Ann. §131285 (West 1991); Cal. Rev. & Tax. Code Ann. §674 (West Supp. 1996); Colo. Rev. Stat. §24-103-202 (Supp. 1995); Conn. Gen. Stat. §4a-57 (Supp. 1996); Del. Code Ann., Tit. 9, §671 (1989); id., Tit. 29, §6903(a) (1991); Fla. Stat. §190.033 (Supp. 1996); id., §287.057 (1991 and Supp. 1996); Ga. Code Ann. §2-10-10 (1990); id., §§32-10-7, 32-10-68 (1991 and Supp. 1995); Haw. Rev. Stat. §103D-302 (Supp. 1995); Idaho Code §§33-1510 (1995); id., §43-2508 (Supp. 1995); id., §50-1710 (1994); id., §67-5711C (1995); id., §67-5718 (1995 and 1996 Idaho Sess. Laws, ch. 198); Ill. Comp. Stat., ch. 50, §20/20 (1993); id., ch. 65, §5/8-10-3 (1993); id., ch. 70,§§205/25, 225/25, 265/25, 280/1-24, 280/2-24, 290/26, 310/5-24, 320/1-25, 320/2-25, 325/1-24, 325/2-24, 325/3-24, 325/5-24, 325/6-24, 325/7-24, 325/8-24, 340/25, 2305/11, 2405/11, 2805/14, 2905/5-4 (1993 and Supp. 1996); Ind. Code §§2-6-1.5-2, 10-7-2-28, 4-13.6-5-2, 8-16-3.5-5.5 (Supp. 1995); Iowa Code §18.6 (1995); Kan. Stat. Ann. §49-417(a) (Supp. 1990); id., §§75-3739 to 75-3741 (1989, Supp. 1990, and 1996 Kan. Sess. Laws); Ky. Rev. Stat. Ann. §162.070 (Baldwin 1990); La. Rev. Stat. Ann. §39:1594 (West 1989); Me. Rev. Stat. Ann., Tit. 5, §§1743, 1743-A (1989); Md. Ann. Code, Art. 25, §3(l) (Supp. 1995, and 1996 Md. Laws, ch. 66); id., Art. 25A, §5(F) (Supp. 1995); Md. Nat. Res. Code Ann. §§3-103(g)(3), 8-1005(c) (Supp. 1995); Mass. Gen. Laws, ch. 149, §§44A-44M (1989 and Supp. 1996); Mich. Comp. Laws Ann. §247.661c

(West Supp. 1996); Minn. Stat. §16B.07 (1988 and Supp. 1996); Miss. Code Ann. §27-35-101 (1995); id., §§31-7-13, 37-151-17 (Supp. 1995); Mo. Rev. Stat. §§34.040.1, 34.042.1, 68.055.1 (Supp. 1996); Mont. Code Ann. §§7-3-1323, 7-5-2301, 7-5-2302, 7-5-4302, 7-14-2404 (1995); Neb. Rev. Stat. §§81-885.55, 84-1603 (1994); Nev. Rev. Stat. §332.065 (1984); N. H. Rev. Stat. Ann. §28:8 (1988); id., §186-C:22(VI) (Supp. 1995); id., §228:4 (1993); N. J. Stat. Ann. §28:1-7 (West 1981); N. M. Stat. Ann. §13-1-102 (1992); N. Y. Alt. County Govt. Law §401 (McKinney 1993); N. Y. Gen. Mun. Law §103 (McKinney 1986 and Supp. 1996); N. C. Gen. Stat. §133-10.1 (1995); id., §143-49 (1993); N. D. Cent. Code §54-44.4-05 (Supp. 1995); Ohio Rev. Code Ann. §§307.90, 511.12 (1994); id., §3381.11 (1995); Okla. Stat., Tit. 11, §24-114 (1994); id., Tit. 52, §318 (1991); id., Tit. 61, §101 (1989); Ore. Rev. Stat. §279.015 (1991); 53 Pa. Cons. Stat. §23308.1 (Supp. 1996); R. I. Gen. Laws §45-55-5 (Supp 1995); S. C. Code Ann. §11-35-1520 (Supp. 1995); S. D. Codified Laws §§5-18-2, 5-18-3 (1994); id., §5-18-9 (Supp. 1996); id., §9-42-5 (1995); id., §11-7-44 (1995); id., §13-49-16, 42-7A%5 (1991); Tenn. Code Ann. §§12-3-202, 12-3-203, 12-3-1007 (1992 and Supp. 1995); Tex. Educ. Code Ann. §51.907 (1987); Tex. Loc. Govt. Code Ann. §§252.021, 262.023, 262.027, 271.027, 375.221 (1988 and Supp. 1996); Utah Code Ann. §17A-2-1195 (1991); Vt. Stat. Ann., Tit. 29, §152(12) (1986); Va. Code Ann. §§11-41, 11-41.1 (1993); Wash. Rev. Code §§28A.160.140, 36.32.250 (Supp. 1996); W. Va. Code §§4-7-7, 5-6-7 (1994); Wis. Stat. §30.32 (1989 and Supp. 1995); id., §60.47 (1988 and Supp. 1995); Wyo. Stat. §35-2-429 (1994).

2 See, e.g., 41 U.S.C. §§ 252a(b), 403(11) (certain federal contracting laws rendered inapplicable "to a contract or subcontract that is not greater than" $100,000); Cal. Pub. Cont. Code Ann. §10507.7 (West Supp. 1996) (lowest responsible bidder requirement for certain goods and materials only applicable to "contracts involving an [annual] expenditure of more than fifty thousand dollars"); Ill. Comp. Stat., ch. 50, §20/20 (1993) (lowest responsible bidder requirement for certain construction contracts not applicable to contracts for more than $5,000); N. Y. Gen. Mun. Law §103.1 (McKinney Supp. 1996) (not covering public work contracts for $20,000 or less or purchase contracts for $10,000 or less); S. D. Codified Laws §5-18-3 (Supp. 1996) (requiring competitive bidding process for certain public improvement contracts "involv[ing] the expenditure of twenty five thousand dollars or more"); Texas Local Govt. Code Ann. §262.023(a) (Supp. 1996) (applying only to "a contract that will require an expenditure exceeding $15,000").

3 See, e. g., Idaho Code §33-1510 (1995); N. J. Stat. Ann. §28:1-7 (1981); Ohio Rev. Code Ann. §511.12 (Supp. 1995); Okla. Stat., Tit. 52, §318 (1991); Utah Code Ann. §17A-2-1195 (1991).

4 See, e.g., Del. Code Ann., Tit. 29, §6903(a)(2) (1991); Fla. Stat. §287.057(3)(a) (Supp. 1996); Minn. Stat. §16B.08(6) (1988); N. H. Rev. Stat. Ann. §228:4(I)(e) (1993); Tenn. Code Ann. §§12-3-202(3), 12-3-206 (1992).

5 O'Hare makes a brief attempt to minimize the seriousness of the litigation concern, pointing out that "[t]he amicus brief filed on behalf of respondents' position represents that in the six years since our opinion in [Rutan] . . . only 18 suits alleging First

Amendment violations in employment decisions have been filed against Illinois state officials." Ante, at 11. In fact the brief said "at least eighteen cases," Brief for Illinois State Officials as Amici Curiae, at 3 (emphasis added), and that includes only suits against state officials, and not those against the officials of Illinois' 102 counties or its even more numerous municipalities. Those statistics pertain to employment suits, moreover--and as I have discussed, the contracting suits will be much more numerous.

O'Hare also says that "we have found no reported case in the Tenth Circuit involving a First Amendment patronage claim by an independent contractor in the six years since its Court of Appeals first recognized such claims, see Abercrombie v. Catoosa, 896 F. 2d 1228 (1990)." O'Hare, ante, at 11-12. With respect, Abercrombie (which discussed this issue in two short paragraphs) was such an obscure case that even the District Court in Umbehr, located in the Tenth Circuit, did not cite it, though it discussed cases in other jurisdictions. Umbehr v. McClure, 840 F. Supp. 837 (Kan. 1993). And when the Tenth Circuit reversed the District Court, it did not do so on the basis of Abercrombie-- which, it noted, had "simply assumed that an independent contractor could assert a First Amendment retaliation claim" and had given "little reasoning" to the matter but merely so "suggested, without analysis." 44 F. 3d 876, 880 (1995) (emphasis added). Abercrombie was, in short, such a muffled clarion that even the courts did not hear it, much less the public at large.

6 See, e.g., Cal. Pub. Cont. Code Ann. §§10302, 10507.7, 20803 (West 1985 and Supp. 1996); Ill. Comp. Stat., ch. 50, §§20/20, 25/3; id., ch. 70, §§15/8, 15/9, 205/25, 220/1-24, 220/2-24 (1993); N. Y. Gen. Mun. Law §103.1 (McKinney Supp. 1996).

7 As the dissenters in Rutan v. Republican Party of Ill., 497 U.S. 62 (1990), agreed, "it greatly exaggerates [the constraints entailed by patronage] to call them `coercion' at all, since we generally make a distinction between inducement and compulsion. The public official offered a bribe is not `coerced' to violate the law, and the private citizen offered a patronage job is not `coerced' to work for the party." Id., at 109-110 (Scalia, J., dissenting).

Justice Scalia's dissent in O'Gilvie v. US (Dec 10, 1996)

Justice Scalia, with whom Justice O'Connor and Justice Thomas join, dissenting.

Section 104(a)(2), as it stood at the time relevant to these cases, provided an exclusion from income for "any damages received . . . on account of personal injuries or sickness." 26 U. S. C. § 104(a)(2) (1988 ed.). The Court is of the view that this phrase, in isolation, is just as susceptible of a meaning that includes only compensatory damages as it is of a broader meaning that includes punitive damages as well. Ante, at 82-83. I do not agree. The Court greatly understates the connection between an award of punitive damages and the personal injury complained of, describing it as nothing more than "but-for" causality, ante, at 82. It seems to me that the personal injury is as proximate a cause of the punitive damages as it is of the compensatory damages; in both cases it is the reason the damages are awarded. That is why punitive damages are called damages. To be sure, punitive damages require intentional, blameworthy conduct, which can be said to be a coequal reason they are awarded. But negligent (or intentional) conduct occupies the same role of coequal causality with regard to compensatory damages. Both types of damages are "received on account of" the personal injury.

The nub of the matter, it seems to me, is this: If one were to be asked, by a lawyer from another legal system, "What damages can be received on account of personal injuries in the United States?" surely the correct answer would be "Compensatory damages and punitive damages—the former to compensate for the inflicting of the personal injuries, and the latter to punish for the inflicting of them." If, as the Court asserts, the phrase "damages received on account of personal injuries" can be used to refer only to the former category, that is only because people sometimes can be imprecise. The notion that Congress carefully and precisely used the phrase "damages received on account of personal injuries" to segregate out compensatory damages seems to me entirely fanciful. That is neither the exact nor the ordinary meaning of the phrase, and hence not the one that the statute should be understood to intend.

What I think to be the fair meaning of the phrase in isolation becomes even clearer when the phrase is considered in its statutory context. The Court proceeds too quickly from its erroneous premise of ambiguity to analysis of the history and policy behind § 104(a)(2). Ante, at 84-87. Ambiguity in isolation, even if it existed, would not end the textual inquiry. Statutory construction, we have said, is a "holistic endeavor." United Sav. Assn. of Tex. v. Timbers of Inwood Forest Associates, Ltd., 484 U. S. 365, 371 (1988). "A provision that may seem ambiguous in isolation is often clarified by the remainder of the statutory scheme." Ibid.

Section 104(a)(2) appears immediately after another provision, § 104(a)(1), which parallels § 104(a)(2) in several respects but does not use the critical phrase "on account of":

"(a) [G]ross income does not include— "(1) amounts received under workmen's compensation acts as compensation for personal injuries or sickness; "(2) the amount of any damages received . . . on account of personal injuries or sickness." (Emphasis added.)

Although § 104(a)(1) excludes amounts received "as compensation for" personal injuries or sickness, while § 104(a)(2) excludes amounts received "on account of" personal injuries or sickness, the Court reads the two phrases to mean precisely the same thing. That is not sound textual interpretation. "[W]hen the legislature uses certain language in one part of the statute and different language in another, the court assumes different meanings were intended." 2A N. Singer, Sutherland on Statutory Construction § 46.07 (5th ed. 1992 and Supp. 1996). See, e. g., Russello v. United States, 464 U. S. 16, 23 (1983). This principle of construction has its limits, of course: Use of different terminology in differing contexts might have little significance. But here the contrasting phrases appear in adjoining provisions that address precisely the same subject matter and that even have identical grammatical structure.

The contrast between the two usages is even more striking in the original statute that enacted them. The Revenue Act of 1918 combined subsections (a)(1) and (a)(2) of § 104, together with (a)(3) (which provides an exclusion from income for amounts received through accident or health insurance for personal injuries or sickness), into a single subsection, which provided:

"`Gross income' . . . [d]oes not include . . . :

"(6) Amounts received, through accident or health insurance or under workmen's compensation acts, as compensation for personal injuries or sickness, plus the amount of any damages received . . . on account of such injuries or sickness." § 213(b)(6) of the Revenue Act of 1918, 40 Stat. 1065-1066 (emphasis added).

The contrast between the first exclusion and the second could not be more clear. Had Congress intended the latter provision to cover only damages received "as compensation for" personal injuries or sickness, it could have written "amounts received, through accident or health insurance, under workmen's compensation acts, or in damages, as compensation for personal injuries or sickness." Instead, it tacked on an additional phrase "plus the amount of[, etc.]" with no apparent purpose except to make clear that not only compensatory damages were covered by the exclusion.

The Court maintains, however, that the Government's reading of § 104(a)(2) is "more faithful to [its] history." Ante, at 84. The "history" to which the Court refers is not statutory history of the sort just discussed—prior enactments approved by earlier Congresses and revised or amended by later ones to produce the current text. Indeed, it is not "history" from within even a small portion of Congress, since the House Committee Report the Court cites, standing by itself, is uninformative, saying only that "[u]nder the present law it is doubtful whether . . . damages received on account of [personal] injuries or sickness are required to be included in gross income." H. R. Rep. No. 767, 65th Cong., 2d Sess., 9-10 (1918). The Court makes this snippet of legislative history relevant by citing as pertinent an antecedent Treasury Department decision, which concludes on the basis of recent judicial decisions that amounts received from prosecution or compromise of a personal-injury suit are not taxable because they are a return of capital. Ante, at 85 (citing T. D. 2747, 20 Treas. Dec. Int. Rev. 457 (1918)). One might expect the Court to conclude from this that the Members of Congress (on the unrealistic assumption that they knew about the Executive Branch opinion) meant the statutory language to cover only return of capital, the source of the "doubt" to which the Committee Report referred. But of course the Court cannot draw that logical conclusion, since even if it is applied only to compensatory damages the statute obviously and undeniably covers more than mere return of "human capital," namely, reimbursement for lost income, which would be a large proportion (indeed perhaps the majority) of any damages award. The Court concedes this is so, but asserts that this inconsistency is not enough "to support cutting the statute totally free from its original moorings," ante, at 86, by which I assume it means the Treasury Decision, however erroneous it might have been as to the "capital" nature of compensatory damages. But the Treasury Decision was no more explicitly limited to compensatory damages than is the statute before us. It exempted from taxation "an amount received by an individual as the result of a suit or compromise for personal injuries." T. D. 2747, supra, at 457. The Court's entire thesis of taxability rests upon the proposition that this Treasury Decision, which overlooked the obvious fact that "an amount received . . . as the result of a suit or compromise for personal injuries" almost always includes compensation for lost future income, did not overlook the obvious fact that such an amount sometimes includes "smart money."

So, to trace the Court's reasoning: The statute must exclude punitive damages because the Committee Report must have had in mind a 1918 Treasury Decision, whose text no more supports exclusion of punitive damages than does the text of the statute itself, but which must have meant to exclude punitive damages since it was based on the "return-ofcapital" theory, though, inconsistently with that theory, it did not exclude the much more common category of compensation for lost income. Congress supposedly knew all of this, and a reasonably diligent lawyer could figure it out by mistrusting the inclusive language of the statute, consulting the Committee Report, surmising that the Treasury Decision of 1918 underlay that Report, mistrusting the inclusive language of the Treasury Decision, and discerning that Treasury could have overlooked lost-income compensatories, but could not have overlooked punitives. I think not. The sure and proper guide, it seems to me, is the language of the statute, inclusive by nature and doubly inclusive by contrast with surrounding provisions.

The Court poses the question, ante, at 86, "why Congress might have wanted the exclusion [in § 104(a)(2)] to have covered . . .punitive damages." If an answer is needed (and the text being as clear as it is, I think it is not), surely it suffices to surmise that Congress was following the Treasury Decision, which had inadvertently embraced punitive damages just as it had inadvertently embraced future-income compensatory damages. Or if some reason free of human error must be found, I see nothing wrong with what the Court itself suggests but rejects out of hand: Excluding punitive as well as compensatory damages from gross income "avoids such administrative problems as separating punitive from compensatory portions of a global settlement." Ante, at 88. How substantial that particular problem is is suggested by the statistics which show that 73 percent of tort cases in state court are disposed of by settlement, and between 92 and 99 percent of tort cases in federal court are disposed of by either settlement or some other means (such as summary judgment) prior to trial. See B. Ostrom & N. Kauder, Examining the Work of State Courts, 1994, p. 34 (1996); Administrative Office of the United States Courts, L. Mecham, Judicial Business of the United States Courts: 1995 Report of the Director 162-164. What is at issue, of course, is not just imposing on the parties the necessity of allocating the settlement between compensatory and punitive damages (with the concomitant suggestion of intentional wrongdoing that any allocation to punitive damages entails), but also imposing on the Internal Revenue Service the necessity of reviewing that allocation, since there would always be strong incentive to inflate the tax-free compensatory portion. The Court's only response to the suggestion that this is an adequate reason (if one is required) for including punitive damages in the exemption is that "[t]he administrative problem of distinguishing punitive from compensatory elements is likely to be less serious than, say, distinguishing among the compensatory elements of a settlement." Ante, at 88. Perhaps so; and it may also be more simple than splitting the atom; but that in no way refutes the point that it is complicated enough to explain the inclusion of punitive damages in an exemption that has already abandoned the purity of a "return-of-capital" rationale.

The remaining argument offered by the Court is that our decision in Commissioner v. Schleier, 515 U. S. 323 (1995), came "close to resolving"—in the Government's favor—the question whether § 104(a)(2) permits the exclusion of punitive damages. Ante, at 83. I disagree. In Schleier we were faced with the question whether backpay and liquidated damages under the Age Discrimination in Employment Act of 1967 (ADEA) were "damages received . . . on account of personal injuries or sickness" for purposes of § 104(a)(2)'s exclusion. As the dissent accurately observed, 515 U. S., at 342 (opinion of O'Connor, J.),"the key to the Court's analysis" was the determination that an ADEA cause of action did not necessarily entail "personal injury or sickness," so that the damages awarded for that cause of action could hardly be awarded "on account of personal injuries or sickness." See id., at 330. In the case at hand, we said, "respondent's unlawful termination may have caused some psychological or `personal' injury comparable to the intangible pain and suffering caused by an automobile accident," but "it is clear that no part of respondent's recovery of back wages is attributable to that injury." Ibid. The respondent countered that at least "the liquidated damages portion of his settlement" could be linked to that psychological injury. Id., at 331. And it was in response to that argument that we made the statement which the Court seeks to press into service for today's opinion. ADEA liquidated damages, we said, were punitive in nature, rather than compensatory. Id., at 331-332, and n. 5.

The Court recites this statement as though the point of it was that punitive damages could not be received "on account of" personal injuries, whereas in fact the point was quite different: Since the damages were punishment for the conduct that gave rise to the (non-personal-injury) cause of action, they could not be "linked to" the incidental psychological injury. In the present cases, of course, there is no question that a personal injury occurred and that this personal injury is what entitled petitioners to compensatory and punitive damages. We neither decided nor intimated in Schleier whether punitive damages that are indisputably "linked to" personal injuries or sickness are received "on account of" such injuries or sickness. Indeed, it would have been odd for us to resolve that question (or even come "close to resolving" it) without any discussion of the numerous considerations of text, history, and policy highlighted by today's opinion. If one were to search our opinions for a dictum bearing upon the present issue, much closer is the statement in United States v. Burke, 504 U. S. 229 (1992), that a statute confers "tort or tort type rights" (qualifying a plaintiff's recovery for the § 104(a)(2) exemption) if it entitles the plaintiff to "a jury trial at which `both equitable and legal relief, including compensatory and, under certain circumstances, punitive damages' may be awarded." Id., at 240 (quoting Johnson v. Railway Express Agency, Inc., 421 U. S. 454, 460 (1975)).

But all of this is really by the way. Because the statutory text unambiguously covers punitive damages that are awarded on account of personal injuries, I conclude that petitioners were entitled to deduct the amounts at issue here. This makes it unnecessary for me to reach the question, discussed ante, at 90-92, whether the Government's refund action against the O'Gilvie children was commenced within the 2-year period specified by 26 U. S. C. § 6532(b). I note, however, that the Court's resolution of these cases also does not demand that this issue be addressed, except to the extent of rejecting the proposition that the statutory period begins to run with the mailing of a refund check. So long as that is not the trigger, there is no need to decide whether the proper trigger is receipt of the check or some later event, such as the check's clearance.

For the reasons stated, I respectfully dissent from the judgment of the Court.

Justice Scalia's concurrence and dissent in Ingalls Shipbuilding, Inc. v. Director, Office of Workers' Compensation (Feb 18, 1997)

Justice Scalia, with whom Justice Thomas joins, concurring in part and dissenting in part.

Today's opinion concludes, on the basis of Federal Rule of Appellate Procedure 15(a), that the Director of the Office of Workers' Compensation Programs, a sub agency within the Department of Labor, is a proper respondent in the courts of appeals when review is sought of an order of the Benefits Review Board (BRB), an independent adjudicatory body within that Department. This conclusion is at odds with the plain language of the Rule, and produces a bizarre arrangement that will have troublesome consequences for both agencies and private parties. I respectfully dissent from the Court's judgment on this issue.

Federal Rule of Appellate Procedure 15(a) provides:

"Review of an order of an administrative agency, board, commission, or officer (hereinafter, the term `agency' will include agency, board, commission, or officer) must be obtained by filing [a petition for review]. . . . In each case the agency must be named respondent."

It is clear (and the Court does not say otherwise) that despite the Rule's shorthand use of "agency" in the second sentence, the entity that must be named respondent is the one whose order is under review, whether it is an agency, board, commission, or officer. Thus, in determining whether the Rule authorizes the Director, as representative of the Department of Labor, to appear as a respondent in the courts of appeals, the central question is whether the order under review is that of the Department. The answer to that question is obviously and unavoidably no.

To begin with, the very statute that provides for the judicial review at issue indicates that the order under review is that of the BRB:

"Any person adversely affected or aggrieved by a final order of the Board may obtain a review of that order in the United States court of appeals for the circuit in which the injury occurred . . . . Upon such filing, the court shall have jurisdiction of the proceeding and shall have the power to give a decree affirming, modifying, or setting aside, in whole or in part, the order of the Board . . . ." 44 Stat. 1436-1437, as amended, 33 U.S.C. § 921(c) (emphasis added).

The governing statute elsewhere specifies that the Board is the statutorily created entity responsible for "hear[ing] and determin[ing] appeals . . . taken by any party in interest from decisions with respect to claims of employees under" the Longshore and Harbor Workers' Compensation Act (LHWCA). §921(b)(3). The Board's disposition of those appeals is not subject to review by the Secretary of Labor in his capacity as head of the Department, but must be appealed to the courts pursuant to the review provision quoted above.

Despite the clarity of the statute, the Court concludes that it is "in reality" an order of the Department that is under review in the courts of appeals. Ante, at 18-21. It offers two arguments in support of this proposition. First, it says--relying upon a regulation promulgated by the Secretary, 20 CFR § 801.1 (1996), and upon a statement in the House Report on the LHWCA Amendments of 1972, 86 Stat. 1251--that the Board is "a subdivision of the Department of Labor." Ante, at 20. But of course neither a Secretary's regulation nor a House Committee's report has the power to transform a statutory entity into something it is not. While the Board may be a "subdivision" of the Department of Labor--and thereby subject to the Secretary's authority--for certain purposes, see, e.g., 33 U.S.C. § 921(b)(1) (Secretary appoints Board members); §939(a) ("Except as otherwise specifically provided, the Secretary shall administer the provisions of" the LHWCA); 20 CFR § 802.101 et seq. (1996) (regulations of Secretary establishing rules of procedure for Board), the Court expressly acknowledges that the Board is not a subdivision in the sense that the Secretary, as head of the Department, can direct or override its decisions. Ante, at 19-20. But that sense is the one relevant to the question whether an order of the Board is "in reality" an order of the Department, ante, at 19. Insofar as vindication of the order is concerned, there is no "necessary identity of interest" between the Board and the Department or the Director as its chosen delegate. Shahady v. Atlas Tile & Marble Co., 673 F. 2d 479, 485 (CADC 1982) (emphasis deleted). Indeed, the Department through its delegate may well be hoping to see the Board's order overturned in the court of appeals. See, e.g., Parker v. Director, Office of Workers' Compensation Programs, 75 F. 3d 929, 932-934, 935, n. 7 (CA4), cert. denied, 519 U. S. ___ (1996); Simpson v. Director, Office of Workers' Compensation Programs, 681 F. 2d 81, 82 (CA1 1982), cert. denied sub nom. Bath Iron Works Corp. v. Director, Office of Workers' Compensation Programs, 459 U.S. 1127 (1983). The Court's attribution of the Board's order to the Department contradicts our recognition, only two Terms ago, that it is "quite simply contrary to the whole structure" of the LHWCA to view the Board's adjudicatory functions as the province of (implicitly) the Department as overarching agency and (explicitly) the Director as its delegate. Director, Office of Workers' Compensation Programs v. Newport News

Shipbuilding & Dry Dock Co., 514 U.S. 122, ____ (1995) (slip op., at 12).

The second argument offered in support of the view that the Director is a proper respondent when review is sought of an order of the Board is that (1) Rule 15(a) requires the naming of someone representing the agency, and (2) the Director is certainly a more sensible candidate than the Board. Ante, at 18, 19. The second part of this analysis, the faute de mieux point, is questionable: The Board could readily develop a staff to defend its judgments, and it is hard to imagine a worse defender than an entity that is free to disagree (and often does disagree) with the order under review. Cf. Pittston Stevedoring Corp. v. Dellaventura, 544 F. 2d 35, 42, n. 5 (CA2 1976) (Friendly, J.) (suggesting that Board rather than Director is proper respondent), aff'd on other grounds sub nom. Northeast Marine Terminal Co. v. Caputo, 432 U.S. 249 (1977). But the real flaw in the reasoning is the first step, which assumes that when Rule 15(a) states that the "agency, board, commission, or officer" whose order is under review "must be named respondent," it means to confer upon such entities (or, in the Court's view, their parent agencies) a party status and litigating power they would not otherwise possess--so that a purely adjudicatory body with no policymaking responsibility, which would otherwise not be a party, is suddenly free to step in (perhaps through its parent) to "defend" its judgment. That is not only an unlikely function for the Federal Rules of Appellate Procedure to perform (and thus an unlikely reading of the language of Rule 15(a), which, contrary to the Court's suggestion, see ante, at 17, is far from unambiguous on this point); it is an impermissible function, since it may give appellate courts jurisdiction over a dispute (if it can be called a dispute) that would otherwise be beyond their ken, namely, one in which the victorious private party to the lower court adjudication has no interest in defending it, and only the adjudicator itself (or its parent) appears. That extension of litigation would violate Rule 1(b), which provides that the Federal Rules of Appellate Procedure "shall not be construed to extend or limit the jurisdiction of the courts of appeals as established by law." Fed. Rule App. Proc. 1(b). In the present context, for example, if the victorious employer against whom the employee takes an appeal chooses not to contest it, or ceases to exist while the appeal is pending, the agency's status as a party respondent would permit continued litigation of the appeal. The concern with extending the jurisdiction of the courts of appeals through participation of the Director is more than theoretical; he has in the past sought to continue litigation of claims (at least at the Board level) that the employee and employer preferred not to pursue. E.g., Ingalls Shipbuilding Div., Litton Systems, Inc. v. White, 681 F. 2d 275, 277 (CA5 1982), overruled on other grounds, Newpark Shipbuilding & Repair, Inc. v. Roundtree, 723 F. 2d 399, 407 (CA5 1984).

The Court's response to all of this is that concerns about extension of jurisdiction are "not . . . controlling" in this case, since both private parties are participating. Ante, at 17-18. But of course when we interpret a rule of general application, such as Rule 15(a), we are bound to take into account not only the ramifications of our interpretation for the case before us, but also the ramifications for future cases. Indeed, a different approach would make the meaning we ascribe to the general rule turn on the specifics of the case that first raises the issue. For good reason, that is not our practice. Because interpreting Rule 15(a) to make the Director a party would sometimes extend the jurisdiction of the courts of appeals, and because Rule 1(b) requires that the Rule be construed to avoid that result, the Rule should not be given the meaning that today's opinion accords it.

Invoking Rule 15(a) (and, of course, ignoring the identity of the body that issued the order) is the only imaginable basis for concluding that the Director is always a proper respondent in the courts of appeals, regardless of the outcome below. There is, however, a respectable argument in support of his respondent status when he participates before the Board and prevails. That parties in whose favor the judgment under review runs are ordinarily proper respondents or appellees in the courts of appeals is so obvious that the Federal Rules of Appellate Procedure--which, contrary to the Court's belief, purport to prescribe which parties must be named, not who is a party--do not bother to provide for the naming of such individuals. (That is to say, there is no analogue to Rule 15(a) for them.)

But the Director--even assuming he is entitled to participate as a party before the Board, compare 20 CFR § 802.201(a)(1) (1996) (allowing participation) with Newport News, supra, at ____ (slip op., at 3-4) ("[T]he [LHWCA] does not by its terms . . . grant [the Director] authority to prosecute appeals to the Board")--is not an ordinary prevailing party. An ordinary party in that position would, if he had lost below, have the right to prosecute an appeal. The Director, in contrast, has no such power. Newport News, supra. This inability to appeal reflects the limited character of the interests of the Director affected by the Board's judgment, which include neither his exposure to financial or other liability, nor nullification of one of his own orders, but only legal or policy disagreement with the Board's decision. [n.*] It would be an odd and novel result if the Director, in cases of this nature, could be named as a respondent if he was on the prevailing side below, but could not initiate an appeal if he was on the losing side. I would not reach such a result unless the statute left no choice, which is not the case here.

Finally, I may observe that today's game has really not been worth the candle. The strange and countertextual arrangement that the Court has constructed might perhaps be excused if excluding the Director from party status would do some substantial harm to the scheme of the LHWCA. But it does not. His "significant role" in administering the Act, ante, at 13, does not mean that his participation in proceedings before the courts of appeals is essential. As we emphasized in Newport News, limits on the Director's ability to participate in the judicial review process are of relatively minor consequence because his "power to resolve legal ambiguities in the statute" may always be exercised through his rulemaking authority. 514 U. S., at ____ (slip op., at 13). In addition, the Director is guaranteed the right to file an amicus brief in the court of appeals, with or without the consent of the parties. Fed. Rule App. Proc. 29.

* * *

I think it plain that the intent of Rule 15(a) is not to restructure the Executive Branch, or to convert Article I courts (or their parent agencies) into litigating arms, but rather simply to require that those agencies entitled to party status--i.e., those that would be entitled to intervene in the appeal under the criteria set forth in Rule 15(d)--must be named as respondents. By making the Rule much more than that, and then flatly misidentifying, through sheer will power, the agency whose "order" is at issue, the Court creates a zany system in which an Executive officer from whom the Board has carefully been made independent, and one who will often disagree with--and perhaps even have argued against--the Board's judgment, will be charged with "defending" that judgment in the court of appeals, where, once arrived, he is free instead to maintain an independent attack upon the judgment, even though, as we held in Newport News, he would not have been able to launch that attack by appealing on his own. Today's disposition regarding the Director's status is at odds with the relevant provisions of law and creates the potential for disruption of orderly litigation and settlement of disputes between employers and employees. I respectfully dissent from that portion of the judgment.

Notes

* In my view the Director is akin to an ordinary respondent or appellee when he prevails before the Board in his capacity as administrator of the LHWCA special fund established by 33 U.S.C. § 944. In Newport News, we left open the question whether the Director has standing to appeal an adverse ruling of the Board when he participates in that capacity. 514 U. S., at ___, n. 1 (slip op., at 3, n. 1).

Justice Scalia's dissent in Camps Newfound/Owatonna, Inc. v. Town of Harrison, Maine (May 19, 1997)

Justice SCALIA, with whom The Chief Justice, Justice THOMAS and Justice GINSBURG join, dissenting.

The Court's negative-commerce-clause jurisprudence has drifted far from its moorings. Originally designed to create a national market for commercial activity, it is today invoked to prevent a State from giving a tax break to charities that benefit the State's inhabitants. In my view, Maine's tax exemption, which excuses from taxation only that property used to relieve the State of its burden of caring for its residents, survives even our most demanding commerce-clause scrutiny.

* We have often said that the purpose of our negative commerce-clause jurisprudence is to create a national market. As Justice Jackson once observed, the "vision of the Founders" was "that every farmer and every craftsman shall be encouraged to produce by the certainty that he will have free access to every market in the Nation, that no home embargoes will withhold his exports, and no foreign state will by customs duties or regulations exclude them." H.P. Hood & Sons, Inc. v. Du Mond, 336 U.S. 525, 539, 69 S.Ct. 657, 665, 93 L.Ed. 865 (1949). In our zeal to advance this policy, however, we must take care not to overstep our mandate, for the Commerce Clause was not intended "to cut the States off from legislating on all subjects relating to the health, life, and safety of their citizens, though the legislation might indirectly affect the commerce of the country." Huron Portland Cement Co. v. Detroit, 362 U.S. 440, 443-444, 80 S.Ct. 813, 816, 4 L.Ed.2d 852 (1960).

Our cases have struggled (to put it nicely) to develop a set of rules by which we may preserve a national market without needlessly intruding upon the States' police powers, each exercise of which no doubt has some effect on the commerce of the Nation. See Oklahoma Tax Comm'n v. Jefferson Lines, Inc., 514 U.S. 175, 180-183, 115 S.Ct. 1331, 1335-1336, 131 L.Ed.2d 261 (1995). The rules that we currently use can be simply stated, if not simply applied: Where a State law facially discriminates against interstate commerce, we observe what has sometimes been referred to as a "virtually per se rule of invalidity;" where, on the other hand, a state law is nondiscriminatory, but nonetheless adversely affects interstate commerce, we employ a deferential "balancing test," under which the law will be sustained unless "the burden imposed on interstate commerce is clearly excessive in relation to the putative local benefits," Pike v. Bruce Church, Inc., 397 U.S. 137, 142, 90 S.Ct. 844, 847, 25 L.Ed.2d 174 (1970). See Oregon Waste Systems, Inc. v. Department of Environmental Quality of Ore., 511 U.S. 93, 99, 114 S.Ct. 1345, 1349-1350, 128 L.Ed.2d 13 (1994).

While the "virtually per se rule of invalidity" entails application of the "strictest scrutiny," Hughes v. Oklahoma, 441 U.S. 322, 337, 99 S.Ct. 1727, 1736-1737, 60 L.Ed.2d 250 (1979), it does not necessarily result in the invalidation of facially discriminatory State legislation, see, e.g., Maine v. Taylor, 477 U.S. 131, 106 S.Ct. 2440, 91 L.Ed.2d 110 (1986) (upholding absolute ban on the importation of baitfish into Maine), for "what may appear to be a "discriminatory' provision in the constitutionally prohibited sense-that is, a protectionist enactment-may on closer analysis not be so," New Energy Co. of Ind. v. Limbach, 486 U.S. 269, 278, 108 S.Ct. 1803, 1810, 100 L.Ed.2d 302 (1988). Thus, even a statute that erects an absolute barrier to the movement of goods across state lines will be upheld if "the discrimination is demonstrably justified by a valid factor unrelated to economic protectionism," id., at 274, 108 S.Ct., at 1808, or to put a finer point on it, if the State law "advances a legitimate local purpose that cannot be adequately served by reasonable nondiscriminatory alternatives," id., at 278, 108 S.Ct., at 1810.

In addition to laws that employ suspect means as a necessary expedient to the advancement of legitimate State ends, we have also preserved from judicial invalidation laws that confer advantages upon the State's residents but do so without regulating interstate commerce. We have therefore excepted the State from scrutiny when it participates in markets rather than regulates them-by selling cement, for example, see Reeves, Inc. v. Stake, 447 U.S. 429, 100 S.Ct. 2271, 65 L.Ed.2d 244 (1980), or purchasing auto hulks, see Hughes v. Alexandria Scrap Corp., 426 U.S. 794, 96 S.Ct. 2488, 49 L.Ed.2d 220 (1976), or hiring contractors, see White v. Massachusetts Council of Construction Employers, 460 U.S. 204, 103 S.Ct. 1042, 75 L.Ed.2d 1 (1983). Likewise, we have said that direct subsidies to domestic industry do not run afoul of the Commerce Clause. See New Energy Co., 486 U.S., at 278, 108 S.Ct., at 1810. In sum, we have declared that " the

Commerce Clause does not prohibit all state action designed to give its residents an advantage in the marketplace, but only action of that description in connection with the State's regulation of interstate commerce. " Ibid. (emphasis in original).

II

In applying the foregoing principles to the case before us, it is of course important to understand the precise scope of the exemption created by Me.Rev.Stat. Ann., Tit. 36, §652(1)(A) (Supp.1996-1997). The Court's analysis suffers from the misapprehension that §652(1)(A) "sweeps to cover broad swathes of the nonprofit sector," ante, at __, including nonprofit corporations engaged in quintessentially commercial activities. That is not so. A review of Maine law demonstrates that the provision at issue here is a narrow tax exemption, designed merely to compensate or subsidize those organizations that contribute to the public fisc by dispensing public benefits the State might otherwise provide.

Although Maine allows nonprofit corporations to be organized "for any lawful purpose," Me.Rev.Stat. Ann., Tit. 13-B, §201 (1981 and Supp.1996-1997), the exemption supplied by §652(1)(A) does not extend to all nonprofit organizations, but only to those "benevolent and charitable institutions," §652(1)(A), which are "organized and conducted exclusively for benevolent and charitable purposes," §652(1)(C)(1) (emphasis added), and only to those parcels of real property and items of personal property that are used "solely," §652(1)(A), "to further the organization's charitable purposes," Poland v. Poland Spring Health Institute, Inc., 649 A.2d 1098, 1100 (Me.1994). The Maine Supreme Judicial Court has defined the statutory term "benevolent and charitable institutions" to include only those nonprofits that dispense "charity," which is in turn defined to include only those acts which are

""for the benefit of an indefinite number of persons, either by bringing their minds or hearts under the influence of education or religion, by relieving their bodies from disease, suffering, or constraint, by assisting them to establish themselves in life, or by erecting or maintaining public buildings or works or otherwise lessening the burdens of government. '" Lewiston v. Marcotte Congregate Housing, Inc., 673 A.2d 209, 211 (1996) (emphasis added).

Moreover, the Maine Supreme Judicial Court has further limited the §652(1)(A) exemption by insisting that the party claiming its benefit "bring its claim unmistakably within the spirit and intent of the act creating the exemption," ibid. (internal quotation marks omitted), and by proclaiming that the spirit and intent of §652(1)(A) is to compensate charitable organizations for their contribution to the public fisc. As the Court has explained:

""Any institution which by its charitable activities relieves the government of part of its burden is conferring a pecuniary benefit upon the body politic, and in receiving exemption from taxation it is merely being given a "quid pro quo" for its services in providing something which otherwise the government would have to provide.'" Episcopal Camp Foundation, Inc. v. Hope, 666 A.2d 108, 110 (1995) (quoting Young Men's Christian

Assn. of Germantown v. Philadelphia, 323 Pa. 401, 413, 187 A. 204, 210 (1936)).

Thus, §652(1)(A) exemptions have been denied to organizations that do not provide substantial public benefits, as defined by reference to the state public policy. In one case, for example, an organization devoted to maintaining a wildlife sanctuary was denied exemption on the ground that the preserve's prohibition on deer hunting conflicted with state policy on game management, so that the preserve could not be deemed to provide a public benefit. See Holbrook Island Sanctuary v. Inhabitants of Town of Brooksville, 161 Me. 476, 214 A.2d 660 (1965). Even churches have been denied exemptions, see Pentecostal Assembly of Bangor v. Maidlow, 414 A.2d 891, 893-894 (Me.1980) ("religious purposes are not to be equated with benevolent and charitable purposes").

The Maine Supreme Judicial Court has adhered rigorously to the requirement that the exempt property be used "solely" for charitable purposes. Even when there is no question that the organization owning the property is devoted exclusively to charitable purposes, the entire exemption will be forfeited if even a small fraction of the property is not used in furtherance of those purposes. See Lewiston, supra, at 212-213 (denying exemption to a building 18 percent of which was leased at market rates); Nature Conservancy of Pine Tree State, Inc. v. Bristol, 385 A.2d 39, 43 (Me.1978) (denying exemption to a nature preserve on which the grantors had reserved rights-of-way).

That §652(1)(A) serves to compensate private charities for helping to relieve the State of its burden of caring for its residents should not be obscured by the fact that this particular case involves a summer camp rather than a more traditional form of social service. The statute that the Court strikes down does not speak of "camps" at all, but rather lists as examples of "benevolent and charitable institutions" nonprofit nursing homes, boarding homes, community mental health service facilities and child care centers, see §652(1)(A). Some summer camps fall within the exemption under a 1933 decision of the Supreme Judicial Court which applied it to a tuition-free camp for indigent children, see Camp Emoh Associates v. Inhabitants of Lyman, 132 Me. 67, 166 A. 59, 60, and under a recent 4-to-3 decision which relied heavily on the fact that the camp at issue provided "moral instruction" and training in "social living and civic responsibility," and was not only "nonprofit" but furnished its camping services below cost, see Episcopal Camp Foundation, supra, at 109, 111. What is at issue in this case is not whether a summer camp can properly be regarded as relieving the State of social costs, but rather whether, assuming it can, a distinction between charities serving mainly residents and charities operated principally for the benefit of nonresidents is constitutional. 1

III

I turn next to the validity of this focused tax exemption-applicable only to property used solely for charitable purposes by organizations devoted exclusively to charity-under the negative-commerce-clause principles discussed earlier. The Court readily concludes that, by limiting the class of eligible property to that which is used "principally for the benefit of persons who are Maine residents," the statute "facially discriminates" against interstate commerce. That seems to me not necessarily true. Disparate treatment constitutes discrimination only if the objects of the disparate treatment are, for the relevant purposes, similarly situated. See General Motors Corp. v. Tracy, ante, at _____, 117 S.Ct., at 823-824. And for purposes of entitlement to a tax subsidy from the State, it is certainly reasonable to think that property gratuitously devoted to relieving the State of some of its welfare burden is not similarly situated to property used "principally for the benefit of persons who are not residents of the State," §652(1)(A). As we have seen, the theory underlying the exemption is that it is a quid pro quo for uncompensated expenditures that lessen the State's burden of providing assistance to its residents.

The Court seeks to establish "facial discrimination" by showing that the effect of treating disparate property disparately is to produce higher costs for those users of the property who come from out of State. But that could be regarded as an indirect effect upon interstate commerce produced by a tax scheme that is not facially discriminatory, which means that the proper mode of analysis would be the more lenient "balancing" standard discussed above. We follow precisely this mode of analysis in Tracy, upholding an Ohio law that provides preferential tax treatment to domestic public utilities. Such entities, we conclude, are not "similarly situated" to other fuel distributors; their insulation from out-of-state competition does not violate the negative Commerce Clause because it "serves important interests in health and safety." Tracy, ante, at ----, 117 S.Ct., at 828. The Court in Tracy paints a compelling image of people shivering in their homes in the dead of winter without the assured service that competition-sheltered public utilities provide. See ante, at ----, ---------, 117 S.Ct., at 825, 827-828. No less important, however, is the availability of many of the benefits provided by Maine's private charities and facilitated not by total insulation from competition but by favorable tax treatment: care for the sick and dying, for example, or nursing services for the elderly.

Even if, however, the Maine statute displays "facial discrimination" against interstate commerce, that is not the end of the analysis. The most remarkable thing about today's judgment is that it is rendered without inquiry into whether the purposes of the tax exemption justify its favoritism. Once having concluded that the statute is facially discriminatory, the Court rests. " The Town," it asserts, "has made no effort to defend the statute under the per se rule." Ante, at ___. This seems to me a pointless technicality. The Town has asserted that the State's interest in encouraging private entities to shoulder part of its social-welfare burden validates this provision under the negative Commerce Clause. Whether it does so because the presence of that interest causes the resident-benefiting charities not to be "similarly situated" to the non-resident-benefiting charities, and hence negates "facial discrimination," or rather because the presence of that interest justifies "facial discrimination," is a question that is not only of no consequence but is also probably unanswerable. To strike down this statute because the Town's lawyers put the argument in one form rather than the other is truly senseless. 2

If the Court were to proceed with that further analysis it would have to conclude, in my view, that this is one of those cases in which the "virtually per se rule of invalidity" does not apply. Facially discriminatory or not, the exemption is no more an artifice of economic protectionism than any state law which dispenses public assistance only to the State's residents. 3 Our cases have always recognized the legitimacy of limiting state-provided welfare benefits to bona fide residents. As Justice STEVENS once wrote for a unanimous Court: "Neither the overnight visitor, the unfriendly agent of a hostile power, the resident diplomat, nor the illegal entrant, can advance even a colorable claim to a share in the bounty that a conscientious sovereign makes available to its own citizens." Mathews v. Diaz, 426 U.S. 67, 80, 96 S.Ct. 1883, 1891, 48 L.Ed.2d 478 (1976). States have restricted public assistance to their own bona fide residents since colonial times, see, M. Ierley, With Charity For All, Welfare and Society, Ancient Times to the Present 41 (1984), and such self-interested behavior (or, put more benignly, application of the principle that charity begins at home) is inherent in the very structure of our federal system, cf. Edgar v. MITE Corp., 457 U.S. 624, 644, 102 S.Ct. 2629, 2641-2642, 73 L.Ed.2d 269 (1982) ("the State has no legitimate interest in protecting nonresidents"). We have therefore upheld against equal protection challenge continuing residency requirements for municipal employment, see McCarthy v. Philadelphia Civil Serv. Comm'n, 424 U.S. 645, 96 S.Ct. 1154, 47 L.Ed.2d 366 (1976) (per curiam), and bona fide residency requirements for free primary and secondary schooling, see Martinez v. Bynum, 461 U.S. 321, 103 S.Ct. 1838, 75 L.Ed.2d 879 (1983).

If the negative Commerce Clause requires the invalidation of a law such as §652(1)(A), as a logical matter it also requires invalidation of the laws involved in those cases. After all, the Court today relies not on any discrimination against out-of-state nonprofits, but on the supposed discrimination against nonresident would-be recipients of charity (the nonprofits' "customers"); surely those individuals are similarly discriminated against in the direct distribution of state benefits. The problem, of course, is not limited to municipal employment and free public schooling, but extends also to libraries, orphanages, homeless shelters and refuges for battered women. One could hardly explain the constitutionality of a State's limiting its provision of these to its own residents on the theory that the State is a "market participant." These are traditional governmental functions, far removed from commercial activity and utterly unconnected to any genuine private market.

If, however, a State that provides social services directly may limit its largesse to its own residents, I see no reason why a State that chooses to provide some of its social services indirectly-by compensating or subsidizing private charitable providers-cannot be similarly restrictive. 4 In fact, we have already approved it. In Board of Ed. of Ky. Annual Conference of Methodist Episcopal Church v. Illinois, 203 U.S. 553, 27 S.Ct. 171, 51 L.Ed. 314 (1906), we upheld a state law providing an inheritance tax exemption to in-state charities but denying a similar exemption to out-of-state charities. We recognized that such exemptions are nothing but compensation to private organizations for their assistance in alleviating the State's burden of caring for its less fortunate residents, see id., at 561, 27 S.Ct., at 173. " It cannot be said," we wrote, "that if a State exempts property bequeathed for charitable or educational purposes from taxation it is unreasonable or arbitrary to require the charity to be exercised or the education to be bestowed within her borders and for her people," id., at 563, 27 S.Ct., at 174. 5

It is true that the opinion in Board of Education addressed only the Equal Protection and Privileges and Immunities Clauses of the Fourteenth Amendment, and not the Commerce Clause. A commerce-clause argument was unquestionably raised by the plaintiff in error, however, in both brief, see Brief for Plaintiff in Error, D.T.1906, No. 103, pp. 30-38, and oral argument, see 203 U.S., at 555 (argument of counsel), and the Court could not have reached the disposition it did without rejecting it. " The Court implicitly rejected the argument . . . by refusing to address it." Clemons v. Mississippi, 494 U.S. 738, 747-748, n. 3, 110 S.Ct. 1441, 1448, n. 3, 108 L.Ed.2d 725 (1990). The Commerce Clause objection went undiscussed, I think, because it was (as it is here) utterly contrived: the State's legislated distinction between charity "bestowed within her borders and for her people" and charity bestowed elsewhere or for others did not implicate commerce at all, except to the indirect and permissible extent that innumerable state laws do.

Finally, even if Maine's property tax exemption for local charities constituted facial discrimination against out-of-state commerce, and even if its policy justification (unrelated to economic protectionism) were insufficient to survive our "virtually per se rule of invalidity," cf. Maine v. Taylor, 477 U.S. 131, 106 S.Ct. 2440, 91 L.Ed.2d 110 (1986), there would remain the question whether we should not recognize an additional exception to the negative Commerce Clause, as we have in Tracy. As that case explains, just as a public health justification unrelated to economic protectionism may justify an overt discrimination against goods moving in interstate commerce, "so may health and safety considerations be weighed in the process of deciding the threshold question whether the conditions entailing application of the dormant Commerce Clause are present." ––––– U.S., at ––––, 117 S.Ct., at 828. Today's opinion goes to great length to reject the Town's contention that Maine's property tax exemption does not fall squarely within either the "market participant" or "subsidy" exceptions to the negative Commerce Clause, but never stops to ask whether those exceptions are the only ones that may apply. As we explicitly acknowledge in Tracy -which effectively creates what might be called a "public utilities" exception to the negative Commerce Clause-the "subsidy" and "market participant" exceptions do not exhaust the realm of state actions that we should abstain from scrutinizing under the Commerce Clause. In my view, the provision by a State of free public schooling, public assistance, and other forms of social welfare to only (or principally) its own residents-whether it be accomplished directly or by providing tax exemptions, cash or other property to private organizations that perform the work for the State-implicates none of the concerns underlying our negative-commerce-clause jurisprudence. That is, I think, self-evidently true, despite the Court's effort to label the recipients of the State's philanthropy as "customers," or "clientele," see, e.g., ante, at ___. Because §652(1)(A) clearly serves these purposes and has nothing to do with economic protectionism, I believe that it is beyond scrutiny under the negative Commerce Clause.

* * *

As I have discussed, there are various routes by which the Court could validate the statute at issue here: on the ground that it does not constitute "facial discrimination" against interstate commerce and readily survives the Pike v. Bruce Church balancing test; on the ground that it does constitute "facial discrimination" but is supported by such traditional and important state interests that it survives scrutiny under the "virtually per se rule of invalidity"; or on the ground that there is a "domestic charity" exception (just as there is a "public utility" exception) to the negative Commerce Clause. Whichever route is selected, it seems to me that the quid pro quo exemption at issue here is such a reasonable exercise of the State's taxing power that it is not prohibited by the Commerce Clause in the absence of congressional action. We held as much in Board of Education, and should not overrule that decision.

The State of Maine may have special need for a charitable-exemption limitation of the sort at issue here: its lands and lakes are attractive to various charities of more densely populated Eastern States, which would (if the limitation did not exist) compel the taxpayers of Maine to subsidize their generosity. But the principle involved in our disapproval of Maine's exemption limitation has broad application elsewhere. A State will be unable, for example, to exempt private schools that serve its citizens from State and local real estate taxes unless it exempts as well private schools attended predominantly or entirely by students from out-of-state. A State that provides a tax exemption for real property used exclusively for the purpose of feeding the poor must provide an exemption for the facilities of an organization devoted exclusively to feeding the poor in another country. These results may well be in accord with the parable of the Good Samaritan, but they have nothing to do with the Commerce Clause.

I respectfully dissent.

Notes

1. The Court protests that "there is no "de minimis' defense to a charge of discriminatory taxation under the Commerce Clause," ante, at ___, n. 15-as though that were the point of our emphasizing in this Part II the narrowness of the challenged limitation. It is not. Rather, the point is (1) that Maine's limitation focuses upon a particular state interest that is deserving of exemption from negative-commerce-clause invalidation, and (2) that acknowledging the principle of such an exemption (as developed in Part III below) will not place the "national market" in any peril. What the Court should have gleaned from our discussion, it did not: It persists in misdescribing the exemption we defend as "a categorical exemption of nonprofit activities from dormant Commerce Clause scrutiny." Ante, at ___, n. 21; see also ante, at ___, n. 27.

The Court also makes an attempt to contest on the merits the narrowness of the exemption, suggesting a massive effect upon interstate commerce by reciting the multi-billion-dollar annual revenues of nonprofit nursing homes, child care centers, hospitals and health maintenance organizations. See ante, at __-__, n. 18. But of course most of the services provided by those institutions are provided locally, to local beneficiaries. —(In that regard the summer camp that is the subject of the present suit is most atypical.) The record does not show the number of nonprofit nursing homes, child care centers, hospitals and HMOs in Maine that have been denied the charitable exemption because their property is not used "principally for the benefit of persons who are Maine residents"; but it would be a good bet that the number is zero.

2. I do not understand the Court's contention, ante, at __ & n. 16, that Fulton Corp. v. Faulkner, 516 U.S. ----, 116 S.Ct. 848, 133 L.Ed.2d 796 (1996), provides precedent for such a course. In Fulton, the arguments left unaddressed had not been made in another form, but had not been made at all. There (unlike here) the State conceded facial discrimination, and relied exclusively on the compensatory tax defense, see id., at ----, 116 S.Ct., at 855, which the Court found had not been made out, see id., at ----, 116 S.Ct., at 860. That narrow defense could not possibly have been regarded as an invocation of broader policy justifications such as those asserted here.

3. In a footnote responding to this dissent, the Court does briefly address whether the statute fails the "virtually per se rule of invalidity." It concludes that it does fail because "Maine has ample alternatives short of a facially discriminatory property tax exemption," such as offering direct cash subsidies to parents of resident children or to camps that serve residents. Ante, at __, n. 16 (emphasis added). These are nonregulatory alternatives (and hence immune from negative-commerce-clause attack), but they are not nondiscriminatory alternatives, which is what the exception to the "virtually per se rule of invalidity" requires. See Oregon Waste, 511 U.S., at 101, 114 S.Ct., at 1351 (quoting New Energy Co., 486 U.S., at 278, 108 S.Ct., at 1810). Surely, for example, our decision in Maine v. Taylor, which upheld Maine's regulatory ban on the importation of baitfish, would not have come out the other way if it had been shown that a state subsidy of sales of in-state baitfish could have achieved the same goal-by making the out-of-state fish noncompetitive and thereby excluding them from the market even more effectively than a difficult-to-police ban on importation. Where regulatory discrimination against out-of-state interests is appropriate, the negative Commerce Clause is not designed to push a State into nonregulatory discrimination instead. It permits State regulatory action disfavoring out-of-staters where disfavoring them is indispensable to the achievement of an important and nonprotectionist State objective. As applied to the present case: it is obviously impossible for a State to distribute social welfare benefits only to its residents without discriminating against nonresidents.

4. It is true, of course, that the legitimacy of a State's subsidizing domestic commercial enterprises out of general funds does not establish the legitimacy of a State's giving domestic commercial enterprises preferential tax treatment. See West Lynn Creamery, Inc. v. Healy, 512 U.S. 186, 210-212, 114 S.Ct. 2205, 2220-2221, 129 L.Ed.2d 157 (1994) (SCALIA, J., concurring in judgment). But there is no valid comparison between, on the one hand, the State's giving tax relief to an enterprise devoted to the making of

profit and, on the other hand, the State's giving tax relief to an enterprise which, for the purpose at hand, has the same objective as the State itself (the expenditure of funds for social welfare).

5. The Court attempts to distinguish Board of Education on the ground that the statute upheld in that case treated charities differently based on whether they were incorporated within the State, rather than on whether they dispensed charity within the State, see ante, at __, n. 27. That is quite impossible, inasmuch as we have held that out-of-state incorporation is not a constitutional basis for discriminating between charities. And in the case that announced that holding (invalidating the denial of a property tax exemption to a nonprofit corporation incorporated in another State), we distinguished Board of Education on the ground that the statute at issue there withheld the exemption "by reason of the foreign corporation's failure or inability to benefit the State in the same measure as do domestic nonprofit corporations." WHYY, Inc. v. Glassboro, 393 U.S. 117, 120, 89 S.Ct. 286, 287, 21 L.Ed.2d 242 (1968). The Court's analysis contradicts both the holding of this case and its reading of Board of Education -which is obviously the correct one.

Justice Scalia's dissent in De Buono v. NYSA-ILA Medical and Clinical Service Fund (June 2, 1997)

Justice Scalia, with whom Justice Thomas joins, dissenting.

"[I]t is the duty of this court to see to it that the jurisdiction of the Circuit Court, which is defined and limited by statute, is not exceeded." Louisville & Nashville R. Co. v. Mottley, 211 U.S. 149, 152 (1908). Despite our obligation to examine federal court jurisdiction even if the issue is not raised by either party, ibid., and despite the Court's explicit acknowledgement, ante, at 3, n. 5, of the possibility that jurisdiction over this case is barred by the Tax Injunction Act, 28 U.S.C. § 1341 the Court proceeds to decide the merits of respondents' ERISA pre-emption challenge. The Court offers two grounds for passing over the threshold question of jurisdiction: our "settled practice of according respect to the courts of appeals' greater familiarity with issues of state law," and petitioner's "active participation in nearly four years of federal litigation with no complaint about federal jurisdiction." Ante, at 4, n. 5. In my view, neither of these factors justifies our proceeding without resolving the issue of jurisdiction.

The Tax Injunction Act bars federal court jurisdiction over an action seeking to enjoin a state tax (such as the one at issue here) where "a plain, speedy and efficient remedy may be had in the Courts of such State." 28 U.S.C. § 1341; see Arkansas v. Farm Credit Servs. of Central Ark., post, at 3 (describing the Act as a "jurisdictional rule" and "broad jurisdictional barrier"). The District Court in this case suggested that the Tax Injunction Act might not bar jurisdiction here, since New York courts might not afford respondents a "plain" remedy within the meaning of the Act. See NYSA-ILA Medical and Clinical Services Fund v. Axelrod, No. 92 Civ. 2779 (SDNY, Feb. 18, 1993), App. to Pet. for

Cert. 19a. That suggestion was not, however, based upon the District Court's resolution of any "issues of state law," as today's opinion intimates, ante, at 4, n. 5; rather, it rested upon the District Court's conclusion that uncertainty over the implications of a federal statute-- §502(e)(1) of ERISA, 29 U.S.C. § 1132(e)(1)--might render the availability of a state court remedy not "plain." App. to Pet. for Cert. 19a. [n.*] The Court of Appeals, in turn, made no mention of the jurisdictional issue, presumably because, under controlling Circuit precedent, jurisdiction was secure: The Second Circuit had previously held that state courts could not provide any remedy for ERISA based challenges to state taxes within the meaning of the Tax Injunction Act, since "Congress has divested the state courts of jurisdiction" over ERISA claims. Travelers Ins. Co. v. Cuomo, 14 F. 3d 708, 714 (1993) (citing ERISA §502(e)(1), 29 U.S.C. § 1132(e)(1)), rev'd on other grounds sub nom. New York State Conference of Blue Cross & Blue Shield Plans v. Travelers Ins. Co., 514 U.S. 645 (1995). That holding (like the District Court's discussion of the issue in this case) in no way turns on New York state law, so I am at a loss to understand the Court's invocation of "our settled practice of according respect to the courts' of appeals' greater familiarity with issues of state law," ante, at 4, n. 5, as a basis for overlooking the question whether the Tax Injunction Act bars federal court jurisdiction.

The second factor relied upon by the Court in support of its treatment of the jurisdictional issue is that petitioner dropped the issue after the District Court failed to adopt her interpretation of the Tax Injunction Act. But the fact that petitioner has "active[ly] participat[ed] in nearly four years of federal litigation with no complaint about federal jurisdiction," ibid., cannot possibly confer upon us jurisdiction that we do not otherwise possess. It is our duty to resolve the jurisdictional question, whether or not it has been preserved by the parties. Sumner v. Mata, 449 U.S. 539, 548, n. 2 (1981); Louisville & Nashville R. Co., 211 U. S., at 152. In Sumner we confronted the identical circumstance presented here--a jurisdictional argument raised before the District Court but abandoned before the Court of Appeals--and felt the need to address the jurisdictional issue. 449 U. S., at 547, n. 2.

I have previously noted the split among the Circuits on the question whether the Tax Injunction Act deprives federal courts of jurisdiction over ERISA based challenges to state taxes. See Barnes v. E Systems, Inc. Group Hospital Medical & Surgical Ins. Plan, 501 U.S. 1301, 1302-1303 (1991) (Scalia, J., in chambers). In a prior case, we expressly left the question open, saying that "[w]e express no opinion [on] whether a party [can] sue under ERISA to enjoin or to declare invalid a state tax levy, despite the Tax Injunction Act"; we noted that the answer would depend on whether "state law provide[s] no `speedy and efficient remedy' " and on whether "Congress intended §502 of ERISA to be an exception to the Tax Injunction Act." Franchise Tax Bd. of Cal. v. Construction Laborers Vacation Trust for Southern Cal., 463 U.S. 1, 20, n. 21 (1983). Because I am uncertain of the federal courts' jurisdiction over this case, I would set the jurisdictional issue for briefing and argument, and would resolve that issue before reaching the merits of respondents' ERISA pre-emption claim. Accordingly, I respectfully dissent from today's opinion.

Notes

* That the District Court rested its conclusion on 29 U.S.C. § 1132(e)(1) is demonstrated by the sole authorities it cited in support of that conclusion: Travelers Ins. Co. v. Cuomo, 813 F. Supp. 996 (SDNY 1993), aff'd in part and rev'd in part, 14 F. 3d 708 (CA2 1993), rev'd on other grounds sub nom. New York State Conference of Blue Cross & Blue Shield Plans v. Travelers Ins. Co., 514 U.S. 645 (1995); and National Carriers' Conference Committee v. Heffernan, 440 F. Supp. 1280, 1283 (Conn. 1977). The only argument in Travelers that supports the conclusion reached here is the argument that "[b]ecause ERISA generally confers exclusive jurisdiction on the federal courts [under 29 U.S.C. § 1132(e)(1)], a New York state court might well feel compelled to dismiss a state court action on the grounds that its jurisdiction has been preempted. . . . Thus, at a minimum the availability of a state court remedy is not `plain.' " 813 F. Supp., at 1001 (internal quotation marks and brackets omitted). Likewise, Heffernan (which arose in Connecticut, not New York) offers pertinent reasoning based only on federal law: "Jurisdiction over suits arising under ERISA is, with minor exceptions, vested exclusively in the federal courts. 29 U.S.C. § 1132(e)(1). If this suit were brought before a . . . state court, that court might well feel compelled to dismiss the action on the grounds that its jurisdiction had been preempted by federal legislation and the supremacy clause. Consequently the plaintiff cannot be said to have a `plain, speedy and efficient' remedy in state court . . . ." 440 F. Supp., at 1283 (footnote omitted).

Justice Scalia's dissent in Richardson v. McKnight (June 23, 1997)

Justice Scalia, with whom The Chief Justice, Justice Kennedy and Justice Thomas join, dissenting.

In Procunier v. Navarette, 434 U.S. 555 (1978), we held that state prison officials, including both supervisory and subordinate officers, are entitled to qualified immunity in a suit brought under 42 U.S.C. § 1983. Today the Court declares that this immunity is unavailable to employees of private prison management firms, who perform the same duties as state employed correctional officials, who exercise the most palpable form of state police power, and who may be sued for acting "under color of state law." This holding is supported neither by common law tradition nor public policy, and contradicts our settled practice of determining §1983 immunity on the basis of the public function being performed.

The doctrine of official immunity against damages actions under §1983 is rooted in the assumption that that statute did not abolish those immunities traditionally available at common law. See Buckley v. Fitzsimmons, 509 U.S. 259, 268 (1993). I agree with the Court, therefore, that we must look to history to resolve this case. I do not agree with the Court, however, that the petitioners' claim to immunity is defeated if they cannot provide an actual case, antedating or contemporaneous with the enactment of §1983, in which immunity was successfully asserted by a private prison guard. It is only the absence of such a case, and not any explicit rejection of immunity by any common law court, that the Court relies upon. The opinion observes that private jailers existed in the 19th century, and that they were successfully sued by prisoners. But one could just as easily show that government employed jailers were successfully sued at common law, often with no mention of possible immunity, see Schellenger, Civil liability of sheriff or other officer charged with keeping jail or prison for death or injury of prisoner, 14 A. L. R. 2d 353 (1950) (annotating numerous cases where sheriffs were held liable). Indeed, as far as my research has disclosed, there may be more case law support for immunity in the private jailer context than in the government jailer context. The only pre-§1983 jailer immunity case of any sort that I am aware of is Williams v. Adams, 85 Mass. 171 (1861), decided only 10 years before §1983 became law. And that case, which explicitly acknowledged that the issue of jailer immunity was "novel," ibid, appears to have conferred immunity upon an independent contractor. [n.1]

The truth to tell, Procunier v. Navarette, supra, which established §1983 immunity for state prison guards, did not trouble itself with history, as our later §1983 immunity opinions have done, see, e.g., Burns v. Reed, 500 U.S. 478, 489-490 (1991); Tower v. Glover, 467 U.S. 914, 920 (1984), but simply set forth a policy prescription. At this stage in our jurisprudence it is irrational, and productive of harmful policy consequences, to rely upon lack of case support to create an artificial limitation upon the scope of a doctrine (prison guard immunity) that was itself not based on case support. I say an artificial limitation, because the historical principles on which common law immunity was based, and which are reflected in our jurisprudence, plainly cover the private prison guard if they cover the nonprivate. Those principles are two: (1) immunity is determined by function, not status, and (2) even more specifically, private status is not disqualifying.

"[O]ur cases clearly indicate that immunity analysis rests on functional categories, not on the status of the defendant." Briscoe v. LaHue, 460 U.S. 325, 342 (1983). Immunity "flows not from rank or title or `location within the Government,' but from the nature of the responsibilities of the individual official." Cleavinger v. Saxner, 474 U.S. 193, 201 (1985), quoting Butz v. Economou, 438 U.S. 478 (1978). "Running through our cases, with fair consistency, is a `functional' approach to immunity questions . . . . Under that approach, we examine the nature of the functions with which a particular official or class of officials has been lawfully entrusted, and we seek to evaluate the effect that exposure to particular forms of liability would likely have on the appropriate exercise of those functions." Forrester v. White, 484 U.S. 219, 224 (1988). See also, Buckley, 509 U. S., at 269; Burns, 500 U. S., at 484-486; Malley v. Briggs, 475 U.S. 335, 342-343 (1986); Harlow v. Fitzgerald, 457 U.S. 800, 810-811 (1982); Imbler v. Pachtman, 424 U.S. 409, 420-429 (1976). The parties concede that petitioners perform a prototypically governmental function (enforcement of state imposed deprivation of liberty), and one that gives rise to qualified immunity.

The point that function rather than status governs the immunity determination is demonstrated in a prison guard case virtually contemporaneous with the enactment of §1983. Alamango v. Board of Supervisors of Albany Cty., 32 N. Y. Sup. Ct. 551 (1881), held that supervisors charged under state law with maintaining a penitentiary were immune from prisoner lawsuits. Although they were not formally state officers, the court emphasized the irrelevance of this fact:

"The duty of punishing criminals is inherent in the Sovereign power. It may be committed to agencies selected for that purpose, but such agencies, while engaged in that duty, stand so far in the place of the State and exercise its political authority, and do not act in any private capacity." Id., at 552. [n.2]

Private individuals have regularly been accorded immunity when they perform a governmental function that qualifies. We have long recognized the absolute immunity of grand jurors, noting that like prosecutors and judges they must "exercise a discretionary judgment on the basis of evidence presented to them." Imbler, 424 U. S., at 423, n. 20. "It is the functional comparability of [grand jurors'] judgments to those of the judge that has resulted in [their] being termed `quasi judicial' officers, and their immunities being termed `quasi judicial' as well." Ibid. Likewise, witnesses who testify in court proceedings have enjoyed immunity, regardless of whether they were government employees. "[T]he common law," we have observed, "provided absolute immunity from subsequent damages liability for all persons--governmental or otherwise--who were integral parts of the judicial process." Briscoe, supra, at 335 (emphasis added). I think it highly unlikely that we would deny prosecutorial immunity to those private attorneys increasingly employed by various jurisdictions in this country to conduct high visibility criminal prosecutions. See, e.g., Kaplan, State Hires Private Lawyer for Bryant Family Trial, Los Angeles Times, Apr. 28, 1993, p. B4, col. 2; Estrich, On Building the Strongest Possible Prosecution Team, Los Angeles Times, July 10, 1994, p. M1, col. 1. There is no more reason for treating private prison guards differently.

Later in its opinion, the Court seeks to establish that there are policy reasons for denying to private prison guards the immunity accorded to public ones. As I have indicated above, I believe that history and not judicially analyzed policy governs this matter--but even on its own terms the Court's attempted policy distinction is unconvincing. The Court suggests two differences between civil service prison guards and those employed by private prison firms which preclude any "special" need to give the latter immunity. First, the Court says that "unwarranted timidity" on the part of private guards is less likely to be a concern, since their companies are subject to market pressures that encourage them to be effective in the performance of their duties. If a private firm does not maintain a proper level of order, the Court reasons, it will be replaced by another one--so there is no need for qualified immunity to facilitate the maintenance of order.

This is wrong for several reasons. First of all, it is fanciful to speak of the consequences of "market" pressures in a regime where public officials are the only purchaser, and other people's money the medium of payment. Ultimately, one prison management firm will be selected to replace another prison management firm only if a decision is made by some political official not to renew the contract. See Tenn. Code Ann. §§41-24-103 to 105 (Supp. 1996). This is a government decision, not a market choice. If state officers turn out to be more strict in reviewing the cost and performance of privately managed prisons than of publically managed ones, it will only be because they have chosen to be so. The process can come to resemble a market choice only to the extent that political actors will such resemblance--that is, to the extent that political actors (1) are willing to pay attention to the issue of prison services, among the many issues vying for their attention, and (2) are willing to place considerations of cost and quality of service ahead of such political considerations as personal friendship, political alliances, in state ownership of the contractor, etc. Secondly and more importantly, however, if one assumes a political regime that is bent on emulating the market in its purchase of prison services, it is almost certainly the case that, short of mismanagement so severe as to provoke a prison riot, price (not discipline) will be the predominating factor in such a regime's selection of a contractor. A contractor's price must depend upon its costs; lawsuits increase costs [n.3] ; and "fearless" maintenance of discipline increases lawsuits. The incentive to down play discipline will exist, moreover, even in those states where the politicians' zeal for market emulation and budget cutting has waned, and where prison management contract renewal is virtually automatic: the more cautious the prison guards, the fewer the lawsuits, the higher the profits. In sum, it seems that "market competitive" private prison managers have even greater need than civil service prison managers for immunity as an incentive to discipline.

The Court's second distinction between state and private prisons is that privatization "helps to meet the immunity related need to ensure that talented candidates are not deterred by the threat of damages suits from entering public service" as prison guards. Ante, at 11 (internal quotation marks omitted). This is so because privatization brings with it (or at least has brought with it in the case before us) (1) a statutory requirement for insurance coverage against civil rights claims, which assertedly "increases the likelihood of employee indemnification," and (2) a liberation "from many civil service law restraints" which prevent increased employee risk from being "offset . . . with higher pay or extra benefits," ibid. As for the former (civil rights liability insurance): surely it is the availability of that protection, rather than its actual presence in the case at hand, which decreases (if it does decrease, which I doubt) the need for immunity protection. (Otherwise, the Court would have to say that a private prison management firm that is not required to purchase insurance, and does not do so, is more entitled to immunity; and that a government run prison system that does purchase insurance is less entitled to immunity.) And of course civil rights liability insurance is no less available to public entities than to private employers. But the second factor--liberation from civil service limitations--is the more interesting one. First of all, simply as a philosophical matter it is fascinating to learn that one of the prime justifications for §1983 immunity should be a phenomenon (civil service laws) that did not even exist when §1983 was enacted and the immunity created. Also as a philosophical matter, it is poetic justice (or poetic revenge) that the Court should use one of the principal economic benefits of "prison out sourcing"--namely, the avoidance of civil service salary and tenure encrustations--as the justification for a legal rule rendering out sourcing more expensive. Of course the savings attributable to out sourcing will not be wholly lost as a result of today's holding; they will be transferred in part from the public to prisoner plaintiffs and to lawyers. It is a result that only the American Bar Association and the American Federation of Government Employees could love. But apart from philosophical fascination, this second factor is subject to the same objection as the first: governments need not have civil service salary encrustations (or can exempt prisons from them); and hence governments, no more than private prison employers, have any need for §1983 immunity.

There is one more possible rationale for denying immunity to private prison guards worth discussing, albeit briefly. It is a theory so implausible that the Court avoids mentioning it, even though it was the primary reason given in the Court of Appeals decision that the Court affirms. McKnight v. Rees, 88 F. 3d 417, 424-425 (CA6 1996). It is that officers of private prisons are more likely than officers of state prisons to violate prisoners' constitutional rights because they work for a profit motive, and hence an added degree of deterrence is needed to keep these officers in line. The Court of Appeals offered no evidence to support its bald assertion that private prison guards operate with different incentives than state prison guards, and gave no hint as to how prison guards might possibly increase their employers' profits by violating constitutional rights. One would think that private prison managers, whose §1983 damages come out of their own pockets, as compared with public prison managers, whose §1983 damages come out of the public purse, would, if anything, be more careful in training their employees to avoid constitutional infractions. And in fact, States having experimented with prison privatization commonly report that the overall caliber of the services provided to prisoners has actually improved in scope and quality. Matters Relating To The Federal Bureau Of Prisons: Hearing before the Subcommittee on Crime of the House Committee on the Judiciary, 104th Cong., 1st Sess., 110 (1995).

* * *

In concluding, I must observe that since there is no apparent reason, neither in history nor in policy, for making immunity hinge upon the Court's distinction between public and private guards, the precise nature of that distinction must also remain obscure. Is it privity of contract that separates the two categories--so that guards paid directly by the State are "public" prison guards and immune, but those paid by a prison management company "private" prison guards and not immune? Or is it rather "employee" versus "independent contractor" status--so that even guards whose compensation is paid directly by the State are not immune if they are not also supervised by a state official? Or is perhaps state supervision alone (without direct payment) enough to confer immunity? Or is it (as the Court's characterization of Alamango, see n. 2, supra, suggests) the formal designation of the guards, or perhaps of the guards' employer, as a "state instrumentality" that makes the difference? Since, as I say, I see no sense in the public private distinction, neither do I see what precisely it consists of.

Today's decision says that two sets of prison guards who are indistinguishable in the ultimate source of their authority over prisoners, indistinguishable in the powers that they possess over prisoners, and indistinguishable in the duties that they owe towards prisoners, are to be treated quite differently in the matter of their financial liability. The only sure effect of today's decision--and the only purpose, as far as I can tell--is that it will artificially raise the cost of privatizing prisons. Whether this will cause privatization to be prohibitively expensive, or instead simply divert state funds that could have been saved or spent on additional prison services, it is likely that taxpayers and prisoners will suffer as a consequence. Neither our precedent, nor the historical foundations of §1983, nor the policies underlying §1983, support this result.

I respectfully dissent.

Notes

1 Williams held that prisoners could not recover damages for negligence against the master of a house of correction. That official seems to have been no more a "public officer" than the head of a private company running a prison. For example, the governing statute provided that he was to be paid by the prisoners for his expenses in supporting and employing them, and in event of their default he was given an action indebitatus assumpsit for the sum due, "which shall be deemed to be his own proper debt." Mass. Gen. Stat., ch. 143, §15 (1835). If he failed to distribute to the prisoners those "rations or articles of food, soap, fuel, or other necessaries" directed by the county commissioner (or the mayor and aldermen of Boston), he was subject to a fine. Id., §45. The opinion in Williams says that "[t]he master of the house of correction is not an independent public officer, having the same relations to those who are confined therein that a deputy sheriff has to the parties to a writ committed to him to serve." 85 Mass., at 173.

2 The Court cites Alamango for the proposition that there is "no cause of action against [a] private contractor where [the] contractor [is] designated [a] state instrumentality by statute." Ante, at 6. The opinion in Alamango, however, does not cite any statutory designation of the supervisors as a "state instrumentality," and does not rely on such a designation for its holding. It does identify the Board of Supervisors as "a mere instrumentality selected by the State," 32 N. Y. Sup. Ct., at 552, but the same could be said of the prison management firm here (or the master of the house of corrections in Williams v. Adams, 85 Mass. 171 (1861), see n. 1, supra). If one were to accept the Court's distinguishing of this case, all that would be needed to change the outcome in the present suit is the pointless formality of designating the contractor a "state instrumentality"-- hardly a rational resolution of the question before us.

3 This is true even of successfully defended lawsuits, and even of lawsuits that have been insured against. The Court thinks it relevant to the factor I am currently discussing that the private prison management firm "must buy insurance sufficient to compensate victims of civil rights torts," ante, at 10. Belief in the relevance of this factor

must be traceable, ultimately, to belief in the existence of a free lunch. Obviously, as civil rights claims increase, the cost of civil rights insurance increases.

Justice Scalia's dissent in Regions Hospital v. Shalala (Feb. 24, 1998)

Justice SCALIA, with whom Justice O'CONNOR and Justice THOMAS join, dissenting.

The Medicare Act requires the Secretary to reimburse teaching hospitals for the Graduate Medical Education (GME) costs attributable to Medicare Services. See 42 U.S.C. 1395 et seq. For fiscal years 1965 through 1984, hospitals were entitled to be reimbursed for the actual "reasonable costs" incurred each year. See 42 U.S.C. 1395f(b)(1), 1395x(v)(1)(A). In 1986, however, Congress directed that thereafter reimbursement rates per full-time-equivalent resident would be indexed to each hospital's 1984 GME costs "recognized as reasonable under this subchapter," divided by the number of full-time-equivalent residents that year. See 42 U.S.C. 1395ww(h)(2)(A). 1 The Court today determines that the phrase "recognized as reasonable under this subchapter" can reasonably be construed as an authorization for the Secretary to redetermine a hospital's composite 1984 GME costs, rather than as a reference to a previously made determination; and thus concludes, pursuant to Chevron U.S.A. Inc. v. Natural Resources Defense Council, Inc., 467 U.S. 837, 842, 104 S.Ct. 2778, 2781, 81 L.Ed.2d 694 (1984), that the Secretary's reaudit regulation is lawful, see 42 C.F.R. §413.86(e)(1)(iii) (1996). 2 See, ante, at ___-___. Because I believe that the 1984 GME costs "recognized as reasonable" in 42 U.S.C. 1395ww(h)(2)(A) must be the "reasonable costs" for which the Secretary actually reimbursed the hospitals in 1984, I respectfully dissent.

On April 7, 1986, the enactment date of the provision tying future GME reimbursements to 1984 GME costs, the Secretary had in place a longstanding procedure for determining a hospital's reasonable GME costs. Under that procedure, the three-year window during which the Secretary could revise the 1984 determinations had not yet closed for any hospital entitled to reimbursement, see 42 CFR §405.1885(a) (1985). Indeed, for many hospitals, like Regions, the three-year period had not yet, or had barely, begun to run, since the 1984 costs had not yet, or had only recently, been determined. On February 28, 1986, Regions' fiscal intermediary, see 42 U.S.C. 1395h, determined that Regions had incurred reasonable 1984 GME costs of $9,892,644 (Regions was later reimbursed for that amount); that decision became final under the Secretary's regulations on March 1, 1989. Nonetheless, in 1991, pursuant to the 1989 regulation now before the Court, Regions' fiscal intermediary reopened the prior determination of reasonable 1984 GME costs (albeit for the limited purpose of calculating future reimbursement rates), reducing them to $5,916,868.

In light of the procedures already in place for determining a hospital's reasonable 1984 GME costs when §1395ww(h) was enacted, that provision's reference to a hospital's 1984 GME costs "recognized as reasonable under this subchapter" cannot reasonably be interpreted to authorize the Secretary to determine a hospital's 1984 GME costs anew. It is true, as the Court points out, that in isolation the phrase "recognized as reasonable" is ambiguous: it "might mean costs the Secretary (1) has recognized as reasonable for 1984 GME cost reimbursement purposes, or (2) will recognize as reasonable as a base for future GME calculations." Ante, at __. But as we have insisted, the words of a statute are not to be read in isolation; statutory interpretation is a "holistic endeavor," United Sav. Assn. of Tex. v. Timbers of Inwood Forest Associates, Ltd., 484 U.S. 365, 371, 108 S.Ct. 626, 630, 98 L.Ed.2d 740 (1988). Viewing the words "recognized as reasonable" in their entire context, they cannot reasonably be understood to authorize a new composite cost determination.

To begin with, it should be borne in mind that §1395ww(h)(2)(A) does not provide directly for a determination of composite costs "recognized as reasonable." It provides for a determination of the average per full-time resident of costs recognized as reasonable. If this is to be interpreted as an authorization for a new "recognition of composite-cost reasonableness," so to speak, it is a most oblique and indirect authorization-so oblique and indirect as to be implausible. That new computation of composite costs, rather than the relatively mechanical averaging of those costs per full-time resident, would have been the major feature of the provision, so that one would have expected it to read something like "the Secretary shall determine each hospital's reasonable direct GME costs for the 1984 cost reporting period, and the average amount of those costs attributable to each full-time-equivalent resident."

It is impossible to imagine, moreover, how the words "recognized as" found their way into the provision unless they were meant to refer to the recognition of reasonableness already made under the pre-existing system. The interpretation that the Court accepts treats them "essentially as surplusage-as words of no consequence," Ratzlaf v. United States, 510 U.S. 135, 140-141, 114 S.Ct. 655, 659, 126 L.Ed.2d 615 (1994), which, of course, we avoid when possible.

"We are not at liberty to construe any statute so as to deny effect to any part of its language. It is a cardinal rule of statutory construction that significance and effect shall, if possible, be accorded to every word. As early as in Bacon's Abridgment, sect. 2, it was said that "a statute ought, upon the whole, to be so construed that, if it can be prevented, no clause, sentence, or word shall be superfluous, void, or insignificant.' This rule has been repeated innumerable times." Washington Market Co. v. Hoffman, 101 U.S. 112, 115-116, 25 L.Ed. 782 (1879).

See also United States v. Nordic Village, Inc., 503 U.S. 30, 36, 112 S.Ct. 1011, 1015-16, 117 L.Ed.2d 181 (1992); Federal Election Comm'n v. National Conservative Political Action Comm., 470 U.S. 480, 486, 105 S.Ct. 1459, 1463, 84 L.Ed.2d 455 (1985). If §1395ww(h)(2)(A) conferred a new cost-determination authority upon the Secretary, to be exercised in the future, it would have sufficed (and would have been normal) to direct the Secretary "to determine, for the hospital's cost reporting period that began during fiscal year 1984, the average amount reasonable under this subchapter for direct GME costs of the hospital for each full-time-equivalent resident." The specification of an amount "recognized as reasonable under this subchapter" only makes sense as a reference to a determination made (or to be made) independent of §1395ww(h)(2)(A) itself-i.e., to the amount "recognized" under the procedures already in place for determining the reasonable 1984 GME costs. Indeed, under the Secretary's interpretation the words "recognized as" become not only superfluous but positively misleading, since without them there would be no question that authority for a new determination was being conferred. It is an unacceptable interpretation which causes the critical words of the text to be (1) meaningless and (2) confusing.

That "recognized as" refers to a determination under the pre-existing regime is strongly confirmed by another provision of the statute that enacted §1395ww(h)(2)(A) into law: "The Secretary . . . shall report to specified Committees of the Senate and House of Representatives, not later than December 31, 1987, on whether §1395ww(h) should be revised to provide for greater uniformity in the approved FTE resident amounts established under §1395ww(h)(2), and, if so, how such revisions should be implemented." §9202(e), 100 Stat. 176 (emphases added). This surely envisions that the Secretary will know the amounts established under §1395ww(h)(2)(A) by December 31, 1987-well within the three-year window for revisiting and revising any teaching hospital's actual 1984 reimbursement amounts. The Secretary's assertion that §1395ww(h)(2)(A) confers a new authority to make cost determinations can technically be reconciled with this directive for a December 31, 1987, evaluation only by saying that the new authority was supposed to be exercised before that date. But if it was supposed to be exercised before that date, it was entirely superfluous, since all prior determinations could be revised before that date under the old authority. In short, given the evaluation deadline, the Secretary's interpretation makes no sense.

Most judicial constructions of statutes solve textual problems; today's construction creates textual problems, in order to solve a practical one. The problem to which the Secretary's implausible reading of the statute is the solution is simply this: Though the Secretary had plenty of time, after enactment of §1395ww(h)(2)(A), to correct any erroneous determinations of 1984 GME costs before the three-year revision window closed, she (or more precisely her predecessor) neglected to do so. We obligingly pull her chestnuts from the fire by accepting a reading of the statute that is implausible. The Court asks the following question:

"Had Congress contemplated that the Secretary would not have responded to the 1986 GME Amendment swiftly enough to catch 1984 NAPR errors within the Secretary's three-year reopening period, what would the Legislature have anticipated as the proper administrative course? Error perpetuation until Congress plugged the hole? Or the Secretary's exercise of authority to effectuate the Legislature's overriding purpose in the Medicare scheme: reasonable (not excessive or unwarranted) cost reimbursement?" Ante, at ___.

The answer to that question is easy. But it is the wrong question. Of course it can always be assumed that Congress would prefer whatever would preserve, in light of unforeseen eventualities, "the Legislature's overriding purpose." We are not governed by legislators' "overriding purposes," however, but by the laws that Congress enacts. If one of them is improvident or ill conceived, it is not the province of this Court to distort its fair meaning (or to sanction the Executive's distortion) so that a better law will result. The immediate benefit achieved by such a practice in a particular case is far outweighed by the disruption of legal expectations in all cases -disruption of the rule of law -that government by ex post facto legislative psychoanalysis produces.

I would pronounce the Secretary's reaudit regulation ultra vires and reverse the Court of Appeals.

Notes

1. 42 U.S.C. 1395ww(h)(2)(A) provides that " [t]he Secretary shall determine, for the hospital's cost reporting period that began during fiscal year 1984, the average amount recognized as reasonable under this subchapter for direct graduate medical education costs of the hospital for each full-time-equivalent resident."

2. 42 C.F.R. §413.86(e)(1)(iii) (1996) provides that " [i]f the hospital's cost report for its GME base period is no longer subject to reopening under §405.1885 of this chapter, the intermediary may modify the hospital's base-period costs solely for purposes of computing the per resident amount."

Justice Scalia's dissent in Almendarez-Torres v. US (March 24, 1998)

Justice Scalia, with whom Justice Stevens, Justice Souter, and Justice Ginsburg join, dissenting.

Because Hugo Roman Almendarez-Torres illegally re-entered the United States after having been convicted of an aggravated felony, he was subject to a maximum possible sentence of 20 years imprisonment. See 8 U.S.C. § 1326(b)(2). Had he not been convicted of that felony, he would have been subject to a maximum of only two years. See 8 U.S.C. § 1326(a). The Court today holds that §1326(b)(2) does not set forth a separate offense, and that conviction of a prior felony is merely a sentencing enhancement for the offense set forth in §1326(a). This causes the Court to confront the difficult question whether the Constitution requires a fact which substantially increases the maximum permissible punishment for a crime to be treated as an element of that crime–to be charged in the indictment, and found beyond a reasonable doubt by a jury. Until the Court said so, it was far from obvious that the answer to this question was no; on the basis of our prior law, in fact, the answer was considerably doubtful.

In all our prior cases bearing upon the issue, however, we confronted a criminal statute or state-court criminal ruling that unambiguously relieved the prosecution of the burden of proving a critical fact to the jury beyond a reasonable doubt. In McMillan v. Pennsylvania, 477 U.S. 79 (1986), the statute provided that " 'visibl[e] possess[ion] [of] a firearm' " " 'shall not be an element of the crime[,]' " " but shall be determined at sentencing by " '[t]he court . . . by a preponderance of the evidence,' " id., at 81, n. 1 (quoting 42 Pa. Cons. Stat. §9712 (1982)). In In re Winship, 397 U.S. 358 (1970), it provided that determinations of criminal action in juvenile cases " 'must be based on a preponderance of the evidence,' " id., at 360 (quoting N. Y. Family Court Act §744(b)). In Patterson v. New York, 432 U.S. 197 (1977), the statute provided that extreme emotional disturbance " 'is an affirmative defense,' " id., at 198, n. 2 (quoting N. Y. Penal Law §125.25 (McKinney 1975)). And in Mullaney v. Wilbur, 421 U.S. 684 (1975), Maine's highest court had held that in murder cases malice aforethought was presumed and had to be negated by the defendant, id., at 689 (citing State v. Lafferty, 309 A. 2d 647 (1973)).

In contrast to the provisions involved in these cases, 8 U.S.C. § 1326 does not, on its face, place the constitutional issue before us: it does not say that subsection (b)(2) is merely a sentencing enhancement. The text of the statute supports, if it does not indeed demand, the conclusion that subsection (b)(2) is a separate offense that includes the violation described in subsection (a) but adds the additional element of prior felony conviction. I therefore do not reach the difficult constitutional issue in this case because I adopt, as I think our cases require, that reasonable interpretation of §1326 which avoids the problem. Illegal re-entry simpliciter (§1326(a)) and illegal reentry after conviction of an aggravated felony (§1326(b)(2)) are separate criminal offenses. Prior conviction of an aggravated felony being an element of the latter offense, it must be charged in the indictment. Since it was not, petitioner's sentence must be set aside.

I

"[W]here a statute is susceptible of two constructions, by one of which grave and doubtful constitutional questions arise and by the other of which such questions are avoided, our duty is to adopt the latter." United States ex rel. Attorney General v. Delaware & Hudson Co., supra, at 408. This "cardinal principle," which "has for so long been applied by this Court that it is beyond debate," Edward J. DeBartolo Corp. v. Florida Gulf Coast Building & Constr. Trades Council, 485 U.S. 568, 575 (1988), requires merely a determination of serious constitutional doubt, and not a determination of unconstitutionality. That must be so, of course, for otherwise the rule would "mea[n] that our duty is to first decide that a statute is unconstitutional and then proceed to hold that such ruling was unnecessary because the statute is susceptible of a meaning, which causes it not to be repugnant to the Constitution." United States ex rel. Attorney General v. Delaware & Hudson Co., supra, at 408. The Court contends that neither of the two conditions for application of this rule is present here: that the constitutional question is not doubtful, and that the statute is not susceptible of a construction that will avoid it. I shall address the former point first.1

That it is genuinely doubtful whether the Constitution permits a judge (rather than a jury) to determine by a mere preponderance of the evidence (rather than beyond a reasonable doubt) a fact that increases the maximum penalty to which a criminal defendant is subject, is clear enough from our prior cases resolving questions on the margins of this one. In In re Winship, supra, we invalidated a New York statute under which the burden of proof in a juvenile delinquency proceeding was reduced to proof by a preponderance of the evidence. We held that "the Due Process Clause protects the accused against conviction except upon proof beyond reasonable doubt of every fact necessary to constitute the crime with which he is charged," 397 U.S., at 364, and that the same protection extends to "a juvenile . . . charged with an act which would constitute a crime if committed by an adult," id., at 359.

Five years later, in Mullaney v. Wilbur, supra, we unanimously extended Winship's protections to determinations that went not to a defendant's guilt or innocence, but simply to the length of his sentence. We invalidated Maine's homicide law, under which all intentional murders were presumed to be committed with malice aforethought (and, as such, were punishable by life imprisonment), unless the defendant could rebut this presumption with proof that he acted in the heat of passion (in which case the conviction would be reduced to manslaughter and the maximum sentence to 20 years). We acknowledged that "under Maine law these facts of intent [were] not general elements of the crime of felonious homicide[, but] [i]nstead, [bore] only on the appropriate punishment category." 421 U.S., at 699. Nonetheless, we rejected this distinction between guilt and punishment. "If Winship," we said, "were limited to those facts that constitute a crime as defined by state law, a State could undermine many of the interests that decision sought to protect without effecting any substantive change in its law. It would only be necessary to redefine the elements that constitute different crimes, characterizing them as factors that bear solely on the extent of punishment." Id., at 697—698.

In Patterson v. New York, we cut back on some of the broader implications of Mullaney. Although that case contained, we acknowledged, "some language . . . that ha[d] been understood as perhaps construing the Due Process Clause to require the prosecution to prove beyond a reasonable doubt any fact affecting 'the degree of criminal culpability,' " we denied that we "intend[ed] . . . such far-reaching effect." 432 U.S., at 214—215, n. 15. Accordingly, we upheld in Patterson New York's law casting upon the defendant the burden of proving as an "affirmative defense" to second-degree murder that he " 'acted under the influence of extreme emotional disturbance for which there was a reasonable explanation or excuse,' " id., at 198—199, n. 2, which defense would reduce his crime to manslaughter. We explained that "[p]roof of the nonexistence of all affirmative defenses has never been constitutionally required," and that the State need not "prove beyond a reasonable doubt every fact, the existence or nonexistence of which it is willing to recognize as an exculpatory or mitigating circumstance affecting the degree of culpability or the severity of the punishment." Id., at 207. We cautioned, however, that while our decision might "seem to permit state legislatures to reallocate burdens of proof by labeling as affirmative defenses at least some elements of the crimes now defined in their statutes[,] . . . [t]here are obviously constitutional limits beyond which the States may not go in this regard." Id., at 210.

Finally, and most recently, in McMillan v. Pennsylvania, 477 U.S., at 81, we upheld

Pennsylvania's Mandatory Minimum Sentencing Act, which prescribed a mandatory minimum sentence of five years upon a judge's finding by a preponderance of the evidence that the defendant "visibly possessed a firearm" during the commission of certain enumerated offenses which all carried maximum sentences of more than five years. We observed that "we [had] never attempted to define precisely the constitutional limits noted in Patterson, i.e., the extent to which due process forbids the reallocation or reduction of burdens of proof in criminal cases," but explained that, whatever those limits, Pennsylvania's law did not transgress them, id., at 86, primarily because it "neither alter[ed] the maximum penalty for the crime committed nor create[d] a separate offense calling for a separate penalty; it operate[d] solely to limit the sentencing court's discretion in selecting a penalty within the range already available to it without the special finding of visible possession of a firearm," id., at 87—88.

The feebleness of the Court's contention that here there is no serious constitutional doubt is evidenced by the degree to which it must ignore or distort the analysis of McMillan. As just described, that opinion emphasized—and emphasized repeatedly—that an increase of the maximum penalty was not at issue. Beyond that, it specifically acknowledged that the outcome might have been different (i.e., the statute might have been unconstitutional) if the maximum sentence had been affected:

"Petitioners' claim that visible possession under the Pennsylvania statute is 'really' an element of the offenses for which they are being punished—that Pennsylvania has in effect defined a new set of upgraded felonies—would have at least more superficial appeal if a finding of visible possession exposed them to greater or additional punishment, cf. 18 U.S.C. § 2113(d) (providing separate and greater punishment for bank robberies accomplished through 'use of a dangerous weapon or device'), but it does not." Id., at 88.

The opinion distinguished one of our own precedents on this very ground, noting that the Colorado Sex Offenders Act invalidated in Specht v. Patterson, 386 U.S. 605 (1967), increased a sex offender's sentence from a 10—year maximum to an indefinite term up to and including life imprisonment. 477 U.S., at 88.

Despite all of that, the Court would have us believe that the present statute's alteration of the maximum permissible sentence—which it acknowledges is "the major difference between this case and McMillan," ante, at 20—militates in favor of, rather than against, this statute's constitutionality, because an increase of the minimum sentence (rather than the permissible maximum) is more disadvantageous to the defendant. Ibid. That is certainly an arguable position (it was argued, as the Court has the temerity to note, by the dissent in McMillan). But it is a position which McMillan not only rejected, but upon the converse of which McMillan rested its judgment.

In addition to inverting the consequence of this distinction (between statutes that prescribe a minimum sentence and those that increase the permissible maximum sentence) the Court seeks to minimize the importance of the distinction by characterizing it as merely one of five factors relied on in McMillan, and asserting that the other four factors here are the same. Ante, at 18-19. In fact, however, McMillan did not set forth any five-factor test; the Court selectively recruits "factors" from various parts of the discussion. Its first factor, for example, that " 'the [statute] plainly does not transgress the limits expressly set out in Patterson,' " ante, at 18, quoting from McMillan, 477 U. S, at 86–viz., that it does not "discar[d] the presumption of innocence" or "relieve the prosecution of its burden of proving guilt[,]" id., at 87–merely narrows the issue to the one before the Court, rather than giving any clue to the resolution of that issue. It is no more a factor in solving the constitutional problem before us than is the observation that §1326 is not an ex post facto law and does not effect an unreasonable search or seizure. The Court's second, fourth, and part of its fifth "factors" are in fact all subparts of the crucial third factor (the one that is absent here), since they are all culled from the general discussion in McMillan of how the Pennsylvania statute simply limited a sentencing judge's discretion. We said that, whereas in Mullaney the State had imposed " 'a differential in sentencing ranging from a nominal fine to a mandatory life sentence' " (the Court's "second" factor), Pennsylvania's law "neither alter[ed] the maximum penalty for the crime committed [the Court's "third" factor] nor create[d] a separate offense calling for a separate penalty [the Court's "fourth" factor]; it operate[d] solely to limit the sentencing court's discretion in selecting a penalty within the range already available to it without the special finding of visible possession of a firearm [the Court's "third" factor] . . . . The statute gives no impression of having been tailored to permit the visible possession finding to be a tail which wags the dog of the substantive offense [part of the Court's "fifth" factor]." 477 U.S., at 87—88.

The Court's recruitment of "factors" is, as I have said, selective. Omitted, for example, is McMillan's statement that "petitioners do not contend that the particular factor made relevant [by the statute] . . . has historically been treated 'in the Anglo-American legal tradition' as requiring proof beyond a reasonable doubt." Id., at 90, quoting Patterson, 432 U.S., at 226. Petitioner does make such an assertion in the present case–correctly, as I shall discuss. But even with its selective harvesting, the Court is incorrect in its assertion that "most" of the "factors" it recites, ante, at 19 (and in its implication that all except the third of them) exist in the present case as well. The second of them contrasted the consequence of the fact assumed in Mullaney (extension of the permissible sentence from as little as a nominal fine to as much as a mandatory life sentence) with the consequence of the fact at issue in McMillan (no extension of the permissible sentence at all, but merely a "limit[ation of] the sentencing court's discretion in selecting a penalty within the range already available," 477 U.S., at 88). The present case resembles Mullaney rather than McMillan in this regard, since the fact at issue increases the permissible sentence tenfold. And the only significant part of the fifth "factor"–that the statute in McMillan " 'dictated the precise weight to be given [the statutory] factor,' " ante, at 18, quoting McMillan, 477 U.S., at 89—90–is likewise a point of difference and not of similarity.

But this parsing of various factors is really beside the point. No one can read our pre-McMillan cases, and especially Mullaney (whose limits were adverted to in Patterson but never precisely described) without entertaining a serious doubt as to whether the statute as interpreted by the Court in the present case is constitutional. And no one can read McMillan, our latest opinion on the point, without perceiving that the determinative element in our validation of the Pennsylvania statute was the fact that it merely limited the sentencing judge's discretion within the range of penalty already available, rather than substantially increasing the available sentence. And even more than that: No one can read McMillan without learning that the Court was open to the argument that the Constitution requires a fact which does increase the available sentence to be treated as an element of the crime (such an argument, it said, would have "at least . . . superficial appeal," 477 U.S., at 88). If all that were not enough, there must be added the fact that many State Supreme Courts have concluded that a prior conviction which increases maximum punishment must be treated as an element of the offense under either their state constitutions, see, e.g., State v. McClay, 146 Me. 104, 112, 78 A. 2d 347, 352 (1951); Tuttle v. Commonwealth, 68 Mass. 505, 506 (1854) (prior conviction increasing maximum sentence must be set forth in indictment); State v. Furth, 5 Wash. 2d 1, 11—19, 104 P.2d 925, 930—933 (1940); State ex rel. Lockmiller v. Mayo, 88 Fla. 96, 98—99, 101 So. 228, 229 (1924); Roberson v. State, 362 P.2d 1115, 1118—1119 (Okla. Crim. App. 1961), or as a matter of common law, see, e.g., People ex rel. Cosgriff v. Craig, 195 N. Y. 190, 194—195, 88 N. E. 38, 39 (1909); People v. McDonald, 233 Mich. 98, 102, 105, 206 N. W. 516, 518, 519 (1925); State v. Smith, 129 Iowa 709, 710—715, 106 N. W. 187, 188—189 (1906) ("By the uniform current authority, the fact of prior convictions is to be taken as part of the offense instantly charged, at least to the extent of aggravating it and authorizing an increased punishment"); State v. Pennye, 102 Ariz. 207, 208—209, 427 P.2d 525, 526—527 (1967); State v. Waterhouse, 209 Ore. 424, 428—433, 307 P.2d 327, 329—331 (1957); Robbins v. State, 219 Ark. 376, 380—381, 242 S. W. 2d 640, 643 (1951); State v. Eichler, 248 Iowa 1267, 1270—1273, 83

N. W. 2d 576, 577—579 (1957).2

In the end, the Court cannot credibly argue that the question whether a fact which increases maximum permissible punishment must be found by a jury beyond a reasonable doubt is an easy one. That, perhaps, is why the Court stresses, and stresses repeatedly, the limited subject matter that §1326(b) addresses–recidivism. It even tries, with utter lack of logic, to limit its rejection of the fair reading of McMillan to recidivism cases. "For the reasons just given," it says, "and in light of the particular sentencing factor at issue in this case–recidivism–we should take McMillan's statement [regarding the "superficial appeal" the defendant's argument would have had if the factor at issue increased his maximum sentence] to mean no more than what it said, and therefore not to make a determinative difference here." Ante, at 21 (emphasis added). It is impossible to understand how McMillan could mean one thing in a later case where recidivism is at issue, and something else in a later case where some other sentencing factor is at issue. One might say, of course, that recidivism should be an exception to the general rule set forth in McMillan– but that more forthright characterization would display how doubtful the constitutional question is in light of our prior case law.

In any event, there is no rational basis for making recidivism an exception. The Court is of the view that recidivism need not be proved to a jury beyond a reasonable doubt (a view that, as I shall discuss, is precisely contrary to the common-law tradition) because it " 'goes to punishment only.' " It relies for this conclusion upon our opinion in Graham v. West Virginia, 224 U.S. 616 (1912). See ante, at 19, quoting Graham, supra, at 624; see also ante, at 23. The holding of Graham provides no support for the Court's position. It upheld against due process and double jeopardy objections a state recidivism law under which a defendant's prior convictions were charged and tried in a separate proceeding after he was convicted of the underlying offense. As the Court notes, ante, at 19, the prior convictions were not charged in the same indictment as the underlying offense; but they were charged in an "information" before the defendant was tried for the prior convictions, and, more importantly, the law explicitly preserved his right to a jury determination on the recidivism question. See Graham, supra, at 622–623; see also Oyler v. Boles, 368 U.S. 448, 453 (1962) (same). It is true, however, that if the basis for Graham's holding were accepted, one would have to conclude that recidivism need not be tried to the jury and found beyond a reasonable doubt. The essence of Graham's reasoning was that in the recidivism proceeding the defendant "was not held to answer for an offense," 224 U.S., at 624, since the recidivism charge " 'goes to the punishment only,' " ibid., quoting from McDonald v. Massachusetts, 180 U.S. 311, 312 (1901).

But that basis for dispensing with the protections of jury trial and findings beyond a reasonable doubt was explicitly rejected in Mullaney, which accorded these protections to facts that were "not general elements of the crime of felonious homicide ... [but bore] only on the appropriate punishment category," 421 U.S., at 699. Whatever else Mullaney stands for, it certainly stands for the proposition that what Graham used as the line of demarcation for double jeopardy and some due process purposes (the matter "goes only to the punishment") is not the line of demarcation for purposes of the right to jury trial and to proof beyond a reasonable doubt. So also does McMillan, which even while narrowing Mullaney made it very clear that the mere fact that a certain finding "goes only to the penalty" does not end the inquiry. The Court is certainly correct that the distinctive treatment of recidivism determinations for double jeopardy purposes takes some explaining; but it takes some explaining for the Court no less than for me. And the explanation assuredly is not (what the Court apparently suggests) that recidivism is never an element of the crime. It does much less violence to our jurisprudence, and to the traditional practice of requiring a jury finding of recidivism beyond a reasonable doubt, to explain Graham as a recidivism exception to the normal double jeopardy rule that conviction of a lesser included offense bars later trial for the greater crime. Our double jeopardy law, after all, is based upon traditional American and English practice, see United States v. Dixon, 509 U.S. 688, 704 (1993); United States v. Wilson, 420 U.S. 332, 339–344 (1975), and that practice has allowed recidivism to be charged and tried separately, see Spencer v. Texas, 385 U.S. 554, 566–567 (1967); Graham, supra, at 623, 625–626, 631; McDonald, supra, at 312–313. It has not allowed recidivism to be determined by a judge as more likely than not.

While I have given many arguments supporting the position that the Constitution requires the recidivism finding in this case to be made by a jury beyond a reasonable doubt, I do not endorse that position as necessarily correct. Indeed, that would defeat my whole purpose, which is to honor the practice of not deciding doubtful constitutional questions unnecessarily. What I have tried to establish–and all that I need to establish–is that on the basis of our jurisprudence to date, the answer to the constitutional question is not clear. It is the Court's burden, on the other hand, to establish that its constitutional answer shines forth clearly from our cases. That burden simply cannot be sustained. I think it beyond question that there was, until today's unnecessary resolution of the point, "serious doubt" whether the Constitution permits a defendant's sentencing exposure to be increased tenfold on the basis of a fact that is not charged, tried to a jury, and found beyond a reasonable doubt. If the Court wishes to abandon the doctrine of constitutional doubt, it should do so forthrightly, rather than by declaring certainty on a point that is clouded in doubt.

II

The Court contends that the doctrine of constitutional doubt is also inapplicable because §1326 is not fairly susceptible of the construction which avoids the constitutional problem–i.e., the construction whereby subsection (b)(2) sets forth a separate criminal offense. Ante, at 14. The Court begins its statutory analysis not by examining the text of §1326, but by demonstrating that the "subject matter [of the statute]–prior commission of a serious crime–is as typical a sentencing factor as one might imagine." Ante, at 5. That is eminently demonstrable, sounds powerfully good, but in fact proves nothing at all. It is certainly true that a judge (whether or not bound by the Federal Sentencing Guidelines) is likely to sentence nearer the maximum permitted for the offense if the defendant is a repeat offender. But the same can be said of many, perhaps most, factors that are used to define aggravated offenses. For example, judges will "typically" sentence nearer the maximum that a statute allows if the crime of conviction is committed with a firearm, or in the course of another felony; but that in no way suggests that armed robbery and felony murder are sentencing enhancements rather than separate crimes.

The relevant question for present purposes is not whether prior felony conviction is "typically" used as a sentencing factor, but rather whether, in statutes that provide higher maximum sentences for crimes committed by convicted felons, prior conviction is "typically" treated as a mere sentence enhancement or rather as an element of a separate offense. The answer to that question is the latter. That was the rule at common law, and was the near-uniform practice among the States at the time of the most recent study I am aware of. See Note, Recidivist Procedures, 40 N. Y. U. L. Rev. 332, 333–334 (1965); Note, The Pleading and Proof of Prior Convictions in Habitual Criminal Prosecutions, 33 N. Y. U. L. Rev. 210, 215–216 (1958). At common law, the fact of prior convictions had to be charged in the same indictment charging the underlying crime, and submitted to the jury for determination along with that crime. See, e.g., Spencer v. Texas, 385 U.S. 554, 566 (1967); Massey v. United States, 281 F. 293, 297 (CA8 1922); Singer v. United States, 278 F. 415, 420 (CA3 1922); People v. Sickles, 156 N. Y. 541, 545, 51 N. E. 288, 289 (1898). While several States later altered this procedure by providing a separate proceeding for the determination of prior convictions, at least as late as 1965 all but eight retained the defendant's right to a jury determination on this issue. See Note, Recidivist Procedures, 40 N. Y. U. L. Rev., supra, at 333—334, and 347. I am at a loss to explain the Court's assertion that it has "found no statute that clearly makes recidivism an offense element" added to another crime, ante, at 5—6. There are many such. 3

It is interesting that the Court drags the red herring of recidivism through both parts of its opinion—the "constitutional doubt" part and the "statutory interpretation" part alike. As just discussed, logic demonstrates that the nature of that charge (the fact that it is a "typical" sentencing factor) has nothing to do with what this statute means. And as discussed earlier, the text and reasoning of McMillan, and of the cases McMillan distinguishes, provide no basis for saying that recidivism is exempt from the Court's clear acknowledgment that taking away from the jury facts that increase the maximum sentence is constitutionally questionable. One wonders what state courts, and lower federal courts, are supposed to do with today's mysterious utterances. Are they to pursue logic, and conclude that all ambiguous statutes adding punishment for factors accompanying the principal offense are mere enhancements, or are they illogically to give this special treatment only to recidivism? Are they to deem the reasoning of McMillan superseded for all cases, or does it remain an open and doubtful question, for all cases except those involving recidivism, whether statutory maximums can be increased without the benefit of jury trial? Whatever else one may say about today's opinion, there is no doubt that it has brought to this area of the law more confusion than clarification.

Passing over the red herring, let me turn now to the statute at issue—§1326 as it stood when petitioner was convicted. The author of today's opinion for the Court once agreed that the "language and structure" of this enactment "are subject to two plausible readings," one of them being that recidivism constitutes a separate offense. United States v. Forbes, 16 F.3d 1294, 1298 (CA1 1994) (opinion of Coffin, J., joined by Breyer, C. J.).4 This would surely be enough to satisfy the requirement expressed by Justice Holmes, see United States v. Jin Fuey Moy, 241 U.S. 394, 401 (1916), and approved by the Court, ante, at 13, that the constitutional-doubt-avoiding construction be "fairly possible." Today, however, the Court relegates statutory language and structure to merely two of five "factors" that "help courts determine a statute's objectives and thereby illuminate its text," ante, at 4.

The statutory text reads, in relevant part, as follows:

"Reentry of deported alien; criminal penalties for reentry of certain deported aliens

"(a) Subject to subsection (b) of this section, any alien who [has been deported and thereafter reenters the United States] . . . shall be fined under title 18, or imprisoned not more than 2 years, or both.

"(b) Notwithstanding subsection (a) of this section, in the case of any alien described in such subsection–

"(1) whose deportation was subsequent to a conviction for commission of three or more misdemeanors involving drugs, crimes against the person, or both, or a felony (other than an aggravated felony), such alien shall be fined under title 18, imprisoned not more than 10 years, or both; or

"(2) whose deportation was subsequent to a conviction for commission of an aggravated felony, such alien shall be fined under such title, imprisoned not more than 20 years, or both." 8 U.S.C. § 1326(b).

One is struck at once by the parallel structure of subsections (a) and (b). Neither subsection says that the individual it describes "shall be guilty of a felony," and both subsections say that the individuals they describe "shall be fined under Title 18, or imprisoned not more than [2, 10, or 20] years." If this suffices to define a substantive offense in subsection (a) (as all agree it does), it is hard to see why it would not define a substantive offense in each paragraph of subsection (b) as well. Compare, for example, 21 U.S.C. § 841 which has a subsection (a) entitled "Unlawful acts," and a subsection (b) entitled "Penalties."

The opening phrase of subsection (b) certainly does not indicate that what follows merely supplements or enhances the penalty provision of subsection (a); what follows is to apply "notwithstanding" all of subsection (a), i.e., "in spite of" or "without prevention or obstruction from or by" subsection (a). See, e.g., Webster's New International Dictionary 1669 (2d ed. 1949). The next phrase ("in the case of any alien described in . . . subsection [(a)]") imports by reference the substantive acts attributed to the hypothetical alien (deportation and unauthorized reentry) in subsection (a). Significantly, this phrase does not apply subsection (b) to any alien "convicted under" subsection (a)–which is what one would expect if the provision was merely increasing the penalty for certain subsection (a) convictions. See, e.g., United States v. Davis, 801 F.2d 754, 755–756 (CA5 1986) (noting that "predicat[ing] punishment upon conviction" of another offense is one of the "common indicia of sentence-enhancement provisions"). Instead, subsection (b) applies to an alien "described in" subsection (a)–one who has been deported and has reentered illegally. And finally, subsection (a)'s provision that it applies "[s]ubject to subsection (b)" means that subsection (a) is inapplicable to an alien covered by subsection (b), just as subsection (b) applies "notwithstanding" that the alien would otherwise be covered by subsection (a).5

The Court relies on an earlier version of §1326 to support its interpretation of the statute in its current form. Ante, at 7–8. While I agree that such statutory history is a legitimate tool of construction, the statutory history of §1326 does not support, but rather undermines, the Court's interpretation. That earlier version contained a subsection (a) that, in addition to setting forth penalties (as did the subparts of subsection (b)), contained the phrase (which the subparts of subsection (b) did not) "shall be guilty of a felony, and upon conviction thereof, . . ." With such a formulation, of course, it would be easier to conclude that subsection (a) defines the crime and sets forth the basic penalty, and subsection (b) sets forth merely penalty enhancements. But if that was what the additional language in subsection (a) of the 1988 statute connoted, then what was the elimination of that additional language (in the 1990 version of the statute at issue here) meant to achieve? See §543(b)(3), 104 Stat. 5059. The more strongly the "shall be guilty of a felony" language suggests that subsection (b) of the 1988 statute contained only enhancements, the more strongly the otherwise inexplicable elimination of that language suggests that subsection (b) of the 1990 statute was meant to be parallel with subsection (a)—i.e., that both subsections were meant to set forth not merely penalties but also offenses. 6

After considering the subject matter and statutory language, the third factor the Court considers in arriving at its determination that this statute can only be read as a sentencing enhancement is the title of the 1988 amendment that added subsection (b)(2): "Criminal Penalties for Reentry of Certain Deported Aliens." See §7345, 102 Stat. 4471, cited ante, at 9. Of course, this title pertains to a subsection (b)(2) which, unlike the (b)(2) under which petitioner was convicted, was not parallel with the preceding subsection (a). But even disregarding that, the title of the amendment proves nothing at all. While "Criminal Penalties for Reentry" might normally be more suggestive of an enhancement than of a separate offense, there is good reason to believe it imports no such suggestion here. For the very next provision of the same enactment, which adjusts the substantive requirements for the crime of aiding and abetting the unlawful entry of an alien, is entitled "Criminal Penalties for Aiding or Assisting Certain Aliens to Enter the United States." See §7346, 102 Stat. 4471. Evidently, new substantive offenses that were penalized were simply entitled "Criminal Penalties" for the relevant offense. Moreover, the 1988 amendment kept the original title of §1326 ("Reentry of Deported Alien") intact, leaving it to apply to both subsection (a) and subsection (b). See §7345, supra; §276, 66 Stat. 229.

The Court's fourth factor leading it to conclude that this statute cannot reasonably be construed as establishing substantive offenses is legislative history. See ante, at 9. It is, again, the legislative history of the provision as it existed in 1988, before subsection (a) was stripped of the language "shall be guilty of a felony," thereby making subsections (a) and (b) parallel. Even so, it is of no help to the Court's case. The stray statements that the Court culls from the Congressional Record prove only that the new subsection (b) was thought to increase penalties for unlawful reentry. But there is no dispute that it does that! The critical question is whether it does it by adding penalties to the subsection (a) offense, or by creating additional, more severely punished, offenses. That technical point is not alluded to in any of the remarks the Court recites.

The Court's fifth and last argument in support of its interpretation of the statute is the contention that "the contrary interpretation . . . risks unfairness," ante, at 10, because it would require bringing the existence of the prior felony conviction to the attention of the jury. But it is also "unfair," of course, to deprive the defendant of a jury determination (and a beyond-a-reasonable-doubt burden of proof) on the critical question of the prior conviction. This Court's own assessment of which of those disadvantages is the greater can be of relevance here only insofar as we can presume that that perception would have been shared by the enacting Congress. We usually presume, however, not that an earlier Congress agreed with our current policy judgments, but rather that it agreed with the disposition provided by traditional practice or the common law. See United States v. Texas, 507 U.S. 529, 534 (1993); Astoria Fed. Sav. & Loan Assn. v. Solimino, 501 U.S. 104, 108 (1991); Norfolk Redevelopment and Housing Authority v. Chesapeake & Potomac Telephone Co. of Va., 464 U.S. 30, 35 (1983); Morissette v. United States, 342 U.S. 246, 263 (1952). As noted earlier, the Court's hostility to jury determination of prior convictions is quite simply at odds with the manner in which recidivism laws have historically been treated in this country.

Moreover, even if we were free to resolve this matter according to our current views of what is fair, the Court's judgment that avoiding jury "infection" is more important than affording a jury verdict (beyond a reasonable doubt) does not seem to me sound. The Court is not correct, to begin with, that the fact of prior conviction is "almost never contested," ante, at 10, particularly in unlawful-entry cases. That is clear from the very legislative history of the present statute. Senator Chiles explained that "identifying and prosecuting . . . illegal alien felons is a long and complex process" because "[i]t is not uncommon for an alien who has committed a certain felony to pay his bond and walk, only to be apprehended for a similar crime in the next county but with a new name and identification." 133 Cong. Rec. 8771. He went on to describe two specific aliens, one from whom police "seized 3 passports issued to him in 3 different names, 11 drivers licenses, immigration cards and numerous firearms and stolen property," and the other on whom immigration officials had "5 alien files . . . with 13 aliases, different birth dates and different social security cards." Id., at 8772. He said that "these aliens [were] not exceptions but rather common amongst the 100,000 illegal alien felons in the United States." Ibid. Representative Smith stated that aliens arrested for felonies "often are able to pay expensive bonds and disappear under a new identity often to reappear in court with a different name and a new offense. In some cases, they may return to their native lands and reenter the United States with new names and papers but committing the same crimes." Id., at 28840. And on the other side of the ledger, I doubt whether "infection" of the jury with knowledge of the prior crime is a serious problem. See, e.g., Spencer, supra, at 561 ("The defendants' interests [in keeping prejudicial prior convictions from the jury] are protected by limiting instructions and by the discretion residing with the trial judge to limit or forbid the admission of particularly prejudicial evidence even though admissible under an accepted rule of evidence") (citation omitted); Old Chief v. United States, 519 U.S. ___, ___ (slip op., at 18) (it is an abuse of discretion under Federal Rule of Evidence 403 to disallow defendant's stipulation to prior felony convictions where such convictions are an element of the offense); cf. Brief for National Association of Criminal Defense Lawyers as Amicus Curiae 30 ("In 1996, 98.2% of all Section 1326 defendants pleaded guilty"). If it is a problem, however, there are legislative and even judicial means for dealing with it, short of what today's decision does: taking the matter away from the jury in all cases. See 40 N. Y. U. L. Rev., at 333—334 (describing commonly used procedures under which defendant's right to a jury is invoked only "[i]f [he] denies the existence of prior convictions or stands mute"); Spencer, supra, at 567 (describing the English rule, under which the indictment alleges both the substantive offense and prior conviction, but the jury is not charged on the prior conviction until after it convicts the defendant of the substantive offense).

In sum, I find none of the four nontextual factors relied upon by the Court to support its interpretation ("typicality" of recidivism as a sentencing factor; titles; legislative history; and risk of unfairness) persuasive. What does seem to me significant, however, is a related statutory provision, introduced by a 1996 amendment, which explicitly refers to subsection (b)(2) as setting forth "offenses." See §334, 110 Stat. 3009—635 (instructing United States Sentencing Commission to amend sentencing guidelines "for offenses under . . . 1326(b)"). This later amendment can of course not cause subsection (b)(2) to have meant, at the time of petitioner's conviction, something different from what it then said. But Congress's expressed understanding that subsection (b) creates separate offenses is surely evidence that it is "fairly possible" to read the provision that way.7

I emphasize (to conclude this part of the discussion) that "fairly possible" is all that needs to be established. The doctrine of constitutional doubt does not require that the problem-avoiding construction be the preferable one–the one the Court would adopt in any event. Such a standard would deprive the doctrine of all function. "Adopt the interpretation that avoids the constitutional doubt if that is the right one" produces precisely the same result as "adopt the right interpretation." Rather, the doctrine of constitutional doubt comes into play when the statute is "susceptible of" the problem-avoiding interpretation, Delaware & Hudson Co., 213 U.S., at 408–when that interpretation is reasonable, though not necessarily the best. I think it quite impossible to maintain that this standard is not met by the interpretation of subsection (b) which regards it as creating separate offenses.

* * *

For the foregoing reasons, I think we must interpret the statute before us here as establishing a separate offense rather than a sentence enhancement. It can be argued that, once the constitutional doubts that require this course have been resolved, statutes no less ambiguous than the one before us here will be interpretable as sentence enhancements, so that not much will have been achieved. That begs the question, of course, as to how the constitutional doubt will be resolved. Moreover, where the doctrine of constitutional doubt does not apply, the same result may be dictated by the rule of lenity, which would preserve rather than destroy the criminal defendant's right to jury findings beyond a reasonable doubt. See, e.g., People ex rel. Cosgriff v. Craig, 195 N. Y., at 197, 88 N. E., at 40 ("It is unnecessary in this case to decide how great punishment the legislature may constitutionally authorize Courts of Special Sessions to impose on a conviction without a common-law jury. It is sufficient to say that in cases of doubtful construction or of conflicting statutory provisions, that interpretation should be given which best protects the rights of a person charged with an offense, to a trial according to the common law"). Whichever doctrine is applied for the purpose, it seems to me a sound principle that whenever Congress wishes a fact to increase the maximum sentence without altering the substantive offense, it must make that intention unambiguously clear. Accordingly, I would find that §1326(b)(2) establishes a separate offense, and would reverse the judgment below.

Notes

1. The Court asserts that we have declined to apply the doctrine "in circumstances similar to those here–where a constitutional question, while lacking an obvious answer, does not lead a majority gravely to doubt that the statute is constitutional." Ante, at 14. The cases it cites, however, do not support this contention. In Rust v. Sullivan, 500 U.S. 173 (1991), the Court believed that "[t]here [was] no question but that the statutory prohibition . . . [was] constitutional," id., at 192 (emphasis added). And in United States v. Locke, 471 U.S. 84 (1985), the Court found the doctrine inapplicable not because of lack of constitutional doubt, but because the statutory language did not permit an interpretation that would "avoid a constitutional question," id., at 96. Similarly, in United States v. Monsanto, 491 U.S. 600 (1989), "the language of [the statute was] plain and unambiguous," id. at 606.

2. It would not be, as the Court claims, "anomalous" to require jury trial for a factor increasing the maximum sentence, "in light of existing case law that permits a judge, rather than a jury, to determine the existence of factors that can make a defendant eligible for the death penalty . . . ." Ante, at 23, citing Walton v. Arizona, 497 U.S. 639 (1990); Hildwin v. Florida, 490 U.S. 638 (1989) (per curiam); and Spaziano v. Florida, 468 U.S. 447 (1984). Neither the cases cited, nor any other case, permits a judge to determine the existence of a factor which makes a crime a capital offense. What the cited cases hold is that, once a jury has found the defendant guilty of all the elements of an offense which carries as its maximum penalty the sentence of death, it may be left to the judge to decide whether that maximum penalty, rather than a lesser one, ought to be imposed–even where that decision is constrained by a statutory requirement that certain "aggravating factors" must exist. The person who is charged with actions that expose him to to the death penalty has an absolute entitlement to jury trial on all the elements of the charge.

3. For federal statutes of this sort, see, e.g., 15 U.S.C. § 1264(a), 18 U.S.C. § 924(c), and 18 U.S.C. § 2114(a). In each of these provisions, recidivism is recited in a list of sentence-increasing aggravators that include, for example, intent to defraud or mislead (15 U.S.C. § 1264(a)), use of a firearm that is a machine gun, or a destructive device, or that is equipped with a silencer (18 U.S.C. § 924(c)), and wounding or threatening life with a dangerous weapon (§2114(a)). It would do violence to the text to treat recidivism as a mere

enhancement while treating the parallel provisions as aggravated offenses, which they obviously are.

4. The statutory text at issue in Forbes was in all relevant respects identical to the statute before us here, except that the years of imprisonment for the offenses were less; they were increased by a 1994 amendment, see §130001(b), 108 Stat. 2023.

5. The Court contends that treating subsection (b) as establishing substantive offenses renders the "notwithstanding" and "subject to" provisions redundant, because even without them our lesser included-offense jurisprudence would prevent a defendant from being convicted under both subsections (a) and (b). Ante, at 6. Redundancy, however, consists of the annoying practice of saying the same thing twice, not the sensible practice of saying once, with clarity and conciseness, what the law provides. The author of today's opinion once agreed that "[t]he fact that each subsection makes reference to the other is simply the logical way of indicating the relationship between the arguably two separate crimes." United States v. Forbes, 16 F.3d 1294, 1298 (CA1 1994). But if this be redundancy, it is redundancy that the Court's alternative reading does not cure—unless one believes that, without the "notwithstanding" and "subject to" language, our interpretive jurisprudence would permit the subsection (a) penalty to be added to the subsection (b) penalties.

6. Immediately after stressing the significance of the 1988 version of §1326(a), the Court dismisses the 1990 amendment that eliminated the 1988 language upon which it relies, as a "housekeeping measure" by which "Congress [did not] inten[d] to change, or to clarify, the fundamental relationship between" subsections (a) and (b). Ante, at 9. The Court offers no support for this confident characterization, unless it is the mistaken assumption that statutory changes or clarifications unconfirmed by legislative history are inoperative. "Suffice it to say that legislative history need not confirm the details of changes in the law effected by statutory language before we will interpret that language according to its natural meaning." Morales v. Trans World Airlines, Inc., 504 U.S. 374, 385, n. 2 (1992).

7. The Court is incorrect in its contention that the effective-date provision of the 1996 amendments reflects the opposite congressional understanding. See, ante, at 13. That provision states that the amendments "apply under [subsection (b)] . . . only to violations of [subsection (a)]," occurring on or after the date of enactment. §321(c), 110 Stat. 3009—628. There is no dispute, of course, that if subsection (b) creates separate offenses, one of the elements of the separate offenses is the lesser offense set forth in subsection (a). The quoted language is the clearest and simplest way of saying that that element of the subsection (b) offenses must have occurred after the date of enactment in order for the amendments to be applicable.

Justice Scalia's concurrence and dissent in Clinton v. New York (June 25, 1998)

Justice Scalia, with whom Justice O'Connor joins, and with whom Justice Breyer joins as to Part III, concurring in part and dissenting in part.

Today the Court acknowledges the " 'overriding and time-honored concern about keeping the Judiciary's power within its proper constitutional sphere,' " ante, at 1—2, quoting Raines v. Byrd, 521 U.S. ____, ____ (1997) (slip op., at 8). It proceeds, however, to ignore the prescribed statutory limits of our jurisdiction by permitting the expedited-review provisions of the Line Item Veto Act to be invoked by persons who are not "individual[s]," 2 U.S.C. § 692 (1994 ed., Supp. II); and to ignore the constitutional limits of our jurisdiction by permitting one party to challenge the Government's denial to another party of favorable tax treatment from which the first party might, but just as likely might not, gain a concrete benefit. In my view, the Snake River appellees lack standing to challenge the President's cancellation of the "limited tax benefit," and the constitutionality of that action should not be addressed. I think the New York appellees have standing to challenge the President's cancellation of an "item of new direct spending"; I believe we have statutory authority (other than the expedited-review provision) to address that challenge; but unlike the Court I find the President's cancellation of spending items to be entirely in accord with the Constitution.

I

The Court's unrestrained zeal to reach the merits of this case is evident in its disregard of the statute's expedited-review provision, which extends that special procedure to "[a]ny Member of Congress or any individual adversely affected by [the Act]," §692. With the exception of Mike Cranney, a natural person, the appellees—corporations, cooperatives, and governmental entities—are not "individuals" under any accepted usage of that term. Worse still, the first provision of the United States Code confirms that insofar as this word is concerned, Congress speaks English like the rest of us: "In determining the meaning of any Act of Congress, unless the context indicates otherwise ... the wor[d] 'person' ... include[s] corporations, companies, associations, firms, partnerships, societies, and joint stock companies, as well as individuals." 1 U.S.C. § 1 (emphasis added). And doubly worse, one of the definitional provisions of this very Act expressly distinguishes "individuals" from "persons." A tax law does not create a "limited tax benefit," it says, so long as

"any difference in the treatment of persons is based solely on—

"(I) in the case of businesses and associations, the size or form of the business or association involved;

"(II) in the case of individuals, general demographic conditions, such as income, marital status, number of dependents, or tax return filing status ... ." 2 U.S.C. § 691e(9)(B)(iii) (1994 ed., Supp. II) (emphasis added).

The Court majestically sweeps the plain language of the statute aside, declaring that "[t]here is no plausible reason why Congress would have intended to provide for such special treatment of actions filed by natural persons and to have precluded entirely jurisdiction over comparable cases brought by corporate persons." Ante, at 10. Indeed, the

Court says, it would be "absurd" for Congress to have done so. Ibid. But Congress treats individuals more favorably than corporations and other associations all the time. There is nothing whatever extraordinary—and surely nothing so bizarre as to permit this Court to declare a "scrivener's error"—in believing that individuals will suffer more seriously from delay in the receipt of "vetoed" benefits or tax savings than corporations will, and therefore according individuals (but not corporations) expedited review. It may be unlikely that this is what Congress actually had in mind; but it is what Congress said, it is not so absurd as to be an obvious mistake, and it is therefore the law.

The only individual who has sued, and thus the only appellee who qualifies for expedited review under §692, is Mike Cranney. Since §692 does not confer jurisdiction over the claims of the other appellees, we must dismiss them, unless we have jurisdiction under another statute. In their complaints, appellees sought declaratory relief not only under §692(a), but also under the Declaratory Judgment Act, 28 U.S.C. § 2201 invoking the District Court's jurisdiction under 28 U.S.C. § 1331. After the District Court ruled, the Government appealed directly to this Court, but it also filed a notice of appeal to the Court of Appeals for the District of Columbia. In light of the Government's representation that it desires "[t]o eliminate any possibility that the district court's decision might escape review," Reply Brief for Appellants 2, n. 1, I would deem its appeal to this Court a petition for writ of certiorari before judgment, see 28 U.S.C. § 2101(e), and grant it. Under this Court's Rule 11, "[a] petition for a writ of certiorari to review a case pending in a United States court of appeals, before judgment is entered in that court, will be granted only upon a showing that the case is of such imperative public importance as to justify deviation from normal appellate practice and to require immediate determination in this Court." In light of the public importance of the issues involved, and the little sense it would make for the Government to pursue its appeal against one appellee in this Court and against the others in the Court of Appeals, the entire case, in my view, qualifies for certiorari review before judgment.

II

Not only must we be satisfied that we have statutory jurisdiction to hear this case; we must be satisfied that we have jurisdiction under Article III. "To meet the standing requirements of Article III, '[a] plaintiff must allege personal injury fairly traceable to the defendant's allegedly unlawful conduct and likely to be redressed by the requested relief.' " Raines, 521 U.S., at ____ (slip op., at 6), quoting Allen v. Wright, 468 U.S. 737, 751 (1984).

In the first action before us, appellees Snake River Potato Growers, Inc. (Snake River) and Mike Cranney, Snake River's Director and Vice-Chairman, challenge the constitutionality of the President's cancellation of §968 of the Taxpayer Relief Act of 1997. The Snake River appellees have standing, in the Court's view, because §968 gave them "the equivalent of a statutory 'bargaining chip,' " and "[b]y depriving them of their statutory bargaining chip, the cancellation inflicted a sufficient likelihood of economic injury to establish standing under our precedents." Ante, at 13, 14. It is unclear whether the Court means that deprivation of a "bargaining chip" itself suffices for standing, or that such deprivation suffices in the present case because it creates a likelihood of economic injury. The former is wrong as a matter of law, and the latter is wrong as a matter of fact, on the facts alleged.

For the proposition that "a denial of a benefit in the bargaining process" can suffice for standing the Court relies in a footnote, see ante, at 15, n. 22, on Northeastern Fla. Chapter, Associated Gen. Contractors of America v. Jacksonville, 508 U.S. 656 (1993). There, an association of contractors alleged that a city ordinance according racial preferences in the award of city contracts denied its members equal protection of the laws. Id., at 658—659. The association's members had regularly bid on and performed city contracts, and would have bid on designated set-aside contracts but for the ordinance. Id., at 659. We held that the association had standing even without proof that its members would have been awarded contracts absent the challenged discrimination. The reason, we explained, is that "[t]he 'injury in fact' in an equal protection case of this variety is the denial of equal treatment resulting from the imposition of the barrier, not the ultimate inability to obtain the benefit." Id., at 666, citing two earlier equal protection cases, Turner v. Fouche, 396 U.S. 346, 362 (1970), and Richmond v. J. A. Croson Co., 488 U.S. 469, 493 (1989). In other words, Northeastern Florida did not hold, as the Court suggests, that harm to one's bargaining position is an "injury in fact," but rather that, in an equal protection case, the denial of equal treatment is. Inasmuch as Snake River does not challenge the Line Item Veto Act on equal-protection grounds, Northeastern Florida is inapposite. And I know of no case outside the equal-protection field in which the mere detriment to one's "bargaining position," as opposed to a demonstrated loss of some bargain, has been held to confer standing. The proposition that standing is established by the mere reduction in one's chances of receiving a financial benefit is contradicted by Simon v. Eastern Ky. Welfare Rights Organization, 426 U.S. 26 (1976), which held that low-income persons who had been denied treatment at local hospitals lacked standing to challenge an Internal Revenue Service (IRS) ruling that reduced the amount of charitable care necessary for the hospitals to qualify for tax-exempt status. The situation in that case was strikingly similar to the one before us here: the denial of a tax benefit to a third party was alleged to reduce the chances of a financial benefit to the plaintiffs. And standing was denied.

But even if harm to one's bargaining position were a legally cognizable injury, Snake River has not alleged, as it must, facts sufficient to demonstrate that it personally has suffered that injury. See Warth v. Seldin, 422 U.S. 490, 502 (1975). In Eastern Ky. Welfare Rights, supra, the plaintiffs at least had applied for the financial benefit which had allegedly been rendered less likely of receipt; the present suit, by contrast, resembles a complaint asserting that the plaintiff's chances of winning the lottery were reduced, filed by a plaintiff who never bought a lottery ticket, or who tore it up before the winner was announced. Snake River has presented no evidence to show that it was engaged in bargaining, and that that bargaining was impaired by the President's cancellation of §968. The Court says that Snake River "was engaged in ongoing negotiations with the owner of a processing plant who had expressed an interest in structuring a tax-deferred sale when the President canceled §968," ante, at 13. There is, however, no evidence of "negotiations," only of two "discussions." According to the affidavit of Mike Cranney:

"On or about May 1997, I spoke with Howard Phillips, the principal owner of Idaho Potato Packers, concerning the possibility that, if the Cooperative Tax Act were passed, Snake River Potato Growers might purchase a Blackfoot, Idaho processing facility in a transaction that would allow the deferral of gain. Mr. Phillips expressed an interest in such a transaction if the Cooperative Tax Act were to pass. Mr. Phillips also acknowledged to me that Jim Chapman, our General Manager, had engaged him in a previous discussion concerning this matter." App. 112.

This affidavit would have set forth something of significance if it had said that Phillips had expressed an interest in the transaction "if and only if the Cooperative Tax Act were to pass." But of course it is most unlikely he said that; Idaho Potato Packers (IPP) could get just as much from the sale without the Act as with the Act, so long as the price was right. The affidavit would also have set forth something of significance if it had said that Phillips had expressed an interest in the sale "at a particular price if the Cooperative Tax Act were to pass." But it does not say that either. Nor does it even say that the President's action caused IPP to reconsider. Moreover, it was Snake River, not IPP, that terminated the discussions. According to Cranney, "[t]he President's cancellation of the Cooperative Tax Act caused me to terminate discussions with Phillips about the possibility of Snake River Potato Growers buying the Idaho Potato Packers facility," App. 114. So all we know from the record is that Snake River had two discussions with IPP concerning the sale of its processing facility on the tax deferred basis the Act would allow; that IPP was interested; and that Snake River ended the discussions after the President's action. We do not know that Snake River was prepared to offer a price–tax deferral or no–that would cross IPP's laugh threshold. We do not even know for certain that the tax deferral was a significant attraction to IPP; we know only that Cranney thought it was. On these facts– which never even bring things to the point of bargaining–it is pure conjecture to say that Snake River suffered an impaired bargaining position. As we have said many times, conjectural or hypothetical injuries do not suffice for Article III standing. See Lujan v. Defenders of Wildlife, 504 U.S. 555, 560 (1992).

Nor has Snake River demonstrated, as the Court finds, that "the cancellation inflicted a sufficient likelihood of economic injury to establish standing under our precedents." Ante, at 14. Presumably the economic injury the Court has in mind is Snake River's loss of a bargain purchase of a processing plant. But there is no evidence, and indeed not even an allegation, that before the President's action such a purchase was likely. The most that Snake River alleges is that the President's action rendered it "more difficult for plaintiffs to purchase qualified processors," App. 12. And even if that abstract "increased difficulty" sufficed for injury-in-fact (which it does not), the existence of even that is pure speculation. For all that appears, no owner of a processing plant would have been willing to sell to Snake River at any price that Snake River could afford–and the impossible cannot be made "more difficult." All we know is that a potential seller was "interested" in talking about the subject before the President's action, and that after the President's action Snake River itself decided to proceed no further. If this establishes a "likelihood" that Snake River would have made a bargain purchase but for the President's action, or even a "likelihood" that the President's action rendered "more difficult" a purchase that was realistically within Snake River's grasp, then we must adopt for our standing jurisprudence a new definition of likely: "plausible."

Twice before have we addressed whether plaintiffs had standing to challenge the Government's tax treatment of a third party, and twice before have we held that the speculative nature of a third party's response to changes in federal tax laws defeats standing. In Eastern Ky. Welfare Rights, 426 U.S. 26 (1976), we found it "purely speculative whether the denials of service ... fairly can be traced to [the IRS's] 'encouragement' or instead result from decisions made by the hospitals without regard to the tax implications." Id., at 42—43. We found it "equally speculative whether the desired exercise of the court's remedial powers in this suit would result in the availability to respondents of such services." Id., at 43. In Allen v. Wright, 468 U.S. 737 (1984), we held that parents of black children attending public schools lacked standing to challenge IRS policies concerning tax exemptions for private schools. The parents alleged, inter alia, that "federal tax exemptions to racially discriminatory private schools in their communities impair their ability to have their public schools desegregated." Id., at 752—753. We concluded that "the injury alleged is not fairly traceable to the Government conduct ... challenge[d] as unlawful," id., at 757, and that "it is entirely speculative ... whether withdrawal of a tax exemption from any particular school would lead the school to change its policies." Id., at 758. Likewise, here, it is purely speculative whether a tax-deferral would have prompted any sale, let alone one that reflected the tax benefit in the sale price.

The closest case the Court can appeal to as precedent for its finding of standing is Bryant v. Yellen, 447 U.S. 352 (1980). Even on its own terms, Bryant is distinguishable. As that case came to us, it involved a dispute between a class of some 800 landowners in the Imperial Valley, each of whom owned more than 160 acres, and a group of Imperial Valley residents who wished to purchase lands owned by that class. The point at issue was the application to those lands of a statutory provision that forbade delivery of water from a federal reclamation project to irrigable land held by a single owner in excess of 160 acres, and that limited the sale price of any lands so held in excess of 160 acres to a maximum amount, fixed the Secretary of the Interior, based on fair market value in 1929, before the Valley was irrigated by water from the Boulder Canyon Project. Id., at 366—367. That price would of course be "far below [the lands'] current market values," id., at 367, n. 17. The Court concluded that the would-be purchasers "had a sufficient stake in the outcome of the controversy to afford them standing," id., at 368. It is true, as the Court today emphasizes, that the purchasers had not presented "detailed information about [their] financial resources," but the Court thought that unnecessary only because "purchasers of such land would stand to reap significant gains on resale." Id., at 367, n. 17. Financing, in other words, would be easy to come by. Here, by contrast, not only do we have no notion whether Snake River has the cash in hand to afford IPP's bottom-line price, but we also have no reason to believe that financing of the purchase will be readily available. Potato processing plants, unlike agricultural land in the Imperial Valley, do not have a readily available resale market. On the other side of the equation, it was also much clearer in Bryant that if the suit came out in the would-be purchasers' favor, many of the landowners would be willing to sell. The alternative would be withdrawing the land from agricultural production, whereas sale–even at bargain-basement prices for the land–would at least enable recoupment of the cost of improvements, such as drainage systems. Ibid. In the present case, by contrast, we have no reason to believe that IPP is not operating its processing plant at a profit, and will not continue to do so in the future; Snake River has proffered no evidence that IPP or any other processor would surely have sold if only the President had not cancelled the tax deferral. The only uncertainty in Bryant was whether any of the respondents would wind up as buyers of any of the excess land; that seemed probable enough, since "respondents are residents of the Imperial Valley who desire to purchase the excess land for purposes of farming." Ibid. We have no basis to say that it is "likely" that Snake River would have purchased a processing facility if §968 had not been cancelled.

More fundamentally, however, the reasoning of Bryant should not govern the present case because it represents a crabbed view of the standing doctrine that has been superseded. Bryant was decided at the tail-end of "an era in which it was thought that the only function of the constitutional requirement of standing was 'to assure that concrete adverseness which sharpens the presentation of issues,' " Spencer v. Kemna, 523 U.S. ____, ____ (1998) (slip op., at 9), quoting Baker v. Carr, 369 U.S. 186, 204 (1962). Thus, the Bryant Court ultimately afforded the respondents standing simply because they "had a sufficient stake in the outcome of the controversy," 447 U.S., at 368, not because they had demonstrated injury in fact, causation and redressability. "That parsimonious view of the function of Article III standing has since yielded to the acknowledgement that the constitutional requirement is a 'means of "defin[ing] the role assigned to the judiciary in a tripartite allocation of power," ' and 'a part of the basic charter ... provid[ing] for the interaction between [the federal] government and the governments of the several States,' " Spencer, supra, at ____ (slip op., at 10), quoting Valley Forge Christian College v. Americans United for Separation of Church and State, Inc., 454 U.S. 464, 474, 476 (1982). While Snake River in the present case may indeed have enough of a "stake" to assure adverseness, the matter it brings before us is inappropriate for our resolution because its allegations do not establish an injury in fact, attributable to the Presidential action it challenges, and remediable by this Court's invalidation of that Presidential action.

Because, in my view, Snake River has no standing to bring this suit, we have no jurisdiction to resolve its challenge to the President's authority to cancel a "limited tax benefit."

III

I agree with the Court that the New York appellees have standing to challenge the President's cancellation of §4722(c) of the Balanced Budget Act of 1997 as an "item of new direct spending." See ante, at 11—12. The tax liability they will incur under New York law is a concrete and particularized injury, fairly traceable to the President's action, and avoided if that action is undone. Unlike the Court, however, I do not believe that Executive cancellation of this item of direct spending violates the Presentment Clause.

The Presentment Clause requires, in relevant part, that "[e]very Bill which shall have passed the House of Representatives and the Senate, shall, before it becomes a Law, be presented to the President of the United States; If he approve he shall sign it, but if not he shall return it," U.S. Const., Art. I, §7, cl. 2. There is no question that enactment of the Balanced Budget Act complied with these requirements: the House and Senate passed the bill, and the President signed it into law. It was only after the requirements of the Presentment Clause had been satisfied that the President exercised his authority under the Line Item Veto Act to cancel the spending item. Thus, the Court's problem with the Act is not that it authorizes the President to veto parts of a bill and sign others into law, but rather that it authorizes him to "cancel"–prevent from "having legal force or effect"– certain parts of duly enacted statutes.

Article I, §7 of the Constitution obviously prevents the President from cancelling a law that Congress has not authorized him to cancel. Such action cannot possibly be considered part of his execution of the law, and if it is legislative action, as the Court observes, " 'repeal of statutes, no less than enactment, must conform with Art. I.' " Ante, at 19, quoting from INS v. Chadha, 462 U.S. 919, 954 (1983). But that is not this case. It was certainly arguable, as an original matter, that Art. I, §7 also prevents the President from cancelling a law which itself authorizes the President to cancel it. But as the Court acknowledges, that argument has long since been made and rejected. In 1809, Congress passed a law authorizing the President to cancel trade restrictions against Great Britain and France if either revoked edicts directed at the United States. Act of Mar. 1, 1809, §11, 2 Stat. 528. Joseph Story regarded the conferral of that authority as entirely unremarkable in The Orono, 18 F. Cas. 830 (No. 10, 585) (CCD Mass. 1812). The Tariff Act of 1890 authorized the President to "suspend, by proclamation to that effect" certain of its provisions if he determined that other countries were imposing "reciprocally unequal and unreasonable" duties. Act of Oct. 1, 1890, §3, 26 Stat. 612. This Court upheld the constitutionality of that Act in Field v. Clark, 143 U.S. 649 (1892), reciting the history since 1798 of statutes conferring upon the President the power to, inter alia, "discontinue the prohibitions and restraints hereby enacted and declared," id., at 684, "suspend the operation of the aforesaid act," id., at 685, and "declare the provisions of this act to be inoperative," id., at 688.

As much as the Court goes on about Art. I, §7, therefore, that provision does not demand the result the Court reaches. It no more categorically prohibits the Executive reduction of congressional dispositions in the course of implementing statutes that authorize such reduction, than it categorically prohibits the Executive augmentation of congressional dispositions in the course of implementing statutes that authorize such augmentation–generally known as substantive rulemaking. There are, to be sure, limits upon the former just as there are limits upon the latter–and I am prepared to acknowledge that the limits upon the former may be much more severe. Those limits are established, however, not by some categorical prohibition of Art. I, §7, which our cases conclusively disprove, but by what has come to be known as the doctrine of unconstitutional delegation of legislative authority: When authorized Executive reduction or augmentation is allowed to go too far, it usurps the nondelegable function of Congress and violates the separation of powers.

It is this doctrine, and not the Presentment Clause, that was discussed in the Field opinion, and it is this doctrine, and not the Presentment Clause, that is the issue presented by the statute before us here. That is why the Court is correct to distinguish prior authorizations of Executive cancellation, such as the one involved in Field, on the ground that they were contingent upon an Executive finding of fact, and on the ground that they related to the field of foreign affairs, an area where the President has a special "degree of discretion and freedom," ante, at 27 (citation omitted). These distinctions have nothing to do with whether the details of Art. I, §7 have been complied with, but everything to do with whether the authorizations went too far by transferring to the Executive a degree of political, law-making power that our traditions demand be retained by the Legislative Branch.

I turn, then, to the crux of the matter: whether Congress's authorizing the President to cancel an item of spending gives him a power that our history and traditions show must reside exclusively in the Legislative Branch. I may note, to begin with, that the Line Item Veto Act is not the first statute to authorize the President to "cancel" spending items. In Bowsher v. Synar, 478 U.S. 714 (1986), we addressed the constitutionality of the Balanced Budget and Emergency Deficit Control Act of 1985, 2 U.S.C. § 901 et seq. (1982 ed., Supp. III), which required the President, if the federal budget deficit exceeded a certain amount, to issue a "sequestration" order mandating spending reductions specified by the Comptroller General. §902. The effect of sequestration was that "amounts sequestered ... shall be permanently cancelled," §902(a)(4) (emphasis added). We held that the Act was unconstitutional, not because it impermissibly gave the Executive legislative power, but because it gave the Comptroller General, an officer of the Legislative Branch over whom Congress retained removal power, "the ultimate authority to determine the budget cuts to be made," 478 U.S., at 733, "functions ... plainly entailing execution of the law in constitutional terms." Id., at 732—733 (emphasis added). The President's discretion under the Line Item Veto Act is certainly broader than the Comptroller General's discretion was under the 1985 Act, but it is no broader than the discretion traditionally granted the President in his execution of spending laws.

Insofar as the degree of political, "law-making" power conferred upon the Executive is concerned, there is not a dime's worth of difference between Congress's authorizing the President to cancel a spending item, and Congress's authorizing money to be spent on a particular item at the President's discretion. And the latter has been done since the Founding of the Nation. From 1789–1791, the First Congress made lump-sum appropriations for the entire Government–"sum[s] not exceeding" specified amounts for broad purposes. Act of Sept. 29, 1789, ch. 23, §1, 1 Stat. 95; Act of Mar. 26, 1790, ch. 4, §1, 1 Stat. 104; Act of Feb. 11, 1791, ch. 6, 1 Stat. 190. From a very early date Congress also made permissive individual appropriations, leaving the decision whether to spend the money to the President's unfettered discretion. In 1803, it appropriated $50,000 for the President to build "not exceeding fifteen gun boats, to be armed, manned and fitted out, and employed for such purposes as in his opinion the public service may require," Act of Feb. 28, 1803, ch. 11, §3, 2 Stat. 206. President Jefferson reported that "[t]he sum of fifty thousand dollars appropriated by Congress for providing gun boats remains unexpended. The favorable and peaceable turn of affairs on the Mississippi rendered an immediate execution of that law unnecessary," 13 Annals of Cong. 14 (1803). Examples of appropriations committed to the discretion of the President abound in our history. During the Civil War, an Act appropriated over $76 million to be divided among various items "as the exigencies of the service may require," Act of Feb. 25, 1862, ch. 32, 12 Stat. 344–345. During the Great Depression, Congress appropriated $950 million "for such projects and/or purposes and under such rules and regulations as the President in his discretion may prescribe," Act of Feb. 15, 1934, ch. 13, 48 Stat. 351, and $4 billion for general classes of projects, the money to be spent "in the discretion and under the direction of the President," Emergency Relief Appropriation Act of 1935, 49 Stat. 115. The constitutionality of such appropriations has never seriously been questioned. Rather, "[t]hat Congress has wide discretion in the matter of prescribing details of expenditures for which it appropriates must, of course, be plain. Appropriations and other acts of Congress are replete with instances of general appropriations of large amounts, to be allotted and expended as directed by designated government agencies." Cincinnati Soap Co. v. United States, 301 U.S. 308, 321–322 (1937).

Certain Presidents have claimed Executive authority to withhold appropriated funds even absent an express conferral of discretion to do so. In 1876, for example, President Grant reported to Congress that he would not spend money appropriated for certain harbor and river improvements, see Act of Aug. 14, 1876, ch. 267, 19 Stat. 132, because "[u]nder no circumstances [would he] allow expenditures upon works not clearly national," and in his view, the appropriations were for "works of purely private or local interest, in no sense national," 4 Cong. Rec. 5628. President Franklin D. Roosevelt impounded funds appropriated for a flood control reservoir and levee in Oklahoma. See Act of Aug. 18, 1941, ch. 377, 55 Stat. 638, 645; Hearings on S. 373 before the Ad Hoc Subcommittee on Impoundment of Funds of the Committee on Government Operations and the Subcommittee on Separation of Powers of the Senate Committee on the Judiciary, 93d Cong., 1st Sess., 848–849 (1973). President Truman ordered the impoundment of hundreds of millions of dollars that had been appropriated for military aircraft. See Act of Oct. 29, 1949, ch. 787, 63 Stat. 987, 1013; Public Papers of the Presidents of the United

States, Harry S. Truman, 1949, pp. 538—539 (W. Reid ed. 1964). President Nixon, the Mahatma Ghandi of all impounders, asserted at a press conference in 1973 that his "constitutional right" to impound appropriated funds was "absolutely clear." The President's News Conference of Jan. 31, 1973, 9 Weekly Comp. of Pres. Doc. 109—110 (1973). Our decision two years later in Train v. City of New York, 420 U.S. 35 (1975), proved him wrong, but it implicitly confirmed that Congress may confer discretion upon the executive to withhold appropriated funds, even funds appropriated for a specific purpose. The statute at issue in Train authorized spending "not to exceed" specified sums for certain projects, and directed that such "[s]ums authorized to be appropriated ... shall be allotted" by the Administrator of the Environmental Protection Agency, 33 U.S.C. § 1285 1287 (1970 ed., Supp. III). Upon enactment of this statute, the President directed the Administrator to allot no more than a certain part of the amount authorized. 420 U.S., at 40. This Court held, as a matter of statutory interpretation, that the statute did not grant the Executive discretion to withhold the funds, but required allotment of the full amount authorized. Id., at 44—47.

The short of the matter is this: Had the Line Item Veto Act authorized the President to "decline to spend" any item of spending contained in the Balanced Budget Act of 1997, there is not the slightest doubt that authorization would have been constitutional. What the Line Item Veto Act does instead—authorizing the President to "cancel" an item of spending—is technically different. But the technical difference does not relate to the technicalities of the Presentment Clause, which have been fully complied with; and the doctrine of unconstitutional delegation, which is at issue here, is preeminently not a doctrine of technicalities. The title of the Line Item Veto Act, which was perhaps designed to simplify for public comprehension, or perhaps merely to comply with the terms of a campaign pledge, has succeeded in faking out the Supreme Court. The President's action it authorizes in fact is not a line-item veto and thus does not offend Art. I, §7; and insofar as the substance of that action is concerned, it is no different from what Congress has permitted the President to do since the formation of the Union.

IV

I would hold that the President's cancellation of §4722(c) of the Balanced Budget Act as an item of direct spending does not violate the Constitution. Because I find no party before us who has standing to challenge the President's cancellation of §968 of the Taxpayer Relief Act, I do not reach the question whether that violates the Constitution.

For the foregoing reasons, I respectfully dissent.

Justice Scalia's dissent in Holloway v. US (March 2, 1999)

Justice Scalia, dissenting.

The issue in this case is the meaning of the phrase, in 18 U.S.C. § 2119 "with the intent to cause death or serious bodily harm." (For convenience' sake, I shall refer to it in this opinion as simply intent to kill.) As recounted by the Court, petitioner's accomplice,

Vernon Lennon, "testified that the plan was to steal the cars without harming the victims, but that he would have used his gun if any of the drivers had given him a 'hard time.'" Ante, at 2. The District Court instructed the jury that the intent element would be satisfied if petitioner possessed this "conditional" intent. Today's judgment holds that instruction to have been correct.

I dissent from that holding because I disagree with the following, utterly central, passage of the opinion:

"[A] carjacker's intent to harm his victim may be either 'conditional' or 'unconditional.' The statutory phrase at issue theoretically might describe (1) the former, (2) the latter, or (3) both species of intent." Ante, at 5 (footnote omitted).

I think, to the contrary, that in customary English usage the unqualified word "intent" does not usually connote a purpose that is subject to any conditions precedent except those so remote in the speaker's estimation as to be effectively nonexistent—and it never connotes a purpose that is subject to a condition which the speaker hopes will not occur. (It is this last sort of "conditional intent" that is at issue in this case, and that I refer to in my subsequent use of the term.) "Intent" is "[a] state of mind in which a person seeks to accomplish a given result through a course of action." Black's Law Dictionary 810 (6th ed. 1990). One can hardly "seek to accomplish" a result he hopes will not ensue.

The Court's division of intent into two categories, conditional and unconditional, makes the unreasonable seem logical. But Aristotelian classification says nothing about linguistic usage. Instead of identifying two categories, the Court might just as readily have identified three: unconditional intent, conditional intent, and feigned intent. But the second category, like the third, is simply not conveyed by the word "intent" alone. There is intent, conditional intent, and feigned intent, just as there is agreement, conditional agreement, and feigned agreement—but to say that in either case the noun alone, without qualification, "theoretically might describe" all three phenomena is simply false. Conditional intent is no more embraced by the unmodified word "intent" than a sea lion is embraced by the unmodified word "lion."

If I have made a categorical determination to go to Louisiana for the Christmas holidays, it is accurate for me to say that I "intend" to go to Louisiana. And that is so even though I realize that there are some remote and unlikely contingencies—"acts of God," for example—that might prevent me. (The fact that these remote contingencies are always implicit in the expression of intent accounts for the humorousness of spelling them out in such expressions as "if I should live so long," or "the Good Lord willing and the creek don't rise.") It is less precise, though tolerable usage, to say that I "intend" to go if my purpose is conditional upon an event which, though not virtually certain to happen (such as my continuing to live), is reasonably likely to happen, and which I hope will happen. I might, for example, say that I "intend" to go even if my plans depend upon receipt of my usual and hoped-for end-of-year bonus.

But it is not common usage—indeed, it is an unheard-of usage—to speak of my having an "intent" to do something, when my plans are contingent upon an event that is not virtually certain, and that I hope will not occur. When a friend is seriously ill, for example, I would not say that "I intend to go to his funeral next week." I would have to make it clear that the intent is a conditional one: "I intend to go to his funeral next week if he dies." The carjacker who intends to kill if he is met with resistance is in the same position: he has an "intent to kill if resisted"; he does not have an "intent to kill." No amount of rationalization can change the reality of this normal (and as far as I know exclusive) English usage. The word in the statute simply will not bear the meaning that the Court assigns.

The Government makes two contextual arguments to which I should respond. First, it points out that the statute criminalizes not only carjackings accomplished by "force and violence" but also those accomplished by mere "intimidation." Requiring an unconditional intent, it asserts, would make the number of covered carjackings accomplished by intimidation "implausibly small." Brief for United States 22. That seems to me not so. It is surely not an unusual carjacking in which the criminal jumps into the passenger seat and forces the person behind the wheel to drive off at gunpoint. A carjacker who intends to kill may well use this modus operandi, planning to kill the driver in a more secluded location. Second, the Government asserts that it would be hard to imagine an unconditional-intent-to-kill case in which the first penalty provision of §2119 would apply, i.e., the provision governing cases in which no death or bodily harm has occurred. Brief for United States 23. That is rather like saying that the crime of attempted murder should not exist, because someone who intends to kill always succeeds.

Notwithstanding the clear ordinary meaning of the word "intent," it would be possible, though of course quite unusual, for the word to have acquired a different meaning in the criminal law. The Court does not claim—and falls far short of establishing—such "term-of-art" status. It cites five state cases (representing the majority view among the minority of jurisdictions that have addressed the question) saying that conditional intent satisfies an intent requirement; but it acknowledges that there are cases in other jurisdictions to the contrary. See ante, at 9, n. 9 (citing State v. Irwin, 55 N. C. App. 305, 205 S. E. 2d 345 (1982); State v. Kinnemore, 34 Ohio App. 2d 39, 295 N. E. 2d 680 (1972)); see also Craddock v. State, 204 Miss. 606, 37 So. 2d 778 (1948); McArdle v. State, 372 So. 2d 897 (Ala. Crim. App.), writ denied, 372 S.2d 902 (Ala. 1979). As I understand the Court's position, it is not that the former cases are right and the latter wrong, so that "intent" in criminal statutes, a term of art in that context, includes conditional intent; but rather that "intent" in criminal statutes may include conditional intent, depending upon the statute in question. That seems to me not an available option. It is so utterly clear in normal usage that "intent" does not include conditional intent, that only an accepted convention in the criminal law could give the word a different meaning. And an accepted convention is not established by the fact that some courts have thought so some times. One must decide, I think, which line of cases is correct, and in my judgment it is that which rejects the conditional-intent rule.

There are of course innumerable federal criminal statutes containing an intent requirement, ranging from intent to steal, see 18 U.S.C. § 2113 to intent to defeat the provisions of the Bankruptcy Code, see §152(5), to intent that a vessel be used in hostilities against a friendly nation, see §962, to intent to obstruct the lawful exercise of parental rights, see §1204. Consider, for example, 21 U.S.C. § 841 which makes it a crime to possess certain drugs with intent to distribute them. Possession alone is also a crime, but a lesser one, see §844. Suppose that a person acquires and possesses a small quantity of cocaine for his own use, and that he in fact consumes it entirely himself. But assume further that, at the time he acquired the drug, he told his wife not to worry about the expense because, if they had an emergency need for money, he could always resell it. If conditional intent suffices, this person, who has never sold drugs and has never "intended" to sell drugs in any normal sense, has been guilty of possession with intent to distribute. Or consider 18 U.S.C. § 2390 which makes it a crime to enlist within the United States "with intent to serve in armed hostility against the United States." Suppose a Canadian enlists in the Canadian army in the United States, intending, of course, to fight all of Canada's wars, including (though he neither expects nor hopes for it) a war against the United States. He would be criminally liable. These examples make it clear, I think, that the doctrine of conditional intent cannot reasonably be applied across-the-board to the criminal code. I am unaware that any equivalent absurdities result from reading "intent" to mean what it says—a conclusion strongly supported by the fact that the Government has cited only a single case involving another federal statute, from over two centuries of federal criminal jurisprudence, applying the conditional-intent doctrine (and that in circumstances where it would not at all have been absurd to require real intent).1 The course selected by the Court, of course—"intent" is sometimes conditional and sometimes not—would require us to sift through these many statutes one-by-one, making our decision on the basis of such ephemeral indications of "congressional purpose" as the Court has used in this case, to which I now turn.

Ultimately, the Court rests its decision upon the fact that the purpose of the statute—which it says is deterring carjacking—"is better served by construing the statute to cover both the conditional and the unconditional species of wrongful intent." Ante, at 8. It supports this statement, both premise and conclusion, by two unusually uninformative statements from the legislative history (to stand out in that respect in that realm is quite an accomplishment) that speak generally about strengthening and broadening the carjacking statute and punishing carjackers severely. Ante, at 7, n. 7. But every statute intends not only to achieve certain policy objectives, but to achieve them by the means specified. Limitations upon the means employed to achieve the policy goal are no less a "purpose" of the statute than the policy goal itself. See Director, Office of Workers' Compensation Programs v. Newport News Shipbuilding & Dry Dock Co., 514 U.S. 122, 135—136 (1995). Under the Court's analysis, any interpretation of the statute that would broaden its reach would further the purpose the Court has found. Such reasoning is limitless and illogical.

The Court confidently asserts that "petitioner's interpretation would exclude from the coverage of the statute most of the conduct that Congress obviously intended to prohibit." Ante, at 8. It seems to me that one can best judge what Congress "obviously intended" not by intuition, but by the words that Congress enacted, which in this case require intent (not conditional intent) to kill. Is it implausible that Congress intended to define such a narrow federal crime? Not at all. The era when this statute was passed contained well publicized instances of not only carjackings, and not only carjackings involving violence or the threat of violence (as of course most of them do); but also of carjackings in which the perpetrators senselessly harmed the car owners when that was entirely unnecessary to the crime. I have a friend whose father was killed, and whose mother was nearly killed, in just such an incident–after the car had already been handed over. It is not at all implausible that Congress should direct its attention to this particularly savage sort of carjacking–where killing the driver is part of the intended crime.2

Indeed, it seems to me much more implausible that Congress would have focused upon the ineffable "conditional intent" that the Court reads into the statute, sending courts and juries off to wander through "would-a, could-a, should-a" land. It is difficult enough to determine a defendant's actual intent; it is infinitely more difficult to determine what the defendant planned to do upon the happening of an event that the defendant hoped would not happen, and that he himself may not have come to focus upon. There will not often be the accomplice's convenient confirmation of conditional intent that exists in the present case. Presumably it will be up to each jury whether to take the carjacker ("Your car or your life") at his word. Such a system of justice seems to me so arbitrary that it is difficult to believe Congress intended it. Had Congress meant to cast its carjacking net so broadly, it could have achieved that result–and eliminated the arbitrariness–by defining the crime as "carjacking under threat of death or serious bodily injury." Given the language here, I find it much more plausible that Congress meant to reach–as it said–the carjacker who intended to kill.

In sum, I find the statute entirely unambiguous as to whether the carjacker who hopes to obtain the car without inflicting harm is covered. Even if ambiguity existed, however, the rule of lenity would require it to be resolved in the defendant's favor. See generally United States v. Wiltberger, 5 Wheat. 76, 95 (1820). The Government's statement that the rule of lenity "has its primary application in cases in which there is some doubt whether the legislature intended to criminalize conduct that might otherwise appear to be innocent," Brief for United States 31 (emphasis added), is carefully crafted to conceal the fact that we have repeatedly applied the rule to situations just like this. For example, in Ladner v. United States, 358 U.S. 169 (1958), the statute at issue made it a crime to assault a federal officer with a deadly weapon. The defendant, who fired one shotgun blast that wounded two federal officers, contended that under this statute he was guilty of only one, and not two, assaults. The Court said, in an opinion joined by all eight Justices who reached the merits of the case:

"This policy of lenity means that the Court will not interpret a federal criminal statute so as to increase the penalty that it places on an individual when such an interpretation can be based on no more than a guess as to what Congress intended. If Congress desires to create multiple offenses from a single act affecting more than one federal officer, Congress can make that meaning clear. We thus hold that the single discharge of a shotgun alleged by the petitioner in this case would constitute only a single violation of §254." Id., at 178.

In Bell v. United States, 349 U.S. 81 (1955), the issue was similar: whether transporting two women, for the purpose of prostitution, in the same vehicle and on the same trip, constituted one or two violations of the Mann Act. In an opinion authored by Justice Frankfurter, the Court said:

"When Congress leaves to the Judiciary the task of imputing to Congress an undeclared will, the ambiguity should be resolved in favor of lenity. And this is not out of any sentimental consideration, or for want of sympathy with the purpose of Congress in proscribing evil or antisocial conduct. It may fairly be said to be a presupposition of our law to resolve doubts in the enforcement of a penal code against the imposition of a harsher punishment." Id., at 83.

If that is no longer the presupposition of our law, the Court should say so, and reduce the rule of lenity to an historical curiosity. But if it remains the presupposition, the rule has undeniable application in the present case. If the statute is not, as I think, clear in the defendant's favor, it is at the very least ambiguous and the defendant must be given the benefit of the doubt.

* * *

This seems to me not a difficult case. The issue before us is not whether the "intent" element of some common-law crime developed by the courts themselves–or even the "intent" element of a statute that replicates the common-law definition–includes, or should include, conditional intent. Rather, it is whether the English term "intent" used in a statute defining a brand new crime bears a meaning that contradicts normal usage. Since it is quite impossible to say that longstanding, agreed-upon legal usage has converted this word into a term of art, the answer has to be no. And it would be no even if the question were doubtful. I think it particularly inadvisable to introduce the new possibility of "conditional-intent" prosecutions into a modern federal criminal-law system characterized by plea bargaining, where they will predictably be used for in terrorem effect. I respectfully dissent.

Notes

1. The one case the Government has come up with is Shaffer v. United States, 308 F.2d 654 (CA5 1962), cert. denied, 373 U.S. 939 (1963), which upheld a conviction of assault "with intent to do bodily harm" where the defendant had said that if any persons tried to leave the building within five minutes after his departure "he would shoot their heads off," 308 F.2d, at 655. In my view, and in normal parlance, the defendant did not "intend" to do bodily harm, and there would have been nothing absurd about holding to

that effect.   The Government cites six other federal cases, Brief for United States 14—15, n. 5, but they are so inapposite that they succeed only in demonstrating the weakness of its assertion that conditional intent is the federal rule. Two of them, United States v. Richardson, 27 F. Cas. 798 (No. 16,155) (CCDC 1837), and United States v. Myers, 27 F. Cas. 43 (No. 15,845) (CCDC 1806), involve convictions for simple assault with no specific intent, and do not even contain any dictum bearing upon the present question. A third, United States v. Arrellano, 812 F.2d 1209, 1212, n. 2 (CA9 1987), contains nothing but dictum, since the jury found no intent of any sort. A fourth, United States v. Marks, 29 M. J. 1 (Ct. Mil. App. 1989), involved a defendant who tried to set fire to material that he assertedly believed was flame resistant. The crime he was convicted of, aggravated arson, was, as the court specifically stated, "a general intent crime," id., at 3. And the last two cases, United States v. Dworken, 855 F.2d 12 (CA1 1988), and United States v. Anello, 765 F.2d 253 (CA1), cert. denied, 474 U.S. 996 (1985), both involved conspiracy to possess drugs with intent to distribute. Defendants contended that they could not be convicted because they did not intend to complete the conspired-for transaction unless the quality of the drugs (and, in the case of Dworken, the price as well) was satisfactory. Of course the intent necessary to conspire for a specific-intent crime is not the same as the intent necessary for the crime itself, particularly insofar as antecedent conditions are concerned. And in any event, since it can hardly be thought that the conspirators wanted the quality and price of the drugs to be inadequate, neither case involved the conditional intent that is the subject of the present case.

2. Note that I am discussing what was a plausible congressional purpose in enacting this language–not what I necessarily think was the real one. I search for a plausible purpose because a text without one may represent a "scrivener's error" that we may properly correct. See Green v. Bock Laundry Machine Co., 490 U.S. 504, 528—529 (1989) (Scalia, J., concurring in judgment); see also United States v. X-Citement Video, Inc., 513 U.S. 64, 82 (1994) (Scalia, J., dissenting). There is no need for such correction here; the text as it reads, unamended by a meaning of "intent" that contradicts normal usage, makes total sense. If I were to speculate as to the real reason the "intent" requirement was added by those who drafted it, I think I would select neither the Court's attribution of purpose nor the one I have hypothesized. Like the District Court, see 921 F. Supp. 155, 158 (EDNY 1996), and the Court of Appeals for the Third Circuit, see United States v. Anderson, 108 F.3d 478, 482—483 (1997), I suspect the "intent" requirement was inadvertently expanded beyond the new subsection 2119(3), which imposed the death penalty–where it was thought necessary to ensure the constitutionality of that provision. Of course the actual intent of the draftsmen is irrelevant; we are governed by what Congress enacted.

Justice Scalia's concurrence and dissent in Neder v. US (June 10, 1999)

Justice Scalia, with whom Justice Souter and Justice Ginsburg join, concurring in part and dissenting in part.

I join Parts I and III of the Court's opinion. I do not join Part II, however, and I dissent from the judgment of the Court, because I believe that depriving a criminal defendant of the right to have the jury determine his guilt of the crime charged—which necessarily means his commission of every element of the crime charged—can never be harmless.

I

Article III, §2, cl. 3 of the Constitution provides: "The Trial of all Crimes, except in Cases of Impeachment, shall be by Jury . . . ." The Sixth Amendment provides: "In all criminal prosecutions, the accused shall enjoy the right to a speedy and public trial, by an impartial jury . . . ." When this Court deals with the content of this guarantee—the only one to appear in both the body of the Constitution and the Bill of Rights—it is operating upon the spinal column of American democracy. William Blackstone, the Framers' accepted authority on English law and the English Constitution, described the right to trial by jury in criminal prosecutions as "the grand bulwark of [the Englishman's] liberties . . . secured to him by the great charter." 4 W. Blackstone, Commentaries *349. One of the indictments of the Declaration of Independence against King George III was that he had "subject[ed] us to a Jurisdiction foreign to our Constitution, and unacknowledged by our Laws" in approving legislation "[f]or depriving us, in many Cases, of the Benefits of Trial by Jury." Alexander Hamilton wrote that "[t]he friends and adversaries of the plan of the convention, if they agree in nothing else, concur at least in the value they set upon the trial by jury: Or if there is any difference between them, it consists in this, the former regard it as a valuable safeguard to liberty, the latter represent it as the very palladium of free government." The Federalist No. 83, p. 426 (M. Beloff ed. 1987). The right to trial by jury in criminal cases was the only guarantee common to the 12 state constitutions that predated the Constitutional Convention, and it has appeared in the constitution of every State to enter the Union thereafter. Alschuler & Deiss, A Brief History of the Criminal Jury in the United States, 61 U. Chi. L. Rev. 867, 870, 875, n. 44 (1994). By comparison, the right to counsel—deprivation of which we have also held to be structural error—is a Johnny-come-lately: Defense counsel did not become a regular fixture of the criminal trial until the mid-1800's. See W. Beaney, Right to Counsel in American Courts 226 (1955).

The right to be tried by a jury in criminal cases obviously means the right to have a jury determine whether the defendant has been proved guilty of the crime charged. And since all crimes require proof of more than one element to establish guilt (involuntary manslaughter, for example, requires (1) the killing (2) of a human being (3) negligently), it follows that trial by jury means determination by a jury that all elements were proved. The Court does not contest this. It acknowledges that the right to trial by jury was denied in the present case, since one of the elements was not—despite the defendant's protestation—submitted to be passed upon by the jury. But even so, the Court lets the defendant's sentence stand, because we judges can tell that he is unquestionably guilty.

Even if we allowed (as we do not) other structural errors in criminal trials to be

pronounced "harmless" by judges–a point I shall address in due course–it is obvious that
we could not allow judges to validate this one. The constitutionally required step that was
omitted here is distinctive, in that the basis for it is precisely that, absent voluntary waiver
of the jury right, the Constitution does not trust judges to make determinations of criminal
guilt. Perhaps the Court is so enamoured of judges in general, and federal judges in
particular, that it forgets that they (we) are officers of the Government, and hence proper
objects of that healthy suspicion of the power of government which possessed the Framers
and is embodied in the Constitution. Who knows?–20 years of appointments of federal
judges by oppressive administrations might produce judges willing to enforce oppressive
criminal laws, and to interpret criminal laws oppressively–at least in the view of the
citizens in some vicinages where criminal prosecutions must be brought. And so the
people reserved the function of determining criminal guilt to themselves, sitting as jurors.
It is not within the power of us Justices to cancel that reservation–neither by permitting
trial judges to determine the guilt of a defendant who has not waived the jury right, nor
(when a trial judge has done so anyway) by reviewing the facts ourselves and pronouncing
the defendant without-a-doubt guilty. The Court's decision today is the only instance I
know of (or could conceive of) in which the remedy for a constitutional violation by a trial
judge (making the determination of criminal guilt reserved to the jury) is a repetition of
the same constitutional violation by the appellate court (making the determination of
criminal guilt reserved to the jury).

II

The Court's decision would be wrong even if we ignored the distinctive
character of this constitutional violation. The Court reaffirms the rule that it would be
structural error (not susceptible of "harmless-error" analysis) to " 'vitiat[e] all the jury's
findings.' " Ante, at 8 (quoting Sullivan v. Louisiana, 508 U.S. 275, 281 (1993)). A court
cannot, no matter how clear the defendant's culpability, direct a guilty verdict. See
Carpenters v. United States, 330 U.S. 395, 410 (1947); Rose v. Clark, 478 U.S. 570, 578
(1986); Arizona v. Fulminante, 499 U.S. 279, 294 (1991) (White, J., dissenting). The
question that this raises is why, if denying the right to conviction by jury is structural
error, taking one of the elements of the crime away from the jury should be treated
differently from taking all of them away–since failure to prove one, no less than failure to
prove all, utterly prevents conviction.

The Court never asks, much less answers, this question. Indeed, we do not
know, when the Court's opinion is done, how many elements can be taken away from the
jury with impunity, so long as appellate judges are persuaded that the defendant is surely
guilty. What if, in the present case, besides keeping the materiality issue for itself, the
District Court had also refused to instruct the jury to decide whether the defendant signed
his tax return, see 26 U.S.C. § 7206(1)? If Neder had never contested that element of the
offense, and the record contained a copy of his signed return, would his conviction be
automatically reversed in that situation but not in this one, even though he would be just
as obviously guilty? We do not know. We know that all elements cannot be taken from the

jury, and that one can. How many is too many (or perhaps what proportion is too high) remains to be determined by future improvisation. All we know for certain is that the number is somewhere between tuppence and 19 shillings 11, since the Court's only response to my assertion that there is no principled distinction between this case and a directed verdict is that "our course of constitutional adjudication has not been characterized by this 'in for a penny, in for a pound' approach." See Ante, at 14, n. 1.

The underlying theme of the Court's opinion is that taking the element of materiality from the jury did not render Neder's trial unfair, because the judge certainly reached the "right" result. But the same could be said of a directed verdict against the defendant—which would be per se reversible no matter how overwhelming the unfavorable evidence. See Rose v. Clark, supra, at 578. The very premise of structural-error review is that even convictions reflecting the "right" result are reversed for the sake of protecting a basic right. For example, in Tumey v. Ohio, 273 U.S. 510 (1927), where we reversed the defendant's conviction because he had been tried before a biased judge, the State argued that "the evidence shows clearly that the defendant was guilty and that he was only fined $100, which was the minimum amount, and therefore that he can not complain of a lack of due process, either in his conviction or in the amount of the judgment." Id., at 535. We rejected this argument out of hand, responding that "[n]o matter what the evidence was against him, he had the right to have an impartial judge." Ibid. (emphasis added). The amount of evidence against a defendant who has properly preserved his objection, while relevant to determining whether a given error was harmless, has nothing to do with determining whether the error is subject to harmless-error review in the first place.

The Court points out that in Johnson v. United States, 520 U.S. 461 (1997), we affirmed the petitioner's conviction even though the element of materiality had been withheld from the jury. But the defendant in that case, unlike the defendant here, had not requested a materiality instruction. In the context of such unobjected-to error, the mere deprivation of substantial rights "does not, without more," warrant reversal, United States v. Olano, 507 U.S. 725, 737 (1993), but the appellant must also show that the deprivation "seriously affect[s] the fairness, integrity or public reputation of judicial proceedings," Johnson, supra, at 469 (quoting Olano, supra, at 736) (internal quotation marks omitted). Johnson stands for the proposition that, just as the absolute right to trial by jury can be waived, so also the failure to object to its deprivation at the point where the deprivation can be remedied will preclude automatic reversal.1

Insofar as it applies to the jury-trial requirement, the structural-error rule does not exclude harmless-error analysis—though it is harmless-error analysis of a peculiar sort, looking not to whether the jury's verdict would have been the same without the error, but rather to whether the error did not prevent the jury's verdict. The failure of the court to instruct the jury properly—whether by omitting an element of the offense or by so misdescribing it that it is effectively removed from the jury's consideration—can be harmless, if the elements of guilt that the jury did find necessarily embraced the one omitted or misdescribed. This was clearly spelled out by our unanimous opinion in

Sullivan v. Louisiana, supra, which said that harmless-error review "looks . . . to the basis on which 'the jury actually rested its verdict.' " Id., at 279 (quoting Yates v. Evatt, 500 U.S. 391, 404 (1991)). Where the facts necessarily found by the jury (and not those merely discerned by the appellate court) support the existence of the element omitted or misdescribed in the instruction, the omission or misdescription is harmless.2 For there is then no "gap" in the verdict to be filled by the factfinding of judges. This formulation adequately explains the three cases, see California v. Roy, 519 U.S. 2, 6 (1996) (Scalia, J., concurring); Carella v. California, 491 U.S. 270–273 (1989) (Scalia, J., concurring in judgment); Pope v. Illinois, 481 U.S. 497, 504 (1987) (Scalia, J., concurring),3 that the majority views as "dictat[ing] the answer" to the question before us today. Ante, at 10. In casting Sullivan aside, the majority does more than merely return to the state of confusion that existed in our prior cases; it throws open the gate for appellate courts to trample over the jury's function.

Asserting that "[u]nder our cases, a constitutional error is either structural or it is not," ante, at 11, the Court criticizes the Sullivan test for importing a "case-by-case approach" into the structural-error determination. If that were true, it would seem a small price to pay for keeping the appellate function consistent with the Sixth Amendment. But in fact the Court overstates the cut-and-dried nature of identifying structural error. Some structural errors, like the complete absence of counsel or the denial of a public trial, are visible at first glance. Others, like deciding whether the trial judge was biased or whether there was racial discrimination in the grand jury selection, require a more fact-intensive inquiry. Deciding whether the jury made a finding "functionally equivalent" to the omitted or misdescribed element is similar to structural-error analysis of the latter sort.

III

The Court points out that all forms of harmless-error review "infringe upon the jury's factfinding role and affect the jury's deliberative process in ways that are, strictly speaking, not readily calculable." Ante, at 15. In finding, for example, that the jury's verdict would not have been affected by the exclusion of evidence improperly admitted, or by the admission of evidence improperly excluded, a court is speculating on what the jury would have found. See, e.g., Arizona v. Fulminante, 499 U.S., at 296 (Would the verdict have been different if a coerced confession had not been introduced?); Delaware v. Van Arsdall, 475 U.S. 673, 684 (1986) (Would the verdict have been different if evidence had not been unconstitutionally barred from admission?). There is no difference, the Court asserts, in permitting a similar speculation here. Ante, at 15.

If this analysis were correct—if permitting speculation on whether a jury would have changed its verdict logically demands permitting speculation on what verdict a jury would have rendered—we ought to be able to uphold directed verdicts in cases where the defendant's guilt is absolutely clear. In other words, the Court's analysis is simply a repudiation of the principle that depriving the criminal defendant of a jury verdict is structural error. Sullivan v. Louisiana clearly articulated the line between permissible and impermissible speculation that preserves the well established structural character of the jury-trial right and places a principled and discernible limitation upon judicial intervention: "The inquiry . . . is not whether, in a trial that occurred without the error, a guilty verdict would surely have been rendered, but whether the guilty verdict actually rendered in this trial was surely unattributable to the error." 508 U.S., at 279 (emphasis added). Harmless-error review applies only when the jury actually renders a verdict–that is, when it has found the defendant guilty of all the elements of the crime.

The difference between speculation directed towards confirming the jury's verdict (Sullivan) and speculation directed towards making a judgment that the jury has never made (today's decision) is more than semantic. Consider, for example, the following scenarios. If I order for my wife in a restaurant, there is no sense in which the decision is hers, even if I am sure beyond a reasonable doubt about what she would have ordered. If, however, while she is away from the table, I advise the waiter to stay with an order she initially made, even though he informs me that there has been a change in the accompanying dish, one can still say that my wife placed the

order–even if I am wrong about whether she would have changed her mind in light of the new information. Of course, I may predict correctly in both instances simply because I know my wife well. I doubt, however, that a low-error rate would persuade my wife that my making a practice of the first was a good idea.

It is this sort of allocation of decisionmaking power that the Sullivan standard protects. The right to render the verdict in criminal prosecutions belongs exclusively to the jury; reviewing it belongs to the appellate court. "Confirming" speculation does not disturb that allocation, but "substituting" speculation does. Make no mistake about the shift in standard: Whereas Sullivan confined appellate courts to their proper role of reviewing verdicts, the Court today puts appellate courts in the business of reviewing the defendant's guilt. The Court does not–it cannot–reconcile this new approach with the proposition that denial of the jury-trial right is structural error.

*   *   *

The recipe that has produced today's ruling consists of one part self-esteem, one part panic, and one part pragmatism. I have already commented upon the first ingredient: What could possibly be so bad about having judges decide that a jury would necessarily have found the defendant guilty? Nothing except the distrust of judges that underlies the jury-trial guarantee. As to the ingredient of panic: The Court is concerned that the Sullivan approach will invalidate convictions in innumerable cases where the defendant is obviously guilty. There is simply no basis for that concern. The limited harmless-error approach of Sullivan applies only when specific objection to the erroneous instruction has been made and rejected. In all other cases, the Olano plain-error rule governs, which is similar to the ordinary harmless-error analysis that the Court would apply. I doubt that the criminal cases in which instructions omit or misdescribe elements of the offense over the objection of the defendant are so numerous as to present a massive problem. (If they are, the problem of vagueness in our criminal laws, or of incompetence in our judges, makes the problem under discussion here seem insignificant by comparison.)

And as for the ingredient of pragmatism (if the defendant is unquestionably guilty, why go through the trouble of trying him again?), it suffices to quote Blackstone once again:

"[H]owever convenient [intrusions on the jury right] may appear at first (as, doubtless, all arbitrary powers, well executed are the most convenient), yet, let it again be remembered, that delays and little inconveniences in the forms of justice are the price that all free nations must pay for their liberty in more substantial matters; that these inroads upon this sacred bulwark of the nation are fundamentally opposite to the spirit of our constitution; and that, though begun in trifles, the precedent may gradually increase and spread, to the utter disuse of juries in questions of the most momentous concern." 4 Blackstone, Commentaries *350.

See also Bollenbach v. United States, 326 U.S. 607, 615 (1946). Formal requirements are often scorned when they stand in the way of expediency. This Court, however, has an obligation to take a longer view. I respectfully dissent.

Notes

1. Contrary to Justice Stevens' suggestion, ante, at 3 (Stevens, J., concurring in part and concurring in the judgment), there is nothing "internally inconsistent" about believing that a procedural guarantee is fundamental while also believing that it must be asserted in a timely fashion. It is a universally acknowledged principle of law that one who sleeps on his rights – even fundamental rights – may lose them.

2. Justice Stevens thinks that the jury findings as to the amounts that petitioner failed to report on his tax returns "necessarily included" a finding on materiality, since "'total income' is obviously 'information necessary to a determination of a taxpayer's income tax liability.'" Ante, at 2 (emphasis added). If that analysis were valid, we could simply dispense with submitting the materiality issue to the jury in all future tax cases involving understatement of income; a finding of intentional understatement would be a finding of guilt—no matter how insignificant the understatement might be, and no matter whether it was offset by understatement of deductions as well. But the right to a jury trial on all elements of the offense does not mean the right to a jury trial on only so many elements as are necessary in order logically to deduce the remainder. The jury has the right to apply its own logic (or illogic) to its decision to convict or acquit. At bottom, Justice Stevens' "obviously" represents his judgment that any reasonable jury would have to think that the misstated amounts were material. Cf. Ante, at 13, n. 1. It is, in other words, nothing more than a repackaging of the majority's approach, which allows a judge to determine what a jury "would have found" if asked. And it offers none of the protection that Justice Stevens promises the jury will deliver "against the corrupt or overzealous prosecutor and against the compliant, biased, or eccentric judge." Ante, at 5 (quoting Duncan v. Louisiana, 391 U.S. 145, 156 (1968)).

3. The Court asserts that this "functional equivalent" test does not explain Pope, since "a juror in Rockford, Illinois, who found that the [allegedly obscene] material lacked

value under community standards would not necessarily have found that it did so under presumably broader and more tolerant national standards." Ante, at 11. If the jury had been instructed to measure the material by Rockford, Illinois, standards, I might agree. It was instructed, however, to "judge whether the material was obscene by determining how it would be viewed by ordinary adults in the whole State of Illinois," 481 U.S., at 499 (emphasis added)–which includes, of course, the City of Chicago, that toddlin' town. A finding of obscenity under that standard amounts to a finding of obscenity under a national ("reasonable person") standard. See id., at 504 (Scalia, J., concurring).

Justice Scalia's dissent in Chicago v. Jesus Morales (June 10, 1999)

Justice Scalia, dissenting.

The citizens of Chicago were once free to drive about the city at whatever speed they wished. At some point Chicagoans (or perhaps Illinoisans) decided this would not do, and imposed prophylactic speed limits designed to assure safe operation by the average (or perhaps even subaverage) driver with the average (or perhaps even subaverage) vehicle. This infringed upon the "freedom" of all citizens, but was not unconstitutional.

Similarly, the citizens of Chicago were once free to stand around and gawk at the scene of an accident. At some point Chicagoans discovered that this obstructed traffic and caused more accidents. They did not make the practice unlawful, but they did authorize police officers to order the crowd to disperse, and imposed penalties for refusal to obey such an order. Again, this prophylactic measure infringed upon the "freedom" of all citizens, but was not unconstitutional.

Until the ordinance that is before us today was adopted, the citizens of Chicago were free to stand about in public places with no apparent purpose–to engage, that is, in conduct that appeared to be loitering. In recent years, however, the city has been afflicted with criminal street gangs. As reflected in the record before us, these gangs congregated in public places to deal in drugs, and to terrorize the neighborhoods by demonstrating control over their "turf." Many residents of the inner city felt that they were prisoners in their own homes. Once again, Chicagoans decided that to eliminate the problem it was worth restricting some of the freedom that they once enjoyed. The means they took was similar to the second, and more mild, example given above rather than the first: Loitering was not made unlawful, but when a group of people occupied a public place without an apparent purpose and in the company of a known gang member, police officers were authorized to order them to disperse, and the failure to obey such an order was made unlawful. See Chicago Municipal Code §8—4—015 (1992). The minor limitation upon the free state of nature that this prophylactic arrangement imposed upon all Chicagoans seemed to them (and it seems to me) a small price to pay for liberation of their streets.

The majority today invalidates this perfectly reasonable measure by ignoring our rules governing facial challenges, by elevating loitering to a constitutionally guaranteed right, and by discerning vagueness where, according to our usual standards, none exists.

I

Respondents' consolidated appeal presents a facial challenge to the Chicago Ordinance on vagueness grounds. When a facial challenge is successful, the law in question is declared to be unenforceable in all its applications, and not just in its particular application to the party in suit. To tell the truth, it is highly questionable whether federal courts have any business making such a declaration. The rationale for our power to review federal legislation for constitutionality, expressed in Marbury v. Madison, 1 Cranch 137 (1803), was that we had to do so in order to decide the case before us. But that rationale only extends so far as to require us to determine that the statute is unconstitutional as applied to this party, in the circumstances of this case.

That limitation was fully grasped by Tocqueville, in his famous chapter on the power of the judiciary in American society:

"The second characteristic of judicial power is, that it pronounces on special cases, and not upon general principles. If a judge, in deciding a particular point, destroys a general principle by passing a judgment which tends to reject all the inferences from that principle, and consequently to annul it, he remains within the ordinary limits of his functions. But if he directly attacks a general principle without having a particular case in view, he leaves the circle in which all nations have agreed to confine his authority; he assumes a more important, and perhaps a more useful influence, than that of the magistrate; but he ceases to represent the judicial power.

. . . . .

"Whenever a law which the judge holds to be unconstitutional is invoked in a tribunal of the United States, he may refuse to admit it as a rule ... . But as soon as a judge has refused to apply any given law in a case, that law immediately loses a portion of its moral force. Those to whom it is prejudicial learn that means exist of overcoming its authority; and similar suits are multiplied, until it becomes powerless. ... The political power which the Americans have entrusted to their courts of justice is therefore immense; but the evils of this power are considerably diminished by the impossibility of attacking the laws except through the courts of justice. ... [W]hen a judge contests a law in an obscure debate on some particular case, the importance of his attack is concealed from public notice; his decision bears upon the interest of an individual, and the law is slighted only incidentally. Moreover, although it is censured, it is not abolished; its moral force may be diminished, but its authority is not taken away; and its final destruction can be accomplished only by the reiterated attacks of judicial functionaries." Democracy in America 73, 75—76 (R. Heffner ed. 1956).

As Justice Sutherland described our system in his opinion for a unanimous Court in Massachusetts v. Mellon, 262 U.S. 447, 488 (1923):

"We have no power per se to review and annul acts of Congress on the ground that they are unconstitutional. That question may be considered only when the justification for some direct injury suffered or threatened, presenting a justiciable issue, is made to rest upon such an act. Then the power exercised is that of ascertaining and declaring the law applicable to the controversy. It amounts to little more than the negative power to disregard an unconstitutional enactment, which otherwise would stand in the way of the enforcement of a legal right. . . . If a case for preventive relief be presented the court enjoins, in effect, not the execution of the statute, but the acts of the official, the statute notwithstanding."

And as Justice Brennan described our system in his opinion for a unanimous Court in United States v. Raines, 362 U.S. 17, 21—22 (1960):

"The very foundation of the power of the federal courts to declare Acts of Congress unconstitutional lies in the power and duty of those courts to decide cases and controversies before them. . . . This Court, as is the case with all federal courts, 'has no jurisdiction to pronounce any statute, either of a State or of the United States, void, because irreconcilable with the Constitution, except as it is called upon to adjudge the legal rights of litigants in actual controversies. In the exercise of that jurisdiction, it is bound by two rules, to which it has rigidly adhered, one, never to anticipate a question of constitutional law in advance of the necessity of deciding it; the other never to formulate a rule of constitutional law broader than is required by the precise facts to which it is to be applied'. . . . Kindred to these rules is the rule that one to whom application of a statute is constitutional will not be heard to attack the statute on the ground that impliedly it might also be taken as applying to other persons or other situations in which its application might be unconstitutional. . . . The delicate power of pronouncing an Act of Congress unconstitutional is not to be exercised with reference to hypothetical cases thus imagined."

It seems to me fundamentally incompatible with this system for the Court not to be content to find that a statute is unconstitutional as applied to the person before it, but to go further and pronounce that the statute is unconstitutional in all applications. Its reasoning may well suggest as much, but to pronounce a holding on that point seems to me no more than an advisory opinion—which a federal court should never issue at all, see Hayburn's Case, 2 Dall. 409 (1792), and especially should not issue with regard to a constitutional question, as to which we seek to avoid even nonadvisory opinions, see, e.g., Ashwander v. TVA, 297 U.S. 288, 347 (1936) (Brandeis, J., concurring). I think it quite improper, in short, to ask the constitutional claimant before us: Do you just want us to say that this statute cannot constitutionally be applied to you in this case, or do you want to go for broke and try to get the statute pronounced void in all its applications?

I must acknowledge, however, that for some of the present century we have done just this. But until recently, at least, we have—except in free-speech cases subject to the doctrine of overbreadth, see, e.g., New York v. Ferber, 458 U.S. 747, 769—773 (1982)— required the facial challenge to be a go-for-broke proposition. That is to say, before declaring a statute to be void in all its applications (something we should not be doing in the first place), we have at least imposed upon the litigant the eminently reasonable requirement that he establish that the statute was unconstitutional in all its applications. (I say that is an eminently reasonable requirement, not only because we should not be holding a statute void in all its applications unless it is unconstitutional in all its applications, but also because unless it is unconstitutional in all its applications we do not even know, without conducting an as-applied analysis, whether it is void with regard to the very litigant before us–whose case, after all, was the occasion for undertaking this inquiry in the first place.1)

As we said in United States v. Salerno, 481 U.S. 739, 745 (1987):

"A facial challenge to a legislative Act is, of course, the most difficult challenge to mount successfully, since the challenger must establish that no set of circumstances exists under which the Act would be valid. The fact that [a legislative Act] might operate unconstitutionally under some conceivable set of circumstances is insufficient to render it wholly invalid, since we have not recognized an 'overbreadth' doctrine outside the limited context of the First Amendment." (Emphasis added.)2

This proposition did not originate with Salerno, but had been expressed in a line of prior opinions. See, e.g., Members of City Council of Los Angeles v. Taxpayers for Vincent, 466 U.S. 789, 796 (1984) (opinion for the Court by Stevens, J.) (statute not implicating First Amendment rights is invalid on its face if "it is unconstitutional in every conceivable application"); Schall v. Martin, 467 U.S. 253, 269, n. 18 (1984); Hoffman Estates v. Flipside, Hoffman Estates, Inc., 455 U.S. 489, 494–495, 497 (1982); United States v. National Dairy Products Corp., 372 U.S. 29, 31–32 (1963); Raines, supra, at 21. And the proposition has been reaffirmed in many cases and opinions since. See, e.g., Anderson v. Edwards, 514 U.S. 143, 155–156, n. 6 (1995) (unanimous Court); Babbitt v. Sweet Home Chapter of Communities for Great Oregon, 515 U.S. 687, 699 (1995) (opinion for the Court by Stevens, J.) (facial challenge asserts that a challenged statute or regulation is invalid "in every circumstance"); Reno v. Flores, 507 U.S. 292, 301 (1993); Rust v. Sullivan, 500 U.S. 173, 183 (1991); Ohio v. Akron Center for Reproductive Health, 497 U.S. 502, 514 (1990) (opinion of Kennedy, J.); Webster v. Reproductive Health Servs., 492 U.S. 490, 523–524 (1989) (O'Connor, J., concurring in part and concurring in judgment); New York State Club Assn., Inc. v. City of New York, 487 U.S. 1, 11–12 (1988).3 Unsurprisingly, given the clarity of our general jurisprudence on this point, the Federal Courts of Appeals all apply the Salerno standard in adjudicating facial challenges.4

I am aware, of course, that in some recent facial-challenge cases the Court has, without any attempt at explanation, created entirely irrational exceptions to the "unconstitutional in every conceivable application" rule, when the statutes at issue concerned hot-button social issues on which "informed opinion" was zealously united. See Romer v. Evans, 517 U.S. 620, 643 (1996) (Scalia, J., dissenting) (homosexual rights); Planned Parenthood of Southeastern Pa. v. Casey, 505 U.S. 833, 895 (1992) (abortion rights). But the present case does not even lend itself to such a "political correctness" exception–which, though illogical, is at least predictable. It is not à la mode to favor gang members and associated loiterers over the beleaguered law-abiding residents of the inner city.

When our normal criteria for facial challenges are applied, it is clear that the

Justices in the majority have transposed the burden of proof. Instead of requiring the respondents, who are challenging the Ordinance, to show that it is invalid in all its applications, they have required the petitioner to show that it is valid in all its applications. Both the plurality opinion and the concurrences display a lively imagination, creating hypothetical situations in which the law's application would (in their view) be ambiguous. But that creative role has been usurped from the petitioner, who can defeat the respondents' facial challenge by conjuring up a single valid application of the law. My contribution would go something like this[5]: Tony, a member of the Jets criminal street gang, is standing alongside and chatting with fellow gang members while staking out their turf at Promontory Point on the South Side of Chicago; the group is flashing gang signs and displaying their distinctive tattoos to passersby. Officer Krupke, applying the Ordinance at issue here, orders the group to disperse. After some speculative discussion (probably irrelevant here) over whether the Jets are depraved because they are deprived, Tony and the other gang members break off further conversation with the statement—not entirely coherent, but evidently intended to be rude—"Gee, Officer Krupke, krup you." A tense standoff ensues until Officer Krupke arrests the group for failing to obey his dispersal order. Even assuming (as the Justices in the majority do, but I do not) that a law requiring obedience to a dispersal order is impermissibly vague unless it is clear to the objects of the order, before its issuance, that their conduct justifies it, I find it hard to believe that the Jets would not have known they had it coming. That should settle the matter of respondents' facial challenge to the Ordinance's vagueness.

Of course respondents would still be able to claim that the Ordinance was vague as applied to them. But the ultimate demonstration of the inappropriateness of the Court's holding of facial invalidity is the fact that it is doubtful whether some of these respondents could even sustain an as-applied challenge on the basis of the majority's own criteria. For instance, respondent Jose Renteria—who admitted that he was a member of the Satan Disciples gang—was observed by the arresting officer loitering on a street corner with other gang members. The officer issued a dispersal order, but when she returned to the same corner 15 to 20 minutes later, Renteria was still there with his friends, whereupon he was arrested. In another example, respondent Daniel Washington and several others—who admitted they were members of the Vice Lords gang—were observed by the arresting officer loitering in the street, yelling at passing vehicles, stopping traffic, and preventing pedestrians from using the sidewalks. The arresting officer issued a dispersal order, issued another dispersal order later when the group did not move, and finally arrested the group when they were found loitering in the same place still later. Finally, respondent Gregorio Gutierrez—who had previously admitted to the arresting officer his membership in the Latin Kings gang—was observed loitering with two other men. The officer issued a dispersal order, drove around the block, and arrested the men after finding them in the same place upon his return. See Brief for Petitioner 7, n. 5; Brief for United States as Amicus Curiae 16, n. 11. Even on the majority's assumption that to avoid vagueness it must be clear to the object of the dispersal order ex ante that his conduct is covered by the

Ordinance, it seems most improbable that any of these as-applied challenges would be sustained. Much less is it possible to say that the Ordinance is invalid in all its applications.

II

The plurality's explanation for its departure from the usual rule governing facial challenges is seemingly contained in the following statement: "[This] is a criminal law that contains no mens rea requirement ... and infringes on constitutionally protected rights .... When vagueness permeates the text of such a law, it is subject to facial attack." Ante, at 11 (emphasis added). The proposition is set forth with such assurance that one might suppose that it repeats some well-accepted formula in our jurisprudence: (Criminal law without mens rea requirement) + (infringement of constitutionally protected right) + (vagueness) = (entitlement to facial invalidation). There is no such formula; the plurality has made it up for this case, as the absence of any citation demonstrates.

But no matter. None of the three factors that the plurality relies upon exists anyway. I turn first to the support for the proposition that there is a constitutionally protected right to loiter—or, as the plurality more favorably describes it, for a person to "remain in a public place of his choice." Ibid. The plurality thinks much of this Fundamental Freedom to Loiter, which it contrasts with such lesser, constitutionally unprotected, activities as doing (ugh!) business: "This is not an ordinance that simply regulates business behavior and contains a scienter requirement. . . . It is a criminal law that contains no mens rea requirement . . . and infringes on constitutionally protected rights." Ibid. (internal quotation marks omitted). (Poor Alexander Hamilton, who has seen his "commercial republic" devolve, in the eyes of the plurality, at least, into an "indolent republic," see The Federalist No. 6, p. 56; No. 11, pp. 84—91 (C. Rossiter ed. 1961).)

Of course every activity, even scratching one's head, can be called a "constitutional right" if one means by that term nothing more than the fact that the activity is covered (as all are) by the Equal Protection Clause, so that those who engage in it cannot be singled out without "rational basis." See FCC v. Beach Communications, Inc., 508 U.S. 307, 313 (1993). But using the term in that sense utterly impoverishes our constitutional discourse. We would then need a new term for those activities—such as political speech or religious worship—that cannot be forbidden even with rational basis.

The plurality tosses around the term "constitutional right" in this renegade sense, because there is not the slightest evidence for the existence of a genuine constitutional right to loiter. Justice Thomas recounts the vast historical tradition of criminalizing the activity. Post, at 5—9. It is simply not maintainable that the right to loiter would have been regarded as an essential attribute of liberty at the time of the framing or at the time of adoption of the Fourteenth Amendment. For the plurality, however, the historical practices of our people are nothing more than a speed bump on the road to the "right" result. Its opinion blithely proclaims: "Neither this history nor the scholarly compendia in Justice Thomas' dissent, post, at 5—9, persuades us that the right to engage in loitering that is entirely harmless in both purpose and effect is not a part of the liberty protected by the Due Process Clause." Ante, at 10, n. 20. The entire practice of using the Due Process Clause to add judicially favored rights to the limitations upon democracy set forth in the Bill of Rights (usually under the rubric of so-called "substantive due process") is in my view judicial usurpation. But we have, recently at least, sought to limit the damage by tethering the courts' "right-making" power to an objective criterion. In Washington v. Glucksberg, 521 U.S. 702, 720—721 (1997), we explained our "established method" of substantive due process analysis: carefully and narrowly describing the asserted right, and then examining whether that right is manifested in "[o]ur Nation's history, legal traditions, and practices." See also Collins v. Harker Heights, 503 U.S. 115, 125—126 (1992); Michael H. v. Gerald D., 491 U.S. 110, 122—123 (1989); Moore v. East Cleveland, 431 U.S. 494, 502—503 (1977). The plurality opinion not only ignores this necessary limitation, but it leaps far beyond any substantive-due-process atrocity we have ever committed, by actually placing the burden of proof upon the defendant to establish that loitering is not a "fundamental liberty." It never does marshal any support for the proposition that loitering is a constitutional right, contenting itself with a (transparently inadequate) explanation of why the historical record of laws banning loitering does not positively contradict that proposition,6 and the (transparently erroneous) assertion that the City of Chicago appears to have conceded the point.7 It is enough for the members of the plurality that "history ... [fails to] persuad[e] us that the right to engage in loitering that is entirely harmless in both purpose and effect is not a part of the liberty protected by the Due Process Clause," ante, at 10, n. 20 (emphasis added); they apparently think it quite unnecessary for anything to persuade them that it is.8

It would be unfair, however, to criticize the plurality's failed attempt to establish that loitering is a constitutionally protected right while saying nothing of the concurrences. The plurality at least makes an attempt. The concurrences, on the other hand, make no pretense at attaching their broad "vagueness invalidates" rule to a liberty interest. As far as appears from Justice O'connor's and Justice Breyer's opinions, no police officer may issue any order, affecting any insignificant sort of citizen conduct (except, perhaps, an order addressed to the unprotected class of "gang members") unless the standards for the issuance of that order are precise. No modern urban society—and probably none since London got big enough to have sewers—could function under such a rule. There are innumerable reasons why it may be important for a constable to tell a pedestrian to "move on"—and even if it were possible to list in an ordinance all of the reasons that are known, many are simply unpredictable. Hence the (entirely reasonable) Rule of the City of New York which reads: "No person shall fail, neglect or refuse to comply with the lawful direction or command of any Police Officer, Urban Park Ranger, Parks Enforcement Patrol Officer or other [Parks and Recreation] Department employee, indicated by gesture or otherwise." 56 RCNY §1—03(c)(1) (1996). It is one thing to uphold an "as applied" challenge when a pedestrian disobeys such an order that is unreasonable—or even when a pedestrian asserting some true "liberty" interest (holding a political rally, for instance) disobeys such an order that is reasonable but unexplained. But to say that such a general ordinance permitting "lawful orders" is void in all its applications demands more than a safe and orderly society can reasonably deliver.

Justice Kennedy apparently recognizes this, since he acknowledges that "some police commands will subject a citizen to prosecution for disobeying whether or not the citizen knows why the order is given," including, for example, an order "tell[ing] a pedestrian not to enter a building" when the reason is "to avoid impeding a rescue team." Ante, at 1. But his only explanation of why the present interference with the "right to loiter" does not fall within that permitted scope of action is as follows: "The predicate of an order to disperse is not, in my view, sufficient to eliminate doubts regarding the adequacy of notice under this ordinance." Ibid. I have not the slightest idea what this means. But I do understand that the follow-up explanatory sentence, showing how this principle invalidates the present ordinance, applies equally to the rescue-team example that Justice Kennedy thinks is constitutional–as is demonstrated by substituting for references to the facts of the present case (shown in italics) references to his rescue-team hypothetical (shown in brackets): "A citizen, while engaging in a wide array of innocent conduct, is not likely to know when he may be subject to a dispersal order [order not to enter a building] based on the officer's own knowledge of the identity or affiliations of other persons with whom the citizen is congregating [what is going on in the building]; nor may the citizen be able to assess what an officer might conceive to be the citizen's lack of an apparent purpose [the impeding of a rescue team]." Ibid.

III

I turn next to that element of the plurality's facial-challenge formula which consists of the proposition that this criminal ordinance contains no mens rea requirement. The first step in analyzing this proposition is to determine what the actus reus, to which that mens rea is supposed to be attached, consists of. The majority believes that loitering forms part of (indeed, the essence of) the offense, and must be proved if conviction is to be obtained. See ante, at 2, 6, 9—13, 14—15, 16—18 (plurality and majority opinions); ante, at 2—3, 4 (O'Connor, J., concurring in part and concurring in judgment); ante, at 1—2 (Kennedy, J., concurring in part and concurring in judgment); ante, at 3—4 (Breyer, J., concurring in part and concurring in judgment). That is not what the Ordinance provides. The only part of the Ordinance that refers to loitering is the portion that addresses, not the punishable conduct of the defendant, but what the police officer must observe before he can issue an order to disperse; and what he must observe is carefully defined in terms of what the defendant appears to be doing, not in terms of what the defendant is actually doing. The Ordinance does not require that the defendant have been loitering (i.e., have been remaining in one place with no purpose), but rather that the police officer have observed him remaining in one place without any apparent purpose. Someone who in fact has a genuine purpose for remaining where he is (waiting for a friend, for example, or waiting to hold up a bank) can be ordered to move on (assuming the other conditions of the Ordinance are met), so long as his remaining has no apparent purpose. It is likely, to be sure, that the Ordinance will come down most heavily upon those who are actually loitering (those who really have no purpose in remaining where they are); but that activity is not a condition for issuance of the dispersal order.

The only act of a defendant that is made punishable by the Ordinance—or, indeed, that is even mentioned by the Ordinance—is his failure to "promptly obey" an order to disperse. The question, then, is whether that actus reus must be accompanied by any wrongful intent—and of course it must. As the Court itself describes the requirement, "a person must disobey the officer's order." Ante, at 3 (emphasis added). No one thinks a defendant could be successfully prosecuted under the Ordinance if he did not hear the order to disperse, or if he suffered a paralysis that rendered his compliance impossible. The willful failure to obey a police order is wrongful intent enough.

IV

Finally, I address the last of the three factors in the plurality's facial-challenge formula: the proposition that the Ordinance is vague. It is not. Even under the ersatz overbreadth standard applied in Kolender v. Lawson, 461 U.S. 352, 358 n. 8 (1983), which allows facial challenges if a law reaches "a substantial amount of constitutionally protected conduct," respondents' claim fails because the Ordinance would not be vague in most or even a substantial number of applications. A law is unconstitutionally vague if its lack of definitive standards either (1) fails to apprise persons of ordinary intelligence of the prohibited conduct, or (2) encourages arbitrary and discriminatory enforcement. See, e.g., Grayned v. City of Rockford, 408 U.S. 104, 108 (1972).

The plurality relies primarily upon the first of these aspects. Since, it reasons, "the loitering is the conduct that the ordinance is designed to prohibit," and "an officer may issue an order only after prohibited conduct has already occurred," ante, at 14, 15, the order to disperse cannot itself serve "to apprise persons of ordinary intelligence of the prohibited conduct." What counts for purposes of vagueness analysis, however, is not what the Ordinance is "designed to prohibit," but what it actually subjects to criminal penalty. As discussed earlier, that consists of nothing but the refusal to obey a dispersal order, as to which there is no doubt of adequate notice of the prohibited conduct. The plurality's suggestion that even the dispersal order itself is unconstitutionally vague, because it does not specify how far to disperse (!), see ante, at 15, scarcely requires a response.9 If it were true, it would render unconstitutional for vagueness many of the Presidential proclamations issued under that provision of the United States Code which requires the President, before using the militia or the Armed Forces for law enforcement, to issue a proclamation ordering the insurgents to disperse. See 10 U.S.C. § 334. President Eisenhower's proclamation relating to the obstruction of court-ordered enrollment of black students in public schools at Little Rock, Arkansas, read as follows: "I . . . command all persons engaged in such obstruction of justice to cease and desist therefrom, and to disperse forthwith." Presidential Proclamation No. 3204, 3 CFR 132 (1954—1958 Comp.). See also Presidential Proclamation No. 3645, 3 CFR 103 (1964—1965 Comp.) (ordering those obstructing the civil rights march from Selma to Montgomery, Alabama, to "disperse ... forthwith"). See also Boos v. Barry, 485 U.S. 312, 331 (1988) (rejecting overbreadth/vagueness challenge to a law allowing police officers to order congregations near foreign embassies to disperse); Cox v. Louisiana, 379 U.S. 536, 551 (1965) (rejecting vagueness challenge to the dispersal-order prong of a breach-of-the-peace statute and describing that prong as "narrow and specific").

For its determination of unconstitutional vagueness, the Court relies secondarily–and Justice O'Connor's and Justice Breyer's concurrences exclusively–upon the second aspect of that doctrine, which requires sufficient specificity to prevent arbitrary and discriminatory law enforcement. See ante, at 16 (majority opinion); ante, at 2 (O'Connor, J., concurring in part and concurring in judgment); ante, at 3 (Breyer, J., concurring in part and concurring in judgment). In discussing whether Chicago's Ordinance meets that requirement, the Justices in the majority hide behind an artificial construct of judicial restraint. They point to the Supreme Court of Illinois' statement that the "apparent purpose" standard "provides absolute discretion to police officers to decide what activities constitute loitering," 687 N. E. 2d 53, 63 (1997), and protest that it would be wrong to construe the language of the Ordinance more narrowly than did the State's highest court. Ante, at 17, 19 (majority opinion); ante, at 4—5 (O'Connor, J., concurring in part and concurring in judgment). The "absolute discretion" statement, however, is nothing more than the Illinois Supreme Court's characterization of what the language achieved–after that court refused (as I do) to read in any limitations that the words do not fairly contain. It is not a construction of the language (to which we are bound) but a legal conclusion (to which we most assuredly are not bound).

The criteria for issuance of a dispersal order under the Chicago Ordinance could hardly be clearer. First, the law requires police officers to "reasonably believ[e]" that one of the group to which the order is issued is a "criminal street gang member." This resembles a probable-cause standard, and the Chicago Police Department's General Order 92—4 (1992)–promulgated to govern enforcement of the Ordinance–makes the probable cause requirement explicit.10 Under the Order, officers must have probable cause to believe that an individual is a member of a criminal street gang, to be substantiated by the officer's "experience and knowledge of the alleged offenders" and by "specific, documented and reliable information" such as reliable witness testimony or an individual's admission of gang membership or display of distinctive colors, tattoos, signs, or other markings worn by members of particular criminal street gangs. App. to Pet. for Cert. 67a—69a, 71a—72a.

Second, the Ordinance requires that the group be "remain[ing] in one place with no apparent purpose." Justice O'Connor's assertion that this applies to "any person standing in a public place," ante, at 2, is a distortion. The Ordinance does not apply to "standing," but to "remain[ing]"–a term which in this context obviously means "[to] endure or persist," see American Heritage Dictionary 1525 (1992). There may be some ambiguity at the margin, but "remain[ing] in one place" requires more than a temporary stop, and is clear in most of its applications, including all of those represented by the facts surrounding the respondents' arrests described supra, at 12.

As for the phrase "with no apparent purpose": Justice O'Connor again distorts this adjectival phrase, by separating it from the word that it modifies. "[A]ny person standing on the street," her concurrence says, "has a general 'purpose'–even if it is simply to stand," and thus "the ordinance permits police officers to choose which purposes are permissible." Ante, at 2. But Chicago police officers enforcing the Ordinance are not looking for people with no apparent purpose (who are regrettably in oversupply); they are looking for people who "remain in any one place with no apparent purpose"–that is, who remain there without any apparent reason for remaining there. That is not difficult to perceive.11

The Court's attempt to demonstrate the vagueness of the Ordinance produces the following peculiar statement: "The 'no apparent purpose' standard for making [the decision to issue an order to disperse] is inherently subjective because its application depends on whether some purpose is 'apparent' to the officer on the scene." Ante, at 18. In the Court's view, a person's lack of any purpose in staying in one location is presumably an objective factor, and what the Ordinance requires as a condition of an order to disperse– the absence of any apparent purpose–is a subjective factor. This side of the looking glass, just the opposite is true.

Elsewhere, of course, the Court acknowledges the clear, objective commands of the Ordinance, and indeed relies upon them to paint it as unfair:

"By its very terms, the ordinance encompasses a great deal of harmless behavior. In any public place in the city of Chicago, persons who stand or sit in the company of a gang member may be ordered to disperse unless their purpose is apparent. The mandatory language in the enactment directs the police to issue an order without first making any inquiry about their possible purposes. It matters not whether the reason that a gang member and his father, for example, might loiter near Wrigley Field is to rob an unsuspecting fan or just to get a glimpse of Sammy Sosa leaving the ballpark; in either event, if their purpose is not apparent to a nearby police officer, she may–indeed, she 'shall'–order them to disperse." Ante, at 16.

Quite so. And the fact that this clear instruction to the officers "encompasses a great deal of harmless behavior" would be invalidating if that harmless behavior were constitutionally protected against abridgment, such as speech or the practice of religion. Remaining in one place is not so protected, and so (as already discussed) it is up to the citizens of Chicago–not us–to decide whether the trade-off is worth it.

The Court also asserts–in apparent contradiction to the passage just quoted– that the "apparent purpose" test is too elastic because it presumably allows police officers to treat de minimis "violations" as not warranting enforcement.12 See ante, at 18–19. But such discretion–and, for that matter, the potential for ultra vires action–is no different with regard to the enforcement of this clear ordinance than it is with regard to the enforcement of all laws in our criminal-justice system. Police officers (and prosecutors, see Bordenkircher v. Hayes, 434 U.S. 357, 364 (1978)), have broad discretion over what laws to enforce and when. As we said in Whren v. United States, 517 U.S. 806, 818 (1996), "we are aware of no principle that would allow us to decide at what point a code of law becomes so expansive and so commonly violated that infraction itself can no longer be the ordinary measure of the lawfulness of enforcement."

Justice Breyer's concurrence tries to perform the impossible feat of affirming our unquestioned rule that a criminal statute that is so vague as to give constitutionally inadequate notice to some violators may nonetheless be enforced against those whose conduct is clearly covered, see ante, at 3, citing Parker v. Levy, 417 U.S. 733 (1974), while at the same time asserting that a statute which "delegates too much discretion to a police officer" is invalid in all its applications, even where the officer uses his discretion "wisely," ante, at 2. But the vagueness that causes notice to be inadequate is the very same vagueness that causes "too much discretion" to be lodged in the enforcing officer. Put another way: A law that gives the policeman clear guidance in all cases gives the public clear guidance in all cases as well. Thus, what Justice Breyer gives with one hand, he takes away with the other. In his view, vague statutes that nonetheless give adequate notice to some violators are not unenforceable against those violators because of inadequate notice, but are unenforceable against them "because the policeman enjoys too much discretion in every case," ibid. This is simply contrary to our case-law, including Parker v. Levy, supra.13

V

The plurality points out that Chicago already has several laws that reach the intimidating and unlawful gang-related conduct the Ordinance was directed at. See ante, at 7—8, n. 17. The problem, of course, well recognized by Chicago's City Council, is that the gang members cease their intimidating and unlawful behavior under the watchful eye of police officers, but return to it as soon as the police drive away. The only solution, the council concluded, was to clear the streets of congregations of gangs, their drug customers, and their associates.

Justice O'Connor's concurrence proffers the same empty solace of existing laws useless for the purpose at hand, see ante, at 3—4, but seeks to be helpful by suggesting some measures similar to this ordinance that would be constitutional. It says that Chicago could, for example, enact a law that "directly prohibit[s] the presence of a large collection of obviously brazen, insistent, and lawless gang members and hangers-on on the public ways, that intimidates residents." Ibid., (internal quotation marks omitted). (If the majority considers the present ordinance too vague, it would be fun to see what it makes of "a large collection of obviously brazen, insistent, and lawless gang members.") This prescription of the concurrence is largely a quotation from the plurality–which itself answers the concurrence's suggestion that such a law would be helpful by pointing out that the city already "has several laws that serve this purpose." Ante, at 7—8, n. 17 (plurality opinion) (citing extant laws against "intimidation," "streetgang criminal drug conspiracy," and "mob action"). The problem, again, is that the intimidation and lawlessness do not occur when the police are in sight.

Justice O'Connor's concurrence also proffers another cure: "If the ordinance applied only to persons reasonably believed to be gang members, this requirement might have cured the ordinance's vagueness because it would have directed the manner in which the order was issued by specifying to whom the order could be issued." Ante, at 3 (the Court agrees that this might be a cure, see ante, at 18—19). But the Ordinance already specifies to whom the order can be issued: persons remaining in one place with no apparent purpose in the company of a gang member. And if "remain[ing] in one place with no apparent purpose" is so vague as to give the police unbridled discretion in controlling the conduct of non-gang-members, it surpasses understanding how it ceases to be so vague when applied to gang members alone. Surely gang members cannot be decreed to be outlaws, subject to the merest whim of the police as the rest of us are not.

* * *

The fact is that the present ordinance is entirely clear in its application, cannot be violated except with full knowledge and intent, and vests no more discretion in the police than innumerable other measures authorizing police orders to preserve the public peace and safety. As suggested by their tortured analyses, and by their suggested solutions that bear no relation to the identified constitutional problem, the majority's real quarrel with the Chicago Ordinance is simply that it permits (or indeed requires) too much harmless conduct by innocent citizens to be proscribed. As Justice O'Connor's concurrence says with disapprobation, "the ordinance applies to hundreds of thousands of persons who are not gang members, standing on any sidewalk or in any park, coffee shop, bar, or other location open to the public." Ante, at 2—3 (internal quotation marks omitted).

But in our democratic system, how much harmless conduct to proscribe is not a judgment to be made by the courts. So long as constitutionally guaranteed rights are not affected, and so long as the proscription has a rational basis, all sorts of perfectly harmless activity by millions of perfectly innocent people can be forbidden—riding a motorcycle without a safety helmet, for example, starting a campfire in a national forest, or selling a safe and effective drug not yet approved by the FDA. All of these acts are entirely innocent and harmless in themselves, but because of the risk of harm that they entail, the freedom to engage in them has been abridged. The citizens of Chicago have decided that depriving themselves of the freedom to "hang out" with a gang member is necessary to eliminate pervasive gang crime and intimidation—and that the elimination of the one is worth the deprivation of the other. This Court has no business second-guessing either the degree of necessity or the fairness of the trade.

I dissent from the judgment of the Court.

Notes

1. In other words, a facial attack, since it requires unconstitutionality in all circumstances, necessarily presumes that the litigant presently before the court would be able to sustain an as-applied challenge. See Hoffman Estates v. Flipside, Hoffman Estates, Inc., 455 U.S. 489, 495 (1982) ("A plaintiff who engages in some conduct that is clearly proscribed cannot complain of the vagueness of the law as applied to

the conduct of others. A court should therefore examine the complainant's conduct before analyzing other hypothetical applications of the law"); Parker v. Levy, 417 U.S. 733, 756 (1974) ("One to whose conduct a statute clearly applies may not successfully challenge it for vagueness"). The plurality asserts that in United States v. Salerno, 481 U.S. 739 (1987), which I discuss in text immediately following this footnote, the Court "entertained" a facial challenge even though "the defendants . . . did not claim that the statute was unconstitutional as applied to them." Ante, at 11, n. 22. That is not so. The Court made it absolutely clear in Salerno that a facial challenge requires the assertion that "no set of circumstances exists under which the Act would be valid," 481 U.S., at 745 (emphasis added). The footnoted statement upon which the plurality relies ("Nor have respondents claimed that the Act is unconstitutional because of the way it was applied to the particular facts of their case," id., at 745, n. 3) was obviously meant to convey the fact that the defendants were not making, in addition to their facial challenge, an alternative as-applied challenge–i.e., asserting that even if the statute was not unconstitutional in all its applications it was at least unconstitutional in its particular application to them.

2. Salerno, a criminal case, repudiated the Court's statement in Kolender v. Lawson, 461 U.S. 352, 359, n. 8 (1983), to the effect that a facial challenge to a criminal statute could succeed "even when [the statute] could conceivably have had some valid application." Kolender seems to have confused the standard for First Amendment overbreadth challenges with the standard governing facial challenges on all other grounds. See ibid. (citing the Court's articulation of the standard for First Amendment overbreadth challenges from Hoffman Estates, supra, at 494). As Salerno noted, 481 U.S., at 745, the overbreadth doctrine is a specialized exception to the general rule for facial challenges, justified in light of the risk that an overbroad statute will chill free expression. See, e.g., Broadrick v. Oklahoma, 413 U.S. 601, 612 (1973).

3. The plurality asserts that the Salerno standard for facial challenge "has never been the decisive factor in any decision of this Court." It means by that only this: in rejecting a facial challenge, the Court has never contented itself with identifying only one situation in which the challenged statute would be constitutional, but has mentioned several. But that is not at all remarkable, and casts no doubt upon the validity of the principle that Salerno and these many other cases enunciated. It is difficult to conceive of a statute that would be constitutional in only a single application–and hard to resist mentioning more than one.   The plurality contends that it does not matter whether the Salerno standard is federal law, since facial challenge is a species of third-party standing, and federal limitations upon third-party standing do not apply in an appeal from a state decision which takes a broader view, as the Illinois Supreme Court's opinion did here. Ante, at 11, n. 22. This is quite wrong. Disagreement over the Salerno rule is not a disagreement over the "standing" question of whether the person challenging the statute can raise the rights of third parties: under both Salerno and the plurality's rule he can. The disagreement relates to how many third-party rights he must prove to be infringed by the statute before he can win: Salerno says "all" (in addition to his own rights), the plurality

says "many." That is not a question of standing but of substantive law. The notion that, if Salerno is the federal rule (a federal statute is not totally invalid unless it is invalid in all its applications), it can be altered by a state court (a federal statute is totally invalid if it is invalid in many of its applications), and that that alteration must be accepted by the Supreme Court of the United States is, to put it as gently as possible, remarkable.

4. See, e.g., Abdullah v. Commissioner of Ins. of Commonwealth of Mass., 84 F.3d 18, 20 (CA1 1996); Deshawn E. v. Safir, 156 F.3d 340, 347 (CA2 1998); Artway v. Attorney Gen. of State of N. J., 81 F.3d 1235, 1252, n. 13 (CA3 1996); Manning v. Hunt, 119 F.3d 254, 268—269 (CA4 1997); Causeway Medical Suite v. Ieyoub, 109 F.3d 1096, 1104 (CA5), cert. denied, 522 U.S. 943 (1997); Aronson v. City of Akron, 116 F.3d 804, 809 (CA6 1997); Government Suppliers Consolidating Servs., Inc. v. Bayh, 975 F.2d 1267, 1283 (CA7 1992), cert. denied, 506 U.S. 1053 (1993); Woodis v. Westark Community College, 160 F.3d 435, 438—439 (CA8 1998); Roulette v. Seattle, 97 F.3d 300, 306 (CA9 1996); Public Lands Council v. Babbitt, 167 F.3d 1287, 1293 (CA10 1999); Dimmitt v. Clearwater, 985 F.2d 1565, 1570—1571 (CA11 1993); Time Warner Entertainment Co. v. FCC, 93 F.3d 957, 972 (CADC 1996).

5. With apologies for taking creative license with the work of Messrs. Bernstein, Sondheim, and Laurents. West Side Story, copyright 1959.

6. The plurality's explanation for ignoring these laws is that many of them carried severe penalties and, during the Reconstruction era, they had "harsh consequences on African-American women and children." Ante, at 9—10, n. 20. Those severe penalties and those harsh consequences are certainly regrettable, but they in no way lessen (indeed, the harshness of penalty tends to increase) the capacity of these laws to prove that loitering was never regarded as a fundamental liberty.

7. Ante, at 9, n. 19. The plurality bases its assertion of apparent concession upon a footnote in Part I of petitioner's brief which reads: "Of course, laws regulating social gatherings affect a liberty interest, and thus are subject to review under the rubric of substantive due process .... We address that doctrine in Part II below." Brief for Petitioner 21—22, n. 14. If a careless reader were inclined to confuse the term "social gatherings" in this passage with "loitering," his confusion would be eliminated by pursuing the reference to Part II of the brief, which says, in its introductory paragraph: "[A]s we explain below, substantive due process does not support the court's novel holding that the Constitution secures the right to stand still on the public way even when one is not engaged in speech, assembly, or other conduct that enjoys affirmative constitutional protection." Id., at 39.

8. The plurality says, ante, at 20, n. 35, that since it decides the case on the basis of procedural due process rather than substantive due process, I am mistaken in analyzing its opinion "under the framework for substantive due process set out in Washington v. Glucksberg." Ibid. But I am not analyzing it under that framework. I am simply assuming that when the plurality says (as an essential part of its reasoning) that "the right to loiter for innocent purposes is . . . a part of the liberty protected by the Due Process Clause" it

does not believe that the same word ("liberty") means one thing for purposes of substantive due process and something else for purposes of procedural due process. There is no authority for that startling proposition. See Board of Regents of State Colleges v. Roth, 408 U.S. 564, 572–575 (1972) (rejecting procedural-due-process claim for lack of "liberty" interest, and citing substantive-due-process cases).   The plurality's opinion seeks to have it both ways, invoking the Fourteenth Amendment's august protection of "liberty" in defining the standard of certainty that it sets, but then, in identifying the conduct protected by that high standard, ignoring our extensive case-law defining "liberty," and substituting, instead, all "harmless and innocent" conduct, ante, at 14.

9. I call it a "suggestion" because the plurality says only that the terms of the dispersal order "compound the inadequacy of the notice," and acknowledges that they "might not render the ordinance unconstitutionally vague if the definition of the forbidden conduct were clear." Ante, at 15, 16. This notion that a prescription ("Disperse!") which is itself not unconstitutionally vague can somehow contribute to the unconstitutional vagueness of the entire scheme is full of mystery–suspending, as it does, the metaphysical principle that nothing can confer what it does not possess (nemo dat qui non habet).

10. "Administrative interpretation and implementation of a regulation are ... highly relevant to our [vagueness] analysis, for '[i]n evaluating a facial challenge to a state law, a federal court must ... consider any limiting construction that a state court or enforcement agency has proffered.' " Ward v. Rock Against Racism, 491 U.S. 781, 795–796 (1989) (emphasis added) (quoting Hoffman Estates, 455 U.S., at 494, n. 5). See also Hoffman Estates, 455 U.S., at 504 (administrative regulations "will often suffice to clarify a standard with an otherwise uncertain scope").

11. Justice Breyer asserts that "one always has some apparent purpose," so that the policeman must "interpret the words 'no apparent purpose' as meaning 'no apparent purpose except for . . . .'" Ante, at 1–2. It is simply not true that "one always has some apparent purpose"–and especially not true that one always has some apparent purpose in remaining at rest, for the simple reason that one often (indeed, perhaps usually) has no actual purpose in remaining at rest. Remaining at rest will be a person's normal state, unless he has a purpose which causes him to move. That is why one frequently reads of a person's "wandering aimlessly" (which is worthy of note) but not of a person's "sitting aimlessly" (which is not remarkable at all). And that is why a synonym for "purpose" is "motive": that which causes one to move.

12. The Court also speculates that a police officer may exercise his discretion to enforce the Ordinance and direct dispersal when (in the Court's view) the Ordinance is inapplicable–viz., where there is an apparent purpose, but it is an unlawful one. See ante, at 18. No one in his right mind would read the phrase "without any apparent purpose" to mean anything other than "without any apparent lawful purpose." The implication that acts referred to approvingly in statutory language are "lawful" acts is routine. The Court asserts that the Illinois Supreme Court has forced it into this interpretive inanity because, since it "has not placed any limiting construction on the language in the ordinance, we

must assume that the ordinance means what it says . . . ." Ante, at 19. But the Illinois Supreme Court did not mention this particular interpretive issue, which has nothing to do with giving the Ordinance a "limiting" interpretation, and everything to do with giving it its ordinary legal meaning.

13. The opinion that Justice Breyer relies on, Coates v. Cincinnati, 402 U.S. 611 (1971), discussed ante, at 3—4, did not say that the ordinance there at issue gave adequate notice but did not provide adequate standards for the police. It invalidated that ordinance on both inadequate-notice and inadequate-enforcement-standard grounds, because First Amendment rights were implicated. It is common ground, however, that the present case does not implicate the First Amendment, see ante, at 8—9 (plurality opinion); ante, at 3 (Breyer, J., concurring in part and concurring in judgment).

Justice Scalia's dissent in Troxel v. Granville (June 5, 2000)

Justice Scalia, dissenting.

In my view, a right of parents to direct the upbringing of their children is among the "unalienable Rights" with which the Declaration of Independence proclaims "all Men ... are endowed by their Creator." And in my view that right is also among the "othe[r] [rights] retained by the people" which the Ninth Amendment says the Constitution's enumeration of rights "shall not be construed to deny or disparage." The Declaration of Independence, however, is not a legal prescription conferring powers upon the courts; and the Constitution's refusal to "deny or disparage" other rights is far removed from affirming any one of them, and even farther removed from authorizing judges to identify what they might be, and to enforce the judges' list against laws duly enacted by the people. Consequently, while I would think it entirely compatible with the commitment to representative democracy set forth in the founding documents to argue, in legislative chambers or in electoral campaigns, that the state has no power to interfere with parents' authority over the rearing of their children, I do not believe that the power which the Constitution confers upon me as a judge entitles me to deny legal effect to laws that (in my view) infringe upon what is (in my view) that unenumerated right.

Only three holdings of this Court rest in whole or in part upon a substantive constitutional right of parents to direct the upbringing of their children1—two of them from an era rich in substantive due process holdings that have since been repudiated. See Meyer v. Nebraska, 262 U.S. 390, 399, 401 (1923); Pierce v. Society of Sisters, 268 U.S. 510, 534—535 (1925); Wisconsin v. Yoder, 406 U.S. 205, 232—233 (1972). Cf. West Coast Hotel Co. v. Parrish, 300 U.S. 379 (1937) (overruling Adkins v. Children's Hospital of D. C., 261 U.S. 525 (1923)). The sheer diversity of today's opinions persuades me that the theory of unenumerated parental rights underlying these three cases has small claim to stare decisis protection. A legal principle that can be thought to produce such diverse outcomes in the relatively simple case before us here is not a legal principle that has induced substantial reliance. While I would not now overrule those earlier cases (that has not been urged), neither would I extend the theory upon which they rested to this new context.

Judicial vindication of "parental rights" under a Constitution that does not even mention them requires (as Justice Kennedy's opinion rightly points out) not only a judicially crafted definition of parents, but also—unless, as no one believes, the parental rights are to be absolute—judicially approved assessments of "harm to the child" and judicially defined gradations of other persons (grandparents, extended family, adoptive family in an adoption later found to be invalid, long-term guardians, etc.) who may have some claim against the wishes of the parents. If we embrace this unenumerated right, I think it obvious—whether we affirm or reverse the judgment here, or remand as Justice Stevens or Justice Kennedy would do—that we will be ushering in a new regime of judicially prescribed, and federally prescribed, family law. I have no reason to believe that federal judges will be better at this than state legislatures; and state legislatures have the great advantages of doing harm in a more circumscribed area, of being able to correct their mistakes in a flash, and of being removable by the people.[2]

For these reasons, I would reverse the judgment below.

Notes

1. Whether parental rights constitute a "liberty" interest for purposes of procedural due process is a somewhat different question not implicated here. Stanley v. Illinois, 405 U.S. 645 (1972), purports to rest in part upon that proposition, see id., at 651—652; but see Michael H. v. Gerald D., 491 U.S. 110, 120—121 (1989) (plurality opinion), though the holding is independently supported on equal protection grounds, see Stanley, supra, at 658.

2. I note that respondent is asserting only, on her own behalf, a substantive due process right to direct the upbringing of her own children, and is not asserting, on behalf of her children, their First Amendment rights of association or free exercise. I therefore do not have occasion to consider whether, and under what circumstances, the parent could assert the latter enumerated rights.

Justice Scalia's dissent in Dickerson v. US (June 26, 2000) [Excerpt]

Justice Scalia, with whom Justice Thomas joins, dissenting.

Those to whom judicial decisions are an unconnected series of judgments that produce either favored or disfavored results will doubtless greet today's decision as a paragon of moderation, since it declines to overrule Miranda v. Arizona, 384 U.S. 436 (1966). Those who understand the judicial process will appreciate that today's decision is not a reaffirmation of Miranda, but a radical revision of the most significant element of Miranda (as of all cases): the rationale that gives it a permanent place in our jurisprudence.

Marbury v. Madison, 1 Cranch 137 (1803), held that an Act of Congress will not be enforced by the courts if what it prescribes violates the Constitution of the United States. That was the basis on which Miranda was decided. One will search today's opinion in vain, however, for a statement (surely simple enough to make) that what 18 U.S.C. § 3501 prescribes—the use at trial of a voluntary confession, even when a Miranda warning or its equivalent has failed to be given—violates the Constitution. The reason the statement does not appear is not only (and perhaps not so much) that it would be absurd, inasmuch as §3501 excludes from trial precisely what the Constitution excludes from trial, viz., compelled confessions; but also that Justices whose votes are needed to compose today's majority are on record as believing that a violation of Miranda is not a violation of the Constitution. See Davis v. United States, 512 U.S. 452, 457—458 (1994) (opinion of the Court, in which Kennedy, J., joined); Duckworth v. Eagan, 492 U.S. 195, 203 (1989) (opinion of the Court, in which Kennedy, J., joined); Oregon v. Elstad, 470 U.S. 298 (1985) (opinion of the Court by O'Connor, J.); New York v. Quarles, 467 U.S. 649 (1984) (opinion of the Court by Rehnquist, J.). And so, to justify today's agreed-upon result, the Court must adopt a significant new, if not entirely comprehensible, principle of constitutional law. As the Court chooses to describe that principle, statutes of Congress can be disregarded, not only when what they prescribe violates the Constitution, but when what they prescribe contradicts a decision of this Court that "announced a constitutional rule," ante, at 7. As I shall discuss in some detail, the only thing that can possibly mean in the context of this case is that this Court has the power, not merely to apply the Constitution but to expand it, imposing what it regards as useful "prophylactic" restrictions upon Congress and the States. That is an immense and frightening antidemocratic power, and it does not exist.

It takes only a small step to bring today's opinion out of the realm of power-judging and into the mainstream of legal reasoning: The Court need only go beyond its carefully couched iterations that "Miranda is a constitutional decision," ante, at 8, that "Miranda is constitutionally based," ante, at 10, that Miranda has "constitutional underpinnings," ante, at 10, n. 5, and come out and say quite clearly: "We reaffirm today that custodial interrogation that is not preceded by Miranda warnings or their equivalent violates the Constitution of the United States." It cannot say that, because a majority of the Court does not believe it. The Court therefore acts in plain violation of the Constitution when it denies effect to this Act of Congress.

[. . .]

Petitioner and the United States are right on target, however, in characterizing the Court's actions in a case decided within a few years of Miranda, North Carolina v. Pearce, 395 U.S. 711 (1969). There, the Court concluded that due process would be offended were a judge vindictively to resentence with added severity a defendant who had successfully appealed his original conviction. Rather than simply announce that vindictive sentencing violates the Due Process Clause, the Court went on to hold that "[i]n order to assure the absence of such a [vindictive] motivation, ... the reasons for [imposing the increased sentence] must affirmatively appear" and must "be based upon objective information concerning identifiable conduct on the part of the defendant occurring after the time of the original sentencing proceeding." Id., at 726. The Court later explicitly acknowledged Pearce's prophylactic character, see Michigan v. Payne, 412 U.S. 47, 53 (1973). It is true, therefore, that the case exhibits the same fundamental flaw as does Miranda when deprived (as it has been) of its original (implausible) pretension to announcement of what the Constitution itself required. That is, although the Due Process Clause may well prohibit punishment based on judicial vindictiveness, the Constitution by no means vests in the courts "any general power to prescribe particular devices 'in order to assure the absence of such a motivation,'" 395 U.S., at 741 (Black, J., dissenting). Justice Black surely had the right idea when he derided the Court's requirement as "pure legislation if there ever was legislation," ibid., although in truth Pearce's rule pales as a legislative achievement when compared to the detailed code promulgated in Miranda.1

The foregoing demonstrates that, petitioner's and the United States' suggestions to the contrary notwithstanding, what the Court did in Miranda (assuming, as later cases hold, that Miranda went beyond what the Constitution actually requires) is in fact extraordinary. That the Court has, on rare and recent occasion, repeated the mistake does not transform error into truth, but illustrates the potential for future mischief that the error entails. Where the Constitution has wished to lodge in one of the branches of the Federal Government some limited power to supplement its guarantees, it has said so. See Amdt. 14, §5 ("The Congress shall have power to enforce, by appropriate legislation, the provisions of this article"). The power with which the Court would endow itself under a "prophylactic" justification for Miranda goes far beyond what it has permitted Congress to do under authority of that text. Whereas we have insisted that congressional action under §5 of the Fourteenth Amendment must be "congruent" with, and "proportional" to, a constitutional violation, see City of Boerne v. Flores, 521 U.S. 507, 520 (1997), the Miranda nontextual power to embellish confers authority to prescribe preventive measures against not only constitutionally prohibited compelled confessions, but also (as discussed earlier) foolhardy ones.

[. . .]

Today's judgment converts Miranda from a milestone of judicial overreaching into the very Cheops' Pyramid (or perhaps the Sphinx would be a better analogue) of judicial arrogance. In imposing its Court-made code upon the States, the original opinion at least asserted that it was demanded by the Constitution. Today's decision does not pretend that it is–and yet still asserts the right to impose it against the will of the people's representatives in Congress. Far from believing that stare decisis compels this result, I believe we cannot allow to remain on the books even a celebrated decision–especially a celebrated decision–that has come to stand for the proposition that the Supreme Court has power to impose extraconstitutional constraints upon Congress and the States. This is not the system that was established by the Framers, or that would be established by any sane supporter of government by the people.

I dissent from today's decision, and, until §3501 is repealed, will continue to apply it in all cases where there has been a sustainable finding that the defendant's confession was voluntary.

Justice Scalia's concurrence in Apprendi v. New Jersey (June 26, 2000)

Justice Scalia, concurring.

I feel the need to say a few words in response to Justice Breyer's dissent. It sketches an admirably fair and efficient scheme of criminal justice designed for a society that is prepared to leave criminal justice to the State. (Judges, it is sometimes necessary to remind ourselves, are part of the State—and an increasingly bureaucratic part of it, at that.) The founders of the American Republic were not prepared to leave it to the State, which is why the jury-trial guarantee was one of the least controversial provisions of the Bill of Rights. It has never been efficient; but it has always been free.

As for fairness, which Justice Breyer believes "[i]n modern times," post, at 1, the jury cannot provide: I think it not unfair to tell a prospective felon that if he commits his contemplated crime he is exposing himself to a jail sentence of 30 years—and that if, upon conviction, he gets anything less than that he may thank the mercy of a tenderhearted judge (just as he may thank the mercy of a tenderhearted parole commission if he is let out inordinately early, or the mercy of a tenderhearted governor if his sentence is commuted). Will there be disparities? Of course. But the criminal will never get more punishment than he bargained for when he did the crime, and his guilt of the crime (and hence the length of the sentence to which he is exposed) will be determined beyond a reasonable doubt by the unanimous vote of 12 of his fellow citizens.

In Justice Breyer's bureaucratic realm of perfect equity, by contrast, the facts that determine the length of sentence to which the defendant is exposed will be determined to exist (on a more-likely-than-not basis) by a single employee of the State. It is certainly arguable (Justice Breyer argues it) that this sacrifice of prior protections is worth it. But it is not arguable that, just because one thinks it is a better system, it must be, or is even more likely to be, the system envisioned by a Constitution that guarantees trial by jury. What ultimately demolishes the case for the dissenters is that they are unable to say what the right to trial by jury does guarantee if, as they assert, it does not guarantee—what it has been assumed to guarantee throughout our history—the right to have a jury determine those facts that determine the maximum sentence the law allows. They provide no coherent alternative.

Justice Breyer proceeds on the erroneous and all-too-common assumption that the Constitution means what we think it ought to mean. It does not; it means what it says. And the guarantee that "[i]n all criminal prosecutions, the accused shall enjoy the right to . . . trial, by an impartial jury" has no intelligible content unless it means that all the facts which must exist in order to subject the defendant to a legally prescribed punishment must be found by the jury.

Justice Scalia's dissent in Hill v. Colorado (June 28, 2000)

Justice Scalia, with whom Justice Thomas joins, dissenting.

The Court today concludes that a regulation requiring speakers on the public thoroughfares bordering medical facilities to speak from a distance of eight feet is "not a 'regulation of speech,'" but "a regulation of the places where some speech may occur," ante, at 14; and that a regulation directed to only certain categories of speech (protest, education, and counseling) is not "content-based." For these reasons, it says, the regulation is immune from the exacting scrutiny we apply to content-based suppression of speech in the public forum. The Court then determines that the regulation survives the less rigorous scrutiny afforded content-neutral time, place, and manner restrictions because it is narrowly tailored to serve a government interest–protection of citizens' "right to be let alone"–that has explicitly been disclaimed by the State, probably for the reason that, as a basis for suppressing peaceful private expression, it is patently incompatible with the guarantees of the First Amendment.

None of these remarkable conclusions should come as a surprise. What is before us, after all, is a speech regulation directed against the opponents of abortion, and it therefore enjoys the benefit of the "ad hoc nullification machine" that the Court has set in motion to push aside whatever doctrines of constitutional law stand in the way of that highly favored practice. Madsen v. Women's Health Center, Inc., 512 U.S. 753, 785 (1994) (Scalia, J., concurring in judgment in part and dissenting in part). Having deprived abortion opponents of the political right to persuade the electorate that abortion should be restricted by law, the Court today continues and expands its assault upon their individual right to persuade women contemplating abortion that what they are doing is wrong. Because, like the rest of our abortion jurisprudence, today's decision is in stark contradiction of the constitutional principles we apply in all other contexts, I dissent.

I

Colorado's statute makes it a criminal act knowingly to approach within 8 feet of another person on the public way or sidewalk area within 100 feet of the entrance door of a health care facility for the purpose of passing a leaflet to, displaying a sign to, or engaging in oral protest, education, or counseling with such person. Whatever may be said about the restrictions on the other types of expressive activity, the regulation as it applies to oral communications is obviously and undeniably content-based. A speaker wishing to approach another for the purpose of communicating any message except one of protest, education, or counseling may do so without first securing the other's consent. Whether a speaker must obtain permission before approaching within eight feet–and whether he will be sent to prison for failing to do so–depends entirely on what he intends to say when he gets there. I have no doubt that this regulation would be deemed content-based in an instant if the case before us involved antiwar protesters, or union members seeking to "educate" the public about the reasons for their strike. "[I]t is," we would say, "the content of the speech that determines whether it is within or without the statute's blunt prohibition," Carey v. Brown, 447 U.S. 455, 462 (1980). But the jurisprudence of this Court has a way of changing when abortion is involved.

The Court asserts that this statute is not content-based for purposes of our First Amendment analysis because it neither (1) discriminates among viewpoints nor (2) places restrictions on "any subject matter that may be discussed by a speaker." Ante, at 18. But we have never held that the universe of content-based regulations is limited to those two categories, and such a holding would be absurd. Imagine, for instance, special place-and-manner restrictions on all speech except that which "conveys a sense of contentment or happiness." This "happy speech" limitation would not be "viewpoint-based"–citizens would be able to express their joy in equal measure at either the rise or fall of the NASDAQ, at either the success or the failure of the Republican Party–and would not discriminate on the basis of subject matter, since gratification could be expressed about anything at all. Or consider a law restricting the writing or recitation of poetry–neither viewpoint-based nor limited to any particular subject matter. Surely this Court would consider such regulations to be "content-based" and deserving of the most exacting scrutiny1

"The vice of content-based legislation–what renders it deserving of the high standard of strict scrutiny–is not that it is always used for invidious, thought-control purposes, but that it lends itself to use for those purposes." Madsen, supra, at 794 (opinion of Scalia, J.) (emphasis omitted). A restriction that operates only on speech that communicates a message of protest, education, or counseling presents exactly this risk. When applied, as it is here, at the entrance to medical facilities, it is a means of impeding speech against abortion. The Court's confident assurance that the statute poses no special threat to First Amendment freedoms because it applies alike to "used car salesmen, animal rights activists, fundraisers, environmentalists, and missionaries," ante, at 18, is a wonderful replication (except for its lack of sarcasm) of Anatole France's observation that "[t]he law, in its majestic equality, forbids the rich as well as the poor to sleep under bridges ... ." see J. Bartlett, Familiar Quotations 550 (16th ed. 1992). This Colorado law is no more targeted at used car salesmen, animal rights activists, fund raisers, environmentalists, and missionaries than French vagrancy law was targeted at the rich. We know what the Colorado legislators, by their careful selection of content ("protest, education, and counseling"), were taking aim at, for they set it forth in the statute itself: the "right to protest or counsel against certain medical procedures" on the sidewalks and streets surrounding health care facilities. Col. Rev. Stat. §18—9—122(1) (1999) (emphasis added).

The Court is unpersuasive in its attempt to equate the present restriction with content-neutral regulation of demonstrations and picketing–as one may immediately suspect from the opinion's wildly expansive definitions of demonstrations as " 'public display[s] of sentiment for or against a person or cause,' " and of picketing as an effort " 'to persuade or otherwise influence.' " Ante, at 16—17, quoting Webster's Third New International Dictionary 600, 1710 (1993). (On these terms, Nathan Hale was a demonstrator and Patrick Henry a picket.) When the government regulates "picketing," or "demonstrating," it restricts a particular manner of expression that is, as the author of today's opinion has several times explained, " 'a mixture of conduct and communication.' " Frisby v. Schultz, 487 U.S. 474, 497 (1988) (Stevens, J., dissenting), quoting NLRB v. Retail Store Employees, 447 U.S. 607, 618—619 (1980) (Stevens, J., concurring in part and concurring in result). The latter opinion quoted approvingly Justice Douglas's statement:

"Picketing by an organized group is more than free speech, since it involves patrol of a particular locality and since the very presence of a picket line may induce action of one kind or another, quite irrespective of the nature of the ideas which are being disseminated. Hence those aspects of picketing make it the subject of restrictive regulation." Bakery Drivers v. Wohl, 315 U.S. 769, 776—777 (1942) (concurring opinion).

As Justice Stevens went on to explain, "no doubt the principal reason why handbills containing the same message are so much less effective than labor picketing is that the former depend entirely on the persuasive force of the idea." Retail Store Employees, supra, at 619. Today, of course, Justice Stevens gives us an opinion restricting not only handbilling but even one-on-one conversation of a particular content. There comes a point—and the Court's opinion today passes it—at which the regulation of action intimately and unavoidably connected with traditional speech is a regulation of speech itself. The strictures of the First Amendment cannot be avoided by regulating the act of moving one's lips; and they cannot be avoided by regulating the act of extending one's arm to deliver a handbill, or peacefully approaching in order to speak. All of these acts can be regulated, to be sure; but not, on the basis of content, without satisfying the requirements of our strict-scrutiny First Amendment jurisprudence.

Even with regard to picketing, of course, we have applied strict scrutiny to content-based restrictions. See Carey, 447 U.S., at 461 (applying strict scrutiny to, and invalidating, an Illinois statute that made "permissibility of residential picketing ... dependent solely on the nature of the message being conveyed"). As discussed above, the prohibition here is content-based: those who wish to speak for purposes other than protest, counsel, or education may do so at close range without the listener's consent, while those who wish to speak for other purposes may not. This bears no resemblance to a blanket prohibition of picketing—unless, of course, one uses the fanciful definition of picketing ("an effort to persuade or otherwise influence") newly discovered by today's opinion. As for the Court's appeal to the fact that we often "examine the content of a communication" to determine whether it "constitutes a threat, blackmail, an agreement to fix prices, a copyright violation, a public offering of securities, or an offer to sell goods," ante, at 16, the distinction is almost too obvious to bear mention: Speech of a certain content is constitutionally proscribable. The Court has not yet taken the step of consigning "protest, education, and counseling" to that category.

Finally, the Court is not correct in its assertion that the restriction here is content-neutral because it is "justified without reference to the content of regulated speech," in the sense that "the State's interests in protecting access and privacy, and providing the police with clear guidelines, are unrelated to the content of the demonstrators' speech." Ante, at 14—15 (emphasis added). That is not an accurate statement of our law. The Court makes too much of the statement in Ward v. Rock Against Racism, 491 U.S. 781 (1989), that "[t]he principal inquiry in determining content neutrality ... is whether the government has adopted a regulation of speech because of disagreement with the message it conveys." Id., at 791, quoted ante, at 14. That is indeed "the principal inquiry"–suppression of uncongenial ideas is the worst offense against the First Amendment–but it is not the only inquiry. Even a law that has as its purpose something unrelated to the suppression of particular content cannot irrationally single out that content for its prohibition. An ordinance directed at the suppression of noise (and therefore "justified without reference to the content of regulated speech") cannot be applied only to sound trucks delivering messages of "protest." Our very first use of the "justified by reference to content" language made clear that it is a prohibition in addition to, rather than in place of, the prohibition of facially content-based restrictions. "Selective exclusions from a public forum" we said, "may not be based on content alone, and may not be justified by reference to content alone." Police Dept. of Chicago v. Mosley, 408 U.S. 92, 96 (1972) (emphasis added).

But in any event, if one accepts the Court's description of the interest served by this regulation, it is clear that the regulation is both based on content and justified by reference to content. Constitutionally proscribable "secondary effects" of speech are directly addressed in subsection (2) of the statute, which makes it unlawful to obstruct, hinder, impede, or block access to a health care facility–a prohibition broad enough to include all physical threats and all physically threatening approaches. The purpose of subsection (3), however (according to the Court), is to protect "[t]he unwilling listener's interest in avoiding unwanted communication," ante, at 11. On this analysis, Colorado has restricted certain categories of speech–protest, counseling, and education–out of an apparent belief that only speech with this content is sufficiently likely to be annoying or upsetting as to require consent before it may be engaged in at close range. It is reasonable enough to conclude that even the most gentle and peaceful close approach by a so-called "sidewalk counselor"–who wishes to "educate" the woman entering an abortion clinic about the nature of the procedure, to "counsel" against it and in favor of other alternatives, and perhaps even (though less likely if the approach is to be successful) to "protest" her taking of a human life–will often, indeed usually, have what might be termed the "secondary effect" of annoying or deeply upsetting the woman who is planning the abortion. But that is not an effect which occurs "without reference to the content" of the speech. This singling out of presumptively "unwelcome" communications fits precisely the description of prohibited regulation set forth in Boos v. Barry, 485 U.S. 312, 321 (1988): It "targets the direct impact of a particular category of speech, not a secondary feature that happens to be associated with that type of speech." Ibid. (emphasis added).2

In sum, it blinks reality to regard this statute, in its application to oral communications, as anything other than a content-based restriction upon speech in the public forum. As such, it must survive that stringent mode of constitutional analysis our cases refer to as "strict scrutiny," which requires that the restriction be narrowly tailored to serve a compelling state interest. See United States v. Playboy Entertainment Group, Inc., 529 U.S. ___, ___ (2000) (slip op., at 8); Perry Ed. Assn. v. Perry Local Educators' Assn., 460 U.S. 37, 45 (1983). Since the Court does not even attempt to support the regulation under this standard, I shall discuss it only briefly. Suffice it to say that if protecting people from unwelcome communications (the governmental interest the Court posits) is a compelling state interest, the First Amendment is a dead letter. And if (as I shall discuss at greater length below) forbidding peaceful, nonthreatening, but uninvited speech from a distance closer than eight feet is a "narrowly tailored" means of preventing the obstruction of entrance to medical facilities (the governmental interest the State asserts) narrow tailoring must refer not to the standards of Versace, but to those of Omar the tentmaker. In the last analysis all of this does not matter, however, since as I proceed to discuss neither the restrictions upon oral communications nor those upon handbilling can withstand a proper application of even the less demanding scrutiny we apply to truly content-neutral regulations of speech in a traditional public forum.

II

As the Court explains, under our precedents even a content-neutral, time, place, and manner restriction must be narrowly tailored to advance a significant state interest, and must leave open ample alternative means of communication. Ward, 491 U.S., at 802. It cannot be sustained if it "burden[s] substantially more speech than is necessary to further the government's legitimate interests." Id., at 799.

This requires us to determine, first, what is the significant interest the State seeks to advance? Here there appears to be a bit of a disagreement between the State of Colorado (which should know) and the Court (which is eager to speculate). Colorado has identified in the text of the statute itself the interest it sought to advance: to ensure that the State's citizens may "obtain medical counseling and treatment in an unobstructed manner" by "preventing the willful obstruction of a person's access to medical counseling and treatment at a health care facility." Colo. Rev. Stat. §18—9—122(1) (1999). In its brief here, the State repeatedly confirms the interest squarely identified in the statute under review. See, e.g., Brief for Respondents 15 ("Each provision of the statute was chosen to precisely address crowding and physical intimidation: conduct shown to impede access, endanger safety and health, and strangle effective law enforcement"); id., at 14 ("[T]his provision narrowly addresses the conduct shown to interfere with access through crowding and physical threats"). The Court nevertheless concludes that the Colorado provision is narrowly tailored to serve . . . the State's interest in protecting its citizens' rights to be let alone from unwanted speech.

Indeed, the situation is even more bizarre than that. The interest that the Court makes the linchpin of its analysis was not only unasserted by the State; it is not only completely different from the interest that the statute specifically sets forth; it was explicitly disclaimed by the State in its brief before this Court, and characterized as a "straw interest" petitioners served up in the hope of discrediting the State's case. Id., at 25, n. 19. We may thus add to the lengthening list of "firsts" generated by this Court's relentlessly proabortion jurisprudence, the first case in which, in order to sustain a statute, the Court has relied upon a governmental interest not only unasserted by the State, but positively repudiated.

I shall discuss below the obvious invalidity of this statute assuming, first (in Part A), the fictitious state interest that the Court has invented, and then (in Part B), the interest actually recited in the statute and asserted by counsel for Colorado.

A

It is not without reason that Colorado claimed that, in attributing to this statute the false purpose of protecting citizens' right to be let alone, petitioners were seeking to discredit it. Just three Terms ago, in upholding an injunction against antiabortion activities, the Court refused to rely on any supposed " 'right of the people approaching and entering the facilities to be left alone.' " Schenck v. Pro-Choice Network of Western N. Y., 519 U.S. 357, 383 (1997). It expressed "doubt" that this "right ... accurately reflects our First Amendment jurisprudence." Ibid. Finding itself in something of a jam (the State here has passed a regulation that is obviously not narrowly tailored to advance any other interest) the Court today neatly re-packages the repudiated "right" as an "interest" the State may decide to protect, ante, at 11, n. 24, and then places it onto the scales opposite the right to free speech in a traditional public forum.

To support the legitimacy of its self-invented state interest, the Court relies upon a bon mot in a 1928 dissent (which we evidently overlooked in Schenck). It characterizes the "unwilling listener's interest in avoiding unwanted communication" as an "aspect of the broader 'right to be let alone' " Justice Brandeis coined in his dissent in Olmstead v. United States, 277 U.S. 438, 478. The amusing feature is that even this slim reed contradicts rather than supports the Court's position. The right to be let alone that Justice Brandeis identified was a right the Constitution "conferred, as against the government"; it was that right, not some generalized "common-law right" or "interest" to be free from hearing the unwanted opinions of one's fellow citizens, which he called the "most comprehensive" and "most valued by civilized men." Ibid. (emphasis added). To the extent that there can be gleaned from our cases a "right to be let alone" in the sense that Justice Brandeis intended, it is the right of the speaker in the public forum to be free from government interference of the sort Colorado has imposed here.

In any event, the Court's attempt to disguise the "right to be let alone" as a "governmental interest in protecting the right to be let alone" is unavailing for the simple reason that this is not an interest that may be legitimately weighed against the speakers' First Amendment rights (which the Court demotes to the status of First Amendment "interests," ante, at 9.) We have consistently held that "the Constitution does not permit the government to decide which types of otherwise protected speech are sufficiently offensive to require protection for the unwilling listener or viewer." Erznoznik v.

Jacksonville, 422 U.S. 205, 210 (1975) (emphasis added). And as recently as in Schenck, the Court reiterated that "[a]s a general matter, we have indicated that in public debate our own citizens must tolerate insulting, and even outrageous, speech in order to provide adequate breathing space to the freedoms protected by the First Amendment." 519 U.S., at 383 (internal quotation marks omitted).

The Court nonetheless purports to derive from our cases a principle limiting the protection the Constitution affords the speaker's right to direct "offensive messages" at "unwilling" audiences in the public forum. Ante, at 10. There is no such principle. We have upheld limitations on a speaker's exercise of his right to speak on the public streets when that speech intrudes into the privacy of the home. Frisby, 487 U.S., at 483, upheld a content-neutral municipal ordinance prohibiting picketing outside a residence or dwelling. The ordinance, we concluded, was justified by, and narrowly tailored to advance, the government's interest in the "protection of residential privacy." Id., at 484. Our opinion rested upon the "unique nature of the home"; "the home," we said, "is different." Ibid. The reasoning of the case plainly assumed the nonexistence of the right–common law or otherwise–that the Court relies on today, the right to be free from unwanted speech when on the public streets and sidewalks. The home, we noted, was " 'the one retreat to which men and women can repair to escape from the tribulations of their daily pursuits.' " Ibid. (quoting Carey, 447 U.S., at 471). The limitation on a speaker's right to bombard the home with unwanted messages which we approved in Frisby–

and in Rowan v. Post Office Dept., 397 U.S. 728 (1970), upon which the Court also relies–was predicated on the fact that " 'we are often 'captives' outside the sanctuary of the home and subject to objectionable speech.' " Frisby, supra, at 484 (quoting Rowan, supra,, at 738) (emphasis added). As the universally understood state of First Amendment law is described in a leading treatise: "Outside the home, the burden is generally on the observer or listener to avert his eyes or plug his ears against the verbal assaults, lurid advertisements, tawdry books and magazines, and other 'offensive' intrusions which increasingly attend urban life." L. Tribe, American Constitutional Law §12—19, p. 948 (2d ed. 1988). The Court today elevates the abortion clinic to the status of the home.3

There is apparently no end to the distortion of our First Amendment law that the Court is willing to endure in order to sustain this restriction upon the free speech of abortion opponents. The labor movement, in particular, has good cause for alarm in the Court's extensive reliance upon American Steel Foundries v. Tri-City Central Trades Council, 257 U.S. 184 (1921), an opinion in which the Court held that the Clayton Act's prohibition of injunctions against lawful and peaceful labor picketing did not forbid the injunction in that particular case. The First Amendment was not at issue, and was not so much as mentioned in the opinion, so the case is scant authority for the point the Court wishes to make. The case is also irrelevant because it was "clear from the evidence that from the outset, violent methods were pursued from time to time in such a way as to characterize the attitude of the picketers as continuously threatening." Id., at 200. No such finding was made, or could be made, here. More importantly, however, as far as our future labor cases are concerned: If a "right to be free" from "persistence, importunity, following and dogging," id., at 204, short of actual intimidation was part of our infant First Amendment law in 1921, I am shocked to think that it is there today. The Court's assertion that "[n]one of our decisions has minimized the enduring importance of 'the right to be free' from persistent 'importunity, following and dogging' after an offer to communicate has been declined," ante, at 12, is belied by the fact that this passage from American Steel Foundries has never–not once–found its way into any of the many First Amendment cases this Court has decided since 1921. We will have cause to regret today's injection of this irrelevant anachronism into the mainstream of our First Amendment jurisprudence.

Of course even if one accepted the American Steel Foundries dictum as an accurate expression of First Amendment law, the statute here is plainly not narrowly tailored to protect the interest that dictum describes. Preserving the "right to be free" from "persistent importunity, following and dogging" does not remotely require imposing upon all speakers who wish to protest, educate, or counsel a duty to request permission to approach closer than eight feet. The only way the narrow-tailoring objection can be eliminated is to posit a state-created, First-Amendment-trumping "right to be let alone" as broad and undefined as Brandeis's Olmstead dictum, which may well (why not, if the Court wishes it?) embrace a right not to be spoken to without permission from a distance closer than eight feet. Nothing stands in the way of that solution to the narrow-tailoring problem–except, of course, its utter absurdity, which is no obstacle in abortion cases.

B

I turn now to the real state interest at issue here–the one set forth in the statute and asserted in Colorado's brief: the preservation of unimpeded access to health care facilities. We need look no further than subsection (2) of the statute to see what a provision would look like that is narrowly tailored to serve that interest. Under the terms of that subsection, any person who "knowingly obstructs, detains, hinders, impedes, or blocks another person's entry to or exit from a health care facility" is subject to criminal and civil liability. It is possible, I suppose, that subsection (2) of the Colorado statute will leave unrestricted some expressive activity that, if engaged in from within eight feet, may be sufficiently harassing as to have the effect of impeding access to health care facilities. In subsection (3), however, the State of Colorado has prohibited a vast amount of speech that cannot possibly be thought to correspond to that evil.

To begin with, the 8-foot buffer zone attaches to every person on the public way or sidewalk within 100 feet of the entrance of a medical facility, regardless of whether that person is seeking to enter or exit the facility. In fact, the State acknowledged at oral argument that the buffer zone would attach to any person within 100 feet of the entrance door of a skyscraper in which a single doctor occupied an office on the 18th floor. Tr. of Oral Arg. 41. And even with respect to those who are seeking to enter or exit the facilities, the statute does not protect them only from speech that is so intimidating or threatening as to impede access. Rather, it covers all unconsented-to approaches for the purpose of oral protest, education, or counseling (including those made for the purpose of the most peaceful appeals) and, perhaps even more significantly, every approach made for the purposes of leafletting or handbilling, which we have never considered, standing alone, obstructive or unduly intrusive. The sweep of this prohibition is breathtaking.

The Court makes no attempt to justify on the facts this blatant violation of the narrow-tailoring principle. Instead, it flirts with the creation of yet a new constitutional "first" designed for abortion cases: "[W]hen," it says, "a content-neutral regulation does not entirely foreclose any means of communication, it may satisfy the tailoring requirement even though it is not the least restrictive or least intrusive means of serving the statutory goal." Ante, at 21. The implication is that the availability of alternative means of communication permits the imposition of the speech restriction upon more individuals, or more types of communication, than narrow tailoring would otherwise demand. The Court assures us that "we have emphasized" this proposition "on more than one occasion," ibid. The only citation the Court provides, however, says no such thing. Ward v. Rock Against Racism, 491 U.S., at 798, quoted ante, at 21, n. 32, says only that narrow tailoring is not synonymous with "least restrictive alternative." It does not at all suggest—and to my knowledge no other case does either—that narrow tailoring can be relaxed when there are other speech alternatives.

The burdens this law imposes upon the right to speak are substantial, despite an attempt to minimize them that is not even embarrassed to make the suggestion that they might actually "assist ... the speakers' efforts to communicate their messages," ante, at 22. (Compare this with the Court's statement in a nonabortion case, joined by the author of today's opinion: "The First Amendment mandates that we presume that speakers, not the government, know best both what they want to say and how to say it." Riley v. National Federation of Blind of N. C., Inc., 487 U.S. 781, 790—791 (1988).) The Court displays a willful ignorance of the type and nature of communication affected by the statute's restrictions. It seriously asserts, for example, that the 8-foot zone allows a speaker to communicate at a "normal conversational distance," ante, at 22. I have certainly held conversations at a distance of eight feet seated in the quiet of my chambers, but I have never walked along the public sidewalk—and have not seen others do so—"conversing" at an 8-foot remove. The suggestion is absurd. So is the suggestion that the opponents of abortion can take comfort in the fact that the statute "places no limitation on the number of speakers or the noise level, including the use of amplification equipment," ante, at 21. That is good enough, I suppose, for "protesting"; but the Court must know that most of the "counseling" and "educating" likely to take place outside a health care facility cannot be done at a distance and at a high-decibel level. The availability of a powerful amplification system will be of little help to the woman who hopes to forge, in the last moments before another of her sex is to have an abortion, a bond of concern and intimacy that might enable her to persuade the woman to change her mind and heart. The counselor may wish to walk alongside and to say, sympathetically and as softly as the circumstances allow, something like: "My dear, I know what you are going through. I've been through it myself. You're not alone and you do not have to do this. There are other alternatives. Will you let me help you? May I show you a picture of what your child looks like at this stage of her human development?" The Court would have us believe that this can be done effectively–yea, perhaps even more effectively–by shouting through a bullhorn at a distance of eight feet.

The Court seems prepared, if only for a moment, see ante, at 22—23, to take seriously the magnitude of the burden the statute imposes on simple handbilling and leafletting. That concern is fleeting, however, since it is promptly assuaged by the realization that a leafletter may, without violating the statute, stand "near the path" of oncoming pedestrians and make his "proffe[r] ..., which the pedestrians can easily accept," ante, at 22—23. It does not take a veteran labor organizer to recognize–

although surely any would, see Brief for American Federation of Labor and Congress of Industrial Organization as Amicus Curiae 7—8–that leafletting will be rendered utterly ineffectual by a requirement that the leafletter obtain from each subject permission to approach, or else man a stationary post (one that does not obstruct access to the facility, lest he violate subsection (2) of statute) and wait for passersby voluntarily to approach an outstretched hand. That simply is not how it is done, and the Court knows it–or should. A leafletter, whether he is working on behalf of Operation Rescue, Local 109, or Bubba's Bar-B-Que, stakes out the best piece of real estate he can, and then walks a few steps toward individuals passing in his vicinity, extending his arm and making it as easy as possible for the passerby, whose natural inclination is generally not to seek out such distributions, to simply accept the offering. Few pedestrians are likely to give their "consent" to the approach of a handbiller (indeed, by the time he requested it they would likely have passed by), and even fewer are likely to walk over in order to pick up a leaflet. In the abortion context, therefore, ordinary handbilling, which we have in other contexts recognized to be a "classic for[m] of speech that lie[s] at the heart of the First Amendment," Schenck, 519 U.S., at 377, will in its most effective locations be rendered futile, the Court's implausible assertions to the contrary notwithstanding.

The Colorado provision differs in one fundamental respect from the "content-neutral" time, place, and manner restrictions the Court has previously upheld. Each of them rested upon a necessary connection between the regulated expression and the evil the challenged regulation sought to eliminate. So, for instance, in Ward v. Rock Against Racism, the Court approved the city's control over sound amplification because every occasion of amplified sound presented the evil of excessive noise and distortion disturbing the areas surrounding the public forum. The regulation we upheld in Ward, rather than "bann[ing] all concerts, or even all rock concerts, . . . instead focus[ed] on the source of the evils the city seeks to eliminate . . . and eliminates them without at the same time banning or significantly restricting a substantial quantity of speech that does not create the same evils." 491 U.S., at 799, n. 7. In Members of City Council of Los Angeles v. Taxpayers for Vincent, 466 U.S. 789, 808 (1984), the Court approved a prohibition on signs attached to utility poles which "did no more than eliminate the exact source of the evil it sought to remedy." In Heffron v. International Soc. for Krishna Consciousness, Inc., 452 U.S. 640,

652 (1981), the Court upheld a regulation prohibiting the sale or distribution on the state fairgrounds of any merchandise, including printed or written material, except from a fixed location, because that precisely served the State's interest in "avoiding congestion and maintaining the orderly movement of fair patrons on the fairgrounds."

In contrast to the laws approved in those cases, the law before us here enacts a broad prophylactic restriction which does not "respon[d] precisely to the substantive problem which legitimately concern[ed]" the State, Vincent, supra, at 810–namely (the only problem asserted by Colorado), the obstruction of access to health facilities. Such prophylactic restrictions in the First Amendment context–even when they are content-neutral–are not permissible. "Broad prophylactic rules in the area of free expression are suspect. . . . Precision of regulation must be the touchstone in an area so closely touching our most precious freedoms." NAACP v. Button, 371 U.S. 415, 438 (1963). In United States v. Grace, 461 U.S. 171 (1983), we declined to uphold a ban on certain expressive activity on the sidewalks surrounding the Supreme Court. The purpose of the restriction was the perfectly valid interest in security, just as the purpose of the restriction here is the perfectly valid interest in unobstructed access; and there, as here, the restriction furthered that interest–but it furthered it with insufficient precision and hence at excessive cost to the freedom of speech. There was, we said, "an insufficient nexus" between security and all the expressive activity that was banned, id., at 181–just as here there is an insufficient nexus between the assurance of access and forbidding unconsented communications within eight feet.4

Compare with these venerable and consistent descriptions of our First Amendment law the defenses that the Court makes to the contention that the present statute is overbroad. (To be sure, the Court is assuming its own invented state interest–protection of the "right to be let alone"–rather than the interest that the statute describes, but even so the statements are extraordinary.) "The fact," the Court says, "that the coverage of a statute is broader than the specific concern that led to its enactment is of no constitutional significance." Ante, at 26. That is true enough ordinarily, but it is not true with respect to restraints upon speech, which is what the doctrine of overbreadth is all about. (Of course it is also not true, thanks to one of the other proabortion "firsts" announced by the current Court, with respect to restrictions upon abortion, which–as our decision in Stenberg v. Carhart, post, p. ____, exemplifies–has been raised to First Amendment status, even as speech opposing abortion has been demoted from First Amendment status.) Again, the Court says that the overbreadth doctrine is not applicable because this law simply "does not 'ban' any signs, literature, or oral statements," but "merely regulates the places where communications may occur." Ante, at 27. I know of no precedent for the proposition that time, place, and manner restrictions are not subject to the doctrine of overbreadth. Our decision in Grace, supra, demonstrates the contrary: Restriction of speech on the sidewalks around the Supreme Court was invalidated because it went further than the needs of security justified. Surely New York City cannot require a parade permit and a security bond for any individual who carries a sign on the sidewalks of Fifth Avenue.

The Court can derive no support for its approval of Colorado's overbroad prophylactic measure from our decision in Schenck. To be sure, there we rejected the argument that the court injunction on demonstrating within a fixed buffer zone around clinic entrances was unconstitutional because it banned even " 'peaceful nonobstructive demonstrations.' " 519 U.S., at 381. The Court upheld the injunction, however, only because the "District Court was entitled to conclude," "[b]ased on defendants' past conduct" and "the record in [that] case," that the specific defendants involved would, if permitted within the buffer zone, "continue to do what they had done before: aggressively follow and crowd individuals right up to the clinic door and then refuse to move, or purposefully mill around parking lot entrances in an effort to impede or block the progress of cars." Id., at 382. It is one thing to assume, as in Schenck, that a prophylactic injunction is necessary when the specific targets of that measure have demonstrated an inability or unwillingness to engage in protected speech activity without also engaging in conduct that the Constitution clearly does not protect. It is something else to assume that all those who wish to speak outside health care facilities across the State will similarly abuse their rights if permitted to exercise them. The First Amendment stands as a bar to exactly this type of prophylactic legislation. I cannot improve upon the Court's conclusion in Madsen that "it is difficult, indeed, to justify a prohibition on all uninvited approaches of persons seeking the services of the clinic, regardless of how peaceful the contact may be, without burdening more speech than necessary to prevent intimidation and to ensure access to the clinic. Absent evidence that the protestors' speech is independently proscribable (i.e., 'fighting words' or threats), or is so infused with violence as to be indistinguishable from a threat of physical harm, this provision cannot stand." 512 U.S., at 774 (citation omitted).

The foregoing discussion of overbreadth was written before the Court, in responding to Justice Kennedy, abandoned any pretense at compliance with that doctrine, and acknowledged—indeed, boasted—that the statute it approves "takes a prophylactic approach," ante, at 24, and adopts "[a] bright-line prophylactic rule," ante, at 25.5 I scarcely know how to respond to such an unabashed repudiation of our First Amendment doctrine. Prophylaxis is the antithesis of narrow tailoring, as the previously quoted passage from Button makes clear ("Broad prophylactic rules in the area of free expression are suspect. . . . Precision of regulation must be the touchstone in an area so closely touching our most precious freedoms." 371 U.S., at 438.) If the Court were going to make this concession, it could simply have dispensed with its earlier (unpersuasive) attempt to show that the statute was narrowly tailored. So one can add to the casualties of our whatever-it-takes proabortion jurisprudence the First Amendment doctrine of narrow tailoring and overbreadth. R. I. P.

     * * *

Before it effectively threw in the towel on the narrow-tailoring point, the Court asserted the importance of taking into account " 'the place to which the regulations apply in determining whether these restrictions burden more speech than necessary.' " Ante, at

23 (quoting Madsen, supra, at 772). A proper regard for the "place" involved in this case should result in, if anything, a commitment by this Court to adhere to and rigorously enforce our speech-protective standards. The public forum involved here—the public spaces outside of health care facilities—has become, by necessity and by virtue of this Court's decisions, a forum of last resort for those who oppose abortion. The possibility of limiting abortion by legislative means—even abortion of a live-and-kicking child that is almost entirely out of the womb—has been rendered impossible by our decisions from Roe v. Wade, 410 U.S. 113 (1973), to Stenberg v. Carhart, post, p. ____. For those who share an abiding moral or religious conviction (or, for that matter, simply a biological appreciation) that abortion is the taking of a human life, there is no option but to persuade women, one by one, not to make that choice. And as a general matter, the most effective place, if not the only place, where that persuasion can occur, is outside the entrances to abortion facilities. By upholding these restrictions on speech in this place the Court ratifies the State's attempt to make even that task an impossible one.

Those whose concern is for the physical safety and security of clinic patients, workers, and doctors should take no comfort from today's decision. Individuals or groups intent on bullying or frightening women out of an abortion, or doctors out of performing that procedure, will not be deterred by Colorado's statute; bullhorns and screaming from eight feet away will serve their purposes well. But those who would accomplish their moral and religious objectives by peaceful and civil means, by trying to persuade individual women of the rightness of their cause, will be deterred; and that is not a good thing in a democracy. This Court once recognized, as the Framers surely did, that the freedom to speak and persuade is inseparable from, and antecedent to, the survival of self-government. The Court today rotates that essential safety valve on our democracy one-half turn to the right, and no one who seeks safe access to health care facilities in Colorado or elsewhere should feel that her security has by this decision been enhanced.

It is interesting to compare the present decision, which upholds an utterly bizarre proabortion "request to approach" provision of Colorado law, with Stenberg, post, p. ____, also announced today, which strikes down a live-birth abortion prohibition adopted by 30 States and twice passed by both Houses of Congress (though vetoed both times by the President). The present case disregards the State's own assertion of the purpose of its proabortion law, and posits instead a purpose that the Court believes will be more likely to render the law constitutional. Stenberg rejects the State's assertion of the very meaning of its antiabortion law, and declares instead a meaning that will render the law unconstitutional. The present case rejects overbreadth challenges to a proabortion law that regulates speech, on grounds that have no support in our prior jurisprudence and that instead amount to a total repudiation of the doctrine of overbreadth. Stenberg applies overbreadth analysis to an antiabortion law that has nothing to do with speech, even though until eight years ago overbreadth was unquestionably the exclusive preserve of the First Amendment. See Stenberg, post, at ____ (Thomas, J., dissenting); Janklow v. Planned Parenthood, Sioux Falls Clinic, 517 U.S. 1174, 1177—1181 (1996) (Scalia, J., dissenting from denial of cert.); Ada v. Guam Soc. of Obstetricians & Gynecologists, 506 U.S. 1011, 1013 (1992) (Scalia, J., dissenting from denial of cert.).

Does the deck seem stacked? You bet. As I have suggested throughout this opinion, today's decision is not an isolated distortion of our traditional constitutional principles, but is one of many aggressively proabortion novelties announced by the Court in recent years. See, e.g., Madsen v. Women's Health Center, Inc., 512 U.S. 753 (1994); Schenck v. Pro-Choice Network of Western N. Y., 519 U.S. 357 (1997); Thornburgh v. American College of Obstetricians and Gynecologists, 476 U.S. 747 (1986). Today's distortions, however, are particularly blatant. Restrictive views of the First Amendment that have been in dissent since the 1930's suddenly find themselves in the majority. "Uninhibited, robust, and wide open" debate is replaced by the power of the state to protect an unheard-of "right to be let alone" on the public streets. I dissent.

Notes

1. The Court responds that statutes which restrict categories of speech—as opposed to subject matter or viewpoint—are constitutionally worrisome only if a "significant number of communications, raising the same problem that the statute was enacted to solve, . . . fall outside the statute's scope, while others fall inside." Ante, at 18–19. I am not sure that is correct, but let us assume, for the sake of argument, that it is. The Court then proceeds to assert that "[t]he statutory phrases, 'oral protest, education, or counseling,' distinguish speech activities likely to" present the problem of "harassment, . . . nuisance, . . . persistent importuning, . . . following, . . . dogging, and . . . implied threat of physical touching," from "speech activities [such as my example of 'happy speech'] that are most unlikely to have those consequences," ibid. Well. That may work for "oral protest"; but it is beyond imagining why "education" and "counseling" are especially likely, rather than especially unlikely, to involve such conduct. (Socrates was something of a noodge, but even he did not go that far.) Unless, of course, "education" and "counseling" are code words for efforts to dissuade women from abortion—in which event the statute would not be viewpoint neutral, which the Court concedes makes it invalid.

2. The Court's contention that the statute is content-neutral because it is not a " 'regulation of speech' " but a "regulation of the places where some speech may occur," ante, at 14 (quoting Ward v. Rock Against Racism, 491 U.S. 781, 791 (1989)), is simply baffling. First, because the proposition that a restriction upon the places where speech may occur is not a restriction upon speech is both absurd and contradicted by innumerable cases. See, e.g., Madsen v. Women's Health Center, Inc., 512 U.S. 753 (1994); Burson v. Freeman, 504 U.S. 191 (1992); Frisby v. Schultz, 487 U.S. 474 (1988); Boos v. Barry, 485 U.S. 312 (1988); Heffron v. International Soc. for Krishna Consciousness, Inc., 452 U.S. 640 (1981); Carey v. Brown, 447 U.S. 455 (1980); Grayned v. City of Rockford, 408 U.S. 104 (1972); Police Dept. of Chicago v. Mosley, 408 U.S. 92 (1972). And second, because the fact that a restriction is framed as a "regulation of the places where some speech may occur" has nothing whatever to do with whether the restriction is content-

neutral—which is why Boos held to be content-based the ban on displaying, within 500 feet of foreign embassies, banners designed to " 'bring into public odium any foreign government.' " 485 U.S., at 316.

3. I do not disagree with the Court that "our cases have repeatedly recognized the interests of unwilling listeners" in locations, such as public conveyances, where " 'the degree of captivity makes it impractical for the unwilling viewer or auditor to avoid exposure,' " ante, at 13 (quoting Erzoznick v. City of Jacksonville, 422 U.S. 205 (1975)). But we have never made the absurd suggestion that a pedestrian is a "captive" of the speaker who seeks to address him on the public sidewalks, where he may simply walk quickly by. Erzoznick itself, of course, invalidated a prohibition on the showing of films containing nudity on screens visible from the street, noting that "the burden normally falls upon the viewer to 'avoid further bombardment of [his] sensibilities simply by averting [his] eyes.' " Id., at 210—211 (quoting Cohen v. California, 403 U.S. 15, 21 (1971).

4. The Court's suggestion, ante, at 25, that the restrictions imposed by the Colorado ban are unobjectionable because they "interfer[e] far less with a speaker's ability to communicate," than did the regulations involved in Frisby and Heffron, and in cases requiring "silence" outside of a hospital (by which I presume the Court means Madsen v. Women's Health Center, Inc., 512 U.S. 753 (1994)), misses the point of narrow-tailoring analysis. We do not compare restrictions on speech to some Platonic ideal of speech restrictiveness, or to each other. Rather, our First Amendment doctrine requires us to consider whether the regulation in question burdens substantially more speech than necessary to achieve the particular interest the government has identified and asserted. Ward, 491 U.S., at 799. In each of the instances the Court cites, we concluded that the challenged regulation contained the precision that our cases require and that Colorado's statute (which the Court itself calls "prophylactic," ante, at 24—25) manifestly lacks.

5. Of course the Court greatly understates the scope of the prophylaxis, saying that "the statute's prophylactic aspect is justified by the great difficulty of protecting, say, a pregnant woman from physical harassment with legal rules that focus exclusively on the individual impact of each instance of behavior," ante, at 24—25. But the statute prevents the "physically harassing" act of (shudder!) approaching within closer than eight feet not only when it is directed against pregnant women, but also (just to be safe) when it is directed against 300-pound, male, and unpregnant truck drivers—surely a distinction that is not "difficult to make accurately," ante, at 25.

Justice Scalia's dissent in Rogers v. Tennessee (May 14, 2001)

Justice Scalia, with whom Justice Stevens and Justice Thomas join, and with whom Justice Breyer joins as to Part II, dissenting.

The Court today approves the conviction of a man for a murder that was not murder (but only manslaughter) when the offense was committed. It thus violates a principle—encapsulated in the maxim *nulla poena sine lege*—which "dates from the ancient

Greeks" and has been described as one of the most "widely held value-judgment[s] in the entire history of human thought." J. Hall, General Principles of Criminal Law 59 (2d ed. 1960). Today's opinion produces, moreover, a curious constitution that only a judge could love. One in which (by virtue of the Ex Post Facto Clause) the elected representatives of all the people cannot retroactively make murder what was not murder when the act was committed; but in which unelected judges can do precisely that. One in which the predictability of parliamentary lawmaking cannot validate the retroactive creation of crimes, but the predictability of judicial lawmaking can do so. I do not believe this is the system that the Framers envisioned–or, for that matter, that any reasonable person would imagine.

I

A

To begin with, let us be clear that the law here was altered after the fact. Petitioner, whatever else he was guilty of, was innocent of murder under the law as it stood at the time of the stabbing, because the victim did not die until after a year and a day had passed. The requisite condition subsequent of the murder victim's death within a year and a day is no different from the requisite condition subsequent of the rape victim's raising a "hue and cry" which we held could not retroactively be eliminated in Carmell v. Texas, 529 U.S. 513 (2000). Here, as there, it operates to bar conviction. Indeed, if the present condition differs at all from the one involved in Carmell it is in the fact that it does not merely pertain to the "quantum of evidence" necessary to corroborate a charge, id., at 530, but is an actual element of the crime–a "substantive principle of law," 992 S. W. 2d 393, 399 (Tenn. 1999), the failure to establish which "entirely precludes a murder prosecution," id., at 400. Though the Court spends some time questioning whether the year-and-a-day rule was ever truly established in Tennessee, see ante, at 12—15, the Supreme Court of Tennessee said it was, see 992 S. W. 2d, at 396, 400, and this reasonable reading of state law by the State's highest court is binding upon us.

Petitioner's claim is that his conviction violated the Due Process Clause of the Fourteenth Amendment, insofar as that Clause contains the principle applied against the legislature by the Ex Post Facto Clause of Article I. We first discussed the relationship between these two Clauses in Bouie v. City of Columbia, 378 U.S. 347 (1964). There, we considered Justice Chase to have spoken for the Court in Calder v. Bull, 3 Dall. 386, 390 (1798), when he defined an ex post facto law as, inter alia, one that "aggravates a crime, or makes it greater than it was, when committed." 378 U.S., at 353 (emphasis deleted). We concluded that, "[i]f a state legislature is barred by the Ex Post Facto Clause from passing such a law, it must follow that a State Supreme Court is barred by the Due Process Clause from achieving precisely the same result by judicial construction." Id., at 353—354. The Court seeks to avoid the obvious import of this language by characterizing it as mere dicta. See ante, at 7. Only a concept of dictum that includes the very reasoning of the opinion could support this characterization. The ratio decidendi of Bouie was that the principle applied to the legislature though the Ex Post Facto Clause was contained in the Due

Process Clause insofar as judicial action is concerned. I cannot understand why the Court derives such comfort from the fact that later opinions applying Bouie have referred to the Due Process Clause rather than the Ex Post Facto Clause, see ante, at 7—8; that is entirely in accord with the rationale of the case, which I follow and which the Court discards.

The Court attempts to cabin Bouie by reading it to prohibit only " 'unexpected and indefensible' " judicial law revision, and to permit retroactive judicial changes so long as the defendant has had "fair warning" that the changes might occur. Ante, at 10. This reading seems plausible because Bouie does indeed use those quoted terms; but they have been wrenched entirely out of context. The "fair warning" to which Bouie and subsequent cases referred was not "fair warning that the law might be changed," but fair warning of what constituted the crime at the time of the offense. And Bouie did not express disapproval of "unexpected and indefensible changes in the law" (and thus implicitly approve "expected or defensible changes"). It expressed disapproval of "judicial construction of a criminal statute" that is "unexpected and indefensible by reference to the law which had been expressed prior to the conduct in issue." 378 U.S., at 354 (emphasis added; internal quotation marks omitted). It thus implicitly approved only a judicial construction that was an expected or defensible application of prior cases interpreting the statute. Extending this principle from statutory crimes to common-law crimes would result in the approval of retroactive holdings that accord with prior cases expounding the common law, and the disapproval of retroactive holdings that clearly depart from prior cases expounding the common law. According to Bouie, not just "unexpected and indefensible" retroactive changes in the common law of crimes are bad, but all retroactive changes.

Bouie rested squarely upon "[t]he fundamental principle that 'the required criminal law must have existed when the conduct in issue occurred,' " ibid. (Nulla poena sine lege.) Proceeding from that principle, Bouie said that "a State Supreme Court is barred by the Due Process Clause from achieving precisely the same result [prohibited by the Ex Post Facto Clause] by judicial construction." Id., at 353—354. There is no doubt that "fair warning" of the legislature's intent to change the law does not insulate retroactive legislative criminalization. Such a statute violates the Ex Post Facto Clause, no matter that, at the time the offense was committed, the bill enacting the change was pending and assured of passage–or indeed, had already been passed but not yet signed by the President whose administration had proposed it. It follows from the analysis of Bouie that "fair warning" of impending change cannot insulate retroactive judicial criminalization either.

Nor is there any reason in the nature of things why it should. According to the Court, the exception is necessary because prohibiting retroactive judicial criminalization would "place an unworkable and unacceptable restraint on normal judicial processes," would be "incompatible with the resolution of uncertainty that marks any evolving legal system," and would "unduly impair the incremental and reasoned development of precedent that is the foundation of the common law system." Ante, at 9. That assessment ignores the crucial difference between simply applying a law to a new set of circumstances and changing the law that has previously been applied to the very circumstances before the court. Many criminal cases present some factual nuance that arguably distinguishes them from cases that have come before; a court applying the penal statute to the new fact pattern does not purport to change the law. That, however, is not the action before us here, but rather, a square, head-on overruling of prior law—or, more accurately, something even more extreme than that: a judicial opinion acknowledging that under prior law, for reasons that used to be valid, the accused could not be convicted, but decreeing that, because of changed circumstances, "we hereby abolish the common law rule," 922 S. W. 2d, at 401, and upholding the conviction by applying the new rule to conduct that occurred before the change in law was announced. Even in civil cases, and even in modern times, such retroactive revision of a concededly valid legal rule is extremely rare. With regard to criminal cases, I have no hesitation in affirming that it was unheard-of at the time the original Due Process Clause was adopted. As I discuss in detail in the following section, proceeding in that fashion would have been regarded as contrary to the judicial traditions embraced within the concept of due process of law.

B

The Court's opinion considers the judgment at issue here "a routine exercise of common law decisionmaking," whereby the Tennessee court "brought the law into conformity with reason and common sense," by "laying to rest an archaic and outdated rule." Ante, at 15. This is an accurate enough description of what modern "common law decisionmaking" consists of—but it is not an accurate description of the theoretical model of common-law decisionmaking accepted by those who adopted the Due Process Clause. At the time of the framing, common-law jurists believed (in the words of Sir Francis Bacon) that the judge's "office is jus dicere, and not jus dare; to interpret law, and not to make law, or give law." Bacon, Essays, Civil and Moral, in 3 Harvard Classics 130 (C. Eliot ed. 1909) (1625). Or as described by Blackstone, whose Commentaries were widely read and "accepted [by the framing generation] as the most satisfactory exposition of the common law of England," see Schick v. United States, 195 U.S. 65, 69 (1904), "judicial decisions are the principal and most authoritative evidence, that can be given, of the existence of such a custom as shall form a part of the common law." 1 W. Blackstone, Commentaries on the Laws of England *69 (1765) (hereinafter Blackstone) (emphasis added).

Blackstone acknowledged that the courts' exposition of what the law was could change. Stare decisis, he said, "admits of exception, where the former determination is most evidently contrary to reason . . . ." Ibid. But "in such cases the subsequent judges do not pretend to make a new law, but to vindicate the old one from misrepresentation." Id., at *70. To fit within this category of bad law, a law must be "manifestly absurd or unjust." It would not suffice, he said, that "the particular reason [for the law] can at this distance of time [not be] precisely assigned." "For though [its] reason be not obvious at first view, yet we owe such a deference to former times as not to suppose they acted wholly without consideration." Ibid.1 By way of example, Blackstone pointed to the seemingly unreasonable rule that one cannot inherit the estate of one's half-brother. Though he accepted that the feudal reason behind the law was no longer obvious, he wrote "yet it is not in [a common law judge's] power to alter it." Id., at *70—

*71 (emphasis added).2 Moreover, "the unreasonableness of a custom in modern circumstances will not affect its validity if the Court is satisfied of a reasonable origin." Allen 140—141. "A custome once reasonable and tolerable, if after it become grievous, and not answerable to the reason, whereupon it was grounded, yet is to be . . . taken away by act of parliament." 2 E. Coke, Institutes of the Laws of England *664 (1642) (hereinafter Institutes); see also id., at *97 ("No law, or custome of England can be taken away, abrogated, or adnulled, but by authority of parliament"); Of Oaths before an Ecclesiastical Judge Ex Officio, 12 Co. Rep. *26, *29 (1655) ("[T]he law and custom of England is the inheritance of the subject, which he cannot be deprived of without his assent in Parliament").

There are, of course, stray statements and doctrines found in the historical record that—read out of context—could be thought to support the modern-day proposition that the common law was always meant to evolve. Take, for instance, Lord Coke's statement in the Institutes that "the reason of the law ceasing, the law itself ceases." This maxim is often cited by modern devotees of a turbulently changing common law—often in its Latin form (cessante ratione legis, cessat ipse lex) to create the impression of great venerability. In its original context, however, it had nothing to do with the power of common-law courts to change the law. At the point at which it appears in the Institutes, Coke was discussing the exception granted abbots and mayors from the obligation of military service to the King which attached to land ownership. Such service would be impracticable for a man of the cloth or a mayor. But, said Coke, "if they convey over the lands to any naturall man and his heires," the immunity "by the conveyance over ceaseth." 1 Institutes *70. In other words, the service which attached to the land would apply to any subsequent owner not cloaked in a similar immunity. It was in describing this change that Coke employed the Latin maxim cessante ratione legis, cessat ipse lex. It had to do, not with a changing of the common-law rule, but with a change of circumstances that rendered the common-law rule no longer applicable to the case.

The same is true of the similar quotation from Coke: "[R]atio legis est anima legis, et mutata legis ratione, mutatur et lex"—reason is the soul of the law; the reason of the law being changed, the law is also changed. This is taken from Coke's report of Milborn's Case, 7 Co. Rep. 6b, 7a (1587), a suit involving a town's responsibility for a murder committed within its precincts. The common-law rule had been that a town could be amerced for failure to apprehend a murderer who committed his crime on its streets during the day, but not a murderer who struck after nightfall, when its citizens were presumably asleep. Parliament, however, enacted a statute requiring towns to close their gates at night, and the court reasoned that thereafter a town that left its gates open could be amerced for the nocturnal homicide as well, since the town's violation of the Act was negligence that facilitated the escape. This perhaps partakes more of a new right of action implied from legislation than of any common-law rule. But to the extent it involved the common law, it assuredly did not change the prior rule: A town not in violation of the statute would continue to be immune. Milborn's Case simply held that the rule would not be extended to towns that wrongfully failed to close their gates—which involves no overruling, but nothing more than normal, case-by-case common-law adjudication.

It is true that framing-era judges in this country considered themselves authorized to reject English common-law precedent they found "barbarous" and "ignorant," see 1 Z. Swift, A System of the Laws of the State of Connecticut 46 (1795) (hereinafter Swift); N. Chipman, A Dissertation on the Act Adopting the Common and Statute Laws of England, in Reports and Dissertations 117, 128 (1793) (hereinafter Chipman). That, however, was not an assertion of judges' power to change the common law. For, as Blackstone wrote, the common law was a law for England, and did not automatically transfer to the American Colonies; rather, it had to be adopted. See 1 Blackstone *107—*108 (observing that "the common law of England, as such, has no allowance or authority" in "[o]ur American plantations"); see also 1 Swift 46 ("The English common law is not in itself binding in this state"); id., at 44—45 ("The English common law has never been considered to be more obligatory here, than the Roman law has been in England"). In short, the colonial courts felt themselves perfectly free to pick and choose which parts of the English common law they would adopt.3 As stated by Chipman, at 128, "[i]f no reason can be assigned, in support of rules, or precedents, not already adopted in practice, to adopt such rules, is certainly contrary to the principles of our government" (emphasis added). This discretion not to adopt would not presuppose, or even support, the power of colonial courts subsequently to change the accumulated colonial common law. The absence of belief in that power is demonstrated by the following passage from 1 M. Horwitz, The Transformation of American Law 1780—1860, p. 5 (1977) (hereinafter, Horwitz): "Massachusetts Chief Justice Hutchison could declare in 1767 that 'laws should be established, else Judges and Juries must go according to their Reason, that is, their Will.' It was also imperative 'that the Judge should never be the Legislator: Because, then the Will of the Judge would be the Law: and this tends to a State of Slavery.' " Or, as Judge Swift put it, courts "ought never to be allowed to depart from the well known boundaries of express law, into the wide fields of discretion." 2 Swift 366.

Nor is the framing era's acceptance of common-law crimes support for the proposition that the Framers accepted an evolving common law. The acknowledgment of a new crime, not thitherto rejected by judicial decision, was not a changing of the common law, but an application of it. At the time of the framing, common-law crimes were considered unobjectionable, for " 'a law founded on the law of nature may be retrospective, because it always existed,' " Horwitz, at 7, quoting Blackwell v. Wilkinson, Jefferson's Rep. 73, 77 (Va. 1768) (argument of then-Attorney General John Randolph). Of course, the notion of a common-law crime is utterly anathema today, which leads one to wonder why that is so. The obvious answer is that we now agree with the perceptive chief justice of

Connecticut, who wrote in 1796 that common-law crimes "partak[e] of the odious nature of an ex post facto law." 2 Swift 365—366. But, as Horwitz makes clear, a widespread sharing of Swift's "preoccupation with the unfairness of administering a system of judge-made criminal law was a distinctly post-revolutionary phenomenon, reflecting a profound change in sensibility. For the inarticulate premise that lay behind Swift's warnings against the danger of judicial discretion was a growing perception that judges no longer merely discovered law; they also made it." Horwitz 14—15 (emphases added). In other words, the connection between ex post facto lawmaking and common-law judging would not have become widely apparent until common-law judging became lawmaking, not (as it had been) law declaring. This did not happen, see id., at 1—4, until the 19th century, after the framing.

What occurred in the present case, then, is precisely what Blackstone said—and the Framers believed—would not suffice. The Tennessee Supreme Court made no pretense that the year-and-a-day rule was "bad" law from the outset; rather, it asserted, the need for the rule, as a means of assuring causality of the death, had disappeared with time. Blackstone—and the Framers who were formed by Blackstone—would clearly have regarded that change in law as a matter for the legislature, beyond the power of the court. It may well be that some common-law decisions of the era in fact changed the law while purporting not to. But that is beside the point. What is important here is that it was an undoubted point of principle, at the time the Due Process Clause was adopted, that courts could not "change" the law. That explains why the Constitution restricted only the legislature from enacting ex post facto laws. Under accepted norms of judicial process, an ex post facto law (in the sense of a judicial holding, not that a prior decision was erroneous, but that the prior valid law is hereby retroactively changed) was simply not an option for the courts. This attitude subsisted, I may note, well beyond the founding era, and beyond the time when due process guarantees were extended against the States by the Fourteenth Amendment. In an 1886 admiralty case, for example, this Court said the following: "The rights of persons in this particular under the maritime law of this country are not different from those under the common law, and as it is the duty of courts to declare the law, not to make it, we cannot change this rule." The Harrisburg, 119 U.S. 199, 213—214 (1886), overruled by Moragne v. States Marine Lines, Inc., 398 U.S. 375 (1970).

It is not a matter, therefore, of "[e]xtending the [Ex Post Facto] Clause to courts through the rubric of due process," and thereby "circumvent[ing] the clear constitutional text," ante, at 8. It is simply a matter of determining what due judicial process consists of—and it does not consist of retroactive creation of crimes. The Ex Post Facto Clause is relevant only because it demonstrates beyond doubt that, however much the acknowledged and accepted role of common-law courts could evolve (as it has) in other respects, retroactive revision of the criminal law was regarded as so fundamentally unfair that an alteration of the judicial role which permits that will be a denial of due process. Madison wrote that "ex-post-facto laws . . . are contrary to the first principles of the social compact, and to every principle of social legislation." The Federalist No. 44, p. 282 (C.

Rossiter ed. 1961). I find it impossible to believe, as the Court does, that this strong sentiment attached only to retroactive laws passed by the legislature, and would not apply equally (or indeed with even greater force) to a court's production of the same result through disregard of the traditional limits upon judicial power. Insofar as the "first principles of the social compact" are concerned, what possible difference does it make that "[a] court's opportunity for discrimination" by retroactively changing a law "is more limited than a legislature's, in that it can only act in construing existing law in actual litigation"? Ante, at 9 (internal quotation marks and citation omitted). The injustice to the individuals affected is no less.

II

Even if I agreed with the Court that the Due Process Clause is violated only when there is lack of "fair warning" of the impending retroactive change, I would not find such fair warning here. It is not clear to me, in fact, what the Court believes the fair warning consisted of. Was it the mere fact that "[t]he year and a day rule is widely viewed as an outdated relic of the common law"? Ante, at 11. So are many of the elements of common-law crimes, such as "breaking the close" as an element of burglary, or "asportation" as an element of larceny. See W. LaFave & A. Scott, Criminal Law 631–633, 708–710 (1972). Are all of these "outdated relics" subject to retroactive judicial rescission? Or perhaps the fair warning consisted of the fact that "the year and a day rule has been legislatively or judicially abolished in the vast majority of jurisdictions recently to have addressed the issue." Ante, at 11. But why not count in petitioner's favor (as giving him no reason to expect a change in law) those even more numerous jurisdictions that have chosen not "recently to have addressed the issue"? And why not also count in petitioner's favor (rather than against him) those jurisdictions that have abolished the rule legislatively, and those jurisdictions that have abolished it through prospective rather than retroactive judicial rulings (together, a large majority of the abolitions, see 922 S. W. 2d, at 397, n. 4, 402 (listing statutes and cases))? That is to say, even if it was predictable that the rule would be changed, it was not predictable that it would be changed retroactively, rather than in the prospective manner to which legislatures are restricted by the Ex Post Facto Clause, or in the prospective manner that most other courts have employed.

In any event, as the Court itself acknowledges, "[d]ue process . . . does not require a person to apprise himself of

the common law of all 50 States in order to guarantee that his actions will not subject him to punishment in light of a developing trend in the law that has not yet made its way to his State." Ante, at 12. The Court tries to counter this self-evident point with the statement that "[a]t the same time, however, the fact that a vast number of jurisdictions have abolished a rule that has so clearly outlived its purpose is surely relevant to whether the abolition of the rule in a particular case can be said to be unexpected and indefensible by reference to the law as it then existed," ibid. This retort rests upon the fallacy that I discussed earlier: that "expected or defensible" "abolition" of prior law was approved by Bouie. It was not—and according such conclusive effect to the "defensibility" (by which I presume the Court means the "reasonableness") of the change in law will validate the retroactive creation of many new crimes.

Finally, the Court seeks to establish fair warning by discussing at great length, ante, at 12—15, how unclear it was that the year-and-a-day rule was ever the law in Tennessee. As I have already observed, the Supreme Court of Tennessee is the authoritative expositor of Tennessee law, and has said categorically that the year-and-a-day rule was the law. Does the Court mean to establish the principle that fair warning of impending change exists—or perhaps fair warning can be dispensed with—when the prior law is not crystal clear? Yet another boon

for retroactively created crimes.

I reiterate that the only "fair warning" discussed in our precedents, and the only "fair warning" relevant to the issue before us here, is fair warning of what the law is. That warning, unlike the new one that today's opinion invents, goes well beyond merely "safeguarding defendants against unjustified and unpredictable breaks with prior law," ante, at 10 (emphasis added). It safeguards them against changes in the law after the fact. But even accepting the Court's novel substitute, the opinion's conclusion that this watered-down standard has been met seems to me to proceed on the principle that a large number of almost-valid arguments makes a solid case. As far as I can tell, petitioner had nothing that could fairly be called a "warning" that the Supreme Court of Tennessee would retroactively eliminate one of the elements of the crime of murder.

    * * *

To decide this case, we need only conclude that due process prevents a court from (1) acknowledging the validity, when they were rendered, of prior decisions establishing a particular element of a crime; (2) changing the prior law so as to eliminate that element; and (3) applying that change to conduct that occurred under the prior regime. A court would remain free to apply common-law criminal rules to new fact patterns, see ante, at 9—10, so long as that application is consistent with a fair reading of prior cases. It would remain free to conclude that a prior decision or series of decisions establishing a particular element of a crime was in error, and to apply that conclusion retroactively (so long as the "fair notice" requirement of Bouie is satisfied). It would even remain free, insofar as the ex post facto element of the Due Process Clause is concerned, to "reevaluat[e] and refin[e]" the elements of common-law crimes to its heart's content, so long as it does so prospectively. (The majority of state courts that have abolished the year-and-a-day rule have done so in this fashion.) And, of course (as Blackstone and the Framers envisioned), legislatures would be free to eliminate outmoded elements of common-law crimes for the future by law. But what a court cannot do, consistent with due process, is what the Tennessee Supreme Court did here: avowedly change (to the defendant's disadvantage) the criminal law governing past acts.

For these reasons, I would reverse the judgment of the Supreme Court of Tennessee.

Notes

1. Inquiring into a law's original reasonableness was perhaps tantamount to questioning whether it existed at all. "In holding the origin to have been unreasonable, the Court nearly always doubts or denies the actual origin and continuance of the custom in fact." C. Allen, Law in the Making 140 (3d ed. 1939) (hereinafter Allen).

2. The near-dispositive strength Blackstone accorded stare decisis was not some mere personal predilection. Chancellor Kent was of the same view: "If a decision has been made upon solemn argument and mature deliberation, the presumption is in favor of its correctness; and the community have a right to regard it as a just declaration or exposition of the law, and to regulate their actions and contracts by it." 1 J. Kent, Commentaries *475—*476 (emphasis added). See also Hamilton's statement in The Federalist: "To avoid an arbitrary discretion in the courts, it is indispensable that they should be bound down by strict rules and precedents which serve to define and point out their duty in every particular case that comes before them." The Federalist No. 78, p. 471 (C. Rossiter ed. 1961).

3. In fact, however, "most of the basic departures [from English common law] were accomplished not by judicial decision but by local statute, so that by the time of the American Revolution one hears less and less about the unsuitability of common law principles to the American environment." 1 M. Horwitz, Transformation of American Law 1780—1860, p. 5 (1977).

Justice Scalia's dissent in PGA Tour, Inc. v. Casey Martin (May 29, 2001)

Justice Scalia, with whom Justice Thomas joins, dissenting.

In my view today's opinion exercises a benevolent compassion that the law does not place it within our power to impose. The judgment distorts the text of Title III, the structure of the ADA, and common sense. I respectfully dissent.

I

The Court holds that a professional sport is a place of public accommodation and that respondent is a "custome[r]" of "competition" when he practices his profession. Ante, at 17. It finds, ante, at 18, that this strange conclusion is compelled by the "literal text" of Title III of the Americans with Disabilities Act of 1990 (ADA), 42 U.S.C. § 12101 et seq., by the "expansive purpose" of the ADA, and by the fact that Title II of the Civil Rights Act of 1964, 42 U.S.C. § 2000a(a), has been applied to an amusement park and public golf courses. I disagree.

The ADA has three separate titles: Title I covers employment discrimination, Title II covers discrimination by government entities, and Title III covers discrimination by places of public accommodation. Title II is irrelevant to this case. Title I protects only "employees" of employers who have 15 or more employees, §§12112(a), 12111(5)(A). It does not protect independent contractors. See, e.g., Birchem v. Knights of Columbus, 116 F.3d 310, 312—313 (CA8 1997); cf. Nationwide Mut. Ins. Co. v. Darden, 503 U.S. 318, 322—323

(1992). Respondent claimed employment discrimination under Title I, but the District Court found him to be an independent contractor rather than an employee.

Respondent also claimed protection under §12182 of Title III. That section applies only to particular places and persons. The place must be a "place of public accommodation," and the person must be an "individual" seeking "enjoyment of the goods, services, facilities, privileges, advantages, or accommodations" of the covered place. §12182(a). Of course a court indiscriminately invoking the "sweeping" and "expansive" purposes of the ADA, ante, at 13, 18, could argue that when a place of public accommodation denied any "individual," on the basis of his disability, anything that might be called a "privileg[e]," the individual has a valid Title III claim. Cf. ante, at 14. On such an interpretation, the employees and independent contractors of every place of public accommodation come within Title III: The employee enjoys the "privilege" of employment, the contractor the "privilege" of the contract.

For many reasons, Title III will not bear such an interpretation. The provision of Title III at issue here (§12182, its principal provision) is a public-accommodation law, and it is the traditional understanding of public-accommodation laws that they provide rights for customers. "At common law, innkeepers, smiths, and others who made profession of a public employment, were prohibited from refusing, without good reason, to serve a customer." Hurley v. Irish-American Gay, Lesbian and Bisexual Group of Boston, Inc., 515 U.S. 557, 571 (1995) (internal quotation marks omitted). See also Heart of Atlanta Motel, Inc. v. United States, 379 U.S. 241 (1964). This understanding is clearly reflected in the text of Title III itself. Section 12181(7) lists 12 specific types of entities that qualify as "public accommodations," with a follow-on expansion that makes it clear what the "enjoyment of the goods, services, etc." of those entities consists of—and it plainly envisions that the person "enjoying" the "public accommodation" will be a customer. For example, Title III is said to cover an "auditorium" or "other place of public gathering," §12181(7)(D). Thus, "gathering" is the distinctive enjoyment derived from an auditorium; the persons "gathering" at an auditorium are presumably covered by Title III, but those contracting to clean the auditorium are not. Title III is said to cover a "zoo" or "other place of recreation," §12181(7)(I). The persons "recreat[ing]" at a "zoo" are presumably covered, but the animal handlers bringing in the latest panda are not. The one place where Title III specifically addresses discrimination by places of public accommodation through "contractual" arrangements, it makes clear that discrimination against the other party to the contract is not covered, but only discrimination against "clients or customers of the covered public accommodation that enters into the contractual, licensing or other arrangement." §12182(b)(1)(A)(iv). And finally, the regulations promulgated by the Department of Justice reinforce the conclusion that Title III's protections extend only to customers. "The purpose of the ADA's public accommodations requirements," they say, "is to ensure accessibility to the goods offered by a public accommodation." 28 CFR, Ch. 1, pt. 36, App. B, p. 650 (2000). Surely this has nothing to do with employees and independent contractors.

If there were any doubt left that §12182 covers only clients and customers of places of public accommodation, it is eliminated by the fact that a contrary interpretation would make a muddle of the ADA as a whole. The words of Title III must be read "in their context and with a view to their place in the overall statutory scheme." Davis v. Michigan Dept. of Treasury, 489 U.S. 803, 809 (1989). Congress expressly excluded employers of fewer than 15 employees from Title I. The mom-and-pop grocery store or laundromat need not worry about altering the nonpublic areas of its place of business to accommodate handicapped employees—or about the litigation that failure to do so will invite. Similarly, since independent contractors are not covered by Title I, the small business (or the large one, for that matter) need not worry about making special accommodations for the painters, electricians, and other independent workers whose services are contracted for from time to time. It is an entirely unreasonable interpretation of the statute to say that these exemptions so carefully crafted in Title I are entirely eliminated by Title III (for the many businesses that are places of public accommodation) because employees and independent contractors "enjoy" the employment and contracting that such places provide. The only distinctive feature of places of public accommodation is that they accommodate the public, and Congress could have no conceivable reason for according the employees and independent contractors of such businesses protections that employees and independent contractors of other businesses do not enjoy.

The United States apparently agrees that employee claims are not cognizable under Title III, see Brief for United States as Amicus Curiae 18—19, n. 17, but despite the implications of its own regulations, see 28 CFR, Ch. 1, pt. 36, App. B, p. 650 (2000), appears to believe (though it does not explicitly state) that claims of independent contractors are cognizable. In a discussion littered with entirely vague statements from the legislative history, cf. ante, at 12, the United States argues that Congress presumably wanted independent contractors with private entities covered under Title III because independent contractors with governmental entities are covered by Title II, see Brief for United States as Amicus Curiae 18, and n. 17—a line of reasoning that does not commend itself to the untutored intellect. But since the United States does not provide (and I cannot conceive of) any possible construction of the terms of Title III that will exclude employees while simultaneously covering independent contractors, its concession regarding employees effectively concedes independent contractors as well. Title III applies only to customers.

The Court, for its part, assumes that conclusion for the sake of argument, ante, at 17, but pronounces respondent to be a "customer" of the PGA TOUR or of the golf courses on which it is played. That seems to me quite incredible. The PGA TOUR is a professional sporting event, staged for the entertainment of a live and TV audience, the receipts from whom (the TV audience's admission price is paid by advertisers) pay the expenses of the tour, including the cash prizes for the winning golfers. The professional golfers on the tour are no more "enjoying" (the statutory term) the entertainment that the tour provides, or the facilities of the golf courses on which it is held, than professional baseball players "enjoy" the baseball games in which they play or the facilities of Yankee Stadium. To be sure, professional ballplayers participate in the games, and use the ballfields, but no one in his right mind would think that they are customers of the American League or of Yankee Stadium. They are themselves the entertainment that the customers pay to watch. And professional golfers are no different. It makes not a bit of difference, insofar as their "customer" status is concerned, that the remuneration for their performance (unlike most of the remuneration for ballplayers) is not fixed but contingent–viz., the purses for the winners in the various events, and the compensation from product endorsements that consistent winners are assured. The compensation of many independent contractors is contingent upon their success–real estate brokers, for example, or insurance salesmen.

As the Court points out, the ADA specifically identifies golf courses as one of the covered places of public accommodation. See §12181(7)(L) ("a gymnasium, health spa, bowling alley, golf course, or other place of exercise or recreation"); and the distinctive "goo[d], servic[e], facilit[y], privileg[e], advantag[e], or accommodatio[n]" identified by that provision as distinctive to that category of place of public accommodation is "exercise or recreation." Respondent did not seek to "exercise" or "recreate" at the PGA TOUR events; he sought to make money (which is why he is called a professional golfer). He was not a customer buying recreation or entertainment; he was a professional athlete selling it. That is the reason (among others) the Court's reliance upon Civil Rights Act cases like Daniel v. Paul, 395 U.S. 298 (1969), see ante, at 18-19, is misplaced. A professional golfer's practicing his profession is not comparable to John Q. Public's frequenting "a 232-acre amusement area with swimming, boating, sun bathing, picnicking, miniature golf, dancing facilities, and a snack bar." Daniel, supra, at 301.

The Court relies heavily upon the Q-School. It says that petitioner offers the golfing public the "privilege" of "competing in the Q-School and playing in the tours; indeed, the former is a privilege for which thousands of individuals from the general public pay, and the latter is one for which they vie." Ante, at 14—15. But the Q-School is no more a "privilege" offered for the general public's "enjoyment" than is the California Bar Exam.1 It is a competition for entry into the PGA TOUR–an open tryout, no different in principle from open casting for a movie or stage production, or walk-on tryouts for other professional sports, such as baseball. See, e.g., Amateurs Join Pros for New Season of HBO's "Sopranos," Detroit News, Dec. 22, 2000, p. 2 (20,000 attend open casting for "The Sopranos"); Bill Zack, Atlanta Braves, Sporting News, Feb. 6, 1995 (1,300 would-be players attended an open tryout for the Atlanta Braves). It may well be that some amateur golfers enjoy trying to make the grade, just as some amateur actors may enjoy auditions, and amateur baseball players may enjoy open tryouts (I hesitate to say that amateur lawyers may enjoy taking the California Bar Exam). But the purpose of holding those tryouts is not to provide entertainment; it is to hire. At bottom, open tryouts for performances to be held at a place of public accommodation are no different from open bidding on contracts to cut the grass at a place of public accommodation, or open applications for any job at a place of public accommodation. Those bidding, those applying–and those trying out–are not converted into customers. By the Court's reasoning, a business exists not only to sell goods and services to the public, but to provide the "privilege" of employment to the public; wherefore it follows, like night the day, that everyone who seeks a job is a customer.2

II

Having erroneously held that Title III applies to the "customers" of professional golf who consist of its practitioners, the Court then erroneously answers–or to be accurate simply ignores–a second question. The ADA requires covered businesses to make such reasonable modifications of "policies, practices, or procedures" as are necessary to "afford" goods, services, and privileges to individuals with disabilities; but it explicitly does not require "modifications [that] would fundamentally alter the nature" of the goods, services, and privileges. §12182(b)(2)(A)(ii). In other words, disabled individuals must be given access to the same goods, services, and privileges that others enjoy. The regulations state that Title III "does not require a public accommodation to alter its inventory to include accessible or special goods with accessibility features that are designed for, or facilitate use by, individuals with disabilities." 28 CFR § 36.307 (2000); see also 28 CFR, ch. 1, pt. 36, App. B, p. 650 (2000). As one Court of Appeals has explained:

"The common sense of the statute is that the content of the goods or services offered by a place of public accommodation is not regulated. A camera store may not refuse to sell cameras to a disabled person, but it is not required to stock cameras specially designed for such persons. Had Congress purposed to impose so enormous a burden on the retail sector of the economy and so vast a supervisory responsibility on the federal courts, we think it would have made its intention clearer and would at least have imposed some standards. It is hardly a feasible judicial function to decide whether shoestores should sell single shoes to one-legged persons and if so at what price, or how many Braille books the Borders or Barnes and Noble bookstore chains should stock in each of their stores." Doe v. Mutual of Omaha Ins. Co., 179 F.3d 557, 560 (CA7 1999).

Since this is so, even if respondent here is a consumer of the "privilege" of the PGA TOUR competition, see ante, at 14, I see no basis for considering whether the rules of that competition must be altered. It is as irrelevant to the PGA TOUR's compliance with the statute whether walking is essential to the game of golf as it is to the shoe store's compliance whether "pairness" is essential to the nature of shoes. If a shoe store wishes to sell shoes only in pairs it may; and if a golf tour (or a golf course) wishes to provide only walk-around golf, it may. The PGA TOUR cannot deny respondent access to that game because of his disability, but it need not provide him a game different (whether in its essentials or in its details) from that offered to everyone else.

Since it has held (or assumed) professional golfers to be customers "enjoying" the "privilege" that consists of PGA TOUR golf; and since it inexplicably regards the rules of PGA TOUR golf as merely "policies, practices, or procedures" by which access to PGA TOUR golf is provided, the Court must then confront the question whether respondent's requested modification of the supposed policy, practice, or procedure of walking would "fundamentally alter the nature" of the PGA TOUR game, §12182(b)(2)(A)(ii). The Court attacks this "fundamental alteration" analysis by asking two questions: first, whether the "essence" or an "essential aspect" of the sport of golf has been altered; and second, whether the change, even if not essential to the game, would give the disabled player an advantage over others and thereby "fundamentally alter the character of the competition." Ante, at 20-21. It answers no to both.

Before considering the Court's answer to the first question, it is worth pointing out that the assumption which underlies that question is false. Nowhere is it writ that PGA TOUR golf must be classic "essential" golf. Why cannot the PGA TOUR, if it wishes, promote a new game, with distinctive rules (much as the American League promotes a game of baseball in which the pitcher's turn at the plate can be taken by a "designated hitter")? If members of the public do not like the new rules—if they feel that these rules do not truly test the individual's skill at "real golf" (or the team's skill at "real baseball") they can withdraw their patronage. But the rules are the rules. They are (as in all games) entirely arbitrary, and there is no basis on which anyone—not even the Supreme Court of the United States—can pronounce one or another of them to be "nonessential" if the rulemaker (here the PGA TOUR) deems it to be essential.

If one assumes, however, that the PGA TOUR has some legal obligation to play classic, Platonic golf—and if one assumes the correctness of all the other wrong turns the Court has made to get to this point—then we Justices must confront what is indeed an awesome responsibility. It has been rendered the solemn duty of the Supreme Court of the United States, laid upon it by Congress in pursuance of the Federal Government's power "[t]o regulate Commerce with foreign Nations, and among the several States," U.S. Const., Art. I, §8, cl. 3, to decide What Is Golf. I am sure that the Framers of the Constitution, aware of the 1457 edict of King James II of Scotland prohibiting golf because it interfered with the practice of archery, fully expected that sooner or later the paths of golf and government, the law and the links, would once again cross, and that the judges of this august Court would some day have to wrestle with that age-old jurisprudential question, for which their years of study in the law have so well prepared them: Is someone riding around a golf course from shot to shot really a golfer? The answer, we learn, is yes. The Court ultimately concludes, and it will henceforth be the Law of the Land, that walking is not a "fundamental" aspect of golf.

Either out of humility or out of self-respect (one or the other) the Court should decline to answer this incredibly difficult and incredibly silly question. To say that something is "essential" is ordinarily to say that it is necessary to the achievement of a certain object. But since it is the very nature of a game to have no object except amusement (that is what distinguishes games from productive activity), it is quite impossible to say that any of a game's arbitrary rules is "essential." Eighteen-hole golf courses, 10-foot-high basketball hoops, 90-foot baselines, 100-yard football fields—all are arbitrary and none is essential. The only support for any of them is tradition and (in more modern times) insistence by what has come to be regarded as the ruling body of the sport—both of which factors support the PGA TOUR's position in the present case. (Many, indeed, consider walking to be the central feature of the game of golf—hence Mark Twain's classic criticism of the sport: "a good walk spoiled.") I suppose there is some point at which the rules of a well-known game are changed to such a degree that no reasonable person would call it the same game. If the PGA TOUR competitors were required to dribble a large, inflated ball and put it through a round hoop, the game could no longer reasonably be called golf. But this criterion—destroying recognizability as the same generic game—is surely not the test of "essentialness" or "fundamentalness" that the Court applies, since it apparently thinks that merely changing the diameter of the cup might "fundamentally alter" the game of golf, ante, at 20.

Having concluded that dispensing with the walking rule would not violate federal-Platonic "golf" (and, implicitly, that it is federal-Platonic golf, and no other, that the PGA TOUR can insist upon) the Court moves on to the second part of its test: the competitive effects of waiving this nonessential rule. In this part of its analysis, the Court first finds that the effects of the change are "mitigated" by the fact that in the game of golf weather, a "lucky bounce," and "pure chance" provide different conditions for each competitor and individual ability may not "be the sole determinant of the outcome." Ante, at 25. I guess that is why those who follow professional golfing consider Jack Nicklaus the luckiest golfer of all time, only to be challenged of late by the phenomenal luck of Tiger Woods. The Court's empiricism is unpersuasive. "Pure chance" is randomly distributed among the players, but allowing respondent to use a cart gives him a "lucky" break every time he plays. Pure chance also only matters at the margin—a stroke here or there; the cart substantially improves this respondent's competitive prospects beyond a couple of strokes. But even granting that there are significant nonhuman variables affecting competition, that fact does not justify adding another variable that always favors one player.

In an apparent effort to make its opinion as narrow as possible, the Court relies upon the District Court's finding that even with a cart, respondent will be at least as fatigued as everyone else. Ante, at 28. This, the Court says, proves that competition will not be affected. Far from thinking that reliance on this finding cabins the effect of today's opinion, I think it will prove to be its most expansive and destructive feature. Because step one of the Court's two-part inquiry into whether a requested change in a sport will "fundamentally alter [its] nature," §12182(b)(2)(A)(ii), consists of an utterly unprincipled ontology of sports (pursuant to which the Court is not even sure whether golf's "essence" requires a 3-inch hole), there is every reason to think that in future cases involving requests for special treatment by would-be athletes the second step of the analysis will be determinative. In resolving that second step—determining whether waiver of the "nonessential" rule will have an impermissible "competitive effect"—by measuring the athletic capacity of the requesting individual, and asking whether the special dispensation would do no more than place him on a par (so to speak) with other competitors, the Court guarantees that future cases of this sort will have to be decided on the basis of individualized factual findings. Which means that future cases of this sort will be numerous, and a rich source of lucrative litigation. One can envision the parents of a Little League player with attention deficit disorder trying to convince a judge that their son's disability makes it at least 25% more difficult to hit a pitched ball. (If they are successful, the only thing that could prevent a court order giving the kid four strikes would be a judicial determination that, in baseball, three strikes are metaphysically necessary, which is quite absurd.)

The statute, of course, provides no basis for this individualized analysis that is the Court's last step on a long and misguided journey. The statute seeks to assure that a disabled person's disability will not deny him equal access to (among other things) competitive sporting events—not that his disability will not deny him an equal chance to win competitive sporting events. The latter is quite impossible, since the very nature of competitive sport is the measurement, by uniform rules, of unevenly distributed excellence. This unequal distribution is precisely what determines the winners and losers— and artificially to "even out" that distribution, by giving one or another player exemption from a rule that emphasizes his particular weakness, is to destroy the game. That is why the "handicaps" that are customary in social games of golf—which, by adding strokes to the scores of the good players and subtracting them from scores of the bad ones, "even out" the varying abilities—are not used in professional golf. In the Court's world, there is one set of rules that is "fair with respect to the able-bodied" but "individualized" rules, mandated by the ADA, for "talented but disabled athletes." Ante, at 29. The ADA mandates no such ridiculous thing. Agility, strength, speed, balance, quickness of mind, steadiness of nerves, intensity of concentration—these talents are not evenly distributed. No wild-eyed dreamer has ever suggested that the managing bodies of the competitive sports that test precisely these qualities should try to take account of the uneven distribution of God-given gifts when writing and enforcing the rules of competition. And I have no doubt Congress did not authorize misty-eyed judicial supervision of such a revolution.

* * *

My belief that today's judgment is clearly in error should not be mistaken for a belief that the PGA TOUR clearly ought not allow respondent to use a golf cart. That is a close question, on which even those who compete in the PGA TOUR are apparently divided; but it is a different question from the one before the Court. Just as it is a different question whether the Little League ought to give disabled youngsters a fourth strike, or some other waiver from the rules that makes up for their disabilities. In both cases, whether they ought to do so depends upon (1) how central to the game that they have organized (and over whose rules they are the master) they deem the waived provision to be, and (2) how competitive—how strict a test of raw athletic ability in all aspects of the competition—they want their game to be. But whether Congress has said they must do so depends upon the answers to the legal questions I have discussed above—not upon what this Court sententiously decrees to be "decent, tolerant,

[and] progressive," ante, at 13 (quoting Board of Trustees of Univ. of Ala. v.

Garrett, 531 U.S. 356, 375 (2001) (Kennedy, J., concurring)).

And it should not be assumed that today's decent, tolerant, and progressive judgment will, in the long run, accrue to the benefit of sports competitors with disabilities. Now that it is clear courts will review the rules of sports for "fundamentalness," organizations that value their autonomy have every incentive to defend vigorously the necessity of every regulation. They may still be second-guessed in the end as to the Platonic requirements of the sport, but they will assuredly lose if they have at all wavered in their enforcement. The lesson the PGA TOUR and other sports organizations should take from this case is to make sure that the same written rules are set forth for all levels of play, and never voluntarily to grant any modifications. The second lesson is to end open tryouts. I doubt that, in the long run, even disabled athletes will be well served by these incentives that the Court has created.

Complaints about this case are not "properly directed to Congress," ante, at 27-28, n. 51. They are properly directed to this Court's Kafkaesque determination that professional sports organizations, and the fields they rent for their exhibitions, are "places of public accommodation" to the competing athletes, and the athletes themselves "customers" of the organization that pays them; its Alice in Wonderland determination that there are such things as judicially determinable "essential" and "nonessential" rules of a made-up game; and its Animal Farm determination that fairness and the ADA mean that everyone gets

to play by individualized rules which will assure that no one's lack of ability (or at least no one's lack of ability

so pronounced that it amounts to a disability) will be a handicap. The year was 2001, and "everybody was finally equal." K. Vonnegut, Harrison Bergeron, in Animal Farm and Related Readings 129 (1997).

Notes

1. The California Bar Exam is covered by the ADA, by the way, because a separate provision of Title III applies to "examinations . . . related to applications, licensing, certification, or credentialing for secondary or post-secondary education, professional, or trade purposes." 42 U.S.C. § 12189. If open tryouts were "privileges" under §12182, and participants in the tryouts "customers," §12189 would have been unnecessary.

2. The Court suggests that respondent is not an independent contractor because he "play[s] at [his] own pleasure," and is not subject to PGA TOUR control "over [his] manner of performance," ante, at 18 n. 33. But many independent contractors–composers of movie music, portrait artists, script writers, and even (some would say) plumbers–retain at least as much control over when and how they work as does respondent, who agrees to play in a minimum of 15 of the designated PGA TOUR events, and to play by the rules that the PGA TOUR specifies. Cf. Community for Creative Non-Violence v. Reid, 490 U.S. 730, 751-753 (1989) (discussing independent contractor status of a sculptor). Moreover, although, as the Court suggests in the same footnote, in rare cases a PGA TOUR

winner will choose to forgo the prize money (in order, for example, to preserve amateur status necessary for continuing participation in college play) he is contractually entitled to the prize money if he demands it, which is all that a contractual relationship requires.

Justice Scalia's dissent in Kansas v. Crane (Jan 22, 2002)

Justice Scalia, with whom Justice Thomas joins, dissenting.

Today the Court holds that the Kansas Sexually Violent Predator Act (SVPA) cannot, consistent with so-called substantive due process, be applied as written. It does so even though, less than five years ago, we upheld the very same statute against the very same contention in an appeal by the very same petitioner (the State of Kansas) from the judgment of the very same court. Not only is the new law that the Court announces today wrong, but the Court's manner of promulgating it–snatching back from the State of Kansas a victory so recently awarded–cheapens the currency of our judgments. I would reverse, rather than vacate, the judgment of the Kansas Supreme Court.

I

Respondent was convicted of lewd and lascivious behavior and pleaded guilty to aggravated sexual battery for two incidents that took place on the same day in 1993. In the first, respondent exposed himself to a tanning salon attendant. In the second, 30 minutes later, respondent entered a video store, waited until he was the only customer present, and then exposed himself to the clerk. Not stopping there, he grabbed the clerk by the neck, demanded she perform oral sex on him, and threatened to rape her, before running out of the store. Following respondent's plea to aggravated sexual battery, the State filed a petition in State District Court to have respondent evaluated and adjudicated a sexual predator under the SVPA. That Act permits the civil detention of a person convicted of any of several enumerated sexual offenses, if it is proven beyond a reasonable doubt that he suffers from a "mental abnormality"–a disorder affecting his "emotional or volitional capacity which predisposes the person to commit sexually violent offenses"–or a "personality disorder," either of "which makes the person likely to engage in repeat acts of sexual violence." Kan. Stat. Ann. §§59—29a02(a), (b) (2000 Cum. Supp.).

Several psychologists examined respondent and determined he suffers from exhibitionism and antisocial personality disorder. Though exhibitionism alone would not support classification as a sexual predator, a psychologist concluded that the two in combination did place respondent's condition within the range of disorders covered by the SVPA, "cit[ing] the increasing frequency of incidents involving [respondent], increasing intensity of the incidents, [respondent's] increasing disregard for the rights of others, and his increasing daring and aggressiveness." In re Crane, 269 Kan. 578, 579, 7 P.3d 285, 287 (2000). Another psychologist testified that respondent's behavior was marked by "impulsivity or failure to plan ahead," indicating his unlawfulness "was a combination of willful and uncontrollable behavior," id., at 584—585, 7 P.3d, at 290. The State's experts agreed, however, that "[r]espondent's mental disorder does not impair his volitional control to the degree he cannot control his dangerous behavior." Id., at 581, 7 P.3d, at 288.

Respondent moved for summary judgment, arguing that for his detention to comport with substantive due process the State was required to prove not merely what the statute requires–that by reason of his mental disorder he is "likely to engage in repeat acts of sexual violence"–but also that he is unable to control his violent behavior. The trial court denied this motion, and instructed the jury pursuant to the terms of the statute. Id., at 581, 7 P.3d, at 287–288. The jury found, beyond a reasonable doubt, that respondent was a sexual predator as defined by the SVPA. The Kansas Supreme Court reversed, holding the SVPA unconstitutional as applied to someone, like respondent, who has only an emotional or personality disorder within the meaning of the Act, rather than a volitional impairment. For such a person, it held, the State must show not merely a likelihood that the defendant would engage in repeat acts of sexual violence, but also an inability to control violent behavior. It based this holding solely on our decision in Kansas v. Hendricks, 521 U.S. 346 (1997).

II

Hendricks also involved the SVPA, and, as in this case, the Kansas Supreme Court had found that the SVPA swept too broadly. On the basis of considerable evidence showing that Hendricks suffered from pedophilia, the jury had found, beyond a reasonable doubt, that Hendricks met the statutory standard for commitment. See id., at 355; In re Hendricks, 259 Kan. 246, 247, 912 P.2d 129, 130 (1996). This standard (to repeat) was that he suffered from a "mental abnormality"–a disorder affecting his "emotional or volitional capacity which predisposes [him] to commit sexually violent offenses"–or a "personality disorder," either of which "makes [him] likely to engage in repeat acts of sexual violence." Kan. Stat. Ann. §§59–29a02(a), (b) (2000 Cum. Supp.). The trial court, after determining as a matter of state law that pedophilia was a "mental abnormality" within the meaning of the Act, ordered Hendricks committed. See 521 U.S., at 355–356. The Kansas Supreme Court held the jury finding to be constitutionally inadequate. "Absent ... a finding [of mental illness]," it said, "the Act does not satisfy ... constitutional standard[s]," 259 Kan., at 261, 912 P.2d, at 138. (Mental illness, as it had been defined by Kansas law, required a showing that the detainee "[i]s suffering from a severe mental disorder"; "lacks capacity to make an informed decision concerning treatment"; and "is likely to cause harm to self or others." Kan. Stat. Ann. §59–2902(h) (1994).) We granted the State of Kansas's petition for certiorari.

The first words of our opinion dealing with the merits of the case were as follows: "Kansas argues that the Act's definition of 'mental abnormality' satisfies 'substantive' due process requirements. We agree." Hendricks, 521 U.S., at 356. And the reason it found substantive due process satisfied was clearly stated:

"The Kansas Act is plainly of a kind with these other civil commitment statutes [that we have approved]: It requires a finding of future dangerousness [viz., that the person committed is "likely to engage in repeat acts of sexual violence"], and then links that finding to the existence of a 'mental abnormality' or 'personality disorder' that makes it difficult, if not impossible, for the person to control his dangerous behavior. Kan. Stat. Ann. §59—29a02(b) (1994)." Id., at 358 (emphasis added).

It is the italicized language in the foregoing excerpt that today's majority relies upon as establishing the requirement of a separate finding of inability to control behavior. Ante, at 4.

That is simply not a permissible reading of the passage, for several reasons. First, because the authority cited for the statement—in the immediately following reference to the Kansas Statutes Annotated—is the section of the SVPA that defines "mental abnormality," which contains no requirement of inability to control. What the opinion was obviously saying was that the SVPA's required finding of a causal connection between the likelihood of repeat acts of sexual violence and the existence of a "mental abnormality" or "personality disorder" necessarily establishes "difficulty if not impossibility" in controlling behavior. This is clearly confirmed by the very next sentence of the opinion, which reads as follows:

"The precommitment requirement of a 'mental abnormality' or 'personality disorder' is consistent with the requirements of ... other statutes that we have upheld in that it narrows the class of persons eligible for confinement to those who are unable to control their dangerousness." 521 U.S., at 358.

It could not be clearer that, in the Court's estimation, the very existence of a mental abnormality or personality disorder that causes a likelihood of repeat sexual violence in itself establishes the requisite "difficulty if not impossibility" of control. Moreover, the passage in question cannot possibly be read as today's majority would read it because nowhere did the jury verdict of commitment that we reinstated in Hendricks contain a separate finding of "difficulty, if not impossibility, to control behavior." That finding must (as I have said) have been embraced within the finding of mental abnormality causing future dangerousness. And finally, the notion that the Constitution requires in every case a finding of "difficulty if not impossibility" of control does not fit comfortably with the broader holding of Hendricks, which was that "we have never required state legislatures to adopt any particular nomenclature in drafting civil commitment statutes. Rather, we have traditionally left to legislators the task of defining terms of a medical nature that have legal significance." Id., at 359.

The Court relies upon the fact that "Hendricks underscored the constitutional importance of distinguishing a dangerous sexual offender subject to civil commitment 'from other dangerous persons who are perhaps more properly dealt with exclusively through criminal proceedings.' " Ante, at 4—5 (quoting 521 U.S., at 360). But the SVPA as written—without benefit of a supplemental control finding—already achieves that objective. It conditions civil commitment not upon a mere finding that the sex offender is likely to reoffend, but only upon the additional finding (beyond a reasonable doubt) that the cause of the likelihood of recidivism is a "mental abnormality or personality disorder." Kan. Stat. Ann. §59—29a02(a) (2000 Cum. Supp.). Ordinary recidivists choose to reoffend and are therefore amenable to deterrence through the criminal law; those subject to civil commitment under the SVPA, because their mental illness is an affliction and not a choice, are unlikely to be deterred. We specifically pointed this out in Hendricks. "Those persons committed under the Act," we said, "are, by definition, suffering from a 'mental abnormality' or a 'personality disorder' that prevents them from exercising adequate control over their behavior. Such persons are therefore unlikely to be deterred by the threat of confinement." 521 U.S., at 362–363.

III

Not content with holding that the SVPA cannot be applied as written because it does not require a separate "lack-of-control determination," ante, at 4, the Court also reopens a question closed by Hendricks: whether the SVPA also cannot be applied as written because it allows for the commitment of people who have mental illnesses other than volitional impairments. "Hendricks," the Court says, "had no occasion to consider" this question. Ante, at 8.

But how could the Court possibly have avoided it? The jury whose commitment we affirmed in Hendricks had not been asked to find a volitional impairment, but had been charged in the language of the statute, which quite clearly covers nonvolitional impairments. And the fact that it did so had not escaped our attention. To the contrary, our Hendricks opinion explicitly and repeatedly recognized that the SVPA reaches individuals with personality disorders, 521 U.S., at 352, 353, 357, 358, and quoted the Act's definition of mental abnormality (§59—29a02(b)), which makes plain that it embraces both emotional and volitional impairments, id., at 352. It is true that we repeatedly referred to Hendricks's "volitional" problems–because that was evidently the sort of mental abnormality that he had. But we nowhere accorded any legal significance to that fact–as we could not have done, since it was not a fact that the jury had been asked to determine. We held, without any qualification, "that the Kansas Sexually Violent Predator Act comports with [substantive] due process requirements," id., at 371, because its "precommitment requirement of a 'mental abnormality' or 'personality disorder' is consistent with the requirements of ... other statutes that we have upheld in that it narrows the class of persons eligible for confinement to those who are unable to control their dangerousness," id., at 358.

The Court appears to argue that, because Hendricks involved a defendant who indeed had a volitional impairment (even though we made nothing of that fact), its narrowest holding covers only that application of the SVPA, and our statement that the SVPA in its entirety was constitutional can be ignored. See ante, at 7—8. This cannot be correct. The narrowest holding of Hendricks affirmed the constitutionality of commitment on the basis of the jury charge given in that case (to wit, the language of the SVPA); and since that charge did not require a finding of volitional impairment, neither does the Constitution.

I cannot resist observing that the distinctive status of volitional impairment which the Court mangles Hendricks to preserve would not even be worth preserving by more legitimate means. There is good reason why, as the Court accurately says, "when considering civil commitment ... we [have not] ordinarily distinguished for constitutional purposes between volitional, emotional, and cognitive impairments," ante, at 7. We have not done so because it makes no sense. It is obvious that a person may be able to exercise volition and yet be unfit to turn loose upon society. The man who has a will of steel, but who delusionally believes that every woman he meets is inviting crude sexual advances, is surely a dangerous sexual predator.

IV

I not only disagree with the Court's gutting of our holding in Hendricks; I also doubt the desirability, and indeed even the coherence, of the new constitutional test which (on the basis of no analysis except a misreading of Hendricks) it substitutes. Under our holding in Hendricks, a jury in an SVPA commitment case would be required to find, beyond a reasonable doubt, (1) that the person previously convicted of one of the enumerated sexual offenses is suffering from a mental abnormality or personality disorder, and (2) that this condition renders him likely to commit future acts of sexual violence. Both of these findings are coherent, and (with the assistance of expert testimony) well within the capacity of a normal jury. Today's opinion says that the Constitution requires the addition of a third finding: (3) that the subject suffers from an inability to control behavior—not utter inability, ante, at 4, and not even inability in a particular constant degree, but rather inability in a degree that will vary "in light of such features of the case as the nature of the psychiatric diagnosis, and the severity of the mental abnormality itself," ante, at 5.

This formulation of the new requirement certainly displays an elegant subtlety of mind. Unfortunately, it gives trial courts, in future cases under the many commitment statutes similar to Kansas's SVPA, not a clue as to how they are supposed to charge the jury! Indeed, it does not even provide a clue to the trial court, on remand, in this very case. What is the judge to ask the jury to find? It is fine and good to talk about the desirability of our "proceeding deliberately and contextually, elaborating generally stated constitutional standards and objectives as specific circumstances require," ante, at 6, but one would think that this plan would at least produce the "elaboration" of what the jury charge should be in the "specific circumstances" of the present case. "Proceeding deliberately" is not synonymous with not proceeding at all.

I suspect that the reason the Court avoids any elaboration is that elaboration which passes the laugh test is impossible. How is one to frame for a jury the degree of "inability to control" which, in the particular case, "the nature of the psychiatric diagnosis, and the severity of the mental abnormality" require? Will it be a percentage ("Ladies and gentlemen of the jury, you may commit Mr. Crane under the SVPA only if you find, beyond a reasonable doubt, that he is 42% unable to control his penchant for sexual violence")? Or a frequency ratio ("Ladies and gentlemen of the jury, you may commit Mr. Crane under the SVPA only if you find, beyond a reasonable doubt, that he is unable to control his penchant for sexual violence 3 times out of 10")? Or merely an adverb ("Ladies and gentlemen of the jury, you may commit Mr. Crane under the SVPA only if you find, beyond a reasonable doubt, that he is appreciably—or moderately, or substantially, or almost totally—unable to control his penchant for sexual violence")? None of these seems to me satisfactory.

But if it is indeed possible to "elaborate" upon the Court's novel test, surely the Court has an obligation to do so in the "specific circumstances" of the present case, so that the trial court will know what is expected of it on remand. It is irresponsible to leave the law in such a state of utter indeterminacy.

* * *

Today's holding would make bad law in any circumstances. In the circumstances under which it is pronounced, however, it both distorts our law and degrades our authority. The State of Kansas, unable to apply its legislature's sexual predator legislation as written because of the Kansas Supreme Court's erroneous view of the Federal Constitution, sought and received certiorari in Hendricks, and achieved a reversal, in an opinion holding that "the Kansas Sexually Violent Predator Act comports with [substantive] due process requirements," 521 U.S., at 371. The Kansas Supreme Court still did not like the law and prevented its operation, on substantive due process grounds, once again. The State of Kansas again sought certiorari, asking nothing more than reaffirmation of our 5-year-old opinion—only to be told that what we said then we now unsay. There is an obvious lesson here for state supreme courts that do not agree with our jurisprudence: ignoring it is worth a try.

A jury determined beyond a reasonable doubt that respondent suffers from antisocial personality disorder combined with exhibitionism, and that this is either a mental abnormality or a personality disorder making it likely he will commit repeat acts of sexual violence. That is all the SVPA requires, and all the Constitution demands. Since we have already held precisely that in another case (which, by a remarkable feat of jurisprudential jujitsu the Court relies upon as the only authority for its decision), I would reverse the judgment below.

Notes

*. As quoted earlier in the Hendricks opinion, see 521 U.S., at 352, §59—29a02(b) defines "mental abnormality" as a "congenital or acquired condition affecting the emotional or volitional capacity which predisposes the person to commit sexually violent offenses in a degree constituting such person a menace to the health and safety of others."

Justice Scalia's dissent in US Airways, Inc. v. Barnett (April 29, 2002)

Justice Scalia, with whom Justice Thomas joins, dissenting.

The question presented asks whether the "reasonable accommodation" mandate of the Americans with Disabilities Act of 1990 (ADA or Act) requires reassignment of a disabled employee to a position that "another employee is entitled to hold ... under the employer's bona fide and established seniority system." Pet. for Cert. i; 532 U.S. 970

(2001). Indulging its penchant for eschewing clear rules that might avoid litigation, see, e.g., Kansas v. Crane, 534 U.S. 407, 423 (2002) (Scalia, J., dissenting); TRW Inc. v. Andrews, 534 U.S. 19, 35-36 (2001) (Scalia, J., concurring in judgment), the Court answers "maybe." It creates a presumption that an exception to a seniority rule is an "unreasonable" accommodation, ante, at 11, but allows that presumption to be rebutted by showing that the exception "will not likely make a difference," ante, at 13.

The principal defect of today's opinion, however, goes well beyond the uncertainty it produces regarding the relationship between the ADA and the infinite variety of seniority systems. The conclusion that any seniority system can ever be overridden is merely one consequence of a mistaken interpretation of the ADA that makes all employment rules and practices—even those which (like a seniority system) pose no distinctive obstacle to the disabled—subject to suspension when that is (in a court's view) a "reasonable" means of enabling a disabled employee to keep his job. That is a far cry from what I believe the accommodation provision of the ADA requires: the suspension (within reason) of those employment rules and practices that the employee's disability prevents him from observing.

I

The Court begins its analysis by describing the ADA as declaring that an employer may not "discriminate against a qualified individual with a disability." Ante, at 4. In fact the Act says more: an employer may not "discriminate against a qualified individual with a disability because of the disability of such individual." 42 U.S.C. § 12112(a) (1994 ed.) (emphasis added). It further provides that discrimination includes "not making reasonable accommodations to the known physical or mental limitations of an otherwise qualified individual with a disability." §12112(b)(5)(A) (emphasis added).

Read together, these provisions order employers to modify or remove (within reason) policies and practices that burden a disabled person "because of [his] disability." In other words, the ADA eliminates workplace barriers only if a disability prevents an employee from overcoming them—those barriers that would not be barriers but for the employee's disability. These include, for example, work stations that cannot accept the employee's wheelchair, or an assembly-line practice that requires long periods of standing. But they do not include rules and practices that bear no more heavily upon the disabled employee than upon others—even though an exemption from such a rule or practice might in a sense "make up for" the employee's disability. It is not a required accommodation, for example, to pay a disabled employee more than others at his grade level—even if that increment is earmarked for massage or physical therapy that would enable the employee to work with as little physical discomfort as his co-workers. That would be "accommodating" the disabled employee, but it would not be "making ... accommodatio[n] to the known physical or mental limitations" of the employee, §12112(b)(5)(A), because it would not eliminate any workplace practice that constitutes an obstacle because of his disability.

So also with exemption from a seniority system, which burdens the disabled and nondisabled alike. In particular cases, seniority rules may have a harsher effect upon the disabled employee than upon his co-workers. If the disabled employee is physically capable of performing only one task in the workplace, seniority rules may be, for him, the difference between employment and unemployment. But that does not make the seniority system a disability-related obstacle, any more than harsher impact upon the more needy disabled employee renders the salary system a disability-related obstacle. When one departs from this understanding, the ADA's accommodation provision becomes a standardless grab bag—leaving it to the courts to decide which workplace preferences (higher salary, longer vacations, reassignment to positions to which others are entitled) can be deemed "reasonable" to "make up for" the particular employee's disability.

Some courts, including the Ninth Circuit in the present case, have accepted respondent's contention that the ADA demands accommodation even with respect to those obstacles that have nothing to do with the disability. Their principal basis for this position is that the definition of "reasonable accommodation" includes "reassignment to a vacant position." §12111(9)(B). This accommodation would be meaningless, they contend, if it required only that the disabled employee be considered for a vacant position. The ADA already prohibits employers from discriminating against the disabled with respect to "hiring, advancement, or discharge ... and other terms, conditions, and privileges of employment." §12112(a). Surely, the argument goes, a disabled employee must be given preference over a nondisabled employee when a vacant position appears. See Smith v. Midland Brake, Inc., 180 F.3d 1154, 1164—1165 (CA10 1999) (en banc); Aka v. Washington Hospital Center, 156 F.3d 1284, 1304—1305 (CADC 1998) (en banc). Accord, EEOC Enforcement Guidance: Reasonable Accommodation and Undue Hardship Under the Americans with Disabilities Act, 3 BNA EEOC Compliance Manual, No. 246, p. N:2479 (Mar. 1, 1999).

This argument seems to me quite mistaken. The right to be given a vacant position so long as there are no obstacles to that appointment (including another candidate who is better qualified, if "best qualified" is the workplace rule) is of considerable value. If an employee is hired to fill a position but fails miserably, he will typically be fired. Few employers will search their organization charts for vacancies to which the low-performing employee might be suited. The ADA, however, prohibits an employer from firing a person whose disability is the cause of his poor performance without first seeking to place him in a vacant job where the disability will not affect performance. Such reassignment is an accommodation to the disability because it removes an obstacle (the inability to perform the functions of the assigned job) arising solely from the disability. Cf. Bruff v. North Mississippi Health Services, Inc., 244 F.3d 495, 502 (CA5 2001). See also 3 BNA EEOC Compliance Manual, supra, at N:2478 ("[A]n employer who does not normally transfer employees would still have to reassign an employee with a disability").

The phrase "reassignment to a vacant position" appears in a subsection describing a variety of potential "reasonable accommodation[s]":

"(A) making existing facilities used by employees readily accessible to and usable by individuals with disabilities; and

"(B) job restructuring, part-time or modified work schedules, reassignment to a vacant position, acquisition or modification of equipment or devices, appropriate adjustment or modifications of examinations, training materials or policies, the provision of qualified readers or interpreters, and other similar accommodations for individuals with disabilities." §12111(9) (emphasis added).

Subsection (A) clearly addresses features of the workplace that burden the disabled because of their disabilities. Subsection (B) is broader in scope but equally targeted at disability-related obstacles. Thus it encompasses "modified work schedules" (which may accommodate inability to work for protracted periods), "modification of equipment and devices," and "provision of qualified readers or interpreters." There is no reason why the phrase "reassignment to a vacant position" should be thought to have a uniquely different focus. It envisions elimination of the obstacle of the current position (which requires activity that the disabled employee cannot tolerate) when there is an alternate position freely available. If he is qualified for that position, and no one else is seeking it, or no one else who seeks it is better qualified, he must be given the position. But "reassignment to a vacant position" does not envision the elimination of obstacles to the employee's service in the new position that have nothing to do with his disability—for example, another employee's claim to that position under a seniority system, or another employee's superior qualifications. Cf. 29 CFR pt. 1630, App. §1630.2(o), p. 357 (2001) (explaining "reasonable accommodation" as "any change in the work environment or in the way things are customarily done that enables an individual with a disability to enjoy equal employment opportunities" (emphasis added)); Aka v. Washington Hospital Center, 156 F.3d at 1314–1315 (Silberman, J., dissenting) (interpreting "reassignment to a vacant position" consistently with the other accommodations listed in §12111(9), none of which "even alludes to the possibility of a preference for the disabled over the nondisabled").

Unsurprisingly, most Courts of Appeals addressing the issue have held or assumed that the ADA does not mandate exceptions to a "legitimate, nondiscriminatory policy" such as a seniority system or a consistent policy of assigning the most qualified person to a vacant position. See, e.g., EEOC v. Sara Lee Corp., 237 F.3d 349, 353–355 (CA4 2001) (seniority system); EEOC v. Humiston-Keeling, Inc., 227 F.3d 1024, 1028–1029 (CA7 2000) (policy of assigning the most qualified applicant); Burns v. Coca-Cola Enterprises, Inc., 222 F.3d 247, 257–258 (CA6 2000) (policy of reassigning employees only if they request a transfer to an advertised vacant position); Cravens v. Blue Cross and Blue Shield of Kansas City, 214 F.3d 1011, 1020 (CA8 2000) (assuming reassignment is not required if it would violate legitimate, nondiscriminatory policies); Duckett v. Dunlop Tire Corp., 120 F.3d 1222, 1225 (CA11 1997) (policy of not reassigning salaried workers to production positions covered by a collective-bargaining unit); Daugherty v. El Paso, 56 F.3d 695, 700 (CA5 1995) (policy of giving full-time employees priority over part-time employees in assigning vacant positions).

Even the EEOC, in at least some of its regulations, acknowledges that the ADA clears away only obstacles arising from a person's disability and nothing more. According to the agency, the term "reasonable accommodation" means

"(i) [m]odifications or adjustments to a job application process that enable a qualified applicant with a disability to be considered for the position such qualified applicant desires; or

"(ii) [m]odifications or adjustments to the work environment ... that enable a qualified individual with a disability to perform the essential functions of that position; or

"(iii) [m]odifications or adjustments that enable a covered entity's employee with a disability to enjoy equal benefits and privileges of employment as are enjoyed by its other similarly situated employees without disabilities." 29 CFR § 1630.2(o) (2001) (emphasis added).

See also 29 CFR pt. 1630, App. §1630.9, p. 364 (2001) ("reasonable accommodation requirement is best understood as a means by which barriers to ... equal employment opportunity ... are removed or alleviated").

Sadly, this analysis is lost on the Court, which mistakenly and inexplicably concludes, ante, at 6, that my position here is the same as that attributed to US Airways. In rejecting the argument that the ADA creates no "automatic exemption" for neutral workplace rules such as "break-from-work" and furniture budget rules, ante, at 5-6, the Court rejects an argument I have not made.

II

Although, as I have said, the uncertainty cast upon bona fide seniority systems is the least of the ill consequences produced by today's decision, a few words on that subject are nonetheless in order. Since, under the Court's interpretation of the ADA, all workplace rules are eligible to be used as vehicles of accommodation, the one means of saving seniority systems is a judicial finding that accommodation through the suspension of those workplace rules would be unreasonable. The Court is unwilling, however, to make that finding categorically, with respect to all seniority systems. Instead, it creates (and "creates" is the appropriate word) a rebuttable presumption that exceptions to seniority rules are not "reasonable" under the ADA, but leaves it free for the disabled employee to show that under the "special circumstances" of his case, an exception would be "reasonable." Ante, at 13. The employee would be entitled to an exception, for example, if he showed that "one more departure" from the seniority rules "will not likely make a difference." Ante, at 13.

I have no idea what this means. When is it possible for a departure from seniority rules to "not likely make a difference"? Even when a bona fide seniority system has multiple exceptions, employees expect that these are the only exceptions. One more unannounced exception will invariably undermine the values ("fair, uniform treatment," "job security," "predictable advancement," etc.) that the Court cites as its reasons for believing seniority systems so important that they merit a presumption of exemption. See ante, at 12.

One is tempted to impart some rationality to the scheme by speculating that the Court's burden-shifting rule is merely intended to give the disabled employee an opportunity to show that the employer's seniority system is in fact a sham—a system so full of exceptions that it creates no meaningful employee expectations. The rule applies, however, even if the seniority system is "bona fide and established," Pet. for Cert i. And the Court says that "to require the typical employer to show more than the existence of a seniority system might well undermine the employees' expectations of consistent, uniform treatment ... ." Ante, at 12. How could deviations from a sham seniority system "undermine the employees' expectations"?

I must conclude, then, that the Court's rebuttable presumption does not merely give disabled employees the opportunity to unmask sham seniority systems; it gives them a vague and unspecified power (whenever they can show "special circumstances") to undercut bona fide systems. The Court claims that its new test will not require exceptions to seniority systems "in the run of cases," ante, at 11, but that is belied by the disposition of this case. The Court remands to give respondent an opportunity to show that an exception to petitioner's seniority system "will not likely make a difference" to employee expectations, ante, at 13, despite the following finding by the District Court:

"[T]he uncontroverted evidence shows that [petitioner's] seniority system has been in place for 'decades' and governs over 14,000 ... Agents. Moreover, seniority policies such as the one at issue in this case are common to the airline industry. Given this context, it seems clear that [petitioner's] employees were justified in relying upon the policy. As such, any significant alteration of that policy would result in undue hardship to both the company and its non-disabled employees." App. to Pet. for Cert. 96a.

   * * *

Because the Court's opinion leaves the question whether a seniority system must be disregarded in order to accommodate a disabled employee in a state of uncertainty that can be resolved only by constant litigation; and because it adopts an interpretation of the ADA that incorrectly subjects all employer rules and practices to the requirement of reasonable accommodation; I respectfully dissent.

Justice Scalia's dissent in Atkins v. Virginia (June 20, 2002)

Justice Scalia, with whom the Chief Justice and Justice Thomas join, dissenting.

Today's decision is the pinnacle of our Eighth Amendment death-is-different jurisprudence. Not only does it, like all of that jurisprudence, find no support in the text or history of the Eighth Amendment; it does not even have support in current social attitudes regarding the conditions that render an otherwise just death penalty inappropriate. Seldom has an opinion of this Court rested so obviously upon nothing but the personal views of its members.

   I

I begin with a brief restatement of facts that are abridged by the Court but important to understanding this case. After spending the day drinking alcohol and smoking marijuana, petitioner Daryl Renard Atkins and a partner in crime drove to a convenience store, intending to rob a customer. Their victim was Eric Nesbitt, an airman from Langley Air Force Base, whom they abducted, drove to a nearby automated teller machine, and forced to withdraw $200. They then drove him to a deserted area, ignoring his pleas to leave him unharmed. According to the co-conspirator, whose testimony the jury evidently credited, Atkins ordered Nesbitt out of the vehicle and, after he had taken only a few steps, shot him one, two, three, four, five, six, seven, eight times in the thorax, chest, abdomen, arms, and legs.

The jury convicted Atkins of capital murder. At resentencing (the Virginia Supreme Court affirmed his conviction but remanded for resentencing because the trial court had used an improper verdict form, 257 Va. 160, 179, 510 S. E. 2d 445, 457 (1999)), the jury heard extensive evidence of petitioner's alleged mental retardation. A psychologist testified that petitioner was mildly mentally retarded with an IQ of 59, that he was a "slow learne[r]," App. 444, who showed a "lack of success in pretty much every domain of his life," id., at 442, and that he had an "impaired" capacity to appreciate the criminality of his conduct and to conform his conduct to the law, id., at 453. Petitioner's family members offered additional evidence in support of his mental retardation claim (e.g., that petitioner is a "follower," id., at 421). The State contested the evidence of retardation and presented testimony of a psychologist who found "absolutely no evidence other than the IQ score ... indicating that [petitioner] was in the least bit mentally retarded" and concluded that petitioner was "of average intelligence, at least." Id., at 476.

The jury also heard testimony about petitioner's 16 prior felony convictions for robbery, attempted robbery, abduction, use of a firearm, and maiming. Id., at 491—522. The victims of these offenses provided graphic depictions of petitioner's violent tendencies: He hit one over the head with a beer bottle, id., at 406; he slapped a gun across another victim's face, clubbed her in the head with it, knocked her to the ground, and then helped her up, only to shoot her in the stomach, id., at 411—413. The jury sentenced petitioner to death. The Supreme Court of Virginia affirmed petitioner's sentence. 260 Va. 375, 534 S. E. 2d 312 (2000).

II

As the foregoing history demonstrates, petitioner's mental retardation was a central issue at sentencing. The jury concluded, however, that his alleged retardation was not a compelling reason to exempt him from the death penalty in light of the brutality of his crime and his long demonstrated propensity for violence. "In upsetting this particularized judgment on the basis of a constitutional absolute," the Court concludes that no one who is even slightly mentally retarded can have sufficient "moral responsibility to be subjected to capital punishment for any crime. As a sociological and moral conclusion that is implausible; and it is doubly implausible as an interpretation of the United States Constitution." Thompson v. Oklahoma, 487 U.S. 815, 863—864 (1988) (Scalia, J., dissenting).

Under our Eighth Amendment jurisprudence, a punishment is "cruel and unusual" if it falls within one of two categories: "those modes or acts of punishment that had been considered cruel and unusual at the time that the Bill of Rights was adopted," Ford v. Wainwright, 477 U.S. 399, 405 (1986), and modes of punishment that are inconsistent with modern "standards of decency," as evinced by objective indicia, the most important of which is "legislation enacted by the country's legislatures," Penry v. Lynaugh, 492 U.S. 302, 330–331 (1989).

The Court makes no pretense that execution of the mildly mentally retarded would have been considered "cruel and unusual" in 1791. Only the severely or profoundly mentally retarded, commonly known as "idiots," enjoyed any special status under the law at that time. They, like lunatics, suffered a "deficiency in will" rendering them unable to tell right from wrong. 4 W. Blackstone, Commentaries on the Laws of England 24 (1769) (hereinafter Blackstone); see also Penry, 492 U.S., at 331–332 ("[T]he term 'idiot' was generally used to describe persons who had a total lack of reason or understanding, or an inability to distinguish between good and evil"); id., at 333 (citing sources indicating that idiots generally had an IQ of 25 or below, which would place them within the "profound" or "severe" range of mental retardation under modern standards); 2 A. Fitz-Herbert, Natura Brevium 233B (9th ed. 1794) (originally published 1534) (An idiot is "such a person who cannot account or number twenty pence, nor can tell who was his father or mother, nor how old he is, etc., so as it may appear that he hath no understanding of reason what shall be for his profit, or what for his loss"). Due to their incompetence, idiots were "excuse[d] from the guilt, and of course from the punishment, of any criminal action committed under such deprivation of the senses." 4 Blackstone 25; see also Penry, supra, at 331. Instead, they were often committed to civil confinement or made wards of the State, thereby preventing them from "go[ing] loose, to the terror of the king's subjects." 4 Blackstone 25; see also S. Brakel, J. Parry, & B. Weiner, The Mentally Disabled and the Law 12–14 (3d ed. 1985); 1 Blackstone 292–296; 1 M. Hale, Pleas of the Crown 33 (1st Am. ed. 1847). Mentally retarded offenders with less severe impairments–those who were not "idiots"–suffered criminal prosecution and punishment, including capital punishment. See, e.g., I. Ray, Medical Jurisprudence of Insanity 65, 87–92 (W. Overholser ed. 1962) (recounting the 1834 trial and execution in Concord, New Hampshire, of an apparent "imbecile"–imbecility being a less severe form of retardation which "differs from idiocy in the circumstance that while in [the idiot] there is an utter destitution of every thing like reason, [imbeciles] possess some intellectual capacity, though infinitely less than is possessed by the great mass of mankind"); A. Highmore, Law of Idiocy and Lunacy 200 (1807) ("The great difficulty in all these cases, is to determine where a person shall be said to be so far deprived of his sense and memory as not to have any of his actions imputed to him: or where notwithstanding some defects of this kind he still appears to have so much reason and understanding as will make him accountable for his actions ...").

The Court is left to argue, therefore, that execution of the mildly retarded is inconsistent with the "evolving standards of decency that mark the progress of a maturing society." Trop v. Dulles, 356 U.S. 86, 101 (1958) (plurality opinion) (Warren, C. J.). Before today, our opinions consistently emphasized that Eighth Amendment judgments regarding the existence of social "standards" "should be informed by objective factors to the maximum possible extent" and "should not be, or appear to be, merely the subjective views of individual Justices." Coker v. Georgia, 433 U.S. 584, 592 (1977) (plurality opinion); see also Stanford, supra, at 369; McCleskey v. Kemp, 481 U.S. 279, 300 (1987); Enmund v. Florida, 458 U.S. 782, 788 (1982). "First" among these objective factors are the "statutes passed by society's elected representatives," Stanford v. Kentucky, 492 U.S. 361, 370 (1989); because it "will rarely if ever be the case that the Members of this Court will have a better sense of the evolution in views of the American people than do their elected representatives," Thompson, supra, at 865 (Scalia, J., dissenting).

The Court pays lipservice to these precedents as it miraculously extracts a "national consensus" forbidding execution of the mentally retarded, ante, at 12, from the fact that 18 States–less than half (47%) of the 38 States that permit capital punishment (for whom the issue exists)–have very recently enacted legislation barring execution of the mentally retarded. Even that 47% figure is a distorted one. If one is to say, as the Court does today, that all executions of the mentally retarded are so morally repugnant as to violate our national "standards of decency," surely the "consensus" it points to must be one that has set its righteous face against all such executions. Not 18 States, but only seven–18% of death penalty jurisdictions–have legislation of that scope. Eleven of those that the Court counts enacted statutes prohibiting execution of mentally retarded defendants convicted after, or convicted of crimes committed after, the effective date of the legislation;1 those already on death row, or consigned there before the statute's effective date, or even (in those States using the date of the crime as the criterion of retroactivity) tried in the future for murders committed many years ago, could be put to death. That is not a statement of absolute moral repugnance, but one of current preference between two tolerable approaches. Two of these States permit execution of the mentally retarded in other situations as well: Kansas apparently permits execution of all except the severely mentally retarded; 2 New York permits execution of the mentally retarded who commit murder in a correctional facility. N. Y. Crim. Proc. Law §400.27.12(d) (McKinney 2001); N. Y. Penal Law §125.27 (McKinney 202).

But let us accept, for the sake of argument, the Court's faulty count. That bare number of States alone–18–should be enough to convince any reasonable person that no "national consensus" exists. How is it possible that agreement among 47% of the death penalty jurisdictions amounts to "consensus"? Our prior cases have generally required a much higher degree of agreement before finding a punishment cruel and unusual on "evolving standards" grounds. In Coker, supra, at 595—596, we proscribed the death penalty for rape of an adult woman after finding that only one jurisdiction, Georgia, authorized such a punishment. In Enmund, supra, at 789, we invalidated the death penalty for mere participation in a robbery in which an accomplice took a life, a punishment not permitted in 28 of the death penalty States (78%). In Ford, 477 U.S., at

408, we supported the common-law prohibition of execution of the insane with the observation that "[t]his ancestral legacy has not outlived its time," since not a single State authorizes such punishment. In Solem v. Helm, 463 U.S. 277, 300 (1983), we invalidated a life sentence without parole under a recidivist statute by which the criminal "was treated more severely than he would have been in any other State." What the Court calls evidence of "consensus" in the present case (a fudged 47%) more closely resembles evidence that we found inadequate to establish consensus in earlier cases. Tison v. Arizona, 481 U.S. 137, 154, 158 (1987), upheld a state law authorizing capital punishment for major participation in a felony with reckless indifference to life where only 11 of the 37 death penalty States (30%) prohibited such punishment. Stanford, supra, at 372, upheld a state law permitting execution of defendants who committed a capital crime at age 16 where only 15 of the 36 death penalty States (42%) prohibited death for such offenders.

Moreover, a major factor that the Court entirely disregards is that the legislation of all 18 States it relies on is still in its infancy. The oldest of the statutes is only 14 years old; 3 five were enacted last year; 4 over half were enacted within the past eight years.5 Few, if any, of the States have had sufficient experience with these laws to know whether they are sensible in the long term. It is "myopic to base sweeping constitutional principles upon the narrow experience of [a few] years." Coker, 433 U.S., at 614 (Burger, C. J., dissenting); see also Thompson, 487 U.S., at 854—855 (O'Connor, J., concurring in judgment).

The Court attempts to bolster its embarrassingly feeble evidence of "consensus" with the following: "It is not so much the number of these States that is significant, but the consistency of the direction of change." Ante, at 10 (emphasis added). But in what other direction could we possibly see change? Given that 14 years ago all the death penalty statutes included the mentally retarded, any change (except precipitate undoing of what had just been done) was bound to be in the one direction the Court finds significant enough to overcome the lack of real consensus. That is to say, to be accurate the Court's "consistency-of-the-direction-of-change" point should be recast into the following unimpressive observation: "No State has yet undone its exemption of the mentally retarded, one for as long as 14 whole years." In any event, reliance upon "trends," even those of much longer duration than a mere 14 years, is a perilous basis for constitutional adjudication, as Justice O'Connor eloquently explained in Thompson:

"In 1846, Michigan became the first State to abolish the death penalty ... . In succeeding decades, other American States continued the trend towards abolition ... . Later, and particularly after World War II, there ensued a steady and dramatic decline in executions ... . In the 1950's and 1960's, more States abolished or radically restricted capital punishment, and executions ceased completely for several years beginning in 1968... .

In 1972, when this Court heard arguments on the constitutionality of the death penalty, such statistics might have suggested that the practice had become a relic, implicitly rejected by a new societal consensus ... . We now know that any inference of a societal consensus rejecting the death penalty would have been mistaken. But had this Court then declared the existence of such a consensus, and outlawed capital punishment, legislatures would very likely not have been able to revive it. The mistaken premise of the decision would have been frozen into constitutional law, making it difficult to refute and even more difficult to reject." 487 U.S., at 854—855.

Her words demonstrate, of course, not merely the peril of riding a trend, but also the peril of discerning a consensus where there is none.

The Court's thrashing about for evidence of "consensus" includes reliance upon the margins by which state legislatures have enacted bans on execution of the retarded. Ante, at 11. Presumably, in applying our Eighth Amendment "evolving-standards-of-decency" jurisprudence, we will henceforth weigh not only how many States have agreed, but how many States have agreed by how much. Of course if the percentage of legislators voting for the bill is significant, surely the number of people represented by the legislators voting for the bill is also significant: the fact that 49% of the legislators in a State with a population of 60 million voted against the bill should be more impressive than the fact that 90% of the legislators in a state with a population of 2 million voted for it. (By the way, the population of the death penalty States that exclude the mentally retarded is only 44% of the population of all death penalty States. U.S. Census Bureau, Statistical Abstract of the United States 21 (121st ed. 2001).) This is quite absurd. What we have looked for in the past to "evolve" the Eighth Amendment is a consensus of the same sort as the consensus that adopted the Eighth Amendment: a consensus of the sovereign States that form the Union, not a nose count of Americans for and against.

Even less compelling (if possible) is the Court's argument, ante, at 11, that evidence of "national consensus" is to be found in the infrequency with which retarded persons are executed in States that do not bar their execution. To begin with, what the Court takes as true is in fact quite doubtful. It is not at all clear that execution of the mentally retarded is "uncommon," ibid., as even the sources cited by the Court suggest, see ante, at 11, n. 20 (citing D. Keyes, W. Edwards, & R. Perske, People with Mental Retardation are Dying Legally, 35 Mental Retardation (Feb. 1997) (updated by Death Penalty Information Center; available at http://www.advocacyone.org/ deathpenalty.html) (June 12, 2002) (showing that 12 States executed 35 allegedly mentally retarded offenders during the period 1984—2000)). See also Bonner & Rimer, Executing the Mentally Retarded Even as Laws Begin to Shift, N. Y. Times, Aug. 7, 2000 p. A1 (reporting that 10% of death row inmates are retarded). If, however, execution of the mentally retarded is "uncommon"; and if it is not a sufficient explanation of this that the retarded comprise a tiny fraction of society (1% to 3%), Brief for American Psychological Association et al. as Amici Curiae 7; then surely the explanation is that mental retardation is a constitutionally mandated mitigating factor at sentencing, Penry, 492 U.S., at 328. For that reason, even if there were uniform national sentiment in favor of executing the retarded in appropriate cases, one would still expect execution of the mentally retarded to be "uncommon." To adapt to the present case what the Court itself said in Stanford, 492

U.S., at 374: "[I]t is not only possible, but overwhelmingly probable, that the very considerations which induce [today's majority] to believe that death should never be imposed on [mentally retarded] offenders ... cause prosecutors and juries to believe that it should rarely be imposed."

But the Prize for the Court's Most Feeble Effort to fabricate "national consensus" must go to its appeal (deservedly relegated to a footnote) to the views of assorted professional and religious organizations, members of the so-called "world community," and respondents to opinion polls. Ante, at 11—12, n. 21. I agree with the Chief Jus-tice, ante, at 4—8 (dissenting opinion), that the views of professional and religious organizations and the results of opinion polls are irrelevant.6 Equally irrelevant are the practices of the "world community," whose notions of justice are (thankfully) not always those of our people. "We must never forget that it is a Constitution for the United States of America that we are expounding. ... [W]here there is not first a settled consensus among our own people, the views of other nations, however enlightened the Justices of this Court may think them to be, cannot be imposed upon Americans through the Constitution." Thompson, 487 U.S., at 868—869, n. 4 (Scalia, J., dissenting).

III

Beyond the empty talk of a "national consensus," the Court gives us a brief glimpse of what really underlies today's decision: pretension to a power confined neither by the moral sentiments originally enshrined in the Eighth Amendment (its original meaning) nor even by the current moral sentiments of the American people. " '[T]he Constitution,' " the Court says, "contemplates that in the end our own judgment will be brought to bear on the question of the acceptability of the death penalty under the Eighth Amendment.' " Ante, at 7 (quoting Coker, 433 U.S., at 597) (emphasis added). (The unexpressed reason for this unexpressed "contemplation" of the Constitution is presumably that really good lawyers have moral sentiments superior to those of the common herd, whether in 1791 or today.) The arrogance of this assumption of power takes one's breath away. And it explains, of course, why the Court can be so cavalier about the evidence of consensus. It is just a game, after all. "[I]n the end," it is the feelings and intuition of a majority of the Justices that count—"the perceptions of decency, or of penology, or of mercy, entertained ... by a majority of the small and unrepresentative segment of our society that sits on this Court." Thompson, supra, at 873 (Scalia, J., dissenting).

The genuinely operative portion of the opinion, then, is the Court's statement of the reasons why it agrees with the contrived consensus it has found, that the "diminished capacities" of the mentally retarded render the death penalty excessive. Ante, at 13—17. The Court's analysis rests on two fundamental assumptions: (1) that the Eighth Amendment prohibits excessive punishments, and (2) that sentencing juries or judges are unable to account properly for the "diminished capacities" of the retarded. The first assumption is wrong, as I explained at length in Harmelin v. Michigan, 501 U.S. 957, 966—990 (1991) (opinion of Scalia, J.). The Eighth Amendment is addressed to always-

and-everywhere "cruel" punishments, such as the rack and the thumbscrew. But where the punishment is in itself permissible, "[t]he Eighth Amendment is not a ratchet, whereby a temporary consensus on leniency for a particular crime fixes a permanent constitutional maximum, disabling the States from giving effect to altered beliefs and responding to changed social conditions." Id., at 990. The second assumption–inability of judges or juries to take proper account of mental retardation–is not only unsubstantiated, but contradicts the immemorial belief, here and in England, that they play an indispensable role in such matters:

"[I]t is very difficult to define the indivisible line that divides perfect and partial insanity; but it must rest upon circumstances duly to be weighed and considered both by the judge and jury, lest on the one side there be a kind of inhumanity towards the defects of human nature, or on the other side too great an indulgence given to great crimes … ." 1 Hale, Pleas of the Crown, at 30.

Proceeding from these faulty assumptions, the Court gives two reasons why the death penalty is an excessive punishment for all mentally retarded offenders. First, the "diminished capacities" of the mentally retarded raise a "serious question" whether their execution contributes to the "social purposes" of the death penalty, viz., retribution and deterrence. Ante, at 13–14. (The Court conveniently ignores a third "social purpose" of the death penalty–"incapacitation of dangerous criminals and the consequent prevention of crimes that they may otherwise commit in the future," Gregg v. Georgia, 428 U.S. 153, 183, n. 28 (1976) (joint opinion of Stewart, Powell, and Stevens, JJ.). But never mind; its discussion of even the other two does not bear analysis.) Retribution is not advanced, the argument goes, because the mentally retarded are no more culpable than the average murderer, whom we have already held lacks sufficient culpability to warrant the death penalty, see Godfrey v. Georgia, 446 U.S. 420, 433 (1980) (plurality opinion). Ante, at 14–15. Who says so? Is there an established correlation between mental acuity and the ability to conform one's conduct to the law in such a rudimentary matter as murder? Are the mentally retarded really more disposed (and hence more likely) to commit willfully cruel and serious crime than others? In my experience, the opposite is true: being childlike generally suggests innocence rather than brutality.

Assuming, however, that there is a direct connection between diminished intelligence and the inability to refrain from murder, what scientific analysis can possibly show that a mildly retarded individual who commits an exquisite torture-killing is "no more culpable" than the "average" murderer in a holdup-gone-wrong or a domestic dispute? Or a moderately retarded individual who commits a series of 20 exquisite torture-killings? Surely culpability, and deservedness of the most severe retribution, depends not merely (if at all) upon the mental capacity of the criminal (above the level where he is able to distinguish right from wrong) but also upon the depravity of the crime–which is precisely why this sort of question has traditionally been thought answerable not by a categorical rule of the sort the Court today imposes upon all trials, but rather by the sentencer's weighing of the circumstances (both degree of retardation and depravity of crime) in the particular case. The fact that juries continue to sentence mentally retarded offenders to death for extreme crimes shows that society's moral outrage sometimes demands execution of retarded offenders. By what principle of law, science, or logic can the Court pronounce that this is wrong? There is none. Once the Court admits (as it does) that mental retardation does not render the offender morally blameless, ante, at 13—14, there is no basis for saying that the death penalty is never appropriate retribution, no matter how heinous the crime. As long as a mentally retarded offender knows "the difference between right and wrong," ante, at 13, only the sentencer can assess whether his retardation reduces his culpability enough to exempt him from the death penalty for the particular murder in question.

As for the other social purpose of the death penalty that the Court discusses, deterrence: That is not advanced, the Court tells us, because the mentally retarded are "less likely" than their non-retarded counterparts to "process the information of the possibility of execution as a penalty and ... control their conduct based upon that information." Ante, at 15. Of course this leads to the same conclusion discussed earlier— that the mentally retarded (because they are less deterred) are more likely to kill–which neither I nor the society at large believes. In any event, even the Court does not say that all mentally retarded individuals cannot "process the information of the possibility of execution as a penalty and . . . control their conduct based upon that information"; it merely asserts that they are "less likely" to be able to do so. But surely the deterrent effect of a penalty is adequately vindicated if it successfully deters many, but not all, of the target class. Virginia's death penalty, for example, does not fail of its deterrent effect simply because some criminals are unaware that Virginia has the death penalty. In other words, the supposed fact that some retarded criminals cannot fully appreciate the death penalty has nothing to do with the deterrence rationale, but is simply an echo of the arguments denying a retribution rationale, discussed and rejected above. I am not sure that a murderer is somehow less blameworthy if (though he knew his act was wrong) he did not fully appreciate that he could die for it; but if so, we should treat a mentally retarded murderer the way we treat an offender who may be "less likely" to respond to the death penalty because he was abused as a child. We do not hold him immune from capital punishment, but require his background to be considered by the sentencer as a mitigating factor. Eddings v. Oklahoma, 455 U.S. 104, 113—117 (1982).

The Court throws one last factor into its grab bag of reasons why execution of the retarded is "excessive" in all cases: Mentally retarded offenders "face a special risk of wrongful execution" because they are less able "to make a persuasive showing of mitigation," "to give meaningful assistance to their counsel," and to be effective witnesses. Ante, at 16. "Special risk" is pretty flabby language (even flabbier than "less likely")–and I suppose a similar "special risk" could be said to exist for just plain stupid people, inarticulate people, even ugly people. If this unsupported claim has any substance to it (which I doubt) it might support a due process claim in all criminal prosecutions of the mentally retarded; but it is hard to see how it has anything to do with an Eighth

Amendment claim that execution of the mentally retarded is cruel and unusual. We have never before held it to be cruel and unusual punishment to impose a sentence in violation of some other constitutional imperative.

* * *

Today's opinion adds one more to the long list of substantive and procedural requirements impeding imposition of the death penalty imposed under this Court's assumed power to invent a death-is-different jurisprudence. None of those requirements existed when the Eighth Amendment was adopted, and some of them were not even supported by current moral consensus. They include prohibition of the death penalty for "ordinary" murder, Godfrey, 446 U.S., at 433, for rape of an adult woman, Coker, 433 U.S., at 592, and for felony murder absent a showing that the defendant possessed a sufficiently culpable state of mind, Enmund, 458 U.S., at 801; prohibition of the death penalty for any person under the age of 16 at the time of the crime, Thompson, 487 U.S., at 838 (plurality opinion); prohibition of the death penalty as the mandatory punishment for any crime, Woodson v. North Carolina, 428 U.S. 280, 305 (1976) (plurality opinion), Sumner v. Shuman, 483 U.S. 66, 77–78 (1987); a requirement that the sentencer not be given unguided discretion, Furman v. Georgia, 408 U.S. 238 (1972) (per curiam), a requirement that the sentencer be empowered to take into account all mitigating circumstances, Lockett v. Ohio, 438 U.S. 586, 604 (1978) (plurality opinion), Eddings v. Oklahoma, supra, at 110; and a requirement that the accused receive a judicial evaluation of his claim of insanity before the sentence can be executed, Ford, 477 U.S., at 410–411 (plurality opinion). There is something to be said for popular abolition of the death penalty; there is nothing to be said for its incremental abolition by this Court.

This newest invention promises to be more effective than any of the others in turning the process of capital trial into a game. One need only read the definitions of mental retardation adopted by the American Association of Mental Retardation and the American Psychiatric Association (set forth in the Court's opinion, ante, at 2–3, n. 3) to realize that the symptoms of this condition can readily be feigned. And whereas the capital defendant who feigns insanity risks commitment to a mental institution until he can be cured (and then tried and executed), Jones v. United States, 463 U.S. 354, 370, and n. 20 (1983), the capital defendant who feigns mental retardation risks nothing at all. The mere pendency of the present case has brought us petitions by death row inmates claiming for the first time, after multiple habeas petitions, that they are retarded. See, e.g., Moore v. Texas, 535 U.S. ___ (2002) (Scalia, J., dissenting from grant of applications for stay of execution).

Perhaps these practical difficulties will not be experienced by the minority of capital-punishment States that have very recently changed mental retardation from a mitigating factor (to be accepted or rejected by the sentencer) to an absolute immunity. Time will tell–and the brief time those States have had the new disposition in place (an average of 6.8 years) is surely not enough. But if the practical difficulties do not appear, and if the other States share the Court's perceived moral consensus that all mental retardation renders the death penalty inappropriate for all crimes, then that majority will presumably follow suit. But there is no justification for this Court's pushing them into the experiment–and turning the experiment into a permanent practice–on constitutional pretext. Nothing has changed the accuracy of Matthew Hale's endorsement of the common law's traditional method for taking account of guilt-reducing factors, written over three centuries ago:

"[Determination of a person's incapacity] is a matter of great difficulty, partly from the easiness of counterfeiting this disability ... and partly from the variety of the degrees of this infirmity, whereof some are sufficient, and some are insufficient to excuse persons in capital offenses. ...

"Yet the law of England hath afforded the best method of trial, that is possible, of this and all other matters of fact, namely, by a jury of twelve men all concurring in the same judgment, by the testimony of witnesses ..., and by the inspection and direction of the judge." 1 Hale, Pleas of the Crown, at 32–33.

Notes

1. See Ariz. Rev. Stat. Ann. §13–703.02(I) (Supp. 2001); Ark. Code Ann. §5–4–618(d)(1) (1997); Reams v. State, 322 Ark. 336, 340, 909 S. W. 2d 324, 326–327 (1995); Fla. Stat. §921.137(8) (Supp. 2002); Ga. Code Ann. §17–7–131(j) (1997); Ind. Code §35–36–9–6 (1998); Rondon v. State, 711 N. E. 2d 506, 512 (Ind. 1999); Kan. Stat. Ann. §§21–4623(d), 21–4631(c) (1995); Ky. Rev. Stat. Ann. §532.140(3) (1999); Md. Ann. Code, Art. 27, §412(g) (1996); Booth v. State, 327 Md. 142, 166–167, 608 A. 2d 162, 174 (1992); Mo. Rev. Stat. §565.030(7) (Supp. 2001); N. Y. Crim. Proc. Law §400.27.12(c) (McKinney Supp. 2002); 1995 Sess. N. Y. Laws, ch. 1, §38; Tenn. Code Ann. §39–13–203(b) (1997); Van Tran v. State, 66 S. W. 2d 790, 798–799 (Tenn. 2001).

2. The Kansas statute defines "mentally retarded" as "having significantly subaverage general intellectual functioning ... to an extent which substantially impairs one's capacity to appreciate the criminality of one's conduct or to conform one's conduct to the requirements of law." Kan. Stat. Ann. §21–4623(e) (2001). This definition of retardation, petitioner concedes, is analogous to the Model Penal Code's definition of a "mental disease or defect" excusing responsibility for criminal conduct, see ALI, Model Penal Code §4.01 (1985), which would not include mild mental retardation. Reply Brief for petitioner 3, n. 4.

3. Ga. Code Ann. §17–7–131(j).

4. Ariz. Rev. Stat. Ann. §13–703.02; Conn. Gen. Stat. §53a–46a(h); Fla. Stat. Ann. §921.137; Mo. Rev. Stat. §§565.030(4)–(7); N. C. Gen. Stat. §15A–2005.

5. In addition to the statutes cited n. 3 supra, see S. D. Codified Laws §23A–27A–26.1 (enacted 2000); Neb. Rev. Stat. §§28–105.01(2)–(5) (1998); N. Y. Crim. Proc. Law §400.27(12) (1995); Ind. Code §35–36–9–6 (1994); Kan. Stat. Ann. §21–4623 (1994).

6. And in some cases positively counter-indicative. The Court cites, for example,

the views of the United States Catholic Conference, whose members are the active Catholic Bishops of the United States. See ante, at 12, n. 21 (citing Brief for United States Catholic Conference et al. as Amici Curiae in McCarver v. North Carolina, O. T. 2001, No. 00–8727, p. 2). The attitudes of that body regarding crime and punishment are so far from being representative, even of the views of Catholics, that they are currently the object of intense national (and entirely ecumenical) criticism.

Justice Scalia's dissent in Columbus v. Ours Garage & Wrecker Service, Inc. (June 20, 2002)

Justice Scalia, with whom Justice O'Connor joins, dissenting.

The dispute in the present case arises from the fact that a reference to "State" power or authority can be meant to include all that power or authority, including the portion exercised by political subdivisions (as, for example, in the ordinary reference to "the State's police power"); but can also be meant to include only that power or authority exercised at the state level (as, for example, in the phrase "State and local governmental authority"). The issue is whether, when 49 U.S.C. § 14501(c)(2)(A) (1994 ed., Supp. V) excepts from the preclusionary command of §14501(c)(1) "the safety regulatory authority of a State with respect to motor vehicles," it means to except the safety regulatory authority of cities and counties as well. In my view it plainly does not.

I

There are four exceptions to the preclusionary rule of §14501(c)(1), which read as follows:

"(2) Matters not covered.–[The preemption rule]–

"(A) shall not restrict the safety regulatory authority of a State with respect to motor vehicles, the authority of a State to impose highway route controls or limitations based on the size or weight of the motor vehicle or the hazardous nature of the cargo, or the authority of a State to regulate motor carriers with regard to minimum amounts of financial responsibility relating to insurance requirements and self-insurance authorization;

"(B) does not apply to the transportation of household goods; and

"(C) does not apply to the authority of a State or a political subdivision of a State to enact or enforce a law, regulation, or other provision relating to the price of for-hire motor vehicle transportation by a tow truck, if such transportation is performed without the prior consent or authorization of the owner or operator of the motor vehicle.

"(3) State standard transportation practices.–

"(A) Continuation.–[The preemption rule] shall not affect any authority of a State, political subdivision of a State, or political authority of 2 or more States to enact or enforce a law, regulation, or other provision, with respect to the intrastate transportation of property by motor carriers, related to–[inter alia] uniform cargo liability rules, ... if such law, regulation, or provision meets the requirements of subparagraph (B)." §§14501(c)(2),

(3) (emphases added).

It is impossible to read this text without being struck by the fact that the term "political subdivision of a State" is added to the term "State" in some of the exceptions, §§14501(c)(2)(C), (c)(3), but not in the exception at issue here, §14501(c)(2)(A). " 'Where Congress includes particular language in one section of a statute but omits it in another section of the same Act, it is generally presumed that Congress acts intentionally and purposely in the disparate inclusion or exclusion.' " Russello v. United States, 464 U.S. 16, 23 (1983). The only way to impart some purpose and intent here is to assume that the word "State" is used in its narrower sense, so that political subdivisions are not covered by the term. The Court admits that the rule applied in Russello "supports an argument of some force," ante, at 7, that the exception for the "safety regulatory authority of a State" does not include local safety regulation.

But while the Russello argument is strong, it alone does not fully describe the clarity with which §14501(c)(2)(A) excludes political subdivisions. For the clarity begins not just with the various exceptions, but with the very preemption rule to which the exceptions are appended. That rule reads:

"Except as provided [in §§14501(c)(2), (3)], a State, political subdivision of a State, or political authority of 2 or more States may not enact or enforce a law, regulation, or other provision having the force and effect of law related to a price, route, or service of any motor carrier ... or any motor private carrier, broker, or freight forwarder with respect to the transportation of property." 49 U.S.C. § 14501(c)(1).

Since the law-making power of a political subdivision of a State is a subset of the law-making power of the State, Hess v. Port Authority Trans-Hudson Corporation, 513 U.S. 30, 47 (1994); Wisconsin Public Intervenor v. Mortier, 501 U.S. 597, 607—608 (1991), the preemption rule would have precisely the same scope if it omitted the reference to "political subdivision of a State." It is a well-established principle of statutory construction (and of common sense) that when such a situation occurs, when "two words or expressions are coupled together, one of which generically includes the other, it is obvious that the more general term is used in a meaning excluding the specific one." J. Sutherland, Statutes and Statutory Construction §266, p. 349 (1891). The only conceivable reason for this specification of "political subdivision" apart from "State" is to establish, in the rule, the two separate categories of state power—state power exercised through political subdivisions and state power exercised by the State directly—that are later treated differently in the exceptions to the rule.

The situation is comparable to the following hypothetical using the term "football" (which may be used to include soccer, see Webster's New International Dictionary 983 (2d ed. 1950)): Assume a statute which says that "football and soccer shall not be played on the town green" (§14501(c)(1)), except that "football and soccer may be played on Saturdays" (§14501(c)(2)(C)), "football and soccer may be played on summer nights" (14501(c)(3)(A)), and "football may be played on Mondays" (§14501(c)(2)(A)). In today's opinion, the Court says soccer may be played on Mondays. I think it clear that soccer is not to be regarded as a subset of football but as a separate category. And the same is true of "political subdivision" here.

II

The Court reaches the opposite conclusion merely because §14501(c) exhibits uneven drafting. First the Court notes that §14501(c)(2)(A) does not "trac[k] the language and structure of the general preemption rule." Ante, at 8. Whereas other exceptions to the rule refer to the authority of a State or other political entity "to enact or enforce a law, regulation, or other provision," §14501(c)(2)(A) merely refers to the "safety regulatory authority of a State." Second, the Court notes that another exception to the preemption rule, §14501(c)(2)(B), is "stated with similar economy." Ante, at 8. It addresses merely the subject of regulation (transportation of household goods) instead of both the subject and the source of regulation (a State, political subdivision, or political authority of 2 or more States). This has, the Court notes, the same effect as its neighbor, §14501(c)(2)(C), of permitting both state and local regulation.1 Ibid. These inconsistencies in the statute's drafting style, the Court contends, undermine the conclusion we would ordinarily draw from the absence of the term "political subdivision" in §14501(c)(2)(A). Ante, at 9.

The weakness of this argument should be self-evident. How can inconsistencies of style, on points that have nothing to do with the issue of separating state and local authority, cause the text's crystal-clear distinction between state and local authority to disappear? It would certainly reflect more orderly draftsmanship if the statute consistently used the formulation "to enact or enforce a law, regulation, or other provision," rather than replacing it in §14501(c)(2)(A) with the equivalent phrase "regulatory authority of a State"; and if the statute referred to subject matter alone (à la §14501(c)(2)(B)) either never at all, or else whenever the exception applied to all three categories of States, subdivisions of States, and political authorities of 2 or more States. But it is impossible to imagine how this imperfect draftsmanship in unrelated matters casts any doubt upon the precise meaning of the subject-matter-plus-source provisions where they appear. Unless the Court is appealing to some hitherto unknown canon of interpretation–perhaps (borrowed from the law of evidence) *negligens in uno, negligens in omnibus*–the diverse styles of §14501(c)'s exceptions have nothing to do with whether we should take seriously the references to States and subdivisions of States where they appear.

What is truly anomalous here is not the fact that the terminology of §14501(c) is diverse with regard to presently irrelevant matters, but the fact that the Court has today come up with a judicial interpretation of §14501(c) that renders the term "political subdivision of a State," which appears throughout, utterly superfluous throughout. Although the Court claims that the "Russello presumption ... grows weaker with each difference in the formulation of the provisions under inspection," ante, at 9, it cites no authority for that proposition–nor could it, because we have routinely applied the Russello presumption in cases where a statute employs different "verbal formulation[s]" in sections that include particular language and in sections that omit such language. See, e.g., Barnhart v. Sigmon Coal Co., 534 U.S. 438, ___ (2002) (slip op., at 12–13); Duncan v.

Walker, 533 U.S. 167, 173–174 (2001); Hohn v. United States, 524 U.S. 236, 249–250 (1998); United States v. Gonzales, 520 U.S. 1, 5 (1997).

III

Lacking support in the text of the statute, the Court invokes federalism concerns to justify its decision. "Absent a basis more reliable than statutory language insufficient to demonstrate a 'clear and manifest purpose' to the contrary," the Court reasons, "federal courts should resist attribution to Congress of a design to disturb a State's decision on the division of authority between the State's central and local units over safety on municipal streets and roads." Ante, at 13. Well of course we think there is "clear and manifest purpose here"; but besides that, the Court's federalism concerns are overblown. To begin with, it should not be thought that the States' power to control the relationship between themselves and their political subdivisions–their "traditional prerogative ... to delegate" (or to refuse to delegate) "their authority to their constituent parts," ante, at 2–has hitherto been regarded as sacrosanct. To the contrary. To take only a few examples,2 the Federal Government routinely gives directly to municipalities substantial grants of funds that cannot be reached or directed by "the politicians upstate" (or "downstate"), see, e.g., Office of Management and Budget, 2001 Catalog of Federal Domestic Assistance AEI–1 to AEI–29; Lawrence County v. Lead-Deadwood School Dist. No. 40–1, 469 U.S. 256, 270 (1985); and many significant federal programs require laws or regulations that must be adopted by the state government and cannot be delegated to political subdivisions, see, e.g., 42 U.S.C. § 1396a(a) (1994 ed. and Supp. V) (Medicaid); 23 U.S.C. § 153 158 (Federal-Aid Highway System); 42 U.S.C. § 7407(a), 7410 (1994 ed.) (Clean Air Act).3 This "interference" of the Federal Government with the States' "traditional prerogative ... to delegate their authority to their constituent parts" has long been a subject of considerable debate and controversy. See, e.g., Hills, Dissecting the State: The Use of Federal Law to Free State and Local Officials from State Legislatures' Control, 97 Mich. L. Rev. 1201 (1999).

With such major impositions as these already on the books, treating §14501(c)(1) as some extraordinary federal obstruction of state allocation of power is absurd. That provision preempts the authority of political subdivisions to regulate "a price, route, or service of any motor carrier ... or any motor private carrier, broker, or freight forwarder with respect to the transportation of property." (Emphasis added.) The italicized language massively limits the scope of preemption to include only laws, regulations, and other provisions that single out for special treatment "motor carriers of property." §14501(c). States and political sub-divisions remain free to enact and enforce general traffic safety laws, general restrictions on the weight of cars and trucks that may enter highways or pass over bridges, and other regulations that do not target motor carriers "with respect to the transportation of property." In addition, the exception contained in §14501(c)(2)(A) allows a State–but not a political subdivision–to apply special safety rules (rules adopted under its "safety regulatory authority") to motor carriers of property.4

This relatively modest burden on the "historic powers of the States" to delegate authority to political subdivisions, Gregory v. Ashcroft, 501 U.S. 452, 461 (1991) (internal quotation marks omitted), is unambiguously imposed by the statute. The Court repeatedly emphasizes the fact that §14501(c)(2)(A) declares that §14501(c)(1) shall "not restrict the safety regulatory authority of a State," ante, at 11, 13–which, it says, "includes the choice to delegate ... to localities," ante, at 13. This entirely begs the question, which is precisely whether the statute's reference to the authority of a "State" includes authority possessed by a municipality on delegation from the State. As I have described, the text and structure of the statute leave no doubt that it does not–that "State" does not include "subdivision of a State." Even when we are dealing with the traditional powers of the States, "[e]vidence of pre-emptive purpose is sought in the text and structure of the statute at issue." CSX Transp., Inc. v. Easterwood, 507 U.S. 658, 664 (1993) (emphasis added); see also Rice v. Santa Fe Elevator Corp., 331 U.S. 218, 230 (1947).

* * *

I believe the text and structure of §14501(c) show plainly that "the safety regulatory authority of a State" does not encompass the authority of a political subdivision. For this reason, I respectfully dissent.

Notes

1. Not only is this point (as the text proceeds to discuss) irrelevant in principle; it is misleading in its description of fact, suggesting that the two neighboring sections produce the same result with different language. It is true enough that §14501(c)(2)(C), like §14501(c)(2)(B), permits both state and local regulation. But 14501(c)(2)(C), unlike §14501(c)(2)(B), also permits regulation by a "political authority of 2 or more States."

2. The Court thinks these examples are "hardly comparable" to §14501(c) because many involve Spending Clause legislation. Ante, at 11–12. A sufficient answer is that one of them does not, see 42 U.S.C. § 7410 (1994 ed.) (Clean Air Act), and that other examples not involving Spending Clause legislation could be added, see, e.g., 33 U.S.C. § 1313(d), 1362(3) (Clean Water Act). But in any event, a siphoning off of the States' "historic powers" to delegate has equally been achieved, whether it has come about through the coercion of deprivation of Spending Clause funds or through other means. The point is that it is not unusual for Congress to interfere in this matter.

3. The Court thinks the Clean Air Act is a bad example merely because a State can rely on political subdivisions to enforce the State's implementation plan. Ante, at 12–13, n. 4; see 42 U.S.C. § 7407(a), 7410(a)(2)(E)(iii). So what? Only States may adopt implementation plans; this duty cannot be delegated to localities. Moreover, as I explain n. 4, infra, the statute at issue here is no different. Under 49 U.S.C. § 14501(c)(1) and (c)(2)(A), a State may enact regulations pursuant to its "safety regulatory authority" and rely on localities to enforce those regulations.

4. This interpretation of the statutory scheme "introduces an interpretive conundrum of another kind," the Court asserts, because §14501(c)(1) declares that a

political subdivision may not "enact or enforce" laws, regulations, or other provisions relating to motor carriers of property. Ante, at 9. In the Court's view, if the term "State" does not include "subdivision of a State," §14501(c)(1) will prevent a State from relying on localities to "enforce" rules adopted under its "safety regulatory authority." Ibid. But the conclusion that §14501(c)(1) prevents a political subdivision from enforcing regulations enacted by the State can only be reached by ignoring (for this issue) the rule that the Court is so insistent upon elsewhere: that federal interference with the "historic powers of the States" must be evinced by a "plain statement," Gregory v. Ashcroft, 501 U.S. 452, 461 (1991). A natural reading of the phrase "a ... political subdivision of a State . . . may not enact or enforce a law"–and a reading faithful to Gregory's plain statement rule–is that a political subdivision may not enact new laws or enforce its previously enacted laws. The Court believes this reading "raises the startling possibility," ante, at 10, n. 3, that §14501(c)(1) prevents States but not political subdivisions from enforcing previously enacted State regulations relating to motor carriage of property. I think not. A possibility so startling (and unlikely to occur) is well enough precluded by the rule that a statute should not be interpreted to produce absurd results. The municipalities' reserved power to enforce state law does not include the power to enforce state law that the State has no continuing power to enact or enforce.

Justice Scalia's dissent in Barnhart v. Peabody Coal Co. (Jan 15, 2003)

Justice Scalia, with whom Justice O'Connor and Justice Thomas join, dissenting.

The Court's holding today confers upon the Commissioner of Social Security an unexpiring power to assign retired coal miners to signatory operators under 26 U.S.C. § 9706(a). In my view, this disposition is irreconcilable with the text and structure of the Coal Industry Retiree Health Benefit Act of 1992 (Coal Act or Act), and finds no support in our precedents. I respectfully dissent.

I

The respondents contend that the Commissioner improperly assigned them responsibility for 600 coal miners under §9706(a). Section 9706(a) provides, in pertinent part:

"[T]he Commissioner of Social Security shall, before October 1, 1993, assign each coal industry retiree who is an eligible beneficiary to a signatory operator which (or any related person with respect to which) remains in business in the following order:

"(1) First, to the signatory operator which–

"(A) was a signatory to the 1978 coal wage agreement or any subsequent coal wage agreement, and

"(B) was the most recent signatory operator to employ the coal industry retiree in the coal industry for at least 2 years.

"(2) Second, if the retiree is not assigned under paragraph (1), to the signatory operator which—

"(A) was a signatory to the 1978 coal wage agreement or any subsequent coal wage agreement, and

"(B) was the most recent signatory operator to employ the coal industry retiree in the coal industry.

"(3) Third, if the retiree is not assigned under paragraph (1) or (2), to the signatory operator which employed the coal industry retiree in the coal industry for a longer period of time than any other signatory operator prior to the effective date of the 1978 coal wage agreement."

The Commissioner failed to complete the task of assigning each eligible beneficiary to a signatory operator before October 1, 1993. As a result, many eligible beneficiaries were "unassigned," and their benefits were financed, for a time, by the United Mine Workers of America 1950 Pension Plan (UMWA Pension Plan) and the Abandoned Mine Land Reclamation Fund. See §§9705(a)(3)(B), 9705(b)(2).

The Commissioner blames her failure to meet the statutory deadline on the "magnitude of the task" and the lack of appropriated funds. Brief for Petitioners Trustees of the UMWA Combined Benefit Fund 15. It should not be thought, however, that these cases are about letting the Commissioner complete a little unfinished business that barely missed the deadline. They concern some 600 post-October 1, 1993, assignments to these respondents, the vast majority of which were made between 1995 and 1997, years after the statutory deadline had passed. App. 98—121. Respondents contend that these assignments are unlawful, and unless Congress has conferred upon the Commissioner the power that she claims—an unexpiring authority to assign eligible beneficiaries to signatory operators— the respondents must prevail. Section 9706(a) of the Coal Act does not provide such an expansive power, and the other provisions of the Act confirm this.

II

It is well established that an agency's power to regulate private entities must be grounded in a statutory grant of authority from Congress. See FDA v. Brown & Williamson Tobacco Corp., 529 U.S. 120, 161 (2000); Bowen v. Georgetown Univ. Hospital, 488 U.S. 204, 208 (1988); Louisiana Pub. Serv. Comm'n v. FCC, 476 U.S. 355, 374 (1986). This principle has special importance with respect to the extraordinary power the Commissioner asserts here: to compel coal companies to pay miners (and their families) health benefits that they never contracted to pay. We have held that the Commissioner's use of this power under §9706(a), even when exercised before October 1, 1993, violates the Constitution to the extent it imposes severe retroactive liability on certain coal companies. See Eastern Enterprises v. Apfel, 524 U.S. 498 (1998). When an agency exercises a power that so tests constitutional limits, we have all the more obligation to assure that it is rooted in the text of a statute.

The Court holds that the Commissioner retains the power to act after October 1, 1993, because Congress did not " 'specify a consequence for noncompliance' " with the statutory deadline. Ante, at 8. This makes no sense. When a power is conferred for a limited time, the automatic consequence of the expiration of that time is the expiration of the power. If a landowner authorizes someone to cut Christmas trees "before December 15," there is no doubt what happens when December 15 passes: The authority to cut terminates. And the situation is not changed when the authorization is combined with a mandate—as when the landowner enters a contract which says that the other party "shall cut all Christmas trees on the property before December 15." Even if time were not of the essence of that contract (as it is of the essence of §9706(a), for reasons I shall discuss in Part III, infra) no one would think that the contractor had continuing authority—not just for a few more days or weeks—but perpetually, to harvest trees.1

The Court points out, ante, at 10—11, that three other provisions of the Coal Act combine the word "shall" with a statutory deadline that in its view is extendible:

(1) Section 9705(a)(1)(A) states that the UMWA Pension Plan "shall transfer to the Combined Fund . . . $70,000,000 on   February 1, 1993";

(2) §9704(h) says the trustees for the Combined Fund "shall, not later than 60 days" after the enactment date, furnish certain information regarding benefits to the Commissioner; and

(3) §9702(a)(1) provides that certain individuals described   in §9702(b)(1) "shall designate" the trustees for the Combined Fund "not later than 60 days . . . after the enactment date."

I agree that the actions mandated by the first two of these deadlines can be taken after the deadlines have expired (though perhaps not forever after, which is what the Court claims for the deadline of §9706(a)). The reason that is so, however, does not at all apply to §9706(a). In those provisions, the power to do what is mandated does not stem from the mere implication of the mandate itself. The private entities involved have the power to do what is prescribed, quite apart from the statutory command that they do it by a certain date: The UMWA Pension Plan has the power to transfer funds,2 and the trustees of the Combined Fund have the power to provide the specified information, whether the statute commands that they do so or not. The only question is whether the late exercise of an unquestionably authorized act will produce the consequences that the statute says will follow from a timely exercise of that act. It is as though, to pursue the tree-harvesting analogy, a contract provided that the landowner will harvest and deliver trees by December 15; even after December 15 passes, he can surely harvest and deliver trees, and the only issue is whether the December 15 date is so central to the contract that late delivery does not have the contractual consequence of requiring the other side's counterperformance. The Commissioner of Social Security, by contrast, being not a private entity but a creature of Congress, has no authority to assign beneficiaries to operators except insofar as such authority is implicit in the mandate; but the mandate (and hence the implicit authority) expired on October 1, 1993.

The last of these three provisions does confer a power that is not otherwise available to the private entities involved: the power to appoint initial trustees to the board of the Combined Fund. I do not, however, think it as clear as the Court does—indeed, I think it quite debatable—whether that power survives the deadline. If it be thought utterly essential that all the trustees be in place, it seems to me just as reasonable to interpret the provision for appointment of successor trustees (§9702(b)(2)) to include the power to fill vacancies arising from initial failure to appoint, as to interpret the initial appointment power to extend beyond its specified termination date. The provision surely does not establish the Court's proposition that time-limited mandates include continuing authority.

III

None of the cases on which the Court relies is even remotely in point. In Brock v. Pierce County, 476 U.S. 253 (1986), the agency action in question was authorized by an explicit statutory grant of authority, separate and apart from the provision that contained the time-limited mandate. Title 29 U.S.C. § 816(d)(1) (1976 ed., Supp. V) (now repealed), gave the Secretary of Labor "authority to . . . order such sanctions or corrective actions as are appropriate." Another provision of the statute, former §816(b), required the Secretary, when investigating a complaint that a recipient is misusing funds, to "make the final determination . . . regarding the truth of the allegation . . . not later than 120 days after receiving the complaint." We held that the Secretary's failure to meet the 120-day deadline did not prevent him from ordering repayment of misspent funds. Respondent had not, we said, shown anything that caused the Secretary to "lose its power to act," 476 U.S., at 260 (emphasis added). Here, by contrast, the Commissioner never had power to act apart from the mandate, which expired after October 1, 1993.

In United States v. James Daniel Good Real Property, 510 U.S. 43 (1993), federal statutes authorized the Government to bring a forfeiture action within a 5-year limitation period. 21 U.S.C. § 881(a)(7); 19 U.S.C. § 1621. We held that that power was not revoked by the Government's failure to comply with some of the separate "internal timing requirements" set forth in §§1602—1604. Because those provisions failed to specify a consequence for noncompliance, we refused to "impose [our] own coercive sanction" of terminating the Government's authority to bring a forfeiture action. James Daniel Good, supra, at 63. The authorization separate from the defaulted obligation was not affected. There is no authorization separate from the defaulted obligation here.

In United States v. Montalvo-Murillo, 495 U.S. 711 (1990), the statute at issue, 18 U.S.C. § 3142(e), gave courts power to order pretrial detention "after a hearing pursuant to the provisions of subsection (f) of this section." One of those provisions was that the hearing "shall be held immediately upon the person's first appearance before the judicial officer . . . ." §3142(f). The court had failed to hold a hearing immediately upon the respondent's first appearance, yet we held that the authority to order pretrial detention was unaffected. As we explained: "It is conceivable that some combination of procedural irregularities could render a detention hearing so flawed that it would not constitute 'a hearing pursuant to the provisions of subsection (f)' for purposes of §3142(e)," 495 U.S., at 717 (emphasis added), but the mere failure to comply with the first-appearance requirement did not alone have that effect. Once again, the case holds that an authorization separate from the defaulted obligation is not affected; and there is no authorization separate from the defaulted obligation here.

The contrast between these cases and the present ones demonstrates why the Court's extended discussion of whether Congress specified consequences for the Commissioner's failure to comply with the October 1 deadline, ante, at 12—14, is quite beside the point. A specification of termination of authority may be needed where there is a separate authorization to be canceled; it is utterly superfluous where the only authorization is contained in the time-limited mandate that has expired.

IV

That the Commissioner lacks authority to assign eligible beneficiaries after the statutory deadline is confirmed by other provisions of the Coal Act that are otherwise rendered incoherent.

A

The calculation of "death benefit premiums" and "unassigned beneficiaries premiums" owed by coal operators is based on an assigned operator's "applicable percentage," which is defined in §9704(f) as "the percentage determined by dividing the number of eligible beneficiaries assigned under section 9706 to such operator by the total number of eligible beneficiaries assigned under section 9706 to all such operators (determined on the basis of assignments as of October 1, 1993)." (Emphasis added.) The statute specifies only two circumstances in which adjustments may be made to an assigned operator's "applicable percentage": (1) when changes to the assignments "as of October 1, 1993," result from the appeals process set out in §9706(f), see §9704(f)(2)(A); and (2) when an assigned operator goes out of business, see §9704(f)(2)(B). No provision allows adjustments to account for post-October 1, 1993, initial assignments. This is perfectly consistent with the view that the §9706(a) power to assign does not extend beyond October 1, 1993; it is incompatible with the Court's holding to the contrary.

The Court's response to this structural dilemma is nothing short of astonishing. The Court concludes that the applicable percentage based on assignments as of October 1, 1993, may be adjusted to account for the subsequent initial assignments, notwithstanding the statutory command that the applicable percentage be determined "on the basis of assignments as of October 1, 1993," and notwithstanding the statute's provision of two, and only two, exceptions to this command that do not include post-October 1, 1993, initial assignments. "The enunciation of two exceptions," the Court says, "does not imply an exclusion of a third unless there is reason to think the third was at least considered." Ante, at 20. Here, "[s]ince Congress apparently never thought that initial assignments would be late, . . .the better inference is that what we face . . . is nothing more than a case unprovided for." Id., at 18—19 (referred to id., at 20). This is an unheard-of limitation upon the accepted principle of construction inclusio unius, exclusio alterius. See, e.g., O'Melveny & Myers v. FDIC, 512 U.S. 79, 86 (1994); Leatherman v. Tarrant County Narcotics Intelligence and Coordination Unit, 507 U.S. 163, 168 (1993). It is also an absurd limitation, since it means that the more unimaginable an unlisted item is, the more likely it is not to be excluded. Does this new maxim mean, for example, that exceptions to the hearsay rule beyond those set forth in the Federal Rules of Evidence must be recognized if it is unlikely that Congress (or perhaps the Rules committee) "considered" those unnamed exceptions? Our cases do not support such a proposition. See, e.g., Williamson v. United States, 512 U.S. 594 (1994); United States v. Salerno, 505 U.S. 317 (1992).3 There is no more reason to make a "case unprovided for" exception to the clear import of an exclusive listing than there is to make such an exception to any other clear textual disposition. In a way, therefore, the Court's treatment of this issue has ample precedent—in those many wrongly decided cases that replace what the legislature said, with what courts thinks the legislature would have said (i.e., in the judges' estimation should have said) if it had only "considered" unanticipated consequences of what it did say (of which the courts disapprove). In any event, the relevant question here is not whether §9704(f)(2) excludes other grounds for adjustments to the applicable percentage, but rather whether anything in the statute affirmatively authorizes them. The answer to that question is no—an answer that should not surprise the Court, given its acknowledgment that Congress "did not foresee a failure to make timely assignments." Ante, at 20.

B

Post-October 1, 1993, initial assignments can also not be reconciled with the Coal Act's provisions regarding appointments to the board of trustees. Section 9702(b)(1)(B) establishes for the Combined Fund a board of seven members, one of whom is to be "designated by the three employers . . . who have been assigned the greatest number of eligible beneficiaries under section 9706." The Act provides for an "initial trustee" to fill this position pending completion of the assignment process, but §9702(b)(3)(B) permits this initial trustee to serve only "until November 1, 1993." It is evident, therefore, that the "three employers . . . who have been assigned the greatest number of eligible beneficiaries under section 9706" must be known by November 1, 1993. It is simply inconceivable that the three appointing employers were to be unknown (and the post left unfilled) until the Commissioner completes an open-ended assignment process—whenever that might be; or that the designated trustee is constantly to change, as the identity of the "three employers . . . who have been assigned the greatest number of eligible beneficiaries under section 9706" constantly changes.

V

At bottom, the Court's reading of the Coal Act—its confident filling in of provisions to cover "cases not provided for"—rests upon its perception that the statute's overriding goal is accuracy in assignments. That is a foundation of sand. The Coal Act is demonstrably not a scheme that requires, or even attempts to require, a perfect match between each beneficiary and the coal operator most responsible for that beneficiary's health care. It provides, at best, rough justice; seemingly unfair and inequitable provisions abound.

When, for example, an operator goes out of business, §9704(f)(2)(B) provides that beneficiaries previously assigned to that operator must go into the unassigned pool for purposes of calculating the "applicable percentage." It makes no provision for them to be reassigned to another operator, even if another operator might qualify under §§9706(a)(1)—(3). That is hardly compatible with a scheme that is keen on "accuracy of assignments," and that envisions perpetual assignment authority in the Commissioner.

To account for the existence of §9704(f)(2)(B), the Court retreats to the more nuanced position that the Coal Act prefers accuracy over finality only "in the first assignment," ante, at 19, n. 12. Why it should have this strange preference for perfection in virgin assignments is a mystery. One might understand insisting upon as perfect a match-up as possible up to October 1, 1993, and then prohibiting future changes, both by way of initial assignment or otherwise; that would assure an initial system that is as near perfect as possible, but abstain from future adjustments that upset expectations and render sales of companies more difficult. But what is the conceivable reason for insistence upon perfection in initial assignments, whether made before the deadline or afterward?4 As it is, however, the Act does not insist upon accuracy in initial assignments, not even in those made before the deadline. For each assigned beneficiary, only one signatory operator is held responsible for health benefits, even if that miner had worked for other signatory operators that should in perfect fairness share the responsibility.

The reality is that the Coal Act reflects a compromise between the goals of perfection in assignments and finality. It provides some accuracy in initial assignments along with some repose to signatory operators, who are given full notice of their obligations by October 1, 1993, and can plan their business accordingly without the surprise of new (and retroactive) liabilities imposed by the Commissioner. It is naive for the Court to rely on guesses as to what Congress would have wanted in legislation as complicated as this, the culmination of a long, drawn-out legislative battle in which, as we put it in Barnhart v. Sigmon Coal Co., 534 U.S. 438, 461 (2002), "highly interested parties attempt[ed] to pull the provisions in different directions." The best way to be faithful to the resulting compromise is to follow the statute's text, as I have done above—not to impute to Congress one statutory objective favored by the majority of this Court at the expense of other, equally plausible, statutory objectives.

* * *

I think it clear from the text of §9706(a) and other provisions of the Coal Act that the Commissioner lacks authority to assign eligible beneficiaries to signatory operators on or after October 1, 1993. I respectfully dissent from the Court's judgment to the contrary.

Notes

1. This interpretation of §9706(a) does not "assum[e] away the very question to be decided," as the Court accuses, ante, at 8, n. 6. It is no assumption at all, but rather the consequence of the proposition that the scope of an agency's power is determined by the text of the statutory grant of authority. Because §9706(a)'s power to "assign . . . eligible beneficiar[ies]" is prefaced by the phrase "before October 1, 1993," the statutory date is intertwined with the grant of authority; it is part of the very definition of the

Commissioner's power. If the statute provided that the Commissioner "shall, on or after October 1, 1993," assign each eligible beneficiary to a signatory operator, it would surely be beyond dispute that pre-October 1, 1993, assignments were ineffective. No different conclusion should obtain here, where the temporal scope of the Commissioner's authority is likewise defined according to a clear and unambiguous date. If this is (as the Court charges) "formalism," ante, at 8—9, n. 6, it is only because language is a matter of form. Here the form that Congress chose presumptively represents the political compromise that Congress arrived at.

   2. Private entities, unlike administrative agencies, do not need authorization from Congress in order to act—they have the power to take all action within the scope of their charter, unless and until the law forbids it. The Court suggests that the Employee Retirement Income Security Act of 1974 (ERISA) may actually forbid the UMWA Pension Plan from transferring its pension surplus to the benefit fund. Ante, at 11, n. 8. But if this is true, that does not convert §9705(a)(1) into a power-conferring statutory provision in the mold of §9706(a). It instead means that the UMWA Pension Plan is subject to contradictory statutory mandates, and the relevant question becomes whether, and to what extent, §9705(a)(1) implicitly repealed the provisions of ERISA as applied to the UMWA Pension Plan. Resolving that question would be no small task, given our disinclination to find implied repeals, see Morton v. Mancari, 417 U. S. 535, 551 (1974), and I will not speculate on it. Instead, I am content to go along with the Court's assumption that nothing in §9705(a)(1), or in the rest of the Coal Act, prevents the UMWA Pension Plan from transferring money to the Combined Fund after the statutory deadline, and to emphasize that nothing in this concession lends support to the Court's interpretation of §9706(a).

   3. The most enduring consequence of today's opinion may well be its gutting of the ancient canon of construction. It speaks volumes about the dearth of precedent for the Court's position that the principal case it relies upon, ante, at 18, is Chevron U. S. A. Inc. v. Echazabal, 536 U. S. 73 (2002). The express language of the statute interpreted in that case demonstrated that the single enumerated example of a "qualification standard" was illustrative rather than exhaustive: "The term 'qualification standards' may include a requirement that an individual shall not pose any direct threat to the health or safety of other individuals in the workplace." 42 U. S. C. § 12113(b) (emphasis added). Little wonder that the Court did not find in that text "an omission [that] bespeaks a negative implication," 536 U. S., at 81. And of course the opinion said nothing about the requirement (central to the Court's analysis today) that it be "fair to suppose that Congress considered the unnamed possibility," ante, at 18.

   4. The Court points to §9706(f)'s review process in support of its view that the Coal Act envisions "accuracy 'in inital assignments, whether made before the deadline or afterward.' " Ante, at 19, n. 12 (emphasis deleted). In fact it shows the opposite—reflecting the statute's trade-offs between the competing objectives of accuracy in assignments and finality. Sections 9706(f)(1) and (f)(2) provide time limits for coal operators to request

reconsideration by the Commissioner; errors discovered after these time limits have passed are forever closed from correction. (Unless, of course, the Court chooses, in the interest of accuracy in assignments, to ignore those time limits, just as it has ignored the time limit of §9706(a).)

Justice Scalia's concurrence and dissent in Grutter v. Bollinger (June 23, 2003)

Justice Scalia, with whom Justice Thomas joins, concurring in part and dissenting in part.

I join the opinion of The Chief Justice. As he demonstrates, the University of Michigan Law School's mystical "critical mass" justification for its discrimination by race challenges even the most gullible mind. The admissions statistics show it to be a sham to cover a scheme of racially proportionate admissions.

I also join Parts I through VII of Justice Thomas's opinion. I find particularly unanswerable his central point: that the allegedly "compelling state interest" at issue here is not the incremental "educational benefit" that emanates from the fabled "critical mass" of minority students, but rather Michigan's interest in maintaining a "prestige" law school whose normal admissions standards disproportionately exclude blacks and other minorities. If that is a compelling state interest, everything is.

I add the following: The "educational benefit" that the University of Michigan seeks to achieve by racial discrimination consists, according to the Court, of " 'cross-racial understanding,' " ante, at 18, and " 'better prepar[ation of] students for an increasingly diverse workforce and society,' " ibid., all of which is necessary not only for work, but also for good "citizenship," ante, at 19. This is not, of course, an "educational benefit" on which students will be graded on their Law School transcript (Works and Plays Well with Others: B+) or tested by the bar examiners (Q: Describe in 500 words or less your cross-racial understanding). For it is a lesson of life rather than law—essentially the same lesson taught to (or rather learned by, for it cannot be "taught" in the usual sense) people three feet shorter and twenty years younger than the full-grown adults at the University of Michigan Law School, in institutions ranging from Boy Scout troops to public-school kindergartens. If properly considered an "educational benefit" at all, it is surely not one that is either uniquely relevant to law school or uniquely "teachable" in a formal educational setting. And therefore: If it is appropriate for the University of Michigan Law School to use racial discrimination for the purpose of putting together a "critical mass" that will convey generic lessons in socialization and good citizenship, surely it is no less appropriate—indeed, particularly appropriate—for the civil service system of the State of Michigan to do so. There, also, those exposed to "critical masses" of certain races will presumably become better Americans, better Michiganders, better civil servants. And surely private employers cannot be criticized—indeed, should be praised—if they also "teach" good citizenship to their adult employees through a patriotic, all-American system of racial discrimination in hiring. The nonminority individuals who are deprived of a legal education, a civil service job, or any job at all by reason of their skin color will surely understand.

Unlike a clear constitutional holding that racial preferences in state educational institutions are impermissible, or even a clear anticonstitutional holding that racial preferences in state educational institutions are OK, today's Grutter-Gratz split double header seems perversely designed to prolong the controversy and the litigation. Some future lawsuits will presumably focus on whether the discriminatory scheme in question contains enough evaluation of the applicant "as an individual," ante, at 24, and sufficiently avoids "separate admissions tracks" ante, at 22, to fall under Grutter rather than Gratz. Some will focus on whether a university has gone beyond the bounds of a " 'good faith effort' " and has so zealously pursued its "critical mass" as to make it an unconstitutional de facto quota system, rather than merely " 'a permissible goal.' " Ante, at 23 (quoting Sheet Metal Workers v. EEOC, 478 U. S 421, 495 (1986) (O'Connor, J., concurring in part and dissenting in part)). Other lawsuits may focus on whether, in the particular setting at issue, any educational benefits flow from racial diversity. (That issue was not contested in Grutter; and while the opinion accords "a degree of deference to a university's academic decisions," ante, at 16, "deference does not imply abandonment or abdication of judicial review," Miller-El v. Cockrell, 537 U.S. 322, 340 (2003).) Still other suits may challenge the bona fides of the institution's expressed commitment to the educational benefits of diversity that immunize the discriminatory scheme in Grutter. (Tempting targets, one would suppose, will be those universities that talk the talk of multiculturalism and racial diversity in the courts but walk the walk of tribalism and racial segregation on their campuses–through minority-only student organizations, separate minority housing opportunities, separate minority student centers, even separate minority-only graduation ceremonies.) And still other suits may claim that the institution's racial preferences have gone below or above the mystical Grutter-approved "critical mass." Finally, litigation can be expected on behalf of minority groups intentionally short changed in the institution's composition of its generic minority "critical mass." I do not look forward to any of these cases. The Constitution proscribes government discrimination on the basis of race, and state-provided education is no exception.

*. Part VII of Justice Thomas's opinion describes those portions of the Court's opinion in which I concur. See post, at 27—31.

Justice Scalia's dissent in Lawrence v. Texas (June 26, 2003) [Excerpt]

Justice Scalia, with whom The Chief Justice and Justice Thomas join, dissenting.
[. . .]
Let me be clear that I have nothing against homosexuals, or any other group, promoting their agenda through normal democratic means. Social perceptions of sexual and other morality change over time, and every group has the right to persuade its fellow

citizens that its view of such matters is the best. That homosexuals have achieved some success in that enterprise is attested to by the fact that Texas is one of the few remaining States that criminalize private, consensual homosexual acts. But persuading one's fellow citizens is one thing, and imposing one's views in absence of democratic majority will is something else. I would no more require a State to criminalize homosexual acts–or, for that matter, display any moral disapprobation of them–than I would forbid it to do so. What Texas has chosen to do is well within the range of traditional democratic action, and its hand should not be stayed through the invention of a brand-new "constitutional right" by a Court that is impatient of democratic change. It is indeed true that "later generations can see that laws once thought necessary and proper in fact serve only to oppress," ante, at 18; and when that happens, later generations can repeal those laws. But it is the premise of our system that those judgments are to be made by the people, and not imposed by a governing caste that knows best.

One of the benefits of leaving regulation of this matter to the people rather than to the courts is that the people, unlike judges, need not carry things to their logical conclusion. [. . .]

Justice Scalia's concurrence and dissent in McConnell v. FEC (Dec 10, 2003)

Justice Scalia, concurring with respect to BCRA Titles III and IV, dissenting with respect to BCRA Titles I and V, and concurring in the judgment in part and dissenting in part with respect to BCRA Title II.

With respect to Titles I, II, and V: I join in full the dissent of The Chief Justice; I join the opinion of Justice Kennedy, except to the extent it upholds new §323(e) of the Federal Election Campaign Act of 1971 (FECA) and §202 of the Bipartisan Campaign Reform Act of 2002 (BCRA) in part; and because I continue to believe that Buckley v. Valeo, 424 U.S. 1 (1976) (per curiam), was wrongly decided, I also join Parts I, II—A, and II—B of the opinion of Justice Thomas. With respect to Titles III and IV, I join The Chief Justice's opinion for the Court. Because these cases are of such extraordinary importance, I cannot avoid adding to the many writings a few words of my own.

This is a sad day for the freedom of speech. Who could have imagined that the same Court which, within the past four years, has sternly disapproved of restrictions upon such inconsequential forms of expression as virtual child pornography, Ashcroft v. Free Speech Coalition, 535 U.S. 234 (2002), tobacco advertising, Lorillard Tobacco Co. v. Reilly, 533 U.S. 525 (2001), dissemination of illegally intercepted communications, Bartnicki v. Vopper, 532 U.S. 514 (2001), and sexually explicit cable programming, United States v. Playboy Entertainment Group, Inc., 529 U.S. 803 (2000), would smile with favor upon a law that cuts to the heart of what the First Amendment is meant to protect: the right to criticize the government. For that is what the most offensive provisions of this legislation are all about. We are governed by Congress, and this legislation prohibits the criticism of Members of Congress by those entities most capable of giving such criticism loud voice: national political parties and corporations, both of the commercial and the not-for-profit sort. It forbids pre-election criticism of incumbents by corporations, even not-for-profit corporations, by use of their general funds; and forbids national-party use of "soft" money to fund "issue ads" that incumbents find so offensive.

To be sure, the legislation is evenhanded: It similarly prohibits criticism of the candidates who oppose Members of Congress in their reelection bids. But as everyone knows, this is an area in which evenhandedness is not fairness. If all electioneering were evenhandedly prohibited, incumbents would have an enormous advantage. Likewise, if incumbents and challengers are limited to the same quantity of electioneering, incumbents are favored. In other words, any restriction upon a type of campaign speech that is equally available to challengers and incumbents tends to favor incumbents.

Beyond that, however, the present legislation targets for prohibition certain categories of campaign speech that are particularly harmful to incumbents. Is it accidental, do you think, that incumbents raise about three times as much "hard money"—the sort of funding generally not restricted by this legislation—as do their challengers? See FEC, 1999—2000 Financial Activity of All Senate and House Campaigns (Jan. 1, 1999—Dec. 31, 2000) (last modified on May 15, 2001), http://www.fec.gov/press/051501congfinact/tables/allcong2000.xls (all Internet ma-terials as visited Dec. 4, 2003, and available in Clerk of Court's case file). Or that lobbyists (who seek the favor of incumbents) give 92 percent of their money in "hard" contributions? See U.S. Public Interest Research Group (PIRG), The Lobbyist's Last Laugh: How K Street Lobbyists Would Benefit from the McCain-Feingold Campaign Finance Bill 3 (July 5, 2001), http://www.pirg.org/democracy/democracy.asp?id2=5068. Is it an oversight, do you suppose, that the so-called "millionaire provisions" raise the contribution limit for a candidate running against an individual who devotes to the campaign (as challengers often do) great personal wealth, but do not raise the limit for a candidate running against an individual who devotes to the campaign (as incumbents often do) a massive election "war chest"? See BCRA §§304, 316, and 319. And is it mere happenstance, do you estimate, that national-party funding, which is severely limited by the Act, is more likely to assist cash-strapped challengers than flush-with-hard-money incumbents? See A. Gierzynski & D. Breaux, The Financing Role of Parties, in Campaign Finance in State Legislative Elections 195—200 (J. Thompson & S. Moncrief eds. 1998). Was it unintended, by any chance, that incumbents are free personally to receive some soft money and even to solicit it for other organizations, while national parties are not? See new FECA §§323(a) and (e).

I wish to address three fallacious propositions that might be thought to justify some or all of the provisions of this legislation—only the last of which is explicitly embraced by the principal opinion for the Court, but all of which underlie, I think, its approach to these cases.

(a) Money is Not Speech

It was said by congressional proponents of this legislation, see 143 Cong. Rec. 20746 (1997) (remarks of Sen. Boxer), 145 Cong. Rec. S12612 (Oct. 14, 1999) (remarks of

Sen. Cleland), 147 Cong. Rec. S2436 (Mar. 19, 2001) (remarks of Sen. Dodd), with support from the law reviews, see, e.g., Wright, Politics and the Constitution: Is Money Speech?, 85 Yale L. J. 1001 (1976), that since this legislation regulates nothing but the expenditure of money for speech, as opposed to speech itself, the burden it imposes is not subject to full First Amendment scrutiny; the government may regulate the raising and spending of campaign funds just as it regulates other forms of conduct, such as burning draft cards, see United States v. O'Brien, 391 U.S. 367 (1968), or camping out on the National Mall, see Clark v. Community for Creative Non-Violence, 468 U.S. 288 (1984). That proposition has been endorsed by one of the two authors of today's principal opinion: "The right to use one's own money to hire gladiators, [and] to fund 'speech by proxy,' ... [are] property rights . . . not entitled to the same protection as the right to say what one pleases." Nixon v. Shrink Missouri Government PAC, 528 U.S. 377, 399 (2000) (Stevens, J., concurring). Until today, however, that view has been categorically rejected by our jurisprudence. As we said in Buckley, 424 U.S., at 16, "this Court has never suggested that the dependence of a communication on the expenditure of money operates itself to introduce a nonspeech element or to reduce the exacting scrutiny required by the First Amendment."

Our traditional view was correct, and today's cavalier attitude toward regulating the financing of speech (the "exacting scrutiny" test of Buckley, see ibid., is not uttered in any majority opinion, and is not observed in the ones from which I dissent) frustrates the fundamental purpose of the First Amendment. In any economy operated on even the most rudimentary principles of division of labor, effective public communication requires the speaker to make use of the services of others. An author may write a novel, but he will seldom publish and distribute it himself. A freelance reporter may write a story, but he will rarely edit, print, and deliver it to subscribers. To a government bent on suppressing speech, this mode of organization presents opportunities: Control any cog in the machine, and you can halt the whole apparatus. License printers, and it matters little whether authors are still free to write. Restrict the sale of books, and it matters little who prints them. Predictably, repressive regimes have exploited these principles by attacking all levels of the production and dissemination of ideas. See, e.g., Printing Act of 1662, 14 Car. II, c. 33, §§1, 4, 7 (punishing printers, importers, and booksellers); Printing Act of 1649, 2 Acts and Ordinances of the Interregnum 245, 246, 250 (punishing authors, printers, booksellers, importers, and buyers). In response to this threat, we have interpreted the First Amendment broadly. See, e.g., Bantam Books, Inc. v. Sullivan, 372 U.S. 58, 65, n. 6 (1963) ("The constitutional guarantee of freedom of the press embraces the circulation of books as well as their publication ...").

Division of labor requires a means of mediating exchange, and in a commercial society, that means is supplied by money. The publisher pays the author for the right to sell his book; it pays its staff who print and assemble the book; it demands payments from booksellers who bring the book to market. This, too, presents opportunities for repression: Instead of regulating the various parties to the enterprise individually, the government can suppress their ability to coordinate by regulating their use of money. What good is the right to print books without a right to buy works from authors? Or the right to publish newspapers without the right to pay deliverymen? The right to speak would be largely ineffective if it did not include the right to engage in financial transactions that are the incidents of its exercise.

This is not to say that any regulation of money is a regulation of speech. The government may apply general commercial regulations to those who use money for speech if it applies them evenhandedly to those who use money for other purposes. But where the government singles out money used to fund speech as its legislative object, it is acting against speech as such, no less than if it had targeted the paper on which a book was printed or the trucks that deliver it to the bookstore.

History and jurisprudence bear this out. The best early examples derive from the British efforts to tax the press after the lapse of licensing statutes by which the press was first regulated. The Stamp Act of 1712 imposed levies on all newspapers, including an additional tax for each advertisement. 10 Anne, c. 18, §113. It was a response to unfavorable war coverage, "obvious[ly] ... designed to check the publication of those newspapers and pamphlets which depended for their sale on their cheapness and sensationalism." F. Siebert, Freedom of the Press in England, 1476–1776, pp. 309–310 (1952). It succeeded in killing off approximately half the newspapers in England in its first year. Id., at 312. In 1765, Parliament applied a similar Act to the Colonies. 5 Geo. III, c. 12, §1. The colonial Act likewise placed exactions on sales and advertising revenue, the latter at 2s. per advertisement, which was "by any standard . . . excessive, since the publisher himself received only from 3 to 5s. and still less for repeated insertions." A. Schlesinger, Prelude to Independence: The Newspaper War on Britain, 1764–1776, p. 68 (1958). The founding generation saw these taxes as grievous incursions on the freedom of the press. See, e.g., 1 D. Ramsay, History of the American Revolution 61–62 (L. Cohen ed. 1990); J. Adams, A Dissertation on the Canon and Feudal Law (1765), reprinted in 3 Life and Works of John Adams 445, 464 (C. Adams ed. 1851). See generally Grosjean v. American Press Co., 297 U.S. 233, 245–249 (1936); Schlesinger, supra, at 67–84.

We have kept faith with the Founders' tradition by prohibiting the selective taxation of the press. Minneapolis Star & Tribune Co. v. Minnesota Comm'r of Revenue, 460 U.S. 575 (1983) (ink and paper tax); Grosjean, supra (advertisement tax). And we have done so whether the tax was the product of illicit motive or not. See Minneapolis Star & Tribune Co., supra, at 592. These press-taxation cases belie the claim that regulation of money used to fund speech is not regulation of speech itself. A tax on a newspaper's advertising revenue does not prohibit anyone from saying anything; it merely appropriates part of the revenue that a speaker would otherwise obtain. That is even a step short of totally prohibiting advertising revenue–which would be analogous to the total prohibition of certain campaign-speech contributions in the present cases. Yet it is unquestionably a violation of the First Amendment.

Many other cases exemplify the same principle that an attack upon the funding of speech is an attack upon speech itself. In Schaumburg v. Citizens for a Better

Environment, 444 U.S. 620 (1980), we struck down an ordinance limiting the amount charities could pay their solicitors. In Simon & Schuster, Inc. v. Members of N. Y. State Crime Victims Bd., 502 U.S. 105 (1991), we held unconstitutional a state statute that appropriated the proceeds of criminals' biographies for payment to the victims. And in Rosenberger v. Rector and Visitors of Univ. of Va., 515 U.S. 819 (1995), we held unconstitutional a university's discrimination in the disbursement of funds to speakers on the basis of viewpoint. Most notable, perhaps, is our famous opinion in New York Times Co. v. Sullivan, 376 U.S. 254 (1964), holding that paid advertisements in a newspaper were entitled to full First Amendment protection:

"Any other conclusion would discourage newspapers from carrying 'editorial advertisements' of this type, and so might shut off an important outlet for the promulgation of information and ideas by persons who do not themselves have access to publishing facilities–who wish to exercise their freedom of speech even though they are not members of the press. The effect would be to shackle the First Amendment in its attempt to secure 'the widest possible dissemination of information from diverse and antagonistic sources.'" Id., at 266 (citations omitted).

This passage was relied on in Buckley for the point that restrictions on the expenditure of money for speech are equivalent to restrictions on speech itself. 424 U.S., at 16–17. That reliance was appropriate. If denying protection to paid-for speech would "shackle the First Amendment," so also does forbidding or limiting the right to pay for speech.

It should be obvious, then, that a law limiting the amount a person can spend to broadcast his political views is a direct restriction on speech. That is no different from a law limiting the amount a newspaper can pay its editorial staff or the amount a charity can pay its leafletters. It is equally clear that a limit on the amount a candidate can raise from any one individual for the purpose of speaking is also a direct limitation on speech. That is no different from a law limiting the amount a publisher can accept from any one shareholder or lender, or the amount a newspaper can charge any one advertiser or customer.

(b) Pooling Money is Not Speech

Another proposition which could explain at least some of the results of today's opinion is that the First Amendment right to spend money for speech does not include the right to combine with others in spending money for speech. Such a proposition fits uncomfortably with the concluding words of our Declaration of Independence: "And for the support of this Declaration, . . . we mutually pledge to each other our Lives, our Fortunes and our sacred Honor." (Emphasis added.) The freedom to associate with others for the dissemination of ideas–not just by singing or speaking in unison, but by pooling financial resources for expressive purposes–is part of the freedom of speech.

"Our form of government is built on the premise that every citizen shall have the right to engage in political expression and association. This right was enshrined in the First Amendment of the Bill of Rights. Exercise of these basic freedoms in America has traditionally been through the media of political associations. Any interference with the freedom of a party is simultaneously an interference with the freedom of its adherents." NAACP v. Button, 371 U.S. 415, 431 (1963) (internal quotation marks omitted).

"The First Amendment protects political association as well as political expression. The constitutional right of association explicated in NAACP v. Alabama, 357 U.S. 449, 460 (1958), stemmed from the Court's recognition that '[e]ffective advocacy of both public and private points of view, particularly controversial ones, is undeniably enhanced by group association.' Subsequent decisions have made clear that the First and Fourteenth Amendments guarantee ' "freedom to associate with others for the common advancement of political beliefs and ideas," ' ... ." Buckley, supra, at 15.

We have said that "implicit in the right to engage in activities protected by the First Amendment" is "a corresponding right to associate with others in pursuit of a wide variety of political, social, economic, educational, religious, and cultural ends." Roberts v. United States Jaycees, 468 U.S. 609, 622 (1984). That "right to associate . . . in pursuit" includes the right to pool financial resources.

If it were otherwise, Congress would be empowered to enact legislation requiring newspapers to be sole proprietorships, banning their use of partnership or corporate form. That sort of restriction would be an obvious violation of the First Amendment, and it is incomprehensible why the conclusion should change when what is at issue is the pooling of funds for the most important (and most perennially threatened) category of speech: electoral speech. The principle that such financial association does not enjoy full First Amendment protection threatens the existence of all political parties.

(c) Speech by Corporations Can Be Abridged

The last proposition that might explain at least some of today's casual abridgment of free-speech rights is this: that the particular form of association known as a corporation does not enjoy full First Amendment protection. Of course the text of the First Amendment does not limit its application in this fashion, even though "[b]y the end of the eighteenth century the corporation was a familiar figure in American economic life." C. Cooke, Corporation, Trust and Company 92 (1951). Nor is there any basis in reason why First Amendment rights should not attach to corporate associations—and we have said so. In First Nat. Bank of Boston v. Bellotti, 435 U.S. 765 (1978), we held unconstitutional a state prohibition of corporate speech designed to influence the vote on referendum proposals. We said:

"[T]here is practically universal agreement that a major purpose of [the First] Amendment was to protect the free discussion of governmental affairs. If the speakers here were not corporations, no one would suggest that the State could silence their proposed speech. It is the type of speech indispensable to decision-making in a democracy, and this is no less true because the speech comes from a corporation rather than an individual. The inherent worth of the speech in terms of its capacity for informing the public does not depend upon the identity of its source, whether corporation, association, union, or individual." Id., at 776—777 (internal quotation marks, footnotes, and citations omitted).

In NAACP v. Button, supra, at 428—429, 431, we held that the NAACP could assert First Amendment rights "on its own behalf, . . . though a corporation," and that the activities of the corporation were "modes of expression and association protected by the First and Fourteenth Amendments." In Pacific Gas & Elec. Co. v. Public Util. Comm'n of Cal., 475 U.S. 1, 8 (1986), we held unconstitutional a state effort to compel corporate speech. "The identity of the speaker," we said, "is not decisive in determining whether speech is protected. Corporations and other associations, like individuals, contribute to the 'discussion, debate, and the dissemination of information and ideas' that the First Amendment seeks to foster." And in Buckley, 424 U.S. 1, we held unconstitutional FECA's limitation upon independent corporate expenditures.

The Court changed course in Austin v. Michigan Chamber of Commerce, 494 U.S. 652 (1990), upholding a state prohibition of an independent corporate expenditure in support of a candidate for state office. I dissented in that case, see id., at 679, and remain of the view that it was error. In the modern world, giving the government power to exclude corporations from the political debate enables it effectively to muffle the voices that best represent the most significant segments of the economy and the most passionately held social and political views. People who associate—who pool their financial resources—for purposes of economic enterprise overwhelmingly do so in the corporate form; and with increasing frequency, incorporation is chosen by those who associate to defend and promote particular ideas—such as the American Civil Liberties Union and the National Rifle Association, parties to these cases. Imagine, then, a government that wished to suppress nuclear power—or oil and gas exploration, or automobile manufacturing, or gun ownership, or civil liberties—and that had the power to prohibit corporate advertising against its proposals. To be sure, the individuals involved in, or benefited by, those industries, or interested in those causes, could (given enough time) form political action committees or other associations to make their case. But the organizational form in which those enterprises already exist, and in which they can most quickly and most effectively get their message across, is the corporate form. The First Amendment does not in my view permit the restriction of that political speech. And the same holds true for corporate electoral speech: A candidate should not be insulated from the most effective speech that the major participants in the economy and major incorporated interest groups can generate.

But what about the danger to the political system posed by "amassed wealth"? The most direct threat from that source comes in the form of undisclosed favors and payoffs to elected officials—which have already been criminalized, and will be rendered no more discoverable by the legislation at issue here. The use of corporate wealth (like individual wealth) to speak to the electorate is unlikely to "distort" elections—especially if disclosure requirements tell the people where the speech is coming from. The premise of the First Amendment is that the American people are neither sheep nor fools, and hence fully capable of considering both the substance of the speech presented to them and its proximate and ultimate source. If that premise is wrong, our democracy has a much greater problem to overcome than merely the influence of amassed wealth. Given the premises of democracy, there is no such thing as too much speech.

But, it is argued, quite apart from its effect upon the electorate, corporate speech in the form of contributions to the candidate's campaign, or even in the form of independent expenditures supporting the candidate, engenders an obligation which is later paid in the form of greater access to the officeholder, or indeed in the form of votes on particular bills. Any quid-pro-quo agreement for votes would of course violate criminal law, see 18 U.S.C. § 201 and actual payoff votes have not even been claimed by those favoring the restrictions on corporate speech. It cannot be denied, however, that corporate (like noncorporate) allies will have greater access to the officeholder, and that he will tend to favor the same causes as those who support him (which is usually why they supported him). That is the nature of politics–if not indeed human nature–and how this can properly be considered "corruption" (or "the appearance of corruption") with regard to corporate allies and not with regard to other allies is beyond me. If the Bill of Rights had intended an exception to the freedom of speech in order to combat this malign proclivity of the officeholder to agree with those who agree with him, and to speak more with his supporters than his opponents, it would surely have said so. It did not do so, I think, because the juice is not worth the squeeze. Evil corporate (and private affluent) influences are well enough checked (so long as adequate campaign-expenditure disclosure rules exist) by the politician's fear of being portrayed as "in the pocket" of so-called moneyed interests. The incremental benefit obtained by muzzling corporate speech is more than offset by loss of the information and persuasion that corporate speech can contain. That, at least, is the assumption of a constitutional guarantee which prescribes that Congress shall make no law abridging the freedom of speech.

But let us not be deceived. While the Government's briefs and arguments before this Court focused on the horrible "appearance of corruption," the most passionate floor statements during the debates on this legislation pertained to so-called attack ads, which the Constitution surely protects, but which Members of Congress analogized to "crack cocaine," 144 Cong. Rec. S868 (Feb. 24, 1998) (remarks of Sen. Daschle), "drive-by shooting[s]," id., at S879 (remarks of Sen. Durbin), and "air pollution," 143 Cong. Rec. 20505 (1997) (remarks of Sen. Dorgan). There is good reason to believe that the ending of negative campaign ads was the principal attraction of the legislation. A Senate sponsor said, "I hope that we will not allow our attention to be distracted from the real issues at hand–how to raise the tenor of the debate in our elections and give people real choices. No one benefits from negative ads. They don't aid our Nation's political dialog." Id., at 20521–20522 (remarks of Sen. McCain). He assured the body that "[y]ou cut off the soft money, you are going to see a lot less of that [attack ads]. Prohibit unions and corporations, and you will see a lot less of that. If you demand full disclosure for those who pay for those ads, you are going to see a lot less of that . . . ." 147 Cong. Rec. S3116 (Mar. 29, 2001) (remarks of Sen. McCain). See also, e.g., 148 Cong. Rec. S2117 (Mar. 20, 2002) (remarks of Sen. Cantwell) ("This bill is about slowing the ad war. . . . It is about slowing political advertising and making sure the flow of negative ads by outside interest groups does not continue to permeate the airwaves"); 143 Cong. Rec. 20746 (1997) (remarks of Sen. Boxer) ("These so-called issues ads are not regulated at all and mention candidates by name. They directly attack candidates without any accountability. It is brutal.... . We have an opportunity in the McCain-Feingold bill to stop that . . ."); 145 Cong. Rec. S12606–S12607 (Oct. 14, 1999) (remarks of Sen. Wellstone) ("I think these issue advocacy ads are a nightmare. I think all of us should hate them.... . [By passing the legislation], [w]e could get some of this poison politics off television").

Another theme prominent in the legislative debates was the notion that there is too much money spent on elections. The first principle of "reform" was that "there should be less money in politics." 147 Cong. Rec. S3236 (Apr. 2, 2001) (remarks of Sen. Murray). "The enormous amounts of special interest money that flood our political system have become a cancer in our democracy." 148 Cong. Rec. S2151 (Mar. 20, 2002) (remarks of Sen. Kennedy). "[L]arge sums of money drown out the voice of the average voter." 148 Cong. Rec. H373 (Feb. 13, 2002) (remarks of Rep. Langevin). The system of campaign finance is "drowning in money." Id., at H404 (remarks of Rep. Menendez). And most expansively:

"Despite the ever-increasing sums spent on campaigns, we have not seen an improvement in campaign discourse, issue discussion or voter education. More money does not mean more ideas, more substance or more depth. Instead, it means more of what voters complain about most. More 30-second spots, more negativity and an increasingly longer campaign period." 148 Cong. Rec. S2150 (Mar. 20, 2002) (remarks of Sen. Kerry).

Perhaps voters do detest these 30-second spots–though I suspect they detest even more hour-long campaign-debate interruptions of their favorite entertainment programming. Evidently, however, these ads do persuade voters, or else they would not be so routinely used by sophisticated politicians of all parties. The point, in any event, is that it is not the proper role of those who govern us to judge which campaign speech has "substance" and "depth" (do you think it might be that which is least damaging to incumbents?) and to abridge the rest.

And what exactly are these outrageous sums frittered away in determining who will govern us? A report prepared for Congress concluded that the total amount, in hard and soft money, spent on the 2000 federal elections was between $2.4 and $2.5 billion. J. Cantor, CRS Report for Congress, Campaign Finance in the 2000 Federal Elections: Overview and Estimates of the Flow of Money (2001). All campaign spending in the United States, including state elections, ballot initiatives, and judicial elections, has been estimated at $3.9 billion for 2000, Nelson, Spending in the 2000 Elections, in Financing the 2000 Election 24, Tbl. 2–1 (D. Magleby ed. 2002), which was a year that "shattered spending and contribution records," id., at 22. Even taking this last, larger figure as the benchmark, it means that Americans spent about half as much electing all their Nation's officials, state and federal, as they spent on movie tickets ($7.8 billion); about a fifth as much as they spent on cosmetics and perfume ($18.8 billion); and about a sixth as much as they spent on pork (the nongovernmental sort) ($22.8 billion). See U.S. Dept. of Commerce, Bureau of Economic Analysis, Tbl. 2.6U (Col. AS; Rows 356, 214, and 139), http:// www.bea.doc.gov/bea/dn/206u.csv. If our democracy is drowning from this much spending, it cannot swim.

* * *

Which brings me back to where I began: This litigation is about preventing criticism of the government. I cannot say for certain that many, or some, or even any, of the Members of Congress who voted for this legislation did so not to produce "fairer" campaigns, but to mute criticism of their records and facilitate reelection. Indeed, I will stipulate that all those who voted for the Act believed they were acting for the good of the country. There remains the problem of the Charlie Wilson Phenomenon, named after Charles Wilson, former president of General Motors, who is supposed to have said during the Senate hearing on his nomination as Secretary of Defense that "what's good for General Motors is good for the country."* Those in power, even giving them the benefit of the greatest good will, are inclined to believe that what is good for them is good for the country. Whether in prescient recognition of the Charlie Wilson Phenomenon, or out of fear of good old-fashioned, malicious, self-interested manipulation, "[t]he fundamental approach of the First Amendment . . . was to assume the worst, and to rule the regulation of political speech 'for fairness' sake' simply out of bounds." Austin, 494 U.S., at 693 (Scalia, J., dissenting). Having abandoned that approach to a limited extent in Buckley, we abandon it much further today.

We will unquestionably be called upon to abandon it further still in the future. The most frightening passage in the lengthy floor debates on this legislation is the following assurance given by one of the cosponsoring Senators to his colleagues:

"This is a modest step, it is a first step, it is an essential step, but it does not even begin to address, in some ways, the fundamental problems that exist with the hard money aspect of the system." 148 Cong. Rec. S2101 (Mar. 20, 2002) (statement of Sen. Feingold).

The system indeed. The first instinct of power is the retention of power, and, under a Constitution that requires periodic elections, that is best achieved by the suppression of election-time speech. We have witnessed merely the second scene of Act I of what promises to be a lengthy tragedy. In scene 3 the Court, having abandoned most of the First Amendment weaponry that Buckley left intact, will be even less equipped to resist the incumbents' writing of the rules of political debate. The federal election campaign laws, which are already (as today's opinions show) so voluminous, so detailed, so complex, that no ordinary citizen dare run for office, or even contribute a significant sum, without hiring an expert advisor in the field, can be expected to grow more voluminous, more detailed, and more complex in the years to come—and always, always, with the objective of reducing the excessive amount of speech.

*. * It is disillusioning to learn that the fabled quote is inaccurate. Wilson actually said: "[F]or years I thought what was good for our country was good for General Motors, and vice versa. The difference did not exist." Hearings before the Senate Committee on Armed Services, 83d Cong., 1st Sess., 26 (1953).

Justice Scalia's dissent in Rasul v. Bush (June 28, 2004)

Justice Scalia, with whom The Chief Justice and Justice Thomas join, dissenting.

The Court today holds that the habeas statute, 28 U.S.C. § 2241 extends to aliens detained by the United States military overseas, outside the sovereign borders of the United States and beyond the territorial jurisdictions of all its courts. This is not only a novel holding; it contradicts a half-century-old precedent on which the military undoubtedly relied, Johnson v. Eisentrager, 339 U.S. 763 (1950). The Court's contention that Eisentrager was somehow negated by Braden v. 30th Judicial Circuit Court of Ky., 410 U.S. 484 (1973)—a decision that dealt with a different issue and did not so much as mention Eisentrager—is implausible in the extreme. This is an irresponsible overturning of settled law in a matter of extreme importance to our forces currently in the field. I would leave it to Congress to change §2241, and dissent from the Court's unprecedented holding.

I

As we have repeatedly said: "Federal courts are courts of limited jurisdiction. They possess only that power authorized by Constitution and statute, which is not to be expanded by judicial decree. It is to be presumed that a cause lies outside this limited jurisdiction . . . ." Kokkonen v. Guardian Life Ins. Co. of America, 511 U.S. 375, 377 (1994) (citations omitted). The petitioners do not argue that the Constitution independently requires jurisdiction here.1 Accordingly, this case turns on the words of §2241, a text the Court today largely ignores. Even a cursory reading of the habeas statute shows that it presupposes a federal district court with territorial jurisdiction over the detainee. Section 2241(a) states:

"Writs of habeas corpus may be granted by the Supreme Court, any justice thereof, the district courts and any circuit judge within their respective jurisdictions." (Emphasis added).

It further requires that "[t]he order of a circuit judge shall be entered in the records of the district court of the district wherein the restraint complained of is had." 28 U.S.C. § 2241(a) (emphases added). And §2242 provides that a petition "addressed to the Supreme Court, a justice thereof or a circuit judge . . . shall state the reasons for not making application to the district court of the district in which the applicant is held." (Emphases added). No matter to whom the writ is directed, custodian or detainee, the statute could not be clearer that a necessary requirement for issuing the writ is that some federal district court have territorial jurisdiction over the detainee. Here, as the Court allows, see ante, at 10, the Guantanamo Bay detainees are not located within the territorial jurisdiction of any federal district court. One would think that is the end of this case.

The Court asserts, however, that the decisions of this Court have placed a gloss on the phrase "within their respective jurisdictions" in §2241 which allows jurisdiction in this case. That is not so. In fact, the only case in point holds just the opposite (and just what the statute plainly says). That case is Eisentrager, but to fully understand its implications for the present dispute, I must also discuss our decisions in the earlier case of Ahrens v. Clark, 335 U.S. 188 (1948), and the later case of Braden.

In Ahrens, the Court considered "whether the presence within the territorial jurisdiction of the District Court of the person detained is prerequisite to filing a petition for a writ of habeas corpus." 335 U.S., at 189 (construing 28 U.S.C. § 452 the statutory precursor to §2241). The Ahrens detainees were held at Ellis Island, New York, but brought their petitions in the District Court for the District of Columbia. Interpreting "within their respective jurisdictions," the Court held that a district court has jurisdiction to issue the writ only on behalf of petitioners detained within its territorial jurisdiction. It was "not sufficient . . . that the jailer or custodian alone be found in the jurisdiction." 335 U.S., at 190.

Ahrens explicitly reserved "the question of what process, if any, a person confined in an area not subject to the jurisdiction of any district court may employ to assert federal rights." Id., at 192, n. 4. That question, the same question presented to this Court today, was shortly thereafter resolved in Eisentrager insofar as noncitizens are concerned. Eisentrager involved petitions for writs of habeas corpus filed in the District Court for the District of Columbia by German nationals imprisoned in Landsberg Prison, Germany. The District Court, relying on Ahrens, dismissed the petitions because the petitioners were not located within its territorial jurisdiction. The Court of Appeals reversed. According to the Court today, the Court of Appeals "implicitly conceded that the District Court lacked jurisdiction under the habeas statute as it had been interpreted in Ahrens," and "[i]n essence . . . concluded that the habeas statute, as construed in Ahrens, had created an unconstitutional gap that had to be filled by reference to 'fundamentals.' " Ante, at 9. That is not so. The Court of Appeals concluded that there was statutory jurisdiction. It arrived at that conclusion by applying the canon of constitutional avoidance: "[I]f the existing jurisdictional act be construed to deny the writ to a person entitled to it as a substantive right, the act would be unconstitutional. It should be construed, if possible, to avoid that result." Eisentrager v. Forrestal, 174 F.2d 961, 966 (CADC 1949). In cases where there was no territorial jurisdiction over the detainee, the Court of Appeals held, the writ would lie at the place of a respondent with directive power over the detainee. "It is not too violent an interpretation of 'custody' to construe it as including those who have directive custody, as well as those who have immediate custody, where such interpretation is necessary to comply with constitutional requirements. . . . The statute must be so construed, lest it be invalid as constituting a suspension of the writ in violation of the constitutional provision." Id., at 967 (emphasis added).2

This Court's judgment in Eisentrager reversed the Court of Appeals. The opinion was largely devoted to rejecting the lower court's constitutional analysis, since the doctrine of constitutional avoidance underlay its statutory conclusion. But the opinion had to pass judgment on whether the statute granted jurisdiction, since that was the basis for the judgments of both lower courts. A conclusion of no constitutionally conferred right would obviously not support reversal of a judgment that rested upon a statutorily conferred right.3　　　And absence of a right to the writ under the clear wording of the habeas statute is what the Eisentrager opinion held: "Nothing in the text of the Constitution extends such a right, nor does anything in our statutes." 339 U.S., at 768 (emphasis added). "[T]hese prisoners at no relevant time were within any territory over which the United States is sovereign, and the scenes of their offense, their capture, their trial and their punishment were all beyond the territorial jurisdiction of any court of the United States." Id., at 777–778. See also id., at 781 (concluding that "no right to the writ of habeas corpus appears"); id., at 790 (finding "no basis for invoking federal judicial power in any district"). The brevity of the Court's statutory analysis signifies nothing more than that the Court considered it obvious (as indeed it is) that, unaided by the canon of constitutional avoidance, the statute did not confer jurisdiction over an alien detained outside the territorial jurisdiction of the courts of the United States.

　　Eisentrager's directly-on-point statutory holding makes it exceedingly difficult for the Court to reach the result it desires today. To do so neatly and cleanly, it must either argue that our decision in Braden overruled Eisentrager, or admit that it is overruling Eisentrager. The former course would not pass the laugh test, inasmuch as Braden dealt with a detainee held within the territorial jurisdiction of a district court, and never mentioned Eisentrager. And the latter course would require the Court to explain why our almost categorical rule of stare decisis in statutory cases should be set aside in order to complicate the present war, and, having set it aside, to explain why the habeas statute does not mean what it plainly says. So instead the Court tries an oblique course: "Braden," it claims, "overruled the statutory predicate to Eisentrager's holding," ante, at 11 (emphasis added), by which it means the statutory analysis of Ahrens. Even assuming, for the moment, that Braden overruled some aspect of Ahrens, inasmuch as Ahrens did not pass upon any of the statutory issues decided by Eisentrager, it is hard to see how any of that case's "statutory predicate" could have been impaired.

　　But in fact Braden did not overrule Ahrens; it distinguished Ahrens. Braden dealt with a habeas petitioner incarcerated in Alabama. The petitioner filed an application for a writ of habeas corpus in Kentucky, challenging an indictment that had been filed against him in that Commonwealth and naming as respondent the Kentucky court in which the proceedings were pending. This Court held that Braden was in custody because a detainer had been issued against him by Kentucky, and was being executed by Alabama, serving as an agent for Kentucky. We found that jurisdiction existed in Kentucky for Braden's petition challenging the Kentucky detainer, notwithstanding his physical confinement in Alabama. Braden was careful to distinguish that situation from the general rule established in Ahrens.

　　"A further, critical development since our decision in Ahrens is the emergence of new classes of prisoners who are able to petition for habeas corpus because of the adoption of a more expansive definition of the 'custody' requirement of the habeas statute. The overruling of McNally v. Hill, 293 U.S. 131 (1934), made it possible for prisoners in custody under one sentence to attack a sentence which they had not yet begun to serve. And it also enabled a petitioner held in one State to attack a detainer lodged against him by another State. In such a case, the State holding the prisoner in immediate confinement acts as agent for the demanding State, and the custodian State is presumably indifferent to the resolution of the prisoner's attack on the detainer. Here, for example, the petitioner is confined in Alabama, but his dispute is with the Commonwealth of Kentucky, not the State of Alabama. Under these circumstances, it would serve no useful purpose to apply the Ahrens rule and require that the action be brought in Alabama." 410 U.S., at 498—499 (citations and footnotes omitted; emphases added).

This cannot conceivably be construed as an overturning of the Ahrens rule in other circumstances. See also Braden, supra, at 499—500 (noting that Ahrens does not establish "an inflexible jurisdictional rule dictating the choice of an inconvenient forum even in a class of cases which could not have been foreseen at the time of that decision" (emphasis added)). Thus, Braden stands for the proposition, and only the proposition, that where a petitioner is in custody in multiple jurisdictions within the United States, he may seek a writ of habeas corpus in a jurisdiction in which he suffers legal confinement, though not physical confinement, if his challenge is to that legal confinement. Outside that class of cases, Braden did not question the general rule of Ahrens (much less that of Eisentrager). Where, as here, present physical custody is at issue, Braden is inapposite, and Eisentrager unquestionably controls.4

The considerations of forum convenience that drove the analysis in Braden do not call into question Eisentrager's holding. The Braden opinion is littered with venue reasoning of the following sort: "The expense and risk of transporting the petitioner to the Western District of Kentucky, should his presence at a hearing prove necessary, would in all likelihood be outweighed by the difficulties of transporting records and witnesses from Kentucky to the district where petitioner is confined." 410 U.S., at 494. Of course nothing could be more inconvenient than what the Court (on the alleged authority of Braden) prescribes today: a domestic hearing for persons held abroad, dealing with events that transpired abroad.

Attempting to paint Braden as a refutation of Ahrens (and thereby, it is suggested, Eisentrager), today's Court imprecisely describes Braden as citing with approval post-Ahrens cases in which "habeas petitioners" located overseas were allowed to proceed (without consideration of the jurisdictional issue) in the District Court for the District of Columbia. Ante, at 10. In fact, what Braden said is that "[w]here American citizens confined overseas (and thus outside the territory of any district court) have sought relief in habeas corpus, we have held, if only implicitly, that the petitioners' absence from the district does not present a jurisdictional obstacle to consideration of the claim." 410 U.S., at 498 (emphasis added). Of course "the existence of unaddressed jurisdictional defects has no precedential effect," Lewis v. Casey, 518 U.S. 343, 352, n. 2 (1996) (citing cases), but we need not "overrule" those implicit holdings to decide this case. Since Eisentrager itself made an exception for such cases, they in no way impugn its holding. "With the citizen," Eisentrager said, "we are now little concerned, except to set his case apart as untouched by this decision and to take measure of the difference between his status and that of all categories of aliens." 339 U.S., at 769. The constitutional doubt that the Court of Appeals in Eisentrager had erroneously attributed to the lack of habeas for an alien abroad might indeed exist with regard to a citizen abroad–justifying a strained construction of the habeas statute, or (more honestly) a determination of constitutional right to habeas. Neither party to the present case challenges the atextual extension of the habeas statute to United States citizens held beyond the territorial jurisdictions of the United States courts; but the possibility of one atextual exception thought to be required by the Constitution is no justification for abandoning the clear application of the text to a situation in which it raises no constitutional doubt.

The reality is this: Today's opinion, and today's opinion alone, overrules Eisentrager; today's opinion, and today's opinion alone, extends the habeas statute, for the first time, to aliens held beyond the sovereign territory of the United States and beyond the territorial jurisdiction of its courts. No reasons are given for this result; no acknowledgment of its consequences made. By spurious reliance on Braden the Court evades explaining why stare decisis can be disregarded, and why Eisentrager was wrong. Normally, we consider the interests of those who have relied on our decisions. Today, the Court springs a trap on the Executive, subjecting Guantanamo Bay to the oversight of the federal courts even though it has never before been thought to be within their jurisdiction–and thus making it a foolish place to have housed alien wartime detainees.

II

In abandoning the venerable statutory line drawn in Eisentrager, the Court boldly extends the scope of the habeas statute to the four corners of the earth. Part III of its opinion asserts that Braden stands for the proposition that "a district court acts 'within [its] respective jurisdiction' within the meaning of §2241 as long as 'the custodian can be reached by service of process.' " Ante, at 10. Endorsement of that proposition is repeated in Part IV. Ante, at 16 ("Section 2241, by its terms, requires nothing more [than the District Court's jurisdiction over petitioners' custodians]").

The consequence of this holding, as applied to aliens outside the country, is breathtaking. It permits an alien captured in a foreign theater of active combat to bring a §2241 petition against the Secretary of Defense. Over the course of the last century, the United States has held millions of alien prisoners abroad. See, e.g., Department of Army, G. Lewis & J. Mewha, History of Prisoner of War Utilization by the United States Army 1776–1945, Pamphlet No. 20–213, p. 244 (1955) (noting that, "[b]y the end of hostilities [in World War II], U.S. forces had in custody approximately two million enemy soldiers"). A great many of these prisoners would no doubt have complained about the circumstances of their capture and the terms of their confinement. The military is currently detaining over 600 prisoners at Guantanamo Bay alone; each detainee undoubtedly has complaints–

real or contrived–about those terms and circumstances. The Court's unheralded expansion of federal-court jurisdiction is not even mitigated by a comforting assurance that the legion of ensuing claims will be easily resolved on the merits. To the contrary, the Court says that the "[p]etitioners' allegations . . . unquestionably describe 'custody in violation of the Constitution or laws or treaties of the United States.' " Ante, at 15, n. 15 (citing United States v. Verdugo-Urquidez, 494 U.S. 259, 277–278 (1990) (Kennedy, J., concurring)). From this point forward, federal courts will entertain petitions from these prisoners, and others like them around the world, challenging actions and events far away, and forcing the courts to oversee one aspect of the Executive's conduct of a foreign war.

Today's carefree Court disregards, without a word of acknowledgment, the dire warning of a more circumspect Court in Eisentrager:

"To grant the writ to these prisoners might mean that our army must transport them across the seas for hearing. This would require allocation for shipping space, guarding personnel, billeting and rations. It might also require transportation for whatever witnesses the prisoners desired to call as well as transportation for those necessary to defend legality of the sentence. The writ, since it is held to be a matter of right, would be equally available to enemies during active hostilities as in the present twilight between war and peace. Such trials would hamper the war effort and bring aid and comfort to the enemy. They would diminish the prestige of our commanders, not only with enemies but with wavering neutrals. It would be difficult to devise more effective fettering of a field commander than to allow the very enemies he is ordered to reduce to submission to call him to account in his own civil courts and divert his efforts and attention from the military offensive abroad to the legal defensive at home. Nor is it unlikely that the result of such enemy litigiousness would be conflict between judicial and military opinion highly comforting to enemies of the United States." 339 U.S., at 778–779.

These results should not be brought about lightly, and certainly not without a textual basis in the statute and on the strength of nothing more than a decision dealing with an Alabama prisoner's ability to seek habeas in Kentucky.

III

Part IV of the Court's opinion, dealing with the status of Guantanamo Bay, is a puzzlement. The Court might have made an effort (a vain one, as I shall discuss) to distinguish Eisentrager on the basis of a difference between the status of Landsberg Prison in Germany and Guantanamo Bay Naval Base. But Part III flatly rejected such an approach, holding that the place of detention of an alien has no bearing on the statutory availability of habeas relief, but "is strictly relevant only to the question of the appropriate forum." Ante, at 11. That rejection is repeated at the end of Part IV: "In the end, the answer to the question presented is clear. . . . No party questions the District Court's jurisdiction over petitioners' custodians. . . . Section 2241, by its terms, requires nothing more." Ante, at 15–16. Once that has been said, the status of Guantanamo Bay is entirely irrelevant to the issue here. The habeas statute is (according to the Court) being applied domestically, to "petitioners' custodians," and the doctrine that statutes are presumed to have no extraterritorial effect simply has no application.

Nevertheless, the Court spends most of Part IV rejecting respondents' invocation of that doctrine on the peculiar ground that it has no application to Guantanamo Bay. Of course if the Court is right about that, not only §2241 but presumably all United States law applies there—including, for example, the federal cause of action recognized in Bivens v. Six Unknown Fed. Narcotics Agents, 403 U.S. 388 (1971), which would allow prisoners to sue their captors for damages. Fortunately, however, the Court's irrelevant discussion also happens to be wrong.

The Court gives only two reasons why the presumption against extraterritorial effect does not apply to Guantanamo Bay. First, the Court says (without any further elaboration) that "the United States exercises 'complete jurisdiction and control' over the Guantanamo Bay Naval Base [under the terms of a 1903 lease agreement], and may continue to exercise such control permanently if it so chooses [under the terms of a 1934 Treaty]." Ante, at 12; see ante, at 2—3. But that lease agreement explicitly recognized "the continuance of the ultimate sovereignty of the Republic of Cuba over the [leased areas]," Lease of Lands for Coaling and Naval Stations, Feb. 23, 1903, U.S.-Cuba, Art. III, T. S. No. 418, and the Executive Branch—whose head is "exclusively responsible" for the "conduct of diplomatic and foreign affairs," Eisentrager, supra, at 789—affirms that the lease and treaty do not render Guantanamo Bay the sovereign territory of the United States, see Brief for Respondents 21.

The Court does not explain how "complete jurisdiction and control" without sovereignty causes an enclave to be part of the United States for purposes of its domestic laws. Since "jurisdiction and control" obtained through a lease is no different in effect from "jurisdiction and control" acquired by lawful force of arms, parts of Afghanistan and Iraq should logically be regarded as subject to our domestic laws. Indeed, if "jurisdiction and control" rather than sovereignty were the test, so should the Landsberg Prison in Germany, where the United States held the Eisentrager detainees.

The second and last reason the Court gives for the proposition that domestic law applies to Guantanamo Bay is the Solicitor General's concession that there would be habeas jurisdiction over a United States citizen in Guantanamo Bay. "Considering that the statute draws no distinction between Americans and aliens held in federal custody, there is little reason to think that Congress intended the geographical coverage of the statute to vary depending on the detainee's citizenship." Ante, at 12—13. But the reason the Solicitor General conceded there would be jurisdiction over a detainee who was a United States citizen had nothing to do with the special status of Guantanamo Bay: "Our answer to that question, Justice Souter, is that citizens of the United States, because of their constitutional circumstances, may have greater rights with respect to the scope and reach of the Habeas Statute as the Court has or would interpret it." Tr. of Oral Arg. 40. See also id., at 27—28. And that position—the position that United States citizens throughout the world may be entitled to habeas corpus rights—is precisely the position that this Court adopted in Eisentrager, see 339 U.S., at 769—770, even while holding that aliens abroad did not have habeas corpus rights. Quite obviously, the Court's second reason has no force whatever.

The last part of the Court's Part IV analysis digresses from the point that the presumption against extraterritorial application does not apply to Guantanamo Bay. Rather, it is directed to the contention that the Court's approach to habeas jurisdiction—applying it to aliens abroad—is "consistent with the historical reach of the writ." Ante, at 13. None of the authorities it cites comes close to supporting that claim. Its first set of authorities involves claims by aliens detained in what is indisputably domestic territory. Ante, at 13, n. 11. Those cases are irrelevant because they do not purport to address the territorial reach of the writ. The remaining cases involve issuance of the writ to " 'exempt jurisdictions' " and "other dominions under the sovereign's control." Ante, at 13—14, and nn. 12—13. These cases are inapposite for two reasons: Guantanamo Bay is not a sovereign dominion, and even if it were, jurisdiction would be limited to subjects.

"Exempt jurisdictions"—the Cinque Ports and Counties Palatine (located in modern-day England)—were local franchises granted by the Crown. See 1 W. Holdsworth, History of English Law 108, 532 (7th ed. rev. 1956); 3 W. Blackstone, Commentaries *78—*79 (hereinafter Blackstone). These jurisdictions were "exempt" in the sense that the Crown had ceded management of municipal affairs to local authorities, whose courts had exclusive jurisdiction over private disputes among residents (although review was still available in the royal courts by writ of error). See id., at *79. Habeas jurisdiction nevertheless extended to those regions on the theory that the delegation of the King's authority did not include his own prerogative writs. Ibid.; R. Sharpe, Law of Habeas Corpus 188—189 (2d ed. 1989) (hereinafter Sharpe). Guantanamo Bay involves no comparable local delegation of pre-existing sovereign authority.

The cases involving "other dominions under the sovereign's control" fare no better. These cases stand only for the proposition that the writ extended to dominions of the Crown outside England proper. The authorities relating to Jersey and the other Channel Islands, for example, see ante, at 14, n. 13, involve territories that are "dominions of the crown of Great Britain" even though not "part of the kingdom of England," 1 Blackstone *102—*105, much as were the colonies in America, id., at *104—*105, and Scotland, Ireland, and Wales, id., at *93. See also King v. Cowle, 2 Burr. 834, 853—854, 97 Eng. Rep. 587, 598 (K. B. 1759) (even if Berwick was "no part of the realm of England," it was still a "dominion of the Crown"). All of the dominions in the cases the Court cites—and all of the territories Blackstone lists as dominions, see 1 Blackstone *93—*106—are the sovereign territory of the Crown: colonies, acquisitions and conquests, and so on. It is an enormous extension of the term to apply it to installations merely leased for a particular use from another nation that still retains ultimate sovereignty.

The Court's historical analysis fails for yet another reason: To the extent the writ's "extraordinary territorial ambit" did extend to exempt jurisdictions, outlying dominions, and the like, that extension applied only to British subjects. The very sources the majority relies on say so: Sharpe explains the "broader ambit" of the writ on the ground that it is "said to depend not on the ordinary jurisdiction of the court for its effectiveness, but upon the authority of the sovereign over all her subjects." Sharpe, supra, at 188 (emphasis added). Likewise, Blackstone explained that the writ "run[s] into all parts of the king's dominions" because "the king is at all times entitled to have an account why the liberty of any of his subjects is restrained." 3 Blackstone *131 (emphasis added). Ex parte Mwenya, [1960] 1 Q. B. 241 (C. A.), which can hardly be viewed as evidence of the historic scope of the writ, only confirms the ongoing relevance of the sovereign-subject relationship to the scope of the writ. There, the question was whether "the Court of Queen's Bench can be debarred from making an order in favour of a British citizen unlawfully or arbitrarily detained" in Northern Rhodesia, which was at the time a protectorate of the Crown. Id., at 300 (Lord Evershed M. R.). Each judge made clear that the detainee's status as a subject was material to the resolution of the case. See id., at 300, 302 (Lord Evershed, M. R.); id., at 305 (Romer, L. J.) ("[I]t is difficult to see why the sovereign should be deprived of her right to be informed through her High Court as to the validity of the detention of her subjects in that territory"); id., at 311 (Sellers, L. J.) ("I am not prepared to say, as we are solely asked to say on this appeal, that the English courts have no jurisdiction in any circumstances to entertain an application for a writ of habeas corpus ad subjiciendum in respect of an unlawful detention of a British subject in a British protectorate"). None of the exempt-jurisdiction or dominion cases the Court cites involves someone not a subject of the Crown.

The rule against issuing the writ to aliens in foreign lands was still the law when, in In re Ning Yi-Ching, 56 T. L. R. 3 (Vacation Ct. 1939), an English court considered the habeas claims of four Chinese subjects detained on criminal charges in Tientsin, China, an area over which Britain had by treaty acquired a lease and "therewith exercised certain rights of administration and control." Id., at 4. The court held that Tientsin was a foreign territory, and that the writ would not issue to a foreigner detained there. The Solicitor-General had argued that "[t]here was no case on record in which a writ of habeas corpus had been obtained on behalf of a foreign subject on foreign territory," id., at 5, and the court "listened in vain for a case in which the writ of habeas corpus had issued in respect of a foreigner detained in a part of the world which was not a part of the King's dominions or realm," id., at 6.5

In sum, the Court's treatment of Guantanamo Bay, like its treatment of §2241, is a wrenching departure from precedent.6

      * * *

Departure from our rule of stare decisis in statutory cases is always extraordinary; it ought to be unthinkable when the departure has a potentially harmful effect upon the Nation's conduct of a war. The Commander in Chief and his subordinates had every reason to expect that the internment of combatants at Guantanamo Bay would not have the consequence of bringing the cumbersome machinery of our domestic courts into military affairs. Congress is in session. If it wished to change federal judges' habeas jurisdiction from what this Court had previously held that to be, it could have done so.

And it could have done so by intelligent revision of the statute,7 instead of by today's clumsy, countertextual reinterpretation that confers upon wartime prisoners greater habeas rights than domestic detainees. The latter must challenge their present physical confinement in the district of their confinement, see Rumsfeld v. Padilla, ante, whereas under today's strange holding Guantanamo Bay detainees can petition in any of the 94 federal judicial districts. The fact that extraterritorially located detainees lack the district of detention that the statute requires has been converted from a factor that precludes their ability to bring a petition at all into a factor that frees them to petition wherever they wish–and, as a result, to forum shop. For this Court to create such a monstrous scheme in time of war, and in frustration of our military commanders' reliance upon clearly stated prior law, is judicial adventurism of the worst sort. I dissent.

Notes

1. See Tr. of Oral Arg. 5 ("Question: And you don't raise the issue of any potential jurisdiction on the basis of the Constitution alone. We are here debating the jurisdiction under the Habeas Statute, is that right? [Answer]: That's correct. . .").

2. The parties' submissions to the Court in Eisentrager construed the Court of Appeals' decision as I do. See Pet. for Cert., O. T. 1949, No. 306, pp. 8–9 ("[T]he court felt constrained to construe the habeas corpus jurisdictional statute–despite its reference to the 'respective jurisdictions' of the various courts and the gloss put on that terminology in the Ahrens and previous decisions–to permit a petition to be filed in the district court with territorial jurisdiction over the officials who have directive authority over the immediate jailer in Germany"); Brief for Respondent, O. T. 1949, No. 306, p. 9 ("Respondent contends that the U.S. Court of Appeals . . . was correct in its holding that the statute, 28 U.S.C. 2241 provides that the U.S. District Court for the District of Columbia has jurisdiction to entertain the petition for a writ of habeas corpus in the case at bar"). Indeed, the briefing in Eisentrager was mainly devoted to the question of whether there was statutory jurisdiction. See, e.g., Brief for Petitioner, O. T. 1949, No. 306, pp. 15–59; Brief for Respondent, O. T. 1949, No. 306, pp. 9–27, 38–49.

3. The Court does not seriously dispute my analysis of the Court of Appeals' holding in Eisentrager. Instead, it argues that this Court in Eisentrager "understood the Court of Appeals' decision to rest on constitutional and not statutory grounds." Ante, at 10, n. 8. That is inherently implausible, given that the Court of Appeals' opinion clearly reached a statutory holding, and that both parties argued the case to this Court on that basis, see n. 2, supra. The only evidence of misunderstanding the Court adduces today is the Eisentrager Court's description of the Court of Appeals' reasoning as "that, although no statutory jurisdiction of such cases is given, courts must be held to possess it as part of the judicial power of the United States . . . ." 339 U.S., at 767. That is no misunderstanding, but an entirely accurate description of the Court of Appeals' reasoning–the penultimate step of that reasoning rather than its conclusion. The Court of Appeals went on to hold that, in light of the constitutional imperative, the statute should

be interpreted as supplying jurisdiction. See Eisentrager v. Forrestal, 174 F.2d 961, 965—967 (CADC 1949). This Court in Eisentrager undoubtedly understood that, which is why it immediately followed the foregoing description with a description of the Court of Appeals' conclusion tied to the language of the habeas statute: "[w]here deprivation of liberty by an official act occurs outside the territorial jurisdiction of any District Court, the petition will lie in the District Court which has territorial jurisdiction over officials who have directive power over the immediate jailer." 339 U.S., at 767.

4. The Court points to Court of Appeals cases that have described Braden as "overruling" Ahrens. See ante, at 11, n. 9. Even if that description (rather than what I think the correct one, "distinguishing") is accepted, it would not support the Court's view that Ahrens was overruled with regard to the point on which Eisentrager relied. The ratio decidendi of Braden does not call into question the principle of Ahrens applied in Eisentrager: that habeas challenge to present physical confinement must be made in the district where the physical confinement exists. The Court is unable to produce a single authority that agrees with its conclusion that Braden overruled Eisentrager. Justice Kennedy recognizes that Eisentrager controls, ante, at 1 (opinion concurring in judgment), but misconstrues that opinion. He thinks it makes jurisdiction under the habeas statute turn on the circumstances of the detainees' confinement—including, apparently, the availability of legal proceedings and the length of detention, see ante, at 3—4. The Eisentrager Court mentioned those circumstances, however, only in the course of its constitutional analysis, and not in its application of the statute. It is quite impossible to read §2241 as conditioning its geographic scope upon them. Among the consequences of making jurisdiction turn upon circumstances of confinement are (1) that courts would always have authority to inquire into circumstances of confinement, and (2) that the Executive would be unable to know with certainty that any given prisoner-of-war camp is immune from writs of habeas corpus. And among the questions this approach raises: When does definite detention become indefinite? How much process will suffice to stave off jurisdiction? If there is a terrorist attack at Guantanamo Bay, will the area suddenly fall outside the habeas statute because it is no longer "far removed from any hostilities," ante, at 3? Justice Kennedy's approach provides enticing law-school-exam imponderables in an area where certainty is called for.

5. The Court argues at some length that Ex parte Mwenya, [1960] 1 Q. B. 241 (C. A.), calls into question my reliance on In re Ning Yi-Ching. See ante, at 15, n. 14. But as I have explained, see supra, at 17—18, Mwenya dealt with a British subject and the court went out of its way to explain that its expansive description of the scope of the writ was premised on that fact. The Court cites not a single case holding that aliens held outside the territory of the sovereign were within reach of the writ.

6. The Court grasps at two other bases for jurisdiction: the Alien Tort Statute (ATS), 28 U.S.C. § 1350 and the federal-question statute, 28 U.S.C. § 1331. The former is not presented to us. The ATS, while invoked below, was repudiated as a basis for jurisdiction by all petitioners, either in their petition for certiorari, in their briefing before

this Court, or at oral argument. See Pet. for Cert. in No. 03—334, p. 2, n. 1 ("Petitioners withdraw any reliance on the Alien Tort Claims Act …"); Brief for Petitioners in No. 03—343, p. 13; Tr. of Oral Arg. 6. With respect to §1331, petitioners assert a variety of claims arising under the Constitution, treaties, and laws of the United States. In Eisentrager, though the Court's holding focused on §2241, its analysis spoke more broadly: "We have pointed out that the privilege of litigation has been extended to aliens, whether friendly or enemy, only because permitting their presence in the country implied protection. No such basis can be invoked here, for these prisoners at no relevant time were within any territory over which the United States is sovereign, and the scenes of their offense, their capture, their trial and their punishment were all beyond the territorial jurisdiction of any court of the United States." 339 U.S., at 777—778. That reasoning dooms petitioners' claims under §1331, at least where Congress has erected a jurisdictional bar to their raising such claims in habeas.

7. It could, for example, provide for jurisdiction by placing Guantanamo Bay within the territory of an existing district court; or by creating a district court for Guantanamo Bay, as it did for the Panama Canal Zone, see 22 U.S.C. § 3841(a) (repealed 1979).

Justice Scalia's dissent in Koons Buick Pontiac GMC v. Nigh (November 30, 2004)

Justice Scalia, dissenting.

The Court views this case as a dispute about the meaning of "subparagraph" in 15 U.S.C. § 1640(a)(2)(A). I think it involves more than that. For while I agree with the construction of that word adopted by the Court, see ante, at 8—10, by Justice Kennedy, see ante, at 1—2 (concurring opinion), and by Justice Thomas, see ante, at 1—2 (opinion concurring in judgment), I disagree with the conclusion that the Court believes follows. The ultimate question here is not the meaning of "subparagraph," but the scope of the exception which contains that term. When is "liability under this subparagraph" limited by the $100/$1,000 brackets? In answering that question, I would give dispositive weight to the structure of §1640(a)(2)(A), which indicates that the exception is part of clause (ii) and thus does not apply to clause (i).

After establishing the fact that "subparagraph" refers to a third-level subdivision within a section, denominated by a capital letter (here subparagraph (A)), see ante, at 8—10, the Court's analysis proceeds in five steps. First, the Court presumes that this fact determines the scope of the exception. See ante, at 10. It does not. In context, the reference to "liability under this subparagraph" is indeterminate. Since it is not a freestanding limitation, but an exception to the liability imposed by clause (ii), it is quite possible to read it as saying that, in the consumer-lease cases covered by clause (ii), "the liability under this subparagraph" would be subject to the $100/$1,000 brackets. Using "subparagraph" in that way would hardly be nonsensical, since the only liability under subparagraph (A) that applies to consumer-lease cases is the amount of damages specified by clause (ii). In other words, if the exception is part of clause (ii), then "liability under this subparagraph" is actually synonymous with "liability under this clause," cf. ibid., in the sense that either phrase would have the same effect were it to appear in clause (ii). As a result, the term "subparagraph" cannot end our inquiry.

The structure of subparagraph (A) provides the best indication of whether the exception is part of clause (ii). In simplified form, the subparagraph reads: "(i) ... , (ii) ... , or (iii) ... ." Clauses (i), (ii), and (iii) are separated by commas, and an "or" appears before clause (iii). It is reasonable to conclude that the exception—which appears between "(ii)" and the comma that precedes "or (iii)"–is part of clause (ii). In fact, the Court admits in passing that the exception appears "in clause (ii)." Ibid. (emphasis added); see also ante, at 1 (Stevens, J., concurring) (referring to "the ceiling contained in (ii)" (emphasis added)). Yet the Court's holding necessarily assumes that the exception somehow stands outside of clause (ii)–someplace where its reference to "subparagraph" can have a different effect than "clause" would. The Court effectively requires the exception to be either part of clauses (i) and (ii) simultaneously, or a part of subparagraph (A) that is not within any of the individual clauses. The legislative drafting manuals cited by the Court, see ante, at 9, and n. 4, reveal how unnatural such an unanchored subdivision would be. See L. Filson, The Legislative Drafter's Desk Reference 223 (1992) ("If a section or other statutory unit contains subdivisions of any kind, it should never contain subdivisions of any other kind unless they are parts of one of those subdivisions" (emphasis added)); House Legislative Counsel's Manual on Drafting Style, HLC No. 104—1, p. 24 (1995) ("If there is a subdivision of the text of a unit, there should not be a different kind of subdivision of that unit unless the latter is part of the 1st subdivision" (emphasis added)); Senate Office of the Legislative Counsel, Legislative Drafting Manual 10—11 (1997) (explaining how to avoid "using a cut-in followed by flush language," that is, inserting a clause that is supposed to apply to (a)(1) and (a)(2) after (2) rather than between (a) and (a)(1)).

In its second step, the Court notes that, before 1995, the exception was generally read as applying to both clauses (i) and (ii). See ante, at 10—11. But the prior meaning is insufficient to reveal the meaning of the current version. As Justice Thomas points out, the placement of the exception "at the end of (A)" used to "indicat[e] that it was meant to refer to the whole of (A)." Ante, at 3 (opinion concurring in judgment). That inference, however, is no longer available, since Congress eliminated the "or" between clauses (i) and (ii) and added clause (iii). If the "or" were still there, it might just be possible to conceive of clauses (i) and (ii) as a sub-list to which the exception attached as a whole. But one simply does not find a purportedly universal exception at the end of the second item in a three-item list.

The Court's third step addresses clause (iii), which is not directly implicated by the facts of this case. The Court concludes that the underlying measure of damages in clause (i) (twice the finance charge) "continues to apply" to actions governed by the newly created clause (iii). Ante, at 11. That conclusion does not follow from merely reading the exception in clause (ii) to apply to clause (i), but it is necessary because, by reading "subparagraph" in the exception to have the effect of extending the exception to all of subparagraph (A), the Court has caused that exception to conflict with the higher limit in clause (iii). To remedy this, the Court proceeds (see ante, at 11, n. 9) to do further violence to §1640(a)(2)(A), simply reading out its division into clauses (i), (ii), and (iii) entirely.1

It is not sound statutory construction to create a conflict by ignoring one feature of a statute and then to solve the problem by ignoring yet another. My construction of the exception in clause (ii) avoids the conflict altogether.

In its fourth step, the Court returns to the application of the $100/$1,000 brackets to clause (i). The Court finds "scant indication that Congress meant to alter the meaning of clause (i)" in 1995 and compares this to " 'Sir Arthur Conan Doyle's "dog that didn't bark." ' " Ante, at 11 (quoting Church of Scientology of Cal. v. IRS, 484 U.S. 9, 17—18 (1987)). I hardly think it "scant indication" of intent to alter that Congress amended the text of the statute by moving the exception from the end of the list to the middle, making it impossible, without doing violence to the text, to read the exception as applying to the entire list. Needless to say, I also disagree with the Court's reliance on things that the sponsors and floor managers of the 1995 amendment failed to say.2 I have often criticized the Court's use of legislative history because it lends itself to a kind of ventriloquism. The Congressional Record or committee reports are used to make words appear to come from Congress's mouth which were spoken or written by others (individual Members of Congress, congressional aides, or even enterprising lobbyists). The Canon of Canine Silence that the Court invokes today introduces a reverse—and at least equally dangerous—phenomenon, under which courts may refuse to believe Congress's own words unless they can see the lips of others moving in unison. See Morales v. Trans World Airlines, Inc., 504 U.S. 374, 385, n. 2 (1992) ("[L]egislative history need not confirm the details of changes in the law effected by statutory language before we will interpret that language according to its natural meaning").

In its fifth and final step, the Court asserts that it would be "anomalous" for liability to be "uncapped by the [$1,000] limit" when real property secures an open-end loan but capped by the $2,000 limit when it secures a closed-end loan, and that it would be "passing strange" for damages to be "substantially lower" under clause (iii) than under clause (i). Ante, at 12, and n. 10. The lack of a $1,000 limit does not, of course, make liability under clause (i) limitless. In all cases under clause (i), the damages are twice the finance charge, and the 1-year statute of limitations, 15 U.S.C. § 1640(e), naturally limits the amount of damages that can be sought.

More importantly, Congress would have expected the amounts financed (and thus the finance charges) under clause (i) to be generally much lower than those under clause (iii). In cases (like this one) where loans are not secured by real property, the amount financed can be no greater than $25,000. §1603(3). Where loans are secured by real property, clause (iii) includes both first mortgages and second mortgages (or home equity loans), which are far more common and significantly larger than the open-end home equity lines of credit (HELOCs) that are still covered by clause (i). In 1994, 64% of home-owning households had first or second mortgages, but only 7% had HELOCs with outstanding balances. Survey Research Center, Univ. of Michigan, National Survey of Home Equity Loans 25 (Oct. 1998) (Table 1) (hereinafter National Survey). The mean first mortgage balance was $66,884; the mean second mortgage balance was $16,199; and the mean HELOC outstanding balance was $18,459. Ibid.3 Assuming a 10% interest rate (which would have been higher than a typical HELOC in 1994, see Canner and Luckett, Home Equity Lending: Evidence from Recent Surveys, 80 Fed. Res. Bull. 571, 582 (1994)), a year of finance charges on the mean HELOC would still have been less than $2,000— which, when doubled, would still be less than two times the maximum damages under clause (iii), a disproportion no greater than what Congress has explicitly prescribed between clauses (ii) and (iii). In addition, very large outstanding balances on HELOCs are comparatively rare. In 2001, roughly 94% of them were less than the median outstanding mortgage principal of $69,227. See U.S. Census Bureau, American Housing Survey for the United States: 2001, pp. 150, 152 (Oct. 2002) (Table 3—15) (hereinafter American Housing Survey).4 Approximately 2% of HELOC balances were $100,000 or more (compared with approximately 32% of mortgages). See ibid. Because closed-end loans are many times more common, and typically much larger, than open-end ones, the finance charges would generally be much higher under clause (iii) than under clause (i), providing a reason for Congress to focus more intently on limiting damages in clause (iii). As for the difference between clause (i) and the $1,000 cap in clause (ii): Consumer leases (principally car leases) are obviously a distinctive category and a special damages cap (which differs from clause (iii) as well as from clause (i)) no more demands an explanation than does the fact that damages for those leases are tied to monthly payments rather than to finance charges. As Justice Stevens acknowledges, applying the $1,000 cap to clause (ii) but not clause (i) is a "plausible policy decision." Ante, at 1 (concurring opinion). The Court should not fight the current structure of the statute merely to vindicate the suspicion that Congress actually made—but neglected to explain clearly—a different policy decision.

As the Court noted earlier this year: "If Congress enacted into law something different from what it intended, then it should amend the statute to conform it to its intent. It is beyond our province to rescue Congress from its drafting errors, and to provide for what we might think is the preferred result." Lamie v. United States Trustee, 540 U.S. 526, 542 (2004) (internal quotation marks and alteration omitted). I would apply the exception only to the clause with which it is associated and affirm the judgment of the Court of Appeals.

Notes

1. In footnote 7, the Court asserts that its new reading merely requires one to pretend that "Congress had not added '(iii)' when it raised the cap on recovery." That is not so—not, at least, if the Court adheres to the sound drafting principles that supposedly

form the basis for its opinion. See supra, at 2—3. To adhere to those and also to apply both the limitation of clause (ii) and the limitation of clause (iii) to clause (i), one must "pretend" that Congress not only had not added "(iii)" but also had eliminated "(i)" and "(ii)." Otherwise, those limits which are recited in clause (ii) would apply only to that clause.

 2. The things that were said about the 1995 amendment are characteristically unhelpful. Rep. McCollum said: "[T]he bill raises the statutory damages for individual actions from \$1,000 to \$2,000." 141 Cong. Rec. 26576 (1995); see also id., at 26898 (remarks of Sen. Mack) (same). Two weeks later, he "clarif[ied]" his remarks by specifying that the amendments "apply solely to loans secured by real estate." Id., at 27703 (statement of Reps. McCollum and Gonzalez). Taken literally, these floor statements could mean that the new \$2,000 limit applies either to all "individual actions" under subparagraph (A), or to all "loans secured by real estate" under clauses (i) and (iii). Neither option is consistent with the Court's conclusion that there is a \$1,000 limit under clause (i).

 3. The medians were, of course, lower than the means: \$49,000 for first mortgages, \$11,000 for second mortgages, and \$15,000 for HELOCs. National Survey 25 (Table 1).

 4. The 1994 survey did not report on the range of amounts owed on HELOCs. In 2001, however, the Census Bureau's Housing Survey began reporting detailed data about HELOCs—in figures presumably comparable to the 1994 data recited above, since the median outstanding balance and median interest rate for HELOCs had not dramatically changed. (The 2001 medians were \$17,517 and 8%. See American Housing Survey 152, 154 (Table 3—15).)

Justice Scalia's concurrence in Gonzales v. Raich (June 6, 2005)

 Justice Scalia, concurring in the judgment.

 I agree with the Court's holding that the Controlled Substances Act (CSA) may validly be applied to respondents' cultivation, distribution, and possession of marijuana for personal, medicinal use. I write separately because my understanding of the doctrinal foundation on which that holding rests is, if not inconsistent with that of the Court, at least more nuanced.

 Since Perez v. United States, 402 U.S. 146 (1971), our cases have mechanically recited that the Commerce Clause permits congressional regulation of three categories: (1) the channels of interstate commerce; (2) the instrumentalities of interstate commerce, and persons or things in interstate commerce; and (3) activities that "substantially affect" interstate commerce. Id., at 150; see United States v. Morrison, 529 U.S. 598, 608—609 (2000); United States v. Lopez, 514 U.S. 549, 558—559 (1995); Hodel v. Virginia Surface Mining & Reclamation Assn., Inc., 452 U.S. 264, 276—277 (1981). The first two categories are self-evident, since they are the ingredients of interstate commerce itself. See Gibbons

v. Ogden, 9 Wheat. 1, 189–190 (1824). The third category, however, is different in kind, and its recitation without explanation is misleading and incomplete.

It is misleading because, unlike the channels, instrumentalities, and agents of interstate commerce, activities that substantially affect interstate commerce are not themselves part of interstate commerce, and thus the power to regulate them cannot come from the Commerce Clause alone. Rather, as this Court has acknowledged since at least United States v. Coombs, 12 Pet. 72 (1838), Congress's regulatory authority over intrastate activities that are not themselves part of interstate commerce (including activities that have a substantial effect on interstate commerce) derives from the Necessary and Proper Clause. Id., at 78; Katzenbach v. McClung, 379 U.S. 294, 301–302 (1964); United States v. Wrightwood Dairy Co., 315 U.S. 110, 119 (1942); Shreveport Rate Cases, 234 U.S. 342, 353 (1914); United States v. E. C. Knight Co., 156 U.S. 1, 39–40 (1895) (Harlan, J., dissenting).1 And the category of "activities that substantially affect interstate commerce," Lopez, supra, at 559, is incomplete because the authority to enact laws necessary and proper for the regulation of interstate commerce is not limited to laws governing intrastate activities that substantially affect interstate commerce. Where necessary to make a regulation of interstate commerce effective, Congress may regulate even those intrastate activities that do not themselves substantially affect interstate commerce.

I

Our cases show that the regulation of intrastate activities may be necessary to and proper for the regulation of interstate commerce in two general circumstances. Most directly, the commerce power permits Congress not only to devise rules for the governance of commerce between States but also to facilitate interstate commerce by eliminating potential obstructions, and to restrict it by eliminating potential stimulants. See NLRB v. Jones & Laughlin Steel Corp., 301 U.S. 1, 36–37 (1937). That is why the Court has repeatedly sustained congressional legislation on the ground that the regulated activities had a substantial effect on interstate commerce. See, e.g., Hodel, supra, at 281 (surface coal mining); Katzenbach, supra, at 300 (discrimination by restaurants); Heart of Atlanta Motel, Inc. v. United States, 379 U.S. 241, 258 (1964) (discrimination by hotels); Mandeville Island Farms v. American Crystal Sugar Co., 334 U.S. 219, 237 (1948) (intrastate price-fixing); Board of Trade of Chicago v. Olsen, 262 U.S. 1, 40 (1923) (activities of a local grain exchange); Stafford v. Wallace, 258 U.S. 495, 517, 524–525 (1922) (intrastate transactions at stockyard). Lopez and Morrison recognized the expansive scope of Congress's authority in this regard: "[T]he pattern is clear. Where economic activity substantially affects interstate commerce, legislation regulating that activity will be sustained." Lopez, supra, at 560; Morrison, supra, at 610 (same).

This principle is not without limitation. In Lopez and Morrison, the Court— conscious of the potential of the "substantially affects" test to " 'obliterate the distinction between what is national and what is local,' " Lopez, supra, at 566–567 (quoting A. L. A. Schechter Poultry Corp. v. United States, 295 U.S. 495, 554 (1935)); see also Morrison, supra, at 615–616–rejected the argument that Congress may regulate noneconomic activity based solely on the effect that it may have on interstate commerce through a remote chain of inferences. Lopez, supra, at 564—566; Morrison, supra, at 617—618. "[I]f we were to accept [such] arguments," the Court reasoned in Lopez, "we are hard pressed to posit any activity by an individual that Congress is without power to regulate." Lopez, supra, at 564; see also Morrison, supra, at 615—616. Thus, although Congress's authority to regulate intrastate activity that substantially affects interstate commerce is broad, it does not permit the Court to "pile inference upon inference," Lopez, supra, at 567, in order to establish that noneconomic activity has a substantial effect on interstate commerce.

As we implicitly acknowledged in Lopez, however, Congress's authority to enact laws necessary and proper for the regulation of interstate commerce is not limited to laws directed against economic activities that have a substantial effect on interstate commerce. Though the conduct in Lopez was not economic, the Court nevertheless recognized that it could be regulated as "an essential part of a larger regulation of economic activity, in which the regulatory scheme could be undercut unless the intrastate activity were regulated." 514 U.S., at 561. This statement referred to those cases permitting the regulation of intrastate activities "which in a substantial way interfere with or obstruct the exercise of the granted power." Wrightwood Dairy Co., 315 U.S., at 119; see also United States v. Darby, 312 U.S. 100, 118—119 (1941); Shreveport Rate Cases, 234 U.S., at 353. As the Court put it in Wrightwood Dairy, where Congress has the authority to enact a regulation of interstate commerce, "it possesses every power needed to make that regulation effective." 315 U.S., at 118—119.

Although this power "to make ... regulation effective" commonly overlaps with the authority to regulate economic activities that substantially affect interstate commerce,2 and may in some cases have been confused with that authority, the two are distinct. The regulation of an intrastate activity may be essential to a comprehensive regulation of interstate commerce even though the intrastate activity does not itself "substantially affect" interstate commerce. Moreover, as the passage from Lopez quoted above suggests, Congress may regulate even noneconomic local activity if that regulation is a necessary part of a more general regulation of interstate commerce. See Lopez, supra, at 561. The relevant question is simply whether the means chosen are "reasonably adapted" to the attainment of a legitimate end under the commerce power. See Darby, supra, at 121.

In Darby, for instance, the Court explained that "Congress, having ... adopted the policy of excluding from interstate commerce all goods produced for the commerce which do not conform to the specified labor standards," 312 U.S., at 121, could not only require employers engaged in the production of goods for interstate commerce to conform to wage and hour standards, id., at 119—121, but could also require those employers to keep employment records in order to demonstrate compliance with the regulatory scheme, id., at 125. While the Court sustained the former regulation on the alternative ground that the activity it regulated could have a "great effect" on interstate commerce, id., at 122—123, it affirmed the latter on the sole ground that "[t]he requirement for records even of the intrastate transaction is an appropriate means to a legitimate end," id., at 125.

As the Court said in the Shreveport Rate Cases, the Necessary and Proper Clause does not give "Congress ... the authority to regulate the internal commerce of a State, as such," but it does allow Congress "to take all measures necessary or appropriate to" the effective regulation of the interstate market, "although intrastate transactions ... may thereby be controlled." 234 U.S., at 353; see also Jones & Laughlin Steel Corp., 301 U.S., at 38 (the logic of the Shreveport Rate Cases is not limited to instrumentalities of commerce).

II

Today's principal dissent objects that, by permitting Congress to regulate activities necessary to effective interstate regulation, the Court reduces Lopez and Morrison to "little more than a drafting guide." Post, at 5 (opinion of O'Connor, J.). I think that criticism unjustified. Unlike the power to regulate activities that have a substantial effect on interstate commerce, the power to enact laws enabling effective regulation of interstate commerce can only be exercised in conjunction with congressional regulation of an interstate market, and it extends only to those measures necessary to make the interstate regulation effective. As Lopez itself states, and the Court affirms today, Congress may regulate noneconomic intrastate activities only where the failure to do so "could ... undercut" its regulation of interstate commerce. See Lopez, supra, at 561; ante, at 15, 21, 22. This is not a power that threatens to obliterate the line between "what is truly national and what is truly local." Lopez, supra, at 567–568.

Lopez and Morrison affirm that Congress may not regulate certain "purely local" activity within the States based solely on the attenuated effect that such activity may have in the interstate market. But those decisions do not declare noneconomic intrastate activities to be categorically beyond the reach of the Federal Government. Neither case involved the power of Congress to exert control over intrastate activities in connection with a more comprehensive scheme of regulation; Lopez expressly disclaimed that it was such a case, 514 U.S., at 561, and Morrison did not even discuss the possibility that it was. (The Court of Appeals in Morrison made clear that it was not. See Brzonkala v. Virginia Polytechnic Inst., 169 F.3d 820, 834–835 (CA4 1999) (en banc).) To dismiss this distinction as "superficial and formalistic," see post, at 6 (O'Connor, J., dissenting), is to misunderstand the nature of the Necessary and Proper Clause, which empowers Congress to enact laws in effectuation of its enumerated powers that are not within its authority to enact in isolation. See McCulloch v. Maryland, 4 Wheat. 316, 421–422 (1819).

And there are other restraints upon the Necessary and Proper Clause authority. As Chief Justice Marshall wrote in McCulloch v. Maryland, even when the end is constitutional and legitimate, the means must be "appropriate" and "plainly adapted" to that end. Id., at 421. Moreover, they may not be otherwise "prohibited" and must be "consistent with the letter and spirit of the constitution." Ibid. These phrases are not merely hortatory. For example, cases such as Printz v. United States, 521 U.S. 898 (1997), and New York v. United States, 505 U.S. 144 (1992), affirm that a law is not " 'proper for carrying into Execution the Commerce Clause' " "[w]hen [it] violates [a constitutional] principle of state sovereignty." Printz, supra, at 923–924; see also New York, supra, at 166.

III

The application of these principles to the case before us is straightforward. In the CSA, Congress has undertaken to extinguish the interstate market in Schedule I controlled substances, including marijuana. The Commerce Clause unquestionably permits this. The power to regulate interstate commerce "extends not only to those regulations which aid, foster and protect the commerce, but embraces those which prohibit it." Darby, 312 U.S., at 113. See also Hipolite Egg Co. v. United States, 220 U.S. 45, 58 (1911); Lottery Case, 188 U.S. 321, 354 (1903). To effectuate its objective, Congress has prohibited almost all intrastate activities related to Schedule I substances–both economic activities (manufacture, distribution, possession with the intent to distribute) and noneconomic activities (simple possession). See 21 U.S.C. § 841(a), 844(a). That simple possession is a noneconomic activity is immaterial to whether it can be prohibited as a necessary part of a larger regulation. Rather, Congress's authority to enact all of these prohibitions of intrastate controlled-substance activities depends only upon whether they are appropriate means of achieving the legitimate end of eradicating Schedule I substances from interstate commerce.

By this measure, I think the regulation must be sustained. Not only is it impossible to distinguish "controlled substances manufactured and distributed intrastate" from "controlled substances manufactured and distributed interstate," but it hardly makes sense to speak in such terms. Drugs like marijuana are fungible commodities. As the Court explains, marijuana that is grown at home and possessed for personal use is never more than an instant from the interstate market–and this is so whether or not the possession is for medicinal use or lawful use under the laws of a particular State.3 See ante, at 23–30. Congress need not accept on faith that state law will be effective in maintaining a strict division between a lawful market for "medical" marijuana and the more general marijuana market. See id., at 26–27, and n. 38. "To impose on [Congress] the necessity of resorting to means which it cannot control, which another government may furnish or withhold, would render its course precarious, the result of its measures uncertain, and create a dependence on other governments, which might disappoint its most important designs, and is incompatible with the language of the constitution." McCulloch, supra, at 424.

Finally, neither respondents nor the dissenters suggest any violation of state sovereignty of the sort that would render this regulation "inappropriate," id., at 421– except to argue that the CSA regulates an area typically left to state regulation. See post, at 6–7, 11 (opinion of O'Connor, J.); post, at 8–9 (opinion of Thomas, J.); Brief for Respondents 39–42. That is not enough to render federal regulation an inappropriate means. The Court has repeatedly recognized that, if authorized by the commerce power, Congress may regulate private endeavors "even when [that regulation] may pre-empt express state-law determinations contrary to the result which has commended itself to the collective wisdom of Congress." National League of Cities v. Usery, 426 U.S. 833, 840

(1976); see Cleveland v. United States, 329 U.S. 14, 19 (1946); McCulloch, supra, at 424. At bottom, respondents' state-sovereignty argument reduces to the contention that federal regulation of the activities permitted by California's Compassionate Use Act is not sufficiently necessary to be "necessary and proper" to Congress's regulation of the interstate market. For the reasons given above and in the Court's opinion, I cannot agree.

***

I thus agree with the Court that, however the class of regulated activities is subdivided, Congress could reasonably conclude that its objective of prohibiting marijuana from the interstate market "could be undercut" if those activities were excepted from its general scheme of regulation. See Lopez, 514 U.S., at 561. That is sufficient to authorize the application of the CSA to respondents.

Notes

1. See also Garcia v. San Antonio Metropolitan Transit Authority, 469 U.S. 528, 584—585 (1985) (O'Connor, J., dissenting) (explaining that it is through the Necessary and Proper Clause that "an intrastate activity 'affecting' interstate commerce can be reached through the commerce power").

2. Wickard v. Filburn, 317 U.S. 111 (1942), presented such a case. Because the unregulated production of wheat for personal consumption diminished demand in the regulated wheat market, the Court said, it carried with it the potential to disrupt Congress's price regulation by driving down prices in the market. Id., at 127—129. This potential disruption of Congress's interstate regulation, and not only the effect that personal consumption of wheat had on interstate commerce, justified Congress's regulation of that conduct. Id., at 128—129.

3. The principal dissent claims that, if this is sufficient to sustain the regulation at issue in this case, then it should also have been sufficient to sustain the regulation at issue in United States v. Lopez, 514 U.S. 549 (1995). See post, at 11—12 (arguing that "we could have surmised in Lopez that guns in school zones are 'never more than an instant from the interstate market' in guns already subject to federal regulation, recast Lopez as a Necessary and Proper Clause case, and thereby upheld the Gun-Free School Zones Act"). This claim founders upon the shoals of Lopez itself, which made clear that the statute there at issue was "not an essential part of a larger regulation of economic activity." Lopez, supra, at 561 (emphasis added). On the dissent's view of things, that statement is inexplicable. Of course it is in addition difficult to imagine what intelligible scheme of regulation of the interstate market in guns could have as an appropriate means of effectuation the prohibition of guns within 1000 feet of schools (and nowhere else). The dissent points to a federal law, 18 U.S.C. § 922(b)(1), barring licensed dealers from selling guns to minors, see post, at 12, but the relationship between the regulatory scheme of which §922(b)(1) is a part (requiring all dealers in firearms that have traveled in interstate commerce to be licensed, see §922(a)) and the statute at issue in Lopez approaches the nonexistent—which is doubtless why the Government did not attempt to justify the statute

on the basis of that relationship.

Justice Scalia's dissent in Gonzales v. Oregon (Jan 17, 2006) [Notes omitted]

Justice Scalia, with whom Chief Justice Roberts and Justice Thomas join, dissenting.

The Court concludes that the Attorney General lacked authority to declare assisted suicide illicit under the Controlled Substances Act (CSA), because the CSA is concerned only with "illicit drug dealing and trafficking," ante, at 23 (emphasis added). This question-begging conclusion is obscured by a flurry of arguments that distort the statute and disregard settled principles of our interpretive jurisprudence.

Contrary to the Court's analysis, this case involves not one but three independently sufficient grounds for reversing the Ninth Circuit's judgment. First, the Attorney General's interpretation of "legitimate medical purpose" in 21 CFR § 1306.04 (2005) (hereinafter Regulation) is clearly valid, given the substantial deference we must accord it under Auer v. Robbins, 519 U.S. 452, 461 (1997), and his two remaining conclusions follow naturally from this interpretation. See Part I, infra. Second, even if this interpretation of the Regulation is entitled to lesser deference or no deference at all, it is by far the most natural interpretation of the Regulation–whose validity is not challenged here. This interpretation is thus correct even upon de novo review. See Part II, infra. Third, even if that interpretation of the Regulation were incorrect, the Attorney General's independent interpretation of the statutory phrase "public interest" in 21 U.S.C. § 824(a) and 823(f), and his implicit interpretation of the statutory phrase "public health and safety" in §823(f)(5), are entitled to deference under Chevron U. S. A. Inc. v. Natural Resources Defense Council, Inc., 467 U.S. 837 (1984), and they are valid under Chevron. See Part III, infra. For these reasons, I respectfully dissent.

I

The Interpretive Rule issued by the Attorney General (hereinafter Directive) provides in relevant part as follows:

"For the reasons set forth in the OLC Opinion, I hereby determine that assisting suicide is not a 'legitimate medical purpose' within the meaning of 21 CFR § 1306.04 (2001), and that prescribing, dispensing, or administering federally controlled substances to assist suicide violates the CSA. Such conduct by a physician registered to dispense controlled substances may 'render his registration ... inconsistent with the public interest' and therefore subject to possible suspension or revocation under 21 U.S.C. [§]824(a)(4)." 66 Fed. Reg. 56608 (2001).

The Directive thus purports to do three distinct things: (1) to interpret the phrase "legitimate medical purpose" in the Regulation to exclude physician-assisted suicide; (2) to determine that prescribing, dispensing, and administering federally controlled substances to assist suicide violates the CSA; and (3) to determine that participating in physician-assisted suicide may render a practitioner's registration "inconsistent with the public interest" within the meaning of 21 U.S.C. § 823(f) and 824(a)(4) (which incorporates §823(f) by reference). The Court's analysis suffers from an unremitting failure to distinguish among these distinct propositions in the Directive.

As an initial matter, the validity of the Regulation's interpretation of "prescription" in §829 to require a "legitimate medical purpose" is not at issue. Respondents conceded the validity of this interpretation in the lower court, see Oregon v. Ashcroft, 368 F.3d 1118, 1133 (CA9 2004), and they have not challenged it here. By its assertion that the Regulation merely restates the statutory standard of 21 U.S.C. § 830(b)(3)(A)(ii), see ante, at 10, the Court likewise accepts that the "legitimate medical purpose" interpretation for prescriptions is proper. See also ante, at 11 (referring to "legitimate medical purpose" as a "statutory phrase"). It is beyond dispute, then, that a "prescription" under §829 must issue for a "legitimate medical purpose."

A

Because the Regulation was promulgated by the Attorney General, and because the Directive purported to interpret the language of the Regulation, see 66 Fed. Reg. 56608, this case calls for the straightforward application of our rule that an agency's interpretation of its own regulations is "controlling unless plainly erroneous or inconsistent with the regulation." Auer, supra, at 461 (internal quotation marks omitted). The Court reasons that Auer is inapplicable because the Regulation "does little more than restate the terms of the statute itself." Ante, at 9. "Simply put," the Court asserts, "the existence of a parroting regulation does not change the fact that the question here is not the meaning of the regulation but the meaning of the statute." Ante, at 10.

To begin with, it is doubtful that any such exception to the Auer rule exists. The Court cites no authority for it, because there is none. To the contrary, our unanimous decision in Auer makes clear that broadly drawn regulations are entitled to no less respect than narrow ones. "A rule requiring the Secretary to construe his own regulations narrowly would make little sense, since he is free to write the regulations as broadly as he wishes, subject only to the limits imposed by the statute." 519 U.S., at 463 (emphasis added).

Even if there were an antiparroting canon, however, it would have no application here. The Court's description of 21 CFR § 1306.04 (2005) as a regulation that merely "paraphrase[s] the statutory language," ante, at 10, is demonstrably false. In relevant part, the Regulation interprets the word "prescription" as it appears in 21 U.S.C. § 829 which governs the dispensation of controlled substances other than those on Schedule I (which may not be dispensed at all). Entitled "[p]rescriptions," §829 requires, with certain exceptions not relevant here, "the written prescription of a practitioner" (usually a medical doctor) for the dispensation of Schedule II substances (§829(a)), "a written or oral prescription" for substances on Schedules III and IV (§829(b)), and no prescription but merely a "medical purpose" for the dispensation of Schedule V substances (§829(c)).

As used in this section, "prescription" is susceptible of at least three reasonable interpretations. First, it might mean any oral or written direction of a practitioner for the dispensation of drugs. See United States v. Moore, 423 U.S. 122, 137, n. 13 (1975) ("On its face §829 addresses only the form that a prescription must take... . [Section] 829 by its terms does not limit the authority of a practitioner"). Second, in light of the requirement of a "medical purpose" for the dispensation of Schedule V substances, see §829(c), it might mean a practitioner's oral or written direction for the dispensation of drugs that the practitioner believes to be for a legitimate medical purpose. See Webster's New International Dictionary 1954 (2d ed. 1950) (hereinafter Webster's Second) (defining "prescription" as "[a] written direction for the preparation and use of a medicine"); id., at 1527 (defining "medicine" as "[a]ny substance or preparation used in treating disease") (emphases added). Finally, "prescription" might refer to a practitioner's direction for the dispensation of drugs that serves an objectively legitimate medical purpose, regardless of the practitioner's subjective judgment about the legitimacy of the anticipated use. See ibid.

The Regulation at issue constricts or clarifies the statute by adopting the last and narrowest of these three possible interpretations of the undefined statutory term: "A prescription for a controlled substance to be effective must be issued for a legitimate medical purpose ... ." 21 CFR § 1306.04(a) (2005). We have previously acknowledged that the Regulation gives added content to the text of the statute: "The medical purpose requirement explicit in subsection (c) [of §829] could be implicit in subsections (a) and (b). Regulation §[1]306.04 makes it explicit." Moore, supra, at 137, n. 13.1

The Court points out that the Regulation adopts some of the phrasing employed in unrelated sections of the statute. See ante, at 10. This is irrelevant. A regulation that significantly clarifies the meaning of an otherwise ambiguous statutory provision is not a "parroting" regulation, regardless of the sources that the agency draws upon for the clarification. Moreover, most of the statutory phrases that the Court cites as appearing in the Regulation, see ibid. (citing 21 U.S.C. § 812(b) (" 'currently accepted medical use' "), 829(c) (" 'medical purpose' "), 802(21) (" 'in the course of professional practice' ")), are inapposite because they do not "parrot" the only phrase in the Regulation that the Directive purported to construe. See 66 Fed. Reg. 56608 ("I hereby determine that assisting suicide is not a 'legitimate medical purpose' within the meaning of 21 CFR § 1306.04 ..."). None of them includes the key word "legitimate," which gives the most direct support to the Directive's theory that §829(c) presupposes a uniform federal standard of medical practice.2

Since the Regulation does not run afowl (so to speak) of the Court's newly invented prohibition of "parroting"; and since the Directive represents the agency's own interpretation of that concededly valid regulation; the only question remaining is whether that interpretation is "plainly erroneous or inconsistent with the regulation"; otherwise, it is "controlling." Auer, supra, at 461 (internal quotation marks omitted). This is not a difficult question. The Directive is assuredly valid insofar as it interprets "prescription" to require a medical purpose that is "legitimate" as a matter of federal law—since that is an interpretation of "prescription" that we ourselves have adopted. Webb v. United States, 249 U.S. 96 (1919), was a prosecution under the Harrison Act of a doctor who wrote prescriptions of morphine "for the purpose of providing the user with morphine sufficient to keep him comfortable by maintaining his customary use," id., at 99. The dispositive issue in the case was whether such authorizations were "prescriptions" within the meaning of §2(b) of the Harrison Act, predecessor to the CSA. Ibid. We held that "to call such an order for the use of morphine a physician's prescription would be so plain a perversion of meaning that no discussion of the subject is required." Id., at 99–100. Like the Directive, this interprets "prescription" to require medical purpose that is legitimate as a matter of federal law. And the Directive is also assuredly valid insofar as it interprets "legitimate medical purpose" as a matter of federal law to exclude physician-assisted suicide, because that is not only a permissible but indeed the most natural interpretation of that phrase. See Part II, infra.

B

Even if the Regulation merely parroted the statute, and the Directive therefore had to be treated as though it construed the statute directly, see ante, at 11, the Directive would still be entitled to deference under Chevron. The Court does not take issue with the Solicitor General's contention that no alleged procedural defect, such as the absence of notice-and-comment rulemaking before promulgation of the Directive, renders Chevron inapplicable here. See Reply Brief for Petitioners 4 (citing Barnhart v. Walton, 535 U.S. 212, 219–222 (2002); 5 U.S.C. § 553(b)(3)(A) (exempting interpretive rules from notice-and-comment rulemaking)). Instead, the Court holds that the Attorney General lacks interpretive authority to issue the Directive at all, on the ground that the explicit delegation provision, 21 U.S.C.A. §821 (Supp. 2005), limits his rulemaking authority to "registration and control," which (according to the Court) are not implicated by the Directive's interpretation of the prescription requirement. See ante, at 12–14.

Setting aside the implicit delegation inherent in Congress's use of the undefined term "prescription" in §829, the Court's reading of "control" in §821 is manifestly erroneous. The Court urges, ante, at 12–13, that "control" is a term defined in part A of the subchapter (entitled "Introductory Provisions") to mean "to add a drug or other substance ... to a schedule under part B of this subchapter," 21 U.S.C. § 802(5) (emphasis added). But §821 is not included in "part B of this subchapter," which is entitled "Authority to Control; Standards and Schedules," and consists of the sections related to scheduling, 21 U.S.C.A. §§811–814 (main ed. and Supp. 2005), where the statutory definition is uniquely appropriate. Rather, §821 is found in part C of the subchapter, §§821–830, entitled "Registration of Manufacturers, Distributors, and Dispensers of Controlled Substances," which includes all and only the provisions relating to the "manufacture, distribution, and dispensing of controlled substances," §821. The artificial definition of "control" in §802(5) has no conceivable application to the use of that word in §821. Under that definition, "control" must take a substance as its direct object, see 21 U.S.C. § 802(5) ("to add a drug or other substance ... to a schedule")–and that is how "control" is consistently used throughout part B. See, e.g., §§811(b) ("proceedings ... to control a drug or other substance"), 811(c) ("each drug or other substance proposed to be controlled or removed from the schedules"), 811(d)(1) ("If control is required ... the Attorney General shall issue an order controlling such drug ..."), 812(b) ("Except where control is required ... a drug or other substance may not be placed in any schedule ..."). In §821, by contrast, the term "control" has as its object, not "a drug or other substance," but rather the processes of "manufacture, distribution, and dispensing of controlled substances." It could not be clearer that the artificial definition of "control" in §802(5) is inapplicable. It makes no sense to speak of "adding the manufacturing, distribution, and dispensing of substances to a schedule." We do not force term-of-art definitions into contexts where they plainly do not fit and produce nonsense. What is obviously intended in §821 is the ordinary meaning of "control"–namely, "[t]o exercise restraining or directing influence over; to dominate; regulate; hence, to hold from action; to curb," Webster's Second 580. "Control" is regularly used in this ordinary sense elsewhere in part C of the subchapter. See, e.g., 21 U.S.C. § 823(a)(1), (b)(1), (d)(1), (e)(1), (h)(1) ("maintenance of effective controls against diversion"); §§823(a)(5), (d)(5) ("establishment of effective control against diversion"); §823(g)(2)(H)(i) ("to exercise supervision or control over the practice of medicine"); §830(b)(1)(C) ("a listed chemical under the control of the regulated person"); §830(c)(2)(D) ("chemical control laws") (emphases added).

When the word is given its ordinary meaning, the Attorney General's interpretation of the prescription requirement of §829 plainly "relat[es] to the ... control of the ... dispensing of controlled substances," 21 U.S.C. A. §821 (Supp. 2005) (emphasis added), since a prescription is the chief requirement for "dispensing" such drugs, see §829. The same meaning is compelled by the fact that §821 is the first section not of part B of the subchapter, which deals entirely with "control" in the artificial sense, but of part C, every section of which relates to the "registration and control of the manufacture, distribution, and dispensing of controlled substances," §821. See §§822 (persons required to register), 823 (registration requirements), 824 (denial, revocation, or suspension of registration), 825 (labeling and packaging), 826 (production quotas for controlled substances), 827 (recordkeeping and reporting requirements of registrants), 828 (order forms), 829 (prescription requirements), 830 (regulation of listed chemicals and certain machines). It would be peculiar for the first section of this part to authorize rulemaking for matters covered by the previous part. The only sensible interpretation of §821 is that it gives the Attorney General interpretive authority over the provisions of part C, all of which "relat[e] to the registration and control of the manufacture, distribution, and dispensing of controlled substances." These provisions include both the prescription requirement of §829, and the criteria for registration and deregistration of §§823 and 824 (as relevant below, see Part III, infra).3

C

In sum, the Directive's construction of "legitimate medical purpose" is a perfectly valid agency interpretation of its own regulation; and if not that, a perfectly valid agency interpretation of the statute. No one contends that the construction is "plainly erroneous or inconsistent with the regulation," Bowles v. Seminole Rock & Sand Co., 325

U.S. 410, 414 (1945), or beyond the scope of ambiguity in the statute, see Chevron, 467 U.S., at 843. In fact, as explained below, the Directive provides the most natural interpretation of the Regulation and of the statute. The Directive thus definitively establishes that a doctor's order authorizing the dispensation of a Schedule II substance for the purpose of assisting a suicide is not a "prescription" within the meaning of §829.

Once this conclusion is established, the other two conclusions in the Directive follow inevitably. Under our reasoning in Moore, writing prescriptions that are illegitimate under §829 is certainly not "in the [usual] course of professional practice" under §802(21) and thus not "authorized by this subchapter" under §841(a). See 423 U.S., at 138, 140–141. A doctor who does this may thus be prosecuted under §841(a), and so it follows that such conduct "violates the Controlled Substances Act," 66 Fed. Reg. 56608. And since such conduct is thus not in "[c]ompliance with applicable ... Federal ... laws relating to controlled substances," 21 U.S.C. § 823(f)(4), and may also be fairly judged to "threaten the public health and safety," §823(f)(5), it follows that "[s]uch conduct by a physician registered to dispense controlled substances may 'render his registration ... inconsistent with the public interest' and therefore subject to possible suspension or revocation under 21 U.S.C. [§]824(a)(4)." 66 Fed. Reg. 56608 (emphases added).

II

Even if the Directive were entitled to no deference whatever, the most reasonable interpretation of the Regulation and of the statute would produce the same result. Virtually every relevant source of authoritative meaning confirms that the phrase "legitimate medical purpose"4 does not include intentionally assisting suicide. "Medicine" refers to "[t]he science and art dealing with the prevention, cure, or alleviation of disease." Webster's Second 1527. The use of the word "legitimate" connotes an objective standard of "medicine," and our presumption that the CSA creates a uniform federal law regulating the dispensation of controlled substances, see Mississippi Band of Choctaw Indians v. Holyfield, 490 U.S. 30, 43 (1989), means that this objective standard must be a federal one. As recounted in detail in the memorandum for the Attorney General that is attached as an appendix to the Directive (OLC Memo), virtually every medical authority from Hippocrates to the current American Medical Association (AMA) confirms that assisting suicide has seldom or never been viewed as a form of "prevention, cure, or alleviation of disease," and (even more so) that assisting suicide is not a "legitimate" branch of that "science and art." See OLC Memo, App. to Pet. for Cert. 113a–130a. Indeed, the AMA has determined that " '[p]hysician-assisted suicide is fundamentally incompatible with the physician's role as a healer.' " Washington v. Glucksberg, 521 U.S. 702, 731 (1997). "[T]he overwhelming weight of authority in judicial decisions, the past and present policies of nearly all of the States and of the Federal Government, and the clear, firm and unequivocal views of the leading associations within the American medical and nursing professions, establish that assisting in suicide ... is not a legitimate medical purpose." OLC Memo, supra, at 129a. See also Glucksberg, supra, at 710, n. 8 (prohibitions or condemnations of assisted suicide in 50 jurisdictions, including 47 States, the District of Columbia, and 2

Territories).

In the face of this "overwhelming weight of authority," the Court's admission that "[o]n its own, this understanding of medicine's boundaries is at least reasonable," ante, at 26 (emphasis added), tests the limits of understatement. The only explanation for such a distortion is that the Court confuses the normative inquiry of what the boundaries of medicine should be—which it is laudably hesitant to undertake—with the objective inquiry of what the accepted definition of "medicine" is. The same confusion is reflected in the Court's remarkable statement that "[t]he primary problem with the Government's argument ... is its assumption that the CSA impliedly authorizes an Executive officer to bar a use simply because it may be inconsistent with one reasonable understanding of medical practice." Ibid. (emphasis added). The fact that many in Oregon believe that the boundaries of "legitimate medicine" should be extended to include assisted suicide does not change the fact that the overwhelming weight of authority (including the 47 States that condemn physician-assisted suicide) confirms that they have not yet been so extended. Not even those of our Eighth Amendment cases most generous in discerning an "evolution" of national standards would have found, on this record, that the concept of "legitimate medicine" has evolved so far. See Roper v. Simmons, 543 U.S. 551, 564—567 (2005).

The Court contends that the phrase "legitimate medical purpose" cannot be read to establish a broad, uniform federal standard for the medically proper use of controlled substances. Ante, at 22. But it also rejects the most plausible alternative proposition, urged by the State, that any use authorized under state law constitutes a "legitimate medical purpose." (The Court is perhaps leery of embracing this position because the State candidly admitted at oral argument that, on its view, a State could exempt from the CSA's coverage the use of morphine to achieve euphoria.) Instead, the Court reverse-engineers an approach somewhere between a uniform national standard and a state-by-state approach, holding (with no basis in the CSA's text) that "legitimate medical purpose" refers to all uses of drugs unrelated to "addiction and recreational abuse." Ante, at 27. Thus, though the Court pays lipservice to state autonomy, see ante, 23—24, its standard for "legitimate medical purpose" is in fact a hazily defined federal standard based on its purposive reading of the CSA, and extracted from obliquely relevant sections of the Act. In particular, relying on its observation that the criteria for scheduling controlled substances are primarily concerned with "addiction or abnormal effects on the nervous system," ante, at 26—27 (citing 21 U.S.C. § 811(c)(7), 812(b), 811(f), 801a), the Court concludes that the CSA's prescription requirement must be interpreted in light of this narrow view of the statute's purpose.

Even assuming, however, that the principal concern of the CSA is the curtailment of "addiction and recreational abuse," there is no reason to think that this is its exclusive concern. We have repeatedly observed that Congress often passes statutes that sweep more broadly than the main problem they were designed to address. "[S]tatutory prohibitions often go beyond the principal evil to cover reasonably comparable evils, and it is ultimately the provisions of our laws rather than the principal concerns of our legislators by which we are governed." Oncale v. Sundowner Offshore Services, Inc., 523 U.S. 75, 79 (1998). See also H. J. Inc. v. Northwestern Bell Telephone Co., 492 U.S. 229, 248 (1989).

The scheduling provisions of the CSA on which the Court relies confirm that the CSA's "design," ante, at 23, is not as narrow as the Court asserts. In making scheduling determinations, the Attorney General must not only consider a drug's "psychic or physiological dependence liability" as the Court points out, ante, at 26 (citing 21 U.S.C. § 811(c)(7)), but must also consider such broad factors as "[t]he state of current scientific knowledge regarding the drug or other substance," §811(c)(3), and (most notably) "[w]hat, if any, risk there is to the public health," §811(c)(6). If the latter factor were limited to addiction-related health risks, as the Court supposes, it would be redundant of §811(c)(7). Moreover, in making registration determinations regarding manufacturers and distributors, the Attorney General "shall" consider "such other factors as may be relevant to and consistent with the public health and safety," §§823(a)(6), (b)(5), (d)(6), (e)(5) (emphasis added)–over and above the risk of "diversion" of controlled substances, §§823(a)(1), (a)(5), (b)(1), (d)(1), (d)(5), (e)(1). And, most relevant of all, in registering and deregistering physicians, the Attorney General "may deny an application for such registration if he determines that the issuance of such registration would be inconsistent with the public interest," §823(f); see also §824(a)(4), and in making that determination "shall" consider "[s]uch other conduct which may threaten the public health and safety," §823(f)(5). All of these provisions, not just those selectively cited by the Court, shed light upon the CSA's repeated references to the undefined term "abuse." See §§811(a)(1)(A), (c)(1), (c)(4), (c)(5); §§812(b)(1)(A), (b)(2)(A), (b)(3)(A), (b)(4)(A), (b)(5)(A).

By disregarding all these public-interest, public-health, and public-safety objectives, and limiting the CSA to "addiction and recreational abuse," the Court rules out the prohibition of anabolic-steroid use for bodybuilding purposes. It seeks to avoid this consequence by invoking the Anabolic Steroids Control Act of 1990, 104 Stat. 4851. Ante, at 27. But the only effect of that legislation is to make anabolic steroids controlled drugs under Schedule III of the CSA. If the only basis for control is (as the Court says) "addiction and recreational abuse," dispensation of these drugs for bodybuilding could not be proscribed.

Although, as I have described, the Court's opinion no more defers to state law than does the Directive, the Court relies on two provisions for the conclusion that "[t]he structure and operation of the CSA presume and rely upon a functioning medical profession regulated under the States' police powers," ante, at 23–namely the registration provisions of §823(f) and the nonpre-emption provision of §903. Reliance on the former is particularly unfortunate, because the Court's own analysis recounts how Congress amended §823(f) in 1984 in order to liberate the Attorney General's power over registration from the control of state regulators. See ante, at 14; 21 U.S.C. § 823(f); see also Brief for Petitioners 34—35. And the nonpre-emption clause is embarrassingly inapplicable, since it merely disclaims field pre-emption, and affirmatively prescribes federal pre-emption whenever state law creates a conflict.5 In any event, the Directive does not purport to pre-empt state law in any way, not even by conflict pre-emption— unless the Court is under the misimpression that some States require assisted suicide. The Directive merely interprets the CSA to prohibit, like countless other federal criminal provisions, conduct that happens not to be forbidden under state law (or at least the law of the State of Oregon).

With regard to the CSA's registration provisions, 21 U.S.C. § 823(f), 824(a), the Court argues that the statute cannot fairly be read to " 'hide elephants in mouseholes' " by delegating to the Attorney General the power to determine the legitimacy of medical practices in " 'vague terms or ancillary provisions.' " Ante, at 20 (quoting Whitman v. American Trucking Assns., Inc., 531 U.S. 457, 468 (2001)). This case bears not the remotest resemblance to Whitman, which held that "Congress ... does not alter the fundamental details of a regulatory scheme in vague terms or ancillary provisions." Ibid. (emphasis added). The Attorney General's power to issue regulations against questionable uses of controlled substances in no way alters "the fundamental details" of the CSA. I am aware of only four areas in which the Department of Justice has exercised that power to regulate uses of controlled substances unrelated to "addiction and recreational abuse" as the Court apparently understands that phrase: assisted suicide, aggressive pain management therapy, anabolic-steroid use, and cosmetic weight-loss therapy. See, e.g., In re Harline, 65 Fed. Reg. 5665, 5667 (2000) (weight loss); In re Tecca, 62 Fed. Reg. 12842, 12846 (1997) (anabolic steroids); In re Roth, 60 Fed. Reg. 62262, 62263, 62267 (1995) (pain management). There is no indication that enforcement in these areas interferes with the prosecution of "drug abuse" as the Court understands it. Unlike in Whitman, the Attorney General's additional power to address other forms of drug "abuse" does absolutely nothing to undermine the central features of this regulatory scheme. Of course it was critical to our analysis in Whitman that the language of the provision did not bear the meaning that respondents sought to give it. See 531 U.S., at 465. Here, for the reasons stated above, the provision is most naturally interpreted to incorporate a uniform federal standard for legitimacy of medical practice.6

Finally, respondents argue that the Attorney General must defer to state-law judgments about what constitutes legitimate medicine, on the ground that Congress must speak clearly to impose such a uniform federal standard upon the States. But no line of our clear-statement cases is applicable here. The canon of avoidance does not apply, since the Directive does not push the outer limits of Congress's commerce power, compare Solid Waste Agency of Northern Cook Cty. v. Army Corps of Engineers, 531 U.S. 159, 172 (2001) (regulation of isolated ponds), with United States v. Sullivan, 332 U.S. 689, 698 (1948) (regulation of labeling of drugs shipped in interstate commerce), or impinge on a core aspect of state sovereignty, cf. Atascadero State Hospital v. Scanlon, 473 U.S. 234, 242 (1985) (sovereign immunity); Gregory v. Ashcroft, 501 U.S. 452, 460 (1991) (qualifications of state government officials). The clear-statement rule based on the presumption against pre-emption does not apply because the Directive does not pre-empt any state law, cf. id., at 456—457; Rush Prudential HMO, Inc. v. Moran, 536 U.S. 355, 359 (2002). And finally, no clear statement is required on the ground that the Directive intrudes upon an area traditionally reserved exclusively to the States, cf. BFP v. Resolution Trust Corporation, 511 U.S. 531, 544 (1994) (state regulation of titles to real property), because the Federal Government has pervasively regulated the dispensation of drugs for over 100 years. See generally Brief for Pro-Life Legal Defense Fund et al. as Amici Curiae 3—15. It would be a novel and massive expansion of the clear-statement rule to apply it in a commerce case not involving pre-emption or constitutional avoidance, merely because Congress has chosen to prohibit conduct that a State has made a contrary policy judgment to permit. See Sullivan, supra, at 693.

III

Even if the Regulation did not exist and "prescription" in §829 could not be interpreted to require a "legitimate medical purpose," the Directive's conclusion that "prescribing, dispensing, or administering federally controlled substances ... by a physician ... may 'render his registration ... inconsistent with the public interest' and therefore subject to possible suspension or revocation under 21 U.S.C. [§]824(a)(4)," 66 Fed. Reg. 56608, would nevertheless be unassailable in this Court.

Sections 823(f) and 824(a) explicitly grant the Attorney General the authority to register and deregister physicians, and his discretion in exercising that authority is spelled out in very broad terms. He may refuse to register or deregister if he determines that registration is "inconsistent with the public interest," 21 U.S.C. § 823(f), after considering five factors, the fifth of which is "[s]uch other conduct which may threaten the public health and safety," §823(f)(5). See also In re Arora, 60 Fed. Reg. 4447, 4448 (1995) ("It is well established that these factors are to be considered in the disjunctive, i.e., the Deputy Administrator may properly rely on any one or a combination of factors, and give each factor the weight he deems appropriate"). As the Court points out, these broad standards were enacted in the 1984 amendments for the specific purpose of freeing the Attorney General's discretion over registration from the decisions of state authorities. See ante, at 13.

The fact that assisted-suicide prescriptions are issued in violation of §829 is of course sufficient to support the Directive's conclusion that issuing them may be cause for deregistration: such prescriptions would violate the fourth factor of §823(f), namely "[c]ompliance with applicable ... Federal ... laws relating to controlled substances," 21 U.S.C. § 823(f)(4). But the Attorney General did not rely solely on subsection (f)(4) in reaching his conclusion that registration would be "inconsistent with the public interest"; nothing in the text of the Directive indicates that. Subsection (f)(5) ("[s]uch other conduct which may threaten the public health and safety") provides an independent, alternative basis for the Directive's conclusion regarding deregistration–provided that the Attorney General has authority to interpret "public interest" and "public health and safety" in §823(f) to exclude assisted suicide.

Three considerations make it perfectly clear that the statute confers authority to interpret these phrases upon the Attorney General. First, the Attorney General is solely and explicitly charged with administering the registration and deregistration provisions. See §§823(f), 824(a). By making the criteria for such registration and deregistration such obviously ambiguous factors as "public interest" and "public health and safety," Congress implicitly (but clearly) gave the Attorney General authority to interpret those criteria– whether or not there is any explicit delegation provision in the statute. "Sometimes the legislative delegation to an agency on a particular question is implicit rather than explicit. In such a case, a court may not substitute its own construction of a statutory provision for a reasonable interpretation made by the administrator of an agency." Chevron, 467 U.S., at 844. The Court's exclusive focus on the explicit delegation provisions is, at best, a fossil of our pre-Chevron era; at least since Chevron, we have not conditioned our deferral to agency interpretations upon the existence of explicit delegation provisions. United States v. Mead Corp., 533 U.S. 218, 229 (2001), left this principle of implicit delegation intact.

Second, even if explicit delegation were required, Congress provided it in §821, which authorizes the Attorney General to "promulgate rules and regulations ... relating to the registration and control of the manufacture, distribution, and dispensing of controlled substances ... ." (Emphasis added.) Because "dispensing" refers to the delivery of a controlled substance "pursuant to the lawful order of, a practitioner," 21 U.S.C. § 802(10), the deregistration of such practitioners for writing impermissible orders "relat[es] to the registration ... of the ... dispensing" of controlled substances, 21 U.S.C. A. §821 (Supp. 2005).

Third, §821 also gives the Attorney General authority to promulgate rules and regulations "relating to the ... control of the ... dispensing of controlled substances." As discussed earlier, it is plain that the ordinary meaning of "control" must apply to §821, so that the plain import of the provision is to grant the Attorney General rulemaking authority over all the provisions of part C of the CSA, 21 U.S.C. A. §§821–830 (main ed. and Supp. 2005). Registering and deregistering the practitioners who issue the prescriptions necessary for lawful dispensation of controlled substances plainly "relat[es] to the ... control of the ... dispensing of controlled substances." §821 (Supp. 2005).

The Attorney General is thus authorized to promulgate regulations interpreting §§823(f) and 824(a), both by implicit delegation in §823(f) and by two grounds of explicit delegation in §821. The Court nevertheless holds that this triply unambiguous delegation cannot be given full effect because "the design of the statute," ante, at 18, evinces the intent to grant the Secretary of Health and Human Services exclusive authority over scientific and medical determinations. This proposition is not remotely plausible. The Court cites as authority for the Secretary's exclusive authority two specific areas in which his medical determinations are said to be binding on the Attorney General–with regard to the "scientific and medical evaluation" of a drug's effects that precedes its scheduling, §811(b), and with regard to "the appropriate methods of professional practice in the medical treatment of the narcotic addiction of various classes of narcotic addicts," 42

U.S.C. § 290bb—2a; see also 21 U.S.C. § 823(g) (2000 ed. and Supp. II). See ante, at 17—19. Far from establishing a general principle of Secretary supremacy with regard to all scientific and medical determinations, the fact that Congress granted the Secretary specifically defined authority in the areas of scheduling and addiction treatment, without otherwise mentioning him in the registration provisions, suggests, to the contrary, that Congress envisioned no role for the Secretary in that area—where, as we have said, interpretive authority was both implicitly and explicitly conferred upon the Attorney General.

Even if we could rewrite statutes to accord with sensible "design," it is far from a certainty that the Secretary, rather than the Attorney General, ought to control the registration of physicians. Though registration decisions sometimes require judgments about the legitimacy of medical practices, the Department of Justice has seemingly had no difficulty making them. See In re Harline, 65 Fed. Reg. 5665; In re Tecca, 62 Fed. Reg. 12842; In re Roth, 60 Fed. Reg. 62262. But unlike decisions about whether a substance should be scheduled or whether a narcotics addiction treatment is legitimate, registration decisions are not exclusively, or even primarily, concerned with "medical [and] scientific" factors. See 21 U.S.C. § 823(f). Rather, the decision to register, or to bring an action to deregister, an individual physician implicates all the policy goals and competing enforcement priorities that attend any exercise of prosecutorial discretion. It is entirely reasonable to think (as Congress evidently did) that it would be easier for the Attorney General occasionally to make judgments about the legitimacy of medical practices than it would be for the Secretary to get into the business of law enforcement. It is, in other words, perfectly consistent with an intelligent "design of the statute" to give the Nation's chief law enforcement official, not its chief health official, broad discretion over the substantive standards that govern registration and deregistration. That is especially true where the contested "scientific and medical" judgment at issue has to do with the legitimacy of physician-assisted suicide, which ultimately rests, not on "science" or "medicine," but on a naked value judgment. It no more depends upon a "quintessentially medical judgmen[t]," ante, at 20, than does the legitimacy of polygamy or eugenic infanticide. And it requires no particular medical training to undertake the objective inquiry into how the continuing traditions of Western medicine have consistently treated this subject. See OLC Memo, App. to Pet. for Cert. 113a—130a. The Secretary's supposedly superior "medical expertise" to make "medical judgments," ante, at 19—20, is strikingly irrelevant to the case at hand.

The Court also reasons that, even if the CSA grants the Attorney General authority to interpret §823(f), the Directive does not purport to exercise that authority, because it "does not undertake the five-factor analysis" of §823(f) and does not "on its face purport to be an application of the registration provision in §823(f)." Ante, at 14 (emphasis added). This reasoning is sophistic. It would be improper—indeed, impossible—for the Attorney General to "undertake the five-factor analysis" of §823(f) and to "appl[y] the registration provision" outside the context of an actual enforcement proceeding. But of course the Attorney General may issue regulations to clarify his interpretation of the five factors, and to signal how he will apply them in future enforcement proceedings. That is what the Directive plainly purports to do by citing §824(a)(4), and that is why the Directive's conclusion on deregistration is couched in conditional terms: "Such conduct by a physician ... may 'render his registration ... inconsistent with the public interest' and therefore subject to possible suspension or revocation under 21 U.S.C. [§]824(a)(4)." 66 Fed. Reg. 56608 (emphasis added).

It follows from what we have said that the Attorney General's authoritative interpretations of "public interest" and "public health and safety" in §823(f) are subject to Chevron deference. As noted earlier, the Court does not contest that the absence of notice-and-comment procedures for the Directive renders Chevron inapplicable. And there is no serious argument that "Congress has directly spoken to the precise question at issue," or that the Directive's interpretations of "public health and safety" and "inconsistent with the public interest" are not "permissible." Chevron, 467 U.S., at 842—843. On the latter point, in fact, the condemnation of assisted suicide by 50 American jurisdictions supports the Attorney General's view. The Attorney General may therefore weigh a physician's participation in assisted suicide as a factor counseling against his registration, or in favor of deregistration, under §823(f).

In concluding to the contrary, the Court merely presents the conclusory assertion that "it is doubtful the Attorney General could cite the 'public interest' or 'public health' to deregister a physician simply because he deemed a controversial practice permitted by state law to have an illegitimate medical purpose." Ante, at 17. But why on earth not?—especially when he has interpreted the relevant statutory factors in advance to give fair warning that such a practice is "inconsistent with the public interest." The Attorney General's discretion to determine the public interest in this area is admittedly broad—but certainly no broader than other congressionally conferred Executive powers that we have upheld in the past. See, e.g., National Broadcasting Co. v. United States, 319 U.S. 190, 216—217 (1943) ("public interest"); New York Central Securities Corp. v. United States, 287 U.S. 12, 24—25 (1932) (same); see also Mistretta v. United States, 488 U.S. 361, 415—416 (1989) (Scalia, J., dissenting).

*   *   *

In sum, the Directive's first conclusion—namely that physician-assisted suicide is not a "legitimate medical purpose"—is supported both by the deference we owe to the agency's interpretation of its own regulations and by the deference we owe to its interpretation of the statute. The other two conclusions—(2) that prescribing controlled drugs to assist suicide violates the CSA, and (3) that such conduct is also "inconsistent with the public interest"—are inevitable consequences of that first conclusion. Moreover, the third conclusion, standing alone, is one that the Attorney General is authorized to make.

The Court's decision today is perhaps driven by a feeling that the subject of assisted suicide is none of the Federal Government's business. It is easy to sympathize with that position. The prohibition or deterrence of assisted suicide is certainly not among the enumerated powers conferred on the United States by the Constitution, and it is within the realm of public morality (bonos mores) traditionally addressed by the so-called police power of the States. But then, neither is prohibiting the recreational use of drugs or discouraging drug addiction among the enumerated powers. From an early time in our national history, the Federal Government has used its enumerated powers, such as its power to regulate interstate commerce, for the purpose of protecting public morality–for example, by banning the interstate shipment of lottery tickets, or the interstate transport of women for immoral purposes. See Hoke v. United States, 227 U.S. 308, 321–323 (1913); Lottery Case, 188 U.S. 321, 356 (1903). Unless we are to repudiate a long and well-established principle of our jurisprudence, using the federal commerce power to prevent assisted suicide is unquestionably permissible. The question before us is not whether Congress can do this, or even whether Congress should do this; but simply whether Congress has done this in the CSA. I think there is no doubt that it has. If the term "legitimate medical purpose" has any meaning, it surely excludes the prescription of drugs to produce death.

For the above reasons, I respectfully dissent from the judgment of the Court.

Justice Scalia's dissent in Massachusetts v. EPA (April 2, 2007) [Notes omitted]

Justice Scalia, with whom The Chief Justice, Justice Thomas, and Justice Alito join, dissenting.

I join The Chief Justice's opinion in full, and would hold that this Court has no jurisdiction to decide this case because petitioners lack standing. The Court having decided otherwise, it is appropriate for me to note my dissent on the merits.

I

A

The provision of law at the heart of this case is §202(a)(1) of the Clean Air Act (CAA), which provides that the Administrator of the Environmental Protection Agency (EPA) "shall by regulation prescribe ... standards applicable to the emission of any air pollutant from any class or classes of new motor vehicles or new motor vehicle engines, which in his judgment cause, or contribute to, air pollution which may reasonably be anticipated to endanger public health or welfare." 42 U. S. C. §7521(a)(1) (emphasis added). As the Court recognizes, the statute "condition[s] the exercise of EPA's authority on its formation of a 'judgment.' " Ante, at 30. There is no dispute that the Administrator has made no such judgment in this case. See ante, at 32 ("We need not and do not reach the question whether on remand EPA must make an endangerment finding"); 68Fed. 52929 (2003) ("[N]o Administrator has made a finding under any of the CAA's regulatory provisions that CO_2 meets the applicable statutory criteria for regulation").

The question thus arises: Does anything require the Administrator to make a "judgment" whenever a petition for rulemaking is filed? Without citation of the statute or any other authority, the Court says yes. Why is that so? When Congress wishes to make private action force an agency's hand, it knows how to do so. See, e.g., Brock v. Pierce County, 476 U. S. 253, 254–255 (1986) (discussing the Comprehensive Employment and Training Act (CETA), 92 Stat. 1926, 29 U. S. C. §816(b) (1976 ed., Supp. V), which "provide[d] that the Secretary of Labor 'shall' issue a final determination as to the misuse of CETA funds by a grant recipient within 120 days after receiving a complaint alleging such misuse"). Where does the CAA say that the EPA Administrator is required to come to a decision on this question whenever a rulemaking petition is filed? The Court points to no such provision because none exists.

Instead, the Court invents a multiple-choice question that the EPA Administrator must answer when a petition for rulemaking is filed. The Administrator must exercise his judgment in one of three ways: (a) by concluding that the pollutant does cause, or contribute to, air pollution that endangers public welfare (in which case EPA is required to regulate); (b) by concluding that the pollutant does not cause, or contribute to, air pollution that endangers public welfare (in which case EPA is not required to regulate); or (c) by "provid[ing] some reasonable explanation as to why it cannot or will not exercise its discretion to determine whether" greenhouse gases endanger public welfare, ante, at 30, (in which case EPA is not required to regulate).

I am willing to assume, for the sake of argument, that the Administrator's discretion in this regard is not entirely unbounded—that if he has no reasonable basis for deferring judgment he must grasp the nettle at once. The Court, however, with no basis in text or precedent, rejects all of EPA's stated "policy judgments" as not "amount[ing] to a reasoned justification," ante, at 31, effectively narrowing the universe of potential reasonable bases to a single one: Judgment can be delayed only if the Administrator concludes that "the scientific uncertainty is [too] profound." Ibid. The Administrator is precluded from concluding for other reasons "that it would … be better not to regulate at this time." Ibid.<footcall num="1"> Such other reasons—perfectly valid reasons—were set forth in the agency's statement.

"We do not believe … that it would be either effective or appropriate for EPA to establish [greenhouse gas] standards for motor vehicles at this time. As described in detail below, the President has laid out a comprehensive approach to climate change that calls for near-term voluntary actions and incentives along with programs aimed at reducing scientific uncertainties and encouraging technological development so that the government may effectively and efficiently address the climate change issue over the long term.

.   .   .   .   .

"[E]stablishing [greenhouse gas] emission standards for U. S. motor vehicles at this time would … result in an inefficient, piecemeal approach to addressing the climate change issue. The U. S. motor vehicle fleet is one of many sources of [greenhouse gas] emissions both here and abroad, and different [greenhouse gas] emission sources face different technological and financial challenges in reducing emissions. A sensible regulatory scheme would require that all significant sources and sinks of [greenhouse gas] emissions be considered in deciding how best to achieve any needed emission reductions.

"Unilateral EPA regulation of motor vehicle [greenhouse gas] emissions could also weaken U. S. efforts to persuade developing countries to reduce the [greenhouse gas] intensity of their economies. Considering the large populations and growing economies of some developing countries, increases in their [greenhouse gas] emissions could quickly overwhelm the effects of [greenhouse gas] reduction measures in developed countries. Any potential benefit of EPA regulation could be lost to the extent other nations decided to let their emissions significantly increase in view of U. S. emissions reductions. Unavoidably, climate change raises important foreign policy issues, and it is the President's prerogative to address them." 68 Fed. Reg. 52929–52931 (footnote omitted).

The Court dismisses this analysis as "rest[ing] on reasoning divorced from the statutory text." Ante, at 30. "While the statute does condition the exercise of EPA's authority on its formation of a 'judgment,' ... that judgment must relate to whether an air pollutant 'cause[s], or contribute[s] to, air pollution which may reasonably be anticipated to endanger public health or welfare.' " Ibid. True but irrelevant. When the Administrator makes a judgment whether to regulate greenhouse gases, that judgment must relate to whether they are air pollutants that "cause, or contribute to, air pollution which may reasonably be anticipated to endanger public health or welfare." 42 U. S. C. §7521(a)(1). But the statute says nothing at all about the reasons for which the Administrator may defer making a judgment—the permissible reasons for deciding not to grapple with the issue at the present time. Thus, the various "policy" rationales, ante, at 31, that the Court criticizes are not "divorced from the statutory text," ante, at 30, except in the sense that the statutory text is silent, as texts are often silent about permissible reasons for the exercise of agency discretion. The reasons the EPA gave are surely considerations executive agencies regularly take into account (and ought to take into account) when deciding whether to consider entering a new field: the impact such entry would have on other Executive Branch programs and on foreign policy. There is no basis in law for the Court's imposed limitation.

EPA's interpretation of the discretion conferred by the statutory reference to "its judgment" is not only reasonable, it is the most natural reading of the text. The Court nowhere explains why this interpretation is incorrect, let alone why it is not entitled to deference under Chevron U. S. A. Inc. v. Natural Resources Defense Council, Inc., 467 U. S. 837 (1984) . As the Administrator acted within the law in declining to make a "judgment" for the policy reasons above set forth, I would uphold the decision to deny the rulemaking petition on that ground alone.

B

Even on the Court's own terms, however, the same conclusion follows. As mentioned above, the Court gives EPA the option of determining that the science is too uncertain to allow it to form a "judgment" as to whether greenhouse gases endanger public welfare. Attached to this option (on what basis is unclear) is an essay requirement: "If," the Court says, "the scientific uncertainty is so profound that it precludes EPA from making a reasoned judgment as to whether greenhouse gases contribute to global warming, EPA must say so." Ante, at 31. But EPA has said precisely that—and at great length, based on information contained in a 2001 report by the National Research Council (NRC) entitled Climate Change Science: An Analysis of Some Key Questions:

"As the NRC noted in its report, concentrations of [greenhouse gases (GHGs)] are increasing in the atmosphere as a result of human activities (pp. 9–12). It also noted that '[a] diverse array of evidence points to a warming of global surface air temperatures' (p. 16). The report goes on to state, however, that '[b]ecause of the large and still uncertain level of natural variability inherent in the climate record and the uncertainties in the time histories of the various forcing agents (and particularly aerosols), a [causal] linkage between the buildup of greenhouse gases in the atmosphere and the observed climate changes during the 20th century cannot be unequivocally established. The fact that the magnitude of the observed warming is large in comparison to natural variability as simulated in climate models is suggestive of such a linkage, but it does not constitute proof of one because the model simulations could be deficient in natural variability on the decadal to century time scale' (p. 17).

"The NRC also observed that 'there is considerable uncertainty in current understanding of how the climate system varies naturally and reacts to emissions of [GHGs] and aerosols' (p. 1). As a result of that uncertainty, the NRC cautioned that 'current estimate of the magnitude of future warming should be regarded as tentative and subject to future adjustments (either upward or downward).' Id. It further advised that '[r]educing the wide range of uncertainty inherent in current model predictions of global climate change will require major advances in understanding and modeling of both (1) the factors that determine atmospheric concentrations of [GHGs] and aerosols and (2) the so-called "feedbacks" that determine the sensitivity of the climate system to a prescribed increase in [GHGs].' Id.

"The science of climate change is extraordinarily complex and still evolving. Although there have been substantial advances in climate change science, there continue to be important uncertainties in our understanding of the factors that may affect future climate change and how it should be addressed. As the NRC explained, predicting future climate change necessarily involves a complex web of economic and physical factors including: Our ability to predict future global anthropogenic emissions of GHGs and aerosols; the fate of these emissions once they enter the atmosphere (e.g., what percentage are absorbed by vegetation or are taken up by the oceans); the impact of those emissions that remain in the atmosphere on the radiative properties of the atmosphere; changes in critically important climate feedbacks (e.g., changes in cloud cover and ocean circulation); changes in temperature characteristics (e.g., average temperatures, shifts in daytime and evening temperatures); changes in other climatic parameters (e.g., shifts in precipitation, storms); and ultimately the impact of such changes on human health and welfare (e.g., increases or decreases in agricultural productivity, human health impacts). The NRC noted, in particular, that '[t]he understanding of the relationships between weather/climate and human health is in its infancy and therefore the health consequences of climate change are poorly understood' (p. 20). Substantial scientific uncertainties limit our ability to assess each of these factors and to separate out those changes resulting from natural variability from those that are directly the result of increases in anthropogenic GHGs.

"Reducing the wide range of uncertainty inherent in current model predictions will require major advances in understanding and modeling of the factors that determine atmospheric concentrations of greenhouse gases and aerosols, and the processes that determine the sensitivity of the climate system." 68 Fed. Reg. 52930.

I simply cannot conceive of what else the Court would like EPA to say.

II

A

Even before reaching its discussion of the word "judgment," the Court makes another significant error when it concludes that "§202(a)(1) of the Clean Air Act authorizes EPA to regulate greenhouse gas emissions from new motor vehicles in the event that it forms a 'judgment' that such emissions contribute to climate change." Ante, at 25 (emphasis added). For such authorization, the Court relies on what it calls "the Clean Air Act's capacious definition of 'air pollutant.'" Ante, at 30.

"Air pollutant" is defined by the Act as "any air pollution agent or combination of such agents, including any physical, chemical, ... substance or matter which is emitted into or otherwise enters the ambient air." 42 U. S. C. §7602(g). The Court is correct that "[c]arbon dioxide, methane, nitrous oxide, and hydrofluorocarbons," ante, at 26, fit within the second half of that definition: They are "physical, chemical, ... substance[s] or matter which [are] emitted into or otherwise ente[r] the ambient air." But the Court mistakenly believes this to be the end of the analysis. In order to be an "air pollutant" under the Act's definition, the "substance or matter [being] emitted into ... the ambient air" must also meet the first half of the definition—namely, it must be an "air pollution agent or combination of such agents." The Court simply pretends this half of the definition does not exist.

The Court's analysis faithfully follows the argument advanced by petitioners, which focuses on the word "including" in the statutory definition of "air pollutant." See Brief for Petitioners 13–14. As that argument goes, anything that follows the word "including" must necessarily be a subset of whatever precedes it. Thus, if greenhouse gases qualify under the phrase following the word "including," they must qualify under the phrase preceding it. Since greenhouse gases come within the capacious phrase "any physical, chemical, ... substance or matter which is emitted into or otherwise enters the ambient air," they must also be "air pollution agent[s] or combination[s] of such agents," and therefore meet the definition of "air pollutant[s]."

That is certainly one possible interpretation of the statutory definition. The word "including" can indeed indicate that what follows will be an "illustrative" sampling of the general category that precedes the word. Federal Land Bank of St. Paul v. Bismarck Lumber Co., 314 U. S. 95, 100 (1941). Often, however, the examples standing alone are broader than the general category, and must be viewed as limited in light of that category. The Government provides a helpful (and unanswered) example: "The phrase 'any American automobile, including any truck or minivan,' would not naturally be construed to encompass a foreign-manufactured [truck or] minivan." Brief for Federal Respondent 34. The general principle enunciated—that the speaker is talking about American automobiles—carries forward to the illustrative examples (trucks and minivans), and limits them accordingly, even though in isolation they are broader. Congress often uses the word "including" in this manner. In 28 U. S. C. §1782(a), for example, it refers to "a proceeding in a foreign or international tribunal, including criminal investigations conducted before formal accusation." Certainly this provision would not encompass criminal investigations underway in a domestic tribunal. See also, e.g., 2 U. S. C. §54(a) ("The Clerk of the House of Representatives shall, at the request of a Member of the House of Representatives, furnish to the Member, for official use only, one set of a privately published annotated version of the United States Code, including supplements and pocket parts"); 22 U. S. C. §2304(b)(1) ("the relevant findings of appropriate international organizations, including nongovernmental organizations").

 In short, the word "including" does not require the Court's (or the petitioners') result. It is perfectly reasonable to view the definition of "air pollutant" in its entirety: An air pollutant can be "any physical, chemical, ... substance or matter which is emitted into or otherwise enters the ambient air," but only if it retains the general characteristic of being an "air pollution agent or combination of such agents." This is precisely the conclusion EPA reached: "[A] substance does not meet the CAA definition of 'air pollutant' simply because it is a 'physical, chemical, ... substance or matter which is emitted into or otherwise enters the ambient air.' It must also be an 'air pollution agent.' " 68 Fed. Reg. 52929, n. 3. See also id., at 52928 ("The root of the definition indicates that for a substance to be an 'air pollutant,' it must be an 'agent' of 'air pollution' "). Once again, in the face of textual ambiguity, the Court's application of Chevron deference to EPA's interpretation of the word "including" is nowhere to be found.2 Evidently, the Court defers only to those reasonable interpretations that it favors.

 B

 Using (as we ought to) EPA's interpretation of the definition of "air pollutant," we must next determine whether greenhouse gases are "agent[s]" of "air pollution." If so, the statute would authorize regulation; if not, EPA would lack authority.

 Unlike "air pollutants," the term "air pollution" is not itself defined by the CAA; thus, once again we must accept EPA's interpretation of that ambiguous term, provided its interpretation is a "permissible construction of the statute." Chevron, 467 U. S., at 843. In this case, the petition for rulemaking asked EPA for "regulation of [greenhouse gas] emissions from motor vehicles to reduce the risk of global climate change." 68 Fed. Reg.

52925. Thus, in deciding whether it had authority to regulate, EPA had to determine whether the concentration of greenhouse gases assertedly responsible for "global climate change" qualifies as "air pollution." EPA began with the commonsense observation that the "[p]roblems associated with atmospheric concentrations of CO_2," id., at 52927, bear little resemblance to what would naturally be termed "air pollution":

"EPA's prior use of the CAA's general regulatory provisions provides an important context. Since the inception of the Act, EPA has used these provisions to address air pollution problems that occur primarily at ground level or near the surface of the earth. For example, national ambient air quality standards (NAAQS) established under CAA section 109 address concentrations of substances in the ambient air and the related public health and welfare problems. This has meant setting NAAQS for concentrations of ozone, carbon monoxide, particulate matter and other substances in the air near the surface of the earth, not higher in the atmosphere.... CO_2, by contrast, is fairly consistent in concentration throughout the world's atmosphere up to approximately the lower stratosphere." Id., at 52926–52927.

In other words, regulating the buildup of CO_2 and other greenhouse gases in the upper reaches of the atmosphere, which is alleged to be causing global climate change, is not akin to regulating the concentration of some substance that is polluting the air.

We need look no further than the dictionary for confirmation that this interpretation of "air pollution" is eminently reasonable. The definition of "pollute," of course, is "[t]o make or render impure or unclean." Webster's New International Dictionary 1910 (2d ed. 1949). And the first three definitions of "air" are as follows: (1) "[t]he invisible, odorless, and tasteless mixture of gases which surrounds the earth"; (2) "[t]he body of the earth's atmosphere; esp., the part of it near the earth, as distinguished from the upper rarefied part"; (3) "[a] portion of air or of the air considered with respect to physical characteristics or as affecting the senses." Id., at 54. EPA's conception of "air pollution"—focusing on impurities in the "ambient air" "at ground level or near the surface of the earth"—is perfectly consistent with the natural meaning of that term.

In the end, EPA concluded that since "CAA authorization to regulate is generally based on a finding that an air pollutant causes or contributes to air pollution," 68 Fed. Reg. 52928, the concentrations of CO_2 and other greenhouse gases allegedly affecting the global climate are beyond the scope of CAA's authorization to regulate. "[T]he term 'air pollution' as used in the regulatory provisions cannot be interpreted to encompass global climate change." Ibid. Once again, the Court utterly fails to explain why this interpretation is incorrect, let alone so unreasonable as to be unworthy of Chevron deference.

*   *   *

The Court's alarm over global warming may or may not be justified, but it ought not distort the outcome of this litigation. This is a straightforward administrative-law case, in which Congress has passed a malleable statute giving broad discretion, not to us but to an executive agency. No matter how important the underlying policy issues at stake, this Court has no business substituting its own desired outcome for the reasoned judgment of the responsible agency.

Justice Scalia's concurrence and dissent in FEC v. Wisconsin Right to Life (June 25, 2007) [Notes omitted]

Justice Scalia, with whom Justice Kennedy and Justice Thomas join, concurring in part and concurring in the judgment.

A Moroccan cartoonist once defended his criticism of the Moroccan monarch (lse majesté being a serious crime in Morocco) as follows: " 'I'm not a revolutionary, I'm just defending freedom of speech.... I never said we had to change the king—no, no, no, no! But I said that some things the king is doing, I do not like. Is that a crime?' "1 Well, in the United States (making due allowance for the fact that we have elected representatives instead of a king) it is a crime, at least if the speaker is a union or a corporation (including not-for-profit public-interest corporations) and if the representative is identified by name within a certain period before a primary or congressional election in which he is running. That is the import of §203 of the Bipartisan Campaign Reform Act of 2002 (BCRA), the constitutionality of which we upheld three Terms ago in McConnell v. Federal Election Comm'n, 540 U. S. 93 (2003). As an element essential to that determination of constitutionality, our opinion left open the possibility that a corporation or union could establish that, in the particular circumstances of its case, the ban was unconstitutional because it was (to pursue the analogy) only the king's policies and not his tenure in office that was criticized. Today's cases present the question of what sort of showing is necessary for that purpose. For the reasons I set forth below, it is my view that no test for such a showing can both (1) comport with the requirement of clarity that unchilled freedom of political speech demands, and (2) be compatible with the facial validity of §203 (as pronounced in McConnell). I would therefore reconsider the decision that sets us the unsavory task of separating issue-speech from election-speech with no clear criterion.

I

Today's cases originated in the efforts of Wisconsin Right to Life, Inc. (WRTL), a Wisconsin nonprofit, nonstock ideological advocacy corporation, to lobby Wisconsin voters concerning the filibustering of the President's judicial nominees. The problem for WRTL was that, under §203 of BCRA, it would have been unlawful to air its television and radio ads within 30 days before the September 14, 2004, primary or within 60 days before the November 2, 2004, general election because the ads named Senator Feingold, who was then seeking reelection. Section 203(a) of BCRA amended §316(b)(2) of the Federal Election Campaign Act Amendments of 1974, which prohibited corporations and unions from "mak[ing] a contribution or expenditure in connection with any election to any political office, or in connection with any primary election ... for any political office." 2 U. S. C. §441b(a). Prior to BCRA, that section covered only expenditures for communications that expressly advocated the election or defeat of a candidate (in campaign-finance speak, so-called "express advocacy"). McConnell, supra, at 204. As amended, however, that section was broadened to cover "electioneering communication[s]," §441b(b)(2) (2000 ed., Supp. IV), which include "any broadcast, cable, or satellite communication" that "refers to a clearly identified candidate for Federal office" and that is aired within 60 days before a general election, or 30 days before a primary election, in the jurisdiction in which the candidate is running. §434(f)(3) (2000 ed., Supp. IV).2 Under the new law, a corporation or union wishing to air advertisements covered by the definition of "electioneering communication" is prohibited by §203 from doing so unless it first creates a separate segregated fund run by a "political action committee," commonly known as a "PAC." §441b(b)(2)(C) (2000 ed., Supp. IV). Three Terms ago, in McConnell, supra, this Court upheld most of BCRA's provisions against constitutional challenge, including §203. The Court found that the "vast majority" of ads aired during the 30-day and 60-day periods before elections were "the functional equivalent of express advocacy," id., at 206, but suggested that "pure issue ads," id., at 207, or "genuine issue ads," id., at 206, would be protected.

 The question in these cases is whether §203 can be applied to WRTL's ads consistently with the First Amendment . Last Term, this Court unanimously held, in Wisconsin Right to Life, Inc. v. Federal Election Comm'n, 546 U. S. 410, 411–412 (2006) (per curiam) (WRTL I), that as-applied challenges to §203 are available. The District Court in these cases subsequently held that §203 is unconstitutional as applied to the three ads at issue. The Court today affirms the judgment of the District Court. While I agree with that result, I disagree with the principal opinion's reasons.

 II

 A proper explanation of my views in these cases requires some discussion of the case law leading up to McConnell. I begin with the seminal case of Buckley v. Valeo, 424 U. S. 1 (1976) (per curiam), wherein this Court considered the constitutionality of various political contribution and expenditure limitations contained in the Federal Election Campaign Act of 1971 (FECA), 86 Stat. 3, as amended, 88 Stat. 1263. Buckley set forth a now-familiar framework for evaluating the constitutionality of campaign-finance regulations. The Court began with the recognition that contributing money to, and spending money on behalf of, political candidates implicates core First Amendment protections, and that restrictions on such contributions and expenditures "operate in an area of the most fundamental First Amendment activities." 424 U. S., at 14. The Court also recognized, however, that the Government has a compelling interest in "prevention of corruption and the appearance of corruption." Id., at 25. The "corruption" to which the Court repeatedly referred was of the "quid pro quo" variety, whereby an individual or entity makes a contribution or expenditure in exchange for some action by an official. Id., at 26, 27, 45, 47.

 The Court then held that FECA's contribution limitations passed constitutional muster because they represented a "marginal restriction upon the contributor's ability to engage in free communication," id., at 20–21, and were thus subject to a lower level of scrutiny, id., at 25. The Court invalidated, however, FECA's limitation on independent expenditures (i.e., expenditures made to express one's own positions and not in coordination with a campaign). Id., at 39–51. In the Court's view, expenditure limitations restrict speech that is " 'at the core of our electoral process and of the First Amendment freedoms,' " id., at 39, and require the highest scrutiny, id., at 44–45.

The independent-expenditure restriction at issue in Buckley limited the amount of money that could be spent " 'relative to a clearly identified candidate.' " Id., at 41 (quoting 18 U. S. C. §608(e)(1) (1970 ed., Supp. IV) (repealed 1976)). Before striking down the expenditure limitation, the Court narrowly construed §608(e)(1), in light of vagueness concerns, to cover only express advocacy—that is, advertising that "in express terms advocate[s] the election or defeat of a clearly identified candidate for federal office" by use of such words of advocacy "as 'vote for,' 'elect,' 'support,' 'cast your ballot for,' 'Smith for Congress,' 'vote against,' 'defeat,' 'reject.' " 424 U. S., at 44, and n. 52. This narrowing construction excluded so-called "issue advocacy"—for example, an ad that refers to a clearly identified candidate's position on an issue, but does not expressly advocate his election or defeat. Even as narrowly construed to cover only express advocacy, however, §608(e)(1) was held to be unconstitutional because the narrowed prohibition was too narrow to be effective and (quite apart from that shortcoming) independent expenditures did not pose a serious enough threat of corruption. Id., at 45–46. Notably, the Court also found the Government's interest in "equalizing the relative ability of individuals and groups to influence the outcome of elections" insufficient to support limitations on independent expenditures. Id., at 48.

Buckley might well have been the last word on limitations on independent expenditures. Some argued, however, that independent expenditures by corporations should be treated differently. That argument should have been foreclosed by Buckley for several reasons: (1) the particular provision at issue in Buckley, §608(e)(1) of FECA, was directed to expenditures not just by "individuals," but by "persons," with " 'persons' " specifically defined to include " 'corporation[s],' " id., at 23, 39, n. 45; (2) the plaintiffs in Buckley included corporations, id., at 8; and (3) Buckley, id., at 50–51, cited a case that involved limitations on corporations in support of its striking down the restriction at issue, Miami Herald Publishing Co. v. Tornillo, 418 U. S. 241 (1974) . Moreover, pre-Buckley cases had accorded corporations full First Amendment protection. See, e.g., NAACP v. Button, 371 U. S. 415, 428–429, 431 (1963) (holding that the corporation's activities were "modes of expression and association protected by the First and Fourteenth Amendment s"); Grosjean v. American Press Co., 297 U. S. 233, 244 (1936) (holding that corporations are guaranteed the "freedom of speech and of the press ... safeguarded by the due process of law clause of the Fourteenth Amendment "). See also Pacific Gas & Elec. Co. v. Public Util. Comm'n of Cal., 475 U. S. 1, 8 (1986) (plurality opinion) ("The identity of the speaker is not decisive in determining whether speech is protected"; "[c]orporations and other associations, like individuals, contribute to the 'discussion, debate, and the dissemination of information and ideas' that the First Amendment seeks to foster").

Indeed, one would have thought the coup de grâce to the argument that corporations can be treated differently for these purposes was dealt by First Nat. Bank of Boston v. Bellotti, 435 U. S. 765 (1978), decided just two years after Buckley. In that case, the Court struck down a Massachusetts statute that prohibited corporations from spending money in connection with a referendum unless the referendum materially affected the corporation's property, business, or assets. As the Court explained: The principle that such advocacy is "at the heart of the First Amendment's protection" and is "indispensable to decisionmaking in a democracy" is "no less true because the speech comes from a corporation rather than an individual." 435 U. S., at 776–777. And the Court rejected the arguments that corporate participation "would exert an undue influence on the outcome of a referendum vote"; that corporations would "drown out other points of view" and "destroy the confidence of the people in the democratic process," id., at 789; and that the prohibition was needed to protect corporate shareholders "by preventing the use of corporate resources in furtherance of views with which some shareholders may disagree," id., at 792–793.3

    The Court strayed far from these principles, however, in one post-Buckley case: Austin v. Michigan Chamber of Commerce, 494 U. S. 652 (1990) . This was the only pre-McConnell case in which this Court had ever permitted the Government to restrict political speech based on the corporate identity of the speaker. Austin upheld state restrictions on corporate independent expenditures in support of, or in opposition to, any candidate in elections for state office. 494 U. S., at 654–655. The statute had been modeled after the federal statute that BCRA §203 amended, which had been construed to reach only express advocacy, id., at 655, n. 1. And the ad at issue in Austin used the magical and forbidden words of express advocacy: "Elect Richard Bandstra." Id., at 714 (App. to opinion of Kennedy, J., dissenting). How did the Court manage to reach this result without overruling Bellotti? It purported to recognize a different class of corruption: "the corrosive and distorting effects of immense aggregations of wealth that are accumulated with the help of the corporate form and that have little or no correlation to the public's support for the corporation's political ideas." Austin, supra, at 660.

    Among the many problems with this "new" theory of corruption was that it actually constituted "the same 'corrosive and distorting effects of immense aggregations of wealth,' found insufficient to sustain a similar prohibition just a decade earlier," in Bellotti. McConnell, 540 U. S., at 325 (opinion of Kennedy, J.) (quoting Austin, supra, at 660; citation omitted). Indeed, Buckley itself had cautioned that "[t]he First Amendment's protection against governmental abridgment of free expression cannot properly be made to depend on a person's financial ability to engage in public discussion." 424 U. S., at 49. However, two Members of Austin's 6-to-3 majority appear to have thought it significant that Austin involved express advocacy whereas Bellotti involved issue advocacy. 494 U. S., at 675–676 (Brennan, J., concurring); id., at 678 (Stevens, J., concurring).4

    Austin was a significant departure from ancient First Amendment principles. In my view, it was wrongly decided. The flawed rationale upon which it is based is examined at length elsewhere, including in a dissenting opinion in Austin that a Member of the 5-to-

4 McConnell majority had joined, see Austin, 494 U. S., at 695–713 (opinion of Kennedy, J., joined by O'Connor, J.). See also id., at 679–695 (Scalia, J., dissenting); McConnell, 540 U. S., at 257–259 (opinion of Scalia, J.); id., at 325–330 (opinion of Kennedy, J.); id., at 273–275 (opinion of Thomas, J.). But at least Austin was limited to express advocacy, and nonexpress advocacy was presumed to remain protected under Buckley and Bellotti, even when engaged in by corporations.

Three Terms ago the Court extended Austin's flawed rationale to cover an even broader class of speech. In McConnell, the Court rejected a facial overbreadth challenge to BCRA §203's restrictions on corporate and union advertising, which were not limited to express advocacy but covered vast amounts of nonexpress advocacy (embraced within the term "electioneering communications"). 540 U. S., at 203–209. The Court held that, at least in light of the availability of the PAC option, the compelling governmental interest that supported restrictions on corporate expenditures for express advocacy also justified the extension of those restrictions to "electioneering communications," the "vast majority" of which were intended to influence elections. Id., at 206. Of course, the compelling interest to which the Court referred was " 'the corrosive and distorting effects of immense aggregations of [corporate] wealth,' " id., at 205 (quoting Austin, supra, at 660). "The justifications for the regulation of express advocacy," the Court explained, "apply equally" to ads run during the BCRA blackout period "to the extent ... [those ads] are the functional equivalent of express advocacy." 540 U. S., at 206 (emphasis added). The Court found that the "vast majority" of ads aired during the 30- and 60-day periods before elections fit that description. Finally, the Court concluded that, "[e]ven ... assum[ing] that BCRA will inhibit some constitutionally protected corporate and union speech" (i.e., "pure issue ads," id., at 207, or "genuine issue ads," id., at 206, and n. 88), its application to such ads was insubstantial, and thus the statute was not overbroad, id., at 207. But McConnell did not foreclose as-applied challenges to §203, WRTL I, 546 U. S., at 411–412, which brings me back to the present cases.

III

The question is whether WRTL meets the standard for prevailing in an as-applied challenge to BCRA §203. Answering that question obviously requires the Court to articulate the standard. The most obvious one, and the one suggested by the Federal Election Commission (FEC) and intervenors, is the standard set forth in McConnell itself: whether the advertisement is the "functional equivalent of express advocacy." McConnell, supra, at 206. See also Brief for Appellant FEC 18 (arguing that WRTL's "advertisements are the functional equivalent of the sort of express advocacy that this Court has long recognized may be constitutionally regulated"); Reply Brief for Appellant Sen. John McCain et al. in No. 06–970, p. 14 ("[C]ourts should apply the standard articulated in McConnell; Congress may constitutionally restrict corporate funding of ads that are the 'functional equivalent of express advocacy' for or against a candidate"). Intervenors flesh out the standard somewhat further: "[C]ourts should ask whether the ad's audience would reasonably understand the ad, in the context of the campaign, to promote or attack the candidate." Id., at 15. The District Court instead articulated a five-factor test that looks to whether the ad under review "(1) describes a legislative issue that is either currently the subject of legislative scrutiny or likely to be the subject of such scrutiny in the near future; (2) refers to the prior voting record or current position of the named candidate on the issue described; (3) exhorts the listener to do anything other than contact the candidate about the described issue; (4) promotes, attacks, supports, or opposes the named candidate; and (5) refers to the upcoming election, candidacy, and/or political party of the candidate." 466 F. Supp. 2d 195, 207 (DC 2006). The backup definition of "electioneering communications" contained in BCRA itself, see n. 2, supra, offers another possibility. It covers any communication that "promotes or supports a candidate for that office ... (regardless of whether the communication expressly advocates a vote for or against a candidate) and which also is suggestive of no plausible meaning other than an exhortation to vote for or against a specific candidate." And the principal opinion in this case offers a variation of its own (one bearing a strong likeness to BCRA's backup definition): whether "the ad is susceptible of no reasonable interpretation other than as an appeal to vote for or against a specific candidate." Ante, at 16.

There is a fundamental and inescapable problem with all of these various tests. Each of them (and every other test that is tied to the public perception, or a court's perception, of the import, the intent, or the effect of the ad) is impermissibly vague and thus ineffective to vindicate the fundamental First Amendment rights of the large segment of society to which §203 applies. Consider the application of these tests to WRTL's ads: There is not the slightest doubt that these ads had an issue-advocacy component. They explicitly urged lobbying on the pending legislative issue of appellate-judge filibusters. The question before us is whether something about them caused them to be the "functional equivalent" of express advocacy, and thus constitutionally subject to BCRA's criminal penalty. Does any of the tests suggested above answer this question with the degree of clarity necessary to avoid the chilling of fundamental political discourse? I think not.

The "functional equivalent" test does nothing more than restate the question (and make clear that the electoral advocacy need not be express). The test which asks how the ad's audience "would reasonably understand the ad" provides ample room for debate and uncertainty. The District Court's five-factor test does not (and could not possibly) specify how much weight is to be given to each factor—and includes the inherently vague factor of whether the ad "promotes, attacks, supports, or opposes the named candidate." (Does attacking the king's position attack the king?) The tests which look to whether the ad is "susceptible of no plausible meaning" or "susceptible of no reasonable interpretation" other than an exhortation to vote for or against a specific candidate seem tighter. They ultimately depend, however, upon a judicial judgment (or is it—worse still—a jury judgment?) concerning "reasonable" or "plausible" import that is far from certain, that rests upon consideration of innumerable surrounding circumstances which the speaker may not even be aware of, and that lends itself to distortion by reason of the decisionmaker's subjective evaluation of the importance or unimportance of the challenged speech. In this critical area of political discourse, the speaker cannot be compelled to risk felony prosecution with no more assurance of impunity than his prediction that what he says will be found susceptible of some "reasonable interpretation other than as an appeal to vote for or against a specific candidate." Under these circumstances, "[m]any persons, rather than undertake the considerable burden (and sometimes risk) of vindicating their rights through case-by-case litigation, will choose simply to abstain from protected speech—harming not only themselves but society as a whole, which is deprived of an uninhibited marketplace of ideas." Virginia v. Hicks, 539 U. S. 113, 119 (2003) (citation omitted).

It will not do to say that this burden must be accepted—that WRTL's antifilibustering, constitutionally protected speech can be constrained—in the necessary pursuit of electoral "corruption." We have rejected the "can't-make-an-omelet-without-breaking-eggs" approach to the First Amendment, even for the infinitely less important (and less protected) speech category of virtual child pornography. In Ashcroft v. Free Speech Coalition, 535 U. S. 234 (2002), the Government argued:

"the possibility of producing images by using computer imaging makes it very difficult for it to prosecute those who produce pornography by using real children. Experts ... may have difficulty in saying whether the pictures were made by using real children or by using computer imaging. The necessary solution ... is to prohibit both kinds of images." Id., at 254–255.

The Court rejected the principle that protected speech may be banned because it is difficult to distinguish from unprotected speech. Ibid. "[T]hat protected speech may be banned as a means to ban unprotected speech," it said, "turns the First Amendment upside down." Id., at 255. The same principle must be applied here. Indeed, it must be applied a fortiori, since laws targeting political speech are the principal object of the First-Amendment guarantee. The fact that the line between electoral advocacy and issue advocacy dissolves in practice is an indictment of the statute, not a justification of it.

Buckley itself compels the conclusion that these tests fall short of the clarity that the First Amendment demands. Recall that Buckley narrowed the ambiguous phrase "any expenditure ... relative to a clearly identified candidate" to mean any expenditure "advocating the election or defeat of a candidate." 424 U. S., at 42 (internal quotation marks omitted). But that construction alone did not eliminate the vagueness problem because "the distinction between discussion of issues and candidates and advocacy of election or defeat of candidates may often dissolve in practical application." Ibid. Any effort to distinguish between the two based on intent of the speaker or effect of the speech on the listener would " 'pu[t] the speaker ... wholly at the mercy of the varied understanding of his hearers,' " would " 'offe[r] no security for free discussion,' " and would " 'compe[l] the speaker to hedge and trim.' " Id., at 43 (quoting Thomas v. Collins, 323 U. S. 516, 535 (1945)). In order to avoid these "constitutional deficiencies," the Court was compelled to narrow the statutory language even further to cover only advertising that used the magic words of express advocacy. 424 U. S., at 43–44.

If a permissible test short of the magic-words test existed, Buckley would surely have adopted it. Especially since a consequence of the express-advocacy interpretationwas the invalidation ofthe entire limitation on independent expenditures, in part because the statute (as thus narrowed) could not be an effective limitation on expenditures for electoral advocacy. (It would be "naiv[e]," Buckley said, to pretend that persons and groups would have difficulty "devising expenditures that skirted the restriction on express advocacy of election or defeat but nevertheless benefited the candidate's campaign." Id., at 45.) Why did Buckley employ such a "highly strained" reading of the statute, McConnell, 540 U. S., at 280 (opinion of Thomas, J.), when broader readings, more faithful to the text, were available that might not have resulted in such underinclusiveness? In particular, after going to the trouble of narrowing the statute to cover "advocacy of [the] election or defeat of a candidat[e]," why not do what the principal opinion in these cases does, which is essentially to preface that phrase with the phrase "susceptible of no reasonable interpretation other than as"? Ante, at 16. There is only one plausible explanation: The Court eschewed narrowing constructions that would have been more faithful to the text and more effective at capturing campaign speech because those tests were all too vague. We cannot now adopt a standard held to be facially vague on the theory that it is somehow clear enough for constitutional as-applied challenges. If Buckley foreclosed such vagueness in a statutory test, it also must foreclose such vagueness in an as-applied test.

Though the principal opinion purports to recognize the "imperative for clarity" in this area of First Amendment law, its attempt to distinguish its test from the test found to be vague in Buckley falls far short. It claims to be "not so sure" that Buckley rejected its test because Buckley's holding did not concern "what the constitutional standard was in the abstract, divorced from specific statutory language." Ante, at 21, n. 7. Forget about abstractions: Thespecific statutory language at issue in Buckley was interpreted to mean " 'advocating the election or defeat of a candidate,' " and that is materially identical to the operative language in the principal opinion's test. The principal opinion's protestation that Buckley's vagueness holding "d[id] not dictate a constitutional test," ante, at 21, n. 7, is utterly compromised by the fact that the principal opinion itself relies on the very same vagueness holding to reject an intent-and-effect test in this case. See ante, at 13–14 (citing Buckley, supra, at 43–44). It is the same vagueness holding, and the principal opinion cannot invoke it on page 13 of its opinion and disclaim it on page 22. Finally, the principal opinion quotes McConnell for the proposition that "[t]he Buckley Court's 'express advocacy restriction was an endpoint of statutory interpretation, not a first principle of constitutional law.' " Ante, at 21, n. 7 (quoting McConnell, 540 U. S., at 190). I am not sure why this cryptic statement is at all relevant, since we are discussing here the principle of constitutional law that underlay Buckley's express-advocacy restriction. In any case, the statement is assuredly not a repudiation of Buckley's vagueness holding, since overbreadth and not vagueness was the issue in McConnell.[5]

What, then, is to be done? We could adopt WRTL's proposed test, under which §203 may not be applied to any ad (1) that "focuses on a current legislative branch matter, takes a position on the matter, and urges the public to ask a legislator to take a particular position or action with respect to the matter," and (2) that "does not mention any election, candidacy, political party, or challenger, or the official's character, qualifications, or fitness for office," (3) whether or not it "say[s] that the public official is wrong or right on the issue," so long as it does not expressly say he is "wrong for [the] office." Brief for Appellee 56–57 (footnote omitted).6 Or we could of course adopt the Buckley test of express advocacy. The problem is that, although these tests are clear, they are incompatible with McConnell's holding that §203 is facially constitutional, which was premised on the finding that a vast majority of ads proscribed by §203 are "sham issue ads," 540 U. S., at 185, that fall outside the First Amendment's protection. Indeed, any clear rule that would protect all genuine issue ads would cover such a substantial number of ads prohibited by §203 that §203 would be rendered substantially overbroad. The Government claims that even the amorphous test adopted by the District Court "call[s] into question a substantial percentage of the statute's applications," Tr. of Oral Arg. 4,7 and that any test providing relief to WRTL is incompatible with McConnell's facial holding because WRTL's ads are in the "heartland" of what Congress meant to prohibit, Brief for Appellant FEC 18, 28, 36, n. 9. If that is so, then McConnell cannot be sustained.

Like the Buckley Court and the parties to these cases, I recognize the practical reality that corporations can evade the express-advocacy standard. I share the instinct that "[w]hat separates issue advocacy and political advocacy is a line in the sand drawn on a windy day." See McConnell, supra, at 126, n. 16 (internal quotation marks omitted); Brief for Appellant FEC 30; Brief for Appellant Sen. John McCain et al. in No. 06–970, p. 35. But the way to indulge that instinct consistently with the First Amendment is either to eliminate restrictions on independent expenditures altogether or to confine them to one side of the traditional line—the express-advocacy line, set in concrete on a calm day by Buckley, several decades ago. Section 203's line is bright, but it bans vast amounts of political advocacy indistinguishable from hitherto protected speech.

The foregoing analysis shows that McConnell was mistaken in its belief that as-applied challenges could eliminate the unconstitutional applications of §203. They can do so only if a test is adopted which contradicts the holding of McConnell—that §203 is facially valid because the vast majority of pre-election issue ads can constitutionally be proscribed. In light of the weakness in Austin's rationale, and in light of the longstanding acceptance of the clarity of Buckley's express-advocacy line, it was adventurous for McConnell to extend Austin beyond corporate speech constituting express advocacy. Today's cases make it apparent that the adventure is a flop, and that McConnell's holding concerning §203 was wrong.8

IV

Which brings me to the question of stare decisis. "Stare decisis is not an inexorable command" or " 'a mechanical formula of adherence to the latest decision.' " Payne v. Tennessee, 501 U. S. 808, 828 (1991) (quoting Helvering v. Hallock, 309 U. S. 106, 119 (1940)). It is instead " 'a principle of policy,' " Payne, supra, at 828, and this

Court has a "considered practice" not to apply that principle of policy "as rigidly in constitutional as in nonconstitutional cases." Glidden Co. v. Zdanok, 370 U. S. 530, 543 (1962) . This Court has not hesitated to overrule decisions offensive to the First Amendment (a "fixed star in our constitutional constellation," if there is one, West Virginia Bd. of Ed. v. Barnette, 319 U. S. 624, 642 (1943))—and to do so promptly where fundamental error was apparent. Just three years after our erroneous decision in Minersville School Dist. v. Gobitis, 310 U. S. 586 (1940), the Court corrected the error in Barnette. Overruling a constitutional case decided just a few years earlier is far from unprecedented.9

Of particular relevance to the stare decisis question in these cases is the impracticability of the regime created by McConnell. Stare decisis considerations carry little weight when an erroneous "governing decisio[n]" has created an "unworkable" legal regime. Payne, supra, at 827. As described above, the McConnell regime is unworkable because of the inability of any acceptable as-applied test to validate the facial constitutionality of §203—that is, its inability to sustain proscription of the vast majority of issue ads. We could render the regime workable only by effectively overruling McConnell without saying so—adopting a clear as-applied rule protective of speech in the "heartland" of what Congress prohibited. The promise of an administrable as-applied rule that is both effective in the vindication of First Amendment rights and consistent with McConnell's holding is illusory.

It is not as though McConnell produced a settled body of law. Indeed, it is far more accurate to say that McConnell unsettled a body of law. Not until 1947, with the enactment of the Taft-Hartley amendments to the Federal Corrupt Practices Act, 1925, did Congress even purport to regulate campaign-related expenditures of corporations and unions. See United States v. CIO, 335 U. S. 106, 107, 113–115 (1948) . In the three decades following, this Court expressly declined to pronounce upon the constitutionality of such restrictions on independent expenditures. See Pipefitters v. United States, 407 U. S. 385, 400 (1972); United States v. Automobile Workers, 352 U. S. 567, 591–592 (1957); CIO, supra, at 110, 124. When the Court finally did turn to that question, it struck them down. See Buckley, 424 U. S. 1 . Our subsequent pre-McConnell decisions, with the lone exception of Austin, disapproved limits on independent expenditures. The modest medicine of restoring First Amendment protection to nonexpress advocacy—speech that was protected until three Terms ago—does not unsettle an established body of law.

Neither do any of the other considerations relevant to stare decisis suggest adherence to McConnell. These cases do not involve property or contract rights, where reliance interests are involved. Payne, supra, at 828. And McConnell's §203 holding has assuredly not become "embedded" in our "national culture." Dickerson v. United States, 530 U. S. 428, 443–444 (2000) (declining to overrule Miranda v. Arizona, 384 U. S. 436 (1966), in part because it had become embedded in our national culture). If §203 has had any cultural impact, it has been to undermine the traditional and important role of grassroots advocacy in American politics by burdening the "budget-strapped nonprofit entities upon which many of our citizens rely for political commentary and advocacy." McConnell, 540 U. S., at 340 (opinion of Kennedy, J.).

Perhaps overruling this one part of McConnell with respect to one part of BCRA would not "ai[d] the legislative effort to combat real or apparent corruption." Id., at 194.But the First Amendment was not designed to facilitate legislation, even wise legislation. Indeed, the assessment of former House Minority Leader Richard Gephardt, a proponent of campaign-finance reform, may well be correct. He said that " '[w]hat we have is two important values in direct conflict: freedom of speech and our desire for healthy campaigns in a healthy democracy,' " and " '[y]ou can't have both.' " Gibbs, The Wake-Up Call, Time, Feb. 3, 1997, pp. 22, 25. (He was referring, presumably, to incumbents' notions of healthy campaigns.) If he was wrong, however, and the two values can coexist, it is pretty clear which side of the equation this institution is primarily responsible for. It is perhaps our most important constitutional task to assure freedom of political speech. And when a statute creates a regime as unworkable and unconstitutional as today's effort at as-applied review proves §203 to be, it is our responsibility to decline enforcement.

> *   *   *

There is wondrous irony to be found in both the genesis and the consequences of BCRA. In the fact that the institutions it was designed to muzzle—unions and nearly all manner of corporations—for all the "corrosive and distorting effects" of their "immense aggregations of wealth," were utterly impotent to prevent the passage of this legislation that forbids them to criticize candidates (including incumbents). In the fact that the effect of BCRA has been to concentrate more political power in the hands of the country's wealthiest individuals and their so-called 527 organizations, unregulated by §203. (In the 2004 election cycle, a mere 24 individuals contributed an astounding total of $142 million to 527s. S. Weissman & R. Hassan, BCRA and the 527 Groups, in The Election After Reform 79, 92—96 (M. Malbin ed. 2006).) And in the fact that while these wealthy individuals dominate political discourse, it is this small, grass-roots organization of Wisconsin Right to Life that is muzzled.

I would overrule that part of the Court's decision in McConnell upholding §203(a) of BCRA. Accordingly, I join Parts I and II of today's principal opinion and otherwise concur only in the judgment.

Justice Scalia's dissent in Washington State Grange v. Washington State Republican Party (March 18, 2008)

Justice Scalia, with whom Justice Kennedy joins, dissenting.

The electorate's perception of a political party's beliefs is colored by its perception of those who support the party; and a party's defining act is the selection of a candidate and advocacy of that candidate's election by conferring upon him the party's endorsement. When the state-printed ballot for the general election causes a party to be associated with candidates who may not fully (if at all) represent its views, it undermines both these vital aspects of political association. The views of the self-identified party supporter color perception of the party's message, and that self-identification on the ballot, with no space for party repudiation or party identification of its own candidate, impairs the party's advocacy of its standard bearer. Because Washington has not demonstrated that this severe burden upon parties' associational rights is narrowly tailored to serve a compelling interest—indeed, because it seems to me Washington's only plausible interest is precisely to reduce the effectiveness of political parties—I would find the law unconstitutional.

I

I begin with the principles on which the Court and I agree. States may not use election regulations to undercut political parties' freedoms of speech or association. See U. S. Term Limits, Inc. v. Thornton, 514 U. S. 779, 833–834 (1995). Thus, when a State regulates political parties as a part of its election process, we consider "the 'character and magnitude' " of the burden imposed on the party's associational rights and "the extent to which the State's concerns make the burden necessary." Timmons v. Twin Cities Area New Party, 520 U. S. 351, 358 (1997). Regulations imposing severe burdens must be narrowly tailored to advance a compelling state interest. Ibid.

Among the First Amendment rights that political parties possess is the right to associate with the persons whom they choose and to refrain from associating with persons whom they reject. Democratic Party of United States v. Wisconsin ex rel. La Follette, 450 U. S. 107, 122 (1981). Also included is the freedom to choose and promote the " 'standard bearer who best represents the party's ideologies and preferences.' " Eu v. San Francisco County Democratic Central Comm., 489 U. S. 214, 224 (1989).

When an expressive organization is compelled to associate with a person whose views the group does not accept, the organization's message is undermined; the organization is understood to embrace, or at the very least tolerate, the views of the persons linked with them. We therefore held, for example, that a State severely burdened the right of expressive association when it required the Boy Scouts to accept an openly gay scoutmaster. The scoutmaster's presence "would, at the very least, force the organization to send a message, both to the youth members and the world, that the Boy Scouts accepts homosexual conduct as a legitimate form of behavior." Boy Scouts of America v. Dale, 530 U. S. 640, 653 (2000).

A political party's expressive mission is not simply, or even primarily, to persuade voters of the party's views. Parties seek principally to promote the election of candidates who will implement those views. See, e.g., Tashjian v. Republican Party of Conn., 479 U. S. 208, 216 (1986); Storer v. Brown, 415 U. S. 724, 745 (1974); M. Hershey & P. Beck, Party Politics in America13(10th ed. 2003). That is achieved in large part by marking candidates with the party's seal of approval. Parties devote substantial resources to making their names trusted symbols of certain approaches to governance. See, e.g., App. 239 (Declaration of Democratic Committee Chair Paul J. Berendt); J. Aldrich, Why Parties? 48–49 (1995). They then encourage voters to cast their votes for the candidates that carry the party name. Parties' efforts to support candidates by marking them with the party trademark, so to speak, have been successful enough to make the party name, in the words of one commentator, "the most important resource that the party possesses." Cain, Party Autonomy and Two-Party Electoral Competition, 149 U. Pa. L. Rev. 793, 804 (2001). And all evidence suggests party labels are indeed a central consideration for most voters. See, e.g., id., at 804, n. 34; Rahn, The Role of Partisan Stereotypes in Information Processing About Political Candidates, 37Am. J. Pol. Sci. 472 (1993); Klein & Baum, Ballot Information and Voting Decisions in Judicial Elections, 54 Pol. Research Q. 709 (2001).

II

A

The State of Washington need not like, and need not favor, political parties. It is entirely free to decline running primaries for the selection of party nominees and to hold nonpartisan general elections in which party labels have no place on the ballot. See California Democratic Party v. Jones, 530 U. S. 567, 585–586 (2000) . Parties would then be left to their own devices in both selecting and publicizing their candidates. But Washington has done more than merely decline to make its electoral machinery available for party building. Recognizing that parties draw support for their candidates by giving them the party imprimatur, Washington seeks to reduce the effectiveness of that endorsement by allowing any candidate to use the ballot for drawing upon the goodwill that a party has developed, while preventing the party from using the ballot to reject the claimed association or to identify the genuine candidate of its choice. This does not merely place the ballot off limits for party building; it makes the ballot an instrument by which party building is impeded, permitting unrebutted associations that the party itself does not approve.

These cases cannot be decided without taking account of the special role that a state-printed ballot plays in elections. The ballot comes into play "at the most crucial stage in the electoral process—the instant before the vote is cast." Anderson v. Martin, 375 U. S. 399, 402 (1964) . It is the only document that all voters are guaranteed tosee, and it is "the last thing the voter sees before he makes his choice," Cook v. Gralike, 531 U. S. 510, 532 (2001) (Rehnquist, C. J., concurring in judgment). Thus, we have held that a State cannot elevate a particular issue to prominence by making it the only issue for which the ballot sets forth the candidates' positions. Id., at 525–526 (opinion of the Court). And we held unconstitutional California's election system, which listed as the party's candidate on the general election ballot the candidate selected in a state-run "blanket primary" in which all citizens could determine who would be the party's nominee. Jones, 530 U. S., at 586. It was not enough to sustain the law that the party remained free to select its preferred candidate through another process, and could denounce or campaign against the candidate carrying the party's name on the general election ballot. Forced association with the party on the general election ballot was fatal. Id., at 575–577.

The Court makes much of the fact that the party names shown on the Washington ballot may be billed as mere statements of candidate "preference." See ante, at 11–14. To be sure, the party is not itself forced to display favor for someone it does not wish to associate with, as the Boy Scouts were arguably forced to do by employing the homosexual scoutmaster in Dale, and as the political parties were arguably forced to do by lending their ballot-endorsement as party nominee in Jones. But thrusting an unwelcome, self-proclaimed association upon the party on the election ballot itself is amply destructive of the party's associational rights. An individual's endorsement of a party shapes the voter's view of what the party stands for, no less than the party's endorsement of an individual shapes the voter's view of what the individual stands for. That is why party nominees are often asked (and regularly agree) to repudiate the support of persons regarded as racial extremists. On Washington's ballot, such repudiation is impossible. And because the ballot is the only document voters are guaranteed to see, and the last thing they see before casting their vote, there is "no meansof replying" that "would be equally effective with the voter." Cook, supra, at 532 (Rehnquist, C. J., concurring in judgment).

Not only is the party's message distorted, but its goodwill is hijacked. There can be no dispute that candidate acquisition of party labels on Washington's ballot—even if billed as self-identification—is a means of garnering the support of those who trust and agree with the party. The "I prefer the D's" and "I prefer the R's" will not be on the ballot for esthetic reasons; they are designed to link candidates to unwilling parties (or at least parties who are unable to express their revulsion) and to encourage voters to cast their ballots based in part on the trust they place in the party's name and the party's philosophy. These harms will be present no matter how Washington's law is implemented. There is therefore "no set of circumstances" under which Washington's law would not severely burden political parties, see United States v. Salerno, 481 U. S. 739, 745 (1987), and no good reason to wait until Washington has undermined its political parties to declare that it is forbidden to do so.

B

The Chief Justice would wait to see if the law is implemented in a manner that no more harms political parties than allowing a person to state that he " 'like[s] Campbell's soup' " would harm the Campbell Soup Company. See ante, at 3 (concurring opinion). It is hard to know how to respond. First and most fundamentally, there is simply no comparison between statements of "preference" for an expressive association and statements of "preference" for soup. The robust First Amendment freedom to associate belongs only to groups "engage[d] in 'expressive association,' " Dale, 530 U. S., at 648. The Campbell Soup Company does not exist to promote a message, and "there is only minimal constitutional protection of the freedom of commercial association," Roberts v. United States Jaycees, 468 U. S. 609, 634 (1984) (O'Connor, J., concurring in part and concurring in judgment).

Second, I assuredly do not share The Chief Justice's view that the First Amendment will be satisfied so long as the ballot "is designed in such a manner that no reasonable voter would believe that the candidates listed there are nominees or members of, or otherwise associated with, the parties the candidates claimed to 'prefer.' " Ante, at 3.

To begin with, it seems to me quite impossible for the ballot to satisfy a reasonable voter that the candidate is not "associated with" the party for which he has expressed a preference. He has associated himself with the party by his very expression of a preference—and that indeed is the whole purpose of allowing the preference to be expressed. If all The Chief Justice means by "associated with" is that the candidate "does not speak on the party's behalf or with the party's approval," ibid., none of my analysis in this opinion relies upon that misperception, nor upon the misperception that the candidate is a member or the nominee of the party. Avoiding those misperceptions is far from enough. Is it enough to say on the ballot that a notorious and despised racist who says that the party is his choice does not speak with the party's approval? Surely not. His unrebutted association of that party with his views distorts the image of the party nonetheless. And the fact that the candidate who expresses a "preference" for one or another party is shown not to be the nominee of that party does not deprive him of the boost from the party's reputation which the party wishes to confer only on its nominee. The Chief Justice claims that "the content of the ballots in the pertinent respect is yet to be determined," ibid. I disagree. We know all we need to know about the form of ballot. When pressed, Washington's Attorney General assured us at oral argument that the ballot will not say whether the party for whom the candidate expresses a preference claims or disavows him. (Of course it will not, for that would enable the party expression that it is the very object of this legislation to impair.)

And finally, while The Chief Justice earlier expresses his awareness that the special character of the ballot is what makes these cases different, ante, at 2, his Campbell's Soup example seems to forget that. If we must speak in terms of soup, Washington's law is like a law that encourages Oscar the Grouch (Sesame Street's famed bad-taste resident of a garbage can) to state a "preference" for Campbell's at every point of sale, while barring the soup company from disavowing his endorsement, or indeed using its name at all, in those same crucial locations. Reserving the most critical communications forum for statements of "preference" by a potentially distasteful speaker alters public perceptions of the entity that is "preferred"; and when this privileged connection undermines not a company's ability to identify and promote soup but an expressive association's ability to identify and promote its message and its standard bearer, the State treads on the constitutionally protected freedom of association.

The majority opinion and The Chief Justice's concurrence also endorse a wait-and-see approach on the grounds that it is not yet evident how the law will affect voter perception of the political parties. But contrary to the Court's suggestion, it is not incumbent on the political parties to adduce "evidence," ante, at 15, that forced association affects their ability to advocate for their candidates and their causes. We have never put expressive groups to this perhaps-impossible task. Rather, we accept their own assessments of the matter. The very cases on which The Chief Justice relies for a wait-and-see approach, ante, at 1–2, establish as much. In Dale, for example, we did not require the Boy Scouts to prove that forced acceptance of the openly homosexual scoutmaster would distort their message. See 530 U. S., at 653 (citing La Follette, 450 U. S., at 123–124). Nor in Hurley v. Irish-American Gay, Lesbian and Bisexual Group of Boston, Inc., 515 U. S. 557 (1995),did we require the organizers of the St. Patrick's Day Parade to demonstrate that including a gay contingent in the parade would distort their message. See id., at 577. Nor in Jones, 530 U. S. 567, did we require the political parties to demonstrate either that voters would incorrectly perceive the "nominee" labels on the ballot to be the products of party elections or that the labels would change voter perceptions of the party. It does not take a study to establish that when statements of party connection are the sole information listed next to candidate names on the ballot, those statements will affect voters' perceptions of what the candidate stands for, what the party stands for, and whom they should elect.

III

Since I conclude that Washington's law imposes a severe burden on political parties' associational rights, I would uphold the law only if it were "narrowly tailored" to advance "a compelling state interest." Timmons, 520 U. S., at 358. Neither the Court's opinion nor the State's submission claims that Washington's law passes such scrutiny. The State argues only that it "has a rational basis" for "providing voters with a modicum of relevant information about the candidates," Brief for Petitioners in No. 06–730, pp. 48–49. This is the only interest the Court's opinion identifies as well. Ante, at 15.

But "rational basis" is the least demanding of our tests; it is the same test that allows individuals to be taxed at different rates because they are in different businesses. See Allied Stores of Ohio, Inc. v. Bowers, 358 U. S. 522, 526–527 (1959) . It falls far, far short of establishing the compelling state interest that the First Amendment requires. And to tell the truth, here even the existence of a rational basis is questionable. Allowing candidates to identify themselves with particular parties on the ballot displays the State's view that adherence to party philosophy is "an important—perhaps paramount— consideration in the citizen's choice." Anderson, 375 U. S., at 402. If that is so, however, it seems to me irrational not to allow the party to disclaim that self-association, or to identify its own endorsed candidate.

It is no mystery what is going on here. There is no state interest behind this law except the Washington Legislature's dislike for bright-colors partisanship, and its desire to blunt the ability of political parties with noncentrist views to endorse and advocate their own candidates. That was the purpose of the Washington system that this enactment was adopted to replace—a system indistinguishable from the one we invalidated in Jones, which required parties to allow nonmembers to join in the selection of the candidates shown as their nominees on the election ballot. (The system was held unconstitutional in Democratic Party of Washington State v. Reed, 343 F. 3d 1198 (CA9 2003).) And it is the obvious purpose of Washington legislation enacted after this law, which requires political parties to repeat a candidate's self-declared party "preference" in electioneering communications concerning the candidate—even if the purpose of the communication is to criticize the candidate and to disavow any con-nection between him and the party.

Wash. Rev. Code §42.17.510(1) (2006); see also Wash. Admin. Code §390–18–020 (2007).

Even if I were to assume, however, that Washington has a legitimate interest in telling voters on the ballot (above all other things) that a candidate says he favors a particular political party; and even if I were further to assume (per impossibile) that that interest was a compelling one; Washington would still have to "narrowly tailor" its law to protect that interest with minimal intrusion upon the parties' associational rights. There has been no attempt to do that here. Washington could, for example, have permitted parties to disclaim on the general-election ballot the asserted association or to designate on the ballot their true nominees. The course the State has chosen makes sense only as an effort to use its monopoly power over the ballot to undermine the expressive activities of the political parties.

*   *   *

The right to associate for the election of candidates is fundamental to the operation of our political system, and state action impairing that association bears a heavy burden of justification. Washington's electoral system permits individuals to appropriate the parties' trademarks, so to speak, at the most crucial stage of election, thereby distorting the parties' messages and impairing their endorsement of candidates. The State's justification for this (to convey a "modicum of relevant information") is not only weak but undeserving of credence. We have here a system which, like the one it replaced, does not merely refuse to assist, but positively impairs, the legitimate role of political parties. I dissent from the Court's conclusion that the Constitution permits this sabotage.

Justice Scalia's dissent in Boumediene v. Bush (June 12, 2008) [Notes omitted]

Justice SCALIA, with whom THE CHIEF JUSTICE, Justice THOMAS, and Justice ALITO join, dissenting.

Today, for the first time in our Nation's history, the Court confers a constitutional right to habeas corpus on alien enemies detained abroad by our military forces in the course of an ongoing war. THE CHIEF JUSTICE's dissent, which I join, shows that the procedures prescribed by Congress in the Detainee Treatment Act provide the essential protections that habeas corpus guarantees; there has thus been no suspension of the writ, and no basis exists for judicial intervention beyond what the Act allows. My problem with today's opinion is more fundamental still: The writ of habeas corpus does not, and never has, run in favor of aliens abroad; the Suspension Clause thus has no application, and the Court's intervention in this military matter is entirely ultra vires.

I shall devote most of what will be a lengthy opinion to the legal errors contained in the opinion of the Court. Contrary to my usual practice, however, I think it appropriate to begin with a description of the disastrous consequences of what the Court has done today.

I

America is at war with radical Islamists. The enemy began by killing Americans and American allies abroad: 241 at the Marine barracks in Lebanon, 19 at the Khobar Towers in Dhahran, 224 at our embassies in Dar es Salaam and Nairobi, and 17 on the USS Cole in Yemen. See National Commission on Terrorist Attacks Upon the United States, The 9/11 Commission Report, pp. 60-61, 70, 190 (2004). On September 11, 2001, the enemy brought the battle to American soil, killing 2,749 at the Twin Towers in New York City, 184 at the Pentagon in Washington, D. C., and 40 in Pennsylvania. See id., at 552, n. 188. It has threatened further attacks against our homeland; one need only walk about buttressed and barricaded Washington, or board a plane anywhere in the country, to know that the threat is a serious one. Our Armed Forces are now in the field against the enemy, in Afghanistan and Iraq. Last week, 13 of our countrymen in arms were killed.

The game of bait-and-switch that today's opinion plays upon the Nation's Commander in Chief will make the war harder on us. It will almost certainly cause more Americans to be killed. That consequence would be tolerable if necessary to preserve a time-honored legal principle vital to our constitutional Republic. But it is this Court's blatant abandonment of such a principle that produces the decision today. The President relied on our settled precedent in Johnson v. Eisentrager, 339 U.S. 763, 70 S.Ct. 936, 94 L.Ed. 1255 (1950), when he established the prison at Guantanamo Bay for enemy aliens. Citing that case, the President's Office of Legal Counsel advised him "that the great weight of legal authority indicates that a federal district court could not properly exercise habeas jurisdiction over an alien detained at [Guantanamo Bay]." Memorandum from Patrick F. Philbin and John C. Yoo, Deputy Assistant Attorneys General, Office of Legal Counsel, to William J. Haynes II, General Counsel, Dept. of Defense, p. 1 (Dec. 28, 2001). Had the law been otherwise, the military surely would not have transported prisoners there, but would have kept them in Afghanistan, transferred them to another of our foreign military bases, or turned them over to allies for detention. Those other facilities might well have been worse for the detainees themselves.

In the long term, then, the Court's decision today accomplishes little, except perhaps to reduce the well-being of enemy combatants that the Court ostensibly seeks to protect. In the short term, however, the decision is devastating. At least 30 of those prisoners hitherto released from Guantanamo Bay have returned to the battlefield. See S.Rep. No. 110-90, pt. 7, p. 13 (2007) (minority views of Sens. Kyl, Sessions, Graham, Cornyn, and Coburn) (hereinafter Minority Report). Some have been captured or killed. See ibid.; see also Mintz, Released Detainees Rejoining the Fight, Washington Post, Oct. 22, 2004, pp. A1, A12. But others have succeeded in carrying on their atrocities against innocent civilians. In one case, a detainee released from Guantanamo Bay masterminded the kidnaping of two Chinese dam workers, one of whom was later shot to death when used as a human shield against Pakistani commandoes. See Khan & Lancaster, Pakistanis Rescue Hostage; 2nd Dies, Washington Post, Oct. 15, 2004, p. A18. Another former detainee promptly resumed his post as a senior Taliban commander and murdered a United Nations engineer and three Afghan soldiers. Mintz, supra. Still another murdered an Afghan judge. See Minority Report 13. It was reported only last month that a released detainee carried out a suicide bombing against Iraqi soldiers in Mosul, Iraq. See White, Ex-Guantanamo Detainee Joined Iraq Suicide Attack, Washington Post, May 8, 2008, p. A18.

These, mind you, were detainees whom the military had concluded were not enemy combatants. Their return to the kill illustrates the incredible difficulty of assessing who is and who is not an enemy combatant in a foreign theater of operations where the environment does not lend itself to rigorous evidence collection. Astoundingly, the Court today raises the bar, requiring military officials to appear before civilian courts and defend their decisions under procedural and evidentiary rules that go beyond what Congress has specified. As THE CHIEF JUSTICE's dissent makes clear, we have no idea what those procedural and evidentiary rules are, but they will be determined by civil courts and (in the Court's contemplation at least) will be more detainee-friendly than those now applied, since otherwise there would no reason to hold the congressionally prescribed procedures unconstitutional. If they impose a higher standard of proof (from foreign battlefields) than the current procedures require, the number of the enemy returned to combat will obviously increase.

But even when the military has evidence that it can bring forward, it is often foolhardy to release that evidence to the attorneys representing our enemies. And one escalation of procedures that the Court is clear about is affording the detainees increased access to witnesses (perhaps troops serving in Afghanistan?) and to classified information. See ante, at 2269-2270. During the 1995 prosecution of Omar Abdel Rahman, federal prosecutors gave the names of 200 unindicted co-conspirators to the "Blind Sheik's" defense lawyers; that information was in the hands of Osama Bin Laden within two weeks. See Minority Report 14-15. In another case, trial testimony revealed to the enemy that the United States had been monitoring their cellular network, whereupon they promptly stopped using it, enabling more of them to evade capture and continue their atrocities. See id., at 15.

And today it is not just the military that the Court elbows aside. A mere two Terms ago in Hamdan v. Rumsfeld, 548 U.S. 557, 126 S.Ct. 2749, 165 L.Ed.2d 723 (2006), when the Court held (quite amazingly) that the Detainee Treatment Act of 2005 had not stripped habeas jurisdiction over Guantanamo petitioners' claims, four Members of today's five-Justice majority joined an opinion saying the following:

"Nothing prevents the President from returning to Congress to seek the authority [for trial by military commission] he believes necessary.

"Where, as here, no emergency prevents consultation with Congress, judicial insistence upon that consultation does not weaken our Nation's ability to deal with danger. To the contrary, that insistence strengthens the Nation's ability to determine—through democratic means—how best to do so. The Constitution places its faith in those democratic means." Id., at 636, 126 S.Ct. 2749 (BREYER, J., concurring).[1]

Turns out they were just kidding. For in response, Congress, at the President's request, quickly enacted the Military Commissions Act, emphatically reasserting that it did not want these prisoners filing habeas petitions. It is therefore clear that Congress and the Executive—both political branches—have determined that limiting the role of civilian courts in adjudicating whether prisoners captured abroad are properly detained is important to success in the war that some 190,000 of our men and women are now fighting. As the Solicitor General argued, "the Military Commissions Act and the Detainee Treatment Act . . . represent an effort by the political branches to strike an appropriate balance between the need to preserve liberty and the need to accommodate the weighty and sensitive governmental interests in ensuring that those who have in fact fought with the enemy during a war do not return to battle against the United States." Brief for Federal Respondents 10-11 (internal quotation marks omitted).

But it does not matter. The Court today decrees that no good reason to accept the judgment of the other two branches is "apparent." Ante, at 2261. "The Government," it declares, "presents no credible arguments that the military mission at Guantanamo would be compromised if habeas corpus courts had jurisdiction to hear the detainees' claims." Ibid. What competence does the Court have to second-guess the judgment of Congress and the President on such a point? None whatever. But the Court blunders in nonetheless. Henceforth, as today's opinion makes unnervingly clear, how to handle enemy prisoners in this war will ultimately lie with the branch that knows least about the national security concerns that the subject entails.

II

A

The Suspension Clause of the Constitution provides: "The Privilege of the Writ of Habeas Corpus shall not be suspended, unless when in Cases of Rebellion or Invasion the public Safety may require it." Art. I, § 9, cl. 2. As a court of law operating under a written Constitution, our role is to determine whether there is a conflict between that Clause and the Military Commissions Act. A conflict arises only if the Suspension Clause preserves the privilege of the writ for aliens held by the United States military as enemy combatants at the base in Guantanamo Bay, located within the sovereign territory of Cuba.

We have frequently stated that we owe great deference to Congress's view that a law it has passed is constitutional. See, e.g., Department of Labor v. Triplett, 494 U.S. 715, 721, 110 S.Ct. 1428, 108 L.Ed.2d 701 (1990); United States v. National Dairy Products Corp., 372 U.S. 29, 32, 83 S.Ct. 594, 9 L.Ed.2d 561 (1963); see also American Communications Assn. v. Douds, 339 U.S. 382, 435, 70 S.Ct. 674, 94 L.Ed. 925 (1950) (Jackson, J., concurring in part and dissenting in part). That is especially so in the area of foreign and military affairs; "perhaps in no other area has the Court accorded Congress greater deference." Rostker v. Goldberg, 453 U.S. 57, 64-65, 101 S.Ct. 2646, 69 L.Ed.2d 478 (1981). Indeed, we accord great deference even when the President acts alone in this area. See Department of Navy v. Egan, 484 U.S. 518, 529-530, 108 S.Ct. 818, 98 L.Ed.2d 918 (1988); Regan v. Wald, 468 U.S. 222, 243, 104 S.Ct. 3026, 82 L.Ed.2d 171 (1984).

In light of those principles of deference, the Court's conclusion that "the common law [does not] yiel[d] a definite answer to the questions before us," ante, at 2251, leaves it no choice but to affirm the Court of Appeals. The writ as preserved in the Constitution could not possibly extend farther than the common law provided when that Clause was written. See Part III, infra. The Court admits that it cannot determine whether the writ historically extended to aliens held abroad, and it concedes (necessarily) that Guantanamo Bay lies outside the sovereign territory of the United States. See ante, at 2251-2252; Rasul v. Bush, 542 U.S. 466, 500-501, 124 S.Ct. 2686, 159 L.Ed.2d 548 (2004) (SCALIA, J., dissenting). Together, these two concessions establish that it is (in the Court's view) perfectly ambiguous whether the common-law writ would have provided a remedy for these petitioners. If that is so, the Court has no basis to strike down the Military Commissions Act, and must leave undisturbed the considered judgment of the coequal branches.[2]

How, then, does the Court weave a clear constitutional prohibition out of pure interpretive equipoise? The Court resorts to "fundamental separation-of-powers principles" to interpret the Suspension Clause. Ante, at 2253. According to the Court, because "the writ of habeas corpus is itself an indispensable mechanism for monitoring the separation of powers," the test of its extraterritorial reach "must not be subject to manipulation by those whose power it is designed to restrain." Ante, at 2259.

That approach distorts the nature of the separation of powers and its role in the constitutional structure. The "fundamental separation-of-powers principles" that the Constitution embodies are to be derived not from some judicially imagined matrix, but from the sum total of the individual separation-of-powers provisions that the Constitution sets forth. Only by considering them one-by-one does the full shape of the Constitution's separation-of-powers principles emerge. It is nonsensical to interpret those provisions themselves in light of some general "separation-of-powers principles" dreamed up by the Court. Rather, they must be interpreted to mean what they were understood to mean when the people ratified them. And if the understood scope of the writ of habeas corpus was "designed to restrain" (as the Court says) the actions of the Executive, the understood limits upon that scope were (as the Court seems not to grasp) just as much "designed to restrain" the incursions of the Third Branch. "Manipulation" of the territorial reach of the writ by the Judiciary poses just as much a threat to the proper separation of powers as "manipulation" by the Executive. As I will show below, manipulation is what is afoot here. The understood limits upon the writ deny our jurisdiction over the habeas petitions brought by these enemy aliens, and entrust the President with the crucial wartime determinations about their status and continued confinement.

B

The Court purports to derive from our precedents a "functional" test for the extraterritorial reach of the writ, ante, at 2258, which shows that the Military Commissions Act unconstitutionally restricts the scope of habeas. That is remarkable because the most pertinent of those precedents, Johnson v. Eisentrager, 339 U.S. 763, 70 S.Ct. 936, 94 L.Ed. 1255, conclusively establishes the opposite. There we were confronted with the claims of 21 Germans held at Landsberg Prison, an American military facility located in the American zone of occupation in postwar Germany. They had been captured in China, and an American military commission sitting there had convicted them of war crimes—collaborating with the Japanese after Germany's surrender. Id., at 765-766, 70 S.Ct. 936. Like petitioners here, the Germans claimed that their detentions violated the Constitution and international law, and sought a writ of habeas corpus. Writing for the Court, Justice Jackson held that American courts lacked habeas jurisdiction:

"We are cited to [sic] no instance where a court, in this or any other country where the writ is known, has issued it on behalf of an alien enemy who, at no relevant time and in no stage of his captivity, has been within its territorial jurisdiction. Nothing in the text of the Constitution extends such a right, nor does anything in our statutes." Id., at 768, 70 S.Ct. 936.

Justice Jackson then elaborated on the historical scope of the writ:

"The alien, to whom the United States has been traditionally hospitable, has been accorded a generous and ascending scale of rights as he increases his identity with our society . . . .

"But, in extending constitutional protections beyond the citizenry, the Court has been at pains to point out that it was the alien's presence within its territorial jurisdiction that gave the Judiciary power to act." Id., at 770-771, 70 S.Ct. 936.

Lest there be any doubt about the primacy of territorial sovereignty in determining the jurisdiction of a habeas court over an alien, Justice Jackson distinguished two cases in which aliens had been permitted to seek habeas relief, on the ground that the prisoners in those cases were in custody within the sovereign territory of the United States. Id., at 779-780, 70 S.Ct. 936 (discussing Ex parte Quirin, 317 U.S. 1, 63 S.Ct. 1, 87 L.Ed. 3 (1942), and In re Yamashita, 327 U.S. 1, 66 S.Ct. 340, 90 L.Ed. 499 (1946)). "By reason of our sovereignty at that time over [the Philippines]," Jackson wrote, "Yamashita stood much as did Quirin before American courts." 339 U.S., at 780, 70 S.Ct. 936.

Eisentrager thus held—held beyond any doubt—that the Constitution does not ensure habeas for aliens held by the United States in areas over which our Government is not sovereign.[3]

The Court would have us believe that Eisentrager rested on "[p]ractical considerations," such as the "difficulties of ordering the Government to produce the prisoners in a habeas corpus proceeding." Ante, at 2257. Formal sovereignty, says the Court, is merely one consideration "that bears upon which constitutional guarantees apply" in a given location. Ante, at 2258. This is a sheer rewriting of the case. Eisentrager mentioned practical concerns, to be sure—but not for the purpose of determining under what circumstances American courts could issue writs of habeas corpus for aliens abroad. It cited them to support its holding that the Constitution does not empower courts to issue writs of habeas corpus to aliens abroad in any circumstances. As Justice Black accurately said in dissent, "the Court's opinion inescapably denies courts power to afford the least bit of protection for any alien who is subject to our occupation government abroad, even if he is neither enemy nor belligerent and even after peace is officially declared." 339 U.S., at 796, 70 S.Ct. 936.

The Court also tries to change Eisentrager into a "functional" test by quoting a paragraph that lists the characteristics of the German petitioners:

"To support [the] assumption [of a constitutional right to habeas corpus] we must hold that a prisoner of our military authorities is constitutionally entitled to the writ, even though he (a) is an enemy alien; (b) has never been or resided in the United States; (c) was captured out-side of our territory and there held in military custody as a prisoner of war; (d) was tried and convicted by a Military Commission sitting outside the United States; (e) for offenses against laws of war committed outside the United States; (f) and is at all times imprisoned outside the United States." Id., at 777, 70 S.Ct. 936 (quoted in part, ante, at 2259).

But that paragraph is introduced by a sentence stating that "[t]he foregoing demonstrates how much further we must go if we are to invest these enemy aliens, resident, captured and imprisoned abroad, with standing to demand access to our courts." 339 U.S., at 777, 70 S.Ct. 936 (emphasis added). How much further than what? Further than the rule set forth in the prior section of the opinion, which said that "in extending constitutional protections beyond the citizenry, the Court has been at pains to point out that it was the alien's presence within its territorial jurisdiction that gave the Judiciary power to act." Id., at 771, 70 S.Ct. 936. In other words, the characteristics of the German prisoners were set forth, not in application of some "functional" test, but to show that the case before the Court represented an a fortiori application of the ordinary rule. That is reaffirmed by the sentences that immediately follow the listing of the Germans' characteristics:

"We have pointed out that the privilege of litigation has been extended to aliens, whether friendly or enemy, only because permitting their presence in the country implied protection. No such basis can be invoked here, for these prisoners at no relevant time were within any territory over which the United States is sovereign, and the scenes of their offense, their capture, their trial and their punishment were all beyond the territorial jurisdiction of any court of the United States." Id., at 777-778, 70 S.Ct. 936.

Eisentrager nowhere mentions a "functional" test, and the notion that it is based upon such a principle is patently false.[4]

The Court also reasons that Eisentrager must be read as a "functional" opinion because of our prior decisions in the Insular Cases. See ante, at 2253-2255. It cites our statement in Balzac v. Porto Rico, 258 U.S. 298, 312, 42 S.Ct. 343, 66 L.Ed. 627 (1922), that "`the real issue in the Insular Cases was not whether the Constitution extended to the Philippines or Porto Rico when we went there, but which of its provisions were applicable by way of limitation upon the exercise of executive and legislative power in dealing with new conditions and requirements.'" Ante, at 2254-2255. But the Court conveniently omits Balzac's predicate to that statement: "The Constitution of the United States is in force in Porto Rico as it is wherever and whenever the sovereign power of that government is exerted." 258 U.S., at 312, 42 S.Ct. 343 (emphasis added). The Insular Cases all concerned Territories acquired by Congress under its Article IV authority and indisputably part of the sovereign territory of the United States. See United States v. Verdugo-Urquidez, 494 U.S. 259, 268, 110 S.Ct. 1056, 108 L.Ed.2d 222 (1990); Reid v. Covert, 354 U.S. 1, 13, 77 S.Ct. 1222, 1 L.Ed.2d 1148 (1957) (plurality opinion of Black, J.). None of the Insular Cases stands for the proposition that aliens located outside U.S. sovereign territory have constitutional rights, and Eisentrager held just the opposite with respect to habeas corpus. As I have said, Eisentrager distinguished Yamashita on the ground of "our sovereignty [over the Philippines]," 339 U.S., at 780, 70 S.Ct. 936.

The Court also relies on the "[p]ractical considerations" that influenced our decision in Reid v. Covert, supra. See ante, at 2255-2257. But all the Justices in the majority except Justice Frankfurter limited their analysis to the rights of citizens abroad. See Reid, 354 U.S., at 5-6, 77 S.Ct. 1222 (plurality opinion of Black, J.); id., at 74-75, 77 S.Ct. 1222 (Harlan, J., concurring in result). (Frankfurter limited his analysis to the even narrower class of civilian dependents of American military personnel abroad, see id., at 45, 77 S.Ct. 1222 (opinion concurring in result).) In trying to wring some kind of support out of Reid for today's novel holding, the Court resorts to a chain of logic that does not hold. The members of the Reid majority, the Court says, were divided over whether In re Ross, 140 U.S. 453, 11 S.Ct. 897, 35 L.Ed. 581 (1891), which had (according to the Court) held that under certain circumstances American citizens abroad do not have indictment and jury-trial rights, should be overruled. In the Court's view, the Reid plurality would have overruled Ross, but Justices Frankfurter and Harlan preferred to distinguish it. The upshot: "If citizenship had been the only relevant factor in the case, it would have been necessary for the Court to overturn Ross, something Justices Harlan and Frankfurter were unwilling to do." Ante, at 2257. What, exactly, is this point supposed to prove? To say that "practical considerations" determine the precise content of the constitutional protections American citizens enjoy when they are abroad is quite different from saying that "practical considerations" determine whether aliens abroad enjoy any constitutional protections whatever, including habeas. In other words, merely because citizenship is not a sufficient factor to extend constitutional rights abroad does not mean that it is not a necessary one.

The Court tries to reconcile Eisentrager with its holding today by pointing out that in postwar Germany, the United States was "answerable to its Allies" and did not "pla[n] a long-term occupation." Ante, at 2260, 2260. Those factors were not mentioned in Eisentrager. Worse still, it is impossible to see how they relate to the Court's asserted purpose in creating this "functional" test—namely, to ensure a judicial inquiry into detention and prevent the political branches from acting with impunity. Can it possibly be that the Court trusts the political branches more when they are beholden to foreign powers than when they act alone?

After transforming the a fortiori elements discussed above into a "functional" test, the Court is still left with the difficulty that most of those elements exist here as well with regard to all the detainees. To make the application of the newly crafted "functional" test produce a different result in the present cases, the Court must rely upon factors (d) and (e): The Germans had been tried by a military commission for violations of the laws of war; the present petitioners, by contrast, have been tried by a Combatant Status Review Tribunal (CSRT) whose procedural protections, according to the Court's ipse dixit, "fall well short of the procedures and adversarial mechanisms that would eliminate the need for habeas corpus review." Ante, at 2260. But no one looking for "functional" equivalents would put Eisentrager and the present cases in the same category, much less place the present cases in a preferred category. The difference between them cries out for lesser procedures in the present cases. The prisoners in Eisentrager were prosecuted for crimes after the cessation of hostilities; the prisoners here are enemy combatants detained during an ongoing conflict. See Hamdi v. Rumsfeld, 542 U.S. 507, 538, 124 S.Ct. 2633, 159 L.Ed.2d 578 (2004) (plurality opinion) (suggesting, as an adequate substitute for habeas corpus, the use of a tribunal akin to a CSRT to authorize the detention of American citizens as enemy combatants during the course of the present conflict).

The category of prisoner comparable to these detainees are not the Eisentrager criminal defendants, but the more than 400,000 prisoners of war detained in the United States alone during World War II. Not a single one was accorded the right to have his detention validated by a habeas corpus action in federal court—and that despite the fact that they were present on U.S. soil. See Bradley, The Military Commissions Act, Habeas Corpus, and the Geneva Conventions, 101 Am. J. Int'l L. 322, 338 (2007). The Court's analysis produces a crazy result: Whereas those convicted and sentenced to death for war crimes are without judicial remedy, all enemy combatants detained during a war, at least insofar as they are confined in an area away from the battlefield over which the United States exercises "absolute and indefinite" control, may seek a writ of habeas corpus in federal court. And, as an even more bizarre implication from the Court's reasoning, those prisoners whom the military plans to try by full-dress Commission at a future date may file habeas petitions and secure release before their trials take place.

There is simply no support for the Court's assertion that constitutional rights extend to aliens held outside U.S. sovereign territory, see Verdugo-Urquidez, supra, at 271, 110 S.Ct. 1056, and Eisentrager could not be clearer that the privilege of habeas corpus does not extend to aliens abroad. By blatantly distorting Eisentrager, the Court avoids the difficulty of explaining why it should be overruled. See Planned Parenthood of Southeastern Pa. v. Casey, 505 U.S. 833, 854-855, 112 S.Ct. 2791, 120 L.Ed.2d 674 (1992) (identifying stare decisis factors). The rule that aliens abroad are not constitutionally entitled to habeas corpus has not proved unworkable in practice; if anything, it is the Court's "functional" test that does not (and never will) provide clear guidance for the future. Eisentrager forms a coherent whole with the accepted proposition that aliens abroad have no substantive rights under our Constitution. Since it was announced, no relevant factual premises have changed. It has engendered considerable reliance on the part of our military. And, as the Court acknowledges, text and history do not clearly compel a contrary ruling. It is a sad day for the rule of law when such an important constitutional precedent is discarded without an apologia, much less an apology.

C

What drives today's decision is neither the meaning of the Suspension Clause, nor the principles of our precedents, but rather an inflated notion of judicial supremacy. The Court says that if the extraterritorial applicability of the Suspension Clause turned on formal notions of sovereignty, "it would be possible for the political branches to govern without legal constraint" in areas beyond the sovereign territory of the United States. Ante, at 2258-2259. That cannot be, the Court says, because it is the duty of this Court to say what the law is. Ante, at 2258-2259. It would be difficult to imagine a more question-begging analysis. "The very foundation of the power of the federal courts to declare Acts of Congress unconstitutional lies in the power and duty of those courts to decide cases and controversies properly before them." United States v. Raines, 362 U.S. 17, 20-21, 80 S.Ct. 519, 4 L.Ed.2d 524 (1960) (citing Marbury v. Madison, 1 Cranch 137, 2 L.Ed. 60 (1803); emphasis added). Our power "to say what the law is" is circumscribed by the limits of our statutorily and constitutionally conferred jurisdiction. See Lujan v. Defenders of Wildlife, 504 U.S. 555, 573-578, 112 S.Ct. 2130, 119 L.Ed.2d 351 (1992). And that is precisely the question in these cases: whether the Constitution confers habeas jurisdiction on federal courts to decide petitioners' claims. It is both irrational and arrogant to say that the answer must be yes, because otherwise we would not be supreme.

But so long as there are some places to which habeas does not run—so long as the Court's new "functional" test will not be satisfied in every case—then there will be circumstances in which "it would be possible for the political branches to govern without legal constraint." Or, to put it more impartially, areas in which the legal determinations of the other branches will be (shudder!) supreme. In other words, judicial supremacy is not really assured by the constitutional rule that the Court creates. The gap between rationale and rule leads me to conclude that the Court's ultimate, unexpressed goal is to preserve the power to review the confinement of enemy prisoners held by the Executive anywhere in the world. The "functional" test usefully evades the precedential landmine of Eisentrager but is so inherently subjective that it clears a wide path for the Court to traverse in the years to come.

III

Putting aside the conclusive precedent of Eisentrager, it is clear that the original understanding of the Suspension Clause was that habeas corpus was not available to aliens abroad, as Judge Randolph's thorough opinion for the court below detailed. See 476 F.3d 981, 988-990 (C.A.D.C.2007).

The Suspension Clause reads: "The Privilege of the Writ of Habeas Corpus shall not be suspended, unless when in Cases of Rebellion or Invasion the public Safety may require it." U.S. Const., Art. I, § 9, cl. 2. The proper course of constitutional interpretation is to give the text the meaning it was understood to have at the time of its adoption by the people. See, e.g., Crawford v. Washington, 541 U.S. 36, 54, 124 S.Ct. 1354, 158 L.Ed.2d 177 (2004). That course is especially demanded when (as here) the Constitution limits the power of Congress to infringe upon a preexisting common-law right. The nature of the writ of habeas corpus that cannot be suspended must be defined by the common-law writ that was available at the time of the founding. See McNally v. Hill, 293 U.S. 131, 135-136, 55 S.Ct. 24, 79 L.Ed. 238 (1934); see also INS v. St. Cyr, 533 U.S. 289, 342, 121 S.Ct. 2271, 150 L.Ed.2d 347 (2001) (SCALIA, J., dissenting); D'Oench, Duhme & Co. v. FDIC, 315 U.S. 447, 471, n. 9, 62 S.Ct. 676, 86 L.Ed. 956 (1942) (Jackson, J., concurring).

It is entirely clear that, at English common law, the writ of habeas corpus did not extend beyond the sovereign territory of the Crown. To be sure, the writ had an "extraordinary territorial ambit," because it was a so-called "prerogative writ," which, unlike other writs, could extend beyond the realm of England to other places where the Crown was sovereign. R. Sharpe, The Law of Habeas Corpus 188 (2d ed.1989) (hereinafter Sharpe); see also Note on the Power of the English Courts to Issue the Writ of Habeas to Places Within the Dominions of the Crown, But Out of England, and On the Position of Scotland in Relation to that Power, 8 Jurid. Rev. 157 (1896) (hereinafter Note on Habeas); King v. Cowle, 2 Burr. 834, 855-856, 97 Eng. Rep. 587, 599 (K.B.1759).

But prerogative writs could not issue to foreign countries, even for British subjects; they were confined to the King's dominions—those areas over which the Crown was sovereign. See Sharpe 188; 2 R. Chambers, A Course of Lectures on the English Law 1767-1773, pp. 7-8 (T. Curley ed.1986); 3 W. Blackstone, Commentaries on the Laws of England 131 (1768) (hereinafter Blackstone). Thus, the writ has never extended to Scotland, which, although united to England when James I succeeded to the English throne in 1603, was considered a foreign dominion under a different Crown—that of the King of Scotland. Sharpe 191; Note on Habeas 158.[5] That is why Lord Mansfield wrote that "[t]o foreign dominions, which belong to a prince who succeeds to the throne of England, this Court has no power to send any writ of any kind. We cannot send a habeas corpus to Scotland...." Cowle, supra, at 856, 97 Eng. Rep., at 599-600.

The common-law writ was codified by the Habeas Corpus Act of 1679, which "stood alongside Magna Charta and the English Bill of Rights of 1689 as a towering common law lighthouse of liberty—a beacon by which framing lawyers in America consciously steered their course." Amar, Sixth Amendment First Principles, 84 Geo. L.J. 641, 663 (1996). The writ was established in the Colonies beginning in the 1690's and at least one colony adopted the 1679 Act almost verbatim. See Dept. of Political Science, Okla. State Univ., Research Reports, No. 1, R. Walker, The American Reception of the Writ of Liberty 12-16 (1961). Section XI of the Act stated where the writ could run. It "may be directed and run into any county palatine, the cinque-ports, or other privileged places within the kingdom of England, dominion of Wales, or town of Berwick upon Tweed, and the islands of Jersey or Guernsey." 31 Car. 2, ch. 2. The cinque-ports and counties palatine were so-called "exempt jurisdictions"—franchises granted by the Crown in which local authorities would manage municipal affairs, including the court system, but over which the Crown maintained ultimate sovereignty. See 3 Blackstone 78-79. The other places listed—Wales, Berwick-upon-Tweed, Jersey, and Guernsey—were territories of the Crown even though not part of England proper. See Cowle, supra, at 853-854, 97 Eng. Rep., at 598 (Wales and Berwick-upon-Tweed); 1 Blackstone 104 (Jersey and Guernsey); Sharpe 192 (same).

The Act did not extend the writ elsewhere, even though the existence of other places to which British prisoners could be sent was recognized by the Act. The possibility of evading judicial review through such spiriting-away was eliminated, not by expanding the writ abroad, but by forbidding (in Section XII of the Act) the shipment of prisoners to places where the writ did not run or where its execution would be difficult. See 31 Car. 2, ch. 2; see generally Nutting, The Most Wholesome Law—The Habeas Corpus Act of 1679, 65 Am. Hist. Rev. 527 (1960).

The Habeas Corpus Act, then, confirms the consensus view of scholars and jurists that the writ did not run outside the sovereign territory of the Crown. The Court says that the idea that "jurisdiction followed the King's officers" is an equally credible view. Ante, at 2248. It is not credible at all. The only support the Court cites for it is a page in Boumediene's brief, which in turn cites this Court's dicta in Rasul, 542 U.S., at 482, 124 S.Ct. 2686, mischaracterizing Lord Mansfield's statement that the writ ran to any place that was "under the subjection of the Crown," Cowle, supra, at 856, 97 Eng. Rep., at 599. It is clear that Lord Mansfield was saying that the writ extended outside the realm of England proper, not outside the sovereign territory of the Crown.[6]

The Court dismisses the example of Scotland on the grounds that Scotland had its own judicial system and that the writ could not, as a practical matter, have been enforced there. Ante, at 2250. Those explanations are totally unpersuasive. The existence of a separate court system was never a basis for denying the power of a court to issue the writ. See 9 W. Holdsworth, A History of English Law 124, and n. 6 (3d ed.1944) (citing Ex parte Anderson, 3 El. and El. 487, 121 Eng. Rep. 525 (K. B. 1861)). And as for logistical problems, the same difficulties were present for places like the Channel Islands, where the writ did run. The Court attempts to draw an analogy between the prudential limitations on issuing the writ to such remote areas within the sovereign territory of the Crown and the jurisdictional prohibition on issuing the writ to Scotland. See ante, at 2249-2250. But the very authority that the Court cites, Lord Mansfield, expressly distinguished between these two concepts, stating that English courts had the "power" to send the writ to places within the Crown's sovereignty, the "only question" being the "propriety," while they had "no power to send any writ of any kind" to Scotland and other "foreign dominions." Cowle, 2 Burr., at 856, 97 Eng. Rep., at 599-600. The writ did not run to Scotland because, even after the Union, "Scotland remained a foreign dominion of the prince who succeeded to the English throne," and "union did not extend the prerogative of the English crown to Scotland." Sharpe 191; see also Sir Matthew Hale's The Prerogatives of the King 19 (D. Yale ed.1976).[7]

In sum, all available historical evidence points to the conclusion that the writ would not have been available at common law for aliens captured and held outside the sovereign territory of the Crown. Despite three opening briefs, three reply briefs, and support from a legion of amici, petitioners have failed to identify a single case in the history of Anglo-American law that supports their claim to jurisdiction. The Court finds it significant that there is no recorded case denying jurisdiction to such prisoners either. See ante, at 2250-2251. But a case standing for the remarkable proposition that the writ could issue to a foreign land would surely have been reported, whereas a case denying such a writ for lack of jurisdiction would likely not. At a minimum, the absence of a reported case either way leaves unrefuted the voluminous commentary stating that habeas was confined to the dominions of the Crown.

What history teaches is confirmed by the nature of the limitations that the Constitution places upon suspension of the common-law writ. It can be suspended only "in Cases of Rebellion or Invasion." Art. I, § 9, cl. 2. The latter case (invasion) is plainly limited to the territory of the United States; and while it is conceivable that a rebellion could be mounted by American citizens abroad, surely the overwhelming majority of its occurrences would be domestic. If the extraterritorial scope of habeas turned on flexible, "functional" considerations, as the Court holds, why would the Constitution limit its suspension almost entirely to instances of domestic crisis? Surely there is an even greater justification for suspension in foreign lands where the United States might hold prisoners of war during an ongoing conflict. And correspondingly, there is less threat to liberty when the Government suspends the writ's (supposed) application in foreign lands, where even on the most extreme view prisoners are entitled to fewer constitutional rights. It makes no sense, therefore, for the Constitution generally to forbid suspension of the writ abroad if indeed the writ has application there.

It may be objected that the foregoing analysis proves too much, since this Court has already suggested that the writ of habeas corpus does run abroad for the benefit of United States citizens. "[T]he position that United States citizens throughout the world may be entitled to habeas corpus rights ... is precisely the position that this Court adopted in Eisentrager, see 339 U.S., at 769-770, 70 S.Ct. 936, even while holding that aliens abroad did not have habeas corpus rights." Rasul, supra, at 501, 502, 124 S.Ct. 2686 (SCALIA, J., dissenting) (emphasis deleted). The reason for that divergence is not difficult to discern. The common-law writ, as received into the law of the new constitutional Republic, took on such changes as were demanded by a system in which rule is derived from the consent of the governed, and in which citizens (not "subjects") are afforded defined protections against the Government. As Justice Story wrote for the Court:

"The common law of England is not to be taken in all respects to be that of America. Our ancestors brought with them its general principles, and claimed it as their birthright; but they brought with them and adopted only that portion which was applicable to their situation." Van Ness v. Pacard, 2 Pet. 137, 144, 7 L.Ed. 374 (1829).

See also Hall, The Common Law: An Account of its Reception in the United States, 4 Vand. L.Rev. 791 (1951). It accords with that principle to say, as the plurality opinion said in Reid: "When the Government reaches out to punish a citizen who is abroad, the shield which the Bill of Rights and other parts of the Constitution provide to protect his life and liberty should not be stripped away just because he happens to be in another land." 354 U.S., at 6, 77 S.Ct. 1222; see also Verdugo-Urquidez, 494 U.S., at 269-270, 110 S.Ct. 1056. On that analysis, "[t]he distinction between citizens and aliens follows from the undoubted proposition that the Constitution does not create, nor do general principles of law create, any juridical relation between our country and some undefined, limitless class of noncitizens who are beyond our territory." Id., at 275, 110 S.Ct. 1056 (KENNEDY, J., concurring).

In sum, because I conclude that the text and history of the Suspension Clause provide no basis for our jurisdiction, I would affirm the Court of Appeals even if Eisentrager did not govern these cases.

＊ ＊ ＊

Today the Court warps our Constitution in a way that goes beyond the narrow issue of the reach of the Suspension Clause, invoking judicially brainstormed separation-of-powers principles to establish a manipulable "functional" test for the extraterritorial reach of habeas corpus (and, no doubt, for the extraterritorial reach of other constitutional protections as well). It blatantly misdescribes important precedents, most conspicuously Justice Jackson's opinion for the Court in Johnson v. Eisentrager. It breaks a chain of precedent as old as the common law that prohibits judicial inquiry into detentions of aliens abroad absent statutory authorization. And, most tragically, it sets our military commanders the impossible task of proving to a civilian court, under whatever standards this Court devises in the future, that evidence supports the confinement of each and every enemy prisoner.

The Nation will live to regret what the Court has done today. I dissent.

Justice Scalia's dissent in Dada v. Mukasey (June 16, 2008) [Notes omitted]

Justice SCALIA, with whom THE CHIEF JUSTICE and Justice THOMAS join, dissenting.

The statutory provision at issue here authorizes the Attorney General to permit an alien who has been found deportable, if he so requests, to depart the country voluntarily. This enables the alien to avoid detention pending involuntary deportation, to select his own country of destination, to leave according to his own schedule (within the prescribed period), and to avoid restrictions upon readmission that attend involuntary departure. The statute specifies that the permission "shall not be valid for a period exceeding 60 days," 8 U.S.C. § 1229c(b)(2), and that failure to depart within the prescribed period causes the alien to be ineligible for certain relief, including adjustment of status, for 10 years, § 1229c(d)(1) (2000 ed., Supp. V). Moreover, pursuant to a regulation that the Court accepts as valid, departure (whether voluntary or involuntary) terminates the alien's ability to move for reopening of his removal proceeding, and withdraws any such motion filed before his departure. See 8 CFR § 1003.2(d) (2007). All of these provisions were in effect when petitioner agreed to depart, and the Court cites no statute or regulation currently in force that permits an alien who has agreed voluntarily to depart to change his mind. Yet the Court holds that petitioner must be permitted to renounce that agreement (the opinion dresses this up as "withdraw[ing] the motion for voluntary departure") provided the request is made before the departure period expires. Ante, at 2311. That is "necessary," the Court says, to "preserve the alien's right to pursue reopening," ante, at 2318, forfeiture of which was the known consequence of the departure he had agreed to. The Court's perceived "necessity" does not exist, and the Court lacks the authority to impose its chosen remedy. I respectfully dissent.

The Court is resolute in its belief that there is a "conflict between the right to file a motion to reopen and the provision requiring voluntary departure no later than 60 days." Ante, at 2311. The statute cannot be interpreted to put the alien to the choice of either (1) "remain[ing] in the United States to ensure [his] motion to reopen remains pending, while incurring statutory penalties for overstaying the voluntary departure date" or (2) "avoid[ing] penalties by prompt departure but abandon[ing] the motion to reopen." Ibid. This, according to the Court, would "render the statutory right to seek reopening a nullity in most cases of voluntary departure." Ante, at 2316-2317. Indeed, the problem is of mythological proportions: "[T]he alien who is granted voluntary departure but whose circumstances have changed in a manner cognizable by a motion to reopen is between Scylla and Charybdis: He or she can leave the United States in accordance with the voluntary departure order; but, pursuant to regulation, the motion to reopen will be deemed withdrawn." Ante, at 2318. So certain is the Court of this premise that it is asserted no less than seven times during the course of today's opinion. See ante, at 2311, 2316, 2317-2320.

The premise is false. It would indeed be extraordinary (though I doubt it would justify a judicial rewrite) for a statute to impose that stark choice upon an alien: depart and lose your right to seek reopening, or stay and incur statutory penalties. But that is not the choice this statute imposes. It offers the alien a deal, if he finds it in his interest and wishes to take it: "Agree to depart voluntarily (within the specified period, of course) and you may lose your right to pursue reopening, but you will not suffer detention, you can depart at your own convenience rather than ours, and to the destination that you rather than we select, and you will not suffer the statutory restrictions upon reentry that accompany involuntary departure. If you accept this deal, however, but do not live up to it—if you fail to depart as promised within the specified period—you will become ineligible for cancellation of removal, adjustment of status, and voluntary departure." Seems entirely reasonable to me. Litigants are put to similar voluntary choices between the rock and the whirlpool all the time, without cries for a judicial rewrite of the law. It happens, for example, whenever a criminal defendant is offered a plea bargain that gives him a lesser sentence than he might otherwise receive but deprives him of his right to trial by jury and his right to appeal. It is indeed utterly commonplace that electing to pursue one avenue of relief may require the surrender of certain other remedies.

Petitioner requested and accepted the above described deal, but now—to put the point bluntly but entirely accurately—he wants to back out. The case is as simple as that. Two days before the deadline for his promised voluntary departure, he filed a motion asking the Board of Immigration Appeals (BIA) to reopen his removal proceedings and remand his case to the Immigration Judge for adjustment of status based on his wife's pending visa petition. Administrative Record 3; see id., at 8-21. The motion also asked the BIA to "withdraw his request for voluntary departure" and "instead accep[t] an order of deportation." Id., at 10. After the voluntary departure period expired, the BIA denied petitioner's motion to reopen, explaining that under 8 U.S.C. § 1229c(d) (2000 ed. and Supp. V), "an alien who fails to depart following a grant of voluntary departure... is statutorily barred from applying for certain forms of discretionary relief." App. to Pet. for Cert. 3-4.

It seems to me that the BIA proceeded just as it should have, and just as petitioner had every reason to expect. To be sure, the statute provides for the right to file (and presumably to have ruled upon in due course) a petition to reopen. But it does not forbid the relinquishment of that right in exchange for other benefits that the BIA has discretion to provide. Nor does it suggest any weird departure from the ancient rule that an offer (the offer to depart voluntarily in exchange for specified benefits, and with specified consequences for default) cannot be "withdrawn" after it has been accepted and after the quid pro quo promise (to depart) has been made.

The Court's rejection of this straightforward analysis is inconsistent with its treatment of petitioner's argument that the statute requires automatic tolling of the voluntary departure period while a motion to reopen is pending. With respect to that argument, the Court says:

"Voluntary departure is an agreed-upon exchange of benefits, much like a settlement agreement. In return for anticipated benefits, including the possibility of readmission, an alien who requests voluntary departure represents that he or she `has the means to depart the United States and intends to do so' promptly. Included among the substantive burdens imposed upon the alien when selecting voluntary departure is the obligation to arrange for departure, and actually depart, within the 60-day period." Ante, at 2318-2319 (citations omitted).

Precisely so. But also among the substantive burdens is the inability to receive certain relief through a motion to reopen once the promised departure date has passed; and perhaps paramount among the substantive burdens is that the alien is bound to his agreement. The Court is quite right that the Act does not allow us to require that an alien who agrees to depart voluntarily must receive the benefits of his bargain without the costs. But why does it allow us to convert the alien's statutorily required promise to depart voluntarily into an "option either to abide by the terms, and receive the agreed-upon benefits, of voluntary departure; or, alternatively, to forgo those benefits and remain in the United States to pursue an administrative motion"? Ante, at 2319. And why does it allow us to nullify the provision of § 1229c(d)(1) that failure to depart within the prescribed and promised period causes the alien to be ineligible for certain relief, including adjustment of status (which is what petitioner seeks here) for 10 years?

Of course it is not unusual for the Court to blue-pencil a statute in this fashion, directing that one of its provisions, severable from the rest, be disregarded. But that is done when the blue-penciled provision is unconstitutional. It would be unremarkable, if the Court found that the alien had a constitutional right to reopen, and that conditioning permission for voluntary departure upon waiver of that right was an unconstitutional condition, for the Court to order that the alien cannot be held to his commitment. But that is not the case here. The Court holds that the plain requirement of the statute and of validly adopted regulations cannot be enforced because the statute itself forbids it.

Not so. The Court derives this prohibition from its belief that an alien must, no matter what, be given the full benefit of the right to reopen, even if that means creating an extrastatutory option to renege upon the statutorily contemplated agreement to depart voluntarily. "We must be reluctant to assume," the Court says, "that the voluntary departure statute was designed to remove this important safeguard [of the motion to reopen]," "particularly so when the plain text of the statute reveals no such limitation." Ante, at 2318. But in fact that safeguard is not sacrosanct. The "plain text of the statute" does cause voluntary departure to remove that safeguard for at least 30 days of its 90-day existence, and permits voluntary departure to remove it almost entirely. Section 1229a(c)(7) (2000 ed., Supp. V) generally permits the filing of a motion to reopen "within 90 days of ... entry of a final administrative order of removal." But as I have described, § 1229c(b)(2) (2000 ed.) provides that a grant of voluntary departure issued at the conclusion of removal proceedings "shall not be valid for a period exceeding 60 days." Since motions to reopen cannot be filed after removal or departure, the unquestionable effect of the statutory scheme is to deprive the alien who agrees to voluntary departure of the (sacrosanct) right to reopen for a full third of its existence. And since 60 days is merely the maximum period for a voluntary departure, it is theoretically possible for the right to reopen to be limited to one week, or even one day. Given that reality, it is not at all hard to believe that the statute allows nullification of motions to reopen requesting adjustment of status filed within the 60-day departure period and not ruled upon before departure. Indeed, it seems to me much more likely that the statute allows that than that it allows judicial imposition of the unheard-of rule that a promise to depart is not a promise to depart, and judicial nullification of a statutorily prescribed penalty for failure to depart by the gimmick of allowing the request for voluntary departure to be "withdrawn."

The same analysis makes it true that, even under the Court's reconstructed statute, a removable alien's agreement to depart voluntarily may limit, and in some instances foreclose, his ability to pursue a motion to reopen at a later date. Even if the alien who has agreed to voluntary departure is permitted to renege within the specified departure period, that period can be no longer than 60 days after entry of the order of removal—meaning that he has been deprived of at least 30 days of his right to reopen. Thus, the Court has not "reconciled" statutory provisions; it has simply rewritten two of them to satisfy its notion of sound policy—the requirement of a commitment to depart and the prescription that a failure to do so prevents adjustment of status.

The Court suggests that the statute compels its conclusion because otherwise "[w]hether an alien's motion will be adjudicated within the 60-day statutory period in all likelihood will depend on pure happenstance—namely, the backlog of the particular Board member to whom the motion is assigned" and because "arbitrary results are `not to be presumed lightly.'" Ante, at 2318. It is, however, a happenstance that the alien embraces when he makes his commitment to leave, and its effect upon him is therefore not arbitrary. If he wants to be sure to have his motion to reopen considered, he should not enter into the voluntary departure agreement. A reading of the statute that permits that avoidable happenstance seems to me infinitely more plausible than a reading that turns a commitment to depart into an option to depart.

But the most problematic of all the Court's reasons for allowing petitioner to withdraw his motion to depart voluntarily is its reliance on the Department of Justice's (DOJ) as-yet-unadopted proposal that is in some respects (though not the crucial one) similar to the Court's rule. See ante, at 2319-2320 (citing Proposed Rules, DOJ, Executive Office for Immigration Review, Voluntary Departure: Effect of a Motion To Reopen or Reconsider or a Petition for Review, 72 Fed.Reg. 67674, 67677, and n. 2 (2007)). I shall assume that the proposed rule would be valid, even though it converts the statutory requirement of departure within the prescribed period (on pain of losing the right to seek adjustment of status) into an option to depart.[1] According to the Court, the proposed regulation "`warrants respectful consideration.'" Ante, at 2319-2320. What this evidently means is respectful adoption of that portion of the proposed regulation with which the Court agrees, and sub silentio rejection of that portion it disfavors, namely: "The provisions of this proposed rule will be applied ... only with respect to immigration judge orders issued on or after the effective date of the final rule that grant a period of voluntary departure," 72 Fed.Reg. 67682. See Supp. Brief for Respondent 8-9 (observing that the rule "will not apply to petitioner's case"). Our administrative law jurisprudence is truly in a state of confused degeneration if this pick-and-choose technique constitutes "respectful" consideration.

It must be acknowledged, however, that the Department's proposed regulation has some bearing upon this case: It demonstrates that the agency is actively considering whether the terms it has prescribed for its discretionary grants of voluntary departure are too harsh and should be revised for the future, perhaps along the very lines that the Justices in today's majority would choose if they were the Attorney General. It shows, in other words, that today's interpretive gymnastics may have been performed, not for the enjoyment of innumerable aliens in the future, but for Mr. Dada alone.

    * * *

In the final analysis, the Court's entire approach to interpreting the statutory scheme can be summed up in this sentence from its opinion: "Allowing aliens to withdraw from their voluntary departure agreements ... establishes a greater probability that their motions to reopen will be considered." Ante, at 2320. That is true enough. What does not appear from the Court's opinion, however, is the source of the Court's authority to increase that probability in flat contradiction to the text of the statute. Just as the Government can (absent some other statutory restriction) relieve criminal defendants of their plea agreements for one reason or another, the Government may well be able to let aliens who have agreed to depart the country voluntarily repudiate their agreements. This Court lacks such authority, and nothing in the statute remotely dictates the result that today's judgment decrees. I would affirm the judgment of the Court of Appeals.[2]

Justice Scalia's dissent in Metropolitan Life Ins. v. Glenn (June 19, 2008) [Notes omitted]

JUSTICE SCALIA, with whom JUSTICE THOMAS joins, dissenting.

I agree with the Court that petitioner Metropolitan Life Insurance Company (hereinafter petitioner) has a conflict of interest. A third-party insurance company that administers an ERISA-governed disability plan and that pays for benefits out of its own coffers profits with each benefits claim it rejects. I see no reason why the Court must volunteer, however, that an employer who administers its own ERISA-governed plan "clear[ly]" has a conflict of interest. See ante, at 2348. At least one Court of Appeals has thought that while the insurance-company-administrator has a conflict, the employer-administrator does not. See Colucci v. Agfa Corp. Severance Pay Plan, 431 F.3d 170, 179 (C.A.4 2005). I would not resolve this question until it has been presented and argued, and the Court's unnecessary and uninvited resolution must be regarded as dictum.

The more important question is how the existence of a conflict should bear upon judicial review of the administrator's decision, and on that score I am in fundamental disagreement with the Court. Even if the choice were mine as a policy matter, I would not adopt the Court's totality-of-the-circumstances (so-called) "test," in which the existence of a conflict is to be put into the mix and given some (unspecified) "weight." This makes each case unique, and hence the outcome of each case unpredictable—not a reasonable position in which to place the administrator that has been explicitly given discretion by the creator of the plan, despite the existence of a conflict. See ante, at 2353-2354 (ROBERTS, C.J., concurring in part and concurring in judgment). More importantly, however, this is not a question to be solved by this Court's policy views; our cases make clear that it is to be governed by the law of trusts. Under that law, a fiduciary with a conflict does not abuse its discretion unless the conflict actually and improperly motivates the decision. There is no evidence of that here.

I

Our opinion in Firestone Tire & Rubber Co. v. Bruch, 489 U.S. 101, 109 S.Ct. 948, 103 L.Ed.2d 80 (1989), does not provide the answer to the all-important question in this case, but it does direct us to the answer. It held that federal courts hearing 29 U.S.C. § 1132(a)(1)(B) claims should review the decisions of ERISA-plan administrators the same way that courts have traditionally reviewed decisions of trustees. 489 U.S., at 111, 109 S.Ct.

948. In trust law, the decision of a trustee who was not vested with discretion would be reviewed de novo. Id., at 112-113, 109 S.Ct. 948. Citing the Restatement of Trusts current at the time of ERISA's enactment, Firestone acknowledged that courts traditionally would defer to trustees vested with discretion, but rejected that course in the case at hand because, among other reasons, the Firestone plan did not vest its administrator with discretion. Id., at 111, 109 S.Ct. 948 (citing Restatement (Second) of Trusts § 187 (1957) (hereinafter Restatement)). Accordingly, Firestone had no occasion to consider the scope of, or limitations on, the deference accorded to fiduciaries with discretion. But in sheer dictum quoting a portion of one comment of the Restatement, our opinion said, "[o]f course, if a benefit plan gives discretion to an administrator or fiduciary who is operating under a conflict of interest, that conflict must be weighed as a `facto[r]' in determining whether there is an abuse of discretion.'" 489 U.S., at 115, 109 S.Ct. 948 (quoting Restatement § 187, Comment d).

The Court takes that throwaway dictum literally and builds a castle upon it. See ante, at 2350-2352. But the dictum cannot bear that weight, and the Court's "elucidation" of the sentence does not reveal trust-law practice as much as it reveals the Justices' fondness for a judge-liberating totality-of-the-circumstances "test." The Restatement does indeed list in Comment d certain circumstances (including conflict of interest) that "may be relevant" to deciding whether a trustee has abused his discretion.[1] It does not, however, suggest that they should all be chucked into a brown paper bag and shaken up to determine the answer. Nowhere does it mention the majority's modus operandi of "weighing" all these factors together. To the contrary, the immediately following Comments (e-l) precisely elaborate upon how some of those factors (factor (1), extent of discretion, see Comment j; factor (4), existence of an external standard for judging reasonableness, see Comment i; factors (5) and (6), motives of the trustee and conflict of interest, see Comment g) are relevant—making very clear that each of them can be alone determinative, without the necessity of "weighing" other factors. These later Comments also address other factors not even included in the earlier listing, some of which can be alone determinative. See Comment h, Trustee's failure to use his judgment; Comment k, Limits of power of settlor to confer discretion.

Instead of taking the pain to reconcile the entirety of the Restatement section with the Firestone dictum, the Court treats the dictum like a statutory command, and makes up a standard (if one can call it that) to make sense of the dictum. The opinion is painfully opaque, despite its promise of elucidation. It variously describes the object of judicial review as "determining whether the trustee, substantively or procedurally, has abused his discretion" (ante, at 2350), determining "the lawfulness of benefit denials" (ante, at 2351), and as tantamount to "review of agency factfinding" (ibid.). How a court should go about conducting this review is unclear. The opinion is rife with instruction on what a court should not do. See ante, at 2350-2351. In the final analysis, the Court seems to advance a gestalt reasonableness standard (a "combination-of-factors method of review," the opinion calls it, ante, at 2351), by which a reviewing court, mindful of being deferential, should nonetheless consider all the circumstances, weigh them as it thinks best, then divine whether a fiduciary's discretionary decision should be overturned.[2] Notwithstanding the Court's assurances to the contrary, ante, at 2350, that is nothing but de novo review in sheep's clothing.[3]

Looking to the common law of trusts (which is, after all, what the holding of Firestone binds us to do), I would adopt the entirety of the Restatement's clear guidelines for judicial review. In trust law, a court reviewing a trustee's decision would substitute its own de novo judgment for a trustee's only if it found either that the trustee had no discretion in making the decision, see Firestone, supra, at 111-112, 109 S.Ct. 948, or that the trustee had discretion but abused it, see Restatement § 187. Otherwise, the court would defer to the trustee. Cf. Shelton v. King, 229 U.S. 90, 94-95, 33 S.Ct. 686, 57 L.Ed. 1086 (1913). "Abuse of discretion," as the Restatement uses the term, refers specifically to four distinct failures: The trustee acted dishonestly; he acted with some other improper motive; he failed to use judgment; or he acted beyond the bounds of a reasonable judgment. See Restatement § 187, Comment e.

The Restatement discusses all four of these manners of abusing discretion successively, in Comments f, g, h, and i, describing the aim of a court's inquiry into each. A trustee abuses his discretion by acting dishonestly when, for example, he accepts bribes. See id., § 187, Comment f. A trustee abuses his discretion by failing to use his judgment, when he acts "without knowledge of or inquiry into the relevant circumstances and merely as a result of his arbitrary decision or whim." Id., § 187, Comment h. A trustee abuses his discretion by acting unreasonably when his decision is substantively unreasonable either with regard to his exercise of a discretionary power or with regard to his assessment of whether the preconditions to that exercise have been met.[4] See id., § 187, Comment i. And—most important for this case—a trustee abuses his discretion by acting on an improper motive when he acts "from a motive other than to further the purposes of the trust." Id., § 187, Comment g. Improper motives include "spite or prejudice or to further some interest of his own or of a person other than the beneficiary." Ibid. (emphasis added).

The four abuses of discretion are clearly separate and distinct. Indeed, the circumstances the Restatement identifies as relevant for finding each abuse of discretion are not identified as relevant for finding the other abuses of discretion. For instance, "the existence or non-existence, the definiteness or indefiniteness, of an external standard by which the reasonableness of the trustee's conduct can be judged," id., § 187, Comment d, is alluded to only in the later Comment dealing with abuse of discretion by acting beyond the bounds of reasonable judgment, id., § 187, Comment i. And particularly relevant to the present case, "the existence or nonexistence of an interest in the trustee conflicting with that of the beneficiaries," id., § 187, Comment d, is mentioned only in the later Comment dealing with abuse of discretion by reason of improper motive, id., § 187, Comment g. The other Comments do not even hint that a conflict of interest is relevant to determining whether one of the other three types of abuse of discretion exists.

Common sense confirms that a trustee's conflict of interest is irrelevant to determining the substantive reasonableness of his decision. A reasonable decision is reasonable whether or not the person who makes it has a conflict. If it were otherwise, the consequences would be perverse: A trustee without a conflict could take either of two reasonable courses of action, but a trustee with a conflict, facing the same two choices, would be compelled to take the course that avoids the appearance of self-dealing. He would have to do that even if he thought the other one would better serve the beneficiary's interest, lest his determination be set aside as unreasonable. It makes no sense to say that a lurking conflict of interest, or the mere identity of the trustee, can make a reasonable decision unreasonable, or a well-thought-out, informed decision uninformed or arbitrary. The Restatement echoes the commonsensical view: It explains that a court applying trust law must pretermit its inquiry into whether a trustee abused his discretion by acting unreasonably when there is no standard for evaluating reasonableness, but "[i]n such a case . . . the court will interpose if the trustee act[ed] dishonestly, or from some improper motive." Id., § 187, Comment i. That explanation plainly excludes the court's "weighing" of a trustee's conflict of interest.

A trustee's conflict of interest is relevant (and only relevant) for determining whether he abused his discretion by acting with an improper motive. It does not itself prove that he did so, but it is the predicate for an inquiry into motive, and can be part of the circumstantial evidence establishing wrongful motive. That circumstantial evidence could theoretically include the unreasonableness of the decision—but using it for that purpose would be entirely redundant, since unreasonableness alone suffices to establish an abuse of discretion. There are no gradations of reasonableness, so that one might infer that a trustee acted upon his conflict of interest when he chose a "less reasonable," yet self-serving, course, but not when he chose a "more reasonable," yet self-serving, course. Reasonable is reasonable. A reasonable decision is one over which reasonable minds seeking the "best" or "right" answer could disagree. It is a course that a trustee acting in the best interest of the beneficiary might have chosen. Gradating reasonableness, and making it a "factor" in the improper-motive determination, would have the precise effect of eliminating the discretion that the settlor has intentionally conferred upon the trustee with a conflict, for such a trustee would be foreclosed from making an otherwise reasonable decision. See supra, at 2348-2349.

Respondent essentially asks us to presume that all fiduciaries with a conflict act in their selfish interest, so that their decisions are automatically reviewed with less than total deference (how much less is unspecified). But if one is to draw any inference about a fiduciary from the fact that he made an informed, reasonable, though apparently self-serving discretionary decision, it should be that he suppressed his selfish interest (as the settlor anticipated) in compliance with his duties of good faith and loyalty. See, e.g., Gregory v. Moose, 266 Ark. 926, 933-934, 590 S.W.2d 665, 670-671 (1979) (citing Jarvis v. Boatmen's Nat. Bank of St. Louis, 478 S.W.2d 266, 273 (Mo.1972)). Only such a presumption can vindicate the trust principles and ERISA provisions that permit settlors to appoint fiduciaries with a conflict in the first place. See Pegram v. Herdrich, 530 U.S. 211, 225, 120 S.Ct. 2143, 147 L.Ed.2d 164 (2000).

II

Applying the Restatement's guidelines to this case, I conclude that the only possible basis for finding an abuse of discretion would be unreasonableness of petitioner's determination of no disability. The principal factor suggesting that is the finding of disability by the Social Security Administration (SSA). But ERISA fiduciaries need not always reconcile their determinations with the SSA's, nor is the SSA's conclusion entitled to any special weight. Cf. Black & Decker Disability Plan v. Nord, 538 U.S. 822, 834, 123 S.Ct. 1965, 155 L.Ed.2d 1034 (2003). The SSA's determination may have been wrong, and it was contradicted by other medical opinion.

We did not take this case to make the reasonableness determination, but rather to clarify when a conflict exists, and how it should be taken into account. I would remand to the Court of Appeals for its determination of the reasonableness of petitioner's denial, without regard to the existence of a conflict of interest.

Justice Scalia's dissent in Nunez v. US (June 23, 2008)

Justice SCALIA, with whom THE CHIEF JUSTICE and Justice THOMAS join, dissenting.

Petitioner pleaded guilty to federal narcotics offenses and waived appellate and collateral-review rights. Despite that waiver, he demanded (the Court of Appeals assumed) that his attorney file a notice of appeal; his attorney refused. Petitioner sought habeas relief, claiming that this failure was ineffective assistance of counsel. See 495 F.3d 544, 545 (C.A.7 2007). The District Court denied relief, and the Court of Appeals affirmed, finding that petitioner had waived his right to raise even the ineffective-assistance claim on collateral review. See id., at 546, 548-549. Petitioner has filed a petition for a writ of certiorari, asking us to consider the ineffective-assistance claim. The Government argues in response that the question is not presented because the Court of Appeals' opinion rests on petitioner's collateral-review waiver. I agree with that response, and so would deny the petition for writ of certiorari.

Yet the Government urges us to GVR—to grant the petition, vacate the judgment, and remand the case to the Court of Appeals—because it believes that the Court of Appeals misconstrued the scope of petitioner's collateral-review waiver. A majority of the Court agrees to that course. I do not. In my view we have no power to set aside (vacate) another court's judgment unless we find it to be in error. See Mariscal v. United States, 449 U.S. 405, 407, 101 S.Ct. 909, 66 L.Ed.2d 616 (1981)(Rehnquist, J., dissenting). Even so, I have reluctantly acquiesced in our dubious yet well-entrenched habit of entering a GVR order without an independent examination of the merits when the Government, as respondent, confesses error in the judgment below. See Lawrence v. Chater, 516 U.S. 163, 182-183, 116 S.Ct. 611, 133 L.Ed.2d 545 (1996) (Scalia, J., dissenting). But because "we have no power to vacate a judgment that has not been shown to be (or been conceded to be) in error," Price v. United States, 537 U.S. 1152, 1153, 123 S.Ct. 986, 154 L.Ed.2d 888 (2003) (SCALIA, J., dissenting), I continue to resist GVR disposition when the Government, without conceding that a judgment is in error, merely suggests that the lower court's basis for the judgment is wrong, see Lawrence, supra, at 183, and n. 3, 116 S.Ct. 611 (dissenting opinion); cf. Alvarado v. United States, 497 U.S. 543, 545, 110 S.Ct. 2995, 111 L.Ed.2d 439 (1990) (Rehnquist, C.J., dissenting). That describes this case. The Government's brief is entirely agnostic on the correctness of the Court of Appeals' judgment—i.e., its affirmance of the District Court's denial of habeas relief. Presumably, the Government believes the judgment is correct; it asked the Court of Appeals to affirm the District Court's judgment the first time around, and presumably will do the same on remand.

To make matters worse, the Government's suggestion that the Court of Appeals erred in construing the scope of petitioner's waiver is not even convincing. The collateral-review waiver in petitioner's plea agreement is inartfully worded; it is perhaps susceptible of the Government's reading, but in my view the Court of Appeals' reading is better. In any event, during his plea colloquy petitioner orally agreed to a collateral-review waiver precisely in line with the Court of Appeals' position. Compare Brief for United States 3-4 (plea colloquy) with id., at 16-17 (plea agreement). It is bad enough to upend the judgment of a lower court because the Solicitor General, while not saying the judgment was wrong, opines that the expressed basis for it was wrong; it is absurd to do this when the Solicitor General's gratuitous opinion is dubious on its face.

Finally, we should be especially reluctant to GVR on the Solicitor General's say-so when, if that say-so is correct, the likely consequence will be to create a conflict among the Courts of Appeals. Before resting its judgment on petitioner's collateral-review waiver, the Court of Appeals expressed its unfavorable view of petitioner's ineffective-assistance claim, recognizing, however, that its view contradicted the view of at least six other Courts of Appeals. See 495 F.3d, at 546-548. If, on remand, the Court of Appeals agrees with the Solicitor General that petitioner's collateral-review waiver does not preclude his claim, the court in all likelihood will enter the same judgment by rejecting petitioner's ineffective-assistance claim, thereby creating (absent reversal en banc) a split with those other courts. I had thought that the main purpose of our certiorari jurisdiction was to eliminate circuit splits, not to create them.

For all these reasons, I respectfully dissent from the Court's order.

Justice Scalia's dissent to denial of certiorari in Marlowe v. US (October 14, 2008)

Justice SCALIA, dissenting.

Patrick Marlowe was a prison guard whose failure to provide needed medical care caused a prisoner's death. He was convicted of deprivation of constitutional rights in violation of 18 U.S.C. § 242. Under the then-applicable Sentencing Guidelines, the recommended sentence for civil rights violations was calculated using the base offense level of the crime underlying the civil rights violation. Since Marlowe's jury had not been asked to determine his mental state in connection with the death, the facts resolved by the jury verdict convicted him of no more than involuntary manslaughter through criminal negligence. The base offense level for that crime was 10, which, under the other circumstances of Marlowe's offense, would have produced a recommended sentence of 51 to 63 months. United States Sentencing Commission, Guidelines Manual § 2A1.4 (Nov. 2002). The District Judge, however, determined that Marlowe had possessed the "malice aforethought" required for second-degree murder, which increased the base offense level from 10 to 33, producing a Guidelines-recommended sentence of life. The District Judge sentenced Marlowe to life in prison.

On appeal, the Sixth Circuit applied a presumption of reasonableness to the sentence[1] because, in light of the judge-found fact that Marlowe had possessed the state of mind required for second-degree murder, the sentence was consistent with the Guidelines. United States v. Conatser, 514 F.3d 508, 526-527 (2008).[2] In other words, the Sixth Circuit found the life sentence lawful solely because of the judge-found fact that Marlowe had acted with malice aforethought. This falls short of what we have held the right to trial by jury demands: "Any fact (other than a prior conviction) which is necessary to support a sentence exceeding the maximum authorized by the facts established by a plea of guilty or a jury verdict must be admitted by the defendant or proved to a jury beyond a reasonable doubt." United States v. Booker, 543 U.S. 220, 244, 125 S.Ct. 738, 160 L.Ed.2d 621 (2005).

I would grant the petition for certiorari, so that we may either forthrightly apply Booker or announce that the case is overruled.

Notes

[1] For the reasons set forth in my separate opinion in Rita v. United States, 551 U.S. 338, 368, 127 S.Ct. 2456, 168 L.Ed.2d 203 (2007) (concurring in part and concurring in judgment), I believe that it is improper for courts to review for substantive reasonableness sentences that are within the statutory limits. I give stare decisis effect, however, to the Court's contrary holding in that case.

[2] Only one of the three-judge panel said that she would have upheld the sentence as reasonable even if it had been calculated as an upward departure from the Guidelines-recommended sentence. 514 F.3d, at 528-532 (Moore, J., concurring in part and concurring in judgment). If substantive reasonableness review has any meaning, I doubt that a life sentence for negligent homicide could be sustained.

Justice Scalia's dissent in Oregon v. Ice (Jan 14, 2009)

Justice Scalia, with whom The Chief Justice, Justice Souter, and Justice Thomas join, dissenting.

The rule of Apprendi v. New Jersey, 530 U. S. 466 (2000) , is clear: Any fact—other than that of a prior conviction—that increases the maximum punishment to which a defendant may be sentenced must be admitted by the defendant or proved beyond a reasonable doubt to a jury. Oregon's sentencing scheme allows judges rather than juries to find the facts necessary to commit defendants to longer prison sentences, and thus directly contradicts what we held eight years ago and have reaffirmed several times since. The Court's justification of Oregon's scheme is a virtual copy of the dissents in those cases.

The judge in this case could not have imposed a sentence of consecutive prison terms without making the factual finding that the defendant caused "separate harms" to the victim by the acts that produced two convictions. See 343 Ore. 248, 268, 170 P. 3d 1049, 1060 (2007) (Kistler, J., dissenting). There can thus be no doubt that the judge's factual finding was "essential to" the punishment he imposed. United States v. Booker, 543 U. S. 220, 232 (2005) . That "should be the end of the matter." Blakely v. Washington, 542 U. S. 296, 313 (2004) .

Instead, the Court attempts to distinguish Oregon's sentencing scheme by reasoning that the rule of Apprendi applies only to the length of a sentence for an individual crime and not to the total sentence for a defendant. I cannot understand why we would make such a strange exception to the treasured right of trial by jury. Neither the reasoning of the Apprendi line of cases, nor any distinctive history of the factfinding necessary to imposition of consecutive sentences, nor (of course) logic supports such an odd rule.

We have taken pains to reject artificial limitations upon the facts subject to the jury-trial guarantee. We long ago made clear that the guarantee turns upon the penal consequences attached to the fact, and not to its formal definition as an element of the crime. Mullaney v. Wilbur, 421 U. S. 684, 698 (1975) . More recently, we rejected the contention that the "aggravating circumstances" that qualify a defendant for the death penalty did not have to be found by the jury. "If," we said, "a State makes an increase in a defendant's authorized punishment contingent on the finding of a fact, that fact—no matter how the State labels it—must be found by a jury beyond a reasonable doubt." Ring v. Arizona, 536 U. S. 584, 602 (2002) . A bare three years ago, in rejecting the contention that the facts determining application of the Federal Sentencing Guidelines did not have to be found by the jury, we again set forth the pragmatic, practical, nonformalistic rule in terms that cannot be mistaken: The jury must "find the existence of ' "any particular fact" ' that the law makes essential to [a defendant's] punishment." Booker, supra, at 232 (quoting Blakely, supra, at 301).

This rule leaves no room for a formalistic distinction between facts bearing on the number of years of imprisonment that a defendant will serve for one count (subject to the rule of Apprendi) and facts bearing on how many years will be served in total (now not subject to Apprendi). There is no doubt that consecutive sentences are a "greater punishment" than concurrent sentences, Apprendi, supra, at 494. We have hitherto taken note of the reality that "a concurrent sentence is traditionally imposed as a lesssevere sanction than a consecutive sentence." Ralston v. Robinson, 454 U. S. 201, 216, n. 9 (1981) (emphasis deleted). The decision to impose consecutive sentences alters the single consequence most important to convicted noncapital defendants: their date of release from prison. For many defendants, the difference between consecutive and concurrent sentences is more important than a jury verdict of innocence on any single count: Two consecutive 10-year sentences are in most circumstances a more severe punishment than any number of concurrent 10-year sentences.

To support its distinction-without-a-difference, the Court puts forward the same (the very same) arguments regarding the history of sentencing that were rejected by Apprendi. Here, it is entirely irrelevant that common-law judges had discretion to impose either consecutive or concurrent sentences, ante, at 7; just as there it was entirely irrelevant that common-law judges had discretion to impose greater or lesser sentences (within the prescribed statutory maximum) for individual convictions. There is no Sixth Amendment problem with a system that exposes defendants to a known range of sentences after a guilty verdict: "In a system that says the judge may punish burglary with 10 to 40 years, every burglar knows he is risking 40 years in jail." Blakely, supra, at 309. The same analysis applies to a system where both consecutive and concurrent sentences are authorized after only a jury verdict of guilt; the burglar-rapist knows he is risking consecutive sentences. Our concern here is precisely the same as our concern in Apprendi: What happens when a State breaks from the common-law practice of discretionary sentences and permits the imposition of an elevated sentence only upon the showing of extraordinary facts? In such a system, the defendant "is entitled to" the lighter sentence "and by reason of the Sixth Amendment [,] the facts bearing upon that entitlement must be found by a jury." Blakely, 542 U. S., at 309.

The Court protests that in this case there is no "encroachment" on or "erosion" of the jury's role because traditionally it was for the judge to determine whether there would be concurrent terms. Ante, at 8–9. Alas, this argument too was made and rejected in Apprendi. The jury's role was not diminished, the Apprendi dissent contended, because it was traditionally up to judges, not juries, to determine what the sentence would be. 530 U. S., at 556, 559 (opinion of Breyer, J.). The Court's opinion acknowledged that in the 19th century it was the practice to leave sentencing up to the judges, within limits fixed by law. But, it said, that practice had no bearing upon whether the jury must find the fact where a law conditions the higher sentence upon the fact. The jury's role is diminished when the length of a sentence is made to depend upon a fact removed from its determination. Id., at 482–483. The same is true here.

The Court then observes that the results of the Oregon system could readily be achieved, instead, by a system in which consecutive sentences are the default rulebut judges are permitted to impose concurrent sentences when they find certain facts. Ante, at 9–10. Undoubtedly the Sixth Amendment permits a system in which judges are authorized (or even required) to impose consecutive sentences unless the defendant proves additional facts to the Court's satisfaction. See ibid. But the permissibility of that alternative means of achieving the same end obviously does not distinguish Apprendi,because the same argument (the very same argument) was raised and squarely rejected in that case:

"If the defendant can escape the statutory maximum by showing, for example, that he is a war veteran, then a judge that finds the fact of veteran status is neither exposing the defendant to a deprivation of liberty greater than that authorized by the verdict according to statute, nor is the judge imposing upon the defendant a greater stigma than that accompanying the jury verdict alone. Core concerns animating the jury and burden-of-proof requirements are thus absent from such a scheme." 530 U. S., at 491, n. 16.

Ultimately, the Court abandons its effort to provide analytic support for its decision, and turns to what it thinks to be the " 'salutary objectives' " of Oregon's scheme. Ante, at 9. "Limiting judicial discretion," we are told, promotes sentences proportionate to the gravity of the offense, and reduces disparities in sentence length. Ibid. The same argument (the very same argument) was made and rejected in Booker, see 543 U. S., at 244,and Blakely, see 542 U. S., at 313. The protection of the Sixth Amendment does not turn on this Court's opinion of whether an alternative scheme is good policy, or whether the legislature had a compassionate heart in adopting it. The right to trial by jury and proof beyond a reasonable doubt is a given, and all legislative policymaking—good and bad, heartless and compassionate—must work within the confines of that reality. Of course the Court probably exaggerates the benign effect of Oregon's scheme, as is suggested by the defense bar's vigorous objection, evidenced by the participation of the National Association of Criminal Defense Lawyers as amicus in favor of respondent. Even that exaggeration is a replay of the rejected dissentin one of our prior cases. There the Court responded: "It is hard to believe that the National Association of Criminal Defense Lawyers was somehow duped into arguing for the wrong side." Blakely, supra, at 312.

Finally, the Court summons up the parade of horribles assembled by the amicus brief of 17 States supporting Oregon. It notes that "[t]rial judges often find facts" in connection with "a variety of sentencing determinations other than the length of incarceration," and worries that even their ability to set the length of supervised release, impose community service, or order entry into a drug rehabilitation program, may be called into question. Ante, at 10. But if these courses reduce rather than augment the punishment that the jury verdict imposes, there is no problem. The last horrible the Court invokes is the prospect of bifurcated or even trifurcated trials in order to have the jury find the facts essential to consecutive sentencing without prejudicing the defendant's merits case. Ibid. That is another déjÀ vu and déjÀ rejeté; we have watched it parade past before, in several of our Apprendi-related opinions, and have not saluted. See Blakely, supra, at 336–337 (Breyer, J., dissenting); Apprendi, supra, at 557 (same).

*　*　*

The Court's peroration says that "[t]he jury-trial right is best honored through a 'principled rationale' that applies the rule of the Apprendi cases 'within the central sphere of their concern.' " Ante, at 11 (quoting Cunningham v. California, 549 U. S. 270, 295 (2007) (Kennedy, J., dissenting)). Undoubtedly so. But we have hitherto considered "the central sphere of their concern" to be facts necessary to the increase of the defendant's sentence beyond what the jury verdict alone justifies. "If the jury's verdict alone does not authorize the sentence, if, instead, the judge must find an additional fact to impose the longer term, the Sixth Amendment requirement is not satisfied." Id., at 290 (opinion of the Court). If the doubling or tripling of a defendant's jail time through fact-dependent consecutive sentencing does not meet this description, nothing does. And as for a "principled rationale": The Court's reliance upon a distinction without a difference, and its repeated exhumation of arguments dead and buried by prior cases, seems to me the epitome of the opposite. Today's opinion muddies the waters, and gives cause to doubt whether the Court is willing to stand by Apprendi's interpretation of the Sixth Amendment 's jury-trial guarantee.

Justice Scalia's dissent from denial of certiorari in Sorich v. US (Feb 23, 2009)

The petition for a writ of certiorari is denied.

Justice Scalia, dissenting.

In McNally v. United States, 483 U.S. 350, 107 S.Ct. 2875, 97 L.Ed.2d 292 (1987), this Court held that while "[t]he mail fraud statute clearly protects property rights,... [it] does not refer to the intangible right of the citizenry to good government." Id., at 356, 107 S.Ct. 2875. That holding invalidated the theory that official corruption and misconduct, by depriving citizens of their "intangible right" to the honest and impartial services of government, constituted fraud. Although all of the Federal Courts of Appeals had accepted the theory, see id., at 364, 107 S.Ct. 2875 (STEVENS, J., dissenting), we declined to

"construe the statute in a manner that leaves its outer boundaries ambiguous and involves the Federal Government in setting standards of disclosure and good government for local and state officials," id., at 360, 107 S.Ct. 2875 (majority opinion). "If Congress desires to go further," we said, "it must speak more clearly than it has." Ibid.

Congress spoke shortly thereafter. "For the purposes of this chapter, the term `scheme or artifice to defraud' includes a scheme or artifice to deprive another of the intangible right of honest services." 18 U.S.C. § 1346. Whether that terse amendment qualifies as speaking "more clearly" or in any way lessens the vagueness and federalism concerns that produced this Court's decision in McNally is another matter.

Though it consists of only 28 words, the statute has been invoked to impose criminal penalties upon a staggeringly broad swath of behavior, including misconduct not only by public officials and employees but also by private employees and corporate fiduciaries. Courts have upheld convictions of a local housing official who failed to disclose a conflict of interest, United States v. Hasner, 340 F.3d 1261, 1271 (C.A.11 2003) (per curiam); a businessman who attempted to pay a state legislator to exercise "informal and behind-the-scenes influence on legislation," United States v. Potter, 463 F.3d 9, 18 (C.A.1 2006); students who schemed with their professors to turn in plagiarized work, United

States v. Frost, 125 F.3d 346, 369 (C.A.6 1997); lawyers who made side-payments to insurance adjusters in exchange for the expedited processing of their clients' pending claims, United States v. Rybicki, 354 F.3d 124, 142 (C.A.2 2003) (en banc); and, in the decision we are asked to review here, city employees who engaged in political-patronage hiring for local civil-service jobs, 523 F.3d 702, 705 (C.A.7 2008).

If the "honest services" theory — broadly stated, that officeholders and employees owe a duty to act only in the best interests of their constituents and employers — is taken seriously and carried to its logical conclusion, presumably the statute also renders criminal a state legislator's decision to vote for a bill because he expects it will curry favor with a small minority essential to his reelection; a mayor's attempt to use the prestige of his office to obtain a restaurant table without a reservation; a public employee's recommendation of his incompetent friend for a public contract; and any self-dealing by a corporate officer. Indeed, it would seemingly cover a salaried employee's phoning in sick to go to a ball game. In many cases, moreover, the maximum penalty for violating this statute will be added to the maximum penalty for violating 18 U.S.C. § 666, a federal bribery statute, since violation of the latter requires the additional factor of the employer's receipt of federal funds, while violation of the "honest services" provision requires use of mail or wire services, §§ 1341, 1343. Quite a potent federal prosecutorial tool.

To avoid some of these extreme results, the Courts of Appeals have spent two decades attempting to cabin the breadth of § 1346 through a variety of limiting principles. No consensus has emerged. The Fifth Circuit has held that the statute criminalizes only a deprivation of services that is unlawful under state law, United States v. Brumley, 116 F.3d 728, 735 (1997) (en banc), but other courts have not agreed, see United States v. Martin, 195 F.3d 961, 966 (C.A.7 1999) (Brumley "is contrary to the law in this circuit ... and in the other circuits to have addressed the question"). The Seventh Circuit has construed the statute to prohibit only the abuse of position "for private gain," United States v. Bloom, 149 F.3d 649, 655 (1998), but other Circuits maintain that gain is not an element of the crime at all, e.g., United States v. Panarella, 277 F.3d 678, 692 (C.A.3 2002). Courts have expressed frustration at the lack of any "simple formula specific enough to give clear cut answers to borderline problems." United States v. Urciuoli, 513 F.3d 290, 300 (C.A.1 2008).

It is practically gospel in the lower courts that the statute "does not encompass every instance of official misconduct," United States v. Sawyer, 85 F.3d 713, 725 (C.A.1 1996). The Tenth Circuit has confidently proclaimed that the statute is "not violated by every breach of contract, breach of duty, conflict of interest, or misstatement made in the course of dealing," United States v. Welch, 327 F.3d 1081, 1107 (2003). But why that is so, and what principle it is that separates the criminal breaches, conflicts and misstatements from the obnoxious but lawful ones, remains entirely unspecified. Without some coherent limiting principle to define what "the intangible right of honest services" is, whence it derives, and how it is violated, this expansive phrase invites abuse by headline-grabbing prosecutors in pursuit of local officials, state legislators, and corporate CEOs who engage in any manner of unappealing or ethically questionable conduct.

In the background of the interpretive venture remain the two concerns voiced by this Court in McNally. First, the prospect of federal prosecutors' (or federal courts') creating ethics codes and setting disclosure requirements for local and state officials. Is it the role of the Federal Government to define the fiduciary duties that a town alderman or school board trustee owes to his constituents? It is one thing to enact and enforce clear rules against certain types of corrupt behavior, e.g., 18 U.S.C. § 666(a) (bribes and gratuities to public officials), but quite another to mandate a freestanding, open-ended duty to provide "honest services" — with the details to be worked out case-by-case. See generally Brown, Should Federalism Shield Corruption? — Mail Fraud, State Law and Post-Lopez Analysis, 82 Cornell L.Rev. 225 (1997).

Second and relatedly, this Court has long recognized the "basic principle that a criminal statute must give fair warning of the conduct that it makes a crime." Bouie v. City of Columbia, 378 U.S. 347, 350, 84 S.Ct. 1697, 12 L.Ed.2d 894 (1964). There is a serious argument that § 1346 is nothing more than an invitation for federal courts to develop a common-law crime of unethical conduct. But "the notion of a common-law crime is utterly anathema today," Rogers v. Tennessee, 532 U.S. 451, 476, 121 S.Ct. 1693, 149 L.Ed.2d 697 (2001) (SCALIA, J., dissenting), and for good reason. It is simply not fair to prosecute someone for a crime that has not been defined until the judicial decision that sends him to jail. "How can the public be expected to know what the statute means when the judges and prosecutors themselves do not know, or must make it up as they go along?" Rybicki, supra, at 160 (Jacobs, J., dissenting).

The present case in which certiorari is sought implicates two of the limiting principles that the Courts of Appeals have debated — whether the crime of deprivation of "honest services" requires a predicate violation of state law, and whether it requires the defendant's acquisition of some sort of private gain. The jury was instructed that petitioners, who were employed by the city of Chicago, were obliged, "[a]s part of the honest services they owed the City and the people of the City of Chicago," to abide by a laundry list of "laws, decrees, and policies," including a 1983 civil consent decree entered into by the city which barred patronage hiring for some city jobs. App. to Pet. for Cert. 137-140. The Seventh Circuit approved the instruction, again rejecting the Fifth Circuit's violation-of-state-law principle. "It may well be," the court said, "that merely by virtue of being public officials the defendants inherently owed the public a fiduciary duty to discharge their offices in the public's best interest." 523 F.3d, at 712. And though petitioners received no direct personal benefit from the patronage they doled out on behalf of their political masters, the Seventh Circuit found it sufficient that the patronage appointees — who were not charged in the scheme — accrued private gain. Id., at 709.

Finally, in addition to presenting two of the principal devices the Courts of Appeals have used in an effort to limit § 1346, the case also squarely presents the issue of its constitutionality. The Court of Appeals rebuffed petitioners' argument that if § 1346 really criminalizes all conduct that is not "in the public's best interest" and that benefits someone, it is void for vagueness. The court cited two prior Circuit decisions which, it said, "provided sufficient notice." Id., at 711.

It may be true that petitioners here, like the defendants in other "honest services" cases, have acted improperly. But "[b]ad men, like good men, are entitled to be tried and sentenced in accordance with law." Green v. United States, 365 U.S. 301, 309, 81 S.Ct. 653, 5 L.Ed.2d 670 (1961) (Black, J., dissenting). In light of the conflicts among the Circuits; the longstanding confusion over the scope of the statute; and the serious due process and federalism interests affected by the expansion of criminal liability that this case exemplifies, I would grant the petition for certiorari and squarely confront both the meaning and the constitutionality of § 1346. Indeed, it seems to me quite irresponsible to let the current chaos prevail.

Justice Scalia's dissent in Caperton v. AT Massey Coal (June 8, 2009)

Justice SCALIA, dissenting.

The principal purpose of this Court's exercise of its certiorari jurisdiction is to clarify the law. See this Court's Rule 10. As THE CHIEF JUSTICE's dissent makes painfully clear, the principal consequence of today's decision is to create vast uncertainty with respect to a point of law that can be raised in all litigated cases in (at least) those 39 States that elect their judges. This course was urged upon us on grounds that it would preserve the public's confidence in the judicial system. Brief for Petitioners 16.

The decision will have the opposite effect. What above all else is eroding public confidence in the Nation's judicial system is the perception that litigation is just a game, that the party with the most resourceful lawyer can play it to win, that our seemingly interminable legal proceedings are wonderfully self-perpetuating but incapable of delivering real-world justice. The Court's opinion will reinforce that perception, adding to the vast arsenal of lawyerly gambits what will come to be known as the Caperton claim. The facts relevant to adjudicating it will have to be litigated — and likewise the law governing it, which will be indeterminate for years to come, if not forever. Many billable hours will be spent in poring through volumes of campaign finance reports, and many more in contesting nonrecusal decisions through every available means.

A Talmudic maxim instructs with respect to the Scripture: "Turn it over, and turn it over, for all is therein." 8 The Babylonian Talmud: Seder Nezikin, Tractate Aboth, Ch. V, Mishnah 22, pp. 75-77 (I. Epstein ed.1935) (footnote omitted). Divinely inspired text may contain the answers to all earthly questions, but the Due Process Clause most assuredly does not. The Court today continues its quixotic quest to right all wrongs and repair all imperfections through the Constitution. Alas, the quest cannot succeed — which is why some wrongs and imperfections have been called nonjusticiable. In the best of all possible worlds, should judges sometimes recuse even where the clear commands of our prior due process law do not require it? Undoubtedly. The relevant question, however, is whether we do more good than harm by seeking to correct this imperfection through expansion of our constitutional mandate in a manner ungoverned by any discernable rule. The answer is obvious.

Justice Scalia's dissent in Yeager v. US (June 18, 2009)

Justice SCALIA, with whom Justice THOMAS and Justice ALITO join, dissenting.

The Double Jeopardy Clause of the Fifth Amendment provides that no person shall "be subject for the same offence to be twice put in jeopardy of life or limb." The Court today holds that this proscription, as interpreted in Ashe v. Swenson, 397 U.S. 436, 90 S.Ct. 1189, 25 L.Ed.2d 469 (1970), sometimes bars retrial of hung counts if the jury acquits on factually related counts. Because that result neither accords with the original meaning of the Double Jeopardy Clause nor is required by the Court's precedents, I dissent.

I

Today's opinion begins with the proclamation that this Court has "found more guidance in the common-law ancestry of the [Double Jeopardy] Clause than its brief text." Ante, at 2365. Would that it were so. This case would be easy indeed if our cases had adhered to the Clause's original meaning. The English common-law pleas of auterfoits acquit and auterfoits convict, on which the Clause was based, barred only repeated "prosecution for the same identical act and crime." 4 W. Blackstone, Commentaries on the Laws of England 330 (1769) (emphasis added). See also Grady v. Corbin, 495 U.S. 508, 530-535, 110 S.Ct. 2084, 109 L.Ed.2d 548 (1990) (SCALIA, J., dissenting). As described by Sir Matthew Hale, "a man acquitted for stealing [a] horse" could be later "arraigned and convict[ed] for stealing the saddle, tho both were done at the same time." 2 Pleas of the Crown 246 (1736). Under the common-law pleas, the jury's acquittal of Yeager on the fraud counts would have posed no bar to further prosecution for the distinct crimes of insider trading and money laundering.

But that is water over the dam. In Ashe the Court departed from the original meaning of the Double Jeopardy Clause, holding that it precludes successive prosecutions on distinct crimes when facts essential to conviction of the second crime have necessarily been resolved in the defendant's favor by a verdict of acquittal of the first crime. 397 U.S. at 445-446, 90 S.Ct. 1189.[1] Even if I am to adhere to Ashe on stare decisis grounds, cf. Grady, supra, at 528, 110 S.Ct. 2084 (SCALIA, J., dissenting), today's holding is an illogical extension of that case. Ashe held only that the Clause sometimes bars successive prosecution of facts found during "a prior proceeding." 397 U.S. at 444, 90 S.Ct. 1189. But today the Court bars retrial on hung counts after what was not, under this Court's theory of "continuing jeopardy," Justices of Boston Municipal Court v. Lydon, 466 U.S. 294, 308, 104 S.Ct. 1805, 80 L.Ed.2d 311 (1984), a prior proceeding but simply an earlier stage of the same proceeding.

As an historical matter, the common-law pleas could be invoked only once "there ha[d] been a conviction or an acquittal — after a complete trial." Crist v. Bretz, 437 U.S. 28, 33, 98 S.Ct. 2156, 57 L.Ed.2d 24 (1978). This Court has extended the protections of the

Double Jeopardy Clause by holding that jeopardy attaches earlier: at the time a jury is empanelled and sworn. Id., at 38, 98 S.Ct. 2156. Although one might think that this early attachment would mean that any second trial with a new jury would constitute a second jeopardy, the Court amended its innovation by holding that discharge of a deadlocked jury does not "terminat[e] the original jeopardy," Richardson v. United States, 468 U.S. 317, 325, 104 S.Ct. 3081, 82 L.Ed.2d 242 (1984). Under this continuing-jeopardy principle, retrial after a jury has failed to reach a verdict is not a new trial but part of the same proceeding.[2]

Today's holding is inconsistent with this principle. It interprets the Double Jeopardy Clause, for the first time, to have effect internally within a single prosecution, even though the "`criminal proceedings against [the] accused have not run their full course.'" Lydon, supra, at 308, 104 S.Ct. 1805 (quoting Price v. Georgia, 398 U.S. 323, 326, 90 S.Ct. 1757, 26 L.Ed.2d 300 (1970)). As a conceptual matter, it makes no sense to say that events occurring within a single prosecution can cause an accused to be "twice put in jeopardy." U.S. Const., Amdt. 5. And our cases, until today, have acknowledged that. Ever since Dunn v. United States, 284 U.S. 390, 393, 52 S.Ct. 189, 76 L.Ed. 356 (1932), we have refused to set aside convictions that were inconsistent with acquittals in the same trial; and we made clear in United States v. Powell, 469 U.S. 57, 64-65, 105 S.Ct. 471, 83 L.Ed.2d 461 (1984), that Ashe does not mandate a different result. There is no reason to treat perceived inconsistencies between hung counts and acquittals any differently.

Richardson accentuates the point. Under our cases, if an appellate court reverses a conviction for lack of constitutionally sufficient evidence, that determination constitutes an acquittal which, under the Double Jeopardy Clause, precludes further prosecution. Burks v. United States, 437 U.S. 1, 11, 98 S.Ct. 2141, 57 L.Ed.2d 1 (1978). In Richardson, the defendant sought to prevent retrial after a jury failed to reach a verdict, claiming that the case should not have gone to the jury because the Government failed to present sufficient evidence. 468 U.S. at 322-323, 104 S.Ct. 3081. The Court held that the Double Jeopardy Clause was inapplicable because there had not been an "event, such as an acquittal, which terminate[d] the original jeopardy." Id. at 325, 104 S.Ct. 3081. I do not see why the Double Jeopardy Clause effect of a jury acquittal on a different count should be any different from the Double Jeopardy Clause effect of the prosecution's failure to present a case sufficient to go to the jury on the same count. In both cases, the predicate necessary for Double Jeopardy Clause preclusion of a new prosecution exists: in the former, the factual findings implicit in the jury's verdict of acquittal, in the latter, the State's presentation of a case so weak that it would have demanded a jury verdict of acquittal. In both cases, it seems to me, the Double Jeopardy Clause cannot be invoked because the jeopardy with respect to the retried count has not terminated.

The acquittals here did not, as the majority argues, "unquestionably terminat[e] [Yeager's] jeopardy with respect to the issues finally decided" in those counts. Ante, at 2366 (emphasis added). Jeopardy is commenced and terminated charge by charge, not issue by issue. And if the prosecution's failure to present sufficient evidence at a first trial cannot prevent retrial on a hung count because the retrial is considered part of the same proceeding, then there is no basis for invoking Ashe to prevent retrial in the present case. If a conviction can stand with a contradictory acquittal when both are pronounced at the same trial, there is no reason why an acquittal should prevent the State from pressing for a contradictory conviction in the continuation of the prosecution on the hung counts.

II

The Court's extension of Ashe to these circumstances cannot even be justified based on the rationales underlying that holding. Invoking issue preclusion to bar seriatim prosecutions has the salutary effect of preventing the Government from circumventing acquittals by forcing defendants "to `run the gantlet' a second time" on effectively the same charges. 397 U.S. at 446, 90 S.Ct. 1189. In cases where the prosecution merely seeks to get "one full and fair opportunity to convict" on all charges brought in an initial indictment, Ohio v. Johnson, 467 U.S. 493, 502, 104 S.Ct. 2536, 81 L.Ed.2d 425 (1984), there is no risk of such gamesmanship. We have said that "where the State has made no effort to prosecute the charges seriatim, the considerations of double jeopardy protection implicit in the application of collateral estoppel are inapplicable." Id., at 500 n. 9, 104 S.Ct. 2536.

Moreover, barring retrial when a jury acquits on some counts and hangs on others bears only a tenuous relationship to preserving the finality of "an issue of ultimate fact [actually] determined by a valid and final judgment." Ashe, supra, at 443, 90 S.Ct. 1189. There is no clear, unanimous jury finding here. In the unusual situation in which a factual finding upon which an acquittal must have been based would also logically require an acquittal on the hung count, all that can be said for certain is that the conflicting dispositions are irrational — the result of "mistake, compromise, or lenity." Powell, 469 U.S. at 65, 105 S.Ct. 471. It is at least as likely that the irrationality consisted of failing to make the factual finding necessary to support the acquittal as it is that the irrationality consisted of failing to adhere to that factual finding with respect to the hung count. While I agree that courts should avoid speculation as to why a jury reached a particular result, ante, at 2368, the Court's opinion steps in the wrong direction by pretending that the acquittals here mean something that they in all probability do not.[3] Powell, supra, at 69, 105 S.Ct. 471, concluded that "the best course to take is simply to insulate jury verdicts" from review on grounds of inconsistency. In my view the same conclusion applies to claims that inconsistency will arise from proceeding to conviction on hung counts.

The burdens created by the Court's opinion today are likely to be substantial. The Ashe inquiry will require courts to "examine the record of a prior proceeding, taking into account the pleadings, evidence, charge, and other relevant matter, and conclude whether a rational jury could have grounded its verdict upon an issue other than that which the defendant seeks to foreclose from consideration." 397 U.S. at 446, 90 S.Ct. 1189 (internal quotation marks omitted). What is more, our holding in Abney v. United States, 431 U.S. 651, 97 S.Ct. 2034, 52 L.Ed.2d 651 (1977), ensures that every defendant in Yeager's shoes will be entitled to an immediate interlocutory appeal (and petition for certiorari) whenever his Ashe claim is rejected by the trial court. Abney, supra, at 662, 97 S.Ct. 2034.

     * * *

Until today, this Court has consistently held that retrial after a jury has been unable to reach a verdict is part of the original prosecution and that there can be no second jeopardy where there has been no second prosecution. Because I believe holding that line against this extension of Ashe is more consistent with the Court's cases and with the original meaning of the Double Jeopardy Clause, I would affirm the judgment.

Notes

[1] Because this case arises in federal court, the federal doctrine of issue preclusion might have prevented the Government from retrying Yeager even without Ashe's innovation. See United States v. Oppenheimer, 242 U.S. 85, 87, 37 S.Ct. 68, 61 L.Ed. 161 (1916). But the District Court held that the jury in this case had not necessarily decided that Yeager lacked inside information (the fact that Yeager claims the Government is barred from relitigating), 446 F.Supp.2d 719, 735 (S.D.Tex. 2006), and jurisdiction for this interlocutory appeal of that holding comes by way of the collateral order doctrine, which encompasses claims of former jeopardy, Abney v. United States, 431 U.S. 651, 662, 97 S.Ct. 2034, 52 L.Ed.2d 651 (1977). We have not accorded the same privilege to litigants asserting issue preclusion.

[2] That the Government issued a new indictment after the mistrial in this case does not alter the fact that, for double jeopardy purposes, retrial would have been part of the same, initial proceeding. As a matter of practice, it seems that prosecutors and courts treat retrials after mistrials as part of the same proceeding by filing superseding indictments under the original docket number. See, e.g., Superseding Information in United States v. Pena, Case No. 8:03-cr-476-T-23EAJ (MD Fla., Feb. 17, 2005). The Court implies that the new indictment in this case materially refined the charges, ante, at 2364, but the only relevant changes were dropping of the other defendants and elimination of a few counts and related factual allegations. Compare App. 6-71 with App. 188-200.

[3] The Court claims that a jury's failure to reach a verdict is not relevant evidence, ante, at 2367-2368, but its justifications for that statement are utterly unpersuasive. It is obvious that a failure to reach a verdict on one count "make[s] the existence" of a factual finding on a necessary predicate for both counts substantially "less probable," Fed. Rule Evid. 401; how the Court can believe otherwise is beyond me.

Justice Scalia's dissent in Padilla v. Kentucky (March 31, 2010)

Justice Scalia, with whom Justice Thomas joins, dissenting.

In the best of all possible worlds, criminal defendants contemplating a guilty plea ought to be advised of all serious collateral consequences of conviction, and surely ought not to be misadvised. The Constitution, however, is not an all-purpose tool for judicial construction of a perfect world; and when we ignore its text in order to make it that, we often find ourselves swinging a sledge where a tack hammer is needed.

The Sixth Amendment guarantees the accused a lawyer "for his defense" against a "criminal prosecutio[n]"—not for sound advice about the collateral consequences of conviction. For that reason, and for the practical reasons set forth in Part I of Justice Alito 's concurrence, I dissent from the Court's conclusion that the Sixth Amendment requires counsel to provide accurate advice concerning the potential removal consequences of a guilty plea. For the same reasons, but unlike the concurrence, I do not believe that affirmative misadvice about those consequences renders an attorney's assistance in defending against the prosecution constitutionally inadequate; or that the Sixth Amendment requires counsel to warn immigrant defendants that a conviction may render them removable. Statutory provisions can remedy these concerns in a more targeted fashion, and without producing permanent, and legislatively irreparable, overkill.

*　　*　　*

The Sixth Amendment as originally understood and ratified meant only that a defendant had a right to employ counsel, or to use volunteered services of counsel. See, United States v. Van Duzee , 140 U. S. 169, 173 (1891) ; W. Beaney, Right to Counsel in American Courts 21, 28–29 (1955). We have held, however, that the Sixth Amendment requires the provision of counsel to indigent defendants at government expense, Gideon v. Wainwright , 372 U. S. 335, 344–345 (1963) , and that the right to "the assistance of counsel" includes the right to effective assistance, Strickland v. Washington , 466 U. S. 668, 686 (1984) . Even assuming the validity of these holdings, I reject the significant further extension that the Court, and to a lesser extent the concurrence, would create. We have until today at least retained the Sixth Amendment 's textual limitation to criminal prosecutions. "[W]e have held that 'defence' means defense at trial, not defense in relation to other objectives that may be important to the accused." Rothgery v. Gillespie County, 554 U. S. ____, ____ (2008) (A lito , J., concurring) (slip op., at 4) (summarizing cases). We have limited the Sixth Amendment to legal advice directly related to defense against prosecution of the charged offense—advice at trial, of course, but also advice at postindictment interrogations and lineups, Massiah v. United States , 377 U. S. 201, 205–206 (1964) ; United States v. Wade , 388 U. S. 218, 236–238 (1967) , and in general advice at all phases of the prosecution where the defendant would be at a disadvantage when pitted alone against the legally trained agents of the state, see Moran v. Burbine , 475 U. S. 412, 430 (1986) . Not only have we not required advice of counsel regarding consequences collateral to prosecution, we have not even required counsel appointed to defend against one prosecution to be present when the defendant is interrogated in connection with another possible prosecution arising from the same event. Texas v. Cobb , 532 U. S. 162, 164 (2001) .

There is no basis in text or in principle to extend the constitutionally required advice regarding guilty pleas beyond those matters germane to the criminal prosecution at hand—to wit, the sentence that the plea will produce, the higher sentence that conviction after trial might entail, and the chances of such a conviction. Such matters fall within "the range of competence demanded of attorneys in criminal cases," McMann v. Richardson , 397 U. S. 759, 771 (1970) . See id., at 769–770 (describing the matters counsel and client must consider in connection with a contemplated guilty plea). We have never held, as the logic of the Court's opinion assumes, that once counsel is appointed all professional responsibilities of counsel—even those extending beyond defense against the prosecution—become constitutional commands. Cf. Cobb , supra , at 171, n. 2; Moran , supra , at 430. Because the subject of the misadvice here was not the prosecution for which Jose Padilla was entitled to effective assistance of counsel, the Sixth Amendment has no application.

Adding to counsel's duties an obligation to advise about a conviction's collateral consequences has no logical stopping-point. As the concurrence observes,

"[A] criminal convictio[n] can carry a wide variety of consequences other than conviction and sentencing, including civil commitment, civil forfeiture, the loss of the right to vote, disqualification from public benefits, ineligibility to possess firearms, dishonorable discharge from the Armed Forces, and loss of business or professional licenses. . . . All of those consequences are 'serious,' ... ." Ante , at 2–3 (Alito, J., concurring in judgment).

But it seems to me that the concurrence suffers from the same defect. The same indeterminacy, the same inability to know what areas of advice are relevant, attaches to misadvice. And the concurrence's suggestion that counsel must warn defendants of potential removal consequences, see ante , at 14–15—what would come to be known as the " Padilla warning"—cannot be limited to those consequences except by judicial caprice. It is difficult to believe that the warning requirement would not be extended, for example, to the risk of heightened sentences in later federal prosecutions pursuant to the Armed Career Criminal Act, 18 U. S. C. §924(e). We could expect years of elaboration upon these new issues in the lower courts, prompted by the defense bar's devising of ever-expanding categories of plea-invalidating misadvice and failures to warn—not to mention innumerable evidentiary hearings to determine whether misadvice really occurred or whether the warning was really given.

The concurrence's treatment of misadvice seems driven by concern about the voluntariness of Padilla's guilty plea. See ante , at 12. But that concern properly relates to the Due Process Clauses of the Fifth and Fourteenth Amendment s, not to the Sixth Amendment . See McCarthy v. United States , 394 U. S. 459, 466 (1969) ; Brady v. United States , 397 U. S. 742, 748 (1970) . Padilla has not argued before us that his guilty plea was not knowing and voluntary. If that is, however, the true substance of his claim (and if he has properly preserved it) the state court can address it on remand. 1 But we should not smuggle the claim into the Sixth Amendment .

The Court's holding prevents legislation that could solve the problems addressed by today's opinions in a more precise and targeted fashion. If the subject had not been constitutionalized, legislation could specify which categories of misadvice about matters ancillary to the prosecution invalidate plea agreements, what collateral consequences counsel must bring to a defendant's attention, and what warnings must be given. 2 Moreover, legislation could provide consequences for the misadvice, nonadvice, or failure to warn, other than nullification of a criminal conviction after the witnesses and evidence needed for retrial have disappeared. Federal immigration law might provide, for example, that the near-automatic removal which follows from certain criminal convictions will not apply where the conviction rested upon a guilty plea induced by counsel's misadvice regarding removal consequences. Or legislation might put the government to a choice in such circumstances: Either retry the defendant or forgo the removal. But all that has been precluded in favor of today's sledge hammer.

In sum, the Sixth Amendment guarantees adequate assistance of counsel in defending against a pending criminal prosecution. We should limit both the constitutional obligation to provide advice and the consequences of bad advice to that well defined area.

Notes

1 I do not mean to suggest that the Due Process Clause would surely provide relief. We have indicated that awareness of "direct consequences" suffices for the validity of a guilty plea. See Brady, 397 U. S., at 755 (internal quotation marks omitted). And the required colloquy between a federal district court and a defendant required by Federal Rule of Criminal Procedure 11(b) (formerly Rule 11(c)), which we have said approximates the due process requirements for a valid plea, see Libretti v. United States, 516 U. S. 29, 49–50 (1995) , does not mention collateral consequences. Whatever the outcome, however, the effect of misadvice regarding such consequences upon the validity of a guilty plea should be analyzed under the Due Process Clause.

2 As the Court's opinion notes, ante, at 16–17, n. 15, many States—including Kentucky—already require that criminal defendants be warned of potential removal consequences.

Justice Scalia's concurrence in McDonald v. Chicago (June 28, 2010) [Notes omitted]

Justice Scalia, concurring.

I join the Court's opinion. Despite my misgivings about Substantive Due Process as an original matter, I have acquiesced in the Court's incorporation of certain guarantees in the Bill of Rights "because it is both long established and narrowly limited." Albright v. Oliver, 510 U. S. 266, 275 (1994) (Scalia, J., concurring). This case does not require me to reconsider that view, since straightforward application of settled doctrine suffices to decide it.

I write separately only to respond to some aspects of Justice Stevens' dissent. Not that aspect which disagrees with the majority's application of our precedents to this case, which is fully covered by the Court's opinion. But much of what Justice Stevens writes is a broad condemnation of the theory of interpretation which underlies the Court's opinion, a theory that makes the traditions of our people paramount. He proposes a different theory, which he claims is more "cautiou[s]" and respectful of proper limits on the judicial role. Post, at 57. It is that claim I wish to address.

I

A

After stressing the substantive dimension of what he has renamed the "liberty clause," post, at 4–7, 1 Justice Stevens proceeds to urge readoption of the theory of incorporation articulated in Palko v. Connecticut, 302 U. S. 319, 325 (1937), see post, at 14–20. But in fact he does not favor application of that theory at all. For whether Palko requires only that "a fair and enlightened system of justice would be impossible without" the right sought to be incorporated, 302 U. S., at 325, or requires in addition that the right be rooted in the "traditions and conscience of our people," ibid. (internal quotation marks omitted), many of the rights Justice Stevens thinks are incorporated could not pass muster under either test: abortion, post, at 7 (citing Planned Parenthood of Southeastern Pa. v. Casey, 505 U. S. 833, 847 (1992)); homosexual sodomy, post, at 16 (citing Lawrence v. Texas, 539 U. S. 558, 572 (2003)); the right to have excluded from criminal trials evidence obtained in violation of the Fourth Amendment, post, at 18 (citing Mapp v. Ohio, 367 U. S. 643, 650, 655–657 (1961)); and the right to teach one's children foreign languages, post, at 7 (citing Meyer v. Nebraska, 262 U. S. 390, 399–403 (1923)), among others.

That Justice Stevens is not applying any version of Palko is clear from comparing, on the one hand, the rights he believes are covered, with, on the other hand, his conclusion that the right to keep and bear arms is not covered. Rights that pass his test include not just those "relating to marriage, procreation, contraception, family relationships, and child rearing and education," but also rights against "[g]overnment action that shocks the conscience, pointlessly infringes settled expectations, trespasses into sensitive private realms or life choices without adequate justification, [or] perpetrates gross injustice." Post, at 23 (internal quotation marks omitted). Not all such rights are in, however, since only " some fundamental aspects of personhood, dignity, and the like" are protected, post, at 24 (emphasis added). Exactly what is covered is not clear. But whatever else is in, he knows that the right to keep and bear arms is out, despite its being as "deeply rooted in this Nation's history and tradition," Washington v. Glucksberg, 521 U. S. 702, 721 (1997) (internal quotation marks omitted), as a right can be, see District of Columbia v. Heller, 554 U. S. ___, ___–___, ___–___, ___–___ (2008) (slip op., at 20–21, 26–30, 41–44). I can find no other explanation for such certitude except that Justice Stevens, despite his forswearing of "personal and private notions," post, at 21 (internal quotation marks omitted), deeply believes it should be out.

The subjective nature of Justice Stevens' standard is also apparent from his claim that it is the courts' prerogative—indeed their duty —to update the Due Process Clause so that it encompasses new freedoms the Framers were too narrow-minded to imagine, post, at 19–20, and n. 21. Courts, he proclaims, must "do justice to [the Clause's] urgent call and its open texture" by exercising the "interpretive discretion the latter embodies." Post, at 21. (Why the people are not up to the task of deciding what new rights to protect, even though it is they who are authorized to make changes, see U. S. Const., Art. V, is never explained. 2) And it would be "judicial abdication" for a judge to "tur[n] his back" on his task of determining what the Fourteenth Amendment covers by "outsourc[ing]" the job to "historical sentiment," post, at 20—that is, by being guided by what the American people throughout our history have thought. It is only we judges, exercising our "own reasoned judgment," post, at 15, who can be entrusted with deciding the Due Process Clause's scope—which rights serve the Amendment's "central values," post, at 23—which basically means picking the rights we want to protect and discarding those we do not.

B

<tab>Justice Stevens resists this description, insisting that his approach provides plenty of "guideposts" and "constraints" to keep courts from "injecting excessive subjectivity" into the process. 3 Post, at 21. Plenty indeed—and that alone is a problem. The ability of omnidirectional guideposts to constrain is inversely proportional to their number. But even individually, each lodestar or limitation he lists either is incapable of restraining judicial whimsy or cannot be squared with the precedents he seeks to preserve.

He begins with a brief nod to history, post, at 21, but as he has just made clear, he thinks historical inquiry unavailing, post, at 19–20. Moreover, trusting the meaning of the Due Process Clause to what has historically been protected is circular, see post, at 19, since that would mean no new rights could get in.

<tab>Justice Stevens moves on to the "most basic" constraint on subjectivity his theory offers: that he would "esche[w] attempts to provide any all-purpose, top-down, totalizing theory of 'liberty.' " Post, at 22. The notion that the absence of a coherent theory of the Due Process Clause will somehow curtail judicial caprice is at war with reason. Indeterminacy means opportunity for courts to impose whatever rule they like; it is the problem, not the solution. The idea that interpretive pluralism would reduce courts' ability to impose their will on the ignorant masses is not merely naïve, but absurd. If there are no right answers, there are no wrong answers either.

<tab>Justice Stevens also argues that requiring courts to show "respect for the democratic process" should serve as a constraint. Post, at 23. That is true, but Justice Stevens would have them show respect in an extraordinary manner. In his view, if a right "is already being given careful consideration in, and subjected to ongoing calibration by, the States, judicial enforcement may not be appropriate." Ibid. In other words, a right, such as the right to keep and bear arms, that has long been recognized but on which the States are considering restrictions, apparently deserves less protection, while a privilege the political branches (instruments of the democratic process) have withheld entirely and continue to withhold, deserves more . That topsy-turvy approach conveniently accomplishes the objective of ensuring that the rights this Court held protected in Casey, Lawrence, and other such cases fit the theory—but at the cost of insulting rather than respecting the democratic process.

The next constraint Justice Stevens suggests is harder to evaluate. He describes as "an important tool for guiding judicial discretion" "sensitivity to the interaction between the intrinsic aspects of liberty and the practical realities of contemporary society." Post, at 24. I cannot say whether that sensitivity will really guide judges because I have no idea what it is. Is it some sixth sense instilled in judges when they ascend to the bench? Or does it mean judges are more constrained when they agonize about the cosmic conflict between liberty and its potentially harmful consequences? Attempting to give the concept more precision, Justice Stevens explains that "sensitivity is an aspect of a deeper principle: the need to approach our work with humility and caution." Ibid. Both traits are undeniably admirable, though what relation they bear to sensitivity is a mystery. But it makes no difference, for the first case Justice Stevens cites in support, see ibid., Casey, 505 U. S., at 849, dispels any illusion that he has a meaningful form of judicial modesty in mind.

<tab>Justice Stevens offers no examples to illustrate the next constraint: stare decisis, post, at 25. But his view of it is surely not very confining, since he holds out as a "canonical" exemplar of the proper approach, see post, at 16, 54, Lawrence, which overruled a case decided a mere 17 years earlier, Bowers v. Hardwick, 478 U. S. 186 (1986), see 539 U. S., at 578 (it "was not correct when it was decided, and it is not correct today"). Moreover, Justice Stevens would apply that constraint unevenly: He apparently approves those Warren Court cases that adopted jot-for-jot incorporation of procedural protections for criminal defendants, post, at 11, but would abandon those Warren Court rulings that undercut his approach to substantive rights, on the basis that we have "cut back" on cases from that era before, post, at 12.

<tab>Justice Stevens also relies on the requirement of a "careful description of the asserted fundamental liberty interest" to limit judicial discretion. Post, at 25 (internal quotation marks omitted). I certainly agree with that requirement, see Reno v. Flores, 507 U. S. 292, 302 (1993), though some cases Justice Stevens approves have not applied it seriously, see, e.g., Lawrence, supra, at 562 ("The instant case involves liberty of the person both in its spatial and in its more transcendent dimensions"). But if the "careful description" requirement is used in the manner we have hitherto employed, then the enterprise of determining the Due Process Clause's "conceptual core," post, at 23, is a waste of time. In the cases he cites we sought a careful, specific description of the right at issue in order to determine whether that right, thus narrowly defined, was fundamental . See, e.g., Glucksberg, 521 U. S., at 722–728; Reno, supra, at 302–306; Collins v. Harker Heights, 503 U. S. 115, 125–129 (1992); Cruzan v. Director, Mo. Dept. of Health, 497 U. S. 261, 269–279 (1990); see also Vacco v. Quill, 521 U. S. 793, 801–808 (1997) . The threshold step of defining the asserted right with precision is entirely unnecessary, however, if (as Justice Stevens maintains) the "conceptual core" of the "liberty clause," post, at 23, includes a number of capacious, hazily defined categories. There is no need to define the right with much precision in order to conclude that it pertains to the plaintiff's "ability independently to define [his] identity," his "right to make certain unusually important decisions that will affect his own, or his family's, destiny," or some aspect of his

"[s]elf-determination, bodily integrity, freedom of conscience, intimate relationships, political equality, dignity [or] respect." Ibid. (internal quotation marks omitted). Justice Stevens must therefore have in mind some other use for the careful-description requirement—perhaps just as a means of ensuring that courts "procee[d] slowly and incrementally," post, at 25. But that could be achieved just as well by having them draft their opinions in longhand. 4

II

If Justice Stevens' account of the constraints of his approach did not demonstrate that they do not exist, his application of that approach to the case before us leaves no doubt. He offers several reasons for concluding that the Second Amendment right to keep and bear arms is not fundamental enough to be applied against the States. 5 None is persuasive, but more pertinent to my purpose, each is either intrinsically indeterminate, would preclude incorporation of rights we have already held incorporated, or both. His approach therefore does nothing to stop a judge from arriving at any conclusion he sets out to reach.

<tab>Justice Stevens begins with the odd assertion that "firearms have a fundamentally ambivalent relationship to liberty," since sometimes they are used to cause (or sometimes accidentally produce) injury to others. Post, at 35. The source of the rule that only nonambivalent liberties deserve Due Process protection is never explained— proof that judges applying Justice Stevens' approach can add new elements to the test as they see fit. The criterion, moreover, is inherently manipulable. Surely Justice Stevens does not mean that the Clause covers only rights that have zero harmful effect on anyone . Otherwise even the First Amendment is out. Maybe what he means is that the right to keep and bear arms imposes too great a risk to others' physical well-being. But as the plurality explains, ante, at 35–36, other rights we have already held incorporated pose similarly substantial risks to public safety. In all events, Justice Stevens supplies neither a standard for how severe the impairment on others' liberty must be for a right to be disqualified, nor (of course) any method of measuring the severity.

<tab>Justice Stevens next suggests that the Second Amendment right is not fundamental because it is "different in kind" from other rights we have recognized. Post, at 37. In one respect, of course, the right to keep and bear arms is different from some other rights we have held the Clause protects and he would recognize: It is deeply grounded in our nation's history and tradition. But Justice Stevens has a different distinction in mind: Even though he does "not doubt for a moment that many Americans . . . see [firearms] as critical to their way of life as well as to their security," he pronounces that owning a handgun is not "critical to leading a life of autonomy, dignity, or political equality." 6 Post, at 37–38. Who says? Deciding what is essential to an enlightened, liberty-filled life is an inherently political, moral judgment—the antithesis of an objective approach that reaches conclusions by applying neutral rules to verifiable evidence. 7

No determination of what rights the Constitution of the United States covers would be complete, of course, without a survey of what other countries do. Post, at 40–41.

When it comes to guns, Justice Stevens explains, our Nation is already an outlier among "advanced democracies"; not even our "oldest allies" protect as robust a right as we do, and we should not widen the gap. Ibid. Never mind that he explains neither which countries qualify as "advanced democracies" nor why others are irrelevant. For there is an even clearer indication that this criterion lets judges pick which rights States must respect and those they can ignore: As the plurality shows, ante, at 34–35, and nn. 28–29, this follow-the-foreign-crowd requirement would foreclose rights that we have held (and Justice Stevens accepts) are incorporated, but that other "advanced" nations do not recognize—from the exclusionary rule to the Establishment Clause. A judge applying Justice Stevens' approach must either throw all of those rights overboard or, as cases Justice Stevens approves have done in considering unenumerated rights, simply ignore foreign law when it undermines the desired conclusion, see, e.g., Casey, 505 U. S. 833 (making no mention of foreign law).

<tab>Justice Stevens also argues that since the right to keep and bear arms was codified for the purpose of "prevent[ing] elimination of the militia," it should be viewed as " 'a federalism provision' " logically incapable of incorporation. Post, at 41–42 (quoting Elk Grove Unified School Dist. v. Newdow, 542 U. S. 1, 45 (2004) (Thomas, J., concurring in judgment); some internal quotation marks omitted). This criterion, too, evidently applies only when judges want it to. The opinion Justice Stevens quotes for the "federalism provision" principle, Justice Thomas's concurrence in <font i="1">Newdow, argued that incorporation of the Establishment Clause "makes little sense" because that Clause was originally understood as a limit on congressional interference with state establishments of religion. Id., at 49–51. Justice Stevens, of course, has no problem with applying the Establishment Clause to the States. See, e.g., id., at 8, n. 4 (opinion for the Court by Stevens, J.) (acknowledging that the Establishment Clause "appl[ies] to the States by incorporation into the Fourteenth Amendment "). While he insists that Clause is not a "federalism provision," post, at 42, n. 40, he does not explain why it is not, but the right to keep and bear arms is (even though only the latter refers to a "right of the people"). The "federalism" argument prevents the incorporation of only certain rights.

Justice Stevens next argues that even if the right to keep and bear arms is "deeply rooted in some important senses," the roots of States' efforts to regulate guns run just as deep. Post, at 44 (internal quotation marks omitted). But this too is true of other rights we have held incorporated. No fundamental right—not even the First Amendment —is absolute. The traditional restrictions go to show the scope of the right, not its lack of fundamental character. At least that is what they show (Justice Stevens would agree) for other rights. Once again, principles are applied selectively.

Justice Stevens' final reason for rejecting incorporation of the Second Amendment reveals, more clearly than any of the others, the game that is afoot. Assuming that there is a "plausible constitutional basis" for holding that the right to keep and bear arms is incorporated, he asserts that we ought not to do so for prudential reasons . Post, at 47. Even if we had the authority to withhold rights that are within the Constitution's command (and we assuredly do not), two of the reasons Justice Stevens gives for abstention show just how much power he would hand to judges. The States' "right to experiment" with solutions to the problem of gun violence, he says, is at its apex here because "the best solution is far from clear." Post, at 47–48 (internal quotation marks omitted). That is true of most serious social problems—whether, for example, "the best solution" for rampant crime is to admit confessions unless they are affirmatively shown to have been coerced, but see Miranda v. Arizona, 384 U. S. 436, 444–445 (1966), or to permit jurors to impose the death penalty without a requirement that they be free to consider "any relevant mitigating factor," see Eddings v. Oklahoma, 455 U. S. 104, 112 (1982), which in turn leads to the conclusion that defense counsel has provided inadequate defense if he has not conducted a "reasonable investigation" into potentially mitigating factors, see, e.g., Wiggins v. Smith, 539 U. S. 510, 534 (2003), inquiry into which question tends to destroy any prospect of prompt justice, see, e.g., Wong v. Belmontes, 558 U. S. ____ (2009) (per curiam) (reversing grant of habeas relief for sentencing on a crime committed in 1981). The obviousness of the optimal answer is in the eye of the beholder. The implication of Justice Stevens' call for abstention is that if We The Court conclude that They The People's answers to a problem are silly, we are free to "interven[e]," post, at 47, but if we too are uncertain of the right answer, or merely think the States may be on to something, we can loosen the leash.

A second reason Justice Stevens says we should abstain is that the States have shown they are "capable" of protecting the right at issue, and if anything have protected it too much. Post, at 49. That reflects an assumption that judges can distinguish between a proper democratic decision to leave things alone (which we should honor), and a case of democratic market failure (which we should step in to correct). I would not—and no judge should—presume to have that sort of omniscience, which seems to me far more "arrogant," post, at 41, than confining courts' focus to our own national heritage.

III

Justice Stevens' response to this concurrence, post, at 51–56, makes the usual rejoinder of "living Constitution" advocates to the criticism that it empowers judges to eliminate or expand what the people have prescribed: The traditional, historically focused method, he says, reposes discretion in judges as well. 8 Historical analysis can be difficult; it sometimes requires resolving threshold questions, and making nuanced judgments about which evidence to consult and how to interpret it.

I will stipulate to that. 9 But the question to be decided is not whether the historically focused method is a perfect means of restraining aristocratic judicial Constitution-writing; but whether it is the best means available in an imperfect world. Or indeed, even more narrowly than that: whether it is demonstrably much better than what Justice Stevens proposes. I think it beyond all serious dispute that it is much less subjective, and intrudes much less upon the democratic process. It is less subjective because it depends upon a body of evidence susceptible of reasoned analysis rather than a variety of vague ethico-political First Principles whose combined conclusion can be found to point in any direction the judges favor. In the most controversial matters brought before this Court—for example, the constitutionality of prohibiting abortion, assisted suicide, or homosexual sodomy, or the constitutionality of the death penalty— any historical methodology, under any plausible standard of proof, would lead to the same conclusion. 10 Moreover, the methodological differences that divide historians, and the varying interpretive assumptions they bring to their work, post, at 52–54, are nothing compared to the differences among the American people (though perhaps not among graduates of prestigious law schools) with regard to the moral judgments Justice Stevens would have courts pronounce. And whether or not special expertise is needed to answer historical questions, judges most certainly have no "comparative ... advantage," post, at 24 (internal quotation marks omitted), in resolving moral disputes. What is more, his approach would not eliminate, but multiply, the hard questions courts must confront, since he would not replace history with moral philosophy, but would have courts consider both .

And the Court's approach intrudes less upon the democratic process because the rights it acknowledges are those established by a constitutional history formed by democratic decisions; and the rights it fails to acknowledge are left to be democratically adopted or rejected by the people, with the assurance that their decision is not subject to judicial revision. Justice Stevens ' approach, on the other hand, deprives the people of that power, since whatever the Constitution and laws may say, the list of protected rights will be whatever courts wish it to be. After all, he notes, the people have been wrong before, post, at 55, and courts may conclude they are wrong in the future. Justice Stevens abhors a system in which "majorities or powerful interest groups always get their way," post, at 56, but replaces it with a system in which unelected and life-tenured judges always get their way. That such usurpation is effected unabashedly, see post, at 53—with "the judge's cards ... laid on the table," ibid. —makes it even worse. In a vibrant democracy, usurpation should have to be accomplished in the dark. It is Justice Stevens' approach, not the Court's, that puts democracy in peril.

Justice Scalia's dissent in Michigan v. Bryant (Feb 28, 2011) [Notes omitted]

Justice Scalia, dissenting.

Today's tale—a story of five officers conducting successive examinations of a dying man with the primary purpose, not of obtaining and preserving his testimony regarding his killer, but of protecting him, them, and others from a murderer somewhere on the loose—is so transparently false that professing to believe it demeans this institution. But reaching a patently incorrect conclusion on the facts is a relatively benign judicial mischief; it affects, after all, only the case at hand. In its vain attempt to make the incredible plausible, however—or perhaps as an intended second goal—today's opinion distorts our Confrontation Clause jurisprudence and leaves it in a shambles. Instead of clarifying the law, the Court makes itself the obfuscator of last resort. Because I continue to adhere to the Confrontation Clause that the People adopted, as described in Crawford v. Washington , 541 U. S. 36 (2004) , I dissent.

I

A

The Confrontation Clause of the Sixth Amendment , made binding on the States by the Fourteenth Amendment , Pointer v. Texas , 380 U. S. 400, 403 (1965) , provides that "[i]n all criminal prosecutions, the accused shall enjoy the right ... to be confronted with the witnesses against him." In Crawford , we held that this provision guarantees a defendant his common-law right to confront those "who 'bear testimony' " against him. 541 U. S., at 51. A witness must deliver his testimony against the defendant in person, or the prosecution must prove that the witness is unavailable to appear at trial and that the defendant has had a prior opportunity for cross-examination. Id., at 53–54.

Not all hearsay falls within the Confrontation Clause's grasp. At trial a witness "bears testimony" by providing " '[a] solemn declaration or affirmation . . . for the purpose of establishing or proving some fact.' " Id., at 51 (quoting 2 N. Webster, An American Dictionary of the English Language (1828)). The Confrontation Clause protects defendants only from hearsay statements that do the same. Davis v. Washington , 547 U. S. 813, 823–824 (2006) . In Davis , we explained how to identify testimonial hearsay prompted by police questioning in the field. A statement is testimonial "when the circumstances objectively indicate ... that the primary purpose of the interrogation is to establish or prove past events potentially relevant to later criminal prosecution." Id., at 822 . When, however, the circumstances objectively indicate that the declarant's statements were "a cry for help [o]r the provision of information enabling officers immediately to end a threatening situation," id., at 832, they bear little resemblance to in-court testimony. "No 'witness' goes into court to proclaim an emergency and seek help." Id., at 828.

Crawford and Davis did not address whose perspective matters—the declarant's, the interrogator's, or both—when assessing "the primary purpose of [an] interrogation." In those cases the statements were testimonial from any perspective. I think the same is true here, but because the Court picks a perspective so will I: The declarant's intent is what counts. In-court testimony is more than a narrative of past events; it is a solemn declaration made in the course of a criminal trial. For an out-of-court statement to qualify as testimonial, the declarant must intend the statement to be a solemn declaration rather than an unconsidered or offhand remark; and he must make the statement with the understanding that it may be used to invoke the coercive machinery of the State against the accused. 1 See Friedman, Grappling with the Meaning of "Testimonial," 71 Brooklyn L. Rev. 241, 259 (2005). That is what distinguishes a narrative told to a friend over dinner from a statement to the police. See Crawford , supra, at 51. The hidden purpose of an interrogator cannot substitute for the declarant's intentional solemnity or his understanding of how his words may be used.

A declarant-focused inquiry is also the only inquiry that would work in every fact pattern implicating the Confrontation Clause. The Clause applies to volunteered testimony as well as statements solicited through police interrogation. See Davis , supra , at 822–823, n. 1. An inquiry into an officer's purposes would make no sense when a declarant blurts out "Rick shot me" as soon as the officer arrives on the scene. I see no reason to adopt a different test—one that accounts for an officer's intent—when the officer asks "what happened" before the declarant makes his accusation. (This does not mean the interrogator is irrelevant. The identity of an interrogator, and the content and tenor of his questions, can bear upon whether a declarant intends to make a solemn statement, and envisions its use at a criminal trial. But none of this means that the interrogator's purpose matters.)

In an unsuccessful attempt to make its finding of emergency plausible, the Court instead adopts a test that looks to the purposes of both the police and the declarant. It claims that this is demanded by necessity, fretting that a domestic-violence victim may want her abuser briefly arrested—presumably to teach him a lesson—but not desire prosecution. See ante, at 22. I do not need to probe the purposes of the police to solve that problem. Even if a victim speaks to the police "to establish or prove past events" solely for the purpose of getting her abuser arrested, she surely knows her account is "potentially rel-evant to later criminal prosecution" should one ensue. Davis , supra , at 822.

The Court also wrings its hands over the possibility that "a severely injured victim" may lack the capacity to form a purpose, and instead answer questions "reflexive[ly]." Ante , at 22. How to assess whether a declarant with diminished capacity bore testimony is a difficult question, and one I do not need to answer today. But the Court's proposed answer—to substitute the intentions of the police for the missing intentions of the declarant—cannot be the correct one. When the declarant has diminished capacity, focusing on the interrogators make less sense, not more. The inquiry under Crawford turns in part on the actions and statements of a declarant's audience only because they shape the declarant's perception of why his audience is listening and therefore influence his purpose in making the declaration. See 541 U. S., at 51. But a person who cannot perceive his own purposes certainly cannot perceive why a listener might be interested in what he has to say. As far as I can tell, the Court's substituted-intent theory "has nothing to be said for it except that it can sometimes make our job easier," Jerman v. Carlisle, McNellie, Rini, Kramer & Ulrich, L. P. A. , 559 U. S. ___, ___ (2010) (Scalia , J., concurring in part and concurring in judgment) (slip op., at 2).

The Court claims one affirmative virtue for its focus on the purposes of both the declarant and the police: It "ameliorates problems that ... arise" when declarants have "mixed motives." Ante , at 21. I am at a loss to know how. Sorting out the primary purpose of a declarant with mixed motives is sometimes difficult. But adding in the mixed motives of the police only compounds the problem. Now courts will have to sort through two sets of mixed motives to determine the primary purpose of an interrogation. And the Court's solution creates a mixed-motive problem where (under the proper theory) it does not exist—viz., where the police and the declarant each have one motive, but those motives conflict. The Court does not provide an answer to this glaringly obvious problem, probably because it does not have one.

The only virtue of the Court's approach (if it can be misnamned a virtue) is that it leaves judges free to reach the "fairest" result under the totality of the circumstances. If the dastardly police trick a declarant into giving an incriminating statement against a sympathetic defendant, a court can focus on the police's intent and declare the statement testimonial. If the defendant "deserves" to go to jail, then a court can focus on whatever perspective is necessary to declare damning hearsay nontestimonial. And when all else fails, a court can mix-and-match perspectives to reach its desired outcome. Unfortunately, under this malleable approach "the guarantee of confrontation is no guarantee at all." Giles v. California , 554 U. S. 353, 375 (2008) (plurality).

B

Looking to the declarant's purpose (as we should), this is an absurdly easy case. Roughly 25 minutes after Anthony Covington had been shot, Detroit police responded to a 911 call reporting that a gunshot victim had appeared at a neighborhood gas station. They quickly arrived at the scene, and in less than 10 minutes five different Detroit police officers questioned Covington about the shooting. Each asked him a similar battery of questions: "what happened" and when, App. 39, 126, "who shot" the victim," id., at 22, and "where" did the shooting take place, id., at 132. See also id., at 113. After Covington would answer, they would ask follow-up questions, such as "how tall is" the shooter, id., at 134, "[h]ow much does he weigh," ibid. what is the exact address or physical description of the house where the shooting took place, and what chain of events led to the shooting. The battery relented when the paramedics arrived and began tending to Covington's wounds.

From Covington's perspective, his statements had little value except to ensure the arrest and eventual prosecution of Richard Bryant. He knew the "threatening situation," Davis, 547 U. S., at 832, had ended six blocks away and 25 minutes earlier when he fled from Bryant's back porch. See 483 Mich. 132, 135–136, 768 N.W. 2d 65, 67 (2009); App. 105. Bryant had not confronted him face-to-face before he was mortally wounded, instead shooting him through a door. See 483 Mich. , at 136–137, 768 N.W. 2d, at 67. Even if Bryant had pursued him (unlikely), and after seeing that Covington had ended up at the gas station was unable to confront him there before the police arrived (doubly unlikely), it was entirely beyond imagination that Bryant would again open fire while Covington was surrounded by five armed police officers. And Covington knew the shooting was the work of a drug dealer, not a spree killer who might randomly threaten others. Id., at 135, 137, 768 N.W. 2d, at 67.

Covington's knowledge that he had nothing to fear differs significantly from Michelle McCottry's state of mind during her "frantic" statements to a 911 operator at issue in Davis , 547 U. S., at 827. Her "call was plainly a call for help against a bona fide physical threat" describing "events as they were actually happening ." Ibid. She did not have the luxuries of police protection and of time and space separating her from immediate danger that Covington enjoyed when he made his statements. See id., at 831.

Covington's pressing medical needs do not suggest that he was responding to an emergency, but to the contrary reinforce the testimonial character of his statements. He understood the police were focused on investigating a past crime, not his medical needs. None of the officers asked Covington how he was doing, attempted more than superficially to assess the severity of his wounds, or attempted to administer first aid. 2 They instead primarily asked questions with little, if any, relevance to Covington's dire situation. Police, paramedics, and doctors do not need to know the address where a shooting took place, the name of the shooter, or the shooter's height and weight to provide proper medical care. Underscoring that Covington understood the officers' investigative role, he interrupted their interrogation to ask "when is EMS coming?" App. 57. When, in other words, would the focus shift to his medical needs rather than Bryant's crime?

Neither Covington's statements nor the colloquy between him and the officers would have been out of place at a trial; it would have been a routine direct examination. See Davis , 547 U. S., at 830. Like a witness, Covington recounted in detail how a past criminal event began and progressed, and like a prosecutor, the police elicited that account through structured questioning. Preventing the admission of "weaker substitute[s] for live testimony at trial" such as this, id., at 828 (internal quotation marks omitted), is precisely what motivated the Framers to adopt the Confrontation Clause and what motivated our decisions in Crawford and in Hammon v. Indiana , decided with Davis . Ex parte examinations raise the same constitutional concerns whether they take place in a gas-station parking lot or in a police interrogation room.

C

Worse still for the repute of today's opinion, this is an absurdly easy case even if one (erroneously) takes the interrogating officers' purpose into account. The five officers interrogated Covington primarily to investigate past criminal events. None—absolutely none—of their actions indicated that they perceived an imminent threat. They did not draw their weapons, and indeed did not immediately search the gas station for potential shooters. 3 To the contrary, all five testified that they questioned Covington before conducting any investigation at the scene . Would this have made any sense if they feared the presence of a shooter? Most tellingly, none of the officers started his interrogation by asking what would have been the obvious first question if any hint of such a fear existed: Where is the shooter?

But do not rely solely on my word about the officers' primary purpose. Listen to Sergeant Wenturine, who candidly admitted that he interrogated Covington because he "ha[d] a man here that [he] believe[d] [was] dying [so he was] gonna find out who did this, period." App. 112. In short, he needed to interrogate Covington to solve a crime. Wenturine never mentioned an interest in ending an ongoing emergency.

At the very least, the officers' intentions turned investigative during their 10-minute encounter with Covington, and the conversation "evolve[d] into testimonial statements." Davis , 547 U. S., at 828 (internal quotation marks omitted). The fifth officer to arrive at the scene did not need to run straight to Covington and ask a battery of questions "to determine the need for emergency assistance," Ibid . He could have asked his fellow officers, who presumably had a better sense of that than Covington—and a better sense of what he could do to assist. No, the value of asking the same battery of questions a fifth time was to ensure that Covington told a consistent story and to see if any new details helpful to the investigation and eventual prosecution would emerge. Having the testimony of five officers to recount Covington's consistent story undoubtedly helped obtain Bryant's conviction. (Which came, I may note, after the first jury could not reach a verdict. See 483 Mich., at 137, 768 N.W. 2d, at 67.)

D

A final word about the Court's active imagination. The Court invents a world where an ongoing emergency exists whenever "an armed shooter, whose motive for and location after the shooting [are] unknown, ... mortally wound[s]" one individual "within a few blocks and [25] minutes of the location where the police" ultimately find that victim. Ante , at 27. Breathlessly, it worries that a shooter could leave the scene armed and ready to pull the trigger again. See ante , at 17–18, 27, 30 . Nothing suggests the five officers in this case shared the Court's dystopian 4 view of Detroit, where drug dealers hunt their shooting victim down and fire into a crowd of police officers to finish him off, see ante , at 30, or where spree killers shoot through a door and then roam the streets leaving a trail of bodies behind. Because almost 90 percent of murders involve a single victim, 5 it is much more likely—indeed, I think it certain—that the officers viewed their encounter with Covington for what it was: an investi-gation into a past crime with no ongoing or immediate consequences.

The Court's distorted view creates an expansive exception to the Confrontation Clause for violent crimes. Because Bryant posed a continuing threat to public safety in the Court's imagination, the emergency persisted for confrontation purposes at least until the police learned his "motive for and location after the shooting." Ante , at 27. It may have persisted in this case until the police "secured the scene of the shooting" two-and-a-half hours later. Ante , at 28. (The relevance of securing the scene is unclear so long as the killer is still at large—especially if, as the Court speculates, he may be a spree-killer.) This is a dangerous definition of emergency. Many individuals who testify against a defendant at trial first offer their accounts to police in the hours after a violent act. If the police can plausibly claim that a "potential threat to ... the public" persisted through those first few hours, ante , at 12 (and if the claim is plausible here it is always plausible) a defendant will have no constitutionally protected right to exclude the uncross-examined testimony of such witnesses. His conviction could rest (as perhaps it did here) solely on the officers' recollection at trial of the witnesses' accusations.

The Framers could not have envisioned such a hollow constitutional guarantee. No framing-era confrontation case that I know of, neither here nor in England, took such an enfeebled view of the right to confrontation. For example, King v. Brasier , 1 Leach 199, 200, 168 Eng. Rep. 202, 202–203 (K. B. 1779), held inadmissible a mother's account of her young daughter's statements "immediately on her coming home" after being sexually assaulted. The daughter needed to testify herself. But today's majority presumably would hold the daughter's account to her mother a nontestimonial statement made during an ongoing emergency. She could not have known whether her attacker might reappear to attack again or attempt to silence the lone witness against him. Her mother likely listened to the account to assess the threat to her own safety and to decide whether the rapist posed a threat to the community that required the immediate intervention of the local authorities. Cf. ante , at 29–30. Utter nonsense.

The 16th- and 17th-century English treason trials that helped inspire the Confrontation Clause show that today's decision is a mistake. The Court's expansive definition of an "ongoing emergency" and its willingness to consider the perspective of the interrogator and the declarant cast a more favorable light on those trials than history or our past decisions suggest they deserve. Royal officials conducted many of the ex parte examinations introduced against Sir Walter Raleigh and Sir John Fenwick while investigating alleged treasonous conspiracies of unknown scope, aimed at killing or overthrowing the King. See Brief for National Association of Criminal Defense Lawyers as Amicus Curiae 21–22, and n. 11. Social stability in 16th- and 17th-century England depended mainly on the continuity of the ruling monarch, cf. 1 J. Stephen, A History of the Criminal Law of England 354 (1883), so such a conspiracy posed the most pressing emergency imaginable. Presumably, the royal officials investigating it would have understood the gravity of the situation and would have focused their interrogations primarily on ending the threat, not on generating testimony for trial. I therefore doubt that under the Court's test English officials acted improperly by denying Raleigh and Fenwick the opportunity to confront their accusers "face to face," id., at 326.

Under my approach, in contrast, those English trials remain unquestionably infamous. Lord Cobham did not speak with royal officials to end an ongoing emergency. He was a traitor! He spoke, as Raleigh correctly observed, to establish Raleigh's guilt and to save his own life. See 1 D. Jardine, Criminal Trials 435 (1832). Cobham's statements, when assessed from his perspective, had only a testimonial purpose. The same is true of Covington's statements here.

II

A

But today's decision is not only a gross distortion of the facts. It is a gross distortion of the law—a revisionist narrative in which reliability continues to guide our Confrontation Clause jurisprudence, at least where emergencies and faux emergencies are concerned.

According to today's opinion, the Davis inquiry into whether a declarant spoke to end an ongoing emergency or rather to "prove past events potentially relevant to later criminal prosecution," 547 U. S., at 822, is not aimed at answering whether the declarant acted as a witness. Instead, the Davis inquiry probes the reliability of a declarant's statements, "[i]mplicit[ly]" importing the excited-utterances hearsay exception into the Constitution. Ante , at 14–15. A statement during an ongoing emergency is sufficiently reliable, the Court says, "because the prospect of fabrication ... is presumably significantly diminished," so it "does not [need] to be subject to the crucible of cross-examination." Id., at 14.

Compare that with the holding of Crawford: "Where testimonial statements are at issue, the only indicium of reliability sufficient to satisfy constitutional demands is the one the Constitution actually prescribes: confrontation." 541 U. S., at 68–69. Today's opinion adopts, for emergencies and faux emergencies at least, the discredited logic of White v. Illinois, 502 U. S. 346, and n. 8 (1992), and Idaho v. Wright, 497 U. S. 805, 819–820 (1990). White is, of course, the decision that both Crawford and Davis found most incompatible with the text and history of the Confrontation Clause. See Davis, supra, at 825; Crawford, supra, at 58, n. 8. (This is not to say that that "reliability" logic can actually justify today's result: Twenty-five minutes is plenty of time for a shooting victim to reflect and fabricate a false story.)

The Court announces that in future cases it will look to "standard rules of hearsay, designed to identify some statements as reliable," when deciding whether a statement is testimonial. Ante, at 11–12. Ohio v. Roberts, 448 U. S. 56 (1980) said something remarkably similar: An out-of-court statement is admissible if it "falls within a firmly rooted hearsay exception" or otherwise "bears adequate 'indicia of reliability.' " Id., at 66. We tried that approach to the Confrontation Clause for nearly 25 years before Crawford rejected it as an unworkable standard unmoored from the text and the historical roots of the Confrontation Clause. See 541 U. S., at 54, 60, 63–65, 67–68. The arguments in Raleigh's infamous 17th-century treason trial contained full debate about the reliability of Lord Cobham's ex parte accusations, see Raleigh's Case, 2 How. St. Tr. 1, 14, 17, 19–20, 22–23, 29 (1603); that case remains the canonical example of a Confrontation Clause violation, not because Raleigh should have won the debate but because he should have been allowed cross-examination.

The Court attempts to fit its resurrected interest in reliability into the Crawford framework, but the result is incoherent. Reliability, the Court tells us, is a good indicator of whether "a statement is ... an out-of-court substitute for trial testimony." Ante, at 11. That is patently false. Reliability tells us nothing about whether a statement is testimonial. Testimonial and nontestimonial statements alike come in varying degrees of reliability. An eyewitness's statements to the police after a fender-bender, for example, are both reliable and testimonial. Statements to the police from one driver attempting to blame the other would be similarly testimonial but rarely reliable.

The Court suggests otherwise because it "misunderstands the relationship" between qualification for one of the standard hearsay exceptions and exemption from the confrontation requirement. Melendez-Diaz v. Massachusetts, 557 U. S. ___, ___ (2009) (slip op., at 18). That relationship is not a causal one. Hearsay law exempts business records, for example, because businesses have a financial incentive to keep reliable records. See Fed. Rule Evid. 803(6). The Sixth Amendment also generally admits business records into evidence, but not because the records are reliable or because hearsay law says so. It admits them "because—having been created for the administration of an entity's affairs and not for the purpose of establishing or proving some fact at trial—they are not" weaker substitutes for live testimony. Melendez-Diaz , 557 U. S., at ____ (slip op., at 18). Moreover, the scope of the exemption from confrontation and that of the hearsay exceptions also are not always coextensive. The reliability logic of the business-record exception would extend to records maintained by neutral parties providing litigation-support services, such as evidence testing. The Confrontation Clause is not so forgiving. Business records prepared specifically for use at a criminal trial are testimonial and require confrontation. See ibid.

Is it possible that the Court does not recognize the contradiction between its focus on reliable statements and Crawford 's focus on testimonial ones? Does it not realize that the two cannot coexist? Or does it intend, by following today's illogical roadmap, to resurrect Roberts by a thousand unprincipled distinctions without ever explicitly overruling Crawford? After all, honestly overruling Crawford would destroy the illusion of judicial minimalism and restraint. And it would force the Court to explain how the Justices' preference comports with the meaning of the Confrontation Clause that the People adopted—or to confess that only the Justices' preference really matters.

B

The Court recedes from Crawford in a second significant way. It requires judges to conduct "open-ended balancing tests" and "amorphous, if not entirely subjective," inquiries into the totality of the circumstances bearing upon reliability. 541 U. S., at 63, 68. Where the prosecution cries "emergency," the admissibility of a statement now turns on "a highly context-dependent inquiry," ante , at 16, into the type of weapon the defendant wielded, see ante , at 17 ; the type of crime the defendant committed, see ante , at 12, 16–17; the medical condition of the declarant, see ante , at 17–18; if the declarant is injured, whether paramedics have arrived on the scene, see ante , at 20; whether the encounter takes place in an "exposed public area," ibid .; whether the encounter appears disorganized, see ibid .; whether the declarant is capable of forming a purpose, see ante , at 22; whether the police have secured the scene of the crime, see ante , at 28; the formality of the statement, see ante , at 19; and finally, whether the statement strikes us as reliable, see ante , at 11–12, 14–15. This is no better than the nine-factor balancing test we rejected in Crawford , 541 U. S., at 63. I do not look forward to resolving conflicts in the future over whether knives and poison are more like guns or fists for Confrontation Clause purposes, or whether rape and armed robbery are more like murder or domestic violence.

It can be said, of course, that under Crawford analysis of whether a statement is testimonial requires consideration of all the circumstances, and so is also something of a multifactor balancing test. But the "reliability" test does not replace that analysis; it supplements it. As I understand the Court's opinion, even when it is determined that no emergency exists (or perhaps before that determination is made) the statement would be found admissible as far as the Confrontation Clause is concerned if it is not testimonial.

In any case, we did not disavow multifactor balancing for reliability in Crawford out of a preference for rules over standards. We did so because it "d[id] violence to" the

Framers' design. Id., at 68. It was judges' open-ended determination of what was reliable that violated the trial rights of Englishmen in the political trials of the 16th and 17th centuries. See, e.g., Throckmorton's Case , 1 How. St. Tr. 869, 875–876 (1554); Raleigh's Case , 2 How. St. Tr., at 15–16, 24. The Framers placed the Confrontation Clause in the Bill of Rights to ensure that those abuses (and the abuses by the Admiralty courts in colonial America) would not be repeated in this country. Not even the least dangerous branch can be trusted to assess the reliability of uncross-examined testimony in politically charged trials or trials implicating threats to national security. See Crawford , supra , at 67–68; cf. Hamdi v. Rumsfeld , 542 U. S. 507, 576–578 (2004) (Scalia , J., dissenting).

      *   *   *

Judicial decisions, like the Constitution itself, are nothing more than "parchment barriers," 5 Writings of James Madison 269, 272 (G. Hunt ed. 1901). Both depend on a judicial culture that understands its constitutionally assigned role, has the courage to persist in that role when it means announcing unpopular decisions, and has the modesty to persist when it produces results that go against the judges' policy preferences. Today's opinion falls far short of living up to that obligation—short on the facts, and short on the law.

For all I know, Bryant has received his just deserts. But he surely has not received them pursuant to the procedures that our Constitution requires. And what has been taken away from him has been taken away from us all.

Justice Scalia's dissent in Kasten v. Saint-Gobain Performance Plastics Corporation (March 22, 2011)

Justice Scalia , with whom Justice Thomas joins as to all but footnote 6, dissenting.

The Seventh Circuit found for the employer because it held that the Fair Labor Standards Act of 1938 (FLSA), 29 U. S. C. §215(a)(3), covers only written complaints to the employer. I would affirm the judgment on the ground that §215(a)(3) does not cover complaints to the employer at all.

I

The FLSA's retaliation provision states that it shall be unlawful

"to discharge or in any other manner discriminate against any employee because such employee has filed any complaint or instituted or caused to be instituted any proceeding under or related to this chapter, or has testified or is about to testify in any such proceeding, or has served or is about to serve on an industry committee." Ibid .

The phrase central to the outcome here is "filed any complaint." In the courts below, Kasten asserted a claim for retaliation based solely on allegations that he "filed" oral "complaints" with his employer; Saint-Gobain argued that the retaliation provision protects only complaints that are (1) in writing, and (2) made to judicial or administrative bodies. I agree with at least the second part of Saint-Gobain's contention. The plain meaning of the critical phrase and the context in which appears make clear that the retaliation provision contemplates an official grievance filed with a court or an agency, not oral complaints—or even formal, written complaints—from an employee to an employer.

A

In isolation, the word "complaint" could cover Kasten's objection: It often has an expansive meaning, connoting any "[e]xpression of grief, regret, pain ... or resentment." Webster's New International Dictionary 546 (2d ed. 1934) (hereinafter Webster's). But at the time the FLSA was passed (and still today) the word when used in a legal context has borne a specialized meaning: "[a] formal allegation or charge against a party, made or presented to the appropriate court or officer." Ibid. See also Cambridge Dictionary of American English 172 (2000) ("a formal statement to a government authority that you have a legal cause to complain about the way you have been treated"); 3 Oxford English Dictionary 608 (2d ed. 1989) ("[a] statement or injury or grievance laid before a court or judicial authority ... for purposes of prosecution or of redress").

There are several reasons to think that the word bears its specialized meaning here. First, every other use of the word "complaint" in the FLSA refers to an official filing with a governmental body. Sections 216(b) and (c) both state that the right to bring particular types of actions "shall terminate upon the filing of a complaint" by the Secretary of Labor, and §216(c) clarifies that the statute of limitations begins running in actions to recover unpaid wages "on the date when the complaint is filed." These provisions unquestionably use "complaint" in the narrow legal sense. Identical words used in different parts of a statute are presumed to have the same meaning absent contrary indication, IBP, Inc. v. Alvarez , 546 U. S. 21, 34 (2005) ; Sullivan v. Stroop , 496 U. S. 478, 484 (1990) . It is one thing to expand the meaning of "complaint" in §215(a)(3) to include complaints filed with an agency instead of a court; it is quite something else to wrench it from the legal context entirely, to include an employee's objection to an employer.

Second, the word "complaint" appears as part of the phrase "filed any complaint" and thus draws meaning from the verb with which it is connected. The choice of the word "filed" rather than a broader alternative like "made," if it does not connote (as the Seventh Circuit believed, and as I need not consider) something in writing, at least suggests a degree of formality consistent with legal action and inconsistent (at least in the less regulated work environment of 1938) with employee-to-employer complaints. It is noteworthy that every definition of the verb "filed" that the Court's opinion provides, whether it supports the inclusion of oral content or not, envisions a formal, prescribed process of delivery or submission. Ante , at 4–5 (comparing, for example, Webster's 945 (to file is to "deliver (a paper or instrument) to the proper officer") with 1 Funk & Wagnalls New Standard Dictionary of the English Language 920 (rev. ed. 1938) (to file is to "present in the regular way, as to a judicial or legislative body")).

Moreover, "[t]he law uses familiar legal expressions in their familiar legal sense," Henry v. United States , 251 U. S. 393, 395 (1920) . It is, I suppose, possible to speak of "filing a complaint" with an employer, but that is assuredly not common usage.

Thus, when the antiretaliation provision of the Mine Health and Safety Act used that phrase in a context that includes both complaints to an agency and complaints to the employer, it did not use "filed" alone, but supplemented that with "or made"—and to boot specified "including a complaint notifying the [mine] operator ... of an alleged danger or safety or health violation ... ." 30 U. S. C. §815(c)(1). 1

Third, the phrase "filed any complaint" appears alongside three other protected activities: "institut[ing] or caus[ing] to be instituted any proceeding under or related to this chapter," "testif[ying] in any such proceeding," and "serv[ing] ... on an industry committee." 2 29 U. S. C. §215(a)(3). Since each of these three activities involves an interaction with governmental authority, we can fairly attribute this characteristic to the phrase "filed any complaint" as well. "That several items in a list share an attribute counsel in favor of interpreting the other items as possessing that attribute as well." Beecham v. United States , 511 U. S. 368, 371 (1994) .

And finally, the 1938 version of the FLSA, while creating private rights of action for other employer violations, see §16(b), 52 Stat. 1069, did not create a private right of action for retaliation. That was added in 1977, see §10, 91 Stat. 1252. Until then, only the Administrator of the Wage and Hour Division of the Department of Labor could enforce the retaliation provision. See §11(a), 52 Stat. 1066. It would seem more strange to require the employee to go to the Administrator to establish, and punish retaliation for, his intracompany complaint, than to require the Administrator-protected complaint to be filed with the Administrator in the first place. 3

B

1

The meaning of the phrase "filed any complaint" is clear in light of its context, and there is accordingly no need to rely on abstractions of congressional purpose. Nevertheless, Kasten argues that protecting intracompany complaints best accords with the purpose of the FLSA—"to assure fair compensation to covered employees"—because such purposes are "advanced when internal complaints lead to voluntary compliance." Reply Brief for Petitioner 18. But no legislation pursues its ends at all costs. Rodriguez v. United States , 480 U. S. 522, 525–526 (1987) (per curiam). Congress may not have protected intracompany complaints for the same reason it did not provide a private cause of action for retaliation against complaints: because it was unwilling to expose employers to the litigation, or to the inability to dismiss unsatisfactory workers, which that additional step would entail. Limitation of the retaliation provision to agency complaints may have been an attempt "to achieve the benefits of regulation right up to the point where the costs of further benefits exceed the value of those benefits." Easterbrook, Statutes' Domains, 50 U. Chi. L. Rev. 533, 541 (1983).

2

In deciding whether an oral complaint may be "filed," the Court's opinion examines modern state and federal statutes, which presumably cover complaints filed with an employer. The only relevance of these provisions to whether the FLSA covers such complaints is that none of them achieves that result by use of the term "filed any complaint," and all of them use language that unmistakably includes complaints to employers. See, e.g. , 42 U. S. C. §2000e–3(a) (prohibiting retaliation against employees who "oppos[e] any [unlawful] practice"). Any suggestion that because more recent statutes cover intracompany complaints, a provision adopted in the 1938 Act should be deemed to do so is unacceptable. While the jurisprudence of this Court has sometimes sanctioned a "living Constitution," it has never approved a living United States Code. What Congress enacted in 1938 must be applied according to its terms, and not according to what a modern Congress (or this Court) would deem desirable. 4

3

Kasten argues that this Court should defer to the Department of Labor and Equal Employment Opportunity Commission's (EEOC) interpretations of 29 U. S. C. §215(a)(3). He claims that those agencies have construed §215(a)(3) to protect intracompany complaints "[f]or almost half a century," in litigating positions and enforcement actions. Reply Brief for Petitioner 22. He also argues that although the Department of Labor lacks the authority to issue regulations implementing §215(a)(3), it has such authority for several similarly worded provisions and has interpreted those statutes to include intracompany complaints. Id ., at 20.

Even were §215(a)(3) ambiguous, deference would still be unwarranted. If we are to apply our new jurisprudence that deference is appropriate only when Congress has given the agency authority to make rules carrying the force of law, see Gonzales v. Oregon , 546 U. S. 243, 255–256 (2006) , deference is improper here. The EEOC has no such authority. Although the Secretary of Labor and his subordinates have authority to issue regulations under various provisions of the FLSA, see, e.g. , §203(l); §206(a)(2), they have no general authority to issue regulations interpreting the Act, and no specific authority to issue regulations interpreting §215(a)(3).

Presumably for this reason, the Court's opinion seems to suggest that only so-called Skidmore deference is appropriate, see Skidmore v. Swift & Co. , 323 U. S. 134, 140 (1944) . 5 This doctrine states that agencies' views are " 'entitled to respect' " to the extent they have " 'the power to persuade.' " Christensen v. Harris County , 529 U. S. 576, 587 (2000) (quoting Skidmore , supra, at 140). 6 For the reasons stated above, the agencies' views here lack the "power to persuade."

II

The Court's opinion claims that whether §215(a)(3) covers intracompany complaints is not fairly included in the question presented because the argument, although raised below, was not made in Saint-Gobain's response to Kasten's petition for certiorari. Citing this Court's Rule 15.2 and Caterpillar Inc. v. Lewis , 519 U. S. 61 , n. 13 (1996), the opinion says that this Court does "not normally consider a separate legal question not raised in the certiorari briefs." Ante , at 15.

It regularly does so, however, under the circumstances that obtain here. (Curiously enough, Caterpillar , the case cited by the Court, was one instance.) Rule 15.2 is permissive rather than mandatory: "Any objection to consideration of a question presented based on what occurred in the proceedings below ... may be deemed waived unless called to the Court's attention in the brief in opposition." (Emphasis added.) Accordingly, the Court has often permitted parties to defend a judgment on grounds not raised in the brief in opposition when doing so is "predicate to an intelligent resolution of the question presented, and therefore fairly included therein." Ohio v. Robinette , 519 U. S. 33, 38 (1996) (internal quotation marks omitted); see also Vance v. Terrazas , 444 U. S. 252 , n. 5 (1980).

Kasten's petition for certiorari phrases the question presented as follows: "Is an oral complaint of a violation of the Fair Labor Standards Act protected conduct under the anti-retaliation provision, 29 U. S. C. §215(a)(3)?" Pet. for Cert. i . Surely the word "complaint" in this question must be assigned an implied addressee. It presumably does not include a complaint to Judge Judy. And the only plausible addressee, given the facts of this case, is the employer. Saint-Gobain's rewording of the question presented in its brief in opposition is even more specific: "Has an employee alleging solely that he orally asserted objections to his employer ... 'filed any complaint' within the meaning of [§215(a)(3)]." Brief in Opposition i (emphasis added). Moreover, under this Court's Rule 14.1(a), the question presented is "deemed to comprise every subsidiary question fairly included therein." Whether intracompany complaints are protected is at least subsidiary to Kasten's formulation (and explicitly included in Saint-Gobain's). The question was also decided by the courts below and was briefed before this Court. It is not clear what benefit additional briefing would provide.

Moreover, whether §215(a)(3) covers intracompany complaints is "predicate to an intelligent resolution of the question presented" in this case. The Court's own opinion demonstrates the point. While claiming that it remains an open question whether intracompany complaints are covered, the opinion adopts a test for "filed any complaint" that assumes a "yes" answer—and that makes no sense otherwise. An employee, the Court says, is deemed to have "filed [a] complaint" only when " 'a reasonable, objective person would have understood the employee' to have 'put the employer on notice that the employee is asserting statutory rights under the [Act]." Ante , at 12 (quoting Tr. of Oral Arg. 23, 26). This utterly atextual standard is obviously designed to counter the argument of Saint-Gobain, that if oral complaints are allowed, "employers too often will be left in a state of uncertainty about whether an employee ... is in fact making a complaint ... or just letting off steam." Ante , at 11. Of course, if intracompany complaints were excluded, this concern would be nonexistent: Filing a complaint with a judicial or administrative body is quite obviously an unambiguous assertion of one's rights. There would be no need for lower courts to question whether a complaint is "sufficiently clear and de-tailed," ante , at 12, carries the requisite "degree of formality," ante , at 11, or provides "fair notice," ibid. , whatever those terms may require.

The test the Court adopts amply disproves its contention that "we can decide the oral/written question separately," ante , at 15. And it makes little sense to consider that question at all in the present case if neither oral nor written complaints to employers are protected, cf. United States v. Grubbs , 547 U. S. 90 , n. 1 (2006). This Court should not issue an advisory opinion as to what would have been the scope of a retaliation provision covering complaints to employers if Congress had enacted such a provision.

Notes

1 Kasten and this Court's opinion, ante, at 7, argue that the use of the modifier "any" in the phrase "filed any complaint" suggests that Congress meant to define the word "complaint" expansively. Not so. The modifier "any" does not cause a word that is in context narrow to become broad. The phrase "to cash a check at any bank" does not refer to a river bank, or even a blood bank.

2 Section 5 of the original FLSA, which has since been repealed, charged industry committees with recommending minimum wages for certain industries to the Department of Labor. 52 Stat. 1062. In order to perform this function, industry committees were empowered, among other things, to "hear ... witnesses" and "receive ... evidence." §8(b), id., at 1064.

3 Kasten argues that excluding intracompany complaints would make the phrases "filed any complaint" and "instituted or caused to be instituted any proceeding" redundant. That is not so. An employee may file a complaint with the Administrator that does not result in a proceeding, or has not yet done so when the employer takes its retaliatory action.

4 Moreover, if the substance of the retaliation provision of any other Act could shed light upon what Congress sought to achieve in the FLSA, it would be the relatively contemporaneous provision of the National Labor Relations Act, §8(4), 49 Stat. 453, codified at 29 U. S. C. §158(a)(4), which did not cover retaliation for employee-employer complaints. See NLRB v. Scrivener, 405 U. S. 117 (1972) .

5 Or perhaps not. The actual quantum of deference measured out by the Court's opinion is unclear—seemingly intentionally so. The Court says that it is giving "a degree of weight" to the Secretary and EEOC's views "given Congress' delegation of enforcement powers to federal administrative agencies." Ante, at 12. But it never explicitly states the level of deference applied, and includes a mysterious citation of United States v. Mead Corp., 533 U. S. 218 (2001) , along with a parenthetical saying that "sometimes ... judicial deference [is] intended even in [the] absence of rulemaking authority." Ante, at 13. I say this is mysterious because Mead clearly held that rulemaking authority was necessary for full Chevron deference, see Chevron U. S. A. Inc. v. Natural Resources Defense Council, Inc., 467 U. S. 837 (1984) . I have chosen to interpret the Court as referring to Skidmore deference, rather than Chevron deference or something in-between, in order to minimize the Court's ongoing obfuscation of this once-clear area of administrative law. See Mead, supra, at 245 (Scalia, J., dissenting).

6 In my view this doctrine (if it can be called that) is incoherent, both linguistically and practically. To defer is to subordinate one's own judgment to another's.

If one has been persuaded by another, so that one's judgment accords with the other's, there is no room for deferral—only for agreement. Speaking of "Skidmore deference" to a persuasive agency position does nothing but confuse.

Justice Scalia's dissent in Brown v. Plata (May 23, 2011)

Justice Scalia, with whom Justice Thomas joins, dissenting.

Today the Court affirms what is perhaps the most radical injunction issued by a court in our Nation's history: an order requiring California to release the staggering number of 46,000 convicted criminals.

There comes before us, now and then, a case whose proper outcome is so clearly indicated by tradition and common sense, that its decision ought to shape the law, rather than vice versa. One would think that, before allowing the decree of a federal district court to release 46,000 convicted felons, this Court would bend every effort to read the law in such a way as to avoid that outrageous result. Today, quite to the contrary, the Court disregards stringently drawn provisions of the governing statute, and traditional constitutional limitations upon the power of a federal judge, in order to uphold the absurd.

The proceedings that led to this result were a judicial travesty. I dissent because the institutional reform the District Court has undertaken violates the terms of the governing statute, ignores bedrock limitations on the power of Article III judges, and takes federal courts wildly beyond their institutional capacity.

I

A

The Prison Litigation Reform Act (PLRA) states that "[p]rospective relief in any civil action with respect to prison conditions shall extend no further than necessary to correct the violation of the Federal right of a particular plaintiff or plaintiffs"; that such relief must be "narrowly drawn, [and] exten[d] no further than necessary to correct the violation of the Federal right"; and that it must be "the least intrusive means necessary to correct the violation of the Federal right." 18 U. S. C. §3626(a)(1)(A). In deciding whether these multiple limitations have been complied with, it is necessary to identify with precision what is the "violation of the Federal right of a particular plaintiff or plaintiffs" that has been alleged. What has been alleged here, and what the injunction issued by the Court is tailored (narrowly or not) to remedy is the running of a prison system with inadequate medical facilities. That may result in the denial of needed medical treatment to "a particular [prisoner] or [prisoners]," thereby violating (ac-cording to our cases) his or their Eighth Amendment rights. But the mere existence of the inadequate system does not subject to cruel and unusual punishment the entire prison population in need of medical care, including those who receive it.

The Court acknowledges that the plaintiffs "do not base their case on deficiencies in care provided on any one occasion"; rather, "[p]laintiffs rely on systemwide deficiencies in the provision of medical and mental health care that, taken as a whole, subject sick and mentally ill prisoners in California to 'substantial risk of serious harm' and cause the delivery of care in the prisons to fall below the evolving standards of decency that mark the progress of a maturing society." Ante, at 7, n. 3. But our judge-empowering "evolving standards of decency" jurisprudence (with which, by the way, I heartily disagree, see, e.g., Roper v. Simmons, 543 U. S. 551, 615–616 (2005) (Scalia, J., dissenting)) does not prescribe (or at least has not until today prescribed) rules for the "decent" running of schools, prisons, and other government institutions. It forbids "indecent" treatment of individuals—in the context of this case, the denial of medical care to those who need it . And the persons who have a constitutional claim for denial of medical care are those who are denied medical care—not all who face a "substantial risk" (whatever that is) of being denied medical care.

The Coleman litigation involves "the class of seriously mentally ill persons in California prisons," ante, at 8, and the Plata litigation involves "the class of state prisoners with serious medical conditions," ante, at 9. The plaintiffs do not appear to claim—and it would absurd to suggest—that every single one of those prisoners has personally experienced "torture or a lingering death," ante, at 13 (internal quotation marks omitted), as a consequence of that bad medical system. Indeed, it is inconceivable that anything more than a small proportion of prisoners in the plaintiff classes have personally received sufficiently atrocious treatment that their Eighth Amendment right was violated—which, as the Court recognizes, is why the plaintiffs do not premise their claim on "deficiencies in care provided on any one occasion." Ante, at 7, n. 3. Rather, the plaintiffs' claim is that they are all part of a medical system so defective that some number of prisoners will inevitably be injured by incompetent medical care, and that this number is sufficiently high so as to render the system, as a whole, unconstitutional.

But what procedural principle justifies certifying a class of plaintiffs so they may assert a claim of systemic unconstitutionality? I can think of two possibilities, both of which are untenable. The first is that although some or most plaintiffs in the class do not individually have viable Eighth Amendment claims, the class as a whole has collectively suffered an Eighth Amendment violation. That theory is contrary to the bedrock rule that the sole purpose of classwide adjudication is to aggregate claims that are individually viable. "A class action, no less than traditional joinder (of which it is a species), merely enables a federal court to adjudicate claims of multiple parties at once, instead of in separate suits. And like traditional joinder, it leaves the parties' legal rights and duties intact and the rules of decision unchanged." Shady Grove Orthopedic Associates, P. A. v. Allstate Ins. Co., 559 U. S. ___, ___ (2010) (plurality opinion) (slip op., at 14).

The second possibility is that every member of the plaintiff class has suffered an Eighth Amendment violation merely by virtue of being a patient in a poorly-run prison system, and the purpose of the class is merely to aggregate all those individually viable claims. This theory has the virtue of being consistent with procedural principles, but at the cost of a gross substantive departure from our case law. Under this theory, each and every prisoner who happens to be a patient in a system that has systemic weaknesses—such as "hir[ing] any doctor who had a license, a pulse and a pair of shoes," ante, at 10 (internal quotation marks omitted)—has suffered cruel or unusual punishment, even if that person cannot make an individualized showing of mistreatment. Such a theory of the Eighth Amendment is preposterous. And we have said as much in the past: "If ... a healthy inmate who had suffered no deprivation of needed medical treatment were able to claim violation of his constitutional right to medical care ... simply on the ground that the prison medical facilities were inadequate, the essential distinction between judge and executive would have disappeared: it would have become the function of the courts to assure adequate medical care in prisons." Lewis v. Casey, 518 U. S. 343, 350 (1996) .

Whether procedurally wrong or substantively wrong, the notion that the plaintiff class can allege an Eighth Amendment violation based on "systemwide deficiencies" is assuredly wrong. It follows that the remedy decreed here is also contrary to law, since the theory of systemic unconstitutionality is central to the plaintiffs' case. The PLRA requires plaintiffs to establish that the systemwide injunction entered by the District Court was "narrowly drawn" and "extends no further than necessary" to correct "the violation of the Federal right of a particular plaintiff or plaintiffs." If (as is the case) the only viable constitutional claims consist of individual instances of mistreatment, then a remedy reforming the system as a whole goes far beyond what the statute allows.

It is also worth noting the peculiarity that the vast majority of inmates most generously rewarded by the re-lease order—the 46,000 whose incarceration will be ended—do not form part of any aggrieved class even under the Court's expansive notion of constitutional violation. Most of them will not be prisoners with medical conditions or severe mental illness; and many will undoubtedly be fine physical specimens who have developed intimidating muscles pumping iron in the prison gym.

B

Even if I accepted the implausible premise that the plaintiffs have established a systemwide violation of the Eighth Amendment, I would dissent from the Court's endorsement of a decrowding order. That order is an example of what has become known as a "structural injunction." As I have previously explained, structural injunctions are radically different from the injunctions traditionally issued by courts of equity, and presumably part of "the judicial Power" conferred on federal courts by Article III:

"The mandatory injunctions issued upon termination of litigation usually required 'a single simple act.' H. McClintock, Principles of Equity §15, pp. 32–33 (2d ed. 1948). Indeed, there was a 'historical prejudice of the court of chancery against rendering decrees which called for more than a single affirmative act.' Id., §61, at 160. And where specific performance of contracts was sought, it was the categorical rule that no decree would issue that required ongoing supervision. . . . Compliance with these 'single act' mandates could, in addition to being simple, be quick; and once it was achieved the contemnor's relationship with the court came to an end, at least insofar as the subject of the order was concerned. Once the document was turned over or the land conveyed, the litigant's obligation to the court, and the court's coercive power over the litigant, ceased.... The court did not engage in any ongoing supervision of the litigant's conduct, nor did its order continue to regulate its behavior." Mine Workers v. Bagwell, 512 U. S. 821, 841–842 (1994) (Scalia, J., concurring).

Structural injunctions depart from that historical practice, turning judges into long-term administrators of complex social institutions such as schools, prisons, and police departments. Indeed, they require judges to play a role essentially indistinguishable from the role ordinarily played by executive officials. Today's decision not only affirms the structural injunction but vastly expands its use, by holding that an entire system is unconstitutional because it may produce constitutional violations.

The drawbacks of structural injunctions have been described at great length elsewhere. See, e.g., Lewis, supra, at 385–393 (1996) (Thomas, J., concurring); Missouri v. Jenkins, 515 U. S. 70, 124–133 (1995) (Thomas, J., concurring); Horowitz, Decreeing Organizational Change: Judicial Supervision of Public Institutions, 1983 Duke L. J. 1265. This case illustrates one of their most pernicious aspects: that they force judges to engage in a form of factfinding-as-policymaking that is outside the traditional judicial role. The factfinding judges traditionally engage in involves the determination of past or present facts based (except for a limited set of materials of which courts may take "judicial notice") exclusively upon a closed trial record. That is one reason why a district judge's factual findings are entitled to plain-error review: because having viewed the trial first hand he is in a better position to evaluate the evidence than a judge reviewing a cold record. In a very limited category of cases, judges have also traditionally been called upon to make some predictive judgments: which custody will best serve the interests of the child, for example, or whether a particular one-shot injunction will remedy the plaintiff's grievance. When a judge manages a structural injunction, however, he will inevitably be required to make very broad empirical predictions necessarily based in large part upon policy views—the sort of predictions regularly made by legislators and executive officials, but inappropriate for the Third Branch.

This feature of structural injunctions is superbly illustrated by the District Court's proceeding concerning the decrowding order's effect on public safety. The PLRA requires that, before granting "[p]rospective relief in [a] civil action with respect to prison conditions," a court must "give substantial weight to any adverse impact on public safety or the operation of a criminal justice system caused by the relief." 18 U. S. C. §3626(a)(1)(A). Here, the District Court discharged that requirement by making the "factual finding" that "the state has available methods by which it could readily reduce the prison population to 137.5% design capacity or less without an adverse impact on public safety or the operation of the criminal justice system." Juris. Statement App., O. T. 2009, No. 09-416, p. 253a. It found the evidence "clear" that prison overcrowding would "perpetuate a criminogenic prison system that itself threatens public safety," id., at 186a, and volunteered its opinion that "[t]he population could be reduced even further with the reform of California's antiquated sentencing policies and other related changes to the laws." Id., at 253a. It "reject[ed] the testimony that inmates released early from prison would commit additional new crimes," id., at 200a, finding that "shortening the length of stay through earned credits would give inmates incentives to participate in programming designed to lower recidivism," id., at 204a, and that "slowing the flow of technical parole violators to prison, thereby substantially reducing the churning of parolees, would by itself improve both the prison and parole systems, and public safety." Id., at 209a. It found that "the diversion of offenders to community correctional programs has significant beneficial effects on public safety," id., at 214a, and that "additional rehabilitative programming would result in a significant population reduction while improving public safety," id., at 216a.

The District Court cast these predictions (and the Court today accepts them) as "factual findings," made in reliance on the procession of expert witnesses that testified at trial. Because these "findings" have support in the record, it is difficult to reverse them under a plain-error standard of review. Ante, at 38. And given that the District Court devoted nearly 10 days of trial and 70 pages of its opinion to this issue, it is difficult to dispute that the District Court has discharged its statutory obligation to give "substantial weight to any adverse impact on public safety."

But the idea that the three District Judges in this case relied solely on the credibility of the testifying expert witnesses is fanciful. Of course they were relying largely on their own beliefs about penology and recidivism. And of course different district judges, of different policy views, would have "found" that rehabilitation would not work and that releasing prisoners would increase the crime rate. I am not saying that the District Judges rendered their factual findings in bad faith. I am saying that it is impossible for judges to make "factual findings" without inserting their own policy judgments, when the factual findings are policy judgments. What occurred here is no more judicial factfinding in the ordinary sense than would be the factual findings that deficit spending will not lower the unemployment rate, or that the continued occupation of Iraq will decrease the risk of terrorism. Yet, because they have been branded "factual findings" entitled to deferential review, the policy preferences of three District Judges now govern the operation of California's penal system.

It is important to recognize that the dressing-up of pol-icy judgments as factual findings is not an error peculiar to this case. It is an unavoidable concomitant of institutional-reform litigation. When a district court issues an injunction, it must make a factual assessment of the anticipated consequences of the injunction. And when the injunction undertakes to restructure a social institution, assessing the factual consequences of the injunction is necessarily the sort of predictive judgment that our system of government allocates to other government officials.

But structural injunctions do not simply invite judges to indulge policy preferences. They invite judges to indulge incompetent policy preferences. Three years of law school and familiarity with pertinent Supreme Court precedents give no insight whatsoever into the management of social institutions. Thus, in the proceeding below the District Court determined that constitutionally adequate medical services could be provided if the prison population was 137.5% of design capacity. This was an empirical finding it was utterly unqualified to make. Admittedly, the court did not generate that number entirely on its own; it heard the numbers 130% and 145% bandied about by various witnesses and decided to split the difference. But the ability of judges to spit back or even average-out numbers spoon-fed to them by expert witnesses does not render them competent decisionmakers in areas in which they are otherwise unqualified.

The District Court also relied heavily on the views of the Receiver and Special Master, and those reports play a starring role in the Court's opinion today. The Court notes that "the Receiver and the Special Master filed reports stating that overcrowding posed a significant barrier to their efforts" and deems those reports "persuasive evidence that, absent a reduction in overcrowding, any remedy might prove unattainable and would at the very least require vast expenditures of resources by the State." Ante, at 31–32. The use of these reports is even less consonant with the traditional judicial role than the District Court's reliance on the expert testimony at trial. The latter, even when, as here, it is largely the expression of policy judgments, is at least subject to cross-examination. Relying on the un-cross-examined findings of an investigator, sent into the field to prepare a factual report and give suggestions on how to improve the prison system, bears no resemblance to ordinary judicial decisionmaking. It is true that the PLRA contemplates the appointment of Special Masters (although not Receivers), but Special Masters are authorized only to "conduct hearings and prepare proposed findings of fact" and "assist in the development of remedial plans," 18 U. S. C. §3626(f)(6). This does not authorize them to make factual findings (unconnected to hearings) that are given seemingly wholesale deference. Neither the Receiver nor the Special Master was selected by California to run its prisons, and the fact that they may be experts in the field of prison reform does not justify the judicial imposition of their perspectives on the state.

C

My general concerns associated with judges' running social institutions are magnified when they run prison systems, and doubly magnified when they force prison officials to release convicted criminals. As we have previously recognized:

"[C]ourts are ill equipped to deal with the increasingly urgent problems of prison administration and re- form.... . [T]he problems of prisons in America are complex and intractable, and, more to the point, they are not readily susceptible of resolution by decree.... . Running a prison is an inordinately difficult undertaking that requires expertise, planning, and the com-mitment of resources, all of which are peculiarly within the province of the legislative and executive branches of government. Prison is, moreover, a task that has been committed to the responsibility of those branches, and separation of powers concerns counsel a policy of judicial restraint. Where a state penal system is involved, federal courts have ... additional reason to accord deference to the appropriate prison authorities." Turner v. Safley, 482 U. S. 78, 84–85 (1987) (internal quotation marks omitted).

These principles apply doubly to a prisoner-release order. As the author of today's opinion explained earlier this Term, granting a writ of habeas corpus " 'disturbs the State's significant interest in repose for concluded litigation, denies society the right to punish some admitted offenders, and intrudes on state sovereignty to a degree matched by few exercises of federal judicial authority.' " Harrington v. Richter, 562 U. S. ____, ____ (2011) (slip op., at 13) (quoting Harris v. Reed, 489 U. S. 255, 282 (1989) (Kennedy, J., dissenting)). Recognizing that habeas relief must be granted sparingly, we have reversed the Ninth Circuit's erroneous grant of habeas relief to individual California prisoners four times this Term alone. Cullen v. Pinholster, 563 U. S. ____ (2011); Felkner v. Jackson, 562 U. S. ____ (2011) (per curiam); Swarthout v. Cooke, 562 U. S. ____ (2011) (per curiam); Harrington, supra . And yet here, the Court affirms an order granting the functional equivalent of 46,000 writs of habeas corpus, based on its paean to courts' "substantial flexibility when making these judgments." Ante, at 41. It seems that the Court's respect for state sovereignty has vanished in the case where it most matters.

II

The Court's opinion includes a bizarre coda noting that "[t]he State may wish to move for modification of the three-judge court's order to extend the deadline for the required reduction to five years." Ante, at 46–47. The District Court, it says, "may grant such a request provided that the State satisfies necessary and appropriate preconditions designed to ensure the measures are taken to implement the plan without undue delay"; and it gives vague suggestions of what these preconditions "may include," such as "interim benchmarks." Ante, at 47. It also invites the District Court to "consider whether it is appropriate to order the State to begin without delay to develop a system to identify prisoners who are unlikely to reoffend," and informs the State that it "should devise systems to select those prisoners least likely to jeopardize public safety." Ibid. (What a good idea!)

The legal effect of this passage is unclear—I suspect intentionally so. If it is nothing but a polite remainder to the State and to the District Court that the injunction is subject to modification, then it is entirely unnecessary. As both the State and the District Court are undoubtedly aware, a party is always entitled to move to modify an equitable decree, and the PLRA contains an express provision authorizing District Courts to modify or terminate prison injunctions. See 18 U. S. C. §3626(b).

I suspect, however, that this passage is a warning shot across the bow, telling the District Court that it had better modify the injunction if the State requests what we invite it to request. Such a warning, if successful, would achieve the benefit of a marginal reduction in the inevitable murders, robberies, and rapes to be committed by the released inmates. But it would achieve that at the expense of intellectual bankruptcy, as the Court's "warning" is entirely alien to ordinary principles of appellate review of injunctions. When a party moves for modification of an injunction, the district court is entitled to rule on that motion first, subject to review for abuse of discretion if it declines to modify the order. Horne v. Flores, 557 U. S. ____, ____, ____ (2009) (slip op., at 10, 20). Moreover, when a district court enters a new decree with new benchmarks, the selection of those benchmarks is also reviewed under a deferential, abuse-of-discretion standard of review—a point the Court appears to recognize. Ante, at 45. Appellate courts are not supposed to "affirm" injunctions while preemptively noting that the State "may" request, and the District Court "may" grant, a request to extend the State's deadline to release prisoners by three years based on some suggestions on what appropriate preconditions for such a modification "may" include.

Of course what is really happening here is that the Court, overcome by common sense, disapproves of the results reached by the District Court, but cannot remedy them (it thinks) by applying ordinary standards of appellate review. It has therefore selected a solution unknown in our legal system: A deliberately ambiguous set of suggestions on how to modify the injunction, just deferential enough so that it can say with a straight face that it is "affirming," just stern enough to put the District Court on notice that it will likely get reversed if it does not follow them. In doing this, the Court has aggrandized itself, grasping authority that appellate courts are not supposed to have, and using it to enact a compromise solution with no legal basis other than the Court's say-so. That we are driven to engage in these extralegal activities should be a sign that the entire project of permitting district courts to run prison systems is misbegotten.

But perhaps I am being too unkind. The Court, or at least a majority of the Court's majority, must be aware that the judges of the District Court are likely to call its bluff, since they know full well it cannot possibly be an abuse of discretion to refuse to accept the State's proposed modifications in an injunction that has just been approved (affirmed) in its present form. An injunction, after all, does not have to be perfect; only good enough for government work, which the Court today says this is. So perhaps the coda is nothing more than a ceremonial washing of the hands—making it clear for all to see, that if the terrible things sure to happen as a consequence of this outrageous order do happen, they will be none of this Court's responsibility. After all, did we not want, and indeed even suggest, something better?

III

In view of the incoherence of the Eighth Amendment claim at the core of this case, the nonjudicial features of institutional reform litigation that this case exemplifies, and the unique concerns associated with mass prisoner releases, I do not believe this Court can affirm this injunction. I will state my approach briefly: In my view, a court may not order a prisoner's release unless it determines that the prisoner is suffering from a violation of his constitutional rights, and that his release, and no other relief, will remedy that violation. Thus, if the court determines that a particular prisoner is being denied constitutionally required medical treatment, and the release of that prisoner (and no other remedy) would enable him to obtain medical treatment, then the court can order his release; but a court may not order the release of prisoners who have suffered no violations of their constitutional rights, merely to make it less likely that that will happen to them in the future.

This view follows from the PLRA's text that I discussed at the outset, 18 U. S. C.

§3626(a)(1)(A). "[N]arrowly drawn" means that the relief applies only to the "particular [prisoner] or [prisoners]" whose constitutional rights are violated; "extends no further than necessary" means that prisoners whose rights are not violated will not obtain relief; and "least intrusive means necessary to correct the violation of the Federal right" means that no other relief is available. * *

I acknowledge that this reading of the PLRA would severely limit the circumstances under which a court could issue structural injunctions to remedy allegedly unconstitutional prison conditions, although it would not eliminate them entirely. If, for instance, a class representing all prisoners in a particular institution alleged that the temperature in their cells was so cold as to violate the Eighth Amendment, or that they were deprived of all exercise time, a court could enter a prisonwide injunction ordering that the temperature be raised or exercise time be provided. Still, my approach may invite the objection that the PLRA appears to contemplate structural injunctions in general and mass prisoner-release orders in particular. The statute requires courts to "give substantial weight to any adverse impact on public safety or the operation of a criminal justice system caused by the relief" and authorizes them to appoint Special Masters, §3626 (a)(1)(A), (f), provisions that seem to presuppose the possibility of a structural remedy. It also sets forth criteria under which courts may issue orders that have "the purpose or effect of reducing or limiting the prisoner population," §3626(g)(4).

I do not believe that objection carries the day. In addition to imposing numerous limitations on the ability of district courts to order injunctive relief with respect to prison conditions, the PLRA states that "[n]othing in this section shall be construed to ... repeal or detract from otherwise applicable limitations on the remedial powers of the courts." §3626(a)(1)(C). The PLRA is therefore best understood as an attempt to constrain the discretion of courts issuing structural injunctions—not as a mandate for their use. For the reasons I have outlined, structural injunctions, especially prisoner-release orders, raise grave separation-of-powers concerns and veer significantly from the historical role and institutional capability of courts. It is appropriate to construe the PLRA so as to constrain courts from entering injunctive relief that would exceed that role and capability.

　　*　　*　　*

The District Court's order that California release 46,000 prisoners extends "further than necessary to correct the violation of the Federal right of a particular plaintiff or plaintiffs" who have been denied needed medical care. 18 U. S. C. §3626(a)(1)(A). It is accordingly forbidden by the PLRA—besides defying all sound conception of the proper role of judges.

* * Any doubt on this last score, at least as far as prisoner-release orders are concerned, is eliminated by §3626(a)(3)(E) of the statute, which provides that to enter a prisoner-release order the court must find "by clear and convincing evidence that— (i) crowding is the primary cause of the violation of a Federal right; and (ii) no other relief will remedy the violation of the Federal right."

Justice Scalia's dissent in Sykes v. US (June 9, 2011) [Note omitted]

Justice Scalia, dissenting.

As the Court's opinion acknowledges, this case is "another in a series," ante , at 1. More specifically, it is an at-tempt to clarify, for the fourth time since 2007, what distinguishes "violent felonies" under the residual clause of the Armed Career Criminal Act (ACCA), 18 U. S. C. §924(e)(2)(B)(ii), from other crimes. See James v. United States, 550 U. S. 192 (2007) ; Begay v. United States , 553 U. S. 137 (2008) ; Chambers v. United States , 555 U. S. 122 (2009) . We try to include an ACCA residual-clause case in about every second or third volume of the United States Reports.

As was perhaps predictable, instead of producing a clar-ification of the Delphic residual clause, today's opinion produces a fourth ad hoc judgment that will sow further confusion. Insanity, it has been said, is doing the same thing over and over again, but expecting different results. Four times is enough. We should admit that ACCA's residual provision is a drafting failure and declare it void for vagueness. See Kolender v. Lawson , 461 U. S. 352, 357 (1983) .

I

ACCA defines "violent felony," in relevant part, as "any crime punishable by imprisonment for a term exceeding one year ... that ... is burglary, arson, or extortion, involves use of explosives, or otherwise involves conduct that presents a serious potential risk of physical injury to another." 18 U. S. C. §924(e)(2)(B)(ii). Many years of prison hinge on whether a crime falls within this definition. A felon convicted of possessing a firearm who has three prior violent-felony convictions faces a 15-year mandatory minimum sentence and the possibility of life imprisonment. See §924(e)(1); see United States v. Harrison , 558 F. 3d 1280, 1282, n. 1 (CA11 2009). Without those prior convictions, he would face a much lesser sentence, which could not possibly exceed 10 years. See §924(a)(2).

Vehicular flight is a violent felony only if it falls within ACCA's residual clause; that is, if it "involves conduct that presents a serious potential risk of physical injury to another." §924(e)(2)(B)(ii). Today's opinion says, or initially seems to say, that an offense qualifies as a violent felony if its elements, in the typical case, create a degree of risk " 'comparable to that posed by its closest analog among the enumerated offenses.' " Ante , at 6. That is a quotation from the Court's opinion in the first of our residual-clause trilogy, James , 550 U. S., at 203. I did not join that opinion because I thought it should suffice if the elements created a degree of risk comparable to the least risky of the enumerated offenses, whether or not it was the closest analog. See id. , at 230 (Scalia , J., dissenting). The problem with applying the James standard to the pres- ent case is that the elements of vehicular flight under Indiana law are not analogous to any of the four enumerated offenses. See Ind. Code §35–44–3–3 (2004). Nor is it apparent which of the enumerated offenses most closely resembles, for example, statutory rape, see United States v. Daye ,

571 F. 3d 225, 228–236 (CA2 2009); possession of a sawed-off shotgun, see United States v. Upton , 512 F. 3d 394, 403–405 (CA7 2008); or a failure to report to prison, see Chambers, supra . I predicted this inadequacy of the "closest analog" test in my James dissent. See 550 U. S., at 215.

But as it turns out, the Court's inability to identify an analog makes no difference to the outcome of the present case. For today's opinion introduces the James standard with the words "[f]or instance," ante , at 6. It is (according to the Court) merely one example of how the enumerated crimes (burglary, arson, extortion, and crimes using explosives) "provide guidance." Ibid. And the opinion then proceeds to obtain guidance from the risky-as-the-least-risky test that I suggested (but the Court rejected) in James — finding vehicular flight at least as risky as both arson and burglary. See ante , at 6–9.

But what about the test that determined the outcome in our second case in this "series"—the "purposeful, violent, and aggressive" test of Begay? Fear not. That incompatible variation has been neither overlooked nor renounced in today's tutti-frutti opinion. "In many cases," we are told, it "will be redundant with the inquiry into risk." Ante , at 11. That seems to be the case here—though why, and when it will not be the case, are not entirely clear. The Court's accusation that Sykes "overreads the opinions of this Court," ante , at 10, apparently applies to his interpretation of Begay 's "purposeful, violent, and aggressive" test, which the Court now suggests applies only "to strict liability, negligence, and recklessness crimes," ante , at 11. But that makes no sense. If the test excluded only those unintentional crimes, it would be recast as the "purposeful" test, since the last two adjectives ("violent, and aggressive") would do no work. For that reason, perhaps, all 11 Circuits that have addressed Begay "overrea[d]" it just as Sykes does * — and as does the Government, see Brief for United States 8.

The only case that is not brought forward in today's opinion to represent yet another test is the third and most recent in the trilogy, Chambers , 555 U. S. 122 —which applied both the risky-as-the-least-risky test and the "pur-poseful, violent, and aggressive" test to reach the con-clusion that failure to report for periodic incarceration was not a crime of violence under ACCA. But today's opinion does cite Chambers for another point: Whereas James rejected the risky-as-the-least-risky approach be-cause, among other reasons, no "hard statistics" on risk-iness "have been called to our attention," 550 U. S., at 210; and whereas Begay made no mention of statistics; Chambers explained (as today's opinion points out) that "statistical evidence sometimes 'helps provide a conclusive ... answer' concerning the risks that crimes present," ante , at 8 (quoting Chambers , supra , at 129). Today's opinion then outdoes Chambers in the volume of statistics that it spews forth—statistics compiled by the International Association of Chiefs of Police concerning injuries attributable to police pursuits, ante , at 8; statistics from the Department of Justice concerning injuries attributable to burglaries, ante , at 9; statistics from the U. S. Fire Administration concerning injuries attributable to fires, ibid. , and (by reference to Justice Thomas 's concurrence) statistics from the National Center for Statistics & Analysis, the Pennsylvania State Police Bureau of Research, the FBI Law Enforcement

Bulletin and several articles published elsewhere concerning injuries attributable to police pursuits, ante , at 8 (citing ante , at 4–5 (Thomas , J., concurring in judgment)).

Supreme Court briefs are an inappropriate place to develop the key facts in a case. We normally give parties more robust protection, leaving important factual questions to district courts and juries aided by expert witnesses and the procedural protections of discovery. See Fed. Rule Crim. Proc. 16(a)(1)(F), (G); Fed. Rules Evid. 702–703, 705. An adversarial process in the trial courts can identify flaws in the methodology of the studies that the parties put forward; here, we accept the studies' findings on faith, without examining their methodology at all. The Court does not examine, for example, whether the police-pursuit data on which it relies is a representative sample of all vehicular flights. The data may be skewed towards the rare and riskier forms of flight. See post , at 6, n. 4 (Kagan , J., dissenting). We also have no way of knowing how many injuries reported in that data would have occurred even absent pursuit, by a driver who was driving recklessly even before the police gave chase. Similar questions undermine confidence in the burglary and arson data the Court cites. For example, the Court relies on a U. S. Fire Administration dataset to conclude that 3.3 injuries occur per 100 arsons. See ante , at 9. But a 2001 report from the same U. S. Fire Administration suggests that roughly 1 injury occurs per 100 arsons. See Arson in the United States, Vol. 1 Topical Fire Research Series, No. 8, pp. 1–2 (rev. Dec. 2001), online at http: / / www.usfa.dhs.gov / downloads / pdf / tfrs / v1i8-508.pdf (as visited May 27, 2011, and available in Clerk of Court's case file). The Court does not reveal why it chose one dataset over another. In sum, our statistical analysis in ACCA cases is untested judicial factfinding masquerading as statutory interpretation. Most of the statistics on which the Court relies today come from government-funded studies, and did not make an appearance in this litigation until the Government's merits brief to this Court. See Brief for Petitioner 17; see also Chambers , supra , at 128–129 (demonstrating that the same was true in that case).

But the more fundamental problem with the Court's use of statistics is that, far from eliminating the vagueness of the residual clause, it increases the vagueness. Vagueness, of course, must be measured ex ante — before the Court gives definitive meaning to a statutory provision, not after. Nothing is vague once the Court decrees precisely what it means. And is it seriously to be expected that the average citizen would be familiar with the sundry statistical studies showing (if they are to be believed) that this-or-that crime is more likely to lead to physical injury than what sundry statistical studies (if they are to be believed) show to be the case for burglary, arson, extortion, or use of explosives? To ask the question is to answer it. A few words, then, about unconstitutional vagueness.

II

When I dissented from the Court's judgment in James , I said that the residual clause's "shoddy draftsmanship" put courts to a difficult choice:

"They can (1) apply the ACCA enhancement to virtually all predicate offenses, ... ; (2) apply it case by case in its pristine abstraction, finding it applicable whenever the particular sentencing judge (or the particular reviewing panel) believes there is a 'serious potential risk of physical injury to another' (whatever that means); (3) try to figure out a coherent way of interpreting the statute so that it applies in a relatively predictable and administrable fashion to a smaller subset of crimes; or (4) recognize the statute for the drafting failure it is and hold it void for vagueness ... ." 550 U. S., at 229–230.

My dissent "tried to implement," id. , at 230, the third option; and the Court, I believed, had chosen the second. "Today's opinion," I wrote, "permits an unintelligible crim-inal statute to survive uncorrected, unguided, and unexplained." Id., at 230–231.

My assessment has not been changed by the Court's later decisions in the ACCA "series." Today's opinion, which adds to the "closest analog" test (James) the "purposeful, violent, and aggressive" test (Begay) , and even the risky-as-the-least-risky test that I had proposed as the exclusive criterion, has not made the statute's applica- tion clear and predictable. And all of them together—or even the risky-as-the-least-risky test alone, I am now convinced—never will. The residual-clause series will be endless, and we will be doing ad hoc application of ACCA to the vast variety of state criminal offenses until the cows come home.

That does not violate the Constitution. What does vio-late the Constitution is approving the enforcement of a sentencing statute that does not "give a person of ordinarily intelligence fair notice" of its reach, United States v. Batchelder , 442 U. S. 114, 123 (1979) (internal quotation marks omitted), and that permits, indeed invites, arbitrary enforcement, see Kolender , 461 U. S., at 357. The Court's ever-evolving interpretation of the residual clause will keep defendants and judges guessing for years to come. The reality is that the phrase "otherwise involves conduct that presents a serious potential risk of physical injury to another" does not clearly define the crimes that will subject defendants to the greatly increased ACCA penalties. It is not the job of this Court to impose a clarity which the text itself does not honestly contain. And even if that were our job, the further reality is that we have by now demonstrated our inability to accomplish the task.

We have, I recognize, upheld hopelessly vague criminal statutes in the past— indeed, in the recent past. See, e.g., Skilling v. United States , 561 U. S. ____ (2010). That is regrettable, see id. , at ____ (Scalia, J., concurring in part and concurring in judgment) (slip op., at 1). What sets ACCA apart from those statutes—and what confirms its incurable vagueness—is our repeated inability to craft a principled test out of the statutory text. We have demonstrated by our opinions that the clause is too vague to yield "an intelligible principle," ante , at 13, each attempt to ignore that reality producing a new regime that is less predictable and more arbitrary than the last. ACCA's residual clause fails to speak with the clarity that criminal proscriptions require. See United States v. L. Cohen Grocery Co. , 255 U. S. 81, 89–90 (1921) .

The Court believes that the residual clause cannot be unconstitutionally vague because other criminal prohibitions also refer to the degree of risk posed by a defendant's conduct. See ante , at 14. Even apart from the fact that our opinions dealing with those statutes have not displayed the confusion evident in our four ACCA efforts, this is not the first time I have found the comparison unpersuasive:

"None of the provisions the Court cites ... is similar in the crucial relevant respect: None prefaces its judicially-to-be-determined requirement of risk of physical injury with the word 'otherwise,' preceded by four confusing examples that have little in common with respect to the supposedly defining characteristic. The phrase 'shades of red,' standing alone, does not generate confusion or unpredictability; but the phrase 'fire-engine red, light pink, maroon, navy blue, or colors that otherwise involve shades of red' assuredly does so." James , 550 U. S., at 230, n. 7.

Of course even if the cited statutes were comparable, repetition of constitutional error does not produce constitutional truth.

*   *   *

We face a Congress that puts forth an ever-increasing volume of laws in general, and of criminal laws in particular. It should be no surprise that as the volume increases, so do the number of imprecise laws. And no surprise that our indulgence of imprecisions that violate the Constitution encourages imprecisions that violate the Constitution. Fuzzy, leave-the-details-to-be-sorted-out-by-the-courts legislation is attractive to the Congressman who wants credit for addressing a national problem but does not have the time (or perhaps the votes) to grapple with the nitty-gritty. In the field of criminal law, at least, it is time to call a halt. I do not think it would be a radical step— indeed, I think it would be highly responsible—to limit ACCA to the named violent crimes. Congress can quickly add what it wishes. Because the majority prefers to let vagueness reign, I respectfully dissent.

Justice Scalia's dissent in Gonzalez v. Thaler (Jan 10, 2012) [Notes omitted]

Justice SCALIA, dissenting.

The obvious, undeniable, purpose of 28 U.S.C. § 2253(c) is to spare three-judge courts of appeals the trouble of entertaining (and the prosecution the trouble of defending against) appeals from the denials of relief in habeas and § 2255 proceedings, unless a district or circuit judge has identified an issue on which the applicant has made a substantial showing of a constitutional violation. Where no such constitutional issue has been identified, an appeal on other, nonconstitutional, issues (such as the statute of limitations issue that the Court decides today) will not lie.

Today's opinion transforms this into a provision that allows appeal so long as a district or circuit judge, for whatever reason or for no reason at all, approves it. This makes a hash of the statute. The opinion thinks this alchemy required by the Court's previously expressed desire to "'bring some discipline' to the use of the term `jurisdictional,'" ante, at 648 (quoting Henderson v. Shinseki, 562 U.S. ___, ___, 131 S.Ct. 1197, 1202, 179 L.Ed.2d 159 (2011)). If that is true, discipline has become a code word for eliminating inconvenient statutory limits on our jurisdiction. I would reverse the judgment below for want of jurisdiction.

I

Fair Meaning of the Text

Congress amended § 2253 to its current form in the Antiterrorism and Effective Death Penalty Act of 1996 (AEDPA). In its entirety, the section reads as follows:

"(a) In a habeas corpus proceeding or a proceeding under section 2255 before a district judge, the final order shall be subject to review, on appeal, by the court of appeals for the circuit in which the proceeding is held.

"(b) There shall be no right of appeal from a final order in a proceeding to test the validity of a warrant to remove to another district or place for commitment or trial a person charged with a criminal offense against the United States, or to test the validity of such person's detention pending removal proceedings.

"(c)(1) Unless a circuit justice or judge issues a certificate of appealability, an appeal may not be taken to the court of appeals from—

"(A) the final order in a habeas corpus proceeding in which the detention complained of arises out of process issued by a State court; or

"(B) the final order in a proceeding under section 2255.

"(2) A certificate of appealability may issue under paragraph (1) only if the applicant has made a substantial showing of the denial of a constitutional right.

"(3) The certificate of appealability under paragraph (1) shall indicate which specific issue or issues satisfy the showing required by paragraph (2)."

As the Court acknowledges, ante, at 648-649, all three subsections—(a), (b), and (c)—clearly speak to the jurisdiction of the courts of appeals. Subsection (a) gives appellate jurisdiction to "the court of appeals for the circuit in which the proceeding is held"; subsection (b) carves out certain classes of cases from that appellate jurisdiction; and subsection (c) imposes a procedural hurdle to the exercise of that appellate jurisdiction—a judge's issuance of a certificate of appealability, see Miller-El v. Cockrell, 537 U.S. 322, 336, 123 S.Ct. 1029, 154 L.Ed.2d 931 (2003).

Paragraph 2253(c)(3) says that a certificate of appealability must "indicate" which issue or issues in the case involve a substantial showing of a constitutional violation. Everyone agrees that the certificate issued below contains no such indication. See ante, at 648. It appears, in fact, that the issuing judge never considered whether any of Gonzalez's constitutional claims satisfied paragraph (2). As far as we know, no federal judge has ever determined that Gonzalez "has made a substantial showing of the denial of a constitutional right." § 2253(c)(2). The Court does not even suggest that he has—but it goes on to decide the statute-of-limitations issue in the case.

Its basis for proceeding in this fashion is the remarkable statement that "[a] defective COA is not equivalent to the lack of any COA." Ante, at 649. That is simply not true with respect to a significant defect in a legal document. Would one say that a deed which lacks the words of conveyance is not equivalent to the lack of a deed? Or that a passport which lacks the Secretary of State's affirmance of the bearer's citizenship is not equivalent to the lack of a passport? Minor technical defects are one thing, but a defect that goes to the whole purpose of the instrument is something else. And the whole purpose of the certificate-of-appealability procedure is to make sure that, before a case can proceed to the court of appeals, a judge has made the determination that it presents a substantial showing of the denial of a constitutional right. To call something a valid certificate of appealability which does not contain the central finding that is the whole purpose of a certificate of appealability is quite absurd.

The Court says that "[o]nce a judge has made the determination that a COA is warranted and resources are deployed in briefing and argument, ... the COA has fulfilled [its] gatekeeping function." Ante, at 650. But of course it has not done so— it has performed no gatekeeping function whatever—if "the determination that a COA is warranted" has not been accompanied by the issuing judge's opinion required to support the determination: that there is an issue as to which the applicant has made a "substantial showing of the denial of a constitutional right," § 2253(c)(2). As the very next sentence of today's opinion discloses, what the Court means by "has fulfilled [its] gatekeeping function" is simply that it will not be worth the trouble of going back, since that would "not outweigh the costs of further delay," ante, at 650.

That is doubtless true, and it demonstrates the hollowness of the Court's assurance that "calling a rule nonjurisdictional does not mean that it is not mandatory or that a timely objection can be ignored," ante, at 651. That statement is true enough as a general proposition: Calling the numerosity requirement in Arbaugh v. Y & H Corp., 546 U.S. 500, 126 S.Ct. 1235, 163 L.Ed.2d 1097 (2006), nonjurisdictional, for example, did not eliminate it, where protest was made, as a continuing mandatory requirement for relief on the merits, id., at 516, 126 S.Ct. 1235. Even the time-of-filing requirement in Eberhart v. United States, 546 U.S. 12, 126 S.Ct. 403, 163 L.Ed.2d 14 (2005) (per curiam), continued to have "bite" even though it was held nonjurisdictional: It prevented relief when the failure to observe it was properly challenged, id., at 19, 126 S.Ct. 403. But the Court has managed to create today a "mandatory" requirement which—precisely because it will not be worth the trouble of going back—has no practical, real-world effect.[1] What is the consequence when the issuing judge, over properly preserved objection, produces a COA like the one here, which does not contain the required opinion? None whatever. The habeas petitioner already has what he wants, argument before the court of appeals. The government, for its part, is either confident in its view that there has been no substantial showing of denial of a constitutional right—in which case it is just as easy (if not easier) to win before three judges as it is before one; or else it is not—in which case a crusade to enforce § 2253(c) is likely to yield nothing but additional litigation expenses. As for the three-judge panel of the court of appeals, it remains free, as always, to choose whichever mandatory-but-not-jurisdictional basis it wishes for resolving the case. Cf. Steel Co. v. Citizens for Better Environment, 523 U.S. 83, 93-94, 118 S.Ct. 1003, 140 L.Ed.2d 210 (1998). Why not choose the one that is sure to be final and that might avoid embarrassing a colleague? No one has any interest in enforcing the "mandatory" requirement. Which is perhaps why, as I proceed to discuss, mandatory requirements for court-to-court appeal are always made jurisdictional.

Past Treatment of Similar Provisions

As the Court acknowledges, "`context, including this Court's interpretation of similar provisions in many years past, is relevant to whether a statute ranks a requirement as jurisdictional.'" Ante, at 648-649, n. 3 (quoting Reed Elsevier, Inc. v. Muchnick, 559 U.S. ___, ___, 130 S.Ct. 1237, 1248, 176 L.Ed.2d 18 (2010)). Thus, we have said that a requirement prescribed as a condition to obtaining judicial review of agency action is quite different (nonjurisdictional) from a requirement prescribed as a condition to appeal from one court to another (jurisdictional). See Henderson, 562 U.S., at ___ _ ___, 131 S.Ct., at 1203-1204. We have always— always, without exception—held that procedural conditions for appealing a case from one Article III court to another are jurisdictional. When an appeal is "not taken within the time prescribed by law," the "Court of Appeals [is] without jurisdiction." George v. Victor Talking Machine Co., 293 U.S. 377, 379, 55 S.Ct. 229, 79 L.Ed. 439 (1934) (per curiam); see also United States v. Robinson, 361 U.S. 220, 229-230, 80 S.Ct. 282, 4 L.Ed.2d 259 (1960). When a party's name is not listed in the notice of appeal, as the Federal Rules of Appellate Procedure require, the court has no jurisdiction over that party's appeal. Torres v. Oakland Scavenger Co., 487 U.S. 312, 314-315, 108 S.Ct. 2405, 101 L.Ed.2d 285 (1988).

When this Court reviewed cases by writ of error, the law required that the lower-court record be filed with the Court "before the end of the term next succeeding the issue of the writ." Edmonson v. Bloomshire, 7 Wall. 306, 309, 19 L.Ed. 91 (1869). The Court routinely dismissed cases that did not comply with that requirement. See, e.g., Mesa v. United States, 2 Black 721, 721-722, 17 L.Ed. 350 (1863) (per curiam); Edmonson, supra, at 309-310; Steamer Virginia v. West, 19 How. 182, 183, 15 L.Ed. 594 (1857). The same jurisdictional treatment was accorded to failure to serve notice on the defendant in error within the succeeding term, see, e.g., United States v. Curry, 6 How. 106, 112-113, 12 L.Ed. 363 (1848); Villabolos v. United States, 6 How. 81, 88, 91, 12 L.Ed. 352 (1848), and to failure to file the writ of error with the clerk of the lower court, see, e.g., Credit Co. v. Arkansas Central R. Co., 128 U.S. 258, 261, 9 S.Ct. 107, 32 L.Ed. 448 (1888); Scarborough v. Pargoud, 108 U.S. 567, 2 S.Ct. 877, 27 L.Ed. 824 (1883). Today, when a petition for certiorari in a civil case is not filed within the time prescribed by 28 U.S.C. § 2101(c), this Court lacks jurisdiction. Federal Election Comm'n v. NRA Political Victory Fund, 513 U.S. 88, 90, 115 S.Ct. 537, 130 L.Ed.2d 439 (1994) (citing Missouri v. Jenkins, 495 U.S. 33, 45, 110 S.Ct. 1651, 109 L.Ed.2d 31 (1990)); see also Matton S.S. Co. v. Murphy, 319 U.S. 412, 415, 63 S.Ct. 1126, 87 L.Ed. 1483 (1943) (per curiam).[2]

So strict has been the rule enforcing as jurisdictional those requirements attached to court-from-court appeals, that we have applied it to a requirement contained in a statute not even addressed to the courts. Section 518(a) of Title 28 charges the Solicitor General with "conduct[ing] and argu[ing] suits and appeals in the Supreme Court ... in which the United States is interested." We held that, absent independent statutory authority, an agency's petition for certiorari filed without authorization from the Solicitor

General does not suffice to invoke our jurisdiction. NRA Political Victory Fund, supra, at 98-99.[3]

Jurisdictional enforcement of procedural requirements for appeal has deep roots in our jurisprudence. Chief Justice Taney dismissed an appeal in which the citation was not issued and served in time, because "we have no power to receive an appeal in any other mode than that provided by law." Villabolos, supra, at 90. And Chief Justice Chase wrote, in a case dismissing an appeal for failure to file in time:

"In the Judiciary Act of 1789, and in many acts since, Congress has provided for [appellate courts'] exercise [of jurisdiction] in such cases and classes of cases, and under such regulations as seemed to the legislative wisdom convenient and appropriate. The court has always regarded appeals in other cases as excepted from the grant of appellate power, and has always felt itself bound to give effect to the regulations by which Congress has prescribed the manner of its exercise." Castro v. United States, 3 Wall. 46, 49, 18 L.Ed. 163 (1866).

Jurisdictional Nature of Predecessor Provision

But similarity to a general type of provision that has always been held jurisdictional is not all that supports the jurisdictional character of § 2253(c)(3). Its very predecessor statute made a judge's expression of opinion a condition of appellate jurisdiction. The certificate of probable cause, of which the COA was born, arrived on the scene over 100 years ago in "An Act Restricting in certain cases the right of appeal to the Supreme Court in habeas corpus proceedings," Act of Mar. 10, 1908, ch. 76, 35 Stat. 40:

"[F]rom a final decision by a court of the United States in a proceeding in habeas corpus where the detention complained of is by virtue of process issued out of a State court no appeal to the Supreme Court shall be allowed unless the United States court by which the final decision was rendered or a justice of the Supreme Court shall be of opinion that there exists probable cause for an appeal, in which event, on allowing the same, the said court or justice shall certify that there is probable cause for such allowance."

The last version of this statute, before it was amended to its current form in AEDPA, provided for issuance of the certificate of probable cause by a circuit judge instead of a justice. See § 2253, 62 Stat. 967 (codified at 28 U.S.C. § 2253). Even applying the Court's simplistic rule that the jurisdictional restriction must be contained in the very same paragraph as the procedural requirement, there is no doubt that under this statute a judge's certification that there was probable cause for an appeal was jurisdictional. See, e.g., Ex parte Patrick, 212 U.S. 555, 29 S.Ct. 686, 53 L.Ed. 650 (1908) (per curiam); Bilik v. Strassheim, 212 U.S. 551, 29 S.Ct. 684, 53 L.Ed. 649 (1908) (per curiam). There is no reason whatever to think that Congress rendered the statement of opinion unnecessary for jurisdiction by (1) extending the requirement for it to § 2255 proceedings; (2) requiring the opinion to address a more specific point (not just probable cause for an appeal but presence of an issue presenting a "substantial showing of the denial of a constitutional right")[4]; and (3) giving the document in which the judge is required to express the opinion a name ("certificate of appealability")—so that now a "certificate of appealability" without opinion will suffice. Neither any one of these steps, nor all of them combined, suggest elimination of jurisdictional status for the required expression of opinion.[5] It would be an entirely strange way of achieving that result. It was not a strange way, however, of dividing the now more complex and lengthy provision into manageable subsections.

Stare Decisis Effect of Torres

In addition to the fact that conditions attached to court-to-court appeal have always been held jurisdictional, and the fact that this statute's predecessor was held to be so, we have considered, and found to be jurisdictional, a statute presenting precisely what is at issue here: a provision governing court-to-court appeals which made particular content a required element of a document that the statute said was necessary for jurisdiction; and which did that in a separate section that "excluded the jurisdictional terms," ante, at 651. That case flatly contradicts today's holding. In Torres v. Oakland Scavenger Co., 487 U.S. 312, 108 S.Ct. 2405, 101 L.Ed.2d 285, we dealt with Rule 3(c)(1) of the Federal Rules of Appellate Procedure. Rule 3(a) of those Rules makes a notice of appeal necessary to appellate jurisdiction—just as § 2253(c)(1) makes a certificate of appealability necessary. And Rule 3(c)(1), which, like § 2253(c)(3), does not contain jurisdictional language, says what the requisite notice of appeal must contain—just as § 2253(c)(3) says what the requisite certificate of appealability must contain:

"The notice of appeal must:

"(A) specify the party or parties taking the appeal by naming each one in the caption or body of the notice ...;

"(B) designate the judgment, order, or part thereof being appealed; and

"(C) name the court to which the appeal is taken."

In Torres we held that the Court of Appeals lacked jurisdiction over the appeal of a party not properly named in the notice of appeal. 487 U.S., at 314-315, 108 S.Ct. 2405. The parallel is perfect.

The Court claims that the jurisdictional consequences of Rule 3(c) were "`imposed by the legislature,'" ante, at 652 (quoting Torres, supra, at 318, 108 S.Ct. 2405), which according to the Court's analysis "`clearly state[d],'" ante, at 648 (quoting Arbaugh, 546 U.S., at 515, 126 S.Ct. 1235), that Rule 3(c) is jurisdictional. But the legislature there did precisely what it did here: made a particular document necessary to jurisdiction and then specified what that document must contain.[6] I certainly agree that that is a clear statement that a document with the requisite content is necessary to jurisdiction. But the Court does not. So to distinguish Torres it has to find something else in Rule 3(c) that provided a "clear statement" of what "Congress intended," ante, at 648-649. The best it can come up with, ante, at 652, is an un clear statement, and that not from Congress but from Advisory Committee Notes referred to in the Torres opinion. Such Notes are (of course) "the product of the Advisory Committee, and not Congress," and "they are transmitted to Congress before the rule is enacted into law." United States v. Vonn, 535

U.S. 55, 64, n. 6, 122 S.Ct. 1043, 152 L.Ed.2d 90 (2002). They are, in other words, a species of legislative history. I know of no precedent for the proposition that legislative history can satisfy a clear-statement requirement imposed by this Court's opinions. Does today's distinguishing of Torres mean that legislative history can waive the sovereign immunity of the United States? See United States v. Nordic Village, Inc., 503 U.S. 30, 33-34, 112 S.Ct. 1011, 117 L.Ed.2d 181 (1992). Or abrogate the sovereign immunity of the States? See Atascadero State Hospital v. Scanlon, 473 U.S. 234, 242, 105 S.Ct. 3142, 87 L.Ed.2d 171 (1985). Or give retroactive effect to new legislation? See Greene v. United States, 376 U.S. 149, 160, 84 S.Ct. 615, 11 L.Ed.2d 576 (1964). Or foreclose review of agency actions? See Abbott Laboratories v. Gardner, 387 U.S. 136, 141, 87 S.Ct. 1507, 18 L.Ed.2d 681 (1967). Today's opinion is in this respect a time-bomb.

To make matters worse, the Advisory Committee Note considered by the Torres Court—as "support for [its] view," 487 U.S., at 315, 108 S.Ct. 2405—did not clearly say that Rule 3(c)'s requirements were jurisdictional. It said this:

"'Rule 3 and Rule 4 combine to require that a notice of appeal be filed with the clerk of the district court within the time prescribed for taking an appeal. Because the timely filing of a notice of appeal is "mandatory and jurisdictional," United States v. Robinson, [361 U.S. 220, 224, 80 S.Ct. 282, 4 L.Ed.2d 259 (1960)], compliance with the provisions of those rules is of the utmost importance.'" 487 U.S., at 315 [108 S.Ct. 2405] (quoting 28 U.S.C.App., p. 467; alteration omitted and emphasis added).

To say that timely filing of a notice of appeal is jurisdictional, and that placing within the notice of appeal what Rule 3 says it must contain is "of the utmost importance," does not remotely add up to a clear statement that placing within the notice of appeal what Rule 3 says it must contain is jurisdictional. There is simply no principled basis for saying that Torres satisfies the "clear-statement principle," ante, at 649, except the commonsense notion that when a document is made jurisdictional, and the required contents of that document specified, a document that does not contain those contents cannot confer jurisdiction.[7]

The Court is not willing to say that Torres is no longer good law, but I doubt whether future litigants will be so coy. They know that in the past, to avoid the uncongenial rigidity of the rule that procedures attending court-to-court appeals are jurisdictional, we have performed wondrous contortions to find compliance with those rules. For example, in Smith v. Barry, 502 U.S. 244, 248, 112 S.Ct. 678, 116 L.Ed.2d 678 (1992), we held that an "informal brief" filed after a defective notice of appeal counted as a valid notice of appeal. In Foman v. Davis, 371 U.S. 178, 181, 83 S.Ct. 227, 9 L.Ed.2d 222 (1962), we held that a notice of appeal from the denial of a motion to vacate the judgment was also a notice of appeal from the underlying judgment. And in Houston v. Lack, 487 U.S. 266, 270, 108 S.Ct. 2379, 101 L.Ed.2d 245 (1988), we held that a prisoner's notice of appeal was "filed" when it was delivered to prison authorities for forwarding to the district court. These (shall we say) creative interpretations of the procedural requirements were made necessary by the background principle that is centuries old: "[I]f the mode prescribed for removing cases by writ of error or appeal be too strict and technical, and likely to produce inconvenience or injustice, it is for Congress to provide a remedy by altering the existing laws; not for the court." United States v. Curry, 6 How. 106, 113, 12 L.Ed. 363 (1848). But if we have been willing to expose ourselves to ridicule in order to approve implausible compliance with procedural prerequisites to appeal, surely we may be willing to continue and expand the process of simply converting those obnoxious prerequisites into the now favored "claims processing rules," enabling us to avoid unseemly contortions by simply invoking the ever-judge-friendly principles of equity.

What began as an effort to "`bring some discipline' to the use of the term `jurisdictional,'" ante, at 648 (quoting Henderson, 562, U.S., at ___, 131 S.Ct., at 1202), shows signs of becoming a libertine, liberating romp through our established jurisprudence.

II

A few remaining points raised by the Court's opinion warrant response.

The Court holds that the requirement imposed by paragraph (c)(2) (that a COA may issue "only if the applicant has made a substantial showing of the denial of a constitutional right") is not jurisdictional, and says that "[i]t follows that § 2253(c)(3) is nonjurisdictional as well." Ante, at 649. I need not reach the issue whether (c)(2) is jurisdictional—though it seems to me that the Court disposes rather summarily of the Solicitor General's view that it is. And I need not confront the Court with the back-at-you argument that if (c)(3) is jurisdictional (as I think) then (c)(2) is as well. For whether one runs it backwards or forwards, the argument is a bad one. Assuming that (c)(2) is nonjurisdictional, it does not at all "follow" that (c)(3) is nonjurisdictional as well. Paragraph (c)(3) is jurisdictional not because it is located in subsection (c), but because it describes the required content of a COA. Paragraph (c)(2) does not; it sets forth the criterion for a COA's issuance. A judge may apply that criterion erroneously but still produce a COA that (as paragraph (c)(3) requires) "indicate[s] which specific issue or issues satisfy the showing required by paragraph (2)." It no more follows that the erroneousness of the judge's indication must destroy the jurisdiction that the COA creates, than it followed under the predecessor statute that the erroneousness of the certification of probable cause for an appeal destroyed the jurisdiction that the certification created.[8] The two issues are quite separate: what the judge must find, and what the COA (or certification) must contain.

The Court points out that Gonzalez raised the Sixth Amendment issue in his application for a COA, that "[a] petitioner, having successfully obtained a COA, has no control over how the judge drafts the COA," and that the petitioner, "as in Gonzalez's case, may have done everything required of him by law." Ante, at 650. Perhaps it is true that the defective COA was not at all Gonzalez's fault—though he could have promptly moved to amend it. But no-fault elimination of jurisdiction is not forbidden. In Bowles v. Russell, 551 U.S. 205, 127 S.Ct. 2360, 168 L.Ed.2d 96 (2007), we enforced a time limit on notice of appeal where the district court had purported to extend the time to file and the appellant had complied with the court's order. Id., at 207, 213-214, 127 S.Ct. 2360. It did not matter that the fault lay with the court.

Finally, the Court points out that treating § 2253(c)(3) as jurisdictional would waste a lot of time. "Even if additional screening of already-issued COAs for § 2253(c)(3) defects could further winnow the cases before the courts of appeals, that would not outweigh the costs of further delay from the extra layer of review." Ante, at 650. But that is not an argument directed to the statute before us; it is an argument directed against enforcement of all jurisdictional requirements (all of which, I suspect, are the object of the Court's mounting disfavor). And the argument may not even be true, except in the (presumably rare) case where the jurisdictional prescription is disregarded. Over the long term, the time saved to judges and lawyers by an enforceable requirement that appeals be screened by a single judge may vastly outweigh the time wasted by the occasional need for enforcement. That, it seems to me, is what Congress believed.

* * *

Terminology is destiny. Today's holding, and the erosion of our prior jurisprudence that will perhaps follow upon it, is foreshadowed and facilitated by the unfortunate terminology with which we have chosen to accompany our campaign to "bring some discipline" to determinations of jurisdiction. We have said that the universe of rules placing limitations upon the courts is divided into (1) "claims processing rules," and (2) jurisdiction-removing rules. Unless our prior jurisprudence is to be repudiated, that is a false dichotomy. The requirement that the unsuccessful litigant file a timely notice of appeal, for example, is (if the term is to have any meaning) a claims-processing rule, ordering the process by which claims are adjudicated. Yet as discussed above, that, and all procedures that must be followed to proceed from one court to another, have always been deemed jurisdictional. The proper dichotomy is between claims processing rules that are jurisdictional, and those that are not. To put it otherwise suggests a test for jurisdiction that is not to be found in our cases.[9]

At the end of the day, the indication requirement in § 2253(c)(3) is "`imposed by the legislature and not by the judicial process.'" Torres, 487 U.S., at 318, 108 S.Ct. 2405 (quoting Schiavone v. Fortune, 477 U.S. 21, 31, 106 S.Ct. 2379, 91 L.Ed.2d 18 (1986)). Whether or not its enforcement leads to a harsh result, wastes time in this particular case, or (though the Court does not give this as a reason) prevents us from reaching a circuit conflict we are dying to resolve, we are obliged to enforce it. I respectfully dissent.

Justice Scalia's dissent in Lafler v. Cooper (March 21, 2012) [Notes omitted]

Justice SCALIA, with whom Justice THOMAS joins, and with whom THE CHIEF JUSTICE joins as to all but Part IV, dissenting.

"If a plea bargain has been offered, a defendant has the right to effective assistance of counsel in considering whether to accept it. If that right is denied, prejudice can be shown if loss of the plea opportunity led to a trial resulting in a conviction on more serious charges or the imposition of a more severe sentence." Ante, at 1387.

"The inquiry then becomes how to define the duty and responsibilities of defense counsel in the plea bargain process. This is a difficult question. . . . Bargaining is, by its nature, defined to a substantial degree by personal style. . . . This case presents neither the necessity nor the occasion to define the duties of defense counsel in those respects.. . .." Missouri v. Frye, ante, at 1408, 132 S.Ct. 1399.

With those words from this and the companion case, the Court today opens a whole new field of constitutionalized criminal procedure: plea-bargaining law. The ordinary criminal process has become too long, too expensive, and unpredictable, in no small part as a consequence of an intricate federal Code of Criminal Procedure imposed on the States by this Court in pursuit of perfect justice. See Friendly, The Bill of Rights as a Code of Criminal Procedure, 53 Cal. L.Rev. 929 (1965). The Court now moves to bring perfection to the alternative in which prosecutors and defendants have sought relief. Today's opinions deal with only two aspects of counsel's plea-bargaining inadequacy, and leave other aspects (who knows what they might be?) to be worked out in further constitutional litigation that will burden the criminal process. And it would be foolish to think that "constitutional" rules governing counsel's behavior will not be followed by rules governing the prosecution's behavior in the plea-bargaining process that the Court today announces "`is the criminal justice system,'" Frye, ante, at 1407, 132 S.Ct. 1399 (quoting approvingly from Scott & Stuntz, Plea Bargaining as Contract, 101 Yale L.J. 1909, 1912 (1992) (hereinafter Scott)). Is it constitutional, for example, for the prosecution to withdraw a plea offer that has already been accepted? Or to withdraw an offer before the defense has had adequate time to consider and accept it? Or to make no plea offer at all, even though its case is weak—thereby excluding the defendant from "the criminal justice system"?

Anthony Cooper received a full and fair trial, was found guilty of all charges by a unanimous jury, and was given the sentence that the law prescribed. The Court nonetheless concludes that Cooper is entitled to some sort of habeas corpus relief (perhaps) because his attorney's allegedly incompetent advice regarding a plea offer caused him to receive a full and fair trial. That conclusion is foreclosed by our precedents. Even if it were not foreclosed, the constitutional right to effective plea-bargainers that it establishes is at least a new rule of law, which does not undermine the Michigan Court of Appeals' decision and therefore cannot serve as the basis for habeas relief. And the remedy the Court announces—namely, whatever the state trial court in its discretion prescribes, down to and including no remedy at all—is unheard-of and quite absurd for violation of a constitutional right. I respectfully dissent.

I

This case and its companion, Missouri v. Frye, ____ U.S. ____, 132 S.Ct. 1399, ____ L.Ed.2d ____, raise relatively straightforward questions about the scope of the right to effective assistance of counsel. Our case law originally derived that right from the Due Process Clause, and its guarantee of a fair trial, see United States v. Gonzalez-Lopez, 548

U.S. 140, 147, 126 S.Ct. 2557, 165 L.Ed.2d 409 (2006), but the seminal case of Strickland v. Washington, 466 U.S. 668, 104 S.Ct. 2052, 80 L.Ed.2d 674 (1984), located the right within the Sixth Amendment. As the Court notes, ante, at 1394, the right to counsel does not begin at trial. It extends to "any stage of the prosecution, formal or informal, in court or out, where counsel's absence might derogate from the accused's right to a fair trial." United States v. Wade, 388 U.S. 218, 226, 87 S.Ct. 1926, 18 L.Ed.2d 1149 (1967). Applying that principle, we held that the "entry of a guilty plea, whether to a misdemeanor or a felony charge, ranks as a `critical stage' at which the right to counsel adheres." Iowa v. Tovar, 541 U.S. 77, 81, 124 S.Ct. 1379, 158 L.Ed.2d 209 (2004); see also Hill v. Lockhart, 474 U.S. 52, 58, 106 S.Ct. 366, 88 L.Ed.2d 209 (1985). And it follows from this that acceptance of a plea offer is a critical stage. That, and nothing more, is the point of the Court's observation in Padilla v. Kentucky, 559 U.S. ___, ___, 130 S.Ct. 1473, 1486, 176 L.Ed.2d 284 (2010), that "the negotiation of a plea bargain is a critical phase of litigation for purposes of the Sixth Amendment right to effective assistance of counsel." The defendant in Padilla had accepted the plea bargain and pleaded guilty, abandoning his right to a fair trial; he was entitled to advice of competent counsel before he did so. The Court has never held that the rule articulated in Padilla, Tovar, and Hill extends to all aspects of plea negotiations, requiring not just advice of competent counsel before the defendant accepts a plea bargain and pleads guilty, but also the advice of competent counsel before the defendant rejects a plea bargain and stands on his constitutional right to a fair trial. The latter is a vast departure from our past cases, protecting not just the constitutionally prescribed right to a fair adjudication of guilt and punishment, but a judicially invented right to effective plea bargaining.

It is also apparent from Strickland that bad plea bargaining has nothing to do with ineffective assistance of counsel in the constitutional sense. Strickland explained that "[i]n giving meaning to the requirement [of effective assistance], . . . we must take its purpose— to ensure a fair trial—as the guide." 466 U.S., at 686, 104 S.Ct. 2052. Since "the right to the effective assistance of counsel is recognized not for its own sake, but because of the effect it has on the ability of the accused to receive a fair trial," United States v. Cronic, 466 U.S. 648, 658, 104 S.Ct. 2039, 80 L.Ed.2d 657 (1984), the "benchmark" inquiry in evaluating any claim of ineffective assistance is whether counsel's performance "so undermined the proper functioning of the adversarial process" that it failed to produce a reliably "just result." Strickland, 466 U.S., at 686, 104 S.Ct. 2052. That is what Strickland's requirement of "prejudice" consists of: Because the right to effective assistance has as its purpose the assurance of a fair trial, the right is not infringed unless counsel's mistakes call into question the basic justice of a defendant's conviction or sentence. That has been, until today, entirely clear. A defendant must show "that counsel's errors were so serious as to deprive the defendant of a fair trial, a trial whose result is reliable." Id., at 687, 104 S.Ct. 2052. See also Gonzalez-Lopez, supra, at 147, 126 S.Ct. 2557. Impairment of fair trial is how we distinguish between unfortunate attorney error and error of constitutional significance.[1]

To be sure, Strickland stated a rule of thumb for measuring prejudice which, applied blindly and out of context, could support the Court's holding today: "The defendant must show that there is a reasonable probability that, but for counsel's unprofessional errors, the result of the proceeding would have been different." 466 U.S., at 694, 104 S.Ct. 2052. Strickland itself cautioned, however, that its test was not to be applied in a mechanical fashion, and that courts were not to divert their "ultimate focus" from "the fundamental fairness of the proceeding whose result is being challenged." Id., at 696, 104 S.Ct. 2052. And until today we have followed that course.

In Lockhart v. Fretwell, 506 U.S. 364, 113 S.Ct. 838, 122 L.Ed.2d 180 (1993), the deficient performance at issue was the failure of counsel for a defendant who had been sentenced to death to make an objection that would have produced a sentence of life imprisonment instead. The objection was fully supported by then-extant Circuit law, so that the sentencing court would have been compelled to sustain it, producing a life sentence that principles of double jeopardy would likely make final. See id., at 383-385, 113 S.Ct. 838 (STEVENS, J., dissenting); Bullington v. Missouri, 451 U.S. 430, 101 S.Ct. 1852, 68 L.Ed.2d 270 (1981). By the time Fretwell's claim came before us, however, the Circuit law had been overruled in light of one of our cases. We determined that a prejudice analysis "focusing solely on mere outcome determination, without attention to whether the result of the proceeding was fundamentally unfair or unreliable," would be defective. Fretwell, 506 U.S., at 369, 113 S.Ct. 838. Because counsel's error did not "deprive the defendant of any substantive or procedural right to which the law entitles him," the defendant's sentencing proceeding was fair and its result was reliable, even though counsel's error may have affected its outcome. Id., at 372, 113 S.Ct. 838. In Williams v. Taylor, 529 U.S. 362, 391-393, 120 S.Ct. 1495, 146 L.Ed.2d 389 (2000), we explained that even though Fretwell did not mechanically apply an outcome-based test for prejudice, its reasoning was perfectly consistent with Strickland. "Fretwell's counsel had not deprived him of any substantive or procedural right to which the law entitled him." 529 U.S. at 392, 120 S.Ct. 1495.[2]

Those precedents leave no doubt about the answer to the question presented here.

As the Court itself observes, a criminal defendant has no right to a plea bargain. Ante, at 1395-1396. "[T]here is no constitutional right to plea bargain; the prosecutor need not do so if he prefers to go to trial." Weatherford v. Bursey, 429 U.S. 545, 561, 97 S.Ct. 837, 51 L.Ed.2d 30 (1977). Counsel's mistakes in this case thus did not "deprive the defendant of a substantive or procedural right to which the law entitles him," Williams, supra, at 393, 120 S.Ct. 1495. Far from being "beside the point," ante, at 1406, that is critical to correct application of our precedents. Like Fretwell, this case "concerns the unusual circumstance where the defendant attempts to demonstrate prejudice based on considerations that, as a matter of law, ought not inform the inquiry," 506 U.S., at 373, 113 S.Ct. 838 (O'Connor, J., concurring); he claims "that he might have been denied `a right the law simply does not recognize,'" id., at 375, 113 S.Ct. 838 (same). Strickland, Fretwell, and Williams all instruct that the pure outcome-based test on which the Court relies is an erroneous measure of cognizable prejudice. In ignoring Strickland's "ultimate focus . . . on the fundamental fairness of the proceeding whose result is being challenged," 466 U.S., at 696, 104 S.Ct. 2052, the Court has lost the forest for the trees, leading it to accept what we have previously rejected, the "novel argument that constitutional rights are infringed by trying the defendant rather than accepting his plea of guilty." Weatherford, supra, at 561, 97 S.Ct. 837.

II

Novelty alone is the second, independent reason why the Court's decision is wrong. This case arises on federal habeas, and hence is governed by the Antiterrorism and Effective Death Penalty Act of 1996 (AEDPA). Since, as the Court acknowledges, the Michigan Court of Appeals adjudicated Cooper's ineffective-assistance claim on the merits, AEDPA bars federal courts from granting habeas relief unless that court's decision was "contrary to, or involved an unreasonable application of, clearly established Federal law, as determined by the Supreme Court of the United States." 28 U.S.C. § 2254(d)(1). Yet the Court concludes that § 2254(d)(1) does not bar relief here, because "[b]y failing to apply Strickland to assess the ineffective-assistance-of-counsel claim respondent raised, the state court's adjudication was contrary to clearly established federal law." Ante, at 1390. That is not so.

The relevant portion of the Michigan Court of Appeals decision reads as follows:

"To establish ineffective assistance, the defendant must demonstrate that his counsel's performance fell below an objective standard of reasonableness and that counsel's representation so prejudiced the defendant that he was deprived of a fair trial. With respect to the prejudice aspect of the test, the defendant must demonstrate a reasonable probability that, but for counsel's errors, the result of the proceedings would have been different, and that the attendant proceedings were fundamentally unfair and unreliable.

"Defendant challenges the trial court's finding after a Ginther hearing that defense counsel provided effective assistance to defendant during the plea bargaining process. He contends that defense counsel failed to convey the benefits of the plea offer to him and ignored his desire to plead guilty, and that these failures led him to reject a plea offer that he now wishes to accept. However, the record shows that defendant knowingly and intelligently rejected two plea offers and chose to go to trial. The record fails to support defendant's contentions that defense counsel's representation was ineffective because he rejected a defense based on [a] claim of self-defense and because he did not obtain a more favorable plea bargain for defendant." People v. Cooper, No. 250583 (Mar. 15, 2005), App. to Pet. for Cert. 45a, 2005 WL 599740, [at] *1 (per curiam) (footnote and citations omitted).

The first paragraph above, far from ignoring Strickland, recites its standard with a good deal more accuracy than the Court's opinion. The second paragraph, which is presumably an application of the standard recited in the first, says that "defendant knowingly and intelligently rejected two plea offers and chose to go to trial." This can be regarded as a denial that there was anything "fundamentally unfair" about Cooper's conviction and sentence, so that no Strickland prejudice had been shown. On the other hand, the entire second paragraph can be regarded as a contention that Cooper's claims of inadequate representation were unsupported by the record. The state court's analysis was admittedly not a model of clarity, but federal habeas corpus is a "guard against extreme malfunctions in the state criminal justice systems," not a license to penalize a state court for its opinion-writing technique. Harrington v. Richter, 562 U.S. ___, ___, 131 S.Ct. 770, 786, 178 L.Ed.2d 624 (2011) (internal quotation marks omitted). The Court's readiness to find error in the Michigan court's opinion is "inconsistent with the presumption that state courts know and follow the law," Woodford v. Visciotti, 537 U.S. 19, 24, 123 S.Ct. 357, 154 L.Ed.2d 279 (2002) (per curiam), a presumption borne out here by the state court's recitation of the correct legal standard.

Since it is ambiguous whether the state court's holding was based on a lack of prejudice or rather the court's factual determination that there had been no deficient performance, to provide relief under AEDPA this Court must conclude that both holdings would have been unreasonable applications of clearly established law. See Premo v. Moore, 562 U.S. ___, ___, 131 S.Ct. 733, 740-741, 178 L.Ed.2d 649 (2011). The first is impossible of doing, since this Court has never held that a defendant in Cooper's position can establish Strickland prejudice. The Sixth Circuit thus violated AEDPA in granting habeas relief, and the Court now does the same.

III

It is impossible to conclude discussion of today's extraordinary opinion without commenting upon the remedy it provides for the unconstitutional conviction. It is a remedy unheard-of in American jurisprudence—and, I would be willing to bet, in the jurisprudence of any other country.

The Court requires Michigan to "reoffer the plea agreement" that was rejected because of bad advice from counsel. Ante, at 1391. That would indeed be a powerful remedy—but for the fact that Cooper's acceptance of that reoffered agreement is not conclusive. Astoundingly, "the state trial court can then exercise its discretion in determining whether to vacate the convictions and resentence respondent pursuant to the plea agreement, to vacate only some of the convictions and resentence respondent accordingly, or to leave the convictions and sentence from trial undisturbed." Ibid. (emphasis added).

Why, one might ask, require a "reoffer" of the plea agreement, and its acceptance by the defendant? If the district court finds (as a necessary element, supposedly, of Strickland prejudice) that Cooper would have accepted the original offer, and would thereby have avoided trial and conviction, why not skip the reoffer-and-reacceptance minuet and simply leave it to the discretion of the state trial court what the remedy shall be? The answer, of course, is camouflage. Trial courts, after all, regularly accept or reject plea agreements, so there seems to be nothing extraordinary about their accepting or rejecting the new one mandated by today's decision. But the acceptance or rejection of a plea agreement that has no status whatever under the United States Constitution is worlds apart from what this is: "discretionary" specification of a remedy for an unconstitutional criminal conviction.

To be sure, the Court asserts that there are "factors" which bear upon (and presumably limit) exercise of this discretion—factors that it is not prepared to specify in full, much less assign some determinative weight. "Principles elaborated over time in decisions of state and federal courts, and in statutes and rules" will (in the Court's rosy view) sort all that out. Ante, at 1389. I find it extraordinary that "statutes and rules" can specify the remedy for a criminal defendant's unconstitutional conviction. Or that the remedy for an unconstitutional conviction should ever be subject at all to a trial judge's discretion. Or, finally, that the remedy could ever include no remedy at all.

I suspect that the Court's squeamishness in fashioning a remedy, and the incoherence of what it comes up with, is attributable to its realization, deep down, that there is no real constitutional violation here anyway. The defendant has been fairly tried, lawfully convicted, and properly sentenced, and any "remedy" provided for this will do nothing but undo the just results of a fair adversarial process.

IV

In many—perhaps most—countries of the world, American-style plea bargaining is forbidden in cases as serious as this one, even for the purpose of obtaining testimony that enables conviction of a greater malefactor, much less for the purpose of sparing the expense of trial. See, e.g., World Plea Bargaining 344, 363-366 (S. Thaman ed. 2010). In Europe, many countries adhere to what they aptly call the "legality principle" by requiring prosecutors to charge all prosecutable offenses, which is typically incompatible with the practice of charge-bargaining. See, e.g., id., at xxii; Langbein, Land Without Plea Bargaining: How the Germans Do It, 78 Mich. L.Rev. 204, 210-211 (1979) (describing the "Legalitätsprinzip," or rule of compulsory prosecution, in Germany). Such a system reflects an admirable belief that the law is the law, and those who break it should pay the penalty provided.

In the United States, we have plea bargaining a-plenty, but until today it has been regarded as a necessary evil. It presents grave risks of prosecutorial overcharging that effectively compels an innocent defendant to avoid massive risk by pleading guilty to a lesser offense; and for guilty defendants it often—perhaps usually—results in a sentence well below what the law prescribes for the actual crime. But even so, we accept plea bargaining because many believe that without it our long and expensive process of criminal trial could not sustain the burden imposed on it, and our system of criminal justice would grind to a halt. See, e.g., Alschuler, Plea Bargaining and its History, 79 Colum. L.Rev. 1, 38 (1979).

Today, however, the Supreme Court of the United States elevates plea bargaining from a necessary evil to a constitutional entitlement. It is no longer a somewhat embarrassing adjunct to our criminal justice system; rather, as the Court announces in the companion case to this one, "`it is the criminal justice system.'" Frye, ante, at 1407, 132

S.Ct. 1399 (quoting approvingly from Scott 1912). Thus, even though there is no doubt that the respondent here is guilty of the offense with which he was charged; even though he has received the exorbitant gold standard of American justice—a full-dress criminal trial with its innumerable constitutional and statutory limitations upon the evidence that the prosecution can bring forward, and (in Michigan as in most States[3]) the requirement of a unanimous guilty verdict by impartial jurors; the Court says that his conviction is invalid because he was deprived of his constitutional entitlement to plea-bargain.

I am less saddened by the outcome of this case than I am by what it says about this Court's attitude toward criminal justice. The Court today embraces the sporting-chance theory of criminal law, in which the State functions like a conscientious casino-operator, giving each player a fair chance to beat the house, that is, to serve less time than the law says he deserves. And when a player is excluded from the tables, his constitutional rights have been violated. I do not subscribe to that theory. No one should, least of all the Justices of the Supreme Court.

  * * *

Today's decision upends decades of our cases, violates a federal statute, and opens a whole new boutique of constitutional jurisprudence ("plea-bargaining law") without even specifying the remedies the boutique offers. The result in the present case is the undoing of an adjudicatory process that worked exactly as it is supposed to. Released felon Anthony Cooper, who shot repeatedly and gravely injured a woman named Kali Mundy, was tried and convicted for his crimes by a jury of his peers, and given a punishment that Michigan's elected representatives have deemed appropriate. Nothing about that result is unfair or unconstitutional. To the contrary, it is wonderfully just, and infinitely superior to the trial-by-bargain that today's opinion affords constitutional status. I respectfully dissent.

Justice Scalia's concurrence and dissent in Arizona v. US (June 25, 2012) [Notes omitted]

Justice Scalia, concurring in part and dissenting in part.

The United States is an indivisible "Union of sovereign States." Hinderlider v. La Plata River & Cherry Creek Ditch Co., 304 U. S. 92, 104 (1938). Today's opinion, approving virtually all of the Ninth Circuit's injunction against enforcement of the four challenged provisions of Arizona's law, deprives States of what most would consider the defining characteristic of sovereignty: the power to exclude from the sovereign's territory people who have no right to be there. Neither the Constitution itself nor even any law passed by Congress supports this result. I dissent.

  I

As a sovereign, Arizona has the inherent power to exclude persons from its territory, subject only to those limitations expressed in the Constitution or constitutionally imposed by Congress. That power to exclude has long been recognized as inherent in sovereignty. Emer de Vattel's seminal 1758 treatise on the Law of Nations stated:

"The sovereign may forbid the entrance of his territory either to foreigners in general, or in particular cases, or to certain persons, or for certain particular purposes, according as he may think it advantageous to the state. There is nothing in all this, that does not flow from the rights of domain and sovereignty: every one is obliged to pay respect to the prohibition; and whoever dares violate it, incurs the penalty decreed to render it effectual." The Law of Nations, bk. II,ch. VII, §94, p. 309 (B. Kapossy & R. Whatmore eds. 2008).

See also I R. Phillimore, Commentaries upon International Law, pt. III, ch. X, p. 233 (1854) ("It is a received maxim of International Law that, the Government of a State may prohibit the entrance of strangers into the country"). 1

There is no doubt that "before the adoption of the constitution of the United States" each State had the author-ity to "prevent [itself] from being burdened by an influx of persons." Mayor of New York v. Miln, 11 Pet. 102, 132–133 (1837). And the Constitution did not strip the States of that authority. To the contrary, two of the Constitution's provisions were designed to enable the States to prevent "the intrusion of obnoxious aliens through other States." Letter from James Madison to Edmund Randolph (Aug. 27, 1782), in 1 The Writings of James Madison 226 (1900); accord, The Federalist No. 42, pp. 269–271 (C. Rossiter ed. 1961) (J. Madison). The Articles of Confederation had provided that "the free inhabitants of each of these States, paupers, vagabonds and fugitives from justice excepted, shall be entitled to all privileges and immunities of free citizens in the several States." Articles of Confederation, Art. IV. This meant that an unwelcome alien could obtain all the rights of a citizen of one State simply by first becoming an inhabitant of another. To remedy this, the Constitution's Privileges and Immunities Clause provided that "[t]he Citizens of each State shall be entitled to all Privileges and Immunities of Citizens in the several States." Art. IV, §2, cl. 1 (emphasis added). Butif one State had particularly lax citizenship standards, it might still serve as a gateway for the entry of "obnoxious aliens" into other States. This problem was solved "by authorizing the general government to establish a uniform rule of naturalization throughout the United States." The Federalist No. 42, supra, at 271; see Art. I, §8, cl. 4. In other words, the naturalization power was given to Congress not to abrogate States' power to exclude those they did not want, but to vindicate it.

Two other provisions of the Constitution are an acknowledgment of the States' sovereign interest in protecting their borders. Article I provides that "[n]o State shall, without the Consent of the Congress, lay any Imposts or Duties on Imports or Exports, except what may be absolutely necessary for executing it's inspection Laws." Art. I, §10, cl. 2 (emphasis added). This assumed what everyone assumed: that the States could exclude from their territory dangerous or unwholesome goods. A later portion of the same section provides that "[n]o State shall, without the Consent of Congress, . . . engage in War, unless actually invaded, or in such imminent Danger as will not admit of delay." Art. I, §10, cl. 3 (emphasis added). This limits the States' sovereignty (in a way not relevant here) but leaves intact their inherent power to protect their territory.

Notwithstanding "[t]he myth of an era of unrestricted immigration" in the first 100 years of the Republic, the States enacted numerous laws restricting the immigration of certain classes of aliens, including convicted criminals, indigents, persons with contagious diseases, and (in Southern States) freed blacks. Neuman, The Lost Century of American Immigration (1776–1875), 93 Colum. L. Rev. 1833, 1835, 1841–1880 (1993). State laws not only pro-vided for the removal of unwanted immigrants but also imposed penalties on unlawfully present aliens and those who aided their immigration. 2 Id., at 1883.

In fact, the controversy surrounding the Alien and Sedition Acts involved a debate over whether, under the Constitution, the States had exclusive authority to enact such immigration laws. Criticism of the Sedition Act has become a prominent feature of our First Amendment jurisprudence, see, e.g., New York Times Co. v. Sullivan, 376 U. S. 254–276 (1964), but one of the Alien Acts 3 also aroused controversy at the time:

"Be it enacted by the Senate and House of Representatives of the United States of America in Congress assembled, That it shall be lawful for the President of the United States at any time during the continuance of this act, to order all such aliens as he shall judge dangerous to the peace and safety of the United States, or shall have reasonable grounds to suspect are concerned in any treasonable or secret machinations against the government thereof, to depart out of the territory of the United States . . . ." An Act concerning Aliens, 1Stat. 570, 570–571.

The Kentucky and Virginia Resolutions, written in denunciation of these Acts, insisted that the power to exclude unwanted aliens rested solely in the States. Jefferson's Kentucky Resolutions insisted "that alien friends are under the jurisdiction and protection of the laws of the state wherein they are [and] that no power over them has been delegated to the United States, nor prohibited to the individual states, distinct from their power over citizens." Kentucky Resolutions of 1798, reprinted in J. Powell, Languages of Power: A Sourcebook of Early American Constitutional History 131 (1991). Madison's Virginia Resolutions likewise contended that the Alien Act purported to give the President "a power nowhere delegated to the federal government." Virginia Resolutions of 1798, reprinted in Powell, supra, at 134 (emphasis omitted). Notably, moreover, the Federalist proponents of the Act defended it primarily on the ground that "[t]he removal of aliens is the usual preliminary of hostility" and could therefore be justified in exercise of the Federal Government's war powers. Massachussets Resolutions in Reply to Virginia, reprinted in Powell, supra, at 136.

In Mayor of New York v. Miln, this Court considered a New York statute that required the commander of any ship arriving in New York from abroad to disclose "the name, place of birth, and last legal settlement, age and occupation . . . of all passengers . . . with the intention of proceeding to the said city." 11 Pet., at 130–131. After discussing the sovereign authority to regulate the entrance of foreigners described by De Vattel, the Court said:

"The power . . . of New York to pass this law having undeniably existed at the formation of the constitution, the simply inquiry is, whether by that instrument it was taken from the states, and granted to congress; for if it were not, it yet remains with them." Id., at 132.

And the Court held that it remains. Id., at 139.

II

One would conclude from the foregoing that after the adoption of the Constitution there was some doubt about the power of the Federal Government to control immigration, but no doubt about the power of the States to do so. Since the founding era (though not immediately), doubt about the Federal Government's power has disappeared. Indeed, primary responsibility for immigration policy has shifted from the States to the Federal Government. Congress exercised its power "[t]o establish an uniform Rule of Naturalization," Art. I, §8, cl. 4, very early on, see An Act to establish an uniform Rule of Naturalization, 1Stat. 103. But with the fleeting exception of the Alien Act, Congress did not enact any legislation regulating immigration for the better part of a century. In 1862, Congress passed "An Act to prohibit the 'Coolie Trade' by American Citizens in American Vessels," which prohibited "procuring [Chinese nationals] . . . to be disposed of, or sold, or transferred, for any term of years or for any time what-ever, as servants or apprentices, or to be held to service or labor." 12Stat. 340. Then, in 1875, Congress amended that act to bar admission to Chinese, Japanese, and other Asian immigrants who had "entered into a contract or agreement for a term of service within the United States, for lewd and immoral purposes." An act supplementary to the acts in relation to immigration, ch. 141, 18Stat. 477. And in 1882, Congress enacted the first general immi-gration statute. See An act to regulate Immigration, 22Stat. 214. Of course, it hardly bears mention that Federal immigration law is now extensive.

I accept that as a valid exercise of federal power—not because of the Naturalization Clause (it has no necessary connection to citizenship) but because it is an inherent attribute of sovereignty no less for the United States than for the States. As this Court has said, it is an " 'accepted maxim of international law, that every sovereign nation has the power, as inherent in sovereignty, and essential to self-preservation, to forbid the entrance of foreigners within its dominions.' " Fong Yue Ting v. United States, 149 U. S. 698, 705 (1893) (quoting Ekiu v. United States, 142 U. S. 651, 659 (1892)). That is why there was no need to set forth control of immigration as one of the enumerated powers of Congress, although an acknowledgment of that power (as well as of the States' similar power, subject to federal abridgment) was contained in Art. I, §9, which provided that "[t]he Migration or Importation of such Persons as any of the States now existing shall think proper to admit, shall not be prohibited by the Congress prior to the Year one thousand eight hundred and eight . . . ."

In light of the predominance of federal immigration restrictions in modern times, it is easy to lose sight of the States' traditional role in regulating immigration—and to overlook their sovereign prerogative to do so. I accept as a given that State regulation is excluded by the Constitution when (1) it has been prohibited by a valid federal law, or (2) it conflicts with federal regulation—when, for example, it admits those whom federal regulation would exclude, or excludes those whom federal regulation would admit.

Possibility (1) need not be considered here: there is no federal law prohibiting the States' sovereign power to exclude (assuming federal authority to enact such a law). The mere existence of federal action in the immigration area—and the so-called field preemption arising from that action, upon which the Court's opinion so heavily relies, ante, at 9–11—cannot be regarded as such a prohibition. We are not talking here about a federal law prohibiting the States from regulating bubble-gum advertising, or even the construction of nuclear plants. We are talking about a federal law going to the core of state sovereignty: the power to exclude. Like elimination of the States' other inherent sovereign power, immunity from suit, elimination of the States' sovereign power to exclude requires that "Congress . . . unequivocally expres[s] its intent to abrogate," Seminole Tribe of Fla. v. Florida, 517 U. S. 44, 55 (1996) (internal quotation marks and citation omitted). Implicit "field preemption" will not do.

Nor can federal power over illegal immigration be deemed exclusive because of what the Court's opinion solicitously calls "foreign countries['] concern[s] about the status, safety, and security of their nationals in the United States," ante, at 3. The Constitution gives all those on our shores the protections of the Bill of Rights—but just as those rights are not expanded for foreign nationals because of their countries' views (some countries, for example, have recently discovered the death penalty to be barbaric), neither are the fundamental sovereign powers of the States abridged to accommodate foreign countries' views. Even in its international relations, the Federal Government must live with the inconvenient fact that it is a Union of independent States, who have their own sovereign powers. This is not the first time it has found that a nuisance and a bother in the conduct of foreign policy. Four years ago, for example, the Government importuned us to interfere with thoroughly constitutional state judicial procedures in the criminal trial of foreign nationals because the international community, and even an opinion of the International Court of Justice, disapproved them. See Medellín v. Texas, 552 U. S. 491 (2008) . We rejected that request, as we should reject the Executive's invocation of foreign-affairs considerations here. Though it may upset foreign powers—and even when the Federal Government desperately wants to avoid upsetting foreign powers—the States have the right to protect their borders against foreign nationals, just as they have the right to execute foreign nationals for murder.

What this case comes down to, then, is whether the Arizona law conflicts with federal immigration law—whether it excludes those whom federal law would admit, or admits those whom federal law would exclude. It does not purport to do so. It applies only to aliens who neither possess a privilege to be present under federal law nor have been removed pursuant to the Federal Government's inherent authority. I proceed to consider the challenged provisions in detail.

§2(B)

"For any lawful stop, detention or arrest made by a law enforcement official . . . in the enforcement of any other law or ordinance of a county, city or town or this state where reasonable suspicion exists that the person is an alien and is unlawfully present in the United States, a reasonable attempt shall be made, when practicable, to determine the immigration status of the person, except if the determination may hinder or obstruct an investigation. Any person who is arrested shall have the person's immigration status determined before the person is released. . . ." S. B. 1070, §2(B), as amended, Ariz. Rev. Stat. Ann. §11–1051(B) (West 2012).

The Government has conceded that "even before Section 2 was enacted, state and local officers had state-law authority to inquire of DHS [the Department of Homeland Security] about a suspect's unlawful status and other-wise cooperate with federal immigration officers." Brief for United States 47 (citing App. 62, 82); see also Brief for United States 48–49. That concession, in my view, obviates the need for further inquiry. The Government's conflict-pre-emption claim calls on us "to determine whether, under the circumstances of this particular case, [the State's] law stands as an obstacle to the accomplishment and execution of the full purposes and objectives of Congress." Hines v. Davidowitz, 312 U. S. 52, 67 (1941) (emphasis added). It is impossible to make such a finding without a factual record concerning the manner in which Arizona is implementing these provisions—something the Government's pre-enforcement challenge has pretermitted. "The fact that [a law] might operate unconstitutionally under some conceivable set of circumstances is insufficient to render it wholly invalid, since we have not recognized an 'overbreadth' doctrine outside the limited context of the First Amendment." United States v. Salerno, 481 U. S. 739, 745 (1987) . And on its face, §2(B) merely tells state officials that they are authorized to do something that they were, by the Government's con-cession, already authorized to do.

The Court therefore properly rejects the Government's challenge, recognizing that, "[a]t this stage, without the benefit of a definitive interpretation from the state courts, it would be inappropriate to assume §2B will be construed in a way that creates a conflict with federal law." Ante, at 23. Before reaching that conclusion, however, the Court goes to great length to assuage fears that "state officers will be required to delay the release of some detainees for no reason other than to verify their immigration status." Ante, at 22. Of course, any investigatory detention, including one under §2(B), may become an "unreasonable . . . seizur[e]," U. S. Const., Amdt. IV, if it lasts too long. See Illinois v. Caballes, 543 U. S. 405, 407 (2005) . But that has nothing to do with this case, in which the Government claims that §2(B) is pre-empted by federal immigration law, not that anyone's Fourth Amendment rights have been violated. And I know of no reason why aprotracted detention that does not violate the Fourth Amendment would contradict or conflict with any federal immigration law.

§6

"A peace officer, without a warrant, may arrest a person if the officer has probable cause to believe . . . [t]he person to be arrested has committed any public offense that makes the person removable from the United States." S. B. 1070, §6(A)(5), Ariz. Rev. Stat.

Ann. §13–3883(A)(5) (West Supp. 2011).

This provision of S. B. 1070 expands the statutory list of offenses for which an Arizona police officer may make an arrest without a warrant. See §13–3883. If an officer has probable cause to believe that an individual is "removable" by reason of a public offense, then a warrant is not required to make an arrest. The Government's primary contention is that §6 is pre-empted by federal immigration law because it allows state officials to make arrests "without regard to federal priorities." Brief for United States 53. The Court's opinion focuses on limits that Congress has placed on federal officials' authority to arrest removable aliens and the possibility that state officials will make arrests "to achieve [Arizona's] own immigration policy" and "without any input from the Federal Government." Ante, at 17.

Of course on this pre-enforcement record there is no reason to assume that Arizona officials will ignore federal immigration policy (unless it be the questionable policy of not wanting to identify illegal aliens who have committed offenses that make them removable). As Arizona points out, federal law expressly provides that state officers may "cooperate with the Attorney General in the identification, apprehension, detention, or removal of aliens not lawfully present in the United States," 8 U. S. C. §1357(g)(10)(B); and "cooperation" requires neither identical efforts nor prior federal approval. It is consistent with the Arizona statute, and with the "cooperat[ive]" system that Congress has created, for state officials to arrest a removable alien, contact federal immigration authorities, and follow their lead on what to do next. And it is an assault on logic to say that identifying a removable alien and holding him for federal determination of whether he should be removed "violates the principle that the removal process is entrusted to the discretion of the Federal Government," ante, at18. The State's detention does not represent commencement of the removal process unless the Federal Government makes it so.

But that is not the most important point. The most important point is that, as we have discussed, Arizona is entitled to have "its own immigration policy"—including a more rigorous enforcement policy—so long as that does not conflict with federal law. The Court says, as though the point is utterly dispositive, that "it is not a crime for a removable alien to remain present in the United States," ante, at 15. It is not a federal crime, to be sure. But there is no reason Arizona cannot make it a state crime for a removable alien (or any illegal alien, for that matter) to remain present in Arizona.

The Court quotes 8 U. S. C. §1226(a), which provides that, "[o]n a warrant issued by the Attorney General, an alien may be arrested and detained pending a decision on whether the alien is to be removed from the United States." Section 1357(a)(2) also provides that a federal immigration official "shall have power without warrant . . . to arrest any alien in the United States, if he has reason to believe that the alien so arrested is in the United States in violation of any [federal immigration] law or regulation and is likely to escape before a warrant can be obtained for his arrest." But statutory limitations upon the actions of federal officers in enforcing the United States' power to protect its borders do not on their face apply to the actions of state officers in enforcing the State's power to protect its borders. There is no more reason to read these provisions as implying that state officials are subject to similar limitations than there is to read them as implying that only federal officials may arrest removable aliens. And in any event neither implication would constitute the sort of clear elimination of the States' sovereign power that our cases demand.

The Court raises concerns about "unnecessary harassment of some aliens . . . whom federal officials determine should not be removed." Ante, at 17. But we have no license to assume, without any support in the record, that Arizona officials would use their arrest authority under §6 to harass anyone. And it makes no difference that federal officials might "determine [that some unlawfully present aliens] should not be removed," ibid. They may well determine not to remove from the United States aliens who have no right to be here; but unless and until these aliens have been given the right to remain, Arizona is entitled to arrest them and at least bring them to federal officials' attention, which is all that §6 necessarily entails. (In my view, the State can go further than this, and punish them for their unlawful entry and presence in Arizona.)

The Government complains that state officials might not heed "federal priorities." Indeed they might not, particularly if those priorities include willful blindness or deliberate inattention to the presence of removable aliens in Arizona. The State's whole complaint—the reason this law was passed and this case has arisen—is that the citizens of Arizona believe federal priorities are too lax. The State has the sovereign power to protect its borders more rigorously if it wishes, absent any valid federal prohibition. The Executive's policy choice of lax federal enforcement does not constitute such a prohibition.

§3

"In addition to any violation of federal law, a person is guilty of willful failure to complete or carry an alien registration document if the person is in violation of 8 [U. S. C.] §1304(e) or §1306(a)." S. B. 1070, §3(A), as amended, Ariz. Rev. Stat. Ann. §13–1509(A).

It is beyond question that a State may make violation of federal law a violation of state law as well. We have held that to be so even when the interest protected is a distinctively federal interest, such as protection of the dignity of the national flag, see Halter v. Nebraska, 205 U. S. 34 (1907), or protection of the Federal Government's ability to recruit soldiers, Gilbert v. Minnesota, 254 U. S. 325 (1920) . "[T]he State is not inhibited from making the national purposes its own purposes to the extent of exerting its police power to prevent its own citizens from obstructing the accomplishment of such purposes." Id., at 331 (internal quotation marks omitted). Much more is that so when, as here, the State is protecting its own interest, the integrity of its borders. And we have said that explicitly with regard to illegal immigration: "Despite the exclusive federal control of this Nation's borders, we cannot conclude that the States are without any power to deter the influx of persons entering the United States against federal law, and whose numbers might have a discernible impact on traditional state concerns." Plyler v. Doe, 457 U. S. 202, n. 23 (1982).

The Court's opinion relies upon Hines v. Davidowitz, supra. Ante, at 9–10. But that case did not, as the Court believes, establish a "field preemption" that implicitly eliminates the States' sovereign power to exclude those whom federal law excludes. It held that the States are not permitted to establish "additional or auxiliary" registration requirements for aliens. 312 U. S., at 66–67. But §3 does not establish additional or auxiliary registration requirements. It merely makes a violation of state law the very same failure to register and failure to carry evidence of registration that are violations of federal law. Hines does not prevent the State from relying on the federal registration system as "an available aid in the enforcement of a number of statutes of the state applicable to aliens whose constitutional validity has not been questioned." Id., at 75–76 (Stone, J., dissenting). One such statute is Arizona's law forbidding illegal aliens to collect unemployment benefits, Ariz. Rev. Stat. Ann. §23–781(B) (West 2012). To enforce that and other laws that validly turn on alien status, Arizona has, in Justice Stone's words, an interest in knowing "the number and whereabouts of aliens within the state" and in having "a means of their identification," 312 U. S., at 75. And it can punish the aliens' failure to comply with the provisions of federal law that make that knowledge and identification possible.

In some areas of uniquely federal concern—e.g., fraud in a federal administrative process (Buckman Co. v. Plaintiffs' Legal Comm., 531 U. S. 341 (2001)) or perjury in violation of a federally required oath (In re Loney, 134 U. S. 372 (1890))—this Court has held that a State has no legitimate interest in enforcing a federal scheme. But the federal alien registration system is certainly not of uniquely federal interest. States, private entities, and individuals rely on the federal registration system (including the E-Verify program) on a regular basis. Arizona's legitimate interest in protecting (among other things) its unemployment-benefits system is an entirely adequate basis for making the violation of federal registration and carry requirements a violation of state law as well.

The Court points out, however, ante, at 11, that in some respects the state law exceeds the punishments prescribed by federal law: It rules out probation and pardon, which are available under federal law. The answer is that it makes no difference. Illegal immigrants who violate §3 violate Arizona law. It is one thing to say that the Supremacy Clause prevents Arizona law from excluding those whom federal law admits. It is quite something else to say that a violation of Arizona law cannot be punished more severely than a violation of federal law. Especially where (as here) the State is defending its own sovereign interests, there is no precedent for such a limitation. The sale of illegal drugs, for example, ordinarily violates state law as well as federal law, and no one thinks that the state penalties cannot exceed the federal. As I have discussed, moreover, "field preemption" cannot establish a prohibition of additional state penalties in the area of immigration.

Finally, the Government also suggests that §3 poses an obstacle to the administration of federal immigration law, see Brief for United States 31–33, but "there is no conflict in terms, and no possibility of such conflict, [if] the state statute makes federal law its own," California v. Zook, 336 U. S. 725, 735 (1949).

It holds no fear for me, as it does for the Court, that "[w]ere §3 to come into force, the State would have the power to bring criminal charges against individuals for violating a federal law even in circumstances where federal officials in charge of the comprehensive scheme determine that prosecution would frustrate federal policies." Ante, at 11. That seems to me entirely appropriate when the State uses the federal law (as it must) as the criterion for the exercise of its own power, and the implementation of its own policies of excluding those who do not belong there. What I do fear—and what Arizona and the States that support it fear—is that "federal policies" of nonenforcement will leave the States helpless before those evil effects of illegal immigration that the Court's opinion dutifully recites in its prologue (ante, at 6) but leaves unremedied in its disposition.

§5(C)

"It is unlawful for a person who is unlawfully present in the United States and who is an unauthorized alien to knowingly apply for work, solicit work in a public place or perform work as an employee or independent contractor in this state." S. B. 1070, §5(C), as amended, Ariz. Rev. Stat. Ann. §13–2928(C).

Here, the Court rightly starts with De Canas v. Bica, 424 U. S. 351 (1976), which involved a California law providing that " '[n]o employer shall knowingly employ an alien who is not entitled to lawful residence in the United States if such employment would have an adverse effect on lawful resident workers.' " Id., at 352 (quoting California Labor Code Ann. §2805(a)). This Court concluded that the California law was not pre-empted, as Congress had neither occupied the field of "regulation of employment of illegal aliens" nor expressed "the clear and manifest purpose" of displacing such state regulation. Id., at 356–357 (internal quotation marks omitted). Thus, at the time De Canas was decided, §5(C) would have been indubitably lawful.

The only relevant change is that Congress has since enacted its own restrictions on employers who hire illegal aliens, 8 U. S. C. §1324a, in legislation that also includes some civil (but no criminal) penalties on illegal aliens who accept unlawful employment. The Court concludes from this (reasonably enough) "that Congress made a deliberate choice not to impose criminal penalties on aliens who seek, or engage in, unauthorized employment," ante, at 13. But that is not the same as a deliberate choice to prohibit the States from imposing criminal penalties. Congress's intent with regard to exclusion of state law need not be guessed at, but is found in the law's express pre-emption provision, which excludes "any State or local law impos-ing civil or criminal sanctions (other than through licensing and similar laws) upon those who employ, or recruit or refer for a fee for employment, unauthorized aliens," §1324a(h)(2) (emphasis added). Common sense, reflected in the canon *expressio unius est exclusio alterius*, suggests that the specification of pre-emption for laws punishing "those who employ" implies the lack of pre-emption for other laws, including laws punishing "those who seek or accept employment."

The Court has no credible response to this. It quotes our jurisprudence to the effect that an "express pre-emption provisio[n] does not bar the ordinary working of conflict pre-emption principles." Ante, at 14 (quoting Geier v. American Honda Motor Co., 529 U. S. 861(2000) (internal quotation marks omitted)). True enough—conflict preemption principles. It then goes on say that since "Congress decided it would be inappropriate to impose criminal penalties on aliens who seek or engage in unauthorized employment," "[i]t follows that a state law to the contrary is an obstacle to the regulatory system Congress chose." Ante, at 15. For " '[w]here a comprehensive federal scheme intentionally leaves a portion of the regulated field without controls, then the pre-emptive inference can be drawn.' " Ibid. (quoting Puerto Rico Dept. of Consumer Affairs v. ISLA Petroleum Corp., 485 U.S. 495, 503 (1988)). All that is a classic description not of conflict pre-emption but of field pre-emption, which (concededly) does not occur beyond the terms of an express pre-emption provision.

The Court concludes that §5(C) "would interfere with the careful balance struck by Congress," ante, at 15, (another field pre-emption notion, by the way) but that is easy to say and impossible to demonstrate. The Court relies primarily on the fact that "[p]roposals to make unauthorized work a criminal offense were debated and discussed during the long process of drafting [the Immigration Reform and Control Act of 1986 (IRCA)]," "[b]ut Congress rejected them." Ante, at 14. There is no more reason to believe that this rejection was expressive of a desire that there be no sanctions on employees, than expressive of a desire that such sanctions be left to the States. To tell the truth, it was most likely expressive of what inaction ordinarily expresses: nothing at all. It is a "naïve assumption that the failure of a bill to make it out of committee, or to be adopted when reported to the floor, is the same as a congressional rejection of what the bill contained." Crosby v. National Foreign Trade Council, 530 U. S. 363, 389 (2000) (Scalia, J., concurring in judgment) (internal quotation marks and alterations omitted).

*   *   *

The brief for the Government in this case asserted that "the Executive Branch's ability to exercise discretion and set priorities is particularly important because of the need to allocate scarce enforcement resources wisely." Brief for United States 21. Of course there is no reason why the Federal Executive's need to allocate its scarce enforcement resources should disable Arizona from devoting its resources to illegal immigration in Arizona that in its view the Federal Executive has given short shrift. Despite Congress's prescription that "the immigration laws of the United States should be enforced vigorously and uniformly," IRCA §115, 100Stat. 3384, Arizona asserts without contradiction and with supporting citations:

"[I]n the last decade federal enforcement efforts have focused primarily on areas in California and Texas, leaving Arizona's border to suffer from comparative neglect. The result has been the funneling of an increasing tide of illegal border crossings into Arizona. Indeed, over the past decade, over a third of the Nation's illegal border crossings occurred in Arizona." Brief for Petitioners 2–3 (footnote omitted).

Must Arizona's ability to protect its borders yield to the reality that Congress has provided inadequate funding for federal enforcement—or, even worse, to the Executive's unwise targeting of that funding?

But leave that aside. It has become clear that federal enforcement priorities—in the sense of priorities based on the need to allocate "scarce enforcement resources"—is not the problem here. After this case was argued and while it was under consideration, the Secretary of Homeland Security announced a program exempting from immigration enforcement some 1.4 million illegal immigrants under the age of 30. 4 If an individual unlawfully present in the United States

"• came to the United States under the age of sixteen;

"• has continuously resided in the United States for at least five years . . .,

"• is currently in school, has graduated from high school, has obtained a general education development certificate, or is an honorably discharged veteran . . .,

"• has not been convicted of a [serious crime]; and

"• is not above the age of thirty," 5

then U. S. immigration officials have been directed to "defe[r] action" against such individual "for a period of two years, subject to renewal." 6 The husbanding of scarce enforcement resources can hardly be the justification for this, since the considerable administrative cost of conducting as many as 1.4 million background checks, and ruling on the biennial requests for dispensation that the nonenforcement program envisions, will necessarily be deducted from immigration enforcement. The President said at a news conference that the new program is "the right thing to do" in light of Congress's failure to pass the Administration's proposed revision of the Immigration Act. 7 Perhaps it is, though Arizona may not think so. But to say, as the Court does, that Arizona contradicts federal law by enforcing applications of the Immigration Act that the President declines to enforce boggles the mind.

The Court opinion's looming specter of inutterable horror—"[i]f §3 of the Arizona statute were valid, every State could give itself independent authority to prosecute federal registration violations," ante, at 10—seems to me not so horrible and even less looming. But there has come to pass, and is with us today, the specter that Arizona and the States that support it predicted: A Federal Government that does not want to enforce the immigration laws as written, and leaves the States' borders unprotected against immigrants whom those laws would exclude. So the issue is a stark one. Are the sovereign States at the mercy of the Federal Executive's refusal to enforce the Nation's immigration laws?

A good way of answering that question is to ask: Would the States conceivably have entered into the Union if the Constitution itself contained the Court's holding? Today's judgment surely fails that test. At the Constitutional Convention of 1787, the delegates contended with "the jealousy of the states with regard to their sovereignty." 1 Records of the Federal Convention 19 (M. Farrand ed. 1911) (statement of Edmund Randolph). Through ratification of the fundamental charter that the Convention produced, the States ceded much of their sovereignty to the Federal Government. But much of it remained jealously guarded—as reflected in the innumerable proposals that never left Independence Hall. Now, imagine a provision—perhaps inserted right after Art. I, §8, cl. 4, the Naturalization Clause—which included among the enumerated powers of Congress "To establish Limitations upon Immigration that will be exclusive and that will be enforced only to the extent the President deems appropriate." The delegates to the Grand Convention would have rushed to the exits.

As is often the case, discussion of the dry legalities that are the proper object of our attention suppresses the very human realities that gave rise to the suit. Arizona bears the brunt of the country's illegal immigration problem. Its citizens feel themselves under siege by large numbers of illegal immigrants who invade their property, strain their social services, and even place their lives in jeopardy. Federal officials have been unable to remedy the problem, and indeed have recently shown that they are unwilling to do so. Thousands of Arizona's estimated 400,000 illegal immigrants—including not just children but men and women under 30—are now assured immunity from enforcement, and will be able to compete openly with Ari-zona citizens for employment.

Arizona has moved to protect its sovereignty—not in contradiction of federal law, but in complete compliance with it. The laws under challenge here do not extend or revise federal immigration restrictions, but merely enforce those restrictions more effectively. If securing its territory in this fashion is not within the power of Arizona, we should cease referring to it as a sovereign State. I dissent.

Justice Scalia's dissent in NFIB v. Sebelius (June 28, 2012)

Justice Scalia, Justice Kennedy, Justice Thomas, and Justice Alito, dissenting.

Congress has set out to remedy the problem that the best health care is beyond the reach of many Americans who cannot afford it. It can assuredly do that, by exercising the powers accorded to it under the Constitution. The question in this case, however, is whether the complex structures and provisions of the Patient Protection and Affordable Care Act (Affordable Care Act or ACA) go beyond those powers. We conclude that they do.

This case is in one respect difficult: it presents two questions of first impression. The first of those is whether failure to engage in economic activity (the purchase of health insurance) is subject to regulation under the Commerce Clause. Failure to act does result in an effect on commerce, and hence might be said to come under this Court's "affecting commerce" criterion of Commerce Clause jurisprudence. But in none of its decisions has this Court extended the Clause that far. The second question is whether the congressional power to tax and spend, U. S. Const., Art. I, §8, cl. 1, permits the conditioning of a State's continued receipt of all funds under a massive state-administered federal welfare program upon its acceptance of an expansion to that program. Several of our opinions have suggested that the power to tax and spend cannot be used to coerce state administration of a federal program, but we have never found a law enacted under the spending power to be coercive. Those questions are difficult.

The case is easy and straightforward, however, in another respect. What is absolutely clear, affirmed by the text of the 1789 Constitution, by the Tenth Amendment ratified in 1791, and by innumerable cases of ours in the 220 years since, is that there are structural limits upon federal power—upon what it can prescribe with respect to private conduct, and upon what it can impose upon the sovereign States. Whatever may be the conceptual limits upon the Commerce Clause and upon the power to tax and spend, they cannot be such as will enable the Federal Government to regulate all private conduct and to compel the States to function as administrators of federal programs.

That clear principle carries the day here. The striking case of Wickard v. Filburn, 317 U. S. 111 (1942), which held that the economic activity of growing wheat, even for one's own consumption, affected commerce sufficiently that it could be regulated, always has been regarded as the ne plus ultra of expansive Commerce Clause jurisprudence. To go beyond that, and to say the failure to grow wheat (which is not an economic activity, or any activity at all) nonetheless affects commerce and therefore can be federally regulated, is to make mere breathing in and out the basis for federal prescription and to extend federal power to virtually all human activity.

As for the constitutional power to tax and spend for the general welfare: The Court has long since expanded that beyond (what Madison thought it meant) taxing and spending for those aspects of the general welfare that were within the Federal Government's enumerated powers, see United States v. Butler, 297 U. S. 1–66 (1936). Thus, we now have sizable federal Departments devoted to subjects not mentioned among Congress' enumerated powers, and only marginally related to commerce: the Department of Education, the Department of Health and Human Services, the Department of Housing and Urban Development. The principal practical obstacle that prevents Congress from using the tax-and-spend power to assume all the general-welfare responsibilities traditionally exercised by the States is the sheer impossibility of managing a Federal Government large enough to administer such a system. That obstacle can be overcome by granting funds to the States, allowing them to administer the program. That is fair and constitutional enough when the States freely agree to have their powers employed and their employees enlisted in the federal scheme. But it is a blatant violation of the constitutional structure when the States have no choice.

The Act before us here exceeds federal power both in mandating the purchase of health insurance and in denying nonconsenting States all Medicaid funding. These parts of the Act are central to its design and operation, and all the Act's other provisions would not have been enacted without them. In our view it must follow that the entire statute is inoperative.

I

The Individual Mandate

Article I, §8, of the Constitution gives Congress the power to "regulate Commerce . . . among the several States." The Individual Mandate in the Act commands that every "applicable individual shall for each month beginning after 2013 ensure that the individual, and any dependent of the individual who is an applicable individual, is covered under minimum essential coverage." 26 U. S. C. §5000A(a) (2006 ed., Supp. IV). If this provision "regulates" anything, it is the failure to maintain minimum essential coverage. One might argue that it regulates that failure by requiring it to be accompanied by payment of a penalty. But that failure—that abstention from commerce—is not "Commerce." To be sure, purchasing insurance is "Commerce"; but one does not regulate commerce that does not exist by compelling its existence.

In Gibbons v. Ogden, 9 Wheat. 1, 196 (1824), Chief Justice Marshall wrote that the power to regulate commerce is the power "to prescribe the rule by which commerce is to be governed." That understanding is consistent with the original meaning of "regulate" at the time of the Constitution's ratification, when "to regulate" meant "[t]o adjust by rule, method or established mode," 2 N. Webster, An American Dictionary of the English Language (1828); "[t]o adjust by rule or method," 2 S. Johnson, A Dictionary of the English Language (7th ed. 1785); "[t]o adjust, to direct according to rule," 2 J. Ash, New and Complete Dictionary of the English Language (1775); "to put in order, set to rights, govern or keep in order," T. Dyche & W. Pardon, A New General English Dictionary (16th ed. 1777). 1 It can mean to direct the manner of something but not to direct that something come into being. There is no instance in which this Court or Congress (or anyone else, to our knowledge) has used "regulate" in that peculiar fashion. If the word bore that meaning, Congress' authority "[t]o make Rules for the Government and Regulation of the land and naval Forces," U. S. Const., Art. I, §8, cl. 14, would have made superfluous the later provision for authority "[t]o raise and support Armies," id., §8, cl. 12, and "[t]o provide and maintain a Navy," id., §8, cl. 13.

We do not doubt that the buying and selling of health insurance contracts is commerce generally subject to federal regulation. But when Congress provides that (nearly) all citizens must buy an insurance contract, it goes beyond "adjust[ing] by rule or method," Johnson, supra, or "direct[ing] according to rule," Ash, supra; it directs the creation of commerce.

In response, the Government offers two theories as to why the Individual Mandate is nevertheless constitutional. Neither theory suffices to sustain its validity.

A

First, the Government submits that §5000A is "integral to the Affordable Care Act's insurance reforms" and "necessary to make effective the Act's core reforms." Brief for Petitioners in No. 11–398 (Minimum Coverage Provision) 24 (hereinafter Petitioners' Minimum Coverage Brief). Congress included a "finding" to similar effect in the Act itself. See 42 U. S. C. §18091(2)(H).

As discussed in more detail in Part V, infra, the Act contains numerous health insurance reforms, but most notable for present purposes are the "guaranteed issue" and "community rating" provisions, §§300gg to 300gg–4. The former provides that, with a few exceptions, "each health insurance issuer that offers health insurance coverage in the individual or group market in a State must accept every employer and individual in the State that applies for such coverage." §300gg–1(a). That is, an insurer may not deny coverage on the basis of, among other things, any pre-existing medical condition that the applicant may have, and the resulting insurance must cover that condition. See §300gg–3.

Under ordinary circumstances, of course, insurers would respond by charging high premiums to individuals with pre-existing conditions. The Act seeks to prevent this through the community-rating provision. Simply put, the community-rating provision requires insurers to calculate an individual's insurance premium based on only four factors: (i) whether the individual's plan covers just the individual or his family also, (ii) the "rating area" in which the individual lives, (iii) the individual's age, and (iv) whether the individual uses tobacco. §300gg(a)(1)(A). Aside from the rough proxies of age and tobacco use (and possibly rating area), the Act does not allow an insurer to factor the individual's health characteristics into the price of his insurance premium. This creates a new incentive for young and healthy individuals without pre-existing conditions. The insurance premiums for those in this group will not reflect their own low actuarial risks but will subsidize insurance for others in the pool. Many of them may decide that purchasing health insurance is not an economically sound decision—especially since the guaranteed-issue provision will enable them to purchase it at the same cost in later years and even if they have developed a pre-existing condition. But without the contribution of above-risk premiums from the young and healthy, the community-rating provision will not enable insurers to take on high-risk individuals without a massive increase in premiums.

The Government presents the Individual Mandate as a unique feature of a complicated regulatory scheme governing many parties with countervailing incentives that must be carefully balanced. Congress has imposed an extensive set of regulations on the health insurance industry, and compliance with those regulations will likely cost the industry a great deal. If the industry does not respond by increasing premiums, it is not likely to survive. And if the industry does increase premiums, then there is a serious risk that its products—insurance plans—will become economically undesirable for many and prohibitively ex-pensive for the rest.

This is not a dilemma unique to regulation of the health-insurance industry. Government regulation typically imposes costs on the regulated industry—especially regulation that prohibits economic behavior in which most market participants are already engaging, such as "piecing out" the market by selling the product to different classes of people at different prices (in the present context, providing much lower insurance rates to young and healthy buyers). And many industries so regulated face the reality that, without an artificial increase in demand, they cannot continue on. When Congress is regulating these industries directly, it enjoys the broad power to enact " 'all appropriate legislation' " to " 'protec[t]' " and " 'advanc[e]' " commerce, NLRB v. Jones & Laughlin Steel Corp., 301 U. S. 1–37 (1937) (quoting The Daniel Ball, 10 Wall. 557, 564 (1871)). Thus, Congress might protect the imperiled industry by prohibiting low-cost competition, or by according it preferential tax treatment, or even by granting it a direct subsidy.

Here, however, Congress has impressed into service third parties, healthy individuals who could be but are not customers of the relevant industry, to offset the undesirable consequences of the regulation. Congress' desire to force these individuals to purchase insurance is motivated by the fact that they are further removed from the market than unhealthy individuals with pre-existing conditions, because they are less likely to need extensive care in the near future. If Congress can reach out and command even those furthest removed from an interstate market to participate in the market, then the Commerce Clause becomes a font of unlimited power, or in Hamilton's words, "the hideous monster whose devouring jaws . . . spare neither sex nor age, nor high nor low, nor sacred nor profane." The Federalist No. 33, p. 202 (C. Rossiter ed. 1961).

At the outer edge of the commerce power, this Court has insisted on careful scrutiny of regulations that do not act directly on an interstate market or its participants. In New York v. United States, 505 U. S. 144 (1992), we held that Congress could not, in an effort to regulate the disposal of radioactive waste produced in several different industries, order the States to take title to that waste. Id., at 174–177. In Printz v. United States, 521 U. S.898 (1997), we held that Congress could not, in an effort to regulate the distribution of firearms in the interstate market, compel state law-enforcement officials to perform background checks. Id., at 933–935. In United States v. Lopez, 514 U. S. 549 (1995), we held that Congress could not, as a means of fostering an educated interstate labor market through the protection of schools, ban the possession of a firearm within a school zone. Id., at 559–563. And in United States v. Morrison, 529 U. S. 598 (2000), we held that Congress could not, in an effort to ensure the full participation of women in the interstate economy, subject private individuals and companies to suit for gender-motivated violent torts. Id., at 609–619. The lesson of these cases is that the Commerce Clause, even when supplemented by the Necessary and Proper Clause, is not carte blanche for doing whatever will help achieve the ends Congress seeks by the regulation of commerce. And the last two of these cases show that the scope of the Necessary and Proper Clause is exceeded not only when the congressional action directly violates the sovereignty of the States but also when it violates the background principle of enumerated (and hence limited) federal power.

The case upon which the Government principally relies to sustain the Individual Mandate under the Necessary and Proper Clause is Gonzales v. Raich, 545 U. S. 1 (2005) . That case held that Congress could, in an effort to restrain the interstate market in marijuana, ban the local cultivation and possession of that drug. Id., at 15–22. Raich is no precedent for what Congress has done here. That case's prohibition of growing (cf. Wickard, 317 U. S. 111), and of possession (cf. innumerable federal statutes) did not represent the expansion of the federal power to direct into a broad new field. The mandating of economic activity does, and since it is a field so limitless that it converts the Commerce Clause into a general authority to direct the economy, that mandating is not "consist[ent] with the letter and spirit of the constitution." McCulloch v. Maryland, 4 Wheat. 316, 421 (1819).

Moreover, Raich is far different from the Individual Mandate in another respect. The Court's opinion in Raich pointed out that the growing and possession prohibitions were the only practicable way of enabling the prohibition of interstate traffic in marijuana to be effectively enforced. 545 U. S., at 22. See also Shreveport Rate Cases, 234 U. S. 342 (1914) (Necessary and Proper Clause allows regulations of intrastate transactions if necessary to the regulation of an interstate market). Intrastate marijuana could no more be distinguished from interstate marijuana than, for example, endangered-species trophies obtained before the species was federally protected can be distinguished from trophies obtained afterwards—which made it necessary and proper to prohibit the sale of all such trophies, see Andrus v. Allard, 444 U. S. 51 (1979) .

With the present statute, by contrast, there are many ways other than this unprecedented Individual Mandate by which the regulatory scheme's goals of reducing insurance premiums and ensuring the profitability of insurers could be achieved. For instance, those who did not purchase insurance could be subjected to a surcharge when they do enter the health insurance system. Or they could be denied a full income tax credit given to those who do purchase the insurance.

The Government was invited, at oral argument, to suggest what federal controls over private conduct (other than those explicitly prohibited by the Bill of Rights or other constitutional controls) could not be justified as necessary and proper for the carrying out of a general regulatory scheme. See Tr. of Oral Arg. 27–30, 43–45 (Mar. 27, 2012). It was unable to name any. As we said at the outset, whereas the precise scope of the Commerce Clause and the Necessary and Proper Clause is uncertain, the proposition that the Federal Government cannot do everything is a fundamental precept. See Lopez, 514 U. S., at 564 ("[I]f we were to accept the Government's arguments, we are hard pressed to posit any activity by an in-dividual that Congress is without power to regulate"). Section 5000A is defeated by that proposition.

B

The Government's second theory in support of the Individual Mandate is that §5000A is valid because it is actually a "regulat[ion of] activities having a substantial relation to interstate commerce, . . . i.e., . . . activities that substantially affect interstate commerce." Id., at 558–559. See also Shreveport Rate Cases, supra. This argument takes a few different forms, but the basic idea is that §5000A regulates "the way in which individuals finance their participation in the health-care market." Petitioners' Minimum Coverage Brief 33 (emphasis added). That is, the provision directs the manner in which individuals purchase health care services and related goods (directing that they be purchased through insurance) and is therefore a straightforward exercise of the commerce power.

The primary problem with this argument is that §5000A does not apply only to persons who purchase all, or most, or even any, of the health care services or goods that the mandated insurance covers. Indeed, the main objection many have to the Mandate is that they have no intention of purchasing most or even any of such goods or services and thus no need to buy insurance for those purchases. The Government responds that the health-care market involves "essentially universal participation," id., at 35. The principal difficulty with this response is that it is, in the only relevant sense, not true. It is true enough that everyone consumes "health care," if the term is taken to include the purchase of a bottle of aspirin. But the health care "market" that is the object of the Individual Mandate not only includes but principally consists of goods and services that the young people primarily affected by the Mandate do not purchase. They are quite simply not participants in that market, and cannot be made so (and thereby subjected to regulation) by the simple device of defining participants to include all those who will, later in their lifetime, probably purchase the goods or services covered by the mandated insurance. 2 Such a definition of market participants is unprecedented, and were it to be a premise for the exercise of national power, it would have no principled limits.

In a variation on this attempted exercise of federal power, the Government points out that Congress in this Act has purported to regulate "economic and financial decision[s] to forego [sic] health insurance coverage and [to] attempt to self-insure," 42 U. S. C. §18091(2)(A), since those decisions have "a substantial and deleterious effect on interstate commerce," Petitioners' Minimum Coverage Brief 34. But as the discussion above makes clear, the decision to forgo participation in an interstate market is not itself commercial activity (or indeed any activity at all) within Congress' power to regulate. It is true that, at the end of the day, it is inevitable that each American will affect commerce and become a part of it, even if not by choice. But if every person comes within the Commerce Clause power of Congress to regulate by the simple reason that he will one day engage in commerce, the idea of a limited Government power is at an end.

Wickard v. Filburn has been regarded as the most expansive assertion of the commerce power in our history. A close second is Perez v. United States, 402 U. S. 146 (1971), which upheld a statute criminalizing the eminently local activity of loan-sharking. Both of those cases, however, involved commercial activity. To go beyond that, and to say that the failure to grow wheat or the refusal to make loans affects commerce, so that growing and lending can be federally compelled, is to extend federal power to virtually everything. All of us consume food, and when we do so the Federal Government can prescribe what its quality must be and even how much we must pay. But the mere fact that we all consume food and are thus, sooner or later, participants in the "market" for food, does not empower the Government to say when and what we will buy. That is essentially what this Act seeks to do with respect to the purchase of health care. It exceeds federal power.

C

A few respectful responses to Justice Ginsburg's dissent on the issue of the Mandate are in order. That dissent duly recites the test of Commerce Clause power that our opinions have applied, but disregards the premise the test contains. It is true enough that Congress needs only a " 'rational basis' for concluding that the regulated activity substantially affects interstate commerce," ante, at 15 (emphasis added). But it must be activity affecting commerce that is regulated, and not merely the failure to engage in commerce. And one is not now purchasing the health care covered by the insurance mandate simply because one is likely to be purchasing it in the future. Our test's premise of regulated activity is not invented out of whole cloth, but rests upon the Constitution's requirement that it be commerce which is regulated. If all inactivity affecting commerce is commerce, commerce is everything. Ultimately the dissent is driven to saying that there is really no difference between action and inaction, ante, at 26, a proposition that has never recommended itself, neither to the law nor to common sense. To say, for example, that the inaction here consists of activity in "the self-insurance market," ibid., seems to us wordplay. By parity of reasoning the failure to buy a car can be called participation in the non-private-car-transportation market. Commerce becomes everything.

The dissent claims that we "fai[l] to explain why the individual mandate threatens our constitutional order." Ante, at 35. But we have done so. It threatens that order because it gives such an expansive meaning to the Commerce Clause that all private conduct (including failure to act) becomes subject to federal control, effectively destroying the Constitution's division of governmental powers. Thus the dissent, on the theories proposed for the validity of the Mandate, would alter the accepted constitutional relation between the individual and the National Government. The dissent protests that the Necessary and Proper Clause has been held to include "the power to enact criminal laws, . . . the power to imprison, . . . and the power to create a national bank," ante, at 34–35. Is not the power to compel purchase of health insurance much lesser? No, not if (unlike those other dispositions) its application rests upon a theory that everything is within federal control simply because it exists.

The dissent's exposition of the wonderful things the Federal Government has achieved through exercise of its assigned powers, such as "the provision of old-age and survivors' benefits" in the Social Security Act, ante, at 2, is quite beside the point. The issue here is whether the federal government can impose the Individual Mandate through the Commerce Clause. And the relevant history is not that Congress has achieved wide and wonderful results through the proper exercise of its assigned powers in the past, but that it has never before used the Commerce Clause to compel entry into commerce. 3 The dissent treats the Constitution as though it is an enumeration of those problems that the Federal Government can address—among which, it finds, is "the Nation's course in the economic and social welfare realm," ibid., and more specifically "the problem of the uninsured," ante, at 7. The Constitution is not that. It enumerates not federally soluble problems, but federally available powers. The Federal Government can address whatever problems it wants but can bring to their solution only those powers that the Constitution confers, among which is the power to regulate commerce. None of our cases say anything else. Article I contains no whatever-it-takes-to-solve-a-national-problem power.

The dissent dismisses the conclusion that the power to compel entry into the health-insurance market would include the power to compel entry into the new-car or broccoli markets. The latter purchasers, it says, "will be obliged to pay at the counter before receiving the vehicle or nourishment," whereas those refusing to purchase health-insurance will ultimately get treated anyway, at others' expense. Ante, at 21. "[T]he unique attributes of the health-care market . . . give rise to a significant free-riding problem that does not occur in other markets." Ante, at 28. And "a vegetable-purchase mandate" (or a car-purchase mandate) is not "likely to have a substantial effect on the health-care costs" borne by other Americans. Ante, at 29. Those differences make a very good argument by the dissent's own lights, since they show that the failure to purchase health insurance, unlike the failure to purchase cars or broccoli, creates a national, social-welfare problem that is (in the dissent's view) included among the unenumerated "problems" that the Constitution authorizes the Federal Government to solve. But those differences do not show that the failure to enter the health-insurance market, unlike the failure to buy cars and broccoli, is an activity that Congress can "regulate." (Of course one day the failure of some of the public to purchase American cars may endanger the existence of domestic automobile manufacturers; or the failure of some to eat broccoli may be found to deprive them of a newly discovered cancer-fighting chemical which only that food contains, producing health-care costs that are a burden on the rest of us—in which case, under the theory of Justice Ginsburg's dissent, moving against those inactivities will also come within the Federal Government's unenumerated problem-solving powers.)

II

The Taxing Power

As far as §5000A is concerned, we would stop there. Congress has attempted to regulate beyond the scope of its Commerce Clause authority, 4 and §5000A is therefore invalid. The Government contends, however, as expressed in the caption to Part II of its brief, that "the minimum coverage provision is independently authorized by congress's taxing power." Petitioners' Minimum Coverage Brief 52. The phrase "independently authorized" suggests the existence of a creature never hitherto seen in the United States Reports: A penalty for constitutional purposes that is also a tax for constitutional purposes. In all our cases the two are mutually exclusive. The provision challenged under the Constitution is either a penalty or else a tax. Of course in many cases what was a regulatory mandate enforced by a penalty could have been imposed as a tax upon permissible action; or what was imposed as a tax upon permissible action could have been a regulatory mandate enforced by a penalty. But we know of no case, and the Government cites none, in which the imposition was, for constitutional purposes, both. 5 The two are mutually exclusive. Thus, what the Government's caption should have read was "alternatively, the minimum coverage provision is not a mandate-with-penalty but a tax." It is important to bear this in mind in evaluating the tax argument of the Government and of those who support it: The issue is not whether Congress had the power to frame the minimum-coverage provision as a tax, but whether it did so.

In answering that question we must, if "fairly possible," Crowell v. Benson, 285 U. S. 22, 62 (1932), construe the provision to be a tax rather than a mandate-with-penalty, since that would render it constitutional rather than un-constitutional (*ut res magis valeat quam pereat*). But we cannot rewrite the statute to be what it is not. " ' "[A]l-though this Court will often strain to construe legislation so as to save it against constitutional attack, it must not and will not carry this to the point of perverting the purpose of a statute . . ." or judicially rewriting it.' " Commodity Futures Trading Comm'n v. Schor, 478 U. S. 833, 841 (1986) (quoting Aptheker v. Secretary of State, 378 U. S. 500, 515 (1964), in turn quoting Scales v. United States, 367 U. S. 203, 211 (1961)). In this case, there is simply no way, "without doing violence to the fair meaning of the words used," Grenada County Supervisors v. Brogden, 112 U. S. 261, 269 (1884), to escape what Congress enacted: a mandate that individuals maintain minimum essential coverage, enforced by a penalty.

Our cases establish a clear line between a tax and a penalty: " '[A] tax is an enforced contribution to provide for the support of government; a penalty . . . is an exaction imposed by statute as punishment for an unlawful act.' " United States v. Reorganized CF&I Fabricators of Utah, Inc., 518 U. S. 213, 224 (1996) (quoting United States v. La Franca, 282 U. S. 568, 572 (1931)). In a few cases, this Court has held that a "tax" imposed upon private conduct was so onerous as to be in effect a penalty. But we have never held—never—that a penalty imposed for violation of the law was so trivial as to be in effect a tax. We have never held that any exaction imposed for violation of the law is an exercise of Congress' taxing power—even when the statute calls it a tax, much less when (as here) the statute repeatedly calls it a penalty. When an act "adopt[s] the criteria of wrongdoing" and then imposes a monetary penalty as the "principal consequence on those who transgress its standard," it creates a regulatory penalty, not a tax. Child Labor Tax Case, 259 U. S. 20, 38 (1922) .

So the question is, quite simply, whether the exaction here is imposed for violation of the law. It unquestionably is. The minimum-coverage provision is found in 26 U. S. C. §5000A, entitled "Requirement to maintain minimum essential coverage." (Emphasis added.) It commands that every "applicable individual shall . . . ensure that the individual . . . is covered under minimum essential coverage." Ibid. (emphasis added). And the immediately following provision states that, "[i]f . . . an applicable individual . . . fails to meet the requirement of subsection (a) . . . there is hereby imposed . . . a penalty." §5000A(b) (emphasis added). And several of Congress' legislative "findings" with regard to §5000A confirm that it sets forth a legal requirement and constitutes the assertion of regulatory power, not mere taxing power. See 42 U. S. C. §18091(2)(A) ("The requirement regulates activity . . ."); §18091(2)(C) ("The requirement . . . will add millions of new consumers to the health insurance market . . ."); §18091(2)(D) ("The requirement achieves near-universal coverage"); §18091(2)(H) ("The requirement is an essential part of this larger regulation of economic activity, and the absence of the requirement would undercut Federal regulation of the health insurance market"); §18091(3) ("[T]he Supreme Court of the United States ruled that insurance is interstate commerce subject to Federal regulation").

The Government and those who support its view on the tax point rely on New York v. United States, 505 U. S. 144, to justify reading "shall" to mean "may." The "shall" in that case was contained in an introductory provision—a recital that provided for no legal consequences—which said that "[e]ach State shall be responsible for providing . . . for the disposal of . . . low-level radioactive waste." 42 U. S. C. §2021c(a)(1)(A). The Court did not hold that "shall" could be construed to mean "may," but rather that this preliminary provision could not impose upon the operative provisions of the Act a mandate that they did not contain: "We . . . decline petitioners' invitation to construe §2021c(a)(1)(A), alone and in isolation, as a command to the States independent of the remainder of the Act." New York, 505 U. S., at 170. Our opinion then proceeded to "consider each [of the three operative provisions] in turn." Ibid. Here the mandate—the "shall"—is contained not in an inoperative preliminary recital, but in the dispositive operative provision itself. New York provides no support for reading it to be permissive.

Quite separately, the fact that Congress (in its own words) "imposed . . . a penalty," 26 U. S. C. §5000A(b)(1), for failure to buy insurance is alone sufficient to render that failure unlawful. It is one of the canons of interpretation that a statute that penalizes an act makes it unlawful: "[W]here the statute inflicts a penalty for doing an act, although the act itself is not expressly prohibited, yet to do the act is unlawful, because it cannot be supposed that the Legislature intended that a penalty should be inflicted for a lawful act." Powhatan Steamboat Co. v. Appomattox R. Co., 24 How. 247, 252 (1861). Or in the words of Chancellor Kent: "If a statute inflicts a penalty for doing an act, the penalty implies a prohibition, and the thing is unlawful, though there be no prohibitory words in the statute." 1 J. Kent, Commentaries on American Law 436 (1826).

We never have classified as a tax an exaction imposed for violation of the law, and so too, we never have classified as a tax an exaction described in the legislation itself as a penalty. To be sure, we have sometimes treated as a tax a statutory exaction (imposed for something other than a violation of law) which bore an agnostic label that does not entail the significant constitutional consequences of a penalty—such as "license" (License Tax Cases, 5 Wall. 462 (1867)) or "surcharge" (New York v. United States, supra.). But we have never—never—treated as a tax an exaction which faces up to the critical difference between a tax and a penalty, and explicitly denominates the exaction a "penalty." Eighteen times in §5000A itself and else-where throughout the Act, Congress called the exaction in §5000A(b) a "penalty."

That §5000A imposes not a simple tax but a mandate to which a penalty is attached is demonstrated by the fact that some are exempt from the tax who are not exempt from the mandate—a distinction that would make no sense if the mandate were not a mandate. Section 5000A(d) exempts three classes of people from the definition of "applicable individual" subject to the minimum coverage requirement: Those with religious objections or who participate in a "health care sharing ministry," §5000A(d)(2); those who are "not lawfully present" in the United States, §5000A(d)(3); and those who are incarcerated, §5000A(d)(4). Section 5000A(e) then creates a separate set of exemptions, excusing from liability for the penalty certain individuals who are subject to the minimum coverage requirement: Those who cannot afford coverage, §5000A(e)(1); who earn too little income to require filing a tax return, §5000A(e)(2); who are members of an Indian tribe, §5000A(e)(3); who experience only short gaps in coverage,

§5000A(e)(4); and who, in the judgment of the Secretary of Health and Human Services, "have suffered a hardship with respect to the capability to obtain coverage," §5000A(e)(5). If §5000A were a tax, these two classes of exemption would make no sense; there being no requirement, all the exemptions would attach to the penalty (renamed tax) alone.

In the face of all these indications of a regulatory requirement accompanied by a penalty, the Solicitor General assures us that "neither the Treasury Department nor the Department of Health and Human Services interprets Section 5000A as imposing a legal obligation," Petitioners' Minimum Coverage Brief 61, and that "[i]f [those subject to the Act] pay the tax penalty, they're in compliance with the law," Tr. of Oral Arg. 50 (Mar. 26, 2012). These self-serving litigating positions are entitled to no weight. What counts is what the statute says, and that is entirely clear. It is worth noting, moreover, that these assurances contradict the Government's position in related litigation. Shortly before the Affordable Care Act was passed, the Commonwealth of Virginia enacted Va. Code Ann. §38.2–3430.1:1 (Lexis Supp. 2011), which states, "No resident of [the] Commonwealth . . . shall be required to obtain or maintain a policy of individual insurance coverage except as required by a court or the Department of Social Services . . . ." In opposing Virginia's assertion of standing to challenge §5000A based on this statute, the Government said that "if the minimum coverage provision is unconstitutional, the [Virginia] statute is unnecessary, and if the minimum coverage provision is upheld, the state statute is void under the Supremacy Clause." Brief for Appellant in No. 11–1057 etc. (CA4), p. 29. But it would be void under the Supremacy Clause only if it was contradicted by a federal "require[ment] to obtain or maintain a policy of individual insurance coverage."

Against the mountain of evidence that the minimum coverage requirement is what the statute calls it—a requirement—and that the penalty for its violation is what the statute calls it—a penalty—the Government brings forward the flimsiest of indications to the contrary. It notes that "[t]he minimum coverage provision amends the Internal Revenue Code to provide that a non-exempted individual . . . will owe a monetary penalty, in addition to the income tax itself," and that "[t]he [Internal Revenue Service (IRS)] will assess and collect the penalty in the same manner as assessable penalties under the Internal Revenue Code." Petitioners' Minimum Coverage Brief 53. The manner of collection could perhaps suggest a tax if IRS penalty-collection were unheard-of or rare. It is not. See, e.g., 26 U. S. C. §527(j) (2006 ed.) (IRS-collectible penalty for failure to make campaign-finance disclosures); §5761(c) (IRS-collectible penalty for domestic sales of tobacco products labeled for export); §9707 (IRS-collectible penalty for failure to make required health-insurance premium payments on behalf of mining employees). In Reorganized CF&I Fabricators of Utah, Inc., 518 U. S. 213, we held that an exaction not only enforced by the Commissioner of Internal Revenue but even called a "tax" was in fact a penalty. "[I]f the concept of penalty means anything," we said, "it means punishment for an unlawful act or omission." Id., at 224. See also Lipke v. Lederer, 259 U. S. 557 (1922) (same). Moreover, while the penalty is assessed and collected by the IRS, §5000A is administered both by that agency and by the Department of Health and Human Services (and also the Secretary of Veteran Affairs), see §5000A(e)(1)(D), (e)(5), (f)(1)(A)(v), (f)(1)(E) (2006 ed., Supp. IV), which is responsible for defining its substantive scope—a feature that would be quite extraordinary for taxes.

The Government points out that "[t]he amount of the penalty will be calculated as a percentage of household income for federal income tax purposes, subject to a floor and [a] ca[p]," and that individuals who earn so little money that they "are not required to file income tax returns for the taxable year are not subject to the penalty" (though they are, as we discussed earlier, subject to the mandate). Petitioners' Minimum Coverage Brief 12, 53. But varying a penalty according to ability to pay is an utterly familiar practice. See, e.g., 33 U. S. C. §1319(d) (2006 ed., Supp. IV) ("In determining the amount of a civil penalty the court shall consider . . . the economic impact of the penalty on the violator"); see also 6 U. S. C. §488e(c); 7 U. S. C. §§7734(b)(2), 8313(b)(2); 12 U. S. C. §§1701q–1(d)(3), 1723i(c)(3), 1735f–14(c)(3), 1735f–15(d)(3), 4585(c)(2); 15 U. S. C. §§45(m)(1)(C), 77h–1(g)(3), 78u–2(d), 80a–9(d)(4), 80b–3(i)(4), 1681s(a)(2)(B), 1717a(b)(3), 1825(b)(1), 2615(a)(2)(B), 5408(b)(2); 33 U. S. C. §2716a(a).

The last of the feeble arguments in favor of petitioners that we will address is the contention that what this statute repeatedly calls a penalty is in fact a tax because it contains no scienter requirement. The presence of such a requirement suggests a penalty—though one can imagine a tax imposed only on willful action; but the absence of such a requirement does not suggest a tax. Penalties for absolute-liability offenses are commonplace. And where a statute is silent as to scienter, we traditionally presume a mens rea requirement if the statute imposes a "severe penalty." Staples v. United States, 511 U. S. 600, 618 (1994) . Since we have an entire jurisprudence addressing when it is that a scienter requirement should be inferred from a penalty, it is quite illogical to suggest that a penalty is not a penalty for want of an express scienter requirement.

And the nail in the coffin is that the mandate and penalty are located in Title I of the Act, its operative core, rather than where a tax would be found—in Title IX, containing the Act's "Revenue Provisions." In sum, "the terms of [the] act rende[r] it unavoidable," Parsons v. Bedford, 3 Pet. 433, 448 (1830), that Congress imposed a regulatory penalty, not a tax.

For all these reasons, to say that the Individual Mandate merely imposes a tax is not to interpret the statute but to rewrite it. Judicial tax-writing is particularly troubling. Taxes have never been popular, see, e.g., Stamp Act of 1765, and in part for that reason, the Constitution requires tax increases to originate in the House of Representatives. See Art. I, §7, cl. 1. That is to say, they must originate in the legislative body most accountable to the people, where legislators must weigh the need for the tax against the terrible price they might pay at their next election, which is never more than two years off. The Federalist No. 58 "defend[ed] the decision to give the origination power to the House on the ground that the Chamber that is more accountable to the people should have the primary role in raising revenue." United States v. Munoz-Flores, 495 U. S. 385, 395 (1990) . We have no doubt that Congress knew precisely what it was doing when it rejected an earlier version of this legislation that imposed a tax instead of a requirement-with-penalty. See Affordable Health Care for America Act, H. R. 3962, 111th Cong., 1st Sess., §501 (2009); America's Healthy Future Act of 2009, S. 1796, 111th Cong., 1st Sess., §1301. Imposing a tax through judicial legislation inverts the constitutional scheme, and places the power to tax in the branch of government least accountable to the citizenry.

Finally, we must observe that rewriting §5000A as a tax in order to sustain its constitutionality would force us to confront a difficult constitutional question: whether this is a direct tax that must be apportioned among the States according to their population. Art. I, §9, cl. 4. Perhaps it is not (we have no need to address the point); but the meaning of the Direct Tax Clause is famously unclear, and its application here is a question of first impression that deserves more thoughtful consideration than the lick-and-a-promise accorded by the Government and its supporters. The Government's opening brief did not even address the question—perhaps because, until today, no federal court has accepted the implausible argument that §5000A is an exercise of the tax power. And once respondents raised the issue, the Government devoted a mere 21 lines of its reply brief to the issue. Petitioners' Minimum Coverage Reply Brief 25. At oral argument, the most prolonged statement about the issue was just over 50 words. Tr. of Oral Arg. 79 (Mar. 27, 2012). One would expect this Court to demand more than fly-by-night briefing and argument before deciding a difficult constitutional question of first impression.

III

The Anti-Injunction Act

There is another point related to the Individual Mandate that we must discuss—a point that logically should have been discussed first: Whether jurisdiction over the challenges to the minimum-coverage provision is precluded by the Anti-Injunction Act, which provides that "no suit for the purpose of restraining the assessment or collection of any tax shall be maintained in any court by any person," 26 U. S. C. §7421(a) (2006 ed.).

We have left the question to this point because it seemed to us that the dispositive question whether the minimum-coverage provision is a tax is more appropriately addressed in the significant constitutional context of whether it is an exercise of Congress' taxing power. Having found that it is not, we have no difficulty in deciding that these suits do not have "the purpose of restraining the assessment or collection of any tax." 6

The Government and those who support its position on this point make the remarkable argument that §5000A is not a tax for purposes of the Anti-Injunction Act, see Brief for Petitioners in No. 11–398 (Anti-Injunction Act), butis a tax for constitutional purposes, see Petitioners' Minimum Coverage Brief 52–62. The rhetorical device that tries to cloak this argument in superficial plausibility is the same device employed in arguing that for constitutional purposes the minimum-coverage provision is a tax: confusing the question of what Congress did with the question of what Congress could have done. What qualifies as a tax for purposes of the Anti-Injunction Act, unlike what qualifies as a tax for purposes of the Constitution, is entirely within the control of Congress. Compare Bailey v. George, 259 U. S. 16, 20 (1922) (Anti-Injunction Act barred suit to restrain collections under the Child Labor Tax Law), with Child Labor Tax Case, 259 U. S., at 36–41 (holding the same law unconstitutional as exceeding Congress' taxing power). Congress could have defined "tax" for purposes of that statute in such fashion as to exclude some exactions that in fact are "taxes." It might have prescribed, for example, that a particular exercise of the taxing power "shall not be regarded as a tax for purposes of the Anti-Injunction Act." But there is no such prescription here. What the Government would have us believe in these cases is that the very same textual indications that show this is not a tax under the Anti-Injunction Act show that it is a tax under the Constitution. That carries verbal wizardry too far, deep into the forbidden land of the sophists.

IV

The Medicaid Expansion

We now consider respondents' second challenge to the constitutionality of the ACA, namely, that the Act's dramatic expansion of the Medicaid program exceeds Congress' power to attach conditions to federal grants to the States.

The ACA does not legally compel the States to participate in the expanded Medicaid program, but the Act authorizes a severe sanction for any State that refuses to go along: termination of all the State's Medicaid funding. For the average State, the annual federal Medicaid subsidy is equal to more than one-fifth of the State's expenditures. 7 A State forced out of the program would not only lose this huge sum but would almost certainly find it necessary to increase its own health-care expenditures substantially, requiring either a drastic reduction in funding for other programs or a large increase in state taxes. And these new taxes would come on top of the federal taxes already paid by the State's citizens to fund the Medicaid program in other States.

The States challenging the constitutionality of the ACA's Medicaid Expansion contend that, for these practical reasons, the Act really does not give them any choice at all. As proof of this, they point to the goal and the struc-ture of the ACA. The goal of the Act is to provide near-universal medical coverage, 42 U. S. C. §18091(2)(D), and without 100% State participation in the Medicaid program, attainment of this goal would be thwarted. Even if States could elect to remain in the old Medicaid program, while declining to participate in the Expansion, there would be a gaping hole in coverage. And if a substantial number of States were entirely expelled from the program, the number of persons without coverage would be even higher.

In light of the ACA's goal of near-universal coverage, petitioners argue, if Congress had thought that anything less than 100% state participation was a realistic possibility, Congress would have provided a backup scheme. But no such scheme is to be found anywhere in the more than 900 pages of the Act. This shows, they maintain, that Congress was certain that the ACA's Medicaid offer was one that no State could refuse.

In response to this argument, the Government contends that any congressional assumption about uniform state participation was based on the simple fact that the offer of federal funds associated with the expanded coverage is such a generous gift that no State would want to turn it down.

To evaluate these arguments, we consider the extent of the Federal Government's power to spend money and to attach conditions to money granted to the States.

A

No one has ever doubted that the Constitution authorizes the Federal Government to spend money, but for many years the scope of this power was unsettled. The Constitution grants Congress the power to collect taxes "to . . . provide for the . . . general Welfare of the United States," Art. I, §8, cl. 1, and from "the foundation of the Nation sharp differences of opinion have persisted as to the true interpretation of the phrase" "the general welfare." Butler, 297 U. S., at 65. Madison, it has been said, thought that the phrase "amounted to no more than a reference to the other powers enumerated in the subsequent clauses of the same section," while Hamilton "maintained the clause confers a power separate and distinct from those later enumerated [and] is not restricted in meaning by the grant of them." Ibid.

The Court resolved this dispute in Butler. Writing for the Court, Justice Roberts opined that the Madisonian view would make Article I's grant of the spending power a "mere tautology." Ibid. To avoid that, he adopted Hamilton's approach and found that "the power of Congress to authorize expenditure of public moneys for public purposes is not limited by the direct grants of legislative power found in the Constitution." Id., at 66. Instead, he wrote, the spending power's "confines are set in the clause which confers it, and not in those of section 8 which bestow and define the legislative powers of the Congress." Ibid.; see also Steward Machine Co. v. Davis, 301 U. S. 548–587 (1937); Helvering v. Davis, 301 U. S. 619, 640 (1937).

The power to make any expenditure that furthers "the general welfare" is obviously very broad, and shortly after Butler was decided the Court gave Congress wide leeway to decide whether an expenditure qualifies. See Helvering, 301 U. S., at 640–641. "The discretion belongs to Congress," the Court wrote, "unless the choice is clearly wrong, a display of arbitrary power, not an exercise of judgment." Id., at 640. Since that time, the Court has never held that a federal expenditure was not for "the general welfare."

B

One way in which Congress may spend to promote the general welfare is by making grants to the States. Monetary grants, so-called grants-in-aid, became more frequent during the 1930's, G. Stephens & N. Wikstrom, Ameri-can Intergovernmental Relations—A Fragmented Federal Polity 83 (2007), and by 1950 they had reached $20 billion 8 or 11.6% of state and local government expenditures from their own sources. 9 By 1970 this number had grown to $123.7 billion 10 or 29.1% of state and local government expenditures from their own sources. 11 As of 2010, fed-eral outlays to state and local governments came to over $608 billion or 37.5% of state and local government expenditures. 12

When Congress makes grants to the States, it customarily attaches conditions, and this Court has long held that the Constitution generally permits Congress to do this. See Pennhurst State School and Hospital v. Halderman, 451 U. S. 1, 17 (1981); South Dakota v.

Dole, 483 U. S. 203, 206 (1987); Fullilove v. Klutznick, 448 U. S. 448, 474 (1980) (opinion of Burger, C. J.); Steward Machine, supra, at 593.

C

This practice of attaching conditions to federal funds greatly increases federal power. "[O]bjectives not thought to be within Article I's enumerated legislative fields, may nevertheless be attained through the use of the spending power and the conditional grant of federal funds." Dole, supra, at 207 (internal quotation marks and citation omitted); see also College Savings Bank v. Florida Prepaid Postsecondary Ed. Expense Bd., 527 U. S. 666, 686 (1999) (by attaching conditions to federal funds, Congress may induce the States to "tak[e] certain actions that Congress could not require them to take").

This formidable power, if not checked in any way, would present a grave threat to the system of federalism created by our Constitution. If Congress' "Spending Clause power to pursue objectives outside of Article I's enumerated legislative fields," Davis v. Monroe County Bd. of Ed., 526 U. S. 629, 654 (1999) (Kennedy, J., dissenting) (internal quotation marks omitted), is "limited only by Congress' notion of the general welfare, the reality, given the vast financial resources of the Federal Government, is thatthe Spending Clause gives 'power to the Congress to tear down the barriers, to invade the states' jurisdiction, and to become a parliament of the whole people, subject to no restrictions save such as are self-imposed,' " Dole, supra, at 217 (O'Connor, J., dissenting) (quoting Butler, 297 U. S., at 78). "[T]he Spending Clause power, if wielded without concern for the federal balance, has the potential to obliterate distinctions between national and local spheres of interest and power by permitting the Federal Government to set policy in the most sensitive areas of traditional state concern, areas which otherwise would lie outside its reach." Davis, supra, at 654–655 (Kennedy, J.,dissenting).

Recognizing this potential for abuse, our cases have long held that the power to attach conditions to grants to the States has limits. See, e.g., Dole, supra, at 207–208; id.,at 207 (spending power is "subject to several general restrictions articulated in our cases"). For one thing, any such conditions must be unambiguous so that a State at least knows what it is getting into. See Pennhurst, supra, at 17. Conditions must also be related "to the federal interest in particular national projects or programs," Massachusetts v. United States, 435 U. S. 444, 461 (1978), and the conditional grant of federal funds may not "induce the States to engage in activities that would themselves be unconstitutional," Dole, supra, at 210; see Lawrence County v. Lead-Deadwood School Dist. No. 40–1, 469 U. S.256, 269–270 (1985). Finally, while Congress may seek to induce States to accept conditional grants, Congress may not cross the "point at which pressure turns into compulsion, and ceases to be inducement." Steward Machine, 301 U. S., at 590. Accord, College Savings Bank, supra, at 687; Metropolitan Washington Airports Authority v. Citizens for Abatement of Aircraft Noise, Inc., 501 U. S. 252, 285 (1991) (White, J., dissenting); Dole, supra, at 211.

When federal legislation gives the States a real choice whether to accept or decline a federal aid package, the federal-state relationship is in the nature of a contractual relationship. See Barnes v. Gorman, 536 U. S. 181, 186 (2002); Pennhurst, 451 U. S., at 17. And just as a contract is voidable if coerced, "[t]he legitimacy of Congress' power to legislate under the spending power . . . rests on whether the State voluntarily and knowingly accepts the terms of the 'contract.' " Ibid. (emphasis added). If a federal spending program coerces participation the States have not "exercise[d] their choice"—let alone made an "informed choice." Id., at 17, 25.

Coercing States to accept conditions risks the destruction of the "unique role of the States in our system." Davis, supra, at 685 (Kennedy, J., dissenting). "[T]he Constitution has never been understood to confer upon Congress the ability to require the States to govern according to Congress' instructions." New York, 505 U. S., at 162. Congress may not "simply commandeer the legislative processes of the States by directly compelling them to enact and enforce a federal regulatory program." Id., at 161 (internal quotation marks and brackets omitted). Congress effectively engages in this impermissible compulsion when state participation in a federal spending program is coerced, so that the States' choice whether to enact or administer a federal regulatory program is rendered illusory.

Where all Congress has done is to "encourag[e] state regulation rather than compe[l] it, state governments remain responsive to the local electorate's preferences; state officials remain accountable to the people. [But] where the Federal Government compels States to regulate, the accountability of both state and federal officials is diminished." New York, supra, at 168.

Amici who support the Government argue that forcing state employees to implement a federal program is more respectful of federalism than using federal workers to implement that program. See, e.g., Brief for Service Employees International Union et al. as Amici Curiae in No. 11–398, pp. 25–26. They note that Congress, instead of expanding Medicaid, could have established an entirely federal program to provide coverage for the same group of people. By choosing to structure Medicaid as a cooperative federal-state program, they contend, Congress allows for more state control. Ibid.

This argument reflects a view of federalism that our cases have rejected—and with good reason. When Congress compels the States to do its bidding, it blurs the lines of political accountability. If the Federal Government makes a controversial decision while acting on its own, "it is the Federal Government that makes the decision in full view of the public, and it will be federal officials that suffer the consequences if the decision turns out to be detrimental or unpopular." New York, 505 U. S., at 168. But when the Federal Government compels the States to take unpopular actions, "it may be state officials who will bear the brunt of public disapproval, while the federal officials who devised the regulatory program may remain insulated from the electoral ramifications of their decision." Id., at 169; see Printz, supra, at 930. For this reason, federal officeholders may view this "departur[e] from the federal structure to be in their personal interests . . . as a means of shifting responsibility for the eventual decision." New York, 505 U. S., at 182–183. And even state officials may favor such a "departure from the constitutional plan," since uncertainty concerning responsibility may also permit them to escape accountability. Id., at 182. If a program is popular, state officials may claim credit; if it is unpopular, they may protest that they were merely responding to a federal directive.

Once it is recognized that spending-power legislation cannot coerce state participation, two questions remain: (1) What is the meaning of coercion in this context? (2) Is the ACA's expanded Medicaid coverage coercive? We now turn to those questions.

D

1

The answer to the first of these questions—the meaning of coercion in the present context—is straightforward. As we have explained, the legitimacy of attaching conditions to federal grants to the States depends on the voluntariness of the States' choice to accept or decline the offered package. Therefore, if States really have no choice other than to accept the package, the offer is coercive, and the conditions cannot be sustained under the spending power. And as our decision in South Dakota v. Dole makes clear, theoretical voluntariness is not enough.

In South Dakota v. Dole, we considered whether the spending power permitted Congress to condition 5% of the State's federal highway funds on the State's adoption of a minimum drinking age of 21 years. South Dakota argued that the program was impermissibly coercive, but we disagreed, reasoning that "Congress ha[d] directed only that a State desiring to establish a minimum drinking age lower than 21 lose a relatively small percentage of certain federal highway funds." 483 U. S., at 211. Because "all South Dakota would lose if she adhere[d] to her chosen course as to a suitable minimum drinking age [was] 5%of the funds otherwise obtainable under specified high-way grant programs," we found that "Congress ha[d] offered relatively mild encouragement to the States to enact higher minimum drinking ages than they would otherwise choose." Ibid. Thus, the decision whether to comply with the federal condition "remain[ed] the prerogative of the States not merely in theory but in fact," and so the program at issue did not exceed Congress' power. Id., at 211–212 (emphasis added).

The question whether a law enacted under the spending power is coercive in fact will sometimes be difficult, but where Congress has plainly "crossed the line distinguishing encouragement from coercion," New York, supra, at 175, a federal program that coopts the States' political processes must be declared unconstitutional. "[T]he federal balance is too essential a part of our constitutional structure and plays too vital a role in securing freedom for us to admit inability to intervene." Lopez, 514 U. S., at 578 (Kennedy, J., concurring).

2

The Federal Government's argument in this case at best pays lip service to the anticoercion principle. The Federal Government suggests that it is sufficient if States are "free, as a matter of law, to turn down" federal funds. Brief for Respondents in No. 11–400, p. 17 (emphasis added); see also id., at 25. According to the Federal Government, neither the amount of the offered federal funds nor the amount of the federal taxes extracted from the taxpayers of a State to pay for the program in question is relevant in determining whether there is impermissible coercion. Id., at 41–46.

This argument ignores reality. When a heavy federal tax is levied to support a federal program that offers large grants to the States, States may, as a practical matter, be unable to refuse to participate in the federal program and to substitute a state alternative. Even if a State believes that the federal program is ineffective and inefficient, withdrawal would likely force the State to impose a huge tax increase on its residents, and this new state tax would come on top of the federal taxes already paid by residents to support subsidies to participating States. 13

Acceptance of the Federal Government's interpretation of the anticoercion rule would permit Congress to dictate policy in areas traditionally governed primarily at the state or local level. Suppose, for example, that Congress enacted legislation offering each State a grant equal to the State's entire annual expenditures for primary and secondary education. Suppose also that this funding came with conditions governing such things as school curriculum, the hiring and tenure of teachers, the drawing of school districts, the length and hours of the school day, the school calendar, a dress code for students, and rules for student discipline. As a matter of law, a State could turn down that offer, but if it did so, its residents would not only be required to pay the federal taxes needed to support this expensive new program, but they would also be forced to pay an equivalent amount in state taxes. And if the State gave in to the federal law, the State and its subdivisions would surrender their traditional authority in the field of education. Asked at oral argument whether such a law would be allowed under the spending power, the Solicitor General responded that it would. Tr. of Oral Arg. 44–45 (Mar. 28, 2012).

E

Whether federal spending legislation crosses the line from enticement to coercion is often difficult to determine, and courts should not conclude that legislation is unconstitutional on this ground unless the coercive nature of an offer is unmistakably clear. In this case, however, there can be no doubt. In structuring the ACA, Congress unambiguously signaled its belief that every State would have no real choice but to go along with the Medicaid Expansion. If the anticoercion rule does not apply in this case, then there is no such rule.

1

The dimensions of the Medicaid program lend strong support to the petitioner States' argument that refusing to accede to the conditions set out in the ACA is not a realistic option. Before the ACA's enactment, Medicaid funded medical care for pregnant women, families with dependents, children, the blind, the elderly, and the disabled. See 42 U. S. C. §1396a(a)(10) (2006 ed., Supp. IV). The ACA greatly expands the program's reach, making new funds available to States that agree to extend coverage to all individuals who are under age 65 and have incomes below 133% of the federal poverty line. See §1396a(a)(10)(A)(i)(VIII). Any State that refuses to expand its Medicaid programs in this way is threatened with a severe sanction: the loss of all its federal Medicaid funds. See

§1396c (2006 ed.).

Medicaid has long been the largest federal program of grants to the States. See Brief for Respondents in No. 11–400, at 37. In 2010, the Federal Government directed more than $552 billion in federal funds to the States. See Nat. Assn. of State Budget Officers, 2010 State Expenditure Report: Examining Fiscal 2009–2011 State Spending, p. 7 (2011) (NASBO Report). Of this, more than $233 billion went to pre-expansion Medicaid. See id., at 47. 14 This amount equals nearly 22% of all state expenditures combined. See id., at 7.

The States devote a larger percentage of their budgets to Medicaid than to any other item. Id., at 5. Federal funds account for anywhere from 50% to 83% of each State's total Medicaid expenditures, see §1396d(b) (2006 ed., Supp. IV); most States receive more than $1 billion in federal Medicaid funding; and a quarter receive more than$5 billion, NASBO Report 47. These federal dollars total nearly two thirds—64.6%—of all Medicaid expenditures nationwide. 15 Id., at 46.

The Court of Appeals concluded that the States failed to establish coercion in this case in part because the "states have the power to tax and raise revenue, and therefore can create and fund programs of their own if they do not like Congress's terms." 648 F. 3d 1235, 1268 (CA11 2011); see Brief for Sen. Harry Reid et al. as Amici Curiae in No. 11–400, p. 21 ("States may always choose to decrease expenditures on other programs or to raise revenues"). But the sheer size of this federal spending program in relation to state expenditures means that a State would be very hard pressed to compensate for the loss of federal funds by cutting other spending or raising additional revenue. Arizona, for example, commits 12% of its state expenditures to Medicaid, and relies on the Federal Government to provide the rest: $5.6 billion, equaling roughly one-third of Arizona's annual state expenditures of $17 billion. See NASBO Report 7, 47. Therefore, if Arizona lost federal Medicaid funding, the State would have to commit an additional 33% of all its state expenditures to fund an equivalent state program along the lines of pre-expansion Medicaid. This means that the State would have to allocate 45% of its annual expenditures for that one purpose. See ibid.

The States are far less reliant on federal funding for any other program. After Medicaid, the next biggest federal funding item is aid to support elementary and secondary education, which amounts to 12.8% of total federal outlays to the States, see id., at 7, 16, and equals only 6.6% of all state expenditures combined. See ibid. In Arizona, for example, although federal Medicaid expenditures are equal to 33% of all state expenditures, federal education funds amount to only 9.8% of all state expenditures. See ibid. And even in States with less than average federal Medicaid funding, that funding is at least twice the size of federal education funding as a percentage of state expenditures. Id., at 7, 16, 47.

A State forced out of the Medicaid program would face burdens in addition to the loss of federal Medicaid funding. For example, a nonparticipating State might be found to be ineligible for other major federal funding sources, such as Temporary Assistance for

Needy Families (TANF), which is premised on the expectation that States will participate in Medicaid. See 42 U. S. C. §602(a)(3) (2006 ed.) (requiring that certain beneficiaries of TANF funds be "eligible for medical assistance under the State['s Medicaid] plan"). And withdrawal or expulsion from the Medicaid program would not relieve a State's hospitals of their obligation under federal law to provide care for patients who are unable to pay for medical services. The Emergency Medical Treatment and Active Labor Act, §1395dd, requires hospitals that receive any federal funding to provide stabilization care for indigent patients but does not offer federal funding to assist facilities in carrying out its mandate. Many of these patients are now covered by Medicaid. If providers could not look to the Medicaid program to pay for this care, they would find it exceedingly difficult to comply with federal law unless they were given substantial state support. See, e.g., Brief for Economists as Amici Curiae in No 11–400, p. 11.

For these reasons, the offer that the ACA makes to the States—go along with a dramatic expansion of Medicaid or potentially lose all federal Medicaid funding—is quite unlike anything that we have seen in a prior spending-power case. In South Dakota v. Dole, the total amount that the States would have lost if every single State had refused to comply with the 21-year-old drinking age was approximately $614.7 million—or about 0.19%of all state expenditures combined. See Nat. Assn.of State Budget Officers, 1989 (Fiscal Years 1987–1989 Data) State Expenditure Report 10, 84 (1989), http://www.nasbo.org/publications-data/state-expenditure-report/archives. South Dakota stood to lose, at most, funding that amounted to less than 1% of its annual state expenditures. See ibid. Under the ACA, by contrast, the Federal Government has threatened to withhold 42.3% of all federal outlays to the states, or approximately $233 billion. See NASBO Report 7, 10, 47. South Dakota stands to lose federal funding equaling 28.9% of its annual state expenditures. See id., at 7, 47. Withholding $614.7 million, equaling only 0.19% of all state expenditures combined, is aptly characterized as "relatively mild encouragement," but threatening to withhold $233 billion, equaling 21.86% of all state expenditures combined, is a different matter.

2

What the statistics suggest is confirmed by the goaland structure of the ACA. In crafting the ACA, Congress clearly expressed its informed view that no State could possibly refuse the offer that the ACA extends.

The stated goal of the ACA is near-universal health care coverage. To achieve this goal, the ACA mandates that every person obtain a minimum level of coverage. It attempts to reach this goal in several different ways. The guaranteed issue and community-rating provisions are designed to make qualifying insurance available and affordable for persons with medical conditions that may require expensive care. Other ACA provisions seek to make such policies more affordable for people of modest means. Finally, for low-income individuals who are simply not able to obtain insurance, Congress expanded Medicaid, transforming it from a program covering only members of a limited list of vulnerable groups into a program that provides at least the requisite minimum level of coverage for the poor. See 42 U. S. C. §§1396a(a)(10)(A)(i)(VIII) (2006 ed., Supp. IV), 1396u–7(a), (b)(5), 18022(a). This design was intended to provide at least a specified minimum level of coverage for all Americans, but the achievement of that goal obviously depends on participation by every single State. If any State—notto mention all of the 26 States that brought this suit—chose to decline the federal offer, there would be a gaping hole in the ACA's coverage.

It is true that some persons who are eligible for Medicaid coverage under the ACA may be able to secure private insurance, either through their employers or by obtaining subsidized insurance through an exchange. See 26 U. S. C. §36B(a) (2006 ed., Supp. IV); Brief for Respondents in No. 11–400, at 12. But the new federal subsidies are not available to those whose income is below the federal poverty level, and the ACA provides no means, other than Medicaid, for these individuals to obtain coverage and comply with the Mandate. The Government counters that these people will not have to pay the penalty, see, e.g., Tr. of Oral Arg. 68 (Mar. 28, 2012); Brief for Respondents in No. 11–400, at 49–50, but that argument misses the point: Without Medicaid, these individuals will not have coverage and the ACA's goal of near-universal coverage will be severely frustrated.

If Congress had thought that States might actually refuse to go along with the expansion of Medicaid, Congress would surely have devised a backup scheme so that the most vulnerable groups in our society, those previously eligible for Medicaid, would not be left out in the cold. But nowhere in the over 900-page Act is such a scheme to be found. By contrast, because Congress thought that some States might decline federal funding for the operation of a "health benefit exchange," Congress provided a backup scheme; if a State declines to participate in the operation of an exchange, the Federal Government will step in and operate an exchange in that State. See 42 U. S. C. §18041(c)(1). Likewise, knowing that States would not necessarily provide affordable health insurance for aliens lawfully present in the United States—because Medicaid does not require States to provide such coverage—Congress extended the availability of the new federal insurance subsidies to all aliens. See 26 U. S. C. §36B(c)(1)(B)(ii) (excepting from the income limit individuals who are "not eligible for the medicaid program . . . by reason of [their] alien status"). Congress did not make these subsidies available for citizens with incomes below the poverty level because Congress obviously assumed that they would be covered by Medicaid. If Congress had contemplated that some of these citizens would be left without Medicaid coverage as a result of a State's withdrawal or expulsion from the program, Congress surely would have made them eligible for the tax subsidies provided for low-income aliens.

These features of the ACA convey an unmistakable message: Congress never dreamed that any State would refuse to go along with the expansion of Medicaid. Congress well understood that refusal was not a practical option.

The Federal Government does not dispute the inference that Congress anticipated 100% state participation, but it argues that this assumption was based on the fact that ACA's offer was an "exceedingly generous" gift. Brief for Respondents in No. 11–400, at 50. As the Federal Government sees things, Congress is like the generous benefactor who offers $1 million with few strings attached to 50 randomly selected individuals. Just as this benefactor might assume that all of these 50 individuals would snap up his offer, so Congress assumed that every State would gratefully accept the federal funds (and conditions) to go with the expansion of Medicaid.

This characterization of the ACA's offer raises obvious questions. If that offer is "exceedingly generous," as the Federal Government maintains, why have more than half the States brought this lawsuit, contending that the offer is coercive? And why did Congress find it necessary to threaten that any State refusing to accept this "exceed-ingly generous" gift would risk losing all Medicaid funds? Congress could have made just the new funding provided under the ACA contingent on acceptance of the terms of the Medicaid Expansion. Congress took such an approach in some earlier amendments to Medicaid, separating new coverage requirements and funding from the rest of the program so that only new funding was conditioned on new eligibility extensions. See, e.g., Social Security Amendments of 1972, 86 Stat. 1465.

Congress' decision to do otherwise here reflects its understanding that the ACA offer is not an "exceedingly generous" gift that no State in its right mind would decline. Instead, acceptance of the offer will impose very substantial costs on participating States. It is true that the Federal Government will bear most of the initial costs associated with the Medicaid Expansion, first paying 100% of the costs of covering newly eligible individuals between 2014 and 2016. 42 U. S. C. §1396d(y). But that is just part of the picture. Participating States will be forced to shoulder substantial costs as well, because after 2019 the Federal Government will cover only 90% of the costs associated with the Expansion, see ibid., with state spending projected to increase by at least $20 billion by 2020 as a consequence. Statement of Douglas W. Elmendorf, CBO's Analysis of the Major Health Care Legislation Enacted in March 2010, p. 24 (Mar. 30, 2011); see also R. Bovbjerg, B. Ormond, & V. Chen, Kaiser Commission on Medicaid and the Uninsured, State Budgets under Federal Health Reform: The Extent and Causes of Variations in Estimated Impacts 4, n. 27 (Feb. 2011) (estimating new state spending at $43.2 billion through 2019). After 2019, state spending is expected to increase at a faster rate; the CBO estimates new state spending at $60 billion through 2021. Statement of Douglas W. Elmendorf, supra, at 24. And these costs may increase in the future because of the very real possibility that the Federal Government will change funding terms and reduce the percentage of funds it will cover. This would leave the States to bear an increasingly large percentage of the bill. See Tr. of Oral Arg. 74–76 (Mar. 28, 2012). Finally, after 2015, the States will have to pick up the tab for 50% of all administrative costs associated with implementing the new program, see §§1396b(a)(2)–(5), (7) (2006 ed., Supp. IV), costs that could approach $12 billion between fiscal years 2014 and 2020, see Dept. of Health and Human Services, Center for Medicaid and Medicare Services, 2010 Actuarial Report on the Financial Outlook for Medicaid 30.

In sum, it is perfectly clear from the goal and structure of the ACA that the offer of the Medicaid Expansion was one that Congress understood no State could refuse. The

Medicaid Expansion therefore exceeds Congress' spending power and cannot be implemented.

F

Seven Members of the Court agree that the Medicaid Expansion, as enacted by Congress, is unconstitutional. See Part IV–A to IV–E, supra; Part IV–A, ante, at 45–55 (opinion of Roberts, C. J., joined by Breyer and Kagan, JJ.). Because the Medicaid Expansion is unconstitutional, the question of remedy arises. The most natural remedy would be to invalidate the Medicaid Expansion. However, the Government proposes—in two cursory sentences at the very end of its brief—preserving the Expansion. Under its proposal, States would receive the additional Medicaid funds if they expand eligibility, but States would keep their pre-existing Medicaid funds if they do not expand eligibility. We cannot accept the Government's suggestion.

The reality that States were given no real choice but to expand Medicaid was not an accident. Congress assumed States would have no choice, and the ACA depends on States' having no choice, because its Mandate requires low-income individuals to obtain insurance many of them can afford only through the Medicaid Expansion. Furthermore, a State's withdrawal might subject everyone in the State to much higher insurance premiums. That is because the Medicaid Expansion will no longer offset the cost to the insurance industry imposed by the ACA's insurance regulations and taxes, a point that is explained in more detail in the severability section below. To make the Medicaid Expansion optional despite the ACA's structure and design " 'would be to make a new law, not to enforce an old one. This is no part of our duty.' " Trade-Mark Cases, 100 U. S. 82, 99 (1879).

Worse, the Government's proposed remedy introduces a new dynamic: States must choose between expanding Medicaid or paying huge tax sums to the federal fisc for the sole benefit of expanding Medicaid in other States. If this divisive dynamic between and among States can be introduced at all, it should be by conscious congressional choice, not by Court-invented interpretation. We do not doubt that States are capable of making decisions when put in a tight spot. We do doubt the authority of this Court to put them there.

The Government cites a severability clause codified with Medicaid in Chapter 7 of the United States Code stating that if "any provision of this chapter, or the application thereof to any person or circumstance, is held invalid, the remainder of the chapter, and the application of such provision to other persons or circumstances shall not be affected thereby." 42 U. S. C. §1303 (2006 ed.). But that clause tells us only that other provisions in Chapter 7 should not be invalidated if §1396c, the authorization for the cut-off of all Medicaid funds, is unconstitutional. It does not tell us that §1396c can be judicially revised, to say what it does not say. Such a judicial power would not be called the doctrine of severability but perhaps the doctrine of amendatory invalidation—similar to the amendatory veto that permits the Governors of some States to reduce the amounts appropriated in legislation. The proof that such a power does not exist is the fact that it would not preserve other congressional dispositions, but would leave it up to the Court what the "validated" legislation will contain. The Court today opts for permitting the cut-off of only incremental Medicaid funding, but it might just as well have permitted, say, the cut-off of funds that represent no more than x percent of the State's bud-get. The Court severs nothing, but simply revises §1396c to read as the Court would desire.

We should not accept the Government's invitation to attempt to solve a constitutional problem by rewriting the Medicaid Expansion so as to allow States that reject it to retain their pre-existing Medicaid funds. Worse, the Government's remedy, now adopted by the Court, takes the ACA and this Nation in a new direction and charts a course for federalism that the Court, not the Congress, has chosen; but under the Constitution, that power and authority do not rest with this Court.

V

Severability

The Affordable Care Act seeks to achieve "near-universal" health insurance coverage. §18091(2)(D) (2006 ed., Supp. IV). The two pillars of the Act are the Individual Mandate and the expansion of coverage under Medicaid. In our view, both these central provisions of the Act—the Individual Mandate and Medicaid Expansion—are invalid. It follows, as some of the parties urge, that all other provisions of the Act must fall as well. The following section explains the severability principles that require this conclusion. This analysis also shows how closely interrelated the Act is, and this is all the more reason why it is judicial usurpation to impose an entirely new mechanism for withdrawal of Medicaid funding, see Part IV–F, supra, which is one of many examples of how rewriting the Act alters its dynamics.

A

When an unconstitutional provision is but a part of a more comprehensive statute, the question arises as to the validity of the remaining provisions. The Court's authority to declare a statute partially unconstitutional has been well established since Marbury v. Madison, 1 Cranch 137 (1803), when the Court severed an unconstitutional provision from the Judiciary Act of 1789. And while the Court has sometimes applied "at least a modest presumption in favor of . . . severability," C. Nelson, Statutory Interpretation 144 (2010), it has not always done so, see, e.g., Minnesota v. Mille Lacs Band of Chippewa Indians, 526 U. S. 172–195 (1999).

An automatic or too cursory severance of statutory provisions risks "rewrit[ing] a statute and giv[ing] it an effect altogether different from that sought by the measure viewed as a whole." Railroad Retirement Bd. v. Alton R. Co., 295 U. S. 330, 362 (1935) . The Judiciary, if it orders uncritical severance, then assumes the legislative function; for it imposes on the Nation, by the Court's decree, its own new statutory regime, consisting of policies, risks, and duties that Congress did not enact. That can be a more extreme exercise of the judicial power than striking the whole statute and allowing Congress to address the conditions that pertained when the statute was considered at the outset.

The Court has applied a two-part guide as the framework for severability analysis.

The test has been deemed "well established." Alaska Airlines, Inc. v. Brock, 480 U. S. 678, 684 (1987) . First, if the Court holds a statutory provision unconstitutional, it then determines whether the now truncated statute will operate in the manner Congress intended. If not, the remaining provisions must be invalidated. See id., at 685. In Alaska Airlines, the Court clarified that this first inquiry requires more than ask-ing whether "the balance of the legislation is incapable of functioning independently." Id., at 684. Even if the remaining provisions will operate in some coherent way, that alone does not save the statute. The question is whether the provisions will work as Congress intended. The "relevant inquiry in evaluating severability is whether the statute will function in a manner consistent with the intent of Congress." Id., at 685 (emphasis in original). See also Free Enterprise Fund v. Public Company Accounting Oversight Bd., 561 U. S. ___, ___ (2010) (slip op., at28) (the Act "remains fully operative as a law with these tenure restrictions excised") (internal quotation marks omitted); United States v. Booker, 543 U. S. 220, 227 (2005) ("[T]wo provisions . . . must be invalidated in order to allow the statute to operate in a manner consistentwith congressional intent"); Mille Lacs, supra, at 194 ("[E]m- bodying as it did one coherent policy, [the entire order]is inseverable").

Second, even if the remaining provisions can operate as Congress designed them to operate, the Court must determine if Congress would have enacted them standing alone and without the unconstitutional portion. If Congress would not, those provisions, too, must be invalidated. See Alaska Airlines, supra, at 685 ("[T]he unconstitutional provision must be severed unless the statute cre-ated in its absence is legislation that Congress would not have enacted"); see also Free Enterprise Fund, supra, at ___ (slip op., at 29) ("[N]othing in the statute's text or historical context makes it 'evident' that Congress, faced with the limitations imposed by the Constitution, would have preferred no Board at all to a Board whose members are removable at will"); Ayotte v. Planned Parenthood of Northern New Eng., 546 U. S. 320, 330 (2006) ("Would the legislature have preferred what is left of its statute to no statute at all"); Denver Area Ed. Telecommunications Consortium, Inc. v. FCC, 518 U. S. 727, 767 (1996) (plurality opinion) ("Would Congress still have passed §10(a) had it known that the remaining provisions were invalid" (internal quotation marks and brackets omitted)).

The two inquiries—whether the remaining provisions will operate as Congress designed them, and whether Congress would have enacted the remaining provisions standing alone—often are interrelated. In the ordinary course, if the remaining provisions cannot operate according to the congressional design (the first inquiry), it almost necessarily follows that Congress would not have enacted them (the second inquiry). This close interaction may explain why the Court has not always been precise in distinguishing between the two. There are, however, occasions in which the severability standard's first inquiry (statutory functionality) is not a proxy for the second inquiry (whether the Legislature intended the remaining provisions to stand alone).

B

The Act was passed to enable affordable, "near-universal" health insurance coverage. 42 U. S. C. §18091(2)(D).The resulting, complex statute consists of mandates and other requirements; comprehensive regulation and penalties; some undoubted taxes; and increases in some governmental expenditures, decreases in others. Under the severability test set out above, it must be determined if those provisions function in a coherent way and as Congress would have intended, even when the major provisions establishing the Individual Mandate and Medicaid Expansion are themselves invalid.

Congress did not intend to establish the goal of near-universal coverage without regard to fiscal consequences. See, e.g., ACA §1563, 124Stat. 270 ("[T]his Act will reduce the Federal deficit between 2010 and 2019"). And it did not intend to impose the inevitable costs on any one industry or group of individuals. The whole design of the Act is to balance the costs and benefits affecting each set of regulated parties. Thus, individuals are required to obtain health insurance. See 26 U. S. C. §5000A(a). Insurance companies are required to sell them insurance regardless of patients' pre-existing conditions and to comply with a host of other regulations. And the companies must pay new taxes. See §4980I (high-cost insurance plans);42 U. S. C. §§300gg(a)(1), 300gg–4(b) (community rating); §§300gg–1, 300gg–3, 300gg–4(a) (guaranteed issue); §300gg–11 (elimination of coverage limits); §300gg–14(a) (dependent children up to age 26); ACA §§9010, 10905, 124Stat. 865, 1017 (excise tax); Health Care and Education Reconciliation Act of 2010 (HCERA) §1401, 124Stat. 1059 (excise tax). States are expected to expand Medicaid eligibility and to create regulated marketplaces called ex-changes where individuals can purchase insurance. See 42 U. S. C. §§1396a(a)(10)(A)(i)(VIII) (2006 ed., Supp. IV) (Medicaid Expansion), 18031 (exchanges). Some persons who cannot afford insurance are provided it through the Medicaid Expansion, and others are aided in their purchase of insurance through federal subsidies available on health-insurance exchanges. See 26 U. S. C. §36B (2006 ed., Supp. IV), 42 U. S. C. §18071 (2006 ed., Supp. IV) (federal subsidies). The Federal Government's increased spending is offset by new taxes and cuts in other federal expenditures, including reductions in Medicare and in federal payments to hospitals. See, e.g., §1395ww(r) (Medicare cuts); ACA Title IX, Subtitle A, 124Stat. 847 ("Rev-enue Offset Provisions"). Employers with at least 50employees must either provide employees with adequate health benefits or pay a financial exaction if an employee who qualifies for federal subsidies purchases insurance through an exchange. See 26 U. S. C. §4980H (2006 ed., Supp. IV).

In short, the Act attempts to achieve near-universal health insurance coverage by spreading its costs to individuals, insurers, governments, hospitals, and employers—while, at the same time, offsetting significant portions of those costs with new benefits to each group. For ex-ample, the Federal Government bears the burden of paying billions for the new entitlements mandated by the Medicaid Expansion and federal subsidies for insurance purchases on the exchanges; but it benefits from reductions in the reimbursements it pays to hospitals. Hospitals lose those reimbursements; but they benefit from the decrease in uncompensated care, for under the insurance regulations it is easier for individuals with pre-existing conditions to purchase coverage that increases payments to hospitals. Insurance companies bear new costs imposed by a collection of insurance regulations and taxes, including "guaranteed issue" and "community rating" requirements to give coverage regardless of the insured's pre-existing conditions; but the insurers benefit from the new, healthy purchasers who are forced by the Individual Mandate to buy the insurers' product and from the new low-income Medicaid recipients who will enroll in insurance companies' Medicaid-funded managed care programs. In summary, the Individual Mandate and Medicaid Expansion offset insurance regulations and taxes, which offset reduced reimbursements to hospitals, which offset increases in federal spending. So, the Act's major provisions are interdependent.

The Act then refers to these interdependencies as "shared responsibility." See ACA Subtitle F, Title I, 124Stat. 242 ("Shared Responsibility"); ACA §1501, ibid. (same); ACA §1513, id., at 253 (same); ACA §4980H, ibid. (same). In at least six places, the Act describes the Individual Mandate as working "together with the other pro-visions of this Act." 42 U. S. C. §18091(2)(C) (2006 ed., Supp. IV) (working "together" to "add millions of new consumers to the health insurance market"); §18091(2)(E) (working "together" to "significantly reduce" the economic cost of the poorer health and shorter lifespan of the uninsured); §18091(2)(F) (working "together" to "lower health insurance premiums"); §18091(2)(G) (working "together" to "improve financial security for families"); §18091(2)(I) (working "together" to minimize "adverse selection and broaden the health insurance risk pool to include healthy individuals"); §18091(2)(J) (working "together" to "significantly reduce administrative costs and lower health insurance premiums"). The Act calls the Individual Mandate "an essential part" of federal regulation of health insurance and warns that "the absence of the requirement would undercut Federal regulation of the health insurance market." §18091(2)(H).

C

One preliminary point should be noted before applying severability principles to the Act. To be sure, an argument can be made that those portions of the Act that none of the parties has standing to challenge cannot be held nonseverable. The response to this argument is that our cases do not support it. See, e.g., Williams v. Standard Oil Co. of La., 278 U. S. 235–244 (1929) (holding nonseverable statutory provisions that did not burden the parties). It would be particularly destructive of sound government to apply such a rule with regard to a multifaceted piece of legislation like the ACA. It would take years, perhaps decades, for each of its provisions to be adjudicated separately—and for some of them (those simply expending federal funds) no one may have separate standing. The Federal Government, the States, and private parties ought to know at once whether the entire legislation fails.

The opinion now explains in Part V–C–1, infra, why the Act's major provisions are not severable from the Mandate and Medicaid Expansion. It proceeds from the insurance regulations and taxes (C–1–a), to the reductions in reimbursements to hospitals and other Medicare reductions (C–1–b), the exchanges and their federal subsidies (C–1–c), and the employer responsibility assessment (C–1–d).Part V–C–2, infra, explains why the Act's minor provisions also are not severable.

1

The Act's Major Provisions

Major provisions of the Affordable Care Act—i.e., the insurance regulations and taxes, the reductions in federal reimbursements to hospitals and other Medicare spend-ing reductions, the exchanges and their federal subsidies, and the employer responsibility assessment—cannot remain once the Individual Mandate and Medicaid Expansion are invalid. That result follows from the undoubted inability of the other major provisions to operate as Congress intended without the Individual Mandate and Medicaid Expansion. Absent the invalid portions, the other major provisions could impose enormous risks of unexpected bur-dens on patients, the health-care community, and the federal budget. That consequence would be in absolute conflict with the ACA's design of "shared responsibility," and would pose a threat to the Nation that Congress did not intend.

a

Insurance Regulations and Taxes

Without the Individual Mandate and Medicaid Expansion, the Affordable Care Act's insurance regulations and insurance taxes impose risks on insurance companies and their customers that this Court cannot measure. Those risks would undermine Congress' scheme of "shared responsibility." See 26 U. S. C. §4980I (2006 ed., Supp.IV) (high-cost insurance plans); 42 U. S. C. §§300gg(a)(1) (2006 ed., Supp. IV), 300gg–4(b) (community rating); §§300gg–1, 300gg–3, 300gg–4(a) (guaranteed issue); §300gg–11 (elimination of coverage limits); §300gg–14(a) (dependent children up to age 26); ACA §§9010, 10905, 124Stat. 865, 1017 (excise tax); HCERA §1401, 124Stat. 1059 (excise tax).

The Court has been informed by distinguished economists that the Act's Individual Mandate and Medicaid Expansion would each increase revenues to the insurance industry by about $350 billion over 10 years; that this combined figure of $700 billion is necessary to offset the approximately $700 billion in new costs to the insurance industry imposed by the Act's insurance regulations and taxes; and that the new $700-billion burden would otherwise dwarf the industry's current profit margin. See Brief for Economists as Amici Curiae in No. 11–393 etc. (Severability), pp. 9–16, 10a.

If that analysis is correct, the regulations and taxes will mean higher costs for insurance companies. Higher costs may mean higher premiums for consumers, despite the Act's goal of "lower[ing] health insurance premiums." 42 U. S. C. §18091(2)(F) (2006 ed., Supp. IV). Higher costs also could threaten the survival of health-insurance companies, despite the Act's goal of "effective health insurance markets." §18091(2)(J).

The actual cost of the regulations and taxes may be more or less than predicted. What is known, however, is that severing other provisions from the Individual Mandate and Medicaid Expansion necessarily would impose significant risks and real uncertainties on insurance companies, their customers, all other major actors in the sys-tem, and the government treasury. And what also is known is this: Unnecessary risks and avoidable uncertainties are hostile to economic progress and fiscal stability and thus to the safety and welfare of the Nation and the Nation's freedom. If those risks and uncertainties are to be imposed, it must not be by the Judiciary.

b

Reductions in Reimbursements to Hospitals and Other Reductions in Medicare Expenditures

The Affordable Care Act reduces payments by the Federal Government to hospitals by more than $200 billion over 10 years. See 42 U. S. C. §1395ww(b)(3)(B)(xi)–(xii) (2006 ed., Supp. IV); §1395ww(q); §1395ww(r); §1396r–4(f)(7).

The concept is straightforward: Near-universal coverage will reduce uncompensated care, which will increase hospitals' revenues, which will offset the government's reductions in Medicare and Medicaid reimbursements to hospitals. Responsibility will be shared, as burdens and benefits balance each other. This is typical of the whole dynamic of the Act.

Invalidating the key mechanisms for expanding insurance coverage, such as community rating and the Medicaid Expansion, without invalidating the reductions in Medicare and Medicaid, distorts the ACA's design of "shared responsibility." Some hospitals may be forced to raise the cost of care in order to offset the reductions in reimbursements, which could raise the cost of insurance premiums, in contravention of the Act's goal of "lower[ing] health insurance premiums." 42 U. S. C. §18091(2)(F) (2006 ed., Supp. IV). See also §18091(2)(I) (goal of "lower[ing] health insurance premiums"); §18091(2)(J) (same). Other hospitals, particularly safety-net hospitals that serve a large number of uninsured patients, may be forced to shut down. Cf. National Assn. of Public Hospitals, 2009 Annual Survey: Safety Net Hospitals and Health Systems Fulfill Mission in Uncertain Times 5–6 (Feb. 2011). Like the effect of preserving the insurance regulations and taxes, the precise degree of risk to hospitals is unknowable. It is not the proper role of the Court, by severing part of a statute and allowing the rest to stand, to impose unknowable risks that Congress could neither measure nor predict. And Congress could not have intended that result in any event.

There is a second, independent reason why the reductions in reimbursements to hospitals and the ACA's other Medicare cuts must be invalidated. The ACA's $455 billion in Medicare and Medicaid savings offset the $434-billion cost of the Medicaid Expansion. See CBO Estimate, Table 2 (Mar. 20, 2010). The reductions allowed Congress to find that the ACA "will reduce the Federal deficit between 2010 and 2019" and "will continue to reduce budget deficits after 2019." ACA §§1563(a)(1), (2), 124Stat. 270.

That finding was critical to the ACA. The Act's "shared responsibility" concept extends to the federal budget. Congress chose to offset new federal expenditures with budget cuts and tax increases. That is why the United States has explained in the course of this litigation that "[w]hen Congress passed the ACA, it was careful to ensure that any increased spending, including on Medicaid, was offset by other revenue-raising and cost-saving provisions." Memorandum in Support of Government's Motion for Summary Judgment in No. 3–10–cv–91, p. 41.

If the Medicare and Medicaid reductions would no longer be needed to offset the costs of the Medicaid Expansion, the reductions would no longer operate in the manner Congress intended. They would lose their justification and foundation. In addition, to preserve them would be "to eliminate a significant quid pro quo of the legislative compromise" and create a statute Congress did not enact. Legal Services Corporation v. Velazquez, 531 U. S. 533, 561 (2001) (Scalia, J., dissenting). It is no secret that cutting Medicare is unpopular; and it is most improbable Congress would have done so without at least the assurance that it would render the ACA deficit-neutral. See ACA §§1563(a)(1), (2), 124Stat. 270.

c

Health Insurance Exchanges and Their Federal Subsidies

The ACA requires each State to establish a health-insurance "exchange." Each exchange is a one-stop marketplace for individuals and small businesses to compare community-rated health insurance and purchase the policy of their choice. The exchanges cannot operate in the manner Congress intended if the Individual Mandate, Medicaid Expansion, and insurance regulations cannot remain in force.

The Act's design is to allocate billions of federal dollars to subsidize individuals' purchases on the exchanges. Individuals with incomes between 100 and 400 percent of the poverty level receive tax credits to offset the cost of insurance to the individual purchaser. 26 U. S. C. §36B (2006 ed., Supp. IV); 42 U. S. C. §18071 (2006 ed., Supp. IV). By 2019, 20 million of the 24 million people who will obtain insurance through an exchange are expected to receive an average federal subsidy of $6,460 per person. See CBO, Analysis of the Major Health Care Legislation Enacted in March 2010, pp. 18–19 (Mar. 30, 2011). Without the community-rating insurance regulation, however, the average federal subsidy could be much higher; for community rating greatly lowers the enormous premiums unhealthy individuals would otherwise pay. Federal subsidies would make up much of the difference.

The result would be an unintended boon to insurance companies, an unintended harm to the federal fisc, and a corresponding breakdown of the "shared responsibility" between the industry and the federal budget that Congress intended. Thus, the federal subsidies must be invalidated.

In the absence of federal subsidies to purchasers, insurance companies will have little incentive to sell insurance on the exchanges. Under the ACA's scheme, few, if any, individuals would want to buy individual insurance policies outside of an exchange, because federal subsidies would be unavailable outside of an exchange. Difficulty in attracting individuals outside of the exchange would in turn motivate insurers to enter exchanges, despite the exchanges' onerous regulations. See 42 U. S. C. §18031. That system of incentives collapses if the federal subsidies are invalidated. Without the federal subsidies, individuals would lose the main incentive to purchase insurance inside the exchanges, and some insurers may be unwilling to offer insurance inside of exchanges. With fewer buyers and even fewer sellers, the exchanges would not operate as Congress intended and may not operate at all.

There is a second reason why, if community rating is invalidated by the Mandate and Medicaid Expansion's invalidity, exchanges cannot be implemented in a manner consistent with the Act's design. A key purpose of an exchange is to provide a marketplace of insurance options where prices are standardized regardless of the buyer's pre-existing conditions. See ibid. An individual who shops for insurance through an exchange will evaluate different insurance products. The products will offer different benefits and prices. Congress designed the exchanges so the shopper can compare benefits and prices. But the comparison cannot be made in the way Congress designed if the prices depend on the shopper's pre-existing health conditions. The prices would vary from person to person. So without community rating—which prohibits insurers from basing the price of insurance on pre-existing conditions—the exchanges cannot operate in the manner Congress intended.

d

Employer-Responsibility Assessment

The employer responsibility assessment provides an incentive for employers with at least 50 employees to provide their employees with health insurance options that meet minimum criteria. See 26 U. S. C. §4980H (2006 ed., Supp. IV). Unlike the Individual Mandate,the employer-responsibility assessment does not require employers to provide an insurance option. Instead, it re-quires them to make a payment to the Federal Government if they do not offer insurance to employees and if insurance is bought on an exchange by an employee who qualifies for the exchange's federal subsidies. See ibid.

For two reasons, the employer-responsibility assessment must be invalidated. First, the ACA makes a direct link between the employer-responsibility assessment and the exchanges. The financial assessment against employers occurs only under certain conditions. One of them is the purchase of insurance by an employee on an exchange. With no exchanges, there are no purchases on the exchanges; and with no purchases on the exchanges, there is nothing to trigger the employer-responsibility assessment.

Second, after the invalidation of burdens on individuals (the Individual Mandate), insurers (the insurance regulations and taxes), States (the Medicaid Expansion), the Federal Government (the federal subsidies for exchanges and for the Medicaid Expansion), and hospitals (the reductions in reimbursements), the preservation of the employer-responsibility assessment would upset the ACA's design of "shared responsibility." It would leave employers as the only parties bearing any significant responsibility. That was not the congressional intent.

2

The Act's Minor Provisions

The next question is whether the invalidation of the ACA's major provisions requires the Court to invalidate the ACA's other provisions. It does.

The ACA is over 900 pages long. Its regulations include requirements ranging from a break time and secluded place at work for nursing mothers, see 29 U. S. C. §207(r)(1) (2006 ed., Supp. IV), to displays of nutritional content at chain restaurants, see

21 U. S. C. §343(q)(5)(H).The Act raises billions of dollars in taxes and fees, including exactions imposed on high-income taxpayers, see ACA §§9015, 10906; HCERA §1402, medical devices, see 26 U. S. C. §4191 (2006 ed., Supp. IV), and tanning booths, see §5000B. It spends government money on, among other things, the study of how to spend less government money. 42 U. S. C. §1315a. And it includes a number of provisions that provide benefits to the State of a particular legislator. For example, §10323, 124Stat. 954, extends Medicare coverage to individuals exposed to asbestos from a mine in Libby, Montana. Another provision, §2006, id., at 284, increases Medicaid payments only in Louisiana.

Such provisions validate the Senate Majority Leader's statement, " 'I don't know if there is a senator that doesn't have something in this bill that was important to them. . . . [And] if they don't have something in it important to them, then it doesn't speak well of them. That's what this legislation is all about: It's the art of compromise.' " Pear, In Health Bill for Everyone, Provisions for a Few, N. Y. Times, Jan. 4, 2010, p. A10 (quoting Sen. Reid). Often, a minor provision will be the price paid for support of a major provision. So, if the major provision were unconstitutional, Congress would not have passed the minor one.

Without the ACA's major provisions, many of these minor provisions will not operate in the manner Congress intended. For example, the tax increases are "Revenue Offset Provisions" designed to help offset the cost to the Federal Government of programs like the Medicaid Expansion and the exchanges' federal subsidies. See Title IX, Subtitle A—Revenue Offset Provisions, 124Stat. 847. With the Medicaid Expansion and the exchanges invalidated, the tax increases no longer operate to offset costs, and they no longer serve the purpose in the Act's scheme of "shared responsibility" that Congress intended.

Some provisions, such as requiring chain restaurants to display nutritional content, appear likely to operate as Congress intended, but they fail the second test for severability. There is no reason to believe that Congress would have enacted them independently. The Court has not previously had occasion to consider severability in the con-text of an omnibus enactment like the ACA, which includes not only many provisions that are ancillary to its central provisions but also many that are entirely unrelated— hitched on because it was a quick way to get them passed despite opposition, or because their proponents could exact their enactment as the quid pro quo for their needed support. When we are confronted with such a so-called "Christmas tree," a law to which many nongermane ornaments have been attached, we think the proper rule must be that when the tree no longer exists the ornaments are superfluous. We have no reliable basis for knowing which pieces of the Act would have passed on their own. It is certain that many of them would not have, and it is not a proper function of this Court to guess which. To sever the statute in that manner " 'would be to make a new law, not to enforce an old one. This is not part of our duty.' " Trade-Mark Cases, 100 U. S., at 99.

This Court must not impose risks unintended by Congress or produce legislation

Congress may have lacked the support to enact. For those reasons, the unconstitutionality of both the Individual Mandate and the Medicaid Expansion requires the invalidation of the Affordable Care Act's other provisions.

*   *   *

The Court today decides to save a statute Congress did not write. It rules that what the statute declares to be a requirement with a penalty is instead an option subject to a tax. And it changes the intentionally coercive sanction of a total cut-off of Medicaid funds to a supposedly noncoercive cut-off of only the incremental funds that the Act makes available.

The Court regards its strained statutory interpretation as judicial modesty. It is not. It amounts instead to a vast judicial overreaching. It creates a debilitated, inoperable version of health-care regulation that Congress did not enact and the public does not expect. It makes enactment of sensible health-care regulation more difficult, since Congress cannot start afresh but must take as its point of departure a jumble of now senseless provisions, provisions that certain interests favored under the Court's new design will struggle to retain. And it leaves the public and the States to expend vast sums of money on requirements that may or may not survive the necessary congressional revision.

The Court's disposition, invented and atextual as it is, does not even have the merit of avoiding constitutional difficulties. It creates them. The holding that the Individual Mandate is a tax raises a difficult constitutional question (what is a direct tax?) that the Court resolves with inadequate deliberation. And the judgment on the Medicaid Expansion issue ushers in new federalism concerns and places an unaccustomed strain upon the Union. Those States that decline the Medicaid Expansion must subsidize, by the federal tax dollars taken from their citizens, vast grants to the States that accept the Medicaid Expansion. If that destabilizing political dynamic, so antagonistic to a harmonious Union, is to be introduced at all, it should be by Congress, not by the Judiciary.

The values that should have determined our course today are caution, minimalism, and the understanding that the Federal Government is one of limited powers. But the Court's ruling undermines those values at every turn. In the name of restraint, it overreaches. In the name of constitutional avoidance, it creates new constitutional questions. In the name of cooperative federalism, it undermines state sovereignty.

The Constitution, though it dates from the founding of the Republic, has powerful meaning and vital relevance to our own times. The constitutional protections that this case involves are protections of structure. Structural protections—notably, the restraints imposed by federalism and separation of powers—are less romantic and have less obvious a connection to personal freedom than the provisions of the Bill of Rights or the Civil War Amendments. Hence they tend to be undervalued or even forgotten by our citizens. It should be the responsibility of the Court to teach otherwise, to remind our people that the Framers considered structural protections of freedom the most important ones, for which reason they alone were embodied in the original Constitution and not left to later amendment. The fragmentation of power produced by the structure of our Government is central to liberty, and when we destroy it, we place liberty at peril. Today's decision should have vindicated, should have taught, this truth; instead, our judgment today has disregarded it.

For the reasons here stated, we would find the Act invalid in its entirety. We respectfully dissent.

Notes

1 The most authoritative legal dictionaries of the founding era lack any definition for "regulate" or "regulation," suggesting that the term bears its ordinary meaning (rather than some specialized legal meaning) in the constitutional text. See R. Burn, A New Law Dictionary 281 (1792); G. Jacob, A New Law Dictionary (10th ed. 1782); 2 T. Cunningham, A New and Complete Law Dictionary (2d ed. 1771).

2 Justice Ginsburg is therefore right to note that Congress is "not mandating the purchase of a discrete, unwanted product." Ante, at 22 (opinion concurring in part, concurring in judgment in part, and dissenting in part). Instead, it is mandating the purchase of an unwanted suite of products—e.g., physician office visits, emergency room visits, hospital room and board, physical therapy, durable medical equipment, mental health care, and substance abuse detoxification. See Selected Medical Benefits: A Report from the Dept. of Labor to the Dept. of Health & Human Services (April 15, 2011) (reporting that over two-thirds of private industry health plans cover these goods and services), online at http://www.bls.gov/ncs/ebs/sp/selmedbensreport.pdf (all Inter-net materials as visited June 26, 2012, and available in Clerk of Court's case file).

3 In its effort to show the contrary, Justice Ginsburg's dissent comes up with nothing more than two condemnation cases, which it says demonstrate "Congress' authority under the commerce power to compel an 'inactive' landholder to submit to an unwanted sale." Ante, at 24. Wrong on both scores. As its name suggests, the condemnation power does not "compel" anyone to do anything. It acts in rem, against the property that is condemned, and is effective with or without a transfer of title from the former owner. More important, the power to condemn for public use is a separate sovereign power, explicitly acknowledged in the Fifth Amendment, which provides that "private property [shall not] be taken for public use, without just compensation." Thus, the power to condemn tends to refute rather than support the power to compel purchase of unwanted goods at a prescribed price: The latter is rather like the power to condemn cash for public use. If it existed, why would it not (like the condemnation power) be accompanied by a requirement of fair compensation for the portion of the exacted price that exceeds the goods' fair market value (here, the difference between what the free market would charge for a health-insurance policy on a young, healthy person with no pre-existing conditions, and the government-exacted community-rated premium)?

4 No one seriously contends that any of Congress' other enumerated powers gives it the authority to enact §5000A as a regulation.

5 Of course it can be both for statutory purposes, since Congress can define "tax" and "penalty" in its enactments any way it wishes. That is why United States v. Sotelo, 436 U. S. 268 (1978), does not disprove our statement. That case held that a "penalty" for willful failure to pay one's taxes was included among the "taxes" made non-dischargeable under the Bankruptcy Code. 436 U. S., at 273–275. Whether the "penalty" was a "tax" within the meaning of the Bankruptcy Code had absolutely no bearing on whether it escaped the constitutional limitations on penalties.

6 The amicus appointed to defend the proposition that the Anti-Injunction Act deprives us of jurisdiction stresses that the penalty for failing to comply with the mandate "shall be assessed and collected in the same manner as an assessable penalty under subchapter B of chapter 68," 26 U. S. C. §5000A(g)(1) (2006 ed., Supp. IV), and that such penalties "shall be assessed and collected in the same manner as taxes," §6671(a) (2006 ed.). But that point seems to us to confirm the inapplicability of the Anti-Injunction Act. That the penalty is to be "assessed and collected in the same manner as taxes" refutes the proposition that it is a tax for all statutory purposes, including with respect to the Anti-Injunction Act. Moreover, elsewhere in the Internal Revenue Code, Congress has provided both that a particular payment shall be "assessed and collected" in the same manner as a tax and that no suit shall be maintained to restrain the assessment or collection of the payment. See, e.g., §§7421(b)(1), §6901(a); §6305(a), (b). Thelatter directive would be superfluous if the former invoked the Anti-Injunction Act. Amicus also suggests that the penalty should be treated as a tax because it is an assessable penalty, and the Code's assessment provision authorizes the Secretary of the Treasury to assess "all taxes (in-cluding interest, additional amounts, additions to the tax, and as-sessable penalties) imposed by this title." §6201(a) (2006 ed., Supp.IV). But the fact that such items are included as "taxes" for purposes of assessment does not establish that they are included as "taxes" for purposes of other sections of the Code, such as the Anti-Injunction Act, that do not contain similar "including" language.

7 "State expenditures" is used here to mean annual expenditures from the States' own funding sources, and it excludes federal grants unless otherwise noted.

8 This number is expressed in billions of Fiscal Year 2005 dollars.

9 See Office of Management and Budget, Historical Tables, Budget of the U. S. Government, Fiscal Year 2013, Table 12.1—Summary Comparison of Total Outlays for Grants to State and Local Governments: 1940–2017 (hereinafter Table 12.1), http://www.whitehouse.gov/omb/budget/Historicals; id., Table 15.2—Total Government Expenditures: 1948–2011 (hereinafter Table 15.2).

10 This number is expressed in billions of Fiscal Year 2005 dollars.

11 See Table 12.1; Dept. of Commerce, Bureau of Census, Statistical Abstract of the United States: 2001, p. 262 (Table 419, Federal Grants-in-Aid Summary: 1970 to 2001).

12 See Statistical Abstract of the United States: 2012, p. 268 (Table 431, Federal Grants-in-Aid to State and Local Governments: 1990 to 2011).

13 Justice Ginsburg argues that "[a] State . . . has no claim on the money its

residents pay in federal taxes." Ante, at 59, n. 26. This is true as a formal matter. "When the United States Government taxes United States citizens, it taxes them 'in their individual capacities' as 'the people of America'—not as residents of a particular State." Ante, at 58, n. 26 (quoting U. S. Term Limits, Inc. v. Thornton, 514 U. S. 779, 839 (1995) (Kennedy, J., concurring)). But unless Justice Ginsburg thinks that there is no limit to the amount of money that can be squeezed out of taxpayers, heavy federal taxation diminishes the practical ability of States to collect their own taxes.

14 The Federal Government has a higher number for federal spending on Medicaid. According to the Office of Management and Budget, federal grants to the States for Medicaid amounted to nearly $273 billion in Fiscal Year 2010. See Office of Management and Bud-get, Historical Tables, Budget of the U. S. Government, Fiscal Year 2013, Table 12.3—Total Outlays for Grants to State and Local Gov-ernments by Function, Agency, and Program: 1940–2013, http://www.whitehouse.gov/omb/budget/Historicals. In that Fiscal Year, total federal outlays for grants to state and local governments amounted to over $608 billion, see Table 12.1, and state and local government expenditures from their own sources amounted to $1.6 trillion, see Table 15.2. Using these numbers, 44.8% of all federal outlays to both state and local governments was allocated to Medicaid, amounting to 16.8% of all state and local expenditures from their own sources.

15 The Federal Government reports a higher percentage. According to Medicaid.gov, in Fiscal Year 2010, the Federal Government made Medicaid payments in the amount of nearly $260 billion, representing 67.79% of total Medicaid payments of $383 billion. See www.medicaid.gov/Medicaid-CHIP-Program-Information/By-State/By-State.html.

Justice Scalia's dissent in McQuiggin v. Perkins (May 28, 2013)

Justice Scalia, with whom The Chief Justice and Justice Thomas join, and with whom Justice Alito joins as to Parts I, II, and III, dissenting.

The Antiterrorism and Effective Death Penalty Act of 1996 (AEDPA) provides that a "1-year period of limitation shall apply" to a state prisoner's application for a writ of habeas corpus in federal court. 28 U. S. C. §2244(d)(1). The gaping hole in today's opinion for the Court is its failure to answer the crucial question upon which all else depends: What is the source of the Court's power to fashion what it concedes is an "exception" to this clear statutory command?

That question is unanswered because there is no answer. This Court has no such power, and not one of the cases cited by the opinion says otherwise. The Constitution vests legislative power only in Congress, which never enacted the exception the Court creates today. That inconvenient truth resolves this case.

I

A

"Actual innocence" has, until today, been an exception only to judge-made, prudential barriers to habeas relief, or as a means of channeling judges' statutorily conferred discretion not to apply a procedural bar. Never before have we applied the exception to circumvent a categorical statutory bar to relief. We have not done so because we have no power to do so. Where Congress has erected a constitutionally valid barrier to habeas relief, a court cannot decline to give it effect.

Before AEDPA, the Supreme Court had developed an array of doctrines, see, e.g., Wainwright v. Sykes, 433 U. S. 72, 87 (1977) (procedural default); McCleskey v. Zant, 499 U. S. 467, 489 (1991) (abuse of the writ), to limit the habeas practice that it had radically expanded in the early or mid-20th century to include review of the merits of conviction and not merely jurisdiction of the convicting court, see Stone v. Powell, 428 U. S. 465–478 (1976) (citing Frank v. Mangum, 237 U. S. 309 (1915)); Brown v. Allen, 344 U. S. 443–534 (1953) (Jackson, J., concurring in result); Bator, Finality in Criminal Law and Federal Habeas Corpus for State Prisoners, 76 Harv. L. Rev. 441, 483–499 (1963). For example, the doctrine of procedural default holds that a state prisoner's default of his federal claims "in state court pursuant to an independent and adequate state procedural rule" bars federal habeas review of those claims. Coleman v. Thompson, 501 U. S. 722, 750 (1991) . That doctrine is not a statutory or jurisdictional command; rather, it is a "prudential" rule "grounded in 'considerations of comity and concerns for the orderly administration of criminal justice.' " Dretke v. Haley, 541 U. S. 386–393 (2004) (quoting Francis v. Henderson, 425 U. S. 536–539 (1976)).

And what courts have created, courts can modify. One judge-made exception to procedural default allows a petitioner to proceed where he can demonstrate "cause" for the default and "prejudice." See Coleman, supra, at 750. As relevant here, we have also expressed a willingness to excuse a petitioner's default, even absent a showing of cause, "where a constitutional violation has probably resulted in the conviction of one who is actually innocent." Murray v. Carrier, 477 U. S. 478, 496 (1986) ; see Schlup v. Delo, 513 U. S. 298–327 (1995); House v. Bell, 547 U. S. 518–537 (2006).

There is nothing inherently inappropriate (as opposed to merely unwise) about judge-created exceptions to judge-made barriers to relief. Procedural default, for example, raises "no question of a federal district court's power to entertain an application for a writ of habeas corpus." Francis, supra, at 538. Where a petitioner would, but for a judge-made doctrine like procedural default, have a good habeas claim, it offends no command of Congress's for a federal court to consider the petition. But that free-and-easy approach has no place where a statutory bar to habeas relief is at issue. "[T]he power to award the writ by any of the courts of the United States, must be given by written law," Ex parte Bollman, 4 Cranch 75, 94 (1807) (Marshall, C. J.), and "judgments about the proper scope of the writ are 'normally for Congress to make,' " Felker v. Turpin, 518 U. S. 651, 664 (1996) (quoting Lonchar v. Thomas, 517 U. S. 314, 323 (1996)). One would have thought it too obvious to mention that this Court is duty bound to enforce AEDPA, not amend it.

B

Because we have no "equitable" power to discard statutory barriers to habeas relief, we cannot simply extend judge-made exceptions to judge-made barriers into the statutory realm. The Court's insupportable leap from judge-made procedural bars to all procedural bars, including statutory bars, does all the work in its opinion—and there is not a whit of precedential support for it. McCleskey v. Zant applied a "miscarriage of justice" exception to the judge-made abuse-of-the-writ doctrine. 499 U. S., at 487–489, 495. Coleman v. Thompson and Murray v. Carrier applied it to the judge-made procedural-default doctrine. 501 U. S., at 750; 477 U. S., at 496. Keeney v.Tamayo-Reyes, 504 U. S. 1 (1992) , applied it to a variant of procedural default: a state prisoner's failure adequately to develop material facts in state court. Id., at 8. Kuhlmann v. Wilson, 477 U. S. 436 (1986) , a plurality opinion, applied it to a statute that merely said lower federal courts "need not" entertain successive petitions, thus leaving them with "discretion to entertain successive petitions under some circumstances." Id., at 449, 451 (emphasis added). Not one of the cases on which the Court relies today supports the extraordinary premise that courts can create out of whole cloth an exception to a statutory bar to relief.

The opinion for the Court also trots out post-AEDPA cases to prove the irrelevant point that "[t]he miscarriage of justice exception . . . survived AEDPA's passage." Ante, at 8. What it ignores, yet again, is that after AEDPA's passage, as before, the exception applied only to nonstatutory obstacles to relief. Bousley v. United States and House v. Bell were applications of the judge-made doctrine of procedural default. See Bousley, 523 U. S. 614, 623 (1998) ; id., at 625 (Stevens, J., concurring in part and dissenting in part) ("I agree with the Court's central holding . . . that none of its judge-made rules foreclose petitioner's collateral attack . . ." (emphasis added)); id., at 630 (Scalia, J., dissenting); House, 547 U. S., at 522. Calderon v. Thompson, 523 U. S. 538 (1998) , a non-AEDPA case, involved the courts of appeals' "inherent power to recall their mandates, subject to review for an abuse of discretion," id., at 549; it stands only for the proposition that the miscarriage-of-justice exception is an appropriate " 'means of channeling' " that discretion, id., at 559 (quoting McCleskey, supra, at 496).

The Court's opinion, in its way, acknowledges the dearth of precedential support for its holding. "Prior to AEDPA," it concedes, "this Court had not ruled that a credible claim of actual innocence could supersede a federal statute of limitations." Ante, at 13, n. 2. Its explanation for this lack of precedent is that before AEDPA, "petitions for federal habeas relief were not governed by any statute of limitations." Ibid. That is true but utterly unprobative. There are many statutory bars to relief other than statutes of limitations, and we had never (and before today, have never) created an actual-innocence exception to any of them. The reason why is obvious: Judicially amending a validly enacted statute in this way is a flagrant breach of the separation of powers.

H

The Court has no qualms about transgressing such a basic principle. It does not even attempt to cloak its act of judicial legislation in the pretense that it is merely construing the statute; indeed, it freely admits that its opinion recognizes an "exception" that the statute does not contain. Ante, at 7. And it dismisses, with a series of transparent non sequiturs, Michigan's overwhelming textual argument that the statute provides no such exception and envisions none.

The key textual point is that two provisions of §2244, working in tandem, provide a comprehensive path to relief for an innocent prisoner who has newly discovered evidence that supports his constitutional claim. Section 2244(d)(1)(D) gives him a fresh year in which to file, starting on "the date on which the factual predicate of the claim or claims presented could have been discovered through the exercise of due diligence," while §2244(b)(2)(B) lifts the bar on second or successive petitions. Congress clearly anticipated the scenario of a habeas petitioner with a credible innocence claim and addressed it by crafting an exception (and an exception, by the way, more restrictive than the one that pleases the Court today). One cannot assume that Congress left room for other, judge-made applications of the actual-innocence exception, any more than one would add another gear to a Swiss watch on the theory that the watchmaker surely would have included it if he had thought of it. In both cases, the intricate craftsmanship tells us that the designer arranged things just as he wanted them.

The Court's feeble rejoinder is that its (judicially invented) version of the "actual innocence" exception applies only to a "severely confined category" of cases. Ante, at 10. Since cases qualifying for the actual-innocence exception will be rare, it explains, the statutory path for innocent petitioners will not "be rendered superfluous." Ibid. That is no answer at all. That the Court's exception would not entirely frustrate Congress's design does not weaken the force of the State's argument that Congress addressed the issue comprehensively and chose to exclude dilatory prisoners like respondent. By the Court's logic, a statute banning littering could simply be deemed to contain an exception for cigarette butts; after all, the statute as thus amended would still cover something. That is not how a court respectful of the separation of powers should interpret statutes.

Even more bizarre is the Court's concern that applying AEDPA's statute of limitations without recognizing an atextual actual-innocence exception would "accord greater force to a federal deadline than to a similarly designed state deadline." Ante, at 9; see also ante, at 13, n. 2. The Court terms that outcome "passing strange," ante, at 9, but it is not strange at all. Only federal statutes of limitations bind federal habeas courts with the force of law; a state statute of limitations is given effect on federal habeas review only by virtue of the judge-made doctrine of procedural default. 1 See Coleman, 501 U. S., at 730–731. With its eye firmly fixed on something it likes—a shiny new exception to a statute unloved in the best circles—the Court overlooks this basic distinction, which would not trouble a second-year law student armed with a copy of Hart & Wechsler. The Court simply ignores basic legal principles where they pose an obstacle to its policy-driven, free-form improvisation.

The Court's statutory-construction blooper reel does not end there. Congress's express inclusion of innocence-based exceptions in two neighboring provisions of the Act confirms, one would think, that there is no actual-innocence exception to §2244(d)(1). Section 2244(b)(2)(B), as already noted, lifts the bar on claims presented in second or successive petitions where "the factual predicate for the claim could not have been discovered previously through . . . due diligence" and "the facts underlying the claim . . . would be sufficient to establish by clear and convincing evidence that, but for constitutional error, no reasonable factfinder would have found" the petitioner guilty. Section 2254(e)(2) permits a district court to hold an evidentiary hearing where a diligent state prisoner's claim relies on new facts that "would be sufficient to establish by clear and convincing evidence that but for constitutional error, no reasonable factfinder would have found" him guilty. Ordinarily, we would draw from the express enumeration of these two actual-innocence exceptions the inference that no others were intended.

The Court's twisting path to the contrary conclusion is not easy to follow, but I will try. In the Court's view, the key fact here is that these two provisions of AEDPA codified what had previously been judge-made barriers to relief and applied to them a stricter actual-innocence standard than the courts had been applying. See ante, at 11–12. From this, the Court reasons that Congress made a conscious choice not also to apply the more restrictive actual-innocence standard to the statute of limitations. Ergo, the Court concludes, we are free to apply the more lenient version of the actual-innocence exception. Ante, at 12–13. That clever account ignores the background against which Congress legislated. Of course Congress did not "constrain" application of the actual-innocence exception to the statute of limitations. It felt no need to do so, because it had no reason whatsoever to suspect that any version of the exception would apply to the statute of limitations. The collective efforts of respondent and the majority have turned up not a single instance where this Court has applied the actual-innocence exception to any statutory barrier to habeas relief, much less to a statute of limitations. See Part I–B, supra. What has been said of equitable tolling applies in spades to non-tolling judicial inventions: "Congress cannot intend to incorporate, by silence, various forms of equitable tolling that were not generally recognized in the common law at the time of enactment." Bain & Colella, Interpreting Federal Statutes of Limitations, 37 Creighton L. Rev. 493, 503 (2004).The only conceivable relevance of §§2244(b)(2)(B) and 2254(e)(2) is (1) as we have said, that no other actual-innocence exception was intended, and (2) that if Congress had anticipated that this Court would amend §2244(d)(1) to add an actual-innocence exception (which it surely did not), it would have desired the more stringent formulation and not the expansive formulation applied today, which it specifically rejected for those other provisions.

III

Three years ago, in Holland v. Florida, 560 U. S. ____ (2010), we held that AEDPA's statute of limitations is subject to equitable tolling. That holding offers no support for importing a novel actual-innocence exception. Equit-able tolling—extending the deadline for a filing because of an event or circumstance that deprives the filer, through no fault of his own, of the full period accorded by thestatute—seeks to vindicate what might be considered the genuine intent of the statute. By contrast, suspending the statute because of a separate policy that the court believes should trump it ("actual innocence") is a blatant over-ruling. Moreover, the doctrine of equitable tolling is centuries old, and dates from a time when the separation of the legislative and judicial powers was incomplete. See, e.g., Bree v. Holbech, 2 Doug. 655, 656 (1781) (Mansfield, J.); South-Sea Co. v. Wymondsell, 24 E. R. 1004, 3 P. Wms. 143, 144 (1732); Booth v. Warrington, 2 E. R. 111, 112–113, 4 Bro. P. C. 163, 165–166 (1714); see also Holmberg v. Armbrecht, 327 U. S. 392–397 (1946); Exploration Co. v. United States, 247 U. S. 435–447 (1918); Bailey v. Glover, 21 Wall. 342, 348 (1875); Sherwood v. Sutton, 21 F. Cas. 1303, 1304–1305 (No. 12,782) (CCNH 1828) (Story, J.); Jones v. Conoway, 4 Yeates 109 (Pa. 1804). As Professor Manning has explained, until the Glorious Revolution of 1688, the Crown retained "pretensions to independent legislative authority, and English judges continued to serve as the Crown's agents, in theory and practice a component of the executive. Given these conditions, which distinguish the old English from the American constitutional context, it is not surprising to find a similarly indistinct line between appropriate legislative and judicial functions in matters of interpretation." Manning, Textualism and the Equity of the Statute, 101 Colum. L. Rev. 1, 36–37 (2001) (footnote omitted). Thus, the doctrine of the equity of the statute, of which equitable tolling was an example, was reflected in Blackstone's Commentaries "two-thirds of the way through the eighteenth century." Manning, supra, at 52.

American courts' later adoption of the English equitable-tolling practice need not be regarded as a violation of the separation of powers, but can be seen as a reasonable assumption of genuine legislative intent. Colonial legislatures would have assumed that equitable tolling would attend any statute of limitations they adopted. In any case, equitable tolling surely represents such a reasonable assumption today. "It is hornbook law that limitations periods are customarily subject to equitable tolling, unless tolling would be inconsistent with the text of the relevant statute. Congress must be presumed to draft limitations periods in light of this background principle." Young v. United States, 535 U. S. 43–50 (2002) (internal quotation marks and citations omitted); see Manning, What Divides Textualists from Purposivists? 106 Colum. L. Rev. 70, 81–82, and n. 42 (2006). Congress, being well aware of the longstanding background presumption of equitable tolling, "may provide otherwise if it wishes to do so." Irwin v. Department of Veterans Affairs, 498 U. S. 89, 96 (1990) . The majority and dissenting opinions in Holland disputed whether that presumption had been overcome, but all agreed that the presumption existed and was a legitimate tool for construing statutes of limitations. See Holland, 560 U. S., at ___ (slip op., at 13); id., at ___ (Scalia, J., dissenting) (slip op., at 1).

Here, by contrast, the Court has ambushed Congress with an utterly unprecedented (and thus unforeseeable) maneuver. Congressional silence, "while permitting an inference that Congress intended to apply ordinary background" principles, "cannot show that it intended to apply an unusual modification of those rules." Meyer v. Holley, 537 U. S. 280, 286 (2003) . 2 Because there is no plausible basis for inferring that Congress intended or could have anticipated this exception, its adoption here amounts to a pure judicial override of the statute Congress enacted. "It is wrong for us to reshape" AEDPA "on the very lathe of judge-made habeas jurisprudence it was designed to repair." Stewart v. Martinez-Villareal, 523 U. S. 637, 647 (1998) (Scalia, J., dissenting).

*   *   *

"It would be marvellously inspiring to be able to boast that we have a criminal-justice system in which a claim of 'actual innocence' will always be heard, no matter how late it is brought forward, and no matter how much the failure to bring it forward at the proper time is the defendant's own fault." Bousley, 523 U. S., at 635 (Scalia, J., dissenting). I suspect it is this vision of perfect justice through abundant procedure that impels the Court today. Of course, "we do not have such a system, and no society unwilling to devote unlimited resources to repetitive criminal litigation ever could." Ibid. Until today, a district court could dismiss an untimely petition without delving into the underlying facts. From now on, each time an untimely petitioner claims innocence—and how many prisoners asking to be let out of jail do not?—the district court will be obligated to expend limited judicial resources wading into the murky merits of the petitioner's innocence claim. The Court notes "that tenable actual-innocence gateway pleas are rare." Ante, at 2. That discouraging reality, intended as reassurance, is in truth "the condemnation of the procedure which has encouraged frivolous cases." Brown, 344 U. S., at 537 (Jackson, J., concurring in result).

It has now been 60 years since Brown v. Allen, in which we struck the Faustian bargain that traded the simple elegance of the common-law writ of habeas corpus for federal-court power to probe the substantive merits of state-court convictions. Even after AEDPA's pass through the Augean stables, no one in a position to observe the functioning of our byzantine federal-habeas system can believe it an efficient device for separating the truly deserving from the multitude of prisoners pressing false claims. "[F]loods of stale, frivolous and repetitious petitions inundate the docket of the lower courts and swell our own. . . . It must prejudice the occasional meritorious applicant to be buried in a flood of worthless ones." Id., at 536–537.

The "inundation" that Justice Jackson lamented in 1953 "consisted of 541" federal habeas petitions filed by state prisoners. Friendly, Is Innocence Irrelevant? Collateral Attack on Criminal Judgments, 38 U. Chi. L. Rev. 142, 143 (1970). By 1969, that number had grown to 7,359. Ibid. In the year ending on September 30, 2012, 15,929 such petitions were filed. Administrative Office of the United States Courts, Judicial Business of the United States Courts 3 (Sept. 30, 2012) (Table C–2). Today's decision piles yet more dead weight onto a postconviction habeas system already creaking at its rusted joints.

I respectfully dissent.

Notes

1 If the Court is really troubled by this disparity, there is a way to resolve it that is consistent with the separation of powers: Revise our judge-made procedural-default doctrine to give absolute preclusive effect to state statutes of limitations.

2 The Court concedes that "Congress legislates against the backdrop of existing law," but protests that "[a]t the time of AEDPA's enactment, multiple decisions of this Court applied the miscarriage of justice exception to overcome various threshold barriers to relief." Ante, at 14, n. 3. That is right, of course, but only at an uninformative level of generality; the relevant inquiry is, to which barriers had we applied the exception? Whistling past the graveyard, the Court refuses to engage with this question.

Justice Scalia's dissent in Maryland v. King (June 2, 2013) [Notes omitted]

Justice Scalia, with whom Justice Ginsburg, Justice Sotomayor, and Justice Kagan join, dissenting.

The Fourth Amendment forbids searching a person for evidence of a crime when there is no basis for believing the person is guilty of the crime or is in possession of incriminating evidence. That prohibition is categorical and without exception; it lies at the very heart of the Fourth Amendment. Whenever this Court has allowed a suspicionless search, it has insisted upon a justifying motive apart from the investigation of crime.

It is obvious that no such noninvestigative motive exists in this case. The Court's assertion that DNA is being taken, not to solve crimes, but to identify those in the State's custody, taxes the credulity of the credulous. And the Court's comparison of Maryland's DNA searches to other techniques, such as fingerprinting, can seem apt only to those who know no more than today's opinionhas chosen to tell them about how those DNA searches actually work.

I

A

At the time of the Founding, Americans despised the British use of so-called "general warrants"—warrants not grounded upon a sworn oath of a specific infraction by a particular individual, and thus not limited in scope and application. The first Virginia Constitution declared that "general warrants, whereby any officer or messenger may be commanded to search suspected places without evidence of a fact committed," or to search a person "whose offence is not particularly described and supported by evidence," "are grievous and oppressive, and ought not be granted." Va. Declaration of Rights §10 (1776), in 1 B. Schwartz, The Bill of Rights: A Documentary History 234, 235 (1971). The Maryland Declaration of Rights similarly provided that general warrants were "illegal." Md. Declaration of Rights §XXIII (1776), in id., at 280, 282.

In the ratification debates, Antifederalists sarcastically predicted that the general, suspicionless warrant would be among the Constitution's "blessings." Blessings of the New Government, Independent Gazetteer, Oct. 6, 1787, in 13 Documentary History of the Ratification of the Constitution 345 (J. Kaminski & G. Saladino eds. 1981). "Brutus" of New York asked why the Federal Constitution contained no provision like Maryland's, Brutus II, N. Y. Journal, Nov. 1, 1787, in id., at 524, and Patrick Henry warned that the new Federal Constitution would expose the citizenry to searches and seizures "in the most arbitrary manner, without any evidence or reason." 3 Debates on the Federal Constitution 588 (J. Elliot 2d ed. 1854).

Madison's draft of what became the Fourth Amendment answered these charges by providing that the "rights of the people to be secured in their persons . . . from all unreasonable searches and seizures, shall not be violated by warrants issued without probable cause . . . or not particularly describing the places to be searched." 1 Annals of Cong. 434–435 (1789). As ratified, the Fourth Amendment's Warrant Clause forbids a warrant to "issue" except "upon probable cause," and requires that it be "particula[r]" (which is to say, individualized) to "the place to be searched, and the persons or things to be seized." And we have held that, even when a warrant is not constitution-ally necessary, the Fourth Amendment's general prohibition of "unreasonable" searches imports the same requirement of individualized suspicion. See Chandler v. Miller, 520 U. S. 305, 308 (1997)

.

Although there is a "closely guarded category of constitutionally permissible suspicionless searches," id., at 309, that has never included searches designed to serve "the normal need for law enforcement," Skinner v. Railway Labor Executives' Assn., 489 U. S. 602, 619 (1989) (internal quotation marks omitted). Even the common name for suspicionless searches—"special needs" searches—itself reflects that they must be justified, always, by concerns "other than crime detection." Chandler, supra, at 313–314. We have approved random drug tests of railroad employees, yes—but only because the Government's need to "regulat[e] the conduct of railroad employees to ensure safety" is distinct from "normal law enforcement." Skinner, supra, at 620. So too we have approved suspicionless searches in public schools—but only because there the government acts in furtherance of its "responsibilities . . . as guardian and tutor of children entrusted to its care." Vernonia School Dist. 47J v. Acton, 515 U. S. 646, 665 (1995) .

So while the Court is correct to note (ante, at 8–9) that there are instances in which we have permitted searches without individualized suspicion, "[i]n none of these cases . . . did we indicate approval of a [search] whose primary purpose was to detect evidence of ordinary criminal wrongdoing." Indianapolis v. Edmond, 531 U. S. 32, 38 (2000) . That limitation is crucial. It is only when a governmental purpose aside from crime-solving is at stake that we engage in the free-form "reasonableness" inquiry that the Court indulges at length today. To put it another way, both the legitimacy of the Court's method and the correctness of its outcome hinge entirely on the truth of a single proposition: that the primary purpose of these DNA searches is something other than simply discovering evidence of criminal wrongdoing. As I detail below, that proposition is wrong.

B

The Court alludes at several points (see ante, at 11, 25) to the fact that King was an arrestee, and arrestees may be validly searched incident to their arrest. But the Court does not really rest on this principle, and for good reason: The objects of a search incident to arrest must be either (1) weapons or evidence that might easily be destroyed, or (2) evidence relevant to the crime of arrest. See Arizona v. Gant, 556 U. S. 332–344 (2009); Thornton v. United States, 541 U. S. 615, 632 (2004) (Scalia, J., concurring in judgment). Neither is the object of the search at issue here.

The Court hastens to clarify that it does not mean to approve invasive surgery on arrestees or warrantless searches of their homes. Ante, at 25. That the Court feels the need to disclaim these consequences is as damning a criticism of its suspicionless-search regime as any I can muster. And the Court's attempt to distinguish those hypothetical searches from this real one is unconvincing. We are told that the "privacy-related concerns" in the search of a home "are weighty enough that the search may require a warrant, notwithstanding the diminished expectations of privacy of the arrestee." Ante, at 26. But why are the "privacy-related concerns" not also "weighty" when an intrusion into the body is at stake? (The Fourth Amendment lists "persons" first among the entities protected against unreasonable searches and seizures.) And could the police engage, without any suspicion of wrongdoing, in a "brief and . . . minimal" intrusion into the home of an arrestee—perhaps just peeking around the curtilage a bit? See ante, at 26. Obviously not.

At any rate, all this discussion is beside the point. No matter the degree of invasiveness, suspicionless searches are never allowed if their principal end is ordinary crime-solving. A search incident to arrest either serves other ends (such as officer safety, in a search for weapons) or is not suspicionless (as when there is reason to believe the arrestee possesses evidence relevant to the crime of arrest).

Sensing (correctly) that it needs more, the Court elaborates at length the ways that the search here served the special purpose of "identifying" King. 1 But that seems to me quite wrong—unless what one means by "identifying" someone is "searching for evidence that he has committed crimes unrelated to the crime of his arrest." At points the Court does appear to use "identifying" in that peculiar sense—claiming, for example, that knowing "an arrestee's past conduct is essential to an assessment of the danger he poses." Ante, at 15. If identifying someone means finding out what unsolved crimes he has committed, then identification is indistinguishable from the ordinary law-enforcement aims that have never been thought to justify a suspicionless search. Searching every lawfully stopped car, for example, might turn up information about unsolved crimes the driver had committed, but no one would say that such a search was aimed at "identifying" him, and

no court would hold such a search lawful. I will therefore assume that the Court means that the DNA search at issue here was useful to "identify" King in the normal sense of that word—in the sense that would identify the author of Introduction to the Principles of Morals and Legislation as Jeremy Bentham.

1

The portion of the Court's opinion that explains the identification rationale is strangely silent on the actual workings of the DNA search at issue here. To know those facts is to be instantly disabused of the notion that what happened had anything to do with identifying King.

King was arrested on April 10, 2009, on charges unrelated to the case before us. That same day, April 10, the police searched him and seized the DNA evidence at issue here. What happened next? Reading the Court's opinion, particularly its insistence that the search was necessary to know "who [had] been arrested," ante, at 11, one might guess that King's DNA was swiftly processed and his identity thereby confirmed—perhaps against some master database of known DNA profiles, as is done for fingerprints. After all, was not the suspicionless search here crucial to avoid "inordinate risks for facility staff" or to "existing detainee population," ante, at 14? Surely, then—surely—the State of Maryland got cracking on those grave risks immediately, by rushing to identify King with his DNA as soon as possible.

Nothing could be further from the truth. Maryland officials did not even begin the process of testing King's DNA that day. Or, actually, the next day. Or the day after that. And that was for a simple reason: Maryland law forbids them to do so. A "DNA sample collected from an individual charged with a crime . . . may not be tested or placed in the statewide DNA data base system prior to the first scheduled arraignment date." Md. Pub. Saf. Code Ann. §2–504(d)(1) (Lexis 2011) (emphasis added). And King's first appearance in court was not until three days after his arrest. (I suspect, though, that they did not wait three days to ask his name or take his fingerprints.)

This places in a rather different light the Court's solemn declaration that the search here was necessary so that King could be identified at "every stage of the criminal process." Ante, at 18. I hope that the Maryland officials who read the Court's opinion do not take it seriously. Acting on the Court's misperception of Maryland law could lead to jail time. See Md. Pub. Saf. Code Ann. §2–512(c)–(e) (punishing by up to five years' imprisonment anyone who obtains or tests DNA information except as provided by statute). Does the Court really believe that Marylanddid not know whom it was arraigning? The Court's response is to imagine that release on bail could take so long that the DNA results are returned in time, or perhaps that bail could be revoked if the DNA test turned up incriminating information. Ante, at 16–17. That is no answer at all. If the purpose of this Act is to assess "whether [King] should be released on bail," ante, at 15, why would it possibly forbid the DNA testing process to begin until King was arraigned? Why would Maryland resign itself to simply hoping that the bail decision will drag out long enough that the "identification" can succeed before the arrestee is released? The truth, known to Maryland and increasingly to the reader: this search had nothing to do with establishing King's identity.

It gets worse. King's DNA sample was not received by the Maryland State Police's Forensic Sciences Division until April 23, 2009—two weeks after his arrest. It sat in that office, ripening in a storage area, until the custodians got around to mailing it to a lab for testing on June 25, 2009—two months after it was received, and nearly three since King's arrest. After it was mailed, the data from the lab tests were not available for several more weeks, until July 13, 2009, which is when the test results were entered into Maryland's DNA database, together with information identifying the person from whom the sample was taken. Meanwhile, bail had been set, King had engaged in discovery, and he had requested a speedy trial—presumably not a trial of John Doe. It was not until August 4, 2009—four months after King's arrest—that the forwarded sample transmitted (without identifying information) from the Maryland DNA database to the Federal Bureau of Investigation's national database was matched with a sample taken from the scene of an unrelated crime years earlier.

A more specific description of exactly what happened at this point illustrates why, by definition, King couldnot have been identified by this match. The FBI'sDNA database (known as CODIS) consists of two distinct collections. FBI, CODIS and NDIS Fact Sheet, http://www.fbi.gov/about-us/lab/codis/codis-and-ndis-fact-sheet (all Internet materials as visited May 31, 2013, and available in Clerk of Court's case file). One of them, the one to which King's DNA was submitted, consists of DNA samples taken from known convicts or arrestees. I will refer to this as the "Convict and Arrestee Collection." The other collection consists of samples taken from crime scenes; I will refer to this as the "Unsolved Crimes Collection." The Convict and Arrestee Collection stores "no names or other personal identifiers of the offenders, arrestees, or detainees." Ibid. Rather, it contains only the DNA profile itself, the name of the agency that submitted it, the laboratory personnel who analyzed it, and an identification number for the specimen. Ibid. This is because the submitting state laboratories are expected already to know the identities of the convicts and arrestees from whom samples are taken. (And, of course, they do.)

Moreover, the CODIS system works by checking to see whether any of the samples in the Unsolved Crimes Collection match any of the samples in the Convict and Arrestee Collection. Ibid. That is sensible, if what one wants to do is solve those cold cases, but note what it requires: that the identity of the people whose DNA has been entered in the Convict and Arrestee Collection already be known. 2 If one wanted to identify someone in custody using his DNA, the logical thing to do would be to compare that DNA against the Convict and Arrestee Collection: to search, in other words, the collection that could be used (by checking back with the submittingstate agency) to identify people, rather than the collection of evidence from unsolved crimes, whose perpetrators are by definition unknown. But that is not what was done. And that is because this search had nothing to do with identification.

In fact, if anything was "identified" at the moment that the DNA database returned a match, it was not King—his identity was already known. (The docket for the original criminal charges lists his full name, his race, his sex, his height, his weight, his date of birth, and his address.) Rather, what the August 4 match "identified" was the previously-taken sample from the earlier crime. That sample was genuinely mysterious to Maryland; the State knew that it had probably been left by the victim's attacker, but nothing else. King was not identified by his association with the sample; rather, the sample was identified by its association with King. The Court effectively destroys its own "identification" theory when it acknowledges that the object of this search was "to see what [was] already known about [King]." King was who he was, and volumes of his biography could not make him any more or any less King. No minimally competent speaker of English would say, upon noticing a known arrestee's similarity "to a wanted poster of a previously unidentified suspect," ante, at 13, that the arrestee had thereby been identified. It was the previously unidentified suspect who had been identified—just as, here, it was the previously unidentified rapist.

2

That taking DNA samples from arrestees has nothing to do with identifying them is confirmed not just by actual practice (which the Court ignores) but by the enabling statute itself (which the Court also ignores). The Maryland Act at issue has a section helpfully entitled "Purpose of collecting and testing DNA samples." Md. Pub. Saf. Code Ann. §2–505. (One would expect such a section to play a somewhat larger role in the Court's analysis of the Act's purpose—which is to say, at least some role.) That provision lists five purposes for which DNA samples may be tested. By this point, it will not surprise the reader to learn that the Court's imagined purpose is not among them.

Instead, the law provides that DNA samples are collected and tested, as a matter of Maryland law, "as part of an official investigation into a crime." §2–505(a)(2). (Or, as our suspicionless-search cases would put it: for ordinary law-enforcement purposes.) That is certainly how everyone has always understood the Maryland Act until today. The Governor of Maryland, in commenting on our decision to hear this case, said that he was glad, because "[a]llowing law enforcement to collect DNA samples . . . is absolutely critical to our efforts to continue driving down crime," and "bolsters our efforts to resolve open investigations and bring them to a resolution." Marbella, Supreme Court Will Review Md. DNA Law, Baltimore Sun, Nov. 10, 2012, pp. 1, 14. The attorney general of Maryland remarked that he "look[ed] forward to the opportunity to defend this important crime-fighting tool," and praised the DNA database for helping to "bring to justice violent perpetrators." Ibid. Even this Court's order staying the decision below states that the statute "provides a valuable tool for investigating unsolved crimes and thereby helping to remove violent offenders from the general population"—with, unsurprisingly, no mention of identity. 567 U. S. ___, ___ (2012) (Roberts, C. J., in chambers) (slip op., at 3).

More devastating still for the Court's "identification" theory, the statute does enumerate two instances in which a DNA sample may be tested for the purpose of identification: "to help identify human remains," §2–505(a)(3) (emphasis added), and "to help identify missing individuals," §2–505(a)(4) (emphasis added). No mention of identifying arrestees. Inclusio unius est exclusio alterius. And note again that Maryland forbids using DNA records "for any purposes other than those specified"—it is actually a crime to do so. §2–505(b)(2).

The Maryland regulations implementing the Act confirm what is now monotonously obvious: These DNA searches have nothing to do with identification. For example, if someone is arrested and law enforcement determines that "a convicted offender Statewide DNA Data Base sample already exists" for that arrestee, "the agency is not required to obtain a new sample." Code of Md. Regs., tit. 29, §05.01.04(B)(4) (2011).

But how could the State know if an arrestee has already had his DNA sample collected, if the point of the sample is to identify who he is? Of course, if the DNA sample is instead taken in order to investigate crimes, this restriction makes perfect sense: Having previously placed an identified someone's DNA on file to check against available crime-scene evidence, there is no sense in going to the expense of taking a new sample. Maryland's regulations further require that the "individ-ual collecting a sample . . . verify the identity of the individual from whom a sample is taken by name and,if applicable, State identification (SID) number." §05.01.04(K). (But how?) And after the sample is taken, it continues to be identified by the individual's name, fingerprints, etc., see §05.01.07(B)—rather than (as the Court believes) being used to identify individuals. See §05.01.07(B)(2) ("Records and specimen information shall be identified by . . . [the] [n]ame of the donor" (emphasis added)).

So, to review: DNA testing does not even begin until after arraignment and bail decisions are already made. The samples sit in storage for months, and take weeks to test. When they are tested, they are checked against the Unsolved Crimes Collection—rather than the Convict and Arrestee Collection, which could be used to identify them. The Act forbids the Court's purpose (identification), but prescribes as its purpose what our suspicionless-search cases forbid ("official investigation into a crime"). Against all of that, it is safe to say that if the Court's identification theory is not wrong, there is no such thing as error.

II

The Court also attempts to bolster its identification theory with a series of inapposite analogies. See ante, at 18–23.

Is not taking DNA samples the same, asks the Court, as taking a person's photograph? No—because that is not a Fourth Amendment search at all. It does not involve a physical intrusion onto the person, see Florida v. Jardines, 569 U. S. 1, ____ (2013) (slip op., at 3), and we have never held that merely taking a person's photograph invades any recognized "expectation of privacy," see Katz v. United States, 389 U. S. 347 (1967) . Thus, it is unsurprising that the cases the Court cites as authorizing photo-taking do not even mention the Fourth Amendment. See State ex rel. Bruns v. Clausmier, 154 Ind. 599, 57 N. E. 541 (1900) (libel), Shaffer v. United States, 24 App. D. C. 417 (1904) (Fifth Amendment privilege against self-incrimination).

But is not the practice of DNA searches, the Court asks, the same as taking "Bertillon" measurements—noting an arrestee's height, shoe size, and so on, on the back of a photograph? No, because that system was not, in the ordinary case, used to solve unsolved crimes. It is possible, I suppose, to imagine situations in which such measurements might be useful to generate leads. (If witnesses described a very tall burglar, all the "tall man" cards could then be pulled.) But the obvious primary purpose of such measurements, as the Court's description of them makes clear, was to verify that, for example, the person arrested today is the same person that was arrested a year ago. Which is to say, Bertillon measurements were actually used as a system of identification, and drew their primary usefulness from that task. 3

It is on the fingerprinting of arrestees, however, that the Court relies most heavily. Ante, at 20–23. The Court does not actually say whether it believes that taking a person's fingerprints is a Fourth Amendment search, and our cases provide no ready answer to that question. Even assuming so, however, law enforcement's post-arrest use of fingerprints could not be more different from its post-arrestuse of DNA. Fingerprints of arrestees are taken primarily to identify them (though that process sometimes solves

crimes); the DNA of arrestees is taken to solve crimes(and nothing else). Contrast CODIS, the FBI's nationwide DNA database, with IAFIS, the FBI's IntegratedAutomated Fingerprint Identification System. See FBI, Integrated Automated Fingerprint Identification System, http://www.fbi.gov/about-us/cjis/fingerprints_biometrics/iafis/iafis (hereinafter IAFIS).

The Court asserts that the taking of fingerprints was "constitutional for generations prior to the introduction" of the FBI's rapid computer-matching system. Ante, at 22. This bold statement is bereft of citation to authoritybecause there is none for it. The "great expansion in fingerprinting came before the modern era of Fourth Amendment jurisprudence," and so we were never asked to decide the legitimacy of the practice. United States v. Kincade, 379 F. 3d 813, 874 (CA9 2004) (Kozinski, J., dissenting). As fingerprint databases expanded from convictedcriminals, to arrestees, to civil servants, to immigrants,to everyone with a driver's license, Americans simply "became accustomed to having our fingerprints on filein some government database." Ibid. But it is wrongto suggest that this was uncontroversial at the time, or that this Court blessed universal fingerprinting for"generations" before it was possible to use it effectively for identification.

The Court also assures us that "the delay in processing DNA from arrestees is being reduced to a substantial degree by rapid technical advances." Ante, at 22. The idea, presumably, is that the snail's pace in this case is atypical, so that DNA is now readily usable for identification. The Court's proof, however, is nothing but a pair of press releases—each of which turns out to undercut this argument. We learn in them that reductions in backlog have enabled Ohio and Louisiana crime labs to analyze a submitted DNA sample in twenty days. 5 But that is still longer than the eighteen days that Maryland needed to analyze King's sample, once it worked its way through the State's labyrinthine bureaucracy. What this illustrates is that these times do not take into account the many other sources of delay. So if the Court means to suggest that Maryland is unusual, that may be right—it may qualify in this context as a paragon of efficiency. (Indeed, the Governor of Maryland was hailing the elimination of that State's backlog more than five years ago. See Wheeler, O'Malley Wants to Expand DNA Testing, Baltimore Sun, Jan. 11, 2008, p. 5B.) Meanwhile, the Court's holdingwill result in the dumping of a large number of arrestee samples—many from minor offenders—onto an already overburdened system: Nearly one-third of Americans will be arrested for some offense by age 23. See Brame, Turner, Paternoster, & Bushway, Cumulative Prevalence of Arrest From Ages 8 to 23 in a National Sample, 129 Pediatrics 21 (2011).

The Court also accepts uncritically the Government's representation at oral argument that it is developing devices that will be able to test DNA in mere minutes. At most, this demonstrates that it may one day be possible to design a program that uses DNA for a purpose other than crime-solving—not that Maryland has in fact designed such a program today. And that is the main point, which the Court's discussion of the brave new world of instant DNA analysis should not obscure. The issue before us is not whether DNA can some day be used for identification; nor even whether it can today be used for identification; but whether it was used for identification here.

Today, it can fairly be said that fingerprints really are used to identify people—so well, in fact, that there would

be no need for the expense of a separate, wholly redundant DNA confirmation of the same information. What DNA adds—what makes it a valuable weapon in the law-enforcement arsenal—is the ability to solve unsolved crimes, by matching old crime-scene evidence against the profiles of people whose identities are already known. That is what was going on when King's DNA was taken, and we should not disguise the fact. Solving unsolved crimes is a noble objective, but it occupies a lower place in the American pantheon of noble objectives than the protection of our people from suspicionless law-enforcement searches. The Fourth Amendment must prevail.

*　　*　　*

The Court disguises the vast (and scary) scope of its holding by promising a limitation it cannot deliver. The Court repeatedly says that DNA testing, and entry into a national DNA registry, will not befall thee and me, dear reader, but only those arrested for "serious offense[s]." Ante, at 28; see also ante, at 1, 9, 14, 17, 22, 23, 24 (repeatedly limiting the analysis to "serious offenses"). I cannot imagine what principle could possibly justify this limitation, and the Court does not attempt to suggest any. If one believes that DNA will "identify" someone arrested for assault, he must believe that it will "identify" someone arrested for a traffic offense. This Court does not base its judgments on senseless distinctions. At the end of the day, logic will out. When there comes before us the taking of DNA from an arrestee for a traffic violation, the Court will predictably (and quite rightly) say, "We can find no significant difference between this case and King." Make no mistake about it: As an entirely predictable consequence of today's decision, your DNA can be taken and entered into a national DNA database if you are ever arrested, rightly or wrongly, and for whatever reason.

The most regrettable aspect of the suspicionless search that occurred here is that it proved to be quite unnecessary. All parties concede that it would have been entirely permissible, as far as the Fourth Amendment is concerned, for Maryland to take a sample of King's DNA as a consequence of his conviction for second-degree assault. So the ironic result of the Court's error is this: The only arrestees to whom the outcome here will ever make a difference are those who have been acquitted of the crime of arrest (so that their DNA could not have been taken upon conviction). In other words, this Act manages to burden uniquely the sole group for whom the Fourth Amendment's protections ought to be most jealously guarded: people who are innocent of the State's accusations.

Today's judgment will, to be sure, have the beneficial effect of solving more crimes; then again, so would the taking of DNA samples from anyone who flies on an airplane (surely the Transportation Security Administration needs to know the "identity" of the flying public), applies for a driver's license, or attends a public school. Perhaps the construction of such a genetic panopticon is wise. But I doubt that the proud men who wrote the charter of our liberties would have been so eager to open their mouths for royal inspection.

I therefore dissent, and hope that today's incursion upon the Fourth Amendment, like an earlier one, 6 will some day be repudiated.

Justice Scalia's dissent in US v. Windsor (June 26, 2013) [Notes omitted]

Justice Scalia, with whom Justice Thomas joins, and with whom The Chief Justice joins as to Part I, dissenting.

This case is about power in several respects. It is about the power of our people to govern themselves, and the power of this Court to pronounce the law. Today's opinion aggrandizes the latter, with the predictable consequence of diminishing the former. We have no power to decide this case. And even if we did, we have no power under the Constitution to invalidate this democratically adopted legislation. The Court's errors on both points spring forth from the same diseased root: an exalted conception of the role of this institution in America.

I

A

The Court is eager—hungry—to tell everyone its view of the legal question at the heart of this case. Standing in the way is an obstacle, a technicality of little interest to anyone but the people of We the People, who created it as a barrier against judges' intrusion into their lives. They gave judges, in Article III, only the "judicial Power," a power to decide not abstract questions but real, concrete "Cases" and "Controversies." Yet the plaintiff and the Government agree entirely on what should happen in this lawsuit. They agree that the court below got it right; and they agreed in the court below that the court below that one got it right as well. What, then, are we doing here?

The answer lies at the heart of the jurisdictional portion of today's opinion, where a single sentence lays bare the majority's vision of our role. The Court says that we have the power to decide this case because if we did not, then our "primary role in determining the constitutionality of a law" (at least one that "has inflicted real injury on a plaintiff") would "become only secondary to the President's." Ante, at 12. But wait, the reader wonders—Windsor won below, and so cured her injury, and the President was glad to see it. True, says the majority, but judicial review must march on regardless, lest we "undermine the clear dictate of the separation-of-powers principle that when an Act of Congress is alleged to conflict with the Constitution, it is emphatically the province and duty of the judicial department to say what the law is." Ibid. (internal quotation marks and brackets omitted).

That is jaw-dropping. It is an assertion of judicial supremacy over the people's Representatives in Congress and the Executive. It envisions a Supreme Court standing (or rather enthroned) at the apex of government, empowered to decide all constitutional questions, always and every-where "primary" in its role.

This image of the Court would have been unrecognizable to those who wrote and ratified our national charter. They knew well the dangers of "primary" power, and so created branches of government that would be "perfectly co-ordinate by the terms of their common commission," none of which branches could "pretend to an exclusive or superior right of settling the boundaries between their respective powers." The Federalist, No. 49, p. 314 (C. Rossiter ed. 1961) (J. Madison). The people did this to protect themselves. They did it to guard their right to self-rule against the black-robed supremacy that today's majority finds so attractive. So it was that Madison could confidently state, with no fear of contradiction, that there was nothing of "greater intrinsic value" or "stamped with the authority of more enlightened patrons of liberty" than a government of separate and coordinate powers. Id., No. 47, at 301.

For this reason we are quite forbidden to say what the law is whenever (as today's opinion asserts) " 'an Act of Congress is alleged to conflict with the Constitution.' " Ante, at 12. We can do so only when that allegation will determine the outcome of a lawsuit, and is contradicted by the other party. The "judicial Power" is not, as the major-ity believes, the power " 'to say what the law is,' " ibid., giving the Supreme Court the "primary role in determining the constitutionality of laws." The majority must have in mind one of the foreign constitutions that pronounces such primacy for its constitutional court and allows that primacy to be exercised in contexts other than a lawsuit. See, e.g., Basic Law for the Federal Republic of Germany, Art. 93. The judicial power as Americans have understood it (and their English ancestors before them) is the power to adjudicate, with conclusive effect, disputed government claims (civil or criminal) against private persons, and disputed claims by private persons against the government or other private persons. Sometimes (though not always) the parties before the court disagree not with regard to the facts of their case (or not only with regard to the facts) but with regard to the applicable law—in which event (and only in which event) it becomes the " 'province and duty of the judicial department to say what the law is.' " Ante, at 12.

In other words, declaring the compatibility of state or federal laws with the Constitution is not only not the "primary role" of this Court, it is not a separate, free-standing role at all. We perform that role incidentally—by accident, as it were—when that is necessary to resolve the dispute before us. Then, and only then, does it become " 'the province and duty of the judicial department to say what the law is.' " That is why, in 1793, we politely declined the Washington Administration's request to "say what the law is" on a particular treaty matter that was not the subject of a concrete legal controversy. 3 Correspondence and Public Papers of John Jay 486–489 (H. Johnston ed. 1893). And that is why, as our opinions have said, some questions of law will never be presented to this Court, because there will never be anyone with standing to bring a lawsuit. See Schlesinger v. Reservists Comm. to Stop the War, 418 U. S. 208, 227 (1974); United States v. Richardson, 418 U. S. 166, 179 (1974) . As Justice Brandeis put it, we cannot "pass upon the constitutionality of legislation in a friendly, non-adversary, proceeding"; absent a " 'real, earnest and vital controversy between individuals,' " we have neither any work to do nor any power to do it. Ashwander v. TVA, 297 U. S. 288, 346 (1936) (concurring opinion) (quoting Chicago & Grand Trunk R. Co. v. Wellman, 143 U. S. 339, 345 (1892)). Our authority begins and ends with the need to adjudge the rights of an injured party who stands before us seeking redress. Lujan v. Defenders of Wildlife, 504 U. S. 555, 560 (1992)

.

That is completely absent here. Windsor's injury was cured by the judgment in her favor. And while, in ordinary circumstances, the United States is injured by a directive to pay a tax refund, this suit is far from ordinary. Whatever injury the United States has suffered will surely not be redressed by the action that it, as a litigant, asks us to take. The final sentence of the Solicitor General's brief on the merits reads: "For the foregoing reasons, the judgment of the court of appeals should be affirmed." Brief for United States (merits) 54 (emphasis added). That will not cure the Government's injury, but carve it into stone. One could spend many fruitless afternoons ransacking our library for any other petitioner's brief seeking an affirmance of the judgment against it. 1 What the petitioner United States asks us to do in the case before us is exactly what the respondent Windsor asks us to do: not to provide relief from the judgment below but to say that that judgment was correct. And the same was true in the Court of Appeals: Neither party sought to undo the judgment for Windsor, and so that court should have dismissed the appeal (just as we should dismiss) for lack of jurisdiction. Since both parties agreed with the judgment of the District Court for the Southern District of New York, the suit should have ended there. The further proceedings have been a contrivance, having no object in mind except to elevate a District Court judgment that has no precedential effect in other courts, to one that has precedential effect throughout the Second Circuit, and then (in this Court) precedential effect throughout the United States.

We have never before agreed to speak—to "say what the law is"—where there is no controversy before us. In the more than two centuries that this Court has existed as an institution, we have never suggested that we have the power to decide a question when every party agrees with both its nominal opponent and the court below on that question's answer. The United States reluctantly conceded that at oral argument. See Tr. of Oral Arg. 19–20.

The closest we have ever come to what the Court blesses today was our opinion in INS v. Chadha, 462 U. S. 919 (1983) . But in that case, two parties to the litigation disagreed with the position of the United States and with the court below: the House and Senate, which had intervened in the case. Because Chadha concerned the validity of a mode of congressional action—the one-house legislative veto—the House and Senate were threatened with destruction of what they claimed to be one of their institutional powers. The Executive choosing not to defend that power, 2 we permitted the House and Senate to intervene. Nothing like that is present here.

To be sure, the Court in Chadha said that statutory aggrieved-party status was "not altered by the fact that the Executive may agree with the holding that the statute in question is unconstitutional." Id., at 930–931. But ina footnote to that statement, the Court acknowledged Arti-cle III's separate requirement of a "justiciable case or controversy," and stated that this requirement was satisfied "because of the presence of the two Houses of Congress as adverse parties." Id., at 931, n. 6. Later in its opinion, the Chadha Court remarked that the United States' announced intention to enforce the statute also sufficed to permit judicial review, even absent congressional participation. Id., at 939. That remark is true, as a description of the judicial review conducted in the Court of Appeals, where the Houses of Congress had not intervened. (The case originated in the Court of Appeals, since it sought review of agency action under 8 U. S. C. §1105a(a) (1976 ed.).) There, absent a judgment setting aside the INS order, Chadha faced deportation. This pas-sage of our opinion seems to be addressing that initial standing in the Court of Appeals, as indicated by its quotation from the lower court's opinion, 462 U. S., at 939–940. But if it was addressing standing to pursue the appeal, the remark was both the purest dictum (as congressional intervention at that point made the required adverseness "beyond doubt," id., at 939), and quite incorrect. When a private party has a judicial decree safely in hand to prevent his injury, additional judicial action requires that a party injured by the decree seek to undo it. In Chadha, the intervening House and Senate fulfilled that requirement. Here no one does.

The majority's discussion of the requirements of Article III bears no resemblance to our jurisprudence. It accuses the amicus (appointed to argue against our jurisdiction) of "elid[ing] the distinction between . . . the jurisdictional requirements of Article III and the prudential limits on its exercise." Ante, at 6. It then proceeds to call the requirement of adverseness a "prudential" aspect of standing. Of standing. That is incomprehensible. A plaintiff (or appellant) can have all the standing in the world—satisfying all three standing requirements of Lujan that the majority so carefully quotes, ante, at 7—and yet no Article III controversy may be before the court. Article III requires not just a plaintiff (or appellant) who has standing to complain but an opposing party who denies the validity of the complaint. It is not the amicus that has done the eliding of distinctions, but the majority, calling the quite separate Article III requirement of adverseness between the parties an element (which it then pronounces a "prudential" element) of standing. The question here is not whether, as the majority puts it, "the United States retains a stake sufficient to support Article III jurisdiction," ibid. the question is whether there is any controversy (which requires contradiction) between the United States and Ms. Windsor. There is not.

I find it wryly amusing that the majority seeks to dismiss the requirement of party-adverseness as nothing more than a "prudential" aspect of the sole Article III requirement of standing. (Relegating a jurisdictional requirement to "prudential" status is a wondrous device, enabling courts to ignore the requirement whenever they believe it "prudent"—which is to say, a good idea.) Half a century ago, a Court similarly bent upon announcing its view regarding the constitutionality of a federal statute achieved that goal by effecting a remarkably similar but completely opposite distortion of the principles limiting our jurisdiction. The Court's notorious opinion in Flast v. Cohen, 392 U. S. 83– 101 (1968), held that standing was merely an element (which it pronounced to be a "prudential" element) of the sole Article III requirement of adverseness. We have been living with the chaos created by that power-grabbing decision ever since, see Hein v. Freedom From Religion Foundation, Inc., 551 U. S. 587 (2007), as we will have to live with the chaos created by this one.

The authorities the majority cites fall miles short of supporting the counterintuitive notion that an Article III "controversy" can exist without disagreement between the parties. In Deposit Guaranty Nat. Bank v. Roper, 445 U. S. 326 (1980), the District Court had entered judgment in the individual plaintiff's favor based on the defendant bank's offer to pay the full amount claimed. The plaintiff, however, sought to appeal the District Court's denial of class certification under Federal Rule of Civil Procedure 23. There was a continuing dispute between the parties concerning the issue raised on appeal. The same is true of the other case cited by the majority, Camreta v. Greene, 563 U. S. ____ (2011). There the District Court found that the defendant state officers had violated the Fourth Amendment, but rendered judgment in their favor because they were entitled to official immunity, application of the Fourth Amendment to their conduct not having been clear at the time of violation. The officers sought to appeal the holding of Fourth Amendment violation, which would circumscribe their future conduct; the plaintiff continued to insist that a Fourth Amendment violation had occurred. The "prudential" discretion to which both those cases refer was the discretion to deny an appeal even when a live controversy exists—not the discretion to grant one when it does not. The majority can cite no case in which this Court entertained an appeal in which both parties urged us to affirm the judgment below. And that is because the existence of a controversy is not a "prudential" requirement that we have invented, but an essential element of an Article III case or controversy. The majority's notion that a case between friendly parties can be entertained so long as "adversarial presentation of the issues is assured by the participation of amici curiae prepared to defend with vigor" the other side of the issue, ante, at 10, effects a breathtaking revolution in our Article III jurisprudence.

It may be argued that if what we say is true some Presidential determinations that statutes are unconstitutional will not be subject to our review. That is as it should be, when both the President and the plaintiff agree that the statute is unconstitutional. Where the Executive is enforcing an unconstitutional law, suit will of course lie; but if, in that suit, the Executive admits the unconstitutionality of the law, the litigation should end in an order or a consent decree enjoining enforcement. This suit saw the light of day only because the President enforced the Act (and thus gave Windsor standing to sue) even though he believed it unconstitutional. He could have equally chosen (more appropriately, some would say) neither to enforce nor to defend the statute he believed to be unconstitutional, see Presidential Authority to Decline to Execute Un-constitutional Statutes, 18 Op. Off. Legal Counsel 199 (Nov. 2, 1994)—in which event Windsor would not have been injured, the District Court could not have refereed this friendly scrimmage, and the Executive's determination of unconstitutionality would have escaped this Court's desire to blurt out its view of the law. The matter would have been left, as so many matters ought to be left, to a tug of war between the President and the Congress, which has innumerable means (up to and including impeachment) of compelling the President to enforce the laws it has written. Or the President could have evaded presentation of the constitutional issue to this Court simply by declining to appeal the District Court and Court of Appeals dispositions he agreed with. Be sure of this much: If a President wants to insulate his judgment of unconstitutionality from our review, he can. What the views urged in this dissent produce is not insulation from judicial review but insulation from Executive contrivance.

The majority brandishes the famous sentence from Marbury v. Madison, 1 Cranch 137, 177 (1803) that "[i]t is emphatically the province and duty of the judicial department to say what the law is." Ante, at 12 (internal quotation marks omitted). But that sentence neither says nor implies that it is always the province and duty of the Court to say what the law is—much less that its responsibility in that regard is a "primary" one. The very next sentence of Chief Justice Marshall's opinion makes the crucial qualification that today's majority ignores: "Those who apply the rule to particular cases, must of necessity expound and interpret that rule." 1 Cranch, at 177 (emphasis added). Only when a "particular case" is before us—that is, a controversy that it is our business to resolve under Article III—do we have the province and duty to pronounce the law. For the views of our early Court more precisely addressing the question before us here, the majority ought instead to have consulted the opinion of Chief Justice Taney in Lord v. Veazie, 8 How. 251 (1850):

"The objection in the case before us is . . . that the plaintiff and defendant have the same interest, and that interest adverse and in conflict with the interest of third persons, whose rights would be seriously affected if the question of law was decided in the manner that both of the parties to this suit desire it to be.

"A judgment entered under such circumstances, and for such purposes, is a mere form. The whole proceeding was in contempt of the court, and highly reprehensible . . . . A judgment in form, thus procured, in the eye of the law is no judgment of the court. It is a nullity, and no writ of error will lie upon it. This writ is, therefore, dismissed." Id., at 255–256.

There is, in the words of Marbury, no "necessity [to] expound and interpret" the law in this case; just a desire to place this Court at the center of the Nation's life. 1 Cranch, at 177.

B

A few words in response to the theory of jurisdiction set forth in Justice Alito's dissent: Though less far reaching in its consequences than the majority's conversion of constitutionally required adverseness into a discretionary element of standing, the theory of that dissent similarly elevates the Court to the "primary" determiner of constitutional questions involving the separation of powers, and, to boot, increases the power of the most dangerous branch: the "legislative department," which by its nature "draw[s] all power into its impetuous vortex." The Federalist, No. 48, at 309 (J. Madison). Heretofore in our national his-tory, the President's failure to "take Care that the Laws be faithfully executed," U. S. Const., Art. II, §3, could only be brought before a judicial tribunal by someone whose concrete interests were harmed by that alleged failure. Justice Alito would create a system in which Congress can hale the Executive before the courts not only to vindicate its own institutional powers to act, but to correct a perceived inadequacy in the execution of its laws. 3 This would lay to rest Tocqueville's praise of our judicial system as one which "intimately bind[s] the case made for the law with the case made for one man," one in which legislation is "no longer exposed to the daily aggression of the parties," and in which "[t]he political question that [the judge] must resolve is linked to the interest" of private litigants. A. de Tocqueville, Democracy in America 97 (H. Mansfield & D. Winthrop eds. 2000). That would be replaced by a system in which Congress and the Executive can pop immediately into court, in their institutional capacity, whenever the President refuses to implement a statute he believes to be unconstitutional, and whenever he implements a law in a manner that is not to Congress's liking.

Justice Alito's notion of standing will likewise enormously shrink the area to which "judicial censure, exercised by the courts on legislation, cannot extend," ibid. For example, a bare majority of both Houses could bring into court the assertion that the Executive's implementation of welfare programs is too generous—a failure that no other litigant would have standing to complain about. Moreover, as we indicated in Raines v. Byrd, 521 U. S. 811, 828 (1997), if Congress can sue the Executive for the erroneous application of the law that "injures" its power to legislate, surely the Executive can sue Congress for its erroneous adoption of an unconstitutional law that "injures" the Executive's power to administer—or perhaps for its protracted failure to act on one of his nominations. The opportunities for dragging the courts into disputes hitherto left for political resolution are endless.

Justice Alito's dissent is correct that Raines did not formally decide this issue, but its reasoning does. The opinion spends three pages discussing famous, decades-long disputes between the President and Congress—regarding congressional power to forbid the Presidential removal of executive officers, regarding the legislative veto, regarding congressional appointment of executive officers, and regarding the pocket veto—that would surely have been promptly resolved by a Congress-vs.-the-President lawsuit if the impairment of a branch's powers alone conferred standing to commence litigation. But it does not, and never has; the "enormous power that the judiciary would acquire" from the ability to adjudicate such suits "would have made a mockery of [Hamilton's] quotation of Montesquieu to the effect that 'of the three powers above mentioned . . . the JUDICIARY is next to nothing.' " Barnes v. Kline, 759 F. 2d 21, 58 (CADC 1985) (Bork, J., dissenting) (quoting The Federalist No. 78 (A. Hamilton)).

To be sure, if Congress cannot invoke our authority in the way that Justice Alito proposes, then its only recourse is to confront the President directly. Unimaginable evil this is not. Our system is designed for confrontation. That is what "[a]mbition . . . counteract[ing] ambition," The Federalist, No. 51, at 322 (J. Madison), is all about. If majorities in both Houses of Congress care enough about the matter, they have available innumerable ways to compel executive action without a lawsuit—from refusing to confirm Presidential appointees to the elimination of funding. (Nothing says "enforce the Act" quite like ". . . or you will have money for little else.") But the condition is crucial; Congress must care enough to act against the President itself, not merely enough to instruct its lawyers to ask us to do so. Placing the Constitution's entirely anticipated political arm wrestling into permanent judicial receivership does not do the system a favor. And by the way, if the President loses the lawsuit but does not faithfully implement the Court's decree, just as he did not faithfully implement Congress's statute, what then? Only Congress can bring him to heel by . . . what do you think? Yes: a direct confrontation with the President.

II

For the reasons above, I think that this Court has, and the Court of Appeals had, no power to decide this suit. We should vacate the decision below and remand to the Court of Appeals for the Second Circuit, with instructions to dismiss the appeal. Given that the majority has volunteered its view of the merits, however, I proceed to discuss that as well.

A

There are many remarkable things about the majority's merits holding. The first is how rootless and shifting its justifications are. For example, the opinion starts with seven full pages about the traditional power of States to define domestic relations—initially fooling many readers, I am sure, into thinking that this is a federalism opinion. But we are eventually told that "it is unnecessary to decide whether this federal intrusion on state power is a violation of the Constitution," and that "[t]he State's power in defining the marital relation is of central relevance in this case quite apart from principles of federalism" be-cause "the State's decision to give this class of persons the right to marry conferred upon them a dignity and status of immense import." Ante, at 18. But no one questions the power of the States to define marriage (with the concomitant conferral of dignity and status), so what is the point of devoting seven pages to describing how long and well established that power is? Even after the opinion has formally disclaimed reliance upon principles of federalism, mentions of "the usual tradition of recognizing and accepting state definitions of marriage" continue. See, e.g., ante, at 20. What to make of this? The opinion never explains. My guess is that the majority, while reluctant to suggest that defining the meaning of "marriage" in federal statutes is unsupported by any of the Federal Government's enumerated powers, 4 nonetheless needs some rhetorical basis to support its pretense that today's prohibition of laws excluding same-sex marriage is confined to the Federal Government (leaving the second, state-law shoe to be dropped later, maybe next Term). But I am only guessing.

Equally perplexing are the opinion's references to "the Constitution's guarantee of equality." Ibid. Near the end of the opinion, we are told that although the "equal protection guarantee of the Fourteenth Amendment makes [the] Fifth Amendment [due process] right all the more specific and all the better understood and preserved"—what can that mean?—"the Fifth Amendment itself withdraws from Government the power to degrade or demean in the way this law does." Ante, at 25. The only possible interpretation of this statement is that the Equal Protection Clause, even the Equal Protection Clause as incorporated in the Due Process Clause, is not the basis for today's holding. But the portion of the majority opinion that explains why DOMA is unconstitutional (Part IV) begins by citing Bolling v. Sharpe, 347 U. S. 497 (1954), Department of Agriculture v. Moreno, 413 U. S. 528 (1973), and Romer v. Evans, 517 U. S. 620 (1996) —all of which are equal-protection cases. 5 And those three cases are the only authorities that the Court cites in Part IV about the Constitution's meaning, except for its citation of Lawrence v. Texas, 539 U. S. 558 (2003) (not an equal-protection case) to support its passing assertion that the Constitution protects the "moral and sexual choices" of same-sex couples, ante, at 23.

Moreover, if this is meant to be an equal-protection opinion, it is a confusing one. The opinion does not resolve and indeed does not even mention what had been the central question in this litigation: whether, under the Equal Protection Clause, laws restricting marriage to a man and a woman are reviewed for more than mere rationality. That is the issue that divided the parties and the court below, compare Brief for Respondent Bipartisan Legal Advisory Group of U. S. House of Representatives (merits) 24–28 (no), with Brief for Respondent Windsor (merits) 17–31 and Brief for United States (merits) 18–36 (yes); and compare 699 F. 3d 169, 180–185 (CA2 2012) (yes), with id., at 208–211 (Straub, J., dissenting in part and concurring in part) (no). In accord with my previously expressed skepticism about the Court's "tiers of scrutiny" approach, I would review this classification only for its rationality. See United States v. Virginia, 518 U. S. 515–570 (1996) (Scalia, J., dissenting). As nearly as I can tell, the Court agrees with that; its opinion does not apply strict scrutiny, and its central propositions are taken from rational-basis cases like Moreno. But the Court certainly does not apply anything that resembles that deferential framework. See Heller v. Doe, 509 U. S. 312, 320 (1993) (a classification "'must be upheld . . . if there is any reason-ably conceivable state of facts' " that could justify it).

The majority opinion need not get into the strict-vs.-rational-basis scrutiny question, and need not justify its holding under either, because it says that DOMA is unconstitutional as "a deprivation of the liberty of the person protected by the Fifth Amendment of the Constitution," ante, at 25; that it violates "basic due process" principles, ante, at 20; and that it inflicts an "injury and indignity" of a kind that denies "an essential part of the liberty protected by the Fifth Amendment," ante, at 19. The majority never utters the dread words "substantive due process," perhaps sensing the disrepute into which that doctrine has fallen, but that is what those statements mean. Yet the opinion does not argue that same-sex marriage is "deeply rooted in this Nation's history and tradition," Washington v. Glucksberg, 521 U. S. 702–721(1997), a claim that would of course be quite absurd. So would the further suggestion (also necessary, under our substantive-due-process precedents) that a world in which DOMA exists is one bereft of " 'ordered liberty.' " Id., at 721 (quoting Palko v. Connecticut, 302 U. S. 319, 325 (1937)).

Some might conclude that this loaf could have used a while longer in the oven. But that would be wrong; it is already overcooked. The most expert care in preparation cannot redeem a bad recipe. The sum of all the Court's nonspecific hand-waving is that this law is invalid (maybe on equal-protection grounds, maybe on substantive-due-process grounds, and perhaps with some amorphous federalism component playing a role) because it is motivated by a " 'bare . . . desire to harm' " couples in same-sex marriages. Ante, at 20. It is this proposition with which I will therefore engage.

B

As I have observed before, the Constitution does not forbid the government to enforce traditional moral and sexual norms. See Lawrence v. Texas, 539 U. S. 558, 599 (2003) (Scalia, J., dissenting). I will not swell the U. S. Reports with restatements of that point. It is enough to say that the Constitution neither requires nor forbids our society to approve of same-sex marriage, much as it neither requires nor forbids us to approve of no-fault divorce, polygamy, or the consumption of alcohol.

However, even setting aside traditional moral disapproval of same-sex marriage (or indeed same-sex sex), there are many perfectly valid—indeed, downright boring—justifying rationales for this legislation. Their existence ought to be the end of this case. For they give the lie to the Court's conclusion that only those with hateful hearts could have voted "aye" on this Act. And more importantly, they serve to make the contents of the legislators' hearts quite irrelevant: "It is a familiar principle of constitutional law that this Court will not strike down an otherwise constitutional statute on the basis of an alleged illicit legislative motive." United States v. O'Brien, 391 U. S. 367, 383 (1968) . Or at least it was a familiar principle. By holding to the contrary, the majority has declared open season on any law that (in the opinion of the law's opponents and any panel of like-minded federal judges) can be characterized as mean-spirited.

The majority concludes that the only motive for this Act was the "bare . . . desire to harm a politically unpopular group." Ante, at 20. Bear in mind that the object of this condemnation is not the legislature of some once-Confederate Southern state (familiar objects of the Court's scorn, see, e.g., Edwards v. Aguillard, 482 U. S. 578 (1987)), but our respected coordinate branches, the Congress and Presidency of the United States. Laying such a charge against them should require the most extraordinary evidence, and I would have thought that every attempt would be made to indulge a more anodyne explanation for the statute. The majority does the opposite—affirmatively concealing from the reader the arguments that exist in justification. It makes only a passing mention of the "arguments put forward" by the Act's defenders, and does not even trouble to paraphrase or describe them. See ante, at 21. I imagine that this is because it is harder to maintain the illusion of the Act's supporters as unhinged members of a wild-eyed lynch mob when one first describes their views as they see them.

To choose just one of these defenders' arguments, DOMA avoids difficult choice-of-law issues that will now arise absent a uniform federal definition of marriage. See, e.g., Baude, Beyond DOMA: Choice of State Law in Federal Statutes, 64 Stan. L. Rev. 1371 (2012). Imagine a pair of women who marry in Albany and then move to Alabama, which does not "recognize as valid any marriage of parties of the same sex." Ala. Code §30–1–19(e) (2011). When the couple files their next federal tax return, may it be a joint one? Which State's law controls, for federal-law purposes: their State of celebration (which recognizes the marriage) or their State of domicile (which does not)? (Does the answer depend on whether they were just visiting in Albany?) Are these questions to be answered as a matter of federal common law, or perhaps by borrowing a State's choice-of-law rules? If so, which State's? And what about States where the status of an out-of-state same-sex marriage is an unsettled question under local law? See Godfrey v. Spano, 13 N. Y. 3d 358, 920 N. E. 2d 328 (2009). DOMA avoided all of this uncertainty by specifying which marriages would be recognized for federal purposes. That is a classic purpose for a definitional provision.

Further, DOMA preserves the intended effects of prior legislation against then-unforeseen changes in circumstance. When Congress provided (for example) that a special estate-tax exemption would exist for spouses, this exemption reached only opposite-sex spouses—those being the only sort that were recognized in any State at the time of DOMA's passage. When it became clear that changes in state law might one day alter that balance, DOMA's definitional section was enacted to ensure that state-level experimentation did not automatically alter the basic operation of federal law, unless and until Congress made the further judgment to do so on its own. That is not animus—just stabilizing prudence. Congress has hardly demonstrated itself unwilling to make such further, revising judgments upon due deliberation. See, e.g., Don't Ask, Don't Tell Repeal Act of 2010, 124Stat. 3515.

The Court mentions none of this. Instead, it accuses the Congress that enacted this law and the President who signed it of something much worse than, for example, having acted in excess of enumerated federal powers—or even having drawn distinctions that prove to be irrational. Those legal errors may be made in good faith, errors though they are. But the majority says that the supporters of this Act acted with malice—with the "purpose" (ante, at 25) "to disparage and to injure" same-sex couples. It says that the motivation for DOMA was to "demean," ibid.; to "impose inequality," ante, at 22; to "impose . . . a stigma," ante, at 21; to deny people "equal dignity," ibid.; to brand gay people as "unworthy," ante, at 23; and to "humiliat[e]" their children, ibid. (emphasis added).

I am sure these accusations are quite untrue. To be sure (as the majority points out), the legislation is called the Defense of Marriage Act. But to defend traditional marriage is not to condemn, demean, or humiliate those who would prefer other arrangements, any more than to defend the Constitution of the United States is to condemn, demean, or humiliate other constitutions. To hurl such accusations so casually demeans this institution. In the majority's judgment, any resistance to its holding is beyond the pale of reasoned disagreement. To question its high-handed invalidation of a presumptively valid statute is to act (the majority is sure) with the purpose to "disparage," "injure," "degrade," "demean," and "humiliate" our fellow human beings, our fellow citizens, who are homosexual. All that, simply for supporting an Act that did no more than codify an aspect of marriage that had been unquestioned in our society for most of its existence—indeed, had been unquestioned in virtually all societies for virtually all of human history. It is one thing for a society to elect change; it is another for a court of law to impose change by adjudging those who oppose it hostes humani generis, enemies of the human race.

*　　*　　*

The penultimate sentence of the majority's opinion is a naked declaration that "[t]his opinion and its holding are confined" to those couples "joined in same-sex marriages made lawful by the State." Ante, at 26, 25. I have heard such "bald, unreasoned disclaimer[s]" before. Lawrence, 539 U. S., at 604. When the Court declared a constitutional right to homosexual sodomy, we were assured that the case had nothing, nothing at all to do with "whether the government must give formal recognition to any relationship that homosexual persons seek to enter." Id., at 578. Now we are told that DOMA is invalid because it "demeans the couple, whose moral and sexual choices the Constitution protects," ante, at 23—with an accompanying citation of Lawrence. It takes real cheek for today's majority to assure us, as it is going out the door, that a constitutional requirement to give formal recognition to same-sex marriage is not at issue here—when what has preceded that assurance is a lecture on how superior the majority's moral judgment in favor of same-sex marriage is to the Congress's hateful moral judgment against it. I promise you this: The only thing that will "confine" the Court's holding is its sense of what it can get away with.

I do not mean to suggest disagreement with The Chief Justice's view, ante, p. 2–4 (dissenting opinion), that lower federal courts and state courts can distinguish today's case when the issue before them is state denial of marital status to same-sex couples—or even that this Court could theoretically do so. Lord, an opinion with such scatter-shot rationales as this one (federalism noises among them) can be distinguished in many ways. And deserves to be. State and lower federal courts should take the Court at its word and distinguish away.

In my opinion, however, the view that this Court will take of state prohibition of same-sex marriage is indicated beyond mistaking by today's opinion. As I have said, the real rationale of today's opinion, whatever disappearing trail of its legalistic argle-bargle one chooses to follow, is that DOMA is motivated by " 'bare . . . desire to harm' " couples in same-sex marriages. Supra, at 18. How easy it is, indeed how inevitable, to reach the same conclusion with regard to state laws denying same-sex couples marital status. Consider how easy (inevitable) it is to make the following substitutions in a passage from today's opinion ante, at 22:

"FONT DOMA's FONT This state law's principal effect is to identify a subset of FONT state-sanctioned marriages FONT constitution-ally protected sexual relationships, see Lawrence, and make them unequal. The principal purpose is to impose inequality, not for other reasons like govern-mental efficiency. Responsibilities, as well as rights, enhance the dignity and integrity of the person. And FONT DOMA FONT this state law contrives to deprive some couples FONT married under the laws of their State FONT enjoying constitutionally protected sexual relationships, but not other couples, of both rights and responsibilities."

Or try this passage, from ante, at 22–23:

"FONT [DOMA] FONT This state law tells those couples, and all the world, that their otherwise valid FONT marriages FONT relationships are unworthy of FONT federal FONT state recognition. This places same-sex couples in an unstable position of being in a second-tier FONT marriage FONT relationship. The differentiation demeans the couple, whose moral and sexual choices the Constitution protects, see Lawrence, ..."

Or this, from ante, at 23—which does not even require alteration, except as to the invented number:

"And it humiliates FONT tens of FONT thousands of children now being raised by same-sex couples. The law in question makes it even more difficult for the children to understand the integrity and closeness of their own family and its concord with other families in their community and in their daily lives."

Similarly transposable passages—deliberately transposable, I think—abound. In sum, that Court which finds it so horrific that Congress irrationally and hatefully robbed same-sex couples of the "personhood and dignity" which state legislatures conferred upon them, will of a certitude be similarly appalled by state legislatures' irrational and hateful failure to acknowledge that "personhood and dig-nity" in the first place. Ante, at 26. As far as this Court is concerned, no one should be fooled; it is just a matter of listening and waiting for the other shoe.

By formally declaring anyone opposed to same-sex marriage an enemy of human decency, the majority arms well every challenger to a state law restricting marriage to its traditional definition. Henceforth those challengers will lead with this Court's declaration that there is "no legitimate purpose" served by such a law, and will claim that the traditional definition has "the purpose and effect to disparage and to injure" the "personhood and dignity" of same-sex couples, see ante, at 25, 26. The majority's limiting assurance will be meaningless in the face of language like that, as the majority well knows. That is why the language is there. The result will be a judicial distortion of our society's debate over marriage—a debate that can seem in need of our clumsy "help" only to a member of this institution.

As to that debate: Few public controversies touch an institution so central to the lives of so many, and few inspire such attendant passion by good people on all sides. Few public controversies will ever demonstrate so vividly the beauty of what our Framers gave us, a gift the Court pawns today to buy its stolen moment in the spotlight: a system of government that permits us to rule ourselves. Since DOMA's passage, citizens on all sides of the question have seen victories and they have seen defeats. There have been plebiscites, legislation, persuasion, and loud voices—in other words, democracy. Victories in one place for some, see North Carolina Const., Amdt. 1 (providing that "[m]arriage between one man and one woman is the only domestic legal union that shall be valid or recognized in this State") (approved by a popular vote, 61% to 39%on May 8, 2012), 6 are offset by victories in other places for others, see Maryland Question 6 (establishing "that Maryland's civil marriage laws allow gay and lesbian couples to obtain a civil marriage license") (approved by a popular vote, 52% to 48%, on November 6, 2012). 7 Even in a single State, the question has come out differently on different occasions. Compare Maine Question 1 (permitting "the State of Maine to issue marriage licenses to same-sex couples") (approved by a popular vote, 53% to 47%, on November 6, 2012) 8 with Maine Question 1 (rejecting "the new law that lets same-sex couples marry") (approved by a popular vote, 53% to 47%, on November 3, 2009). 9

In the majority's telling, this story is black-and-white: Hate your neighbor or come along with us. The truth is more complicated. It is hard to admit that one's political opponents are not monsters, especially in a struggle like this one, and the challenge in the end proves more than today's Court can handle. Too bad. A reminder that dis-agreement over something so fundamental as marriage can still be politically legitimate would have been a fit task for what in earlier times was called the judicial temperament. We might have covered ourselves with honor today, by promising all sides of this debate that it was theirs to settle and that we would respect their resolution. We might have let the People decide.

But that the majority will not do. Some will rejoice in today's decision, and some will despair at it; that is the nature of a controversy that matters so much to so many. But the Court has cheated both sides, robbing the winners of an honest victory, and the losers of the peace that comes from a fair defeat. We owed both of them better. I dissent.

Justice Scalia's dissent from denial of application for stay in Brown v. Plata [and Coleman] (August 2, 2013)

The application for stay presented to JUSTICE KENNEDY and by him referred to the Court is denied. JUSTICE ALITO would grant the application for stay.

JUSTICE SCALIA, with whom JUSTICE THOMAS joins, dissenting.

When this case was here two Terms ago, I dissented from the Court's affirmance of the injunction, because the District Court's order that California release 46,000 prisoners violated the clear limitations of the Prison Litigation Reform Act, 18 U. S. C. §3626(a)(1)(A)—"besides defying all sound conception of the proper role of judges."

Brown v. Plata, 563 U. S. ____, ____ (2011) (slip op., at 16). The Court's opinion approving the order concluded with what I described as a "bizarre coda," id., at ____ (slip op., at 12), which said that "[t]he State may wish to move for modification" of the injunction, and that the District Court "may grant such a request provided that the State satisfies necessary and appropriate preconditions," ibid. (internal quotation marks omitted). More specifically, the opinion suggested that modification might be in order if the State makes "significant progress . . . toward remedying the underlying constitutional violations" and "demonstrate[s] that further population reductions are not necessary." Id., at ____ (slip op., at 47). These "deliberately ambiguous . . . suggestions on how to modify the injunction," were, I observed, "just deferential enough so that [the Court] can say with a straight face that it is 'affirming,' just stern enough to put the District Court on notice that it will likely get reversed if it does not follow them." Id., at ____ (slip op., at 13) (dissenting opinion). That was in my view "a compromise solution" that is "unknown in our legal system," which does not permit appellate courts to pre- scribe in advance the exercise of district-court discretion. Id., at ____, ____ (slip op., at 13, 14). I warned, moreover, that "the judges of the District Court are likely to call [the Court's] bluff, since they know full well it cannot possibly be an abuse of discretion to refuse to accept the State's proposed modifications in an injunction that has just been approved (affirmed) in its present form." Id., at ____ (slip op., at 14).

The bluff has been called, and the Court has nary a pair to lay on the table. The State, seeking to invoke the ex ante appellate control of district-court discretion, and to compel the modification decreed by the Court's raised eyebrow, provided evidence that it has made meaningful progress and that population reductions to the level required by the injunction are unnecessary. But the latter argument was made and rejected in the last round, and the former hardly requires (demands) modification of the injunction. It was predictable two Terms ago that the State would make progress—indeed, it promised to do so. If the reality of incremental progress makes the injunction now invalid, the probability (indeed, one might say the certainty) of incremental progress made the injunction an overreach two Terms ago. Surely it is not the case that when a party subject to an injunction makes substantial progress toward compliance it is an abuse of discretion not to revise the injunction.

But as I suggested in my dissent, perhaps the Court never meant to follow through on its revision suggestions. Perhaps they were nothing more than "a ceremonial washing of the hands—making it clear for all to see, that if the terrible things sure to happen as a consequence of this outrageous order do happen, they will be none of this Court's responsibility. After all, did we not want, and indeed even suggest, something better?" Ibid. So also today, it is not our fault that California must now release upon the public nearly 10,000 inmates convicted of serious crimes—about 1,000 for every city larger than Santa Ana—three-quarters of whom are moderate (57%) or high (74%) recidivism risks. Reply in Support of Application 34.

It appears to have become a standard ploy, when this Court vastly expands the

Power of the Black Robe, to hint at limitations that make it seem not so bad. See, e.g., Lawrence v. Texas, 539 U. S. 558, 604 (2003) (SCALIA, J., dissenting); United States v. Windsor, 570 U. S. ___, ___ (2013) (slip op., at 25–26) (SCALIA, J., dissenting). Comes the moment of truth, the hinted-at limitation proves a sham. As for me, I adhere to my original view of this terrible injunction. It goes beyond what the Prison Litigation Reform Act allows, and beyond the power of the courts. I would grant the stay and dissolve the injunction.

Justice Scalia's dissent in Bond v. United States (June 2, 2014) [Notes omitted]

Justice Scalia, with whom Justice Thomas joins, and with whom Justice Alito joins as to Part I, concurring in the judgment.

Somewhere in Norristown, Pennsylvania, a husband's paramour suffered a minor thumb burn at the hands of a betrayed wife. The United States Congress—"every where extending the sphere of its activity, and drawing all power into its impetuous vortex" 1 — has made a federal case out of it. What are we to do?

It is the responsibility of "the legislature, not the Court, . . . to define a crime, and ordain its punishment." United States v. Wiltberger, 5 Wheat. 76, 95 (1820) (Marshall, C. J., for the Court). And it is "emphatically the province and duty of the judicial department to say what the law [including the Constitution] is." Marbury v. Madison, 1 Cranch 137, 177 (1803) (same). Today, the Court shirks its job and performs Congress's. As sweeping and unsettling as the Chemical Weapons Convention Implementation Act of 1998 may be, it is clear beyond doubt that it covers what Bond did; and we have no authority to amend it. So we are forced to decide—there is no way around it—whether the Act's application to what Bond did was constitutional.

I would hold that it was not, and for that reason would reverse the judgment of the Court of Appeals for the Third Circuit.

I. The Statutory Question

A. Unavoidable Meaning of the Text

The meaning of the Act is plain. No person may knowingly "develop, produce, otherwise acquire, transfer directly or indirectly, receive, stockpile, retain, own, possess, or use, or threaten to use, any chemical weapon." 18 U. S. C. §229(a)(1). A "chemical weapon" is "[a] toxic chemical and its precursors, except where intended for a purpose not prohibited under this chapter as long as the type and quantity is consistent with such a purpose." §229F(1)(A). A "toxic chemical" is "any chemical which through its chemical action on life processes can cause death, temporary incapacitation or permanent harm to humans or animals. The term includes all such chemicals, regardless of their origin or of their method of production, and regardless of whether they are produced in facilities, in munitions or elsewhere." §229F(8)(A). A "purpose not prohibited" is "[a]ny peaceful purpose related to an industrial, agricultural, research, medical, or pharmaceutical activity or other activity." §229F(7)(A).

Applying those provisions to this case is hardly complicated. Bond possessed and used "chemical[s] which through [their] chemical action on life processes can cause death, temporary incapacitation or permanent harm." Thus, she possessed "toxic chemicals." And, because they were not possessed or used only for a "purpose not prohibited," §229F(1)(A), they were "chemical weapons." Ergo, Bond violated the Act. End of statutory analysis, I would have thought. 2

The Court does not think the interpretive exercise so simple. But that is only because its result-driven antitextualism befogs what is evident.

B. The Court's Interpretation

The Court's account of the clear-statement rule reads like a really good lawyer's brief for the wrong side, relying on cases that are so close to being on point that someone eager to reach the favored outcome might swallow them. The relevance to this case of United States v. Bass, 404 U. S. 336 (1971), and Jones v. United States, 529 U. S. 848 (2000), is, in truth, entirely made up. In Bass, we had to decide whether a statute forbidding " 'receiv[ing], possess[ing], or transport[ing] in commerce or affecting commerce . . . any firearm' " prohibited possessing a gun that lacked any connection to interstate commerce. 404 U. S., at 337–339. Though the Court relied in part on a federalism-inspired interpretive presumption, it did so only after it had found, in Part I of the opinion, applying traditional interpretive tools, that the text in question was ambiguous, id., at 339–347. Adopting in Part II the narrower of the two possible readings, we said that "unless Congress conveys its purpose clearly, it will not be deemed to have significantly changed the federal-state balance." Id., at 349 (emphasis added). Had Congress "convey[ed] its purpose clearly" by enacting a clear and even sweeping statute, the presumption would not have applied.

Jones is also irrelevant. To determine whether an owner-occupied private residence counted as a " 'property usedin interstate or foreign commerce or in any activity affecting interstate or foreign commerce' " under the federal arson statute, 529 U. S., at 850–851, our opinion examined not the federal-jurisdiction-expanding consequences of answering yes but rather the ordinary meaning of the words—and answered no, id., at 855–857. Then, in a separate part of the opinion, we observed that our reading was consistent with the principle that we should adopt a construction that avoids "grave and doubtful constitutional questions," id., at 857, and, quoting Bass, the principle that Congress must convey its purpose clearly before its laws will be " 'deemed to have significantly changed the federal-state balance,' " 529 U. S., at 858. To say that the best reading of the text conformed to those principles is not to say that those principles can render clear textambiguous. 3

The latter is what the Court says today. Inverting Bass and Jones, it starts with the federalism-related consequences of the statute's meaning and reasons backwards, holding that, if the statute has what the Court considers a disruptive effect on the "federal-state balance" of criminal jurisdiction, ante, at 14, that effect causes the text, even if clear on its face, to be ambiguous. Just ponder what the Court says: "[The Act's] ambiguity derives from the improbably broad reach of the key statutory definition . . . the deeply serious consequences of adopting such a boundless reading; and the lack of any apparent need to do so . . . ." Ibid. (emphasis added). Imagine what future courts can do with that judge-empowering principle: Whatever has improbably broad, deeply serious, and apparently unnecessary consequences . . . is ambiguous!

The same skillful use of oh-so-close-to-relevant cases characterizes the Court's pro forma attempt to find ambiguity in the text itself, specifically, in the term "[c]hemical weapon." The ordinary meaning of weapon, the Court says, is an instrument of combat, and "no speaker in natural parlance would describe Bond's feud-driven act of spreading irritating chemicals on Haynes's door knob and mailbox as 'combat.' " Ante, at 15–16. Undoubtedly so, but undoubtedly beside the point, since the Act supplies its own definition of "chemical weapon," which unquestionably does bring Bond's action within the statutory prohibition. The Court retorts that "it is not unusual to consider the ordinary meaning of a defined term, particularly when there is dissonance between that ordinary meaning and the reach of the definition." Ante, at 16. So close to true! What is "not unusual" is using the ordinary meaning of the term being defined for the purpose of resolving an ambiguity in the definition. When, for example, "draft," a word of many meanings, is one of the words used in a definition of "breeze," we know it has nothing to do with military conscription or beer. The point is illustrated by the almost-relevant case the Court cites for its novel principle, Johnson v. United States, 559 U. S. 133 (2010). There the defined term was "violent felony," which the Act defined as an offense that " 'has as an element the use . . . of physical force against the person of another.' " Id., at 135 (quoting §924(e)(2)(B)(i)). We had to figure out what "physical force" meant, since the statute "d[id] not define" it. Id., at 138 (emphasis added). So we consulted (among other things) the general meaning of the term being defined, "violent felony." Id., at 140.

In this case, by contrast, the ordinary meaning of the term being defined is irrelevant, because the statute's own definition—however expansive—is utterly clear: any "chemical which through its chemical action on life proc-esses can cause death, temporary incapacitation or permanent harm to humans or animals," §229F(8)(A), unless the chemical is possessed or used for a "peaceful purpose," §229F(1)(A), (7)(A). The statute parses itself. There is no opinion of ours, and none written by any court or put forward by any commentator since Aristotle, which says, or even suggests, that "dissonance" between ordinary meaning and the unambiguous words of a definition is to be resolved in favor of ordinary meaning. If that were the case, there would hardly be any use in providing a definition. No, the true rule is entirely clear: "When a statute includes an explicit definition, we must follow that definition, even if it varies from that term's ordinary meaning." Stenberg v. Carhart, 530 U. S. 914, 942 (2000) (emphasis added). Once again, contemplate the judge-empowering consequences of the new interpretive rule the Court today announces: When there is "dissonance" between the statutory definition and the ordinary meaning of the defined word, the latter may prevail.

But even text clear on its face, the Court suggests, must be read against the backdrop of established interpretive presumptions. Thus, we presume "that a criminal statute derived from the common law carries with it the requirement of a culpable mental state—even if no such limitation appears in the text." Ante, at 11. And we presume that "federal statutes do not apply outside the United States." Ibid. Both of those are, indeed, established interpretive presumptions that are (1) based upon realistic assessments of congressional intent, and (2) well known to Congress—thus furthering rather than subverting genuine legislative intent. To apply these presumptions, then, is not to rewrite clear text; it is to interpret words fairly, in light of their statutory context. But there is nothing either (1) realistic or (2) well known about the presumption the Court shoves down the throat of a resisting statute today. Who in the world would have thought that a definition is inoperative if it contradicts ordinary meaning? When this statute was enacted, there was not yet a "Bond presumption" to that effect—though presumably Congress will have to take account of the Bond presumption in the future, perhaps by adding at the end of all its definitions that depart from ordinary connotation "and we really mean it."

C. The Statute as Judicially Amended

I suspect the Act will not survive today's gruesome surgery. A criminal statute must clearly define the conduct it proscribes. If it does not " 'give a person of ordi-nary intelligence fair notice' " of its scope, United States v. Batchelder, 442 U. S. 114, 123 (1979), it denies due process.

The new §229(a)(1) fails that test. Henceforward, a person "shall be fined . . ., imprisoned for any term of years, or both," §229A(a)(1)—or, if he kills someone, "shall be punished by death or imprisoned for life," §229A(a)(2)—whenever he "develop[s], produce[s], otherwise acquire[s], transfer[s] directly or indirectly, receive[s], stockpile[s], retain[s], own[s], possess[es], or use[s], or threaten[s] to use," §229(a)(1), any chemical "of the sort that an ordinary person would associate with instruments of chemical warfare," ante, at 15 (emphasis added). Whether that test is satisfied, the Court unhelpfully (and also illogically) explains, depends not only on the "particular chemicals that the defendant used" but also on "the circumstances in which she used them." Ibid. The "detergent under the kitchen sink" and "the stain remover in the laundry room" are apparently out, ante, at 16—but what if they are deployed to poison a neighborhood water fountain? Poisoning a goldfish tank is also apparently out, ante, at 17, but what if the fish belongs to a Congressman or Governor and the act is meant as a menacing message, a small-time equivalent of leaving a severed horse head in the bed? See ibid. (using the "concerns" driving the Convention—"acts of war, assassination, and terrorism"—as guideposts of statutory meaning). Moreover, the Court's illogical embellishment seems to apply only to the "use" of a chemical, ante, at 15, but "use" is only 1 of 11 kinds of activity that the statute prohibits. What, one wonders, makes something a "chemical weapon" when it is merely "stockpile[d]" or "possess[ed]?" To these questions and countless others, one guess is as bad as another.

No one should have to ponder the totality of the circumstances in order to determine whether his conduct is a felony. Yet that is what the Court will now require of all future handlers of harmful toxins—that is to say, all of us. Thanks to the Court's revisions, the Act, which before was merely broad, is now broad and unintelligible. "[N]o standard of conduct is specified at all." Coates v. Cincinnati, 402 U. S. 611, 614 (1971). Before long, I suspect, courts will be required to say so.

II. The Constitutional Question

Since the Act is clear, the real question this case presents is whether the Act is constitutional as applied to petitioner. An unreasoned and citation-less sentence from our opinion in Missouri v. Holland, 252 U. S. 416 (1920), purported to furnish the answer: "If the treaty is valid"—and no one argues that the Convention is not—"there can be no dispute about the validity of the statute under Article I, §8, as a necessary and proper means to execute the powers of the Government." Id., at 432. 4 Petitioner and her amici press us to consider whether there is anything to this ipse dixit. The Constitution's text and structure show that there is not. 5

A. Text

Under Article I, §8, cl. 18, Congress has the power "[t]o make all Laws which shall be necessary and proper for carrying into Execution the foregoing Powers and all other Powers vested by this Constitution in the Governmentof the United States, or in any Department or Officer thereof." One such "other Powe[r]" appears in Article II, §2, cl. 2: "[The President] shall have Power, by and with the Advice and Consent of the Senate, to make Treaties, provided two thirds of the Senators present concur." Read together, the two Clauses empower Congress to pass laws "necessary and proper for carrying into Execution . . . [the] Power . . . to make Treaties."

It is obvious what the Clauses, read together, do not say. They do not authorize Congress to enact laws for carrying into execution "Treaties," even treaties that do not execute themselves, such as the Chemical Weapons Convention. 6 Surely it makes sense, the Government contends, that Congress would have the power to carry out the obligations to which the President and the Senate have committed the Nation. The power to "carry into Execution" the "Power . . . to make Treaties," it insists, has to mean the power to execute the treaties themselves.

That argument, which makes no pretense of resting on text, unsurprisingly misconstrues it. Start with the phrase "to make Treaties." A treaty is a contract with a foreign nation made, the Constitution states, by the President with the concurrence of "two thirds of the Senators present." That is true of self-executing and non-self-executing treaties alike; the Constitution does not distinguish between the two. So, because the President and the Senate can enter into a non-self-executing compact with a foreign nation but can never by themselves (without the House) give that compact domestic effect through legislation, the power of the President and the Senate "to make" a Treaty cannot possibly mean to "enter into a compact with a foreign nation and then give that compact domestic legal effect." We have said in another context that a right "to make contracts" (a treaty, of course, is a contract) does not "extend . . . to conduct . . . after the contract relation has been established . . . . Such postformation conduct does not involve the right to make a contract, but rather implicates the performance of established contract obligations." Patterson v. McLean Credit Union, 491 U. S. 164, 177 (1989) (emphasis added). Upon the President's agreement and the Senate's ratification, a treaty—no matter what kind—has been made and is not susceptible of any more making.

How might Congress have helped "carr[y]" the power to make the treaty—here, the Chemical Weapons Convention—"into Execution"? In any number of ways. It could have appropriated money for hiring treaty negotiators, empowered the Department of State to appoint those negotiators, formed a commission to study the benefits and risks of entering into the agreement, or paid for a bevy of spies to monitor the treaty-related deliberations of other potential signatories. See G. Lawson & G. Seidman, The Constitution of Empire: Territorial Expansion and American Legal History 63 (2004). The Necessary and Proper Clause interacts similarly with other Article II powers: "[W]ith respect to the executive branch, the Clause would allow Congress to institute an agency to help the President wisely employ his pardoning power . . . . Most important, the Clause allows Congress to establish officers to assist the President in exercising his 'executive Power.' " Calabresi & Prakash, The President's Power to Execute the Laws, 104 Yale L. J. 541, 591 (1994).

But a power to help the President make treaties is not a power to implement treaties already made. See generally Rosenkranz, Executing the Treaty Power, 118 Harv. L. Rev. 1867 (2005). Once a treaty has been made, Congress's power to do what is "necessary and proper" to assist the making of treaties drops out of the picture. To legislate compliance with the United States' treaty obligations, Congress must rely upon its independent (though quite robust) Article I, §8, powers.

B. Structure

"[T]he Constitutio[n] confer[s] upon Congress . . . not all governmental powers, but only discrete, enumerated ones." Printz v. United States, 521 U. S. 898, 919 (1997) . And, of course, "enumeration presupposes something not enumerated." Gibbons v. Ogden, 9 Wheat. 1, 195 (1824). But in Holland, the proponents of unlimited congressional power found a loophole: "By negotiating a treaty and obtaining the requisite consent of the Senate, the President . . . may endow Congress with a source of legislative authority independent of the powers enumerated in Article I." L. Tribe, American Constitutional Law §4–4, pp. 645–646 (3d ed. 2000). Though Holland's change to the Constitution's text appears minor (the power to carry into execution the power to make treaties becomes the power to carry into execution treaties), the change to its structure is seismic.

To see why vast expansion of congressional power is not just a remote possibility, consider two features of the modern practice of treaty making. In our Nation's early history, and extending through the time when Holland was written, treaties were typically bilateral, and addressed only a small range of topics relating to the obli-gations of each state to the other, and to citizens of the other—military neutrality, for example, or military alliance, or guarantee of most-favored-nation trade treatment. See Bradley, The Treaty Power and American Federalism, 97 Mich. L. Rev. 390, 396 (1998). But beginning in the last half of the last century, many treaties were "detailed multilateral instruments negotiated and drafted at international conferences," ibid., and they sought to regulate states' treatment of their own citizens, or even "the activities of individuals and private entities," A. Chayes & A. Chayes, The New Sovereignty: Compliance with International Regulatory Agreements 14 (1995). "[O]ften vague and open-ended," such treaties "touch on almost every aspect of domestic civil, political, and cultural life." Bradley & Goldsmith, Treaties, Human Rights, and Condi-tional Consent, 149 U. Pa. L. Rev. 399, 400 (2000).

Consider also that, at least according to some scholars, the Treaty Clause comes with no implied subject-matter limitations. See, e.g., L. Henkin, Foreign Affairs and the United States Constitution 191, 197 (2d ed. 1996); but see Bradley, supra, at 433–439. On this view, "[t]he Tenth Amendment . . . does not limit the power to make treaties or other agreements," Restatement (Third) of Foreign Relations Law of the United States §302, Comment d, p. 154 (1986), and the treaty power can be used to regulate matters of strictly domestic concern, see id., at Comment c, p. 153; but see post, at 3–16 (Thomas, J., concurring in judgment).

If that is true, then the possibilities of what the Federal Government may accomplish, with the right treaty in hand, are endless and hardly farfetched. It could begin, as some scholars have suggested, with abrogation of this Court's constitutional rulings. For example, the holding that a statute prohibiting the carrying of firearms near schools went beyond Congress's enumerated powers, United States v. Lopez, 514 U. S. 549, 551 (1995), could be reversed by negotiating a treaty with Latvia providing that neither sovereign would permit the carrying of guns near schools. Similarly, Congress could reenact the invalidated part of the Violence Against Women Act of 1994 that provided a civil remedy for victims of gender-motivated violence, just so long as there were a treaty on point—and some authors think there already is, see MacKinnon, The Supreme Court, 1999 Term, Comment, 114 Harv. L. Rev. 135, 167 (2000).

But reversing some of this Court's decisions is the least of the problem. Imagine the United States' entry into an Antipolygamy Convention, which called for—and Congress enacted—legislation providing that, when a spouse of a man with more than one wife dies intestate, the surviv-ing husband may inherit no part of the estate. Constitu-tional? The Federalist answers with a rhetorical ques-tion: "Suppose by some forced constructions of its authority (which indeed cannot easily be imagined) the Federal Legislature should attempt to vary the law of descent in any State; would it not be evident that . . . it had exceeded its jurisdiction and infringed upon that of the State?" The Federalist No. 33, at 206 (A. Hamilton). Yet given the Antipolygamy Convention, Holland would uphold it. Or imagine that, to execute a treaty, Congress enacted a statute prohibiting state inheritance taxes on real prop-erty. Constitutional? Of course not. Again, The Federalist: "Suppose . . . [Congress] should undertake to abrogate a land tax imposed by the authority of a State, would it not be equally evident that this was an invasion of that concurrent jurisdiction in respect to this species of tax which its constitution plainly supposes to exist in the State governments?" No. 33, at 206. Holland would uphold it. As these examples show, Holland places Congress only one treaty away from acquiring a general police power.

The Necessary and Proper Clause cannot bear such weight. As Chief Justice Marshall said regarding it, no "great substantive and independent power" can be "implied as incidental to other powers, or used as a means of executing them." McCulloch v. Maryland, 4 Wheat. 316, 411 (1819); see Baude, Rethinking the Federal Eminent Domain Power, 122 Yale L. J. 1738, 1749–1755 (2013).No law that flattens the principle of state sovereignty, whether or not "necessary," can be said to be "proper." As an old, well-known treatise put it, "it would not be a proper or constitutional exercise of the treaty-making power to provide that Congress should have a general legislative authority over a subject which has not been given it by the Constitution." 1 W. Willoughby, The Constitutional Law of the United States §216, p. 504 (1910).

We would not give the Government's support of the Holland principle the time of day were we confronted with "treaty-implementing" legislation that abrogated the freedom of speech or some other constitutionally protected individual right. We proved just that in Reid v. Covert, 354 U. S. 1 (1957), which held that commitments made in treaties with Great Britain and Japan would not permit civilian wives of American servicemen stationed in those countries to be tried for murder by court-martial. The plurality opinion said that "no agreement with a foreign nation can confer power on the Congress, or on any other branch of Government, which is free from the restraints of the Constitution." Id., at 16.

To be sure, the Reid plurality purported to distinguish the ipse dixit of Holland with its own unsupported ipse dixit. "[T]he people and the States," it said, "have delegated [the treaty] power to the National Government [so] the Tenth Amendment is no barrier." 354 U. S., at 18. The opinion does not say why (and there is no reason why) only the Tenth Amendment, and not the other nine, has been "delegated" away by the treaty power. The distinction between provisions protecting individual liberty, on the one hand, and "structural" provisions, on the other, cannot be the explanation, since structure in general—and especially the structure of limited federal powers—is designed to protect individual liberty. "The federal structure . . . secures the freedom of the individual. . . . By denying any one government complete jurisdiction over all the concerns of public life, federalism protects the liberty of the individual from arbitrary power." Bond v. United States, 564 U. S. ___, ___ (2011) (slip op., at 9–10).

The Government raises a functionalist objection: If the Constitution does not limit a self-executing treaty to the subject matter delineated in Article I, §8, then it makes no sense to impose that limitation upon a statute implementing a non-self-executing treaty. See Tr. of Oral Arg. 32–33. The premise of the objection (that the power to make self-executing treaties is limitless) is, to say the least, arguable. But even if it is correct, refusing to extend that proposition to non-self-executing treaties makes a great deal of sense. Suppose, for example, that the self-aggrandizing Federal Government wishes to take over the law of intestacy. If the President and the Senate find in some foreign state a ready accomplice, they have two options. First, they can enter into a treaty with "stipulations" specific enough that they "require no legislation to make them operative," Whitney v. Robertson, 124 U. S. 190, 194 (1888), which would mean in this example something like a comprehensive probate code. But for that to succeed, the President and a supermajority of the Senate would need to reach agreement on all the details—which, when once embodied in the treaty, could not be altered or superseded by ordinary legislation. The second option—far the better one—is for Congress to gain lasting and flexible control over the law of intestacy by means of a non-self-executing treaty. "[Implementing] legislation is as much subject to modification and repeal by Congress as legislation upon any other subject." Ibid. And to make such a treaty, the President and Senate would need to agree only that they desire power over the law of intestacy.

The famous scholar and jurist Henry St. George Tucker saw clearly the danger of Holland's ipse dixit five years before it was written:

"[The statement is made that] if the treaty-making power, composed of the President and Senate, in discharging its functions under the government, finds that it needs certain legislative powers which Congress does not possess to carry out its desires, it may . . . infuse into Congress such powers, although the Framers of the Constitution omitted to grant them to Congress. . . . Every reputable commentator upon the Constitution from Story down to the present day, has held that the legislative powers of Congress lie in grant and are limited by such grant. . . . [S]hould such a construction as that asserted in the above statement obtain through judicial endorsement, our system of government would soon topple and fall." Limitations on the Treaty-Making Power Under the Constitution of the United States §113, pp. 129–130 (1915).

*   *   *

We have here a supposedly "narrow" opinion which, in order to be "narrow," sets forth interpretive principles never before imagined that will bedevil our jurisprudence (and proliferate litigation) for years to come. The immediate product of these interpretive novelties is a statute that should be the envy of every lawmaker bent on trapping the unwary with vague and uncertain criminal prohibitions. All this to leave in place an ill-considered ipse dixit that enables the fundamental constitutional principle of limited federal powers to be set aside by the President and Senate's exercise of the treaty power. We should not have shirked our duty and distorted the law to preserve that assertion; we should have welcomed and eagerly grasped the opportunity—nay, the obligation—to consider and repudiate it.

Justice Scalia's dissent from the denial of certiorari in Elmbrook School District v. Doe (June 16, 2014)

Justice Scalia, with whom Justice Thomas joins, dissenting from the denial of certiorari.

Some there are—many, perhaps—who are offended by public displays of religion. Religion, they believe, is a personal matter; if it must be given external manifestation, that should not occur in public places where others may be offended. I can understand that attitude: It parallels my own toward the playing in public of rock music or Stravinsky. And I too am especially annoyed when the intrusion upon my inner peace occurs while I am part of a captive audience, as on a municipal bus or in the waiting room of a public agency.

My own aversion cannot be imposed by law because of the First Amendment. See Ward v. Rock Against Racism, 491 U. S. 781, 790 (1989); Erznoznik v. Jacksonville, 422 U. S. 205–211 (1975). Certain of this Court's cases, however, have allowed the aversion to religious displays to be enforced directly through the First Amendment, at least in public facilities and with respect to public ceremonies—this despite the fact that the First Amendment explicitly favors religion and is, so to speak, agnostic about music.

In the decision below, the en banc Court of Appeals for the Seventh Circuit relied on those cases to condemn a suburban Milwaukee school district's decision to hold high-school graduations in a church. We recently confronted and curtailed this errant line of precedent in Town of Greece v. Galloway, 572 U. S. ___ (2014), which upheld under the Establishment Clause the saying of prayers before monthly town-council meetings. Because that case made clear a number of points with which the Seventh Circuit's decision is fundamentally inconsistent, the Court ought, at a minimum, to grant certiorari, vacate the judgment, and remand for reconsideration (GVR).

Endorsement

First, Town of Greece abandoned the antiquated "endorsement test," which formed the basis for the decision below.

In this case, at the request of the student bodies of the two relevant schools, the Elmbrook School District decided to hold its high-school graduation ceremonies at Elmbrook Church, a nondenominational Christian house of worship. The students of the first school to move its ceremonies preferred that site to what had been the usual venue, the school's gymnasium, which was cramped, hot, and uncomfortable. The church offered more space, air conditioning, and cushioned seating. No one disputes that the church was chosen only because of these amenities.

Despite that, the Seventh Circuit held that the choice of venue violated the Establishment Clause, primarily because it failed the endorsement test. That infinitely malleable standard asks whether governmental action has the purpose or effect of "endorsing" religion. See County of Allegheny v. American Civil Liberties Union, Greater Pittsburgh Chapter, 492 U. S. 573–594 (1989). The Seventh Circuit declared that the endorsement test remains part of "the prevailing analytical tool for the analysis of Establishment Clause claims." 687 F. 3d 840, 849 (2012) (internal quotation marks omitted). 1 * And here, "the sheer religiosity of the space created a likelihood that high school students and their younger siblings would perceive a link between church and state." Id., at 853.

In Town of Greece, the Second Circuit had also relied on the notion of endorsement. See 681 F. 3d 20, 30 (2012). We reversed the judgment without applying that test. What is more, we strongly suggested approval of a previous opinion "disput[ing] that endorsement could be the proper [Establishment Clause] test, as it likely would condemn a host of traditional practices that recognize the role religion plays in our society, among them legislative prayer and the 'forthrightly religious' Thanksgiving proclamations issued by nearly every President since Washington." 572 U. S., at ____ (slip op., at 11) (describing County of Allegheny, supra, at 670–671 (Kennedy, J., concurring in judgment in part and dissenting in part)). After Town of Greece, the Seventh Circuit's declaration— which controlled its subsequent analysis—that the endorsement test remains part of "the prevailing analytical tool" for assessing Establishment Clause challenges, 687 F. 3d, at 849 (internal quotation marks omitted), misstates the law.

Coercion

Second, Town of Greece made categorically clear that mere "[o]ffense . . . does not equate to coercion" in any manner relevant to the proper Establishment Clause analysis. 572 U. S., at ____ (slip op., at 21) (opinion of Kennedy, J.). "[A]n Establishment Clause violation is not made out any time a person experiences a sense of affront from the expression of contrary religious views." Ibid. See also id., at ____ (Thomas, J., concurring in part and concurring in judgment) (slip op., at 7–8) (same).

Here, the Seventh Circuit held that the school district's "decision to use Elmbrook Church for graduations was religiously coercive" under Lee v. Weisman, 505 U. S. 577 (1992) , and Santa Fe Independent School Dist. v. Doe, 530 U. S. 290 (2000) . 687 F. 3d, at 854. Lee and Santa Fe, however, are inapposite because they concluded (however unrealistically) that students were coerced to engage in school-sponsored prayer. In this case, it is beyond dispute that no religious exercise whatever occurred. At most, respondents complain that they took offense at being in a religious place. See 687 F. 3d, at 848 (plaintiffs asserted that they " 'felt uncomfortable, upset, offended, unwelcome, and/or angry' because of the religious setting" of the graduations). Were there any question before, Town of Greece made obvious that this is insufficient to state an Establishment Clause violation.

It bears emphasis that the original understanding of the kind of coercion that the Establishment Clause condemns was far narrower than the sort of peer-pressure coercion that this Court has recently held unconstitutional in cases like Lee and Santa Fe. "The coercion that was a hallmark of historical establishments of religion was coercion of religious orthodoxy and of financial support by force of law and threat of penalty." Lee, supra, at 640 (Scalia, J., dissenting). See also Town of Greece, supra, at ____–____ (opinion of Thomas, J.) (slip op., at 5–8).

As the Supreme Court of Wisconsin explained in a 1916 case challenging the siting of public high-school graduations in local churches:

"A man may feel constrained to enter a house of worship belonging to a different sect from the one with which he affiliates, but if no sectarian services are carried on, he is not compelled to worship God contrary to the dictates of his conscience, and is not obligedto do so at all." State ex rel. Conway v. District Board of Joint School Dist. No. 6, 162 Wis. 482, 490, 156 N. W. 477, 480.

History

Last but by no means least, Town of Greece left no doubt that "the Establishment Clause must be interpreted 'by reference to historical practices and understandings.' " 572 U. S., at ____ (slip op., at 7–8). Moreover, "if there is any inconsistency between [a 'test' set out in the opinions of this Court] and . . . historic practice . . . , the inconsistency calls into question the validity of the test, not the historic practice." Id., at ____ (Alito, J., concurring) (slip op., at 12).

In this case, however, the Seventh Circuit's majority opinion said nothing about history at all. And there is good reason to believe that this omission was material. As demonstrated by Conway, the Wisconsin case mentioned above, public schools have long held graduations in churches. This should come as no surprise, given that "[e]arly public schools were often held in rented rooms, church halls and basements, or other buildings that resembled Protestant churches." W. Reese, America's Public Schools 39 (2005). An 1821 Illinois law, for example, provided that a meetinghouse erected by a Presbyterian congregation "may serve to have the gospel preached therein, and likewise may be used for a school-house for the township." Ill. Laws p. 153.

We ought to remand this case to the Seventh Circuit to conduct the historical inquiry mandated by Town of Greece—or we ought to set the case for argument and conduct that inquiry ourselves.

*　　*　　*

It is perhaps the job of school officials to prevent hurt feelings at school events. But that is decidedly not the job of the Constitution. It may well be, as then-Chief Judge Easterbrook suggested, that the decision of the Elmbrook School District to hold graduations under a Latin crossin a Christian church was "unwise" and "offensive." 687F. 3d, at 869 (dissenting opinion). But Town of Greece makes manifest that an establishment of religion it was not.

In addition to being decided incorrectly, this case bears other indicia of what we have come to call "certworthiness." The Seventh Circuit's decision was en banc and prompted three powerful dissents (by then-Chief Judge Easterbrook and Judges Posner and Ripple). And it conflicts with decisions that have long allowed graduation ceremonies to take place in churches, see, e.g., Miller v. Cooper, 56 N. M. 355, 356–357, 244 P. 2d 520, 520–521 (1952); Conway, 162 Wis., at 489–493, 156 N. W., at 479–481, and with decisions upholding other public uses of religious spaces, see, e.g., Bauchman v. West High School, 132 F. 3d 542, 553–556 (CA10 1997) (sanctioning school-choir performances in venues "dominated by crosses and other religious images"); Otero v. State Election Bd. of Okla., 975 F. 2d 738, 740–741 (CA10 1992) (upholding the use of a church as a polling station); Berman v. Board of Elections, 19 N. Y. 2d 744, 745, 226 N. E. 2d 177 (1967) (same).

According to the prevailing standard, a GVR order is potentially appropriate where "intervening developments . . . reveal a reasonable probability that the decision below rests upon a premise that the lower court would reject if given the opportunity for further consideration, and where it appears that such a redetermination may determine the ultimate outcome of the litigation." Lawrence v. Chater, 516 U. S. 163, 167 (1996) (per curiam). The Court has found that standard satisfied on numerous occasions where judgments were far less obviously undermined by a subsequent decision of ours.

For these reasons, we should either grant the petition and set the case for argument or GVR in light of Town of Greece. I respectfully dissent from the denial of certiorari.

Notes

1* More precisely, the court stated that "[t]he three-pronged test set forth by the Supreme Court in Lemon v. Kurtzman, 403 U. S. 602 (1971) , remains the prevailing analytical tool for the analysis of Establishment Clause claims." 687 F. 3d, at 849 (internal quotation marks and citations omitted). It then explained that the endorsement test has become "a legitimate part of Lemon's second prong." Id., at 850.

Justice Scalia's concurrence in NLRB v. Noel Canning (June 26, 2014) [Notes omitted]

Justice Scalia, with whom The Chief Justice, Justice Thomas, and Justice Alito join, concurring in the judgment.

Except where the Constitution or a valid federal law provides otherwise, all "Officers of the United States" must be appointed by the President "by and with the Advice and Consent of the Senate." U. S. Const., Art. II, §2, cl. 2. That general rule is subject to an exception: "The President shall have Power to fill up all Vacancies that may happen during the Recess of the Senate, by granting Commissions which shall expire at the End of their next Session." Id., §2, cl. 3. This case requires us to decide whether the Recess Appointments Clause authorized three appointments made by President Obama to the National Labor Relations Board in January 2012 without the Senate's consent.

To prevent the President's recess-appointment power from nullifying the Senate's role in the appointment process, the Constitution cabins that power in two significant ways. First, it may be exercised only in "the Recess of the Senate," that is, the intermission between two formal legislative sessions. Second, it may be used to fill only those vacancies that "happen during the Recess," that is, offices that become vacant during that intermission. Both conditions are clear from the Constitution's text and structure, and both were well understood at the founding. The Court of Appeals correctly held that the appointments here at issue are invalid because they did not meet either condition.

Today's Court agrees that the appointments were in-valid, but for the far narrower reason that they were made during a 3-day break in the Senate's session. On its way to that result, the majority sweeps away the key textual limitations on the recess-appointment power. It holds, first, that the President can make appointments without the Senate's participation even during short breaks in the middle of the Senate's session, and second, that those appointments can fill offices that became vacant long before the break in which they were filled. The majority justifies those atextual results on an adverse-possession theory of executive authority: Presidents have long claimed the powers in question, and the Senate has not disputed those claims with sufficient vigor, so the Court should not "upset the compromises and working arrangements that the elected branches of Government themselves have reached." Ante, at 9.

The Court's decision transforms the recess-appointment power from a tool carefully designed to fill a narrow and specific need into a weapon to be wielded by future Presidents against future Senates. To reach that result, the majority casts aside the plain, original meaning of the constitutional text in deference to late-arising historical practices that are ambiguous at best. The majority's insistence on deferring to the Executive's untenably broad interpretation of the power is in clear conflict with our precedent and forebodes a diminution of this Court's role in controversies involving the separation of powers and the structure of government. I concur in the judgment only.

I. Our Responsibility

Today's majority disregards two overarching principles that ought to guide our consideration of the questions presented here.

First, the Constitution's core, government-structuring provisions are no less critical to preserving liberty than are the later adopted provisions of the Bill of Rights. Indeed, "[s]o convinced were the Framers that liberty of the person inheres in structure that at first they did not consider a Bill of Rights necessary." Clinton v. City of New York, 524 U. S. 417, 450 (1998) (Kennedy, J., concurring). Those structural provisions reflect the founding generation's deep conviction that "checks and balances were the foundation of a structure of government that would protect liberty." Bowsher v. Synar, 478 U. S. 714, 722 (1986) . It is for that reason that "the claims of individuals—not of Government departments—have been the principal source of judicial decisions concerning separation of powers and checks and balances." Bond v. United States, 564 U. S. ___, ___ (2011) (slip op., at 10); see, e.g., Free Enterprise Fund v. Public Company Accounting Oversight Bd., 561 U. S. 477 (2010); Clinton, supra; Plaut v. Spendthrift Farm, Inc., 514 U. S. 211 (1995); Bowsher, supra; INS v. Chadha, 462 U. S. 919 (1983); Northern Pipeline Constr. Co. v. Marathon Pipe Line Co., 458 U. S. 50 (1982) . Those decisions all rest on the bedrock principle that "the constitutional structure of our Government" is designed first and foremost not to look after the interests of the respective branches, but to "protec[t] individual liberty." Bond, supra, at ___ (slip op., at 11).

Second and relatedly, when questions involving the Constitution's government-structuring provisions are presented in a justiciable case, it is the solemn responsibility of the Judicial Branch " 'to say what the law is.' " Zivotofsky v. Clinton, 566 U. S. ___, ___ (2012) (slip op., at 7) (quoting Marbury v. Madison, 1 Cranch 137, 177 (1803)). This Court does not defer to the other branches' resolution of such controversies; as Justice Kennedy has previously written, our role is in no way "lessened" because it might be said that "the two political branches are adjusting their own powers between themselves." Clinton, supra, at 449 (concurring opinion). Since the separation of powers exists for the protection of individual liberty, its vitality "does not depend" on "whether 'the encroached-upon branch approves the encroachment.' " Free Enterprise Fund, supra, at 497 (quoting New York v. United States, 505 U. S. 144, 182 (1992)); see also Freytag v. Commissioner, 501 U. S. 868–880 (1991); Metropolitan Washington Airports Authority v. Citizens for Abatement of Aircraft Noise, Inc., 501 U. S. 252–277 (1991). Rather, policing the "enduring structure" of constitutional government when the political branches fail to do so is "one of the most vital functions of this Court." Public Citizen v. Department of Justice, 491 U. S. 440, 468 (1989) (Kennedy, J., concurring in judgment).

Our decision in Chadha illustrates that principle. There, we held that a statutory provision authorizing one House of Congress to cancel an executive action taken pursuant to statutory authority—a so-called "legislative veto"—exceeded the bounds of Congress's authority under the Constitution. 462 U. S., at 957–959. We did not hesitate to hold the legislative veto unconstitutional even though Congress had enacted, and the President had signed, nearly 300 similar provisions over the course of 50 years. Id., at 944–945. Just the opposite: We said the other branches' enthusiasm for the legislative veto "sharpened rather than blunted" our review. Id., at 944. Likewise, when the charge is made that a practice "enhances the President's powers beyond" what the Constitution permits, "[i]t is no answer . . . to say that Congress surrendered its authority by its own hand." Clinton, 524 U. S., at 451 (Kennedy, J., concurring). "[O]ne Congress cannot yield up its own powers, much less those of other Congresses to follow. Abdication of responsibility is not part of the constitutional design." Id., at 452 (citations omitted).

Of course, where a governmental practice has been open, widespread, and unchallenged since the early days of the Republic, the practice should guide our interpretation of an ambiguous constitutional provision. See, e.g., Alden v. Maine, 527 U. S. 706–744 (1999); Bowsher, supra, at 723–724; Myers v. United States, 272 U. S. 52–175 (1926); see also Youngstown Sheet & Tube Co. v. Sawyer, 343 U. S. 579, 610 (1952) (Frankfurter, J., concurring) (arguing that "a systematic, unbroken, executive practice, long pursued to the knowledge of the Congress and never before questioned" should inform interpretation of the "Executive Power" vested in the President); Rutan v. Republican Party of Ill., 497 U. S. 62, and n. 1 (1990) (Scalia, J., dissenting). But " '[p]ast practice does not, by itself, create power.' " Medellín v. Texas, 552 U. S. 491, 532 (2008) (quoting Dames & Moore v. Regan, 453 U. S. 654, 686 (1981)). That is a necessary corollary of the principle that the political branches cannot by agreement alter the constitutional structure. Plainly, then, a self-aggrandizing practice adopted by one branch well after the founding, often challenged, and never before blessed by this Court—in other words, the sort of practice on which the majority relies in this case—does not relieve us of our duty to interpret the Constitution in light of its text, structure, and original understanding.

Ignoring our more recent precedent in this area, which is extensive, the majority relies on The Pocket Veto Case, 279 U. S. 655, 689 (1929), for the proposition that when interpreting a constitutional provision "regulating the relationship between Congress and the President," we must defer to the settled practice of the political branches if the provision is " ' "in any respect of doubtful meaning." ' " Ante, at 7; see ante, at 8, 16, 23, 33. The language the majority quotes from that case was pure dictum. The Pocket Veto Court had to decide whether a bill passed by the House and Senate and presented to the President less than 10 days before the adjournment of the first session of a particular Congress, but neither signed nor vetoed by the President, became a law. Most of the opinion analyzed that issue like any other legal question and concluded that treating the bill as a law would have been inconsistent with the text and structure of the Constitution. Only near the end of the opinion did the Court add that its conclusion was "confirmed" by longstanding Presidential practice in which Congress appeared to have acquiesced. 279 U. S., at 688–689. We did not suggest that the case would have come out differently had the longstanding practice been otherwise. 1

II. Intra-Session Breaks

The first question presented is whether "the Recess of the Senate," during which the President's recess-appointment power is active, is (a) the period between two of the Senate's formal sessions, or (b) any break in the Senate's proceedings. I would hold that "the Recess" is the gap between sessions and that the appointments at issue here are invalid because they undisputedly were made during the Senate's session. The Court's contrary conclusion—that "the Recess" includes "breaks in the midst of a session," ante, at 9—is inconsistent with the Constitution's text and structure, and it requires judicial fabrication of vague, unadministrable limits on the recess-appointment power (thus defined) that overstep the judicial role. And although the majority relies heavily on "historical practice," no practice worthy of our deference supports the majority's conclusion on this issue.

A. Plain Meaning

A sensible interpretation of the Recess Appointments Clause should start by recognizing that the Clause uses the term "Recess" in contradistinction to the term "Session." As Alexander Hamilton wrote: "The time within which the power is to operate 'during the recess of the Senate' and the duration of the appointments 'to the end of the next session' of that body, conspire to elucidate the sense of the provision." The Federalist No. 67, p. 455 (J. Cooke ed. 1961).

In the founding era, the terms "recess" and "session" had well-understood meanings in the marking-out of legislative time. The life of each elected Congress typically consisted (as it still does) of two or more formal sessions separated by adjournments "sine die," that is, without a specified return date. See GPO, Congressional Directory, 113th Cong., pp. 524–542 (2013–2014) (hereinafter Congressional Directory) (listing sessions of Congress from 1789 through 2013); 705 F. 3d 490, 512, and nn. 1–2 (CADC 2013) (case below); ante, at 9. The period between two sessions was known as "the recess." See 26 Annals of Cong. 748 (1814) (Sen. Gore) ("The time of the Senate consists of two periods, viz: their session and their recess"). As one scholar has thoroughly demonstrated, "in government practice the phrase 'the Recess' always referred to the gap between sessions." Natelson, The Origins and Meaning of "Vacancies that May Happen During the Recess" in the Constitution's Recess Appointments Clause, 37 Harv. J. L. & Pub. Pol'y 199, 213 (2014) (hereinafter Natelson); see id., at 214–227 (providing dozens of examples). By contrast, other provisions of the Constitution use the verb "adjourn" rather than "recess" to refer to the commencement of breaks during a formal legislative session. See, e.g., Art. I, §5, cl. 1; id., §5, cl. 4. 2

To be sure, in colloquial usage both words, "recess" and "session," could take on alternative, less precise meanings. A session could include any short period when a legislature's members were "assembled for business," and a recess could refer to any brief "suspension" of legislative "business." 2 N. Webster, American Dictionary of the English Language (1828). So the Continental Congress could complain of the noise from passing carriages disrupting its "daily Session," 29 Journals of the Continental Congress 1774–1789, p. 561 (1785) (J. Fitzpatrick ed. 1933), and the House could "take a recess" from 4 o'clock to 6 o'clock, Journal of the House of Representatives, 17th Cong., 2d Sess., p. 259 (1823). But as even the majority acknowledges, the Constitution's use of "the word 'the' in 'the [R]ecess' " tends to suggest "that the phrase refers to the single break separating formal sessions." Ante, at 10.

More importantly, neither the Solicitor General nor the majority argues that the Clause uses "session" in its loose, colloquial sense. And if "the next Session" denotes a formal session, then "the Recess" must mean the break between formal sessions. As every commentator on the Clause until the 20th century seems to have understood, the "Recess" and the "Session" to which the Clause refers are mutually exclusive, alternating states. See, e.g., The Federalist No. 67, at 455 (explaining that appointments would require Senatorial consent "during the session of the Senate" and would be made by the President alone "in their recess"); 1 Op. Atty. Gen. 631 (1823) (contrasting vacancies occurring "during the recess of the Senate" with those occurring "during the session of the Senate"); 2 Op. Atty Gen. 525, 527 (1832) (discussing a vacancy that "took place while the Senate was in session, and not during the recess"). It is linguistically implausible to suppose—as the majority does—that the Clause uses one of those terms ("Recess") informally and the other ("Session") formally in a single sentence, with the result that an event can occur during both the "Recess" and the "Session."

Besides being linguistically unsound, the majority's reading yields the strange result that an appointment made during a short break near the beginning of one official session will not terminate until the end of the following official session, enabling the appointment to last for up to two years. The majority justifies that result by observing that the process of confirming a nominee "may take several months." Ante, at 17. But the average duration of the confirmation process is irrelevant. The Clause's self-evident design is to have the President's unilateral appointment last only until the Senate has "had an opportunity to act on the subject." 3 J. Story, Commentaries on the Constitution of the

United States §1551, p. 410 (1833) (emphasis added).

One way to avoid the linguistic incongruity of the majority's reading would be to read both "the Recess" and "the next Session" colloquially, so that the recess-appointment power would be activated during any temporary suspension of Senate proceedings, but appointments made pursuant to that power would last only until the beginning of the next suspension (which would end the next colloquial session). See, e.g., Rappaport, The Original Meaning of the Recess Appointments Clause, 52 UCLA L. Rev. 1487, 1569 (2005) (hereinafter Rappaport, Original Meaning). That approach would be more linguistically defensible than the majority's. But it would not cure the most fundamental problem with giving "Recess" its colloquial, rather than its formal, meaning: Doing so leaves the recess-appointment power without a textually grounded principle limiting the time of its exercise.

The dictionary definitions of "recess" on which the majority relies provide no such principle. On the contrary, they make clear that in colloquial usage, a recess could include any suspension of legislative business, no matter how short. See 2 S. Johnson, A Dictionary of the English Language 1602 (4th ed. 1773). Webster even provides a stark illustration: "[T]he house of representatives had a recess of half an hour." 2 Webster, supra. The notion that the Constitution empowers the President to make unilateral appointments every time the Senate takes a half-hour lunch break is so absurd as to be self-refuting. But that, in the majority's view, is what the text authorizes.

The boundlessness of the colloquial reading of "the Recess" thus refutes the majority's assertion that the Clause's "purpose" of "ensur[ing] the continued functioning of the Federal Government" demands that it apply to intra-session breaks as well as inter-session recesses. Ante, at 11. The majority disregards another self-evident purpose of the Clause: to preserve the Senate's role in the appointment process—which the founding generation regarded as a critical protection against " 'despotism,' " Freytag, 501 U. S., at 883—by clearly delineating the times when the President can appoint officers without the Senate's consent. Today's decision seriously undercuts that purpose. In doing so, it demonstrates the folly of interpreting constitutional provisions designed to establish "a structure of government that would protect liberty," Bowsher, 478 U. S., at 722, on the narrow-minded assumption that their only purpose is to make the government run as efficiently as possible. "Convenience and efficiency," we have repeatedly recognized, "are not the primary objectives" of our constitutional framework. Free Enterprise Fund, 561 U. S., at 499 (internal quotation marks omitted).

Relatedly, the majority contends that the Clause's supposed purpose of keeping the wheels of government turning demands that we interpret the Clause to maintain its relevance in light of the "new circumstance" of the Senate's taking an increasing number of intra-session breaks that exceed three days. Ante, at 17. Even if I accepted the canard that courts can alter the Constitution's meaning to accommodate changed circumstances, I would be hard pressed to see the relevance of that notion here. The rise of intra-session adjournments has occurred in tandem with the development of modern forms of communication and transportation that mean the Senate "is always available" to consider nominations, even when its Members are temporarily dispersed for an intra-session break. Tr. of Oral Arg. 21 (Ginsburg, J.). The Recess Appointments Clause therefore is, or rather, should be, an anachronism—"essentially an historic relic, something whose original purpose has disappeared." Id., at 19 (Kagan, J.). The need it was designed to fill no longer exists, and its only remaining use is the ignoble one of enabling the President to circumvent the Senate's role in the appointment process. That does not justify "read[ing] it out of the Constitution" and, contra the majority, ante, at 40, I would not do so; but neither would I distort the Clause's original meaning, as the majority does, to ensure a prominent role for the recess-appointment power in an era when its influence is far more pernicious than beneficial.

To avoid the absurd results that follow from its collo-quial reading of "the Recess," the majority is forced to declare that some intra-session breaks—though undisputedly within the phrase's colloquial meaning—are simply "too short to trigger the Recess Appointments Clause." Ante, at 21. But it identifies no textual basis whatsoever for limiting the length of "the Recess," nor does it point to any clear standard for determining how short is too short. It is inconceivable that the Framers would have left the circumstances in which the President could exercise such a significant and potentially dangerous power so utterly indeterminate. Other structural provisions of the Constitution that turn on duration are quite specific: Neither House can adjourn "for more than three days" without the other's consent. Art. I, §5, cl. 4. The President must return a passed bill to Congress "within ten Days (Sundays excepted)," lest it become a law. Id., §7, cl. 2. Yet on the majority's view, when the first Senate considered taking a 1-month break, a 3-day weekend, or a half-hour siesta, it had no way of knowing whether the President would be constitutionally authorized to appoint officers in its absence. And any officers appointed in those circumstances would have served under a cloud, unable to determine with any degree of confidence whether their appointments were valid. 3

Fumbling for some textually grounded standard, the majority seizes on the Adjournments Clause, which bars either House from adjourning for more than three days without the other's consent. Id., §5, cl. 4. According to the majority, that clause establishes that a 3-day break is always "too short" to trigger the Recess Appointments Clause. Ante, at 19. It goes without saying that nothing in the constitutional text supports that disposition. If (as the majority concludes) "the Recess" means a recess in the colloquial sense, then it necessarily includes breaks shorter than three days. And the fact that the Constitution includes a 3-day limit in one clause but omits it from the other weighs strongly against finding such a limit to be implicit in the clause in which it does not appear. In all events, the dramatically different contexts in which the two clauses operate make importing the 3-day limit from the Adjournments Clause into the Recess Appointments Clause "both arbitrary and mistaken." Rappaport, Original Meaning 1556.

And what about breaks longer than three days? The majority says that a break of four to nine days is "presumptively too short" but that the presumption may be rebutted in an "unusual circumstance," such as a "national catastrophe . . . that renders the Senate unavailable but calls for an urgent response." Ante, at 21. The majority must hope that the in terrorem effect of its "presumptively too short" pronouncement will deter future Presidents from making any recess appointments during 4-to-9-day breaks and thus save us from the absurd spectacle of unelected judges evaluating (after an evidentiary hearing?) whether an alleged "catastrophe" was sufficiently "urgent" to trigger the recess-appointment power. The majority also says that "political opposition in the Senate would not qualify as an unusual circumstance." Ibid. So if the Senate should refuse to confirm a nominee whom the President considers highly qualified; or even if it should refuse to confirm any nominee for an office, thinking the office better left vacant for the time being; the President's power would not be triggered during a 4-to-9-day break, no matter how "urgent" the President's perceived need for the officer's assistance. (The majority protests that this "should go without saying—except that Justice Scalia compels us to say it," ibid., seemingly forgetting that the appointments at issue in this very case were justified on those grounds and that the Solicitor General has asked us to view the recess-appointment power as a "safety valve" against Senatorial "intransigence." Tr. of Oral Arg. 21.)

As for breaks of 10 or more days: We are presumably to infer that such breaks do not trigger any "presumpt[ion]" against recess appointments, but does that mean the President has an utterly free hand? Or can litigants seek invalidation of an appointment made during a 10-day break by pointing to an absence of "unusual" or "urgent" circumstances necessitating an immediate appointment, albeit without the aid of a "presumpt[ion]" in their favor? Or, to put the question as it will present itself to lawyers in the Executive Branch: Can the President make an appointment during a 10-day break simply to overcome "political opposition in the Senate" despite the absence of any "national catastrophe," even though it "go[es] without saying" that he cannot do so during a 9-day break? Who knows? The majority does not say, and neither does the Constitution.

4

Even if the many questions raised by the majority's failure to articulate a standard could be answered, a larger question would remain: If the Constitution's text empowers the President to make appointments during any break in the Senate's proceedings, by what right does the majority subject the President's exercise of that power to vague, court-crafted limitations with no textual basis? The majority claims its temporal guideposts are informed by executive practice, but a President's self-restraint cannot "bind his successors by diminishing their powers." Free Enterprise Fund, 561 U. S., at 497; cf. Clinton v. Jones, 520 U. S. 681, 718 (1997) (Breyer, J., concurring in judgment) ("voluntary actions" by past Presidents "tel[l] us little about what the Constitution commands").

An interpretation that calls for this kind of judicial adventurism cannot be correct. Indeed, if the Clause really did use "Recess" in its colloquial sense, then there would be no "judicially discoverable and manageable standard for resolving" whether a particular break was long enough to trigger the recess-appointment power, making that a nonjusticiable political question. Zivotofsky, 566 U. S., at ____ (slip op., at 5) (internal quotation marks omitted).

B. Historical Practice

For the foregoing reasons, the Constitution's text and structure unambiguously refute the majority's freewheeling interpretation of "the Recess." It is not plausible that the Constitution uses that term in a sense that authorizes the President to make unilateral appointments during any break in Senate proceedings, subject only to hazy, atextual limits crafted by this Court centuries after ratification. The majority, however, insists that history "offers strong support" for its interpretation. Ante, at 11. The historical practice of the political branches is, of course, irrelevant when the Constitution is clear. But even if the Constitution were thought ambiguous on this point, history does not support the majority's interpretation.

1. 1789 to 1866

To begin, the majority dismisses the 78 years of history from the founding through 1866 as "not helpful" because during that time Congress took hardly any "significant" intra-session breaks, by which the majority evidently means breaks longer than three days. Ibid. (citing table in Appendix A, which does not include breaks of three or fewer days). In fact, Congress took 11 intra-session breaks of more than three days during that time, see Congressional Directory 524–527, and it appears Presidents made recess appointments during none of them.

More importantly, during those eight decades, Congress must have taken thousands of breaks that were three days or shorter. On the majority's reading, every one of those breaks would have been within the Clause's text—the majority's newly minted limitation not yet having been announced. Yet there is no record of anyone, ever, having so much as mentioned the possibility that the recess-appointment power was activated during those breaks. That would be surprising indeed if the text meant what the majority thinks it means. Cf. Printz v. United States, 521 U. S. 898–908 (1997).

2. 1867 and 1868

The first intra-session recess appointments in our his-tory almost certainly were made by President Andrew John-son in 1867 and 1868. 5 That was, of course, a period of dramatic conflict between the Executive and Congress that saw the first-ever impeachment of a sitting President. The Solicitor General counts 57 intra-session recess appointments during those two years. App. to Brief for Petitioner 1a–9a. But the precise nature and historical understanding of many of those appointments is subject to debate. See, e.g., Brief for Constitutional Law Scholars as Amici Curiae 23–24; Rappaport, Nonoriginalism 27–33. It seems likely that at least 36 of the 57 appointments were made with the understanding that they took place during a recess between sessions. See id., at 27–31.

As for the remainder, the historical record reveals nothing about how they were justified, if at all. There is no indication that Johnson's Attorney General or anyone else considered at the time whether those appointments were made between or during formal legislative sessions or, if the latter, how they could be squared with the constitutional text. The majority drives that point home by citing a judicial opinion that upheld one of the appointments nearly two decades later with no analysis of the question presented here. See ante, at 11 (citing Gould v. United States, 19 Ct. Cl. 593 (1884)). Johnson's intra-session appointments were disavowed by the first Attorney General to address that question, see infra, at 20, and were not followed as precedent by the Executive Branch for more than 50 years, see infra, at 22. Thus, the relevance of those appointments to our constitutional inquiry is severely limited. Cf. Brief for Political Scientists and Historians as Amici Curiae 21 (Johnson's appointments "should be viewed as anomalies" that were "sui generis in the first 130 years of the Republic").

3. 1869 to 1920

More than half a century went by before any other President made an intra-session recess appointment, and there is strong reason to think that during that period neither the Executive nor the Senate believed such a power existed. For one thing, the Senate adjourned for more than 3 days 45 times during that period, and 43 of those adjournments exceeded 10 days (and thus would not even be subject to the majority's "presumption" against the availability of recess appointments). See Congres-sional Directory 527–529. Yet there is no evidence that a single appointment was made during any of those adjournments or that any President before the 20th century even considered making such appointments.

In 1901 Philander Knox, the first Attorney General known to have opined on the question, explicitly stated that the recess-appointment power was limited to the period between formal sessions. 23 Op. Atty. Gen. 599. Knox advised President Theodore Roosevelt that he could not appoint an appraiser of merchandise during an intra-session adjournment. He explained:

"[T]he Constitution and laws make it clear that in our legislative practice an adjournment during a session of Congress means a merely temporary suspension of business from day to day . . . whereas the recess means the period after the final adjournment of Congress for the session, and before the next session begins. . . . It is this period following the final adjournment for the session which is the recess during which the President has power to fill vacancies . . . . Any intermediate temporary adjournment is not such recess, although it may be a recess in the general and ordinary use of that term." Id., at 601. 6

Knox went on to observe that none of the "many elaborate opinions" of previous Attorneys General concerning the recess-appointment power had asserted that the power could be exercised "during a temporary adjournment of the Senate," rather than "during the recess of the Senate between two sessions of Congress." Id., at 602. He acknowledged the contrary example furnished by Johnson's appointments in 1867 and 1868, but noted (with perhaps too much tact) that "[t]he public circumstances producing this state of affairs were unusual and involved results which should not be viewed as precedents." Id.,at 603.

That was where things stood when, in 1903, Roosevelt made a number of controversial recess appointments. At noon on December 7, the Senate moved seamlessly from a special session into a regular one scheduled to begin at that hour. See 37 Cong. Rec. 544; 38 Cong. Rec. 1. Roosevelt claimed to have made the appointments in a "constructive" recess between the two sessions. See Special Session Is Merged Into Regular, N. Y. Times, Dec. 8, 1903, p. 1. He and his allies in the Senate justified the appointments on the theory that "at the moment the gavel falls to summon the regular session into being there is an infinitesimal fraction of a second, which is the recess between the two sessions." Extra Session Muddle, N. Y. Times, Dec. 7, 1903, p. 3. In 1905, the Senate Judiciary Committee published a report criticizing the appointments on the ground that "the Constitution means a real recess, not a constructive one." S. Rep. No. 4389, 58th Cong., 3d Sess., p. 4. The report explained that the recess is "the period of time when the Senate is not sitting in regular or extraordinary session . . . when its members owe no duty of attendance; when its Chamber is empty; when, because of its absence, it can not receive communications from the President or participate as a body in making appointments." Id., at 2 (emphasis deleted).

The majority seeks support in this episode, claiming that the Judiciary Committee embraced a "broad and functional definition of 'recess' " consistent with the one the majority adopts. Ante, at 16. On the contrary, the episode powerfully refutes the majority's theory. Roosevelt's legal justification for his appointments was extremely aggressive, but even he recognized that "the Recess of the Senate" could take place only between formal sessions. If the majority's view of the Clause had been considered plausible, Roosevelt could have strengthened his position considerably by making the appointments during an intra-session break of a few days, or at least a few hours. (Just 10 minutes after the new session began on December 7, the Senate took "a recess for one hour." 38 Cong. Rec. 2.) That he instead strained to declare a dubious inter-session recess of an "infinitesimal fraction of a second" is powerful evidence that the majority's view of "the Recess" was not taken seriously even as late as the beginning of the 20th century.

Yet the majority contends that "to the extent that the Senate or a Senate committee has expressed a view, that view has favored a functional definition of 'recess' [that] encompasses intra-session recesses." Ante, at 14. It rests that contention entirely on the 1905 Judiciary Committee Report. This distorts what the committee said when it denied Roosevelt's claim that there had been a recess. If someone avers that a catfish is a cat, and I respond by pointing out that a catfish lives in water and does not have four legs, I have not endorsed the proposition that every land-dwelling quadruped is a cat. Likewise, when the Judiciary Committee explained that an instantaneous transition from one session to another is not a recess because the Senate is never absent, it did not suggest that the Senate's absence is enough to create a recess. To assume otherwise, as the majority does, is to commit the fallacy of the inverse (otherwise known as denying the antecedent): the incorrect assumption that if P implies Q, then not-P implies not-Q. Contrary to that fallacious assumption, the Judiciary Committee surely believed, consistent with the Executive's clear position at the time, that "the Recess" was limited to (actual, not constructive) breaks between sessions.

4. 1921 to the Present

It is necessary to skip over the first 13 decades of our Nation's history in order to find a Presidential legal ad-viser arguably embracing the majority's interpretation of "the Recess." In 1921 President Harding's Attorney General, Harry Daugherty, advised Harding that he could make recess appointments while the Senate stood adjourned for 28 days during the session because "the term 'recess' must be given a practical construction." 33 Op. Atty. Gen. 20, 25. Daugherty acknowledged Knox's 1901 opinion to the contrary, id., at 21, but he (committing the same fallacy as today's majority) thought the 1905 Judiciary Committee report had come to the opposite conclusion, id., at 23–24. He also recognized the fundamental flaw in this interpretation: that it would be impossible to "accurately dra[w]" a line between intra-session breaks that constitute "the Recess" and those that do not. Id., at 25. But he thought the absence of a standard gave the President "discretion to determine when there is a real and genuine recess." Ibid. While a "palpable abuse of discretion might subject his appointment to review," Daugherty thought that "[e]very presumption [should] be indulged in favor of the validity of whatever action he may take." Ibid. 7

Only after Daugherty's opinion did the flow of intra-session recess appointments start, and for several years it was little more than a trickle. The Solicitor General has identified 22 such appointments made by Presidents Harding, Coolidge, Hoover, and Franklin Roosevelt between 1921 and 1944. App. to Brief for Petitioner 9a–12a. Intra-session recess appointments experienced a brief heyday after World War II, with President Truman making about 150 such appointments to civilian positions and several thousand to military posts from 1945 through 1950. Id., at 12a–27a. (The majority's impressive-sounding claim that "Presidents have made thousands of intra-session recess appointments," ante, at 12, depends entirely on post-war military appointments that Truman made in just two years, 1947 and 1948.) President Eisenhower made only 43 intra-session recess appointments, id., at 27a–30a, after which the practice sank back into relative obscurity. Presidents Kennedy, Lyndon Johnson, and Ford made none, while Nixon made just 7. Id., at 30a–31a. The practice rose again in the last decades of the 20th century: President Carter made 17 intra-session recess appointments, Reagan 72, George H. W. Bush 37, Clinton 53, and George W. Bush 135. Id., at 31a–61a. When the Solicitor General filed his brief, President Obama had made 26. Id., at 62a–64a. Even excluding Truman's military appointments, roughly 90 percent of all the intra-session recess appointments in our history have been made since 1945.

Legal advisers in the Executive Branch during this period typically endorsed the President's authority to make intra-session recess appointments by citing Daugherty's opinion with little or no additional analysis. See, e.g., 20 Opinions of Office of Legal Counsel (Op. OLC) 124, 161 (1996) (finding the question to have been "settled within the executive branch" by Daugherty's "often-cited opinion"). The majority's contention that "opinions of Presidential legal advisers . . . are nearly unanimous in determining that the Clause authorizes [intra-session recess] appointments," ante, at 12, is thus true but

768

misleading: No Presidential legal adviser approved that practice before 1921, and subsequent approvals have rested more on precedent than on independent examination.

The majority is correct that during this period, the Senate "as a body" did not formally repudiate the emerging executive practice. Ante, at 14. And on one occasion, Comptroller General Lindsay Warren cited Daugherty's opinion as representing "the accepted view" on the question, 28 Comp. Gen. 30, 34 (1948), although there is no evidence he consulted any Senators or that his statement reflected their views. But the rise of intra-session recess appointments in the latter half of the 20th century drew sharp criticism from a number of Senators on both sides of the aisle. At first, their objections focused on the length of the intra-session breaks at issue. See, e.g., 130 Cong. Rec. 22774–22776 (1984) (Sen. Sarbanes) (decrying recess appointment during a 3-week intra-session adjournment as "a circumvention of the Senate confirmation power"); id., at 23235 (resolution offered by Sen. Byrd, with 39 cosponsors, urging that no recess appointments occur during intra-session breaks of fewer than 30 days).

Later, many Senators sought to end intra-session recess appointments altogether. In 1993, the Senate Legal Counsel prepared a brief to be filed on behalf of the Senate in Mackie v. Clinton, 827 F. Supp. 56 (DC 1993), vacated in part as moot, 1994 WL 163761 (CADC 1994) (percuriam), but "Republican opposition" blocked the filing. 139 Cong. Rec. 15266–15267. The brief argued that "the recess[-appointment] power is limited to Congress' annual recess between sessions," that no contrary executive practice "of any appreciable magnitude" had existed before "the past fifty years," and that the Senate had not "acquiesced in this steady expansion of presidential power." Id., at 15268, 15270. It explained that some Senators had limited their objections to shorter intra-session breaks out of a desire "to coexist with the Executive" but that "the Executive's subsequent, steady chipping away at the length of recess sufficient for making recess appointments ha[d] demonstrated the need to return to the Framers' original intent and limit the power to intersession adjournments." Id., at 15267, 15272. Senator Kennedy reiterated that position in a brief to this Court in 2004. Brief for Sen. Edward M. Kennedy as Amicus Curiae in Franklin v. United States, O. T. 2004, No. 04–5858, p. 5. Today the partisan tables are turned, and that position is urged on us by the Senate's Republican Members. See Brief for Sen. McConnell et al. as Amici Curiae 26.

*   *   *

What does all this amount to? In short: Intra-session recess appointments were virtually unheard of for the first 130 years of the Republic, were deemed unconstitutional by the first Attorney General to address them, were not openly defended by the Executive until 1921, were not made in significant numbers until after World War II, and have been repeatedly criticized as unconstitutional by Senators of both parties. It is astonishing for the majority to assert that this history lends "strong support," ante, at 11, to its interpretation of the Recess Appointments Clause. And the majority's contention that recent executive practice in this area merits deference because the Senate has not done more to oppose it is utterly divorced from our precedent. "The structural interests protected by the Appointments Clause are not those of any one branch of Government but of the entire Republic," Freytag, 501 U. S., at 880, and the Senate could not give away those protections even if it wanted to. See Chadha, 462 U. S., at 957–958; Clinton, 524 U. S., at 451–452 (Kennedy, J., concurring).

Moreover, the majority's insistence that the Senate gainsay an executive practice "as a body" in order to prevent the Executive from acquiring power by adverse possession, ante, at 14, will systematically favor the expansion of executive power at the expense of Congress. In any con-troversy between the political branches over a separation-of-powers question, staking out a position and defendingit over time is far easier for the Executive Branch thanfor the Legislative Branch. See generally Bradley and Morrison, Historical Gloss and the Separation of Powers, 126 Harv. L. Rev. 411, 439–447 (2012). All Presidents have a high interest in expanding the powers of their office, since the more power the President can wield, the more effectively he can implement his political agenda; whereas individual Senators may have little interest in opposing Presidential encroachment on legislative prerogatives, especially when the encroacher is a President who is the leader of their own party. (The majority would not be able to point to a lack of "formal action" by the Senate "as a body" challenging intra-session recess appointments, ante, at 15–16, had the appointing President's party in the Senate not blocked such action on multiple occasions.) And when the President wants to assert a power and establish a precedent, he faces neither the collective-action problems nor the procedural inertia inherent in the legislative process. The majority's methodology thus all but guarantees the continuing aggrandizement of the Executive Branch.

III. Pre-Recess Vacancies

The second question presented is whether vacancies that "happen during the Recess of the Senate," which the President is empowered to fill with recess appointments, are (a) vacancies that arise during the recess, or (b) all vacancies that exist during the recess, regardless of when they arose. I would hold that the recess-appointment power is limited to vacancies that arise during the recess in which they are filled, and I would hold that the appointments at issue here—which undisputedly filled pre-recess vacancies—are invalid for that reason as well as for the reason that they were made during the session. The Court's contrary conclusion is inconsistent with the Constitution's text and structure, and it further undermines the balance the Framers struck between Presidential and Senatorial power. Historical practice also fails to support the majority's conclusion on this issue.

A. Plain Meaning

As the majority concedes, "the most natural meaning of 'happens' as applied to a 'vacancy' . . . is that the vacancy 'happens' when it initially occurs." Ante, at 22. The majority adds that this meaning is most natural "to a modern ear," ibid., but it fails to show that founding-era ears heard it differently. "Happen" meant then, as it does now, "[t]o fall out; to chance; to come to pass." 1 Johnson, Dictionary of the English Language 913. Thus, a vacancy that happened during the Recess was most reasonably understood as one that arose during the recess. It was, of course, possible in certain contexts for the word "happen" to mean "happen to be" rather than "happen to occur," as in the idiom "it so happens." But that meaning is not at all natural when the subject is a vacancy, a state of affairs that comes into existence at a particular moment in time. 8

In any event, no reasonable reader would have understood the Recess Appointments Clause to use the word "happen" in the majority's "happen to be" sense, and thus to empower the President to fill all vacancies that might exist during a recess, regardless of when they arose. For one thing, the Clause's language would have been a surpassingly odd way of giving the President that power. The Clause easily could have been written to convey that meaning clearly: It could have referred to "all Vacancies that may exist during the Recess," or it could have omitted the qualifying phrase entirely and simply authorized the President to "fill up all Vacancies during the Recess." Given those readily available alternative phrasings, the reasonable reader might have wondered, why would any intelligent drafter intending the majority's reading have inserted the words "that may happen"—words that, as the majority admits, make the majority's desired reading awkward and unnatural, and that must be effectively read out of the Clause to achieve that reading?

For another thing, the majority's reading not only strains the Clause's language but distorts its constitutional role, which was meant to be subordinate. As Hamilton explained, appointment with the advice and consent of the Senate was to be "the general mode of appointing officers of the United States." The Federalist No. 67, at 455. The Senate's check on the President's appointment power was seen as vital because " 'manipulation of official appointments' had long been one of the American revolutionary generation's greatest grievances against executive power." Freytag, 501 U. S., at 883. The unilateral power conferred on the President by the Recess Appointments Clause was therefore understood to be "nothing more than a supplement" to the "general method" of advice and consent. The Federalist No. 67, at 455.

If, however, the Clause had allowed the President to fill all pre-existing vacancies during the recess by granting commissions that would last throughout the following session, it would have been impossible to regard it—as the Framers plainly did—as a mere codicil to the Constitution's principal, power-sharing scheme for filling federal offices. On the majority's reading, the President would have had no need ever to seek the Senate's advice and consent for his appointments: Whenever there was a fair prospect of the Senate's rejecting his preferred nominee, the President could have appointed that individual unilaterally during the recess, allowed the appointment to expire at the end of the next session, renewed the appointment the following day, and so on ad infinitum. (Circumvention would have been especially easy if, as the majority also concludes, the President was authorized to make such appointments during any intra-session break of more than a few days.) It is unthinkable that such an obvious means for the Executive to expand its power would have been overlooked during the ratification debates. 9

The original understanding of the Clause was consistent with what the majority concedes is the text's "most natural meaning." Ante, at 22. In 1792, Attorney General Edmund Randolph, who had been a leading member of the Constitutional Convention, provided the Executive Branch's first formal interpretation of the Clause. He advised President Washington that the Constitution did not authorize a recess appointment to fill the office of Chief Coiner of the United States Mint, which had been created by Congress on April 2, 1792, during the Senate's session. Randolph wrote: "[I]s it a vacancy which has happened during the recess of the Senate? It is now the same and no other vacancy, than that, which existed on the 2nd. of April 1792. It commenced therefore on that day or may be said to have happened on that day." Opinion on Recess Appointments (July 7, 1792), in 24 Papers of Thomas Jefferson 165–166 (J. Catanzariti ed. 1990). Randolph added that his interpretation was the most congruent with the Constitution's structure, which made the recess-appointment power "an exception to the general participation of the Senate." Ibid. (footnote omitted).

President John Adams' Attorney General, Charles Lee, was in agreement. See Letter to George Washington (July 7, 1796) (the President may "fill for a limited time an old office become vacant during [the] recess" (emphasis added)), online at http:// founders.archives.gov/documents/Washington/99-01-02-00702; Letter from James McHenry to John Adams (May 7, 1799) (hereinafter 1799 McHenry Letter) (conveying Lee's advice that certain offices were " 'vacanc[ies] happening during the session, which the President cannot fill, during the recess, by the powers vested in him by the constitution' "), online at http://wardepartmentpapers.org/document.php?id=31766. 10 One of the most prominent early academic commenters on the Constitution read the Clause the same way. See 1 St. George Tucker, Blackstone's Commentaries, App. 342–343 (1803) (assuming the President could appoint during the recess only if "the office became vacant during the recess").

Early Congresses seem to have shared Randolph's and Lee's view. A statute passed by the First Congress authorized the President to appoint customs inspectors "with the advice and consent of the Senate" and provided that "if the appointment . . . shall not be made during the present session of Congress, the President . . . is hereby empowered to make such appointments during the recess of the Senate, by granting commissions which shall expire at the end of their next session." Act of Mar. 3, 1791, §4, 1Stat. 200. That authorization would have been superfluous if the Recess Appointments Clause had been understood to apply to pre-existing vacancies. We have recognized that an action taken by the First Congress "provides 'contemporaneous and weighty evidence' of the Constitution's meaning." Bowsher, 478 U. S., at 723–724. And other statutes passed in the early years of the Republic contained similar authorizations. See App. to Brief for Respondent Noel Canning 1a–17a. 11

Also illuminating is the way the Third Congress interpreted the Constitution's Senate Vacancies Clause, which uses language similar to that of the Recess Appointments Clause. Before the passage of the Seventeenth Amendment, the Constitution provided that "if Vacancies [in the Senate] happen by Resignation, or otherwise, during the Recess of the

Legislature of any State, the Executive thereof may make temporary Appointments until the next Meeting of the Legislature." Art. I, §3, cl. 2. Senator George Read of Delaware resigned in December 1793; the state legislature met in January and February 1794; and the Governor appointed Kensey Johns to fill the seat in March 1794. The Senate refused to seat Johns, resolving that he was "not entitled to a seat in the Senate of the United States; a session of the Legislature of the said State having intervened, between the resignation . . . and the appointment." 4 Annals of Cong. 77–78 (1794). It is thus clear that the phrase "happen . . . during the Recess" in the Senate Vacancies Clause was understood to refer to vacancies that arose, not merely existed, during the recess in which the appointment was made. It is not apparent why the nearly identical language of the Recess Appointments Clause would have been understood differently.

The majority, however, relies heavily on a contrary account of the Clause given by Attorney General William Wirt in 1823. See 1 Op. Atty. Gen 631. Wirt notably began—as does the majority—by acknowledging that his predecessors' reading was "most accordant with the letter of the constitution." Id., at 632. But he thought the "most natural" reading had to be rejected because it would interfere with the "substantial purpose of the constitution," namely, "keep[ing] . . . offices filled." Id., at 631–632. He was chiefly concerned that giving the Clause its plain meaning would produce "embarrassing inconveniences" if a distant office were to become vacant during the Senate's session, but news of the vacancy were not to reach the President until the recess. Id., at 632, 634. The majority fully embraces Wirt's reasoning. Ante, at 22–25.

Wirt's argument is doubly flawed. To begin, the Constitution provides ample means, short of rewriting its text, for dealing with the hypothetical dilemma Wirt posed. Congress can authorize "acting" officers to perform the duties associated with a temporarily vacant office—and has done that, in one form or another, since 1792. See 5 U. S. C. §3345; Act of May 8, 1792, ch. 37, §8, 1Stat. 281; 705 F. 3d, at 511; Rappaport, Original Meaning 1514–1517. And on "extraordinary Occasions" the President can call the Senate back into session to consider a nomination. Art. II, §3. If the Framers had thought those options insufficient and preferred to authorize the President to make recess appointments to fill vacancies arising late in the session, they would have known how to do so. Massachusetts, for example, had authorized its Governor to make certain recess appointments "in case a vacancy shall happen . . . in the recess of the General Court [i.e., the state legislature], or at so late a period in any session of the same Court, that the vacancy . . . shall not be supplied in the same session thereof." 1783 Mass. Acts ch. 12, in Acts and Laws of the Commonwealth of Massachusetts 523 (1890) (emphasis added).

The majority protests that acting appointments, unlike recess appointments, are an "inadequate" solution to Wirt's hypothetical dilemma because acting officers "may have less authority than Presidential appointments." Ante, at 24–25. It cites an OLC opinion which states that "an acting officer . . . is frequently considered merely a caretaker without a mandate to take far-reaching measures." 6 Op. OLC 119, 121 (1982). But just a few lines later, the majority says that "the lack of Senate approval . . . may diminish the recess appointee's ability, as a practical matter, to get a controversial job done." Ante, at 25. The majority does not explain why an acting officer would have less authority "as a practical matter" than a recess appointee. The majority also objects that requiring the President to rely on acting officers would "lessen the President's ability to staff the Executive Branch with people of his own choosing," ante, at 24—a surprising charge, since that is the very purpose of the Constitution's advice-and-consent requirement. As for special sessions, the majority thinks it a sufficient answer to say that they are "burdensome," ibid., an observation that fails to distinguish them from many procedures required by our structural Constitution.

More fundamentally, Wirt and the majority are mistaken to say that the Constitution's " 'substantial purpose' " isto " 'keep . . . offices filled.' " Ibid. (quoting 1 Op. Atty. Gen., at 632). The Constitution is not a road map for maximally efficient government, but a system of "carefully crafted restraints" designed to "protect the people from the improvident exercise of power." Chadha, 462 U. S., at 957, 959. Wirt's and the majority's argumentum ab inconvenienti thus proves far too much. There are many circumstances other than a vacancy that can produce similar inconveniences if they arise late in the session: For example, a natural disaster might occur to which the Executive cannot respond effectively without a supplemental appropriation. But in those circumstances, the Constitution would not permit the President to appropriate funds himself. See Art. I, §9, cl. 7. Congress must either anticipate such eventualities or be prepared to be haled back into session. The troublesome need to do so is not a bug to be fixed by this Court, but a calculated feature of the constitutional framework. As we have recognized, while the Constitution's government-structuring provisions can seem "clumsy" and "inefficient," they reflect "hard choices . . . consciously made by men who had lived under a form of government that permitted arbitrary governmental acts to go unchecked." Chadha, supra, at 959.

B. Historical Practice

For the reasons just given, it is clear that the Constitution authorizes the President to fill unilaterally only those vacancies that arise during a recess, not every vacancy that happens to exist during a recess. Again, however, the majority says "[h]istorical practice" requires the broader interpretation. Ante, at 26. And again the majority is mistaken. Even if the Constitution were wrongly thought to be ambiguous on this point, a fair recounting of the relevant history does not support the majority's interpretation.

1. 1789 to 1822

The majority correctly admits that there is "no undisputed record of Presidents George Washington, John Adams, or Thomas Jefferson" using a recess appointment to fill a pre-recess vacancy. Ibid. That is not surprising in light of Randolph's early conclusion that doing so would be unconstitutional. Adams on one occasion contemplated filling pre-recess vacancies but was dissuaded by, among others, Attorney General Lee, who said the Constitution did not permit him to do so. See 1799 McHenry Letter. 12 And the Solicitor General does not allege that even a single appointment made by Adams filled a pre-recess vacancy. Jefferson, too, at one point thought the Clause "susceptible of" the majority's reading, 1802 Jefferson Letter, but his administration, like Adams', appears never to have adopted that reading.

James Madison's administration seems to have rejected the majority's reading as well. In 1814, Madison wanted to appoint Andrew Jackson to a vacant major-generalship in the Army during the Senate's recess, but he accepted, without contradiction or reservation, his Secretary of War's advice that he lacked the power to do so because the post's previous occupant had resigned before the recess. He therefore ordered that Jackson be given a "brevet of Major General," i.e., a warrant conferring the nominal rank without the salary thereof. Letter from John Armstrong to Madison (May 14, 1814); Letter from Madison to Armstrong (May 17, 1814). In conveying the brevet, Madison's Secretary of War explained to Jackson that " '[t]he vacancy produced by General Hampton's resignation, not having been filled during the late session of the Senate, cannot be supplied constitutionally, during the recess.' " Letter from Armstrong to Jackson (May 22, 1814). A week later, when Madison learned that a different major general had resigned during the recess, he thought that development would enable him to appoint Jackson "at once." Letter from Madison to Armstrong (May 24, 1814); see Letter from Armstrong to Madison (May 20, 1814) (reporting the resignation). 13

The majority discounts that evidence of an occasion when Madison and his advisers actually considered the precise constitutional question presented here. It does so apparently because Madison, in acting on the advice he was given without questioning the interpretation of the recess-appointment power that was offered as the reason for that advice, did not explicitly say "I agree." The majority prefers to focus on five appointments by Madison, unremarked by anyone at the time, that "the evidence suggests" filled pre-recess vacancies. Ante, at 27. Even if the majority is correct about those appointments, there is no indication that any thought was given to their constitutionality, either within or outside the Executive Branch. A handful of appointments that appear to contravene the written opinions of Attorneys General Randolph and Lee and the written evidence of Madison's own beliefs about what the Constitution authorized, and that lack any contemporaneous explanation, are not convincing evidence of the Constitution's original meaning. 14

If Madison or his predecessors made any appointments in reliance on the broader reading, those appointments must have escaped general notice. In 1822, the Senate Committee on Military Affairs declared that the President had "no power to make [appointments] in the recess" where "the vacancies did not happen in the recess." 38 Annals of Cong. 500. The Committee believed its construction had been "heretofore observed" and that "no instance ha[d] before occurred . . . where the President ha[d] felt himself authorized to fill such vacancies, without special authority by law." Ibid.; see also T. Sergeant, Constitutional Law 373 (2d ed. 1830) ("[I]t seemed distinctly understood to be the sense of the senate, that [it] is only in offices that become vacant during the recess, that the president is authorised to exercise the right of appointing").

2. 1823 to 1862

The Executive Branch did not openly depart from Randolph and Lee's interpretation until 1823, when Wirt issued the opinion discussed earlier. Even within that branch, Wirt's view was hotly contested: William Crawford, Monroe's Treasury Secretary, argued "with great pertinacity" that the Clause authorized the President to fill only "vacancies which happen during the recess" and not those "which happen while Congress are in session." 5 Memoirs of John Quincy Adams 486–487 (C. Adams ed. 1875). Wirt's analysis nonetheless gained ground in the Executive Branch over the next four decades; but it did so slowly and fitfully.

In 1830, Attorney General Berrien disagreed with Wirt when he wrote that "[i]f the vacancy exist during the session of the Senate, . . . the President cannot appoint during the recess." 2 Op. Atty. Gen. 333, 334. Two years later, Attorney General Taney endorsed Wirt's view al-though doing so was, as he acknowledged, unnecessary to resolve the issue before him: whether the President could, during the recess, fill a vacancy resulting from the expiration of a prior recess appointment at the end of the Senate's session. 2 Op. Atty Gen. 525, 528 (1832). Addressing the same issue in 1841, Attorney General Legaré appeared to believe the dispositive question was whether the office could be said to have "becom[e] vacant" during the recess. 3 Op. Atty. Gen. 673, 674. And in 1845, Attorney General Mason thought it "well established" that "[i]f vacancies are known to exist during the session of the Senate, and nominations are not then made, they cannot be filled by executive appointments in the recess." 4 Op. Atty. Gen. 361, 363. 15

The tide seemed to turn—as far as the Executive Branch was concerned—in the mid-19th century: Attorney General Cushing in 1855 and Attorney General Bates in 1862 both treated Wirt's position as settled without subjecting it to additional analysis. 7 Op. Atty. Gen. 186, 223; 10 Op. Atty. Gen. 356. Bates, however, entertained "serious doubts" about its validity. Ibid. And as one 19th-century court shrewdly observed in rejecting Wirt's interpretation, the frequency with which Attorneys General during this period were called upon to opine on the question likely "indicate[s] that no settled administrative usage had been . . . established." In re District Attorney of United States, 7 F. Cas. 731, 738 (No. 3,924) (DC Pa. 1868). The Solicitor General identifies only 10 recess appointments made between 1823 and 1863 that filled pre-recess vacancies—about one every four years. App. to Brief for Petitioner 68a–71a. That is hardly an impressive number, and most of the appointments were to minor offices (like Deputy Postmaster for Janesville, Wisconsin, id., at 70a) unlikely to have gotten the Senate's attention. But the Senate did notice when, in 1862, President Lincoln recess-appointed David Davis to fill a seat on this Court that had become vacant before the recess, id., at 71a—and it reacted with vigor.

3. 1863 to 1939

Two months after Lincoln's recess appointment of Davis, the Senate directed the Judiciary Committee "to inquire whether the practice . . . of appointing officers to fill vacancies which have not occurred during the recess of Congress, but which existed at the preceding session of Congress, is in accordance with the Constitution; and if not, what remedy shall be applied." Cong. Globe, 37th Cong., 3d Sess., 100 (1862). The committee responded with a report denouncing Wirt's interpretation of the Clause as "artificial," "forced and unnatural," "unfounded," and a "perversion of language." S. Rep. No. 80, 37th Cong., 3d Sess., pp. 4–6 (1863). Because the majority all but ignores this evidence of the Senate's views, it is worth quoting the report at some length:

"When must the vacancy . . . accrue or spring into existence? May it begin during the session of the Senate, or must it have its beginning during the recess? We think the language too clear to admit of reasonable doubt, and that, upon principles of just construction, this period must have its inceptive point after one session has closed and before another session has begun. . . .

.   .   .   .   .

"We . . . dissent from the construction implied by the substituted reading, 'happened to exist,' for the word 'happen' in the clause. . . . [I]f a vacancy once exists, it has in law happened; for it is in itself an instantaneous event. It implies no continuance of the act that produces it, but takes effect, and is complete and perfect at an indivisible point of time, like the beginning or end of a recess. Once in existence, it has happened, and the mere continuance of the condition of things which the occurrence produces, cannot, without confounding the most obvious distinctions, be taken or treated as the occurrence itself, as Mr. Wirt seems to have done. . . .

"Again, we see no propriety in forcing the language from its popular meaning in order to meet and fulfill one confessedly great purpose, (the keeping the office filled,) while there is plainly another purpose of equal magnitude and importance (fitting qualifications)attached to and inseparable from the former." Id.,at 3–6.

The Committee acknowledged that the broad reading "ha[d] been, from time to time, sanctioned by Attorneys General . . . and that the Executive ha[d], from time to time, practiced upon it," but it said the Executive's practice was entitled to no weight because the Constitution's text was "too plain to admit of a doubt or to need interpretation." Id., at 7.

On the same day the Committee published its scathing report, its chairman, Senator Trumbull, proposed a law barring the payment of any officer appointed during the recess to fill a pre-recess vacancy. Cong. Globe, 37th Cong., 3d Sess., 564. Senator Fessenden spoke in support of the proposal:

"It ought to be understood distinctly, that when an officer does not come within the rules of law, and is appointed in that way in defiance of the wishes of the Senate, he shall not be paid. It may not be in our power to prevent the appointment, but it is in our power to prevent the payment; and when payment is prevented, I think that will probably put an end to the habit of making such appointments." Id., at 565.

The amendment was adopted by the Senate, ibid., and after passing the House became the Pay Act, which provided that "no money shall be paid . . . out of the Treasury, as salary, to any person appointed during the recess of the Senate, to fill a vacancy . . . which . . . existed while the Senate was in session." Act of Feb. 9, 1863, §2, 12Stat. 646

(codified at Rev. Stat. §1761; subsequently codified as amended at 5 U. S. C. §56 (1925–1926 ed.)).

The Pay Act would remain in force without significant modification for nearly eight decades. The Executive Branch, however, refused to acknowledge that the Act embodied the Senate's rejection of the broad reading of "happen." Several Attorneys General continued to treat Wirt's interpretation as settled without so much as mentioning the Act. See 12 Op. Atty. Gen. 32 (1866); 12 Op. Atty. Gen. 449 (1868); 14 Op. Atty. Gen. 562 (1875); 15 Op. Atty. Gen. 207 (1877). And when, 17 years after its passage, Attorney General Devens deigned to acknowledge the Act, he preposterously described it as "conced[ing]" the President's power to make the appointments for which the Act barred payment. 16 Op. Atty. Gen. 522, 531 (1880).

The majority is not that bold. Instead, it relegates the 1863 Judiciary Committee report to a pair of anodyne sentences in which it says only that the committee "dis-agreed with" Wirt's interpretation. Ante, at 30. (With like understatement, one could say that Shakespeare's Mark Antony "disagreed with" Caesar's detractors.) Even more remarkably, the majority goes on to claim that the Senate's passage of the Pay Act on the same day the committee issued its report was not a strong enough statement to impede the constitutionalization-by-adverse-possession of the power asserted by the Executive. Why not? Because, the majority says, some Senators may have disagreed with the report, and because the Senate did not go so far as to make acceptance of a recess appointment that filled a pre-recess vacancy "a federal crime." Ante, at 30–31. That reasoning starkly illustrates the excessive burden the majority places on the Legislative Branch in contests with the Executive over the separation of powers. See supra, at 26.

Despite its minimization by subsequent Attorneys General and by today's majority, there is no reason to doubt that the Pay Act had a deterrent effect. The Solicitor General has identified just 40 recess appointments that filled pre-recess vacancies during the nearly eight decades between the Act's passage in 1863 and its amendment in 1940. App. to Brief for Petitioner 71a–79a. 16

4. 1940 to the Present

The majority finds it highly significant that in 1940, Congress created a few carefully limited exceptions to the Pay Act's prohibition on paying recess appointees who filled pre-recess vacancies. See Act of July 11, 1940, ch. 580, 54Stat. 751, now codified with nonsubstantive amendments at 5 U. S. C. §5503. Under the current version of the Act, "[p]ayment for services may not be made from the Treasury of the United States to an individual appointed during a recess of the Senate to fill a vacancy" that "existed while the Senate was in session" unless either the vacancy arose, or a different individual's nomination to fill the vacancy was rejected, "within 30 days before the end of the session"; or a nomination was pending before the Senate at the end of the session, and the individual nominated was not himself a recess appointee. §5503(a)(1)–(3). And if the President fills a pre-recess vacancy under one of the circumstances specified in the Act, the law requires that he submit a nomination for that office to the Senate "not later than 40 days after the beginning of the next session." §5503(b).

The majority says that by allowing salaries to be paid to recess appointees in these narrow circumstances, "the 1940 Senate (and later Senates) in effect supported" the majority's interpretation of the Clause. Ante, at 32. Nonsense. Even as amended, the Act strictly regulates payment to recess appointees who fill pre-recess vacancies, and it still forbids payment to many officers whose appointments are constitutional under the majority's interpretation. As amici Senators observe, the 1940 amendments "reflect at most a desire not to punish public servants caught in the crossfire" of interbranch conflict. Brief for Sen. McConnell et al. as Amici Curiae 30. Surely that inference is more reasonable than the majority's supposition that Congress, by permitting some of the appointees covered by the Act to be paid, meant to signal that it now believed all of the covered appointments were valid.

Moreover, given the majority's interpretation of the Recess Appointments Clause, it is fairly debatable whether the current version of the Pay Act is constitutional (and a fortiori, whether the pre-1940 version was constitutional). Even as amended, the Act seeks to limit and channelthe President's exercise of the recess-appointment power by prohibiting payment to officers whose appointmentsare (per the majority) within the President's sole constitutional authority if those appointments do not comply with conditions imposed by Congress, and by requiring the President to submit a nominee to the Senate in the first 40 days of the ensuing session. There is a colorable argument— which is routinely made by lawyers in the Executive Branch—that Congress " 'cannot use the appropriations power to control a Presidential power that is beyond its direct control.' " 33 Op. OLC ___, ___ (2009), online at http://www.justice.gov/olc/opiniondocs/ section7054.pdf (quoting 20 Op. OLC 253, 267 (1996)). Consistent with that view, the Office of Legal Counsel has maintained that Congress could not "condition . . . the funding of an officer's salary on being allowed to appoint the officer." 13 Op. OLC 258, 261 (1989).

If that is correct, then the Pay Act's attempt to control the President's exercise of the recess-appointment power at least raises a substantial constitutional question under the majority's reading of the Recess Appointments Clause. See Rappaport, Original Meaning 1544–1546. The Executive has not challenged the Act's constitutionality in this case, and I express no opinion on whether such a challenge would succeed. I simply point out that it is impossible to regard the amended Pay Act as evidence of Senatorial acquiescence in the majority's reading when that reading has the potential to invalidate the Act.

Since the Pay Act was amended, individual Senators have continued to maintain that recess appointments may not constitutionally be used to fill pre-recess vacancies. See, e.g., 130 Cong. Rec. 22780 (statement of seven Senators that a recess appointment to the Federal Reserve Board in 1984 was unconstitutional because the vacancy "did not happen during the recess"); Brief for Sen. McConnell et al. as Amici Curiae 26 (45 Senators taking that view of the Clause). And there is no evidence that the watering-down of the Pay Act produced an immediate flood of recess appointments filling pre-recess vacancies. The

Solicitor General has pointed us to only 40 such appointments between 1940 and the present. App. to Brief for Petitioner 79a–89a.

The majority, however, finds it significant that in two small "random sample[s]" of contemporary recess appointments—24 since 1981 and 21 since 2000—the bulk of the appointments appear to have filled pre-existing vacancies. Ante, at 29. Based on that evidence, the majority thinks it "a fair inference that a large proportion of the recess appointments in the history of the Nation have filled pre-existing vacancies." Ibid. The extrapolation of that sweeping conclusion from a small set of recent data does not bear even the slightest scrutiny. The majority ignores two salient facts: First, from the founding until the mid-19th century, the President's authority to make such appointments was far from settled even within the Executive Branch. Second, from 1863 until 1940, it was illegal to pay any recess appointee who filled a pre-recess vacancy, which surely discouraged Presidents from making, and nominees from accepting, such appointments. Consequently, there is no reason to assume that the majority's sampling—even if it accurately reflects practices during the last three decades—is at all typical of practices that prevailed throughout "the history of the Nation." 17

* * *

In sum: Washington's and Adams' Attorneys General read the Constitution to restrict recess appointments to vacancies arising during the recess, and there is no evidence that any of the first four Presidents consciously departed from that reading. The contrary reading was first defended by an executive official in 1823, was vehemently rejected by the Senate in 1863, was vigorously resisted by legislation in place from 1863 until 1940, and is arguably inconsistent with legislation in place from 1940 to the present. The Solicitor General has identified only about 100 appointments that have ever been made under the broader reading, and while it seems likely that a good deal more have been made in the last few decades, there is good reason to doubt that many were made before 1940 (since the appointees could not have been compensated). I can conceive of no sane constitutional theory under which this evidence of "historical practice"—which is actually evidence of a long-simmering inter-branch conflict—would require us to defer to the views of the Executive Branch.

IV. Conclusion

What the majority needs to sustain its judgment is an ambiguous text and a clear historical practice. What it has is a clear text and an at-best-ambiguous historical practice. Even if the Executive could accumulate power through adverse possession by engaging in a consistent and unchallenged practice over a long period of time, the oft-disputed practices at issue here would not meet that standard. Nor have those practices created any justifiable expectations that could be disappointed by enforcing the Constitution's original meaning. There is thus no ground for the majority's deference to the unconstitutional recess-appointment practices of the Executive Branch.

The majority replaces the Constitution's text with a new set of judge-made rules to govern recess appointments. Henceforth, the Senate can avoid triggering the President's now-vast recess-appointment power by the odd contrivance of never adjourning for more than three days without holding a pro forma session at which it is understood that no business will be conducted. Ante, at 33–34. How this new regime will work in practice remains to be seen. Perhaps it will reduce the prevalence of recess appointments. But perhaps not: Members of the President's party in Congress may be able to prevent the Senate from holding pro forma sessions with the necessary frequency, and if the House and Senate disagree, the President may be able to adjourn both "to such Time as he shall think proper." U. S. Const., Art. II, §3. In any event, the limitation upon the President's appointment power is there not for the benefit of the Senate, but for the protection of the people; it should not be dependent on Senate action for its existence.

The real tragedy of today's decision is not simply the abolition of the Constitution's limits on the recess-appointment power and the substitution of a novel framework invented by this Court. It is the damage done to our separation-of-powers jurisprudence more generally. It is not every day that we encounter a proper case or controversy requiring interpretation of the Constitution's structural provisions. Most of the time, the interpretation of those provisions is left to the political branches—which, in deciding how much respect to afford the constitutional text, often take their cues from this Court. We should therefore take every opportunity to affirm the primacy of the Constitution's enduring principles over the politics of the moment. Our failure to do so today will resonate well beyond the particular dispute at hand. Sad, but true: The Court's embrace of the adverse-possession theory of executive power (a characterization the majority resists but does not refute) will be cited in diverse contexts, including those presently unimagined, and will have the effect of aggrandizing the Presidency beyond its constitutional bounds and undermining respect for the separation of powers.

I concur in the judgment only.

Justice Scalia's dissent from denial of certiorari in Jones v. US (October 14, 2014)

The petition for a writ of certiorari is denied.

Justice Scalia, with whom Justice Thomas and Justice Ginsburg join, dissenting from denial of certiorari.

A jury convicted petitioners Joseph Jones, Desmond Thurston, and Antwuan Ball of distributing very small amounts of crack cocaine, and acquitted them of conspiring to distribute drugs. The sentencing judge, however, found that they had engaged in the charged conspiracy and, relying largely on that finding, imposed sentences that petitioners say were many times longer than those the Guidelines would otherwise have recommended.

Petitioners present a strong case that, but for the judge's finding of fact, their sentences would have been "substantively unreasonable" and therefore illegal. See Rita v. United States, 551 U. S. 338, 372 (2007) (Scalia, J., joined by Thomas, J., concurring in part and concurring in judgment). If so, their constitutional rights were violated. The Sixth Amendment, together with the Fifth Amendment's Due Process Clause, "requires that each element of a crime" be either admitted by the defendant, or "proved to the jury beyond a reasonable doubt." Alleyne v. United States, 570 U. S. ___, ___ (2013) (slip op., at 3). Any fact that increases the penalty to which a defendant is exposed constitutes an element of a crime, Apprendi v. New Jersey, 530 U. S. 466, n. 10, 490 (2000), and "must be found by a jury, not a judge," Cunningham v. California, 549 U. S. 270, 281 (2007) . 1 * We have held that a substantively unreasonable penalty is illegal and must be set aside. Gall v. United States, 552 U. S. 38, 51 (2007) . It unavoidably follows that any fact necessary to prevent a sentence from being substantively unreasonable—thereby exposing the defendant to the longer sentence—is an element that must be either admitted by the defendant or found by the jury. It may not be found by a judge.

For years, however, we have refrained from saying so. In Rita v. United States, we dismissed the possibility of Sixth Amendment violations resulting from substantive reasonableness review as hypothetical and not presented by the facts of the case. We thus left for another day the question whether the Sixth Amendment is violated when courts impose sentences that, but for a judge-found fact, would be reversed for substantive unreasonableness. 551 U. S., at 353; see also id., at 366 (Stevens, J., joined in part by Ginsburg, J., concurring) ("Such a hypothetical case should be decided if and when it arises"). Nonetheless, the Courts of Appeals have uniformly taken our continuing silence to suggest that the Constitution does permit otherwise unreasonable sentences supported by judicial factfinding, so long as they are within the statu-tory range. See, e.g., United States v. Benkahla, 530 F. 3d 300, 312 (CA4 2008); United States v. Hernandez, 633 F. 3d 370, 374 (CA5 2011); United States v. Ashqar, 582 F. 3d 819, 824–825 (CA7 2009); United States v. Treadwell, 593 F. 3d 990, 1017–1018 (CA9 2010); United States v. Redcorn, 528 F. 3d 727, 745–746 (CA10 2008).

This has gone on long enough. The present petition presents the nonhypothetical case the Court claimed to have been waiting for. And it is a particularly appealing case, because not only did no jury convict these defendants of the offense the sentencing judge thought them guilty of, but a jury acquitted them of that offense. Petitioners were convicted of distributing drugs, but acquitted of conspiring to distribute drugs. The sentencing judge found that petitioners had engaged in the conspiracy of which the jury acquitted them. The Guidelines, petitioners claim, recommend sentences of between 27 and 71 months for their distribution convictions. But in light of the conspir-acy finding, the court calculated much higher Guidelines ranges, and sentenced Jones, Thurston, and Ball to 180, 194, and 225 months' imprisonment.

On petitioners' appeal, the D. C. Circuit held that even if their sentences would have been substantively unreasonable but for judge-found facts, their Sixth Amendment rights were not violated. 744 F. 3d 1362, 1369 (2014). We should grant certiorari to put an end to the unbroken string of cases disregarding the Sixth Amendment—or to eliminate the Sixth Amendment difficulty by acknowledging that all sentences below the statutory maximum are substantively reasonable.

Notes

1* With one exception: We held in Almendarez-Torres v. United States, 523 U. S. 224 (1998), that the fact of a prior conviction, even when it increases the sentence to which the defendant is exposed, may be found by a judge. But see id., at 248 (Scalia, J., dissenting); Rangel-Reyes v. United States, 547 U. S. 1200, 1202 (2006) (Thomas, J., dissenting from denial of certiorari).

Justice Scalia's dissent in Alabama Legislative Black Caucus v. Alabama (March 25, 2015)

Justice Scalia, with whom The Chief Justice, Justice Thomas, and Justice Alito join, dissenting.

Today, the Court issues a sweeping holding that will have profound implications for the constitutional ideal of one person, one vote, for the future of the Voting Rights Act of 1965, and for the primacy of the State in managing its own elections. If the Court's destination seems fantastical, just wait until you see the journey.

Two groups of plaintiffs, the Alabama Democratic Conference and the Alabama Legislative Black Caucus, brought separate challenges to the way in which Alabama drew its state legislative districts following the 2010 census. These cases were consolidated before a three-judge District Court. Even after a full trial, the District Court lamented that "[t]he filings and arguments made by the plaintiffs on these claims were mystifying at best." 989 F. Supp. 2d 1227, 1287 (MD Ala. 2013). Nevertheless, the District Court understood both groups of plaintiffs to argue, as relevant here, only that "the Acts as a whole constitute racial gerrymanders." Id., at 1287. It also understood the Democratic Conference to argue that "Senate Districts 7, 11, 22, and 26 constitute racial gerrymanders," id., at 1288, but held that the Democratic Conference lacked standing to bring "any district-specific claims of racial gerrymandering," id., at 1292 (emphasis added). It then found for Alabama on the merits.

The Court rightly concludes that our racial gerrymandering jurisprudence does not allow for statewide claims. Ante, at 5–12. However, rather than holding appellants to the misguided legal theory they presented to the District Court, it allows them to take a mulligan, remanding the case with orders that the District Court consider whether some (all?) of Alabama's 35 majority-minority districts result from impermissible racial gerrymandering. In doing this, the Court disregards the detailed findings and thoroughly reasoned conclusions of the District Court—in particular its determination, reached after watching the development of the case from complaint to trial, that no appellant proved (or even pleaded) district-specific claims with respect to the majority-minority districts. Worse still, the Court ignores the Democratic Conference's express waiver of these claims before this Court. It does this on the basis of a few stray comments, cherry-picked from district-court filings that are more Rorschach brief than Brandeis brief, in which the vague outline of what could be district-specific racial-gerrymandering claims begins to take shape only with the careful, post-hoc nudging of appellate counsel.

Racial gerrymandering strikes at the heart of our democratic process, undermining the electorate's confidence in its government as representative of a cohesive body politic in which all citizens are equal before the law. It is therefore understandable, if not excusable, that the Court balks at denying merits review simply because appellants pursued a flawed litigation strategy. But allowing appellants a second bite at the apple invites lower courts similarly to depart from the premise that ours is an adversarial system whenever they deem the stakes sufficiently high. Because I do not believe that Article III empowers this Court to act as standby counsel for sympathetic litigants, I dissent.

I. The Alabama Democratic Conference

The District Court concluded that the Democratic Conference lacked standing to bring district-specific claims. It did so on the basis of the Conference's failure to present any evidence that it had members who voted in the challenged districts, and because the individual Conference plaintiffs did not claim to vote in them. 989 F. Supp. 2d, at 1292.

A voter has standing to bring a racial-gerrymandering claim only if he votes in a gerrymandered district, or if specific evidence demonstrates that he has suffered the special harms that attend racial gerrymandering. United States v. Hays, 515 U. S. 737–745 (1995). However, the Democratic Conference only claimed to have "chapters and members in almost all counties in the state." Newton Plaintiffs' Proposed Findings of Fact and Conclusions of Law in No. 12–cv–691, Doc. 195–1, pp. 3–4 (Democratic Conference Post-Trial Brief) (emphasis added). Yet the Court concludes that this fact, combined with the Conference's self-description as a " 'statewide political caucus' " that endorses candidates for political office, "supports an inference that the organization has members in all of the State's majority-minority districts, other things being equal." Ante, at 13. The Court provides no support for this theory of jurisdiction by illogical inference, perhaps because this Court has rejected other attempts to peddle more-likely-than-not standing. See Summers v. Earth Island Institute, 555 U. S. 488, 497 (2009) (rejecting a test for organizational standing that asks "whether, accepting [an] organization's self-description of the activities of its members, there is a statistical probability that some of those members are threatened with concrete injury").

The inference to be drawn from the Conference's statements cuts in precisely the opposite direction. What is at issue here is not just counties but voting districts within counties. If the Conference has members in almost every county, then there must be counties in which it does not have members; and we have no basis for concluding (or inferring) that those counties do not contain all of the majority-minority voting districts. Moreover, even in those counties in which the Conference does have members, we have no basis for concluding (or inferring) that those members vote in majority-minority districts. The Conference had plenty of opportunities, including at trial, to demonstrate that this was the case, and failed to do so. This failure lies with the Democratic Conference, and the consequences should be borne by it, not by the people of Alabama, who must now shoulder the expense of further litigation and the uncertainty that attends a resuscitated constitutional challenge to their legislative districts.

Incredibly, the Court thinks that "elementary principles of procedural fairness" require giving the Democratic Conference the opportunity to prove on appeal what it neglected to prove at trial. Ante, at 14. It observes that the Conference had no reason to believe it should provide such information because "the State did not contest its membership in every district," and the opinion cites an affidavit lodged with this Court providing a list of the Conference's members in each majority-minority district in Alabama. Ibid. I cannot imagine why the absence of a state challenge would matter. Whether or not there was such a challenge, it was the Conference's responsibility, as "[t]he party invoking federal jurisdiction," to establish standing. See Lujan v. Defenders of Wildlife, 504 U. S. 555, 561 (1992) . That responsibility was enforceable, challenge or no, by the court: "The federal courts are under an independent obligation to examine their own jurisdiction, and standing 'is perhaps the most important of [the jurisdictional] doctrines.' " FW/PBS, Inc. v. Dallas, 493 U. S. 215–231 (1990) (citations omitted). And because standing is not a "mere pleading requiremen[t] but rather an indispensable part of the plaintiff's case, each element must be supported in the same way as any other matter on which the plaintiff bears the burden of proof, i.e., with the manner and degree of evidence required at the successive stages of the litigation." Defenders of Wildlife, supra, at 561.

The Court points to Parents Involved in Community Schools v. Seattle School Dist. No. 1, 551 U. S. 701, 718 (2007), as support for its decision to sandbag Alabama with the Democratic Conference's out-of-time (indeed, out-of-court) lodging in this Court. The circumstances in that case, however, are far afield. The organization of parents in that case had established organizational standing in the lower court by showing that it had members with children who would be subject to the school district's "integration tiebreaker," which was applied at ninth grade. Brief for Respondents, O. T. 2006, No. 05–908, p. 16. By the time the case reached this Court, however, the youngest of these children had entered high school, and so would no longer be subject to the challenged policy. Ibid. Accordingly, we accepted a lodging that provided names of additional, younger children in order to show that the organization had not lost standing as a result of the long delay that often accompanies federal litigation. Here, by contrast, the Democratic Conference's lodging in the Supreme Court is its first attempt to show that it has members in the majority-minority districts. This is too little, too late.

But that is just the start. Even if the Democratic Conference had standing to bring district-specific racial-gerrymandering claims, there remains the question whether it did bring them. Its complaint alleged three counts: (1) Violation of §2 of the Voting Rights Act, (2) Racial gerrymandering in violation of the Equal Protection Clause, and (3) §1983 violations of the Voting Rights Act and the Fourteenth and Fifteenth Amendments. Complaint in No. 2:12–cv–1081, Doc. 1, pp. 17–18. The racial gerrymandering count alleged that "Alabama Acts 2012-602 and 2012-603 were drawn for the purpose and effect of minimizing the opportunity of minority voters to participate effectively in the political process," and that this "racial gerrymandering by Alabama Acts 2012-602 and 2012-603 violates the rights of Plaintiffs." Id., at 17. It made no reference to specific districts that were racially gerrymandered; indeed, the only particular jurisdictions mentioned anywhere in the complaint were Senate District 11, Senate District 22, Madison County Senate Districts, House District 73, and Jefferson and Montgomery County House Districts. None of the Senate Districts is majority-minority. Nor is House District 73. Jefferson County does, admittedly, contain 8 of the 27 majority-minority House Districts in Alabama, and Montgomery County contains another 4, making a total of 12. But they also contain 14 majority-white House Districts between them. In light of this, it is difficult to understand the Court's statement that appellants' "evidence and . . . arguments embody the claim that individual majority-minority districts were racially gerrymandered." Ante, at 8.

That observation would, of course, make sense if the Democratic Conference had developed such a claim in the course of discovery and trial. But in its post-trial Proposed Findings of Fact and Conclusions of Law, the Conference hewed to its original charge of statewide racial gerrymandering—or, rather, it did so as much as it reasonably could without actually proposing that the Court find any racial gerrymandering, statewide or otherwise. Instead, the Conference chose only to pursue claims that Alabama violated §2 of the Voting Rights Act under two theories. See Democratic Conference Post-Trial Brief 91–103 (alleging a violation of the results prong of Voting Rights Act §2) and 103–124 (alleging a violation of the purpose prong of Voting Rights Act §2).

To be sure, the Conference employed language and presented factual claims at various points in its 126-page post-trial brief that are evocative of a claim of racial gerrymandering. But in clinging to these stray comments to support its conclusion that the Conference made district-specific racial-gerrymandering claims, ante, at 9–10, the Court ignores the context in which these comments appear—the context of a clear Voting Rights Act §2 claim. Voting Rights Act claims and racial-gerrymandering claims share some of the same elements. See League of United Latin American Citizens v. Perry, 548 U. S. 399, 514 (2006) (Scalia, J., concurring in judgment in part and dissenting in part). Thus, allegations made in the course of arguing a §2 claim will often be indistinguishable from allegations that would be made in support of a racial-gerrymandering claim. The appearance of such allegations in one of the Conference's briefs might support reversal if this case came to us on appeal from the District Court's grant of a motion to dismiss. See Johnson v. City of Shelby, 574 U. S. ___, ___ (2014) (per curiam) (slip op., at 1) (noting that the Federal Rules of Civil Procedure "do not countenance dismissal of a complaint for imperfect statement of the legal theory supporting the claim as-serted"). But here the District Court held a full trial be-fore concluding that the Conference failed to make or prove any district-specific racial-gerrymandering claims with respect to the majority-minority districts. In this posture, and on this record, I cannot agree with the Court that the Conference's district-specific evidence, clearly made in the course of arguing a §2 theory, should be read to give rise to district-specific claims of racial gerrymandering with respect to Alabama's majority-minority districts.

The Court attempts to shift responsibility for the Democratic Conference's ill-fated statewide theory from the Conference to the District Court, implying that it was the "legally erroneous" analysis of the District Court, ante, at 12, rather than the arguments made by the Conference, that conjured this "legal unicorn," ante, at 7, so that the Conference did not forfeit the claims that the Court now attributes to it, ante, at 12. I suspect this will come as a great surprise to the Conference. Whatever may have been presented to the District Court, the Conference un-equivocally stated in its opening brief: "Appellants challenge Alabama's race-based statewide redistricting policy, not the design of any one particular election district." Brief for Appellants in No. 13–1138, p. 2 (emphasis added). It drove the point home in its reply brief: "[I]f theCourt were to apply a predominant-motive and narrow-tailoring analysis, that analysis should be applied to the state's policy, not to the design of each particular district one-by-one." Reply Brief in No. 11–1138, p. 7. How could anything be clearer? As the Court observes, the Conference attempted to walk back this unqualified description of its case at oral argument. Ante, at 11–12. Its assertion that what it really meant to challenge was the policy as applied to every district (not every majority-minority district, mind you) is not "clarification," ante, at 12, but an entirely new argument—indeed, the same argument it expressly disclaimed in its briefing. "We will not revive a forfeited argument simply because the petitioner gestures toward it in its reply brief." Republic of Argentina v. NML Capital, Ltd., 573 U. S. ___, ___, n. 2 (2014) (slip op., at 5, n. 2); we certainly should not do so when the issue is first presented at oral argument.

II. The Alabama Legislative Black Caucus

The Court does not bother to disentangle the independent claims brought by the Black Caucus from those of the Democratic Conference, but it strongly implies that both parties asserted racial-gerrymandering claims with respect to Alabama's 35 majority-minority districts. As we have described, the Democratic Conference brought no such claims; and the Black Caucus's filings provide even weaker support for the Court's conclusion.

The Black Caucus complaint contained three counts: (1) Violation of One Person, One Vote, see Reynolds v. Sims, 377 U. S. 533 (1964); (2) Dilution and Isolation of Black Voting Strength in violation of §2 of the Voting Rights Act; and (3) Partisan Gerrymandering. Complaint in No. 2:12–cv–691, Doc. 1, pp. 15–22. The failure to raise any racial-gerrymandering claim was not a mere oversight or the consequence of inartful pleading. Indeed, in its amended complaint the Black Caucus specifically cited this Court's leading racial-gerrymandering case for the proposition that "traditional or neutral districting principles may not be subordinated in a dominant fashion by either racial or partisan interests absent a compelling state interest for doing so." Amended Complaint in No. 2:12–cv–691, Doc. 60, p. 23 (citing Shaw v. Reno, 509 U. S. 630, 642 (1993);

emphasis added). This quote appears in the first paragraph under the "Partisan Gerrymandering" heading, and claims of subordination to racial interests are notably absent from the Black Caucus complaint.

Racial gerrymandering was not completely ignored, however. In a brief introductory paragraph to the amended complaint, before addressing jurisdiction and venue, the Black Caucus alleged that "Acts 2012-602 and 2012-603 are racial gerrymanders that unnecessarily minimize population deviations and violate the whole-county provisions of the Alabama Constitution with both the purpose and effect of minimizing black voting strength and isolating from influence in the Alabama Legislature legislators chosen by African Americans." Amended Complaint, at 3. This was the first and last mention of racial gerrymandering, and like the Democratic Conference's complaint, it focused exclusively on the districting maps as a whole rather than individual districts. Moreover, even this allegation appears primarily concerned with the use of racially motivated districting as a means of violating one person, one vote (by splitting counties), and §2 of the Voting Rights Act (by minimizing and isolating black voters and legislators).

To the extent the Black Caucus cited particular districts in the body of its complaint, it did so only with respect to its enumerated one-person, one-vote, Voting Rights Act, and partisan-gerrymandering counts. See, e.g., id., at 13–14 (alleging that the "deviation restriction and disregard of the 'whole county' requirements . . . facilitated the Republican majority's efforts to gerrymander the district boundaries in Acts 2012–602 and 2012–603 for partisan purposes. By packing the majority-black House and Senate districts, the plans remove reliable Democratic voters from adjacent majority-white districts . . ."); id., at 36 ("The partisan purpose of [one] gerrymander was to remove predominately black Madison County precincts to SD 1, avoiding a potential crossover district"); id., at 44–45 (asserting that "splitting Jefferson County among 11 House and Senate districts" and "increasing the size of its local legislative delegation and the number of other counties whose residents elect members" of the delegation "dilut[es] the votes of Jefferson County residents" by diminishing their ability to control county-level legislation in the state legislature). And even these claims were made with a statewide scope in mind. Id., at 55 ("Viewed in their entirety, the plans in Acts 2012-602 and 2012-603 have the purpose and effect of minimizing the opportunities for black and white voters who support the Democratic Party to elect candidates of their choice").

Here again, discovery and trial failed to produce any clear claims with respect to the majority-minority districts. In a curious inversion of the Democratic Conference's practice of pleading racial gerrymandering and then effectively abandoning the claims, the Black Caucus, which failed to plead racial gerrymandering, did clearly advance the theory after the trial. See Alabama Legislative Black Caucus Plaintiffs' Post-Trial Proposed Findings of Fact and Conclusions of Law in No. 2:12–cv–691, Doc. 194, pp. 48–51 (Black Caucus Post-Trial Brief). The Black Caucus asserted racial-gerrymandering claims in its post-trial brief, but they all had a clear statewide scope. It charged that Alabama "started their line drawing with the majority-black districts" so as to maximize the size of their black majorities, which "impacted the drawing of majority-white districts in nearly every part of the state." Id., at 48–49. "[R]ace was the predominant factor in drafting both plans," id., at 49, which "drove nearly every districting decision," "dilut[ing] the influence of black voters in the majority-white districts," id., at 50.

The Black Caucus did present district-specific evidence in the course of developing its other legal theories. Al-though this included evidence that Alabama manipulated the racial composition of certain majority-minority districts, it also included evidence that Alabama manipulated racial distributions with respect to the districting maps as a whole, id., at 6 ("Maintaining the same high black percentages had a predominant impact on the entire plan"), and with respect to majority-white districts, id., at 10–11 ("Asked why [majority-white] SD 11 was drawn in a semi-donut-shape that splits St. Clair, Talladega, and Shelby Counties, Sen. Dial blamed that also on the need to preserve the black majorities in Jefferson County Senate districts"), and 43–44 ("Sen. Irons' quick, 'primative' [sic] analysis of the new [majority-white] SD 1 convinced her that it was designed to 'shed' the minority population of Sen. Sanford's [majority-white] SD 7 to SD 1" in order to "crack a minority influence district"). The Black Caucus was attacking the legislative districts from every angle. Nothing gives rise to an inference that it ever homed in on majority-minority districts—or, for that matter, any particular set of districts. Indeed, the fair reading of the Black Caucus's filings is that it was presenting illustrative evidence in particular districts—majority-minority, minority-influence, and majority-white—in an effort to make out a claim of statewide racial gerrymandering. The fact that the Court now concludes that this is not a valid legal theory does not justify its repackaging the claims for a second round of litigation.

III. Conclusion

Frankly, I do not know what to make of appellants' arguments. They are pleaded with such opacity that, squinting hard enough, one can find them to contain just about anything. This, the Court believes, justifies demanding that the District Court go back and squint harder, so that it may divine some new means of construingthe filings. This disposition is based, it seems, on the implicit premise that plaintiffs only plead legally correct theories. That is a silly premise. We should not reward the practice of litigation by obfuscation, especially when we are dealing with a well-established legal claim that numerous plaintiffs have successfully brought in the past. See, e.g., Amended Complaint and Motion for Preliminary and Permanent Injunction in Cromartie v. Hunt, No. 4:96–cv–104 (EDNC), Doc. 21, p. 9 ("Under the March 1997 redistricting plan, the Twelfth District and First District have boundaries which were drawn pursuant to a predominantly racial motivation," which were "the fruit of [earlier] racially gerrymandered plans"). Even the complaint in Shaw, which established a cause of action for racial gerrymandering, displayed greater lucidity than appellants', alleging that defendants "creat[ed] two amorphous districts which embody a scheme for segregation of voters by race in order to meet a racial quota" "totally unrelated to considerations of compactness, contiguous, and geographic or jurisdictional communities of interest." Complaint and Motion for

Preliminary and Permanent Injunction and for Temporary Restraining Order in Shaw v. Barr, No. 5:92–cv–202 (EDNC), Doc. 1, pp. 11–12.

The Court seems to acknowledge that appellants never focused their racial-gerrymandering claims on Alabama's majority-minority districts. While remanding to consider whether the majority-minority districts were racially gerrymandered, it admits that plaintiffs "basically claim that the State, in adding so many new minority voters to majority-minority districts (and to others), went too far." Ante, at 3 (emphasis added). It further concedes that appellants "relied heavily upon statewide evidence," and that they "also sought to prove that the use of race to draw the boundaries of the majority-minority districts affected the boundaries of other districts as well." Ante, at 10.

The only reason I see for the Court's selection of the majority-minority districts as the relevant set of districts for the District Court to consider on remand is that this was the set chosen by appellants after losing on the claim they actually presented in the District Court. By playing along with appellants' choose-your-own-adventure style of litigation, willingly turning back the page every time a strategic decision leads to a dead-end, the Court discourages careful litigation and punishes defendants who are denied both notice and repose. The consequences of this unprincipled decision will reverberate far beyond the narrow circumstances presented in this case.

Accordingly, I dissent.

Justice Scalia's dissent in Williams-Yulee v. The Florida Bar (April 29, 2015)

Justice Scalia, with whom Justice Thomas joins, dissenting.

An ethics canon adopted by the Florida Supreme Court bans a candidate in a judicial election from asking anyone, under any circumstances, for a contribution to his campaign. Faithful application of our precedents would have made short work of this wildly disproportionate restriction upon speech. Intent upon upholding the Canon, however, the Court flattens one settled First Amendment principle after another.

I

The first axiom of the First Amendment is this: As a general rule, the state has no power to ban speech on the basis of its content. One need not equate judges with politicians to see that this principle does not grow weaker merely because the censored speech is a judicial candidate's request for a campaign contribution. Our cases hold that speech enjoys the full protection of the First Amendment unless a widespread and longstanding tradition ratifies its regulation. Brown v. Entertainment Merchants Assn., 564 U. S. ____, ___ (2011) (slip op., at 3). No such tradition looms here. Georgia became the first State to elect its judges in 1812, and judicial elections had spread to a large majority of the States by the time of the Civil War. Republican Party of Minn. v. White, 536 U. S. 765, 785 (2002). Yet there appears to have been no regulation of judicial candidates' speech throughout the 19th and early 20th centuries. Ibid. The American Bar Association first proposed ethics rules concerning speech of judicial candidates in 1924, but these rules did not achieve widespread adoption until after the Second World War. Id., at 786.

Rules against soliciting campaign contributions arrived more recently still. The ABA first proposed a canon advising against it in 1972, and a canon prohibiting it only in 1990. See Brief for American Bar Association as Amicus Curiae 2–4. Even now, 9 of the 39 States that elect judges allow judicial candidates to ask for campaign contributions. See id., at 4. In the absence of any long-settled custom about judicial candidates' speech in general or their solicitations in particular, we have no basis for relaxing the rules that normally apply to laws that suppress speech because of content.

One likewise need not equate judges with politicians to see that the electoral setting calls for all the more vigilance in ensuring observance of the First Amendment. When a candidate asks someone for a campaign contribution, he tends (as the principal opinion acknowledges) also to talk about his qualifications for office and his views on public issues. Ante, at 6–7 (plurality opinion). This expression lies at the heart of what the First Amendment is meant to protect. In addition, banning candidates from asking for money personally "favors some candidates over others—incumbent judges (who benefit from their current status) over non-judicial candidates, the well-to-do (who may not need to raise any money at all) over lower-income candidates, and the well-connected (who have an army of potential fundraisers) over outsiders." Carey v. Wolnitzek, 614 F. 3d 189, 204 (CA6 2010). This danger of legislated (or judicially imposed) favoritism is the very reason the First Amendment exists.

Because Canon 7C(1) restricts fully protected speech on the basis of content, it presumptively violates the First Amendment. We may uphold it only if the State meets its burden of showing that the Canon survives strict scrutiny—that is to say, only if it shows that the Canon is narrowly tailored to serve a compelling interest. I do not for a moment question the Court's conclusion that States have different compelling interests when regulating judicial elections than when regulating political ones. Unlike a legislator, a judge must be impartial—without bias for or against any party or attorney who comes before him. I accept for the sake of argument that States have a compelling interest in ensuring that its judges are seen to be impartial. I will likewise assume that a judicial candidate's request to a litigant or attorney presents a danger of coercion that a political candidate's request to a constituent does not. But Canon 7C(1) does not narrowly target concerns about impartiality or its appearance; it applies even when the person asked for a financial contribution has no chance of ever appearing in the candidate's court. And Florida does not invoke concerns about coercion, presumably because the Canon bans solicitations regardless of whether their object is a lawyer, litigant, or other person vulnerable to judicial pressure. So Canon 7C(1) fails exacting scrutiny and infringes the First Amendment. This case should have been just that straightforward.

II

The Court concludes that Florida may prohibit personal solicitations by judicial candidates as a means of preserving "public confidence in the integrity of the judiciary."

Ante, at 8. It purports to reach this destination by applying strict scrutiny, but it would be more accurate to say that it does so by applying the appearance of strict scrutiny.

A

The first sign that mischief is afoot comes when the Court describes Florida's compelling interest. The State must first identify its objective with precision before one can tell whether that interest is compelling and whether the speech restriction narrowly targets it. In White, for example, the Court did not allow a State to invoke hazy concerns about judicial impartiality in justification of an ethics rule against judicial candidates' announcing their positions on legal issues. 536 U. S., at 775. The Court instead separately analyzed the State's concerns about judges' bias against parties, preconceptions on legal issues, and open-mindedness, and explained why each concern (and each for a different reason) did not suffice to sustain the rule. Id., at 775–780.

In stark contrast to White, the Court today relies on Florida's invocation of an ill-defined interest in "public confidence in judicial integrity." The Court at first suggests that "judicial integrity" involves the "ability to administer justice without fear or favor." Ante, at 9. As its opinion unfolds, however, today's concept of judicial integrity turns out to be "a mere thing of wax in the hands of the judiciary, which they may twist, and shape into any form they please." 12 The Works of Thomas Jefferson 137 (P. Ford ed. 1905). When the Court explains how solicitation undermines confidence in judicial integrity, integrity starts to sound like saintliness. It involves independence from any " 'possible temptation' " that " 'might lead' " the judge, "even unknowingly," to favor one party. Ante, at 11 (emphasis added). When the Court turns to distinguishing in-person solicitation from solicitation by proxy, the any-possible-temptation standard no longer helps and thus drops out. The critical factors instead become the "pressure" a listener feels during a solicitation and the "appearance that the candidate will remember who says yes, and who says no." Ante, at 14. But when it comes time to explain Florida's decision to allow candidates to write thank-you notes, the "appearance that the candidate . . . remember[s] who says yes" gets nary a mention. Ante, at 14–15. And when the Court confronts Florida's decision to prohibit mass-mailed solicitations, concern about pressure fades away. Ante, at 18. More outrageous still, the Court at times molds the interest in the perception that judges have integrity into an interest in the perception that judges do not solicit—for example when it says, "all personal solicitations by judicial candidates create a public appearance that undermines confidence in the integrity of the judiciary; banning all personal solicitations by judicial candidates is narrowly tailored to address that concern." Ante, at 19. This is not strict scrutiny; it is sleight of hand.

B

The Court's twistifications have not come to an end; indeed, they are just beginning. In order to uphold Canon 7C(1) under strict scrutiny, Florida must do more than point to a vital public objective brooding overhead. The State must also meet a difficult burden of demonstrating that the speech restriction substantially advances the claimed objective. The State "bears the risk of uncertainty," so "ambiguous proof will not suffice." Entertainment Merchants, 564 U. S., at ____ (slip op., at 12). In an arresting illustration, this Court held that a law punishing lies about winning military decorations like the Congressional Medal of Honor failed exacting scrutiny, because the Government could not satisfy its "heavy burden" of proving that "the public's general perception of military awards is diluted by false claims." United States v. Alvarez, 567 U. S. ____, ____ (2012) (plurality opinion) (slip op., at 14).

Now that we have a case about the public's perception of judicial honor rather than its perception of military honors, the Justices of this Court change the rules. The Court announces, on the basis of its "intuiti[on]," that allowing personal solicitations will make litigants worry that " 'judges' decisions may be motivated by the desire to repay campaign contributions.' " Ante, at 11. But this case is not about whether Yulee has the right to receive campaign contributions. It is about whether she has the right to ask for campaign contributions that Florida's statutory law already allows her to receive. Florida bears the burden of showing that banning requests for lawful contributions will improve public confidence in judges—not just a little bit, but significantly, because "the Government does not have a compelling interest in each marginal percentage point by which its goals are advanced." Entertainment Merchants, supra, at ____, n. 9 (slip op., at 16, n. 9).

Neither the Court nor the State identifies the slightest evidence that banning requests for contributions will substantially improve public trust in judges. Nor does common sense make this happy forecast obvious. The concept of judicial integrity "dates back at least eight centuries," ante, at 9, and judicial elections in America date back more than two centuries, supra, at 1—but rules against personal solicitations date back only to 1972, supra, at 2. The peaceful coexistence of judicial elections and personal solicitations for most of our history calls into doubt any claim that allowing personal solicitations would imperil public faith in judges. Many States allow judicial candidates to ask for contributions even today, but nobody suggests that public confidence in judges fares worse in these jurisdictions than elsewhere. And in any event, if candidates' appeals for money are " 'characteristically intertwined' " with discussion of qualifications and views on public issues, ante, at 7 (plurality opinion), how can the Court be so sure that the public will regard them as improprieties rather than as legitimate instances of campaigning? In the final analysis, Florida comes nowhere near making the convincing demonstration required by our cases that the speech restriction in this case substantially advances its objective.

C

But suppose we play along with the premise that prohibiting solicitations will significantly improve the public reputation of judges. Even then, Florida must show that the ban restricts no more speech than necessary to achieve the objective. See Sable Communications of Cal., Inc. v. FCC, 492 U. S. 115, 126 (1989) .

Canon 7C(1) falls miles short of satisfying this requirement. The Court seems to accept Florida's claim that solicitations erode public confidence by creating the perception that judges are selling justice to lawyers and litigants. Ante, at 9. Yet the Canon prohibits candidates from asking for money from anybody—even from someone who is neither lawyer nor litigant, even from someone who (because of recusal rules) cannot possibly appear before the candidate as lawyer or litigant. Yulee thus may not call up an old friend, a cousin, or even her parents to ask for a donation to her campaign. The State has not come up with a plausible explanation of how soliciting someone who has no chance of appearing in the candidate's court will diminish public confidence in judges.

No less important, Canon 7C(1) bans candidates from asking for contributions even in messages that do not target any listener in particular—mass-mailed letters, flyers posted on telephone poles, speeches to large gatherings, and Web sites addressed to the general public. Messages like these do not share the features that lead the Court to pronounce personal solicitations a menace to public confidence in the judiciary. Consider online solicitations. They avoid " 'the spectacle of lawyers or potentiallitigants directly handing over money to judicial candidates,' " ante, at 12. People who come across online solicitations do not feel "pressure" to comply with the request, ante, at 14. Nor does the candidate's signature on the online solicitation suggest "that the candidate will remember who says yes, and who says no," ibid. Yet Canon 7C(1) prohibits these and similar solicitations anyway. This tailoring is as narrow as the Court's scrutiny is strict.

Perhaps sensing the fragility of the initial claim that all solicitations threaten public confidence in judges, the Court argues that "the lines Yulee asks [it] to draw are unworkable." Ante, at 18. That is a difficulty of the Court's own imagination. In reality, the Court could have chosen from a whole spectrum of workable rules. It could have held that States may regulate no more than solicitation of participants in pending cases, or solicitation of people who are likely to appear in the candidate's court, or even solicitation of any lawyer or litigant. And it could have ruled that candidates have the right to make fundraising appeals that are not directed to any particular listener (like requests in mass-mailed letters), or at least fundraising appeals plainly directed to the general public (like requests placed online). The Supreme Court of Florida has made similar accommodations in other settings. It allows sitting judges to solicit memberships in civic organizations if (among other things) the solicitee is not "likely ever to appear before the court on which the judge serves." Code of Judicial Conduct for the State of Florida 23 (2014) (Judicial Conduct Code). And it allows sitting judges to accept gifts if (among other things) "the donor is not a party or other person . . . whose interests have come or are likely to come before the judge." Id., at 24. It is not too much to ask that the State show election speech similar consideration.

The Court's accusation of unworkability also suffers from a bit of a pot-kettle problem. Consider the many real-world questions left open by today's decision. Does the First Amendment permit restricting a candidate's appearing at an event where somebody else asks for campaign funds on his behalf? See Florida Judicial Ethics Advisory Committee Opinion No. 2012–14 (JEAC Op.). Does it permit prohibiting the candidate's family from making personal solicitations? See ibid. Does it allow prohibiting the candidate from participating in the creation of a Web site that solicits funds, even if the candidate's name does not appear next to the request? See JEAC Op. No. 2008–11. More broadly, could Florida ban thank-you notes to donors? Cap a candidate's campaign spending? Restrict independent spending by people other than the candidate? Ban independent spending by corporations? And how, by the way, are judges supposed to decide whether these measures promote public confidence in judicial integrity, when the Court does not even have a consistent theory about what it means by "judicial integrity"? For the Court to wring its hands about workability under these circumstances is more than one should have to bear.

D

Even if Florida could show that banning all personal appeals for campaign funds is necessary to protect public confidence in judicial integrity, the Court must overpower one last sentinel of free speech before it can uphold Canon 7C(1). Among its other functions, the First Amendment is a kind of Equal Protection Clause for ideas. The state ordinarily may not regulate one message because it harms a government interest yet refuse to regulate other messages that impair the interest in a comparable way. Applying this principle, we invalidated a law that prohibited picketing dwellings but made an exception for picketing about labor issues; the State could not show that labor picketing harmed its asserted interest in residential privacy any less than other kinds of picketing. Carey v. Brown, 447 U. S. 455–465 (1980). In another case, we set aside a ban on showing movies containing nudity in drive-in theaters, because the government did not demonstrate that movies with nude scenes would distract passing drivers any more than, say, movies with violent scenes. Erznoznik v. Jacksonville, 422 U. S. 205–215 (1975).

The Court's decision disregards these principles. The Court tells us that "all personal solicitations by judicial candidates create a public appearance that undermines confidence in the integrity of the judiciary." Ante, at 19. But Canon 7C(1) does not restrict all personal solicitations; it restricts only personal solicitations related to campaigns. The part of the Canon challenged here prohibits personal pleas for "campaign funds," and the Canon elsewhere prohibits personal appeals to attorneys for "publicly stated support." Judicial Conduct Code 38. So although Canon 7C(1) prevents Yulee from asking a lawyer for a few dollars to help her buy campaign pamphlets, it does not prevent her asking the same lawyer for a personal loan, access to his law firm's luxury suite at the local football stadium, or even a donation to help her fight the Florida Bar's charges. What could possibly justify these distinctions? Surely the Court does not believe that requests for campaign favors erode public confidence in a way that requests for favors unrelated to elections do not. Could anyone say with a straight face that it looks worse for a candidate to say "please give my campaign $25" than to say "please give me $25"? 1 *

Fumbling around for a fig-leaf, the Court says that "the First Amendment imposes no freestanding 'underinclusiveness limitation.' " Ante, at 13. This analysis elides the distinction between selectivity on the basis of content and selectivity on other grounds. Because the First Amendment does not prohibit underinclusiveness as such, lawmakers may target a problem only at certain times or in certain places. Because the First

Amendment does prohibit content discrimination as such, lawmakers may not target a problem only in certain messages. Explaining this distinction, we have said that the First Amendment would allow banning obscenity "only in certain media or markets" but would preclude banning "only that obscenity which includes offensive political messages." R. A. V. v. St. Paul, 505 U. S. 377–388 (1992) (emphasis deleted). This case involves selectivity on the basis of content. The Florida Supreme Court has decided to eliminate the appearances associated with "personal appeals for money," ante, at 18, when the appeals seek money for a campaign but not when the appeals seek money for other purposes. That distinction violates the First Amendment. See Erznoznik, supra, at 215.

Even on the Court's own terms, Canon 7C(1) cannot stand. The Court concedes that "underinclusiveness can raise 'doubts about whether the government is in fact pursuing the interest it invokes.' " Ante, at 13. Canon 7C(1)'s scope suggests that it has nothing to do with the appearances created by judges' asking for money, and everything to do with hostility toward judicial campaigning. How else to explain the Florida Supreme Court's decision to ban all personal appeals for campaign funds (even when the solicitee could never appear before the candidate), but to tolerate appeals for other kinds of funds (even when the solicitee will surely appear before the candidate)? It should come as no surprise that the ABA, whose model rules the Florida Supreme Court followed when framing Canon 7C(1), opposes judicial elections—preferring instead a system in which (surprise!) a committee of lawyers proposes candidates from among whom the Governor must make his selection. See White, 536 U. S., at 787.

The Court tries to strike a pose of neutrality between appointment and election of judges, but no one should be deceived. A Court that sees impropriety in a candidate's request for any contributions to his election campaign does not much like judicial selection by the people. One cannot have judicial elections without judicial campaigns, and judicial campaigns without funds for campaigning, and funds for campaigning without asking for them. When a society decides that its judges should be elected, it necessarily decides that selection by the people is more important than the oracular sanctity of judges, their immunity from the (shudder!) indignity of begging for funds, and their exemption from those shadows of impropriety that fall over the proletarian public officials who must run for office. A free society, accustomed to electing its rulers, does not much care whether the rulers operate through statute and executive order, or through judicial distortion of statute, executive order, and constitution. The prescription that judges be elected probably springs from the people's realization that their judges can become their rulers—and (it must be said) from just a deep-down feeling that members of the Third Branch will profit from a hearty helping of humble pie, and from a severe reduction of their great remove from the (ugh!) People. (It should not be thought that I myself harbor such irreverent and revolutionary feelings; but I think it likely—and year by year more likely—that those who favor the election of judges do so.) In any case, hostility to campaigning by judges entitles the people of Florida to amend their Constitution to replace judicial elections with the selection of judges by lawyers' committees; it does not entitle the Florida Supreme Court to adopt, or this Court to endorse, a rule of judicial conduct that abridges candidates' speech in the judicial elections that the Florida Constitution prescribes.

*   *   *

This Court has not been shy to enforce the First Amendment in recent Terms—even in cases that do not involve election speech. It has accorded robust protection to depictions of animal torture, sale of violent video games to children, and lies about having won military medals. See United States v. Stevens, 559 U. S. 460 (2010); Entertainment Merchants, 564 U. S. ____; Alvarez, 567 U. S. ____. Who would have thought that the same Court would today exert such heroic efforts to save so plain an abridgement of the freedom of speech? It is no great mystery what is going on here. The judges of this Court, like the judges of the Supreme Court of Florida who promulgated Canon 7C(1), evidently consider the preservation of public respect for the courts a policy objective of the highest order. So it is—but so too are preventing animal torture, protecting the innocence of children, and honoring valiant soldiers. The Court did not relax the Constitution's guarantee of freedom of speech when legislatures pursued those goals; it should not relax the guarantee when the Supreme Court of Florida pursues this one. The First Amendment is not abridged for the benefit of the Brotherhood of the Robe.

I respectfully dissent.

Notes

1* Neither Florida nor the Court identifies any other ethics rule that would prevent candidates like Yulee from asking for favors unrelated to elections, and I know of none. The Supreme Court of Florida has adopted various rules restricting sitting judges' solicitation and acceptance of favors, but these rules do not bind challengers like Yulee. See, e.g., Canon 4D(2)(a), Judicial Conduct Code 18–19 ("A judge as [a member or officer of an organization] . . . shall not personally or directly participate in the solicitation of funds . . . "); Canon 5D(5), id., at 24 ("A judge shall not accept . . . a gift, bequest, favor or loan . . ."); JEAC Op. No. 2010–14 ("[J]udicial candidates are only governed by Canon 7, and not by the remainder of the Code of Judicial Conduct").

Justice Scalia's concurrence and dissent in City and County of San Francisco v. Sheehan (May 18, 2015)

JUSTICE SCALIA, with whom JUSTICE KAGAN joins, concurring in part and dissenting in part.

The first question presented (QP) in the petition for certiorari was "Whether Title II of the Americans with Disabilities Act [(ADA)] requires law enforcement officers to provide accommodations to an armed, violent, and mentally ill suspect in the course of bringing the suspect into custody." Pet. for Cert. i. The petition assured us (quite accurately), and devoted a section of its argument to the point, that "The Circuits Are In Conflict On This Question." Id., at 18. And petitioners faulted the Ninth Circuit for "holding that the ADA's reasonable accommodation requirement applies to officers facing violent circumstances," a conclusion that was "in direct conflict with the categorical prohibition on such claims adopted by the Fifth and Sixth Circuits." Ibid. Petitioners had expressly advocated for the Fifth and Sixth Circuits' position in the Court of Appeals. See Appellees' Answering Brief in No. 11–16401 (CA9), pp. 35–37 ("[T]he ADA does not apply to police officers' responses to violent individuals who happen to be mentally ill, where officers have not yet brought the violent situation under control").

Imagine our surprise, then, when the petitioners' principal brief, reply brief, and oral argument had nary a word to say about that subject. Instead, petitioners bluntly announced in their principal brief that they "do not assert that the actions of individual police officers [in arresting violent and armed disabled persons] are never subject to scrutiny under Title II," and proclaimed that "[t]he only ADA issue here is what Title II requires of individual officers who are facing an armed and dangerous suspect." Brief for Petitioners 34 (emphasis added). In other words, the issue is not (as the petition had asserted) whether Title II applies to arrests of violent, mentally ill individuals, but rather how it applies under the circumstances of this case, where the plaintiff threatened officers with a weapon. We were thus deprived of the opportunity to consider, and settle, a controverted question of law that has divided the Circuits, and were invited instead to decide an ADA question that has relevance only if we assume the Ninth Circuit correctly resolved the antecedent, unargued question on which we granted certiorari. The Court is correct to dismiss the first QP as improvidently granted.

Why, one might ask, would a petitioner take a position on a Circuit split that it had no intention of arguing, or at least was so little keen to argue that it cast the argument aside uninvited? The answer is simple. Petitioners included that issue to induce us to grant certiorari. As the Court rightly observes, there are numerous reasons why we would not have agreed to hear petitioners' first QP if their petition for certiorari presented it in the same form that it was argued on the merits. See ante, at 7–10. But it is also true that there was little chance that we would have taken this case to decide only the second, fact-bound QP—that is, whether the individual petitioners are entitled to qualified immunity on respondent's Fourth Amendment claim.

This Court's Rule 10, entitled "Considerations Governing Review on Certiorari," says that certiorari will be granted "only for compelling reasons," which include the existence of conflicting decisions on issues of law among federal courts of appeals, among state courts of last resort, or between federal courts of appeals and state courts of last resort. The Rule concludes: "A petition for a writ of certiorari is rarely granted when the asserted error con- sists of erroneous factual findings or the misapplication of a properly stated rule of law." The second QP implicates, at most, the latter. It is unlikely that we would have granted certiorari on that question alone.

But (and here is what lies beneath the present case) when we do grant certiorari on a question for which there is a "compelling reason" for our review, we often also grant certiorari on attendant questions that are not independently "certworthy," but that are sufficiently connected to the ultimate disposition of the case that the efficient administration of justice supports their consideration. In other words, by promising argument on the Circuit conflict that their first question presented, petitioners got us to grant certiorari not only on the first question but also on the second.

I would not reward such bait-and-switch tactics by proceeding to decide the independently "uncertworthy" second question. And make no mistake about it: Today's judgment is a reward. It gives the individual petitioners all that they seek, and spares San Francisco the significant expense of defending the suit, and satisfying any judgment, against the individual petitioners.* I would not encourage future litigants to seek review premised on arguments they never plan to press, secure in the knowledge that once they find a toehold on this Court's docket, we will consider whatever workaday arguments they choose to present in their merits briefs.

There is no injustice in my vote to dismiss both questions as improvidently granted. To be sure, ex post—after the Court has improvidently decided the uncertworthy question—it appears that refusal to reverse the judgment below would have left a wrong unrighted. Ex ante, how- ever—before we considered and deliberated upon the second QP but after petitioners' principal brief made clear that they would not address the Circuit conflict presented by the first QP—we had no more assurance that this question was decided incorrectly than we do for the thousands of other uncertworthy questions we refuse to hear each Term. Many of them have undoubtedly been decided wrongly, but we are not, and for well over a century have not been, a court of error correction. The fair course—the just course—is to treat this now-nakedly uncertworthy question the way we treat all others: by declining to decide it. In fact, there is in this case an even greater reason to decline: to avoid being snookered, and to deter future snookering.

Because I agree with the Court that "certiorari jurisdiction exists to clarify the law," ante, at 9 (emphasis added), I would dismiss both questions presented as improvidently granted.

*San Francisco will still be subject to liability under the ADA if the trial court determines that the facts demanded accommodation. The Court of Appeals vacated the District Court's judgment that the ADA was inapplicable to police arrests of violent and armed disabled persons, and remanded for the accommodation determination.

Justice Scalia's dissent in Comptroller of Treasure of Maryland v. Wynne (May 18, 2015)

Justice Scalia, with whom Justice Thomas joins as to Parts I and II, dissenting.

The Court holds unconstitutional Maryland's refusal to give its residents full credits against income taxes paid to other States. It does this by invoking the negative Commerce Clause, a judge-invented rule under which judges may set aside state laws that they think impose too much of a burden upon interstate commerce. I join the principal dissent, which demonstrates the incompatibility of this decision with our prior negative Commerce Clause cases. Post, at 2–14 (opinion of Ginsburg, J.). Incompatibility, however, is not the test for me—though what is incompatible with our cases a fortiori fails my test as well, as discussed briefly in Part III below. The principal purpose of my writing separately is to point out how wrong our negative Commerce Clause jurisprudence is in the first place, and how well today's decision illustrates its error.

I

The fundamental problem with our negative Commerce Clause cases is that the Constitution does not contain a negative Commerce Clause. It contains only a Commerce Clause. Unlike the negative Commerce Clause adopted by the judges, the real Commerce Clause adopted by the People merely empowers Congress to "regulate Commerce with foreign Nations, and among the several States, and with the Indian Tribes." Art. I, §8, cl. 3. The Clause says nothing about prohibiting state laws that burden commerce. Much less does it say anything about authorizing judges to set aside state laws they believe burden commerce. The clearest sign that the negative Commerce Clause is a judicial fraud is the utterly illogical holding that congressional consent enables States to enact laws that would otherwise constitute impermissible burdens upon interstate commerce. See Prudential Ins. Co. v. Benjamin, 328 U. S. 408–427 (1946). How could congressional consent lift a constitutional prohibition? See License Cases, 5 How. 504, 580 (1847) (opinion of Taney, C. J.).

The Court's efforts to justify this judicial economic veto come to naught. The Court claims that the doctrine "has deep roots." Ante, at 5. So it does, like many weeds. But age alone does not make up for brazen invention. And the doctrine in any event is not quite as old as the Court makes it seem. The idea that the Commerce Clause of its own force limits state power "finds no expression" in discussions surrounding the Constitution's ratification. F. Frankfurter, The Commerce Clause Under Marshall, Taney and Waite 13 (1937). For years after the adoption of the Constitution, States continually made regulations that burdened interstate commerce (like pilotage laws and quarantine laws) without provoking any doubts about their constitutionality. License Cases, supra, at 580–581. This Court's earliest allusions to a negative Commerce Clause came only in dicta—ambiguous dicta, at that—and were vigorously contested at the time. See, e.g., id., at 581–582. Our first clear holding setting aside a state law under the negative Commerce Clause came after the Civil War, more than 80 years after the Constitution's adoption. Case of the State Freight Tax, 15 Wall. 232 (1873). Since then, we have tended to revamp the doctrine every couple of decades upon finding existing decisions unworkable or unsatisfactory. See Quill Corp. v. North Dakota, 504 U. S. 298, 309 (1992) . The negative Commerce Clause applied today has little in common with the negative Commerce Clause of the 19th century, except perhaps for incoherence.

The Court adds that "tariffs and other laws that burdened interstate commerce" were among "the chief evils that led to the adoption of the Constitution." Ante, at 5. This line of reasoning forgets that interpretation requires heeding more than the Constitution's purposes; it requires heeding the means the Constitution uses to achieve those purposes. The Constitution addresses the evils of local impediments to commerce by prohibiting States from imposing certain especially burdensome taxes—"Imposts or Duties on Imports or Exports" and "Dut[ies] of Tonnage"—without congressional consent. Art. I, §10, cls. 2–3. It also addresses these evils by giving Congress a com-merce power under which it may prohibit other burdensome taxes and laws. As the Constitution's text shows, however, it does not address these evils by empowering the judiciary to set aside state taxes and laws that it deems too burdensome. By arrogating this power anyway, our negative Commerce Clause cases have disrupted the balance the Constitution strikes between the goal of protecting commerce and competing goals like preserving local autonomy and promoting democratic responsibility.

II

The failings of negative Commerce Clause doctrine go beyond its lack of a constitutional foundation, as today's decision well illustrates.

1. One glaring defect of the negative Commerce Clause is its lack of governing principle. Neither the Constitution nor our legal traditions offer guidance about how to sepa-rate improper state interference with commerce from permissible state taxation or regulation of commerce. So we must make the rules up as we go along. That is how we ended up with the bestiary of ad hoc tests and ad hoc exceptions that we apply nowadays, including the substantial nexus test, the fair apportionment test, and the fair relation test, Complete Auto Transit, Inc. v. Brady, 430 U. S. 274, 279 (1977) , the interest-on-state-bonds exception, Department of Revenue of Ky. v. Davis, 553 U. S. 328–356 (2008), and the sales-taxes-on-mail-orders exception, Quill Corp., supra, at 314–319.

The internal consistency rule invoked by the Court nicely showcases our ad hocery. Under this rule, a tax violates the Constitution if its hypothetical adoption by all States would interfere with interstate commerce. Ante, at 19. How did this exercise in counterfactuals find its way into our basic charter? The test, it is true, bears some resemblance to Kant's first formulation of the categorical imperative: "Act only according to that maxim whereby you can at the same time will that it should become a universal law" without contradiction. Grounding for the Metaphysics of Morals 30 (J. Ellington transl. 3d ed. 1993). It bears no resemblance, however, to anything in the text or structure of the Constitution. Nor can one discern an obligation of internal consistency from our legal traditions, which show that States have been imposing internally inconsistent taxes for quite a while—until recently with our approval. See, e.g., General Motors Corp. v. Washington, 377 U. S. 436 (1964) (upholding internally inconsistent business activities tax); Hinson v. Lott, 8 Wall. 148 (1869) (upholding internally inconsistent liquor tax). No, the only justification for the test seems to be that this Court disapproves of " 'cross-border tax disadvantage[s]' " when created by internally inconsistent taxes, but is willing to tolerate them when created by "the interaction of . . . internally consistent schemes." Ante, at 19. "Whatever it is we are expounding in this area, it is not a Constitution." American Trucking Assns., Inc. v. Smith, 496 U. S. 167, 203 (1990) (Scalia, J., concurring in judgment).

    2. Another conspicuous feature of the negative Commerce Clause is its instability. Because no principle anchors our development of this doctrine—and because the line between wise regulation and burdensome interference changes from age to economic age—one can never tell when the Court will make up a new rule or throw away an old one. "Change is almost [the doctrine's] natural state, as it is the natural state of legislation in a constantly changing national economy." Ibid.

    Today's decision continues in this proud tradition. Consider a few ways in which it contradicts earlier decisions:

    In an earlier case, the Court conceded that a trucking tax "fail[ed] the 'internal consistency' test," but upheld the tax anyway. American Trucking Assns., Inc. v. Michigan Pub. Serv. Comm'n, 545 U. S. 429, 437 (2005). Now, the Court proclaims that an income tax "fails the internal consistency test," and for that reason strikes it down. Ante, at 21.

    In an earlier case, the Court concluded that "[i]t is not a purpose of the Commerce Clause to protect state residents from their own state taxes" and that residents could "complain about and change the tax through the [State's] political process." Goldberg v. Sweet, 488 U. S. 252, 266 (1989). Now, the Court concludes that the negative Commerce Clause operates "regardless of whether the plaintiff is a resident . . . or nonresident" and that "the notion that [residents] have a complete remedy at the polls is fanciful." Ante, at 11, 12.

    In an earlier case, the Court said that "[t]he difference in effect between a tax measured by gross receipts and one measured by net income . . . is manifest and substantial." United States Glue Co. v. Town of Oak Creek, 247 U. S. 321, 328 (1918). Now, the Court says that the "formal distinction" between taxes on net and gross income "should [not] matter." Ante, at 7.

    In an earlier case, the Court upheld a tax despite its economic similarity to the gross-receipts tax struck down in Central Greyhound Lines, Inc. v. Mealey, 334 U. S. 653 (1948). Oklahoma Tax Comm'n v. Jefferson Lines, Inc., 514 U. S. 175–191 (1995). The Court explained that "economic equivalence alone has . . . not been (and should not be) the touchstone of Commerce Clause jurisprudence." Id., at 196–197, n. 7. Now, the Court strikes down a tax in part because of its economic similarity to the gross-receipts tax struck down in Central Greyhound. Ante, at 7. The Court explains that "we must consider 'not the formal language of the tax statute but rather its practical effect.'" Ante, at 7–8.

    So much for internal consistency.

    3. A final defect of our Synthetic Commerce Clause cases is their incompatibility with the judicial role. The doctrine does not call upon us to perform a conventional judicial function, like interpreting a legal text, discerning a legal tradition, or even applying a stable body of precedents. It instead requires us to balance the needs of commerce against the needs of state governments. That is a task for legislators, not judges.

    Today's enterprise of eliminating double taxation puts this problem prominently on display. The one sure way to eliminate all double taxation is to prescribe uniform national tax rules—for example, to allow taxation of income only where earned. But a program of prescribing a national tax code plainly exceeds the judicial competence. (It may even exceed the legislative competence to come up with a uniform code that accounts for the many political and economic differences among the States.) As an alternative, we could consider whether a State's taxes in practice overlap too much with the taxes of other States. But any such approach would drive us "to the perplexing inquiry, so unfit for the judicial department, what degree of taxation is the legitimate use, and what degree may amount to an abuse of power." McCulloch v. Maryland, 4 Wheat. 316, 430 (1819). The Court today chooses a third approach, prohibiting States from imposing internally inconsistent taxes. Ante, at 19. But that rule avoids double taxation only in the hypothetical world where all States adopt the same internally consistent tax, not in the real world where different States might adopt different internally consistent taxes. For example, if Maryland imposes its income tax on people who live in Maryland regardless of where they work (one internally consistent scheme), while Virginia imposes its income tax on people who work in Virginia regardless of where they live (an-other internally consistent scheme), Marylanders who work in Virginia still face double taxation. Post, at 17–18. Then again, it is only fitting that the Imaginary Commerce Clause would lead to imaginary benefits.

III

For reasons of stare decisis, I will vote to set aside a tax under the negative Commerce Clause if (but only if) it discriminates on its face against interstate commerce or cannot be distinguished from a tax this Court has already held unconstitutional. American Trucking Assns., 545 U. S., at 439 (Scalia, J., concurring in judgment). The income tax before us does not discriminate on its face against interstate commerce; a resident pays no less to Maryland when he works in Maryland than when he works elsewhere. Neither is the tax before us indistinguishable from one that we have previously held unconstitutional. To the contrary, as the principal dissent establishes, our prior cases validate this tax.

*   *   *

Maryland's refusal to give residents full tax credits against income taxes paid to other States has its disadvantages. It threatens double taxation and encourages residents to work in Maryland. But Maryland's law also has its advantages. It allows the State to collect equal revenue from taxpayers with equal incomes, avoids the administrative burdens of verifying tax payments to other States, and ensures that every resident pays the State at least some income tax. Nothing in the Constitution precludes Maryland from deciding that the benefits of its tax scheme are worth the costs.

I respectfully dissent.

Justice Scalia's dissent in Commil USA v. Cisco Systems (May 26, 2015)

Justice SCALIA, with whom THE CHIEF JUSTICE joins, dissenting.

I agree with the Court's rejection of the main argument advanced by Commil and the United States, that induced infringement under 35 U.S.C. § 271(b) does not "requir[e] knowledge of the infringing nature of the induced acts." Brief for United States as Amicus Curiae 9; see also Brief for Petitioner 15-44. I disagree, however, with the Court's holding that good-faith belief in a patent's invalidity is not a defense to induced infringement.

Infringing a patent means invading a patentee's exclusive right to practice his claimed invention. Crown Die & Tool Co. v. Nye Tool & Machine Works, 261 U.S. 24, 40, 43 S.Ct. 254, 67 L.Ed. 516 (1923) (quoting 3 W. Robinson, Law of Patents § 937, pp. 122-123 (1890)). Only valid patents confer this right to exclusivity—invalid patents do not. FTC v. Actavis, Inc., 570 U.S. ___, ___, 133 S.Ct. 2223, 2230-2231, 186 L.Ed.2d 343 (2013). It follows, as night the day, that only valid patents can be infringed. To talk of infringing an invalid patent is to talk nonsense.

Induced infringement, we have said, "requires knowledge that the induced acts constitute patent infringement." Global-Tech Appliances, Inc. v. SEB S. A., 563 U.S. ___, ___, 131 S.Ct. 2060, 2068, 179 L.Ed.2d 1167 (2011). Because only valid patents can be infringed, anyone with a good-faith belief in a patent's invalidity necessarily believes the patent cannot be infringed. And it is impossible for anyone who believes that a patent cannot be infringed to induce actions that he knows will infringe it. A good-faith belief that a patent is invalid is therefore a defense to induced infringement of that patent.

The Court makes four arguments in support of the contrary position. None seems to me persuasive. First, it notes that the Patent Act treats infringement and validity as distinct issues. Ante, at 1928 - 1929. That is true. It is also irrelevant. Saying that infringement cannot exist without a valid patent does not "conflate the issues of infringement and validity," ante, at 1928, any more than saying that water cannot exist without oxygen "conflates" water and oxygen. Recognizing that infringement requires validity is entirely consistent with the "long-accepted truth . . . that infringement and invalidity are separate matters under patent law." Ibid.

The Court next insists that permitting the defense at issue would undermine the statutory presumption of validity. Ante, at 1928 - 1929. It would do no such thing. By reason of the statutory presumption of validity, § 282(a), patents can be held invalid only by "clear and convincing evidence." Microsoft Corp. v. i4i Ltd. Partnership, 564 U.S. ___, ___, 131 S.Ct. 2238, 2242, 180 L.Ed.2d 131 (2011). This presumption is not weakened by treating a good-faith belief in invalidity as a defense to induced infringement. An alleged inducer who succeeds in this defense does not thereby call a patent's validity into question. He merely avoids liability for a third party's infringement of a valid patent, in no way undermining that patent's presumed validity.

Next, the Court says that "invalidity is not a defense to infringement, it is a defense to liability." Ante, at 1929. That is an assertion, not an argument. Again, to infringe a patent is to invade the patentee's right of exclusivity. An invalid patent confers no such right. How is it possible to interfere with rights that do not exist? The Court has no answer.

That brings me to the Court's weakest argument: that there are "practical reasons not to create a defense based on a good-faith belief in invalidity." Ante, at 1929 (emphasis added); see also ibid. ("Creating a defense of belief in invalidity, furthermore, would have negative consequences" (emphasis added)). Ours is not a common-law court. Erie R. Co. v. Tompkins, 304 U.S. 64, 78, 58 S.Ct. 817, 82 L.Ed. 1188 (1938). We do not, or at least should not, create defenses to statutory liability—and that is not what this dissent purports to do. Our task is to interpret the Patent Act, and to decide whether it makes a good-faith belief in a patent's invalidity a defense to induced infringement. Since, as we said in Global-Tech, supra, the Act makes knowledge of infringement a requirement for induced-infringement liability; and since there can be no infringement (and hence no knowledge of infringement) of an invalid patent; good-faith belief in invalidity is a defense. I may add, however, that if the desirability of the rule we adopt were a proper consideration, it is by no means clear that the Court's holding, which increases the in terrorem power of patent trolls, is preferable. The Court seemingly acknowledges that consequence in Part III of its opinion.

For the foregoing reasons, I respectfully dissent.

Justice Scalia's dissent in Kingsley v. Hendrickson (June 22, 2015)

JUSTICE SCALIA, with whom THE CHIEF JUSTICE and JUSTICE THOMAS join, dissenting.

The Constitution contains no freestanding prohibition of excessive force. There are, however, four constitutional provisions that we have said forbid the use of excessive force in certain circumstances. The Fourth Amendment prohibits it when it makes a search or seizure "unreasonable." The Eighth Amendment prohibits it when it constitutes "cruel and unusual" punishment. The Fifth and Fourteenth Amendments prohibit it (or, for that matter, any use of force) when it is used to "deprive" someone of "life, liberty, or property, without due process of law."

This is a Fourteenth Amendment case. The Fifth Amendment applies only to federal actors; Kingsley forfeited any argument under the Fourth Amendment by failing to raise it below; and he acknowledges that the Eighth Amendment standard is inapplicable, Brief for Petitioner 27, n. 8. The only question before us is whether a pretrial detainee's due process rights are violated when "the force purposely or knowingly used against him [is] objectively unreasonable." Ante, at 6. In my view, the answer is no. Our cases hold that the intentional infliction of punishment upon a pretrial detainee may violate the Fourteenth Amendment; but the infliction of "objectively unreasonable" force, without more, is not the intentional infliction of punishment.

In Bell v. Wolfish, 441 U. S. 520 (1979), we held that the Due Process Clause forbids holding pretrial detainees in conditions that "amount to punishment." Id., at 535. Conditions amount to punishment, we explained, when they are "imposed for the purpose of punishment." Id., at 538. Acting with the intent to punish means taking a "`deliberate act intended to chastise or deter.'" Wilson v. Seiter, 501 U. S. 294, 300 (1991) (quoting Duckworth v. Franzen, 780 F. 2d 645, 652 (CA7 1985)); see also Bell, supra, at 537-538. The Court in Bell recognized that intent to punish need not be "expressed," 441 U. S. at 538, but may be established with circumstantial evidence. More specifically, if the condition of confinement being challenged "is not reasonably related to a legitimate goal— if it is arbitrary or purposeless—a court permissibly may infer that the purpose of the governmental action is punishment." Id., at 539. We endorsed the same inference when we applied Bell's intent-to-punish test in challenges brought by pretrial detainees against jailhouse security policies, id., at 560-562; Block v. Rutherford, 468 U. S. 576, 583-584 (1984), and statutes permitting pretrial detention, Schall v. Martin, 467 U. S. 253, 255, 269 (1984); United States v. Salerno, 481 U. S. 739, 741, 746-747 (1987).

In light of these cases, I agree with the Court that "the Due Process Clause protects a pretrial detainee from the use of excessive force that amounts to punishment." Graham v. Connor, 490 U. S. 386, 395, n. 10 (1989) (citing Bell, supra, at 535-539). I disagree, however, that any intentional application of force that is objectively unreasonable in degree is a use of excessive force that "amount[s] to punishment." Bell, 441 U. S., at 535. The Court reaches that conclusion by misreading Bell as forbidding States to take any harmful action against pretrial detainees that is not "reasonably related to a legitimate goal." Id., at 539.

Bell endorsed this "reasonable relation" inference in the context of a challenge to conditions of a confinement— specifically, challenges to the State's policy of housing two people in each cell, id., at 528, and various security policies, id., at 548-549, 553, 555, 558, 560-562. The conditions in which pretrial detainees are held, and the security policies to which they are subject, are the result of considered deliberation by the authority imposing the detention. If those conditions and policies lack any reasonable relationship to a legitimate, nonpunitive goal, it is logical to infer a punitive intent. And the same logic supports finding a punitive intent in statutes authorizing detention that lacks any reasonable relationship to a valid government interest. Schall, supra, at 269; Salerno, supra, at 746-747.

It is illogical, however, automatically to infer punitive intent from the fact that a prison guard used more force against a pretrial detainee than was necessary. That could easily have been the result of a misjudgment about the degree of force required to maintain order or protect other inmates, rather than the product of an intent to punish the detainee for his charged crime (or for any other behavior). An officer's decision regarding how much force to use is made "in haste, under pressure, and frequently without the luxury of a second chance," Hudson v. McMillian, 503 U. S. 1, 6 (1992) (internal quotation marks omitted), not after the considered thought that precedes detention-policy determinations like those at issue in Bell, Block, Schall, and Salerno. That an officer used more force than necessary might be evidence that he acted with intent to punish, but it is no more than that.

In sum: Bell makes intent to punish the focus of its dueprocess analysis. Objective reasonableness of the force used is nothing more than a heuristic for identifying this intent. That heuristic makes good sense for considered decisions by the detaining authority, but is much weaker in the context of excessive-force claims. Kingsley does not argue that respondents actually intended to punish him, and his reliance on Bell to infer such an intent is misplaced.

Kingsley claims that "the protections of due process . . . extend beyond the narrow context of `punishment.'" Brief for Petitioner 15. Unquestionably. A State would plainly violate the Due Process Clause if it extended a detainee's confinement because it believed him mentally ill (not as "punishment"), without giving him the constitutionally guaranteed processes that must precede the deprivation of liberty. But Kingsley does not claim deprivation of liberty in that normal sense of that word—the right to walk about free. He claims that the Due Process Clause confers, on pretrial detainees, a substantive "liberty" interest that consists of freedom from objectively unreasonable force. Kingsley seeks relief, in other words, under the doctrine of "substantive due process," through which we have occasionally recognized "liberty" interests other than freedom from incarceration or detention, that "cannot be limited at all, except by provisions that are `narrowly tailored to serve a compelling state interest.'" Kerry v. Din, ante, at 6 (plurality opinion) (quoting Reno v. Flores, 507 U. S. 292, 301-302 (1993)).

Even if one believed that the right to process can confer the right to substance in particular cases, Kingsley's interest is not one of the "fundamental liberty interests" that substantive due process protects. We have said that that doctrine protects only those liberty interests that, carefully described, are "objectively, deeply rooted in this Nation's history and tradition, and implicit in the concept of ordered liberty, such that neither liberty nor justice would exist if they were sacrificed." Washington v. Glucksberg, 521 U. S. 702, 720-721 (1997) (citations and internal quotation marks omitted). Carefully described, the liberty interest Kingsley asserts is the right of pretrial detainees to be free from the application of force that is more than is objectively required to further some legitimate, nonpunitive, governmental interest. He does not argue (nor could he) that this asserted interest could pass the test announced in Glucksberg.

I conclude by emphasizing that our Constitution is not the only source of American law. There is an immense body of state statutory and common law under which individuals abused by state officials can seek relief. Kingsley himself, in addition to suing respondents for excessive force under 42 U. S. C. §1983, brought a statelaw claim for assault and battery. 744 F. 3d 443, 446, n. 6 (CA7 2014). The Due Process Clause is not "a font of tort law to be superimposed upon" that state system. Daniels v. Williams, 474 U. S. 327, 332 (1986) (quoting Paul v. Davis, 424 U. S. 693, 701 (1976)). Today's majority overlooks this in its tender-hearted desire to tortify the Fourteenth Amendment.

Justice Scalia's dissent in King v. Burwell (June 25, 2015)

Justice Scalia, with whom Justice Thomas and Justice Alito join, dissenting.

The Court holds that when the Patient Protection and Affordable Care Act says "Exchange established by the State" it means "Exchange established by the State or the Federal Government." That is of course quite absurd, and the Court's 21 pages of explanation make it no less so.

I

The Patient Protection and Affordable Care Act makes major reforms to the American health-insurance market. It provides, among other things, that every State "shall . . . establish an American Health Benefit Exchange"—a marketplace where people can shop for health-insurance plans. 42 U. S. C. §18031(b)(1). And it provides that if a State does not comply with this instruction, the Secretary of Health and Human Services must "establish and operate such Exchange within the State." §18041(c)(1).

A separate part of the Act—housed in §36B of the Internal Revenue Code—grants "premium tax credits" to subsidize certain purchases of health insurance made on Exchanges. The tax credit consists of "premium assistance amounts" for "coverage months." 26 U. S. C. §36B(b)(1). An individual has a coverage month only when he is covered by an insurance plan "that was enrolled in through an Exchange established by the State under [§18031]." §36B(c)(2)(A). And the law ties the size of the premium assistance amount to the premiums for health plans which cover the individual "and which were enrolled in through an Exchange established by the State under [§18031]." §36B(b)(2)(A). The premium assistance amount further depends on the cost of certain other insurance plans "offered through the same Exchange." §36B(b)(3)(B)(i).

This case requires us to decide whether someone who buys insurance on an Exchange established by the Secretary gets tax credits. You would think the answer would be obvious—so obvious there would hardly be a need for the Supreme Court to hear a case about it. In order to receive any money under §36B, an individual must enroll in an insurance plan through an "Exchange established by the State." The Secretary of Health and Human Services is not a State. So an Exchange established by the Secretary is not an Exchange established by the State—which means people who buy health insurance through such an Exchange get no money under §36B.

Words no longer have meaning if an Exchange that is not established by a State is "established by the State." It is hard to come up with a clearer way to limit tax credits to state Exchanges than to use the words "established by the State." And it is hard to come up with a reason to include the words "by the State" other than the purpose of limiting credits to state Exchanges. "[T]he plain, obvious, and rational meaning of a statute is always to be preferred to any curious, narrow, hidden sense that nothing but the exigency of a hard case and the ingenuity and study of an acute and powerful intellect would discover." Lynch v. Alworth-Stephens Co., 267 U. S. 364, 370 (1925) (internal quotation marks omitted). Under all the usual rules of interpretation, in short, the Government should lose this case. But normal rules of interpretation seem always to yield to the overriding principle of the present Court: The Affordable Care Act must be saved.

II

The Court interprets §36B to award tax credits on both federal and state Exchanges. It accepts that the "most natural sense" of the phrase "Exchange established by the State" is an Exchange established by a State. Ante, at 11. (Understatement, thy name is an opinion on the Afford-able Care Act!) Yet the opinion continues, with no semblance of shame, that "it is also possible that the phrase refers to all Exchanges—both State and Federal." Ante, at 13. (Impossible possibility, thy name is an opinion on the Affordable Care Act!) The Court claims that "the context and structure of the Act compel [it] to depart from what would otherwise be the most natural reading of the pertinent statutory phrase." Ante, at 21.

I wholeheartedly agree with the Court that sound interpretation requires paying attention to the whole law, not homing in on isolated words or even isolated sections. Context always matters. Let us not forget, however, why context matters: It is a tool for understanding the terms of the law, not an excuse for rewriting them.

Any effort to understand rather than to rewrite a law must accept and apply the presumption that lawmakers use words in "their natural and ordinary signification." Pensacola Telegraph Co. v. Western Union Telegraph Co., 96 U. S. 1, 12 (1878) . Ordinary connotation does not always prevail, but the more unnatural the proposed interpretation of a law, the more compelling the contex-tual evidence must be to show that it is correct. Today's interpretation is not merely unnatural; it is unheard of. Who would ever have dreamt that "Exchange established by the State" means "Exchange established by the State or the Federal Government"? Little short of an express statutory definition could justify adopting this singular reading. Yet the only pertinent definition here provides that "State" means "each of the 50 States and the District of Columbia." 42 U. S. C. §18024(d). Because the Secretary is neither one of the 50 States nor the District of Columbia, that definition positively contradicts the eccentric theory that an Exchange established by the Secretary has been established by the State.

Far from offering the overwhelming evidence of meaning needed to justify the Court's interpretation, other contextual clues undermine it at every turn. To begin with, other parts of the Act sharply distinguish between the establishment of an Exchange by a State and the establishment of an Exchange by the Federal Government. The States' authority to set up Exchanges comes from one provision, §18031(b); the Secretary's authority comes from an entirely different provision, §18041(c). Funding for States to establish Exchanges comes from one part of the law, §18031(a); funding for the Secretary to establish Exchanges comes from an entirely different part of the law, §18121. States generally run state-created Ex-changes; the Secretary generally runs federally created Exchanges. §18041(b)–(c). And the Secretary's authority to set up an Exchange in a State depends upon the State's "[f]ailure to establish [an] Exchange." §18041(c) (emphasis added). Provisions such as these destroy any pretense that a federal Exchange is in some sense also established by a State.

Reading the rest of the Act also confirms that, as relevant here, there are only two ways to set up an Exchange in a State: establishment by a State and establishment by the

Secretary. §§18031(b), 18041(c). So saying that an Exchange established by the Federal Government is "established by the State" goes beyond giving words bizarre meanings; it leaves the limiting phrase "by the State" with no operative effect at all. That is a stark violation of the elementary principle that requires an interpreter "to give effect, if possible, to every clause and word of a statute." Montclair v. Ramsdell, 107 U. S. 147, 152 (1883) . In weighing this argument, it is well to remember the difference between giving a term a meaning that duplicates another part of the law, and giving a term no meaning at all. Lawmakers sometimes repeat themselves—whether out of a desire to add emphasis, a sense of belt-and-suspenders caution, or a lawyerly penchant for doublets (aid and abet, cease and desist, null and void). Lawmakers do not, however, tend to use terms that "have no operation at all." Marbury v. Madison, 1 Cranch 137, 174 (1803). So while the rule against treating a term as a redundancy is far from categorical, the rule against treating it as a nullity is as close to absolute as interpretive principles get. The Court's reading does not merely give "by the State" a duplicative effect; it causes the phrase to have no effect whatever.

Making matters worse, the reader of the whole Act will come across a number of provisions beyond §36B that refer to the establishment of Exchanges by States. Adopting the Court's interpretation means nullifying the term "by the State" not just once, but again and again throughout the Act. Consider for the moment only those parts of the Act that mention an "Exchange established by the State" in connection with tax credits:

The formula for calculating the amount of the tax credit, as already explained, twice mentions "an Exchange established by the State." 26 U. S. C. §36B(b)(2)(A), (c)(2)(A)(i).

The Act directs States to screen children for eligibility for "[tax credits] under section 36B" and for "anyother assistance or subsidies available for coverage obtained through" an "Exchange established by the State." 42 U. S. C. §1396w–3(b)(1)(B)–(C).

The Act requires "an Exchange established by the State" to use a "secure electronic interface" to determine eligibility for (among other things) tax credits. §1396w–3(b)(1)(D).

The Act authorizes "an Exchange established by the State" to make arrangements under which other state agencies "determine whether a State resident is eligible for [tax credits] under section 36B." §1396w–3(b)(2).

The Act directs States to operate Web sites that allow anyone "who is eligible to receive [tax credits] under section 36B" to compare insurance plans offered through "an Exchange established by the State." §1396w–3(b)(4).

One of the Act's provisions addresses the enrollment of certain children in health plans "offered through an Exchange established by the State" and then dis-cusses the eligibility of these children for tax credits. §1397ee(d)(3)(B).

It is bad enough for a court to cross out "by the State" once. But seven times?

Congress did not, by the way, repeat "Exchange established by the State under [§18031]" by rote throughout the Act. Quite the contrary, clause after clause of the law uses a more general term such as "Exchange" or "Exchange established under [§18031]."

See, e.g., 42 U. S. C. §§18031(k), 18033; 26 U. S. C. §6055. It is common sense that any speaker who says "Exchange" some of the time, but "Exchange established by the State" the rest of the time, probably means something by the contrast.

Equating establishment "by the State" with establishment by the Federal Government makes nonsense of other parts of the Act. The Act requires States to ensure (on pain of losing Medicaid funding) that any "Exchange established by the State" uses a "secure electronic interface" to determine an individual's eligibility for various benefits (including tax credits). 42 U. S. C. §1396w–3(b)(1)(D). How could a State control the type of electronic interface used by a federal Exchange? The Act allows a State to control contracting decisions made by "an Exchange established by the State." §18031(f)(3). Why would a State get to control the contracting decisions of a federal Exchange? The Act also provides "Assistance to States to establish American Health Benefit Exchanges" and directs the Secretary to renew this funding "if the State . . . is making progress . . . toward . . . establishing an Exchange." §18031(a). Does a State that refuses to set up an Exchange still receive this funding, on the premise that Exchanges established by the Federal Government are really established by States? It is presumably in order to avoid these questions that the Court concludes that federal Exchanges count as state Exchanges only "for purposes of the tax credits." Ante, at 13. (Contrivance, thy name is an opinion on the Affordable Care Act!)

It is probably piling on to add that the Congress that wrote the Affordable Care Act knew how to equate two different types of Exchanges when it wanted to do so. The Act includes a clause providing that "[a] territory that . . . establishes . . . an Exchange . . . shall be treated as a State" for certain purposes. §18043(a) (emphasis added). Tellingly, it does not include a comparable clause providing that the Secretary shall be treated as a State for purposes of §36B when she establishes an Exchange.

Faced with overwhelming confirmation that "Exchange established by the State" means what it looks like it means, the Court comes up with argument after feeble argument to support its contrary interpretation. None of its tries comes close to establishing the implausible conclusion that Congress used "by the State" to mean "by the State or not by the State."

The Court emphasizes that if a State does not set up an Exchange, the Secretary must establish "such Exchange." §18041(c). It claims that the word "such" implies that federal and state Exchanges are "the same." Ante, at 13. To see the error in this reasoning, one need only consider a parallel provision from our Constitution: "The Times, Places and Manner of holding Elections for Senators and Representatives, shall be prescribed in each State by the Legislature thereof; but the Congress may at any time by Law make or alter such Regulations." Art. I, §4, cl. 1 (emphasis added). Just as the Affordable Care Act directs States to establish Exchanges while allowing the Secretary to establish "such Exchange" as a fallback, the Elections Clause directs state legislatures to prescribe election regulations while allowing Congress to make "such Regulations" as a fallback. Would anybody refer to an election regulation made by Congress as a "regulation prescribed by the state legislature"? Would anybody say that a federal election law and a state election law are in all respects equivalent? Of course not. The word "such" does not help the Court one whit. The Court's argument also overlooks the rudimentary principle that a specific provision governs a general one. Even if it were true that the term "such Exchange" in §18041(c) implies that federal and state Exchanges are the same in general, the term "established by the State" in §36B makes plain that they differ when it comes to tax credits in particular.

The Court's next bit of interpretive jiggery-pokery involves other parts of the Act that purportedly presuppose the availability of tax credits on both federal and state Exchanges. *Ante*, at 13–14. It is curious that the Court is willing to subordinate the express words of the section that grants tax credits to the mere implications of other provisions with only tangential connections to tax credits. One would think that interpretation would work the other way around. In any event, each of the provisions mentioned by the Court is perfectly consistent with limiting tax credits to state Exchanges. One of them says that the minimum functions of an Exchange include (alongside several tasks that have nothing to do with tax credits) setting up an electronic calculator that shows "the actual cost of coverage after the application of any premium tax credit." 42 U. S. C. §18031(d)(4)(G). What stops a federal Exchange's electronic calculator from telling a customer that his tax credit is zero? Another provision requires an Exchange's outreach program to educate the public about health plans, to facilitate enrollment, and to "distribute fair and impartial information" about enrollment and "the availability of premium tax credits." §18031(i)(3)(B). What stops a federal Exchange's outreach program from fairly and impartially telling customers that no tax credits are available? A third provision requires an Exchange to report information about each insurance plan sold—including level of coverage, premium, name of the insured, and "amount of any advance payment" of the tax credit. 26 U. S. C. §36B(f)(3). What stops a federal Exchange's report from confirming that no tax credits have been paid out?

The Court persists that these provisions "would make little sense" if no tax credits were available on federal Exchanges. *Ante*, at 14. Even if that observation were true, it would show only oddity, not ambiguity. Laws often include unusual or mismatched provisions. The Affordable Care Act spans 900 pages; it would be amazing if its provisions all lined up perfectly with each other. This Court "does not revise legislation . . . just because the text as written creates an apparent anomaly." *Michigan v. Bay Mills Indian Community*, 572 U. S. ___, ___ (2014) (slip op., at 10). At any rate, the provisions cited by the Court are not particularly unusual. Each requires an Exchange to perform a standardized series of tasks, some aspects of which relate in some way to tax credits. It is entirely natural for slight mismatches to occur when, as here, lawmakers draft "a single statutory provision" to cover "different kinds" of situations. *Robers v. United States*, 572 U. S. ___, ___ (2014) (slip op., at 4). Lawmakers need not, and often do not, "write extra language specifically exempting, phrase by phrase, applications in respect to which a portion of a phrase is not needed." *Ibid.*

Roaming even farther afield from §36B, the Court turns to the Act's provisions about "qualified individuals." Ante, at 10–11. Qualified individuals receive favored treatment on Exchanges, although customers who are not qualified individuals may also shop there. See Halbig v. Burwell, 758 F. 3d 390, 404–405 (CADC 2014). The Court claims that the Act must equate federal and state establishment of Exchanges when it defines a qualified individual as someone who (among other things) lives in the "State that established the Exchange," 42 U. S. C. §18032(f)(1)(A). Otherwise, the Court says, there would be no qualified individuals on federal Exchanges, contradicting (for example) the provision requiring every Exchange to takethe " 'interests of qualified individuals' " into accountwhen selecting health plans. Ante, at 11 (quoting §18031(e)(1)(b)). Pure applesauce. Imagine that a university sends around a bulletin reminding every professor to take the "interests of graduate students" into account when setting office hours, but that some professors teach only undergraduates. Would anybody reason that the bulletin implicitly presupposes that every professor has "graduate students," so that "graduate students" must really mean "graduate or undergraduate students"? Surely not. Just as one naturally reads instructions aboutgraduate students to be inapplicable to the extent a particular professor has no such students, so too would one naturally read instructions about qualified individuals to be inapplicable to the extent a particular Exchange has no such individuals. There is no need to rewrite the term "State that established the Exchange" in the definition of "qualified individual," much less a need to rewrite the separate term "Exchange established by the State" in a separate part of the Act.

Least convincing of all, however, is the Court's attempt to uncover support for its interpretation in "the structure of Section 36B itself." Ante, at 19. The Court finds it strange that Congress limited the tax credit to state Exchanges in the formula for calculating the amount of the credit, rather than in the provision defining the range of taxpayers eligible for the credit. Had the Court bothered to look at the rest of the Tax Code, it would have seen that the structure it finds strange is in fact quite common. Consider, for example, the many provisions that initially make taxpayers of all incomes eligible for a tax credit, only to provide later that the amount of the credit is zero if the taxpayer's income exceeds a specified threshold. See, e.g., 26 U. S. C. §24 (child tax credit); §32 (earned-income tax credit); §36 (first-time-homebuyer tax credit). Or consider, for an even closer parallel, a neighboring provision that initially makes taxpayers of all States eligible for a credit, only to provide later that the amount of the credit may be zero if the taxpayer's State does not satisfy certain requirements. See §35 (health-insurance-costs tax credit). One begins to get the sense that the Court's insistence on reading things in context applies to "established by the State," but to nothing else.

For what it is worth, lawmakers usually draft tax-credit provisions the way they do—i.e., the way they drafted §36B—because the mechanics of the credit require it. Many Americans move to new States in the middle of the year. Mentioning state Exchanges in the definition of "coverage month"—rather than (as the Court proposes) in the provisions concerning taxpayers' eligibility for the credit—accounts for taxpayers who live in a State with a state Exchange for a part of the year, but a State with a federal Exchange for the rest of the year. In addition, §36B awards a credit with respect to insurance plans "which cover the taxpayer, the taxpayer's spouse, or any dependent . . . of the taxpayer and which were enrolled in through an Exchange established by the State." §36B(b)(2)(A) (emphasis added). If Congress had mentioned state Exchanges in the provisions discussing taxpayers' eligibility for the credit, a taxpayer who buys insurance from a federal Exchange would get no money, even if he has a spouse or dependent who buys insurance from a state Exchange—say a child attending college in a different State. It thus makes perfect sense for "Exchange established by the State" to appear where it does, rather than where the Court suggests. Even if that were not so, of course, its location would not make it any less clear.

The Court has not come close to presenting the compelling contextual case necessary to justify departing from the ordinary meaning of the terms of the law. Quite the contrary, context only underscores the outlandishness of the Court's interpretation. Reading the Act as a whole leaves no doubt about the matter: "Exchange established by the State" means what it looks like it means.

III

For its next defense of the indefensible, the Court turns to the Affordable Care Act's design and purposes. As relevant here, the Act makes three major reforms. The guaranteed-issue and community-rating requirements prohibit insurers from considering a customer's health when deciding whether to sell insurance and how much to charge, 42 U. S. C. §§300gg, 300gg–1; its famous individ-ual mandate requires everyone to maintain insurance coverage or to pay what the Act calls a "penalty," 26 U. S. C. §5000A(b)(1), and what we have nonetheless called a tax, see National Federation of Independent Business v. Sebelius, 567 U. S. ___, ___ (2012) (slip op., at 39); and its tax credits help make insurance more affordable. The Court reasons that Congress intended these three reforms to "work together to expand insurance coverage"; and because the first two apply in every State, so must the third. Ante, at 16.

This reasoning suffers from no shortage of flaws. To begin with, "even the most formidable argument concerning the statute's purposes could not overcome the clarity [of] the statute's text." Kloeckner v. Solis, 568 U. S. ___, ___, n. 4 (2012) (slip op., at 14, n. 4). Statutory design and purpose matter only to the extent they help clarify an otherwise ambiguous provision. Could anyone maintain with a straight face that §36B is unclear? To mention just the highlights, the Court's interpretation clashes with a statutory definition, renders words inoperative in at least seven separate provisions of the Act, overlooks the contrast between provisions that say "Exchange" and those that say "Exchange established by the State," gives the same phrase one meaning for purposes of tax credits but an entirely different meaning for other purposes, and (let us not forget) contradicts the ordinary meaning of the words Congress used. On the other side of the ledger, the Court has come up with nothing more than a general provision that turns out to be controlled by a specific one, a handful of clauses that are consistent with either understanding of establishment by the State, and a resemblance between the tax-credit provision and the rest of the Tax Code. If that is all it takes to make something ambiguous, everything is ambiguous.

Having gone wrong in consulting statutory purpose at all, the Court goes wrong again in analyzing it. The purposes of a law must be "collected chiefly from its words," not "from extrinsic circumstances." Sturges v. Crowninshield, 4 Wheat. 122, 202 (1819) (Marshall, C. J.). Only by concentrating on the law's terms can a judge hope to uncover the scheme of the statute, rather than some other scheme that the judge thinks desirable. Like it or not, the express terms of the Affordable Care Act make only two of the three reforms mentioned by the Court applicable in States that do not establish Exchanges. It is perfectly possible for them to operate independently of tax credits. The guaranteed-issue and community-rating requirements continue to ensure that insurance companies treat all customers the same no matter their health, and the individual mandate continues to encourage people to maintain coverage, lest they be "taxed."

The Court protests that without the tax credits, the number of people covered by the individual mandate shrinks, and without a broadly applicable individual mandate the guaranteed-issue and community-rating requirements "would destabilize the individual insurance market." Ante, at 15. If true, these projections would show only that the statutory scheme contains a flaw; they would not show that the statute means the opposite of what it says. Moreover, it is a flaw that appeared as well in other parts of the Act. A different title established a long-term-care insurance program with guaranteed-issue and community-rating requirements, but without an individual mandate or subsidies. §§8001–8002, 124Stat. 828–847 (2010). This program never came into effect "only because Congress, in response to actuarial analyses predicting that the [program] would be fiscally unsustainable, repealed the provision in 2013." Halbig, 758 F. 3d, at 410. How could the Court say that Congress would never dream of combining guaranteed-issue and community-rating requirements with a narrow individual mandate, when it combined those requirements with no individual mandate in the context of long-term-care insurance?

Similarly, the Department of Health and Human Services originally interpreted the Act to impose guaranteed-issue and community-rating requirements in the Federal Territories, even though the Act plainly does not make the individual mandate applicable there. Ibid.; see 26 U. S. C. §5000A(f)(4); 42 U. S. C. §201(f). "This combination, predictably, [threw] individual insurance markets in the territories into turmoil." Halbig, supra, at 410. Responding to complaints from the Territories, the Department at first insisted that it had "no statutory authority" to address the problem and suggested that the Territories "seek legislative relief from Congress" instead. Letter from G. Cohen, Director of the Center for Consumer Information and Insurance Oversight, to S. Igisomar, Secretary of Commerce of the Commonwealth of Northern Mariana Islands (July 12, 2013). The Department changed its mind a year later, after what it described as "a careful review of [the] situation and the relevant statutory language." Letter from M. Tavenner,

Administrator of the Centers for Medicare and Medicaid Services, to G. Francis, Insurance Commissioner of the Virgin Islands (July 16, 2014). How could the Court pronounce it "implausible" for Congress to have tolerated instability in insurance markets in States with federal Exchanges, ante, at 17, when even the Government maintained until recently that Congress did exactly that in American Samoa, Guam, the Northern Mariana Islands, Puerto Rico, and the Virgin Islands?

Compounding its errors, the Court forgets that it is no more appropriate to consider one of a statute's purposes in isolation than it is to consider one of its words that way. No law pursues just one purpose at all costs, and no statutory scheme encompasses just one element. Most relevant here, the Affordable Care Act displays a congressional preference for state participation in the establishment of Exchanges: Each State gets the first opportunity to set up its Exchange, 42 U. S. C. §18031(b); States that take up the opportunity receive federal funding for "activities . . . related to establishing" an Exchange, §18031(a)(3); and the Secretary may establish an Exchange in a State only as a fallback, §18041(c). But setting up and running an Exchange involve significant burdens—meeting strict deadlines, §18041(b), implementing requirements related to the offering of insurance plans, §18031(d)(4), setting up outreach programs, §18031(i), and ensuring that the Exchange is self-sustaining by 2015, §18031(d)(5)(A). A State would have much less reason to take on these burdens if its citizens could receive tax credits no matter who establishes its Exchange. (Now that the Internal Revenue Service has interpreted §36B to authorize tax credits everywhere, by the way, 34 States have failed to set up their own Exchanges. Ante, at 6.) So even if making credits available on all Exchanges advances the goal of improving healthcare markets, it frustrates the goal of encouraging state involvement in the implementation of the Act. This is what justifies going out of our way to read "established by the State" to mean "established by the State or not established by the State"?

Worst of all for the repute of today's decision, the Court's reasoning is largely self-defeating. The Court predicts that making tax credits unavailable in States that do not set up their own Exchanges would cause disastrous economic consequences there. If that is so, however, wouldn't one expect States to react by setting up their own Exchanges? And wouldn't that outcome satisfy two of the Act's goals rather than just one: enabling the Act's reforms to work and promoting state involvement in the Act's implementation? The Court protests that the very existence of a federal fallback shows that Congress expected that some States might fail to set up their own Exchanges. Ante, at 19. So it does. It does not show, however, that Congress expected the number of recalcitrant States to be particularly large. The more accurate the Court's dire economic predictions, the smaller that number is likely to be. That reality destroys the Court's pretense that applying the law as written would imperil "the viability of the entire Affordable Care Act." Ante, at 20. All in all, the Court's arguments about the law's purpose and design are no more convincing than its arguments about context.

IV

Perhaps sensing the dismal failure of its efforts to show that "established by the State" means "established by the State or the Federal Government," the Court tries to palm off the pertinent statutory phrase as "inartful drafting." Ante, at 14. This Court, however, has no free-floating power "to rescue Congress from its drafting errors." Lamie v. United States Trustee, 540 U. S. 526, 542 (2004) (internal quotation marks omitted). Only when it is patently obvious to a reasonable reader that a drafting mistake has occurred may a court correct the mistake. The occurrence of a misprint may be apparent from the face of the law, as it is where the Affordable Care Act "creates three separate Section 1563s." Ante, at 14. But the Court does not pretend that there is any such indication of a drafting error on the face of §36B. The occurrence of a misprint may also be apparent because a provision decrees an absurd result—a consequence "so monstrous, that all mankind would, without hesitation, unite in rejecting the application." Sturges, 4 Wheat., at 203. But §36B does not come remotely close to satisfying that demanding standard. It is entirely plausible that tax credits were restricted to state Exchanges deliberately—for example, in order to encourage States to establish their own Exchanges. We therefore have no authority to dismiss the terms of the law as a drafting fumble.

Let us not forget that the term "Exchange established by the State" appears twice in §36B and five more times in other parts of the Act that mention tax credits. What are the odds, do you think, that the same slip of the pen occurred in seven separate places? No provision of the Act—none at all—contradicts the limitation of tax credits to state Exchanges. And as I have already explained, uses of the term "Exchange established by the State" beyond the context of tax credits look anything but accidental. Supra, at 6. If there was a mistake here, context suggests it was a substantive mistake in designing this part of the law, not a technical mistake in transcribing it.

V

The Court's decision reflects the philosophy that judges should endure whatever interpretive distortions it takes in order to correct a supposed flaw in the statutory machinery. That philosophy ignores the American people's decision to give Congress "[a]ll legislative Powers" enumerated in the Constitution. Art. I, §1. They made Congress, not this Court, responsible for both making laws and mending them. This Court holds only the judicial power—the power to pronounce the law as Congress has enacted it. We lack the prerogative to repair laws that do not work out in practice, just as the people lack the ability to throw us out of office if they dislike the solutions we concoct. We must always remember, therefore, that "[o]ur task is to apply the text, not to improve upon it." Pavelic & LeFlore v. Marvel Entertainment Group, Div. of Cadence Industries Corp., 493 U. S. 120, 126 (1989) .

Trying to make its judge-empowering approach seem respectful of congressional authority, the Court asserts that its decision merely ensures that the Affordable Care Act operates the way Congress "meant [it] to operate." Ante, at 17. First of all, what makes the Court so sure that Congress "meant" tax credits to be available everywhere? Our only evidence of what Congress meant comes from the terms of the law, and those terms show beyond all question that tax credits are available only on state Exchanges. More importantly, the Court forgets that ours is a government of laws and not of men. That means we are governed by the terms of our laws, not by the unenacted will of our lawmakers. "If Congress enacted into law something different from what it intended, then it should amend the statute to conform to its intent." Lamie, supra, at 542. In the meantime, this Court "has no roving license . . . to disregard clear language simply on the view that . . . Congress 'must have intended' something broader." Bay Mills, 572 U. S., at ____ (slip op., at 11).

Even less defensible, if possible, is the Court's claim that its interpretive approach is justified because this Act "does not reflect the type of care and deliberation that one might expect of such significant legislation." Ante, at 14–15. It is not our place to judge the quality of the care and deliberation that went into this or any other law. A law enacted by voice vote with no deliberation whatever is fully as binding upon us as one enacted after years of study, months of committee hearings, and weeks of debate. Much less is it our place to make everything come out right when Congress does not do its job properly. It is up to Congress to design its laws with care, and it is up to the people to hold them to account if they fail to carry out that responsibility.

Rather than rewriting the law under the pretense of interpreting it, the Court should have left it to Congress to decide what to do about the Act's limitation of tax credits to state Exchanges. If Congress values above everything else the Act's applicability across the country, it could make tax credits available in every Exchange. If it prizes state involvement in the Act's implementation, it could continue to limit tax credits to state Exchanges while taking other steps to mitigate the economic consequences predicted by the Court. If Congress wants to accommodate both goals, it could make tax credits available everywhere while offering new incentives for States to set up their own Exchanges. And if Congress thinks that the present design of the Act works well enough, it could do nothing. Congress could also do something else altogether, entirely abandoning the structure of the Affordable Care Act. The Court's insistence on making a choice that should be made by Congress both aggrandizes judicial power and encourages congressional lassitude.

Just ponder the significance of the Court's decision to take matters into its own hands. The Court's revision of the law authorizes the Internal Revenue Service to spend tens of billions of dollars every year in tax credits on federal Exchanges. It affects the price of insurance for millions of Americans. It diminishes the participation of the States in the implementation of the Act. It vastly expands the reach of the Act's individual mandate, whose scope depends in part on the availability of credits. What a parody today's decision makes of Hamilton's assurances to the people of New York: "The legislature not only commands the purse but prescribes the rules by which the duties and rights of every citizen are to be regulated. The judiciary, on the contrary, has no influence over . . . the purse; no direction . . . of the wealth of society, and can take no active resolution whatever. It may truly be said to have neither force nor will but merely judgment." The Federalist

No. 78, p. 465 (C. Rossiter ed. 1961).

    *   *   *

Today's opinion changes the usual rules of statutory interpretation for the sake of the Affordable Care Act. That, alas, is not a novelty. In National Federation of Independent Business v. Sebelius, 567 U. S. ____, this Court revised major components of the statute in order to save them from unconstitutionality. The Act that Congress passed provides that every individual "shall" maintain insurance or else pay a "penalty." 26 U. S. C. §5000A. This Court, however, saw that the Commerce Clause does not authorize a federal mandate to buy health insurance. So it rewrote the mandate-cum-penalty as a tax. 567 U. S., at ____–____ (principal opinion) (slip op., at 15–45). The Act that Congress passed also requires every State to accept an expansion of its Medicaid program, or else risk losing all Medicaid funding. 42 U. S. C. §1396c. This Court, however, saw that the Spending Clause does not authorize this coercive condition. So it rewrote the law to withhold only the incremental funds associated with the Medicaid expansion. 567 U. S., at ____–____ (principal opinion) (slip op., at 45–58). Having transformed two major parts of the law, the Court today has turned its attention to a third. The Act that Congress passed makes tax credits available only on an "Exchange established by the State." This Court, however, concludes that this limitation would prevent the rest of the Act from working as well as hoped. So it rewrites the law to make tax credits available everywhere. We should start calling this law SCOTUScare.

Perhaps the Patient Protection and Affordable Care Act will attain the enduring status of the Social Security Act or the Taft-Hartley Act; perhaps not. But this Court's two decisions on the Act will surely be remembered through the years. The somersaults of statutory interpretation they have performed ("penalty" means tax, "further [Medicaid] payments to the State" means only incremental Medicaid payments to the State, "established by the State" means not established by the State) will be cited by litigants endlessly, to the confusion of honest jurisprudence. And the cases will publish forever the discouraging truth that the Supreme Court of the United States favors some laws over others, and is prepared to do whatever it takes to uphold and assist its favorites.

I dissent.

Justice Scalia's dissent in Obergefell v. Hodges (June 26, 2015) [Excerpt]

Justice Scalia, with whom Justice Thomas joins, dissenting.

I join The Chief Justice's opinion in full. I write separately to call attention to this Court's threat to American democracy.

The substance of today's decree is not of immense personal importance to me. The law can recognize as marriage whatever sexual attachments and living arrangements it wishes, and can accord them favorable civil consequences, from tax treatment to rights of inheritance. [. . .]

Justice Scalia's dissent to denial of certiorari of Rapelje v. Blackston (November 30, 2015)

The petition for a writ of certiorari is denied.

Justice Scalia, with whom Justice Thomas and Justice Alito join, dissenting from denial of certiorari.

A criminal defendant "shall enjoy the right . . . to be confronted with the witnesses against him." U. S. Const., Amdt. 6. We have held that this right entitles the accused to cross-examine witnesses who testify at trial, and to exclude certain out-of-court statements that the defendant did not have a prior opportunity to cross-examine. Crawford v. Washington, 541 U. S. 36–51 (2004); Davis v. Alaska, 415 U. S. 308–317 (1974). We have never held—nor would the verb "to confront" support the holding—that confrontation includes the right to admit out-of-court statements into evidence. Nevertheless, the Sixth Circuit held not only that the Confrontation Clause guarantees the right to admit such evidence but that our cases have "clearly established" as much. We should grant certiorari and summarily reverse.

Respondent Junior Fred Blackston was convicted in Michigan state court of first-degree murder on the strength of the testimony of five people, some of whom participated in the crime. For reasons not relevant here, the court ordered a new trial. Before Blackston's retrial, however, two of the five witnesses signed written statements recanting their trial testimony. The prosecution called them at the second trial, but they refused to answer any questions. The trial court therefore pronounced them "unavailable" and, pursuant to a venerable hearsay ex-ception, see Mich. Rule Evid. 804(b)(1) (2012); cf. 5 J. Wigmore, Evidence §1370, p. 55 (J. Chadbourn rev. 1974), allowed their earlier testimony to be read to the jury. But the court refused to admit into evidence their written recantations.

Blackston was once again convicted of first-degree murder and sentenced to life imprisonment. Affirming the conviction, the Supreme Court of Michigan held that the trial court's exclusion of the recantations was not error and, even if it was, was harmless beyond a reasonable doubt. 481 Mich. 451, 751 N. W. 2d 408 (2008).

This petition for federal habeas relief followed. The District Court conditionally granted the writ, finding that the exclusion of the recantations violated Blackston's Sixth and Fourteenth Amendment rights. 907 F. Supp. 2d 878 (ED Mich. 2012). A divided Sixth Circuit panel affirmed. 780 F. 3d 340 (2015). In the Court of Appeals' view, "[t]here is a clearly established right to impeach the credibility of an adverse witness using the witness's own inconsistent statements." Id., at 348. The recantations, reasoned the court, were inconsistent statements that had obvious impeachment value.

The Antiterrorism and Effective Death Penalty Act of 1996 (AEDPA) prohibits federal courts from granting habeas relief unless the state court's decision "involved an unreasonable application of . . . clearly established Federal law, as determined by the Supreme Court of the United States." 28 U. S. C. § 2254(d)(1) (emphasis added). As the dissenting judge below pointed out, no case of ours establishes, clearly or otherwise, that the Confrontation Clause bestows a right to admit this kind of evidence. 780 F. 3d, at 363–364 (opinion of Kethledge, J.). In fact we long ago suggested just the opposite. Mattox v. United States, 156 U. S. 237–250 (1895). Each of the cases the Sixth Circuit relied on involved the defendant's attempting during cross-examination to impeach testifying witnesses, not unavailable declarants. See Olden v. Kentucky, 488 U. S. 227, 230 (1988) (per curiam); Delaware v. Van Arsdall, 475 U. S. 673, 676 (1986) ; Alford v. United States, 282 U. S. 687, 693 (1931) . And just recently we said in Nevada v. Jackson, 569 U. S. ___, ___ (2013) (per curiam) (slip op., at 7), that "this Court has never held that the Confrontation Clause entitles a criminal defendant to introduce extrinsic evidence for impeachment purposes." The Sixth Circuit thought the recantations here intrinsic, not extrinsic, and so beyond Jackson's ambit. That is quite irrelevant. The pertinent question under AEDPA is whether our cases have clearly established a right, not whether they have failed to clearly foreclose it.

There may well be a plausible argument why the recantations ought to have been admitted under state law. See Mich. Rule Evid. 806. But nothing in our precedents clearly establishes their admissibility as a matter of federal constitutional law. AEDPA "provides a remedy for instances in which a state court unreasonably applies this Court's precedent; it does not require state courts to extend that precedent or license federal courts to treat the failure to do so as error." White v. Woodall, 572 U. S. ___, ___ (2014) (slip op., at 11). By framing the confrontation right at a high level of generality (making it the right "to impeach the credibility of an adverse witness"), the Sixth Circuit in effect "transform[ed] . . . [an] imaginative extension of existing case law into 'clearly established' " law. Jackson, supra, at ___ (slip op., at 7). That will not do.

The Sixth Circuit seems to have acquired a taste for disregarding AEDPA. E.g., Woods v. Donald, 575 U. S. ___ (2015) (per curiam); White v. Woodall, supra; Burt v. Titlow, 571 U. S. ___ (2013); Metrish v. Lancaster, 569 U. S. ___ (2013); Howes v. Fields, 565 U. S. ___ (2012). We should grant certiorari to discourage this appetite.

Justice Scalia's dissent in FERC v. Electric Power Supply Assn. (Jan 25, 2016, revised January 28, 2016)

Justice SCALIA, with whom Justice THOMAS joins, dissenting.

I believe the Federal Power Act (FPA or Act), 16 U.S.C. § 791a et seq., prohibits the Federal Energy Regulatory Commission (FERC) from regulating the demand response of retail purchasers of power. I respectfully dissent from the Court's holding to the contrary.

I

A

I agree with the majority that FERC has the authority to regulate practices "affecting" wholesale rates. §§ 824d(a), 824e(a); Mississippi Power & Light Co. v. Mississippi ex rel. Moore, 487 U.S. 354, 371, 108 S.Ct. 2428, 101 L.Ed.2d 322 (1988). I also agree that this so-called "affecting" jurisdiction cannot be limitless. And I suppose I could even live with the Court's "direct effect" test as a reasonable limit. Ante, at 773. But as the majority recognizes, ante, at 775, that extratextual limit on the "affecting" jurisdiction merely supplements, not supplants, limits that are already contained in the statutory text and structure. I believe the Court misconstrues the primary statutory limit. (Like the majority, I think that deference under Chevron U.S.A. Inc. v. Natural Resources Defense Council, Inc., 467 U.S. 837, 104 S.Ct. 2778, 81 L.Ed.2d 694 (1984), is unwarranted because the statute is clear.)

The Act grants FERC authority to regulate the "generation ... [and] transmission of electric energy in interstate commerce and the sale of such energy at wholesale." § 824(a). Yet the majority frames the issue thusly: "[T]o uphold the [r]ule, we also must determine that it does not regulate retail electricity sales." Ante, at 775. That formulation inverts the proper inquiry. The pertinent question under the Act is whether the rule regulates sales "at wholesale." If so, it falls within FERC's regulatory authority. If not, the rule is unauthorized whether or not it happens to regulate "retail electricity sales"; for, with exceptions not material here, the FPA prohibits FERC from regulating "any other sale of electric energy" that is not at wholesale. § 824(b)(1) (emphasis added). (The majority wisely ignores FERC's specious argument that the demand-response rule does not regulate any sale, wholesale or retail. See Brief for Petitioner in No. 14-840, p. 39. Paying someone not to conclude a transaction that otherwise would without a doubt have been concluded is most assuredly a regulation of that transaction. Cf. Gonzales v. Raich, 545 U.S. 1, 39-40, 125 S.Ct. 2195, 162 L.Ed.2d 1 (2005) (SCALIA, J., concurring in judgment).)

Properly framing the inquiry matters not because I think there exists "some undefined category of ... electricity sales" that is "non-retail [and] non-wholesale," ante, at 775, n. 7,[1] but because a proper framing of the inquiry is important to establish the default presumption regarding the scope of FERC's authority. While the majority would find every sale of electric energy to be within FERC's authority to regulate unless the transaction is demonstrably a retail sale, the statute actually excludes from FERC's jurisdiction all sales of electric energy except those that are demonstrably sales at wholesale.

So what, exactly, is a "sale of electric energy at wholesale"? We need not guess, for the Act provides a definition: "a sale of electric energy to any person for resale." § 824(d) (emphasis added). No matter how many times the majority incants and italicizes the word "wholesale," ante, at 776-777, nothing can change the fact that the vast majority of (and likely all) demand-response participants — "[a]ggregators of multiple users of electricity, as well as large-scale individual users like factories or big-box stores," ante, at 770 — do not resell electric energy; they consume it themselves. FERC's own definition of demand response is aimed at energy consumers, not resellers. 18 CFR § 35.28(b)(4) (2015).

It is therefore quite beside the point that the challenged "[r]ule addresses — and addresses only — transactions occurring on the wholesale market," ante, at 776. For FERC's regulatory authority over electric-energy sales depends not on which "market" the "transactions occu[r] on" (whatever that means), but rather on the identity of the putative purchaser. If the purchaser is one who resells electric energy to other customers, the transaction is one "at wholesale" and thus within FERC's authority. If not, then not. Or so, at least, says the statute. As we long ago said of the parallel provision in the Natural Gas Act, 15 U.S.C. § 717, "[t]he line of the statute [i]s thus clear and complete. It cut[s] sharply and cleanly between sales for resale and direct sales for consumptive uses. No exceptions [a]re made in either category for particular uses, quantities, or otherwise." Panhandle Eastern Pipe Line Co. v. Public Serv. Comm'n of Ind., 332 U.S. 507, 517, 68 S.Ct. 190, 92 L.Ed. 128 (1947). The majority makes no textual response to this plain reading of the statute.

The demand-response bidders here indisputably do not resell energy to other customers. It follows that the rule does not regulate electric-energy sales "at wholesale," and 16 U.S.C. § 824(b)(1) therefore forbids FERC to regulate these demand-response transactions. See New York v. FERC, 535 U.S. 1, 17, 122 S.Ct. 1012, 152 L.Ed.2d 47 (2002). That is so whether or not those transactions "directly affect" wholesale rates; as we recently said in another context, we will not adopt a construction that "needlessly produces a contradiction in the statutory text." Shapiro v. McManus, 577 U.S. ____, ____, 136 S.Ct. 450, 454, 193 L.Ed.2d 279 (2015). A faithful application of that principle would compel the conclusion that FERC may not "do under [§§ 824d(a) and 824e(a)] what [it] is forbidden to do under [§ 824(b)(1)]." Id., at ____, 136 S.Ct., at 455.

B

The analysis could stop there. But the majority is wrong even on its own terms, for the rule at issue here does in fact regulate "retail electricity sales," which are indisputably "matters ... subject to regulation by the States" and therefore off-limits to FERC. § 824(a); see FPC v. Conway Corp., 426 U.S. 271, 276, 96 S.Ct. 1999, 48 L.Ed.2d 626 (1976); Panhandle Eastern Pipe Line Co., supra, at 517-518, 68 S.Ct. 190. The demand-response participants are retail customers — they purchase electric energy solely for their own consumption. And FERC's demand-response scheme is intentionally "designed to induce lower consumption of electric energy" — in other words, to induce a reduction in "retail electricity sales" — by offering "incentive payments" to those customers. 18 CFR § 35.28(b)(4). The incentive payments effectively increase the retail price of electric energy for participating customers because they must now account for the opportunity cost of using, as opposed to abstaining from using, more energy. In other words, it literally costs them more to buy energy on the retail market. In the court below, FERC conceded that offering credits to retail customers to reduce their electricity consumption "would be an impermissible intrusion into the retail market" because it would in effect regulate retail rates. 753 F.3d 216, 223 (C.A.D.C.2014). Demand-response incentive payments are identical in substance.

The majority resists this elementary economic conclusion (notwithstanding its own exhortation to "think back to Econ 101," ante, at 769). Why? Because its self-proclaimed "common-sensical" view dictates otherwise. Ante, at 778. Maybe the easiest way to see the majority's error is to take its own example: an airline passenger who rejects a $300 voucher for taking a later flight. Consider the following formulation of that example, indistinguishable in substance from the majority's formulation. (Indistinguishable because the hypothetical passenger has exactly the same options and outcomes available to him.) Suppose the airline said to the passenger: "We have proactively canceled your ticket and refunded $400 to your account; and because we have inconvenienced you, we have also deposited an extra $300. The money is yours to use as you like. But if you insist on repurchasing a ticket on the same flight, you must not only pay us $400, but return the $300 too." Now what is the effective price of the ticket? Sometimes an allegedly commonsensical intuition is just that — an intuition, often mistaken.

Moving closer to home, recall that demand-response participants must choose either to purchase a unit of energy at the prevailing retail price (say $10) or to withhold from purchasing that unit and receive instead an incentive payment (of say $5). The two options thus present a choice between having a unit of energy, on the one hand, and having $15 more in the bank, on the other. To repeat: take the energy, be $15 poorer; forgo the energy, be $15 richer. Is that not the very definition of price? See Black's Law Dictionary 1380 (10th ed. 2014) ("[t]he amount of money or other consideration asked for or given in exchange for something else"). In fact, is that not the majority's definition of price? Ante, at 777 ("the amount of money a consumer will hand over in exchange for power").

In any event, the majority appears to recognize that the effective price is indeed $15 — just as the effective price of the airline ticket in the hypothetical is $700. Ante, at 778, n. 9. That recognition gives away the game. For FERC is prohibited not just from directly setting or modifying retail prices; it is prohibited from regulating retail sales, no matter the means. Panhandle Eastern Pipe Line Co., supra, at 517, 68 S.Ct. 190. Whether FERC sets the "real" retail price (to use the majority's idiosyncratic terminology, ante, at 778, n. 9) or the "effective" retail price is immaterial; either way, the rule — by design — induces demand-response participants to forgo retail electric-energy purchases they otherwise would have made. As noted, even FERC conceded that offering credits to retail customers would impermissibly regulate retail sales. The majority blithely overlooks this concession in favor of its own myopic view of retail pricing — all the while evading the inconvenient fact that fiddling with the effective retail price of electric energy, be it through incentive payments or hypothetical credits, regulates retail sales of electric energy no less than does direct ratesetting.

C

The majority cites dicta in several of our opinions expressing the assumption that state jurisdiction and federal jurisdiction under FERC cover the field, so that there is no regulatory "gap"; one entity or the other "must have jurisdiction to regulate each and every practice that takes place in the electricity markets." Ante, at 780. The cases that express such a principle, with respect to the Federal Power Act and its companion the Natural Gas

Act, base it (no surprise) on legislative history. See, e.g., FPC v. Louisiana Power & Light Co., 406 U.S. 621, 631, 92 S.Ct. 1827, 32 L.Ed.2d 369 (1972); FPC v. Transcontinental Gas Pipe Line Corp., 365 U.S. 1, 19, 81 S.Ct. 435, 5 L.Ed.2d 377 (1961); Panhandle Eastern Pipe Line Co., 332 U.S., at 517-518, and n. 13, 68 S.Ct. 190.

One would expect the congressional proponents of legislation to assert that it is "comprehensive" and leaves no stone unturned. But even if one is a fan of legislative history, surely one cannot rely upon such generalities in determining what a statute actually does. Whether it is "comprehensive" and leaves not even the most minor regulatory "gap" surely depends on what it says and not on what its proponents hoped to achieve. I cannot imagine a more irrational interpretive principle than the following, upon which the majority evidently relies:

"[W]hen a dispute arises over whether a given transaction is within the scope of federal or state regulatory authority, we are not inclined to approach the problem negatively, thus raising the possibility that a `no man's land' will be created. That is to say, in a borderline case where congressional authority is not explicit we must ask whether state authority can practicably regulate a given area and, if we find that it cannot, then we are impelled to decide that federal authority governs." Transcontinental Gas Pipe Line Corp., supra, at 19-20, 81 S.Ct. 435 (citation omitted).

That extravagant and otherwise-unheard-of method of establishing regulatory jurisdiction was not necessary to the judgments that invoked it, and should disappear in the Court's memory hole.

Suppose FERC decides that eliminating the middleman would benefit the public, and therefore promulgates a rule allowing electric-energy generators to sell directly to retail consumers across state lines and fixing generation, transmission, and retail rates for such sales. I think it obvious this hypothetical scheme would be forbidden to FERC. Yet just as surely the States could not enact it either, for only FERC has authority to regulate "the transmission of electric energy in interstate commerce." 16 U.S.C. § 824(b)(1); see also New York, 535 U.S., at 19-20, 122 S.Ct. 1012. Is this a regulatory "gap"? Has the generator-to-consumer sales scheme fallen into a regulatory "no man's land"? Must FERC therefore be allowed to implement this scheme on its own? Applying the majority's logic would yield nothing but "yesses." Yet the majority acknowledges that neither FERC nor the States have regulatory jurisdiction over this scheme. Ante, at 780, n. 10. Such sales transactions, involving a mix of retail and wholesale players — as the demand-response scheme does — can be regulated (if at all) only by joint action. I would not call that a "problem," ante, at 780; I would call it an inevitable consequence of the federal-state division created by the FPA.

The majority is evidently distraught that affirming the decision below "would ... extinguish the wholesale demand response program in its entirety." Ante, at 781. Alarmist hyperbole. Excluding FERC jurisdiction would at most eliminate this particular flavor of FERC-regulated demand response. Nothing prevents FERC from tweaking its demand-response scheme by requiring incentive payments to be offered to wholesale customers, rather than retail ones. Brief for Respondent Electric Power Supply Assn. (EPSA) et al. 47-48; Brief for Respondents Midwest Load-Serving Entities 10-11. And retail-level demand response programs, run by the States, do and would continue to exist. See Brief for Respondent EPSA et al. 46-47; Brief for Respondents Midwest Load-Serving Entities 6-11. In fact Congress seemed to presuppose that States, not FERC, would run such programs: The relevant provisions of the Energy Policy Act of 2005, 119 Stat. 594 et seq., are intended "to encourage States to coordinate, on a regional basis, State energy policies to provide reliable and affordable demand response services." § 1252(e)(1), id., at 965, codified at 16 U.S.C. § 2642 note (emphasis added). That statute also imposes several duties on the Secretary of Energy to assist States in implementing demand-response programs. §§ 1252(e)(2), (e)(3), 119 Stat. 965-966. In context, § 1252(f) of the 2005 Act is therefore best read as directing the Secretary to eliminate "unnecessary barriers" to States' adopting and implementing demand-response systems — and not, as the majority contends, as "praising wholesale demand response" systems to be deployed and regulated by FERC, ante, at 770 (emphasis added).

Moreover, the rule itself allows States to forbid their retail customers to participate in the existing demand-response scheme. 18 CFR § 35.28(g)(1)(i)(A); see Brief for Petitioner in No. 14-840, at 43. The majority accepts FERC's argument that this is merely a matter of grace, and claims that it puts the "finishing blow" to respondents' argument that 16 U.S.C. § 824(b)(1) prohibits the scheme. Ante, at 779. Quite the contrary. Remember that the majority believes FERC's authority derives from 16 U.S.C. §§ 824d(a) and 824e(a), the grants of "affecting" jurisdiction. Yet those provisions impose a duty on FERC to ensure that "all rules and regulations affecting or pertaining to [wholesale] rates or charges shall be just and reasonable." § 824d(a) (emphasis added); see § 824e(a) (similar); Conway Corp., 426 U.S., at 277-279, 96 S.Ct. 1999. If inducing retail customers to participate in wholesale demand response transactions is necessary to render wholesale rates "just and reasonable," how can FERC, consistent with its statutory mandate, permit States to thwart such participation? See Brief for United States as Amicus Curiae 20-21, in Hughes v. Talen Energy Marketing, LLC, No. 14-614 etc., now pending before the Court (making an argument similar to ours); cf. New England Power Co. v. New Hampshire, 455 U.S. 331, 339-341, 102 S.Ct. 1096, 71 L.Ed.2d 188 (1982). Although not legally relevant, the fact that FERC — ordinarily so jealous of its regulatory authority, see Brief for United States as Amicus Curiae in No. 14-614 etc. — is willing to let States opt out of its demand-response scheme serves to highlight just how far the rule intrudes into the retail electricity market.

II

Having found the rule to be within FERC's authority, the Court goes on to hold that FERC's choice of compensating demand-response bidders with the "locational marginal price" is not arbitrary and capricious. There are strong arguments that it is. Brief for Robert L. Borlick et al. as Amici Curiae 5-34. Since, however, I believe FERC's rule is ultra vires I have neither need nor desire to analyze whether, if it were not ultra vires, it would be reasonable.

      * * *

For the foregoing reasons, I respectfully dissent.

Notes

[1] Although the majority dismisses this possibility, in fact it appears to think that demand response is in that category: It rejects the conclusion that the demand-response rule regulates retail sales, ante, at 775-779, yet also implicitly rejects the conclusion that it regulates wholesale sales — otherwise why rely on FERC's "affecting" jurisdiction to rescue the rule's legitimacy?

Made in the USA
Las Vegas, NV
18 July 2023

74934099R00453